Lecture Notes in Artificial Intelligence 3229

Edited by J. G. Carbonell and J. Siekmann

Subseries of Lecture Notes in Computer Science

Preface

Logics have, for many years, laid claim to providing a formal basis for the study and development of applications and systems in artificial intelligence. With the depth and maturity of formalisms, methodologies and logic-based systems today, this claim is stronger than ever. The European Conference on Logics in Artificial Intelligence (or Journées Européennes sur la Logique en Intelligence Artificielle, JELIA) began back in 1988, as a workshop, in response to the need for a European forum for the discussion of emerging work in this field. Since then, JELIA has been organized biennially, with English as its official language, previous meetings taking place in Roscoff, France (1988), Amsterdam, Netherlands (1990), Berlin, Germany (1992), York, UK (1994), Évora, Portugal (1996), Dagstuhl, Germany (1998), Málaga, Spain (2000) and Cosenza, Italy (2002). The increasing interest in this forum, its international level with growing participation from researchers outside Europe, and the overall technical quality have turned JELIA into a major biennial forum for the discussion of logic-based approaches to artificial intelligence.

The 9th European Conference on Logics in AI, JELIA 2004, took place in Lisbon, Portugal, between the 27th and the 30th of September 2004, and was hosted by the Universidade Nova de Lisboa. Its technical program comprised 3 invited talks, by Francesca Rossi, Franz Baader, and Bernhard Nebel, and the presentation of 52 refereed technical articles selected by the Program Committee among the 144 that were submitted, a number which in our opinion clearly indicates that the research area of logics in AI is one with a great and increasing interest.

It is our stance that the use of logics in AI will be further advanced if implemented logical-based systems receive appropriate exposure, implementation and testing methodologies are discussed by the community, and the performance and scope of applicability of these systems are presented and compared. To further promote this research, the JELIA 2004 technical programme also included a special session devoted to presentations and demonstrations of 15 implementations, selected among 25 submissions, for solving or addressing problems of importance to areas in the scope of JELIA.

We would like to thanks the authors of all the 169 contributions that were submitted to JELIA 2004, the members of the Program Committee and the additional experts who helped on the reviewing process, for contributing and ensuring the high scientific quality of JELIA 2004.

September 2004

José Júlio Alferes
João Leite

Conference Organization

The conference was organized by the Departamento de Informática, Faculdade de Ciências e Tecnologia, Universidade Nova de Lisboa, under the auspicies of the Portuguese Association for AI, APPIA.

Conference Chair

João Leite   Universidade Nova de Lisboa, Portugal

Program Chair

José Júlio Alferes   Universidade Nova de Lisboa, Portugal

Program Committee

José Júlio Alferes	Universidade Nova de Lisboa, Portugal
Franz Baader	TU Dresden, Germany
Chitta Baral	Arizona State University, USA
Salem Benferhat	Université d'Artois, France
Alexander Bochman	Holon Academic Institute of Technology, Israel
Rafael Bordini	University of Durham, UK
Gerhard Brewka	University of Leipzig, Germany
Walter Carnielli	Universidade Estadual de Campinas, Brazil
Luis Fariñas del Cerro	Université Paul Sabatier, France
Mehdi Dastani	Universiteit Utrecht, The Netherlands
James Delgrande	Simon Fraser University, Canada
Jürgen Dix	TU Clausthal, Germany
Roy Dyckhoff	University of St Andrews, UK
Thomas Eiter	TU Wien, Austria
Patrice Enjalbert	Université de Caen, France
Michael Fisher	University of Liverpool, UK
Ulrich Furbach	University Koblenz-Landau, Germany
Michael Gelfond	Texas Tech University, USA
Sergio Greco	Università della Calabria, Italy
James Harland	Royal Melbourne Institute of Technology, Australia
João Leite	Universidade Nova de Lisboa, Portugal
Maurizio Lenzerini	Università di Roma "La Sapienza", Italy
Nicola Leone	Università della Calabria, Italy
Vladimir Lifschitz	University of Texas at Austin, USA
Maarten Marx	Universiteit van Amsterdam, The Netherlands
John-Jules Meyer	Universiteit Utrecht, The Netherlands
Bernhard Nebel	Universität Freiburg, Germany

Ilkka Niemelä	Helsinki University of Technology, Finland
Manuel Ojeda-Aciego	Universidad de Málaga, Spain
David Pearce	Universidad Rey Juan Carlos, Spain
Luís Moniz Pereira	Universidade Nova de Lisboa, Portugal
Henri Prade	Université Paul Sabatier, France
Henry Prakken	Universiteit Utrecht, The Netherlands
Luc de Raedt	Universität Freiburg, Germany
Ken Satoh	National Institute of Informatics, Japan
Renate Schmidt	University of Manchester, UK
Terrance Swift	SUNY at Stony Brook, USA
Francesca Toni	Imperial College London, UK
Paolo Torroni	Università di Bologna, Italy
Mirek Truszczynski	University of Kentucky, USA
Hudson Turner	University of Minnesota, USA
Wiebe van der Hoek	University of Liverpool, UK
Toby Walsh	University College Cork, Ireland
Mary-Anne Williams	University of Technology, Sydney, Australia
Michael Zakharyaschev	King's College London, UK

Additional Referees

Aditya Ghose	Clare Dixon	Huib Aldewereld
Agustín Valverde Ramos	Davide Grossi	Ian Pratt-Hartmann
Alessandra Di Pierro	Dmitry Tishkovsky	James McKinna
Alessandro Provetti	Emilia Oikarinen	Jan Broersen
Alfredo Burrieza Muñiz	Evelina Lamma	Jérôme Lang
Álvaro Freitas Moreira	Francesco M. Donini	Jerszy Karczmarczuk
A. El Fallah-Segrouchni	Francesco Scarcello	Jesús Medina Moreno
Anatoli Deghtyarev	Franck Dumoncel	J. F. Lima Alcântara
Andrea Calí	Françoise Clérin	Joris Hulstijn
Andrea Schalk	Frank Wolter	Jürg Kohlas
Andreas Herzig	Gabriel Aguilera Venegas	Jurriaan van Diggelen
Anni-Yasmin Turhan	Gerald Pfeifer	Ken Kaneiwa
Antonino Rotolo	Gérard Becher	Kostas Stathis
Antônio C. Rocha Costa	Gerard Vreeswijk	Kristian Kersting
Antonis C. Kakas	Giacomo Terreni	Laure Vieu
Bihn Tran	Gianni Amati	Leila Amgoud
Bob Pokorny	Giovambattista Ianni	Lengning Liu
Boris Konev	Giuseppe De Giacomo	Leon van der Torre
Carlos Ivan Chesnevar	Greg Wheeler	Luigi Palopoli
Carlos Uzcategui	Hans Tompits	Luís da Cunha Lamb
Carsten Fritz	Hans-Jürgen Ohlbach	Lutz Strassburger
Carsten Lutz	Heinrich Wansing	M. Birna van Riemsdijk
Chiaki Sakama	Herbert Wiklicky	Maartijn van Otterlo
Claire Lefevre	Hisashi Hayashi	Manfred Jaeger

Marc Denecker
Marcello Balduccini
M. Gago-Fernandez
Marta Cialdea
Martin Giese
Matteo Baldoni
Maurice Pagnucco
Michael Winikoff
Nelson Rushton
Norbert E. Fuchs
Ofer Arieli
Olivier Gasquet
Pablo Cordero Ortega
Paola Bruscoli
Paolo Ferraris
Paolo Liberatore

Pasquale Rullo
Peep Küngas
Peter Baumgartner
Phan Minh Dung
Philippe Balbiani
Philippe Besnard
Pierangelo Dell'Acqua
Piero Bonatti
Ralf Küsters
Renata Vieira
Robert Kowalski
Roman Kontchakov
Roman Schindlauer
Sergei Odintsov
Souhila Kaci
Stefan Woltran

Stephen Read
Tiberiu Stratulat
Tom Kelsey
Tommi Syrjänen
Ulle Endriss
Ullrich Hustadt
Uwe Waldmann
Victor Marek
Vincent Louis
Vincenzo Pallotta
Viviana Patti
Wolfgang Faber
Youssef Chahir
Yves Moinard

Secretariat

Filipa Mira Reis

Sílvia Marina Costa

Organizing Committee

António Albuquerque
Duarte Alvim
Eduardo Barros

Jamshid Ashtari
Joana Lopes

Miguel Morais
Sérgio Lopes

Sponsoring Institutions

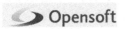

Table of Contents

Invited Talks

Multi-agent Systems

Logic Programming and Nonmonotonic Reasoning

Reasoning Under Uncertainty

Logic Programming

Actions and Causation

Complexity Issues

Description Logics

Belief Revision

Modal, Spacial, and Temporal Logics

Theorem Proving

Applications

Representing and Reasoning with Preferences*

Francesca Rossi

University of Padova, Italy
frossi@math.unipd.it

Many problems in AI require us to represent and reason about preferences. You may, for example, prefer to schedule all your meetings after 10am. Or you may prefer to buy a faster computer than one with a larger disk.

In this talk, I will describe various formalisms proposed for representing preferences. More precisely, I will talk about soft constraints [1] and CP nets [2], which are, respectively, quantitative and qualitative formalisms to handle preferences.

I will then discuss how we can reason about preferences, possibly in the presence of both hard and soft constraints [3]. In this line of work, I will show how CP nets can be paired to a set of hard or soft statements and how the best solutions according to given modelling of the preferences can be obtained.

I will also consider preference aggregation in the context of multi agent systems, I will propose several semantics for preference aggregation based on voting theory, and I will consider the notion of fairness in this context [4]. Fairness is a property which is not possible to obtain (due to Arrow's impossibility theorem) if preferences are described via total orders. In our more general context of possibly partially ordered preferences, a similar result holds for a class of partial orders.

References

1. S. Bistarelli, U. Montanari, and F. Rossi. Semiring-based Constraint Solving and Optimization. *Journal of the ACM*, 44(2):201–236, March 1997.
2. C. Domshlak and R. Brafman. CP-nets - Reasoning and Consistency Testing. Proc. KR-02, 2002, pp.121–132.
3. C. Domshlak, F. Rossi, K.B. Venable, and T. Walsh. Reasoning about soft constraints and conditional preferences: complexity results and approximation techniques. Proc. IJCAI-03, 2003.
4. F. Rossi, K. B. Venable, T. Walsh. mCP nets: representing and reasoning with preferences of multiple agents. Proc. AAAI 2004, San Jose, CA, USA, July 2004.

---

* Joint work with Toby Walsh, Steve Prestwich, and Brent Venable.

J.J. Alferes and J. Leite (Eds.): JELIA 2004, LNAI 3229, p. 1, 2004.
© Springer-Verlag Berlin Heidelberg 2004

Engineering of Logics for the Content-Based Representation of Information

Franz Baader

Theoretical Computer Science
TU Dresden
Germany
baader@tcs.inf.tu-dresden.de

Abstract. The content-based representation of information, which tries to represent the meaning of the information in a machine-understandable way, requires representation formalisms with a well-defined formal semantics. This semantics can elegantly be provided by the use of a logic-based formalism. However, in this setting there is a fundamental tradeoff between the expressivity of the representation formalism and the efficiency of reasoning with this formalism. This motivates the "engineering of logics", i.e., the design of logical formalisms that are tailored to specific representation tasks. The talk will illustrate this approach with the example of so-called Description Logics and their application for databases and as ontology languages for the semantic web.

Storage and transfer of information as well as interfaces for accessing this information have undergone a remarkable evolution. Nevertheless, information systems are still not "intelligent" in the sense that they "understand" the information they store, manipulate, and present to their users. A case in point is the World Wide Web and search engines allowing to access the vast amount of information available there. Web-pages are mostly written for human consumption and the mark-up provides only rendering information for textual and graphical information. Search engines are usually based on keyword search and often provide a huge number of answers, many of which are completely irrelevant, whereas some of the more interesting answers are not found. In contrast, the vision of a "Semantic Web" [4] aims for machine-understandable web resources, whose content can then be comprehended and processed both by automated tools, such as search engines, and by human users.

The content-based representation of information requires representation formalisms with a well-defined formal semantics since otherwise there cannot be a common understanding of the represented information. This semantics can elegantly be provided by a translation into an appropriate logic or the use of a logic-based formalism in the first place. This logical approach has the additional advantage that logical inferences can then be used to reason about the represented information, thus detecting inconsistencies and computing implicit information. However, in this setting there is a fundamental tradeoff between the

J.J. Alferes and J. Leite (Eds.): JELIA 2004, LNAI 3229, pp. 2–3, 2004.

expressivity of the representation formalism on the one hand, and the efficiency of reasoning with this formalism on the other hand [8].

This motivates the "engineering of logics", i.e., the design of logical formalisms that are tailored to specific representation tasks. This also encompasses the formal investigation of the relevant inference problems, the development of appropriate inferences procedures, and their implementation, optimization, and empirical evaluation.

The talk will illustrate this approach with the example of so-called Description Logics [1] and their application for conceptual modeling of databases [6,5] and as ontology languages for the Semantic Web [2,3,7].

References

1. Franz Baader, Diego Calvanese, Deborah McGuinness, Daniele Nardi, and Peter F. Patel-Schneider, editors. *The Description Logic Handbook: Theory, Implementation, and Applications.* Cambridge University Press, 2003.
2. Franz Baader, Ian Horrocks, and Ulrike Sattler. Description logics for the semantic web. *KI – Künstliche Intelligenz*, 4, 2002.
3. Franz Baader, Ian Horrocks, and Ulrike Sattler. Description logics. In Steffen Staab and Rudi Studer, editors, *Handbook on Ontologies*, International Handbooks in Information Systems, pages 3–28. Springer–Verlag, Berlin, Germany, 2003.
4. T. Berners-Lee, J. Hendler, and O. Lassila. The semantic Web. *Scientific American*, 284(5):34–43, 2001.
5. Alex Borgida, Maurizio Lenzerini, and Riccardo Rosati. Description logics for databases. In *[1]*, pages 462–484. 2003.
6. Enrico Franconi and Gary Ng. The i.com tool for intelligent conceptual modeling. In *Proc. of the 7th Int. Workshop on Knowledge Representation meets Databases (KRDB 2000)*, pages 45–53, 2000.
7. Ian Horrocks, Peter F. Patel-Schneider, and Frank van Harmelen. From SHIQ and RDF to OWL: The making of a web ontology language. *Journal of Web Semantics*, 1(1):7–26, 2003.
8. Hector J. Levesque and Ron J. Brachman. A fundamental tradeoff in knowledge representation and reasoning. In Ron J. Brachman and Hector J. Levesque, editors, *Readings in Knowledge Representation*, pages 41–70. Morgan Kaufmann, Los Altos, 1985.

Formal Methods in Robotics

Bernhard Nebel

Albert-Ludwigs-Universität Freiburg

AI research in robotics started out with the hypothesis that logical modelling and reasoning plays a key role. This assumption was seriously questioned by behaviour-based and "Nouvelle AI" approaches. The credo by this school of thinking is that explicit modelling of the environment and reasoning about it is too brittle and computationally too expensive. Instead a purely reactive approach is favoured.

With the increase of computing power we have seen over the last two decades, the argument about the computational costs is not really convincing any more. Furthermore, also the brittleness argument ceases to be convincing, once we start to incorporate probabilities and utilities. I will argue that it is indeed feasible to use computation intensive approaches based on explicit models of the environments to control a robot – and achieve competitive performance.

Most of the time one has to go beyond purely logical approaches, though, because it is necessary to be better than an opponent. For this reason, decision theory and game theory become important ingredients. However, purely logical approaches can have its place if we want to guarantee worst-case properties. I will demonstrate these claims using examples from our robotic soccer team, our foosball robot and our simulated rescue agent team.

J.J. Alferes and J. Leite (Eds.): JELIA 2004, LNAI 3229, p. 4, 2004.
© Springer-Verlag Berlin Heidelberg 2004

Games for Cognitive Agents

Mehdi Dastani[1] and Leendert van der Torre[2]

[1] Utrecht University mehdi@cs.uu.nl
[2] CWI torre@cwi.nl

Abstract. Strategic games model the interaction among simultaneous decisions of agents. The starting point of strategic games is a set of players (agents) having strategies (decisions) and preferences on the game's outcomes. In this paper we do not assume the decisions and preferences of agents to be given in advance, but we derive them from the agents' mental attitudes. We specify such agents, define a mapping from their specification to the specification of the strategic game they play. We discuss a reverse mapping from the specification of strategic games that agents play to a specification of those agents. This mapping can be used to specify a group of agents that can play a strategic game, which shows that the notion of agent system specification is expressive enough to play any kind of game.

1 Introduction

There are several approaches in artificial intelligence, cognitive science, and practical reasoning (within philosophy) to the decision making of individual agents. Most of these theories have been developed independently of classical decision theory based on the expected utility paradigm (usually identified with the work of Neumann and Morgenstern [11] and Savage [9]) and classical game theory. In these approaches, the decision making of individual autonomous agents is described in terms of other concepts than maximizing utility. For example, since the early 40s there is a distinction between classical decision theory and artificial intelligence based on utility aspiration levels and goal based planning (as pioneered by Simon [10]). Qualitative decision theories have been developed based on beliefs (probabilities) and desires (utilities) using formal tools such as modal logic [1]. Also, these beliefs-desires models have been extended with intentions or BDI models [3,8]. Moreover, in cognitive science and philosophy the decision making of individual agents is described in terms of concepts from folk psychology like beliefs, desires and intentions. In these studies, the decision making of individual agents is characterized in terms of a rational balance between these concepts, and the decision making of a group of agents is described in terms of concepts generalized from those used for individual agents, such as joint goals, joint intentions, joint commitments, etc. Moreover, new concepts are introduced at this social level, such as norms (a central concept in most social theories). We are interested in the relation between AI theories of decision making, and their classical counterparts.

We introduce a rule based qualitative decision theory for agents with beliefs and desires. Like classical decision theory but in contrast to several proposals in the BDI approach [3,8], the theory does not incorporate decision processes, temporal reasoning, and scheduling. We also ignore probabilistic decisions. In particular, we explain how

J.J. Alferes and J. Leite (Eds.): JELIA 2004, LNAI 3229, pp. 5–17, 2004.

decisions and preferences of individual agents can be derived from their beliefs and desires. We specify groups of agents and discuss the interaction between their decisions and preferences. The problems we address are: 1) How can we map the specification of the agent system to the specification of the strategic game that they play? This mapping considers agent decisions as agent strategies and decision profiles (a decision for each agent) as the outcomes of the strategic game. 2) How can we map the specification of a strategic game to the specification of the agent system that plays the game? This mapping provides the mental attitudes of agents that can play a strategic game. We show that the mapping which is composed by a mapping from the specification of a strategic games to the specification of an agent system and back is the identity relation, while the mapping composed of a mapping from the specification of an agent system to the specification of a strategic game and back is not necessarily the identity relation.

The layout of this paper is as follows. In section 2 we introduce the rule based qualitative decision theory. In section 3 we define a mapping from the specification of the agent system to the specification of the strategic game they play. In section 4, we discuss the reverse mapping from the specification of a strategic game to the specification of the agent system that plays the game.

2   Agents, Decisions, and Preferences

The specification of agent systems introduced in this section is developed for agents that have conditional beliefs and desires. The architecture and the behavior of this type of agent is studied in [2]. Here, we analyze this type of agent from a decision and game theoretic point of view by studying possible decisions of individual agents and the interaction between these decisions. We do so by defining an agent system specification that indicates possible decisions of individual agents and possible decision profiles (i.e., multiagent decisions). We show how we can derive agent decision profiles and preferences from an agent system specification. In this section, we first define the specification of multiagent systems. Then, we study possible and feasible individual and multiagent decisions within an agent system specification. Finally, we discuss agents' preference ordering defined on the set of individual and multiagent decisions.

2.1   Agent System Specification

The starting point of any theory of decision is a distinction between choices made by the decision maker and choices imposed on it by its environment. For example, a software upgrade agent (decision maker) may have the choice to upgrade a computer system at a particular time of the day. The software company (the environment) may in turn allow/disallow such an upgrade at a particular time. Therefore, we assume n disjoint sets of propositional atoms $A = A_1 \cup \ldots \cup A_n$ with typical elements $a, b, c, \ldots$ (agents' decision variables [6] or controllable propositions [1]) and a set of propositional atoms W with typical elements $p, q, r, \ldots$ (the world parameters or uncontrollable propositions) such that $A \cap W = \emptyset$. In the sequel, the propositional languages that are built up from A_i, A, W, and $A \cup W$ atoms are denoted by L_{A_i}, L_A, L_W, and L_{AW}, respectively. Finally, we use variables $x, y, \ldots$ to stand for any sentences of the languages L_{A_i}, L_A, L_W, and L_{AW}.

An agent system specification given in Definition 1 contains a set of agents and for each agent a description of its decision problem. The agent's decision problem is defined in terms of its beliefs and desires, which are formalized as belief and desire rules, a preference ordering on the powerset of the set of desire rules, a set of facts, and an initial decision (or prior intentions). An initial decision reflects that the agent has already made a decision (intention) in an earlier stage. One may argue that it is not realistic to define the preference ordering on the power set of the set of desire rules since this implies that for each agent its preference on all combinations of its individual desires should be specified beforehand. As it is explained elsewhere [4,5], it is possible to define the preference ordering on the set of desire rules and then lift this ordering to the powerset of the set of desire rules. We have chosen to define the preference ordering on the powerset of the set of desire rules to avoid additional complexity which is not related to the main focus of this paper. The preference ordering is also assumed to be a preorder (i.e. reflexive, transitive, and complete). Again, although this assumption is quite strong for realistic applications, we can use it since the main claim of this paper is not a theory for realistic applications. Finally, we assume that agents are autonomous, in the sense that there are no priorities between desires of distinct agents.

Definition 1 (Agent system specification). *An agent system specification is a tuple* $AS = \langle S, F, B, D, \geq, \lambda^0 \rangle$ *that contains a set of agents* $S = \{\alpha_1, \ldots, \alpha_n\}$, *and for each agent* α_i *a finite set of facts* $F_i \subseteq L_W$ ($F = \langle F_1, \ldots, F_n \rangle$), *a finite set of belief rules* $B_i \subseteq L_{AW} \times L_W$ ($B = \langle B_1, \ldots, B_n \rangle$), *a finite set of desire rules* $D_i \subseteq L_{AW} \times L_{AW}$ ($D = \langle D_1, \ldots, D_n \rangle$), *a relation* $\geq_i$ *on the powerset of* D_i, *i.e.* $\geq_i \subseteq Pow(D_i) \times Pow(D_i)$ ($\geq = \langle \geq_1, \ldots, \geq_n \rangle$) *which is reflexive, transitive, and complete, and a finite initial decision* $\lambda_i^0 \subseteq L_{A_i}$ ($\lambda^0 = \langle \lambda_1^0, \ldots, \lambda_n^0 \rangle$).

In general, a belief rule is an ordered pair $x \Rightarrow y$ with $x \in L_{AW}$ and $y \in L_W$. This belief rule should be interpreted as 'the agent believes y in context x'. A desire rule is an ordered pair $x \Rightarrow y$ with $x \in L_{AW}$ and $y \in L_{AW}$. This desire rule should be interpreted as 'the agent desires y in context x'. It implies that the agent's beliefs are about the world ($x \Rightarrow p$), and not about the agent's decisions. These beliefs can be about the effects of decisions made by the agent ($a \Rightarrow p$) as well as beliefs about the effects of parameters set by the world ($p \Rightarrow q$). Moreover, the agent's desires can be about the world ($x \Rightarrow p$, desire-to-be), but also about the agent's decisions ($x \Rightarrow a$, desire-to-do). These desires can be triggered by parameters set by the world ($p \Rightarrow y$) as well as by decisions made by the agent ($a \Rightarrow y$). Modelling mental attitudes such as beliefs and desires in terms of rules can be called modelling conditional mental attitudes [2].

2.2 Agent Decisions

In the sequel we consider each agent from an agent system specification as a decision making agent. A decision λ of the agent α_i is any consistent subset of L_{A_i} that contains the initial decision λ_i^0.

Definition 2 (Decisions). *Let* $AS = \langle S, F, B, D, \geq, \lambda^0 \rangle$ *be an agent system specification,* L_{A_i} *be the propositional language built up from* A_i, *and* $\models_{A_i}$ *be satisfiability in propositional logics* L_{A_i}. *An AS decision* λ *is a decision of the agent* α_i *such that* $\lambda_i^0 \subseteq \lambda \subseteq L_{A_i}$ & $\lambda \not\models_{A_i} \bot$. *The set of possible decisions of agent* α_i *is denoted by* Λ_i.

The set of possible decisions Λ_i of an agent α_i contains logically equivalent decisions. Two decisions $\lambda, \lambda' \in \Lambda_i$ are logically equivalent, denoted as $\lambda \equiv \lambda'$, if and only if for all models M of L_{A_i} : $M \models \lambda$ iff $M \models \lambda'$, where $M \models \lambda$ iff $\forall x \in \lambda$ $M \models x$.

Definition 3 (Non-equivalent Decisions). *Let Λ_i be the set of possible decisions of agent α_i. A set of possible logically non-equivalent decisions of agent α_i, denoted as $\widetilde{\Lambda}_i$, is a subset of Λ_i such that: $\forall \lambda \in \Lambda_i \exists \lambda' \in \widetilde{\Lambda}_i$ $\lambda \equiv \lambda'$ & $\forall \lambda, \lambda' \in \widetilde{\Lambda}_i$ $\lambda \not\equiv \lambda'$.*

The decisions of an agent depend on the believed consequences of those decisions. The consequences are generated by applying its belief rules to its input facts together with those decisions. In our framework the decisions are formalized based on the notion of extension.

Definition 4 (Belief Extension). *Let Cn_A, Cn_W and Cn_{AW} be the consequence sets for theories from L_A, L_W, and L_{AW}, respectively, and $\models_A$, $\models_W$ and $\models_{AW}$ be satisfiability, in propositional logics L_A, L_W, and L_{AW}, respectively. Let B_i be a set of belief rules of agent α_i, $\lambda_i \in \Lambda_i$ be one of its possible decisions, and $F_i \subseteq L_A$ be its set of facts. The belief consequences of $F_i \cup \lambda_i$ of agent α_i are: $B_i(F_i \cup \lambda_i) = \{y \mid x \Rightarrow y \in B_i, x \in F_i \cup \lambda_i\}$ and the belief extension of $F_i \cup \lambda_i$ is the set of the consequents of the iteratively B_i-applicable rules: $E_{B_i}(F_i \cup \lambda_i) = \bigcap_{F_i \cup \lambda_i \subseteq X, B_i(Cn_{AW}(X)) \subseteq X} X$.*

We give some properties of the belief extension of facts and possible decisions in Definition 4. First note that $E_{B_i}(F_i \cup \lambda_i)$ is *not* closed under logical consequence. The following proposition shows that $E_{B_i}(F_i \cup \lambda_i)$ is the smallest superset of $F_i \cup \lambda_i$ closed under the belief rules B_i interpreted as inference rules.

Proposition 1. *Let $E^0_{B_i}(F_i \cup \lambda_i) = F_i \cup \lambda_i$ and $E^j_{B_i}(F_i \cup \lambda_i) = E^{j-1}_{B_i}(F_i \cup \lambda_i) \cup B_i(Cn_{AW}(E^{j-1}_{B_i}(F_i \cup \lambda_i)))$ for $j > 0$. We have $E_{B_i}(F_i \cup \lambda_i) = \cup_{j=0}^{\infty} E^j_{B_i}(F_i \cup \lambda_i)$.*

The following example illustrates that extensions can be inconsistent.

Example 1. Let $B_i = \{\top \Rightarrow p, a \Rightarrow \neg p\}$, $F_i = \emptyset$, and $\lambda_i = \{a\}$, where $\top$ stands for any tautology like $p \vee \neg p$. We have $E_{B_i}(\emptyset) = \{p\}$ and $E_{B_i}(F_i \cup \lambda_i) = \{a, p, \neg p\}$, which means that the belief extension of $F_i \cup \lambda_i$ is inconsistent.

Although decisions with inconsistent belief consequences are not feasible decisions, we consider them, besides decisions with consistent consequences, as possible decisions. Feasible decisions are defined by excluding decisions that have inconsistent belief consequences.

Definition 5 (Feasible Decisions). *Let $AS = \langle S, F, B, D, \geq, \lambda^0 \rangle$ be an agent system specification, Λ_i and $\widetilde{\Lambda}_i$ be the set of possible decisions and a set of possible logically non-equivalent decisions for agent $\alpha_i \in S$, respectively. The set of feasible decisions of agent α_i, denoted by Λ_i^f, is the subset of its possible decisions Λ_i that have consistent belief consequences, i.e., $\Lambda_i^f = \{\lambda_i \mid \lambda_i \in \Lambda_i$ & $E_{B_i}(F_i \cup \lambda_i)$ is consistent $\}$. A set of logically non-equivalent feasible decisions of agent α_i, denoted by $\widetilde{\Lambda}_i^f$, is the subset of a set of possible non-equivalent decisions $\widetilde{\Lambda}_i$ that have consistent belief consequences, i.e. $\widetilde{\Lambda}_i^f = \{\lambda_i \mid \lambda_i \in \widetilde{\Lambda}_i$ & $E_{B_i}(F_i \cup \lambda_i)$ is consistent $\}$.*

The following example illustrates the decisions of a single agent.

Example 2. Let $A_1 = \{a, b, c, d\}$, $W = \{p, q\}$ and $AS = \langle S, F, B, D, \geq, \lambda^0 \rangle$ with $S = \{\alpha_1\}$, $F_1 = \emptyset$, $B_1 = \{b \Rightarrow q, c \Rightarrow p, d \Rightarrow \neg p\}$, $D_1 = \{b \Rightarrow p, d \Rightarrow \neg q\}$, $\geq_1 = \emptyset < \{b \Rightarrow p\} < \{d \Rightarrow \neg q\} < \{b \Rightarrow p, d \Rightarrow \neg q\}$, and $\lambda_1^0 = \{a\}$. Note that the consequents of all B_1 rules are sentences of L_W. We have due to the definition of $E_{B_1}(F_1 \cup \lambda_1)$, for example, the following logically non-equivalent decisions.

$$\begin{aligned}
E_{B_1}(F_1 \cup \{a\}) &= \{a\}, & E_{B_1}(F_1 \cup \{a, b\}) &= \{a, b, q\}, \\
E_{B_1}(F_1 \cup \{a, c\}) &= \{a, c, p\}, & E_{B_1}(F_1 \cup \{a, d\}) &= \{a, d, \neg p\}, \\
E_{B_1}(F_1 \cup \{a, b, c\}) &= \{a, b, c, p, q\}, & E_{B_1}(F_1 \cup \{a, b, d\}) &= \{a, b, d, \neg p, q\}, \\
E_{B_1}(F_1 \cup \{a, c, d\}) &= \{a, c, d, p, \neg p\}, & E_{B_1}(F_1 \cup \{a, b, c, d\}) &= \{a, b, c, d, p, \neg p, q\}, \ldots
\end{aligned}$$

Therefore $\{a, c, d\}$ and $\{a, b, c, d\}$ are infeasible AS decisions, because their belief extensions are inconsistent. Continued in Example 4.

2.3 Multiagent Decisions

In the previous subsection, we have defined the set of decisions, sets of logically non-equivalent decisions, the set of feasible decisions, and sets of logically non-equivalent feasible decisions for one single agent. In this section, we concentrate on multiagent decisions, which are also called decision profiles, and distinguish various types of multiagent decisions.

Definition 6. *Let $AS = \langle S, F, B, D, \geq, \lambda^0 \rangle$ be an agent system specification where $S = \{\alpha_1, \ldots, \alpha_n\}$. Let also Λ_i and $\widetilde{\Lambda}_i$ be the set of possible decisions and a set of logically non-equivalent decisions for agent $\alpha_i \in S$, respectively. The set of possible decision profiles and a set of logically non-equivalent AS decision profiles are $\Lambda = \Lambda_1 \times \ldots \times \Lambda_n$ and $\widetilde{\Lambda} = \widetilde{\Lambda}_1 \times \ldots \times \widetilde{\Lambda}_n$, respectively. An AS decision profile (i.e., a multiagent decision) λ is a tuple $\langle \lambda_1, \ldots, \lambda_n \rangle$, where $\lambda_i \in \Lambda_i$ for $1 \leq i \leq n$.*

According to definition 5, the feasibility of decisions of individual agents is formulated in terms of the consistency of the extension that is calculated based on the decision and its own facts and beliefs. In a multiagent setting the feasibility of decisions of a single agent depends also on the decisions of other agents. For example, if an agent decides to open a door while another agent decides to close it, then the combined decision can be considered as infeasible. In order to capture the feasibility of multiagent decisions, we consider the feasibility of decision profiles which depends on whether agents' beliefs, facts, and decisions are private or public.

Definition 7. *Let $AS = \langle S, F, B, D, \geq, \lambda^0 \rangle$ where $S = \{\alpha_1, \ldots, \alpha_n\}$. A decision profile $\lambda = \langle \lambda_1, \ldots, \lambda_n \rangle$ is feasible if $E_B(F \cup \lambda)$ is consistent. Below, eight ways to calculate $E_B(F \cup \lambda)$ are distinguished.*

1. $E_{B_1 \cup \ldots \cup B_n}(F_1 \cup \lambda_1 \cup \ldots F_n \cup \lambda_n)$, *i.e., public beliefs, facts, and decisions*
2. $\bigcup_i E_{B_1 \cup \ldots \cup B_n}(F_1 \cup \ldots F_n \cup \lambda_i)$, *i.e., public beliefs and facts, private decisions*
3. $\bigcup_i E_{B_1 \cup \ldots \cup B_n}(F_i \cup \lambda_1 \cup \ldots \cup \lambda_n)$, *i.e., public beliefs and decisions, private facts*
4. $\bigcup_i E_{B_1 \cup \ldots \cup B_n}(F_i \cup \lambda_i)$, *i.e., public beliefs, private facts and decisions*
5. $\bigcup_i E_{B_i}(F_1 \cup \lambda_1 \cup \ldots F_n \cup \lambda_n)$, *i.e., public facts and decisions, private beliefs*
6. $\bigcup_i E_{B_i}(F_i \cup \lambda_1 \cup \ldots \cup \lambda_n)$, *i.e., public decisions, private beliefs and facts*
7. $\bigcup_i E_{B_i}(F_1 \cup \ldots F_n \cup \lambda_i)$, *i.e., public facts, private beliefs and decisions*
8. $\bigcup_i E_{B_i}(F_i \cup \lambda_i)$, *i.e., private beliefs, facts, and decisions*

Given one of these definitions of $E_B(F \cup \lambda)$, *the set of feasible decisions and a set of logically non-equivalent feasible decisions profiles are denoted by* Λ^f *and* $\widetilde{\Lambda}^f$, *respectively.*

Another way to explain these definitions of the feasibility of decision profiles is in terms of communication between agents. The agents communicate their beliefs, facts, or decisions and through this communication decision profiles become infeasible. The following example illustrates the feasibility of decision profiles according to the eight variations.

Example 3. Let $A_1 = \{a\}$, $A_2 = \{b\}$, $W = \{p\}$ and $AS = \langle \{\alpha_1, \alpha_2\}, F, B, D, \geq, \lambda^0 \rangle$ with $F_1 = F_2 = \emptyset$, $B_1 = \{b \Rightarrow p\}$, $B_2 = \{a \Rightarrow \neg p\}$, $D_1 = D_2 = \emptyset$, $\geq$ is the universal relation, and $\lambda_1^0 = \lambda_2^0 = \emptyset$. Note that the only belief of each agent is about the consequence of the decisions that can be taken by the other agent. The following four AS decision profiles are possible; the numbers associated to the following decision profiles indicate according to which definitions of $E_B(F \cup \lambda)$ the decision profile λ is feasible: $\langle \emptyset, \emptyset \rangle : 1 \ldots 8$ $\langle \{a\}, \emptyset \rangle : 1 \ldots 8$ $\langle \emptyset, \{b\} \rangle : 1 \ldots 8$ $\langle \{a\}, \{b\} \rangle : 7, 8$
Since the consequence of decisions that can be taken by each agent is captured by the belief of the other agent, the decision profile $\langle \lambda_1, \lambda_2 \rangle = \langle \{a\}, \{b\} \rangle$ is only feasible when the two agents do not communicate their beliefs and decisions, i.e.,

7. $E_B(F \cup \lambda) = E_{B_1}(F_1 \cup F_2 \cup \lambda_1) \bigcup E_{B_2}(F_1 \cup F_2 \cup \lambda_2) = \{a\} \bigcup \{b\} = \{a, b\}$.

8. $E_B(F \cup \lambda) = E_{B_1}(F_1 \cup \lambda_1) \bigcup E_{B_2}(F_2 \cup \lambda_2) = \{a\} \bigcup \{b\} = \{a, b\}$.

In all other cases, the decision profile $\langle \{a\}, \{b\} \rangle$ will be infeasible since $E_B(F \cup \lambda) = \{a, p, b, \neg p\}$ is inconsistent.

In general, agents may communicate their beliefs, facts, and decisions only to some, but not all, agents. The set of agents to which an agent communicates its beliefs, facts, and decisions depend on the communication network between agents. In order to define the feasibility of decision profiles in terms of communication, one need to restrict the union operators in various definition of $E_B(F \cup \lambda)$ to subsets of agents that can communicate with each other. In this paper, we do not study this further requirement.

Various definitions of $E_B(F \cup \lambda)$, as proposed in definition 7, are related to each other with respect to the public-/privateness of beliefs, facts, and decisions.

Definition 8. *A definition* $\mathcal{D}$ *of* $E_B(F \cup \lambda)$, *as given in definition 7, is more public than another definition* $\mathcal{D}'$ *of* $E_B(F \cup \lambda)$, *written as* $\mathcal{D}' \sqsubseteq_p \mathcal{D}$, *if and only if all aspects (i.e., beliefs, facts, and decisions) that are public in* $\mathcal{D}'$ *are also public in* $\mathcal{D}$.

The definition results a lattice structure on the eight definitions of $E_B(F \cup \lambda)$, as illustrated in Figure 1. The top of the lattice is the definition of $E_B(F \cup \lambda)$ according to which beliefs, facts, and decisions of agents are communicated to each other, and the bottom of the lattice is the definition of $E_B(F \cup \lambda)$ according to which beliefs, facts, and decisions of agents are not communicated. This lattice shows that the more-public-than relation is the same as subset relation on the public aspects.

Proposition 2. *Let* $\mathcal{D}$ *and* $\mathcal{D}'$ *be two definitions of* $E_B(F \cup \lambda)$ *such that* $\mathcal{D}' \sqsubseteq_p \mathcal{D}$. *The feasibility of decision profiles persists under the* $\sqsubseteq_p$ *relation, i.e., for all decision profiles* λ *and* λ' *if the decision profile* λ *is feasible w.r.t. the definition* $\mathcal{D}$, *then it is also feasible w.r.t. the definition* $\mathcal{D}'$.

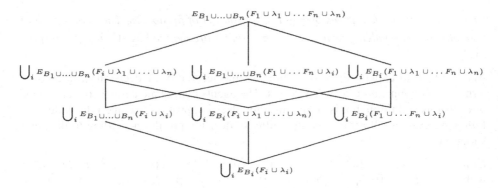

Fig. 1. Different definition for $E_B(F \cup \lambda)$ and their internal structures.

This proposition states that if a decision is feasible when aspects are public, the decision remains feasible when public aspects become private. The following proposition states that communication is relevant for the feasibility of decisions only if the agent system specification consists of more than one agent.

Proposition 3. *Let $AS = \langle S, F, B, D, \geq, \lambda^0 \rangle$ be an agent system specification where $|S| = 1$, i.e., there exists only one agent. If a decision λ is feasible according one definition of $E_B(F \cup \lambda)$, then it is feasible according to all definitions of $E_B(F \cup \lambda)$.*

In this sequel, we proceed with the definition of $E_B(F \cup \lambda)$ where agents' facts, beliefs, and decisions are assumed to be private, i.e., $E_B(F \cup \lambda) = \bigcup_i E_{B_i}(F_i \cup \lambda_i)$.

2.4   Agent Preferences

In this section we introduce a way to compare decisions. Decisions are compared by sets of desire rules that are not reached by the decisions. A desire $x \Rightarrow y$ is unreached by a decision if the expected consequences of the decision imply x but not y[1].

Definition 9 (Comparing decision profiles). *Let $AS = \langle S, F, B, D, \geq, \lambda^0 \rangle$, λ be a AS decision profile, and $E_B(F \cup \lambda) = \bigcup_i E_{B_i}(F_i \cup \lambda_i)$. The unreached desires of λ for agent α_i are: $U_i(\lambda) = \{x \Rightarrow y \in D_i \mid E_B(F \cup \lambda) \models x \text{ and } E_B(F \cup \lambda) \not\models y\}$. Decision profile λ is at least as good as decision profile λ' for agent α_i, written as $\lambda \geq_i^U \lambda'$, iff $U_i(\lambda') \geq_i U_i(\lambda)$. Decision profile λ is equivalent to decision profile λ' for agent α_i, written as $\lambda \approx_i^U \lambda'$, iff $\lambda \geq_i^U \lambda'$ and $\lambda' \geq_i^U \lambda$. Decision profile λ dominates decision profile λ' for agent α_i, written as $\lambda >_i^U \lambda'$, iff $\lambda \geq_i^U \lambda'$ and $\lambda' \not\geq_i^U \lambda$.*

Thus, a decision profile λ is preferred by agent α_i to decision profile λ' if the set of unreached desire rules by λ is less preferred by α_i to the set of unreached desire rules by λ'. Note that the set of unreached desire rules for an infeasible decision is the whole set of desire rules such that all infeasible decision profiles are equally preferred for each agent. The following continuation of Example 2 illustrates the comparison of decisions.

---

[1] The comparison can also be based on the set of violated or reached desires. The desire rule is violated or reached if these consequences imply $x \wedge \neg y$ or $x \wedge y$, respectively.

Example 4 (Continued). In example 2, the agent system specification consists of only one agent such that each decision profile consists only of decisions of one agent. Below are some decision profiles and their corresponding sets of unreached desire rules:

$U_1(\langle\{a\}\rangle) = \emptyset$, $U_1(\langle\{a,b\}\rangle) = \{b \Rightarrow p\}$, $U_1(\langle\{a,c\}\rangle) = \emptyset$,

$U_1(\langle\{a,d\}\rangle) = \{d \Rightarrow \neg q\}$, $U_1(\langle\{a,b,c\}\rangle) = \emptyset$, $U_1(\langle\{a,b,d\}\rangle) = \{b \Rightarrow p, \, d \Rightarrow \neg q\}$,

$U_1(\langle\{a,c,d\}\rangle) = \emptyset$, $U_1(\langle\{a,b,c,d\}\rangle) = \emptyset$, $\ldots$

We thus have for example that the decision profile $\langle\{a,c\}\rangle$ dominates the decision profile $\langle\{a,b\}\rangle$, $\langle\{a,b\}\rangle$ dominates $\langle\{a,d\}\rangle$, and $\langle\{a,d\}\rangle$ dominates $\langle\{a,b,d\}\rangle$, i.e., $\{a,c\} >_1^U \{a,b\} >_1^U \{a,d\} >_1^U \{a,b,d\}$. Moreover, $\langle\{a\}\rangle$, $\langle\{a,c\}\rangle$, and $\langle\{a,b,c\}\rangle$ are equivalent, i.e., $\langle\{a\}\rangle \approx \langle\{a,c\}\rangle \approx \langle\{a,b,c\}\rangle$.

In Example 2, the decision profiles $\langle\{a,c,d\}\rangle$ and $\langle\{a,b,c,d\}\rangle$ are infeasible and therefore have the whole set of desire rules as the set of unreached desire rules. A problem with defining the unreached based ordering on infeasible decisions is that the unreached based ordering cannot differentiate between some feasible decisions, e.g., $\langle\{a,b,c\}\rangle$, and infeasible decisions, e.g., $\langle\{a,c,d\}\rangle$.

The following proposition states that the agent's ordering on decision profiles based on unreached desire rules is a preference ordering.

Proposition 4. *Let* $AS = \langle S, F, B, D, \geq, \lambda^0 \rangle$ *be an agent system specification. For each agent, the ordering on decision profiles based on the set of unreached desire rules is a preorder.*

3   From Agent System Specifications to Game Specifications

In this subsection, we consider interactions between agents based on agent system specifications, their corresponding agent decisions, and the ordering on the decisions as explained in previous subsections. Agents select optimal decisions under the assumption that other agents do likewise. This makes the definition of an optimal decision circular, and game theory therefore restricts its attention to equilibria. For example, a decision is a Nash equilibrium if no agent can reach a better (local) decision by changing its own decision. The most used concepts from game theory are Pareto efficient decisions, dominant decisions and Nash decisions. We first repeat some standard notations from game theory [7].

In the sequel, we consider only strategic games, which is described in [7] as follows: *A strategic game is a model of interactive decision making in which each decision maker chooses his plan of action once and for all, and these choices are made simultaneously.* For strategic games, we use δ_i to denote a decision (strategy) of agent α_i and $\delta = \langle\delta_1, \ldots, \delta_n\rangle$ to denote a decision (strategy) profile containing one decision (strategy) for each agent. We use δ_{-i} to denote the decision profile of all agents except the decision of agent α_i, and (δ_{-i}, δ_i') to denote a decision profile which is the same as δ except that the decision of agent i from δ is replaced with the decision δ_i'. Finally, we use Δ to denote the set of all possible decision profiles for agents $\alpha_1, \ldots, \alpha_n$ and Δ_i to denote the set of possible decisions for agent α_i.

Definition 10 (Strategic Game Specification [7]). *A strategic game specification is a tuple* $\langle N, \Delta, \geq^{gs} \rangle$ *where* $N = \{\alpha_1, \ldots, \alpha_n\}$ *is a set of agents,* $\Delta \subseteq \Delta_1 \times \ldots \times \Delta_n$ *for*

Δ_i is a set of decisions of agent α_i, and $\geq^{gs} = \langle \geq_1^{gs}, \ldots, \geq_n^{gs} \rangle$, for $\geq_i^{gs}$ is the preference order of agent α_i on Δ. The preference order $\geq_i^{gs}$ is reflexive, transitive, and complete.

We now define a mapping $AS2AG$ from the specification of an agent system to the specification of a strategic game. This mapping is based on the correspondence between logically non-equivalent feasible decisions from an agent system specification and agents' decisions in strategic game specifications, and between agents' preference orderings in both specifications. We have chosen to make a correspondence based on the logically non-equivalent decisions (and not possible decisions) since otherwise the resulting strategic game specification contain logically equivalent decisions profiles.

Definition 11 (AS2AG). *Let $S = \{\alpha_1, \ldots, \alpha_n\}$, $AS = \langle S, F, B, D, \geq, \lambda^0 \rangle$, $\widetilde{\Lambda}^f$ be a set of AS logically non-equivalent feasible decision profiles according to Definition 7 and for a given definition of $E_B(F \cup \lambda)$ (i.e., $\bigcup_i E_{B_i}(F_i \cup \lambda_i)$), and $\geq_i^U$ be the AS preference order of agent α_i defined on $\widetilde{\Lambda}^f$ according to definition 9. The strategic game specification of AS is $GS = \langle N, \Delta, \geq^{gs} \rangle$ if there exists a bijjective function g from AS to GS such that $g : S \to N$, $g : \widetilde{\Lambda}^f \to \Delta$, and $g :\geq^U \to \geq^{gs}$.*

Example 5. Let α_1 and α_2 be two agents, $F_1 = F_2 = \emptyset$, and initial decisions $\lambda_1^0 = \lambda_2^0 = \emptyset$. They have the following beliefs en desires: $B_1 = \{a \Rightarrow p\}$, $D_1 = \{\top \Rightarrow p, \top \Rightarrow q\}$, $\emptyset \geq_1 \{\top \Rightarrow q\} \geq_1 \{\top \Rightarrow p\} \geq_1 \{\top \Rightarrow p, \top \Rightarrow q\}$, $B_2 = \{b \Rightarrow q\}$, $D_2 = \{q \Rightarrow \neg p, p \Rightarrow \neg q\}$, $\emptyset \geq_2 \{q \Rightarrow \neg p\} \geq_2 \{p \Rightarrow \neg q\} \geq_2 \{p \Rightarrow \neg q, \Rightarrow \neg p\}$. Let λ be feasible decision profile according to any of the eight formulations of $E_B(F \cup \lambda)$ as proposed in definition 7, and $U_i(\lambda)$ be the set of unreached desires for agent α_i and decision profile λ.

λ	$E_B(F \cup \lambda)$	$U_1(\lambda)$	$U_2(\lambda)$
$\langle \emptyset, \emptyset \rangle$	$\emptyset$	$\{\top \Rightarrow p, \top \Rightarrow q\}$	$\emptyset,$
$\langle \emptyset, \{b\} \rangle$	$\{q\}$	$\{\top \Rightarrow p\}$	$\{q \Rightarrow \neg p\}$
$\langle \{a\}, \emptyset \rangle$	$\{p\}$	$\{\top \Rightarrow q\}$	$\{p \Rightarrow \neg q\}$
$\langle \{a\}, \{b\} \rangle$	$\{p, q\}$	$\emptyset$	$\{p \Rightarrow \neg q, q \Rightarrow \neg p\}$

According to definition 9 the preference ordering over possible decision profiles for agent α_1 is $\langle \{a\}, \{b\} \rangle \geq_1^U \langle \{a\}, \emptyset \rangle \geq_1^U \langle \emptyset, \{b\} \rangle \geq_1^U \langle \emptyset, \emptyset \rangle$, and for agent α_2 is $\langle \emptyset, \emptyset \rangle \geq_2^U \langle \emptyset, \{b\} \rangle \geq_2^U \langle \{a\}, \emptyset \rangle \geq_2^U \langle \{a\}, \{b\} \rangle$. Consider now the following mapping from AS to GS based on the bijective function g defined as $g(\alpha_i) = \alpha_i$ $\forall \alpha_i \in S$, $g(\lambda) = \lambda$ $\forall \lambda \in \widetilde{\Lambda}^f$, and $g(\geq_i^U) = \geq_i^U$ for $i = 1, 2$. The resulting strategic game specification of AS is $GS = \langle N, \Delta, \geq^{gs} \rangle$, where $N = \{g(\alpha_i) \mid \alpha_i \in S\}$, $\Delta = \{g(\lambda) \mid \lambda \in \widetilde{\Lambda}^f\}$, and $\geq^{gs} = \langle g(\geq_1^U), g(\geq_2^U) \rangle$.

We now use the mapping from AS to GS and consider different types of decision profiles which are similar to types of decision (strategy) profiles from game theory.

Definition 12. *[7] Let $\widetilde{\Lambda}^f$ be a set of logically non-equivalent feasible decision profiles that is derived from the AS specification of an agent system and GS be the strategic game specification of AS based on the mapping g. A feasible AS decision profile $\lambda \in \widetilde{\Lambda}^f$ is* **Pareto decision** *if $g(\lambda) = \delta$ is a pareto decision in GS, i.e., if there is no $\delta' \in \Delta$ for which $\delta_i' >_i^{gs} \delta_i$ for all agents $\alpha_i \in N$. A feasible AS is* **strongly Pareto decision** *if $g(\lambda) = \delta$ is a strongly Pareto decision in GS, i.e., if there is no $\delta' \in \Delta$ for which $\delta_i' \geq_i^{gs} \delta_i$ for all*

agents α_i and $\delta'_j >^{gs}_j \delta_j$ for some agents α_j. A feasible AS is **weak dominant decision**
if $g(\lambda) = \delta$ is a weak dominant decision in GS, i.e., if for all $\delta' \in \Delta$ and for every agent
α_i it holds: $(\delta'_{-i}, \delta_i) \geq^{gs}_i (\delta'_{-i}, \delta'_i)$. A feasible AS is **strong dominant decision** *if for*
all $\delta' \in \Delta$ and for every agent α_i it holds: $(\delta'_{-i}, \delta_i) >^{gs}_i (\delta'_{-i}, \delta'_i)$. Finally, a feasible
AS is **Nash decision** *if $g(\lambda) = \delta$ is a Nash decision in GS, i.e., if for all agents α_i it*
holds: $(\delta_{-i}, \delta_i) \geq^{gs}_i (\delta_{-i}, \delta'_i)$ for all $\delta'_i \in \Delta_i$.

It is a well known fact that Pareto decisions exist (for finite games), whereas dominant
decisions do not have to exist. Consider the strategic game specification GS which is
derived from the agent system specification AS in Example 5. None of the decision
profiles in GS are dominant decisions.

Starting from an agent system specification, we can derive the strategic game specification and in this game specification we can use standard techniques to for example find
the Pareto decisions. The problem with this approach is that the translation from an agent
system specification to a strategic game specification is computationally expensive. For
example, a compact agent representation with only a few belief and desire rules may
lead to a huge set of decisions if the number of decision variables is high. A challenge of
qualitative game theory is therefore whether we can bypass the translation to strategic
game specification, and define properties directly on the agent system specification. For
example, are there particular properties of agent system specification for which we can
prove that there always exists a dominant decision for its corresponding derived game
specification? An example is the case in which the agents have the same individual agent
specification, because in that case the game reduces to single agent decision making.
In this paper we do not pursue this challenge, but we consider the expressive power of
agent specifications.

4   From Game Specifications to Agent Specifications

In this section the question is raised whether the notion of agent system specification is
expressive enough for strategic game specifications, that is, whether for each possible
strategic game specification there is an agent system specification that can be mapped on
it. We prove this property in the following way. First, we define a mapping from strategic
game specifications to agent system specifications. Second, we show that the composite
mapping from strategic game specifications to agent system specifications and back to
strategic game specifications is the identity relation. The second step shows that if a
strategic game specification GS is mapped in step 1 on agent system specification AS,
then this agent system specification AS can be mapped on GS. Thus, it shows that there
is a mapping from agent system specifications to strategic game specifications for every
strategic game specification GS.

Unlike the second step, the composite mapping from agent system specifications to
strategic game specifications and back to agent system specifications is not the identity
relation. This is a direct consequence of the fact that there are distinct agent system
specifications that are mapped on the same strategic game specification. For example,
agent system specifications in which the variable names are uniformly substituted by new
names. The mapping from strategic game specifications to agent system specifications
consists of the following steps. 1) The set of agents from strategic game specification

is the set of agents for the agent system specification. 2) For each agent in the agent system specification a set of decision variables is introduced that will generate the set of decisions of the agent in the strategic game specification. 3) For each agent in the agent system specification a set of desire rules and a preference ordering on the powerset of the set of desire rules are introduced, such that they generate the preference order on decision profiles for the agent in the strategic game specification.

According to definition 10, the ingredients of the specification of strategic games are agents identifiers, agents decisions, and the preference ordering of each agent on decision profiles. For each decision $\delta_i \in \Delta_i$ of each agent α_i in a strategic game specification GS we introduce a separate decision variable d_i for the corresponding agent α_i in the agent system specification AS. The set of introduced decision variables for agent α_i is denoted by A_i. The propositional language L_{A_i}, which is based on A_i, specifies the set of possible AS decisions for agent α_i. However, L_{A_i} specifies more AS decisions than GS decisions since it can combine decision variables with conjunction and negation. In order to avoid additional decisions for each agent, we design the initial decisions for each agent such that possible decisions are characterized by one and only one decision variable. In particular, the initial decision λ_i^0 of agent α_i is specified as follows: $\lambda_i^0 = \{\bigvee_k d^k , d \to \neg d' \mid d^k \in A_i \ \& \ d \neq d' \ \& \ d, d' \in A_i\}$. Moreover, the set of decision profiles of strategic game specifications is a subset of all possible decision profiles, i.e., $\Delta \subseteq \Delta_1 \times \ldots \times \Delta_n$. This implies that we need to exclude AS decision profiles that correspond with the excluded decision profiles in GS. For this reason, we introduce belief rules for relevant agents to make excluded decision profile infeasible in AS. For example, suppose in a strategic game specification with two agents α_1 and α_2 the decision profile is excluded, i.e., $\langle \delta_1, \delta_2 \rangle \notin \Delta$, and that d_i is the introduced decision variable for δ_i for $i = \{1, 2\}$. Then, we introduce a new parameter $p \in W$ and add one belief formula for each agent as follows: $d_1 \Rightarrow p \in B_1 \ \& \ d_2 \Rightarrow \neg p \in B_2$. Note that in this example the decision profile (d_1, d_2) in AS is not a feasible decision profile anymore.

We use the preference ordering $\geq_i^{gs}$ of each agent α_i, defined on the set of decision profiles Δ of the strategic game specification, and introduce a set of desire rules D_i together with a preference ordering $\geq_i$ on the powerset of D_i for agent α_i. The set of desire rules for an agent and its corresponding preference ordering are designed in such a way that if the set of unreached desire rules for a decision in the agent system specification are more preferred than the set of unreached desire rules for a second decision, then the first decision is less preferred than the second one (see definition 9).

Definition 13. *Let $GS = \langle N, \Delta, \geq^{gs} \rangle$ be a strategic game specification where $N = \{\alpha_1, \ldots, \alpha_n\}$ is the set of agents, $\Delta \subseteq \Delta_1 \times \ldots \times \Delta_n$ is the set of decision profiles, $\geq^{gs} = \langle \geq_1^{gs}, \ldots, \geq_n^{gs} \rangle$ consists of the preference orderings of agents on Δ, and $\bigvee \neg d_{-i} = \neg d_1 \vee \ldots \vee \neg d_{i-1} \vee \neg d_{i+1} \ldots \vee \neg d_n$. Then, $AS = \langle S, \emptyset, B, D, \geq, \lambda^0 \rangle$ is the agent system specification derived from GS, where $B = \langle B_1, \ldots, B_n \rangle, D = \langle D_1, \ldots, D_n \rangle, \lambda^0 = \langle \lambda_1^0, \ldots, \lambda_n^0 \rangle, \geq = \langle \geq_1, \ldots, \geq_n \rangle, S = N, A_i = \{d \mid d \text{ is a decision variable for } \delta \in \Delta_i\}, W = \{p_1, \ldots, p_n\}$ with parameter for each infeasible decision profile, $\lambda_i^0 = \{\bigvee_k d^k, d \to \neg d' \mid d^k \in A_i \ \& \ d \neq d' \ \& \ d, d' \in A_i\}, (d_i \Rightarrow p) \in B_i \& (d_j \Rightarrow \neg p) \in B_j \forall \langle \delta_1, \ldots, \delta_n \rangle \notin \Delta$ (where $d_i \in A_i, d_j \in A_j, 1 \leq i \neq j \leq n, p \in W$, and d_i, d_j are the decision variables for δ_i and δ_i, respectively), and $D_i = \{d_i \Rightarrow \bigvee \neg d_{-i} \mid \forall \delta =$*

$\langle \delta_1, \ldots, \delta_n \rangle \in \Delta\}$ *(where d_i, d_{-i} are the decision variables for δ_i and δ_{-i}, respectively).*
The preference relation $\geq_i$ defined on $Pow(D_i)$ is characterized as follows: 1) $s \geq_i \emptyset$ for
all $s \in Pow(D_i)$, 2) $\{d_i \Rightarrow \bigvee \neg d_{-i}\} \geq_i \{d'_i \Rightarrow \bigvee \neg d'_{-i}\}$ iff $\delta' \geq_i^{gs} \delta$ (where (d_{-i}, d_i)
and (d'_{-i}, d'_i) are the decision profiles for δ and δ', respectively), and 3) $s' \geq_i s$ for all
$s, s' \in Pow(D_i)$ & $|s| \leq 1$ & $|s'| > 1$.

In this definition, the set D_i is designed in the context of ordering on decisions based on unreached desire rules, as it is defined in Definition 9. In particular, for agent α_i we define for each decision variable a desire rule that will be unreached as the only desire rule by exactly one decision profile. This is the construction of D_i in this definition. Then, we use the reverse of the preference ordering from the strategic game specification, which was defined on decision profiles, to order the unreached (singletons) sets of desire rules. Since each decision profile has exactly one unreached desire rule, the preference ordering $\geq_i^{gs}$ on decision profiles can be directly used as a preference ordering on unreached sets of desire rules, which in turn is the reverse of the preference ordering $\geq_i$ defined on the powerset of the set D_i of desire rules. This is realized by the last three items of this definition. The first item indicates that any desire rule is more preferred than no desire rule $\emptyset$. The second item indicates that if a decision profile δ' is preferred over a decision profile δ according to the unreached desire rules, then the desire rules that are unreached by δ are preferred over the desire rules that are unreached by δ'. Finally, the last item guarantees that the characterized preference ordering $\geq_i$ is complete by indicating that all other sets of of desire rules are preferred over the singletons of desire rules (sets consisting of only one desire rule) and the empty set of desire rules.

The following proposition shows that the mapping from strategic game specifications to agent system specifications leads to the desired identity relation for the composite relation.

Proposition 5. *Let GS be a strategic game specification as in Definition 10. Moreover, let AS be the derived agent system specification as defined in Definition 13. The application of the mapping from agent system specification to strategic game specification, as defined in Definition 11, maps AS to GS.*

Proof. Assume any particular GS. Construct the AS as above. Now apply Definition 9. The unreached desires of decision δ for agent α_i are $U_i(\delta) = \{x \Rightarrow y \in D \mid E_B(F \cup \delta) \models x$ and $E_B(F \cup \delta) \not\models y\}$. The subset ordering on these sets of unreached desires reflects exactly the original ordering on decisions.

The following theorem follows directly from the proposition.

Theorem 1. *The set of agent system specifications with empty set of facts is expressive enough for strategic game specifications.*

Proof. Follows from construction in Proposition 5.

The above construction raises the question whether other sets of agent system specifications are complete too, such as for example the set of agent system specifications in which the set of desires contains only desire-to-be desires. We leave these questions for further research.

5   Concluding Remarks

In this paper we introduce agent system specifications based on belief and desire rules, and we show how various kinds of strategic games can be played (depending on whether the beliefs, desires and decisions are public or private), and we show how for each possible strategic game an agent specification can be defined that plays that game. The agent system specification we propose is relatively simple, but the extension of the results to more complex agent system specifications seems straightforward. We believe that such results give new insights in the alternative theories which are now developed in artificial intelligence, agent theory and cognitive science.

Our work is typical for a line of research knows as qualitative decision theory which aims at closing the gap between on the one hand classical decision and game theory, and on the other hand alternative theories developed in artificial intelligence, agent theory and cognitive science. Our main result is in our opinion not the particular technical results of this paper, but their illustration how the classical and alternative theories can use each others' results. Our motivation comes from the analysis of rule-based agent architectures, which have recently been introduced.

There are several topics for further research. The most interesting question is whether belief and desire rules are fundamental, or whether they in turn can be represented by some other construct. Other topics for further research are the development of an incremental any-time algorithm to find optimal decisions, the development of computationally attractive fragments of the logic, and heuristics of the optimization problem.

References

1. C. Boutilier. Toward a logic for qualitative decision theory. In *Proceedings of the KR'94*, pages 75–86, 1994.
2. J. Broersen, M. Dastani, J. Hulstijn, and L. van der Torre. Goal generation in the BOID architecture. *Cognitive Science Quarterly. Special issue on 'Desires, goals, intentions, and values: Computational architectures'*, 2(3-4):428–447, 2002.
3. P.R. Cohen and H.J. Levesque. Intention is choice with commitment. *Artificial Intelligence*, 42:213–261, 1990.
4. M. Dastani and L. van der Torre. Decisions and games for BD agents. In *Proceedings of The Workshop on Game Theoretic and Decision Theoretic Agents, Canada*, pages 37–43, 2002.
5. M. Dastani and L. van der Torre. What is a normative goal? Towards Goal-based Normative Agent Architectures. In *Regulated Agent-Based Systems, Postproceedings of RASTA'02*, pages 210–227. Springer, 2004.
6. J. Lang. Conditional desires and utilities - an alternative approach to qualitative decision theory. In *In Proceedings of the European Conference on Artificial Intelligence (ECAI'96)*, pages 318–322, 1996.
7. Martin J. Osborne and Ariel Rubenstein. *A Course in Game Theory*. The MIT Press, Cambridge, Massachusetts, 1994.
8. A. Rao and M. Georgeff. Modeling rational agents within a BDI architecture. In *Proceedings of the KR91*, pages 473–484, 1991.
9. L. Savage. *The foundations of statistics*. Wiley, New York, 1954.
10. H. A. Simon. *The Sciences of the Artificial*. MIT Press, Cambridge, MA, 1981.
11. J. von Neumann and O. Morgenstern. *Theory of Games and Economic Behavior*. Princeton University Press, Princeton, NJ, 1 edition, 1944.

Knowledge-Theoretic Properties of Strategic Voting

Samir Chopra[1], Eric Pacuit[2], and Rohit Parikh[3]

[1] Department of Computer Science
Brooklyn College of CUNY
Brooklyn, New York 11210
schopra@sci.brooklyn.cuny.edu
[2] Department of Computer Science
CUNY Graduate Center
New York, NY 10016
epacuit@cs.gc.cuny.edu
[3] Departments of Computer Science, Mathematics and Philosophy
Brooklyn College and CUNY Graduate Center
New York, NY 10016
ripbc@cunyvm.cuny.edu

Abstract. Results in social choice theory such as the Arrow and Gibbard-Satterthwaite theorems constrain the existence of rational collective decision making procedures in groups of agents. The Gibbard-Satterthwaite theorem says that no voting procedure is *strategy-proof*. That is, there will always be situations in which it is in a voter's interest to misrepresent its true preferences i.e., vote strategically. We present some properties of strategic voting and then examine – via a bimodal logic utilizing epistemic and strategizing modalities – the knowledge-theoretic properties of voting situations and note that unless the voter *knows* that it should vote strategically, and how, i.e., knows what the *other* voters' preferences are and *which* alternate preference P' it should use, the voter will not strategize. Our results suggest that opinion polls in election situations effectively serve as the first $n-1$ stages in an n stage election.

1 Introduction

A comprehensive theory of multi-agent interactions must pay attention to results in social choice theory such as the Arrow and Gibbard-Satterthwaite theorems [1, 7,17]. These impossibility results constrain the existence of rational collective decision making procedures. Work on formalisms for belief merging already reflects the attention paid to social choice theory [9,6,12,11,13]. In this study we turn our attention to another aspect of social aggregation scenarios: the role played by the states of knowledge of the agents. The study of strategic interactions in game theory reflects the importance of states of knowledge of the players. In this paper, we bring these three issues—states of knowledge, strategic interaction and social aggregation operations—together.

J.J. Alferes and J. Leite (Eds.): JELIA 2004, LNAI 3229, pp. 18–30, 2004.

The Gibbard-Satterthwaite theorem is best explained as follows[1]. Let S be a social choice function whose domain is an n-tuple of preferences $P_1 \ldots P_n$, where $\{1, \ldots, n\}$ are the voters, M is the set of choices or candidates and each P_i is a linear order over M. S takes $P_1 \ldots P_n$ as input and produces some element of M - the winner. Then the theorem says that there must be situations where it 'profits' a voter to vote *strategically*. Specifically, if P denotes the actual preference ordering of voter i, Y denotes the profile consisting of the preference orderings of all the other voters then the theorem says that there must exist P, Y, P' such that $S(P', Y) >_P S(P, Y)$. Here $>_P$ indicates: better according to P. Thus in the situation where the voter's actual ordering is P and all the orderings of the other voters (together) are Y then voter i is better off saying its ordering is P' rather than what it actually is, namely P. In particular, if the vote consists of voting for the highest element of the preference ordering, it should vote for the highest element of P' rather than of P.

Of course, the agent might be *forced* to express a different preference. For example, if an agent, whose preferences are $B > C > A$, is only presented C, A as choices, then the agent will pick C. This 'vote' differs from the agent's true preference, but should not be understood as 'strategizing' in the true sense.

A real-life example of strategizing was noticed in the 2000 US elections when some supporters of Ralph Nader voted for their second preference, Gore,[2] in a vain attempt to prevent the election of George W. Bush. In that case, Nader voters decided that (voting for the maximal element of) a Gore-Nader-Bush expression of their preferences would be closer to their desired ordering of Nader-Gore-Bush than the Bush-Gore-Nader ordering that would result if they voted for their actual top choice. Similar examples of strategizing have occurred in other electoral systems over the years ([4] may be consulted for further details on the application of game-theoretic concepts to voting scenarios). The Gibbard-Satterthwaite theorem points out that situations like the one pointed out above *must* arise.

What interests us in this paper are the *knowledge-theoretic properties* of the situation described above. We note that unless the voter with preference P *knows* that it should vote strategically, and how, i.e., knows that the other voters' preference is Y and that it should vote according to $P' \neq P$, the theorem is not 'effective'. That is, the theorem only applies in those situations where a certain level of knowledge exists amongst voters. Voters completely or partially ignorant about other voters' preferences would have little incentive to change their actual preference at election time. In the 2000 US elections, many Nader voters changed their votes *because* opinion polls had made it clear that Nader stood no chance of winning, and that Gore would lose as a result of their votes going to Nader.

---

[1] Later we use a different formal framework; we have chosen to use this more transparent formalism during the introduction for ease of exposition.

[2] Surveys show that had Nader not run, 46% of those who voted for him would have voted for Gore, 23% for Bush and 31% would have abstained. Hereafter, when we refer to Nader voters we shall mean those Nader voters who did or would have voted for Gore.

We develop a logic for reasoning about the knowledge that agents have of their own preferences and other agents' preferences, in a setting where a social aggregation function is defined and kept fixed throughout. We attempt to formalize the intuition that agents, knowing an aggregation function, and hence its outputs for input preferences, will strategize if they know a) enough about other agents' preferences and b) that the output of the aggregation function of a changed preference will provide them with a more favorable result, one that is closer to their true preference. We will augment the standard epistemic modality with a modality for strategizing. This choice of a bimodal logic brings with it a greater transparency in understanding the states that a voter will find itself in when there are two possible variances in an election: the preferences of the voters and the states of knowledge that describe these changing preferences.

Our results will suggest that election-year opinion polls are a way to effectively turn a one-shot game, i.e., an election, into a many-round game that may induce agents to strategize. Opinion polls make voters' preferences public in an election year and help voters decide on their strategies on the day of the election. For the rest of the paper, we will refer to opinion polls also as elections.

The outline of the paper is as follows. In Section 2 we define a formal voting system and prove some preliminary results about strategic voting. In Section 3 we demonstrate the dependency of strategizing on the voters' states of knowledge. In Section 4 we develop a bimodal logic for reasoning about strategizing in voting scenarios.

2   A Formal Voting Model

There is a wealth of literature on formal voting theory. This section draws upon discussions in [4,5]. The reader is urged to consult these for further details.

Let $\mathcal{O} = \{o_1, \ldots, o_m\}$ be a set of candidates, $\mathcal{A} = \{1, \ldots, n\}$ be a set of agents or voters. We assume that each voter has a preference over the elements of $\mathcal{O}$, i.e., a reflexive, transitive and connected relation on $\mathcal{O}$. For simplicity we assume that each voter's preference is strict. A voter i's *strict preference relation* on $\mathcal{O}$ will be denoted by P_i. We represent each P_i by a function $P_i : \mathcal{O} \to \{1, \ldots, m\}$, where we say that a voter *strictly prefers* o_j to o_k iff $P_i(o_j) > P_i(o_k)$. We will write $P_i = (o_1, \ldots, o_n)$ iff $P_i(o_1) > P_i(o_2) > \cdots > P_i(o_n)$. Henceforth, for ease of readability we will use **Pref** to denote preferences over $\mathcal{O}$. A *preference profile* is an element of $(\mathbf{Pref})^n$. Given each agent's preference an *aggregation function* returns the social preference ordering over $\mathcal{O}$.

Definition 1 (Aggregation Function). *An* **aggregation function** *is a function from preference profiles to preferences:*

$$\mathrm{Ag} : \mathbf{Pref}^n \to \mathbf{Pref}$$

In voting scenarios such as elections, agents are not expected to announce their actual preference relation, but rather to select a vote that 'represents' their preference. Each voter chooses a vote v, the aggregation function tallies the votes of each candidate and selects a winner (or winners if electing more than one candidate). There are two components to any voting procedure. First, the type of votes that voters can cast. For example, in *plurality voting* voters can only vote for a single candidate so votes v are simply singleton subsets of $\mathcal{O}$, whereas in *approval voting* voters select a set of candidates so votes v are any subset of $\mathcal{O}$. Following [5], given a set of $\mathcal{O}$ of candidates, let $\mathcal{B}(\mathcal{O})$ be the set of feasible votes, or *ballots*. The second component of any voting procedure is the way in which the votes are tallied to produce a winner (or winners if electing more than one candidate). We assume that the voting aggregation function will select exactly one winner, so ties are always broken[3]. Note that elements of the set $\mathcal{B}(\mathcal{O})^n$ represent votes cast by the agents. An element $\vec{v} \in \mathcal{B}(\mathcal{O})^n$ is called a *vote profile*. A tallying function $\mathrm{Ag}_v : \mathcal{B}(\mathcal{O})^n \to \mathcal{O}$ maps vote profiles to candidates.

Given agent i's preference P_i, let $S(v, P_i)$ mean that the vote v is a sincere vote corresponding to P_i. For example, in plurality voting, the only sincere vote is a vote for the maximally ranked candidate under P_i. By contrast, in approval voting, there could be many sincere votes, i.e., those votes where, if candidate o is approved, so is any higher ranking o'. Then $\mathcal{B}(\mathcal{O})_i = \{v | S(v, P_i)\}$ is the set of votes which faithfully represent i's preference. The voter i is said to *strategize* if i selects a vote v that is not in the set $\mathcal{B}(\mathcal{O})_i$.

In what follows we assume that when an agent votes, the agent is selecting a preference in the set **Pref** instead of an element of $\mathcal{B}(\mathcal{O})$. A vote is a preference; a vote profile is a *vector* of preferences, denoted by $\vec{P}$.[4]

Assume that the agents' true preferences are $\vec{P}^* = (P_1^*, \ldots, P_n^*)$ and *fixed* for the remaining discussion. Given a profile $\vec{P}$ of *actual* votes, we ask whether agent i will change its vote if given another chance to express its preference. Let $\vec{P}_{-i}$ be the vector of all *other* agents' preferences. Then given $\vec{P}_{-i}$ and i's true preference P_i^*, there will be a (nonempty) set X_i of those preferences that are i's best response to $\vec{P}_{-i}$. Suppose that $f_i(\vec{P}_{-i})$ selects one such best response from X_i.[5] Then $f(\vec{P}) = (f_1(\vec{P}_{-1}), \ldots, f_n(\vec{P}_{-n}))$. We call f a *strategizing* function. If $\vec{P}$ is a fixed point of f (i.e., $f(\vec{P}) = \vec{P}$), then $\vec{P}$ is a *stable* outcome. In other words, such a fixed point $\vec{P}$ of f is a Nash equilibrium. We define f^n recursively by $f^1(\vec{P}) = f(\vec{P})$, $f^n = f(f^{n-1}(\vec{P}))$, and say that f is **stable at level** n if $f^n(\vec{P})) = f^{n-1}(\vec{P})$. It is clear that if f is stable at level n, then f is stable at all levels m where $m \geq n$. Also, if the initial preference of the $\vec{P}$ is a fixed point of f then all levels are stable.

Putting everything together, we can now define a voting model.

Definition 2 (Voting Model). *Given a set of agents $\mathcal{A}$, candidates $\mathcal{O}$, a* **voting model** *is a 5-tuple $\langle \mathcal{A}, \mathcal{O}, \{P_i^*\}_{i \in \mathcal{A}}, \mathrm{Ag}, f \rangle$, where P_i^* is voter i's true pref-*

---

[3] [2] shows that the Gibbard-Satterthwaite theorem holds when ties are permitted.

[4] This does not quite work for approval voting where P does not fully determine the sincere vote v, but we will ignore this issue here, as it does not apply in the case of plurality elections, whether of one, or of many 'winners'.

[5] Note that P_i may itself be a member of X_i in which case we shall assume that $f(P_i) = P_i$.

erence; Ag *is an aggregation function with domain and range as defined above;*
f is a strategizing function.

Note that in our definition above, we use aggregation functions rather than
tallying functions (which pick a winning candidate). This is because we can
view tallying functions as selecting a 'winner' from the output of an aggregation
function. So in our model, the result of an election is a *ranking* of the candidates.
This allows our results to apply not only to conventional plurality voting, but
also to those situations where more than one candidate is to be elected. They
require some modification to apply to approval voting, as the ballot is not then
determined by the preference ordering but also needs a cut-off point between
approved and 'dis-approved' candidates.

The following example demonstrates the type of analysis that can be modeled
using a strategizing function.

Example 1. Suppose that there are four candidates $\mathcal{O} = \{o_1, o_2, o_3, o_4\}$ and five
groups of voters: A, B, C, D and E. Suppose that the sizes of the groups are
given as follows: $|A| = 40$, $|B| = 30$, $|C| = 15$, $|D| = 8$ and $|E| = 7$. We assume
that all the agents in each group have the same true preference and that they
all vote the same way. Suppose that the tallying function is plurality vote. We
give the agents' true preferences and the summary of the four elections in the
table below. The winner in each round is in boldface.

$$P_A^* = (o_1, o_4, o_2, o_3)$$
$$P_B^* = (o_2, o_1, o_3, o_4)$$
$$P_C^* = (o_3, o_2, o_4, o_1)$$
$$P_D^* = (o_4, o_1, o_2, o_3)$$
$$P_E^* = (o_3, o_1, o_2, o_4)$$

Size	Group	I	II	III	IV
40	A	$\mathbf{o_1}$	o_1	o_4	$\mathbf{o_1}$
30	B	o_2	$\mathbf{o_2}$	$\mathbf{o_2}$	o_2
15	C	o_3	$\mathbf{o_2}$	$\mathbf{o_2}$	o_2
8	D	o_4	o_4	o_1	o_4
7	E	o_3	o_3	o_1	$\mathbf{o_1}$

The above table can be justified by assuming that all agents use the following
protocol. If the current winner is o, then agent i will switch its vote to some
candidate o' provided 1) i prefers o' to o, and 2) the current total for o' plus
agent i's votes for o' is greater than the current total for o. By this protocol
an agent (thinking only one step ahead) will only switch its vote to a candidate
which is currently not the winner.

In round I, everyone reports their top choice and o_1 is the winner. C likes o_2
better than o_1 and its own total plus B's votes for o_2 exceed the current votes
for o_1. Hence by the protocol, C will change its vote to o_2. A will not change its
vote in round II since its top choice is the winner. D and E also remain fixed
since they do not have an alternative like o' required by the protocol. In round
III, group A changes its vote to o_4 since it is preferred to the current winner
(o_2) and its own votes plus D's current votes for o_4 exceed the current votes
for o_2. B and C do not change their votes. For B's top choice o_2 is the current
winner and as for C, they have no o' better than o_2 which satisfies condition 2).

Ironically, Group D and E change their votes to o_1 since it is prefered to the current winner is o_2 and group A is currently voting for o_1. Finally, in round IV, group A notices that E is voting for o_1 which A prefers to o_4 and so changes its votes back to o_1. The situation stabilizes with o_1 which, as it happens, is also the Condorcet winner.

Much more can be said about the above analysis, but this is a topic for a different paper. We now point out that for every aggregation function Ag and any strategizing f, there *must* be instances in which f never stabilizes:

Theorem 1. *For any given tallying function* Ag_v, *there exists an initial vector of preferences such that* f *never stablizes.*

This follows easily from the Gibbard-Satterthwaite theorem. Suppose not, then we show that there is a strategy-proof tallying function contradicting the Gibbard-Satterthwaite theorem. Suppose that Ag_v is an arbitrary tallying function and $\vec{P}^*$ the vector of true preferences. Suppose there always is a level k at which f stabilizes given the agents' true preferences $\vec{P}^*$. But then define Ag' to be the outcome of applying Ag_v to $f^k(\vec{P}^*)$ where $\vec{P}^*$ are the agents' true preferences. Then given some obvious conditions on the strategizing function f, Ag' will be a strategy-proof tallying function contradicting the Gibbard-Satterthwaite theorem. Hence there *must be* situations in which f never stabilizes.

Since our candidate and agent sets are finite, if f does not stabilize then f **cycles**. We say that f has a cycle of length n if there are n different votes $\vec{P}_1, \ldots \vec{P}_n$ such that $f(\vec{P}_i) = \vec{P}_{i+1}$ for all $1 \leq i \leq n-1$ and $f(\vec{P}_n) = \vec{P}_1$.

3   Dependency on Knowledge

Suppose that agent i knows the preferences of the other agents, and that no other agent knows agent i's preference (and agent i knows *this*). Then i is in a very privileged position, where its preferences are completely secret, but it knows it can strategize using the preferences of the other agents. In this case, i will always know *when* to strategize and when the new outcome is 'better' than the current outcome. But if i only knows the preferences of a certain subset B of the set $\mathcal{A}$ of agents, then there still may be a set of possible outcomes that it could force. Since i only knows the preferences of the agents in the set B, any strategy P will generate a set of possible outcomes. Suppose that there are two strategies P and P' that agent i is choosing between. Then the agent is choosing between two different sets of possible outcomes. Some agents may only choose to strategize if they are *guaranteed* a better outcome. Other agents may strategize if there is even a small chance of getting a better outcome and no chance of getting a worse outcome. We will keep this process of choosing a strategy abstract, and only assume that every agent will in fact choose one of the strategies available to it. Let S_i be agent i's strategy choice function, which accepts the votes of a group of agents and returns a preference P that may result in a better outcome for agent i given the agents report their current preference. We will assume that if $B = \emptyset$ then S_i picks P_i^*. That is, agents will vote according to their true preferences unless there is more information.

As voting takes place or polls reveal potential voting patterns, the facts that each agent knows will change. We assume that certain agents may be in a more privileged position than other agents. As in [14], define a **knowledge graph** to be any graph with $\mathcal{A}$ as its set of vertices. If there is an edge from i to j, then we assume that agent i knows agent j's current vote, i.e., how agent j voted in the current election. Let $\mathcal{K} = (\mathcal{A}, E_{\mathcal{K}})$ be a knowledge graph ($E_{\mathcal{K}}$ is the set of edges of $\mathcal{K}$). We assume that $i \in \mathcal{A}$ knows the current votes of all agents accessible from i. Let $B_i = \{j \mid$ there is an edge from i to j in $\mathcal{K}\}$. Then S_i will select the strategy that agent i would prefer given how agents in B_i voted currently.

We clarify the relationship between a knowledge graph and the existence of a cycle in the knowledge graph $\mathcal{K} = (\mathcal{A}, E_{\mathcal{K}})$ by the following:

Theorem 2. *Fix a voting model $\langle \mathcal{A}, \mathcal{O}, \{P_i^*\}_{i \in \mathcal{A}}, \mathrm{Ag}, f \rangle$ and a knowledge graph $\mathcal{K} = (\mathcal{A}, E_{\mathcal{K}})$. If $\mathcal{K}$ is directed and acyclic then the strategizing function f will stabilize at level k, where k is the height of the graph $\mathcal{K}$; f can cycle only if the associated knowledge graph has a cycle.*

Proof. Since $\mathcal{K}$ is a directed acyclic graph, there is at least one agent i such that $B_i = \emptyset$. By assumption such an agent will vote according to P_i^* at every stage. Let

$$A_0 = \{i \mid i \in \mathcal{A} \text{ and } B_i = \emptyset\}$$

and

$$A_k = \{i \mid \text{ if there is } (i,j) \in E_{\mathcal{K}}, \text{then } j \in A_l \text{ for } l < k\}$$

Given (by induction on k) that the agents in A_{k-1} stabilized by level $k - 1$, an agent $i \in A_k$ need only wait $k - 1$ rounds, then choose the strategy according to S_i. □

The following is an example of a situation in which the associated strategizing function never stabilizes:

Example 2. Consider three candidates $\{a, b, c\}$ and 100 agents connected by a complete knowledge graph. Suppose that 40 agents prefer $a > b > c$ (group I), 30 prefer $b > c > a$ (group II) and 30 prefer $c > a > b$ (group III). If we assume that the voting rule is simple majority, then after reporting their initial preferences, candidate a will be the winner with 40 votes. The members of group II dislike a the most, and will strategize in the next election by reporting $c > b > a$ as their preference. So, in the second round, c will win. But now, members of group I will report $b > a > c$ as their preference, in an attempt to draw support away from their lowest ranked candidate. c will still win the third election, but by changing their preferences (and making them public) group I sends a signal to group II that it should report its true preference - this will enable group I to have its second preferred candidate b come out winner. This cycling will continue indefinitely; b will win for two rounds, then a for two rounds, then c for two, etc.

4   An Epistemic Logic for Voting Models

In this section we define an epistemic logic for reasoning about voting models. In Example 2, it is clear that voters are reasoning about the states of knowledge of other voters and furthermore, an agent reasons about the change in states of knowledge of other voters on receipt of information on votes cast by them. We now sketch the details of a logic $\mathcal{KV}$ for reasoning about knowledge and the change of knowledge in a fixed voting model $\mathcal{V}$.

4.1   The Logic $\mathcal{KV}$ - Syntax

In this section we will assume that each vote is an expressed preference, which may or not be the true preference of an agent. So the expression 'preference' without the qualifier 'true' will simply mean an agent's current vote. We assume that for each preference P there is a symbol P that represents it. There are then two types of primitive propositions in $\mathcal{L}(\mathcal{KV})$. First, there are statements with the content "agent i's preference is P". Let P_i represent such statements. Secondly, we include statements with the content "P is the current outcome of the aggregation function". Let P_O represent such statements.

Our language includes the standard boolean connectives, an epistemic modality K_i indexed by each agent i plus an additional modality $\Diamond_i$ (similarly indexed). Formulas in $\mathcal{L}(\mathcal{KV})$ take the following syntactic form:

$$\phi := p \mid \neg\phi \mid \phi \wedge \psi \mid K_i\phi \mid \Diamond_i\phi$$

where p is a primitive proposition, $i \in \mathcal{A}$. We use the standard definitions for $\vee, \rightarrow$ and the duals $L_i, \Box_i$. $K_i\phi$ is read as "agent i knows ϕ; $\Diamond_i\phi$ is read as "after agent i strategizes, ϕ becomes true".

4.2   The Logic $\mathcal{KV}$ - Semantics

Before specifying a semantics we make some brief remarks on comparing preferences. Strategizing means reporting a preference different from your true preference. An agent will strategize if by reporting a preference other than its true preference, the outcome is 'closer' to its true preference than the outcome it would have obtained had it reported its true preference originally. Given preferences P, Q, R, we use the notation $P \sqsubseteq_R Q$ to indicate that P is at least as compatible with R as Q is. Given the above ternary relation, we can be more precise about when an agent will strategize. Given two preferences P and Q, we will say that an agent whose true preference is R prefers P to Q if $P \sqsubseteq_R Q$ holds. That is, i prefers P to Q if P is at least as 'close' to i's true preference as Q is.

We assume the following conditions on $\sqsubseteq$. For arbitrary preferences P, Q, R, S:

1. (Minimality) $R \sqsubseteq_R P$
2. (Reflexivity) $P \sqsubseteq_R P$

3. (Transitivity) If $P \sqsubseteq_R Q$ and $Q \sqsubseteq_R S$, then $P \sqsubseteq_R S$.
4. (Pareto Invariance) Suppose that $R = (o_1, \ldots, o_m)$ and $P = (o'_1, \ldots, o'_m)$ and Q is obtained from P by swapping o'_i and o'_j for some $i \neq j$. If $R(o'_i, o'_j)$ and $P(o'_i, o'_j)$, i.e., R agrees with P on o'_i, o'_j and disagrees with Q, then P must be at least as close to R as Q ($P \sqsubseteq_R Q$).

(Minimality) ensures that a true preference is always the most desired outcome. (Reflexivity) and (Transitivity) carry their usual meanings. As for Pareto invariance, note that swapping o'_i, o'_j may also change other relationships. Our example below will show that this is not a problem.

The following is an example of an ordering $\sqsubseteq_R$ satisfying the above conditions. Let $R = (o_1, \ldots, o_m)$. For each vector P, suppose that $c_P(o_i)$ is the count of o_i in vector P, i.e., the numeric position of o_i numbering from the right. For any vector P, let $V_R(P) = c_R(o_1)c_P(o_1) + \cdots + c_R(o_m)c_P(o_m)$. This assigns the following value to R, $V_R(R) = m^2 + (m-1)^2 + \cdots + 1^2$. We say that P is closer to R than Q iff $V_R(P)$ is greater than $V_R(Q)$. This creates a strict ordering over preferences, which can be weakened to a partial order by composing V_R with a weakly increasing function.[6]

Let $\mathcal{V} = \langle \mathcal{A}, \mathcal{O}, \{P_i^*\}_{i \in \mathcal{A}}, \mathrm{Ag}, f \rangle$ be a fixed voting model. We define a Kripke structure for our bi-modal language based on $\mathcal{V}$. States in this structure are vectors of preferences[7] together with the outcome of the aggregation function. The set of states W is defined as follows:

$$W = \{(\vec{P}, O) \mid \vec{P} \in \mathbf{Pref}^n, \ \mathrm{Ag}(\vec{P}) = O\}$$

Intuitively, given a state $(\vec{P}, O)$, $\vec{P}$ represents the preferences that are reported by the agents and O is the outcome of the aggregation function applied to $\vec{P}$. So states of the world will be complete descriptions of stages of elections.

Our semantics helps clarify our decision to use two modalities. Let $(\vec{P}, O)$ be an element of W. To understand the strategizing modality, note that when an agent strategizes it only changes the ith component of $\vec{P}$, i.e., the accessible worlds for this modality are those in which the remaining components of $\vec{P}$ are fixed. For the knowledge modality note that all agents know how they voted, which implies that accessible worlds for this modality are those in which the ith component of $\vec{P}$ remains fixed while others vary.

We now define accessibility relations for each modality. Since the second component of a state can be calculated using Ag we write $\vec{P}$ for $(\vec{P}, O)$. For the knowledge modality, we assume that the agents know how they voted and so define for each $i \in \mathcal{A}$ and preferences $\vec{P}, \vec{Q}$:

$$(\vec{P}, O)R_i(\vec{Q}, O') \quad \text{iff} \quad P_i = Q_i$$

The above relation does not take into account the fact that some agents may be in a more privileged position than other agents, formally represented by the

---

[6] Plurality cannot be produced this way, but other functions satisfying 1–4 can easily be found that do.

[7] Defining Kripke structures over agents' preferences has been studied by other authors. [18] has a similar semantics in a different context.

knowledge graph from the previous section. If we have fixed a knowledge graph, then agent i not only knows how it itself voted, but also the (current) preferences of each of the agents reachable from it in the knowledge graph. Let $\mathcal{K} = (\mathcal{A}, E_{\mathcal{K}})$ be a knowledge graph, and recall that B_i is the set of nodes reachable from i. Given two vectors of preferences $\vec{P}$ and $\vec{Q}$ and a group of agents $G \subseteq \mathcal{A}$, we say $P_G = Q_G$ iff $P_i = Q_i$ for each $i \in G$. We can now define an epistemic relation based on $\mathcal{K}$:

$$(\vec{P}, O) R_i^{\mathcal{K}} (\vec{Q}, O') \quad \text{iff} \quad P_i = Q_i \text{ and } P_{B_i} = Q_{B_i}$$

Clearly for each agent i and knowledge graph $\mathcal{K}$, $R_i^{\mathcal{K}}$ is an equivalence relation; hence each K_i is an **S5** modal operator. The exact logic for the strategizing modalities depends on the properties of the ternary relation $\sqsubseteq$.

For the strategizing modalities, we define a relation $A_i \subseteq W \times W$ as follows. Given preferences $\vec{P}, \vec{Q}$:

$$(\vec{P}, O) A_i (\vec{Q}, O') \quad \text{iff} \quad P_{-i} = Q_{-i} \text{ and } O' \sqsubseteq_{P_i^*} O$$

where P_{-i} is all components of $\vec{P}$ except for the ith component. So, $(\vec{P}, O)$ and $(\vec{Q}, O')$ are A_i related iff they have the same jth component for all $j \neq i$ and agent i prefers outcome O' to outcome O relative to i's true preference P_i^*.

An **election** is a sequence of states. We say that an election $E = (s_1, s_2, \ldots, s_n)$ *respects* the strategizing function f if $f(s_i) = s_{i+1}$ for $i = 1, \ldots, n - 1$. We assume always that f is such that $f(s) = s$ unless the agent *knows* that it can strategize and get a better outcome, and *how* it should so strategize. A model for $\mathcal{V}$ is a tuple $\mathbb{M} = \langle W, R_i, A_i, V \rangle$ where $V : W \to 2^{\Phi_0}$ (where Φ_0 is the set of primitive propositions). We assume that all relations R_i are based on a given knowledge graph $\mathcal{K}$. Let $(\vec{P}, O) \in W$ be any state; we define truth in a model as follows:

1. $(\vec{P}, O) \models p$ iff $p \in V(\vec{P}, O)$ and $p \in \Phi_0$
2. $(\vec{P}, O) \models \neg \phi$ iff $(\vec{P}, O) \not\models \phi$
3. $(\vec{P}, O) \models \phi \wedge \psi$ iff $(\vec{P}, O) \models \phi$ and $\vec{P} \models \psi$
4. $(\vec{P}, O) \models K_i \phi$ iff for all $(\vec{Q}, O')$ such that $(\vec{P}, O) R_i^{\mathcal{K}} (\vec{Q}, O')$, $(\vec{Q}, O') \models \phi$
5. $(\vec{P}, O) \models \Diamond_i \phi$ iff there is $(\vec{Q}, O')$ such that $(\vec{P}, O) A_i (\vec{Q}, O')$ and $(\vec{Q}, O') \models \phi$

Nothing in our definition of a model forces primitive propositions to have their intended meaning. We therefore make use of the following definition.

Definition 3. *A valuation function V is an* **appropriate valuation** *for a model $\mathbb{M}$ iff V satisfies the following conditions. Let $\mathcal{V} = \langle \mathcal{A}, \mathcal{O}, \{P_i^*\}_{i \in \mathcal{A}}, \mathrm{Ag}, f \rangle$ be a voting model and $\mathbb{M}$ a model based on $\mathcal{V}$. Let $(\vec{P}, O) \in W$ be any state. Then:*

1. *For each $i \in \mathcal{A}$, $\mathsf{P}_i \in V(\vec{P}, O)$ iff P represents the preference P_i.*
2. *For each P_O, $\mathsf{P}_O \in V(\vec{P}, O)$ iff P represents O.*

We assume that valuation functions are appropriate for the corresponding model.

The following formula implies strategizing for an individual agent. It says that agent i knows that the outcome is P_O and by reporting a different preference a preferred outcome can be achieved.

$$K_i(P_O \wedge \Diamond_i \top)$$

We are now in a position to present our last main result.

Theorem 3. *Given a voting system* $\mathcal{V} = \langle \mathcal{A}, \mathcal{O}, \{P_i^*\}_{i \in \mathcal{A}}, \mathrm{Ag}, f \rangle$, *a knowledge graph* $\mathcal{K}$ *and a model* $\mathbb{M}$ *for* $\mathcal{V}$, *let* E *be an election that respects the strategizing function* f. *If there is a state* $\vec{P}$ *such that* $E_l = \vec{P}$ *for some* l *and* $\vec{P} \models \neg K_i(P_O \wedge \Diamond_i \top)$ *for all* i, *then* $\vec{P}$ *is a fixed point of* f. *Equivalently, Given an election* E *that respects* f *and some* k *such that* $E_{k+1} \neq E_k$, *i.e.,* E_k *is not a fixed point of* f, *then* $\exists i \in \mathcal{A}$ *such that:*

$$E_k \models K_i(P_O \wedge \Diamond_i \top)$$

That is, if an agent strategizes at some stage in the election then the agent knows that this strategizing will result in a preferred outcome.

5   Conclusion

We have explored some properties of strategic voting and noted that the Gibbard-Satterthwaite theorem only applies in those situations where agents can obtain the appropriate knowledge. Note that our example in the Introduction showed how strategizing can lead to a rational outcome in elections. In our example the Condorcet winner - the winner in pairwise head-to-head contests - was picked via strategizing. Since our framework makes it possible to view opinion polls as the $n-1$ stages of an n-stage election, it implies that communication of voters' preferences and the results of opinion polls can play an important role in ensuring rational outcomes to elections. A similar line of reasoning in a different context can be found in [15]. Put another way, while the Gibbard-Satterthwaite theorem implies that we are stuck with voting mechanisms susceptible to strategizing, our work indicates ways for voters to avoid irrational outcomes using such mechanisms. Connections such as those explored in this paper are also useful in deontic contexts [10,16] i.e., an agent can only be obligated to take some action if the agent is in possession of the requisite knowledge.

For future work, we note that in this study, we left the definition of the agents' strategy choice function informal, thus assuming that agents have some way of deciding which preference to report if given a choice. This can be made more formal. We could then study the different strategies available to the agents. For example, some agents may only choose to strategize if they are *guaranteed* to get a better outcome, whereas other agents might strategize even if there is only a small chance of getting a better outcome.

Another question suggested by this framework is: what are the effects of different levels of knowledge of the current preferences on individual strategy choices? Suppose that among agent i and agent j, both i and j's true preferences are common knowledge. Now when agent i is trying to decide whether or not to strategize, i knows that j will be able to simulate i's reasoning. Thus if i chooses a strategy based on j's true preference, i knows that j will choose a strategy based on i's choice of strategy, and so i must choose a strategy based on j's response to i's original strategy. We conjecture that if there is only pairwise common knowledge among the agents of the agents' true preferences, then the announcement of the agents' true preferences is a stable announcement.

On a technical note, the logic of knowledge we developed uses **S5** modalities. We would like to develop a logic that uses **KD45** modalities - i.e., a logic of belief. This is because beliefs raise the interesting issue that a voter - or groups of voters - can have possibly inconsistent beliefs about other voters' preferences, while this variation is not possible in the knowledge case. Another area of exploration will be connections with other distinct approaches to characterize game theoretic concepts in modal logic such as [8,3,18]. Lastly, a deeper formal understanding of the relationship between the knowledge and strategizing modalities introduced in this paper will become possible after the provision of an appropriate axiom system for $\mathcal{KV}$. Our work is a first step towards clarifying the knowledge-theoretic properties of voting, but some insight into the importance of states of knowledge and the role of opinion polls is already at hand.

References

1. K. J. Arrow. *Social choice and individual values (2nd ed.)*. Wiley, New York, 1963.
2. Jean-Pierre Benoit. Strategic manipulation in games when lotteries and ties are permitted. *Journal of Economic Theory*, 102:421–436, 2002.
3. Giacomo Bonanno. Modal logic and game theory: two alternative approaches. *Risk Decision and Policy*, 7:309–324, 2002.
4. Steven J. Brams. Voting Procedures. In *Handbook of Game Theory*, volume 2, pages 1055–1089. Elsevier, 1994.
5. Steven J. Brams and Peter C. Fishburn. Voting Procedures. In *Handbook of Social Choice and Welfare*. North-Holland, 1994.
6. Patricia Everaere, Sebastien Konieczny, and Pierre Marquis. On merging strategy-proofness. In *Proceedings of KR 2004*. Morgan-Kaufmann, 2004.
7. Allan Gibbard. Manipulation of Voting Schemes: A General Result. *Econometrica*, 41(4):587–601, 1973.
8. Paul Harrenstein, Wiebe van der Hoek, John-Jules Meyer, and Cees Witteveen. A modal characterization of nash equilibira. *Fundamenta Informaticae*, 57(2-4):281–321, 2002.
9. Sébastien Konieczny and Ramón Pino-Pérez. On the logic of merging. In A. G. Cohn, L. Schubert, and S. C. Shapiro, editors, *Principles of Knowledge Representation and Reasoning: Proceedings of the Sixth International Conference (KR '98)*, pages 488–498, San Francisco, California, 1998. Morgan Kaufmann.
10. Alessio Lomuscio and Marek Sergot. Deontic interpreted systems. *Studia Logica*, 75, 2003.

11. Pedrito Maynard-Zhang and Daniel Lehmann. Representing and aggregating conflicting beliefs. *Journal of Artificial Intelligence*, 19:155–203, 2003.
12. Pedrito Maynard-Zhang and Yoav Shoham. Belief fusion: Aggregating pedigreed belief states. *Journal of Logic, Language and Information*, 10(2):183–209, 2001.
13. Thomas Meyer, Aditya Ghose, and Samir Chopra. Social choice theory, merging and elections. In *Proceedings of Sixth European Conference on Symbolic and Quantitative Approaches to Reasoning with Uncertainty, ECSQARU-2001*. Springer-Verlag, 2001.
14. Eric Pacuit and Rohit Parikh. A logic of communication graphs. In *Proceedings of DALT-04*. Springer-Verlag, 2004.
15. Rohit Parikh. Social software. *Synthese*, 132, 2002.
16. Rohit Parikh, Eric Pacuit, and Eva Cogan. The logic of knowledge based obligations. In *Proceedings of DALT-2004*. Springer Verlag, 2004.
17. Mark Satterthwaite. *The Existence of a Strategy Proof Voting Procedure: a Topic in Social Choice Theory*. PhD thesis, University of Wisconsin, 1973.
18. J. van Benthem. Rational dynamics and epistemic logic in games. Technical report, ILLC, 2003.

The CIFF Proof Procedure for Abductive Logic Programming with Constraints

U. Endriss[1], P. Mancarella[2], F. Sadri[1], G. Terreni[2], and F. Toni[1,2]

[1] Department of Computing, Imperial College London
{ue,fs,ft}@doc.ic.ac.uk
[2] Dipartimento di Informatica, Università di Pisa
{paolo,terreni,toni}@di.unipi.it

Abstract. We introduce a new proof procedure for abductive logic programming and present two soundness results. Our procedure extends that of Fung and Kowalski by integrating abductive reasoning with constraint solving and by relaxing the restrictions on allowed inputs for which the procedure can operate correctly. An implementation of our proof procedure is available and has been applied successfully in the context of multiagent systems.

1 Introduction

Abduction has found broad application as a tool for hypothetical reasoning with incomplete knowledge, which can be handled by labelling some pieces of information as *abducibles*, i.e. as possible hypotheses that can be assumed to hold, provided that they are consistent with the given knowledge base. Abductive Logic Programming (ALP) combines abduction with logic programming enriched by *integrity constraints* to further restrict the range of possible hypotheses. Important applications of ALP include planning [10], requirements specification analysis [8], and agent communication [9]. In recent years, a variety of proof procedures for ALP have been proposed, including the IFF procedure of Fung and Kowalski [4]. Here, we extend this procedure in two ways, namely (1) by integrating abductive reasoning with constraint solving (in the sense of CLP, not to be confused with integrity constraints), and (2) by relaxing the *allowedness* conditions given in [4] to be able to handle a wider class of problems.

Our interest in extending IFF in this manner stems from applications developed in the SOCS project, which investigates the use of computational logic-based techniques in the context of multiagent systems for global computing. In particular, we use ALP extended with constraint solving to give computational models for an agent's *planning*, *reactivity* and *temporal reasoning* capabilities [5]. We found that our requirements for these applications go beyond available state-of-the-art ALP proof procedures. While ACLP [6], for instance, permits the use of constraint predicates (unlike IFF), its syntax for integrity constraints is too restrictive to express the planning knowledge bases (using a variant of the abductive event calculus [10]) used in SOCS. In addition, many procedures put strong, sometimes unnecessary, restrictions on the use of variables. The procedure proposed in this paper, which we call CIFF, manages to overcome these restrictions

J.J. Alferes and J. Leite (Eds.): JELIA 2004, LNAI 3229, pp. 31–43, 2004.

to a degree that has allowed us to apply it successfully to a wide range of problems. We have implemented CIFF in Prolog;[1] the system forms an integral part of the PROSOCS platform for programming agents in computational logic [11].

In the next section we are going to set out the ALP framework used in this paper and discuss the notion of allowedness. Section 3 then specifies the CIFF proof procedure which we propose as a suitable reasoning engine for this framework. Two soundness results for CIFF are presented in Section 4 and Section 5 concludes. An extended version of this paper that, in particular, contains detailed proofs of our results is available as a technical report [3].

2   Abductive Logic Programming with Constraints

We use classical first-order logic, enriched with a number of special predicate symbols with a fixed semantics, namely the equality symbol =, which is used to represent the unifiability of terms (i.e. as in standard logic programming), and a number of constraint predicates. We assume the availability of a sound and complete constraint solver for this constraint language. In principle, the exact specification of the constraint language is independent from the definition of the CIFF procedure, because we are going to use the constraint solver as a *black box* component.[2] However, the constraint language has to include a relation symbol for equality (we are going to write $t_1 =_c t_2$) and it must be closed under complements. In general, the complement of a constraint Con will be denoted as $\overline{Con}$ (but we are going to write $t_1 \neq_c t_2$ for the complement of $t_1 =_c t_2$). The range of admissible arguments to constraint predicates again depends on the specifics of the chosen constraint solver. A typical choice for a constraint system would be an arithmetic constraint solver over integers providing predicates such as $\leq$ and $>$ and allowing for terms constructed from variables, integers and function symbols representing operations such as addition and multiplication.

Abductive logic programs. An *abductive logic program* is a pair $\langle Th, IC \rangle$ consisting of a *theory Th* and a finite set of *integrity constraints IC*. We present theories as sets of so-called iff-definitions:

$$p(X_1, \ldots, X_k) \leftrightarrow D_1 \vee \cdots \vee D_n$$

The predicate symbol p must not be a *special* predicate (constraints, =, $\top$ and $\bot$) and there can be at most one iff-definition for every predicate symbol. Each of the disjuncts D_i is a conjunction of literals. Negative literals are written as implications (e.g. $q(X, Y) \rightarrow \bot$). The variables $X_1, \ldots, X_k$ are implicitly universally quantified with the scope being the entire definition. Any other variable is implicitly existentially quantified, with the scope being the disjunct in which it occurs. A theory may be regarded as the (selective) completion of a normal logic program (i.e. of a logic program allowing for negative subgoals in a rule) [2]. Any predicate that is neither defined nor special is called an *abducible*.

---

[1] The CIFF system is available at http://www.doc.ic.ac.uk/~ue/ciff/.

[2] Our implementation uses the built-in finite domain solver of Sicstus Prolog [1], but the modularity of the system would also support the integration of a different solver.

In this paper, the integrity constraints in the set IC (not to be confused with constraint predicates) are implications of the following form:

$$L_1 \wedge \cdots \wedge L_m \;\rightarrow\; A_1 \vee \cdots \vee A_n$$

Each of the L_i must be a literal (with negative literals again being written in implication form); each of the A_i must be an atom. Any variables are implicitly universally quantified with the scope being the entire implication.

A *query* Q is a conjunction of literals. Any variables in Q are implicitly existentially quantified. They are also called the *free* variables. In the context of the CIFF procedure, we are going to refer to a triple $\langle Th, IC, Q \rangle$ as an *input*.

Semantics. A theory provides definitions for certain predicates, while integrity constraints restrict the range of possible interpretations. A query may be regarded as an *observation* against the background of the world knowledge encoded in a given abductive logic program. An *answer* to such a query would then provide an *explanation* for this observation: it would specify which instances of the abducible predicates have to be assumed to hold for the observation to hold as well. In addition, such an explanation should also validate the integrity constraints. This is formalised in the following definition:

Definition 1 (Correct answer). *A correct answer to a query Q with respect to an abductive logic program $\langle Th, IC \rangle$ is a pair $\langle \Delta, \sigma \rangle$, where Δ is a finite set of ground abducible atoms and σ is a substitution for the free variables occurring in Q, such that $Th \cup Comp(\Delta) \models IC \wedge Q\sigma$.*

Here $\models$ is the usual consequence relation of first-oder logic with the restriction that constraint predicates have to be interpreted according to the semantics of the chosen constraint system and equalities evaluate to *true* whenever their two arguments are unifiable. $Comp(\Delta)$ stands for the *completion* of the set of abducibles in Δ, i.e. any ground atom not occurring in Δ is assumed to be *false*. If we have $Th \cup IC \models \neg Q$ (i.e. if Q is false for all instantiations of the free variables), then we say that there exists no correct answer to the query Q given the abductive logic program $\langle Th, IC \rangle$.

Example 1. Consider the following abductive logic program:

$$
\begin{aligned}
Th: \quad & p(T) \;\leftrightarrow\; q(X, T') \wedge T'{<}T \wedge T{<}8 \\
& q(X, T) \;\leftrightarrow\; X{=}a \wedge s(T) \\
IC: \quad & r(T) \;\rightarrow\; p(T)
\end{aligned}
$$

The set of abducible predicates is $\{r, s\}$. The query $r(6)$, for instance, should succeed; a possible *correct answer* would be the set $\{r(6), s(5)\}$, with an empty substitution. Intuitively, given the query $r(6)$, the integrity constraint in IC would fire and force the atom $p(6)$ to hold, which in turn requires $s(T')$ for some $T' < 6$ to be true (as can be seen by *unfolding* first $p(6)$ and then $q(X, T')$). □

Allowedness. Fung and Kowalski [4] require inputs $\langle Th, IC, Q \rangle$ to meet a number of so-called *allowedness conditions* to be able to guarantee the correct operation of their proof procedure. These conditions are designed to avoid constellations with particular (problematic) patterns of quantification. Unfortunately, it is difficult to formulate appropriate allowedness conditions that guarantee a correct execution of the proof procedure without imposing too many unnecessary restrictions. This is a well-known problem, which is further aggravated for languages that include constraint predicates. Our proposal is to tackle the issue of allowedness *dynamically*, i.e. at runtime, rather than adopting a static and overly strict set of conditions. In this paper, we are only going to impose the following *minimal allowedness conditions:*[3]

  - An integrity constraint $A \rightarrow B$ is allowed iff every variable in it also occurs in a positive literal within its antecedent A.
  - An iff-definition $p(X_1, \ldots, X_k) \leftrightarrow D_1 \vee \cdots \vee D_n$ is allowed iff every variable other than $X_1, \ldots, X_k$ occurring in a disjunct D_i also occurs inside a positive literal within the same D_i.

The crucial allowedness condition is that for integrity constraints: it ensures that, also after an application of the *negation rewriting* rule (which moves negative literals in the antecedent of an implication to its consequent), every variable occurring in the consequent of an implication is also present in its antecedent. The allowedness condition for iff-definitions merely allows us to maintain this property of implications when the *unfolding* rule (which, essentially, replaces a defined predicate with its definition) is applied to atoms in the antecedent of an implication. We do not need to impose any allowedness conditions on queries.

3   The CIFF Proof Procedure

We are now going to formally introduce the CIFF proof procedure. The *input* $\langle Th, IC, Q \rangle$ to the procedure consists of a theory Th, a set of integrity constraints IC, and a query Q. There are three possible *outputs:* (1) the procedure succeeds and indicates an answer to the query Q; (2) the procedure fails, thereby indicating that there is no answer; and (3) the procedure reports that computing an answer is not possible, because a critical part of the input is not allowed.

The CIFF procedure manipulates, essentially, a set of formulas that are either atoms or implications. The theory Th is kept in the background and is only used to *unfold* defined predicates as they are being encountered. In addition to atoms and implications the aforementioned set of formulas may contain disjunctions of atoms and implications to which the *splitting* rule may be applied, i.e. which give rise to different branches in the proof search tree. The sets of formulas manipulated by the procedure are called *nodes*. A node is a set (representing a conjunction)[4] of formulas (atoms, implications, or disjunctions thereof) which

---

[3] Note that the CIFF procedure could easily be adapted to work also on inputs not conforming even to these minimal conditions, but then it would not be possible anymore to represent quantification implicitly.

[4] If a proof rule introduces a conjunction into a node, this conjunction is understood to be broken up into its subformulas right away.

are called *goals*. A proof is initialised with the node containing the integrity constraints *IC* and the literals of the query *Q*. The proof procedure then repeatedly manipulates the current node of goals by rewriting goals in the node, adding new goals to it, or deleting superfluous goals from it. Most of this section is concerned with specifying these *proof rules* in detail.

The structure of our proof rules guarantee that the following *quantification invariants* hold for every node in a derivation:

- No implication contains a universally quantified variable that is not also contained in one of the positive literals in its antecedent.
- No atom contains a universally quantified variable.
- No atom inside a disjunction contains a universally quantified variable.

In particular, these invariants subsume the *minimal allowedness conditions* discussed in the previous section. The invariants also allow us to keep quantification implicit throughout a CIFF derivation by determining the quantification status of any given variable. Most importantly, any variable occurring in either the original query or an atomic conjunct in a node must be existentially quantified.

Notation. In the sequel, we are frequently going to write $\vec{t}$ for a "vector" of terms such as $t_1, \ldots, t_k$. For instance, we are going to write $p(\vec{t})$ rather than $p(t_1, \ldots, t_k)$. To simplify presentation, we assume that there are no two predicates that have the same name but different arities. We are also going to write $\vec{t} = \vec{s}$ as a shorthand for $t_1 = s_1 \wedge \cdots \wedge t_k = s_k$ (with the implicit assumption that the two vectors have the same length), and $[\vec{X}/\vec{t}]$ for the substitution $[X_1/t_1, \ldots, X_k/t_k]$. Note that X and Y always represent variables. Furthermore, in our presentation of proof rules, we are going to abstract from the order of conjuncts in the antecedent of an implication: the critical subformula is always represented as the first conjunct. That is, by using a pattern such as $X = t \wedge A \rightarrow B$ we are referring to any implication with an antecedent that has a conjunct of the form $X = t$. A represents the remaining conjunction, which may also be "empty", that is, the formula $X = t \rightarrow B$ is a special case of the general pattern $X = t \wedge A \rightarrow B$. In this case, the residue $A \rightarrow B$ represents the formula B.

Proof rules. For each of the proof rules in our system, we specify the type of formula(s) which may trigger the rule (*"given"*), a number of side *conditions* that need to be met, and the required *action* (such as replacing the given formula by a different one). Executing this action yields one or more successor nodes and the current node can be discarded. The first rule replaces a defined predicate occurring as an atom in the node by its defining disjunction:

Unfolding atoms

Given: $p(\vec{t})$
Cond.: $[p(\vec{X}) \leftrightarrow D_1 \vee \cdots \vee D_n] \in Th$
Action: replace by $(D_1 \vee \cdots \vee D_n)[\vec{X}/\vec{t}]$

Note that any variables in $D_1 \vee \cdots \vee D_n$ other than those in $\vec{X}$ are existentially quantified with respect to the definition, i.e. they must be new to the node and they will be existentially quantified in the successor node.

Unfolding predicates in the antecedent of an implication yields one new implication for every disjunct in the defining disjunction:

Unfolding within implications

Given: $p(\vec{t}) \wedge A \rightarrow B$

Cond.: $[p(\vec{X}) \leftrightarrow D_1 \vee \cdots \vee D_n] \in Th$

Action: replace by $D_1[\vec{X}/\vec{t}] \wedge A \rightarrow B, \ldots, D_n[\vec{X}/\vec{t}] \wedge A \rightarrow B$

Observe that variables in any of the D_i that have been existentially quantified in the definition of $p(\vec{t})$ are going to be universally quantified in the corresponding new implication (because they appear within the antecedent).

The next rule is the *propagation* rule, which allows us to resolve an atom in the antecedent of an implication with a matching atom in the node. Unlike most rules, this rule does not *replace* a given formula, but it merely *adds* a new one. This is why we require explicitly that propagation cannot be applied again to the same pair of formulas. Otherwise the procedure would be bound to loop.

Propagation

Given: $p(\vec{t}) \wedge A \rightarrow B$ and $p(\vec{s})$

Cond.: the rule has not yet been applied to this pair of formulas

Action: add $\vec{t} = \vec{s} \wedge A \rightarrow B$

The *splitting* rule gives rise to (not just a single but) a whole set of successor nodes, one for each of the disjuncts in $A_1 \vee \cdots \vee A_n$, each of which gives rise to a different branch in the derivation:

Splitting

Given: $A_1 \vee \cdots \vee A_n$

Cond.: none

Action: replace by one of $A_1, \ldots, A_n$

The next rule is a logical simplification that moves negative literals in the antecedent to the consequent of an implication:

Negation rewriting

Given: $(A \rightarrow \bot) \wedge B \rightarrow C$

Cond.: none

Action: replace by $B \rightarrow A \vee C$

There are two further logical simplification rules:

Logical simplification (trivial condition)

Given: $\top \wedge A \rightarrow B$

Cond.: none

Action: replace by $A \rightarrow B$

Logical simplification (redundant formulas)

Given: either $\bot \rightarrow A$ or $\top$

Cond.: none

Action: delete formula

The following *factoring* rule can be used to separate cases in which particular abducible atoms unify from those in which they do not:

Factoring

Given: $p(\vec{t})$ and $p(\vec{s})$

Cond.: p abducible; the rule has not yet been applied to $p(\vec{t})$ and $p(\vec{s})$

Action: replace by $[p(\vec{t}) \wedge p(\vec{s}) \wedge (\vec{t} = \vec{s} \rightarrow \bot)] \vee [p(\vec{t}) \wedge \vec{t} = \vec{s}]$

The next few rules deal with equalities. The first two of these involve simplifying equalities according to the following rewrite rules:

(1) Replace $f(t_1, \ldots, t_k) = f(s_1, \ldots, s_k)$ by $t_1 = s_1 \wedge \cdots \wedge t_k = s_k$.
(2) Replace $f(t_1, \ldots, t_k) = g(s_1, \ldots, s_l)$ by $\bot$ if f and g are distinct or $k \neq l$.
(3) Replace $t = t$ by $\top$.
(4) Replace $X = t$ by $\bot$ if t contains X.
(5) Replace $t = X$ by $X = t$ if X is a variable and t is not.
(6) Replace $Y = X$ by $X = Y$ if X is a univ. quant. variable and Y is not.
(7) Replace $Y = X$ by $X = Y$ if X and Y are exist. quant. variables and X occurs in a constraint predicate, but Y does not.

Rules (1)–(4) essentially implement the term reduction part of the unification algorithm of Martelli and Montanari [7]. Rules (5)–(7) ensure that completely rewritten equalities are always presented in a normal form, thereby simplifying the formulation of our proof rules.

Equality rewriting for atoms

Given: $t_1 = t_2$

Cond.: the rule has not yet been applied to this equality

Action: replace by the result of rewriting $t_1 = t_2$

Equality rewriting for implications

Given: $t_1 = t_2 \wedge A \rightarrow B$

Cond.: the rule has not yet been applied to this equality

Action: replace by $C \wedge A \rightarrow B$ where C is the result of rewriting $t_1 = t_2$

The following two *substitution rules* also handle equalities:

Substitution rule for atoms

Given: $X = t$

Cond.: $X \notin t$; the rule has not yet been applied to this equality

Action: apply substitution $[X/t]$ to entire node except $X = t$ itself

Substitution rule for implications

Given: $X = t \wedge A \rightarrow B$

Cond.: X univ. quant.; $X \notin t$; t contains no univ. quant. variables *or* $X \notin B$

Action: replace by $(A \rightarrow B)[X/t]$

The purpose of the third side condition (of t not containing any universally quantified variables or X not occurring within B) is to maintain the quantification invariant that any universally quantified variable in the consequent of an implication is also present in the antecedent of the same implication.

    If neither *equality rewriting* nor a *substitution rule* are applicable, then an equality may give rise to a *case analysis*:

Case analysis for equalities

Given: $X = t \wedge A \rightarrow B$ (exception: do not apply to $X = t \rightarrow \perp$)
Cond.: X exist. quant.; $X \notin t$; t is not a univ. quant. variable
Action: replace by $X = t$ and $A \rightarrow B$, or replace by $X = t \rightarrow \perp$

Case analysis should not be applied to formulas of the form $X = t \rightarrow \perp$ (despite this being an instance of the pattern $X = t \wedge A \rightarrow B$), because this would lead to a loop (with respect to the second successor node). Also note that, if the third of the above side conditions was not fulfilled and if t was a universally quantified variable, then *equality rewriting* could be applied to obtain $t = X \wedge A \rightarrow B$, to which we could then apply the *substitution rule for implications*.

Observe that the above rule gives rise to two successor nodes (rather than a disjunction). This is necessary, because the term t may contain variables that would be quantified differently on the two branches, i.e. a new formula with a disjunction in the matrix would not (necessarily) be logically equivalent to the disjunction of the two (quantified) subformulas. In particular, in the first successor node all variables in t will become existentially quantified. To see this, consider the example of the implication $X = f(Y) \wedge A \rightarrow B$ and assume X is existentially quantified, while Y is universally quantified. We can distinguish two cases: (1) either X represents a term whose main functor is f, or (2) this is not the case. In case (1), there *exists* a value for Y such that $X = f(Y)$, and furthermore $A \rightarrow B$ must hold. Otherwise, i.e. in case (2), $X = f(Y)$ will be false for *all* values of Y.

Case analysis for constraints

Given: $Con \wedge A \rightarrow B$
Cond.: Con is a constraint predicate without univ. quant. variables
Action: replace by $[Con \wedge (A \rightarrow B)] \vee \overline{Con}$

Observe that the conditions on quantification are a little stricter for *case analysis for constraints* than they were for *case analysis for equalities*. Now all variables involved need to be existentially quantified. This simplifies the presentation of the rule a little, because no variables change quantification. In particular, we can replace the implication in question by a disjunction (to which the splitting rule may be applied in a subsequent step).

While case analysis is used to separate constraints from other predicates, the next rule provides the actual *constraint solving* step itself. It may be applied to any set of constraints in a node, but to guarantee soundness, eventually, it has to be applied to the set of *all* constraint atoms.

Constraint solving

Given: constraint predicates $Con_1, \ldots, Con_n$
Cond.: $\{Con_1, \ldots, Con_n\}$ is not satisfiable
Action: replace by $\perp$

If $\{Con_1, \ldots, Con_n\}$ is found to be satisfiable it may also be replaced with an equivalent but simplified set (in case the constraint solver used offers this feature). To simplify presentation, we assume that the constraint solver will fail (rather than come back with an undefined answer) whenever it is presented with an ill-defined constraint such as, say, $bob \leq 5$ (in the case of an arithmetic solver). For inputs that are "well-typed", however, such a situation will never arise.

Our next two rules ensure that (dis)equalities that affect the satisfiability of the constraints in a node are correctly rewritten using the appropriate constraint predicates. Here we refer to a variable as a *constraint variable* (with respect to a particular node) iff that variable occurs inside a constraint atom in that node. For the purpose of stating the next two rules in a concise manner, we call a term *c-atomic* iff it is either a variable or a ground element of the constraint domain (e.g. an integer in the case of an arithmetic domain).

Equality-constraint rewriting

Given: $X = t$

Cond.: X is a constraint variable

Action: replace by $X =_c t$ if t is c-atomic; replace by $\perp$ otherwise

---

Disequality-constraint rewriting

Given: $X = t \rightarrow \perp$

Cond.: X is a constraint variable

Action: replace by $X \neq_c t$ if t is c-atomic; delete formula otherwise

---

For example, if we are working with an arithmetic constraint domain, then the formula $X = bob \rightarrow \perp$ would be deleted from the node as it holds vacuously whenever X also occurs within a constraint predicate.

We call a formula of the form $t_1 = t_2 \rightarrow \perp$ a *disequality* provided no universally quantified variables occur in either t_1 or t_2. The next rule is used to identify nodes containing formulas with problematic quantification, which could cause difficulties in extracting an abductive answer:

Dynamic allowedness rule (DAR)

Given: $A \rightarrow B$ (exception: do not apply to disequalities)

Cond.: A consists of equalities and constraints alone; no other rule applies

Action: label node as *undefined*

In view of the second side condition, recall that the only rules applicable to an implication with only equalities and constraints in the antecedent are the equality rewriting and substitution rules for implications and the two case analysis rules.

Answer extraction. A node containing $\perp$ is called a *failure node*. If all branches in a derivation terminate with failure nodes, then the derivation is said to fail (the intuition being that there exists no answer to the query). A node to which no more rules can be applied is called a *final node*. A final node that is not a failure node and that has not been labelled as *undefined* is called a *success node*.

Definition 2 (Extracted answer). *An extracted answer for a final success node N is a triple $\langle \Delta, \Phi, \Gamma \rangle$, where Δ is the set of abducible atoms, Φ is the set of equalities and disequalities, and Γ is the set of constraint atoms in N.*

An *extracted* answer in itself is not yet a *correct* answer in the sense of Definition 1, but —as we shall see— it does *induce* such a correct answer. The basic idea is to first define a substitution σ that is consistent with both the (dis)equalities in Φ and the constraints in Γ, and then to ground the set of abducibles Δ by applying σ to it. The resulting set of ground abducible atoms together with the substitution σ then constitutes a correct answer to the query (i.e., an extracted answer will typically give rise to a whole range of correct answers). To argue that this is indeed possible, i.e. to show that the described procedure of deriving answers to a query is a *sound* operation, will be the subject of the next section.

Example 2. We show the derivation for the query $r(6)$ given the abductive logic program of Example 1. Recall that CIFF is initiated with the node N_0 composed of the query and the integrity constraints in *IC*.

N_0: $r(6) \wedge [r(T) \rightarrow p(T)]$ [initial node]
N_1: $r(6) \wedge [T = 6 \rightarrow p(T)] \wedge [r(T) \rightarrow p(T)]$ [by propagation]
N_2: $r(6) \wedge p(6) \wedge [r(T) \rightarrow p(T)]$ [by substitution]
N_3: $r(6) \wedge q(X, T') \wedge T' < 6 \wedge 6 < 8 \wedge [r(T) \rightarrow p(T)]$ [by unfolding]
N_4: $r(6) \wedge q(X, T') \wedge T' < 6 \wedge [r(T) \rightarrow p(T)]$ [by constraint solving]
N_5: $r(6) \wedge X = a \wedge s(T') \wedge T' < 6 \wedge [r(T) \rightarrow p(T)]$ [by unfolding]

No more rules can be applied to the node N_5 and it neither contains $\bot$ nor has it been labelled as *undefined*. Hence, it is a success node and we get an *extracted answer* with $\Delta = \{r(6), s(T')\}$, $\Phi = \{X = a\}$ and $\Gamma = \{T' < 6\}$, of which the *correct answer* given in Example 1 is an instance. $\square$

4   Soundness Results

In this section we are going to present the soundness of the CIFF procedure with respect to the semantics of a correct answer to a given query. Due to space restrictions, we have to restrict ourselves to short sketches of the main ideas involved. Full proofs may be found in [3]. Our results extend those of Fung and Kowalski for the original IFF procedure in two respects: (1) they apply to abductive logic programs with constraints, and (2) they do not rely on a static (and overly strict) definition of allowedness.

For an abductive proof procedure, we can distinguish two types of soundness results: *soundness of success* and *soundness of failure*. The first one establishes the correctness of derivations that are successful (soundness of success): whenever the CIFF procedure terminates successfully then the *extracted* answer (consisting of a set of abducible atoms, a set of equalities and disequalities, and a set of constraints) gives rise to a *true* answer according to the semantics of ALP (i.e. a ground set of abducible atoms and a substitution). Note that for this result to apply, it suffices that a single final success node can be derived. This node will give rise to a correct answer, even if there are other branches in the derivation that do not terminate or for which the DAR has been triggered. The second soundness result applies to derivations that fail (soundness of failure): it states that whenever the CIFF procedure fails then there is indeed no answer according to the semantics. This result applies only when *all* branches in a derivation have failed; if there are branches that do not terminate or for which the DAR has been triggered, then we cannot draw any conclusions regarding the existence of an answer to the query (assuming there are no success nodes).

The proofs of both these results heavily rely on the fact that our proof rules are *equivalence preserving:*

Lemma 1 (Equivalence preservation). *If N is a node in a derivation with respect to the theory Th, and $\mathcal{N}$ is the disjunction of the immediate successor nodes of N in that derivation, then $Th \models N \leftrightarrow \mathcal{N}$.*

Note that the disjunction $\mathcal{N}$ will have only a single disjunct whenever the rule applied to N is neither splitting nor case analysis for equalities. Equivalence preservation is easily verified for most of our proof rules. Considering that $IC \wedge Q$ is the initial node of any derivation, the next lemma then follows by induction over the number of proof steps leading to a final success node:

Lemma 2 (Final nodes entail initial node). *If N is a final success node for the input $\langle Th, IC, Q \rangle$, then $Th \models N \rightarrow (IC \wedge Q)$.*

Our third lemma provides the central argument in showing that it is possible to extract a correct abductive answer from a final success node:

Lemma 3 (Answer extraction). *If N is a final success node and Δ is the set of abducible atoms in N, then there exists a substitution σ such that $Comp(\Delta\sigma) \models N\sigma$.*

The first step in proving this lemma is to show that any formulas in N that are not directly represented in the extracted answer must be implications where the antecedent includes an abducible atom and no negative literals. We can then show that implications of this type are logical consequences of $Comp(\Delta\sigma)$ by distinguishing two cases: either *propagation* has been applied to the implication in question, or it has not. In the latter case, the claim holds vacuously (because the antecedent is not *true*); in the former case we use an inductive argument over the number of abducible atoms in the antecedent.

The full proof of Lemma 3 makes reference to all proof rules except *factoring.* Indeed, factoring is not required to ensure soundness. However, as can easily be verified, factoring is equivalence preserving in the sense of Lemma 1; that is, our soundness results apply both to the system with and to the system without the factoring rule. We are now ready to state these soundness results:

Theorem 1 (Soundness of success). *If there exists a successful derivation for the input $\langle Th, IC, Q \rangle$, then there exists a correct answer for that input.*

Theorem 2 (Soundness of failure). *If there exists a derivation for the input $\langle Th, IC, Q \rangle$ that terminates and where all final nodes are failure nodes, then there exists no correct answer for that input.*

Theorem 1 follows from Lemmas 2 and 3, while Theorem 2 can be proved by induction over the number of proof steps in a derivation, using Lemma 1 in the induction step. We should stress that these soundness results only apply in cases where the DAR has not been triggered and the CIFF procedure has terminated with a defined outcome, namely either *success* or *failure*. Hence, such results are only interesting if we can give some assurance that the DAR is "appropriate": In a similar but ill-defined system where an (inappropriate) allowedness rule would simply label all nodes as *undefined*, it would still be possible to prove the same soundness theorems, but they would obviously be of no practical relevance.

The reason why our rule is indeed appropriate is that extracting an answer from a node labelled as *undefined* by the DAR would either require us to extend the definition of a correct answer to allow for *infinite* sets of abducible atoms or at least involve the enumeration of *all* the solutions to a set of constraints. We shall demonstrate this by means of two simple examples. First, consider the following implication:

$$X = f(Y) \rightarrow p(X)$$

If both X and Y are universally quantified, then this formula will trigger the DAR. Its meaning is that the predicate p is true whenever its argument is of the form $f(\_)$. Hence, an "answer" induced by a node containing this implication would have to include the infinite set $\{p(f(t_1)), p(f(t_2)), \ldots\}$, where $t_1, t_2, \ldots$ stand for the terms in the Herbrand universe. This can also be seen by considering that, if we were to ignore the side conditions on quantification of the *substitution rule for implications*, the above implication could be rewritten as $p(f(Y))$, with Y still being universally quantified.

For the next example, assume that our constraint language includes the predicate $<$ with the usual interpretation over integers:

$$3 < X \wedge X < 100 \rightarrow p(X)$$

Again, if the variable X is universally quantified, this formula will trigger the DAR. While it would be possible to extract a finite answer from a node including this formula, this would require us to enumerate all solutions to the constraint $3 < X \wedge X < 100$; that is, a correct answer would have to include the set of atoms $\{p(4), p(5), \ldots, p(99)\}$. In cases where the set of constraints concerned has an infinite number of solutions, even in theory, it is not possible to extract a correct answer (as it would be required to be both ground and finite).

5   Conclusion

We have introduced a new proof procedure for ALP that extends the IFF procedure in a non-trivial way by integrating abductive reasoning with constraint solving. Our procedure shares the advantages of the IFF procedure [4], but covers a larger class of inputs: (1) predicates belonging to a suitable constraint language may be used, and (2) the allowedness conditions have been reduced to a minimum. Both these extension are important requirements for our applications of ALP to modelling and implementing autonomous agents [5,11]. In cases where no answer is possible due to allowedness problems, the CIFF procedure will report this dynamically. However, if an answer is possible despite such problems, CIFF will report a defined answer. For instance, one node may give rise to a positive answer while another has a non-allowed structure, or a derivation may fail correctly for reasons that are independent of a particular non-allowed integrity constraint. For inputs conforming to any appropriate *static* allowedness definition, the DAR will never be triggered.

We have proved two soundness results for CIFF: *soundness of success* and *soundness of failure*. Together these two results also capture some aspect of completeness: For any class of inputs that are known to be allowed (in the sense of never triggering the DAR) and for which termination can be guaranteed (for instance, by imposing suitable acyclicity conditions [12]) the CIFF procedure will terminate successfully whenever there exists a correct answer according to the semantics. We hope to investigate the issues of termination and completeness further in our future work. Another interesting issue for future work on CIFF would be to investigate different strategies for proof search and other optimisation techniques. Such research could then inform an improvement of our current implementation and help to make it applicable to more complex problems.

Acknowledgements. This work was partially funded by the IST-FET programme of the European Commission under the IST-2001-32530 SOCS project, within the Global Computing proactive initiative. The last author was also supported by the Italian MIUR programme "Rientro dei cervelli".

References

[1] M. Carlsson, G. Ottosson, and B. Carlson. An open-ended finite domain constraint solver. In *Proc. PLILP-1997*, 1997.

[2] K. L. Clark. Negation as failure. In *Logic and Data Bases*. Plenum Press, 1978.

[3] U. Endriss, P. Mancarella, F. Sadri, G. Terreni, and F. Toni. The CIFF proof procedure: Definition and soundness results. Technical Report 2004/2, Department of Computing, Imperial College London, May 2004.

[4] T. H. Fung and R. A. Kowalski. The IFF proof procedure for abductive logic programming. *Journal of Logic Programming*, 33(2):151–165, 1997.

[5] A. C. Kakas, P. Mancarella, F. Sadri, K. Stathis, and F. Toni. The KGP model of agency. In *Proc. ECAI-2004*, 2004. To appear.

[6] A. C. Kakas, A. Michael, and C. Mourlas. ACLP: Abductive constraint logic programming. *Journal of Logic Programming*, 44:129–177, 2000.

[7] A. Martelli and U. Montanari. An efficient unification algorithm. *ACM Transactions on Programming Languages and Systems*, 4(2):258–282, 1982.

[8] A. Russo, R. Miller, B. Nuseibeh, and J. Kramer. An abductive approach for analysing event-based requirements specifications. In *Proc. ICLP-2002*. Springer-Verlag, 2002.

[9] F. Sadri, F. Toni, and P. Torroni. An abductive logic programming architecture for negotiating agents. In *Proc. JELIA-2002*. Springer-Verlag, 2002.

[10] M. Shanahan. An abductive event calculus planner. *Journal of Logic Programming*, 44:207–239, 2000.

[11] K. Stathis, A. Kakas, W. Lu, N. Demetriou, U. Endriss, and A. Bracciali. PROSOCS: A platform for programming software agents in computational logic. In *Proc. AT2AI-2004*, 2004.

[12] I. Xanthakos. *Semantic Integration of Information by Abduction*. PhD thesis, Department of Computing, Imperial College London, 2003.

Hierarchical Decision Making by Autonomous Agents

Stijn Heymans, Davy Van Nieuwenborgh*, and Dirk Vermeir**

Dept. of Computer Science
Vrije Universiteit Brussel, VUB
Pleinlaan 2, B1050 Brussels, Belgium
{sheymans,dvnieuwe,dvermeir}@vub.ac.be

Abstract. Often, decision making involves autonomous agents that are structured in a complex hierarchy, representing e.g. authority. Typically the agents share the same body of knowledge, but each may have its own, possibly conflicting, preferences on the available information.

We model the common knowledge base for such preference agents as a logic program under the extended answer set semantics, thus allowing for the defeat of rules to resolve conflicts. An agent can express its preferences on certain aspects of this information using a partial order relation on either literals or rules. Placing such agents in a hierarchy according to their position in the decision making process results in a system where agents cooperate to find solutions that are jointly preferred.

We show that a hierarchy of agents with either preferences on rules or on literals can be transformed into an equivalent system with just one type of preferences. Regarding the expressiveness, the formalism essentially covers the polynomial hierarchy. E.g. the membership problem for a hierarchy of depth n is Σ^P_{n+2}-complete. We illustrate an application of the approach by showing how it can easily express a generalization of weak constraints, i.e. "desirable" constraints that do not need to be satisfied but where one tries to minimize their violation.

1   Introduction

In *answer set programming*[16,2] one uses a logic program to modularly describe the requirements that must be fulfilled by the solutions to a particular problem, i.e. the answer sets of the program must correspond to the intended solutions of the problem. The technique has been successfully applied to the area of agents and multi-agent systems[3, 8,26]. While [3] and [8] use the basic answer set semantics to represent the agents domain knowledge, [26] applies an extension of the semantics incorporating preferences among choices in a program.

The idea of extending answer set semantics with some kind of preference relation is not new. We can identify two directions for these preferences relations on programs. On the one hand, we can equip a logic program with a preference relation on the rules

* Supported by the FWO.
** This work was partially funded by the Information Society Technologies programme of the European Commission, Future and Emerging Technologies under the IST-2001-37004 WASP project.

J.J. Alferes and J. Leite (Eds.): JELIA 2004, LNAI 3229, pp. 44–56, 2004.

[18,17,15,10,7,5,27,1,22], while on the other hand we can consider a preference relation on the (extended) literals in the program: [21] proposes explicit preferences while [4,6] encodes dynamic preferences within the program.

The traditional answer set semantics is not universal, i.e. programs may not have any answer sets at all. This behavior is not always feasible, e.g. a route planner agent may contain inconsistent information regarding some particular regions in Europe, which should not stop it from providing travel directions in general. The extended answer set semantics from [22,23] allows for the *defeat* of problematic rules. Take, for example, the program consisting of $a \leftarrow b$, $b \leftarrow$ and $\neg a \leftarrow$. Clearly this program has no answer sets. It has, however, extended answer sets $\{a, b\}$, where the rule $\neg a \leftarrow$ is defeated by the applied $a \leftarrow b$, and $\{\neg a, b\}$, where $a \leftarrow b$ is defeated by $\neg a \leftarrow$.

However, not all extended answer sets may be equally preferred by the involved parties: users traveling in "error free" regions of Europe do not mind faults in answers concerning the problematic regions, in contrast to users traveling in these latter regions that want to get a "best" approximation. Therefore, we extend the above semantics by equipping programs with a preference relation over either the rules or the literals in a program. Such a preference relation can be used to induce a partial order on the extended answers, the minimal elements of which will be preferred.

Different agents may exhibit different, possibly contradicting, preferences, that need to be reconciled into commonly accepted answer sets, while taking into account the relative authority of each agent.

For example, sending elderly workers on early pension, reducing the wages, or sacking people are some of the measures that an ailing company may consider. On the other hand, management may be asked to sacrifice expense accounts and/or company cars. Demanding efforts from the workers without touching the management leads to a bad image for the company. Negotiations between three parties are planned: shareholders, management and unions. The measures under consideration, together with the influence on the company's image are represented by the extended answer sets

$$M_1 = \{bad\_image, pension\} \qquad M_4 = \{\neg bad\_image, expense, sack\}$$
$$M_2 = \{bad\_image, wages\} \qquad M_5 = \{\neg bad\_image, car, wages\}$$
$$M_3 = \{\neg bad\_image, expense, wages\} \ .$$

The union representative, who is not allowed to reduce the options of the management, has a preference for the pension option over the wages reduction over the sacking option of people, not taking into account the final image of the company, i.e. $pension < wages < sack < \{bad\_image, \neg bad\_image\}$. This preference strategy will result in M_1 being better than M_2, while M_3 is preferred upon M_4. Furthermore, M_5 is incomparable w.r.t. the other options. Thus M_1, M_3 and M_5 are the choices to be defended by the union representative. Management, on the other hand, would rather give up its expense account than its car, regardless of company image, i.e. $expense < car < \{bad\_image, \neg bad\_image\}$, yielding M_1, M_3 and M_4 as negotiable decisions for the management.

Finally, the shareholders take only into account the decisions that are acceptable to both the management and the unions, i.e. M_1 and M_3, on which they apply their own preference $\neg bad\_image < bad\_image$, i.e. they do not want their company to get a bad image. As a result, $M_3 \sqsubset M_1$, yielding that M_3 is the preferred way to go to save the company, taking into account each party's preferences.

Decision processes like the one above are supported by *agent hierarchies*, where a program, representing the shared world of agents, is equipped with a tree of preference relations on either rules or literals, representing the hierarchy of agents preferences. Semantically, preferred extended answer sets for such systems will result from first optimizing w.r.t. the lowest agents in the hierarchy, then grouping the results according to the hierarchy and let the agents on the next level optimize these results, etc. Thus, each agent applies its preferences on a selection of the preferred answers of the agents immediately below it in the hierarchy, where the lowest agents apply their preferences directly on the extended answer sets of the shared program.

Reconsidering our example results in the system depicted below, i.e. union and management prefer directly, and independently, among all possible solutions, while the shareholders only choose among the solutions preferred by both union and management, obtaining a preferred solution for the complete system.

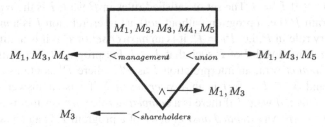

Such agent hierarchies turn out to be rather expressive. More specifically, we show that such systems can solve arbitrary complete problems of the polynomial hierarchy. We also demonstrate how systems with combined preferences, i.e. either on literals or on rules, can effectively be reduced to systems with only one kind of preference.

Finally, we introduce a generalization of weak constraints[9], which are constraints that should be satisfied but may be violated if there are no other options, i.e. violations of weak constraints should be minimized. Weak constraints have useful applications in areas like planning, abduction and optimizations from graph theory[13,11]. We allow for a hierarchy of agents having their individual preferences on the weak constraints they wish to satisfy in favor of others. We show that the original semantics of [9] can be captured by a single preference agent.

The remainder of the paper is organized as follows. In Section 2, we present the extended answer set semantics together with the hierarchy of preference agents, enabling hierarchical decision making. The complexity of the proposed semantics is discussed in Section 3. Before concluding and giving directions for further research in Section 5, we present in Section 4 a generalization of weak constraints and show how the original semantics can be implemented. Due to lack of space, detailed proofs have been omitted.

2   Agent Hierarchies

We give some preliminaries concerning the extended answer set semantics[22]. A *literal* is an atom a or a negated atom $\neg a$. An *extended literal* is a literal or a literal preceded by the *negation as failure*-symbol *not*. A program is a countable set of rules of the form $\alpha \leftarrow \beta$ with α a set of literals, $|\alpha| \leq 1$, and β a set of extended literals. If $\alpha = \emptyset$, we call the rule a *constraint*. The set α is the *head* of the rule while β is called the *body*. We will often denote rules either as $a \leftarrow \beta$ or, in the case of constraints, as $\leftarrow \beta$. For a set X of literals, we take $\neg X = \{\neg l \mid l \in X\}$ where $\neg\neg a$ is a; X is *consistent* if $X \cap \neg X = \emptyset$. The positive part of the body is $\beta^+ = \{l \mid l \in \beta, l \text{ literal}\}$, the negative part is $\beta^- = \{l \mid not\ l \in \beta\}$, e.g. for $\beta = \{a, not\ \neg b, not\ c\}$, we have that $\beta^+ = \{a\}$ and $\beta^- = \{\neg b, c\}$. The *Herbrand Base* $\mathcal{B}_P$ of a program P is the set of all atoms that can be formed using the language of P. Let $\mathcal{L}_P$ be the set of literals and $\mathcal{L}_P^*$ the set of extended literals that can be formed with P, i.e. $\mathcal{L}_P = \mathcal{B}_P \cup \neg\mathcal{B}_P$ and $\mathcal{L}_P^* = \mathcal{L}_P \cup \{not\ l \mid l \in \mathcal{L}_P\}$. An *interpretation* I of P is any consistent subset of $\mathcal{L}_P$. For a literal l, we write $I \models l$, if $l \in I$, which extends for extended literals *not l* to $I \models not\ l$ if $I \not\models l$. In general, for a set of extended literals X, $I \models X$ if $I \models x$ for every extended literal $x \in X$. A rule $r : a \leftarrow \beta$ is *satisfied* w.r.t. I, denoted $I \models r$, if $I \models a$ whenever $I \models \beta$, i.e. r is *applied* whenever it is *applicable*. A constraint $\leftarrow \beta$ is satisfied w.r.t. I if $I \not\models \beta$. The set of satisfied rules in P w.r.t. I is the *reduct* P_I. For a *simple* program P (i.e. a program without *not*), an interpretation I is a *model* of P if I satisfies every rule in P, i.e. $P_I = P$; it is an *answer set* of P if it is a minimal model of P, i.e. there is no model J of P such that $J \subset I$. For programs P containing *not*, we define the *GL-reduct* w.r.t. an interpretation I as P^I, where P^I contains $\alpha \leftarrow \beta^+$ for $\alpha \leftarrow \beta$ in P and $\beta^- \cap I = \emptyset$. I is an *answer set* of P if I is an answer set of P^I. A rule $a \leftarrow \beta$ is *defeated* w.r.t. I if there is a *competing* rule $\neg a \leftarrow \gamma$ that is applied w.r.t. I, i.e. $\{\neg a\} \cup \gamma \subseteq I$. An *extended answer set* I of a program P is an answer set of P_I such that all rules in $P \backslash P_I$ are *defeated*.

Example 1. Take a program P expressing an intention to vote for either the Democrats or the Greens. Voting for the Greens will, however, weaken the Democrats, possibly resulting in a Republican victory. Furthermore, you have a Republican friend who may benefit from a Republican victory.

$$dem\_vote \leftarrow \qquad\qquad \neg dem\_vote \leftarrow$$
$$green\_vote \leftarrow not\ dem\_vote \qquad rep\_win \leftarrow green\_vote$$
$$fr\_benefit \leftarrow rep\_win \qquad \neg fr\_benefit \leftarrow rep\_win$$

This program results in 3 different extended answer sets $M_1 = \{dem\_vote\}$, $M_2 = \{\neg dem\_vote, green\_vote, rep\_win, fr\_benefit\}$, and $M_3 = \{\neg dem\_vote, green\_vote, rep\_win, \neg fr\_benefit\}$.

As mentioned in the introduction, the background knowledge for *agents* will be described by a program P. Agents can express individual preferences either on extended literals or on rules of P, corresponding to *literal* and *rule* agents respectively.

Definition 1. *Let P be a program. A **rule agent** (RA) $\mathcal{A}$ for P is a well-founded strict partial[1] order $<$ on rules in P. The order $<$ induces a relation $\sqsubseteq$ among interpretations M and N of P, such that $M \sqsubseteq N$ iff $\forall r_2 \in P_N \backslash P_M \cdot \exists r_1 \in P_M \backslash P_N \cdot r_1 < r_2$.*

---

[1] A strict partial order on X is an anti-reflexive and transitive relation on X. A strict partial order on a finite X is *well-founded*, i.e. every subset of X has a minimal element w.r.t. $<$.

A *literal agent (LA) for* P *is a strict well-founded partial order* $<$ *on* $\mathcal{L}_P^*$, *and* $M \sqsubseteq N$ *iff* $\forall n \in \{l \in \mathcal{L}_P^* \mid N \models l \wedge M \not\models l\}, \exists m \in \{l \in \mathcal{L}_P^* \mid M \models l \wedge N \not\models l\} \cdot m < n$.

The extended answer sets of an agent for P *correspond to the extended answer sets for* P. *As usual, we have* $M \sqsubset N$ *iff* $M \sqsubseteq N$ *and not* $N \sqsubseteq M$. *A **preferred answer set** M is an extended answer set that is minimal w.r.t.* $\sqsubset$ *among the extended answer sets.*

Note that a RA $<$ for P corresponds to an *ordered logic program* (OLP) $\langle P, < \rangle$ from [22].

We refer to the order of an agent $\mathcal{A}$ with $<_\mathcal{A}$ and $\sqsubseteq_\mathcal{A}$. Intuitively, for rule agents, an extended answer set M is "better" than N if each rule that is satisfied by N but not by M is countered by a better rule satisfied by M and not by N. Similarly, for literal agents we have that $M \sqsubseteq N$ if every extended literal that is true in N, but not in M, is countered by a better one true in M but not in N.

E.g., define a rule agent $fr\_benefit \leftarrow rep\_win < \neg fr\_benefit \leftarrow rep\_win$ for the program P in Example 1, indicating that one rather satisfies the former rule than the latter. We have, with $P_{M_1} = P \setminus \{\neg dem\_vote \leftarrow \}$, $P_{M_2} = P \setminus \{demo\_vote \leftarrow , \neg fr\_benefit \leftarrow rep\_win\}$ and $P_{M_3} = P \setminus \{demo\_vote \leftarrow , fr\_benefit \leftarrow rep\_win\}$, that $M_2 \sqsubset M_3$, yielding that M_1 and M_2 are the only preferred answer sets.

A literal agent might insist on voting for the Democrats: $demo\_vote < \mathcal{L}_P^* \setminus \{demo\_vote\}$, making M_1 its only preferred answer set.

The cooperation of agents for a program P is established by arranging them in a tree-structure[2], such that decisions are made bottom-up, starting with agents that have no successors, all the way up in the hierarchy to the root agent, each agent processing the results of its successor agents. Formally, an *agent hierarchy* (AH) is a pair $\langle P, T \rangle$ where P is a program and T is a finite and/or-tree of agents $\mathcal{A}$ for P.

We will denote the root agent $\mathcal{A}$ of the tree T with $\mathcal{A}_\varepsilon$. The m successors of an agent $\mathcal{A}_x$ are denoted as $\mathcal{A}_{x \cdot 1}, \ldots, \mathcal{A}_{x \cdot m}$. An agent without successors is called an *independent agent*, other agents are *dependent*. An agent associated with an and-node (or-node) will be called an *and-agent* (*or-agent*). We define what it means for an extended answer set to be *preferable* by a certain agent in the hierarchy.

Definition 2. *Let* $\langle P, T \rangle$ *be an AH. An extended answer set M of P is **preferable** by an independent agent $\mathcal{A}$ of T if M is a preferred answer set of $\mathcal{A}$ for P. An extended answer set M of P is preferable by a dependent and-agent (or-agent) $\mathcal{A}_x$, with m successors, if*

- *M is preferable by every (some) $\mathcal{A}_{x \cdot i}$, $1 \leq i \leq m$, and*
- *there is no N, preferable by every (some) $\mathcal{A}_{x \cdot j}$, $1 \leq j \leq m$, such that $N \sqsubset_{\mathcal{A}_x} M$.*

*An extended answer set M of P is **preferred** if it is preferable by $\mathcal{A}_\varepsilon$.*

Rule agents (OLPs) are rather convenient to formulate diagnostic problems[24,25], using "normal" and "fault" model rules to describe the system under consideration, where the former are preferred over the latter. Examples of this approach can be found in [24,25], where it also has been shown that the OLP semantics yields minimal possible explanations. However, to decide which explanations to check first, an engineer typically

---

[2] For simplicity we restrict ourselves to trees, however, the results remain valid for any well-founded strict partial order of agents that has a unique maximal agent.

uses another preference order, preferring e.g. explanations that are cheaper to verify. Such a situation can be modelled by an agent hierarchy containing an extra agent "above" the diagnostic RA. More generally, one may imagine situations where multiple engineers each have their own experience (expressed by preference) and where the head of the group has to take the final decision on which possible explanations to check first, taking into account the proposals of her colleagues. Such systems can easily be expressed using the proposed framework.

Reasoning w.r.t. agent hierarchies, containing both rule and literal agents, can be reduced to reasoning w.r.t. rule agent hierarchies (RAHs) or literal agent hierarchies (LAHs), i.e. hierarchies containing only rule or literal agents.

We show the reduction from RAs to LAs and vice versa. For the reduction of RAs for P to LAs, we introduce for every rule r in P a corresponding atom that is in an answer set iff r is satisfied. Intuitively, the newly introduced atoms will be ordered according to the original order on the rules they correspond with.

Theorem 1. *Let P be a program and $R = \{r_i \leftarrow not\ b \mid r_i : \alpha \leftarrow \beta \in P, b \in \beta^+\} \cup \{r_i \leftarrow b \mid r_i : \alpha \leftarrow \beta \in P, b \in \beta^-\} \cup \{r_i \leftarrow a \mid r_i : a \leftarrow \beta \in P\}$ with a new atom r_i for each rule r_i in P. M is a preferred answer set of a RA $\mathcal{A}^r$ for P iff $M' = M \cup \{r_i \mid r_i \in P_M\}$ is a preferred answer set of the LA $\mathcal{A}^l$ for $P \cup R$ where $\{r_i\} <_{\mathcal{A}^l} \mathcal{L}_P <_{\mathcal{A}^l} not(\mathcal{L}_{P \cup R})$ with additionally $r_i <_{\mathcal{A}^l} r_j$ iff $r_i <_{\mathcal{A}^r} r_j$.*

Moreover, preferred answer sets of a LA for P are in one to one correspondence with the preferred answer sets of a LA for $P \cup R$ by simply ignoring the newly added atoms r_i.

Theorem 2. *Let P be a program and R as in Theorem 1. M is a preferred answer set of a LA $\mathcal{A}$ for P iff $M' = M \cup \{r_i \mid r_i \in P_M\}$ is a preferred answer set of the LA $\mathcal{A}'$ for $P \cup R$ where $<_{\mathcal{A}'}$ is equal to $<_{\mathcal{A}}$ with additionally $k <_{\mathcal{A}'} \mathcal{L}^*_{P \cup R} \backslash \mathcal{L}^*_P$ for every extended literal k appearing in $<_{\mathcal{A}}$.*

The opposite simulation of a LA by a RA can be done by introducing for each literal l and its extended version $not\ l$ rules $l' \leftarrow$ and $\neg l' \leftarrow$ and ordering those rules according to the order on the extended literals.

Theorem 3. *Let P be a program and $L = \{l' \leftarrow; \neg l' \leftarrow \mid l \in \mathcal{L}_P\} \cup \{\leftarrow l', not\ l; \leftarrow \neg l', l \mid l \in \mathcal{L}_P\}$. M is a preferred answer set of a LA $\mathcal{A}^l$ for P iff $M' = M \cup \{(\neg)l' \mid l \in \mathcal{L}_P, M \models (not)l\}$ is a preferred answer set of the RA $\mathcal{A}^r$ for $P \cup L$ with $L <_{\mathcal{A}^r} P$ and additionally $(\neg)l' \leftarrow <_{\mathcal{A}^r} (\neg)k' \leftarrow$ iff $(not)l <_{\mathcal{A}^l} (not)k$.*

Example 2. Take a LA $\mathcal{A}^l$ for P where P consists of the rules $b \leftarrow a$, $a \leftarrow$, and $\neg a \leftarrow$, and $\neg a <_{\mathcal{A}^l} \{a, b, not\ \neg a\}$. This agent has two extended answer sets $\{\neg a\}$ and $\{a, b\}$, of which the first one is preferred. The corresponding RA $\mathcal{A}^r$ is defined by the following program[3]

$b \leftarrow a$	$a \leftarrow$	$\neg a \leftarrow$	
$a' \leftarrow$	$b' \leftarrow$	$(\neg a)' \leftarrow$	$(\neg b)' \leftarrow$
$\neg a' \leftarrow$	$\neg b' \leftarrow$	$\neg(\neg a)' \leftarrow$	$\neg(\neg b)' \leftarrow$
$\leftarrow a', not\ a$	$\leftarrow b', not\ b$	$\leftarrow (\neg a)', not\ \neg a$	$\leftarrow (\neg b)', not\ \neg b$
$\leftarrow \neg a', a$	$\leftarrow \neg b', b$	$\leftarrow \neg(\neg a)', \neg a$	$\leftarrow \neg(\neg b)', \neg b$

[3] Rules below the line are smaller than the ones above w.r.t. $<_{\mathcal{A}^r}$.

and $(\neg a)' \leftarrow <_{A^r} \{a' \leftarrow, b' \leftarrow, \neg(\neg a)' \leftarrow\}$. This RA has the preferred answer set $\{\neg a, (\neg a)', \neg a', \neg b', \neg(\neg b)'\} = \{\neg a\} \cup \{(\neg)l' \mid \{\neg a\} \models (not)l\}$.

Similarly to Theorem 2, we have that RAs for P can be simulated by RAs for $P \cup L$.

Theorem 4. *Let P be a program and L as in Theorem 3. M is a preferred answer set of a RA $\mathcal{A}$ for P iff $M' = M \cup \{(\neg)l' \mid l \in \mathcal{L}_P, M \models (not)l\}$ is a preferred answer set of a RA $\mathcal{A}'$ for $P \cup L$ where $<_{\mathcal{A}'}$ is equal to $<_{\mathcal{A}}$ with additionally $r <_{\mathcal{A}'} L$ for every r appearing in $<_{\mathcal{A}}$.*

Theorem 1 and 2 allow the simulation of an arbitrary AH by a LAH. This is done by extending the program P with the set of rules R as in Theorem 1, and by transforming the rule agents to literal agents (Theorem 1), while the literal agents are adapted according to Theorem 2.

Theorem 5. *Let $\langle P, T \rangle$ be an AH. M is a preferred answer set of $\langle P, T \rangle$ iff $M' = M \cup \{r_i \mid r_i \in P_M\}$ is a preferred answer set of the LAH $\langle P \cup R, T' \rangle$, with T' defined as T but with every rule or literal agent replaced by a literal agent as in Theorems 1 and 2.*

Similarly, but now with Theorems 3 and 4, we can reduce arbitrary AHs to RAHs.

Theorem 6. *Let $\langle P, T \rangle$ be an AH. M is a preferred answer set of $\langle P, T \rangle$ iff $M' = M \cup \{(\neg)l' \mid l \in \mathcal{L}_P, M \models (not)l\}$ is a preferred answer set of the RAH $\langle P \cup L, T' \rangle$, with T' defined as T but with every rule or literal agent replaced by a rule agent as in Theorems 3 and 4.*

3   Complexity

We briefly recall some relevant notions of complexity theory (see e.g. [20,2] for a nice introduction). The class P (NP) represents the problems that are deterministically (non-deterministically) decidable in polynomial time, while $coNP$ contains the problems whose complement are in NP.

The polynomial hierarchy, denoted PH, is made up of three classes of problems, i.e. Δ_k^P, Σ_k^P and Π_k^P, $k \geq 0$, which are defined as $\Delta_0^P = \Sigma_0^P = \Pi_0^P = P$, $\Delta_{k+1}^P = P^{\Sigma_k^P}$, $\Sigma_{k+1}^P = NP^{\Sigma_k^P}$, and $\Pi_{k+1}^P = co\Sigma_{k+1}^P$. The class $P^{\Sigma_k^P}$ ($NP^{\Sigma_k^P}$) represents the problems decidable in deterministic (nondeterministic) polynomial time using an oracle for problems in Σ_k^P, where an oracle is a subroutine capable of solving Σ_k^P problems in unit time. The class PH is defined by $PH = \bigcup_{k=0}^{\infty} \Sigma_k^P$. Note that $\Sigma_k^P \subseteq \Sigma_k^P \cup \Pi_k^P \subseteq \Delta_{k+1}^P \subseteq \Sigma_{k+1}^P$. In the following, we will usually omit the P-superscript to avoid cluttered up lines. A language L is called complete for a complexity class C if both L is in C and L is hard for C. Showing that L is hard is normally done by reducing a known complete decision problem to a decision problem in L.

First of all, checking whether an interpretation I is an extended answer set of a program P is in P, because (a) checking if each rule in P is either satisfied or defeated w.r.t. I, (b) applying the GL-reduct on P_I w.r.t. I, i.e. computing $(P_I)^I$, and (c) checking whether the positive program $(P_I)^I$ has I as its unique minimal model, can all be done in polynomial time.

For an agent $\mathcal{A}$ and a program P, checking whether M is not a preferred answer set is in NP, because one can guess a set $N \sqsubset_{\mathcal{A}} M$ in polynomial time, and subsequently verify that N is an extended answer set of P, which can also be done in P.

On the other hand, the complexity of checking whether an extended answer set M is not preferable by a certain agent $\mathcal{A}_x$ in a hierarchy $\langle P, T \rangle$ depends on the location of the agent in the tree T. For an agent $\mathcal{A}_x$ in T, we denote with $d(\mathcal{A}_x)$ the length of the longest path from $\mathcal{A}_x$ to an independent agent $\mathcal{A}_{x \cdot y}$, $y \in \mathbb{N}^{\star}$, i.e. $d(\mathcal{A}_x) = \max_{\mathcal{A}_{x \cdot y}} |y|$ over independent agents $\mathcal{A}_{x \cdot y}$, where $|y|$ is the length of the string y. We define the depth of T as the longest path from the root, i.e. $d(T) = d(\mathcal{A}_\varepsilon)$.

Lemma 1. *Let $\langle P, T \rangle$ be an AH[4], and let M be an extended answer set of P. Checking whether M is not preferable by $\mathcal{A}_x$ is in $\Sigma_{d(\mathcal{A}_x)+1}$.*

Proof. The proof is by induction. In the base case, i.e. $\mathcal{A}_x$ is an independent agent, we have that $d(\mathcal{A}_x) = 0$. Checking whether M is not preferable by $\mathcal{A}_x$ means checking whether M is not a preferred answer set of the agent $\mathcal{A}_x$ for P, which is in $NP = \Sigma_1 = \Sigma_{d(\mathcal{A}_x)+1}$.

For the induction step, checking that M is not preferable by a dependent and-agent (or-agent) $\mathcal{A}_x$ with m successors can be done by (a) checking that M is (or is not) preferable by every (some) $\mathcal{A}_{x \cdot i}$, $1 \le i \le m$. Since checking whether M is (or is not) preferable by an $\mathcal{A}_{x \cdot i}$ can be done, by the induction hypothesis, in $\Sigma_{d(\mathcal{A}_{x \cdot i})+1}$, we have that checking whether M is preferable by an $\mathcal{A}_{x \cdot i}$ is also in $C \equiv \Sigma_{\max_{1 \le i \le m} d(\mathcal{A}_{x \cdot i})+1}$, and (b) guessing, if M is preferable by every (some) $\mathcal{A}_{x \cdot i}$, $1 \le i \le m$, an interpretation $N \sqsubset_{\mathcal{A}_x} M$ and checking that it is not the case that N is not preferable by every (some) $\mathcal{A}_{x \cdot i}$, $1 \le i \le m$, which is again in C due to the induction hypothesis.

As a result, at most $2m$ calls are made to a C-oracle and at most one guess is made, yielding that the problem itself is in $NP^C = \Sigma_{\max_{1 \le i \le m} d(\mathcal{A}_{x \cdot i})+1+1} = \Sigma_{d(\mathcal{A}_x)+1}$. $\square$

Using the above yields the following theorem about the complexity of AHs.

Theorem 7. *Let $\langle P, T \rangle$ be an AH and l a literal. Deciding whether there is a preferred answer set containing l is in $\Sigma_{d(T)+2}$. Deciding whether every preferred answer set contains l is in $\Pi_{d(T)+2}$.*

Proof. The first task can be performed by an NP-algorithm that guesses an interpretation $M \ni l$ and checks that it is not the case that M is not preferable up to the root agent $\mathcal{A}_\varepsilon$. Due to Lemma 1, the latter is in $\Sigma_{d(\mathcal{A}_\varepsilon)+1} = \Sigma_{d(T)+1}$, so the former is in $NP^{\Sigma_{d(T)+1}} = \Sigma_{d(T)+2}$.

By the previous, finding a preferred answer set M not containing l, i.e. $l \notin M$, is in $\Sigma_{d(T)+2}$. Hence, the complement of the problem is in $\Pi_{d(T)+2}$. $\square$

Consider a LAH $\langle P, T \rangle$ where the tree T is a linear order containing n literal agents $\{\mathcal{A}_\varepsilon, \mathcal{A}_1, \mathcal{A}_{11}, \ldots \mathcal{A}_{11\ldots 1}\}$, i.e. *a linear LAH*. Deciding whether there is a preferred answer set of a linear LAH, containing a literal, is Σ_{n+1}-complete, i.e. $\Sigma_{d(T)+2}$-complete, as is shown in [19]. Furthermore, deciding whether every preferred answer set of a linear LAH contains a literal, is $\Pi_{d(T)+2}$-complete [19]. Hardness for AHs follows then immediately from the hardness of linear LAHs.

---

[4] The depth of the tree is assumed to be bounded by a constant.

Theorem 8. *The problem of deciding, given an AH $\langle P, T \rangle$ and a literal l, whether there exists a preferred answer set containing l is $\Sigma_{d(T)+2}$-hard. Deciding whether every preferred answer set contains l is $\Pi_{d(T)+2}$-hard.*

Proof. Checking whether there is a preferred answer set containing l for a linear LAH $\langle P, T \rangle$ is $\Sigma_{d(T)+2}$-complete, and since a linear LAH is a AH, the result follows.

The second problem can be similarly shown to be $\Pi_{d(T)+2}$-hard.   □

The following is immediate from Theorem 7 and 8.

Corollary 1. *The problem of deciding, given an arbitrary AH $\langle P, T \rangle$ and a literal l, whether there is a preferred answer set containing l is $\Sigma_{d(T)+2}$-complete. On the other hand, deciding whether every preferred answer set contains l is $\Pi_{d(T)+2}$-complete.*

4 Relationship with Weak Constraints

Weak constraints were introduced in [9] as a relaxation of the concept of a constraint. Intuitively, a weak constraint is allowed to be violated, but only as a last resort, meaning that one tries to minimize the number of violated constraints. Additionally, weak constraints may be hierarchically layered by means of a totally ordered set of sets of weak constraints $W = \{W_1, W_2, \ldots, W_n\}$, where it is assumed that $W_i < W_{i+1}, 1 \leq i < n$, if the weak constraints in W_i are more important than the ones in W_{i+1}. Intuitively, one first chooses the answer sets that minimize the number of violated constraints in the most important W_1, and then, among those, one chooses the extended answer sets that minimize the number of violated constraints in W_2, etc.

Formally, a *weak logic program* (WLP) is a pair $\langle P, W \rangle$ where P is a program, and W is a totally ordered set of sets of weak constraints, specified syntactically as constraints $\leftarrow \beta$.

Definition 3. *Let $\langle P, W = \{W_1, \ldots, W_n\} \rangle$ be a WLP. An extended answer set M of P is **preferable** up to W_1 if no extended answer set N of P exists such that $|V_{W_1}^N| < |V_{W_1}^M|$, where $V_{W_i}^X$ are the weak constraints in W_i that are violated by an interpretation X. An extended answer set M of P is preferable up to W_i, $1 < i \leq n$, if*

- *M is preferable up to W_{i-1}, and*
- *there is no N, preferable up to W_{i-1}, such that $|V_{W_i}^N| < |V_{W_i}^M|$.*

*An extended answer set M of P is **preferred** if it is preferable up to W_n.*

In [9] a $Datalog^{not}$-program LP is used[5] disallowing empty heads and classical negation, but allowing for a set of *strong* constraints S. Clearly, this is subsumed by Definition 3, by taking $P = LP \cup S$, and noting that the extended answer set semantics reduces to the answer set semantics, due to the absence of classical negation. Although the preferred models are defined in [9] by means of an object function that has to be minimized, they are equivalent[12] to the ones resulting from Definition 3.

---

[5] The general mechanism is introduced with $Datalog^{\vee,not}$-programs, which allow for disjunction in the head.

The semantics of weak constraints, with preferability up to certain levels, appears very similar to our preferability notion in an agent hierarchy. However, due to the use of cardinality, deciding whether a literal l is contained in some preferred answer set of a WLP is Δ_2^P-complete. As $\Delta_2^P \subseteq \Sigma_2^P$, agent hierarchies of depth 0 suffice to capture WLPs. More specifically, we show that a single agent can solve the problem.

Example 3. Take the weak logic program $\langle P, \{W_1, W_2\}\rangle$, with the program P consisting of rules $a \leftarrow$, $\neg a \leftarrow$, $b \leftarrow$, and $\neg b \leftarrow$, and $W_1 = \{ \leftarrow a\}$, $W_2 = \{ \leftarrow \neg a, \leftarrow \neg b\}$. We have 4 extended answer sets $M_1 = \{a, b\}$, $M_2 = \{a, \neg b\}$, $M_3 = \{\neg a, b\}$, and $M_4 = \{\neg a, \neg b\}$ of which M_3 and M_4 are preferable up to W_1, and only M_3 is preferable up to W_2. Indeed $|V_{W_1}^{M_1}| = |V_{W_1}^{M_2}| = 1$, $|V_{W_1}^{M_3}| = |V_{W_1}^{M_4}| = 0$, $|V_{W_2}^{M_1}| = 0$, $|V_{W_2}^{M_2}| = |V_{W_2}^{M_3}| = 1$, and $|V_{W_2}^{M_4}| = 2$. We define the set WC as the rules $c_1^1 \leftarrow a$, $c_1^2 \leftarrow \neg a$, and $c_2^2 \leftarrow \neg b$, identifying the weak constraints and the level on which they appear, and rules counting the number of violated constraints in a W_i, for $0 \leq l \leq k$,

$$co(1, 0, w_i) \leftarrow not\ c_1^i \qquad co(2, l, w_2) \leftarrow co(1, l, w_2), not\ c_2^2$$
$$co(1, 1, w_i) \leftarrow c_1^i \qquad co(2, l+1, w_2) \leftarrow co(1, l, w_2), c_2^2$$

Intuitively, the third argument in a $co/3$ literal identifies the particular W_i we are looking at, the first argument shows the number of constraints in W_i that have already been considered, and the second argument effectively counts the number of violated constraints in W_i. Further, WC also contains the rules defining the number of violated constraints in each set of weak constraints, $i \in \{0,1\}$, $j \in \{0,1,2\}$: $co(i, w_1) \leftarrow co(1, i, w_1)$ and $co(j, w_2) \leftarrow co(2, j, w_2)$.

The order $<$ on literals is defined as follows $co(0, w_1) < co(1, w_1) < co(0, w_2) < co(1, w_2) < co(2, w_2) < R$, with R the extended literals $\mathcal{L}_{P \cup WC}^*$ without the $co/2$ atoms. Intuitively, the w_1 constraints are more important than the w_2 constraints, and hence appear below them, and, among each w_i, one rather has a low count than a high count, since this implies less violated constraints. One can check that the preferred answer set of the literal agent $\mathcal{A} = <$ for $P \cup WC$ is $M_3' = M_3 \cup \{c_1^2, co(1, 0, w_1), co(1, 1, w_2), co(2, 1, w_2), co(0, w_1), co(1, w_2)\}$.

Formally, we have the following result, where the weak constraints in a W_j are assumed to be numbered and explicitly tagged with a superscript identifying W_j, i.e. $W_j = \{ \leftarrow \beta_1^j, \ldots, \leftarrow \beta_n^j\}$.

Theorem 9. *Let $\langle P, W = \{W_1, \ldots, W_n\}\rangle$ be a weak logic program. M is a preferred answer set of $\langle P, W\rangle$ iff, for all $1 \leq j \leq n$,*

$$M' = M \cup \{c_i^j \mid M \models \beta_i^j\} \cup \{co(1, \alpha, w_j) \mid c_1^j \notin M' \Rightarrow \alpha = 0, c_1^j \in M' \Rightarrow \alpha = 1\}$$
$$\cup \{co(k+1, \alpha, w_j) \mid co(k, l, w_j) \in M', 0 \leq l \leq k < |W_j| \wedge$$
$$[c_{k+1}^j \notin M' \Rightarrow \alpha = l, c_{k+1}^j \in M' \Rightarrow \alpha = l+1]\}$$
$$\cup \{co(m, w_j) \mid co(|W_j|, m, w_j) \in M'\}$$

is a preferred answer set of the literal agent $\mathcal{A}$ for $P \cup WC$ where WC, for all $1 \leq j \leq n$, consists of the rules $c_i^j \leftarrow \beta_i^j$, $co(1, 0, w_j) \leftarrow not\ c_1^j$, $co(1, 1, w_j) \leftarrow c_1^j$ and

$$co(k+1, l, w_j) \leftarrow co(k, l, w_j), not\ c_{k+1}^j\ with\ 0 \leq l \leq k < |W_j|$$
$$co(k+1, l+1, w_j) \leftarrow co(k, l, w_j), c_{k+1}^j$$

together with the rules $co(m, w_j) \leftarrow co(|W_j|, m, w_j)$, $0 \leq m \leq |W_j|$, *and the order* $<_A$ *defined as* $co(0, w_1) <_A co(1, w_1) <_A \ldots <_A co(|W_1|, w_1) <_A \ldots <_A$ $co(0, w_n) <_A co(1, w_n) <_A \ldots <_A co(|W_n|, w_n)$.

A more general approach, in the spirit of rule and literal agents, is to allow agents to prefer the satisfaction of certain weak constraints over the satisfaction of other ones. A weak logic program then becomes a pair $\langle P, W \rangle$, where P is a program and W is a set of constraints. A *weak agent* for $\langle P, W \rangle$ corresponds to a well-founded strict partial order on W, which induces an order $\sqsubseteq$ among interpretations M and N of P such that, $M \sqsubseteq N$ iff $\forall w_2 \in W_N \backslash W_M \cdot \exists w_1 \in W_M \backslash W_N \cdot w_1 < w_2$, where W_X are the weak constraints in W that are satisfied by X, mirroring Definition 1 for rule agents (note that the latter are different from weak agents since RAs require the satisfaction of all constraints in all extended answer sets).

The extended answer sets of P are, by definition, the extended answer sets of a weak agent $\mathcal{A}$ for $\langle P, W \rangle$, and preferred answer sets are defined as the minimal extended answers sets w.r.t. $\sqsubseteq$. Note that a preferred answer set M of a weak agent $\mathcal{A}$ for $\langle P, W \rangle$ has a minimal set of violated constraints, i.e. there is no extended answer set N of $\mathcal{A}$ such that $W \backslash W_N \subset W \backslash W_M$.

For a program P, define the extended program $E(P)$ as P with the rules $a \leftarrow \beta$ replaced by $a \leftarrow \beta, not \neg a$. From Theorem 4 in [22] we have that the extended answer sets of P are exactly the answer sets of $E(P)$. We can then rewrite a weak agent as a rule agent by introducing for each weak constraint $w :\ \leftarrow \beta$ rules $w \leftarrow \beta$ and $\neg w \leftarrow \beta$ such that w is in an answer set if the constraint is violated.

Theorem 10. *Let $\mathcal{A}^w$ be a weak agent for a WLP $\langle P, W \rangle$. M is a preferred answer set of $\mathcal{A}^w$ for $\langle P, W \rangle$ iff $M' = M \cup \{w \mid w \in W, M \not\models w\}$ is a preferred answer set of the RA $\mathcal{A}^r$ for $E(P) \cup WC$ with $WC = \{w \leftarrow \beta; \neg w \leftarrow \beta; \leftarrow \beta, not\ w \mid w :\ \leftarrow \beta \in W\}$ and $\neg w_1 \leftarrow \beta_1 <_{\mathcal{A}^r} \neg w_2 \leftarrow \beta_2$ iff $w_1 <_{\mathcal{A}^w} w_2$.*

Moreover, weak agents are as expressive as rule agents.

Theorem 11. *Let P be a program and $\mathcal{A}^r$ a RA for P. M is a preferred answer set of $\mathcal{A}^r$ for P iff M is a preferred answer set of the weak agent $\mathcal{A}^w$ for the WLP $\langle P, W \rangle$, with $W = \{ \leftarrow \beta, not\ \alpha \mid \alpha \leftarrow \beta \in P \}$ and $\leftarrow \beta_1, not\ \alpha_1 <_{\mathcal{A}^w} \leftarrow \beta_2, not\ \alpha_2$ iff $\alpha_1 \leftarrow \beta_1 <_{\mathcal{A}^r} \alpha_2 \leftarrow \beta_2$.*

Weak agents, placed in a hierarchy, then allow for an intuitive decision making process based on satisfaction and violation of weak constraints. The complexity of weak agent hierarchies can easily be deduced from the reductions from and to rule agent hierarchies, with Theorem 10 and 11 and their extensions for hierarchies.

Theorem 12. *The problem of deciding, given a weak agent hierarchy $\langle \langle P, W \rangle, T \rangle$ and a literal l, whether there is a preferred answer set containing l is $\Sigma_{d(T)+2}$-complete. On the other hand, deciding whether every preferred answer set contains l is $\Pi_{d(T)+2}$-complete.*

5 Conclusions and Directions for Further Research

In this paper, we introduced a system suitable to model hierarchical decision making. We equip agents with a preference relation on the available knowledge and allow them to cooperate with each other in a hierarchical fashion. Preferred solutions of these systems naturally correspond to preferred decisions regarding the problem.

Initially, we defined two types of preference agents: rule agents express a preference over rules, while literal agents use a preference over extended literals they rather prefer upon others in a solution. We showed that mixed AHs, containing both types of agents, can be reduced to hierarchies consisting only of rule or literal agents. It turns out that these AHs cover the polynomial hierarchy.

Finally, we showed that layered weak constraints can be easily simulated by a single agent. Furthermore, we generalized the concept of layered weak constraints to weak agent hierarchies, which are equivalent to rule agent hierarchies.

Future work comprises a dedicated implementation of the approach, using existing answer set solvers. E.g., we could generate an extended answer set which is then improved recursively by a set of augmented programs, corresponding to the agents in the hierarchy, generating strictly better solutions. A fixpoint of this procedure then corresponds to a preferred answer set of the system.

References

1. José Júlio Alferes and Luís Moniz Pereira. Updates plus preferences. In Manual Ojeda-Aciego, Inma P. de Guzmán, Gerhard Brewka, and Luíz Moniz Pereira, editors, *European Workshop, JELIA 2000*, volume 1919 of *Lecture Notes in Artificial Intelligence*, pages 345–360, Malaga, Spain, September–October 2000. Springer Verlag.
2. Chitta Baral. *Knowledge Representation, Reasoning and Declarative Problem Solving*. Cambridge Press, 2003.
3. Chitta Baral and Michael Gelfond. Reasoning agents in dynamic domains. In *Logic-based artificial intelligence*, pages 257–279. Kluwer Academic Publishers, 2000.
4. G. Brewka. Logic programming with ordered disjunction. In *Proceedings of the 18th National Conference on Artificial Intelligence and Fourteenth Conference on Innovative Applications of Artificial Intelligence*, pages 100–105, Edmonton, Canada, July 2002. AAAI Press.
5. Gerhard Brewka and Thomas Eiter. Preferred answer sets for extended logic programs. *Artificial Intelligence*, 109(1-2):297–356, April 1999.
6. Gerhard Brewka, Ilkka Niemela, and Tommi Syrjanen. Implementing ordered disjunction using answer set solvers for normal programs. In Flesca et al. [14], pages 444–455.
7. Francesco Buccafurri, Wolfgang Faber, and Nicola Leone. Disjunctive logic programs with inheritance. In Danny De Schreye, editor, *Logic Programming: The 1999 International Conference*, pages 79–93, Las Cruces, New Mexico, December 1999. MIT Press.
8. Francesco Buccafurri and Georg Gottlob. Multiagent compromises, joint fixpoints, and stable models. In Antonis C. Kakas and Fariba Sadri, editors, *Computational Logic: Logic Programming and Beyond, Essays in Honour of Robert A. Kowalski, Part I*, volume 2407 of *Lecture Notes in Computer Science*, pages 561–585. Springer, 2002.
9. Francesco Buccafurri, Nicola Leone, and Pasquale Rullo. Strong and weak constraints in disjunctive datalog. In *Proceedings of the 4th International Conference on Logic Programming (LPNMR '97)*, pages 2–17, 1997.
10. Francesco Buccafurri, Nicola Leone, and Pasquale Rullo. Disjunctive ordered logic: Semantics and expressiveness. In Anthony G. Cohn, Lenhard K. Schubert, and Stuart C. Shapiro, editors, *Proceedings of the 6th International Conference on Principles of Knowledge Representation and Reasoning*, pages 418–431, Trento, June 1998. Morgan Kaufmann.

11. Francesco Buccafurri, Nicola Leone, and Pasquale Rullo. Enhancing disjunctive datalog by constraints. *Knowledge and Data Engineering*, 12(5):845–860, 2000.
12. Wolfgang Faber. Disjunctive datalog with strong and weak constraints: Representational and computational issues. Master's thesis, Institut for Informationssysteme, Technische Universität Wien, 1998.
13. Wolfgang Faber, Nicola Leone, and Gerald Pfeifer. Representing school timetabling in a disjunctive logic programming language. In *Proceedings of the 13th Workshop on Logic Programming (WLP '98)*, 1998.
14. Sergio Flesca, Sergio Greco, Nicola Leone, and Giovambattista Ianni, editors. *European Conference on Logics in Artificial Intelligence (JELIA '02)*, volume 2424 of *Lecture Notes in Artificial Intelligence*, Cosenza, Italy, September 2002. Springer Verlag.
15. D. Gabbay, E. Laenens, and D. Vermeir. Credulous vs. Sceptical Semantics for Ordered Logic Programs. In J. Allen, R. Fikes, and E. Sandewall, editors, *Proceedings of the 2nd International Conference on Principles of Knowledge Representation and Reasoning*, pages 208–217, Cambridge, Mass, 1991. Morgan Kaufmann.
16. Michael Gelfond and Vladimir Lifschitz. The stable model semantics for logic programming. In Robert A. Kowalski and Kenneth A. Bowen, editors, *Logic Programming, Proceedings of the Fifth International Conference and Symposium*, pages 1070–1080, Seattle, Washington, August 1988. The MIT Press.
17. Robert A. Kowalski and Fariba Sadri. Logic programs with exceptions. In David H. D. Warren and Peter Szeredi, editors, *Proceedings of the 7th International Conference on Logic Programming*, pages 598–613, Jerusalem, 1990. The MIT Press.
18. Els Laenens and Dirk Vermeir. A logical basis for object oriented programming. In Jan van Eijck, editor, *European Workshop, JELIA 90*, volume 478 of *Lecture Notes in Artificial Intelligence*, pages 317–332, Amsterdam, The Netherlands, September 1990. Springer Verlag.
19. Davy Van Nieuwenborgh, Stijn Heymans, and Dirk Vermeir. On programs with linearly ordered multiple preferences, 2004. Accepted at ICLP '04.
20. Christos H. Papadimitriou. *Computational Complexity*. Addison Wesley, 1994.
21. Chiaki Sakama and Katsumi Inoue. Representing priorities in logic programs. In Michael J. Maher, editor, *Proceedings of the 1996 Joint International Conference and Symposium on Logic Programming*, pages 82–96, Bonn, September 1996. MIT Press.
22. Davy Van Nieuwenborgh and Dirk Vermeir. Preferred answer sets for ordered logic programs. In Flesca et al. [14], pages 432–443.
23. Davy Van Nieuwenborgh and Dirk Vermeir. Order and negation as failure. In Catuscia Palamidessi, editor, *ICLP*, volume 2916 of *Lecture Notes in Computer Science*, pages 194–208. Springer, 2003.
24. Davy Van Nieuwenborgh and Dirk Vermeir. Ordered diagnosis. In *Proceedings of the 10th International Conference on Logic for Programming, Artificial Intelligence, and Reasoning (LPAR2003)*, volume 2850 of *Lecture Notes in Artificial Intelligence*, pages 244–258, Almaty, Kazachstan, 2003. Springer Verlag.
25. Davy Van Nieuwenborgh and Dirk Vermeir. Ordered programs as abductive systems. In *Proceedings of the APPIA-GULP-PRODE Conference on Declarative Programming (AGP2003)*, pages 374–385, Regio di Calabria, Italy, 2003.
26. Marina De Vos and Dirk Vermeir. Logic programming agents playing games. In *Research and Development in Intelligent Systems XIX (ES2002)*, BCS Conference Series, pages 323–336. Springer-Verlag, 2002.
27. Kewen Wang, Lizhu Zhou, and Fangzhen Lin. Alternating fixpoint theory for logic programs with priority. In *Proceedings of the First International Conference on Computational Logic (CL2000)*, volume 1861 of *Lecture Notes in Computer Science*, pages 164–178, London, UK, July 2000. Springer.

Verifying Communicating Agents
by Model Checking in a Temporal Action Logic[*]

Laura Giordano[1], Alberto Martelli[2], and Camilla Schwind[3]

[1] Dipartimento di Informatica, Università del Piemonte Orientale, Alessandria
[2] Dipartimento di Informatica, Università di Torino, Torino
[3] MAP, CNRS, Marseille, France

Abstract. In this paper we address the problem of specifying and verifying systems of communicating agents in a Dynamic Linear Time Temporal Logic (DLTL). This logic provides a simple formalization of the communicative actions in terms of their effects and preconditions. Furthermore it allows to specify interaction protocols by means of temporal constraints representing permissions and commitments. Agent programs, when known, can be formulated in DLTL as complex actions (regular programs). The paper addresses several kinds of verification problems including the problem of compliance of agents to the protocol, and describes how they can be solved by model checking in DLTL using automata.

1 Introduction

The specification and the verification of the behavior of interacting agents is one of the central issues in the area of multi-agent systems. In this paper we address the problem of specifying and verifying systems of communicating agents in a Dynamic Linear Time Temporal Logic (DLTL).

The extensive use of temporal logics in the specification and verification of distributed systems has led to the development of many techniques and tools for automating the verification task. Recently, temporal logics have gained attention in the area of reasoning about actions and planning [2,10,12,17,5], and they have also been used in the specification and in the verification of systems of communicating agents. In particular, in [21] agents are written in MABLE, an imperative programming language, and the formal claims about the system are expressed using a quantified linear time temporal BDI logic and can be automatically verified by making use of the SPIN model checker. Guerin in [13] defines an agent communication framework which gives agent communication a grounded declarative semantics. In such a framework, temporal logic is used for formalizing temporal properties of the system.

In this paper we present a theory for reasoning about communicative actions in a multiagent system which is based on the Dynamic Linear Time Temporal

---

[*] This research has been partially supported by the project PRIN 2003 "Logic-based development and verification of multi-agent systems", and by the European Commission within the 6th Framework Programme project REWERSE number 506779

J.J. Alferes and J. Leite (Eds.): JELIA 2004, LNAI 3229, pp. 57–69, 2004.

Logic (*DLTL*) [15], which extends LTL by strengthening the *until* operator by indexing it with the regular programs of dynamic logic. As a difference with [21] we adopt a social approach to agent communication [1,7,19,13], in which communicative actions affect the "social state" of the system, rather than the internal (mental) states of the agents. The social state records social facts, like the permissions and the commitments of the agents. The dynamics of the system emerges from the interactions of the agents, which must respect these permissions and commitments (if they are compliant with the protocol). The social approach allows a high level specification of the protocol, and does not require the rigid specification of the allowed action sequences. It is well suited for dealing with "open" multiagent systems, where the history of communications is observable, but the internal states of the single agents may not be observable.

Our proposal relies on the theory for reasoning about action developed in [10] which is based on DLTL and which allows reasoning with incomplete initial states and dealing with postdiction, ramifications as well as with nondeterministic actions. It allows a simple formalization of the communicative actions in terms of their effects and preconditions as well as the specification of an interaction protocol to constrain the behaviors of autonomous agents.

In [11] we have presented a proposal for reasoning about communicating agents in the Product Version of DLTL, which allows to describe the behavior of a network of sequential agents which coordinate their activities by performing common actions together. Here we focus on the non-product version of DLTL, which appears to be a simpler choice and also a more reasonable choice when a social approach is adopted. In fact, the Product Version of DLTL does not allow to describe global properties of a system of agents, as it keeps the local states of the agents separate. Instead, the "social state" of the system is inherently global and shared by all of the agents. Moreover, we will see that the verification tasks described in [11] can be conveniently represented in DLTL without requiring the product version. The verification of the compliance of an agent to the protocol, the verification of protocol properties, the verification that an agent is (is not) respecting its social facts (commitments and permissions) at runtime are all examples of tasks which can be formalized either as validity or as satisfiability problems in DLTL. Such verification tasks can be automated by making use of Büchi automata. In particular, we make use of the tableau-based algorithm presented in [9] for constructing a Büchi automaton from a DLTL formula. The construction of the automata can be done on-the-fly, while checking for the emptiness of the language accepted by the automaton. As for LTL, the number of states of the automata is, in the worst case, exponential in the size of the input formula.

2   Dynamic Linear Time Temporal Logic

In this section we shortly define the syntax and semantics of DLTL as introduced in [15]. In such a linear time temporal logic the next state modality is indexed by actions. Moreover, (and this is the extension to LTL) the until operator is indexed by programs in Propositional Dynamic Logic (PDL).

Let Σ be a finite non-empty alphabet. The members of Σ are actions. Let Σ^* and Σ^ω be the set of finite and infinite words on Σ, where $\omega = \{0, 1, 2, \ldots\}$. Let $\Sigma^\infty = \Sigma^* \cup \Sigma^\omega$. We denote by σ, σ' the words over Σ^ω and by τ, τ' the words over Σ^*. Moreover, we denote by $\leq$ the usual prefix ordering over Σ^* and, for $u \in \Sigma^\infty$, we denote by $prf(u)$ the set of finite prefixes of u.

We define the set of programs (regular expressions) $Prg(\Sigma)$ generated by Σ as follows:

$$Prg(\Sigma) ::= a \mid \pi_1 + \pi_2 \mid \pi_1; \pi_2 \mid \pi^*$$

where $a \in \Sigma$ and π_1, π_2, π range over $Prg(\Sigma)$. A set of finite words is associated with each program by the mapping $[[]] : Prg(\Sigma) \to 2^{\Sigma^*}$, which is defined as follows:

- $[[a]] = \{a\}$;
- $[[\pi_1 + \pi_2]] = [[\pi_1]] \cup [[\pi_2]]$;
- $[[\pi_1; \pi_2]] = \{\tau_1 \tau_2 \mid \tau_1 \in [[\pi_1]] \text{ and } \tau_2 \in [[\pi_2]]\}$;
- $[[\pi^*]] = \bigcup [[\pi^i]]$, where
  - $[[\pi^0]] = \{\varepsilon\}$
  - $[[\pi^{i+1}]] = \{\tau_1 \tau_2 \mid \tau_1 \in [[\pi]] \text{ and } \tau_2 \in [[\pi^i]]\}$, for every $i \in \omega$.

Let $\mathcal{P} = \{p_1, p_2, \ldots\}$ be a countable set of atomic propositions. The set of formulas of DLTL(Σ) is defined as follows:

$$\text{DLTL}(\Sigma) ::= p \mid \neg\alpha \mid \alpha \vee \beta \mid \alpha \mathcal{U}^\pi \beta$$

where $p \in \mathcal{P}$ and α, β range over DLTL(Σ).

A model of DLTL(Σ) is a pair $M = (\sigma, V)$ where $\sigma \in \Sigma^\omega$ and $V : prf(\sigma) \to 2^\mathcal{P}$ is a valuation function. Given a model $M = (\sigma, V)$, a finite word $\tau \in prf(\sigma)$ and a formula α, the satisfiability of a formula α at τ in M, written $M, \tau \models \alpha$, is defined as follows:

- $M, \tau \models p$ iff $p \in V(\tau)$;
- $M, \tau \models \neg\alpha$ iff $M, \tau \not\models \alpha$;
- $M, \tau \models \alpha \vee \beta$ iff $M, \tau \models \alpha$ or $M, \tau \models \beta$;
- $M, \tau \models \alpha \mathcal{U}^\pi \beta$ iff there exists $\tau' \in [[\pi]]$ such that $\tau\tau' \in prf(\sigma)$ and $M, \tau\tau' \models \beta$. Moreover, for every τ'' such that $\varepsilon \leq \tau'' < \tau'^1$, $M, \tau\tau'' \models \alpha$.

A formula α is satisfiable iff there is a model $M = (\sigma, V)$ and a finite word $\tau \in prf(\sigma)$ such that $M, \tau \models \alpha$.

The formula $\alpha \mathcal{U}^\pi \beta$ is true at τ if "α until β" is true on a finite stretch of behavior which is in the linear time behavior of the program π.

The derived modalities $\langle\pi\rangle$ and $[\pi]$ can be defined as follows: $\langle\pi\rangle\alpha \equiv \top \mathcal{U}^\pi \alpha$ and $[\pi]\alpha \equiv \neg\langle\pi\rangle\neg\alpha$.

---

[1] We define $\tau \leq \tau'$ iff $\exists \tau''$ such that $\tau\tau'' = \tau'$. Moreover, $\tau < \tau'$ iff $\tau \leq \tau'$ and $\tau \neq \tau'$.

Furthermore, if we let $\Sigma = \{a_1, \ldots, a_n\}$, the $\mathcal{U}$, O (next), $\diamond$ and $\square$ operators of LTL can be defined as follows: $O\alpha \equiv \bigvee_{a \in \Sigma} \langle a \rangle \alpha$, $\alpha \mathcal{U} \beta \equiv \alpha \mathcal{U}^{\Sigma^*} \beta$, $\diamond \alpha \equiv \top \mathcal{U} \alpha$, $\square \alpha \equiv \neg \diamond \neg \alpha$, where, in $\mathcal{U}^{\Sigma^*}$, Σ is taken to be a shorthand for the program $a_1 + \ldots + a_n$. Hence both LTL(Σ) and PDL are fragments of DLTL(Σ). As shown in [15], DLTL(Σ) is strictly more expressive than LTL(Σ). In fact, DLTL has the full expressive power of the monadic second order theory of ω-sequences.

3   Action Theories

In this section we recall the action theory developed in [10] that we use for specifying the interaction between communicating agents.

Let $\mathcal{P}$ be a set of atomic propositions, the *fluent names*. A *fluent literal l* is a fluent name f or its negation $\neg f$. Given a fluent literal l, such that $l = f$ or $l = \neg f$, we define $|l| = f$. We will denote by Lit the set of all fluent literals.

A *domain description D* is defined as a tuple $(\Pi, \mathcal{C})$, where Π is a set of *action laws* and *causal laws*, and $\mathcal{C}$ is a set of *constraints*.

Action laws in Π have the form: $\square(\alpha \rightarrow [a]\beta)$, with $a \in \Sigma$ and α, β arbitrary formulas, meaning that executing action a in a state where precondition α holds causes the effect β to hold.

Causal laws in Π have the form: $\square((\alpha \wedge \bigcirc \beta) \rightarrow \bigcirc \gamma)$, meaning that if α holds in a state and β holds in the next state, then γ also holds in the next state. Such laws are intended to expresses "causal" dependencies among fluents.

Constraints in $\mathcal{C}$ are arbitrary temporal formulas of $DLTL$. In particular, the set of constraints $\mathcal{C}$ contains all the temporal formulas which might be needed to constrain the behaviour of a protocol, including the value of fluents in the initial state. The set of constraints $\mathcal{C}$ also includes the precondition laws.

Precondition laws have the form: $\square(\alpha \rightarrow [a]\perp)$, meaning that the execution of an action a is not possible if α holds (i.e. there is no resulting state following the execution of a if α holds). Observe that, when there is no precondition law for an action, the action is executable in all states.

Action laws and causal laws describe the changes to the state. All other fluents which are not changed by the actions are assumed to persist unaltered to the next state. To cope with the *frame problem*, the laws in Π, describing the (immediate and ramification) effects of actions, have to be distinguished from the constraints in $\mathcal{C}$ and given a special treatment. In [10], to deal with the frame problem, a completion construction is defined which, given a domain description, introduces frame axioms for all the frame fluents in the style of the successor state axioms introduced by Reiter [18] in the context of the situation calculus. The completion construction is applied only to the action laws and causal laws in Π and not to the constraints. In the following we call $Comp(\Pi)$ the completion of a set of laws Π and we refer to [10] for the details on the completion construction.

Test actions allow the choice among different behaviours to be controlled. As $DLTL$ does not include test actions, we introduce them in the language as atomic actions in the same way as done in [10]. More precisely, we introduce an atomic action ϕ? for each proposition ϕ we want to test. The test action ϕ? is executable in any state in which ϕ holds and it has no effect on the state. Therefore, we introduce the following laws which rule the modality $[\phi?]$:

$$\Box(\neg\phi \to [\phi?]\bot)$$
$$\Box((\langle\phi?\rangle\top \to (L \leftrightarrow [\phi?]L)), \text{ for all fluent literals } L.$$

The first law is a precondition law, saying that action ϕ? is only executable in a state in which ϕ holds. The second law describes the effects of the action on the state: the execution of the action ϕ? leaves the state unchanged. We assume that, for all test actions occurring in a domain description, the corresponding action laws are implicitly added.

As a difference from [10], in this paper we will use, besides boolean fluents, *functional fluents*, i.e. fluents which take a value in a (finite) set. We use the notation $f = V$ to say that fluent f has value V. It is clear however, that functional fluents can be easily represented by making use of multiple (and mutually exclusive) boolean fluents.

4   Contract Net Protocol

In the social approach [7,13,19,22] an interaction protocol is specified by describing the effects of communicative actions on the social state, and by specifying the permissions and the commitments that arise as a result of the current conversation state. In our action theory the effects of communicative actions will be modelled by *action laws*. Permissions, which determine when an action can be taken by each agent, can be modelled by *precondition laws*. Commitment policies, which rule the dynamic of commitments, can be described by *causal laws* which establish the causal dependencies among fluents. The specification of a protocol can be further constrained through the addition of suitable *temporal formulas*, and also the agents' programs can be modelled, by making use of complex actions (regular programs).

As a running example we will use the Contract Net protocol [6].

Example 1. The Contract Net protocol begins with an agent (the manager) broadcasting a task announcement (call for proposals) to other agents viewed as potential contractors (the participants). Each participant can reply by sending either a proposal or a refusal. The manager must send an accept or reject message to all those who sent a proposal. When a contractor receives an acceptance it is committed to perform the task. For lack of space we will leave out the final step of the protocol.

Let us consider first the simplest case where we have only two agents: the manager (M) and the participant (P). The two agents share all the communicative actions, which are: *cfp(T)* (the manager issues a call for proposals for task T), *accept* and *reject* whose sender is the manager, and *refuse* and *propose* whose sender is the participant.

The social state will contain the following domain specific fluents: *task* (a functional fluent whose value is the task which has been announced, or *nil* if the task has not yet been announced), *replied* (the participant has replied), *proposal* (the participant has sent a proposal) and *acc_rej* (the manager has sent an accept or reject message). Such fluents describe observable facts concerning the execution of the protocol.

We also introduce special fluents to represent *base-level commitments* of the form $C(i, j, \alpha)$, meaning that agent i is committed to agent j to bring about α, where α is an arbitrary formula, or they can be *conditional commitments* of the form $CC(i, j, \beta, \alpha)$ (agent i is committed to agent j to bring about α, if the condition β is brought about)[2]. For modelling the Contract Net example we introduce the following commitments

$C(P, M, replied)$ and $C(M, P, acc\_rej)$

and conditional commitments

$CC(P, M, task \neq nil, replied)$ and $CC(M, P, proposal, acc\_rej)$.

Some reasoning rules have to be defined for cancelling commitments when they have been fulfilled and for dealing with conditional commitments. We introduce the following *causal laws*:

$\Box(\bigcirc\alpha \rightarrow \bigcirc\neg C(i, j, \alpha))$
$\Box(\bigcirc\alpha \rightarrow \bigcirc\neg CC(i, j, \beta, \alpha))$
$\Box((CC(i, j, \beta, \alpha) \wedge \bigcirc\beta) \rightarrow \bigcirc(C(i, j, \alpha) \wedge \neg CC(i, j, \beta, \alpha)))$

A commitment (or a conditional commitment) to bring about α is cancelled when α holds, and a conditional commitment $CC(i, j, \beta, \alpha)$ becomes a base-level commitment $C(i, j, \alpha)$ when β has been brought about.

Let us now describe the effects of communicative actions by the following *action laws*:

$\Box[cfp(T)]task = T$
$\Box[cfp(T)]CC(M, P, proposal, acc\_rej)$
$\Box[accept]acc\_rej$
$\Box[reject]acc\_rej$
$\Box[refuse]replied$
$\Box[propose](replied \wedge proposal)$

The laws for action $cfp(T)$ add to the social state the information that a call for proposal has been done for the task T, and that, if the manager receives a proposal, it is committed to accept or reject it.

The permissions to execute communicative actions in each state are determined by social facts. We represent them by precondition laws. Preconditions on the execution of action *accept* can be expressed as:

---

[2] The two kinds of base-level and conditional commitments we allow are essentially those introduced in [22]. Such choice is different from the one in [13] and in [11], where agents are committed to execute an action rather than to achieve a condition.

$$\Box(\neg proposal \lor acc\_rej \rightarrow [accept]\bot)$$

meaning that action *accept* cannot be executed only if a proposal has not been done, or if the manager has already replied. Similarly we can give the *precondition laws* for the other actions:

$$\Box(\neg proposal \lor acc\_rej \rightarrow [reject]\bot)$$
$$\Box(task = nil \lor replied \rightarrow [refuse]\bot)$$
$$\Box(task = nil \lor replied \rightarrow [propose]\bot)$$
$$\Box(task \neq nil \rightarrow [cfp(T)]\bot).$$

The precondition law for action *propose* (*refuse*) says that a proposal can only be done if $task \neq nil$, that is, if a task has already been announced and the participant has not already replied. The last law says that the manager cannot issue a new call for proposal if $task \neq nil$, that is, if a task has already been announced.

In the following we will denote $Perm_i$ (permissions of agent i) the set of all the precondition laws of the protocol pertaining to the actions of which agent i is the sender.

Assume now that we want the participant to be committed to reply to the task announcement. We can express it by adding the following conditional commitment to the initial state of the protocol: $CC(P, M, task \neq nil, replied)$. Furthermore the manager is committed initially to issue a call for proposal for a task. We can define the *initial state Init* of the protocol as follows:

$$\{task = nil, \neg replied, \neg proposal, CC(P, M, task \neq nil, replied),$$
$$C(M, P, task \neq nil)\}$$

In the following we will be interested in those execution of the protocol in which all commitments have been fulfilled. We can express the condition that the commitment $C(i, j, \alpha)$ will be fulfilled by the following constraint:

$$\Box(C(i, j, \alpha) \rightarrow \Diamond\alpha)$$

We will call Com_i the set of constraints of this kind for all commitments of agent i. Com_i states that agent i will fulfill all the commitments of which he is the debtor.

Given the above rules, the domain description $D = (\Pi, \mathcal{C})$ of a protocol is defined as follows: Π is the set of the action and causal laws given above, and $\mathcal{C} = Init \land \bigwedge_i(Perm_i \land Com_i)$ is the set containing the constraints on the initial state, the permissions $Perm_i$ and the commitments Com_i of all the agents (the agents P and M, in this example).

Given a domain description D, let the completed domain description $Comp(D)$ be the set of formulas $(Comp(\Pi) \land Init \land \bigwedge_i(Perm_i \land Com_i))$. The runs of the system according the protocol are the linear models of $Comp(D)$. Observe that in these protocol runs all permissions and commitments have been fulfilled. However, if Com_j is not included for some agent j, the runs may contain commitments which have not been fulfilled by j.

5   Verification

Given the DLTL specification of a protocol by a domain description, we describe the different kinds of verification problems which can be addressed.

First, given an execution history describing the interactions of the agents, we want to verify the compliance of that execution to the protocol. This verification is carried out at runtime. We are given a history $\tau = a_1, \ldots, a_n$ of the communicative actions executed by the agents, and we want to verify that the history τ is the prefix of a run of the protocol, that is, it respects the permissions and commitments of the protocol. This problem can be formalized by requiring that the formula

$$(Comp(\Pi) \wedge Init \wedge \bigwedge_i (Perm_i \wedge Com_i)) \wedge < a_1; a_2; \ldots; a_n > \top$$

(where i ranges on all the agents involved in the protocol) is satisfiable. In fact, the above formula is satisfiable if it is possible to find a run of the protocol starting with the action sequence $a_1, \ldots, a_n$.

A second problem is that of proving a property φ of a protocol. This can be formulated as the validity of the formula

$$(Comp(\Pi) \wedge Init \wedge \bigwedge_i (Perm_i \wedge Com_i)) \rightarrow \varphi. \tag{1}$$

Observe that, to prove the property φ, all the agents are assumed to be compliant with the protocol.

A further problem is to verify that an agent is compliant with the protocol, given the program executed by the agent itself. In our formalism we can specify the behavior of an agent by making use of complex actions (regular programs). Consider for instance the following program π_P for the participant:

$[\neg done?; ((cfp(T); eval\_task; (\neg ok?; refuse; exit + ok?; propose)) + (reject; exit) + (accept; do\_task; exit))]^*; done?$

The participant cycles and reacts to the messages received by the manager: for instance, if the manager has issued a call for proposal, the participant can either refuse or make a proposal according to his evaluation of the task; if the manager has accepted the proposal, the participant performs the task; and so on.

The state of the agent is obtained by adding to the fluents of the protocol the following local fluents: *done*, which is initially false and is made true by action *exit*, and *ok* which says if the agent must make a bid or not. The local actions are *eval_task*, which evaluates the task and sets the fluent *ok* to true or false, *do_task* and *exit*. Furthermore, *done?* and *ok?* are test actions.

The program of the contractor can be specified by a domain description $Prog_P = (\Pi_P, C_P)$, where Π_P is a set of action laws describing the effects of the private actions of the contractor, for instance:

$\square[exit]done$
$\square(task = t1 \rightarrow [eval\_task]ok)$
$\square(task = t2 \rightarrow [eval\_task]\neg ok)$

and, $\mathcal{C}_P = \{\langle \pi_P \rangle \top, \neg done, \neg ok\}$ contains the constraints on the initial values of fluents $(\neg done, \neg ok)$ as well as the formula $\langle \pi_P \rangle \top$ stating that the program of the participant is executable in the initial state.

We want now to prove that the participant is compliant with the protocol, i.e. that all executions of program π_P satisfy the specification of the protocol. This property cannot be proved by considering only the program π_P. In fact, it is easy to see that the correctness of the property depends on the behavior of the manager. For instance, if the manager begins with an *accept* action, the participant will execute the sequence of actions $accept; do\_task; exit$ and stop, which is not a correct execution of the protocol. Thus we have to take into account also the behavior of the manager. Since we don't know its internal behavior, we will assume that the manager respects its public behavior, i.e. that it respects its permissions and commitments in the protocol specification.

The verification that the participant is compliant with the protocol can be formalized as a validity check. Let $D = (\Pi, \mathcal{C})$ be the domain description describing the protocol, as defined above. The formula

$$(Comp(\Pi) \wedge Init \wedge Perm_M \wedge Com_M \wedge Comp(\Pi_P) \wedge \mathcal{C}_P) \rightarrow (Perm_P \wedge Com_P)$$

is valid if in all the behaviors of the system, in which the participant executes its program π_P and the manager (whose internal program is unknown) respects the protocol specification (in particular, its permissions and commitments), the permissions and commitment of the participant are also satisfied.

6   Contract Net with N Participants

Let us assume now that we have N potential contractors. The above formulation of the protocol can be extended by introducing a fluent $replied(i)$, $proposal(i)$ and $acc\_rej(i)$ for each participant i, and similarly for the commitments. Furthermore we introduce the communicative actions $refuse(i)$, and $propose(i)$, which are sent from participant i to the manager, and $reject(i)$ and $accept(i)$, which are sent from the manager to participant i. We assume action $cfp(T)$ to be shared by all agents (broadcast by the manager).

The theory describing the new version of the protocol can be easily obtained from the one given above. For instance the precondition laws for $accept(i)$ and $reject(i)$ must be modified so that these actions will be executed only after all participants have replied to the manager, i.e.:

$$\square((\neg proposal(i) \vee acc\_rej(i) \vee \bigvee_{j=1,N} \neg replied(j)) \rightarrow [accept(i)]\bot)$$

and the same for $reject(i)$.

The verification problems mentioned before can be formulated using the same approach. For instance, the verification that the protocol satisfies a given property φ can be expressed as the validity of the formula (1) above, where i ranges

over the N participants and the manager. To prove compliance of a participant
with the protocol, we need to restrict the protocol to the actions and the fluents
shared between the manager and this participant (i.e. we need to take the projection of the protocol on agent i and the agents with whom i interacts). Then
the problem can be formulated as in the case of a single participant.

We have not considered here the formulation of the problem in which proposals must be submitted within a given deadline. This would require adding to
the system a further agent *clock*.

7 Model Checking

The above verification and satisfiability problems can be solved by extending the
standard approach for verification and model-checking of Linear Time Temporal
Logic, based on the use of Büchi automata. As described in [15], the satisfiability
problem for DLTL can be solved in deterministic exponential time, as for LTL,
by constructing for each formula $\alpha \in DLTL(\Sigma)$ a Büchi automaton $\mathcal{B}_\alpha$ such
that the language of ω-words accepted by $\mathcal{B}_\alpha$ is non-empty if and only if α
is satisfiable. Actually a stronger property holds, since there is a one to one
correspondence between models of the formula and infinite words accepted by
$\mathcal{B}_\alpha$. The size of the automaton can be exponential in the size of α, while emptiness
can be detected in a time linear in the size of the automaton.

The validity of a formula α can be verified by constructing the Büchi au-
tomaton $\mathcal{B}_{\neg\alpha}$ for $\neg\alpha$: if the language accepted by $\mathcal{B}_{\neg\alpha}$ is empty, then α is valid,
whereas any infinite word accepted by $\mathcal{B}_{\neg\alpha}$ provides a counterexample to the
validity of α.

For instance, let CN be the completed domain description of the Contract
Net protocol, that is $CN = (Comp(\Pi) \wedge Init \wedge \bigwedge_i (Perm_i \wedge Com_i))$. Then
every infinite word accepted by $\mathcal{B}_{CN}$ corresponds to a possible execution of the
protocol. To prove a property φ of the protocol, we can build the automaton
$\mathcal{B}_{\neg\varphi}$ and check that the language accepted by the product of $\mathcal{B}_{CN}$ and $\mathcal{B}_{\neg\varphi}$ is
empty.

The construction given in [15] is highly inefficient since it requires to build
an automaton with an exponential number of states, most of which will not be
reachable from the initial state. A more efficient approach for constructing a
Büchi automaton from a DLTL formula makes use of a tableau-based algorithm
[9]. The construction of the states of the automaton is similar to the standard
construction for LTL [8], but the possibility of indexing until formulas with
regular programs puts stronger constraints on the fulfillment of until formulas
than in LTL, requiring more complex acceptance conditions. The construction
of the automaton can be done on-the-fly, while checking for the emptiness of the
language accepted by the automaton. Given a formula φ, the algorithm builds a
graph $\mathcal{G}(\varphi)$ whose nodes are labelled by sets of formulas. States and transitions
of the Büchi automaton correspond to nodes and arcs of the graph. The algorithm makes use of an auxiliary tableau-based function which expands the set
of formulas at each node. As for LTL, the number of states of the automaton is,

in the worst case, exponential in the size if the input formula, but in practice it is much smaller. For instance, the automaton obtained from the Contract Net protocol has about 20 states.

LTL is widely used to prove properties of (possibly concurrent) programs by means of *model checking* techniques. The property is represented as an LTL formula φ, whereas the program generates a Kripke structure (the model), which directly corresponds to a Büchi automaton where all the states are accepting, and which describes all possible computations of the program. The property can be proved as before by taking the product of the model and of the automaton derived from $\neg\varphi$, and by checking for emptiness of the accepted language.

In principle, with DLTL we do not need to use model checking, because programs and domain descriptions can be represented in the logic itself, as we have shown in the previous section. However representing everything as a logical formula can be rather inefficient from a computational point of view. In particular all formulas of the domain description are universally quantified, and this means that our algorithm will have to propagate them from each state to the next one, and to expand them with the tableau procedure at each step.

Therefore we have adapted model checking to the proof of the formulas given in the previous section, as follows. Let us assume that the negation of a formula to be proved can be represented as $F \wedge \varphi$, where $F = Comp(\Pi) \wedge Init$ contains the completion of the action and causal laws in the domain description and the initial state, and φ the rest of the formula. For instance, in the verification of the compliance of the participant, the negation of the formula to be proved is $(Comp(\Pi) \wedge Init \wedge Perm_M \wedge Com_M \wedge Comp(\Pi_P) \wedge \neg(Perm_P \wedge Com_P))$ and thus $\varphi = (Perm_M \wedge Com_M \wedge Comp(\Pi_P) \wedge \neg(Perm_P \wedge Com_P))$. We can derive from F an automaton describing all possible computations, whose states are sets of fluents, which we consider as the model. In particular, we can obtain from the domain description a function $trans_a(S)$, for each action a, for transforming a state in the next one, and then build this automaton by repeatedly applying these functions starting from the initial state. We can then proceed by taking the product of the model and of the automaton derived from φ, and by checking for emptiness of the accepted language.

Note that, although this automaton has an exponential number of states, we can build it step by step by following the construction of the algorithm on-the-fly. The state of the product automaton will consist of two parts $< S_1, S_2 >$, where S_1 is a set of fluents representing a state of the model, and S_2 is a set of formulas. The initial state will be $< I, \varphi >$, where I is the initial set of fluents. A successor state through a transition a will be obtained as $< trans_a(S_1), S_2' >$ where S_2' is derived from S_2 by the on-the-fly algorithm. If the two parts of a state are inconsistent, the state is discarded.

8   Conclusions

We have shown that DLTL is a suitable formalism for specifying and verifying a system of communicating agents. Our approach provides a unified framework for describing different aspects of multi-agent systems. Programs are expressed as regular expressions, (communicative) actions can be specified by means of action and precondition laws, properties of social facts can be specified by means of causal laws and constraints, and temporal properties can be expressed by means of the *until* operator. We have addressed several kinds of verification problems, including the problem of compliance of agents to the protocol, and described how they can be solved by developing automata-based model checking techniques for DLTL. A preliminary implementation of a model checker based on the algorithm in [9] is being tested in the verification of the properties of various protocols.

The issue of developing semantics for agent communication languages has been examined in [20], by considering in particular the problem of giving a *verifiable* semantics, i.e. a semantics *grounded* on the computational models. Guerin and Pitt [13,14] define an agent communication framework which gives agent communication a grounded declarative semantics. The framework introduces different languages: a language for agent programming, a language for specifying agent communication and social facts, and a language for expressing temporal properties. Our approach instead provides a unified framework for describing multiagent systems using DLTL.

While in this paper we follow a social approach to the specification and verification of systems of communicating agents, [4,3,16,21] have adopted a mentalistic approach. The goal of [3] is to extend model checking to make it applicable to multi-agent systems, where agents have BDI attitudes. This is achieved by using a new logic which is the composition of two logics, one formalizing temporal evolution and the other formalizing BDI attitudes. In [16,21] agents are written in MABLE, an imperative programming language, and have a mental state. MABLE systems may be augmented by the addition of formal claims about the system, expressed using a quantified, linear time temporal BDI logic. Instead [4] deals with programs written in AgentSpeak(F), a variation of the BDI logic programming language AgentSpeak(L). Properties of MABLE or AgentSpeak programs can be verified by means of the SPIN model checker. These papers do not deal with the problem of proving properties of protocols.

Yolum and Singh [22] developed a social approach to protocol specification and execution. In this approach, commitments are formalized in a variant of event calculus. By using an event calculus planner it is possible to determine execution paths that respect the protocol specification. Alberti et al. address a similar problem, by expressing protocols in a logic-based formalism based on Social Integrity Constraints. In [1] they present a system that, during the evolution of a society of agents, verifies the compliance of the agents' behavior to the protocol.

References

1. M. Alberti, D. Daolio and P. Torroni. Specification and Verification of Agent Interaction Protocols in a Logic-based System. *SAC'04*, March 2004.
2. F. Bacchus and F. Kabanza. Planning for temporally extended goals. in *Annals of Mathematics and AI*, 22:5–27, 1998.

3. M. Benerecetti, F. Giunchiglia and L. Serafini. Model Checking Multiagent Systems. *Journal of Logic and Computation.* Special Issue on Computational Aspects of Multi-Agent Systems, 8(3):401-423. 1998.
4. R. Bordini, M. Fisher, C. Pardavila and M. Wooldridge. Model Checking AgentSpeak. *AAMAS 2003*, pp. 409–416, 2003.
5. D. Calvanese, G. De Giacomo and M.Y.Vardi. Reasoning about Actions and Planning in LTL Action Theories. In Proc. *KR'02*, 2002.
6. FIPA Contract Net Interaction Protocol Specification, 2002. Available at http://www.fipa.org.
7. N. Fornara and M. Colombetti. Defining Interaction Protocols using a Commitment-based Agent Communication Language. *Proc. AAMAS'03*, Melbourne, pp. 520–527, 2003.
8. R. Gerth, D. Peled, M.Y.Vardi and P. Wolper. Simple On-the-fly Automatic verification of Linear Temporal Logic. In *Proc. 15th Work. Protocol Specification, Testing and Verification*, Warsaw, June 1995, North Holland.
9. L. Giordano and A. Martelli. On-the-fly Automata Construction for Dynamic Linear Time Temporal Logic. *TIME 04*, June 2004.
10. L. Giordano, A. Martelli, and C. Schwind. Reasoning About Actions in Dynamic Linear Time Temporal Logic. In FAPR'00 - Int. Conf. on Pure and Applied Practical Reasoning, London, September 2000. Also in *The Logic Journal of the IGPL*, Vol. 9, No. 2, pp. 289-303, March 2001.
11. L. Giordano, A. Martelli, and C. Schwind. Specifying and Verifying Systems of Communicating Agents in a Temporal Action Logic. In *Proc. AI*IA'03*, Pisa, pp. 262–274, Springer LNAI 2829, September 2003.
12. F. Giunchiglia and P. Traverso. Planning as Model Checking. In *Proc. The 5th European Conf. on Planning (ECP'99)*, pp.1–20, Durham (UK), 1999.
13. F. Guerin. Specifying Agent Communication Languages. PhD Thesis, Imperial College, London, April 2002.
14. F. Guerin and J. Pitt. Verification and Compliance Testing. *Communications in Multiagent Systems*, Springer LNAI 2650, pp. 98–112, 2003.
15. J.G. Henriksen and P.S. Thiagarajan. Dynamic Linear Time Temporal Logic. in *Annals of Pure and Applied logic*, vol.96, n.1-3, pp.187–207, 1999
16. M.P. Huget and M. Wooldridge. Model Checking for ACL Compliance Verification. *ACL 2003*, Springer LNCS 2922, pp. 75–90, 2003.
17. M.Pistore and P.Traverso. Planning as Model Checking for Extended Goals in Non-deterministic Domains. Proc. IJCAI'01, Seattle, pp.479-484, 2001.
18. R. Reiter. The frame problem in the situation calculus: a simple solution (sometimes) and a completeness result for goal regression. In *Artificial Intelligence and Mathematical Theory of Computation: Papers in Honor of John McCarthy*, V. Lifschitz, ed.,pages 359–380, Academic Press, 1991.
19. M. P. Singh. A social semantics for Agent Communication Languages. In *IJCAI-98 Workshop on Agent Communication Languages*, Springer, Berlin, 2000.
20. M. Wooldridge. Semantic Issues in the Verification of Agent Communication Languages. *Autonomous Agents and Multi-Agent Systems*, vol. 3, pp. 9-31, 2000.
21. M. Wooldridge, M. Fisher, M.P. Huget and S. Parsons. Model Checking Multi-Agent Systems with MABLE. In *AAMAS'02*, pp. 952–959, Bologna, Italy, 2002.
22. P. Yolum and M.P. Singh. Flexible Protocol Specification and Execution: Applying Event Calculus Planning using Commitments. In *AAMAS'02*, pp. 527–534, Bologna, Italy, 2002.

Qualitative Action Theory
A Comparison of the Semantics of Alternating-Time Temporal Logic and the Kutschera-Belnap Approach to Agency

Stefan Wölfl

Institut für Informatik, Albert-Ludwigs-Universität Freiburg
Georges-Köhler-Allee, 79110 Freiburg, Germany
woelfl@informatik.uni-freiburg.de

Abstract. Qualitative action theory deals with purely qualitative descriptions and formal representations of agency, i.e., agents and their possibilities for intervening in the causal flow of events. This means that, contrary to game theory, qualitative action theory abstains from any metric evaluation of the outcomes of actions.

In this paper we present and compare two qualitative approaches to action theory that have been discussed in the literature. The first one coming from philosophical action theory is the Kutschera-Belnap approach, which is the semantic basis of so-called Stit-logics. The second approach is the semantics of Alur, Henzinger, and Kupferman's Alternating-time Temporal Logic (ATL). In computer science, ATL has been introduced as an extension of Computational Tree Logic (CTL) to allow for modeling systems that interact with their environment. Surprisingly, although both approaches are very close in spirit, a systematic analysis of the mutual dependencies between these approaches does not exist.

The paper aims at bringing together these two research streams, which seem to have been developed independently in philosophy and computer science. In particular, we will investigate the assumptions with which both approaches may be considered equivalent. Finally, further research on this topic promises interesting results that translate between the approaches presented here.

1 Introduction

Qualitative action theory deals with purely qualitative descriptions and formal representations of agency, i.e., agents and their possibilities for intervening in the causal flow of events. Qualitative theories of agency are typically situated in a setting that is well-known in game-theory: there are agents (or players) and each agent has choices concerning how to act (possible moves in the play), where the set of choices an agent has may depend on the current state. Contrary to game theory, however, qualitative action theory abstains from any metric evaluation of the outcomes of the actions. This means, in particular, that qualitative action theory does not aim at a theory of how to act *rationally* in a specific situation,

J.J. Alferes and J. Leite (Eds.): JELIA 2004, LNAI 3229, pp. 70–81, 2004.
© Springer-Verlag Berlin Heidelberg 2004

but rather restricts consideration to purely descriptive questions such as: what possibilities does an agent have, and how could the world look like, when all the agents behave in a certain manner.

Qualitative action theory (in the narrow sense) restricts consideration to concepts that are definable by causal notions and by terms describing the possible choices of agents. Examples of such *core concepts* include the concept of *action*, the concept of *bringing-it-about-that*, and the concept of *strategy*. In the wider sense qualitative action theory also takes into account concepts referring to doxastic and/or voluntative aspects of agency, such as *beliefs*, *intentions*, *reasons*, *goals*, and *aims*.

In this paper we focus on two qualitative (core) approaches to action theory discussed in the literature. The first one, coming from philosophical action theory, is the Kutschera-Belnap approach to agency. Historically, the first approach using game-theoretical notions for analyses in philosophical action theory was presented by Lennart Åqvist [3]. Based on Åqvist's and Georg H. von Wright's work on agency and Roman Ingarden's work on causality, Franz von Kutschera developed in the 1980s an approach to agency that took the idea seriously that agency is only explainable in the context of an indeterministic theory (cf. [14]). Kutschera presented formal models for representing agency, and he also developed a semantics for action logics. Further developments were contributed by, among others, Nuel D. Belnap, Brian F. Chellas, John F. Horty, and Michael Perloff. In particular, Belnap contributed many philosophical investigations regarding an indeterminist view of agency. He developed a formal semantics that allows for modeling assertions (as speech acts), promisings, and moral obligations.[1] Based on Kutschera and Belnap's semantics, Ming Xu discussed axiomatizations of action-theoretical concepts. In the literature these logical systems are usually referred to as *stit-logics*.[2]

The second approach discussed in this paper is the semantics of Alur, Henzinger, and Kupferman's Alternating-time Temporal Logic (ATL) [1]. In computer science ATL has been introduced as an extension of Computational Tree Logics (CTL) to allow for modeling systems that interact with their environment. In this context it is worth mentioning that there is a close connection between ATL and M. Pauly's *Coalition Game Logic (CGL)* [15,16], as has been pointed out by Valentin Goranko [11]. In particular, ATL, CGL, and game theory share the assumption of a discrete flow of time, while the Kutschera-Belnap approach (in the sequel abbreviated by *KB-approach*) also allows for dense or continuous flows.

Surprisingly, although the Kutschera-Belnap approach and the ATL approach are very close in spirit, a systematic analysis of the mutual dependencies between these approaches does not exist. This paper aims at bringing together these two research streams, which seem to have developed independently in phi-

---

[1] For discussions of the Kutschera-Belnap approach and for explications of action-theoretical notions in this approach see [4,5], [10], [6,7,8], [12], and [13,14]. A comprising presentation of the current state of discussion may be found in [9].

[2] Cf. [19,20,21,22,23,24] as well as [17].

losophy and computer science. In particular, we will investigate the assumptions with which both approaches may be considered equivalent theories. Finally, further research on this topic promises interesting results that translate between the semantic approaches presented here and the logics defined in terms of these semantics respectively.

2   The Kutschera-Belnap Approach

The basic idea of the Kutschera-Belnap approach can be briefly sketched in the slogan: 'No agency without real choices'. This means that in order to ascribe agency to agents, we must ascribe to them genuine choices for how to act, i. e., choices by which agents can influence the causal flow of events. These choices are *genuine* in that each agent must be able to refrain from what s/he is actually doing. In particular, each agent can realize one of her/his choices independently of what the other agents do at the same moment. Thus, the Kutschera-Belnap approach implicitly assumes that the causal flow of events is not causally determined: If any event were causally determined (by previous events and/or previous circumstances), we would never be able to ascribe genuine choices to agents.

This indeterministic point of view, then, is modeled by tree-like formal structures, i. e., by structures consisting of a set of nodes (called *moments*) and a binary relation defined on this set, which represents the relation of *being-causally-earlier-than*. This relation allows for branching with respect to the future, but not with respect to the past. A (full) branch of such a 'tree' is called *possible history* and represents one of the many possible courses the world might take. The idea is that the future is causally open (in the sense that it is not causally determined by the present and the past), while the past is causally closed (events that occurred in the past are settled, they cannot be made undone). By acting, persons can influence the future, but not the present or the past. But whether an agent can do something or not depends on current circumstances, and these are subject to changes in time. Thus, it may occur that an agent can do something now, but that s/he can not at some later moment. To represent these intuitions within the basic tree-like models, one assigns to each agent at each moment a set of (possible) choices such that each choice is consistent with the choices of all the other agents.

These ideas are captured by the following formal definitions.

Definition 2.1 (Tree). A *tree* is an ordered pair $B = \langle \text{Mom}, \prec \rangle$ consisting of a non-void set Mom (the set of *moments*) and an irreflexive, transitive, and linear-to-the-left relation $\prec$ on Mom (the relation of *earlier-than*). A maximal $\prec$-chain is said to be a *history* in B, and the set of all histories of B is denoted by His. For each moment $m \in \text{Mom}$, let

$$\text{His}\langle m \rangle := \{ h \in \text{His} : m \in h \}$$

denote the set of histories that pass through moment m. Histories h and h' are said to be *undivided* at moment m, $h \perp_m h'$, if there exists a moment $m' \in h \cap h'$

with $m \prec m'$. If h and h' pass through m and if there does not exist any $m' \in h \cap h'$ with $m \prec m'$, then h and h' are said to *split* at m.

Definition 2.2 (Agent Tree). An *agent tree* is a triple $\mathcal{C} = \langle \mathcal{B}, \mathrm{Ag}, \mathrm{Ch} \rangle$, where $\mathcal{B}$ is a tree, Ag is a non-void set of *agents*, and Ch is a map that assigns to each agent $\alpha \in \mathrm{Ag}$ and each moment m of $\mathcal{B}$ a partition $\mathrm{Ch}_\alpha \langle m \rangle$ of $\mathrm{His} \langle m \rangle$ such that the following conditions are satisfied:

(a) If $h \in X \in \mathrm{Ch}_\alpha \langle m \rangle$ and if h and h' are undivided at m, then h' too is in X.

(b) Let m be a moment of $\mathcal{B}$ and suppose that χ is a map that assigns to each agent α an element $\chi(\alpha) \in \mathrm{Ch}_\alpha \langle m \rangle$. Then there exists a history h that is contained in each $\chi(\alpha)$, i.e.,

$$\bigcap_{\alpha \in \mathrm{Ag}} \chi(\alpha) \neq \emptyset.$$

The elements of $\mathrm{Ch}_\alpha \langle m \rangle$ are said to be the *(momentary) choices* of agent α at moment m, and $\mathrm{Ch}_\alpha \langle m \rangle$ is said to be the *choice set* of α at m. An agent α has *non-vacuous choice* at moment m if $\mathrm{Ch}_\alpha \langle m \rangle \neq \{ \mathrm{His} \langle m \rangle \}$, i.e., if α has at least two choices at m.

By saying that each agent's choice set forms a partition, we postulate that at each moment each agent chooses exactly one of her/his alternatives. Condition (a) of definition 2.2 means that an agent cannot separate histories that are undivided. Finally, by condition (b), each agent can choose an alternative in her/his choice set independently of the alternatives chosen by all the other agents (at the same moment). In particular, at a given moment m, no agent can prevent another agent from choosing any of her/his alternatives (at that moment).

Given a moment m and a history $h \in \mathrm{His} \langle m \rangle$, let $\mathrm{ch}_\alpha(m, h)$ denote the unique element of $\mathrm{Ch}_\alpha \langle m \rangle$ that contains h. This means that $\mathrm{ch}_\alpha(m, h)$ is the choice agent α takes in history h at moment m. An agent tree is said to be *agent-complete* if, for all moments $m \in \mathrm{Mom}$ and each pair of histories $h, h' \in \mathrm{His} \langle m \rangle$, it holds:

$$h' \in \bigcap_{\alpha \in \mathrm{Ag}} \mathrm{ch}_\alpha(m, h) \implies h \perp_m h'.$$

The condition of agent completeness was first discussed by Franz von Kutschera [14]. It may be read as: 'No splitting of the tree without the involvement of at least one of the agents.'

3   Alternating-Time Temporal Logic

Alternating-time temporal logic has been introduced to enrich the expressive power of computation tree logics (CTL) for model checking purposes. While CTL is considered a suitable representation for *closed* reactive systems, that is, systems that are completely determined by their current state, ATL aims at *open* systems, that is, systems that allow for interaction with their environment.

Thereto, Alur, Henzinger, and Kupferman [1] introduce the concept of *alternating transition system*, which extends the concept of *transition system* as discussed in CTL. The difference between CTL transition systems and alternating transition systems is characterized as follows: 'While in ordinary transitions systems, each transition corresponds to a possible step of the system, in alternating transition systems, each transition corresponds to a possible move in the game between the system and the environment' [2].

Definition 3.1 (Alternating Transition Frame). An *alternating transition frame* (abbr. by ATF) is a triple $\mathcal{F} = \langle \Sigma, Q, \delta \rangle$, where

(a) Σ is a (non-void) set of *agents*,

(b) Q is a (non-void) set of *states*, and

(c) $\delta \colon Q \times \Sigma \longrightarrow 2^{2^Q}$ is a map that assigns to each state q and each agent α a non-void set of choices, $\delta(q, \alpha)$, i.e., each choice is a set of possible next states,

such that for each state q and for each family $(Q_\alpha)_{\alpha \in \Sigma}$ of choices at q, i.e., $Q_\alpha \in \delta(q, \alpha)$, there exists exactly one state q^* with

$$q^* \in \bigcap_{\alpha \in \Sigma} Q_\alpha.$$

In the sequel, the function δ will be referred to as the *transition function*.

Some notations: Let q and q' be states of an ATF $\mathcal{F}$ and let α be an agent. State q' is said to be an α-*successor* of q if there exists a $Q' \in \delta(q, \alpha)$ with $q' \in Q'$. The set of all α-successors is denoted by $\mathrm{Succ}(q, \alpha)$. State q' is a *successor* of q if, in state q, each agent α has a choice Q_α containing q'. The heuristics of this definition is that q' is a successor of q if and only if, in state q, all the agents of $\mathcal{F}$ can cooperate in such a way that q' becomes the next state.

A *(full) computation* of $\mathcal{F}$ is an infinite sequence of states, $\lambda = (q_i)_{i \in \mathbb{N}}$, where each q_{i+1} is a successor of q_i. A *finite computation* (of length n) is an initial segment $\gamma = (q_1, \ldots, q_n)$ of a full computation. For a finite computation γ let n_γ be the length of γ. A q-*computation* is a computation starting in state q. In the sequel, $\lambda[i]$ will denote the i-th state of λ. The set of all (full) computations of $\mathcal{F}$ will be denoted by $\Lambda_{\mathcal{F}}$ and the set of all finite computations by $\Gamma_{\mathcal{F}}$.

The following example (cf. [1]) may help to illustrate the notions just introduced.

Example 3.2. Consider a system S with two processes α and β. In each state of the system, process α determines the truth value of proposition x and likewise process β that of y. We will assume that the system is completely described by propositions x and y, i.e., $Q = \{q, q_x, q_y, q_{xy}\}$, where q_x denotes the state in which x is true in the system, but y is not, etc. The transition function of the system is defined as follows: If S is in a state, in which x is false, α is free to leave the truth value of x unchanged or to change it to true. Otherwise, α leaves x unchanged. Similarly, if y is false, β can leave the value of y unchanged or make it true, and if y is true, β leaves the truth value of y unchanged. This transition function can be defined formally by:

$$\delta(q, \alpha) = \{\{q, q_y\}, \{q_x, q_{xy}\}\} \qquad \delta(q, \beta) = \{\{q, q_x\}, \{q_y, q_{xy}\}\}$$
$$\delta(q_x, \alpha) = \{\{q_x, q_{xy}\}\} \qquad \delta(q_x, \beta) = \{\{q, q_x\}, \{q_y, q_{xy}\}\}$$
$$\delta(q_y, \alpha) = \{\{q, q_y\}, \{q_x, q_{xy}\}\} \qquad \delta(q_y, \beta) = \{\{q_y, q_{xy}\}\}$$
$$\delta(q_{xy}, \alpha) = \{\{q_x, q_{xy}\}\} \qquad \delta(q_{xy}, \beta) = \{\{q_y, q_{xy}\}\}$$

4   From Alternating Transition Frames to Agent Trees

In what follows we now investigate the conditions with which the semantics of ATL can be embedded into the Kutschera-Belnap approach. To start with, let $\mathcal{F} = \langle \Sigma, Q, \delta \rangle$ be an ATF that satisfies the following two conditions:

(d) For each agent α and each state q, $\delta(q, \alpha)$ is a partition of $\mathrm{Succ}(q, \alpha)$.

(e) For each agent α and each state q, if q' is an α-successor of q, then q' is a β-successor of q for each agent β.

What is the meaning of these conditions? First, condition (d) seems quite plausible when looking at concrete examples of alternating transition frames. For condition (e), let us assume that q' is an α-successor of q, but that there is an agent β such that q' is not a β-successor of q. From this it follows that there does not exist any computation λ with $\lambda[i] = q$ and $\lambda[i+1] = q'$ for some $i \in \mathbb{N}$. But this means that we can withdraw q' from every $Q \in \delta(q, \alpha)$ without loosing any information about the possible runs of the system. If we do that for every agent at the same time, we obtain an ATF that satisfies condition (e).

For example, we could redefine the transition function of example 3.2 as follows:

$$\delta(q, \alpha) = \{\{q, q_y\}, \{q_x, q_{xy}\}\} \qquad \delta(q, \beta) = \{\{q, q_x\}, \{q_y, q_{xy}\}\}$$
$$\delta(q_x, \alpha) = \{\{q_x, q_{xy}\}\} \qquad \delta(q_x, \beta) = \{\{q_x\}, \{q_{xy}\}\}$$
$$\delta(q_y, \alpha) = \{\{q_y\}, \{q_{xy}\}\} \qquad \delta(q_y, \beta) = \{\{q_y, q_{xy}\}\}$$
$$\delta(q_{xy}, \alpha) = \{\{q_{xy}\}\} \qquad \delta(q_{xy}, \beta) = \{\{q_{xy}\}\}$$

This new transition function does not loose any information carried by the old one, but it does satisfy conditions (d) and (e).

Finally, from conditions (d) and (e) it follows that for each agent α and each state q, the choice set $\delta(q, \alpha)$ is a partition of the set of q-successors. In what follows an ATF satisfying these two conditions will be referred to as a *restricted ATF*.

Let now $\mathcal{F} = \langle \Sigma, Q, \delta \rangle$ be an arbitrary ATF. We define a tree $\mathcal{B}^{\mathcal{F}}$ by 'unwinding' $\mathcal{F}$ as follows:

$$\mathrm{Mom}^{\mathcal{F}} := \Gamma_{\mathcal{F}}$$
$$\gamma \prec^{\mathcal{F}} \gamma' :\Longleftrightarrow \gamma[i] = \gamma'[i], \text{ for each } i = 1, \dots, n_\gamma,$$
$$\text{and } n_\gamma < n_{\gamma'}.$$

Lemma 4.1. *The ordered pair $\mathcal{B}^{\mathcal{F}} = \langle \mathrm{Mom}^{\mathcal{F}}, \prec^{\mathcal{F}} \rangle$ is a tree, which has the following properties:*

(a) *There exists a bijective map between the set of computations of $\mathcal{F}$, $\Lambda_{\mathcal{F}}$, and the set of histories of $\mathcal{B}^{\mathcal{F}}$.*

(b) *For each finite computation $\gamma \in \Gamma$, there exists a bijective map between the set of computations with initial segment γ and the set of histories of $\mathcal{B}^{\mathcal{F}}$ that pass through 'moment' γ.*

Proof. First, it is quite obvious that $\prec^{\mathcal{F}}$ is an irreflexive, transitive, and linear-to-the-left relation. Second, if λ is a (full) computation of $\mathcal{F}$, then obviously

$$h_\lambda := \{ (\lambda[1], \dots, \lambda[n]) : n \in \mathbb{N} \}$$

is a maximal $\prec^{\mathcal{F}}$-chain of $\mathcal{B}^{\mathcal{F}}$. Vice versa, let now h be a history of $\mathcal{B}^{\mathcal{F}}$. Then h is a maximal $\prec^{\mathcal{F}}$-chain, i.e., a maximal subset of $\Lambda_{\mathcal{F}}$ that is linearly ordered by $\prec^{\mathcal{F}}$. Let $\gamma = (q_1, \dots, q_n) \in h$ be chosen arbitrarily. Then define $\lambda_h[1] := q_1, \dots, \lambda_h[n] := q_n$. Since q_n has at least one successor, $(q_1, \dots, q_n)$ cannot be the maximal element of h. Hence there exists a $\gamma' = (q'_1, \dots, q'_m) \in h$ with $\gamma \prec^{\mathcal{F}} \gamma'$. Extend λ_h by setting $\lambda_h[n+1] := q'_{n+1}, \dots, \lambda_h[m] := q'_m$. By this step-wise construction, one finally obtains a full computation λ_h.
It can readily be checked that the assignment $h \mapsto \lambda_h$ is the inverse of the mapping $\lambda \mapsto h_\lambda$. From this both claims (a) and (b) follow immediately. □

Let now $\mathcal{F} = \langle \Sigma, Q, \delta \rangle$ be a restricted ATF. For a finite computation γ, let $\Lambda(\gamma)$ be the set of all full computations λ that have γ as initial segment. Define

$$\mathrm{Ag}^{\mathcal{F}} := \Sigma$$
$$X \in \mathrm{Ch}_\alpha^{\mathcal{F}} \langle \gamma \rangle :\Longleftrightarrow \text{ there exists a } Q \in \delta(\gamma[n_\gamma], \alpha) \text{ such that}$$
$$X = \{ h_\lambda : \lambda \in \Lambda(\gamma) \text{ and } \lambda[n_\gamma + 1] \in Q \}.$$

Theorem 4.2. *For each restricted ATF $\mathcal{F} = \langle \Sigma, Q, \delta \rangle$, the triple*

$$\mathcal{C}^{\mathcal{F}} = \left\langle \mathcal{B}^{\mathcal{F}}, \mathrm{Ag}^{\mathcal{F}}, \mathrm{Ch}^{\mathcal{F}} \right\rangle$$

is an agent-complete agent tree.

Proof. From conditions (d) and (e) it follows that each $\delta(q, \alpha)$ is a partition of the set of successors of q. Let γ be a finite computation of $\mathcal{F}$. Then, by applying lemma 4.1(b), we immediately verify that each $\mathrm{Ch}_\alpha^{\mathcal{F}} \langle \gamma \rangle$ is a partition of the set of histories of $\mathcal{B}^{\mathcal{F}}$ that pass through γ. Conditions (a) and (b) of definition 2.2 are easy to check. Finally, $\mathcal{C}^{\mathcal{F}}$ is agent-complete, since for each family $(Q_\alpha)_{\alpha \in \Sigma}$ with $Q_\alpha \in \delta(q, \alpha)$, there exists at most one state $q^* \in \bigcap_{\alpha \in \Sigma} Q_\alpha$. □

5   From Agent Trees to Alternating Transition Frames

Following we will establish an embedding of the semantics of ATL into the KB-approach to agency. The first step in the definition of this embedding is to represent the ATL concept of state in the framework of the KB-approach. However, there does not exist any straight-forward way of defining the notion of state in terms of moments.

To see this, let us assume that we aim at describing a system S with a state set Q. Each $q \in Q$, then, corresponds to a complete description of the system at some time-point. However, when we look at the tree whose branches are the possible computations of the system (as we did in the previous section) the information about possible states of the system has disappeared. Clearly, at each moment (in the sense defined above), the system is in a certain (total) state, but we are *not* able to identify moments that are in the same state.[3]

Definition 5.1 (State Tree). A *state tree* is an ordered triple $\mathcal{B} = \langle \text{Mom}, \prec, \text{Tot} \rangle$ consisting of a non-void set of moments, Mom, an irreflexive, transitive, and linear-to-the left relation on Mom, $\prec$, and a partition Tot of Mom.

The elements of Tot are referred to as *total states*. We say that moments m and m' are in the same (total) state if there exists a $t \in$ Tot such that m and m' are contained in t. For each moment m, let t_m denote the unique total state that contains m.[4] It is worth noting that a total state may have different pasts, while a moment can only have exactly one past.

In what is to follow, we will restrict consideration on discrete trees, more precisely, on trees where each history is order-isomorphic to the set of natural numbers. Such trees will be referred to as *trees over* $\mathbb{N}$. In a tree over $\mathbb{N}$ each moment m has an immediate successor in each history h passing through moment m, which will be denoted by m_h^*.

Let $\mathcal{B}$ be a state tree, and let m be a moment of $\mathcal{B}$. We define

$$\text{Tot}^* \langle m \rangle := \{ t_{m_h^*} : h \in \text{His} \langle m \rangle \},$$

the set of *possible next total states* at moment m.

---

[3] Here and in what is to follow we adopt the following terminology: States correspond to (maybe incomplete) momentary descriptions of a system, while total states correspond to complete momentary descriptions. Thus, states in the sense of the ATL semantics are total states in the sense of the terminology used here.

[4] The concept of state may be introduced in terms of total states as follows: A *state* is a subset of Mom that can be written as a union of total states, i. e.,

$$s \in \text{Stat} \iff \text{there is a } \tau \subseteq \text{Tot with } s = \bigcup \tau.$$

Note that this enables us to speak about the inconsistent state, which is distinct from each total state. Furthermore, Tot and Stat are subsets of 2^{Mom}, and each total state is a state.

Definition 5.2. A state tree is said to be *uniform* if for each $t \in \mathrm{Tot}$ and all $m, m' \in t$,

$$\mathrm{Tot}^* \langle m \rangle = \mathrm{Tot}^* \langle m' \rangle.$$

The underlying idea of uniformity is that the partitioning of moments into total states is respected by the successor relation, i.e., that if m and m' are in the same total state, then m and m' have the same possible next total states. From the point of view of the Kutschera-Belnap approach, uniformity seems a very restrictive condition.

If $\mathcal{F}$ is an ATF, then we can use the defintions of section 4 to define a state tree $\mathcal{B}^{\mathcal{F}} = \langle \mathrm{Mom}^{\mathcal{F}}, \prec^{\mathcal{F}}, \mathrm{Tot}^{\mathcal{F}} \rangle$ by

$$\gamma \simeq \gamma' :\Longleftrightarrow \gamma[n_\gamma] = \gamma'[n_{\gamma'}]$$
$$\mathrm{Tot}^{\mathcal{F}} := \Gamma_{\mathcal{F}}/{\simeq}.$$

Note that there exists a bijective map between the state set of $\mathcal{F}$, Q, and the set $\mathrm{Tot}^{\mathcal{F}}$.

Lemma 5.3. *Let $\mathcal{F}$ be an ATF. Then the tree $\mathcal{B}^{\mathcal{F}}$ is uniform.* $\qquad\square$

Definition 5.4 (Agent state tree). An *agent state tree* is a triple $\mathcal{C} = \langle \mathcal{B}, \mathrm{Ag}, \mathrm{Ch} \rangle$, where $\mathcal{B}$ is a state tree, Ag is a set of agents, and Ch is a choice map as specified in definition 2.2.

Obviously, $\mathrm{Ch}_\alpha \langle m \rangle$ induces a partition of the set of successor moments of m, $\{ m_h^* : m \in h \}$. But, as can be seen from simple examples, $\mathrm{Ch}_\alpha \langle m \rangle$ does not induce a partition of $\mathrm{Tot}^* \langle m \rangle$. Therefore, we need to extend the uniformity condition of the previous paragraph. Define

$$\mathrm{Tot}_\alpha^* \langle m, X \rangle := \{ t_{m_h^*} : m \in h \in X \} = \{ t_{m_h^*} : h \in \mathrm{His} \langle m \rangle \cap X \}$$

where $X \in \mathrm{Ch}_\alpha \langle m \rangle$, i.e., $\mathrm{Tot}_\alpha^* \langle m, X \rangle$ is the set of possible next total states in case that α chooses X at moment m.

Definition 5.5. An agent state tree over $\mathbb{N}$ is said to be *uniform* if the choice map Ch respects uniformity, i.e., if for each agent α, each total state t, and each pair of moments $m, m' \in t$,

$$\{ \mathrm{Tot}_\alpha^* \langle m, X \rangle : X \in \mathrm{Ch}_\alpha \langle m \rangle \} = \{ \mathrm{Tot}_\alpha^* \langle m', X' \rangle : X' \in \mathrm{Ch}_\alpha \langle m' \rangle \}.$$

Note that if an agent state tree is uniform, its underlying state tree is so, too. This follows from the fact that $\mathrm{Tot}^* \langle m \rangle = \bigcup_{X \in \mathrm{Ch}_\alpha \langle m \rangle} \mathrm{Tot}_\alpha^* \langle m, X \rangle$.

Lemma 5.6. *Let $\mathcal{F}$ be a restricted ATF. Then the agent state tree $\mathcal{C}^{\mathcal{F}}$ (as defined in this and the previous section) is uniform.* $\qquad\square$

Let now $\mathcal{C}$ be a uniform agent state tree over $\mathbb{N}$. We set

$$\Sigma^{\mathcal{C}} := \mathrm{Ag}$$

$$Q^{\mathcal{C}} := \mathrm{Tot}$$

$$\delta^{\mathcal{C}}(t, \alpha) := \{\, \mathrm{Tot}^*_\alpha \langle m, X \rangle \; : \; X \in \mathrm{Ch}_\alpha \langle m \rangle \,\}$$

where m is an arbitrarily fixed element of t. This definition is well defined since the tree $\mathcal{C}$ is uniform. Note that $\mathrm{Tot}^*_\alpha \langle m, X \rangle$ is a set of total states. Hence $\mathrm{Tot}^*_\alpha \langle m, X \rangle \in 2^{\mathrm{Tot}}$, and thus $\delta^{\mathcal{C}}(t, \alpha) \in 2^{2^{\mathrm{Tot}}}$.

We are now ready to state our second theorem:

Theorem 5.7. *Let $\mathcal{C}$ be an agent-complete and uniform agent state tree over $\mathbb{N}$. Then*

$$\mathcal{F}^{\mathcal{C}} = \langle \Sigma^{\mathcal{C}}, Q^{\mathcal{C}}, \delta^{\mathcal{C}} \rangle$$

is a restricted alternating transition frame.

Proof. There is almost nothing left to be proven. Let $t \in Q^{\mathcal{C}}$ be a (total) state, and let $(Q_\alpha)_{\alpha \in \Sigma^{\mathcal{C}}}$ be a family with $Q_\alpha \in \delta^{\mathcal{C}}(t, \alpha)$. Choose an arbitrary $m \in t$. Then, for each Q_α, there exists a $\chi(\alpha) \in \mathrm{Ch}_\alpha \langle m \rangle$ with $Q_\alpha = \mathrm{Tot}^*_\alpha \langle m, \chi(\alpha) \rangle$. By applying condition 2.2, there exists a history h that is contained in each $\chi(\alpha)$. Since the tree is agent-complete, h is uniquely determined up to undivided histories. This means that $m^*_{h'} = m^*_h$, for each history $h' \in \bigcap_\alpha \chi(\alpha)$. Since the $\delta^{\mathcal{C}}(t, \alpha)$ do not depend on the particular choice of m in t, there exists exactly one total state that is contained in each Q_α, namely $t_{m^*_h}$. That the frame $\mathcal{F}^{\mathcal{C}}$ is restricted follows from the fact that each $\mathrm{Ch}_\alpha \langle m \rangle$ is a partition of the set of histories that pass through moment m.   □

Finally, if an agent state tree $\mathcal{C}$, as specified in the theorem, is a 'forest' such that each total state is realized in exactly one of its root moments, then there exists a bijection between the set of histories of $\mathcal{C}$ and the set of computations of $\mathcal{F}^{\mathcal{C}}$.

6 Summary and Outlook

In this paper we focused on two approaches to qualitative action theory, the Kutschera-Belnap approach and the semantics of alternating-time temporal logic. Though at first glance both approaches are very close in spirit, they could not be found to be equivalent without modifying the basic semantics respectively. If reasonable conditions on alternating transition frames are enforced, these frames can be shown to induce agent trees. Vice versa, agent trees do induce alternating transition frames if they are enriched with the notion of state and if some uniformity conditions are assumed. However, from the point of view of the Kutschera-Belnap approach, these uniformity constraints seem very special. The best interpretation of them is to read ATL choices (i. e., the elements of the agent-dependent transition function) as *action types* in the following sense: Each agent has a repertoire of 'procedures' that can be performed when the system is in a particular state. Whether this procedure can be performed depends on the current state only and not on one of the many possible pasts the system might have passed through to reach this state. Contrary to this, choices in the Kutschera-Belnap approach are assigned with respect to moments, i. e., with respect to the current state and one particular past of that state.

It is also worthwhile to note that in ATL the notion of strategy is defined in a more KB-like manner, i. e., strategies are not defined with respect to single states only, but are defined with respect to finite computations. More precisely, in the KB-approach a *(strict) strategy* of an agent α is a partial function σ that has as its domain a non-void convex subset of Mom, $\mathrm{dom}\,(\sigma)$, and that assigns to each $m \in \mathrm{dom}\,(\sigma)$, a choice $\sigma(m) \in \mathrm{Ch}_\alpha\langle m\rangle$. In the ATL-approach a *strategy* of α is a map that assigns to each finite computation γ a choice $Q \in \delta(\gamma[n_\gamma], \alpha)$. The close relationship between these two notions of strategy should now be obvious.

The results presented in this paper provide the start point of an interesting research topic: What are the connections between the *logics* that are defined with respect to the semantic concepts presented here? But an answer to this question would go far beyond the scope of this paper.

Acknowledgement. This work has been partially supported by the *Deutsche Forschungsgemeinschaft (DFG)*. I am grateful for helpful discussions with Valentin Goranko and Alberto Zanardo.

References

1. Alur, R., Henzinger, T.A., Kupferman, O.: Alternating-time temporal logic. In: Proceedings of the 38th Symposium on Foundations of Computer Science. (1997)
2. Alur, R., Henzinger, T.A., Kupferman, O.: Alternating-time temporal logic. Journal of the ACM (JACM) **49** (2002) 672–713
3. Åqvist, L.: A new approach to the logical theory of actions and causality. In Stenlund, S., ed.: Logical Theory and Semantic Analysis: Essays Dedicated to Stig Kanger on His Fiftieth Birthday. D. Reidel, Dordrecht (1974) 73–91
4. Belnap, N.D.: Backwards and forwards in the modal logic of agency. Philosophy and Phenomenological Research **51** (1991) 777–807
5. Belnap, N.D.: Before refraining: Concepts for agency. Erkenntnis **34** (1991) 137–169
6. Belnap, N.D., Perloff, M.: Seeing to it that: A canonical form for agentives. In Kyburg, Jr., H.E., Loui, R.P., Carlson, G.N., eds.: Knowledge Representation and Defeasible Reasoning. Kluwer Academic Publisher, Dordrecht (1990) 175–199
7. Belnap, N.D., Perloff, M.: The way of the agent. Studia Logica **51** (1992) 463–484
8. Belnap, N., Perloff, M.: In the realm of agents. Annals of Mathematics and Artificial Intelligence **9** (1993) 25–48
9. Belnap, N.D., Perloff, M., Xu, M.: Facing the Future: Agents and their Choices in our Indeterminist World. Oxford University Press, New York (2001)
10. Chellas, B.F.: Time and modality in the logic of agency. Studia Logica **51** (1992) 485–517

11. Goranko, V.: Coalition games and alternating temporal logic. In: Proceedings of the 8th Conference on Theoretical Aspects of Rationality and Knowledge (TARK VIII), Morgan Kaufmann (2001) 259–272
12. Horty, J.F., Belnap, N.D.: The deliberative stit: A study of action, omission, ability, and obligation. Journal of Philosophical Logic **24** (1995) 583–644
13. Kutschera, F.v.: Grundbegriffe der Handlungslogik. In Lenk, H., ed.: Handlungstheorien interdisziplinär I. Fink, München (1980) 67–106
14. Kutschera, F.v.: Bewirken. Erkenntnis **24** (1986) 253–281
15. Pauly, M.: A modal logic for coalition power in games. *Journal of Logic and Computation* (2000)
16. Pauly, M.: A logical framework for coalitional effectivity in dynamic procedures. In: Proceedings in the 4th Conference on Logic and the Foundations of Game and Decision Theory (LOFT4), Torino (2000)
17. Wölfl, S.: Propositional Q-logic. Journal of Philosophical Logic **31** (2002) 387–414
18. Wölfl, S.: Review of Nuel Belnap, Michael Perloff, and Ming Xu's *Facing the Future*. Notre Dame Philosophical Reviews (2002). Published at: http://ndpr/icaap.org/content/archives/2002/8/wolfl-belnap.html.
19. Xu, M.: Decidability of stit theory with a single agent and refref equivalence. Studia Logica **53** (1994) 259–298
20. Xu, M.: Doing and refraining from refraining. Journal of Philosophical Logic **23** (1994) 621–632
21. Xu, M.: Decidability of deliberative stit theories with multiple agents. In Gabbay, D.M., Ohlbach, H.J., eds.: Temporal Logic, Berlin, Springer (1994) 332–348 Lecture Notes in Artificial Intelligence: 827.
22. Xu, M.: Busy choice sequences, refraining formulas, and modalities. Studia Logica **54** (1995) 267–301
23. Xu, M.: On the basic logic of stit with a single agent. Journal of Symbolic Logic **60** (1995) 459–483
24. Xu, M.: Axioms for deliberative stit. Journal of Philosophical Logic **27** (1998) 505–552

Practical Reasoning for Uncertain Agents

Nivea de C. Ferreira, Michael Fisher, and Wiebe van der Hoek

University of Liverpool, Department of Computer Science, UK
{niveacf, michael, wiebe}@csc.liv.ac.uk

Abstract. Logical formalisation of agent behaviour is desirable, not only in order to provide a clear semantics of agent-based systems, but also to provide the foundation for sophisticated reasoning techniques to be used on, and by, the agents themselves. The possible worlds semantics offered by modal logic has proved to be a successful framework in which to model mental attitudes of agents such as beliefs, desires and intentions. The most popular choices for modeling the informational attitudes involves annotating the agent with an *S5*-like logic for knowledge, or a *KD45*-like logic for belief. However, using these logics in their standard form, an agent cannot distinguish situations in which the evidence for a certain fact is 'equally distributed' over its alternatives, from situations in which there is only one, almost negligible, counterexample to the 'fact'. Probabilistic modal logics are a way to address this, but they easily end up being both computationally and conceptually complex, for example often lacking the property of compactness. In this paper, we propose a probabilistic modal logic $P_F KD45$, in which the probabilities of the possible worlds range over a finite domain of values, while still allowing the agent to reason about infinitely many options. In this way, the logic remains compact, implying that the agent still has to consider only finitely many possibilities for probability distributions during a reasoning task. We demonstrate a sound, compact and complete axiomatisation for $P_F KD45$ and show that it has several appealing features. Then, we discuss an implemented decision procedure for the logic, and provide a small example. Finally we show that, rather than specifying them beforehand, the finite set of possible probabilities can be obtained directly from the problem specification.

1 Introduction

In both reasoning *about* agents and in reasoning *within* agents, it is vital to choose tools that allow the representation of information at an appropriate level of abstraction, yet being simple enough to be mechanised. Logical formalisations of such informational aspects have been particularly successful, often using modal logics such as *S5* for knowledge, or *KD45* for belief. However, it is clear that, in realistic scenarios, such descriptions need to incorporate uncertainty. Without such descriptive flexibility, logical approaches cannot effectively represent real-world concerns and so cannot be used as the basis for practical reasoning in agents acting with uncertain information. While there have been some steps

J.J. Alferes and J. Leite (Eds.): JELIA 2004, LNAI 3229, pp. 82–94, 2004.
© Springer-Verlag Berlin Heidelberg 2004

in developing logics of uncertainty or logics of probability (see Section 6) many of these (for example, probabilistic modal logics) are both computationally and conceptually complex. In particular, a significant drawback is that many such approaches lack the property of *compactness*[1].

In this paper we present a new probabilistic modal logic (called $P_F KD45$) that builds upon the natural framework of Kripke models (the basis of modal logics), while allowing reasoning about uncertainty. Importantly, in this logic, the probabilities of the possible worlds range over a finite domain of values, while still allowing the agent to reason about infinitely many options. In this way, the logic remains compact, ensuring that the agent only has to consider finitely many possibilities for probability distributions during a reasoning task.

The $P_F KD45$ logic extends, in some aspects, the system $P_F D$ previously introduced in [9], which in turn was inspired by the system from [3]. The basic modal operator $P^>$ allows us to write formulas such as $P^>_{0.5}\varphi$, meaning that the "agent believes φ with probability strictly greater than 0.5". The operators (which have self-explanatory meaning) $P^\geq$, $P^<$, $P^\leq$ and $P^=$ can then be defined in terms of the above basis. Since probabilities range from 0 to 1, $P^\geq_1$ corresponds to the modal operator $\Box$ or B. An important property of the logic is that it only allows probability measures (for each world) that are within a finite base set F. Although this semantically restricts probability assignments to a finite range, it is still possible to *express and reason about* arbitrary probabilities, since there is no restriction in the *language* that mirrors this semantic restriction. But again, in the *logic*, a particular axiom (Axiom $A7$; see later) ensures that arbitrary values collapse to values in the set F. The main motivation for using F is the restoration of compactness for the logic.

Logics that allow us to express that $Prob(\varphi) \sim x$ are, in general, not compact. Witness the set of premises Γ

$$\{Prob(q) > \alpha \mid \alpha \in Q \cap [0,1)\} \tag{1}$$

Here, we have $\Gamma \models Prob(q) = 1$, and yet there is no finite subset of Γ that proves this conclusion. This has a computational counterpart: a mechanical device verifying whether a set of premises $\{Prob(\varphi) \sim x\}$ is satisfiable in $Q \cap [0,1]$ in principle has to check an infinite number of assignments of probabilities to formulas φ. The advantage of the $P_F KD45$ logic is that the range of allowed probabilities is within a finite base set $F \subseteq [0,1]$.

Although the use of the base set F causes a logical restriction, it is possible to highlight some interesting aspects (cf.[9]). For instance, it we take $F = \{0,1\}$, we have classical modal logic. Alternatively, Driankov's linguistic estimates (as in [2]) *impossible, extremely unlikely, very low chance, small chance, it may, meaningful chance, most likely, extremely likely, certain* would be modelled by a 9-element F. In other words, the granularity of F can be chosen according to the intended application of the agent. However, since one of our main interests is to use the $P_F KD45$ logic for describing and implementing uncertain agents, then

---

[1] Compactness in the sense that inference in terms of infinite sets coincides with inference over finite sets.

having a mechanism for directly *calculating* the set F is very desirable. For this purpose, the basic idea is to have F determined by a set of arbitrary probability values which are directly extracted from the original agent specification. (Further discussion concerning this aspect will be provided in Section 6.)

In summary, contrary to many other logical approaches to probabilistic reasoning, our logic is both compact and conceptually simple. Thus, it represents a strong candidate for representing and reasoning about uncertainty within computational agents.

The paper is organised as follows. In Section 2 we present a description of the language and, in Section 3, we provide its semantics and establish its properties. Since the focus of $P_F D$ was not on a doxastic interpretation of modalities, we also include two additional properties in the $P_F KD45$ Logic (axioms $A8$ and $A9$; see later), in order to represent $KD45$-like belief. For instance, this allows us to have a probability distribution independent of worlds, and thus ensure that nested belief formulas are equivalent to formulas without nesting. Such issues are considered in more detail in Section 3. A decision procedure for the logic has been developed and implemented, and this is presented in Section 4. Due to space restrictions, only a small motivating example showing the versatility of the approach is provided in Section 5. Finally, related work and final remarks are presented in Section 6.

2   Language Description

The language L of $P_F KD45$ consists of a countable set of propositional symbols, the logical connectives $\neg$ and $\vee$ (with standard definitions for $\bot, \top, \wedge, \rightarrow, \leftrightarrow$), and parentheses. We also define a modal operator $P_x^>$, where x is a real number within the interval $[0, 1]$.

Definition 1. *A set F is a* base *for a logic $P_F KD45$ if it satisfies:*

1. *F is finite;*
2. *$\{0, 1\} \subseteq F \subseteq [0, 1]$;*
3. *$x, y \in F$ and $(x + y \leq 1) \Rightarrow (x + y) \in F$;*
4. *$x \in F \Rightarrow (1 - x) \in F$.*

The logic is defined relative to a fixed base set $F = \{x_0, x_1, ..., x_n\} \subseteq [0, 1]$. It is assumed that $x_i < x_{i+1}$, if $i < n$ (implying $0 = x_0$ and $x_n = 1$). The basic operator is $P_x^>$, with intended meaning of $P_x^> \varphi$ being: "φ is believed to have a probability strictly greater than x".

The following abbreviations are used (from now on, x and y represent arbitrary values over $[0, 1]$, and x_i, x_{i+1} are elements of the base set F.):

D1. $P_x^{\geq} \varphi \equiv \neg P_{1-x}^> \neg \varphi$
D2. $P_x^< \varphi \equiv P_{1-x}^> \neg \varphi$
D3. $P_x^{\leq} \varphi \equiv \neg P_{1-x}^< \neg \varphi$
D4. $P_x^= \varphi \equiv \neg P_x^> \varphi \wedge \neg P_x^< \varphi$

The inference rules ($R1$ and $R2$) and axioms ($A1$–$A9$) of $P_F KD45$ are:

$R1$ From φ and $\varphi \Rightarrow \psi$ infer ψ (modus ponens)

$R2$ From φ infer $P_1^{\geq}\varphi$ (necessitation rule)

$A1$ All propositional tautologies

$A2$ $P_1^{\geq}(\varphi \to \psi) \to [(P_x^{>}\varphi \to P_x^{>}\psi) \wedge (P_x^{>}\varphi \to P_x^{\geq}\psi) \wedge (P_x^{\geq}\varphi \to P_x^{\geq}\psi)]$

$A3$ $P_1^{\geq}(\varphi \to \psi) \to (P_x^{\geq}\varphi \to P_y^{>}\psi)$ (where $y < x$)

$A4$ $P_0^{\geq}\varphi$

$A5$ $P_{x+y}^{>}(\varphi \vee \psi) \to (P_x^{>}\varphi \vee P_y^{>}\psi)$ (where $x + y \in [0, 1]$)

$A6$ $P_1^{\geq}\neg(\varphi \wedge \psi) \to ((P_x^{>}\varphi \wedge P_y^{\geq}\psi) \to P_{x+y}^{>}(\varphi \vee \psi))$ (where $x + y \in [0, 1]$)

$A7$ $P_{x_i}^{>}\varphi \to P_{x_{i+1}}^{\geq}\varphi$

$A8$ $(P_0^{>}P_x^{\geq}\varphi \to P_x^{\geq}\varphi) \wedge (P_0^{>}P_x^{\leq}\varphi \to P_x^{\leq}\varphi)$

$A9$ $(P_x^{\geq}\varphi \to P_1^{\geq}P_x^{\geq}\varphi) \wedge (P_x^{\leq}\varphi \to P_1^{\geq}P_x^{\leq}\varphi)$

The axioms $A1$–$A6$ all reflect basic properties of probabilities. Axiom $A7$ reflects the peculiarity of having a base set F: it says that, if a probability is bigger than a certain value in F, it must be at least the next value. Axioms $A8$ and $A9$ are included to emphasize the relationship with the modal logic $KD45$ and they make our agents doxastically introspective. The intuition behind these additional axioms is as follows. Axiom $A8$ denotes that, if the agent assigns a positive probability to some probabilistic judgement, then it incorporates this judgement. Axiom $A9$ states that the agent is absolutely sure about its own probabilistic beliefs (the focus of [9] was not on a doxastic interpretation of the modalities, and these introspective properties were not included).

Lemma 1. *The following theorems are derivable in $P_F KD45$:*
$\vdash P_1^{\leq}\varphi$ *and* $\vdash P_1^{\geq}\varphi \equiv P_1^{=}\varphi$

Remark 1. We can define a *belief* operator, 'B', using $B\varphi = P_1^{\geq}\varphi$, and can then infer the following.

a) 1. $\vdash \varphi \Rightarrow \vdash B\varphi$
    2. $\vdash B(\varphi \to \psi) \to (B\varphi \to B\psi)$
    3. $\vdash \neg B\bot$
    4. $B\varphi \to BB\varphi$
    5. $\neg B\varphi \to B\neg B\varphi$

b) We say that a formula in L is *modal* if it is built from atomic propositions, using only the logical connectives and the modal operator B. We claim that for all modal formulas, φ, $P_F KD45 \vdash \varphi$ iff $KD45 \vdash \varphi$.

   Proof. The $\Leftarrow$ part follows from **a** above; the $\Rightarrow$ part will be obvious from the semantics for $P_F KD45$ given later[2].

---

[2] Due to space limitations, full proofs are generally omitted, but can found in the associated technical report [1].

Below we present some further theorems of $P_F KD45$, though only give one example proof. We also utilise some additional notation:

- $(\varphi \bigtriangledown \psi)$ means $((\varphi \vee \psi) \wedge \neg(\varphi \wedge \psi))$, i.e. exclusive OR;
- $x\uparrow = min\{y \in F \mid y > x\}$ and $x\downarrow = max\{y \in F \mid y < x\}$.

Now, for all φ, ψ in the language and all $x \in [0, 1]$:

$T1.$ $(P_x^{\geq}\varphi \leftrightarrow (P_x^{>}\varphi \vee P_x^{=}\varphi)) \wedge (P_x^{\leq}\varphi(P_x^{<}\varphi \vee P_x^{=}\varphi))$

$T2.$ $P_x^{>}\varphi \bigtriangledown P_x^{=}\varphi \bigtriangledown P_x^{<}\varphi$

$T3.$ $\neg(P_x^{=}\varphi \wedge P_y^{=}\varphi)$ $\hspace{3cm}$ $(y \neq x)$

$T4.$ $(\neg P_x^{<}\varphi \leftrightarrow P_x^{\geq}\varphi) \wedge (\neg P_x^{>}\varphi \leftrightarrow P_x^{\leq}\varphi)$

$T5.$ $P_x^{=}\varphi \leftrightarrow (P_x^{\geq}\varphi \wedge P_x^{\leq}\varphi)$

$T6.$ $P_x^{>}\varphi \rightarrow P_y^{>}\varphi$ $\hspace{4cm}$ $y \leq x$

$T7.$ $P_x^{=}\varphi \leftrightarrow P_{1-x}^{=}\neg\varphi$

The following lemma shows the benefit of having a finite base F: it guarantees that we can express in the language that every formula has a probability.

Lemma 2. *For all $\varphi \in L$, the following is a $P_F KD45$-theorem:*
$P_{x_0}^{=}\varphi \bigtriangledown P_{x_1}^{=}\varphi \bigtriangledown ... \bigtriangledown P_{x_n}^{=}\varphi$ *(recall: $F = \{0 = x_0, x_1, ..., x_n = 1\}$)*

$T8.$ $P_x^{>}\varphi \rightarrow P_{x_i}^{=}\varphi \bigtriangledown P_{x_{i+1}}^{=}\varphi \bigtriangledown ... \bigtriangledown P_{x_n}^{=}\varphi,$ $\hspace{1cm}$ with $x_i = x\uparrow$;

$T9.$ $P_x^{<}\varphi \rightarrow P_{x_0}^{=}\varphi \bigtriangledown P_{x_1}^{=}\varphi \bigtriangledown ... \bigtriangledown P_{x_i}^{=}\varphi,$ $\hspace{1cm}$ with $x_i = x\downarrow$;

$T10.$ $(P_x^{>}\varphi \leftrightarrow P_{x\uparrow}^{\geq}\varphi) \wedge (P_y^{<}\varphi \leftrightarrow P_{y\downarrow}^{\leq}\varphi)$ $\hspace{1cm}$ $x \in [0, 1), y \in (0, 1]$

$T11.$ $[P_1^{\geq}\neg(\varphi \wedge \psi) \wedge P_x^{=}\varphi] \rightarrow [P_y^{=}\psi \leftrightarrow P_{x+y}^{=}(\varphi \vee \psi)]$ $\hspace{0.5cm}$ $x, y, x + y \in [0, 1]$

$T12$ $P_0^{>}P_x^{\sim}\varphi \rightarrow P_x^{\sim}\varphi,$ $\hspace{3cm}$ $\sim$ is one of $\{<, \leq, =, >\geq\}$

$T13$ $P_x^{\sim}\varphi \rightarrow P_1^{\geq}P_x^{\sim}\varphi,$ $\hspace{3cm}$ $\sim$ is one of $\{<, \leq, =, >\geq\}$

3 Semantics and Properties

Formulas $\varphi \in L$ are interpreted on Probabilistic Kripke Models over F.

Definition 2. *For each base set, F, $\mathcal{P}_F KD45$ is the class of all models $M = \langle W, P_F, \pi \rangle$ for which:*

- *W is a non-empty set (of worlds);*
- *P_F is a function $P_F : W \rightarrow F$, satisfying $\sum_{w \in W} P_F(w) = 1$*
- *π is a valuation: $W \times L \rightarrow \{true, false\}$*
- *The truth definition for formulas is defined in a standard way, the modal clause reading:*

$$(M, w) \models P_x^{\geq}(\varphi) \text{ iff } \sum_{w' \text{ s.t. } (M,w')\models\varphi} P_F(w') \geq x$$

Note that the probability distribution is independent of the world. Let us call such a structure $\mathcal{P}_F\mathcal{K}D45$.

One can relate this semantics to a more standard Kripke semantics as follows. Given $M = \langle W, P_F, \pi \rangle$, first choose an arbitrary world w in the model M. Then, let W' be $\{w\} \cup \{w' \mid P_F(w') > 0\}$. Finally, define $R'(x, y)$ iff $P_F(y) > 0$, i.e., a world is accessible (from any world) if, and only if, its probability is positive. Let $M'_w = \langle W', R', \pi' \rangle$ be the model thus obtained, with π' being the restriction of π to W. The following gives a semantic motivation for coining our system P_FKD45:

Proposition 1. *Given a P_FKD45 model $M = \langle W, P_F, \pi \rangle$ and a world w, let $M'_w = \langle W', R', \pi' \rangle$ be obtained as described above. Moreover, let a purely modal formula from P_FKD45 be a formula in which all modal operators are $P_1^{\geq}$, or, equivalently, B. Then:*

1. *for every purely modal formula φ, we have $M, w \models \varphi$ iff $M'_w \models \varphi$;*
2. *the accessibility relation R' is serial, transitive and Euclidean.*

Lemma 3. *P_FKD45 is sound with respect to $\mathcal{P}_F\mathcal{K}D45$, i. e., $P_FKD45 \vdash \varphi \Rightarrow \mathcal{P}_F\mathcal{K}D45 \models \varphi$.*

3.1 Completeness

Let φ be a consistent formula of P_FKD45. We will show how to construct a model that satisfies φ. Let Ψ be the set of sub-formulas of φ closed under a single negation and satisfying, for any $\sim$ within $\{<, >, \leq, \geq, =\}$, $(P_x^{\sim} \in \Psi \Rightarrow \{P_{x_i}^{=} | x_i \in F\} \subseteq \Psi)$. With Ψ being finite, say $|\Psi| = k$, we can define the Ψ-maximal consistent sets as $\Gamma_1, \Gamma_2, ..., \Gamma_n, n \leq 2^k$. Let γ_i be the conjunction of formulas in $\Gamma_i, i \leq n$. Then, we have:

i. $\vdash \neg(\gamma_i \wedge \gamma_j)$, where $i \neq j$;
ii. $\vdash (\gamma_1 \vee ... \vee \gamma_n)$
iii. $\vdash \psi \leftrightarrow \gamma_{\psi 1} \vee ... \vee \gamma_{\psi x}$, where $\gamma_{\psi 1} \vee ... \vee \gamma_{\psi x}$ are exactly those γ's which contain ψ as a conjunct, for each $\psi \in \Psi$.

Since φ is consistent and, by construction of the Γ's, there is at least one Γ_φ such that $\varphi \in \Gamma_\varphi$. Given this Γ_φ, we construct a set $\Phi \supseteq \Gamma_\varphi$ as follows. From Theorem $T8$, we know that for every consistent set Γ and formula ψ, at least one set of the sequence

$$\Gamma \cup \{P_0^= \psi\}, \Gamma \cup \{P_{x_1}^= \psi\}, ..., \Gamma \cup \{P_{x_{n-1}}^= \psi\}, \Gamma \cup \{P_1^= \psi\} \tag{2}$$

is also consistent. Now, we obtain Φ from Γ_φ as follows:

1. let $\Phi_0 = \Gamma_\varphi$ (this set is consistent);
2. for $i = 1$ to n, we know that there is some $x \in F$ such that $\Phi_{i-1} \cup \{P_x^= \gamma_i\}$ will be consistent, and we make the corresponding choice for Φ_i.

We let Φ be Φ_n; this is a consistent extension of Γ_φ, which contains a probability in F for every 'world' Γ_i $(i \leq n)$. We are now ready to define our canonical model $M^c = \langle W^c, P^c_F, \pi^c \rangle$ as follows:

1. $W^c = \{\Gamma_\varphi\} \cup \{\Gamma_i \mid \exists x > 0 P^=_x \gamma_i \in \Phi\}$.
2. $P^c_F(\Gamma_i) = x \Leftrightarrow P^=_x \gamma_i \in \Phi$
3. $\pi(\Gamma_i)(p) = true$ iff $p \in \Gamma_i$

Lemma 4 (Coincidence Lemma). *For all $\psi \in \Psi$ and $\Gamma \in W^c$*

$$M^c, \Gamma \models \psi \text{ iff } \psi \in \Gamma$$

Theorem 1 (Soundness and Completeness, Finite Models). *For any formula φ, we have $\mathcal{P}_F\mathcal{KD}45 \models \varphi$ iff $\mathcal{P}_F\mathcal{KD}45 \vdash \varphi$. Moreover, every consistent formula has a finite model.*

3.2   Nested Beliefs

Considering $P_F\mathcal{KD}45$ as a language for representing properties within individual agents, we next show that *nested* belief formulas can be removed, i. e,. any nested belief formula is equivalent to some formula given without nesting.

Lemma 5 (Independence of Probability Distribution). *Let $M = \langle W, P_F, \pi \rangle$ be a $\mathcal{P}_F\mathcal{KD}45$ model. Then:*

$$\exists w \in W(M, w) \models P^{\geq}_\gamma \beta \Leftrightarrow \forall u \in W, (M, u) \models P^{\geq}_\gamma \beta.$$

We now demonstrate that nested beliefs are superfluous, in $P_F\mathcal{KD}45$. This result is a generalisation of [10, Theorem 1.7.6.4], where it is proved for $S5$, which means that their result still goes through when weakening the logic to $KD45$, and even when having probabilistic operators.

Definition 3. *We say that a formula ψ is in* normal form *if it is a disjunction of conjunctions of the form $\delta = \omega \wedge P^{\geq}_{\gamma_1} \beta_1 \wedge P^{\geq}_{\gamma_2} \beta_2 \wedge ... \wedge P^{\geq}_{\gamma_n} \beta_n \wedge P^{>}_{\kappa_1} \alpha_1 \wedge P^{>}_{\kappa_2} \alpha_2 \wedge ... \wedge P^{>}_{\kappa_k} \alpha_k$, where $\omega, \beta_i, \alpha_j$, $(i \leq n, j \leq k)$ are all purely propositional formulas. The formula δ is called the* canonical conjunction *and the sub-formulas $P^{\geq}_{\gamma_i} \beta_i$ and $P^{>}_{\kappa_j} \alpha_j$ are called* prenex formulas.*

Lemma 6. *If ψ is in normal form and contains a prenex formula σ, then ψ may be supposed to have the form $\pi \vee (\lambda \wedge \sigma)$ where π, λ and σ are in normal form.*

Proof. ψ is in normal form, so $\psi = \delta_1 \vee \delta_2 \vee ... \vee \delta_m$, where $\delta_{i's}$ are canonical conjunctions. Suppose σ occurs in δ_m. Then σ must be some conjunct $P^{\geq}_\gamma$, so that δ_m can be written as $(\lambda \wedge \sigma)$. Taking π to be $(\delta_1 \vee \delta_2 \vee ... \vee \delta_{m-1})$ gives the desired result $\psi = \pi \vee (\lambda \wedge \sigma)$.

This lemma guarantees that prenex formulas can always be moved to the outermost level.

Lemma 7 (Removal of Nested Beliefs). *We have, in* $\mathcal{P}_F\mathcal{KD}45$:

$$P_\alpha^\geq(\pi \vee (\lambda \wedge P_\gamma^\geq \beta)) \leftrightarrow (P_\alpha^\geq(\pi \vee \lambda) \wedge P_\gamma^\geq \beta) \vee (P_\alpha^\geq \pi \wedge \neg P_\gamma^\geq \beta) \tag{3}$$

$$P_\alpha^\geq(\pi \vee (\lambda \wedge P_\gamma^> \beta)) \leftrightarrow (P_\alpha^\geq(\pi \vee \lambda) \wedge P_\gamma^> \beta) \vee (P_\alpha^\geq \pi \wedge \neg P_\gamma^> \beta) \tag{4}$$

Proof. We sketch the proof of (3). As $(M,s) \models P_\gamma^\geq \beta \vee P_\gamma^\geq \beta$, there are two possible cases to consider.

First Case. Assuming $(M,s) \models P_\gamma^\geq \beta$ we aim to show that

$$P_\alpha^\geq(\pi \vee (\lambda \wedge P_\gamma^\geq \beta)) \leftrightarrow (P_\alpha^\geq(\pi \vee \lambda) \wedge P_\gamma^\geq \beta) \tag{5}$$

For $\to$, note that $(\pi \vee (\lambda \wedge P_\gamma^\geq \beta)) \to (\pi \vee \lambda)$ is a tautology. Hence, the truth of $P_\alpha^\geq(\pi \vee (\lambda \wedge P_\gamma^\geq \beta))$ in s implies that of $P_\alpha^\geq(\pi \vee \lambda)$ in s (using $A2$). This, together with $(M,s) \models P_\gamma^\geq \beta$ leads to

$$(M,s) \models P_\alpha^\geq(\pi \vee (\lambda \wedge P_\gamma^\geq \beta)) \to (P_\alpha^\geq(\pi \vee \lambda) \wedge P_\gamma^\geq \beta) \tag{6}$$

and this is valid for any state since $(M,s) \models P_\gamma^\geq \beta \iff \forall u \in S, (M,u) \models P_\gamma^\geq \beta$.

Concerning the converse, from $P_\alpha^\geq(\pi \vee \lambda) \wedge P_\gamma^\geq \beta$ we have that both $P_\alpha^\geq(\pi \vee \lambda)$ and $P_\gamma^\geq \beta$ are true in all $u \in S$. λ is true. $(\forall u)$ $(M,u) \models \lambda \iff \lambda \wedge P_\gamma^\geq \beta$ is also true. So,

$$(M,s) \models (P_\alpha^\geq(\pi \vee \lambda) \wedge P_\gamma^\geq \beta) \to P_\alpha^\geq(\pi \vee (\lambda \wedge P_\gamma^\geq \beta)) \tag{7}$$

Then, at this point we have:

$$(M,s) \models P_\gamma^\geq \beta \to (P_\alpha^\geq(\pi \vee (\lambda \wedge P_\gamma^\geq \beta)) \leftrightarrow (P_\alpha^\geq(\pi \vee \lambda) \wedge P_\gamma^\geq \beta)) \tag{8}$$

The second case is analogous, giving

$$(M,s) \models \neg P_\gamma^\geq \beta \to (P_\alpha^\geq(\pi \vee (\lambda \wedge P_\gamma^\geq \beta)) \leftrightarrow (P_\alpha^\geq \pi \wedge \neg P_\gamma^\geq \beta)) \tag{9}$$

After considering the two cases we can, finally, use the propositional tautology $[(p \to (q \leftrightarrow (p \wedge r))) \wedge (\neg p \to (q \leftrightarrow (\neg p \wedge s)))] \to [(q \leftrightarrow ((r \wedge p) \vee (s \wedge \neg p)))]$, together with (8) and (9) to conclude (3).

We can this way bring all the probabilistic operators to the outermost level:[3]

Theorem 2. *Every formula φ is equivalent to a formula ψ in normal form, i. e., a formula without nesting of probabilistic operators.*

---

[3] This result seems parallel to a result [7, Theorem 3.1.30] about a language with quantifiers, which proof is given with induction on φ.

4   Decision Procedure

As previously explained, the semantic definition for $P_F KD45$-formulas is based on Probabilistic Kripke Models. For each world w there is a set of worlds that w considers possible and each one of these possible worlds is specified according to the formulas it satisfies. For instance, if in the actual world w $P_1^{\geq}p$ holds, the probability values assigned to the possible worlds where p is true sum up to 1 (which, in this case, guarantees that all the worlds where p is false have probability zero).

In other words, by definition, the probability of a formula is given by the sum of the probability values assigned to the worlds that satisfy this formula, and satisfiability of a propositional formula is given by the assignment of truth-values to its symbols. So, by evaluating formulas, we identify the worlds where those formulas are satisfied. As a result, we can obtain the values that, once assigned to the set of possible worlds, can satisfy the modal formula present in the agent's specification.

The idea is to convert the set of formulas into constraint (in)equations. The inequation components represent all the possible truth valuations for the propositional symbols. A finite set of formulas is given, and a finite set of constraint (in)equations will be generated; each formula is converted into a set of (in)equational statements.

For instance, consider that the agent specification is expressed by the set of formulas: $\{P_{0.8}^{\geq}p, P_{0.7}^{\geq}q\}$ and $F = \{0, 0.1, 0.2, ..., 0.9, 1\}$. The four possible sets of worlds (characterised by the truth-assignments) are: $p1q1$ (where both p and q hold), $p1q0$ (in which p holds and the negation of q holds), $p0q1$ (in which the q and negation of p hold) and $p0q0$ (where both negations hold).

In the given example, the set of constraints generated is:

$$p0q0 + p0q1 + p1q0 + p1q1 = 1$$
$$p1q0 + p1q1 \geq 0.8$$
$$p0q1 + p1q1 \geq 0.7$$

The first equation expresses the fact that probability values have to sum up to 1. The two inequations represent constraints on the worlds in which p holds and worlds in which q holds, respectively.

Solving the constraint (in)equations determines which are the values in set F that obey the constraints imposed by the formulas and can be, consequently, applied to the set of worlds. Therefore, the decision procedure turns out to be a mechanism for finding all the possible probability assignments for the set of possible worlds that would satisfy the specified formulas, as long as this set of formulas is consistent. Otherwise, no possible assignment exists.

As mentioned above the decision procedure converts the set of formulas into a set of constraint (in)equations. Identifying the propositional symbols is essential for determining the inequation components, and the number of components grows exponentially in the number of propositional symbols. Each formula determines which components constitute each inequation. Finally, the inequations are produced and solved.

Theorem 3 (Decision Procedure). *A formula φ in $P_F KD45$ is satisfiable if, and only if, there is a solution for the set of (in)equations generated from φ within the domain F.*

5   Example

We present a simple example to show what an agent specification might look like in the $P_F KD45$ language. This is a variety of the the common "travel agent" scenario whereby once the travel agent believes you might be interested in a holiday, (s)he sends you information. The basic formulas are given as follows (the finiteness of the domain ensures that this example can indeed be represented in a propositional language).

A. $ask(you, x) \rightarrow P_{0.8}^{\geq} go(you, x)$, i. e., "if you ask for information about the destination x, then I believe that you wish to go to x with probability greater than, or equal to, 0.8"

B. $P_1^{=} [go(you, x) \rightarrow buy(you, holiday, x)]$, i. e., "I believe that, if you wish to go to x, then you will buy a holiday in x"

C. $P_{0.5}^{>} buy(you, holiday, x) \rightarrow sendinfo(you, x)$, i. e., "if I believe that you will buy a holiday for x with probability greater than 0.5, I send information about holidays at x"

D. $ask(you, x)$, i. e., "you ask for information on destination x"

From D and A and $R1$ we have: $P_{[0.8]}^{\geq} go(you, x)$ (Res1).

From Res1, $A3$ and item B: $P_{[0.7]}^{>} buy(you, holiday, x)$ (Res2).

From Res2 and $T6$: $P_{[0.5]}^{>} buy(you, holiday, x)$ (Res3).

From Res3 and item C: $sendinfo(you, x)$

Referring to the decision procedure execution, there are three formulas to be evaluated (the ones that express degrees of beliefs):

1. $P_{0.8}^{\geq} go(you, x)$ (from A)
2. $P_1^{=} [go(you, x) \rightarrow buy(you, holiday, x)]$ (from B)
3. $P_{0.5}^{>} buy(you, holiday, x)$ (from C)

We obtain 6 solutions when solving the first two rules. From this set, all solutions satisfy the antecedent of the third rule (as would be expected by the formal proof given above). Which means that, whatever solution is chosen as a possible value assignment, the antecedent of rule C is true. Or, independently of the assignment, $sendinfo(you, x)$ is a logical consequence of the knowledge theory, and six assignments can be considered as options when building a model for the agent specification.

In this case, the six assignments for $[B0G0, B0G1, B1G0, B1G1]$ are: $[0, 0, 0, 1]$, $[0, 0, .1, .9]$, $[0, 0, .2, .8]$, $[.1, 0, 0, .9]$, $[.1, 0, .1, .8]$ and $[.2, 0, 0, .8]$

(where "B" represents buy(...) and "G" go(...)).

5.1   Limiting F

In this section, we elaborate on ways to automatically *generate* an appropriate
base set for a formula. In particular, we will look at sets F that are generated
by some number $\frac{1}{d}$. For such an F, we will write $F = \frac{1}{d}$. In general we have
that satisfiability is preserved when considering bigger sets F: if $F \subseteq F'$, then
$\mathcal{P}_F\mathcal{KD}45$- satisfiability implies $\mathcal{P}_{F'}\mathcal{KD}45$- satisfiability. As a consequence, we
have that a formula φ is $\mathcal{P}_F\mathcal{KD}45$-satisfiable for some F if, and only if, it is
$\mathcal{P}_{F'}\mathcal{KD}45$-satisfiable for some *generated* F'. So, given a formula φ, can we generate a F which is sufficient for satisfiability of φ? If we succeed in this, the user
of the specification language $\mathcal{P}_F KD45$ need not bother about a specific F, but
instead can leave the system to generate it.

To get a feeling for how sensitive the matter of satisfiability is against the
choice of F, suppose we have three atoms p, q and r, and let $L(p, q, r)$ be the
set of conjunctions of literals over them: $L = \{(\neg)p \wedge (\neg)q \wedge (\neg)r\}$ and let our
constraint φ be:

$$\bigwedge_{\psi \in L(p,q,r)} (P_0^> \psi \wedge P_{0.5}^< \psi) \tag{10}$$

If $F = \frac{1}{4}$, there is no model for (10), since every combination of atoms ψ would
have a probability of $\frac{1}{4}$, giving the disjunction $\bigvee_\psi \in L(p, q, r)\psi$ a 'probability'
of 2, which is, of course, not possible. One easily verifies that (10) is satisfiable
for a set F generated by $\frac{1}{d}$ iff $d \geq 8$, giving enough 'space' for each of the ψ's.

A range F with few elements easily gives rise to unsatisfiability. Axiom $A7$
forces one to make 'big jumps' between constraints: if we have $P_{r_i}^> \varphi$ for a certain
$r_i \in F$, we are forced to assign φ at least the next probability in F, viz., r_{i+1}.

We now sketch a way to construct an F from the formula φ in a most cautious
way. Consider the formula φ. Rewrite all the occurrences of $P_x^\sim \psi$ in φ in such a
way, that they all have a common denominator d: every $P_x^\sim \psi$ gets rewritten as a
$P_{\frac{m}{d}}^\gtrless \psi$. Let $x_1, \ldots x_m$ be all the boolean combinations of atoms from φ ($m = 2^k$).
The formula φ gives rise to a number of v inequalities I:

$$I(d) = \begin{cases} \kappa_{1_1} x_1 + \kappa_{1_2} x_2 + \ldots + \kappa_{1_m} x_m \sim_1 \frac{n_1}{d} \\ \ldots \qquad\qquad\qquad\qquad\qquad \sim \ \ldots \\ \kappa_{v_1} x_1 + \kappa_{v_2} x_2 + \ldots + \kappa_{v_m} x_m \sim_k \frac{k_1}{d} \end{cases}$$

Since solutions of $I(d)$ are obtained by taking linear combinations of the inequalities: it is clear that they are (as linear combinations of the right hand sides) of
the form $\frac{n}{d}$, for some n. Now, take the first x_i that is not yet determined, say
the tightest constraint on x_i says that is is between $\frac{n_i}{d}$ and $\frac{n_i+t}{d}$ for certain n
and t. Then we can safely add the constraint $x_i = \frac{n_i+t}{2d}$ to $I(d)$ and obtain a set
of inequalities $I(2d)$. Doing this iteratively gives us the following:

Conjecture 1. Let φ be a formula in our language, with denominator d. Then, φ
is satisfiable for some F iff φ if satisfiable for $F_\varphi = \frac{1}{2 \cdot d \cdot 2^k}$, where k is the number
of atoms occurring in φ.

6   Related Work and Conclusion

Several methods have been developed to deal with uncertain information, often being split between numerical (or quantitative) or symbolic (or qualitative) ones [12]. $P_F KD45$ is a system that combines logic and probability. In this sense, it is related to other work that showed how this combination would be possible in different ways [6]. One of those possible approaches is the interpretation of the modal belief operator according to the concept of 'likelihood' (as in [8]). In this logic, instead of using numbers to express uncertainty one would have expressions like "p is likely to be a consistent hypothesis" (as a state is taken as a set of hypotheses "true for now"). That is, a qualitative notion of likelihood rather than explicit probabilities.

$P_F KD45$ was designed for reasoning with (exact) probabilities. Its Probabilistic Kripke Model semantics is similar to the one presented in [5,4]. In their formalism, a formula is typically a boolean combination of expressions of the form $a_1 w(\varphi_1) + ... + a_k w(\varphi_k) \geq c$, where $a_1, ..., a_k, c$ are integers, and each φ_i is propositional. The restriction of having φ's as purely propositional does not apply to $P_F KD45$. Besides, the system in [5,4] includes, as axioms, all the formulas of linear inequalities; consequently, their proofs of completeness rely on results in the area of linear programming. Our logic is conceptually simpler. Finally, $P_F KD45$ differs mainly from other systems for representing beliefs and probability by allowing only a finite range of probability values, an assumption that at the same time imposes restrictions about the values that can be assigned to the possible worlds and permits the restoration of compactness for the logic.

Maybe the work closest to ours is that of [11]. It considers languages for first order probabilities, and the compactness of $P_F KD45$ easily follows from [11, Theorem 11]. They also consider the case in which all the worlds are assigned the same probability function, but for a language that forbids iteration.

In this paper, we presented $P_F KD45$, a simple and compact logic combining modal logic with probability. Despite the inclusion of new axioms and slight changes in the semantics, it was shown how the logic preserves important results about soundness, completeness, finite model and decidability of the previous system $P_F D$ [9]. In addition, new results about nested beliefs have been presented, a decision procedure for the logic has been developed, and brief examples were given showing how the language can serve as an appropriate basis concerning the informational attitudes of an agent specification language. In summary, we proposed not only a complete axiomatization for the logic, but also a decision procedure that permits us to verify satisfiability of $P_F KD45$-formulas.

The use of a finite range F of probability values is a peculiar, and important, property of our logic. Although the use of a base F causes a logical restriction, it seems possible to chose its granularity according to the intended agent's application. Besides, as discussed earlier in Section 1, the compactness that it brings has significant benefits. Furthermore, a finite range of probability values reduces the computational effort required when building a model for the agent description.

Finally, this work on $P_F KD45$ represents one step towards our main goal: an agent programming language capable of specifying and implementing agents that deal with uncertain information, together with new mechanisms for handling such uncertainty in executable specifications. Future work will concentrate on developing an executable framework combining the probabilistic approach of $P_F KD45$ with the dynamic approach of and Temporal Logics. This will allow us to capture, in our simple an compact approach, the key aspects of uncertain agents working in an uncertain world.

Acknowledgements. The first author gratefully acknowledges support by the Brazilian Government under CAPES-scholarship. The authors thank the anonymous referees for their relevant comments.

References

1. N. de Carvalho Ferreira, M. Fisher and W. van der Hoek, *A Simple Logic for Reasoning about Uncertainty*, Technical Report, Department of Computer Science, University of Liverpool, (2004). Online version:
   http://www.csc.liv.ac.uk/~niveacf/techreport/
2. D. Driankov, 'Reasoning about Uncertainty: Towards a many-valued logic of belief', *IDA annual research report*, 113–120, Linköping University, (1987).
3. M. Fattarosi-Barnaba and G. Amati. 'Modal operators with probabilistic interpretations, I'. *Studia Logica*, **48**:383–393, 1989.
4. R. Fagin and J.Y. Halpern, 'Reasoning about knowledge and probability', *Journal of the ACM*, **41**(2), 340–367, (1994).
5. R. Fagin, J.Y. Halpern, and N. Megiddo, 'A logic for reasoning about probabilities', *Information and Computation*, **87**(1), 277–291, (1990).
6. T. Fernando, 'In conjunction with qualitative probability', *Annals of Pure and Applied Logic*, **92**(3), 217–234, (1998).
7. P. Hájek and T. Havránek, *Mechanizing Hypothesis Formation*, Springer, 1978.
8. J.Y. Halpern and M.O. Rabin, 'A logic to reason about likelihood', *Artificial Intelligence*, **32**(3), 379–405, (1987).
9. W. van der Hoek, 'Some considerations on the logic PFD', *Journal of Applied Non Classical Logics*, **7**(3), 287–307, (1997).
10. J.-J.Ch. Meyer and W. van der Hoek, *Epistemic Logic for AI and Computer Science*, Cambridge University Press, 1995.
11. Z. Ognjanovic and M. Rǎskovic, 'Some first-order probability logics', *Theoretical Computer Science*, 191–212, (2000).
12. S. Parsons and A. Hunter, 'A review of uncertainty handling formalisms', in *Applications of Uncertainty Formalisms*, A. Hunter and S. Parsons (eds), Springer (1998).

Modelling Communicating Agents in Timed Reasoning Logics

Natasha Alechina, Brian Logan, and Mark Whitsey

School of Computer Science and IT, University of Nottingham, UK.
{nza,mtw,bsl}@cs.nott.ac.uk

Abstract. Practical reasoners are resource-bounded—in particular they require time to derive consequences of their knowledge. Building on the Timed Reasoning Logics (TRL) framework introduced in [1], we show how to represent the time required by an agent to reach a given conclusion. TRL allows us to model the kinds of rule application and conflict resolution strategies commonly found in rule-based agents, and we show how the choice of strategy can influence the information an agent can take into account when making decisions at a particular point in time. We prove general completeness and decidability results for TRL, and analyse the impact of communication in an example system consisting of two agents which use different conflict resolution strategies.

1 Introduction

Most research in logics for belief, knowledge and action (see, for example, [12,6,10, 11,16,17,5,13,20,18]) makes the strong assumption that whatever reasoning abilities an agent may have, the results of applying those abilities to a given problem are available immediately. For example, if an agent is capable of reasoning from its observations and some restricted set of logical rules, it derives all the consequences of its rules instantaneously.

While this is a reasonable assumption in some situations, there are many cases where the time taken to do deliberation is of critical importance. Practical agents take time to derive the consequences of their beliefs, and, in a dynamic environment, the time required by an agent to derive the consequences of its observations will determine whether such derivations can play an effective role in action selection. Another example involves more standard analytical reasoning and a classical domain for the application of epistemic logics: verifying cryptographic protocols. An agent intercepting a coded message usually has all the necessary "inference rules" to break the code. The only problem is that if the encoding is decent, it would take the intercepting agent millennia to actually derive the answer. On the other hand, if the encryption scheme is badly designed or the key length is short, the answer can be derived in an undesirably short period of time. The kind of logical results we want to be able to prove are therefore of the form *agent i is capable of reaching conclusion ϕ within time bound t*.

In this paper we show how to model the execution of communicating rule-based agents using Timed Reasoning Logics (TRL). TRL is a context-logic style formalism for describing rule-based resource bounded reasoners who take time to derive the consequences of their knowledge. This paper builds on the work in [1], where we introduced

J.J. Alferes and J. Leite (Eds.): JELIA 2004, LNAI 3229, pp. 95–107, 2004.

TRL. In that paper, we described how our logic can model different rule application and conflict resolution strategies, and proved soundness and completeness of the logic TRL(STEP) which captures the *all rules at each cycle* rule application strategy used by step logic [3] (for another example of a TRL(STEP) logic, see [21]). We also showed how to model a *single rule at each cycle* strategy similar to that employed by the CLIPS [19] rule-based system architecture, and sketched a logic TRL(CLIPS). In this paper, we prove a general soundness and completeness result for TRL, from which soundness and completeness of TRL(CLIPS) follows. We study TRL(CLIPS) in more detail and give a detailed example involving two communicating agents using different CLIPS conflict resolution strategies.

2 Model of an Agent

In this section we outline a simple model of the kind of rule-based agent whose execution cycle we wish to formalise.

A rule-based agent consists of a working memory and one or more sets of condition-action rules. The working memory constitutes the agent's state, and the rules form the agent's program. We assume that agents repeatedly execute a fixed *sense-think-act* cycle. At each tick of the clock, an agent senses its environment and information obtained by sensing is added to the previously derived facts and any a priori knowledge in the agent's working memory. The agent then evaluates the condition-action rules forming its program. The conditions of each rule are matched against the contents of the agent's working memory and a subset of the rules are fired. This typically adds or deletes one or more facts from working memory and/or results in some external actions being performed in the agent's environment. For the purposes of this paper the only external action we assume is a 'communication' action which allows agents to communicate facts currently held in working memory to other agents.

Our interest here is with the rule application and conflict resolution strategy adopted by the agent. In general, the conditions of a rule can be consistently matched against the items in working memory in more than one way, giving rise to a number of distinct *rule instances*. Following standard rule-based system terminology we call the set of rule instances the *conflict set* and the process of deciding which subset of rule instances are to be fired at any given cycle *conflict resolution*. Agents can adopt a wide range of rule application and conflict resolution strategies. For example, they can order the conflict set and fire only the first rule instance in the ordering at each cycle, or they can fire all rule instances in the conflict set on each cycle once, or they can repeatedly compute the conflict set and fire all the rule instances it contains set until no new facts can be derived at the current cycle. We call these three strategies *single rule at each cycle*, *all rules at each cycle*, and *all rules to quiesence* respectively.

3 Timed Reasoning Logics (TRL)

The literature contains many attempts at providing a logic of limited or restricted reasoning. However most of these do not explicitly take account of time. For example, Levesque's [12] logic of implicit and explicit belief restricts an agent's explicit beliefs (the classical possible worlds notion) by allowing non-classical (either incomplete or impossible) worlds to enter an agent's epistemic accessibility relation. Although agents need not then believe all classical tautologies, they remain perfect reasoners in relevance logic. In [7] Fagin & Halpern propose an alternative approach to restricting possible worlds semantics which involves a syntactic *awareness* filter, such that an agent only believes a formula if it (or its subterms) are in his awareness set. Agents are modelled as perfect reasoners whose beliefs are restricted to some syntactic class compatible with the awareness filter. Konolige [10] represents beliefs as sentences belonging to an agent's belief set, which is closed under the agent's deduction rules. A deduction model assigns a set of rules to each agent, allowing representation of agents with differing reasoning capacities within a single system. However the deduction model tells us what a set of agents will believe after an indefinitely long period of deliberation.

The only logical research we are aware of which represents reasoning as a process that explicitly requires time is *step logic* [2,4,3]. However, until recently, step logic lacked adequate semantics. In [15] Nirkhe, Kraus & Perlis propose a possible-worlds type semantics for step logic. However this re-introduces logical omniscience: once an agent learns that ϕ, it simultaneously knows all logically equivalent statements. In more recent work [9], Grant, Kraus & Perlis propose a semantics for step logic which does not result in logical omniscience, and prove soundness and completeness results for families of theories describing timed reasoning. However, their logic for reasoning about time-limited reasoners is first-order and hence undecidable (even if the agents described are very simple).

The approach we describe in this paper, Timed Reasoning Logics (TRL), avoids the problem of logical omniscience and is at the same time decidable. TRL is a context-logic style formalism for describing rule-based resource bounded reasoners who take time to derive the consequences of their knowledge. Not surprisingly, in order to avoid logical omniscience, a logic for reasoning about beliefs has to introduce syntactic objects representing formulas in its semantics. In [9], domains of models of the meta-logic for reasoning about agents contain objects corresponding to formulas of the agent's logic. We have chosen a different approach, where models correspond to sets of agent's states together with a transition relation (similar to [5]). States are identified with finite sets of formulas and the transition relation is computed using the agent rules.

This paper builds on the work in [1], where we introduced TRL. In this section, we give a slightly more general formulation of TRL than that given in [1], and prove its soundness and completeness.

3.1 TRL Syntax

Our choice of syntax is influenced both by step logics and context logics and by Gabbay's Labelled Deductive Systems [8]. To be able to reason about steps in deliberation and the time deliberation takes, we need a set of steps, or logical time points, which we will assume to be the set of natural numbers. To be able to reason about several agents, we also have a non-empty set of agents or reasoners $A = \{a, b, c, i, j, i_1, \ldots, i_n \ldots\}$.

Different agents may use different languages. To be able to model changes in the agent's language, such as acquiring new names for things etc., we also index the language by time points: at time t, agent i speaks the language $\mathcal{L}_t^i$.

Well formed formulas in the agent's languages $\mathcal{L}_t^i$ are defined in the usual way. For example, if $\mathcal{L}_0^a$ (the agent a's language at time 0) is a simple propositional logic with propositional variables $p_0, p_1, \ldots, p_n$, then a well formed formula ϕ of $\mathcal{L}_0^a$ is defined as

$$\phi = p_i | \neg \phi | \phi \rightarrow \phi | \phi \wedge \phi | \phi \vee \phi$$

As in context logic, we use labelled formulas to distinguish between beliefs of different agents at different times. If i is an agent, t is a moment of time, and ϕ a well-formed formula of the language $\mathcal{L}_i^t$, then $(i, t) : \phi$ is a well-formed labelled formula of TRL.

The general form of an inference rule in TRL is:

$$\frac{(i_1, t) : \phi_1, \ \ldots, \ (i_n, t) : \phi_n}{(i, t+1) : \phi}$$

with a possible side condition of the form: provided that $(i_1, t) : \phi_1, \ldots, (i_n, t) : \phi_n$ and the set Δ_t of all formulas derived at the previous stage in the derivation (see Definition 1 below) satisfy some property. For example, a side condition for a defeasible rule may be that some formula is *not in* Δ_t.

A significant restriction on the format of possible TRL rules is that *only finitely many formulas labelled t should be derivable* starting with a finite set of labelled formulas Γ, for any t. For example, supposing we had an operator B_a for "agent a believes that", then the following negative introspection rule:

$$(a, t+1) : \neg B_a \phi \quad \text{given that} \quad (a, t) : \phi \notin \Delta_t$$

cannot be introduced in unrestricted form since it would generate infinitely many formulas at step $t+1$.

A simple example of a TRL rule is an inference rule corresponding to a rule in the agent's program. If agent a's program contains the rule

$$A(x), B(x) \rightarrow C(x)$$

then the corresponding inference rule in TRL would be

$$\frac{(a, t) : A(x), \ (a, t) : B(x)}{(a, t+1) : C(x)}$$

Depending on the agent's rule application strategy, the TRL inference rule may have a side condition stating, for example, that it may only be applied if no other rule is applicable.

Another kind of rule which we will see later is used to model communication between agents. For example,

$$\frac{(a, t) : \phi}{(b, t+1) : B_a \phi}$$

expresses the fact that whenever a believes ϕ, at the next step b believes $B_a \phi$. In this paper, we do not explicitly model message passing. Instead we assume that whenever an agent derives a fact of a certain form it communicates this fact to other agents. The message arrives at the next tick of the clock, and is 'observed' immediately. In the example above, whenever a derives ϕ, it sends a message containing ϕ to b, which arrives at $t + 1$. This model corresponds to perfect broadcast communication with a fixed one tick delay.

The derivability relation in a TRL logic may be non-monotonic due to the agent's rule application strategy (e.g. only one of the rules is applied at each cycle) or to the presence of defeasible rules. Before we give a formal definition of derivability, we need a couple of auxiliary definitions. Let R be a set of TRL rules and Δ a finite set of labelled formulas. Then by $R(\Delta)$ we denote the set of all labelled formulas derivable from Δ by one application of a rule in R. Formally, $R(\Delta)$ is the set of all labelled formulas $(i, t + 1) : \phi$ such that there is a rule in R of the form

$$\frac{(i_1, t) : \phi_1, \dots, (i_n, t) : \phi_n}{(i, t + 1) : \phi}$$

and $(i_1, t) : \phi_1, \dots, (i_n, t) : \phi_n \in \Delta$ and any side condition of the rule, holds for $(i_1, t) : \phi_1, \dots, (i_n, t) : \phi_n$ and Δ. Finally, given a set of labelled formulas Γ, we write Γ_k for the subset of Γ labelled by time point k (formulas in Γ of the form $(j, k) : \psi$ for any agent j).

Definition 1. *Given a set of TRL rules R, a labelled formula $(i, t) : \phi$ is derivable using R from a set of labelled formulas Γ:*

$$\Gamma \vdash_R (i, t) : \phi$$

if there exists a sequence of finite sets of labelled formulas

$$\Delta_0, \Delta_1, \dots, \Delta_t,$$

such that $(i, t) : \phi \in \Delta_t$ and

1. *Δ_0 is the union of Γ_0 and all axioms in R labelled by time 0 (i.e., $(j, 0)$ for some agent j).*
2. *Δ_k is the union of Γ_k and $R(\Delta_{k-1})$.*

3.2 TRL Semantics

We identify the local state of agent i at time t, m_t^i, with a finite set $\{\phi_1, \dots, \phi_n\}$ of formulas of the agent's language at time t, i.e. $\mathcal{L}_t^i$. At this point, we don't require anything else in addition to finiteness. In particular, this set may be empty or inconsistent.

A TRL model is a set of local TRL states. Each local state in a TRL model is indexed by an element of the index set $I = A \times \mathbb{N}$, which is the set of pairs (i, t), where i is an agent and t is the step number. In addition, a TRL model should satisfy constraints which make it a valid representation of a run of a multi-agent system. To formulate those constraints, we need the additional notions of observation and inference, which constrain how the next state of an agent will look.

Each agent has a program—a set of rules which it uses to derive its next state given its current state and any new beliefs it obtains by observing the world. We therefore equip each model with an *obs* function and a set of *inf$_i$* functions (one for each agent i). Intuitively, *obs* models observations, which we take to include inter-agent communication, and takes a step t and an agent i as arguments and returns a finite set of formulas in the agent's language at that step. This set is added to the agent's state at the same step (we thus model observations as being believed instantaneously). Each inf_i models agent i's computation of a new state by mapping a finite set of formulas in the language $\mathcal{L}_t^i$ to another finite set of formulas in the language $\mathcal{L}_{t+1}^i$. Intuitively, inf_i takes the tokens in agent i's state at time t, applies the rules in i's program to them to obtain a new set of tokens, which, together with i's observations at time $t + 1$, constitute its state at time $t + 1$.

Definition 2 (TRL Model). *Let A be a set of agents and $\{\mathcal{L}_t^i : i \in A, t \in \mathbb{N}\}$ a set of agent languages. A TRL model M is a tuple $\langle obs, inf_i, \{m_t^i : i \in A, t \in \mathbb{N}\}\rangle$ where obs is a function which maps a pair (i, t) to a finite set of formulas in $\mathcal{L}_t^i$, inf_i is a function from finite sets of formulas in $\mathcal{L}_t^i$ to finite sets of formulas in $\mathcal{L}_{t+1}^i$, and each m_t^i is a finite set of formulas in $\mathcal{L}_t^i$ such that $m_{t+1}^i = inf_i(m_t^i) \cup obs(i, t + 1)$.*

Definition 3 (Satisfaction and Logical Entailment). *A labelled formula $(i, t) : \phi$ is true in a model, written $M \models (i, t) : \phi$, iff $\phi \in m_t^i$ (the state indexed by (i, t) in M contains ϕ). A labelled formula $(i, t) : \phi$ is valid, $\models (i, t) : \phi$, iff for all models M, $M \models (i, t) : \phi$. Let Γ be a set of labelled formulas. Γ logically entails $(i, t) : \phi$, $\Gamma \models (i, t) : \phi$, if in all models where Γ is true, $(i, t) : \phi$ is true.*

3.3 Soundness and Completeness of TRL

In this section we prove a general soundness and completeness result for TRL systems. We are going to show that given a set of TRL rules R (the only condition on R is that starting from a finite set of premises, it only produces a finite set of consequences labelled t, for any t) and a set of TRL models S, describing possible runs of a multi-agent system, R is sound and complete with respect to S if, and only if, S is the set of models which *conform* to R in the sense defined below.

Definition 4. *A TRL model M conforms to a set of TRL rules R if for every rule in R of the form*

$$\frac{(i_1, t) : \phi_1, \ldots, (i_n, t) : \phi_n}{(i, t + 1) : \psi}$$

possibly with some side condition on Δ_t, M satisfies the property that if for all premises of the rule, $\phi_k \in m_t^k$, and the side condition of the rule holds for $\bigcup_{j \in A} m_t^j$ substituted for Δ_t, then $\psi \in m_{t+1}^i$.

Before proving the main theorem, we need one more notion, similar to the notion of a knowledge-supported model in [9]:

Definition 5. *[Minimal Model] A TRL model M conforming to a set of TRL rules R is a minimal model for a set of labelled formulas Γ if for every i, t and ϕ, $\phi \in m_t^i$ iff one of the following holds:*

1. there is a rule in R of the form

$$\frac{(i_1, t) : \phi_1, \ldots, (i_n, t) : \phi_n}{(i, t+1) : \phi}$$

for all premises of the rule, $\phi_k \in m_{t-1}^k$ and the side condition of the rule holds for $\bigcup_{j \in A} m_{t-1}^j$ (in other words, ϕ is in m_t^i because the model conforms to R)

2. or $(i, t) : \phi \in \Gamma$ in which case $\phi \in obs(m_t^i)$.

A minimal model for Γ only satisfies the formulas in Γ and their logical consequences.

Lemma 1. *Let M be a minimal model for Γ conforming to R. Then for every formula ϕ, $\phi \in m_t^i$ iff $\Gamma \vdash_R (i, t) : \phi$.*

Proof. The proof goes by induction on t. If $t = 0$, then the only way $\phi \in m_0^i$ is because $\phi \in obs(i, 0)$ hence $(i, 0) : \phi \in \Gamma$ so $\Gamma \vdash_R (i, 0) : \phi$. Inductive hypothesis: suppose that for all agents j and all $s \leq t$, $\phi \in m_s^j$ iff $\Gamma \vdash_R (j, s) : \phi$. Let $\phi \in m_{t+1}^i$. Then either $(i, t+1) : \phi \in \Gamma$ hence $\Gamma \vdash_R (i, t+1) : \phi$, or there is a rule in R of the form

$$\frac{(i_1, t) : \phi_1, \ldots, (i_n, t) : \phi_n}{(i, t+1) : \psi}$$

such that $\psi = \phi$ and $\phi_1, \ldots, \phi_n \in m_t^i$ (and the side condition of the rule holds for the set of formulas in the union of all states at time t). By the inductive hypothesis, $\Gamma \vdash_R (i_k, t) : \phi_k$. Hence by this same rule, $\Gamma \vdash_R (i, t+1) : \phi$.

Theorem 1. *Given a set of TRL rules R, for any finite set of labelled formulas Γ and a labelled formula ϕ, $\Gamma \vdash_R \phi$ iff $\Gamma \models_{\mathcal{R}} \phi$ where $\mathcal{R}$ is the set of all models conforming to R.*

Proof. Soundness ($\Gamma \models_{\mathcal{R}} \phi \Rightarrow \Gamma \vdash_R \phi$) is standard: clearly, in a model conforming to R the rules in R preserve validity.

Completeness: suppose $\Gamma \models_{\mathcal{R}} \phi$. Consider a minimal model for Γ, M_Γ, conforming to R. Since $\Gamma \models_{\mathcal{R}} \phi$ and our particular model M_Γ conforms to R and satisfies Γ, $M_\Gamma \models \phi$. From Lemma 1, $\Gamma \vdash_R \phi$.

Theorem 2. *Given a set of TRL rules R, for any finite set of labelled formulas Γ and a labelled formula ϕ, it is decidable whether $\Gamma \vdash_R \phi$ or $\Gamma \models_{\mathcal{R}} \phi$ where $\mathcal{R}$ is the set of all models conforming to R.*

Proof. From Theorem 1 above, the questions whether $\Gamma \vdash_R (i, t) : \phi$ and whether $\Gamma \models_{\mathcal{R}} (i, t) : \phi$, where $\mathcal{R}$ is the set of models conforming to R, are equivalent. Consider a minimal model M_Γ for Γ. If $\Gamma \models_{\mathcal{R}} (i, t) : \phi$, then $\phi \in m_t^i$ in M_Γ. On the other hand, from Lemma 1, if $\phi \in m_t^i$ then $\Gamma \vdash_R (i, t) : \phi$. Hence $\phi \in m_t^i$ iff $\Gamma \vdash_R (i, t) : \phi$ iff $\Gamma \models_{\mathcal{R}} (i, t) : \phi$.

It is easy to see that given that Γ is finite and rules in R only produce a finite number of new formulas at each step, the initial segment of M (up to step t) can be constructed in time bounded by a tower of exponentials in $|\Gamma|$ of height t (but nevertheless bounded). Then we can inspect m_t^i to see if ϕ is there.

4   TRL(CLIPS)

As an example of a logical model of an agent based on TRL, we show how to model a simple system consisting of two communicating agents. The agents use a CLIPS-style [19] *single rule at each cycle* rule application strategy. However each agent uses a different CLIPS conflict resolution strategy. We show that the adoption of different conflict resolution strategies by each agent can result in a reduction in the time required to derive information for action selection.

CLIPS has been used to build a number of agent-based systems (see, e.g., [14]). In CLIPS each rule has a *salience* reflecting its importance in problem solving. At each cycle, all rules are matched against the facts in working memory and any new rule instances are added to the conflict set. Rule matching is refractory, i.e., rules don't match against the same set of premises more than once. New rule instances are placed above all rule instances of lower salience and below all rules of higher salience. If rule instances have equal salience, ties are broken by the conflict resolution strategy. CLIPS supports a variety of conflict resolution strategies including *depth, breadth, simplicity, complexity, lex, mea,* and *random.* The default strategy, called *depth,* gives preference to new rule instances; *breadth* places older rule instances higher. Once the conflict set has been computed, CLIPS fires the highest ranking rule instance in the conflict set at each cycle.

Consider an agent with the following set of rules using the *depth* conflict resolution strategy:

```
R1: tiger(x) -> large-carnivore(x)
R2: large-carnivore(x) -> dangerous(x)
```

R1 has greater salience than R2. If the agent's working memory contains the following fact:

```
0:tiger(c)
```

then at the next cycle the agent would derive

```
1:large-carnivore(c)
```

Assume that at this cycle the agent observes a second tiger, and a corresponding fact is asserted into working memory:

```
1:tiger(d)
```

Instances of R1 have greater salience than instances of R2, so on the following cycle the agent will derive

```
2:large-carnivore(d)
```

Both "large-carnivore(c)" and "large-carnivore(d)" match R2, but "large-carnivore(d)" will be preferred since it it is a more recent instance of R2 than "large-carnivore(c)". On the following cycle the agent will derive

```
3:dangerous(d)
```

Finally the agent derives:

```
4:dangerous(c)
```

This is trivial example. However, in general, the time at which a fact is derived can be significant. For example, in developing an agent we may wish to ensure that it responds to dangers as soon as they are perceived rather than after classifying objects in the environment. In our short example, the delay in identifying danger is just one step, but it is easy to modify the example to make the delay arbitrarily long (by introducing n new tigers instead of one at cycle 1).

It is easy to see that the TRL logic corresponding to the *single rule at each cycle* strategy is non-monotonic. For instance, in the example above, $\{0:\texttt{tiger(c)}\} \vdash 2:\texttt{dangerous(c)}$, but $\{0:\texttt{tiger(c)}, 1:\texttt{tiger(d)}\} \not\vdash 2:\texttt{dangerous(c)}$.

To reflect salience of rules, we assume that there is a partial order $\leq_{j,r}$ on the set of rules $\mathcal{R}_j = \{R_1, \ldots, R_n\}$ which correspond to the rules of agent j's program. Note that the logic will contain more rules describing agent j in addition to $\mathcal{R}_j$; e.g. rules which model observation, or the fact that formulas persist in the state. To determine which rule instance will be fired at a given step in a TRL(CLIPS) derivation, we need to compute a 'conflict set' of sets of premises matching rules in $\mathcal{R}_j$, order it by a total order, and fire the rule with the premises which come top in that order. The total order on the conflict set is determined by the agent's conflict resolution strategy.

To be more formal, let Δ_t be the set of all formulas derived at step t. Let $C_{j,t}$ be the the conflict set for j at t, namely $C_{j,t} = \{\langle (j,t) : \phi_1, \ldots, (j,t) : \phi_n, R_i \rangle : (j,t) : \phi_{1\ldots n} \in \Delta_t, R_i \in \mathcal{R}_j$, and $(j,t) : \phi_1, \ldots, (j,t) : \phi_n$ match $R_i\}$.

Define the order $<_{depth}$ (depth order on $C_{j,t}$, to be read as 'lower in the depth order') as follows:

$$\langle (j,t) : \phi_1, \ldots, (j,t) : \phi_n, R_i \rangle <_{depth} \langle (j,t) : \psi_1, \ldots, (j,t) : \psi_n, R_m \rangle$$

iff

1. $R_i \leq_{r,j} R_m$ (R_i has lower salience); or
2. $R_i =_{r,j} R_m$, but $\langle (j,t) : \phi_1, \ldots, (j,t) : \phi_n, R_i \rangle$ is an earlier rule instance, that is, for some Δ_s with $s < t$, $\langle (j,s) : \phi_1, \ldots, (j,s) : \phi_n, R_i \rangle \in C_{j,s}$ and $\langle (j,s) : \psi_1, \ldots, (j,s) : \psi_n, R_m \rangle \notin C_{j,s}$; or
3. $(j,t) : \phi_1, \ldots, (j,t) : \phi_n$ and $(j,t) : \psi_1, \ldots, (j,t) : \psi_n$ match rules of the same salience and were added to the conflict set at the same time, but $(j,t) : \phi_1, \ldots, (j,t) : \phi_n$ is lower in some arbitrary, e.g., lexicographic, order.

For the breadth order $<_{breadth}$, we reverse the second clause of the definition; now the premises which belong to a conflict set $C_{j,s}$ for the earliest time s are higher in the order.

We introduce meta-logical abbreviation $top_{j,depth}(\phi_1, \ldots, \phi_m, \Delta_t)$ and $top_{j,breadth}(\phi_1, \ldots, \phi_m, \Delta_t)$ to indicate that the set of premises $\phi_1, \ldots, \phi_m$ is the highest in the $<_{depth}$ ($<_{breadth}$) order among the conflict set $C_{j,t}$ of formulas from Δ_t.

Finally, we need to account for the refractoriness of the CLIPS rule application strategy: any rule instance is only used once in the TRL(CLIPS) derivation. To be precise, for any rule R_j and a set of premises $(i, t) : \phi_1, \ldots, (i, t) : \phi_n$ matching this rule, if at some step $s < t$ the rule R_j was fired with a set of premises which were the same but for step label (e.g. $(i, s) : \phi_1, \ldots, (i, s) : \phi_n$), then $(i, t) : \phi_1, \ldots, (i, t) : \phi_n$ are excluded from the conflict set $C_{i,t}$.

The rules of a *single rule at each cycle* agent i using the *depth* strategy then become (for $\phi_1, \ldots, \phi_n \rightarrow \psi$):

$$\frac{(i, t) : \phi_1, \ldots, (i, t) : \phi_n, \Delta_t}{(i, t + 1) : \psi}$$

provided $top_{i,depth}((i, t) : \phi_1, \ldots, (i, t) : \phi_n, \Delta_t)$, namely the premises of the rule are maximal in the $<_{depth}$ order in the conflict set for i at t. In what follows, we refer to such a proviso as 'standard proviso for depth order'. For example, the agent a from the example above has a rule:

$$\frac{(a, t) : Tiger(x), \Delta_t}{(a, t + 1) : Large\text{-}Carnivore(x)}$$

provided $top_{a,depth}((a, t) : Tiger(x), \Delta_t)$

For monotonic agents (who keep all the facts they derived earlier) we have an additional monotonicity rule which does not have a side condition, is always applicable, and is excluded from the ordering of the internal agent rules proper:

$$\frac{(i, t) : \phi}{(i, t + 1) : \phi}$$

To give an example of an observation rule, suppose that the agent a gets some of its information about the world from agent b. In particular, if b decides that something is nearby, then at the next step a also decides that it is nearby:

$$\frac{(b, t) : Near(x)}{(a, t + 1) : Near(x)}$$

This rule also does not have any side conditions.

The notion of derivation in TRL(CLIPS) is a special case of TRL derivation as given in Definition 1.

4.1   Example

In this section we give a worked example of a derivation in TRL(CLIPS). Our example involves two agents, a and b. They have the same set of rules with the same salience order and start with the same set of observations, but a uses the *depth* strategy, while b uses the *breadth* conflict resolution strategy. We show that they both can reach the same conclusion, (classify a tiger as a dangerous object), however if they communicate, they can reach this conclusion faster.

The rules corresponding to the program rules of agent a are (with the standard proviso for depth order):

$$\frac{(a, t) : Large(x), (a, t) : Carnivore(x), (a, t) : Near(x), (a, t) : Free(x), \Delta_t}{(a, t + 1) : Dangerous(x)} \ R1$$

$$\frac{(a,t) : Bengal\text{-}Tiger(x), \Delta_t}{(a,t+1) : Tiger(x)} \; R2$$

$$\frac{(a,t) : Tiger(x), \Delta_t}{(a,t+1) : Large(x)} \; R3$$

$$\frac{(a,t) : Tiger(x), \Delta_t}{(a,t+1) : Carnivore(x)} \; R4$$

$$\frac{(a,t) : Distance < 5m(x), \Delta_t}{(a,t+1) : Near(x)} \; R5$$

$$\frac{(a,t) : \neg Caged(x), \Delta_t}{(a,t+1) : Free(x)} \; R6$$

The rules for agent b are the same, with $top_{a,depth}$ replaced with $top_{b,breadth}$. The salience order on rules is $R1 \geq_r R2 \geq_r \{R3, R4, R5, R6\}$.

In addition, both agents have the monotonicity rule and the following communication rules:

$$\frac{(a,t) : Large(x)}{(b,t+1) : Large(x)}$$

$$\frac{(a,t) : Carnivore(x)}{(b,t+1) : Carnivore(x)}$$

$$\frac{(b,t) : Near(x)}{(a,t+1) : Near(x)}$$

$$\frac{(b,t) : Free(x)}{(a,t+1) : Free(x)}$$

Suppose both agents start with the same set of observations, corresponding to a sighting of a Bengal tiger at a distance less than 5 meters, and apparently uncaged: $(a,0) : Bengal\text{-}Tiger(c), (a,0) : Distance < 5m(c), (a,0) : \neg Caged(c), (b,0) : Bengal\text{-}Tiger(c), (b,0) : Distance < 5m(c), (b,0) : \neg Caged(c)$. At this step, both agent's conflict sets are the same: all formulas match one of the rules, but the highest salience rule is R2, in the case of a matched by $(a,0) : Bengal\text{-}Tiger(c)$. The other two rule instances in $C_{a,0}$ are $(a,0) : Distance < 5m(c)$ matching R5 and $(a,0) : \neg Caged(c)$ matching R6 (similarly for $C_{b,0}$). So at the next step, Δ_1 contains $(a,1) : Bengal\text{-}Tiger(c), (a,1) : Distance < 5m(c), (a,1) : \neg Caged(c)$, by the monotonicity rule, and $(a,1) : Tiger(c)$ by R2, and corresponding formulas for b. From step 1, the conflict sets of the two agents diverge: agent a places a new rules instance, $(a,1) : Tiger(c)$ which matches R3, at the top of the conflict set, while agent b favours one of the old rule instances, let's say R5. The new formulas in Δ_2 are $(a,2) : Large(c)$, and $(b,2) : Near(c)$.

At this stage, the top rule instance for a is $(a,2) : Tiger(c)$ matching R4, while the top rule instance for b is $(b,2) : \neg Caged(c)$ matching R6. In addition, both agents have now derived formulas of the kind they communicate to each other; so at the next step, a will discover that c is nearby and b will discover that c is large. The new formulas in Δ_3 are $(a,3) : Carnivore(c), (a,3) : Near(c), (b,3) : Free(c), (b,3) : Large(c)$.

At the next step, both agents will acquire the facts $(a, 4)$: $Large(c)$, $(a, 4)$: $Carnivore(c)$, $(a, 3)$: $Near(c)$, $(a, 4)$: $Free(c)$, and will match the rule with the top salience, R1, to derive $(a, 5)$: $Dangerous(c)$ (similarly for b). The reader will easily verify that it would have taken the agents longer to derive $Dangerous(c)$ without communication.

5   Conclusion

In this paper we showed how to model the execution of communicating rule-based agents using Timed Reasoning Logics (TRL). Our framework allow us to model agents at a fine-grained level, so that we can prove, for example, that the agent will use so many computation cycles to arrive at a given conclusion.

In previous work [1], we showed how to model a *single rule at each cycle* strategy similar to that employed by the CLIPS [19] rule-based system architecture, and sketched a logic TRL(CLIPS). In this paper, we prove a general soundness and completeness result for TRL, from which soundness and completeness of TRL(CLIPS) follows. We study TRL(CLIPS) in more detail and give a detailed example involving two communicating agents using CLIPS rule application strategy. The example is quite simple, but it demonstrates that we can compare different agent designs and prove properties of various conflict resolution strategies in the presence of communication between agents.

In the future, we plan to add a more fine-grained analysis of action and communication to the TRL framework. It would also be interesting to investigate more systematically the impact of communication on the time required by agents to reach a given conclusion.

References

1. N. Alechina, B. Logan, and M. Whitsey. A complete and decidable logic for resource-bounded agents. In *Proceedings of the Third International Joint Conference on Autonomous Agents and Multi-Agent Systems (AAMAS 2004)*. ACM Press, July 2004.
2. J. Drapkin and D. Perlis. A preliminary excursion into Step-Logics. *Proceedings of the SIGART International Symposium on Methodologies for Intelligent Systems*, pages 262–269, 1986.
3. J. Elgot-Drapkin, M. Miller, and D. Perlis. Memory, reason and time: the Step-Logic approach. In R. Cummins and J. Pollock, editors, *Philosophy and AI: Essays at the Interface*, pages 79–103. MIT Press, Cambridge, Mass., 1991.
4. J. Elgot-Drapkin and D. Perlis. Reasoning situated in time I: Basic concepts. *Journal of Experimental and Theoretical Artificial Intelligence*, 2(1):75–98, 1990.
5. R. Fagin, J. Y. Halpern, Y. Moses, and M. Y. Vardi. *Reasoning about Knowledge*. MIP Press, Cambridge, Mass., 1995.
6. R. Fagin and J.Y. Halpern. Belief, awareness and limited reasoning. In *Proceedings of the Ninth International Joint Conference on Artificial Intelligence (IJCAI-85)*, pages 491–501, Los Angeles, CA, 1985.
7. R. Fagin and J.Y. Halpern. Belief, awareness and limited reasoning. *Artificial Intelligence*, 34:39–76, 1988.
8. Dov M. Gabbay. *Labeled Deductive Systems: Volume I - Foundations*. Oxford University Press, 1996.

9. John Grant, Sarit Kraus, and Donald Perlis. A logic for characterizing multiple bounded agents. *Autonomous Agents and Multi-Agent Systems*, 3(4):351–387, 2000.
10. K. Konolige. *A Deduction Model of Belief.* Morgan Kaufman, 1986.
11. G. Lakemeyer. Steps towards a first-order logic of explicit and implict belief. In J. Y. Halpern, editor, *Theoretical Aspects of Reasoning About Knowledge: Proceedings of the 1986 Conference*, pages 325–340, San Francisco, 1986. Morgan Kaufmann.
12. H.J. Levesque. A logic of implicit and explicit belief. In *Proceedings of the Fourth National Conference on Artificial Intelligence (AAAI '84)*, pages 198–202, 1984.
13. R. C. Moore. *Logic and Representations.* Number 39 in CSLI Lecture Notes. CSLI Publications, 1995.
14. NASA. *Proceedings of the Third Conference on CLIPS (CLIPS'94)*, Lyndon B. Johnson Space Center, September 1994.
15. M. Nirkhe, S. Kraus, and D. Perlis. Thinking takes time: a modal active-logic for reasoning in time. Technical Report CS-TR-3249, University of Maryland, Department of Computer Science, 1994.
16. R. Parikh. Knowledge and the problem of logical omniscience. In *Methodologies for Intelligent Systems, Proceedings of the Second International Symposium*, pages 432–439. North-Holland, 1987.
17. A. S. Rao and M. P. Georgeff. Modeling rational agents within a BDI-architecture. In *Proceedings of the Second International Conference on Principles of Knowledge Representation and Reasoning (KR'91)*, pages 473–484, 1991.
18. M. P. Singh. Know-How. In Michael Wooldridge and Anand Rao, editors, *Foundations of Rational Agency*, pages 81–104. Kluwer, Dordrecht, 1999.
19. Software Technology Branch, Lyndon B. Johnson Space Center, Houston. *CLIPS Reference Manual: Version 6.21*, June 2003.
20. W. van der Hoek, B. van Linder, and J-J. Ch. Meyer. An integrated modal approach to rational agents. In M. Wooldridge and A. Rao, editors, *Foundations of Rational Agency*, pages 133–168. Kluwer, Dordrecht, 1999.
21. M. Whitsey. Timed reasoning logics: An example. In *Proceedings of the Logic and Communication in Multi-Agent Systems Workshop (LCMAS 2004)*. Loria, 2004.

On the Relation Between ID-Logic and Answer Set Programming*

Maarten Mariën, David Gilis, and Marc Denecker

Department of Computer Science, Katholieke Universiteit Leuven, Belgium
{Maarten.Marien,David.Gilis,Marc.Denecker}@cs.kuleuven.ac.be

Abstract. This paper is an analysis of two knowledge representation extensions of logic programming, namely Answer Set Programming and ID-Logic. Our aim is to compare both logics on the level of declarative reading, practical methodology and formal semantics. At the level of methodology, we put forward the *thesis* that in many (but not all) existing applications of ASP, an ASP program is used to encode definitions and assertions, similar as in ID-Logic. We illustrate this thesis with an example and present a formal result that supports it, namely an equivalence preserving translation from a class of ID-Logic theories into ASP. This translation can be exploited also to use the current efficient ASP solvers to reason on ID-Logic theories and it has been used to implement a model generator for ID-Logic.

1 Introduction

This paper is a comparison of Answer Set Programming [9,12], more precisely, of General Logic Programming [8] or Stable Logic Programming [11], and ID-Logic [2,6]. Both logics can be considered as extensions of logic programming for knowledge representation. The basic formal result of this paper is an equivalence preserving translation from an important class of ID-Logic theories to ASP. This result leads to improved understanding of these logics in different ways. Not only does it give insight in the formal relationships between the logics, but it also leads to improved understanding of the methodology of ID-Logic and ASP and allows to compare them. Moreover, this result can be exploited to use the current generation of efficient ASP solvers to reason on or perform problem solving using ID-Logic theories. In fact, we discuss an existing model generator for ID-Logic which we built using this translation and the Smodels system.

ID-Logic is an extension of classical first order logic that allows for a uniform representation of various forms of definitions, including non-inductive definitions, monotone inductive definitions (e.g. the transitive closure of a graph) and non-monotone forms of inductive definitions such as iterated induction and induction over well-founded posets (e.g. the standard definition of truth of a formula in a

* Works supported by FWO-Vlaanderen, European Framework 5 Project WASP, and by GOA/2003/08.

J.J. Alferes and J. Leite (Eds.): JELIA 2004, LNAI 3229, pp. 108–120, 2004.

structure). An ID-Logic theory consists of a set of FOL sentences, called assertions, and definitions. A definition is represented as a set of definitional rules of the form $\forall \bar{x}(A \leftarrow \alpha)$ where A is an atom, $\leftarrow$ the so-called definitional implication (to be distinguished from material implication, $\subset$) and α a FOL formula (thus negation in ID-Logic is classical negation). A definition defines a set of *defined predicates*, namely those occurring in the head of rules, in terms of other *open predicates*, which appear only in the body of rules. Note that an ID-Logic theory never contains a definitional rule; it only may contain *sets* of such rules. The formal semantics is an integration of classical logic semantics and the *well-founded semantics* for definitions. Formally, Abductive Logic Programming under well-founded semantics can be seen as the subformalism of ID-Logic consisting of theories with only one definition and imposing the Domain Closure Axiom and the Unique Name Axioms. In [4], a extension called NMID-logic was proposed allowing for arbitrary boolean combinations of definitions and FOL formulas. The same paper explores the use of this logic for knowledge representation in the context of situation calculus.

The second formalism that we consider here is General Logic Programming [8] or Stable Logic Programming as it was called in [11,12]. A program in this formalism consists of *general program rules* of the form $A \leftarrow Body$ where A is an atom and $Body$ is a conjunction of literals B or **not** B where B is an atom. The semantics is the stable model semantics. The formalism is a subformalism of Answer Set Programming (ASP), without the *strong negation* and the *disjunction* in the head. Despite these limitations, most applications of ASP can be represented in it or in its extension with weight constraints [12]. The formalism is generally seen as a sublogic of default logic and negation as failure as a default negation operator *"it is possible to assume that A is false"*.

Both logics show considerable differences on the conceptual, syntactical and semantical level. Yet, if we compare examples and methodologies, striking similarities show up. To illustrate this, we take a representation of the wellknown notion of hamiltonian cycles of a graph. (See Figure 1, where we implicitly assume that the unique names axioms and the domain closure axioms hold.)

There is an apparent similarity on the level of clauses and structure of the theory. In both theories, four different parts can be distinguished:

- *data*, representing the graph by a set of atomic clauses in ASP or by two definitions of $Vertex/1$ and $Edge/2$ in ID-Logic.
- ASP rules to *open up* predicates, here only the predicate $in/2$. In ASP, this can be done also using a disjunction (as in dlv) or using a weight constraint (as in Smodels). Often, such rules specify also a *domain* for the opened predicate. The domain of $in/2$ is the predicate $edge/2$ which means that $in/2$ is a subset of $edge/1$. As ID-Logic is an extension of classical logic, predicates are open per default; the *domain declaration* is formalised by an implication.
- *definitions*, here only of the concept of reachable vertices (through hamiltonian edges).

ID-Logic	ASP (taken from [11])
$\left.\begin{array}{l} Vertex(U) \leftarrow \\ \dots \\ Edge(U,V) \leftarrow \\ \dots \end{array}\right\}$ $\left\{ InitialVtx(U) \leftarrow \right\}$	$vertex(u) \leftarrow$ $\dots$ $edge(u,v) \leftarrow$ $\dots$ $initialvtx(u) \leftarrow$
	$in(V1,V2) \leftarrow$ $\quad edge(V1,V2), \textbf{not } out(V1,V2)$ $out(V1,V2) \leftarrow$ $\quad edge(V1,V2), \textbf{not } in(V1,V2)$
$\left.\begin{array}{l} \forall x,y(Reached(x) \leftarrow \\ \quad In(y,x) \wedge InitialVtx(y)) \\ \forall x,y(Reached(x) \leftarrow \\ \quad In(y,x) \wedge Reached(y)) \end{array}\right\}$	$reached(V2) \leftarrow$ $\quad in(V1,V2), reached(V1)$ $reached(V2) \leftarrow$ $\quad in(V1,V2), initialvtx(V1)$
$\forall x,y(In(x,y) \supset Edge(x,y))$ $\forall x,y,z((In(x,y) \wedge In(x,z)) \supset (y=z))$ $\forall x,y,z((In(y,x) \wedge In(z,x)) \supset (y=z))$ $\forall x(Vertex(x) \supset Reached(x))$	$f \leftarrow in(V2,V1), in(V3,V1),$ $\quad \textbf{not } V2 = V3, \textbf{not } f$ $f \leftarrow in(V1,V2), in(V1,V3),$ $\quad \textbf{not } V2 = V3, \textbf{not } f$ $f \leftarrow \textbf{not } reached(X), \textbf{not } f$

Fig. 1. Hamiltonian circuit

- *assertions*, (called constraints in ASP) representing the basic properties of hamiltonian cycles.

Note that negation as failure in the ASP program corresponds to classical negation in the ID-Logic theory. This shows that in this type of ASP programs, negation as failure is to be interpreted as classical negation.

The role of *definitional* and *assertional knowledge* for knowledge representation has long been recognised in AI [18,1] and was the motivation for *Description logics*. The distinction between both sorts of knowledge is a fundamental one which sheds light on certain aspects of ASP methodology that are otherwise hard to explain. For example, we need to express that in a hamiltonian cycle, all vertices are reachable. In ID-Logic this property is expressed by the FOL axiom $\forall x(Vertex(x) \supset Reached(x))$. In the ASP program, this is expressed by the constraint $f \leftarrow \textbf{not } reached(X), \textbf{not } f$. Consider an alternative representation by the rule $reached(X) \leftarrow vertex(X)$. If we use this representation, we actually get models in which *no* edge belongs to the hamiltonian cycle. How can we explain this? The reason is that ASP interprets $reached(X) \leftarrow vertex(X)$ as an additional definitional rule, while in fact, it represents assertional knowledge. The only correct way to represent such knowledge in ASP, is by constraints such as $f \leftarrow \text{not } reached(X), \text{not } f$.

In our experience, the pattern of four parts consisting of data, declarations of open predicates, definitions and assertions, can be found in most applications of Stable Logic Programming. Other examples can be found in [13,14], in which different LP-approaches to KR are compared. The thesis that we want to launch in this paper, is that *SLP can be interpreted as a language for representing definitions and assertions* and moreover that *this explains most applications and the methodology that is commonly used in ASP*.

Of course, this thesis cannot be formalised or formally proven. However, the rest of this paper is concerned with a formal translation from ID-Logic with Unique Names Axioms and the Domain Closure Axiom to general logic programs which provides strong support for the thesis. The translation sheds light on how assertions and definitions are implicitly encoded in ASP. The main problem for proving the correctness of this translation is the use of well-founded semantics in ID-Logic versus stable semantics in ASP: basically we will show that the non-determinism of multiple stable models of many ASP programs derives from the combination of open predicates with deterministic definitions on top of them.

As a final remark, we do *not* claim that all ASP programs can be understood as encodings of ID-Logic theories. Certain ASP programs should be understood as autoepistemic theories or default theories, and not as ID-Logic theories. An example taken from [7] is the following rule:

$$check\_status(X) \leftarrow person(X), \text{not } orphan(X), \text{not } \neg orphan(X)$$

The intended declarative reading of this rule is that the status of a person should be checked if it is *unknown* whether it is an orphan or not. In this rule, the negation as failure has indeed a non-objective modality; such a modality is not available in ID-Logic. What this also shows is that in different applications and subsets of ASP, negation as failure and the rule operator have different meanings. This ambiguity is investigated in [4].

2 Preliminaries

2.1 Logic Programs

We first introduce some terminology and basic concepts. A vocabulary τ is a set of constant, function, predicate and variable symbols. The Herbrand universe of τ, consisting of all terms of τ is denoted $\mathcal{HU}(\tau)$. A Herbrand interpretation of τ is a set of ground atoms of τ, containing all atoms that are true. A 3-valued Herbrand interpretation will be defined here as a pair (I, J) of Herbrand interpretations such that $I \subseteq J$. Intuitively, an atom A is true in (I, J) if it is true in I, it is false in (I, J) if it is false in J and otherwise, it is undefined in (I, J). A pair (I, J) is viewed here as a tuple of underestimate I and overestimate J.

A general logic program (in τ) is a set of clauses of the form $A \leftarrow A_1 \wedge \ldots \wedge A_i \wedge$ not $A_{i+1} \wedge \ldots \wedge$ not A_n, with A, A_i all atoms (in τ). We allow infinite programs and infinitary rules (i.e. i and n can be infinite). A definite logic program P is a general logic program without negative literals. A definite logic program has a least Herbrand model denoted $\mathcal{LHM}(P)$.

The grounding of a general logic program P is defined as usual, as the set of all rules that can be obtained by instantiating variables in rules of P by ground terms. Also usual, the grounding is seen as a propositional logic program.

We recall the stable semantics [8] and well-founded semantics [17] of general logic programs. As usual, we define these semantics for propositional programs only. Semantics of predicate programs are defined through their grounding.

Given a general logic program P in τ and a Herbrand interpretation I. The *reduct* P_I is the program obtained from P by deleting

- each rule that has a negative literal not $q_i, q_i \in I$ in the body
- all negative literals in the body of the remaining rules.

Since P_I is a definite logic program, $\mathcal{LHM}(P_I)$ exists.

We define the *Gelfond-Lifschitz* operator GL_P associated to program P as the operator of Herbrand interpretations which maps an interpretation I to $\mathcal{LHM}(P_I)$.

A *stable model* of P is defined as a fixpoint of GL_P, i.e. as a Herbrand interpretation I such that $I = \mathcal{LHM}(P_I)$.

To define the notion of *well-founded model* of P, we follow the approach of [3]. The operator GL_P is antimonotone, i.e. if $I \subseteq J$ then $GL_P(I) \supseteq GL_P(J)$. As a consequence, GL_P^2 is a monotone lattice operator and has a least fixpoint $lfp(GL_P^2)$ and a largest fixpoint $gfp(GL_P^2)$. The pair $(lfp(GL_P^2), gfp(GL_P^2))$ is the well-founded model of P. It holds that for each stable model I, $lfp(GL_P^2) \subseteq I \subseteq gfp(GL_P^2)$.

2.2   ID-Logic

As mentioned in the introduction, an ID-Logic theory T in τ is a set of FOL sentences and definitions. Each definition D is a set of rules of the form $\forall \bar{x}(A \leftarrow \alpha)$ where A is an atom and α a FOL formula. Each definition D has a set $Def(D)$ of defined predicates, i.e., those appearing in the head of a rule. (The defined predicates may explicitly be mentioned in front of the rule set, as in $P/n, Q/m ::= \{\ldots\}$, which simultaneously defines the predicate P with arity n, and the predicate Q with arity m. The empty definition of a predicate P/n can be represented by $P/n ::= \{\}$.) The set $\tau \setminus Def(D)$ is called the set of open symbols of D and is denoted $Open(D)$.

The semantics of ID-Logic is based on an extension of the well-founded semantics to arbitrary (non-Herbrand) interpretations. This extension associates with each definition D and an arbitrary interpretation I_o of $Open(D)$ a unique (possibly 3-valued) well-founded model I_o^D, called the *well-founded model of* D *extending* I_o. A τ-interpretation I is a model of D if I is two-valued and $I = (I|_{Open(D)})^D$. Here, $I|_{Open(D)}$ denotes the restriction of I to the open symbols of D. Formally, an interpretation I is a model of an ID-Logic theory iff it is a model of each of its FOL sentences and a model of each of its definitions D. For details we refer to [2,6].

Example 1. Consider the ID-Logic definition $\{P \leftarrow Q\}$. There are two interpretations of the open predicate Q of this definition: one where $Q = t$, one where $Q = f$. The corresponding well-founded models of the definition are resp. $\{P, Q\}$ and $\emptyset$. By a symmetric argument, these interpretations are also the two models of the definition $\{Q \leftarrow P\}$. Consequently, the theory $T_1 = [\{P \leftarrow Q\}, \{Q \leftarrow P\}]$ has models $\{P, Q\}$ and $\emptyset$.

On the other hand, the theory $T_2 = [\{P \leftarrow Q, \; Q \leftarrow P\}]$ has only one model: $\emptyset$. The definition has no open predicates and its well-founded model is $\emptyset$.

From a knowledge representation perspective, the use of Herbrand interpretations boils down to the use of the *Domain Closure Axiom* and the *Unique Name Axioms*. Those are not imposed by FOL nor by ID-Logic but they can be expressed in ID-Logic [6]. However, in the context of this paper we will only consider ID-Logic theories which (implicitly) contain these axioms. So, all models are Herbrand models (modulo isomorphism).

A crucial notion is that of totality: a definition D is *total* in an interpretation I_o of $Open(D)$ iff the well-founded model I_o^D of D extending I_o is 2-valued. A definition D is *total* in a theory T_o in $Open(D)$ if D is total in each model of T_o. A definition D is total if it is total in the empty theory, that is if D is total in each interpretation I_o of $Open(D)$. Intuitively, a definition D is total in I_o if the definition allows to determine the truth values of all the defined atoms in the context of I_o.

3   The Transformation

We first present a formal transformation for a restricted subclass of ID-Logic theories which comprises the example of Section 1. In the next subsection, we extend the transformation to more general cases.

We will use the following notion of equivalence. Let τ_1, τ_2 be vocabularies extending τ, and T_1 and T_2 theories in respectively τ_1, τ_2; then T_1 and T_2 are *equivalent in* τ (denoted $T_1 \equiv_\tau T_2$) if for each τ_1-model M_1 of T_1, there exists a τ_2-model M_2 of T_2 such that $M_1|_\tau = M_2|_\tau$ and vice versa. The theories T_1 and T_2 do not necessarily belong to the same logic, e.g., T_1 might be an ID-Logic theory and T_2 a stable logic program.

3.1   A First Transformation

The class of ID-Logic theories T considered here in this section have a similar structure as the example of Section 1. They consist of the following components:

- definitions $D_{P/m}$ to represent data, defining certain predicates by exhaustive enumeration. Such definitions consist of ground atomic rules;
- one domain declaration $\forall \bar{x}(P(\bar{x}) \supset C_P(\bar{x}))$ for each predicate P/n, open in all definitions of T; C_P is a conjunction of literals and will be called the domain of P/n. An example is the FOL axiom $\forall x, y(In(x, y) \supset Edge(x, y))$;
- a set of definitions $D_1, \ldots, D_n$ defining other concepts; the bodies of all rules are conjunctions of literals;
- a set of FOL formulas in the clausal form $\forall(A_1 \wedge \ldots A_n \supset B_1 \vee \ldots \vee B_m)$, where A_i, B_j are atoms.

In addition, the definitions of T should satisfy some other conditions. To express these conditions, we need the following concept. The dependency relation $P/n \leq Q/m$ of T is the least transitive relation between predicate symbols containing all pairs $(P/n, Q/m)$ such that Q/m appears in the head and P/n in the body of some rule of some definition $D \in T$. We call an ID-Logic theory T *stratified* if each predicate is defined in at most one definition of T and any two predicates P/n and Q/m are defined in the same definition of T whenever $P/n \leq Q/m$ and $Q/m \leq P/n$. Given this concept, T should also satisfy the following conditions:

- T is a stratified ID-Logic theory;
- each definition $D \in T$ is total.

A theory T satisfying the above conditions can be easily transformed into a stable logic program P_T. We describe this transformation in two steps:

- The first step transforms the ID-Logic theory T in an ID-Logic theory $T' = T_a \cup \{D_T\}$, where T_a consists of all FOL axioms of T and $D_T = \bigcup_{D \in T} D$, with $Def(D_T) = \bigcup_{D \in T} Def(D)$. So, all definitions are merged. Notice that this theory is formally an abductive logic program under the well-founded semantics (where the abducible predicates correspond to $Open(D_T)$).
- In the second step we replace $\neg$ by **not**, and $\wedge$ by ",", in the definition D_T. Also, we switch case of constant, functor and variable symbols. Using the method of Satoh and Iwayama [15] to transform an abductive logic program into a stable logic program, we then interpret D_T as a set of ASP rules, and add to this set the rules

$$P(\bar{X}) \leftarrow C_P(\bar{X}), \text{not } P^*(\bar{X}),$$
$$P^*(\bar{X}) \leftarrow C_P(\bar{X}), \text{not } P(\bar{X})$$

for each predicate $P/n \in Open(D_T)$. Finally, for each clause $\forall(A_1 \wedge \ldots A_n \supset B_1 \vee \ldots \vee B_m) \in T_a$, we add one rule to the set:

$$f \leftarrow A_1, \ldots, A_n, \text{not } B_1, \ldots, \text{not } B_m, \text{not } f.$$

Theorem 1. *An Herbrand interpretation M is a model of T if and only if there is a stable model M' of P_T such that $M = M'|_\tau$.*

Proof. (sketch) The theory T satisfies the conditions of the modularity theorem of [5]. As a consequence, the ID-Logic theories T an T' are equivalent and the definition D_T is total. The ID-Logic theory T' is formally an abductive logic program under the well-founded semantics. Moreover, because of the totality of D_T, all well-founded models are 2-valued, and hence the well-founded and stable semantics coincide. The correctness of the last step of the transformation (i.e. from an abductive logic program under the stable semantics to a stable logic program) was proven in [15].

Example 2. The ID-Logic theory of section 1 satisfies the conditions specified in this section. The only non-trivial condition is the totality of the definition of *Reached*. This definition is a monotone definition (no negative literals with defined predicates in the body of rules) and such definitions are total [5]. The only difference between the translation of this theory and the ASP theory from Fig. 1, is that our translation uses the constraint "$f \leftarrow Vertex(x), \text{not } Reached(x), \text{not } f$", while the original ASP theory uses "$f \leftarrow \text{not } reached(X), \text{not } f$" instead.

3.2   Extending the Transformation

This section presents an extension of the transformation to a broader class of ID-Logic theories, by providing three separately applicable transformations to theories from the class considered in Section 3.1:

- a transformation from non-stratifiable to stratifiable ID-Logic theories;
- a transformation from arbitrary FOL axioms to clausal axioms;
- a transformation from rules with FOL formulas in the body to conjunctive rules.

Non-stratifiable theories. The previous section imposed that no predicate should be defined in more than one definition, and if predicates P/n and Q/m depend on each other, then they are defined in the same definition. If these conditions are not satisfied, then merging together all definitions into one is not equivalence preserving. Example 1 already illustrated this for a non-stratified theory (the theories $[\{P \leftarrow Q\}, \{Q \leftarrow P\}]$ and $[\{P \leftarrow Q, Q \leftarrow P\}]$ are not equivalent); the next example shows the problem with multiple definitions for the same concept.

Example 3. Consider the ID-Logic theory

$$T = \begin{bmatrix} \{\forall x (Person(x) \leftarrow Man(x) \vee Woman(x))\}, \\ \{\forall x (Person(x) \leftarrow Child(x) \vee Adult(x))\} \end{bmatrix}$$

This theory contains two definitions for the predicate *Person*. These definitions constrain each other; for example, T logically entails the formula $\forall x (Man(x) \vee Woman(x) \equiv Child(x) \vee Adult(x))$. If the definitions are merged, this formula is not longer entailed.

The problems shown are easy to avoid by renaming the defined predicates before merging. We create a new ID-Logic theory $T^{(1)}$ consisting of the following parts:

- for each definition $D \in T$, a definition D' obtained from D by replacing any occurrence of $P \in Def(D)$ by P^D, where P^D is a new predicate;
- all assertions of T;
- formulas $\forall \bar{x}(P(\bar{x}) \equiv P^D(\bar{x}))$ for each definition D and predicate P defined in D.

Theorem 2. *The theory $T^{(1)}$ is a stratified theory. It holds that $T \equiv_\tau T^{(1)}$ (where τ is T's vocabulary). Moreover if each definition of T is total, then each definition of $T^{(1)}$ is total.*

Example 4. The theory T_1 from example 1 is transformed by this first step into

$$
T_1^{(1)} = \begin{bmatrix} \{P^{D_1} \leftarrow Q\} & P^{D_1} \equiv P \\ \{Q^{D_2} \leftarrow P\} & Q^{D_2} \equiv Q \end{bmatrix}
$$

Transforming FOL formulas in clausal form. The standard transformation of FOL formulas into clausal form cannot be used in this context. The reason is that we assume the Unique Names Axioms while the transformation to CNF introduces skolem function symbols to which the Unique Names Axioms do not apply. Instead, the following variant transformation can be used. Each FOL formula can be brought in the form:

$$
\forall(F_1 \vee \ldots \vee F_n \vee G_1 \vee \ldots \vee G_m)
$$

where each F_i is a literal and each G_i is an existentially quantified formula $\exists x H_i$.

Let $\bar{x}_i$ be all free variables of G_i. We introduce for each $G_j, 1 \leq j \leq m$ a new predicate P_i/n_i where n_i is the number of variables in $\bar{x}_i$, and translate the above FOL formula in:

$$
\forall(F_1 \vee \ldots \vee F_n \vee P_1(\bar{x}_1) \vee \ldots \vee P_m(\bar{x}_n))
$$

combined with definitions

$$
\{\forall \bar{x}_i(P_i(\bar{x}_i) \leftarrow G_i)\}
$$

Let T be an arbitrary ID-Logic theory, and $T^{(2)}$ be the ID-Logic theory obtained by applying the above transformation.

Theorem 3. *It holds that $T \equiv_\tau T^{(2)}$ where τ is the vocabulary of T (without the new symbols P_i/n_i).*

Creating conjunctive bodies. We now discuss how to transform definitional rules with FOL bodies to rules with conjunctions of literals in the body. The transformation is basically the one proposed by Lloyd and Topor [10], with the exception of the rule for removing universal quantifiers in bodies. Rules of the form

$$\forall (H \leftarrow \boldsymbol{F} \wedge (\forall x V(x)) \wedge \boldsymbol{G})$$

are transformed by Lloyd and Topor into a pair of rules

$$\forall (H \leftarrow \boldsymbol{F} \wedge \neg P'(y_1, \ldots, y_m) \wedge \boldsymbol{G})$$

$$\forall (P'(y_1, \ldots, y_m) \leftarrow \neg V(x))$$

where $y_1, \ldots, y_m$ are the free variables of $\forall x V(x)$ and P' is a new predicate. However, if a predicate depending on H occurs in $V(x)$, this transformation is not equivalence preserving in general. Instead, we replace this rule with

$$\forall (H \leftarrow \boldsymbol{F} \wedge V(C_1) \wedge V(C_2) \wedge \ldots \wedge \boldsymbol{G}).$$

where $C_1, C_2, \ldots$ are all terms in the Herbrand universe. Of course, this transformation rule may produce infinitary rules in case the Herbrand Universe is infinite.

The set of all rewrite rules are presented in Figure 2, where $\boldsymbol{F}$ and $\boldsymbol{G}$ denote arbitrary FOL formulae.

By applying the above rewrite rules on an arbitrary ID-Logic-definition D until none is applicable anymore, we obtain a definition D' such that all bodies are conjunctions of literals. The following theorem holds.

Theorem 4. *The definitions D and D' are logically equivalent. Moreover, if D is total then so is D'.*

At this point, we can transform any ID-Logic-theory T into an equivalent ID-Logic-theory $T^{(3)}$ which is stratified and such that all bodies of definitional rules are conjunctions of literals. More precisely, it holds that $T \equiv_\tau T^{(3)}$. Moreover, if all definitions of T are total, then all definitions of $T^{(3)}$ are total. Consequently, the conditions of theorem 1 hold and $T^{(3)}$ can be transformed into an equivalent stable logic program $P_{T^{(3)}}$. We find that $T \equiv_\tau P_{T^{(3)}}$.

4   A Model Generator for ID-Logic

The above transformation, apart from showing the commonalities between methodology of ASP and of ID-Logic, also provides us with an effective means to compute models for a subclass of ID-Logic theories with total definitions: we first translate them, and then apply a stable model generator, such as lparse/Smodels, to the translation.

Since the general tranformation may produce infinitary rules, and/or rules which have to be grounded w.r.t. $\mathcal{HU}(\tau)$, we further restrict the class of ID-Logic theories.

replace	by
$\forall \bar{x}\,(H \leftarrow \boldsymbol{F} \wedge (\exists y_1 \ldots y_m V) \wedge \boldsymbol{G})$	$\forall \bar{x}, y_1, \ldots y_m : (H \leftarrow \boldsymbol{F} \wedge V \wedge \boldsymbol{G})$
$\forall \bar{x}\,(H \leftarrow \boldsymbol{F} \wedge \neg(\exists y_1 \ldots y_m V) \wedge \boldsymbol{G})$	$\forall \bar{x}\,(H \leftarrow \boldsymbol{F} \wedge \forall y_1 \ldots y_m \neg V \wedge \boldsymbol{G})$
$\forall \bar{x}\,(H \leftarrow \boldsymbol{F} \wedge \neg(\forall y_1 \ldots y_m V) \wedge \boldsymbol{G})$	$\forall \bar{x}, y_1, \ldots y_m\,(H \leftarrow \boldsymbol{F} \wedge \neg V \wedge \boldsymbol{G})$
$\forall \bar{x}(H \leftarrow \boldsymbol{F} \wedge (V \equiv W) \wedge \boldsymbol{G})$	$\forall \bar{x}(H \leftarrow \boldsymbol{F} \wedge ((V \wedge W) \vee (\neg V \wedge \neg W)) \wedge \boldsymbol{G})$
$\forall \bar{x}(H \leftarrow \boldsymbol{F} \wedge (V \subset W) \wedge \boldsymbol{G})$	$\forall \bar{x}(H \leftarrow \boldsymbol{F} \wedge V \wedge \boldsymbol{G})$ $\forall \bar{x}(H \leftarrow \boldsymbol{F} \wedge \neg W \wedge \boldsymbol{G})$
$\forall \bar{x}(H \leftarrow \boldsymbol{F} \wedge \neg(V \subset W) \wedge \boldsymbol{G})$	$\forall \bar{x}(H \leftarrow \boldsymbol{F} \wedge \neg V \wedge W \wedge \boldsymbol{G})$
$\forall \bar{x}(H \leftarrow \boldsymbol{F} \wedge (V \vee W) \wedge \boldsymbol{G})$	$\forall \bar{x}(H \leftarrow \boldsymbol{F} \wedge V \wedge \boldsymbol{G})$ $\forall \bar{x}(H \leftarrow \boldsymbol{F} \wedge W \wedge \boldsymbol{G})$
$\forall \bar{x}(H \leftarrow \boldsymbol{F} \wedge \neg(V \vee W) \wedge \boldsymbol{G})$	$\forall \bar{x}(H \leftarrow \boldsymbol{F} \wedge \neg V \wedge \neg W \wedge \boldsymbol{G})$
$\forall \bar{x}(H \leftarrow \boldsymbol{F} \wedge \neg(V \wedge W) \wedge \boldsymbol{G})$	$\forall \bar{x}(H \leftarrow \boldsymbol{F} \wedge \neg V \wedge \boldsymbol{G})$ $\forall \bar{x}(H \leftarrow \boldsymbol{F} \wedge \neg W \wedge \boldsymbol{G})$
$\forall \bar{x}(H \leftarrow \boldsymbol{F} \wedge \neg\neg V \wedge \boldsymbol{G})$	$\forall \bar{x}(H \leftarrow \boldsymbol{F} \wedge V \wedge \boldsymbol{G})$

Fig. 2. Lloyd-Topor transformations for obtaining conjunctive bodies

Definition 1 (Restricted definitions). *We define that a definition D is restricted in an ID-Logic theory T, by the following inductive rules:*

- *D is a definition by exhaustive enumeration (of ground facts), or*
- *D satisfies the following conditions:*
    - *all bodies are conjunctions of literals, and each predicate of the body is defined in a restricted definition in T,*
    - *each variable occuring in the head of a rule also occurs in a positive literal of the body of this rule, and*
    - *there is no other definition in T defining predicates defined in D*

We denote the predicates of an ID-Logic theory T defined in a restricted definition with $Restricted(T)$. If the definitions of restricted predicates are finite, the extension of each restricted predicate is finite and can be computed easily. Consequently, each conjunction R of atoms from $Restricted(T)$ has a finite and computable extension.

To avoid the infinitary rules which are produced in the presence of recursion over $\forall$, we restrict the use of $\forall$ to formulas of the form "$\forall \bar{x}(R(\bar{x}) \supset F(\bar{x}))$", where R is a conjunction of restricted atoms, and all free variables of $F(\bar{x})$ occur in $R(\bar{x})$. A rule "$\forall \bar{y}(H \leftarrow \boldsymbol{F} \wedge \forall \bar{x}(R(\bar{x}) \supset F(\bar{x})) \wedge \boldsymbol{G})$" can be transformed into "$\forall \bar{y}(H \leftarrow \boldsymbol{F} \wedge F(\bar{C}_1) \wedge \ldots \wedge F(\bar{C}_n) \wedge \boldsymbol{G})$, where $C_1, \ldots, C_n$ are all elements of the extension of R. (Of course, we only do so if F contains a predicate depending on H, otherwise we can just use Lloyd-Topor's transformation.)

Definition 2 (Strongly range-restricted ID-Logic theory). *An ID-Logic theory T is* strongly range-restricted *if the following conditions hold (below, $R(\bar{x})$ denotes a conjunction of restricted atoms):*

- *any definition in it is total;*
- *all quantifiers in assertions and bodies of rules are restricted to formulas of the form $\forall\bar{x}(R(\bar{x}) \supset F(\bar{x}))$ and $\exists\bar{x}(R(\bar{x}) \wedge F(\bar{x}))$;*
- *for each open predicate P there is one domain declaration $\forall\bar{x}(P(\bar{x}) \supset R(\bar{x}))$;*
- *each definitional rule is of the form $\forall\bar{x}(P(\bar{x}) \leftarrow R(\bar{x}) \wedge F)$;*

Theorem 5. *A strongly range-restricted ID-Logic theory is transformed by our transformation to a strongly range-restricted [16] general logic program.*

Note that lparse/Smodels requires *strongly range-restricted* programs. Therefore, by requiring strongly range-restrictedness of our ID-Logic theories, we can calculate ID-Logic models using lparse/Smodels.

We have devised an implementation of our transformation, which, when applied on theories from this class, and combined with lparse/Smodels, computes ID-Logic models.

5 Conclusions

We presented a general tranformation from ID-Logic theories to stable logic programs. This transformation illustrates the fundamental distinction between definitional and assertional knowledge and shows how these can be encoded in Stable Logic Programming. We believe our transformation truthfully corresponds to the way many ASP programs in many applications are developed. This way, the transformation sheds light on the methodologies of ID-Logic and ASP.

Also, the transformation has enabled us to create an ID-Logic model generator, by applying our transformation on an ID-Logic theory, and using an existing ASP model generator to find the models of the resulting program.

References

1. R. J. Brachman and H.J. Levesque. Competence in Knowledge Representation. In *Proc. of the National Conference on Artificial Intelligence*, pages 189–192, 1982.
2. M. Denecker. Extending classical logic with inductive definitions. In J. Lloyd et al., editor, *First International Conference on Computational Logic (CL2000)*, volume 1861 of *Lecture Notes in Artificial Intelligence*, Springer, pages 703–717, 2000.
3. M. Denecker, V.W. Marek and M. Truszczyński. Approximating operators, stable operators, well-founded fixpoints and applications in non-monotonic reasoning. In *Logic-based Artificial Intelligence*, (J. Minker ed.), Kluwer Academic Publishers, pages 127–144, 2000.
4. M. Denecker. What's in a model? Epistemological analysis of Logic Programming. In *Proceedings of Ninth International Conference on Principles of Knowledge Representation and Reasoning, Delta Whistler Resort, Canada*, 2004.

5. M. Denecker and E. Ternovska. A logic of non-monotone inductive definitions and its modularity properties. In *Logic Programming and Nonmonotonic Reasoning: 7th International Conference* (V. Lifschitz and I. Niemelä, eds.), vol 2923, Lecture Notes in Computer Science, pages 47–60, 2004

6. M. Denecker and E. Ternovska. Inductive Situation Calculus. In *Proceedings of Ninth International Conference on Principles of Knowledge Representation and Reasoning, Delta Whistler Resort, Canada*, 2004.

7. M. Gelfond. Representing knowledge in A-Prolog. In A. Kakas and F. Sadri, editors, *Computational Logic: Logic Programming and Beyond; Essays in honour of Robert A. Kowalski, Part II*, number 2407 in Lecture Notes in Computer Science, pages 413–451. Springer Verlag, 2002.

8. M. Gelfond and V. Lifschitz. Logic Programs with Classical Negation. In D.H.D. Warren and P. Szeredi, editors, *Proc. of the 7th International Conference on Logic Programming 90*, page 579. MIT Press, 1990.

9. M. Gelfond and V. Lifschitz. Classical negation in logic programs and disjunctive databases. *New Generation Computing*, pages 365–387, 1991.

10. J. W. Lloyd and R. W. Topor. Making Prolog more Expressive. *Journal of Logic Programming*, 3:225-240, 1984.

11. V.W. Marek and M. Truszczyński. Stable models and an alternative logic programming paradigm. In K.R. Apt, V. Marek, M. Truszczyński, and D.S. Warren, editors, *The Logic Programming Paradigm: a 25 Years Perspective*, pages 375–398. Springer-Verlag, 1999.

12. I. Niemelä. Logic programs with stable model semantics as a constraint programming paradigm. *Annals of Mathematics and Artificial Intelligence*, 25(3,4):241–273, 1999.

13. N. Pelov, E. De Mot, and M. Denecker. Logic programming approaches for representing and solving constraint satisfaction problems: a comparison. *Proceedings of the 7th International Conference on Logic for Programming and Automated Reasoning*, (M. Parigot and A. Voronkov, eds.), vol 1955, Lecture Notes in Artificial Intelligence, pages 225–239, 2000

14. N. Pelov, E. De Mot, and M. Bruynooghe. A comparison of logic programming approaches for representation and solving of constraint satisfaction problems. *Proceedings of the 8th International Workshop on Nonmonotonic Reasoning*, (C. Baral and M. Truszczyńsky, eds.), pages 1–10, 2000.

15. K. Satoh and N. Iwayama. Computing Abduction by Using the TMS. In *Proceedings of ICLP'91*, pages 505–518, 1991.

16. T. Syrjänen. Implementation of Local Grounding for Logic Programs with Stable Model Semantics. *Helsinki University of Technology, Technical Report*, 1998

17. Allen Van Gelder, Kenneth A. Ross, John S. Schlipf. The Well-Founded Semantics for General Logic Programs. *Journal of the ACM* 38(3):620-650, 1991.

18. W. Woods. What's in a Link: Foundations for Semantic Networks. In D. Bobrow and A. Collins, editors, *Representation and understanding: Studies in cognitive science*. Academic Press, New York, 1975. Also in Brachman and Levesque, *Readings in Knowledge Representation*, Morgan Kaufman, 1985.

An Implementation of Statistical Default Logic

Gregory R. Wheeler and Carlos Damásio

Centro de Inteligência Artificial (CENTRIA)
Departamento de Informática, Universidade Nova de Lisboa
2829-516 Caparica, Portugal
{greg,cd}@di.fct.unl.pt

Abstract. Statistical Default Logic (SDL) is an expansion of classical
(i.e., Reiter) default logic that allows us to model common inference
patterns found in standard inferential statistics, e.g., hypothesis testing
and the estimation of a population's mean, variance and proportions.
This paper presents an embedding of an important subset of SDL theories, called *literal statistical default theories*, into stable model semantics.
The embedding is designed to compute the signature set of literals that
uniquely distinguishes each extension on a statistical default theory at a
pre-assigned error-bound probability.

1 Introduction

Standard statistical inference is non-monotonic. Parameters of a target population may be estimated by measures taken on a sample that, after testing for bias,
serve as a defeasible estimate of the population's corresponding parameters. For
example, we may estimate the age of a population by identifying the mean age
of a representative sample drawn from the population. However, classifying a
sample as representative is not straightforward since *knowing* that a sample is
representative is to be in the position of not needing to use inferential statistics.

The fit between a statistic and a target parameter is defeasible because a
sample, however carefully selected, may fail to be representative of the target
population. Consider the estimation of a population's mean age. Textbooks advise that drawing a sample at random is a good procedure for selecting representative samples [2],[12],[8]. But of course drawing a sample at random does
not guarantee that it is representative. Suppose a random sample selects only
subscribers to *Rolling Stone*, a magazine covering popular culture catering to
young adults. Suppose also that the population whose age we are interested in
estimating is of a particular medium-sized city. Our background knowledge concerning the constitution of cities would make us suspect that the sample we've
drawn does not give us a close estimate of the city's mean age even though the
sample was drawn at random.

In [7] it was shown that key assumptions employed in standard inferential
statistical practice, such as the random sampling assumption, actually function
like default justifications. In [16] an expanded default logic, called *statistical default logic*, was introduced to capture the defeasible structure of basic statistical

J.J. Alferes and J. Leite (Eds.): JELIA 2004, LNAI 3229, pp. 121–133, 2004.
© Springer-Verlag Berlin Heidelberg 2004

inference. The resulting logic provides a knowledge representation framework for representing standard statistical argument forms and sequences composed of statistical and deductive inference steps.[1]

In this paper we present an embedding of an important fragment of statistical logic into answer-set programming. The structure of the paper is as follows. First we will present a brief motivation for statistical default logic from a knowledge representation point of view, highlighting the structural similarity between a standard statistical inference and statistical default inference forms. Next we will present an example of a statistical default extension. (Refer to [16] for details.) We then present an embedding of a fragment of statistical default logic into answer-set programming. This embedding faithfully captures the central and new notion in statistical default logic, namely that of terminating admissible inference sequences at a specified threshold level. Finally, we highlight the novelty of these results by comparing them to existing probabilistic logic programming frameworks.

2   Representing Statistical Inference Within Statistical Default Logic

We assume here familiarity with classical default logic [15]. Statistical default logic [16] extends classical default logic by associating with each element in a default theory, both formulae from a propositional language and defaults, a real number $0 \leq \epsilon \leq 1$ called an *error-bound parameter*.

A *statistical default* is an inference form that explicitly acknowledges the *upper limit* of the probability of applying that default rule and accepting a false statement.[2]

Definition 1. *A statistical default is an ordered pair consisting of a classical propositional default in the first coordinate an error bound parameter ϵ in the second coordinate, displayed as*

$$\frac{\alpha : \beta_1, ..., \beta_n}{\gamma} \epsilon. \tag{1}$$

Expression (1) is called an ϵ-*bounded statistical default* (s-default, for short), where ϵ expresses the upper limit on the probability of applying (1) and accepting that γ is true when γ is false. We say that the error-parameter ϵ is an ϵ-*bound* for the s-default displayed in expression (1).

The logic also replaces sentences in the propositional language with sentence-ϵ pairs, called *bounded sentences*.

---

[1] Representing statistical argument forms by defaults is distinct from [1], which studied the representation of statistical statements rather than statistical inference.

[2] A trivial corollary of the probability of error $\hat{\alpha}$ for a statistical inference is the upper limit of the probability of error, denoted by ϵ. So, if $\hat{\alpha} = 0.03$ is understood to mean that the probability of committing a Type I error is 0.03, then $\epsilon = 0.03$ is understood to mean that the probability of committing a Type I error is no more than 0.03.

Definition 2. *Bounded sentence: A sentence ϕ bounded by ϵ is an ordered pair $\langle \phi, \epsilon \rangle$, written $(\phi)_\epsilon$ for short, where ϕ is a sentence in the propositional language $\mathcal{L}$ and $\epsilon \in [0, 1]$. $(\phi)_\epsilon \equiv \phi$, if $\epsilon = 0$.*

Whereas a classical default theory $\Delta = \langle F, D \rangle$ consists of a set F of first-order formulae and a countable set D of defaults, a statistical default theory $\Delta_s = \langle W, S \rangle$ is defined as a pair consisting of a set W of bounded sentences and a set S of statistical defaults.

Note that a Reiter default is a special case of an s-default, namely when $\epsilon = 0$ and classical default logic is a special case of statistical default logic, namely when the ϵ-bound of every bounded sentence and every s-default is zero. We refer readers to [16] for the main results of statistical default logic.

Following [7], we demonstrate how to use an s-default to represent the key structural features of an inference of the mean age of a population, X. This problem is an instance of an inference of the mean of a normal distribution when the standard deviation is known. Suppose we draw a sample s on X and calculate the mean age of s, $\overline{s} = 24$ years. It is reasonable for us to infer that the mean age of X is in the interval 288 months (24 years) $\pm 1.96\sigma$, where σ is the standard deviation of age in months derived from the cardinality of s. Given the s-default rule schemata $(\alpha : \beta_1, ..., \beta_n /_{[\epsilon]} \gamma)$, we may suppose that

α : The calculated mean age of s is 288 months $\wedge$ Measurement errors are distributed normally with mean zero and variance σ^2.

γ : The age of X is within two standard deviations of 288 months.

β_1 : This is the only statistic we have for X.

β_2 : There is no prior statistical knowledge of the distribution of age in the class that s belongs to that would lead to a conflicting inference.

β_3 : There is no information concerning the condition of the sample that preëmpts the information provided by the calculation of s.

$\epsilon = 0.05$.

Notice that we could collect additional statistics of the age of X and undermine the conclusion drawn from *this* rule. Surely if we have two statistics, we should use a distribution for the average of the two values (in most cases) and that uses a smaller variance.

Whether this, or one of the other justifications $\beta_1, ..., \beta_3$ is triggered does not undermine the prerequisite. It remains the case that the calculated mean age of s is 288 months and that the distribution of errors is normal, with a mean of zero and its characteristic variance. It is the consequent, the conclusion that claims that the mean age of the population X is 288 months $\pm 2\sigma$ months, that is blocked. Notice that it is blocked when we have additional not necessarily non-contrary information.

Justification β_2 says that if there is prior statistical information regarding the mean age of X, then that information should take precedence over any conclusion drawn from the measurement report. For instance, if we are dealing with a population with known descriptive statistics (e.g., given by a census), this knowledge should be taken account of: we typically would not infer that the estimate based upon s supersedes the census description of X, for suitably small populations not affected by data recording errors. If we already have knowledge of the age of X this knowledge should block the application of this particular default rule.

The last default, β_3, concerns general conditions that should be in place to get a good estimation of the population's mean age. For instance, if the sampling procedure is carried out from a direct-mail advertiser's database, we should ensure that the database is not biased with respect to age. We don't accept this as an explicit assumption, since s belongs to infinite reference classes. Rather, if we know that s is a member of a biased class with respect to age—such as readers of *Rolling Stone*—we have grounds to block the application of the default. The point isn't that knowing all members of s are *Rolling Stone* readers entails that s fails to be representative, but that knowing that s is drawn exclusively from the class of *Rolling Stone* readers is sufficient to doubt that the statistical model fits—that is, there is reason to doubt that s is an estimate of X within two standard deviations of the true mean age of the population.

3   Statistical Default Extensions

Extensions for statistical default logic are constructed in the usual way, except that the operator 'terminates' when inference reaches a specified threshold and a function $Crop()$ is called on the resulting set of bounded sentences, returning the set of wffs without their corresponding ϵ-bound. For details the reader is referred to [16].

Consider the following two examples.

Example 1.   Let $\Delta_s^1 = \langle W, S_1 \rangle$ be a statistical default theory, where $W = \emptyset$ and S_1 contains four s-defaults:

$$S_1 = \left\{ \frac{:A}{A} 0.01, \frac{:B}{B} 0.01, \frac{A:B,C}{C} 0.01, \frac{A \wedge B:\neg C}{\neg C} 0.01 \right\}$$

For an error-bound parameter $\epsilon_1 = 0.02$, there is one statistical default extension Π^1 where $Crop(\Pi^1)$ contains

$$A, B, A \wedge B, C.$$

The bounded sentence A at ϵ_A is included in extension Π^1 by applying the default $\frac{:A}{A}$ and bounded sentence B at ϵ_B is included by applying the default $\frac{:B}{B}$, where each inference has an error bound of 0.01, so $(A)_{0.01}$ and $(B)_{0.01}$. $(A \wedge B)_{\epsilon_{A \wedge B}}$ is included in the extension, since the sum of the error bounds of conjoining A and B is 0.02, that is $(A \wedge B)_{0.02}$. The bounded sentence C at ϵ_C is included by using A, whose error bound is 0.01, to apply the default $\frac{A:B,C}{C}$, whose error bound is also 0.01. Hence $(C)_{0.02}$. The default $\frac{A \wedge B:\neg C}{\neg C}$ cannot be applied because the resulting conclusion $\neg C$ would have an error bound of 0.03, $(\neg C)_{0.03}$ which is above the designated threshold $\epsilon_1 = 0.02$.

For a threshold parameter $\epsilon_2 = 0.03$, there are two statistical default extensions: Π^1, which is the same as described above, and Π^2, where $Crop(\Pi^2)$ contains

$$A, B, A \wedge B, \neg C.$$

The default rule that could not be applied before is now applicable with respect to ϵ_2, giving rise to the second extension Π^2.[3]

Example 2. Now let $\Delta_s^2 = \langle W, S_2 \rangle$ be a statistical default theory, where $W = \emptyset$ and S_2 contains six s-defaults:

$$S_2 = \left\{ \tfrac{:\neg B, C}{C} 0.00, \tfrac{:C}{C} 0.02, \tfrac{C:B}{B} 0.01, \tfrac{:\neg B}{\neg B} 0.03, \tfrac{:\neg B, A}{A} 0.01, \tfrac{:\neg A}{\neg A} 0.01 \right\}$$

For an error-bound parameter $\epsilon_1 = 0.02$, there is no statistical default extension, since while both $\tfrac{:\neg B, C}{C} 0.00, \tfrac{:C}{C} 0.02$ yield C only the bounded sentence $\langle C, 0.00 \rangle$ from $\tfrac{:\neg B, C}{C} 0.00$ may be substituted for the antecedent of $\tfrac{C:B}{B} 0.01$ which in turn is applicable in extensions consistent with B. But $\tfrac{:\neg B, C}{C} 0.00$ is applicable only in extensions consistent with $\neg B$.

For an error-bound parameter $\epsilon_2 = 0.03$, there are three extensions. We will continue the convention of example 1 of distinguishing them by focusing on the literals of each extension; this will also serve our purposes in the remainder of the paper. However, because this example highlights the role that error-bounds play in constructing extensions we will display the extensions first in uncropped form, then in cropped form.

$\Pi_1 \supseteq \{\langle C, 0.00 \rangle, \langle C, 0.02 \rangle, \langle \neg B, 0.03 \rangle, \langle A, 0.01 \rangle\}$
$\Pi_2 \supseteq \{\langle C, 0.00 \rangle, \langle C, 0.02 \rangle, \langle \neg B, 0.03 \rangle, \langle \neg A, 0.01 \rangle\}$
$\Pi_3 \supseteq \{\langle C, 0.02 \rangle, \langle B, 0.01 \rangle, \langle \neg A, 0.01 \rangle\}$

And the three corresponding cropped extensions are:

$Crop(\Pi_1) \supseteq \{C, B, A\}$
$Crop(\Pi_2) \supseteq \{C, \neg B, \neg A\}$
$Crop(\Pi_3) \supseteq \{C, B, \neg A\}$

We may think of each of these sets of literals as *signatures* of their corresponding statistical default extensions. In what remains we propose an implementation of statistical default logic that computes the signatures of each extension of a statistical default theory.

4   Computing Statistical Default Extensions

In this section we describe an embedding of an important subset of statistical default theories into stable model semantics [6]. This embedding is designed to compute the signatures of each statistical default extension. Resorting to the available engines for computing Stable Model and Answer Set engines [14],[4]

---

[3] The complete cropped extensions Π^1, when $\epsilon = 0.02$, Π^1 and Π^2, when $\epsilon = 0.03$, are as follows: $\Pi^1_{\epsilon = 0.02} = \{A, B, A \wedge B, C\}$; $\Pi^1_{\epsilon = 0.03} = \{A, B, A \wedge B, C, A \wedge C, B \wedge C\}$; $\Pi^2_{\epsilon = 0.03} = \{A, B, A \wedge B, \neg C\}$.

we indirectly provide an efficient implementation of statistical default logic. We start by recalling the Stable Model semantics of Gelfond and Lifschitz [5].

A (normal) logic program is a set of rules[4] of the form:

$$h \; : - \; a_1, \ldots, a_m, not \; a_{m+1}, \ldots, not \; a_n$$

where h, and $a_i (0 \leq i \leq n)$ are atoms of a given first-order language. Atom h is the head of the rule, whilst $a_1, \ldots, a_m, not \; a_{m+1}, \ldots, not \; a_n$ is the body. We say that $not \; a_j$ is a default negated atom. A fact is a rule with an empty body and is succinctly represented by h. A rule with free variables stands for all its ground instances.

Definition 3. *Let P be a (ground) normal logic program and M a set of ground atoms in the language of P (i.e. a subset of the Herbrand base of P). The reduct P^M is the default negation free program obtained from P by:*

1. *Removing all rules of P having a default negated atom not a in the body such that $a \in M$.*
2. *Removing all occurrences of default negated atoms in the bodies of the remaining rules.*

The set M is a stable model of P iff M is the least Herbrand model of P^M.

The Answer Set Semantics [6] generalizes the Stable Model Semantics for the so called extended logic programs. Extended logic programs consist of rules:

$$l \; : - \; l_1, \ldots, l_m, not \; l_{m+1}, \ldots, not \; l_n$$

where l and l_is are literals, i.e. atoms (say, a) or the explicit negation of atoms (say, $\neg a$). The semantics is given now by special sets of ground literals, the answer sets, extending Definition 3. The reduct operation for extended logic programs is defined similarly, but the fixpoint equation must be changed to take into account that the reduct program is no longer a Horn program. Essentially, it interprets a explicit negated literal $\neg a$ as a new atom, unrelated to a, and the least model is computed as before. A special condition is then added to treat the case of the set of all literals. The reader is referred to [6], [11] for details.

The relationships of stable model and answer set semantics with default logic are very well understood. See for instance [11] for a full account. In the rest of this section we extend the existing results to statistical default logic in order to compute statistical default extensions via stable model logic programming engines. A first difficulty lies in the impossibility of representation of real numbers. Furthermore, the existing implementations have support only for arithmetic over the natural/integer numbers. The following condition allows the translation of the arithmetic operations over real numbers into corresponding operations over natural numbers:

---

[4] We use $: -$ instead of $\leftarrow$ in order to respect the syntax used in the existing implementations.

Definition 4. *Let p be a non-zero natural number. A statistical default theory $\Delta_s = \langle W, S \rangle$ is precision limited by p, if every error bound ϵ in W and S is a rational number $\epsilon = \frac{e}{p}$, for some natural number e such that $0 \le e \le p$.*

We cannot translate arbitrary statistical default theories, due to the difficulties of handling statistical inferences with disjunctive formulae with the proposed embedding. Thus, we restrict ourselves to the following types of theories:

Definition 5. *A literal statistical default theory is a statistical default theory $\Delta_s = \langle W, S \rangle$ such that:*

1. *Every bounded sentence in W is of the form $\langle l, \epsilon \rangle$, where l is a literal.*
2. *Every statistical default in S is of the form*

$$\frac{l_1 \wedge \ldots \wedge l_m : j_1, ..., j_n}{c}_\epsilon$$

where $l_1, \ldots, l_m, j_1, \ldots, j_n$ and c are all literals.

Before we proceed, we require the following auxiliary notation. Given a literal $l = a(t_1, \ldots, t_m)$ or $l = \neg a(t_1, \ldots, t_m)$, by $l[e]$ it is meant, respectively, the new atom $a(t_1, \ldots, t_m, e)$ or $neg\_a(t_1, \ldots, t_m, e)$. This function adds a new argument for propagation of error-bounds, and introduces a new predicate name for negated atoms. Similarly, by $crop(l)$ we mean the new atom $crop\_a(t_1, \ldots, t_m)$ or $crop\_neg\_a(t_1, \ldots, t_m)$.

Definition 6. *Consider the literal statistical default theory $\Delta_s = \langle W, S \rangle$ precision limited by p. Construct the logic program $P_s^\Delta(error, p)$ as follows, where $error \le p$ is a natural number such that:*

1. *A bounded sentence $\langle l, \epsilon \rangle$ in W is translated into the fact:*

$$l[0].$$

2. *For every literal l in the language add the rule*

$$crop(l) \; :- \; l[E].$$

3. *Every statistical default in S of the form*

$$\frac{: j_1, ..., j_n}{c}_\epsilon$$

is translated into the rule, where $eps = \epsilon \times p$:

$$c[eps] \; :- \; eps <= error, not\ crop(\neg j_1), \ldots, not\ crop(\neg j_n).$$

4. *Every statistical default in S of the form*

$$\frac{l_1 \wedge \ldots \wedge l_m : j_1, ..., j_n}{c}_\epsilon$$

is translated into the rule:

$$c[A_m] : -\ l_1[E_1], \ldots, l_m[E_m],$$
$$A_1 = eps + E_1, \ldots, A_m = A_{m-1} + E_m, A_m <= error,$$
$$not\ crop(\neg j_1), \ldots, not\ crop(\neg j_n).$$

where $eps = \epsilon \times p$, *and* $E_1, \ldots, E_m$ *and* $A_1, \ldots, A_m$ *are new free variables.*

Complete the program P_s^Δ *with the following closure rules, for every combination of atoms* a *and* b *in the language:*

$$a[E] : -\ b[E_1], \neg b[E_2], E = E1 + E2, E <= error.$$
$$\neg a[E] : -\ b[E_1], \neg b[E_2], E = E1 + E2, E <= error.$$

For simplicity, we assume that the sum operation, as well as the equality and arithmetic comparison predicates are built-in. Theoretically, this can be captured by an infinite set of ground facts of the form $X = Y + Z$, such that variables are substituted by natural numbers x, y, z obeying the equation; the same applies to facts of the form $X <= Y$, where X and Y are instantiated with two natural numbers $x \le y$.

The translation is self-explanatory. The first case takes care of the theory W; by design of statistical default logic, it is assumed that the knowledge W is considered to be error free. The rules introduced in the 2nd step implement the crop operation. The translation of statistical defaults is now immediate, where error-bounds are propagated from the bodies to the head of rules, taking into account the global threshold *error* and the error-bound of the default. The justifications are translated into default negations of the complements, as usual in the relationships of default logic with answer set semantics. The last sets of rules encode the explosive behavior of statistical default logic in face of contradiction, which differs from the one of Answer Set Semantics. The major result is the following:

Theorem 1. *Consider a literal statistical default theory* $\Delta_s = \langle W, S \rangle$ *with error-bound parameter* ϵ, *and precision limited by* p, *and let error* $= \epsilon \times p$ *be a natural number. Then, a set of ground literals* $\{l_1, \ldots, l_i, \ldots\}$ *is contained in* $Crop(\Pi)$, *where* Π *is a statistical default extension* Π *of* Δ_s, *iff there is a stable model of program* $P_s^\Delta(error, p)$ *containing* $\{crop(l_1), \ldots, crop(l_i), \ldots\}$.

By resorting to the known translation of extended logic programming under the answer set semantics into default logic [11] and the relationship of statistical default logic with Reiter's default logic we obtain the following corollary:

Corollary 1. *Let* P *be a extended logic program and construct the statistical default theory* $\Delta_P = \langle \emptyset, S \rangle$ *by including in* S *a default*

$$\frac{l_1 \wedge \ldots \wedge l_m : \neg l_{m+1}, \ldots, \neg l_n}{l} 0.0$$

for each rule

$$l\ : -\ l_1, \ldots, l_m, not\ l_{m+1}, \ldots, not\ l_n$$

in the extended logic program. Then, M is an answer set of P iff Π is a statistical default extension of Δ_P such that $Cn(M) = Crop(\Pi)$, where Cn is the first-order consequences operator.

We conclude by illustrating the embedding:

Example 3. Consider the theory of Example 1 with error-bound threshold of 0.03, and precision limited by 100. The translated normal logic program is:

```
crop_a :- a(_).
crop_b :- b(_).
crop_c :- c(_).
crop_neg_a :- neg_a(_).
crop_neg_b :- neg_b(_).
crop_neg_c :- neg_c(_).

a(1) :- 1 <= 3, not crop_neg_a.
b(1) :- 1 <= 3, not crop_neg_b.

c(A1) :- a(E1), A1 = 1 + E1, A1 <= 3,
            not crop_neg_b, not crop_neg_c.

neg_c(A2) :- a(E1), b(E2),
               A1 = 1 + E1, A2 = A1 + E2, A2 <= 3, not crop_c.

a(E) :- a(E1), neg_a(E2), E = E1 + E2, E <= 3.
neg_a(E) :- a(E1), neg_a(E2), E = E1 + E2, E <= 3.
a(E) :- b(E1), neg_b(E2), E = E1 + E2, E <= 3.
neg_a(E) :- b(E1), neg_b(E2), E = E1 + E2, E <= 3.
a(E) :- c(E1), neg_c(E2), E = E1 + E2, E <= 3.
neg_a(E) :- c(E1), neg_c(E2), E = E1 + E2, E <= 3.

b(E) :- a(E1), neg_a(E2), E = E1 + E2, E <= 3.
neg_b(E) :- a(E1), neg_a(E2), E = E1 + E2, E <= 3.
b(E) :- b(E1), neg_b(E2), E = E1 + E2, E <= 3.
neg_b(E) :- b(E1), neg_b(E2), E = E1 + E2, E <= 3.
b(E) :- c(E1), neg_c(E2), E = E1 + E2, E <= 3.
neg_b(E) :- c(E1), neg_c(E2), E = E1 + E2, E <= 3.

c(E) :- a(E1), neg_a(E2), E = E1 + E2, E <= 3.
neg_c(E) :- a(E1), neg_a(E2), E = E1 + E2, E <= 3.
c(E) :- b(E1), neg_b(E2), E = E1 + E2, E <= 3.
neg_c(E) :- b(E1), neg_b(E2), E = E1 + E2, E <= 3.
c(E) :- c(E1), neg_c(E2), E = E1 + E2, E <= 3.
neg_c(E) :- c(E1), neg_c(E2), E = E1 + E2, E <= 3.
```

The stable models of the above program are:

{a(1), b(1), neg_c(3), crop_a, crop_b, crop_neg_c}

{a(1), b(1), c(2), crop_a, crop_b, crop_c}

which correspond exactly to the signature statistical default extensions of Example 1.

Example 4. Consider the theory of Example 2 with error-bound threshold of 0.03, and precision limited by 100. The translated logic program is:

```
crop_a :- a(_).
crop_b :- b(_).
crop_c :- c(_).
crop_neg_a :- neg_a(_).
crop_neg_b :- neg_b(_).
crop_neg_c :- neg_c(_).

a(1) :- 1 <= 3, not crop_b, not crop_neg_a.
neg_a(1) :- 1 <= 3, not crop_a.

b(A1) :- c(E1), A1 = 1 + E1, A1 <= 3, not crop_neg_b.
neg_b(3) :- 3 <= 3, not crop_b.

c(0) :- 0 <= 3, not crop_b, not crop_neg_c.
c(2) :- 2 <= 3, not crop_neg_c.

a(E) :- a(E1), neg_a(E2), E = E1 + E2, E <= 3.
neg_a(E) :- a(E1), neg_a(E2), E = E1 + E2, E <= 3.
a(E) :- b(E1), neg_b(E2), E = E1 + E2, E <= 3.
neg_a(E) :- b(E1), neg_b(E2), E = E1 + E2, E <= 3.
a(E) :- c(E1), neg_c(E2), E = E1 + E2, E <= 3.
neg_a(E) :- c(E1), neg_c(E2), E = E1 + E2, E <= 3.

b(E) :- a(E1), neg_a(E2), E = E1 + E2, E <= 3.
neg_b(E) :- a(E1), neg_a(E2), E = E1 + E2, E <= 3.
b(E) :- b(E1), neg_b(E2), E = E1 + E2, E <= 3.
neg_b(E) :- b(E1), neg_b(E2), E = E1 + E2, E <= 3.
b(E) :- c(E1), neg_c(E2), E = E1 + E2, E <= 3.
neg_b(E) :- c(E1), neg_c(E2), E = E1 + E2, E <= 3.

c(E) :- a(E1), neg_a(E2), E = E1 + E2, E <= 3.
neg_c(E) :- a(E1), neg_a(E2), E = E1 + E2, E <= 3.
c(E) :- b(E1), neg_b(E2), E = E1 + E2, E <= 3.
neg_c(E) :- b(E1), neg_b(E2), E = E1 + E2, E <= 3.
c(E) :- c(E1), neg_c(E2), E = E1 + E2, E <= 3.
neg_c(E) :- c(E1), neg_c(E2), E = E1 + E2, E <= 3.
```

The stable models of the above program are:

{neg_a(1), neg_b(3), c(0), c(2), crop_neg_a, crop_neg_b, crop_c}

{neg_a(1), b(3), c(2), crop_neg_a, crop_b, crop_c}

{a(1), neg_b(3), c(0), c(2), crop_a, crop_neg_b, crop_c}

which correspond exactly to the signature statistical default extensions of Example 2.

5   Comparisons

Literal statistical default theories have interesting connections to existing probabilistic logic programming frameworks, namely the *Stable Semantics for Probabilistic Deductive Databases* [13]. A default $\frac{l_1 \wedge \ldots l_m : j_1, \ldots, j_n}{c} \epsilon$, with $\epsilon < 1$ in a literal statistical default theory can be translated into a general probabilistic logic program of Ng and Subrahmanian [13] of the form[5]:

$$eps: [1 - \epsilon, 1] \leftarrow$$
$$prereq: [V, 1] \leftarrow (eps \wedge l_1 \wedge \ldots \wedge l_m): [V, 1]$$
$$c: [V, 1] \qquad \leftarrow prereq: [1 - error, 1] \bigwedge prereq: [V, 1] \bigwedge$$
$$not \, \neg j_1 : [1 - error, 1] \bigwedge \ldots \bigwedge not \, \neg j_n : [1 - error, 1]$$

Note that V is an annotation variable, and *error* is the fixed error-bound threshold parameter. The translation of the closure rules is immediate and there is no need to introduce crop sentences, since this is already accommodated in the tests $not \, \neg j_i : [1 - error, 1]$ and $prereq: [1 - error, 1]$.

The translation is justified by the observation that a literal l with error-bound ϵ is equivalent to saying that the probability of l is in the interval $[1 - \epsilon, 1]$. Now, if the error-bound of a literal l_1 (resp. l_2) is ϵ_1 (resp. ϵ_2) this means that the probability of l_1 is between $[1 - \epsilon_1, 1]$ (resp. l_2 between $[1 - \epsilon_2], 1]$). Thus the probability of $l_1 \wedge l_2$ is between $[1 - (\epsilon_1 + \epsilon_2), 1]$, if $\epsilon_1 + \epsilon_2 \leq 1$. Now, the conjunction symbol in $(eps \wedge l_1 \wedge \ldots \wedge l_m): [V, 1])$ corresponds to the conjunctive ignorance probabilistic strategy of *Hybrid Probabilistic Logic Programs* [3], which combines the probability intervals $[a_1, b_1]$ and $[a_2, b_2]$ according to:

$$[a_1, b_1] \wedge [a_2, b_2] = [\max(0, a_1 + a_2 - 1), \min(b_1, b_2)]$$

By applying the ignorance strategy to the previous intervals for l_1 and l_2 we obtain the expected result:

$$[1 - \epsilon_1, 1] \wedge [1 - \epsilon_2, 1] = [\max(0, (1 - \epsilon_1) + (1 - \epsilon_2) - 1), \min(1, 1)]$$
$$= [\max(0, 1 - \epsilon_1 - \epsilon_2), 1] = [\max(0, 1 - (\epsilon_1 + \epsilon_2)), 1]$$

---

[5] The authors use $\neg$ instead of *not* to represent default negation. We use here *not* in order to avoid confusion with the previous translations.

It is now obvious that the framework of [13] is expressive enough to capture literal statistical default theories. However, the authors do not present in [13] any translation into stable model semantics, which we have provided here. Furthermore, the more recent Hybrid Probabilistic Logic Programming framework [3] does not provide a default negation construction and thus cannot embed literal statistical default theories.

A translation of disjunctive logic programs with probabilistic semantics into stable models is presented in [9], but assumes positively correlated interpretations, i.e. the probability of $A \wedge B$ is given by the minimum of the probability of A and the probability of B. Since SDL is intended to be quite general and therefore adopts an ignorance strategy for combination, this framework does not appear to be able to capture statistical default theories. Lukasiewicz also proposed an approach for reasoning from statistical and subjective knowledge, based on the combination of probabilistic conditional constraints with default reasoning [10], but the relationships to our work remain to be studied.

6   Conclusions

In this paper we have presented an embedding of Literal Statistical Default theories into stable model semantics. The embedding is designed to compute the signature set of literals that uniquely distinguishes each extension on a statistical default theory. We also offered a comparison of this work to existing probabilistic logic programming frameworks, highlighting the new contribution of our results.[6]

References

[1] Bacchus, F., A. Grove, J. Halpern and D. Koller. 1993. "Statistical Foundations for Default Reasoning," *Proceedings of The International Joint Conference on Artificial Intelligence 1993 (IJCAI-93)*, 563-569.

[2] Cramér, H. 1946. *Mathematical Methods of Statistics*, Princeton: Princeton University Press.

[3] Dekhtyar, A. and V.S. Subrahmanian, 2000. "Hybrid Probabilistic Programs", *Journal of Logic Programming*, 43(3): 187-250.

[4] Eiter, T., N. Leone, C. Mateis, G. Pfeifer and F. Scarcello. 1998 "The KR system: Progress Report, Comparisons and Benchmarks," *KR '98: Principles of Knowledge Representation and Reasoning*, Cohen, A., L. Schubert and S. Shaprio [eds.]. San Francisco: Morgan Kaufmann.

[5] Gelfond, M. and V. Lifschitz 1988. "The Stable Model Semantics for Logic Programming," *Proceedings of the 5th International Conference on Logic Programming*, [ed.] Kowalski, R. and K. Bowen. Cambridge: MIT Press. pp.1070-1080.

[6] Gelfond, M. and V. Lifschitz 1990. "Logic Programs with Classical Negation," *Proceedings of the 7th International Conference on Logic Programming*, Warren, D. and P. Szeredi [eds.]. Cambridge: MIT Press, 579-597.

[6] This research was supported by grant *SES 990-6128* from the *National Science Foundation* and *SFRH/BPD-13699-2003* from *Fundação para Ciência e a Tecnologia*.

[7] Kyburg, H. E., Jr. and C. M. Teng.1999. "Statistical Inference as Default Logic," *International Journal of Pattern Recognition and Artificial Intelligence*, 13(2): 267-283.

[8] Larsen, R. J. and M. L. Marx. 2001. *An Introduction to Mathematical Statistics*, Upper Saddle River, NJ: Prentice Hall.

[9] Lukasiewicz, T. 2001. "Fixpoint Characterizations for Many-Valued Disjunctive Logic Programs with Probabilistic Semantics", appearing in *Proceedings of the 6th International Conference on Logic Programming and Nonmonotonic Reasoning (LPNMR-01)*, Vienna, Austria, September 2001. Volume 2173 of Lecture Notes in Artificial Intelligence, Springer, 336-350.

[10] Lukasiewicz, T. 2002. "Probabilistic Default Reasoning with Conditional Constraints", *Annals of Mathematics and Artificial Intelligence*, 34(1-3): 35-88.

[11] Marek and Truszczyński 1993. *Nonmonotonic Logic*, Berlin: Springer-Verlag.

[12] Moore, 1979. *Statistics*, San Francisco: W. H. Freeman Press.

[13] Ng, Ramond and V. S. Subrahmanian. 1994. "Stable semantics for probabilistic deductive databases", *Information and Computation*, 110(1): 42-83.

[14] Niemelä, I. and P. Simons. 1996. "Efficient Implementation of the Well-founded and Stable Model Semantics," *Proceedings of the Joint International Conference and Symposium on Logic Programming*, Maher, M. [ed.]. Cambridge: MIT Press.

[15] Reiter, R. 1980. "A Logic for Default Reasoning," *Artificial Intelligence*, 13: 81-132.

[16] Wheeler, G. R. 2004. "A Resource Bounded Default Logic", in James Delgrande and Torsten Schuaub (eds.) *Proceedings of the 10th International Workshop on Non-monotonic Reasoning (NMR-2004)*, Whistler, British Columbia, 416-422.

Capturing Parallel Circumscription with Disjunctive Logic Programs*

Tomi Janhunen and Emilia Oikarinen

Helsinki University of Technology, Laboratory for Theoretical Computer Science
P.O. Box 5400, FIN-02015 HUT, Finland
Tomi.Janhunen@hut.fi, Emilia.Oikarinen@hut.fi

Abstract. The stable model semantics of disjunctive logic programs is based on classical models which are minimal with respect to subset inclusion. As a consequence, every atom appearing in a disjunctive program is false by default. This is sometimes undesirable from the knowledge representation point of view and a more refined control of minimization is called for. Such features are already present in Lifschitz's parallel circumscription where certain atoms are allowed to vary or to have fixed values while all other atoms are minimized. In this paper, it is formally shown that the expressive power of minimal models is properly increased in the presence of varying atoms. In spite of this, we show how parallel circumscription can be embedded into disjunctive logic programming in a relatively systematic fashion using a linear and faithful, but *non-modular* translation. This enables the conscious use of varying atoms in disjunctive logic programs — leading to more elegant and concise problem representations in various domains.

1 Introduction

In disjunctive logic programming, a rule-based language which allows disjunctions in the heads of rules is used for knowledge representation. Along the development of efficient implementations such as dlv [15] and GnT [13], various problems have been formalized as disjunctive logic programs. The semantics of disjunctive logic programs is determined by *stable models* [8,20] which are minimal with respect to subset inclusion. This makes every atom appearing in a disjunctive logic program false by default. In many cases, this is highly desirable, but certain problems become awkward to formalize if all atoms are blindly subject to minimization. This suggests a revision of the stable model semantics in order to incorporate atoms that are not false by default.

The need of atoms, which are not subject to minimization, has already been realized in conjunction with *normal logic programs* which form a special case of disjunctive logic programs. Simons [23] introduces *choice rules* which allow the definition of atoms not being false by default. The same effect can be obtained by allowing negation as failure in the heads of disjunctive rules [9]: a rule of the form $a \vee \sim a$ represents the fact that a can be true or false. As shown by the first author [11], negation as failure can be removed from the heads of disjunctive rules using a linear transformation. This

---

* The research reported in this paper has been partially funded by the Academy of Finland (project #53695) and the European Commission (contract IST-FET-2001-37004).

implies that choice rules can be effectively expressed using disjunctive rules. However, it is important to realize that atoms definable in this way are essentially *fixed* atoms in the sense of *parallel circumscription* [16] which is based on a refined notion of minimality.

In addition to fixed atoms and those subject to minimization, parallel circumscription incorporates yet another category of atoms, namely atoms that are allowed to *vary*. As demonstrated by Lifschitz's ostrich example [16], varying atoms tend to increase the knowledge representation capabilities of ordinary circumscription [18] where all atoms are subject to minimization. Unfortunately, varying atoms are not yet well-supported in disjunctive logic programming, although serious attempts to embed parallel circumscription into disjunctive logic programming have already been made. The approach by Gelfond and Lifschitz [7] is restricted to the stratifiable case and the one by Sakama and Inoue [22] involves *characteristic clauses* which imply an exponential time/space complexity in the worst case. Quite recently, Lee and Lin [14] characterize parallel circumscription in terms of *loop formulas* and then embed parallel circumscription in disjunctive logic programming using them. However, the number of loops can be exponential in the worst case. Thus it remains open whether an efficient translation from parallel circumscription into disjunctive logic programs is feasible in the general case.

The goal of this paper is to develop such a translation — enabling the conscious use of varying atoms in disjunctive logic programs. We proceed as follows. In Section 2, we review the syntax and semantics of disjunctive logic programs and present the notion of *visible equivalence* to enable natural comparisons of programs. Then the effects of varying and fixed atoms on the expressiveness of positive disjunctive programs are studied in Section 3. The key result is that varying atoms lead to a proper increase in expressive power which we believe to explain the above mentioned difficulties in translating parallel circumscription. A linear but non-modular translation for removing varying atoms is presented in Section 4. This paper is concluded by Section 5 where we also sketch potential applications of varying atoms in disjunctive logic programming.

2   Disjunctive Logic Programs Revisited

In this section, we review the basic concepts of disjunctive logic programming in the propositional case. A *disjunctive logic program* (DLP) Π is a set of *rules* of the form

$$a_1 \vee \cdots \vee a_n \leftarrow b_1, \ldots, b_m, \sim c_1, \ldots, \sim c_k, \qquad (1)$$

where $n, m, k \geq 0$ and $a_1, \ldots, a_n, b_1, \ldots, b_m,$ and $c_1, \ldots, c_k$ are propositional atoms. The *head* of the rule $a_1 \vee \cdots \vee a_n$ is interpreted disjunctively while the rest forming the *body* of the rule is interpreted conjunctively. The symbol "$\sim$" denotes *negation as failure to prove*; or *default negation* for short. Intuitively, a rule of the form (1) acts as an inference rule: any of the head atoms $a_1, \ldots, a_n$ can be inferred given that the positive body atoms $b_1, \ldots, b_m$ can be inferred and the negative body atoms $c_1, \ldots, c_k$ cannot.

We define *literals* in the standard way using $\sim$ as the connective for negation. For any set of atoms A, we define a set of negative literals $\sim A = \{\sim a \mid a \in A\}$. Since the order of atoms is insignificant in a rule (1), we use a shorthand $A \leftarrow B, \sim C$ where A, B and C are the sets of atoms involved in (1). If necessary, we separate rules with full stops and we drop the symbol "$\leftarrow$" in case of an empty body. An empty head ($n = 0$) is denoted by "$\perp$" and a rule with an empty head is called an *integrity constraint*. A DLP Π is *positive* if and only if $k = 0$ holds for every rule (1) of Π. We remind the reader that positive DLPs (PDLPs) can be viewed as propositional theories in conjunctive normal form (CNF) which can be obtained in linear time using new atoms.

2.1   Semantics: Minimal and Stable Models

We define the *Herbrand base* $\mathrm{Hb}(\Pi)$ of a DLP Π as a set of atoms which contains all atoms appearing in Π. Due to flexibility of this definition, we view $\mathrm{Hb}(\Pi)$ as the *symbol table* of Π so that it contributes to the length of Π in symbols, denoted by $\|\Pi\|$. Following the ideas from [12], we partition $\mathrm{Hb}(\Pi)$ into two parts $\mathrm{Hb_v}(\Pi)$ and $\mathrm{Hb_h}(\Pi)$ which determine the *visible* and the *hidden* parts of $\mathrm{Hb}(\Pi)$, respectively. The visibility of atoms becomes important in Section 2.2 where the equivalence of DLPs is of interest, but for now we concentrate on defining the semantics of propositional DLPs.

An *interpretation* $I \subseteq \mathrm{Hb}(\Pi)$ of Π determines which atoms $a \in \mathrm{Hb}(\Pi)$ are true ($a \in I$) and which are false ($a \notin I$). An interpretation I is a (classical) *model* of Π, denoted by $I \models \Pi$, if and only if for every rule $A \leftarrow B, \sim C$ of Π, $B \subseteq I$ and $C \cap I = \emptyset$ imply $A \cap I \neq \emptyset$, i.e. the satisfaction of the rule body implies that one of the head atoms must also be true. It is customary to distinguish *minimal models* of a DLP Π, i.e. models $M \models \Pi$ for which there are no other models $N \models \Pi$ such that $N \subset M$. The set of minimal models of Π is denoted by $\mathrm{MM}(\Pi)$. If Π is a positive DLP, then $\mathrm{MM}(\Pi)$ determines the standard minimal model semantics of Π. Unfortunately, minimal models do not properly capture intuitions behind DLPs involving default negation, but *stable models* [8,20] provide a reasonable semantics for such programs.

Definition 1. *Given a DLP Π and an interpretation $M \subseteq \mathrm{Hb}(\Pi)$, the Gelfond-Lifschitz reduct of Π is a positive DLP*

$$\Pi^M = \{A \leftarrow B \mid A \leftarrow B, \sim C \in \Pi \text{ and } M \cap C = \emptyset\}. \qquad (2)$$

An interpretation $M \subseteq \mathrm{Hb}(\Pi)$ is a stable model of Π if and only if $M \in \mathrm{MM}(\Pi^M)$.

Given a DLP Π, we let $\mathrm{SM}(\Pi)$ denote the set of stable models of Π. Any two DLPs Π and Π' are considered to be *equivalent* under the stable model semantics, denoted by $\Pi \equiv \Pi'$, if and only if $\mathrm{SM}(\Pi) = \mathrm{SM}(\Pi')$. For instance, we have $\Pi \equiv \Pi'$ for $\Pi = \{a \vee b. \}$ and $\Pi' = \{a \leftarrow \sim b.\ b \leftarrow \sim a. \}$, as $\mathrm{SM}(\Pi) = \{\{a\}, \{b\}\} = \mathrm{SM}(\Pi')$. The preceding definition of $\equiv$ is justifiable from the viewpoint of formalizing a problem at hand as a DLP Π: the stable models of the program Π are often supposed to be in a one-to-one correspondence with the solutions of the problem. If $\Pi \equiv \Pi'$ holds for two programs $\Pi \neq \Pi'$ formalizing the same problem, then the same solutions are obtained.

2.2   Visible Equivalence

A drawback of the relation $\equiv$ is that it does not take the visibility of atoms into account. It is typical that a DLP Π contains atoms formalizing certain auxiliary concepts local to Π. Such atoms carry little relevance for other programs. This is why we adopt a slightly more general notion of equivalence [12] which treats the visible part $\mathrm{Hb_v}(\Pi)$ of the Herbrand base $\mathrm{Hb}(\Pi)$ as the *program interface* of Π. The key idea is that the hidden atoms in $\mathrm{Hb_h}(\Pi) = \mathrm{Hb}(\Pi) \setminus \mathrm{Hb_v}(\Pi)$ can be viewed local to Π and hence negligible as far as the equivalence of Π with other programs is concerned. The definition below is given relative to the sets of interpretations $\mathrm{SEM}(\Pi)$ and $\mathrm{SEM}(\Pi')$ which determine the semantics of Π and Π', respectively. We need this kind of flexibility in Section 3 when we compare PDLPs which are (possibly) based on different semantics than the stable semantics. The reader may assume $\mathrm{SEM}(\Pi) = \mathrm{SM}(\Pi)$ unless otherwise stated.

Definition 2. *Two DLPs Π and Π' are* visibly equivalent, *denoted by $\Pi \equiv_\mathrm{v} \Pi'$, if and only if $\mathrm{Hb_v}(\Pi) = \mathrm{Hb_v}(\Pi')$ and there is a bijection $f : \mathrm{SEM}(\Pi) \to \mathrm{SEM}(\Pi')$ such that for all interpretations $M \in \mathrm{SEM}(\Pi)$, $M \cap \mathrm{Hb_v}(\Pi) = f(M) \cap \mathrm{Hb_v}(\Pi')$.*

It is easy to verify that $\equiv_\mathrm{v}$ is an equivalence relation. To compare $\equiv_\mathrm{v}$ with $\equiv$, we note that these two relations coincide given that $\mathrm{Hb_h}(\Pi) = \mathrm{Hb_h}(\Pi') = \emptyset$ and $\mathrm{Hb}(\Pi) = \mathrm{Hb}(\Pi')$. The latter condition is actually of little account, as it can be readily satisfied e.g. by extending Herbrand bases with "useless" rules of the form $a \leftarrow a$.

Example 1. Consider logic programs $\Pi = \{a \leftarrow b.\ a \leftarrow c.\ b \leftarrow \sim c.\ c \leftarrow \sim b.\ \}$ and $\Pi' = \{a \leftarrow d, \sim e.\ a \leftarrow e, \sim d.\ d \vee e.\ \}$ with $\mathrm{Hb_v}(\Pi) = \mathrm{Hb_v}(\Pi') = \{a\}$. The stable models of Π are $M_1 = \{a, b\}$ and $M_2 = \{a, c\}$ whereas for Π' they are $N_1 = \{a, d\}$ and $N_2 = \{a, e\}$. Thus $\Pi \not\equiv \Pi'$ is clearly the case, but we have a bijection $f : \mathrm{SM}(\Pi) \to \mathrm{SM}(\Pi')$ which maps M_i to N_i for $i \in \{1, 2\}$. Hence $\Pi \equiv_\mathrm{v} \Pi'$. $\square$

3   Parallel Circumscription and Its Expressive Power

In this section, we analyze the expressive power of Lifschitz's *parallel circumscription* [16] by studying the effects of denying varying atoms and/or fixed atoms on the expressiveness of minimal models. In analogy to Section 2, we formulate parallel circumscription in the propositional case. Rather than using arbitrary propositional sentences to formulate propositional theories, we assume that the syntax of PDLPs is used. As discussed already in the introduction, parallel circumscription is based on a notion of minimality which partitions atoms in three disjoint categories.

Definition 3. *Let Π be a PDLP and let $V \subseteq \mathrm{Hb}(\Pi)$ and $F \subseteq \mathrm{Hb}(\Pi)$ be two sets of atoms satisfying $V \cap F = \emptyset$. A model $M \models \Pi$ is $\langle V, F \rangle$-minimal $\iff \not\exists N \models \Pi$ such that (i) $N \setminus (V \cup F) \subset M \setminus (V \cup F)$ and (ii) $N \cap F = M \cap F$.*

The idea is that the atoms in $\mathrm{Hb}(\Pi) \setminus (V \cup F)$ are subject to minimization in analogy to Section 2.1. However, while such a minimization takes place, the truth values of the atoms in V may *vary* freely and the truth values of the atoms in F are kept *fixed*. The set of all $\langle V, F \rangle$-minimal models of Π is denoted by $\mathrm{MM}_{V,F}(\Pi)$. It is customary in disjunctive logic programming that all atoms are subject to minimization, i.e. $\langle \emptyset, \emptyset \rangle$-minimal models of a positive DLP Π are of interest. Under this restriction, the first condition of Definition 3 is equivalent to $N \subset M$ while the second condition becomes void. Thus $\mathrm{MM}(\Pi) = \mathrm{MM}_{\emptyset,\emptyset}(\Pi)$. In the sequel, we are interested in the problem of determining $\langle V, F \rangle$-minimal models for a given *positive* DLP Π. Note that $V \subseteq \mathrm{Hb}(\Pi)$

and $F \subseteq \mathrm{Hb}(\Pi)$ are separately specified for each program Π and are thus viewed as parts of the respective programs. For now, we concentrate on answering the following question: is it possible to remove fixed and varying atoms by translating a PDLP involving such atoms into another PDLP not containing such atoms?

3.1 PFM Translation Functions

To answer the preceding question, we apply an analysis method [11,12] which is based on the existence of polynomial, faithful and modular translation functions between classes of logic programs. These properties are formalized in Definition 5 below, but first we state conditions on which two DLPs Π and Π' are viewed as separate program modules that can be combined together to form a larger program $\Pi \sqcup \Pi'$.[1]

Definition 4. *Two PDLPs Π and Π' satisfy module conditions if and only if $\Pi \cap \Pi' = \emptyset$, $\mathrm{Hb}_v(\Pi) = \mathrm{Hb}_v(\Pi')$, $\mathrm{Hb}_h(\Pi) \cap \mathrm{Hb}(\Pi') = \emptyset$, $\mathrm{Hb}(\Pi) \cap \mathrm{Hb}_h(\Pi') = \emptyset$.*

The intuition behind the conditions listed in Definition 4 is that the program modules Π and Π' possess identical program interfaces for mutual interaction and they do not share rules nor hidden atoms. If Π and Π' share rules, then $\Pi \setminus \Pi'$, $\Pi' \setminus \Pi$, and $\Pi \cap \Pi'$ might be identified as disjoint program modules, if admitted by the other conditions.

Definition 5. *Let C and C' be two classes of logic programs. A translation function $\mathrm{Tr} : C \to C'$ is defined to be*

1. **polynomial**, *iff for all programs $\Pi \in C$, the translation $\mathrm{Tr}(\Pi) \in C'$ can be computed in time (and hence also space) polynomial to $\|\Pi\|$;*
2. **faithful**, *iff for all programs $\Pi \in C$, $\Pi \equiv_v \mathrm{Tr}(\Pi)$;*
3. **modular**, *iff for all programs $\Pi \in C$ and $\Pi' \in C$ satisfying module conditions, the translation $\mathrm{Tr}(\Pi \sqcup \Pi') = \mathrm{Tr}(\Pi) \sqcup \mathrm{Tr}(\Pi')$ where the translations $\mathrm{Tr}(\Pi)$ and $\mathrm{Tr}(\Pi')$ satisfy module conditions.*

It can be shown that these three properties are preserved under compositions [12]. In particular, the modularity condition differs from the one used in [11]. This is to support translation functions between classes of logic programs (or like) that do not share syntax. Moreover, the module conditions in Definition 4 are more liberal than those used by Eiter et al. [6] which enables richer interaction between program modules.

In the sequel, we use the existence of a polynomial, faithful and modular (PFM) translation function as a criterion when comparing classes of logic programs by expressive power. A class of logic programs C is *at least as expressive as* another class C' iff there is a PFM translation function $\mathrm{Tr} : C' \to C$. We write $C' \leq_{\mathrm{PFM}} C$ to denote such a relationship. If both $C \leq_{\mathrm{PFM}} C'$ and $C' \leq_{\mathrm{PFM}} C$ hold, then C and C' are regarded as *equally expressive* classes, denoted by $C =_{\mathrm{PFM}} C'$. In certain cases, we succeed to find a counter-example to establish a negative relationship $C \nleq_{\mathrm{PFM}} C'$.[2] If, in addition, $C' \leq_{\mathrm{PFM}} C$ holds, then C is *strictly* more expressive than C', denoted by $C' <_{\mathrm{PFM}} C$. Finally, two classes may also turn out to be *incomparable* in terms of PFM translation functions, denoted by $C \neq_{\mathrm{PFM}} C'$, if and only if both $C' \nleq_{\mathrm{PFM}} C$ and $C \nleq_{\mathrm{PFM}} C'$ hold.

---

[1] The symbol $\sqcup$ denotes disjoint union.

[2] Sometimes we do not need all the three properties to form a counter-example and we may drop the respective letters from the notation. E.g. $C \nleq_{\mathrm{FM}} C'$ implies $C \nleq_{\mathrm{PFM}} C'$ in general.

3.2 Expressiveness Analysis

In this section, we apply the classification method presented in Section 3.1 to analyze $\mathcal{D}^+_{\mathrm{mvf}}$ which is defined as the class of PDLPs involving atoms being minimized (m), varying atoms (v), and fixed atoms (f). The semantics of a PDLP Π from this class is determined by $\mathrm{MM}_{V,F}(\Pi)$ rather than $\mathrm{SM}(\Pi) = \mathrm{MM}(\Pi)$; recall that Π has the sets $V \subseteq \mathrm{Hb}(\Pi)$ and $F \subseteq \mathrm{Hb}(\Pi)$ associated with it. We obtain six subclasses of $\mathcal{D}^+_{\mathrm{mvf}}$ by insisting that one or two of the sets $\mathrm{Hb}(\Pi) \setminus (V \cup F)$, V, and F are empty for PDLPs included in the subclass. Such a restriction corresponds to denying minimized/varying/fixed atoms and we drop the corresponding letter(s) from the notation when referring to the respective subclass of $\mathcal{D}^+_{\mathrm{mvf}}$. For instance, $\mathcal{D}^+_{\mathrm{m}}$ denotes the class of PDLPs under the standard semantics according to which all atoms are subject to minimization, i.e. the sets V and F are both empty for all PDLPs Π within this class.

We begin the analysis with fixed atoms. It is a well-known fact that they can be eliminated in general [3], but our interest in this respect is to check that the elimination can be accomplished using a PFM translation function.

Theorem 1. $\mathcal{D}^+_{\mathrm{mfv}} \leq_{\mathrm{PFM}} \mathcal{D}^+_{\mathrm{mv}}$ and $\mathcal{D}^+_{\mathrm{mf}} \leq_{\mathrm{PFM}} \mathcal{D}^+_{\mathrm{m}}$.

Proof. (sketch) Let Π be a PDLP, and V and F the sets of varying and fixed atoms, respectively. The class $\mathcal{D}^+_{\mathrm{mf}}$ can be covered by further assuming $V = \emptyset$. De Kleer and Konolige [3] propose the following technique to remove F. A new atom $f' \notin \mathrm{Hb}(\Pi)$ is introduced for each $f \in F$. The translation $\mathrm{Tr}_{\mathrm{KK}}(\Pi) = \Pi \cup \{f \vee f'.\ \bot \leftarrow f, f'.\ |\ f \in F\}$ with the set of atoms $(\mathrm{Hb}(\Pi) \setminus V) \cup \{f' \mid f \in F\}$ subject to minimization. The visible Herbrand base $\mathrm{Hb}_{\mathrm{v}}(\mathrm{Tr}_{\mathrm{KK}}(\Pi))$ can be defined as $\mathrm{Hb}_{\mathrm{v}}(\Pi)$.

It is easy to see that $\mathrm{Tr}_{\mathrm{KK}}$ is linear. For the faithfulness of $\mathrm{Tr}_{\mathrm{KK}}$, we note that $\langle V, F \rangle$-minimal models M of Π are in a bijective relationship with the $\langle V, \emptyset \rangle$-minimal models $M' = M \cup \{f' \mid f \in F$ and $f \notin M\}$ of $\mathrm{Tr}_{\mathrm{KK}}(\Pi)$. For the modularity of $\mathrm{Tr}_{\mathrm{KK}}$, we suppose that two PDLPs Π and Π' with the sets of varying atoms V and V' and the sets of fixed atoms F and F', respectively, satisfy the module conditions. It is clear that $\mathrm{Tr}_{\mathrm{KK}}(\Pi)$ and $\mathrm{Tr}_{\mathrm{KK}}(\Pi')$ are disjoint and $\mathrm{Tr}_{\mathrm{KK}}(\Pi \sqcup \Pi') = \mathrm{Tr}_{\mathrm{KK}}(\Pi) \sqcup \mathrm{Tr}_{\mathrm{KK}}(\Pi')$, as Π and Π' as well as F and F' are disjoint by the module conditions. Moreover, we have $\mathrm{Hb}_{\mathrm{v}}(\mathrm{Tr}_{\mathrm{KK}}(\Pi)) = \mathrm{Hb}_{\mathrm{v}}(\mathrm{Tr}_{\mathrm{KK}}(\Pi'))$ by definition, because $\mathrm{Hb}_{\mathrm{v}}(\Pi) = \mathrm{Hb}_{\mathrm{v}}(\Pi')$ by the module conditions. Finally, the translations $\mathrm{Tr}_{\mathrm{KK}}(\Pi)$ and $\mathrm{Tr}_{\mathrm{KK}}(\Pi')$ do not share hidden atoms as the modules Π and Π' do not. $\square$

Thus $\mathcal{D}^+_{\mathrm{mv}} \subseteq \mathcal{D}^+_{\mathrm{mfv}}$ and $\mathcal{D}^+_{\mathrm{m}} \subseteq \mathcal{D}^+_{\mathrm{mf}}$ imply $\mathcal{D}^+_{\mathrm{mv}} =_{\mathrm{PFM}} \mathcal{D}^+_{\mathrm{mfv}}$ and $\mathcal{D}^+_{\mathrm{m}} =_{\mathrm{PFM}} \mathcal{D}^+_{\mathrm{mf}}$.

Theorem 2. $\mathcal{D}^+_{\mathrm{mv}} \not\leq_{\mathrm{FM}} \mathcal{D}^+_{\mathrm{m}}$

Proof. Let us assume that there is a polynomial and faithful translation function $\mathrm{Tr} : \mathcal{D}^+_{\mathrm{mv}} \to \mathcal{D}^+_{\mathrm{m}}$ that effectively removes varying atoms. Then consider two disjoint logic programs $\Pi_1 = \{a \vee b.\}$ and $\Pi_2 = \{\bot \leftarrow b, a.\}$ based on $\mathrm{Hb}(\Pi_1) = \mathrm{Hb}(\Pi_2) = \{a, b\}$ with all atoms visible, i.e. $\mathrm{Hb}_{\mathrm{h}}(\Pi_1) = \mathrm{Hb}_{\mathrm{h}}(\Pi_2) = \emptyset$. Then let us define $V_1 = \{a\}$ and $V_2 = \{b\}$ as the sets of varying atoms associated with Π_1 and Π_2, respectively. As regards Π_1 and Π_2, it is straightforward to verify that

1. the only $\langle V_1, \emptyset \rangle$-minimal model of Π_1 is $M_1 = \{a\}$;

2. the program Π_2 has two $\langle V_2, \emptyset \rangle$-minimal models $M_2 = \{b\}$ and $M_3 = \emptyset$; and
3. the program $\Pi_1 \sqcup \Pi_2$ has two $\langle V_1 \sqcup V_2, \emptyset \rangle$-minimal models M_1 and M_2.

On the other hand, the translations $\mathrm{Tr}(\Pi_1, V_1)$, $\mathrm{Tr}(\Pi_2, V_2)$, and $\mathrm{Tr}(\Pi_1 \sqcup \Pi_2, V_1 \sqcup V_2)$ are PDLPs whose all atoms are subject to minimization. Since Tr is faithful, we know that $\mathrm{Tr}(\Pi_1, V_1)$ has a $\langle \emptyset, \emptyset \rangle$-minimal model N such that $N \cap \mathrm{Hb}(\Pi_1) = M_1$, and $\mathrm{Tr}(\Pi_1 \sqcup \Pi_2, V_1 \sqcup V_2)$ has two $\langle \emptyset, \emptyset \rangle$-minimal models N_1 and N_2 such that $N_1 \cap \mathrm{Hb}(\Pi_1 \sqcup \Pi_2) = M_1 = \{a\}$ and $N_2 \cap \mathrm{Hb}(\Pi_1 \sqcup \Pi_2) = M_2 = \{b\}$.

Using the modularity of Tr, we obtain $\mathrm{Tr}(\Pi_1 \sqcup \Pi_2, V_1 \sqcup V_2) = \mathrm{Tr}(\Pi_1, V_1) \sqcup \mathrm{Tr}(\Pi_2, V_2)$. Since $N_2 \models \mathrm{Tr}(\Pi_1 \sqcup \Pi_2, V_1 \sqcup V_2)$, we obtain $N_2 \models \mathrm{Tr}(\Pi_1, V_1)$. It follows that $N' \models \mathrm{Tr}(\Pi_1, V_1)$ holds for the restricted model $N' = N_2 \cap \mathrm{Hb}(\mathrm{Tr}(\Pi_1, V_1))$ from which the local atoms of $\mathrm{Tr}(\Pi_2, V_2)$ have been removed. Recall that $\mathrm{Hb}(\Pi_1) \subseteq \mathrm{Hb}(\mathrm{Tr}(\Pi_1, V_1))$ by the faithfulness of Tr. Because $N' \models \mathrm{Tr}(\Pi_1, V_1)$ and N is the unique $\langle \emptyset, \emptyset \rangle$-minimal model of $\mathrm{Tr}(\Pi_1, V_1)$, we obtain $N \subseteq N'$. A contradiction, since $a \in N$ but $a \notin N'$. To conclude, such a translation function Tr does not exist.   □

It follows that $\mathcal{D}_\mathrm{m}^+ <_\mathrm{PFM} \mathcal{D}_\mathrm{mv}^+$, since $\mathcal{D}_\mathrm{m}^+$ is a subclass of $\mathcal{D}_\mathrm{mv}^+$. The first condition of Definition 3 implies that the classes $\mathcal{D}_\mathrm{v}^+$, $\mathcal{D}_\mathrm{f}^+$, and $\mathcal{D}_\mathrm{vf}^+$ collapse to classical logic, i.e. the semantics assigned to a PDLP Π is $\mathrm{CM}(\Pi) = \{M \subseteq \mathrm{Hb}(\Pi) \mid M \models \Pi\}$. Moreover, PFM translation functions are easily obtained for each pair of classes. E.g., a translation function from $\mathcal{D}_\mathrm{v}^+$ to $\mathcal{D}_\mathrm{f}^+$ simply exchanges the roles of varying and fixed atoms. This is semantically irrelevant, as no atoms are subject to minimization. Such a translation function is trivially PFM. Hence, we have $\mathcal{D}_\mathrm{v}^+ =_\mathrm{PFM} \mathcal{D}_\mathrm{f}^+ =_\mathrm{PFM} \mathcal{D}_\mathrm{vf}^+$ and there is only one relationship to be further explored.

Theorem 3. $\mathcal{D}_\mathrm{m}^+ \not\leq_\mathrm{FM} \mathcal{D}_\mathrm{v}^+$

Proof. Consider $\Pi_1 = \{a \leftarrow a\}$ and $\Pi_2 = \{a\}$ which have unique $\langle \emptyset, \emptyset \rangle$-minimal models $M_1 = \emptyset$ and $M_2 = \{a\}$, respectively. Assuming the existence of a faithful and modular translation function Tr, we obtain that $\mathrm{Tr}(\Pi_1)$ and $\mathrm{Tr}(\Pi_2)$ have unique classical models N_1 and N_2, respectively, such that $N_i \cap \mathrm{Hb}(\Pi_i) = M_i$ for $i \in \{1, 2\}$. Thus $\mathrm{Tr}(\Pi_1 \sqcup \Pi_2) = \mathrm{Tr}(\Pi_1) \sqcup \mathrm{Tr}(\Pi_2)$ is necessarily inconsistent — contradicting the faithfulness of Tr, as M_2 is the unique $\langle \emptyset, \emptyset \rangle$-minimal model of $\Pi_1 \sqcup \Pi_2$.   □

The resulting expressive power hierarchy is summarized in Figure 1. There are three equivalence classes under PFM The most expressive class corresponds to Lifschitz's parallel circumscription [16] while the class in the middle captures ordinary circumscription proposed by McCarthy [18]. The class at the bottom corresponds to classical logic. translation functions. In spite of certain differences, these results can be understood as a refinement to an analogous hierarchy derived for nonmonotonic logics [10] where the lower end of the hierarchy consists of parallel circumscription and classical logic; the former ranked strictly more expressive than the latter. Let us also note that current disjunctive solvers [15,13] cover the hierarchy up to the class in the middle.

$$\mathcal{D}_\mathrm{mv}^+ =_\mathrm{PFM} \mathcal{D}_\mathrm{mvf}^+$$

$$\vee_\mathrm{PFM} \qquad \vee_\mathrm{PFM}$$

$$\mathcal{D}_\mathrm{m}^+ =_\mathrm{PFM} \mathcal{D}_\mathrm{mf}^+$$

$$\vee_\mathrm{PFM} \qquad \vee_\mathrm{PFM}$$

$$\mathcal{D}_\mathrm{v}^+ =_\mathrm{PFM} \mathcal{D}_\mathrm{f}^+ =_\mathrm{PFM} \mathcal{D}_\mathrm{vf}^+$$

Fig. 1. Hierarchy Implied by the Expressiveness Analysis

4   Eliminating Varying Atoms

In this section, we present a non-modular translation function $\mathrm{Tr_{BLIND}}$ which enables us to remove varying atoms from a PDLP Π in a faithful way, i.e. $\langle V, F \rangle$-minimal models M of Π and the stable models N of its translation are in a bijective relationship such that $M = N \cap \mathrm{Hb}(\Pi)$ holds for each pair of models. For the sake of simplicity, we assume that fixed atoms have already been removed (recall $\mathrm{Tr_{KK}}$ from Theorem 1).

The translation function $\mathrm{Tr_{BLIND}}$ introduces new atoms, which do not appear in $\mathrm{Hb}(\Pi)$, as follows. For each $a \in \mathrm{Hb}(\Pi)$, the complement $\overline{a}$ of a expresses the falsity of a. Moreover, a renamed copy a^* of each $a \in \mathrm{Hb}(\Pi)$ is needed when formulating a test for $\langle V, \emptyset \rangle$-minimality. Likewise, a vector of new atoms $d_1, \ldots, d_n$ is introduced for the set of atoms $P = \mathrm{Hb}(\Pi) \setminus V = \{a_1, \ldots, a_n\}$ subject to minimization. Yet another new atom, namely u, will be used in the translation. Given a set of atoms $A \subseteq \mathrm{Hb}(\Pi)$, we introduce shorthands $\overline{A}$ and A^* for the sets $\{\overline{a} \mid a \in A\}$ and $\{a^* \mid a \in A\}$, respectively.

Definition 6. *Let Π be a PDLP and $V \subseteq \mathrm{Hb}(\Pi)$ a set of varying atoms. Let us define $P = \mathrm{Hb}(\Pi) \setminus V = \{a_1, \ldots, a_n\}$ and a translation $\mathrm{Tr_{BLIND}}(\Pi)$ containing*

1. *rules $a \leftarrow \sim\overline{a}$ and $\overline{a} \leftarrow \sim a$ for each $a \in \mathrm{Hb}(\Pi)$;*
2. *a rule $\bot \leftarrow \sim A, \sim\overline{B}$ for each rule $A \leftarrow B$ in Π;*
3. *a rule $A^* \cup \{u\} \leftarrow B^*$ for each rule $A \leftarrow B$ in Π;*
4. *a rule $d_1 \vee \cdots \vee d_n \vee u$;*
5. *rules $u \leftarrow d_i, \sim a_i$ and $u \leftarrow a_i^*, \sim a_i$ for each $1 \leq i \leq n$;*
6. *rules $u \leftarrow d_i, a_i^*, \sim\overline{a_i}$ and $u \vee d_i \vee a_i^* \leftarrow \sim\overline{a_i}$ for each $1 \leq i \leq n$;*
7. *a rule $a^* \leftarrow u$ for each $a \in \mathrm{Hb}(\Pi)$;*
8. *a rule $d_i \leftarrow u$ for each $1 \leq i \leq n$; and*
9. *a rule $\bot \leftarrow \sim u$.*

The rules included in $\mathrm{Tr_{BLIND}}(\Pi)$ serve the following purposes. (1.) An arbitrary interpretation $M \subseteq \mathrm{Hb}(\Pi)$ is chosen for the PDLP Π. (2.) It is ensured that $M \models \Pi$ holds in the classical sense. (3.) A renamed copy of Π is created to check the $\langle V, \emptyset \rangle$-minimality of M. In analogy to [13], this can be achieved by checking whether

$$\mathrm{Tr_{UNSAT}}(\Pi, P, M) = \Pi \cup \{\bot \leftarrow P \cap M\} \cup \{\bot \leftarrow a \mid a \in P \setminus M\} \qquad (3)$$

is unsatisfiable for M and the set of atoms $P = \{a_1, \ldots, a_n\}$ subject to minimization. This is why the intuitive reading of u is *unsatisfiable* which captures the desired state of affairs, implying the $\langle V, \emptyset \rangle$-minimality of M. (4.) The disjunction $d_1 \vee \cdots \vee d_n$ captures the rule $\bot \leftarrow P \cap M$ from (3). This rule depends dynamically on M and it effectively states the *falsity* of at least one atom a_i that is both subject to minimization ($a_i \in P$) and true in M ($a_i \in M$). (5.) The rules cover the case that a_i is false in M, i.e. $a_i \in P \setminus M$. Conforming to (3), both d_i and a_i^* are implicitly assigned to false, as they imply u. Otherwise, a_i is true in M which activates the rules in (6.) enforcing d_i equivalent to the negation of a_i^*. The net effect of the rules included in (4.) – (6.) is that any *potential* counter-model $N \models \Pi$ for the $\langle V, \emptyset \rangle$-minimality of M, expressed in $\mathrm{Hb}(\Pi)^*$ rather than $\mathrm{Hb}(\Pi)$, must satisfy $N \cap P \subset M \cap P$ ($\iff N \setminus V \subset M \setminus V$).

The rules given in items (7.) – (9.) are directly related to the unsatisfiability check which effectively proves that counter-models like N above do not exist. To implement the test for unsatisfiability, we adopt the technique used earlier by Eiter and Gottlob [5].

Example 2. Consider a program $\Pi = \{f \vee ab.\}$ which is a simplified version of Lifschitz's ostrich example [16]. This program has a unique $\langle\{f\}, \emptyset\rangle$-minimal model $M = \{f\}$. The translation $\mathrm{Tr_{BLIND}}(\Pi)$ includes the following rules: (1.) $f \leftarrow {\sim}\overline{f}$. $\overline{f} \leftarrow {\sim}f$. $ab \leftarrow {\sim}\overline{ab}$. $\overline{ab} \leftarrow {\sim}ab$. (2.) $\perp \leftarrow {\sim}f, {\sim}ab$. (3.) $f^* \vee ab^* \vee u$. (4.) $d \vee u$. (5.) $u \leftarrow d, {\sim}ab$. $u \leftarrow ab^*, {\sim}ab$. (6.) $u \leftarrow d, ab^*, {\sim}\overline{ab}$. $u \vee d \vee ab^* \leftarrow {\sim}\overline{ab}$. (7.) $ab^* \leftarrow u$. $f^* \leftarrow u$. (8.) $d \leftarrow u$. (9.) $\perp \leftarrow {\sim}u$. There is only one stable model for $\mathrm{Tr_{BLIND}}(\Pi)$, i.e. $N = \{f, \overline{ab}, f^*, ab^*, d, u\}$ for which $M = N \cap \{f, ab\}$ holds.   □

Our next objective is to establish that the translation function $\mathrm{Tr_{BLIND}}$ given in Definition 6 is faithful, i.e. the $\langle V, \emptyset\rangle$-minimal models of a PDLP Π are in a bijective relationship with the stable models of $\mathrm{Tr_{BLIND}}(\Pi)$. In analogy to [19], we implement the test for $\langle V, \emptyset\rangle$-minimality through propositional unsatisfiability.

Lemma 1. *Given a PDLP Π and $V \subseteq \mathrm{Hb}(\Pi)$, a model $M \subseteq \mathrm{Hb}(\Pi)$ of Π is $\langle V, \emptyset\rangle$-minimal if and only if $\mathrm{Tr_{UNSAT}}(\Pi, \mathrm{Hb}(\Pi) \setminus V, M)$, as defined in (3), is unsatisfiable.*

We split the translation $\mathrm{Tr_{BLIND}}(\Pi)$ in two parts using the *Splitting Set Theorem* [17] which we formulate for stable models rather than *answer sets* used in [17]. A *splitting set* for a DLP Π is any set $U \subseteq \mathrm{Hb}(\Pi)$ such that for every rule $A \leftarrow B, {\sim}C \in \Pi$, if $A \cap U \neq \emptyset$ then $A \cup B \cup C \subseteq U$. The set of rules $A \leftarrow B, {\sim}C \in \Pi$ such that $A \cup B \cup C \subseteq U$ is the *bottom* of Π relative to U, denoted by $\mathrm{b}_U(\Pi)$. The set $\mathrm{t}_U(\Pi) = \Pi \setminus \mathrm{b}_U(\Pi)$ is the *top* of Π relative to U which can be partially evaluated with respect to an interpretation $X \subseteq U$. The result is a DLP $\mathrm{e}_U(\mathrm{t}_U(\Pi), X)$ defined as $\{A \leftarrow (B\setminus U), {\sim}(C\setminus U) \mid A \leftarrow B, {\sim}C \in \mathrm{t}_U(\Pi), B\cap U \subseteq X \text{ and } (C\cap U)\cap X = \emptyset\}$. Given a splitting set U for a program Π, a *solution* to Π with respect to U is a pair $\langle X, Y\rangle$ such that (i) $X \subseteq U$ is a stable model of $\mathrm{b}_U(\Pi)$ and (ii) $Y \subseteq \mathrm{Hb}(\Pi) \setminus U$ is a stable model of $\mathrm{e}_U(\mathrm{t}_U(\Pi), X)$. Solutions and stable models relate as follows.

Theorem 4 (Splitting Set Theorem [17]). *Let U be a splitting set for a DLP Π and $M \subseteq \mathrm{Hb}(\Pi)$ an interpretation. Then $M \in \mathrm{SM}(\Pi)$ if and only if the pair $\langle X, Y\rangle$ with $X = M \cap U$ and $Y = M \setminus U$ is a solution to Π with respect to U.*

We use the set of atoms $U = \mathrm{Hb}(\Pi) \cup \{\overline{a} \mid a \in \mathrm{Hb}(\Pi)\}$ to split $\mathrm{Tr_{BLIND}}(\Pi)$: the bottom $\mathrm{b}_U(\mathrm{Tr_{BLIND}}(\Pi))$ consists of items 1 and 2 in Definition 6, whereas the partially evaluated top $\mathrm{e}_U(\mathrm{t}_U(\mathrm{Tr_{BLIND}}(\Pi)), X)$ consists of items 3, 4 and 7–9 in Definition 6 as such and the following rules corresponding to rules in items 5 and 6:

5.' $u \leftarrow d_i$ and $u \leftarrow a_i^*$ where $1 \le i \le n$ and $a_i \in P \setminus X$; and
6.' $u \leftarrow d_i, a_i^*$ and $u \vee d_i \vee a_i^*$ where $1 \le i \le n$ and $a_i \in P \cap X$.

Thus $\mathrm{Hb}(\mathrm{e}_U(\mathrm{t}_U(\mathrm{Tr_{BLIND}}(\Pi)), X)) = \{a^* \mid a \in \mathrm{Hb}(\Pi)\} \cup \{d_i \mid 1 \le i \le n\} \cup \{u\}$. We use the notation $\mathrm{E}_U(\Pi, X) = \mathrm{e}_U(\mathrm{t}_U(\mathrm{Tr_{BLIND}}(\Pi)), X)$ for the sake of brevity.

It is shown next that there is one-to-one correspondence between the models in $\mathrm{SM}(\mathrm{b}_U(\mathrm{Tr_{BLIND}}(\Pi)))$ and $\mathrm{CM}(\Pi)$. As a consequence, the stable models of the bottom $\mathrm{b}_U(\mathrm{Tr_{BLIND}}(\Pi))$ are classical models of Π extended to $\mathrm{Hb}(\mathrm{b}_U(\mathrm{Tr_{BLIND}}(\Pi)))$.

Proposition 1. *Let Π be a PDLP.*
The function $\mathrm{Ext_B} : \mathrm{CM}(\Pi) \to 2^{\mathrm{Hb}(\mathrm{b}_U(\mathrm{Tr_{BLIND}}(\Pi)))}$ defined by $\mathrm{Ext_B}(M) = M \cup \{\overline{a} \mid a \in \mathrm{Hb}(\Pi) \setminus M\}$ is a bijection from $\mathrm{CM}(\Pi)$ to $\mathrm{SM}(\mathrm{b}_U(\mathrm{Tr_{BLIND}}(\Pi)))$.

Proof. It is shown below that (i) the image of $CM(\Pi)$ under $\mathrm{Ext_B}$ is a subset of $\mathrm{SM}(b_U(\mathrm{Tr_{BLIND}}(\Pi)))$, (ii) $\mathrm{Ext_B}$ is an injection, and (iii) $\mathrm{Ext_B}$ is a surjection.

(i) Assume that $M \in CM(\Pi)$, i.e. $M \models \Pi$. It is clear that $X \models b_U(\mathrm{Tr_{BLIND}}(\Pi))$ holds for $X = \mathrm{Ext_B}(M)$ and it suffices to prove $X \in \mathrm{MM}(b_U(\mathrm{Tr_{BLIND}}(\Pi))^X)$. Since $M \models \Pi$, the reduct $b_U(\mathrm{Tr_{BLIND}}(\Pi))^X$ contains only the rules $a \leftarrow$ for $\overline{a} \notin X$ and $\overline{a} \leftarrow$ for $a \notin X$. Thus $X \in \mathrm{MM}(b_U(\mathrm{Tr_{BLIND}}(\Pi))^X)$.

(ii) If $M_1 \neq M_2$, then $\mathrm{Ext_B}(M_1) \neq \mathrm{Ext_B}(M_2)$ follows by the definition of $\mathrm{Ext_B}$.

(iii) Consider any $X \in \mathrm{SM}(b_U(\mathrm{Tr_{BLIND}}(\Pi)))$. We need to show that there is $M \in CM(\Pi)$ such that $\mathrm{Ext_B}(M) = X$. Let us establish first that $M \models \Pi$ holds for $M = X \cap \mathrm{Hb}(\Pi)$. Since $X \in \mathrm{SM}(b_U(\mathrm{Tr_{BLIND}}(\Pi)))$ and $b_U(\mathrm{Tr_{BLIND}}(\Pi))$ contains the rules $a \leftarrow \sim\overline{a}$ and $\overline{a} \leftarrow \sim a$ for each $a \in \mathrm{Hb}(\Pi)$, it holds for every $a \in \mathrm{Hb}(\Pi)$ that $\overline{a} \notin X \iff a \in X$. Moreover, since $X \models b_U(\mathrm{Tr_{BLIND}}(\Pi))$, we obtain $X \not\models \sim A \cup \sim\overline{B}$ for all rules $A \leftarrow B \in \Pi$. Thus for each rule $A \leftarrow B$ in Π, there is $a \in A$ such that $a \in X$, or $b \in B$ such that $\overline{b} \in X$ ($\iff b \notin X$). In either case, $M \models A \leftarrow B$ and therefore $M \models \Pi$, i.e. $M \in CM(\Pi)$. It remains to establish that $\mathrm{Ext_B}(M) = X$. Since $M = X \cap \mathrm{Hb}(\Pi)$, we have $\mathrm{Ext_B}(M) = \mathrm{Ext_B}(X \cap \mathrm{Hb}(\Pi)) = (X \cap \mathrm{Hb}(\Pi)) \cup \{\overline{a} \mid a \in \mathrm{Hb}(\Pi) \setminus X\}$. Then $\mathrm{Ext_B}(M) = X$ follows by the fact that $\overline{a} \notin X \iff a \in X$ holds for any $a \in \mathrm{Hb}(\Pi)$. □

Finally, we show the connection between $\mathrm{SM}(\mathrm{E}_U(\Pi, \mathrm{Ext_B}(M))) \neq \emptyset$ and the unsatisfiability of $\mathrm{Tr_{UNSAT}}(\Pi, P, M)$. A similar unsatisfiability check is used in [5].

Proposition 2. *Let Π, V, and $P = \{a_1, \dots, a_n\}$ be defined as in Definition 6 and $\mathrm{Ext_B}$ as in Proposition 1. Moreover, let $M \subseteq \mathrm{Hb}(\Pi)$ be a classical model of Π. Then (i) if $N \in \mathrm{SM}(\mathrm{E}_U(\Pi, \mathrm{Ext_B}(M)))$, then $N = \mathrm{Hb}(\mathrm{E}_U(\Pi, \mathrm{Ext_B}(M)))$, and (ii) $\mathrm{Tr_{UNSAT}}(\Pi, P, M)$ is unsatisfiable if and only if $\mathrm{E}_U(\Pi, \mathrm{Ext_B}(M))$ has a stable model.*

Proof. (i) Assume that $N \in \mathrm{SM}(\mathrm{E}_U(\Pi, \mathrm{Ext_B}(M)))$. Since $N \models \mathrm{E}_U(\Pi, \mathrm{Ext_B}(M))$ and the rule $\perp \leftarrow \sim u$ belongs to $\mathrm{E}_U(\Pi, \mathrm{Ext_B}(M))$, we must have $u \in N$. Furthermore, since the rules $a^* \leftarrow u$ (for all $a \in \mathrm{Hb}(\Pi)$) and $d_i \leftarrow u$ (for all $1 \leq i \leq n$) belong to $\mathrm{E}_U(\Pi, \mathrm{Ext_B}(M))$, it follows that $N = \mathrm{Hb}(\mathrm{E}_U(\Pi, \mathrm{Ext_B}(M)))$.

(ii) "$\Rightarrow$" Assume that $\mathrm{Tr_{UNSAT}}(\Pi, P, M)$ is unsatisfiable. It is easy to see that $N \models \mathrm{E}_U(\Pi, \mathrm{Ext_B}(M))$ holds for $N = \mathrm{Hb}(\mathrm{E}_U(\Pi, \mathrm{Ext_B}(M)))$. Let us then show that $N \in \mathrm{MM}(\mathrm{E}_U(\Pi, \mathrm{Ext_B}(M))^N)$ by assuming the opposite, i.e. there is $N' \subset N$ such that $N' \models \mathrm{E}_U(\Pi, \mathrm{Ext_B}(M))^N$. Let us then assume $u \notin N'$ and define an interpretation $M' = \{a \in \mathrm{Hb}(\Pi) \mid a^* \in N'\}$. The following observations can be made.

- We have $N' \models A^* \leftarrow B^*$ for each rule $A \leftarrow B \in \Pi$. Thus $M' \models \Pi$.
- Since $N' \models u \leftarrow d_i, a_i^*$ and $N' \models u \vee d_i \vee a_i^*$ for all $a_i \in P \cap \mathrm{Ext_B}(M) = P \cap M$, it holds $d_i \in N' \iff a_i^* \notin N'$ for all $a_i \in P \cap M$. Also $N' \models d_1 \vee \cdots \vee d_n$ and $N' \models u \leftarrow d_i$ for all $a_i \in P \setminus \mathrm{Ext_B}(M) = P \setminus M$. Thus there is $a_i \in P \cap M$ such that $d_i \in N'$ and $a_i^* \notin N'$, too. This implies $a_i \notin M'$ and $M' \models \perp \leftarrow P \cap M$.
- Since $N' \models u \leftarrow a_i^*$ for all $a_i \in P \setminus M$, we have $a_i^* \notin N'$ for all $a_i \in P \setminus M$. This implies $M' \models \{\perp \leftarrow a \mid a \in P \setminus M\}$.

Thus $M' \models \text{Tr}_{\text{UNSAT}}(\Pi, P, M)$ which is a contradiction so that $u \in N'$ must be the case. Since $u \in N'$ and the rules $a^* \leftarrow u$ (for all $a \in \text{Hb}(\Pi)$) and $d_i \leftarrow u$ (for all $1 \leq i \leq n$) belong to $\text{E}_U(\Pi, \text{Ext}_B(M))^N$, we must have that $a^* \in N'$ for all $a \in \text{Hb}(\Pi)$ and $d_i \in N'$ for $1 \leq i \leq n$. Thus $N' = N$ contradicting our previous assumption. Therefore $N \in \text{SM}(\text{E}_U(\Pi, \text{Ext}_B(M)))$ is necessarily the case.

(ii) "$\Leftarrow$" Consider any $N \in \text{SM}(\text{E}_U(\Pi, \text{Ext}_B(M)))$. It follows by (i) that $N = \text{Hb}(\text{E}_U(\Pi, \text{Ext}_B(M)))$. Let us then assume that $\text{Tr}_{\text{UNSAT}}(\Pi, P, M)$ is satisfiable, i.e. there is $M' \subseteq \text{Hb}(\Pi)$ such that $M' \models \Pi$, $M' \not\models P \cap M$ and $a \notin M'$ for all $a \in P \setminus M$. It is established in the sequel that $N' \models \text{E}_U(\Pi, \text{Ext}_B(M))^N$ holds for the interpretation N' defined as $(M')^* \cup \{d_i \mid a_i \in M \cap P \text{ and } a_i \notin M'\}$.

- Since $M' \models \Pi$, we have $N' \models A^* \cup \{u\} \leftarrow B^*$ for each rule $A \leftarrow B \in \Pi$.
- Since $M' \not\models P \cap M$, there is $d_i \in N'$ and thus $N' \models d_1 \vee \cdots \vee d_n \vee u$.
- The definition of N' implies $a_i^* \notin N'$ and $d_i \notin N'$ for all $a_i \in P \setminus M$, as $a_i \notin M'$ for all $a_i \in P \setminus M$. Thus $N' \models u \leftarrow d_i$ and $N' \models u \leftarrow a_i^*$ when $a_i \in P \setminus M$.
- Given $a_i \in P \cap M$, we have $d_i \in N' \iff a_i \notin M'$, i.e. $a_i^* \notin N'$ by the definition of N'. Thus $N' \models u \leftarrow d_i, a_i^*$ and $N' \models u \vee d_i \vee a_i^*$ hold whenever $a_i \in P \cap M$.
- Since $u \notin N'$, we have $N' \models a^* \leftarrow u$ for each $a \in \text{Hb}(\Pi)$.
- Since $u \notin N'$, it follows that $N' \models d_i \leftarrow u$ for each $1 \leq i \leq n$.

Now $N' \subset N$ and $N' \models \text{E}_U(\Pi, \text{Ext}_B(M))^N$, contradicting the assumption $N \in \text{SM}(\text{E}_U(\Pi, \text{Ext}_B(M)))$. Thus $\text{Tr}_{\text{UNSAT}}(\Pi, P, M)$ must be unsatisfiable. $\square$

We let $\mathcal{D}$ denote the class of DLPs under the stable model semantics [8,20]. The translation function $\text{Tr}_{\text{BLIND}} : \mathcal{D}_{\text{mv}}^+ \to \mathcal{D}$ is clearly linear. Assuming that the visible Herbrand base $\text{Hb}_v(\text{Tr}_{\text{BLIND}}(\Pi)) = \text{Hb}_v(\Pi)$ by definition, the faithfulness of translation $\text{Tr}_{\text{BLIND}}(\Pi)$ follows by Theorem 4 from Lemma 1, and Propositions 1 and 2.

Theorem 5. $\mathcal{D}_{\text{mv}}^+ \leq_{\text{PF}} \mathcal{D}$.

5   Discussion

The main result of this paper is a linear translation from parallel circumscription into disjunctive logic programs such that a bijective correspondence between the $\langle V, F \rangle$-minimal models of a PDLP Π and the stable models of the respective translation $\text{Tr}_{\text{BLIND}}(\text{Tr}_{\text{KK}}(\Pi))$ is obtained. As suggested by the analysis performed in Section 3, the translation function Tr_{BLIND} is non-modular — reflecting the global nature of varying atoms. In contrast to earlier attempts [7,22,14], our translation does not depend on syntactic restrictions and it has a linear time/space complexity. Cadoli et al. [2] achieve the same complexity, but their transformation has ordinary circumscription as the target formalism, and hence a bijective relationship of models cannot be obtained. However, the translation function Tr_{BLIND} presented in this paper exploits default negation in order to establish faithfulness in the strict sense implied by Definitions 5 and 2.

Our results enable the systematic use of varying atoms in order to develop more compact formulations of problems as disjunctive logic programs. A good example in this respect is the consistency-based diagnosis of digital circuits [21]. Reiter-style *minimal diagnoses* are hard to formalize when all atoms are subject to minimization. Following the ideas from [1], a digital circuit can be modeled as follows. For instance, an *inverter* I is described by a propositional theory $(o_I \leftrightarrow \neg i_I) \vee ab_I$, where the atoms i_I and o_I model the input and the output of I, respectively, and ab_I expresses the fact that I is operating against its specification. This theory can be equivalently formulated as a PDLP $\Pi_I = \{ab_I \leftarrow i_I, o_I.\ i_I \vee o_I \vee ab_I.\}$ and minimal diagnoses correspond to $\langle \{i_I, o_I\}, \emptyset \rangle$-minimal models of Π_I augmented by observations. This line of thinking carries over to larger circuits which have also other gates than inverters as their components. Assuming the availability of varying atoms, the description of the circuit can be formed in a very modular fashion, component-by-component. Then the description can be translated into a valid input for disjunctive solvers like dlv [15] and GnT [13] using the translation function $\mathrm{Tr_{BLIND}}$. On the other hand, we run into severe problems if all atoms are set subject to minimization. For example, the program Π_I which models an inverter I has three $\langle \emptyset, \emptyset \rangle$-minimal models $M_1 = \{i_I\}$, $M_2 = \{o_I\}$, and $M_3 = \{ab_I\}$. The first two minimal models capture natural explanations given no observations on I, but the third minimal model does not correspond to a Reiter-style minimal diagnosis, as I is faulty according to it. Similar spurious minimal models are also obtained for more complex circuits encoded in this way if all atoms are subject to minimization.

Our first experiments with large combinational circuits showed that our approach is not yet competitive with a special purpose engine [1] which exploits 1-fault assumption. The diagnosis front-end of the dlv system also covers Reiter-style minimal diagnoses [4], but models like the one described above are ruled out by syntactic restrictions. Moreover, contrary to $\mathrm{Tr_{BLIND}}$, the translation used in the front-end yields only a *many-to-one* correspondence between stable models and diagnoses.

As a further application of varying atoms, a specific reduction from quantified Boolean formulas (QBFs) to DLPs [13] can be improved to produce all satisfying assignments for a $2, \exists$-QBF $\exists X \forall Y \phi$ given as input. Due to blind minimization, the current reduction does not yield a one-to-one correspondence between the satisfying assignments of $\exists X \forall Y \phi$ and the stable models of the resulting DLP. However, the validity of $\exists X \forall Y \phi$ is properly captured by the reduction.

To conclude, it might be a good idea to implement varying atoms directly in disjunctive solvers. This is a challenge, as existing algorithms [13,15] rely much on the fact that all atoms are subject to minimization. A further question is how varying and fixed atoms should be incorporated into stable models. Is it enough to consider $\langle V, F \rangle$-minimal models of the Gelfond-Lifschitz reduct [8] or should V and F be dynamically determined? Finally, we remind the reader about a reduction from *prioritized circumscription* to parallel circumscription [16] which implies that even prioritized circumscription can be captured with disjunctive programs using the technique from Section 4.

References

1. P. Baumgartner, P. Fröhlich, U. Furbach, and W. Nejdl. Semantically guided theorem proving for diagnosis applications. In *Proceedings of the 15th International Joint Conference on Artificial Intelligence*, pages 460–465, Nagoya, 1997. Morgan Kaufmann.
2. M. Cadoli, T. Eiter, and G. Gottlob. An efficient method for eliminating varying predicates from a circumscription. *Artificial Intelligence*, 54(2):397–410, 1992.

3. J. de Kleer and K. Konolige. Eliminating the fixed predicates from a circumscription. *Artificial Intelligence*, 39(3):391–398, July 1989.
4. T. Eiter, W. Faber, N. Leone, and G. Pfeifer. The diagnosis frontend of the DLV system. *AI Communications*, 12(1-2):99–111, 1999.
5. T. Eiter and G. Gottlob. On the computational cost of disjunctive logic programming: Propositional case. *Annals of Mathematics and Artificial Intelligence*, 15:289–323, 1995.
6. T. Eiter, G. Gottlob, and H. Veith. Modular logic programming and generalized quantifiers. In J. Dix, U. Furbach, and A. Nerode, editors, *Logic Programming and Nonmonotonic Reasoning*, pages 289–308, Dagstuhl Castle, Germany, July 1997. Springer-Verlag. LNAI 1265.
7. M. Gelfond and V. Lifschitz. Compiling circumscriptive theories into logic programs. In *Proceedings of the 7th National Conference on Artificial Intelligence*, pages 455–449, St. Paul, MN, August 1988. AAAI Press.
8. M. Gelfond and V. Lifschitz. Classical negation in logic programs and disjunctive databases. *New Generation Computing*, 9:365–385, 1991.
9. K. Inoue and C. Sakama. Negation as failure in the head. *Journal of Logic Programming*, 35(1):39–78, 1998.
10. T. Janhunen. On the intertranslatability of non-monotonic logics. *Annals of Mathematics and Artificial Intelligence*, 27(1-4):79–128, 1999.
11. T. Janhunen. On the effect of default negation on the expressiveness of disjunctive rules. In T. Eiter, W. Faber, and M. Truszczy«ski, editors, *Logic Programming and Nonmonotonic Reasoning, Proceedings of the 6th International Conference*, pages 93–106, Vienna, Austria, September 2001. Springer-Verlag. LNAI 2173.
12. T. Janhunen. Translatability and intranslatability results for certain classes of logic programs. Series A: Research report 82, Helsinki University of Technology, Laboratory for Theoretical Computer Science, Espoo, Finland, November 2003.
13. T. Janhunen, I. Niemelä, D. Seipel, P. Simons, and J.-H. You. Unfolding partiality and disjunctions in stable model semantics. *ACM Transactions on Computational Logic*, 2004. Accepted for publication, see http://www.acm.org/tocl/accepted.html.
14. J. Lee and F. Lin. Loop formulas for circumscription. In *Proceedings of the 19th National Conference on Artificial Intelligence*, pages 281–286, San Jose, California, July 2004. AAAI.
15. N. Leone, G. Pfeifer, W. Faber, T. Eiter, G. Gottlob, and F. Scarcello. The DLV system for knowledge representation and reasoning. CoRR: cs.AI/0211004 v2, August 2003.
16. V. Lifschitz. Computing circumscription. In *Proceedings of the 9th International Joint Conference on Artificial Intelligence*, pages 121–127, Los Angeles, California, USA, August 1985. Morgan Kaufmann.
17. V. Lifschitz and H. Turner. Splitting a logic program. In *Proceedings of the 11th International Conference on Logic Programming*, pages 23–37. MIT Press, 1994.
18. J. McCarthy. Circumscription — a form of non-monotonic reasoning. *Artificial Intelligence*, 13:27–39, 1980.
19. Ilkka Niemelä. A tableau calculus for minimal model reasoning. In *Analytic Tableaux and Related Methods: Fifth Workshop on Theorem Proving with Analytic Tableaux and Related Methods*, pages 278–294, 1996. LNCS 1071.
20. T.C. Przymusinski. Stable semantics for disjunctive programs. *New Generation Computing*, 9:401–424, 1991.
21. R. Reiter. A theory of diagnosis from first principles. *Artificial Intelligence*, 32:57–95, 1987.
22. C. Sakama and K. Inoue. Embedding circumscriptive theories in general disjunctive programs. In *Proceedings of the 3rd International Conference on Logic Programming and Nonmonotonic Reasoning*, pages 344–357. Springer-Verlag, 1995.
23. P. Simons. Extending the stable model semantics with more expressive rules. In *Proceedings of the 5th International Conference on Logic Programming and Nonmonotonic Reasoning*, pages 305–316, El Paso, Texas, USA, 1999. Springer-Verlag.

Towards a First Order Equilibrium Logic for Nonmonotonic Reasoning

David Pearce[1]* and Agustín Valverde[2]**

[1] Universidad Rey Juan Carlos (Madrid, Spain)
d.pearce@escet.urjc.es
[2] Universidad de Málaga (Málaga, Spain)
a_valverde@ctima.uma.es

Abstract. Equilibrium logic, introduced in [20], is a conservative extension of answer set semantics for logic programs to the full language of propositional logic. In this paper we initiate the study of first-order variants of equilibrium logic. In particular, we focus on a quantified version $\mathbf{QN}_5$ of the propositional many-valued logic $\mathbf{N}_5$ of here-and-there with strong negation, and define the condition of equilibrium via a minimal model construction. We verify Skolem forms and Herbrand theorems for $\mathbf{QN}_5$ and show that, like its propositional counterpart, the quantified version of equilibrium logic also conservatively extends answer set semantics.

1 Introduction

Equilibrium logic, introduced in [20], is a general purpose propositional formalism for nonmonotonic reasoning with two kinds of negation: strong negation, representing explicit falsity, and weak or intuitionistic negation which allows for the expression of default relationships. One of the main features of equilibrium logic is that, under all the usual classes of logic programs, it is equivalent to reasoning under answer set semantics and therefore amounts to a conservative extension of answer set inference to the full propositional language. With the emergence of answer set solvers such as dlv [15], GnT [13], and smodels [29], answer set programming (ASP) now provides a practical and viable environment for knowledge representation and declarative problem solving. AI applications include planning and diagnosis [2], the management of heterogenous data in information systems,[1] the representation of ontologies in the semantic web [4], as well as compact and fully declarative representations of hard combinatorial problems.[2].

Compared to ASP systems, equilibrium logic is much less well-developed as a practical knowledge representation tool. Nevertheless it can be implemented

---

* Partially supported by CICyT project TIC-2003-9001-C02, URJC project PPR-2003-39 and WASP (IST-2001-37004)
** Partially supported by CICyT project TIC-2003-9001-C01 and Junta de Andalucía project TIC-115.
[1] see the INFOMIX project http://sv.mat.unical.it/infomix/
[2] For examples and a thorough introduction to ASP, see [3]

J.J. Alferes and J. Leite (Eds.): JELIA 2004, LNAI 3229, pp. 147–160, 2004.
© Springer-Verlag Berlin Heidelberg 2004

in different ways. For example a reduction to quantified boolean formulas has been presented, allowing for an implementation in QBF-based systems such as QUIP, [26] . In [23,24] proof systems for equilibrium logic are given which form the basis for a prototype implementation currently being developed at the University of Málaga. The paper [25] presents a polynomial translation of a restricted class of theories in equilibrium logic, called *nested programs*, into disjunctive logic programs and describes an implementation extending dlv: here equilibrium logic is equivalent to the answer set semantics for nested programs described in [17] (though it predates the latter). Aside from its potential as a knowledge representation formalism, equilibrium logic has already proved useful in the study of the logical and mathematical foundations of ASP. For example, it provided the basis for characterising the strong equivalence of logic programs in [16] and the uniform equivalence of programs in [27]. Recently it has been used to characterise synonymous theories [28] and to develop and study transformations that preserve the strong equivalence of logic programs and allow for program simplification in the setting of ASP [22].

Our aim this paper is to initiate the study of first-order versions of equilibrium logic. It is far from obvious that there should be a unique, natural, quantified version of equilibrium logic. In searching for suitable candidates we shall be guided by two main methodological considerations. The first is coherence with respect to the logical features present in the propositional case. That is, bearing in mind the underlying monotonic base logic and the minimal model construction that defines equilibrium, we shall be looking for suitable first-order extensions of the base logic and ways to preserve the central idea behind the construction of intended models. The second consideration concerns answer set programming. Currently, answer set solvers implement a grounding procedure to eliminate free variables prior to model generation and testing. In the propositional case, therefore, equilibrium logic agrees with or 'captures' answer set semantics for ground programs. In the first-order case, we would like to maintain this relation for logic programs and ultimately obtain logical methods for analysing and simplifying programs prior to grounding.

In the propositional case equilibrium logic is based on the nonclassical logic $\mathbf{N}_5$ of here-and-there with strong negation. To our knowledge, first-order versions of $\mathbf{N}_5$, or even of the logic of here-and-there, have not previously been studied in the literature. Thus, a good deal of our work in this paper is devoted to considering different first-order versions of $\mathbf{N}_5$ and selecting a candidate to form the basis for first-order equilibrium logic. We present this logic in §2 and call it $\mathbf{QN}_5$. It can be equivalently represented as a 5-valued logic or as the logic of rooted linear Kripke frames with two elements ('here' and 'there') having constant domains. It permits a straightforward definition of the equilibrium model construction and appears to be adequate as a tool for applications in ASP. Since $\mathbf{QN}_5$ is something of an unknown on the logical landscape, we devote space in §3 to examining some of its basic properties. We look at prenex normal forms, Skolem forms and establish Herbrand theorems in various guises. The remainder of the paper is then organised as follows. In §4 we turn to the proof theory of

$\mathbf{QN_5}$, sketching a sound and complete tableaux calculus. In §5 we provide the minimal model construction that defines equilibrium logic in the first-order case. Then we show that it satisfies the main criteria of adequacy that we mentioned informally above. More precisely: (i) on universal theories the selected models coincide with the propositional equilibrium models of the theories' ground versions; (ii) for logic programs the Herbrand equilibrium models coincide with answer sets. Some consequences of this are briefly discussed and in §6 we conclude by considering related work and some of the main issues to be tackled in the future.

2   First-Order $\mathbf{N_5}$ Logics

For the propositional version of equilibrium logic the reader is referred to [20, 21,24,16]. It is based on the the propositional logic $\mathbf{N_5}$ of here-and-there with strong negation that contains the logical constants: $\wedge$, $\vee$, $\rightarrow$, $\neg, \sim$, standing respectively for conjunction, disjunction, implication, weak (or intuitionistic) negation and strong negation. Presented as a Hilbert-style axiomatic system, the axioms and rules of inference for $\mathbf{N_5}$ are those of intuitionistic logic (see eg [31]) together with:

1. the axiom schema of Łukasiewicz [18]

$$(\neg\alpha \rightarrow \beta) \rightarrow (((\beta \rightarrow \alpha) \rightarrow \beta) \rightarrow \beta) \tag{1}$$

   which characterises the 3-valued here-and-there logic of Heyting [12] and Gödel [8] (hence it is sometimes known as Gödel's 3-valued logic).
2. the following axiom schemata involving strong negation taken from the calculus of Vorob'ev [32,33] (where '$\alpha \leftrightarrow \beta$' abbreviates $(\alpha \rightarrow \beta) \wedge (\beta \rightarrow \alpha)$):

   N1. $\sim (\alpha \rightarrow \beta) \leftrightarrow \alpha \wedge \sim\beta$ **N2.** $\sim(\alpha \wedge \beta) \leftrightarrow \sim\alpha\vee \sim \beta$
   N3. $\sim(\alpha \vee \beta) \leftrightarrow \sim\alpha \wedge \sim\beta$ **N4.** $\sim \sim\alpha \leftrightarrow \alpha$
   N5. $\sim\neg\alpha \leftrightarrow \alpha$ **N6.** (for atomic α) $\sim\alpha \rightarrow \neg\alpha$

As one can see, there are three basic components to this picture: intuitionistic logic, the Łukasiewicz axiom (1) and the Vorob'ev axioms for strong negation. The last of these components can be regarded as essentially a defining characteristic of strong negation and should be preserved in any quantified version.

One, straightforward way to obtain quantified $\mathbf{N_5}$ is therefore to take Nelson's constructive predicate logic with strong negation [19,9] and simply add the Łukasiewicz axiom. This would amount to the following system: (i) axioms and rules of first-order intuitionistic logic; (ii) the axiom schema (1); (iii) the Vorob'ev axioms augmented with the following two schemata:

$$\sim\exists x\alpha \leftrightarrow \forall x\sim\alpha \qquad\qquad \sim\forall x\alpha \leftrightarrow \exists x\sim\alpha \tag{2}$$

A second approach to obtaining a quantified version of $\mathbf{N_5}$ may be called the semantical approach. Nelson's constructive logic has a natural and appealing characterisation in terms of Kripke models. This is the one that gives rise to the term here-and-there. The idea is to take the usual Kripke model semantics for intuitionistic logic but to allow for sentences to be not only constructively verified at possible worlds or stages of the model, but also constructively falsified (equivalently their strong negations are verified), see [9]; in addition one restricts attention to 2-element, here-and-there frames. This leads to the following semantics that we denote by **FOHT**.[3]

We consider a first order language built over a set of *constants*, $\mathcal{C}$, a set of *functions*, $\mathcal{F}$, and a set of *predicates*, $\mathcal{P}$. We denote by $\mathrm{Term}(\mathcal{C}, \mathcal{F})$ the set of ground terms defined from $\mathcal{C}$ and $\mathcal{F}$; we denote by $\mathrm{Atom}(\mathcal{C}, \mathcal{F}, \mathcal{P})$ the set of ground atomic formulas defined from $\mathcal{C}$, $\mathcal{F}$ and $\mathcal{P}$ in the usual way; we denote by $\mathrm{Lit}(\mathcal{C}, \mathcal{F}, \mathcal{P})$ the set of ground *literals*, that is, either ground atomic formulas or the strong negation of ground atomic formulas. If L is an atom, we say that $\sim L$ is the *contrary* of L and *vice versa*. We will use the usual notions of free and bound variable, but we essentially only work with closed formulas or sentences.

An **FOHT**-model is a quadruple $\mathcal{M} = \langle D_h, H, D_t, T \rangle$ such that: D_h and D_t are non-empty sets such that $\mathcal{C} \subseteq D_h \subseteq D_t$; H and T are sets of literals in $\mathrm{Lit}(D_t, \mathcal{F}, \mathcal{P})$ such that $H \subseteq T$, T does not contain contrary literals and H does not contain constants from $D_t \smallsetminus D_h$. We shall define the satisfaction relation $\models$ for "worlds" $\omega \in \{h, t\}$ where $h \leq h$, $t \leq t$ and $h \leq t$ (we use the following notation: $\mathcal{T}_h = \mathrm{Term}(D_h, \mathcal{F})$ and $\mathcal{T}_t = \mathrm{Term}(D_t, \mathcal{F})$):

- For every literal L: $\mathcal{M}, h \models L$ iff $L \in H$ and $\mathcal{M}, t \models L$ iff $L \in T$.
- $\mathcal{M}, \omega \models \varphi \wedge \psi$ iff $\mathcal{M}, \omega \models \varphi$ and $\mathcal{M}, \omega \models \psi$.
- $\mathcal{M}, \omega \models \varphi \vee \psi$ iff $\mathcal{M}, \omega \models \varphi$ or $\mathcal{M}, \omega \models \psi$.
- $\mathcal{M}, \omega \models \varphi \rightarrow \psi$ iff for every $\omega' \geq \omega$, if $\mathcal{M}, \omega' \models \varphi$ then $\mathcal{M}, \omega' \models \psi$.
- $\mathcal{M}, \omega \models \neg\varphi$ iff for no $\omega' \geq \omega$, $\mathcal{M}, \omega' \models \varphi$.
- $\mathcal{M}, \omega \models \forall x A(x)$ iff for every $\omega' \geq \omega$ and every $d \in \mathcal{T}_{\omega'}$, $\mathcal{M}, \omega' \models A(d)$.
- $\mathcal{M}, \omega \models \exists x A(x)$ iff $\mathcal{M}, \omega \models A(d)$ for some $d \in \mathcal{T}_\omega$.
- $\mathcal{M}, \omega \models \sim(\varphi \wedge \psi)$ iff $\mathcal{M}, \omega \models \sim\varphi$ or $\mathcal{M}, \omega \models \sim\psi$.
- $\mathcal{M}, \omega \models \sim(\varphi \vee \psi)$ iff $\mathcal{M}, \omega \models \sim\varphi$ and $\mathcal{M}, \omega \models \sim\psi$.
- $\mathcal{M}, \omega \models \sim(\varphi \rightarrow \psi)$ iff $\mathcal{M}, \omega \models \varphi$ and $\mathcal{M}, \omega \models \sim\psi$.
- $\mathcal{M}, \omega \models \sim\neg\psi$ iff $\mathcal{M}, \omega \models \varphi$.
- $\mathcal{M}, \omega \models \sim\sim\psi$ iff $\mathcal{M}, \omega \models \varphi$.
- $\mathcal{M}, \omega \models \sim\forall x A(x)$ iff $\mathcal{M}, \omega \models \sim A(d)$ for some $d \in \mathcal{T}_\omega$.
- $\mathcal{M}, \omega \models \sim\exists x A(x)$ iff for every $\omega' \geq \omega$ and every $d \in \mathcal{T}_{\omega'}$, $\mathcal{M}, \omega' \models \sim A(d)$.

Truth of a formula in a model is defined as follows: for every formula A, $\mathcal{M} \models A$ iff $\mathcal{M}, h \models A$ and $\mathcal{M}, t \models A$. A formula is valid in **FOHT** if it is true in all models.

If we add the assumption of *constant domains*, namely that in each model $D_h = D_t$, a stronger version of **FOHT** is obtained; for example, in the general case the formula $\forall x(A(x) \vee B) \rightarrow (\forall x A(x) \vee B)$ (B is closed) is not valid, as the following counter-model shows: $\langle \{a\}, \{P(a)\}, \{a, b\}, \{P(a), B\} \rangle$. However in all models such that $D_h = D_t$ the formula $\forall x(A(x) \vee B) \rightarrow (\forall x A(x) \vee B)$ holds. We

---

[3] It is still an open question whether this second approach is equivalent to the first. We hope to clarify the matter in a future study.

denote by **FOHT**$_c$ the logic determined by constant domain models of the form $\langle D, H, D, T \rangle$; we denote them simply by $\langle D, H, T \rangle$ and D is called the *domain* of the model.

2.1   Five-Valued Semantics

A third approach to obtaining a first-order version of $\mathbf{N}_5$ is also semantical. In the propositional case the Kripke semantics is easily characterised using a five-valued matrix: the set of truth values is $\mathbf{5} = \{-2, -1, 0, 1, 2\}$ and 2 is the designated value; the connectives are interpreted as follows: $\wedge$ is the minimum function, $\vee$ is the maximum function, $\sim x = -x$,

$$x \rightarrow y = \begin{cases} 2 & \text{if either } x \leq 0 \text{ or } x \leq y \\ y & \text{otherwise} \end{cases} \quad \text{and} \quad \neg x = \begin{cases} 2 & \text{if } x \leq 0 \\ -x & \text{otherwise} \end{cases}$$

If we add quantifiers using the standard approach for many-valued logics, we obtain a semantics which we can denote by $\mathbf{QN}_5$ as follows: a model is a pair $\langle D, \sigma \rangle$ where $D \supseteq \mathcal{C}$ is non-empty and called the *domain* and $\sigma \colon \text{Atom}(D, \mathcal{F}, \mathcal{P}) \rightarrow \mathbf{5}$ is the *assignment*. If $\mathcal{T} = \text{Term}(D, \mathcal{F})$ the model is extended to closed quantified formulas in the following way:

$$\sigma(\forall x A(x)) = \min\{\sigma(A(t)); t \in \mathcal{T}\} \qquad \sigma(\exists x A(x)) = \max\{\sigma(A(t)); t \in \mathcal{T}\}$$

In the propositional case an $\mathbf{N}_5$-model σ as a truth-value assignment can trivially be converted into a Kripke model $\langle H, T \rangle$, and *vice versa* with the conversion rules shown in the following table:

Table 1.

$$\begin{cases} \sigma(p) = 2 & \text{iff} \quad p \in H \\ \sigma(p) = 1 & \text{iff} \quad p \in T, p \notin H \\ \sigma(p) = 0 & \text{iff} \quad p \notin T, \sim p \notin T \end{cases} \qquad \begin{array}{ll} \sigma(p) = -1 & \text{iff} \quad \sim p \in T, \sim p \notin H \\ \sigma(p) = -2 & \text{iff} \quad \sim p \in H \end{array}$$

In the first-order case, however, the Kripke and the many-valued semantics are not equivalent. Since in any many-valued logic the quantifiers are interpreted as supremum and infimum, it follows that the formulas $\forall x(A(x) \vee B)$ and $\forall x A(x) \vee B$ are equivalent, which we have seen is not the case for the Kripke semantics. However, there is full equivalence with respect to the logic of constant domains.

Theorem 1. *There is a bijection f between **FOHT**$_c$-models and $\mathbf{QN}_5$-models such that for any formula A and **FOHT**$_c$-model $\mathcal{M}$, $\mathcal{M} \models A$ iff $f(\mathcal{M})(A) = 2$. Thus in particular a formula A is valid in **FOHT**$_c$ if and only if is valid in $\mathbf{QN}_5$.*

Proof. The bijection is established by the conversion rules in table 1 applied to ground atoms; by induction is easy to prove that these rules are also valid for any ground formula and that allows us to conclude the result.□

In other words we can equivalently work with Kripke models having constant domains or with the five-valued semantics. In what follows we alternate freely between these two representations, depending on which version is simpler or more intuitive for the task at hand.

3   Some Metatheory for $\mathbf{QN}_5$

For the remainder of this paper we are going to explore $\mathbf{QN}_5$ or the equivalent constant domain logic as our basis for defining a quantified version of equilibrium logic. There are several reasons for this choice. First, as we shall see, it is easy to check that $\mathbf{QN}_5$ possesses several properties that are desirable from the perspective of automated deduction. Indeed, as it is obtained from the many-valued propositional logic by standard means, we can in some cases make use of well-known techniques and methods from many-valued logic to prove properties of $\mathbf{QN}_5$ and to describe a complete proof-theory. Secondly, as we shall show in Theorem 8, the many-valued approach is adequate as a first step towards an extension of answer set semantics, and any other generalisations should agree with it. Further extensions should analyse the intended meaning of quantifiers in general first order logic programs, a topic we postpone for future work.

3.1   Prenex and Skolem Forms

Theorem 2. *In* $\mathbf{QN}_5$ *the following equivalences hold for any closed formula* C:

$$\forall x A(x) \land C \equiv \forall x (A(x) \land C) \qquad \exists x A(x) \land C \equiv \exists x (A(x) \land C)$$
$$\forall x A(x) \lor C \equiv \forall x (A(x) \lor C) \qquad \exists x A(x) \lor C \equiv \exists x (A(x) \lor C)$$
$$\exists x A(x) \to C \equiv \forall x (A(x) \to C) \qquad \forall x A(x) \to C \equiv \exists x (A(x) \to C)$$
$$C \to \forall x A(x) \equiv \forall x (C \to A(x)) \qquad C \to \exists x A(x) \equiv \exists x (C \to A(x))$$
$$\neg \exists x A(x) \equiv \forall x \neg A(x) \qquad \neg \forall x A(x) \equiv \exists x \neg A(x)$$

Proof. The properties of conjunction and disjunction are a consequence of the associative and distributive properties of the operators max and min over finite sets. Additionally, implication is decreasing in the first argument and increasing in the second one and weak negation is decreasing; thus, the monotony of max and min allows us to conclude the last equivalences.□
    As a consequence we have:

Corollary 1. *In* $\mathbf{QN}_5$ *every formula is equivalent to a formula in prenex normal form, ie of the form* $Q_1 x_1 \ldots Q_n x_n A(x_1, \ldots, x_n)$, *where* $Q_i \in \{\forall, \exists\}$ *and* $A(x_1, \ldots, x_n)$ *is a quantifier-free formula.*

Next we turn to satisfiability preserving Skolemization and the associated Herbrand theorem. These results proceed by adding new constants and functions to the language, and for this reason we specify the signature of the logic: $\mathbf{QN}_5(\mathcal{C}, \mathcal{F}, \mathcal{P})$ denotes the logic over the language with signature $(\mathcal{C}, \mathcal{F}, \mathcal{P})$.

Lemma 1.   *1.* $\exists y A(y)$ *is satisfiable in* $\mathbf{QN}_5(\mathcal{C}, \mathcal{F}, \mathcal{P})$ *if and only if* $A(a)$ *is satisfiable in* $\mathbf{QN}_5(\mathcal{C} \cup \{a\}, \mathcal{F}, \mathcal{P})$, *where* $a \notin \mathcal{C}$.

2. $\forall x_1 \ldots \forall x_n \exists y A(y, x_1, \ldots, x_n)$ is satisfiable in $\mathbf{QN_5}(\mathcal{C}, \mathcal{F}, \mathcal{P})$ if and only if the formula $\forall x_1 \ldots \forall x_n A(f(x_1, \ldots, x_n), x_1, \ldots, x_n)$ is satisfiable in $\mathbf{QN_5}(\mathcal{C}, \mathcal{F} \cup \{f\}, \mathcal{P})$, where $f \notin \mathcal{F}$

Proof. We demonstrate only item 2, the other one is similar. Let $\langle D, \sigma \rangle$ be a model of $\forall x_1 \ldots \forall x_n \exists y A(y, x_1, \ldots, x_n)$ in $\mathbf{QN_5}(\mathcal{C}, \mathcal{F}, \mathcal{P})$ and $\mathcal{T} = \mathrm{Term}(D, \mathcal{F})$; then

$$2 = \sigma(\forall x_1 \ldots \forall x_n \exists y A(y, x_1, \ldots, x_n)) = \min_{t_1, \ldots, t_n \in \mathcal{T}} (\max_{t \in \mathcal{T}} \sigma(A(t, t_1, \ldots, t_n))$$

and thus $\max_{t \in \mathcal{T}} \sigma(A(t, t_1, \ldots, t_n)) = 2$ for all $t_1, \ldots, t_n \in \mathcal{T}$; so we can define the operator $\Phi \colon \mathrm{Atom}(D, \mathcal{F} \cup \{f\}, \mathcal{P}) \to \mathrm{Atom}(D, \mathcal{F}, \mathcal{P})$ (and this can be extended to general formulas) that works by replacing recursively every term $f(t_1, \ldots, t_n)$ by a term t such that $\sigma(A(t, t_1, \ldots, t_n)) = 2$. Let $\bar{\sigma}$ be an assignment in $\mathbf{QN_5}(C, \mathcal{F} \cup \{f\}, \mathcal{P})$ defined by $\bar{\sigma}(L) = \sigma(\Phi_f(L))$; it is easy to prove by induction that $\bar{\sigma}(B) = \sigma(\Phi_f(B))$ for every closed formula B and so, if $\mathcal{T}' = \mathrm{Term}(D, \mathcal{F} \cup \{f\})$:

$$
\begin{aligned}
\bar{\sigma}(\forall x_1 \ldots \forall x_n A(f(x_1, \ldots, x_n), x_1, \ldots, x_n)) \\
= \min_{t_1, \ldots, t_n \in \mathcal{T}'} \sigma(\Phi(A(f(t_1, \ldots, t_n), t_1, \ldots, t_n))) \\
\geq \min_{t_1, \ldots, t_n \in \mathcal{T}} \sigma(A(\Phi(f(t_1, \ldots, t_n)), t_1, \ldots, t_n)) = 2
\end{aligned}
$$

Conversely, let $\langle D, \sigma \rangle$ be a model of $\forall x_1 \ldots \forall x_n A(f(x_1, \ldots, x_n), x_1, \ldots, x_n)$:

$$\min_{t_1, \ldots, t_n \in \mathcal{T}'} \sigma(A(f(t_1, \ldots, t_n), t_1, \ldots, t_n)) = 2$$

and let $\Phi \colon D' \to \mathcal{T}^n$ be a bijection, where $D' \cap D = \varnothing$, and its extension to the set of atoms, $\Phi \colon \mathrm{Atom}(D \cup D', \mathcal{F}, \mathcal{P}) \to \mathrm{Atom}(D, \mathcal{F} \cup \{f\}, \mathcal{P})$ replacing every $c \in D'$ by $f(\Phi(c))$. Then the model $\langle D \cup D', \tau \rangle$ is defined by $\tau(L) = \sigma(\Phi(L))$. $\square$

Definition 1. Let A be a formula, $\mathcal{C}_A$ the set of constants in A and $\mathcal{F}_A$ the set of functions in A. The Herbrand models of A are the models in $\mathbf{QN_5}(\mathcal{C}_A, \mathcal{F}_A, \mathcal{P})$ with domain $\mathcal{C}_A$. $H_A = \mathrm{Term}(\mathcal{C}_A, \mathcal{F}_A)$ is called the Herbrand universe of A.

Lemma 2. If $A(x_1, \ldots, x_n)$ is quantifier-free, then $B = \forall x_1 \ldots \forall x_n A(x_1, \ldots, x_n)$ is satisfiable iff it has a Herbrand model.

Proof. If $\langle D, \sigma \rangle$ is a model of B then $H_B = \mathrm{Term}(\mathcal{C}_B, \mathcal{F}_B) \subseteq \mathrm{Term}(D, \mathcal{F}) = \mathcal{T}$. Then the restriction τ of σ to H_B is a model of B:

$$\tau(B) = \min_{t_1, \ldots, t_n \in H_B} \tau(A(t_1, \ldots, t_n)) \geq \min_{t_1, \ldots, t_n \in \mathcal{T}} \sigma(A(t_1, \ldots, t_n)) = 2 \qquad \square$$

Theorem 3 (Herbrand's theorem for satisfiability). Let A be a formula in $\mathbf{QN_5}$, then there is an algorithm for converting A into a prenex formula A^*, with only universal quantifiers, such that A is satisfiable iff and only if A^* is satisfiable by an Herbrand model (of A^*).

Proof. First, the equivalences of Theorem 2 are applied to obtain a prenex formula, A', equivalent with A; then the transformations in Lemma 3 are applied to eliminate every existential quantifier in the prefix of A' (from left to right) introducing fresh constants and functions. The resulting formula is the formula A^* that we are looking for. Applying Lemma 2 concludes the proof.□

Next we turn to validity-preserving Skolemization and its associated Herbrand theorem. We omit the details of the proofs because they are similar to the previous results.

Lemma 3. *1. $\forall y A(y)$ is valid in $\mathbf{QN}_5(\mathcal{C}, \mathcal{F}, \mathcal{P})$ if and only if for some $a \notin \mathcal{C}$, $A(a)$ is valid in $\mathbf{QN}_5(\mathcal{C} \cup \{a\}, \mathcal{F}, \mathcal{P})$.*

2. $\exists x_1 \ldots \exists x_n \forall y A(y, x_1, \ldots, x_n)$ is valid in $\mathbf{QN}_5(\mathcal{C}, \mathcal{F}, \mathcal{P})$ if and only if the formula $\exists x_1 \ldots \exists x_n A(f(x_1, \ldots, x_n), x_1, \ldots, x_n)$ is valid in $\mathbf{QN}_5(\mathcal{C}, \mathcal{F} \cup \{f\}, \mathcal{P})$, where $f \notin \mathcal{F}$

Lemma 4. *If $A(x_1, \ldots, x_n)$ is quantifier free, then $\Phi = \exists x_1 \ldots \exists x_n A(x_1, \ldots, x_n)$ is valid iff it is true in every Herbrand model.*

Theorem 4 (Herbrand's theorem for validity). *Let A be a formula in $\mathbf{QN}_5$; then there is an algorithm to convert A into a prenex formula A^*, with only existential quantifiers, such that A is valid if and only if A^* is true in every Herbrand model (of A^*).*

4   Tableaux System for $\mathbf{QN}_5$

The many-valued semantics allows us to describe a tableaux system for $\mathbf{QN}_5$ based on *signed formulas*; in [24] a propositional tableaux calculus was introduced and will be extended here to the quantified version. The nodes in the tableaux are closed formulas labelled with a set of truth values, $S{:}\varphi$ (this construction is called a *signed formula*). In fact, we only need the following signs:

Table 2. Tableaux expansion rules in $\mathbf{N}_5$ for $\rightarrow$, $\forall$ and $\exists$. For $\wedge$, $\vee$, $\sim$ and $\neg$, the standard expansion rules for regular connectives are applied.

$$
\begin{array}{|c|c|c|c|}
\hline
\dfrac{\{2\}{:}\varphi \rightarrow \psi}{\{\leq 0\}{:}\varphi \mid \{2\}{:}\psi \mid \{\leq 1\}{:}\varphi} & \dfrac{\{\leq,1\}{:}\varphi \rightarrow \psi}{\{\geq 1\}{:}\varphi \quad \{2\}{:}\varphi} & \dfrac{\{\geq 1\}{:}\varphi \rightarrow \psi}{\{\leq 0\}{:}\varphi \mid \{\geq 1\}{:}\psi} & \dfrac{\{\leq 0\}{:}\varphi \rightarrow \psi}{\{\geq 1\}{:}\varphi} \\
\hline
\end{array}
$$

$$
\dfrac{\{2\}{:}\varphi \rightarrow \psi}{\{\leq 0\}{:}\varphi \;\Big|\; \{2\}{:}\psi \;\Big|\; \begin{array}{c}\{\leq 1\}{:}\varphi \\ \{\geq 1\}{:}\psi\end{array}}
\qquad
\dfrac{\{\leq,1\}{:}\varphi \rightarrow \psi}{\begin{array}{c}\{\geq 1\}{:}\varphi \quad \{2\}{:}\varphi \\ \{\leq 0\}{:}\psi \mid \{\leq 1\}{:}\psi\end{array}}
\qquad
\dfrac{\{\geq 1\}{:}\varphi \rightarrow \psi}{\{\leq 0\}{:}\varphi \mid \{\geq 1\}{:}\psi}
\qquad
\dfrac{\{\leq 0\}{:}\varphi \rightarrow \psi}{\begin{array}{c}\{\geq 1\}{:}\varphi \\ \{\leq 0\}{:}\psi\end{array}}
$$

$$
\dfrac{\{\geq 0\}{:}\varphi \rightarrow \psi}{\{\leq 0\}{:}\varphi \mid \{\geq 0\}{:}\psi}
\qquad
\dfrac{\{\leq -1\}{:}\varphi \rightarrow \psi}{\begin{array}{c}\{\geq 1\}{:}\varphi \\ \{\leq -1\}{:}\psi\end{array}}
\qquad
\dfrac{\{\geq -1\}{:}\varphi \rightarrow \psi}{\{\leq 0\}{:}\varphi \mid \{\geq -1\}{:}\psi}
\qquad
\dfrac{\{-2\}{:}\varphi \rightarrow \psi}{\begin{array}{c}\{\geq 1\}{:}\varphi \\ \{-2\}{:}\psi\end{array}}
$$

$$
\dfrac{\{\leq i\}{:}\exists x \phi(x)}{\{\leq i\}{:}\phi(t)}
\qquad
\dfrac{\{\geq i\}{:}\exists x \phi(x)}{\{\geq i\}{:}\phi(d)}
\qquad
\dfrac{\{\geq i\}{:}\forall x \phi(x)}{\{\geq i\}{:}\phi(t)}
\qquad
\dfrac{\{\leq i\}{:}\forall x \phi(x)}{\{\leq i\}{:}\varphi(d)}
$$

where d is fresh parameter and t is any term.

$\{\leq i\} = \{j \in 5 \mid j \leq i\}$, $\{\geq i\} = \{j \in 5 \mid j \geq i\}$ (we abbreviate $\{-2\} = \{\leq -2\}$ and $\{2\} = \{\geq 2\}$).

As usual, we define recursively the concept of tableau: an initial tableau is defined and then expansion rules are provided to generate further tableaux. More details on tableaux systems for many-valued logics and a general method for proving their soundness and completeness can be found in [10].

Definition 2. *Let* $\Pi = \{\varphi_1, \ldots, \varphi_n\}$ *be a set of formulas and* ψ *a formula.*

1. *The tree*
$$\begin{cases} \{2\}{:}\varphi_1 \\ \quad\cdots \\ \{2\}{:}\varphi_n \\ \{\leq 1\}{:}\psi \end{cases}$$
is called the initial tableau *for* (Π, ψ).

2. *If* $\mathfrak{T}$ *is a tableau for* (Π, ψ) *and* $\mathfrak{T}'$ *is the tree obtained from* $\mathfrak{T}$ *applying one of the expansion rules in Table 2, then* $\mathfrak{T}'$ *is a tableau for* (Π, ψ).
3. *A branch* B *in a tableau* $\mathfrak{T}$ *is called* closed *if it contains a variable* p *with two signs,* $S{:}p$, $S'{:}p$, *such that* $S \cap S' = \varnothing$.
4. *A tableau* $\mathfrak{T}$ *is called* closed *if every branch is closed.*

Theorem 5 (Soundness and completeness of the tableaux system).
The inference $\varphi_1, \ldots, \varphi_n \models \psi$ *is valid if and only if there exists a closed tableau for* $(\{\varphi_1, \ldots, \varphi_n\}, \psi)$.

5   Equilibrium in Quantified N_5

In the propositional case equilibrium logic is most easily characterised by a simple minimal model condition on $\mathbf{N}_5$ Kripke models. If we mirror this condition in the quantified case, we are led to consider a partial ordering $\trianglelefteq$ on $\mathbf{FOHT}_c$ models.

Definition 3. *Given any two* $\mathbf{FOHT}_c$ *models* $\mathcal{M} = \langle D, H, T\rangle$ *and* $\mathcal{M}' = \langle D', H', T'\rangle$, *we set* $\mathcal{M} \trianglelefteq \mathcal{M}$ *if* $D = D', T = T'$ *and* $H \subseteq H'$.

Definition 4. *Let* Π *be a set of first-order* $\mathbf{N}_5$ *formulas and* $\langle D, H, T\rangle$ *a model of* Π.

1. $\langle D, H, T\rangle$ *is said to be* total *if* $H = T$.
2. $\langle D, H, T\rangle$ *is said to be an* equilibrium *model of* Π *if it is minimal under* $\trianglelefteq$ *among models of* Π, *and it is total.*

In other words a model $\langle D, H, T\rangle$ of Π is in equilibrium if it is total and there is no model $\langle D, H', T\rangle$ of Π with $H' \subset H$.

The same property can be equivalently expressed using the many-valued semantics. Let Π be a set of formulas in $(\mathcal{C}, \mathcal{F}, \mathcal{P})$. In $\mathbf{QN}_5$, the model σ of Π is total if $\sigma(L) \in \{-2, 0, 2\}$ for all ground literal L; and the ordering $\sigma_1 \trianglelefteq \sigma_2$ among models σ_1 and σ_2 of Π holds iff for every literal L in $\mathrm{Lit}(\mathcal{C}, \mathcal{F}, \mathcal{P})$ the following properties hold:

1. $\sigma_1(L) = 0$ if and only if $\sigma_2(L) = 0$.
2. If $\sigma_1(L) \geq 1$, then $\sigma_1(L) \leq \sigma_2(L)$
3. If $\sigma_1(L) \leq -1$, then $\sigma_1(L) \geq \sigma_2(L)$

This yields characterisations of total model and equilibrium model, clearly equivalent to the earlier one.

5.1   Equilibrium Logic and Answer Set Semantics

We assume that the reader is familiar with answer set semantics for logic programs as described in [7,17]. In the propositional case equilibrium logic generalises answer set semantics in the following sense. For all the usual classes of logic programs, including normal, disjunctive and nested programs, equilibrium models correspond to answer sets. The 'translation' from the syntax of programs to $\mathbf{N}_5$ propositional formulas is the trivial one, eg. a ground rule of a disjunctive program of the form

$$K_1 \vee \ldots \vee K_k \leftarrow L_1, \ldots, L_m, not L_{m+1}, \ldots, not L_n$$

where the L_i and K_j are literals corresponds to the $\mathbf{N}_5$ sentence

$$L_1 \wedge \ldots \wedge L_m \wedge \neg L_{m+1} \wedge \ldots \wedge \neg L_n \to K_1 \vee \ldots \vee K_k$$

Theorem 6 ([20,16]). *For any ground logic program Π, an $\mathbf{N}_5$ model $\langle T, T \rangle$ is an equilibrium model of Π if and only if T is an answer set of Π.*

Two propositional theories Π and Π' are said to be *logically equivalent*, in symbols $\Pi \equiv \Pi'$, if they have the same $\mathbf{N}_5$ models, and simply *equivalent* if they have the same equilibrium models. They are said to be *strongly* equivalent, in symbols $\Pi \equiv_s \Pi'$, if, for any Σ, $\Pi \cup \Sigma$ is equivalent to $\Pi' \cup \Sigma$. An important property is the following.

Theorem 7 ([16]). *Any two theories Π and Π' are strongly equivalent iff they are logically equivalent, ie. $\Pi \equiv_s \Pi'$ iff $\Pi \equiv \Pi'$.*

Let us now turn to the situation in the first-order case. We are going to consider *universal* theories. A first-order $\mathbf{N}_5$ theory Π in some signature $(\mathcal{C}, \mathcal{F}, \mathcal{P})$ is said to be *universal* if Π is $\mathbf{QN}_5$ equivalent to a set of sentences in prenex form all of whose quantifiers are universal. Let Π be a universal theory (assumed to be presented in prenex form) in a signature $(\mathcal{C}, \mathcal{F}, \mathcal{P})$. Let $D \supseteq \mathcal{C}$.

We define the *grounding* of Π with respect to D as $g(\Pi, D) = \bigcup_{B \in \Pi} g(B, D)$

where

$$g(\forall x_1 \ldots \forall x_n A(x_1, \ldots, x_n), D) = \{A(t_1, \ldots, t_n); t_1, \ldots, t_n \in \text{Term}(D, \mathcal{F})\}$$

Clearly, any grounding of a first-order theory Π can be represented as a (possibly infinite) theory in propositional $\mathbf{N}_5$ logic and so we can now relate the quantified version of equilibrium logic for universal theories to the propositional equilibrium logic of their ground versions.

Lemma 5. *Let Π be a universal theory in $(\mathcal{C}, \mathcal{F}, \mathcal{P})$. Then $\langle D, H, T \rangle \models \Pi$ iff $\langle H, T \rangle$ is a propositional $\mathbf{N}_5$-model of $g(\Pi, D)$.*

Proof. Assume that the sentences of Π are presented in prenex form with universal quantifiers. By the semantics for $\mathbf{QN}_5$ we have that

$$2 = \sigma(\forall x_1 \ldots \forall x_n A(x_1, \ldots, x_n)) = \min\{\sigma(A(t_1, \ldots, t_n)) \mid t_1, \ldots, t_n \in \mathcal{T}\}$$
$$\Leftrightarrow \sigma(A(t_1, \ldots, t_n)) = 2 \text{ for all } t_1, \ldots, t_n \in \mathcal{T}^n$$
$$\Leftrightarrow \sigma \models g(\forall x_1 \ldots \forall x_n A(x_1, \ldots, x_n), D) \qquad \square$$

From this and the definition of equilibrium model we obtain immediately:

Theorem 8. *Let Π be a universal theory in $(\mathcal{C}, \mathcal{F}, \mathcal{P})$ and let $\langle D, T, T \rangle$ be a total model of Π. Then $\langle D, T, T \rangle$ is an equilibrium model of Π iff $\langle T, T \rangle$ is a propositional equilibrium model of $g(\Pi, D)$.*

Combining this property with that of Theorem 6 we can relate quantified equilibrium logic to the answer set semantics of logic programs. The rules of any logic program are interpreted as holding for all values of the free variables in the Herbrand universe. Hence any program (disjunctive, nested, etc) for which answer set semantics is defined can be regarded as the universal closure of the translation of the program *rules* into first-order $\mathbf{N}_5$. Therefore we can identify the equilibrium models of a logic program with the equilibrium models of the universal closure of Π, which is clearly a universal theory. If we make the standard *domain closure assumption*, then it is natural to restrict attention to the Herbrand models of a program Π. Recall that by Lemma 2 every consistent universal theory has an Herbrand model. We obtain:

Corollary 2. *Let Π be a logic program in the signature $(\mathcal{C}, \mathcal{F}, \mathcal{P})$. A total Herbrand model $\langle \mathcal{C}, T, T \rangle$ of the universal closure of Π is an equilibrium model of Π iff T is an answer set of Π.*

Proof. Immediate from Theorem 8 together with the fact that the answer sets of a program Π with variables are identified with the answer sets of the grounding of Π with respect to the Herbrand universe of Π. The latter coincides with $g(\Pi, \mathcal{C})$ defined above. Applying Theorem 6 completes the argument. $\square$

Let Π_1 and Π_2 be $\mathbf{QN}_5$ equivalent theories in $(\mathcal{C}, \mathcal{F}, \mathcal{P})$. Then clearly the ground versions of Π_1 and Π_2 are equivalent in propositional $\mathbf{N}_5$, for any groundings. This leads to the following observation which follows from Lemma 5 and Theorem 7.

Corollary 3. *Let Π_1, Π_2 be logic programs (with variables) in the signature $(\mathcal{C}, \mathcal{F}, \mathcal{P})$. Π_1 and Π_2 are $\mathbf{QN}_5$ equivalent iff for any $D \supseteq \mathcal{C}$, $g(\Pi_1, D) \equiv_s g(\Pi_2, D)$.*

The latter condition amounts to a kind of strong equivalence for open programs, for which logical equivalence in $\mathbf{QN}_5$ provides a necessary and sufficient condition. Corollaries 2 and 3 also suggest that, as hoped, the logic $\mathbf{QN}_5$ may play a role not only in extending ASP but also in its implementation. In particular, any transformation of a program with variables that leads to an $\mathbf{QN}_5$-equivalent program preserves answer sets in a strong sense. This suggests that logical inference in $\mathbf{QN}_5$ may be used as a tool for program transformation and simplification prior to grounding.

6   Related Work and Concluding Remarks

Unlike in the propositional case ([14]), the study of intermediate predicate logics with strong negation is largely uncharted territory. A recent exception is the work of [11] who investigate the constant domain Kripke semantics for certain special cases, including general linear frames, but not specifically treating the two-element frames of the here-and-there logic. The authors are interested in an extension of the strong negation axioms and this may be one reason why they are led to develop a quite complex and non-standard proof theory. In the literature on many-valued logics, it seems that the Gödel predicate logics have mainly been studied in the infinite-valued or fuzzy case, see eg. [1], rather than in the three-valued case, even without the addition of strong negation. To our knowledge in none of these areas have nonmonotonic logics been previously built on the underlying nonclassical base logic.

Our work in this paper is a natural development out of our previous work on propositional equilibrium logic. By choosing as a first step the many-valued semantics, we were able to extend both the model theory and the tableaux-based proof theory for propositional $\mathbf{N}_5$ in a natural manner. We showed that the resulting first-order logic, $\mathbf{QN}_5$, enjoys several properties, including Skolem forms and Herbrand theorems, that are important in automated reasoning. Moreover in this logic equilibrium models admit a very simple characterisation. As we saw, they bear a natural relation to the old equilibrium semantics in the propositional case, when ground versions of universal theories are considered. In the same manner the new logic extends answer set semantics for all the usual kinds of logic programs.

In this paper we have not attempted to provide algorithms for computing equilibrium models, and this remains a major challenge for the future. Among previous work we know of on first-order representations of stable models, the most important appears to be that of Eiter, Lu and Subrahmanian [5]. That work does provide some algorithms for computing first-order stable models and some discussion of implementation methodology. These are issues that we hope to address in the future. However, even at this early stage, there is an important difference in our approach compared to that of [5]: ours is anchored in a logical approach to stable reasoning rather than a purely operational one. Consequently, even if many details of the underlying logic remain open for further study, we can already be fairly confident that proof methods and techniques of automated deduction in nonclassical logics will be useful for computing and for understanding the first-order nonmonotonic systems we are interested in. Even now we have seen how inference in $\mathbf{QN}_5$ might be applied for program simplification.

Aside from work on proof theory and algorithms, we expect future research to tackle a range of other issues including the metatheory of $\mathbf{QN}_5$, alternative definitions of equilibrium, other characterisations and properties of the equilibrium logic and examples of how it might be applied beyond the sphere of logic programs.

References

1. M. Baaz, A. Ciabattoni, and C.G. Fermüller. Herbrand's theorem for Prenex Gödel logic and its consequences for theorem proving. In *Proc. of LPAR 2001*, LNCS 2250, pp. 201–216. Springer, 2001.
2. M. Balduccini, M. Gelfond, R. Watson, and M. Nogueira. The USA-Advisor: A case study in answer set planning. In *Proc. of LPNMR 2001*, LNCS 2173, pp. 439–444. Springer, 2001.
3. C. Baral. *Knowlewdge Representation, Reasoning and Declarative Problem Solving*. Cambridge University Press, 2003.
4. F. Calimeri, S. Galizia, M. Ruffolo, and P. Rullo. Enhancing disjunctive logic programming for ontology specification. In *Proc. of International Joint Conference on Declarative Programming, AGP'03*. Univ. degli Studi di Reggio Calabria, Italy, September 2003.
5. T. Eiter, J. Lu, and V.S. Subrahmanian. A first-order representation of stable models. *AI Communications*, 1:53–73, 1998.
6. M. Gelfond and V. Lifschitz. The stable model semantics for logic programming. In *Proc. of ICLP'88*, pp. 1070–1080, 1988. The MIT Press.
7. M. Gelfond and V. Lifschitz. Classical negation in logic programs and disjunctive databases. *New Generation Computing*, 9:365–385, 1991.
8. K. Gödel. Zum intuitionistischen aussagenkalkül. *Anzeiger der Akademie der Wissenschaften Wien, mathematisch, naturwissenschaftliche Klasse*, 69:65–66, 1932.
9. Y. Gurevich. Intuitionistic logic with strong negation. *Studia Logica*, 36(1–2):49–59, 1977.
10. R. Hähnle. *Automated Deduction in Multiple-Valued Logics*, volume 10 of *International Series of Monographs on Computer Science*. Oxford University Press, 1994.
11. I. Hasuo and R. Kashima. Kripke completeness of first-order constructive logics with strong negation. *Logic Journal of the IGPL*, 11(6):615–646, 2003.
12. A. Heyting. Die formalen regeln der intuitionistischen logik. *Sitzungsberichte der Preussischen Akademie der Wissenschaften, Physikalisch-mathematische Klasse*, pp. 42–56, 1930.
13. T. Janhumen, I. Niemelä, D. Seipel, P. Simons, and J.-H. You. Unfolding partiality and disjunctions in stable model semantics. CoRR: cs.AI/0303009, March 2003.
14. M. Kracht. On extensions of intermediate logics by strong negation. *Journal of Philosophical Logic*, 27(1):49–73, 1998.
15. N. Leone, G. Pfeifer, W. Faber, T. Eiter, G. Gottlob, S. Perri, and F. Scarcello. The dlv system for knowledge representation and reasoning. CoRR: cs.AI/0211004, September 2003.
16. V. Lifschitz, D. Pearce, and A. Valverde. Strongly equivalent logic programs. *ACM Transactions on Computational Logic*, 2(4):526–541, October 2001.
17. V. Lifschitz, L.R. Tang, and H. Turner. Nested expressions in logic programs. *Annals of Mathematics and Artificial Intelligence*, 25(3–4):369–389, 1999.

18. J. Łukasiewicz. Die logik und das grundlagenproblem. In *Les entretiens de Zûrich sur les fondements et la méthode des sciences mathématiques (Zûrich, 1938)*, pp. 82–100, 1941.

19. D. Nelson. Constructible falsity. *Journal of Symbolic Logic*, 14(2):16–26, 1949.

20. D. Pearce. A new logical characterization of stable models and answer sets. In *Proc. of NMELP 96*, LNCS 1216, pp. 57–70. Springer, 1997.

21. D. Pearce. From here to there: Stable negation in logic programming. In Dov Gabbay and Heinrich Wansing, editors, *What is Negation?*, pp. 161–181. Kluwer Academic Pub., 1999.

22. D. Pearce. Simplifying logic programs under answer set semantics. In Vladimir Lifschtiz and Bart Demoen, editors, *Proc. of ICLP04*. Springer, 2004 (to appear).

23. D. Pearce, I.P. de Guzmán, and A. Valverde. Computing equilibrium models using signed formulas. In *Proc. of CL2000*, LNCS 1861, pp. 688–703. Springer, 2000.

24. D. Pearce, I.P. de Guzmán, and A. Valverde. A tableau calculus for equilibrium entailment. In *Proc. of TABLEAUX 2000*, LNAI 1847, pp. 352–367. Springer, 2000.

25. D. Pearce, V. Sarsakov, T. Schaub, H. Tompits, and S. Woltran. A polynomial translation of logic programs with nested expressions into disjunctive logic programs: Preliminary report. In *Proc. of ICLP 2002*, LNCS 2401, pp. 405–420. Springer, 2002.

26. D. Pearce, H. Tompits, and S. Woltran. Encodings for equilibrium logic and logic programs with nested expressions. In *Proc. of EPIA 2001*, LNCS 2258, pp. 306–320. Springer, 2001.

27. D. Pearce and A. Valverde. Uniform equivalence for equilibrium logic and logic programs. In *Proc. of LPNMR'04*, LNAI 2923, pp. 194–206. Springer, 2004.

28. D. Pearce and A. Valverde. Synonymous theories in answer set programming and equilibrium logic. In *Proc. of ECAI 2004 (Valencia, Spain)*, 2004 (to appear).

29. P. Simons, I. Niemelä, and T. Soininen. Extending and implementing the stable model semantics. *Artificial Intelligence*, 138(1–2):181–234, 2002.

30. Y.S. Smetanich. On completeness of a propositional calculus with an additional operation of one variable (in russian). *Trudy Moscovskogo Matematiceskogo Obscestova*, 9:357–372, 1960.

31. D. van Dalen. Intuitionistic logic. In Dov Gabbay and Franz Guenther, editors, *Handbook of Philosophical Logic, Volume III: Alternatives in Classical Logic*, Dordrecht, 1986. D. Reidel Publishing Co.

32. N.N. Vorob'ev. A constructive propositional calculus with strong negation (in russian). *Doklady Akademii Nauk SSR*, 85:465–468, 1952.

33. N.N. Vorob'ev. The problem of deducibility in constructive propositional calculus with strong negation (in russian). *Doklady Akademii Nauk SSR*, 85:689–692, 1952.

Characterizations for Relativized Notions of Equivalence in Answer Set Programming[*]

Stefan Woltran

Institut für Informationssysteme 184/3,Technische Universität Wien,
Favoritenstraße 9-11, A-1040 Vienna, Austria
stefan@kr.tuwien.ac.at

Abstract. Recent research in nonmonotonic logic programming focuses on alternative notions of equivalence. In particular, strong and uniform equivalence are both proposed as useful tools to optimize (parts of) a logic program. More specifically, given a set P of program rules and a possible optimization Q, strong (resp. uniform) equivalence requires that adding any set S of rules (resp. facts) to P and Q simultaneously results in equivalent programs, i.e., $P \cup S$ and $Q \cup S$ possess the same stable models. However, in practice it is often necessary to relax this condition in such a way, that dedicated internal atoms in P or Q are no longer allowed to occur in the possible extensions S. In this paper, we consider these relativized notions of both uniform and strong equivalence and provide semantical characterizations by generalizing the notions of UE- and SE-modelhood. These new characterizations capture all notions of equivalence including ordinary equivalence in a uniform way. Finally, we analyze the complexity of the introduced equivalence tests for the important classes of normal and disjunctive logic programs. As a by-product, we reduce the tests for relativized equivalences to ordinary equivalence between two programs. These reductions may serve as a basis for implementation.

1 Introduction

Recent research in nonmonotonic logic programming focuses on different notions of equivalence between two logic programs. Besides the traditional notion of (ordinary) equivalence, i.e., checking whether two programs P and Q possess the same stable models, the more restrictive notions of strong [15,29,23,17,4,3] and uniform equivalence [6, 24,7,8] have been investigated. Formally, two programs P and Q are strongly equivalent (resp. uniformly equivalent), if, for any set S of rules (resp. atoms), the programs $P \cup S$ and $Q \cup S$ are equivalent in the ordinary sense. These notions have been proposed as a useful tool to change or optimize parts of logic programs avoiding an analysis of the whole program [29,22,7]. Indeed, if a program P contains a subprogram Q which is strongly equivalent to a program Q', then one may replace Q in P by Q', in particular if the resulting program is simpler to evaluate than the original one. Semantical characterizations as strong-equivalence models (SE-models [29]) or uniform-equivalence models (UE-models [6]) provide valuable tools for these purposes.

---

[*] Supported by the Austrian Science Fund (FWF) under project P15068-INF and by the European Commission under projects FET-2001-37004 WASP and IST-2001-33570 INFOMIX.

However, in practice it is often convenient to relax the condition that *arbitrary* rules or facts are considered to be assigned to S. In particular, one wants to *exclude* dedicated atoms from the possible extension S. Such atoms may play the role of internal atoms in the compared program modules Q and Q', and are not considered to appear anywhere else in the complete program P.

Formally, we define *strong* (resp. *uniform*) *equivalence relative to a given set of atoms* A between two programs P and Q as the test whether, for all sets of rules S over A (resp. facts $S \subseteq A$), $P \cup S$ and $Q \cup S$ have the same stable models.[1]

Relativizing uniform equivalence has already been considered in the context of DAT-ALOG, where the notions of uniform equivalence and (DATALOG)-equivalence are as follows: Two DATALOG programs P and Q are uniformly equivalent [18,26] iff, for any set A of atoms, $P \cup A$ and $Q \cup A$ have the same output; P and Q are (DATALOG)-equivalent iff, for any set S of external atoms (an atom is external if it does not occur in any rule head), $P \cup S$ and $Q \cup S$ have the same output. Interestingly, uniform equivalence between DATALOG (Horn) programs is decidable [26], while DATALOG-equivalence is known to be undecidable [27] for this class of programs. Indeed, the latter notion can be seen as a special case of relativized uniform equivalence. This observation motivates to analyze the computational complexity of relativized notions of equivalence also in the propositional case, which we are interested in here.

Our main results can be summarized as follows:

1. For both strong and uniform relativized equivalence we provide suitable *semantical characterizations* by generalizing SE-models as well as UE-models. Our new characterizations of relativized SE- and UE-models allow to capture all considered notions of equivalence (including ordinary equivalence) in a uniform way.
2. We show that relativized strong equivalence shares an important property with general strong equivalence, viz. that constraining the rules in the possible extensions to a very simple syntactical form does not lead to a different concept.
3. We provide a reduction of the tests for relativized equivalences to ordinary equivalence between two programs. This may serve as a basis for implementation.
4. Concerning complexity, we show that relativized uniform equivalence has the same worst-case complexity as general uniform equivalence, for both normal (coNP-completeness) and disjunctive logic programs (Π_2^P-completeness); and that relativized strong equivalence has the same worst-case complexity as general strong equivalence in the case of normal logic programs, namely coNP-completeness.
5. Between disjunctive logic programs P and Q, the complexity of strong equivalence relative to a set of atoms A is shown to remain in coNP, whenever the number of atoms in P and Q not contained in A is bounded by a constant; in general, the task is Π_2^P-complete.

A general notion of equivalence has also been introduced by Inoue and Sakama [12]. In their framework, called *update equivalence*, one can exactly specify a set of arbitrary rules which may be added to the programs under consideration and, furthermore, a set of rules which may be deleted. However, for this explicit enumeration of rules it seems more

---

[1] The notion of strong equivalence relative to a given set of atoms was suggested by Lin in [17] but not further investigated.

complicate to suitably extend the important characterizations of (generalized variants of) SE-models and UE-models in a reasonable way to that approach.

2   Preliminaries

We deal with propositional disjunctive logic programs, containing *rules* r (over a set of atoms At) of the form

$$a_1 \vee \cdots \vee a_l \leftarrow b_1, \ldots, b_m, not\, b_{m+1}, \ldots, not\, b_n, \tag{1}$$

($l \geq 0$, $n \geq m \geq 0$), where all a_i, b_j are from At, and *not* denotes default negation. A rule r is *normal*, if $l \leq 1$; *unary* if $l = 1$ and $m = n \leq 1$; a *fact*, if $l = 1$ and $m = n = 0$. For facts, we sometimes write a instead of $a \leftarrow$. The *head* of r is the set $H(r) = \{a_1, \ldots, a_l\}$; the *body* of r is $B(r) = \{b_1, \ldots, b_m, not\, b_{m+1}, \ldots, not\, b_n\}$. We also define $B^+(r) = \{b_1, \ldots, b_m\}$ and $B^-(r) = \{b_{m+1}, \ldots, b_n\}$.

A *disjunctive logic program* (DLP) over At, or simply a *program*, is a finite set of rules over At. A DLP P is called a *normal logic program* (NLP) (resp. *unary program*) if every rule in P is normal (resp. unary). The set of all atoms occurring in a program P is denoted by $atm(P)$.

We recall the stable-model semantics for DLPs [11,25]. Let I be an *interpretation*, i.e., a set of atoms. An atom a is *true under* I iff $a \in I$, and *false under* I otherwise. I *satisfies* a rule r, denoted $I \models r$, iff $I \cap H(r) \neq \emptyset$, whenever $B^+(r) \subseteq I$ and $I \cap B^-(r) = \emptyset$ jointly hold. Furthermore, I is a *model* of a program P, denoted $I \models P$, iff $I \models r$, for all $r \in P$. Note that the empty program has any interpretation as its model. The *Gelfond-Lifschitz reduct* of a program P *relative to* a set of atoms I is the program $P^I = \{H(r) \leftarrow B^+(r) \mid r \in P, B^-(r) \cap I = \emptyset\}$. An interpretation I is a *stable model* of a program P iff I is a *minimal model* (under set inclusion) of P^I. An equivalent characterization of stable models is as follows: I is a stable model of a program P, iff $I \models P$ and for each $J \subset I$, $J \not\models P^I$. The set of all stable models of P is denoted by $\mathcal{SM}(P)$.

Under stable semantics, two DLPs P and Q are regarded as equivalent, denoted $P \equiv Q$, iff $\mathcal{SM}(P) = \mathcal{SM}(Q)$. The more restrictive forms of *strong equivalence* and *uniform equivalence* are as follows:

Definition 1. *Let P and Q be two DLPs. Then,*

(i)   *P and Q are strongly equivalent, denoted $P \equiv_s Q$, iff, for any set R of rules, $P \cup R \equiv Q \cup R$;*

(ii)   *P and Q are uniformly equivalent, denoted $P \equiv_u Q$, iff, for any set F of facts, $P \cup F \equiv Q \cup F$.*

As an example, consider the two programs

$$P = \{a \vee b \leftarrow; a \leftarrow b; b \leftarrow a; \leftarrow not\, c\}; \quad \text{and}$$
$$P' = \{a \leftarrow not\, b; b \leftarrow not\, a; a \leftarrow b; b \leftarrow a; \leftarrow not\, c\}.$$

The only difference between P and P' is that $a \vee b \leftarrow$ is replaced by the two rules $a \leftarrow not\, b; b \leftarrow not\, a$. Although, P and P' are equivalent (both have no stable model, since c cannot be derived), it can be checked that $P \not\equiv_u P'$ holds. Thus, $P \not\equiv_s P'$ holds, as well. In particular, it suffices to add a fact c; then, $P \cup \{c\}$ has $\{a, b, c\}$ as a stable model, while $P' \cup \{c\}$ has no stable model.

Both uniform and strong equivalence enjoy interesting semantical characterizations [15,28,29,6].

Definition 2. *A pair (X, Y) of interpretations such that $X \subseteq Y$ is called an SE-interpretation. An SE-interpretation (X, Y) is an SE-model of a program P, if $Y \models P$ and $X \models P^Y$.*

Proposition 1 ([28,29]). *Two programs P and Q are strongly equivalent iff they possess the same set of SE-models.*

Recently, the following pendant to SE-models, characterizing uniform equivalence for (finite) logic programs, has been defined [6].

Definition 3. *Let P be a program and (X, Y) an SE-model of P. Then, (X, Y) is an UE-model of P iff, for every SE-model (X', Y) of P, it holds that $X \subset X'$ implies $X' = Y$.*

Proposition 2 ([6]). *Two programs P and Q are uniformly equivalent iff they possess the same set of UE-models.*

To check strong or uniform equivalence between two programs P and Q, it is obviously sufficient to consider SE-interpretations (X, Y) over $atm(P \cup Q)$, i.e., with $X \subseteq Y \subseteq atm(P \cup Q)$. We implicitly make use of this simplification when convenient.

Recall our example programs P and P'. The SE-models (over $\{a, b, c\}$) of the program P are given by[2] (abc, abc), (ab, abc); whilst the program P' has two additional SE-models (c, abc), $(\emptyset, abc)$. Hence, P and P' are not strongly equivalent. Concerning uniform equivalence, note that the pair $(\emptyset, abc)$ is not an UE-model of P', since (ab, abc) (or (c, abc), alternatively) is an SE-model of P' preventing $(\emptyset, abc)$ to be a UE-model of P' by definition. Still, P and P' have different UE-models, i.e., (abc, abc), (ab, abc) for P and additionally (c, abc) for P'. By Proposition 2, this yields $P \not\equiv_u P'$ as claimed above.

Finally, we review the complexity results for equivalence testing in logic programming for the propositional case.

Proposition 3. *For normal logic programs, the problems of ordinary, strong, or uniform equivalence are complete for the class coNP. In the case of disjunctive logic programs, the complexity remains coNP-complete for strong equivalence, while deciding uniform or ordinary equivalence is Π_2^P-complete for DLPs.*

The results for ordinary equivalence can be obtained from results by Marek and Truszczyński [19] for normal logic programs (cf. also [1]) and by Eiter and Gottlob for disjunctive logic programs [9] (for an explicit proof we refer to [21]). Complexity of uniform equivalence has been analyzed by Eiter and Fink [6] and the results concerning strong equivalence have been shown by several authors [23,29,17].

---

[2] We write abc instead of $\{a, b, c\}$, a instead of $\{a\}$, etc.

3   Relativizing Strong and Uniform Equivalence

In what follows, we formally introduce the notions of relativized strong equivalence (RSE) and relativized uniform equivalence (RUE).

Definition 4. *Let P and Q be programs and let A be a set of atoms. Then,*

(i)   *P and Q are strongly equivalent relative to A, denoted $P \equiv_s^A Q$, iff $P \cup R \equiv Q \cup R$, for all programs R over A;*

(ii)   *P and Q are uniformly equivalent relative to A, denoted $P \equiv_u^A Q$, iff $P \cup F \equiv Q \cup F$, for all facts $F \subseteq A$.*

Observe that the range of applicability of these notions covers ordinary equivalence (by setting $A = \emptyset$) between two programs P, Q, and *general* strong (resp. uniform) equivalence (whenever $atm(P \cup Q) \subseteq A$). Also the following relation holds: For any set A of atoms, let $A' = A \cap atm(P \cup Q)$. Then, $P \equiv_e^A Q$ holds, iff $P \equiv_e^{A'} Q$ holds, for $e \in \{s, u\}$.

Recall our example programs P and P'. In the previous section, we have seen that these programs are neither uniformly equivalent nor strongly equivalent to each other. With the concepts of RSE and RUE at hand, we are able to draw a more fine-grained picture. In particular, we can choose any A with $c \notin A$, and get $P \equiv_s^A P'$ and $P \equiv_u^A P'$. In the next section, we will present a model-theoretic characterization to verify this claim.

For technical reasons, we also introduce the following concepts:

Definition 5. *Let P and Q be programs, and let A be a set of atoms. Then,*

(i)   *$P \models_s^A Q$, iff $\mathcal{SM}(P \cup R) \subseteq \mathcal{SM}(Q \cup R)$, for all programs R over A;*

(ii)   *$P \models_u^A Q$, iff $\mathcal{SM}(P \cup F) \subseteq \mathcal{SM}(Q \cup F)$, for all $F \subseteq A$.*

Hence, $P \equiv_e^A Q$ holds, iff $P \models_e^A Q$ and $Q \models_e^A P$ jointly hold, for $e \in \{s, u\}$.

Our first main result lists some properties for relativized strong equivalence. Among them, we show that RSE shares an important property with general strong equivalence: In particular, from the proofs of the results in [15,29], it appears that for strong equivalence, only the addition of unary rules is crucial. That is, by constraining the rules in the set R in Definition 1 to unary ones does not lead to a different concept.

Lemma 1. *For programs P, Q, and a set of atoms A, the following propositions are equivalent:*

(1)   *$P \not\models_s^A Q$;*

(2)   *there exists a unary program U over A, such that $\mathcal{SM}(P \cup U) \not\subseteq \mathcal{SM}(Q \cup U)$;*

(3)   *there exists an interpretation Y, such that (a) $Y \models P$; (b) for each $Y' \subset Y$ with $(Y' \cap A) = (Y \cap A)$, $Y' \not\models P^Y$ holds; and (c) $Y \models Q$ implies existence of an $X \subset Y$, such that $X \models Q^Y$ and, for each $X' \subset Y$ with $(X' \cap A) = (X \cap A)$, $X' \not\models P^Y$ holds.*

Proof. (1) implies (3): Suppose an interpretation Y and a set R of rules over A, such that $Y \in \mathcal{SM}(P \cup R)$ and $Y \notin \mathcal{SM}(Q \cup R)$. From $Y \in \mathcal{SM}(P \cup R)$, we get $Y \models P \cup R$ and, for each $Z \subset Y$, $Z \not\models P^Y \cup R^Y$. Thus (a) holds, and since $Y' \models R^Y$ holds, for each Y' with $(Y' \cap A) = (Y \cap A)$, (b) holds as well. From $Y \notin \mathcal{SM}(Q \cup R)$, we get that either $Y \not\models Q \cup R$ or there exists an interpretation $X \subset Y$, such that $X \models Q^Y \cup R^Y$. Note that $Y \not\models Q \cup R$ implies $Y \not\models Q$, since from above, we have $Y \models R$. Thus, in the case of $Y \not\models Q \cup R$, (c) holds; otherwise we get that $X \models Q^Y$. Now since $X \models R^Y$, we know that, for each $X' \subset Y$ with $(X' \cap A) = (X \cap A)$, $X' \not\models P^Y$ has to hold, otherwise $Y \notin \mathcal{SM}(P \cup R)$. Hence, (c) is satisfied.

(3) implies (2): Suppose an interpretation Y, such that Conditions (a–c) hold. We have two cases: First, if $Y \not\models Q$, consider the unary program $U = (Y \cap A)$. By Conditions (a) and (b), it is easily seen that $Y \in \mathcal{SM}(P \cup U)$, and from $Y \not\models Q$, $Y \notin \mathcal{SM}(Q \cup U)$ follows. So suppose, $Y \models Q$. By (c), there exists an $X \subset Y$, such that $X \models Q^Y$. Consider the program $U = (X \cap A) \cup \{p \leftarrow q \mid p, q \in (Y \setminus X) \cap A\}$. Again, U is unary over A. Clearly, $Y \models Q \cup U$ and $X \models Q^Y \cup U$. Thus $Y \notin \mathcal{SM}(Q \cup U)$. It remains to show that $Y \in \mathcal{SM}(P \cup U)$. We have $Y \models P \cup U$. Towards a contradiction, suppose a $Z \subset Y$, such that $Z \models P^Y \cup U$. By definition of U, $Z \supseteq (X \cap A)$. If $(Z \cap A) = (X \cap A)$, Condition (c) is violated; if $(Z \cap A) = (Y \cap A)$, Condition (b) is violated. Thus, $(X \cap A) \subset (Z \cap A) \subset (Y \cap A)$. But then, $Z \not\models U$, since there exists at least one rule $p \leftarrow q$ in U, such that $q \in Z$ and $p \notin Z$. Contradiction.

(2) implies (1) holds by definition. $\qquad\qquad\square$

Corollary 1. *For programs P, Q, and a set of atoms A, $P \equiv_s^A Q$ holds iff, for each unary program U over A, $P \cup U \equiv Q \cup U$ holds.*

4   A Characterization for Relativized Strong Equivalence

In this section, we provide a semantical characterization of RSE by generalizing the notion of SE-models. Hence, our aim is to capture the problem $P \equiv_s^A Q$ in pure model-theoretic terms. Moreover, having found a suitable notion of *relativized SE-models*, we expect that a corresponding pendant for RUE can be derived in the same manner as general UE-models are defined over general SE-models.

We introduce the following notion.

Definition 6. *Let A be a set of atoms. A pair of interpretations (X, Y) is a (relativized) A-SE-interpretation iff either $X = Y$ or $X \subset (Y \cap A)$. Moreover, (X, Y) is a (relativized) A-SE-model of a program P iff*

(i) $Y \models P$;
(ii)   for all $Y' \subset Y$ with $(Y' \cap A) = (Y \cap A)$, $Y' \not\models P^Y$; and
(iii) $X \subset Y$ implies existence of a $X' \subseteq Y$ with $(X' \cap A) = X$, such that $X' \models P^Y$ holds.

Compared to SE-models, this definition is more involved. This is due to the fact, that we have to take care of two different effects when relativizing strong equivalence. The first one is as follows: Suppose a program P has among its SE-models the pairs (Y, Y) and (Y', Y) with $(Y' \cap A) = (Y \cap A)$ and $Y' \subset Y$. Regardless of the rules R over A we add to P, $Y' \not\models (P \cup R)^Y$ always implies $Y \not\models P \cup R$. In other words, Y is not a stable model of $P \cup R$, for any R over A. Hence, in this situation, we do not pay attention to any original SE-model from P of the form (Z, Y). This motivates Condition (ii). Condition (iii) deals with a different effect: Suppose P has SE-models (X, Y) and (X', Y), with $(X \cap A) = (X' \cap A) \subset (Y \cap A)$. Again, it is not possible to eliminate just one of these two SE-models by adding rules over A. Such SE-models which do not differ with respect to A, are collected into a single A-SE-model $((X \cap A), Y)$.

The different role of these two independent conditions becomes even more apparent in the following cases. On the one hand, setting $A = \emptyset$, the A-SE-models of a program P collapse with the stable models of P. More precisely, all such $\emptyset$-SE-models have to be of the form (Y, Y), and it holds that (Y, Y) is an $\emptyset$-SE-model of a DLP P iff Y is a stable model of P. This is easily seen by the fact that under $A = \emptyset$, Conditions (i) and (ii) in Definition 6 exactly coincide with the characterization of stable models. Therefore, A-SE-model-checking for DLPs is not possible in polynomial time in the general case; otherwise we get that checking whether a DLP has some stable model is NP-complete; which is in contradiction to known results [9], provided the polynomial hierarchy does not collapse. On the other hand, if each atom from P is contained in A, then the A-SE-models of P coincide with the SE-models (over A) of P. The conditions in Definition 6 are hereby instantiated as follows: A pair (X, Y) is an A-SE-interpretation iff $X \subseteq Y$, and by (i) we get $Y \models P$, (ii) is trivially satisfied, and (iii) states $X \models P^Y$.

Next, we list some immediate observations.

Lemma 2. *Let P be a program and A be a set of atoms. We have the following relations between A-SE-models and SE-models.*

- *If (Y, Y) is an A-SE-model of P, then (Y, Y) is an SE-model of P.*
- *If (X, Y) is an A-SE-model of P, then (X', Y) is an SE-model of P, for some X' with $X' = (X \cap A)$.*

Let us compute the relativized SE-models of our example programs P and P' already used in previous sections. Indeed, we expect that $P \equiv_s^A P'$ holds exactly if the A-SE-models of P and P' coincide. By above lemma, it suffices to consider the SE-models of a program and check whether they result in corresponding A-SE-models. P has got two SE-models, (abc, abc) and (ab, abc). Hence, Condition (ii) in Definition 6 is satisfied, only if $c \in A$. In this case, P possesses two A-SE-models (abc, abc) and (X, abc) where $X = A \cap \{a, b\}$. In each other case P' has no A-SE-model, since there is a $Y' \subset Y$ with $(Y' \cap A) = (Y \cap A)$, such that $Y' \models P^Y$, for $Y = \{a, b, c\}$. This is similar for P'. In particular, P' has SE-models $(abc, abc), (ab, abc), (c, abc), (\emptyset, abc)$. Thus, whenever $c \in A$, (c, abc) remains to be an A-SE-model of P', yielding different A-SE-models for P and P'. Otherwise, i.e., $c \notin A$, P' has no A-SE-models. Therefore, the A-SE-models of P and P' coincide, whenever $c \notin A$.

For a further example, consider the programs

$$Q = \{a \vee b \leftarrow; \ a \leftarrow c; \ b \leftarrow c; \ \leftarrow not\, c; \ c \leftarrow a, b\};$$
$$Q' = \{a \leftarrow not\, b; \ b \leftarrow not\, a; \ a \leftarrow c; \ b \leftarrow c; \ \leftarrow not\, c; \ c \leftarrow a, b\}.$$

Thus, Q' results from Q by replacing the disjunctive rule $a \vee b \leftarrow$ by the two rules $a \leftarrow not\, b; \ b \leftarrow not\, a$.

Table 1. Comparing the A-SE-models for example programs Q and Q'.

A	A-SE-models of Q	A-SE-models of Q'
$\{a,b,c\}$	$(abc, abc), (a, abc), (b, abc)$	$(abc, abc), (a, abc), (b, abc), (\emptyset, abc)$
$\{a,b\}$	$(abc, abc), (a, abc), (b, abc)$	$(abc, abc), (a, abc), (b, abc), (\emptyset, abc)$
$\{a,c\}$	$(abc, abc), (a, abc), (\emptyset, abc)$	$(abc, abc), (a, abc), (\emptyset, abc)$
$\{b,c\}$	$(abc, abc), (\emptyset, abc), (b, abc)$	$(abc, abc), (b, abc), (\emptyset, abc)$
$\{a\}$	-	-
$\{b\}$	-	-
$\{c\}$	$(abc, abc), (\emptyset, abc)$	$(abc, abc), (\emptyset, abc)$
$\emptyset$	-	-

Table 1 lists, for each $A \subseteq \{a, b, c\}$, the A-SE-models of Q and Q', respectively. The first row of the table gives the SE-models (over $\{a, b, c\}$) for Q and Q'. Observe that we have $Q \not\equiv_s Q'$. The second row shows that, for $A = \{a, b\}$, $Q \not\equiv_s^A Q'$, as well. Indeed, adding $R = \{a \leftarrow b; \ b \leftarrow a\}$ yields $\{a, b, c\}$ as stable model of $Q \cup R$, whereas $Q' \cup R$ has no stable model. For all other $A \subset \{a, b, c\}$, the A-SE-models of Q and Q' coincide. Basically, there are two different reasons. First, for $A = \{a, c\}$, $A = \{b, c\}$, or $A = \{c\}$, Condition (iii) from Definition 6 comes into play. In those cases, at least one of the SE-interpretations (a, abc) or (b, abc) is "switched" to $(\emptyset, abc)$, and thus the original difference between the SE-models disappears when considering A-SE-models. In the remaining cases, i.e., $A \subset \{a, b\}$, Condition (ii) prevents any (X, abc) to be an A-SE-model. Then, neither Q nor Q' possesses any A-SE-model.

The general result is as follows. In particular, we show that A-SE-models capture the notion of $\equiv_s^A$ in the same manner as SE-models capture $\equiv_s$.

Theorem 1. *For programs P, Q, and a set of atoms A, $P \equiv_s^A Q$ holds iff P and Q possess the same A-SE-models.*

Proof. First suppose $P \not\equiv_s^A Q$ and wlog consider $P \not\models_s^A Q$. By Lemma 1, there exists an interpretation Y, such that (a) $Y \models P$; (b) for each $Y' \subset Y$ with $(Y' \cap A) = (Y \cap A)$, $Y' \not\models P^Y$; and (c) $Y \not\models Q$ or there exists an interpretation $X \subset Y$, such that $X \models Q^Y$ and, for each $X' \subset Y$ with $(X' \cap A) = (X \cap A)$, $X' \not\models P^Y$. First suppose $Y \not\models Q$, or $Y \models Q$ and $(X \cap A) = (Y \cap A)$. Then (Y, Y) is an A-SE-model of P but not of Q. Otherwise, i.e., $Y \models Q$ and $(X \cap A) \subset (Y \cap A)$, $((X \cap A), Y)$ is an A-SE-model of Q. But, by Condition (c), $((X \cap A), Y)$ is not an A-SE-model of P.

For the converse direction of the theorem, suppose a pair (Z, Y), such that wlog (Z, Y) is an A-SE-model of P but not of Q. First, let $Z = Y$. We show $P \not\models_s^A Q$. Since (Y, Y) is an A-SE-model of P, we get from Definition 6, that $Y \models P$ and, for each $Y' \subset Y$ with $(Y \cap A) = (Y' \cap A)$, $Y' \not\models P^Y$. Thus, Conditions (a) and (b) in Part (3) of Lemma 1 are satisfied for P by Y. On the other hand, (Y, Y) is not an A-SE-model of Q. By Definition 6, either $Y \not\models Q$, or there exists a $Y' \subset Y$, with $(Y' \cap A) = (Y \cap A)$, such that $Y' \models Q^Y$. Therefore, Condition (c) from Lemma 1 is satisfied by either $Y \not\models Q$ or, if $Y \models Q$, by setting $X = Y'$. We apply Lemma 1 and get $P \not\models_s^A Q$. Consequently, $P \not\equiv_s^A Q$. So suppose, $Z \neq Y$. We show that then $Q \not\models_s^A P$ holds. First, observe that whenever (Z, Y) is an A-SE-model of P, then also (Y, Y) is an A-SE-model of P. Hence, the case where (Y, Y) is not an A-SE-model of Q is already shown. So, suppose (Y, Y) is an A-SE-model of Q. We have $Y \models Q$ and, for each $Y' \subset Y$ with $(Y' \cap A) = (Y \cap A)$, $Y' \not\models Q^Y$. This satisfies Conditions (a) and (b) in Lemma 1 for Q. However, since (Z, Y) is not an A-SE-model of Q, for each $X' \subset Y$ with $(X' \cap A) = Z$, $X' \not\models Q^Y$ holds. Since (Z, Y) in turn is an A-SE-model of P, there exists an $X'' \subset Y$ with $(X'' \cap A) = Z$, such that $X'' \models P^Y$. These observations imply that (c) holds in Lemma 1. We apply the lemma and get $Q \not\equiv_s^A P$. Hence, $P \not\equiv_s^A Q$. □

5   Characterizing Relativized Uniform Equivalence

In this section, we present a characterization for deciding $\equiv_u^A$, i.e., uniform equivalence relative to a set of atoms A. As mentioned before, we aim at defining relativized A-UE-models over A-SE-models in the same manner as general UE-models are defined over general SE-models, following Definition 3. We thus define the following concept.

Definition 7. *Let A be a set of atoms and P be a program. A pair (X, Y) is a (relativized) A-UE-model of P iff it is an A-SE-model of P and, for every A-SE-model (X', Y) of P, $X \subset X'$ implies $X' = Y$.*

We suitably adapt parts of Lemma 1.

Lemma 3. *For programs P and Q, and a set of atoms A, $P \not\equiv_u^A Q$ holds iff there exists an interpretation Y, such that (a) $Y \models P$; (b) for each $Y' \subset Y$ with $(Y' \cap A) = (Y \cap A)$, $Y' \not\models P^Y$ holds; and (c) $Y \models Q$ implies existence of an $X \subset Y$, such that $X \models Q^Y$ and, for each X' with $(X \cap A) \subseteq X' \subset Y$, $X' \not\models P^Y$ holds.*

Proof. For the only-if direction, suppose sets of atoms Y and $F \subseteq A$, such that $Y \in \mathcal{SM}(P \cup F)$ and $Y \notin \mathcal{SM}(Q \cup F)$. We get $Y \models P \cup F$ and, for each $Z \subset Y$, $Z \not\models P^Y \cup F$. Conditions (a) and (b) thus hold. Since $Y \notin \mathcal{SM}(Q \cup F)$, either $Y \not\models Q \cup F$ or there exists an interpretation $F \subseteq X \subset Y$, such that $X \models Q^Y$. $Y \not\models Q \cup F$ implies $Y \not\models Q$, since $Y \models P \cup F$; otherwise, i.e., $X \models Q^Y$, we know from $Z \not\models P^Y \cup F$ that, for each X' with $(X \cap A) \subseteq X' \subset Y$, $X' \not\models P^Y$ has to hold; otherwise $Y \notin \mathcal{SM}(P \cup F)$. Hence, (c) is satisfied.

For the if-direction, suppose a set Y, such that Conditions (a–c) hold. We have two cases: First, if $Y \not\models Q$, we set $F = (Y \cap A)$. By (a) and (b), we derive $Y \in \mathcal{SM}(P \cup F)$. Since $Y \not\models Q$, $Y \notin \mathcal{SM}(Q \cup F)$ follows, and we are done. So suppose $Y \models Q$ and existence of an $X \subset Y$, such that $X \models Q^Y$. We set $F = (X \cap A)$. Clearly, $Y \models Q \cup F$ and $X \models Q^Y \cup F$. Thus $Y \notin \mathcal{SM}(Q \cup F)$. It remains to show that $Y \in \mathcal{SM}(P \cup F)$. We have $Y \models P \cup F$. By Condition (c), each X' with $(X \cap A) \subseteq X' \subset Y$ satisfies $X' \not\models P^Y$. For each other $X' \subset Y$, we have $X' \subset (X \cap A)$, and thus $X' \not\models F$ by definition of F. Hence, $X' \not\models P^Y \cup R$ holds for each $X' \subset Y$, yielding $Y \in \mathcal{SM}(P \cup F)$. □

Next, we can derive the desired characterization for relativized uniform equivalence.

Theorem 2. *For programs P, Q, and a set of atoms A, $P \equiv_u^A Q$ holds iff P and Q possess the same A-UE-models.*

Proof. First suppose $P \not\equiv_u^A Q$ and wlog consider $P \not\models_u^A Q$. By Lemma 3, there exists an interpretation Y, such that (a) $Y \models P$; (b) for each $Y' \subset Y$ with $(Y' \cap A) = (Y \cap A)$, $Y' \not\models P^Y$; and (c) $Y \not\models Q$ or there exists an interpretation $X \subset Y$, such that $X \models Q^Y$ and, for each X' with $(X \cap A) \subseteq X' \subset Y$, $X' \not\models P^Y$. If $Y \not\models Q$ or $Y \models Q$ and $(X \cap A) = (Y \cap A)$, then (Y, Y) is an A-SE-model of P but not of Q. Consequently, also the A-UE-models of P and Q differ. Otherwise, i.e., $Y \models Q$ and $(X \cap A) \subset (Y \cap A)$, $((X \cap A), Y)$ is an A-SE-model of Q. But Condition (c) guarantees, that any A-SE-model (X', Y) of P with $(X \cap A) \subseteq X'$ satisfies $X' = Y$. Thus, we get an A-UE-model (X', Y) of Q with $(X \cap A) \subseteq X' \subset Y$, which cannot be an A-UE-model of P.

For the converse direction, suppose wlog a pair (Z, Y) is an A-UE-model of P but not of Q. The case of $Z = Y$ proceeds similar as in the proof of Theorem 1, since (Y, Y) is an A-UE-model of a program iff (Y, Y) is an A-SE-model of it. So suppose, $Z \neq Y$. Since (Z, Y) is an A-UE-model of P, (Y, Y) is an A-UE-models of P, as well. We further assume that (Y, Y) is an A-UE-model of Q; the other case is already shown. We thus have $Y \models P \cup Q$ and, for each $Y' \subset Y$ with $(Y' \cap A) = (Y \cap A)$, $Y' \not\models P^Y$ and $Y' \not\models Q^Y$; i.e., Conditions (a) and (b) from Lemma 3 hold in both cases $P \not\models_u^A Q$ and $Q \not\models_u^A P$. There are two possible reasons for (Z, Y) not being an A-UE-model of Q: (Z, Y) is an A-SE-model of Q, but there exists a Z' with $Z \subset Z' \subset Y$, such that (Z', Y) is an A-SE-model of Q, as well; or the A-SE-interpretation (Z, Y) is not an A-SE-model of Q. First, suppose there exists a Z' with $Z \subset Z' \subset Y$, such that (Z', Y) is an A-SE-model of Q. Then, (c) holds since there exists an X with $(X \cap A) = Z'$, such that $X \models Q^Y$, and, for each X' with $Z' \subseteq X' \subset Y$, $X' \not\models P^Y$ holds by assumption that (Z, Y) is an A-UE-model of P. By Lemma 3, we get $P \not\models_u^A Q$. Second, suppose no Z' with $Z \subset Z' \subset Y$ yields an A-SE-model (Z', Y) of Q and (Z, Y) is not an A-SE-model of Q. Then, (c) holds for Q since there exists an X with $(X \cap A) = Z$, such that $X \models P^Y$, and no X' with $Z \subseteq X' \subset Y$ satisfies $X' \models Q^Y$. By Lemma 3, we get $Q \not\models_u^A P$. We thus have either $P \not\models_u^A Q$ or $Q \not\models_u^A P$. Both cases imply $P \not\equiv_u^A Q$. □

Recall our example programs Q and Q' from above. Via the first row in the table (i.e., for $A = \{a, b, c\}$, yielding the respective SE-models), it easily checked by Proposition 2 that Q and Q' are uniformly equivalent. In fact, the SE-model $(\emptyset, abc)$ of Q' is not a UE-model of Q', due to the presence of the SE-model (a, abc), or alternatively because of (b, abc). Note that $Q \equiv_u Q'$ implies $Q \equiv_u^A Q'$ for any A. Inspecting the remaining lines in the table, it can be checked that, for any A, the sets of A-UE-models of Q and Q' are equal, as expected.

As a final remark, we mention that A-UE-models enjoy the same property as A-SE-models for characterizing stable models. In particular, we have a one-to-one correspondence between the $\emptyset$-UE-models of a program P and the stable models of P.

6   Complexity and Implementation Issues

In this section, we first present a method to decide RSE and RUE via reductions to ordinary equivalence tests. Afterwards we utilize these reductions in order to examine the computational complexity of RSE and RUE. We remark that the forthcoming reductions also hold for the general forms of uniform and strong equivalence. These reductions have so far not been presented in the literature we are aware of.[3] We note that the presented method is relevant in practice by composing our reductions with implementations to check equivalence between programs [14,21].

Theorem 3. *Let P_1 and P_2 be programs and A be a set of atoms. Moreover, let p_a and $\bar{p}_a$ be new atoms for each $a \in A$, and define*

$$P_i' = \{p_a \leftarrow not\ \bar{p}_a; \bar{p}_a \leftarrow not\ p_a \mid a \in A\} \cup$$
$$\{a \leftarrow p_a \mid a \in A\} \cup$$
$$P_i;$$

for $i = 1, 2$. Then, $P_1 \equiv_u^A P_2$ iff $P_1' \equiv P_2'$.

Intuitively, the first two rules guess any truth assignment to the atoms p_a. Then, whenever p_a is contained in the guess, a is derived. Hence, the added rules "simulate" each possible extension of facts to the P_i's simultaneously. A formal proof is easily obtained by using the well-known splitting-theorem [10,16]. A similar procedure can be given for RSE making use of the restriction to unary rules, following Corollary 1.

Theorem 4. *Let P_1 and P_2 be programs and A be a set of atoms. Moreover, let $p_{a,b}$ and $\bar{p}_{a,b}$ be new atoms for any $a, b \in A$, and define*

$$P_i' = \{p_{a,b} \leftarrow not\ \bar{p}_{a,b}; \bar{p}_{a,b} \leftarrow not\ p_{a,b} \mid a, b \in A\} \cup$$
$$\{a \leftarrow p_{a,a} \mid a \in A\} \cup \{a \leftarrow b, p_{a,b} \mid a, b \in A, a \neq b\} \cup$$
$$P_i;$$

for $i = 1, 2$. Then, $P_1 \equiv_s^A P_2$ iff $P_1' \equiv P_2'$.

Here, we guess any set of unary rules over A via truth assignments to atoms $p_{a,b}$. Note that $p_{a,a}$ refers to the fact $a \leftarrow$ rather than to the (tautological) rule $a \leftarrow a$.

The program P' as defined in Theorem 3 is clearly constructible in polynomial time from P. Moreover, P' is normal whenever P is normal. This observation gives the respective membership results for RUE in the forthcoming theorem. Hardness follows, for instance, from the complexity results for ordinary equivalence, following Proposition 3. Similarly, this argumentation holds for relativized strong equivalence.

Theorem 5. *Given two programs P and Q, a set of atoms A, and $e \in \{s, u\}$, deciding whether $P \equiv_e^A Q$ is Π_2^P-complete. If P and Q are normal, then $P \equiv_e^A Q$ is coNP-complete.*

However, it is worthful to pay additional attention to the case of strong equivalence relative to A between DLPs. Compared to the other cases, the complexity between the two ends of the range for A differs. As mentioned earlier, for $A = \emptyset$, we have $P \equiv_s^A Q$ iff $P \equiv Q$. The latter test is Π_2^P-complete, hence Π_2^P-completeness for $P \equiv_s^A Q$ is derived. On the other end, for $A = atm(P \cup Q)$, we have $P \equiv_s^A Q$ iff $P \equiv_s Q$. The latter test is coNP-complete, and thus is less involving. We identify the following frontier between coNP- and Π_2^P-hardness for RSE.

---

[3] Alternative methods—which reduce the general variants of uniform and strong equivalence to the consistency problem of stable logic programming—can be found, e.g., in [8].

Theorem 6. *For DLPs P and Q, and a set of atoms A, the test for $P \equiv_s^A Q$ is coNP-complete, whenever the cardinality of the set $atm(P \cup Q) \setminus A$ is bounded by a constant.*

Proof. The proof is shown via the complementary problem, which is in NP. It suffices to show that the test for $P \not\equiv_s^A Q$ is in NP. We guess an interpretation Y and check Conditions (a–c) from Lemma 1. Suppose the cardinality of the set $(atm(P \cup Q)) \setminus A$ is bounded by a constant k. Then, we need in the worst case one additional guess for X and $2^{k+1} + 3$ entailment tests to check the conditions, by unfolding the universal quantifications in Conditions (b) and (c). Entailment tests can be done in polynomial time. This shows membership in coNP for bounded k. Hardness follows from the coNP-completeness of strong equivalence. □

7   Conclusion

In this paper, we introduced relativized variants of strong and uniform equivalence between logic programs. Moreover, we suitably adapted the important notions of SE-models and UE-models in order to provide a uniform semantical characterization.

We showed that for normal logic programs, relativizing equivalence does not increase the computational complexity compared to the original notions of strong (resp. uniform) equivalence. This holds in the case of RUE between disjunctive logic programs, as well. In the case of $P \equiv_s^A Q$ between DLPs, however, we witnessed an increase of the computational complexity, whenever the number of atoms $atm(P \cup Q) \setminus A$ is unbounded; otherwise, $P \equiv_s^A Q$ is coNP-complete. Note that this result is acceptable in a practical setting, since it is often sufficient to exclude from A only a small number of (internal) atoms occurring in the considered programs in order to check $P \equiv_s^A Q$.

Our ongoing and future work concerns the application of these newly introduced relativized SE- and UE-models for program transformation rules as presented in [2], complementing recent research within this area [8,22]. Moreover, we investigate whether criteria for disjunction elimination [7] can be suitably generalized to relativized SE-models. Finally, we plan to extend our results to further classes of logic programs, viz. extended logic programs containing strong negation, nested logic programs, and to the function-free first-order (DATALOG) case. Moreover, we consider to explore how our results can be applied for optimizations of algorithms used in disjunctive logic programming engines such as DLV [5] and smodels+GnT [13].

Acknowledgments. The author would like to thank Chiaki Sakama, Thomas Eiter, and Hans Tompits, as well as the anonymous referees for their valuable comments which helped improving the paper.

References

1. N. Bidoit and C. Froidevaux. General Logical Databases and Programs: Default Logic Semantics and Stratification. *Information and Computation*, 91:15–54, 1991.
2. S. Brass and J. Dix. Semantics of (Disjunctive) Logic Programs Based on Partial Evaluation. *Journal of Logic Programming*, 38(3):167–213, 1999.

3. P. Cabalar. A Three-Valued Characterization for Strong Equivalence of Logic Programs. In *Proc. AAAI-02*, pg. 106–111. AAAI Press/MIT Press, 2002.
4. D. de Jongh and L. Hendriks. Characterizations of Strongly Equivalent Logic Programs in Intermediate Logics. *Theory and Practice of Logic Programming*, 3(3):259–270, 2003.
5. T. Eiter, W. Faber, N. Leone, and G. Pfeifer. Declarative Problem-Solving Using the DLV System. In *Logic-Based Artificial Intelligence*, pg. 79–103. Kluwer Academic, 2000.
6. T. Eiter and M. Fink. Uniform Equivalence of Logic Programs under the Stable Model Semantics. In *Proc. ICLP-03*, LNCS 2916, pg. 224–238. Springer, 2003.
7. T. Eiter, M. Fink, H. Tompits, and S. Woltran. On Eliminating Disjunctions in Stable Logic Programming. In *Proc. KR-04*, pg. 447–585. AAAI-Press, 2004.
8. T. Eiter, M. Fink, H. Tompits, and S. Woltran. Simplifying Logic Programs under Uniform and Strong Equivalence. In *Proc. LPNMR-04*, LNCS 2923, pg. 87–99. Springer, 2004.
9. T. Eiter and G. Gottlob. On the Computational Cost of Disjunctive Logic Programming: Propositional Case. *Annals of Math. and Artificial Intelligence*, 15(3/4):289–323, 1995.
10. T. Eiter, G. Gottlob, and H. Mannila. Disjunctive Datalog. *ACM Transactions on Database Systems*, 22:364–418, 1997.
11. M. Gelfond and V. Lifschitz. Classical Negation in Logic Programs and Disjunctive Databases. *New Generation Computing*, 9:365–385, 1991.
12. K. Inoue and C. Sakama. Equivalence of Logic Programs under Updates. In *Proc. JELIA-04*. This volume.
13. T. Janhunen, I. Niemelä, P. Simons, and J.-H. You. Partiality and Disjunctions in Stable Model Semantics. In *Proc. KR-00*, pg. 411–419. Morgan Kaufmann, 2000.
14. T. Janhunen and E. Oikarinen. LPEQ and DLPEQ - Translators for Automated Equivalence Testing of Logic Programs. In *Proc. LPNMR-04*, LNCS 2923, pg. 336–340. Springer, 2004.
15. V. Lifschitz, D. Pearce, and A. Valverde. Strongly Equivalent Logic Programs. *ACM Transactions on Computational Logic*, 2(4):526–541, 2001.
16. V. Lifschitz and H. Turner. Splitting a Logic Program. In *Proc. ICLP-94*, pg. 23–38. 1994.
17. F. Lin. Reducing Strong Equivalence of Logic Programs to Entailment in Classical Propositional Logic. In *Proc. KR-02*, pg. 170–176. Morgan Kaufmann, 2002.
18. M. J. Maher. Equivalences of Logic Programs. In Minker [20], pg. 627–658.
19. W. Marek and M. Truszczyński. Autoepistemic Logic. *J. of the ACM*, 38(3):588–619, 1991.
20. J. Minker, editor. *Foundations of Deductive Databases and Logic Programming*. Morgan Kaufmann, 1988.
21. E. Oikarinen and T. Janhunen. Verifying the Equivalence of Logic programs in the Disjunctive Case. In *Proc. LPNMR-04*, LNCS 2923, pg. 180–193. Springer, 2004.
22. M. Osorio, J. A. Navarro, and J. Arrazola. Equivalence in Answer Set Programming. In *Proc. LOPSTR-01*, LNCS 2372, pg. 57–75. Springer, 2001.
23. D. Pearce, H. Tompits, and S. Woltran. Encodings for Equilibrium Logic and Logic Programs with Nested Expressions. In *Proc. EPIA-01*, LNCS 2258, pg. 306–320. Springer, 2001.
24. D. Pearce and A. Valverde. Uniform Equivalence for Equilibrium Logic and Logic Programs. In *Proc. LPNMR-04*, LNCS 2923, pg. 194–206. Springer, 2004.
25. T. Przymusinski. Stable Semantics for Disjunctive Programs. *New Generation Computing Journal*, 9:401–424, 1991.
26. Y. Sagiv. Optimizing Datalog Programs. In Minker [20], pg. 659–698.
27. O. Shmueli. Equivalence of Datalog Queries is Undecidable. *Journal of Logic Programming*, 15(3):231–242, 1993.
28. H. Turner. Strong Equivalence for Logic Programs and Default Theories (Made Easy). In *Proc. LPNMR-01*, LNCS 2173, pg. 81–92, Springer, 2001.
29. H. Turner. Strong Equivalence Made Easy: Nested Expressions and Weight Constraints. *Theory and Practice of Logic Programming*, 3(4–5):602–622, 2003.

Equivalence of Logic Programs Under Updates

Katsumi Inoue[1] and Chiaki Sakama[2]

[1] National Institute of Informatics
2-1-2 Hitotsubashi, Chiyoda-ku, Tokyo 101-8430, Japan
ki@nii.ac.jp
[2] Department of Computer and Communication Sciences
Wakayama University, Sakaedani, Wakayama 640-8510, Japan
sakama@sys.wakayama-u.ac.jp

Abstract. This paper defines a general framework for testing equivalence of logic programs with respect to two parameters. Given two sets of rules $\mathcal{Q}$ and $\mathcal{R}$, two logic programs P_1 and P_2 are said to be *update equivalent with respect to* $(\mathcal{Q}, \mathcal{R})$ if $(P_1 \setminus Q) \cup R$ and $(P_2 \setminus Q) \cup R$ have the same answer sets for any two logic programs $Q \subseteq \mathcal{Q}$ and $R \subseteq \mathcal{R}$. The notion of update equivalence is suitable to take program updates into account when two logic programs are compared. That is, the notion of relativity stipulates the languages of updates, and two parameters $\mathcal{Q}$ and $\mathcal{R}$ correspond to the languages for deletion and addition, respectively. Clearly, the notion of strong equivalence is a special case of update equivalence where $\mathcal{Q}$ is empty and $\mathcal{R}$ is the set of all rules in the language. In fact, the notion of update equivalence is strong enough to capture many other notions such as weak equivalence, update equivalence on common rules, and uniform equivalence. We also discuss computation and complexity of update equivalence.

1 Introduction

The notion of equivalence in logic programming has recently become important. Because a logic program is used to represent knowledge of a problem domain, we often have to consider whether two logic programs P_1 and P_2 represent the same knowledge. For example, one logic program P_1 may be viewed as a specification of knowledge in some domain, and another representation P_2 may be expected to be a compact form of P_1 which can easily be computed.

Strong equivalence [11] is one of the most widely recognized criteria for equivalence of logic programs. Two logic programs P_1 and P_2 are said to be *strongly equivalent* if for any logic program R, $P_1 \cup R$ and $P_2 \cup R$ have the same answer sets. On the other hand, two programs are *weakly equivalent* if they agree with their answer sets. The notion of strong equivalence was introduced earlier by Maher [15] for definite programs under the name of *equivalence as program segments*. Recently, strong equivalence has been studied both logically and computationally for answer set programming [11,18,17,14,21,2,4].

In [11], it is argued that strong equivalence can be used to simplify a part of a logic program without looking at the other part. For example, $\{\, p \leftarrow p \,\}$

J.J. Alferes and J. Leite (Eds.): JELIA 2004, LNAI 3229, pp. 174–186, 2004.
© Springer-Verlag Berlin Heidelberg 2004

and $\emptyset$ are strongly equivalent, so that the rule in the former set can always be eliminated from any program. On the other hand, the two weakly equivalent programs $\{p \leftarrow not\,q\}$ and $\{p \leftarrow \}$ are not strongly equivalent, so the rule in the former cannot be replaced by the rule in the latter. Hence, strong equivalence takes the influence of addition of a rule set to each program into account.

However, strong equivalence cannot capture the *negative* influence, i.e., deletion of a rule set from each program. For example, $P_1 = \{p \leftarrow , q \leftarrow not\,p\}$ and $P_2 = \{p \leftarrow \}$ are strongly equivalent. According to the above discussion, the two rules in P_1 can be replaced by the rule of P_2, which implies that the rule $q \leftarrow not\,p$ can be eliminated from P_1. However, the process of program development is not always monotonic. We often revise and update our previous rules and delete some part of a program in exchange for additional new rules. In such a case, eliminating a rule like $q \leftarrow not\,p$ is harmful, and it should be kept for later uses because q should be derived whenever p is removed. Strong equivalence does not take such a possibility of removal into account.

In this paper, we consider a much stronger notion of equivalence which is tolerant of both addition and removal. Given two sets of rules $\mathcal{Q}$ and $\mathcal{R}$, two logic programs P_1 and P_2 are said to be *update equivalent with respect to* $(\mathcal{Q}, \mathcal{R})$ if $(P_1 \setminus Q) \cup R$ and $(P_2 \setminus Q) \cup R$ have the same answer sets for any two logic programs $Q \subseteq \mathcal{Q}$ and $R \subseteq \mathcal{R}$. Clearly, the notion of strong equivalence is a special case of update equivalence where $\mathcal{Q}$ is empty and $\mathcal{R}$ is the set of all rules in the language. In the above example, P_1 and P_2 are not update equivalent with respect to $(\mathcal{P}, \mathcal{P})$ where $\mathcal{P}$ is the set of all rules in the language of P_1 and P_2. This is because the removal of $p \leftarrow$ from both programs involves derivation of q in P_1. For another example, $P_3 = \{p \leftarrow , q \leftarrow p\}$ and $P_4 = \{p \leftarrow , q \leftarrow \}$ are strongly equivalent, but are not update equivalent with respect to $(\mathcal{P}, \mathcal{P})$ because the removal of $p \leftarrow$ differentiates their answer sets. Non-equivalence of P_3 and P_4 is explained as follows. While the reason why q is true in P_3 is justified by the rule $q \leftarrow p$ and the truth of p, both p and q hold as facts in P_4. So q depends on p in P_3, and the loss of p affects the loss of q, but no such dependency exists in P_4. This contrasts well with the case that the weakly equivalent programs $\{p \leftarrow not\,q\}$ and $\{p \leftarrow \}$ are not strongly equivalent, where the truth of p is factual in the latter but it is justified by the default rule in the former. In other words, strong equivalence distinguishes derivation of literals through negation as failure from derivation without involving negation as failure. This asymmetric property of strong equivalence is not always natural from the viewpoint of nonmonotonic reasoning.

Without any restriction on $\mathcal{Q}$ and $\mathcal{R}$, two logic programs are called *strongly update equivalent* if they are update equivalent with respect to $(\mathcal{P}, \mathcal{P})$. Surprisingly, only a small class of strongly equivalent logic programs becomes strongly update equivalent. In fact, we prove that two logic programs are strongly update equivalent only if they only differ in additional valid (or tautological) rules. However, a slightly modified definition assures that most modular transformations of rules proposed in the literature preserve *update equivalence on common rules*. As a related work, Eiter *et al.* [3] discuss another generalization of strong equivalence in the context of updating logic programs. However, the effect of removal in equivalence of logic programs has never been analyzed so far. Leite [10] introduces another update equivalence in the context of dynamic logic programming, but it is not a generalization of strong equivalence.

For update equivalence, often we can restrict the languages of changing parts $(\mathcal{Q}, \mathcal{R})$ to some subsets of the whole language of programs. Such restriction is practicably interesting because logic programs and *deductive databases* are usually divided into invariable and variable parts such that only variable parts are changed in updates [19]. This notion of equivalence is partially considered in [14] as *relative equivalence* and in [2] as *uniform equivalence*.

The rest of this paper is organized as follows. Section 2 reviews the answer set semantics and previous definitions of equivalence. Section 3 defines relative update equivalence. Section 4 shows the necessary and sufficient condition of strong update equivalence, and also considers update equivalence on common rules. Section 5 discusses the application of relative update equivalence to database updates. Section 6 shows a translation from relative update equivalence into relative strong equivalence, and considers the time complexity of update equivalence. Section 7 concludes the paper.

2   Background

A *(logic) program* is represented in a *general extended disjunctive program* (GEDP) [13,7], which consists of a finite number of *rules* of the form:

$$L_1; \cdots; L_k; not\, L_{k+1}; \cdots; not\, L_l \leftarrow L_{l+1}, \ldots, L_m, not\, L_{m+1}, \ldots, not\, L_n \quad (1)$$

where each L_i is a literal ($n \geq m \geq l \geq k \geq 0$), and *not* is *negation as failure* (NAF). The symbol ; represents a disjunction. For any literal L, the literal complimentary to L is written as $\overline{L}$, that is, when A is an atom, $\overline{A} = \neg A$ and $\overline{\neg A} = A$. A rule with variables stands for the set of its ground instances. The left-hand side of the rule is the *head*, and the right-hand side is the *body*. For each rule r of the form (1), $head^+(r)$, $head^-(r)$, $body^+(r)$ and $body^-(r)$ denote the sets of literals $\{L_1, \ldots, L_k\}$, $\{L_{k+1}, \ldots, L_l\}$, $\{L_{l+1}, \ldots, L_m\}$, and $\{L_{m+1}, \ldots, L_n\}$, respectively. A rule r is an *integrity constraint* if $head^+(r) = \emptyset$. Any rule with the empty body $H \leftarrow$ is called a *fact* and is also written as H without the symbol $\leftarrow$ as long as no confusion arises. A GEDP is an *extended disjunctive program* (EDP) [5] if it contains no NAF in the head of any rule (i.e., $k = l$).

The semantics of a program is given by its *answer sets*. First, let P be a GEDP without NAF (i.e., $k = l$ and $m = n$) and $S \subseteq Lit$, where Lit is the set of all ground literals in the language of P. Then, S is an *answer set* of P if S is a minimal set satisfying the conditions:

1. For each ground rule r of the form $L_1; \cdots; L_l \leftarrow L_{l+1}, \ldots, L_m$ from P, $body^+(r) \subseteq S$ implies $head^+(r) \cap S \neq \emptyset$;
2. If S contains a pair of complementary literals L and $\overline{L}$, then $S = Lit$.

Second, given *any* GEDP P (with NAF) and $S \subseteq Lit$, consider the GEDP (without NAF) P^S obtained as follows: a rule $L_1; \cdots; L_k \leftarrow L_{l+1}, \ldots, L_m$ is in P^S if there is a ground rule r of the form (1) from P such that $head^-(r) \subseteq S$ and $body^-(r) \cap S = \emptyset$. Then, S is an *answer set* of P if S is an answer set of P^S.

An answer set is *consistent* if it is not Lit. A program is *consistent* if it has a consistent answer set. An answer set S of P is *minimal* if there is no other answer set S' of P such that $S' \subset S$. Every answer set of any EDP is minimal [5], but the minimality of answer sets no longer holds for GEDPs [13]. The set of all answer sets of P is written as $\mathcal{AS}(P)$.

The notions of weak and strong equivalence are defined as follows.

Definition 2.1. Let P_1, P_2, and R be programs.

(1) P_1 and P_2 are *(weakly) equivalent* if $\mathcal{AS}(P_1) = \mathcal{AS}(P_2)$.
(2) P_1 and P_2 are *equivalent relative to R* [8] if $\mathcal{AS}(P_1 \cup R) = \mathcal{AS}(P_2 \cup R)$.
(3) P_1 and P_2 are *strongly equivalent* [11] if P_1 and P_2 are equivalent relative to any program.

Obviously, two strongly equivalent programs are weakly equivalent, and in fact they are equivalent relative to $\emptyset$.

3   Relative Update Equivalence

Relative update equivalence of logic programs is an elaboration of strong equivalence of logic programs under the two additional concepts: (a) deletion of rules as well as addition, and (b) the restriction of languages for deletion and addition.

Definition 3.1. Suppose that P_1, P_2, $\mathcal{Q}$, and $\mathcal{R}$ are sets of rules with a common underlying language. P_1 and P_2 are *update equivalent with respect to $(\mathcal{Q}, \mathcal{R})$* if $\mathcal{AS}((P_1 \setminus Q) \cup R) = \mathcal{AS}((P_2 \setminus Q) \cup R)$[1] for any programs $Q \subseteq \mathcal{Q}$ and $R \subseteq \mathcal{R}$.

Each rule in $\mathcal{Q}$ is called a *removable rule*, while each rule in $\mathcal{R}$ is called an *insertable rule*. A removable or insertable rule is called an *updatable rule*.

When two programs are update equivalent with respect to some pair $(\mathcal{Q}, \mathcal{R})$, they are called *relatively update equivalent*, or *update equivalent* for short. As it is seen by its name, (relative) update equivalence enables us to give the semantics for equivalence of logic programs with respect to updates. That is, P_1 and P_2 are regarded as equivalent programs in the sense that they are equivalent after any program $Q \subseteq \mathcal{Q}$ is deleted and then any program $R \subseteq \mathcal{R}$ is inserted. Consideration of such update equivalence is meaningful and important because

---

[1] For removing rules containing variables from a program, the set difference operation is semantically defined on ground programs as $P \backslash Q = ground(P) \backslash ground(Q)$, where $ground(P)$ is the ground instances of elements from P. For example, when x is a variable and a is a constant, $\{p(a)\} \backslash \{p(x)\} = \emptyset$, and $\{p(x)\} \backslash \{p(a)\} = \{p(y) \mid y \neq a\}$. Similarly, the union $P \cup Q$ and the intersection $P \cap Q$ are respectively defined as $ground(P) \cup ground(Q)$ and $ground(P) \cap ground(Q)$, e.g., $\{p(a)\} \cup \{p(x)\} = \{p(x)\}$.

it guarantees equivalence of two different programs dynamically in the face of any common change of these programs.[2]

In the special case, both Q and $\mathcal{R}$ are given as the set of all rules in the language of programs, that is, any rule can be either deleted or added in updates. This case is further investigated in Section 4. Often, however, we want to consider update equivalence with respect to $(Q, \mathcal{R})$ in which Q and $\mathcal{R}$ are given as some distinguished sets of updatable rules. Such restriction to updates is practicably interesting because logic programs and *deductive databases* are usually divided into invariable and variable parts such that only variable parts are updatable [19]. *Abductive logic programming* [9,6] is another example where Q and $\mathcal{R}$ are defined as distinguished sets of *abducibles*. Such applications of relative update equivalence are investigated in Section 5.

A similar notion using some distinguished set of insertable rules can also be defined for strong equivalence.[3]

Definition 3.2. Suppose that P_1 and P_2 are programs, and that $\mathcal{R}$ is a set of insertable rules. P_1 and P_2 are *strongly equivalent with respect to* $\mathcal{R}$ if $\mathcal{AS}(P_1 \cup R) = \mathcal{AS}(P_2 \cup R)$ holds for any program $R \subseteq \mathcal{R}$.

4   Strong Update Equivalence

In the general notion of relative update equivalence, we can restrict updatable rules to some distinguished rules in the language. In this section, we consider the special case of update equivalence where such restriction is not specified.

Definition 4.1. Two programs P_1 and P_2 are *strongly update equivalent (S-update equivalent*, for short) if $\mathcal{AS}((P_1 \setminus Q) \cup R) = \mathcal{AS}((P_2 \setminus Q) \cup R)$ holds for any programs Q and R.

For example, two programs $\{p \leftarrow p\}$ and $\emptyset$ are S-update equivalent. Obviously, two S-update equivalent programs are strongly equivalent, and in fact they are equivalent for $Q = \emptyset$ and for any program R. By definition, two S-update equivalent programs are update equivalent with respect to any pair $(Q, \mathcal{R})$ of updatable rules.

4.1   Characterization of S-Update Equivalence

One important problem is how two strongly update equivalent programs are different from each other. With regard to this problem, we can show that two S-update equivalent programs are almost identical; the difference between the

---

[2] Eiter *et al.* [3] have also discussed a notion of update equivalence. The focuses in [3] are different from ours in that the semantics of updates are captured by Kripke structures and that finitary characterization of updates are described.

[3] For strong equivalence, Lin [14] has also mentioned the idea of relative equivalence by defining equivalence between two logic programs with respect to a set of atoms. Our definition is more general than Lin's as a set of rules is taken into account.

two always consists of valid rules. Here, a valid rule is a rule that never changes the answer sets of any program if the rule is added to the program.

Definition 4.2. A rule r is *valid* if $\{r\}$ is strongly equivalent to $\emptyset$.

Lemma 4.1. *Let U be a program. If U and $\emptyset$ are strongly equivalent, then U is a set of valid rules.*

Lemma 4.2. *Let P be a program, and V a set of valid rules. Then, P and $P \cup V$ are S-update equivalent.*

The *symmetric difference* $P_1 \Delta P_2$ of two programs P_1 and P_2 is defined as $P_1 \Delta P_2 = (P_1 \setminus P_2) \cup (P_2 \setminus P_1)$. The next theorem shows that update equivalence of P_1 and P_2 is determined by the validity of $P_1 \Delta P_2$.

Theorem 4.3. *Two programs P_1 and P_2 are S-update equivalent if and only if $P_1 \Delta P_2$ is a set of valid rules.*

Proof. Suppose that P_1 and P_2 are S-update equivalent. Then, for any program R, $\mathcal{AS}((P_1 \setminus P_2) \cup R) = \mathcal{AS}((P_2 \setminus P_2) \cup R)$, that is, $\mathcal{AS}((P_1 \setminus P_2) \cup R) = \mathcal{AS}(R)$. Hence, $P_1 \setminus P_2$ is strongly equivalent to $\emptyset$. By Lemma 4.1, $P_1 \setminus P_2$ is a set of valid rules. The same argument can be applied to $P_2 \setminus P_1$.

Conversely, suppose that $P_1 \setminus P_2$ and $P_2 \setminus P_1$ are sets of valid rules. By Lemma 4.2, P_2 and $P_2 \cup (P_1 \setminus P_2)$ are S-update equivalent, that is, P_2 and $P_2 \cup P_1$ are S-update equivalent. Similarly, P_1 and $P_1 \cup P_2$ are S-update equivalent. Therefore, P_2 and P_1 are S-update equivalent.   □

The next theorem completely characterizes valid rules by their syntax.

Theorem 4.4. *A rule r of the form (1) is valid if and only if it satisfies one of the following:*

(i) $head^+(r) \cap body^+(r) \neq \emptyset$.
(ii) $head^-(r) \cap body^-(r) \neq \emptyset$.
(iii) $body^+(r) \cap body^-(r) \neq \emptyset$.
(iv) $head^+(r) \cup body^-(r) \neq \emptyset$ *and there are two literals L_1 and L_2 in $head^-(r) \cup body^+(r)$ such that $\overline{L_1} = L_2$.*

Proof. Let R be any program, and S any answer set of R. If a rule r satisfies one of (i), (ii), and (iii), then it is easy to show that $\mathcal{AS}(R^S) = \mathcal{AS}((R \cup \{r\})^S)$. By $S \in \mathcal{AS}(R^S)$, S is also an answer set of $R \cup \{r\}$. Next, suppose that r satisfies (iv). Let L_1 and L_2 be a complementary pair of literals in the condition (iv).

   (I) Firstly consider the case that S is consistent. (I-a) If $L_1, L_2 \in body^+(r)$, then $body^+(r) \not\subseteq S$ because S is consistent. So no literal is derived through the rule in $\{r\}^S$. (I-b) If $L_1, L_2 \in head^-(r)$, then $head^-(r) \not\subseteq S$ because S is consistent. Then $\{r\}^S = \emptyset$. (I-c) If $L_1 \in body^+(r)$ and $L_2 \in head^-(r)$, then either (c-1) $L_1 \notin S$ and $L_2 \notin S$, or (c-2) $L_1 \in S$ and $L_2 \notin S$, or (c-3) $L_1 \notin S$ and $L_2 \in S$. If (c-1) or (c-2), $head^-(r) \not\subseteq S$ and thus $\{r\}^S = \emptyset$. If (c-3), $body^+(r) \not\subseteq S$ and hence no literal is derived through the rule in $\{r\}^S$. In either case, $\mathcal{AS}(R^S) = \mathcal{AS}((R \cup \{r\})^S)$ holds.

(II) Secondly suppose that $S = Lit$. In this case, $head^-(r) \cup body^+(r) \subseteq S$, that is, $head^-(r) \subseteq S$ and $body^+(r) \subseteq S$. On the other hand, $head^+(r) \cup body^-(r) \neq \emptyset$ implies that either (II-a) $head^+(r) \neq \emptyset$ or (II-b) $body^-(r) \neq \emptyset$ holds. If (II-a), r is satisfied by S, that is, $body^+(r) \subseteq S$ implies $head^+(r) \cap S \neq \emptyset$. If (II-b), $\{r\}^S = \emptyset$ holds. In either case, $\mathcal{AS}(R^S) = \mathcal{AS}((R \cup \{r\})^S)$ holds. Thus, $S = Lit$ is also an answer set of $R \cup \{r\}$. Hence, r is valid.

Conversely, suppose that r satisfies none of (i), (ii), (iii), and (iv). Then,

$$head^+(r) \cap body^+(r) = \emptyset, \tag{2}$$

$$head^-(r) \cap body^-(r) = \emptyset, \tag{3}$$

$$body^+(r) \cap body^-(r) = \emptyset, \tag{4}$$

and either

$$head^+(r) \cup body^-(r) = \emptyset \tag{5}$$

or there is no complementary pair of literals L_1 and L_2 in $head^-(r) \cup body^+(r)$. Let $S = head^-(r) \cup body^+(r)$.

(I) Suppose that S is consistent. In this case, there is no complementary literals L_1 and L_2 in $S = head^-(r) \cup body^+(r)$. Then, $body^-(r) \cap S = \emptyset$ by (3) and (4). Also by $head^-(r) \subseteq S$, $\{r\}^S \neq \emptyset$ holds. By $body^+(r) \subseteq S$, there is a literal $L \in head^+(r)$ such that $L \notin S$ by (2). Now, let R be the program exactly consisting of the facts of S, i.e., $R = S$. Obviously, $R^S = S$. Then, $L \in S'$ for some answer set $S' \in \mathcal{AS}(\{r\}^S \cup R)$, while $L \notin S$ for the answer set $S \in \mathcal{AS}(\emptyset \cup R)$. Hence, $\{r\}$ and $\emptyset$ are not strongly equivalent.

(II) Suppose that S is inconsistent. In this case, there is a pair of complementary literals L_1 and L_2 in $head^-(r) \cup body^+(r)$. Then, $head^+(r) \cup body^-(r) = \emptyset$ holds by (5), that is, $head^+(r) = body^-(r) = \emptyset$. Thus the rule r is an integrity constraint with no NAF in the body. Again, let $R = S$. Then, the unique answer set of R is Lit. However, Lit is not an answer set of $R \cup \{r\}^{Lit}$ because Lit cannot satisfy the rule of $\{r\}^{Lit}$ so that there is no answer set of $R \cup \{r\}$. Hence, $\{r\}$ and $\emptyset$ are not strongly equivalent. By (I) and (II), r is not valid. $\qquad\square$

The conditions (i) and (iii) in Theorem 4.4 are considered in the context of EDPs without classical negation in [1], in which rules satisfying (i) and (iii) are called *tautologies* and *contradictions*, respectively. The condition (ii) is similar to (i) and is meaningful only for the class of GEDPs with NAF in heads. The condition (iv) is necessary for extended programs with classical negation. In other words, (i), (ii) or (iii) is the necessary and sufficient condition for a rule in a program without classical negation to be valid. According to Theorem 4.4, the following rules are all valid:

$$p \leftarrow p, q, \qquad q \leftarrow p, not\, p, \qquad q;\ not\, p \leftarrow \neg p, \qquad \leftarrow p, \neg p, not\, q.$$

However, the following conditions are excluded from the definition of valid rules.

(v) $head^+(r) \cap head^-(r) \neq \emptyset$.

(vi) there are two literals L_1 and L_2 in $head^+(r)$ such that $\overline{L_1} = L_2$.

(vii) $head^+(r) = body^-(r) = \emptyset$ and there are two literals L_1 and L_2 in $head^-(r) \cup body^+(r)$ such that $\overline{L_1} = L_2$.

An example for the case (v) is $p; not\, p \leftarrow$, which has two answer sets $\emptyset$ and $\{p\}$. Similarly, for the case (vi), $p; \neg p \leftarrow$ has two answer sets $\{p\}$ and $\{\neg p\}$. For the case (vii), the integrity constraint $\leftarrow p, \neg p$ eliminates the answer set Lit if it is added to $\{p \leftarrow, \neg p \leftarrow\}$ as in the proof of Theorem 4.4.

4.2 Update Equivalence on Common Rules

Theorem 4.3 implies that only valid rules can be safely eliminated from a program under the situation that any update can occur. This is a rather unexpected result. In fact, we cannot even show S-update equivalence of $\{p; p \leftarrow q\}$ and $\{p \leftarrow q\}$, although the latter rule is just a *merged* form of the former. The main reason why such two programs P_1 and P_2 are not S-update equivalent is that, when a rule r_1 in $P_1 \setminus P_2$ is removed, r_1 is syntactically different from the semantically equivalent rule r_2 in $P_2 \setminus P_1$. Thus, removing $Q = \{r_1\}$ from P_1 and P_2 results in elimination of r_1 from P_1 while r_2 remains in P_2.

A rational solution is to exclude removal of rules from $P_1 \Delta P_2$ in testing update equivalence. In other words, a removal-addition pair (Q, R) is considered for any program R and any set Q of rules from $P_1 \cap P_2$.

Definition 4.3. Two programs P_1 and P_2 are *update equivalent on common rules* (*C-update equivalent*, for short) if $\mathcal{AS}((P_1 \setminus Q) \cup R) = \mathcal{AS}((P_2 \setminus Q) \cup R)$ holds for any pair (Q, R) of programs such that Q consists of rules from $P_1 \cap P_2$ and R is any set of rules.

Update equivalence on common rules is a restricted version of S-update equivalence, and hence update equivalence implies C-update equivalence. Many important program transformations proposed in the literature preserve C-update equivalence. For example, the previous program $\{p; p \leftarrow q\}$ is C-update equivalent to its merged form $\{p \leftarrow q\}$. In [7], it is shown that any rule of the form
$not\, L_1; \cdots; not\, L_l \leftarrow L_{l+1}, \ldots, L_m, not\, L_{m+1}, \ldots, not\, L_n$
can be transformed to an integrity constraint of the form
$\leftarrow L_1, \ldots, L_l, L_{l+1}, \ldots, L_m, not\, L_{m+1}, \ldots, not\, L_n$
without changing the answer sets. Such a *modular* transformation preserves C-update equivalence as well as strong equivalence [11]. In fact, whenever $P_1 \cap P_2$ is empty, P_1 and P_2 are C-update equivalent if and only if P_1 and P_2 are strongly equivalent. The next theorem generalizes this fact.

Theorem 4.5. *Two programs P_1 and P_2 are C-update equivalent if and only if $P_1 \setminus P_2$ and $P_2 \setminus P_1$ are strongly equivalent.*

Proof. Let $P = P_1 \cap P_2$. If P_1 and P_2 are C-update equivalent, then $\mathcal{AS}((P_1 \setminus P) \cup R) = \mathcal{AS}((P_2 \setminus P) \cup R)$ holds for any program R. Then, $P_1 \setminus P$ and $P_2 \setminus P$ are strongly equivalent. That is, $P_1 \setminus P_2$ and $P_2 \setminus P_1$ are strongly equivalent.

Conversely, suppose that $P_1 \setminus P_2$ and $P_2 \setminus P_1$ are strongly equivalent. Then, $P_1 \setminus P$ and $P_2 \setminus P$ are strongly equivalent. That is, $\mathcal{AS}((P_1 \setminus P) \cup R) = \mathcal{AS}((P_2 \setminus P) \cup R)$

holds for any program R. Here, $R = (R \cap P) \cup (R \backslash P)$. Let Q be the program such that $R \cap P = P \backslash Q$, and R' be the program $R \backslash P$. Then, $(P_i \backslash P) \cup R = (P_i \backslash Q) \cup R'$ holds for $i = 1, 2$. Hence, $\mathcal{AS}((P_1 \backslash Q) \cup R') = \mathcal{AS}((P_2 \backslash Q) \cup R')$ holds. Since R is any program, Q can be any subset of P and R' can also be any program. This implies that P_1 and P_2 are C-update equivalent.   □

On the other hand, an *unfold/fold transformation* [20] does not preserve C-update equivalence. For example, $\{p \leftarrow q, \quad q \leftarrow r\}$ and $\{p \leftarrow r, \quad q \leftarrow r\}$ are weakly equivalent, but are not even strongly equivalent because the addition of q causes the truth of p in the former only. In Section 1, we have seen that $\{p \leftarrow, \quad q \leftarrow not\, p\}$ is strongly equivalent to $\{p \leftarrow \}$. However, these two programs are not C-update equivalent because removing the common $p \leftarrow$ derives q in the former. Although it is claimed that strong equivalence allows us to replace the former rules with the latter, we regard that such a transformation is not tolerant of program updates.[4] Hence, C-update equivalence gives us a better criterion of program transformation than strong equivalence under the situation that updates may occur.

The relationship between several notions of equivalence in logic programs can be summarized in the form of relative update equivalence as follows.

Proposition 4.6. *Let P_1 and P_2 be programs such that $P_1 \subset \mathcal{P}$ and $P_2 \subset \mathcal{P}$ where $\mathcal{P}$ is the set of all rules in the language of P_1 and P_2.*

(1) P_1 *and* P_2 *are S-update equivalent iff they are update equivalent wrt* $(\mathcal{P}, \mathcal{P})$. *iff they are update equivalent wrt* $(P_1 \cup P_2, \mathcal{P})$.
(2) P_1 *and* P_2 *are C-update equivalent iff they are update equivalent wrt* $(P_1 \cap P_2, \mathcal{P})$.
(3) P_1 *and* P_2 *are strongly equivalent iff they are update equivalent wrt* $(\emptyset, \mathcal{P})$.
(4) P_1 *and* P_2 *are weakly equivalent iff they are update equivalent wrt* $(\emptyset, \emptyset)$.

Note in Proposition 4.6 (1) that the removal rules in S-update equivalence can be set to the union of two given programs, $P_1 \cup P_2$, rather than the set of all rules $\mathcal{P}$ in the language. This is because any rule in $\mathcal{P} \backslash (P_1 \cup P_2)$ has no effect if it is removed from either P_1 or P_2, that is, both P_1 and P_2 are unchanged by such a removal.

5   Uniform Equivalence

In database updates, updates are permitted only on variable data. Representing a database as a logic program P, P is usually divided into two parts: $P = Int(P) \cup Ext(P)$, where $Int(P) \cap Ext(P) = \emptyset$. Here, $Ext(P)$ denotes the set of facts in P called an *extensional database*, and the set of non-facts $Int(P) = P \backslash Ext(P)$ is called an *intensional database*. In databases, $Ext(P)$ can be considered as variable data while $Int(P)$ is regarded as invariable knowledge. Similarly, the

---

[4] Unlike strong equivalence, RED⁻, NONMIN, WGPPE and S-IMP in [4] fail to preserve C-update equivalence (thereby, S-update equivalence).

set of all literals in the language is divided into the *extensional literals* $\mathcal{E}$ and the *intensional literals* $\mathcal{I}$ as: $Lit = \mathcal{I} \cup \mathcal{E}$, where $\mathcal{I} \cap \mathcal{E} = \emptyset$. Here, $\mathcal{I}$ is the set of all literals with the predicates appearing in heads of $Int(P)$, and $\mathcal{E}$ is the set of all other literals. Then, two databases P_1 and P_2 are *equivalent* in the sense of Sagiv [19] if P_1 and P_2 are strongly equivalent with respect to $\mathcal{E}$.

Sagiv [19] also considers *uniform equivalence* of two Datalog programs which can be defined as follows. Two programs P_1 and P_2 are *uniformly equivalent* if the output of P_1 agrees with that of P_2 for any input from $Lit = \mathcal{I} \cup \mathcal{E}$, where the output of P is defined as $\{ S \cap \mathcal{I} \mid S \in \mathcal{AS}(P \cup R), R \subseteq Lit \}$.

Uniform equivalence implies Sagiv's equivalence. In fact, uniform equivalence takes an input literal set R not only from the extensional part $\mathcal{E}$ but also from the intensional one $\mathcal{I}$. Since it is obvious that the extensional part in each answer set S, i.e., $\mathcal{E} \cap S$, is always the same between the two, it turns out that two programs are uniformly equivalent if and only if they are strongly equivalent with respect to Lit. Sagiv uses the notion of uniform equivalence for minimizing Datalog programs. Eiter and Fink [2] consider uniform equivalence for normal and extended disjunctive programs. The notion of (uniform) equivalence can also be generalized to update equivalence as follows.

Definition 5.1. Let P_1 and P_2 be programs. Suppose that $\mathcal{I}$ and $\mathcal{E}$ are the sets of intentional and extensional literals, respectively, which are common to both P_1 and P_2. Then, P_1 and P_2 are *extensionally update equivalent* if they are update equivalent with respect to $(\mathcal{E}, \mathcal{E})$. On the other hand, P_1 and P_2 are *uniformly update equivalent* if they are update equivalent with respect to (Lit, Lit).

Example 5.1. Suppose that two databases P_1 and P_2 are given as

$$P_1 = \{ p \leftarrow a, q, \qquad q \leftarrow not\, b, \quad b \leftarrow \},$$
$$P_2 = \{ p \leftarrow a, not\, b, \quad q \leftarrow not\, b, \quad b \leftarrow \},$$

where $\mathcal{E} = \{a, b\}$ and $\mathcal{I} = \{p, q\}$. Then, P_1 and P_2 are extensionally update equivalent, but are not uniformly update equivalent. In fact, P_1 and P_2 are update equivalent with respect to $(\mathcal{E}, \mathcal{E})$, but are not with respect to (Lit, Lit) because $\mathcal{AS}(P_1 \cup \{a, q\}) = \{\{a, b, p, q\}\}$ while $\mathcal{AS}(P_2 \cup \{a, q\}) = \{\{a, b, q\}\}$.

A database P is *disjunctive* if disjunctions appear in P. Usually, $Ext(P)$ also contains disjunctive facts in disjunctive databases. Let $\mathcal{D}(\mathcal{E})$ be the set of all disjunctions of literals from $\mathcal{E}$. Then, *disjunctively update equivalence* of two databases is defined as update equivalence with respect to $(\mathcal{D}(\mathcal{E}), \mathcal{D}(\mathcal{E}))$. This can also be represented by the notion of *disjunctive explanations* in [8].

Often, updates on the invariable part are translated into updates on the variable part in databases. This type of updates is called *view updates*. The view update problem in databases is concerned with the problem of translating an update request on intentional literals in $\mathcal{I}$ into updates on extensional literals $\mathcal{E}$. This problem can be characterized by *extended abduction* [6], and we will consider equivalence with respect to abductive updates in another paper.

6   Computation and Complexity

This section considers the computational aspects of update equivalence.

We first show a translation of relative update equivalence into relative strong equivalence, which is similar to the transformation proposed in [6,8].

Given two tested programs P_1 and P_2 and the updatable rules Q and R, we convert the update equivalence problem (P_1, P_2, Q, R) into the strong equivalence problem $(K_1, K_2, K) = (\nu(P_1), \nu(P_2), \mu(Q) \cup R)$, where K_1 and K_2 are programs and K is a set of insertable rules. To this end, any removable rule r in Q is associated with a unique literal δ_r (the *name* of r) through negation as failure as $not\, \delta_r$. In this way, the deletion of r is realized by the addition of δ_r to the program. Then, the translations ν and μ are defined as:

$$\nu(P_i) = (P_i \setminus Q) \cup \{ (H \leftarrow B, not\, \delta_r) \mid r = (H \leftarrow B) \in P_i \cap Q \}, \quad (i = 1, 2)$$
$$\mu(Q) = \{ \delta_r \mid r \in Q \}.$$

Theorem 6.1. *Suppose that (P_1, P_2, Q, R) is converted to (K_1, K_2, K) as above. P_1 and P_2 are update equivalent with respect to (Q, R) if and only if K_1 and K_2 are strongly equivalent with respect to K.*

Notice that the translation ν is modular. Without loss of generality, we can assume that the removable rules Q are finite and are included in $P_1 \cup P_2$; if $Q \not\subseteq P_1 \cup P_2$, we can substitute Q with $Q \cap (P_1 \cup P_2)$ without changing the result of equivalence testing. See also Proposition 4.6 (1). Then, the translations ν and μ can always be computed in linear time.

Example 6.1. Two programs $\{ p \leftarrow not\, q, \leftarrow q \}$ and $\{ p \leftarrow , \leftarrow q \}$ are strongly equivalent. However, they are neither S-update equivalent nor C-update equivalent. In fact, removing the common constraint $\leftarrow q$ and adding $q \leftarrow$ cause the deletion of p in the former only. Let us verify this fact. The constraint $\leftarrow q$ is converted to $\leftarrow q, not\, \delta_{\leftarrow q}$, so the addition of $\{ \delta_{\leftarrow q}, q \}$ to both converted programs causes the same effect. On the other hand, if the constraint $\leftarrow q$ as well as other rules are not removable, no rule is converted, and hence they become update equivalent with respect to $(\emptyset, R)$ for any R, that is, they are (relatively) strongly equivalent.

Theorem 6.1 reduces testing relative update equivalence to testing relative strong equivalence. At the moment, however, no sophisticated procedure is known for testing relative strong equivalence,[5] although some useful methods exist for testing non-relative strong equivalence [18,14,21]. In fact, we can show that update equivalence in general is harder than strong equivalence as follows.

To establish the computational complexity of relative update equivalence of propositional programs, we can use Proposition 4.6 (4) and the result by Turner [21] that deciding weak equivalence of two GEDPs is Π_2^P-hard.

---

[5] Woltran [22] recently showed that strong/uniform equivalence *wrt all rules over some alphabet* can be reduced to weak equivalence. We can also show that strong equivalence *wrt a finite set of rules* can be reduced to weak equivalence.

Theorem 6.2. *The problem of checking relative update equivalence of two propositional programs is Π_2^P-hard in general.*

By contrast, checking S-update equivalence of two programs P_1 and P_2 can be done in polynomial time by Theorems 4.3 and 4.4. That is, we check whether each rule in $P_1 \Delta P_2$ is valid or not. If every rule in $P_1 \Delta P_2$ is valid, P_1 and P_2 are S-update equivalent; otherwise, they are not S-update equivalent.

Theorem 6.3. *S-update equivalence of two propositional programs can be decided in polynomial time.*

Now, we compare the notions of weak, strong, and update equivalence in the non-relative versions from the complexity viewpoint. In [21], it is shown that deciding strong equivalence of two GEDPs is in coNP and that deciding weak equivalence of two GEDPs is Π_2^P-hard. Hence, the strength of S-update equivalence is reflected in the time complexity of the respective decision problems: unless the polynomial hierarchy collapses, deciding S-update equivalence is easier than deciding strong equivalence, which in turn is easier than weak equivalence.

Although the notion of S-update equivalence seems too strong to be practical, C-update equivalence is more attractive. In fact, Theorem 4.5 indicates that C-update equivalence is much closer to strong equivalence.

Theorem 6.4. *The problem of checking C-update equivalence of two propositional programs is coNP-complete.*

7   Conclusion

We have proposed update equivalence in logic programming, investigated its properties, considered several variants, and presented their applications. We have completely characterized each case of update equivalence. Although the condition for S-update equivalence is very strong, one for C-update equivalence is rather practical. We have also shown that most previously proposed notions of equivalence in logic programming and deductive databases can be characterized by relative update equivalence. The notion of update equivalence can thus be used to guarantee the correctness of a program transformation in a dynamic setting, and is helpful to optimize logic programs for various applications.

We can consider more general form of programs allowing *nested expressions* [12]. There are some formalizations of strong equivalence of two nested logic programs in non-standard logics [18,17,21]. While we have shown that relative update equivalence can be converted to relative strong equivalence, more direct connections between these logics and update equivalence are also worth investigating. Another future work is to characterize many transformation techniques in logic programming in terms of subclasses of relative update equivalence. New transformations preserving relative update equivalence should also be developed.

References

1. S. Brass and J. Dix. Characterization of the disjunctive stable semantics by partial evaluation. *Journal of Logic Programming*, 32(3):207–228, 1997.
2. T. Eiter and M. Fink. Uniform equivalence of logic programs under the stable model semantics. In: *Proc. of ICLP 2003*, LNCS 2916, pp. 224–238, Springer, 2003.
3. T. Eiter, M. Fink, G. Sabbatini, and H. Tompits. Reasoning about evolving non-monotonic knowledge bases. In: *Proc. of LPAR 2001*, LNAI 2250, pp. 407–421, Springer, 2001.
4. T. Eiter, M. Fink, H. Tompits, and S. Woltran. Simplifying logic programs under uniform and strong equivalence. In: *Proc. of LPNMR 2004*, LNAI 2923, pp. 87–99, Springer, 2004.
5. M. Gelfond and V. Lifschitz. Classical negation in logic programs and disjunctive databases. *New Generation Computing*, 9:365–385, 1991.
6. K. Inoue. A simple characterization of extended abduction. In *Proc. of the 1st International Conference on Computational Logic*, LNAI 1861, pp. 718–732, Springer, 2000.
7. K. Inoue and C. Sakama. Negation as failure in the head. *Journal of Logic Programming*, 35(1):39–78, 1998.
8. K. Inoue and C. Sakama. Disjunctive explanations. In: *Proc. of ICLP 2002*, LNCS 2401, pp. 317–332, Springer, 2002.
9. A. C. Kakas, R. A. Kowalski, and F. Toni. The role of abduction in logic programming. In: D. M. Gabbay, C. J. Hogger and J. A. Robinson (eds.), *Handbook of Logic in Artificial Intelligence and Logic Programming*, volume 5, pp. 235–324, Oxford University Press, 1998.
10. J. A. Leite. *Evolving Knowledge Bases*. IOS Press, 2003.
11. V. Lifschitz, D. Pearce, and A. Valverde. Strongly equivalent logic programs. *ACM Transactions on Computational Logic*, 2:526–541, 2001.
12. V. Lifschitz, L. R. Tang, and H. Turner. Nested expressions in logic programs. *Annals of Mathematics and Artificial Intelligence*, 25:369–389, 1999.
13. V. Lifschitz and T. Y. C. Woo. Answer sets in general nonmonotonic reasoning (preliminary report). In: *Proc. of KR '92*, pp. 603–614, Morgan Kaufmann, 1992.
14. F. Lin. Reducing strong equivalence of logic programs to entailment in classical propositional logic. In: *Proc. of KR 2002*, pp. 170–176, Morgan Kaufmann, 2002.
15. M. J. Maher. Equivalence of logic programs. In: [16], pp. 627–658, 1988.
16. J. Minker (ed.). *Foundations of Deductive Databases and Logic Programming*. Morgan Kaufmann, 1988.
17. M. Osorio, J. A. Navarro, and J. Arrazola. Equivalence in answer set programming. In: *Proc. of LOPSTR 2001*, LNCS 2372, pp. 57–75, Springer, 2001.
18. D. Pearce, H. Tompits, and S. Woltran. Encodings for equilibrium logic and logic programs with nested expressions. In: *Proc. of EPIA 2001*, LNCS 2258, pp. 306–320, Springer, 2001.
19. Y. Sagiv. Optimizing Datalog programs. In: [16], pp. 659–668, 1988.
20. H. Tamaki and T. Sato. Unfold/fold transformation of logic programs. In: *Proc. of the 2nd International Conference on Logic Programming*, pp. 127–138, 1984.
21. H. Turner. Strong equivalence made easy: nested expressions and weight constraints. *Theory and Practice of Logic Programming*, 3(4–5):609–622, 2003.
22. S. Woltran. Characterizations for relativized notions of equivalence in answer set programming. In: *Proc. of JELIA '04*, LNAI, this volume, 2004.

Cardinality Constraint Programs

Tommi Syrjänen*

Helsinki University of Technology, Dept. of Computer Science and Eng.,
Laboratory for Theoretical Computer Science,
P.O.Box 5400, FIN-02015 HUT, Finland
Tommi.Syrjanen@hut.fi

Abstract. We define the class of cardinality constraint logic programs
and provide a formal stable model semantics for them. The class extends
normal logic programs by allowing the use of cardinality constraints and
conditional literals. We identify a decidable subset, omega-restricted programs, of the class. We show how the formal semantics can be extended
to allow the use of evaluated function symbols, such as arithmetic built-
in operators. The omega-restricted cardinality constraint programs have
been implemented in the Smodels system.

1 Introduction

When we use Answer Set Programming (ASP) to solve a problem, we encode it
using some logical framework so that the solutions correspond with the models
of the system, and then use a solver of the chosen formalism to find them.
What differentiates ASP from the traditional logic programming is that an ASP
solution is a set of literals instead of a proof tree of Prolog and its derivatives.

Most ASP systems use the stable model semantics [6] of logic programs as
their underlying semantics ([12,4,1]) but systems based on propositional logic
([5]) also exist. Most logic program -based systems have some extensions to the
basic inference rules. For example, dlv [4] allows disjunctive rules and SMOD-
ELS [12] has cardinality and weight constraint literals.

The usual way to define a semantics for ASP is to start with variable-free
(ground) programs and then say that the variables are just short-hand constructs
for denoting sets of rules. This approach has the advantage that you do not have
to alter the basic semantics to use variables and in most cases it is easy to see
what set of ground rules correspond to a rule with variables. However, the things
get more complex when we allow the use of function symbols, especially when
some of function symbols are built-ins that should be evaluated (like $+$, $-$) and
some are uninterpreted Herbrand terms.

In this work we examine in detail how formal stable model semantics can be
defined for non-ground logic programs with cardinality constraints and conditional literals, and explain the motivation why the definitions are done the way
they are. We do it in four steps: 1) we define the semantics for ground programs;

---

* This work has been supported by the Academy of Finland (project 53695).

J.J. Alferes and J. Leite (Eds.): JELIA 2004, LNAI 3229, pp. 187–199, 2004.

2) add variables to them; 3) define some syntactic sugar to make the language easier to use; and 4) identify a decidable subset that corresponds to the language used in the SMODELS system.[1] Finally, we show how interpreted built-in functions fit into the formal semantics. This work is based on [11] and extends [10]. Non-ground cardinality and weight constraints have been examined also earlier ([9,8]). This work has two major differences from the precious work: (1) we allow the default negation of cardinality constraint literals; and (2) the treatment of conditional literals is now more precise.

In the language definition we identify basic primitives and the more complex constructs are then translated into programs that use only those primitives. The main criteria that we use in selecting the primitives are:

1. A program with variables can always be replaced by a ground program that has the same set stable models;
2. When an extended program is translated into basic primitives no new atoms should be generated;
3. It should be possible to translate a complex program with variables without having to instantiate the program first; and
4. All translations should be linear in size.

The first criterion means that we keep the standard interpretation of variables as short-hand notation for sets of ground rules as this makes defining the semantics more convenient. If function symbols are used, then the corresponding ground program is infinite. The second criterion is included since we want to keep a very close link between the original extended program and the translated simple one. It also allows us to manipulate the programs by combining or splitting them without having to worry about possible clashes introduced by the new atoms. The third criterion is connected to the first one with the idea being that we can always see the intended meaning of the program without having to create the potentially infinite instantiation. A translation is linear if the number of new literals and rules is some constant times the size of the original construct.

2   Language

A *term* is either a *variable* or a *function term* $f(t_1, \ldots, t_k)$ where f is a k-ary function symbol and $t_1, \ldots, t_k$ are terms. A 0-ary function symbol is a *constant*. A term is *ground* if it does not contain any variables.

An *atom* is of the form $p(t_1, \ldots, t_k)$ where p is a k-ary predicate symbol and $t_1, \ldots, t_k$ are terms. An atom is ground iff all terms in it are ground. In the following we use A to denote an atom if we are not interested in its arguments, and pred(A) to denote its predicate symbol. The symbol $\top$ denotes a special atom that is always true. A *basic literal* is either an atom A (positive) or its negation not A (negative). We use L to denote a basic literal and $\overline{L}$ its complement when their arguments are not relevant. A *conditional literal* L_c is of the form:

$$X.L : A \tag{1}$$

---

[1] However, the current version of SMODELS recognizes a slightly simpler language.

where the *main literal* L is a basic literal, the *condition* A is an atom, and X is a set of *local variables*. If $X = \emptyset$, we denote (1) simply as $L : A$, and if X is a singleton set we write it without braces. All variables that occur in L_c that are not local are *global*. Intuitively $L : A$ can be seen as a conjunction that is evaluated in two phases: first A is checked, and if it is true, then the truth value of L determines the truth value of the whole construct. A conditional literal is positive if L is, and it is negative otherwise. A *literal* is either a basic literal or a conditional literal. We use the notation $\mathcal{L}$ to denote literals.

A *cardinality constraint* C is of the form:

$$C = \mathrm{Card}(b, S) \tag{2}$$

where b is an integral *bound* and S is a set of literals. The basic intuition is that C is true if the number of true literals $\mathcal{L} \in S$ is greater than or equal to b.[2] The set of positive literals in S is denoted by $\mathrm{pos}(C)$ and the set of negative literals by $\mathrm{neg}(C)$. A *cardinality constraint literal* $\mathcal{C}$ is either a cardinality constraint C or its negation not C.

A *basic rule* is of the form:

$$A \leftarrow \mathcal{C}_1, \dots, \mathcal{C}_n \tag{3}$$

where the *head* A is an atom, and $\mathcal{C}_i$ in its *body* are cardinality constraint literals. The rule (3) encodes the fact that if all literals in the body are true, then the head must also be true. If the body is empty ($n = 0$), then we call a basic rule a *fact*. As above, $\mathrm{pos}(R)$ and $\mathrm{neg}(R)$ denote the sets of positive and negative cardinality constraint literals in the rule body.

We immediately define a two shorthand notations that are used in our examples: 1) a basic literal L in a rule body denotes the constraint literal $\mathrm{Card}(1, \{L\})$; and 2) an empty head is replaced by a new atom f that does not occur anywhere in the program and a rule $f' \leftarrow f, \mathrm{not}\ f'$ that causes a contradiction if f is true to the program. Thus, such a rule acts as a constraint on the models and a model candidate that makes its body true is rejected.

A *choice rule* has the form:

$$\{A\} \leftarrow \mathcal{C}_1, \dots, \mathcal{C}_n \tag{4}$$

where A and $\mathcal{C}_i$ are defined as above. The intuition is that if the rule body is true, then A may be true but it does not have to be true. A cardinality constraint program is a set of rules.

For each formula (term, literal, cardinality constraint, or rule) F, $\mathrm{Var}(F)$ denotes the set of variables that occur in it.

These definitions conclude our basic language. In Section 4 we define several extended language constructs that are then translated to the basic language.

---

[2] In SMODELS syntax this written as $b\ S$

3   Stable Model Semantics

3.1   Ground Programs

In this section we define the stable model semantics for the basic cardinality constraint programs. We do the definition in stages, starting from the simplest possible programs and then extend the definitions to cover the full basic language. In the definition we will be using the notation $M \models F$ to denote that a set of ground atoms M satisfies the formula F. In particular, for an atom A, $M \models A$ iff $A \in M$ and $M \models$ not A iff $A \notin M$. In case of a cardinality constraint $\mathrm{Card}(b, S)$ where S contains only basic literals, $M \models \mathrm{Card}(b, S)$ iff $b \leq |\{L \in S \mid M \models L\}|$, and $M \models$ not $\mathrm{Card}(b, S)$ iff $M \not\models \mathrm{Card}(b, S)$.

In the simplest case the rules have only basic literals and positive cardinality constraint literals in their bodies. We call these *simple* rules. They are essentially equivalent to the extended programs presented in [8].

Definition 1. *Let $C = \mathrm{Card}(b, S)$ be a ground cardinality constraint and M be a set of ground atoms. Then, the reduct C^M is the cardinality constraint:*

$$C^M = \mathrm{Card}(b', \mathrm{pos}(C)) \tag{5}$$

where $b' = b - |\{L \in \mathrm{neg}(C) \mid M \models L\}|$. The reduct R^M of a ground simple basic rule $R = A \leftarrow C_1, \ldots, C_n$ is the singleton set of rules:

$$R^M = \{A \leftarrow C_1^M, \ldots, C_n^M\} \tag{6}$$

and the reduct of a ground simple choice rule $R = \{A\} \leftarrow C_1, \ldots, C_n$ is the set of rules:

$$R^M = \begin{cases} \{A \leftarrow C_1^M, \ldots, C_n^M\}, & \text{if } A \in M \\ \emptyset, & \text{otherwise} . \end{cases} \tag{7}$$

A reduct of a set P of ground simple rules is the set:

$$P^M = \bigcup_{R \in P} R^M . \tag{8}$$

Example 1. Consider the rule $R = \{a\} \leftarrow \mathrm{Card}(2, \{b, \text{not } c\})$ and let $M = \{a\}$. Then, $R^M = \{a \leftarrow \mathrm{Card}(1, \{b\})\}$.

Note that all rules that belong to a reduct of a program P are basic rules and all basic literals that occur in them are positive. Such rules are monotonous [8] so the reduct P^M has a unique least model that we denote with $\mathbf{MM}(P^M)$. The least model is the least fixpoint of the operator T_P where $T_P(S) = \{A \mid A \leftarrow C_1^M, \ldots, C_n^M \in P^M$ and $S \models C_1^M, \ldots, C_n^M\}$ [8]. If this least model happens to coincide with M, then M is a stable model of P.

Definition 2. *Let P be a ground simple cardinality constraint program. A set of ground atoms M is a* stable model *of P if and only if:*

$$\mathbf{MM}(P^M) = M . \tag{9}$$

Next, we extend the semantics by allowing ground conditional literals as well as negative cardinality constraints. We add an extra step, *expansion*, that is done before reduction and at this point all conditional literals $L : A$ are either replaced by L if A is true or removed altogether if A is false.

Definition 3. *Let M be a ground set of atoms. Then, the* expansion *of a ground basic literal L with respect to M is* $E(L, M) = \{L\}$, *and the expansion of a ground conditional literal $L_c = L : A$ is*

$$E(L_c, M) = \begin{cases} \{L\}, & A \in M \\ \emptyset, & \text{otherwise} . \end{cases} \tag{10}$$

The expansion of a ground cardinality constraint $\text{Card}(b, S)$ *with respect to M is the cardinality constraint:*

$$\text{Card}(b, \bigcup_{\mathcal{L} \in S} E(\mathcal{L}, M)) . \tag{11}$$

Example 2. Let $C = \text{Card}(1, \{a : \top, \text{not } b, c : d, e : f\})$ and $M = \{d\}$. Then, $E(C, M) = \text{Card}(1, \{a, \text{not } b, c\})$.

We obtain the reduct of a ground rule by first expanding all constraint literals in its body, and then removing the negative constraints from its body in a way that is analogous to the original Gelfond-Lifschitz -reduction [6].

Definition 4. *Let $R = A \leftarrow C_1, \ldots, C_n, \text{not } C'_1, \ldots, \text{not } C'_m$ be a basic cardinality constraint rule and M a set of ground atoms. Then, the* reduct R^M *is:*

$$R^M = \begin{cases} \{A \leftarrow E(C_1, M)^M, \ldots, E(C_n, M)^M\}, & M \models E(C'_1, M)^M, \ldots, \\ & \qquad\qquad E(C'_m, M)^M \tag{12} \\ \emptyset, & \text{otherwise} . \end{cases}$$

Let $R = \{A\} \leftarrow C_1, \ldots, C_n, \text{not } C'_1, \ldots, \text{not } C'_m$ be a choice rule. Then,

$$R^M = \begin{cases} \{A \leftarrow E(C_1, M)^M, \ldots, E(C_n, M)^M\}, & M \models E(C'_1, M)^M, \ldots, \\ & \qquad\qquad E(C'_m, M)^M \\ & \text{and } A \in M \tag{13} \\ \emptyset, & \text{otherwise} . \end{cases}$$

As was the case with the simple programs, M is a stable model of P if and only if $P = \mathbf{MM}(P^M)$.

Example 3. Let P be the program:

$$\{a\} \leftarrow \text{not } \text{Card}(1, \{b : a\})$$
$$\{b\} \leftarrow \text{Card}(1, \{\text{not } a\})$$

Now P has three stable models: $M_1 = \emptyset$, $M_2 = \{a\}$, and $M_3 = \{b\}$. In the case of M_2, the reduct $P^M = \{a \leftarrow\}$ since $M_2 \models \text{not } \text{Card}(1, \{b : a\})^M = \text{not } \text{Card}(1, \{b\})$.

3.2 Programs with Variables

A rule with variables denotes the set of ground rules that can be obtained by replacing each variable by terms of the Herbrand universe of the program. As there are two types of variables, local and global, the instantiation is defined in two parts. First, the local variables in conditional literals are replaced by their instantiations, and then the same is done for the global variables.

The *Herbrand universe* $\mathbf{HU}(P)$ of a cardinality constraint program P is the set of all ground terms that can be constructed using the function terms that occur in P.

Definition 5. *A substitution is a function $\sigma_{V,U} : V \to U$ that maps a set of variables V to an universe U. The set of all substitutions from V to U is denoted by $\mathrm{Sub}(V, U)$.*

A substitution *applied* to a variable v is the term:

$$v\sigma_{V,U} = \begin{cases} \sigma_{V,U}(v), & v \in V \\ v, & \text{otherwise,} \end{cases} \tag{14}$$

and a substitution applied to a function term $t = f(t_1, \dots, t_n)$ is the term $t\sigma = f(t_1\sigma, \dots, t_n\sigma)$. For atoms and literals the substitution is applied similarly to the case of function terms, that is, their arguments are substituted.

Definition 6. *Let P be a program and $L_c = X.L : A$ be a conditional literal that occurs in it. Then, the* local instantiation $I(L_c, P)$ *of L_c is the set:*

$$I(L_c, P) = \{L\sigma : A\sigma \mid \sigma \in \mathrm{Sub}(X, \mathbf{HU}(P))\} . \tag{15}$$

The local instantiation of a basic literal L is the set $I(L, P) = \{L\}$, and the local instantiation of a cardinality constraint $C = \mathrm{Card}(b, S)$ is the constraint $I(C, P) = \mathrm{Card}(b, \bigcup_{\mathcal{L} \in P} I(\mathcal{L}, P))$.

Definition 7. *The* instantiation *of a rule $R = A \leftarrow C_1, \dots, C_n$ is the set of rules:*

$$\mathbf{HI}(R, P) = \{A\sigma \leftarrow I(C_1, P)\sigma, \dots, I(C_n, P)\sigma \mid \sigma \in \mathrm{Sub}(\mathrm{Var}(P), \mathbf{HU}(P))\} \tag{16}$$

The Herbrand instantiation *of a program P is the set of rules:*

$$\mathbf{HI}(P) = \bigcup_{R \in P} \mathbf{HI}(R, P) . \tag{17}$$

Example 4. Consider the following encoding H of the Hamilton cycle problem:

$$\{hc(X, Y)\} \leftarrow arc(X, Y)$$
$$\leftarrow \mathrm{Card}(2, \{Y.hc(X, Y) : arc(X, Y)\}), vtx(X)$$
$$r(Y) \leftarrow \mathrm{Card}(1, \{start(X), r(X)\}), hc(X, Y), arc(X, Y)$$
$$\leftarrow vtx(X), \mathrm{not}\ r(X).$$

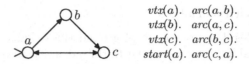

$$vtx(a). \quad arc(a,b).$$
$$vtx(b). \quad arc(a,c).$$
$$vtx(c). \quad arc(b,c).$$
$$start(a). \quad arc(c,a).$$

Fig. 1. Sample graph for the Hamilton cycle problem

The first rule asserts that each arc of the graph may belong in the Hamiltonian cycle, and the second one ensures that at most one arc may leave from any vertex of the graph. The third rule computes the the the set of visited vertices starting from an initial vertex, and the last rule ensures that all vertices belong to the cycle.

Next we add to the program the datacorresponding to the graph that is presented in Figure 1. Then, the local instantiations of the constraint literal in the second rule is: $\{hc(X,a) : arc(X,a), hc(X,b) : arc(X,b), hc(X,b) : arc(X,b)\}$, so the instantiation of the rule is:

$$\leftarrow \text{Card}(2, \{hc(a,a) : arc(a,a), hc(a,b) : arc(a,b), hc(a,c) : arc(a,c)\}), vtx(a)$$
$$\leftarrow \text{Card}(2, \{hc(b,a) : arc(b,a), hc(b,b) : arc(b,b), hc(b,c) : arc(b,c)\}), vtx(b)$$
$$\leftarrow \text{Card}(2, \{hc(c,a) : arc(c,a), hc(c,b) : arc(c,b), hc(c,c) : arc(c,c)\}), vtx(c) \ .$$

4   The Extended Language

In this section we define several additional syntactic constructs for cardinality constraint programs. They are seen as notational shortcuts for larger basic language constructs. We have found that these extensions are useful in practice for modeling several different problem domains.

Upper Bounds for Constraints. We allow a cardinality constraint to have also an upper bound u. The intuition is that a constraint $C_u = \text{Card}(b, u, S)$ is true iff the number of satisfied literals in it is between the bounds, inclusive. We can express C_u in basic syntax by replacing it with two constraint literals: $\text{Card}(b, S)$ and not $\text{Card}(u + 1, S)$. The intuition is that C_u is true if the lower bound is met but it is not the case that the number of satisfied literals is strictly greater than the upper bound.

Conditional Literals in Rule Bodies. We need a more complex translation if we want to use a conditional literal $X.L : A$. An intuitive semantics for such literal is universal quantification; the non-ground conditional literal should be true if $L\sigma$ is true when $A\sigma$ is. Thus, we replace it by a negative constraint literal:

$$\text{not Card}(1, \{\overline{L} : A\}) \ . \tag{18}$$

This construct is analogous to the classical equality of $\forall x.p(x)$ and $\neg\exists x\neg p(x)$. However, in Section 5 we see that it differs from the classical case in one important sense.

Positive Cardinality Constraint Literals in Rule Heads. Thus far we have had only atoms in rule heads. However, many problems have natural representations where there are cardinality constraints in the heads so we want to allow them with the restriction that all literals that occur in the head are positive. A rule:

$$\text{Card}(b, u, \{X_1.A_1 : D_1, \ldots, X_n.A_n : D_n\}) \leftarrow body \qquad (19)$$

is translated into $n + 2$ rules:

$$\{A'_i\} \leftarrow D'_i, body$$
$$\leftarrow \text{not } \text{Card}(b, \{X_1.A_1 : D_1, \ldots, X_n.A_n : D_n\}), body \qquad (20)$$
$$\leftarrow \text{Card}(u + 1, \{X_1.A_1 : D_1, \ldots, X_n.A_n : D_n\}), body$$

where A'_i and D'_i are obtained by renaming all local variables that occur in them. The first rule allows us to include any atom A_i in the model when the *body* is true while the next two rules ensure that the number of such atoms is between the bounds. In the first rule we effectively change local variables into global ones but this does not cause any problems since they stay local variables in the other two rules. If there is no upper bound, then the third rule is not necessary. Note also that if $b = 0$, then the second rule is trivially satisfied, so we obtain in that case behavior that is identical with choice rules.

Example 5. The rule $\text{Card}(1, 2, \{X.a(X) : b(X)\}) \leftarrow c(X)$ is translated to

$$\{a(Y)\} \leftarrow b(Y), c(X)$$
$$\leftarrow \text{not } \text{Card}(1, \{X.a(X) : b(X)\}), c(X)$$
$$\leftarrow \text{Card}(3, \{X.a(X) : b(X)\}), c(X) \ .$$

5   Discussion on the Basic and Extended Languages

In this section we examine the motivations for the definitions in the previous two sections. The very first question is: why cardinality literals and no literals for other aggregate types? The immediate reason is that they form a simple and well-understood base so the semantics stays relatively clear and intuitive. This simple case can then be extended to more complex aggregates when necessary.

Another, not as obvious reason is that cardinality constraints can be used everywhere where a basic literal can occur in normal programs, including in rule heads in the case of the full language. This means that we can use the full power of non-monotonic reasoning with them. A common approach for defining the stable model semantics for aggregates is to use them like negative literals in the reduct: if an aggregate is satisfied by the model candidate, it is removed, but if it is unsatisfied, the whole rule is discarded [7]. However, this makes it possible for an aggregate to justify itself in the model even when all basic literals in it are positive and ground. For example, if this approach is taken in the program:

$$a \leftarrow \text{Card}(1, \{a\}) \ ,$$

then $M = \{a\}$ is a valid stable model as $M \models \text{Card}(1, \{a\})$ even though the only justification for a is a itself.

Note that our semantics allows a circular justification in case where an atom depends on itself via double negation, as in

$$a \leftarrow \text{not Card}(1, \{\text{not } a\}) \ .$$

This example shows that $\text{Card}(1, \{a\})$ and not $\text{Card}(1, \{\text{not } a\})$ are not equivalent even though they are indistinguishable in the classical sense. This situation is analogous to the normal programs where $a \leftarrow a$ and $a \leftarrow \text{not } noa; noa \leftarrow \text{not } a$ have different stable models.

Positive cycles are also the reason why the basic language does not have conditional literals in rule heads. Consider the hypothetical rule $R = \{a : a\} \leftarrow$ that encodes the silly condition that a may be true if a is true. Now, if we expanded the condition before taking the reduct, then $\{a\}$ would be a model of R even though the only justification for a is that a is true.

The combination of local variables and conditional literals is interesting in the sense that you can use them to implement existential quantification in rule bodies. In effect, a cardinality constraint $\text{Card}(1, \{X.a(X) : b(X)\})$ encodes an existential quantification $\exists x.(a(x) \land b(x))$. A straightforward way to encode such a quantification using only normal programs, would need a new atom to do it. Similarly, we get an universal quantification $\forall x.(b(x) \rightarrow a(x))$ using not $\text{Card}(1, \{X.\text{not } a(X) : b(X)\})$. Encoding the universal quantification without conditional literals is tricky as you have to separate the cases where $b(X)$ is never true, so the implication is trivially true, from the cases where $b(X)$ is sometimes true.

6   Omega-Restricted Programs

If a logic program has function symbols in it, then its Herbrand instantiation is infinite and deciding whether it has a stable model or not becomes undecidable even when only Horn rules are used [3]. Also, even if the instantiation is finite, it may be exponential in size so constructing it may be intractable. Fortunately, in most cases most of the rules of the instantiation have trivially unsatisfiable bodies so we may leave them out without affecting the set of stable models.

Next we identify a decidable subset of cardinality constraint programs, namely ω-*restricted* programs [10]. The basic idea is to enforce syntactic restrictions on the programs so that it can be guaranteed that their all stable models are finite. The predicate symbols of a program are arranged into a stratification where more complex predicates are defined in terms of simpler ones. The stratification extends the usual definition of stratification [2] by adding a new level, the ω-stratum, to contain the unstratifiable part of the program.

A constraint literal is *simple* if it is of the form $\text{Card}(1, \{A : \top\})$. Intuitively, a rule is ω-restricted if each variable that occurs in it occurs also in some positive simple constraint literal whose main predicate is on a strictly lower stratum than the head of the rule. This condition ensures that stable models stay finite.

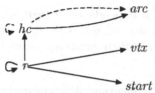

Fig. 2. The Dependency graph of the Hamilton cycle program

6.1 Dependency Graphs

We start by defining a few helper notations. The set $bbody^+(R)$ contains all positive basic literals and main literals of positive conditional literals that occur within positive cardinality constraint literals of the body of R. Thus,

$$bbody^+(R) = \bigcup_{C \in pos(R)} \{L \mid L \in pos(C) \text{ or } X.L : A \in pos(C)\} ,$$

while $bbody^-(R)$ contains all other basic and main literals. Finally, $simple(R)$ denotes the set of simple constraint literals in the body of R.

Definition 8. *A dependency graph of a program P is a triple $D_P = \langle V, E^+, E^- \rangle$ where V is the set of predicate symbols occurring in P, and $E^+, E^- \subseteq V \times V$ are the sets of positive and negative dependency edges, where $\langle p, q \rangle \in E^+$ iff there exists a rule $R \in P$ where p occurs in the head and q occurs in $bbody^+(R)$, and $\langle p, q \rangle \in E^-$ if at least one of the following conditions hold:*

1. *p occurs in a head of a rule $R \in P$ and $q \in bbody^-(R)$;*
2. *there is a conditional literal in P where p occurs as the main literal and q as the condition; or*
3. *$p = q$ and p occurs in the head of a choice rule.*

A dependency path of a program P is a sequence $\langle p_1, \ldots, p_n \rangle$ of predicate symbols such that $\langle p_i, p_{i+1} \rangle \in E^+ \cup E^-$ for all $1 \leq i < n$. A path is negative if for some i, $\langle p_i, p_{i+1} \rangle \in E^-$.

Intuitively, a predicate p depends on q if we cannot know the value of p without knowing the value of q. The definition of E^+ is straightforward, but the one for E^- is more involved. The first case of its definition correspond directly with the E^+ case. The second one is used to ensure that each time when we instantiate a conditional literal $X.L : A$, we already know the extension of A so we can leave out those instances of L that have unsatisfied conditions. The last case is an artificial definition that prevents us from mistakingly concluding that p has a fixed extension if one of its rules is a choice rule.

Example 6. The dependency graph of the Hamilton cycle program is shown in Figure 2. The solid lines are positive arcs and the dashed lines are negative.

Definition 9. *A predicate* p *depends on a predicate* q *(denoted* $q \prec p$*) in a program* P *iff there exists a dependency path* $\langle p, \ldots, q \rangle$ *in* D_P*. The dependence is* negative *(denoted* $q \prec_- p$*) iff there exists a negative dependency path* $\langle p, \ldots, q \rangle$ *in* D_P*.*

Next, we define the ω-stratification. A predicate has to be on at least as high stratum as the predicates that it depends on positively, and it has to be on a higher stratum if the dependency is negative unless both predicates are on the ω-stratum.

Definition 10. *An* ω-*stratification of a program* P *is a function* $\mathcal{S} : \mathcal{P}(P) \to \mathbb{N} \cup \{\omega\}$ *such that:*

1. $\forall p, q \in \mathcal{P}(P)$*: if* $q \prec p$*, then* $\mathcal{S}(p) \geq \mathcal{S}(q)$*;*
2. $\forall p, q, \in \mathcal{P}(p)$*: if* $q \prec_- p$*, then* $\mathcal{S}(p) > \mathcal{S}(q)$ *or* $\mathcal{S}(p) = \mathcal{S}(q) = \omega$*.*

An ω-*stratification is* strict *iff:*

1. *if* $q \prec p$*,* $p \not\prec q$ *and* $\mathcal{S}(p) < \omega$*, then* $\mathcal{S}(p) > \mathcal{S}(q)$*; and*
2. *if* $\mathcal{S}(p) = \omega$*, then there exists* $q \in \mathcal{P}(P)$ *such that* $\mathcal{S}(q) = \omega$ *and* $q \prec_- p$*.*

In [11] it is proved that every cardinality constraint program has a strict stratification and that all strict stratifications of a program are essentially equivalent.

Example 7. The Hamilton cycle program has the following strict ω-stratification: $\mathcal{S}(vtx) = \mathcal{S}(arc) = \mathcal{S}(start) = 0$, $\mathcal{S}(r) = \mathcal{S}(hc) = \omega$.

Definition 11. *The* ω-*valuation* Ω *of a rule* R *under an* ω-*stratification* $\mathcal{S}$ *is* $\Omega(R, \mathcal{S}) = \mathcal{S}(pred(head(R)))$ *and the valuation of a global variable* V *in a rule* R *is:*

$$\Omega(V, R, \mathcal{S}) = \min(\{\mathcal{S}(pred(A)) \mid A : \top \in simple(R)\} \cup \{\omega\}) \qquad (21)$$

Definition 12. *A conditional literal* $X.L : A$ *is* ω-*restricted under a stratification* $\mathcal{S}$ *iff* $\mathcal{S}(L) > \mathcal{S}(A)$ *and* $X \subseteq \mathrm{Var}(A)$*. A rule* R *is* ω-*restricted if all conditional literals in it are* ω-*restricted, and for all* $V \in \mathrm{Var}(R)$*,* $\Omega(V, R, \mathcal{S}) < \Omega(R, \mathcal{S})$*. A program* P *is* ω-*restricted if there exists a strict* ω-*stratification* $\mathcal{S}$ *such that all rules in* P *are* ω-*restricted under* $\mathcal{S}$*.*

Example 8. The rule $\{hc(X, Y)\} \leftarrow arc(X, Y)$ is ω-restricted under the stratification defined in Example 7 since $\Omega(R, \mathcal{S}) = \omega > \Omega(X, R, \mathcal{S}) = \Omega(Y, R, \mathcal{S}) = 0$.

Example 9. The rule $a(f(X)) \leftarrow a(X)$ is not ω-restricted since for each stratification $\mathcal{S}$, $\Omega(R, \mathcal{S}) = \Omega(X, R, \mathcal{S})$.

If a predicate belongs to a finite stratum in one strict stratification, then it does so in all such stratifications [11]. We call those predicates *domain predicates*.

Theorem 1. *The existence of a stable model of a finite ω-restricted cardinality constraint program is decidable.*

Proof. (Sketch, details are shown in [11]) We can construct a strict ω-stratification of a program P by finding the strongly connected components of its dependency graph [11]. After that, we can show by induction that at each stratum starting from the first one the stable model induced by the rules on that stratum is finite. At the first stratum all rules are ground so the models are trivially finite. In the following strata each variable that occurs in a rule occurs in a simple literal that belongs to an earlier stratum so each rule has only a finite number of instances with satisfiable bodies. As the dependency graph contains a finite number of nodes, the number of different non-empty strata is also finite.

7   Adding Interpreted Function Symbols

A practical ASP system has to have direct support for interpreted function symbols such as arithmetical operators. Otherwise, encoding problems involving arithmetics becomes cumbersome very quickly. In this work we take the approach that we add an interpretation function $\mathcal{I}$ that canonizes Herbrand terms. For example, with arithmetic addition we want to have $\mathcal{I}(+(5,2)) = 7$ where $+(5,2)$ is a Herbrand term formed from function symbols $+$, 5, and 2.

Definition 13. *Let P be a cardinality constraint program. Then, an evaluator is a function $\mathcal{I} : \mathbf{HU}(P) \to \mathbf{HU}(P)$.*

We also use $\mathcal{I}(F)$ to denote the formula that is obtained from F by evaluating all terms in it. For example, $\mathcal{I}(a(t_1,\dots,t_n)) = a(\mathcal{I}(t_1),\dots,\mathcal{I}(t_n))$. Next, we alter the definition of the instantiation of a rule so that all terms in it get evaluated.

Definition 14. *The instantiation of a rule $R = A \leftarrow C_1,\dots,C_n$ is the set of rules:*

$$\mathbf{HI}(R,P) = \{\mathcal{I}(A\sigma) \leftarrow \mathcal{I}(I(C_1,P)\sigma),\dots,\mathcal{I}(I(C_n,P)\sigma) \mid \\ \sigma \in \mathrm{Sub}(\mathrm{Var}(P),\mathbf{HU}(P))\} \tag{22}$$

In practice we can often save computational effort by evaluating a function as soon as we know its arguments.

We do not impose any requirements to the evaluation function E in this work. The most practical way to construct it is to have the logic programming tool to provide a number of built-in functions that implement the common arithmetic operations, and then suppose that any other function symbol has the Herbrand interpretation $E(x) = x$ for all $x \in \mathbf{HU}$. In the case that the user tries to use the built-ins in an undefined way, such as writing the term $2 + f(a)$, we have three possible ways to handle it: 1) we may revert back to the Herbrand interpretation; 2) add an explicit error term $\mathbf{e}$ and return that as an answer; or 3) add some high-level type checking into the tool and reject the whole program as erroneous whenever undefined operations occur.

8   Conclusions

We defined the class of cardinality constraint programs that allows the use of cardinality constraint and conditional literals. The language is a superset of normal logic programs. These constructs make it possible to express universal and existential quantifications in rule bodies. We also identified a decidable subset of it, ω-restricted programs, and showed how to formalize built-in functions.

A direct line of further research is to identify other types of aggregate literals that behave in a similar way to cardinality constraints, that is, aggregates that can be used as first-class literals in rules.

References

1. Christian Anger, Kathrin Konczak, and Thomas Linke. Nomore : A system for non-monotonic reasoning under answer set semantics. In *Proceedings of LPNMR'01*, pages 406–410, September 2001.
2. A. Chandra and D. Harel. Horn clause queries and generalizations. *Journal of Logic Programming*, 1:1–15, 1985.
3. Evgeny Dantsin, Thomas Eiter, Georg Gottlob, and Andrei Voronkov. Complexity and expressive power of logic programming. *ACM Comput. Surv.*, 33(3), 374–425, 2001.
4. Tina Dell'Armi, Wolfgang Faber, Giuseppe Ielpa, Christoph Koch, Nicola Leone, Simona Perri, and Gerald Pfeifer. System description: Dlv. In *Proceedings of LPNMR'01*, Vienna, Austria, September 2001. Springer-Verlag.
5. D. East and M Truszczyński. Propositional satisfiability in answer-set programming. In *Proceedings of KI 2001*, pages 138–153, 2001.
6. M. Gelfond and V. Lifschitz. The stable model semantics for logic programming. In *Proceedings of ICLP'88*, pages 1070–1080. The MIT Press, August 1988.
7. David B. Kemp and Peter J. Stuckey. Semantics of logic programs with aggregates. In *Proceedings of ILP'91*, pages 387–401. MIT Press, 1991.
8. Ilkka Niemelä and Patrik Simons. Extending the Smodels system with cardinality and weight constraints. In Jack Minker, editor, *Logic-Based Artificial Intelligence*, pages 491–521. Kluwer Academic Publishers, 2000.
9. Patrik Simons, Ilkka Niemelä, and Timo Soininen. Extending and implementing the stable model semantics. *Artificial Intelligence*, 138(1–2):181–234, 2002.
10. Tommi Syrjänen. Omega-restricted logic programs. In *Proceedings of LPNMR'01*, Vienna, Austria, September 2001. Springer-Verlag.
11. Tommi Syrjänen. Logic programming with cardinality constraints. Research Report A 86, Helsinki University of Technology, Laboratory for Theoretical Computer Science, Helsinki, Finland, December 2003.
12. Tommi Syrjänen and Ilkka Niemelä. The Smodels system. In *Proceedings of LPNMR'01*, Vienna, Austria, September 2001. Springer-Verlag.

Recursive Aggregates in Disjunctive Logic Programs: Semantics and Complexity[*]

Wolfgang Faber[1], Nicola Leone[2], and Gerald Pfeifer[1]

[1] Institut für Informationssysteme, TU Wien, A-1040 Wien, Austria
faber@kr.tuwien.ac.at, gerald@pfeifer.com
[2] Department of Mathematics, University of Calabria, I-87030 Rende (CS), Italy
leone@unical.it

Abstract. The addition of aggregates has been one of the most relevant enhancements to the language of answer set programming (ASP). They strengthen the modeling power of ASP, in terms of concise problem representations. While many important problems can be encoded using nonrecursive aggregates, some relevant examples lend themselves for the use of recursive aggregates. Previous semantic definitions typically agree in the nonrecursive case, but the picture is less clear for recursion. Some proposals explicitly avoid recursive aggregates, most others differ, and many of them do not satisfy desirable criteria, such as minimality or coincidence with answer sets in the aggregate-free case.

In this paper we define a semantics for disjunctive programs with *arbitrary* aggregates (including monotone, antimonotone, and nonmonotone aggregates). This semantics is a fully declarative, genuine generalization of the answer set semantics for disjunctive logic programming (DLP). It is defined by a natural variant of the Gelfond-Lifschitz transformation, and treats aggregate and non-aggregate literals in a uniform way. We prove that our semantics guarantees the minimality (and therefore the incomparability) of answer sets, and demonstrate that it coincides with the standard answer set semantics on aggregate-free programs. Finally we analyze the computational complexity of this language, paying particular attention to the impact of syntactical restrictions on programs.

1 Introduction

Aggregates significantly enhance the language of answer set programming (ASP), allowing for natural and concise modeling of many problems. Nonrecursive (also called stratified) aggregates have clear semantics and capture a large class of meaningful problem specifications. However, there are relevant problems for which recursive (unstratified) aggregate formulations are natural; the *Company Control* problem, illustrated next, is a typical example, cf. [1,2,3,4].

Example 1. We are given a set of facts for predicate $company(X)$, denoting the companies involved, and a set of facts for predicate $ownsStk(C1, C2, Perc)$, denoting the percentage of shares of company $C2$, which is owned by company $C1$. Then, company

---

[*] This work was supported by the European Commission under projects IST-2002-33570 INFOMIX, IST-2001-37004 WASP, and IST-2001-33570 COLOGNET.

J.J. Alferes and J. Leite (Eds.): JELIA 2004, LNAI 3229, pp. 200–212, 2004.
© Springer-Verlag Berlin Heidelberg 2004

$C1$ controls company $C2$ if the sum of the shares of $C2$ owned either directly by $C1$ or by companies, which are controlled by $C1$, is more than 50%. This problem has been encoded as the following program $\mathcal{P}_{ctrl}$ by many authors in the literature [1,2,3,4].[1]

$controlsStk(C1, C1, C2, P) :- ownsStk(C1, C2, P).$
$controlsStk(C1, C2, C3, P) :- company(C1), controls(C1, C2), ownsStk(C2, C3, P).$
$controls(C1, C3) :- company(C1), company(C3),$
$$\#\mathtt{sum}\{P, C2 : controlsStk(C1, C2, C3, P)\} > 50.$$

Intuitively, $controlsStk(C1, C2, C3, P)$ denotes that company $C1$ controls $P\%$ of $C3$ shares "through" company $C2$ (as $C1$ controls $C2$, and $C2$ owns $P\%$ of $C3$ shares). Predicate $controls(C1, C2)$ encodes that company $C1$ controls company $C2$. For two companies, say, $c1$ and $c3$, $controls(c1, c3)$ is derived if the sum of the elements in the *multiset* $\{P \mid \exists C2 : controlsStk(c1, C2, c3, P)\}$ is greater than 50. Note that in the DLV syntax this multiset is expressed by $\{P, C2 : controlsStk(c1, C2, c3, P)\}$ where the variable $C2$ avoids that duplicate occurrences of P are eliminated.

The encoding of *Company Control* contains a recursive aggregate (since predicate *controlsStk* in the aggregate depends on the head predicate *controls*). Unfortunately, however, recursive aggregates are not easy to handle, and their semantics is not always straightforward.

Example 2. Consider the following two programs:

$$P_1 : \{p(a) :- \#\mathtt{count}\{X : p(X)\} > 0.\} \qquad P_2 : \{p(a) :- \#\mathtt{count}\{X : p(X)\} < 1.\}$$

In both cases $p(a)$ is the only atom for p which might be true, so, intuitively, one may expect that $\#\mathtt{count}\{X : p(X)\} > 0$ is true iff $p(a)$ is true; while $\#\mathtt{count}\{X : p(X)\} < 1$ should be true iff $p(a)$ is false. Thus, the above programs should, respectively, behave like the following standard programs:

$$P_1' : \{p(a) :- p(a).\} \qquad P_2' : \{p(a) :- \mathtt{not}\ p(a).\}$$

This is not always the case in the literature, and there is a debate on the best semantics for recursive aggregates.

There have been several attempts for defining a suitable semantics for aggregates [2,6, 7,4,8]. However, while previous semantic definitions typically agree in the nonrecursive case, the picture is not so clear for recursion. Some proposals explicitly avoid recursive aggregates, most others differ, and many of them do not satisfy desirable criteria, such as minimality[2]. Relevant progress towards a suitable semantics for recursive aggregates has been recently made in [4,8], where the authors provide a semantics which guarantees minimality and extends standard answer sets. However, both definitions are given operationally and do not cover *all* language fragments. The first proposal disregards disjunctive programs, while the latter covers *only* monotone aggregates.

---

[1] Throughout this paper, we adopt the concrete syntax of the DLV language [5] to express aggregates in the examples.

[2] The subset-minimality of answer sets, which holds in the aggregate-free case and for the main nonmonotonic logics [9], also guarantees that answer sets are incomparable, and allows to define the transitive closure – which becomes impossible if minimality is lost [4].

In this paper, we make a step forward and provide a fully declarative semantics which works also for disjunctive programs and arbitrary aggregates. The main contributions of the paper are the following:

- We provide a definition of the answer sets semantics for disjunctive programs with arbitrary aggregates (including monotone aggregates, antimonotone aggregates, and aggregates which are neither monotone nor antimonotone). This semantics is fully declarative and is given in the standard way for answer sets, by a generalization of the well-known Gelfond-Lifschitz transformation.
- We study the properties of the proposed semantics, and show the following results:
  - Our answer sets are subset-minimal models, and therefore they are incomparable to each other, which is generally seen as an important property of nonmonotonic semantics [10,4].
  - For aggregate-free programs, our semantics coincides with the standard answer set semantics.
  - From a semantic viewpoint, monotone aggregate literals correspond to positive standard literals, while antimonotone aggregates correspond to negative standard literals. We provide a rewriting from standard logic programs with negation to positive programs with antimonotone aggregate atoms.
- We carry out an in-depth analysis of the computational complexity of disjunctive programs with aggregates and fragments thereof. As long as the values of aggregates are computable in polynomial time, their addition does not increase the complexity of the full DLP language. However, the complexity of some fragments of DLP is affected by aggregates. Interestingly, monotone aggregates never alter the complexity, while antimonotone aggregates cause a complexity gap in many cases (see Section 4); arbitrary aggregates behave precisely like antimonotone aggregates from the complexity viewpoint in the studied cases.

2   The DLP^A Language

In this section, we provide a formal definition of the syntax and semantics of the DLP^A language – an extension of Disjunctive Logic Programming (DLP) by set-oriented functions (also called aggregate functions). We assume that the reader is familiar with standard DLP; we refer to atoms, literals, rules, and programs of DLP, as *standard atoms, standard literals, standard rules*, and *standard programs,* respectively. For further background, see [11,12].

2.1   Syntax

Set Terms. A (DLP^A) *set term* is either a symbolic set or a ground set. A *symbolic set* is a pair $\{Vars : Conj\}$, where *Vars* is a list of variables and *Conj* is a conjunction of standard literals.[3] A *ground set* is a set of pairs of the form $\langle \bar{t} : Conj \rangle$, where $\bar{t}$ is a list of constants and *Conj* is a ground (variable free) conjunction of standard literals.

---

[3] Intuitively, a symbolic set $\{X : a(X, Y), \text{not } p(Y)\}$ stands for the set of X-values making $a(X, Y), \text{not } p(Y)$ true, i.e., $\{X \mid \exists Y s.t.\ a(X, Y), \text{not } p(Y)\ is\ true\}$.

Aggregate Functions. An *aggregate function* is of the form $f(S)$, where S is a set term, and f is an *aggregate function symbol*. Intuitively, an aggregate function can be thought of as a (possibly partial) function mapping multisets[4] of constants to a constant.

Example 3. The aggregate functions currently supported by the DLV system are: #min (minimal term, undefined for empty set), #max (maximal term, undefined for empty set), #count (number of terms), #sum (sum of non-negative integers), and #times (product of positive integers).

Aggregate Literals. An *aggregate atom* is $f(S) \prec T$, where $f(S)$ is an aggregate function, $\prec \in \{=, <, \leq, >, \geq\}$ is a predefined comparison operator, and T is a term (variable or constant) referred to as guard.

Example 4. The following aggregate atoms in DLV notation, where the latter contains a ground set and could be a ground instance of the former:

$$\#\texttt{max}\{Z : r(Z), \texttt{not } a(Z, V)\} > Y$$
$$\#\texttt{max}\{\langle 2 : r(2), \texttt{not } a(2, x)\rangle, \langle 2 : r(2), \texttt{not } a(2, y)\rangle\} > 1$$

An *atom* is either a standard (DLP) atom or an aggregate atom. A *literal* L is an atom A or an atom A preceded by the default negation symbol not; if A is an aggregate atom, L is an *aggregate literal*.

DLP^A Programs. A *(DLP^A) rule* r is a construct

$$a_1 \vee \cdots \vee a_n :- b_1, \cdots, b_k, \texttt{not } b_{k+1}, \cdots, \texttt{not } b_m.$$

where $a_1, \cdots, a_n$ are standard atoms, $b_1, \cdots, b_m$ are atoms, and $n \geq 0$, $m \geq k \geq 0$, $n + m > 0$. The disjunction $a_1 \vee \cdots \vee a_n$ is referred to as the *head* of r, while the conjunction $b_1, ..., b_k, \texttt{not } b_{k+1}, ..., \texttt{not } b_m$ is the *body* of r. A *(DLP^A) program* is a set of DLP^A rules.

Syntactic Properties. A *global* variable of a rule r is a variable appearing in a standard atom of r; all other variables are *local* variables.

    Safety. A rule r is *safe* if the following conditions hold: (i) each global variable of r appears in a positive standard literal in the body of r; (ii) each local variable of r appearing in a symbolic set $\{Vars : Conj\}$ appears in a positive literal in $Conj$; (iii) each guard of an aggregate atom of r is a constant or a global variable. A program $\mathcal{P}$ is safe if all $r \in \mathcal{P}$ are safe. In the following we assume that DLP^A programs are safe.

Example 5. Consider the following rules with DLV aggregates:

$$p(X) :- q(X, Y, V), \#\texttt{max}\{Z : r(Z), \texttt{not } a(Z, V)\} > Y.$$
$$p(X) :- q(X, Y, V), \#\texttt{sum}\{Z : \texttt{not } a(Z, S)\} > Y.$$
$$p(X) :- q(X, Y, V), \#\texttt{min}\{Z : r(Z), \texttt{not } a(Z, V)\} > T.$$

The first rule is safe, while the second is not, since both local variables Z and S violate condition (ii). The third rule is not safe either, since the guard T violates condition (iii).

---

[4] Note that aggregate functions are evaluated on the valuation of a (ground) set w.r.t. an interpretation, which is a multiset, cf. Section 2.2.

Stratification. A DLP^A program $\mathcal{P}$ is *aggregate-stratified* if there exists a function $|| \ ||$, called *level mapping*, from the set of (standard) predicates of $\mathcal{P}$ to ordinals, such that for each pair a and b of standard predicates, occurring in the head and body of a rule $r \in \mathcal{P}$, respectively: (i) if b appears in an aggregate atom, then $||b|| < ||a||$, and (ii) if b occurs in a standard atom, then $||b|| \leq ||a||$.

Example 6. Consider the program consisting of a set of facts for predicates a and b, plus the following two rules:

$$q(X) :- p(X), \#\text{count}\{Y : a(Y, X), b(X)\} \leq 2. \qquad p(X) :- q(X), b(X).$$

The program is aggregate-stratified, as the level mapping $||a|| = ||b|| = 1$, $||p|| = ||q|| = 2$ satisfies the required conditions. If we add the rule $b(X) :- p(X)$, then no such level-mapping exists and the program becomes aggregate-unstratified.

Intuitively, aggregate-stratification forbids recursion through aggregates. While the semantics of aggregate-stratified programs is more or less agreed upon, different and disagreeing semantics for aggregate-unstratified programs have been defined in the past, cf. [4]. In the following we shall provide a novel characterization which directly extends well-known formulations of semantics for aggregate-free programs.

2.2 Semantics

Universe and Base. Given a DLP^A program $\mathcal{P}$, let $U_\mathcal{P}$ denote the set of constants appearing in $\mathcal{P}$, and $B_\mathcal{P}$ the set of standard atoms constructible from the (standard) predicates of $\mathcal{P}$ with constants in $U_\mathcal{P}$. Given a set X, let $\overline{2}^X$ denote the set of all multisets over elements from X. Without loss of generality, we assume that aggregate functions map to $\mathbb{I}$ (the set of integers).

Example 7. Let us now describe the domains of the aggregate functions in DLV (where $\mathbb{N}$ and $\mathbb{N}^+$ denote the set of non-negative integers and positive integers, respectively): $\#\text{count}$ is defined over $\overline{2}^{U_\mathcal{P}}$, $\#\text{sum}$ over $\overline{2}^{\mathbb{N}}$, $\#\text{times}$ over $\overline{2}^{\mathbb{N}^+}$,[5] $\#\text{min}$ and $\#\text{max}$ are defined over $\overline{2}^{\mathbb{N}} - \{\emptyset\}$.

Instantiation. A *substitution* is a mapping from a set of variables to $U_\mathcal{P}$. A substitution from the set of global variables of a rule r (to $U_\mathcal{P}$) is a *global substitution for* r; a substitution from the set of local variables of a symbolic set S (to $U_\mathcal{P}$) is a *local substitution for S*. Given a symbolic set without global variables $S = \{Vars : Conj\}$, the *instantiation of S* is the following ground set of pairs $inst(S)$:
$\{\langle \gamma(Vars) : \gamma(Conj) \rangle \mid \gamma \text{ is a local substitution for } S\}$.[6]
A *ground instance* of a rule r is obtained in two steps: (1) a global substitution σ for r is first applied over r; (2) every symbolic set S in $\sigma(r)$ is replaced by its instantiation $inst(S)$. The instantiation $Ground(\mathcal{P})$ of a program $\mathcal{P}$ is the set of all possible instances of the rules of $\mathcal{P}$.

---

[5] $\#\text{sum}$ and $\#\text{times}$ applied over an empty set return 0 and 1, respectively.

[6] Given a substitution σ and a DLP^A object Obj (rule, set, etc.), we denote by $\sigma(Obj)$ the object obtained by replacing each variable X in Obj by $\sigma(X)$.

Example 8. Consider the following program $\mathcal{P}_1$:

$q(1) \vee p(2,2).$ $\qquad$ $q(2) \vee p(2,1).$ $\qquad$ $t(X) :\!-q(X), \#\text{sum}\{Y : p(X,Y)\} > 1.$

The instantiation $Ground(\mathcal{P}_1)$ is the following:

$q(1) \vee p(2,2).$ $\qquad$ $t(1) :\!-q(1), \#\text{sum}\{\langle 1 : p(1,1)\rangle, \langle 2 : p(1,2)\rangle\} > 1.$
$q(2) \vee p(2,1).$ $\qquad$ $t(2) :\!-q(2), \#\text{sum}\{\langle 1 : p(2,1)\rangle, \langle 2 : p(2,2)\rangle\} > 1.$

Interpretation. An *interpretation* for a DLP$^{\mathcal{A}}$ program $\mathcal{P}$ is a set of standard ground atoms $I \subseteq B_{\mathcal{P}}$. The truth valuation $I(A)$, where A is a standard ground literal or a standard ground conjunction, is defined in the usual way. An interpretation also provides a meaning to (ground) sets, aggregate functions and aggregate literals, namely a multiset, a value, and a truth value, respectively. Let $f(S)$ be a an aggregate function. The valuation $I(S)$ of S w.r.t. I is the multiset of the first constant of the elements in S whose conjunction is true w.r.t. I. More precisely, let $I(S)$ denote the multiset $[t_1 \mid \langle t_1, ..., t_n : Conj\rangle \in S \wedge Conj$ *is true w.r.t.* $I]$ The valuation $I(f(S))$ of an aggregate function $f(S)$ w.r.t. I is the result of the application of f on $I(S)$. If the multiset $I(S)$ is not in the domain of f, $I(f(S)) = \bot$ (where $\bot$ is a fixed symbol not occurring in $\mathcal{P}$).

An instantiated aggregate atom $A = f(S) \prec k$ is *true w.r.t.* I if: (i) $I(f(S)) \neq \bot$, and, (ii) $I(f(S)) \prec k$ holds; otherwise, A is false. An instantiated aggregate literal not $A = \text{not } f(S) \prec k$ is *true w.r.t.* I if (i) $I(f(S)) \neq \bot$, and, (ii) $I(f(S)) \prec k$ does not hold; otherwise, A is false. A rule r is *satisfied w.r.t.* I if some head atom is true w.r.t. I whenever all body literals are true w.r.t. I.

Example 9. Consider the atom $A = \#\text{sum}\{\langle 1 : p(2,1)\rangle, \langle 2 : p(2,2)\rangle\} > 1$ from Example 8. Let S be the ground set in A. For the interpretation $I = \{q(2), p(2,2), t(2)\}$, $I(S) = [2]$, the application of $\#\text{sum}$ over $[2]$ yields 2, and A is therefore true w.r.t. I, since $2 > 1$. I is a model of the program of Example 8.

Definition 1. *A ground literal ℓ is* monotone, *if for all interpretations I, J, such that $I \subseteq J$, ℓ is true w.r.t. I implies that ℓ is true w.r.t. J. A ground literal ℓ is* antimonotone, *if for all interpretations I, J, such that $I \subseteq J$, ℓ is true w.r.t. J implies that ℓ is true w.r.t. I. A ground literal ℓ is* nonmonotone, *if it is neither monotone nor antimonotone.*

Note that positive standard literals are monotone, whereas negative standard literals are antimonotone. Aggregate literals may be monotone, antimonotone or nonmonotone, regardless whether they are positive or negative.

Example 10. All ground instances of the following aggregate literals are monotone

$\#\text{count}\{Z : r(Z)\} > 1$ $\qquad\qquad$ not $\#\text{count}\{Z : r(Z)\} < 1$

while the following are antimonotone:

$\#\text{count}\{Z : r(Z)\} < 1$ $\qquad\qquad$ not $\#\text{count}\{Z : r(Z)\} > 1$

Nonmonotone literals include the sum over (possibly negative) integers and the average. Also, most monotone or antimonotone functions combined with the equality operator yield nonmonotone literals.

2.3 Answer Sets

We will next define the notion of answer sets for DLP$^{\mathcal{A}}$ programs. While usually this is done by first defining the notion of answer sets for positive programs (coinciding with the minimal model semantics) and then for negative programs by a stability condition on a reduct, once aggregates have to be considered, the notions of positive and negative literals are in general not clear. If only monotone and antimonotone aggregate atoms were considered, one could simply treat monotone literals like positive literals and antimonotone literals like negative ones, and follow the standard approach, as hinted at in [4]. Since we also consider nonmonotone aggregates, such a categorization is not feasible, and we rely on a definition which always employs a stability condition on a reduct.

The subsequent definitions are directly based on models: An interpretation M is a model of a DLP$^{\mathcal{A}}$ program $\mathcal{P}$ if all $r \in Ground(\mathcal{P})$ are satisfied w.r.t. M. An interpretation M is a subset-minimal model of $\mathcal{P}$ if no $I \subset M$ is a model of $Ground(\mathcal{P})$.

Next we provide the transformation by which the reduct of a ground program w.r.t. an interpretation is formed. Note that this definition is a generalization of the Gelfond-Lifschitz transformation for DLP programs (see Theorem 3).

Definition 2. *Given a ground DLP$^{\mathcal{A}}$ program $\mathcal{P}$ and an interpretation I, let $\mathcal{P}^I$ denote the transformed program obtained from $\mathcal{P}$ by deleting rules in which a body literal is false w.r.t. I.*

Example 11. Consider Example 2: $Ground(P_1) = \{p(a){:}{-}\#\mathtt{count}\{\langle a : p(a)\rangle\} > 0.\}$ and $Ground(P_2) = \{p(a){:}{-}\#\mathtt{count}\{\langle a : p(a)\rangle\} < 1.\}$, and interpretation $I_1 = \{p(a)\}$, $I_2 = \emptyset$. Then, $Ground(P_1)^{I_1} = Ground(P_1)$, $Ground(P_1)^{I_2} = \emptyset$, and $Ground(P_2)^{I_1} = \emptyset$, $Ground(P_2)^{I_2} = Ground(P_2)$ hold.

We are now ready to formulate the stability criterion for answer sets.

Definition 3 (Answer Sets for DLP$^{\mathcal{A}}$ Programs). *Given a DLP$^{\mathcal{A}}$ program $\mathcal{P}$, an interpretation A of $Ground(\mathcal{P})$ is an answer set if it is a subset-minimal model of $Ground(\mathcal{P})^A$.*

Note that any answer set A of $\mathcal{P}$ is also a model of $\mathcal{P}$ because $Ground(\mathcal{P})^A \subseteq Ground(\mathcal{P})$, and rules in $Ground(\mathcal{P}) - Ground(\mathcal{P})^A$ are satisfied w.r.t. A.

Example 12. For the programs of Example 2, I_2 of Example 11 is the only answer set of P_1 (because I_1 is not a minimal model of $Ground(P_1)^{I_1}$), while P_2 admits no answer set (I_1 is not a minimal model of $Ground(P_2)^{I_1}$, and I_2 is not a model of $Ground(P_2) = Ground(P_2)^{I_2}$.

For Example 1 and the following input facts

$company(a)$. $company(b)$. $company(c)$.
$ownsStk(a, b, 40)$. $ownsStk(c, b, 20)$. $ownsStk(a, c, 40)$. $ownsStk(b, c, 20)$.

only the set $A = \{controlsStk(a, a, b, 40), controlsStk(a, a, c, 40), controlsStk(b, b, c, 20),$ $controlsStk(c, c, b, 20)\}$ (omitting facts) is an answer set, which means that no company controls another company. Note that $A_1 = A \cup \{controls(a, b), controls(a, c),$ $controlsStk(a, b, c, 20), controlsStk(a, c, b, 20)\}$ is not an answer set, which is reasonable, since there is no basis for the truth of literals in $A_1 - A$.

This definition is a generalization and simplification of the definitions given in [13, 10]. In particular, different to [10], we define answer sets directly on top of the notion of models of DLP$^\mathcal{A}$ programs, rather than transforming them to a positive program.

3 Semantic Properties

A generally desirable and important property of nonmonotonic semantics is minimality [10,4], in particular a semantics should refine the notion of minimal models. We now show that our semantics has this property.

Theorem 1. *Answer Sets of a* DLP$^\mathcal{A}$ *program* $\mathcal{P}$ *are subset-minimal models of* $\mathcal{P}$.

Proof. Our proof is by contradiction: Assume that I_1 is a model of $\mathcal{P}$, I_2 is an answer set of $\mathcal{P}$ and that $I_1 \subset I_2$.[7] Since I_2 is an answer set of $\mathcal{P}$, it is a subset-minimal model of $Ground(\mathcal{P})^{I_2}$ by Definition 3. Therefore, I_1 is not a model of $Ground(\mathcal{P})^{I_2}$ (otherwise, I_2 would not be a subset-minimal model of $Ground(\mathcal{P})^{I_2}$). Thus, some rule $r \in Ground(\mathcal{P})^{I_2}$ is not satisfied w.r.t. I_1. Since $Ground(\mathcal{P})^{I_2} \subseteq Ground(\mathcal{P})$, r is also in $Ground(\mathcal{P})$ and therefore I_1 cannot be a model of $\mathcal{P}$, contradicting the assumption.

Corollary 1. *Answer sets of a* DLP$^\mathcal{A}$ *program* $\mathcal{P}$ *are incomparable (w.r.t. set inclusion) among each other.*

Theorem 1 can be refined for DLP$^\mathcal{A}$ programs containing only monotone literals.

Theorem 2. *The answer sets of a* DLP$^\mathcal{A}$ *program* $\mathcal{P}$, *where* $\mathcal{P}$ *contains only monotone literals, are precisely the minimal models of* $\mathcal{P}$.

Proof. Let $\mathcal{P}$ be a DLP$^\mathcal{A}$ program containing only monotone literals, and I be a minimal model of $\mathcal{P}$. Clearly, I is also a model of $\mathcal{P}^I$. We again proceed by contradiction and show that no $J \subset I$ is a model of $\mathcal{P}^I$: Assume that such a model J of $\mathcal{P}$ exists and satisfies all rules in $Ground(\mathcal{P})^I$. All rules in $Ground(\mathcal{P}) - Ground(\mathcal{P})^I$ are satisfied by I because their body is false w.r.t. I. But since $\mathcal{P}$ contains only monotone literals, each false literal in I is also false in $J \subset I$, and hence J also satisfies all rules in $Ground(\mathcal{P}) - Ground(\mathcal{P})^I$ and would therefore be a model of $\mathcal{P}$, contradicting the assumption that I is a minimal model. Together with Theorem 1, the result follows.

Clearly, a very desirable feature of a semantics for an extended language is that it properly extends agreed-upon semantics of the base language, so that the semantics are equal on the base language. Therefore we next show that for DLP programs, our semantics coincides with the standard answer set semantics. Note that not all semantics which have been proposed for programs with aggregates meet this requirement, cf. [4].

Theorem 3. *Given a* DLP *program* $\mathcal{P}$, *an interpretation* I *is an answer set of* $\mathcal{P}$ *according to Definition 3 iff it is an answer set of* $\mathcal{P}$ *according to the standard definition via the classic Gelfond-Lifschitz transformation [11].*

---

[7] Throughout the paper, $\subset$ denotes *strict* set inclusion.

Proof. ($\Rightarrow$): Assume that I is an answer set w.r.t. Definition 3, i.e. I is a minimal model of $Ground(\mathcal{P})^I$. Let us denote the standard Gelfond-Lifschitz transformed program by $GL(Ground(\mathcal{P}), I)$. For each $r \in Ground(\mathcal{P})^I$ some $r' \in GL(Ground(\mathcal{P}), I)$ exists, which is obtained from r by removing all negative literals. Since $r \in Ground(\mathcal{P})^I$, all negative literals of r are true in I, and also in all $J \subseteq I$. For rules of which an $r'' \in GL(Ground(\mathcal{P}), I)$ exists but no corresponding rule in $Ground(\mathcal{P})^I$, some positive body literal of r'' is false w.r.t. I (hence r'' is not included in $Ground(\mathcal{P})^I$), and also false w.r.t. all $J \subseteq I$. Therefore (i) I is a model of $GL(Ground(\mathcal{P}), I)$ and (ii) no $J \subset I$ is a model of $GL(Ground(\mathcal{P}), I)$, as it would also be a model of $Ground(\mathcal{P})^I$ and I thus would not be a minimal model of $Ground(\mathcal{P})^I$. Hence I is a minimal model of $GL(Ground(\mathcal{P}), I)$ whenever it is a minimal model of $Ground(\mathcal{P})^I$.

($\Leftarrow$): Now assume that I is a standard answer set of $\mathcal{P}$, that is, I is a minimal model of $GL(Ground(\mathcal{P}), I)$. By similar reasoning as in ($\Rightarrow$) a rule $r \in GL(Ground(\mathcal{P}), I)$ with true body w.r.t. I has a corresponding rule $r' \in Ground(\mathcal{P})^I$ which contains the negative body of the original rule $r^o \in Ground(\mathcal{P})$, which is true w.r.t. all $J \subseteq I$. Any rule $r'' \in GL(Ground(\mathcal{P}), I)$ with false body w.r.t. I is not contained in $Ground(\mathcal{P})^I$, but it is satisfied in each $J \subseteq I$. Therefore (i) I is a model of $Ground(\mathcal{P})^I$ and (ii) no $J \subset I$ is a model of $Ground(\mathcal{P})^I$ (otherwise J would also be a model of $GL(Ground(\mathcal{P}), I)$). As a consequence, I is a minimal model of $Ground(\mathcal{P})^I$ whenever it is a minimal model of $GL(Ground(\mathcal{P}), I)$.

4 Computational Complexity

4.1 Complexity Framework

We analyze the complexity of DLP^A on **Cautious Reasoning**, a main reasoning task in nonmonotonic formalisms, amounting to the following decisional problem: Given a DLP^A program $\mathcal{P}$ and a standard ground atom A, is A true in all answer sets of $\mathcal{P}$?

We consider propositional (i.e., variable-free) DLP^A programs, and polynomial-time computable aggregate functions (note that all sample aggregate functions appearing in this paper fall into this class).

4.2 Overview of Complexity Results

Table 1 summarizes the complexity results derived in the next sections. The rows specify the allowance of negation (not); the columns specify the allowance of aggregates, namely: M_s = stratified monotone aggregates, M = full (possibly recursive) monotone aggregates, A_s = stratified antimonotone aggregates, A = full antimonotone aggregates, N_s = stratified nonmonotone aggregates, and N = full nonmonotone aggregates.

The good news is that the addition of aggregates does not increase the complexity of disjunctive logic programming. Cautious reasoning on the full DLP^A language, including all considered types of aggregates (monotone, antimonotone, and nonmonotone) even unstratified, remains Π_2^P-complete, as for standard DLP.

The most "benign" aggregates, from the complexity viewpoint, are the monotone ones, whose addition does never cause any complexity increase, even for negation-free programs, and even for unstratified monotone aggregates.

Table 1. The Complexity of Cautious Reasoning on Disjunctive Programs with Aggregates

	$\emptyset$	$\{M_s\}$	$\{M\}$	$\{A_s\}$	$\{N_s\}$	$\{M_s, A_s, N_s\}$	$\{A\}$	$\{N\}$	$\{M, A, N\}$
negation-free	co-NP	co-NP	co-NP	Π_2^P	Π_2^P	Π_2^P	Π_2^P	Π_2^P	Π_2^P
with negation	Π_2^P	Π_2^P	Π_2^P	Π_2^P	Π_2^P	Π_2^P	Π_2^P	Π_2^P	Π_2^P

On negation-free programs, the addition of either antimonotone or nonmonotone aggregates increases the complexity, jumping from co-NP to Π_2^P. In all other cases, the complexity remains the same as for standard programs.

4.3   Proofs of Hardness Results

An important observation is that negation can be rewritten to an antimonotone aggregate. It is therefore possible to turn aggregate-free programs with negation into corresponding positive programs with aggregates.

Definition 4. *Given an (aggregate-free) DLP program* $\mathcal{P}$*, let* $\Gamma(\mathcal{P})$ *be the DLP^A program, which is obtained by replacing each negative literal* not a *in* $\mathcal{P}$ *by* #count$\{\langle\epsilon :$ $a\rangle\} < 1$*, where* ϵ *is an arbitrary constant.*

Theorem 4. *Each aggregate-free DLP program* $\mathcal{P}$ *can be transformed into an equivalent positive DLP^A program* $\Gamma(\mathcal{P})$ *with aggregate literals (all of which are antimonotone). If* $\mathcal{P}$ *is stratified w.r.t. negation, then* $\Gamma(\mathcal{P})$ *is aggregate-stratified (i.e., all aggregates in* $\Gamma(\mathcal{P})$ *are nonrecursive).*

Proof. Note that for any interpretation I, not a is true w.r.t. I iff #count$\{\langle\epsilon : a\rangle\} < 1$ is true w.r.t. I, and that #count$\{\langle\epsilon : a\rangle\} < 1$ is an antimonotone aggregate literal. By virtue of Theorem 3, our answer sets semantics (as in Definition 3) is equivalent to the standard answer set semantics. Thus, since the valuation of literals is equal in $\mathcal{P}$ and $\Gamma(\mathcal{P})$, both programs have the same answer sets.

Since aggregates take the place of negative literals, if the latter are nonrecursive in $\mathcal{P}$ (i.e., $\mathcal{P}$ is stratified w.r.t. negation), the former are nonrecursive as well (i.e., $\Gamma(\mathcal{P})$ is aggregate-stratified).

Theorem 5. *Let* $\mathcal{P}$ *be a DLP program. Then (i)* $\Gamma(\mathcal{P})$ *has the same size (i.e., number of rules and literals) as* $\mathcal{P}$*, and (ii)* $\Gamma(\mathcal{P})$ *is LOGSPACE computable from* $\mathcal{P}$*.*

Proof. The $\Gamma(\mathcal{P})$ transformation replaces each negative literal by an aggregate atom; and it does not add any further literal to the program. Therefore it does not increase the program size. It is easy to see that $\Gamma(\mathcal{P})$ can be computed by a LOGSPACE Turing Machine. Indeed, $\Gamma(\mathcal{P})$ can be generated by dealing with one rule of $\mathcal{P}$ at a time, without storing any intermediate data apart from a fixed number of indices.

Finally, we state the relation between antimonotone and nonmonotone literals.

Theorem 6. *Each* DLP^A *program, whose aggregates are all antimonotone, can be transformed into an equivalent program, whose aggregates are all nonmonotone.*

Proof. W.l.o.g. we will consider a ground program $\mathcal{P}$. We transform each antimonotone aggregate literal l containing the aggregate atom $f(S) \prec k$ to l' containing $f^l(S') \prec k$. We introduce three fresh constants τ, ϵ, and ν and a new predicate symbol Π. Let f^l be undefined for the multisets $[\tau]$ and $[\tau, \epsilon, \nu]$ and return a value making l true for $[\tau, \epsilon]$ (such a value does always exist); otherwise f^l is equal to f. Furthermore, S' is obtained by adding $\langle \tau : \Pi(\tau) \rangle$, $\langle \epsilon : \Pi(\epsilon) \rangle$, and $\langle \nu : \Pi(\nu) \rangle$ to the ground set S. The transformed program $\mathcal{P}'$ contains only nonmonotone aggregates and is equivalent to $\mathcal{P}$.

Theorem 7. *Each field of Table 1 states the proper hardness of the corresponding fragment of* DLP$^\mathcal{A}$.

Proof. The hardness results for all fields in the second row of Table 1 stem from the Π_2^P-hardness of disjunctive programs with negation [14].[8] The same result, together with Theorems 4 and 5, entails Π_2^P-hardness of all the DLP$^\mathcal{A}$ fragments admitting antimonotone aggregates. Π_2^P-hardness of all the DLP$^\mathcal{A}$ fragments with nonmonotone aggregates then follows from Theorem 6. Finally, the results in the first three entries in the first row stem from the co-NP-hardness of positive disjunctive programs [14].

4.4 Proofs of Membership Results

In the membership proofs, we will implicitly use the following lemma:

Lemma 1. *Given an interpretation I for a* DLP$^\mathcal{A}$ *program $\mathcal{P}$, the truth valuation of an aggregate atom L is computable in polynomial time.*

Proof. Let $L = f(T) \prec k$. To determine the truth valuation of L, we have to: (i) compute the valuation $I(T)$ of the ground set T w.r.t. I, (ii) apply the aggregate function f on $I(T)$, and (iii) compare the result of $f(I(T))$ with k w.r.t. $\prec$.

Computing the valuation of a ground set T only requires scanning each element $\langle t_1, ..., t_n : Conj \rangle$ of T, adding t_1 to the result multiset if $Conj$ is true w.r.t. I. This is evidently polynomial, as is the application of the aggregate function on $I(T)$ in our framework (see Section 4.1). The comparison with k, finally, is straightforward.

Lemma 2. *Let $\mathcal{P}$ be a negation-free* DLP$^\mathcal{A}$ *program, whose aggregates are all monotone. A standard ground atom A is not a cautious consequence of $\mathcal{P}$, if and only if there exists a model M of $\mathcal{P}$ which does not contain A.*[9]

Proof. Observe first that, since $\mathcal{P}$ does not contain negation and only monotone aggregate literals, each literal appearing in $\mathcal{P}$ is monotone.

($\Leftarrow$): The existence of a model M of $\mathcal{P}$ not containing A, implies the existence of a minimal model M' of $\mathcal{P}$ (with $M' \subseteq M$) not containing A. By virtue of Theorem 2, M' is an answer set of $\mathcal{P}$. Therefore, A is not a cautious consequence of $\mathcal{P}$.

($\Rightarrow$): Since A is not a cautious consequence of $\mathcal{P}$, by definition of cautious reasoning, there exists an answer set M of $\mathcal{P}$ which does not contain A. By definition of answer sets, M is also a model of $\mathcal{P}$, as remarked after Definition 3.

---

[8] Recall that even for stratified negation cautious reasoning on disjunctive programs is Π_2^P-hard.

[9] Note that M can be *any* model, possibly non-minimal, of $\mathcal{P}$.

Theorem 8. *Cautious reasoning over negation-free disjunctive programs, whose aggregates are all monotone, is in co-NP.*

Proof. By Lemma 2 we can check whether a ground atom A *is not* a cautious consequence of a program $\mathcal{P}$ as follows: (i) Guess an interpretation M of $\mathcal{P}$, (ii) check that M is a model and $a \notin M$. The check is clearly polynomial-time computable, and the problem is therefore in co-NP.

Lemma 3. *Checking whether an interpretation M is an answer set of an arbitrary DLP$^{\mathcal{A}}$ program $\mathcal{P}$ is in co-NP.*

Proof. To prove that M is not an answer set of $\mathcal{P}$, we guess an interpretation M' of $\mathcal{P}$, and check that (at least) one of the following conditions hold: (i) M' is a model of $\mathcal{P}^M$, and $M' \subset M$, or (ii) M is not a model of $\mathcal{P}^M$. The checking of both conditions above is clearly in polynomial time, and the problem is therefore in co-NP.

Theorem 9. *Cautious reasoning over arbitrary DLP$^{\mathcal{A}}$ programs is in Π_2^P.*

Proof. We verify that a ground atom A is not a cautious consequence of a DLP$^{\mathcal{A}}$ program $\mathcal{P}$ as follows: Guess an interpretation $M \subseteq B_{\mathcal{P}}$ and check that (1) M is an answer set for $\mathcal{P}$, and (2) A is not true w.r.t. M. Task (2) is clearly polynomial, while (1) is in co-NP by virtue of Lemma 3. The problem therefore lies in Π_2^P.

5   Related Work and Conclusions

There have been considerable efforts to define semantics for logic programs with recursive aggregates, but most works do not consider disjunctive programs or do not cover all kinds of aggregates. In [4] a partial stable semantics for non-disjunctive programs with aggregates has been defined, for which the "standard" total stable semantics is a special case, while in [8] a stable semantics for disjunctive programs with has been given; but only monotone aggregates are considered. These semantics guarantee the same benign properties as ours, namely minimality and coincidence with answer sets in the aggregate-free case. On the respective language fragment, [4] intuitively coincides with our semantics (but a formal demonstration is still to be done). For [8] there is a slight difference when an aggregate function in a negative literal is undefined. E.g., the program $\{cheap :-$ not $\#\max\{X : salary(X)\} > 1000\}$ without facts for salary would yield the answer set $\{cheap\}$ w.r.t. [8], while our semantics admits only $\emptyset$.

A thorough discussion of pros and cons for the various approaches for recursive aggregates has been given in [4,15], so we will only briefly compare our approach with previous ones on typical examples.

The approaches of [2,6,7] basically all admit non-minimal answer sets. In particular, program P_1 of Example 2 would have $\emptyset$ and $\{p(a)\}$ as answer sets. As shown in Example 12 (also by Theorem 1), the semantics proposed in this paper only admits $\emptyset$.

The approach of [13] is defined on non-disjunctive programs with particular kinds of aggregates (called cardinality and weight constraints), which basically correspond to programs with *count* and *sum* functions. As shown in [4], the program $\{a:-\#\text{sum}\{\langle 1 : $ not $a\rangle\} \leq 0.\}$ admits two stable models, $\emptyset$ and $\{a\}$, according to [13], whereas our semantics only allows for $\emptyset$ as an answer set. An extension to this approach has been presented in [10], which allows for arbitrary aggregates in non-disjunctive programs.

Finally, the work in [16] deals with the more abstract concept of generalized quantifiers, and the semantics therein shares several properties with ours.

Concluding, we proposed a declarative semantics for disjunctive programs with arbitrary aggregates. We demonstrated that our semantics is endowed with desirable properties. Importantly, we proved that aggregate literals do not increase the computational complexity of disjunctive programs in our approach. Future work concerns the design of efficient algorithms for the implementation of our proposal in the DLV system. Upon completion of this paper, we have learned that yet another semantics has been independently proposed in [15]; studying the relationship to it is also a subject for future work.

We would like to thank the anonymous reviewers for their useful comments.

References

1. Mumick, I.S., Pirahesh, H., Ramakrishnan, R.: The magic of duplicates and aggregates. In: VLDB'90 (1990) 264–277
2. Kemp, D.B., Stuckey, P.J.: Semantics of Logic Programs with Aggregates. In: ISLP'91, MIT Press (1991) 387–401
3. Ross, K.A., Sagiv, Y.: Monotonic Aggregation in Deductive Databases. JCSS **54** (1997) 79–97
4. Pelov, N., Denecker, M., Bruynooghe, M.: Partial stable models for logic programs with aggregates. In: LPNMR-7. LNCS 2923., Springer (2004) 207–219
5. Dell'Armi, T., Faber, W., Ielpa, G., Leone, N., Pfeifer, G.: Aggregate Functions in Disjunctive Logic Programming: Semantics, Complexity, and Implementation in DLV. In: IJCAI 2003, Acapulco, Mexico, Morgan Kaufmann (2003) 847–852
6. Gelfond, M.: Representing Knowledge in A-Prolog. In: Computational Logic. Logic Programming and Beyond. LNCS 2408. Springer (2002) 413–451
7. Dell'Armi, T., Faber, W., Ielpa, G., Leone, N., Pfeifer, G.: Aggregate Functions in DLV. In: ASP'03, Messina, Italy (2003) 274–288 Online at http://CEUR-WS.org/Vol-78/.
8. Pelov, N., Truszczyński, M.: Semantics of disjunctive programs with monotone aggregates - an operator-based approach. In: NMR 2004. (2004) 327–334
9. Marek, V.W., Remmel, J.B.: On Logic Programs with Cardinality Constraints. In: NMR'2002 (2002) 219–228
10. Marek, V.W., Remmel, J.B.: Set Constraints in Logic Programming. In: LPNMR-7. LNCS, Springer (2004) 167–179
11. Gelfond, M., Lifschitz, V.: Classical Negation in Logic Programs and Disjunctive Databases. New Generation Computing **9** (1991) 365–385
12. Eiter, T., Faber, W., Leone, N., Pfeifer, G.: Declarative Problem-Solving Using the DLV System. In Minker, J., ed.: Logic-Based Artificial Intelligence. Kluwer (2000) 79–103
13. Niemelä, I., Simons, P., Soininen, T.: Stable Model Semantics of Weight Constraint Rules. In: LPNMR'99. Number 1730 in Lecture Notes in AI (LNAI), Springer (1999) 107–116
14. Dantsin, E., Eiter, T., Gottlob, G., Voronkov, A.: Complexity and Expressive Power of Logic Programming. ACM Computing Surveys **33** (2001) 374–425
15. Pelov, N.: Semantics of Logic Programs with Aggregates. PhD thesis, Katholieke Universiteit Leuven, Leuven, Belgium (2004)
16. Eiter, T., Gottlob, G., Veith, H.: Modular Logic Programming and Generalized Quantifiers. In: LPNMR'97. LNCS 1265, Springer (1997) 290–309

A Logic for Reasoning About Coherent Conditional Probability: A Modal Fuzzy Logic Approach

Enrico Marchioni[1,2] and Lluís Godo[1]

[1] Institut d'Investigació en Intel·ligència Artificial
Campus UAB, 08193 Bellaterra, Spain
{enrico,godo}@iiia.csic.es
[2] Departamento de Lógica, Universidad de Salamanca
Campus Unamuno, 37007 Salamanca, Spain
marchioni@usal.es

Abstract. In this paper we define a logic to reason about coherent conditional probability, in the sense of de Finetti. Under this view, a conditional probability $\mu(\cdot \mid \cdot)$ is a primitive notion that applies over conditional events of the form "φ given ψ", where ψ is not the impossible event. Our approach exploits an idea already used by Hájek and colleagues to define a logic for (unconditional) probability in the frame of fuzzy logics. Namely, in our logic for each pair of classical propositions φ and ψ, we take the probability of the conditional event "φ given ψ", $\varphi|\psi$ for short, as the truth-value of the (fuzzy) modal proposition $P(\varphi \mid \psi)$, read as "$\varphi|\psi$ is probable". Based on this idea we define a fuzzy modal logic FCP(ŁΠ), built up over the many-valued logic ŁΠ$\frac{1}{2}$ (a logic which combines the well-known Łukasiewicz and Product fuzzy logics), which is shown to be complete with respect to the class of probabilistic Kripke structures induced by coherent conditional probabilities. Finally, we show that checking coherence of a probability assessment to an arbitrary family of conditional events is tantamount to checking consistency of a suitable defined theory over the logic FCP(ŁΠ).

1 Introduction: Conditional Probability and Fuzzy Logic

Reasoning under uncertainty is a key issue in many areas of Artificial Intelligence. From a logical point of view, uncertainty basically concerns formulas that can be either true or false, but their truth-value is unknown due to incompleteness of the available information. Among the different models uncertainty, probability theory is no doubt the most relevant. One may find in the literature a number of logics to reason about probability, some of them rather early. We may cite [1,6,7,9,10,14,16,18,19,20,21,22,23,24] as some of the most relevant references. Besides, it is worth mentioning the recent book [15] by Halpern, where a deep investigation of uncertainty (not only probability) representations and uncertainty logics is presented.

J.J. Alferes and J. Leite (Eds.): JELIA 2004, LNAI 3229, pp. 213–225, 2004.
© Springer-Verlag Berlin Heidelberg 2004

Nearly almost all the probability logics in the above references are based on classical two-valued logic (except for [10]). In this paper we develop a propositional *fuzzy* logic of (conditional) probability for which completeness results are provided. In [13] a new approach, further elaborated in [12] and in [11], was proposed to axiomatize logics of uncertainty in the framework of fuzzy logic. The basic idea consists in considering, for each classical (two-valued) proposition φ, a (fuzzy) modal proposition $P\varphi$ which reads "φ is probable" and taking as truth-degree of $P\varphi$ the probability of φ. Then one can define theories about the $P\varphi$'s over a particular fuzzy logic including, as axioms, formulas corresponding to the basic postulates of probability theory. The advantage of such an approach is that algebraic operations needed to compute with probabilities (or with any other uncertainty model) are embedded in the connectives of the many-valued logical framework, resulting in clear and elegant formalizations.

In reasoning with probability, a crucial issue concerns the notion of *conditional probability*. Traditionally, given a probability measure μ on an algebra of possible worlds W, if the agent observes that the actual world is in $A \subseteq W$, then the updated probability measure $\mu(\cdot \mid A)$, called conditional probability, is defined as $\mu(B \mid A) = \mu(B \cap A)/\mu(A)$, provided that $\mu(A) > 0$. If $\mu(A) = 0$ the conditional probability remains then undefined. This yields both philosophical and logical problems.

For instance, in [11] statements about conditional probability are handled by introducing formulas $P(\varphi \mid \psi)$ standing for $P\psi \rightarrow_\Pi P(\varphi \wedge \psi)$. Such a definition exploits the properties of Product logic implication $\rightarrow_\Pi$, whose truth function behaves like a truncated division:

$$e(\Phi \rightarrow_\Pi \Psi) = \begin{cases} 1, & \text{if } e(\Phi) \leq e(\Psi) \\ e(\Psi)/e(\Phi), & \text{otherwise.} \end{cases}$$

With such a logical modelling, whenever the probability of the conditioning event χ is 0, $P(\varphi \mid \chi)$ takes as truth-value 1. Therefore, this yields problems when dealing with zero probabilities.

To overcome such difficulties, an alternative approach (that goes back to the 30's with de Finetti, and later to the 60's with Rényi and Popper among others) proposes to consider conditional probability and conditional events as basic notions, not derived from the notion of unconditional probability. Coletti and Scozzafava's book [4] includes a rich elaboration of different issues of reasoning with *coherent* conditional probability, i.e. the conditional probability in the sense of de Finetti. We take from there the following definition (cf. [4]).

Definition 1. *Let $\mathcal{G}$ be a Boolean algebra and let $\mathcal{B} \subseteq \mathcal{G}$ be closed with respect to finite unions (additive set). Let $\mathcal{B}^0 = \mathcal{B} \setminus \{\emptyset\}$. A conditional probability on the set $\mathcal{G} \times \mathcal{B}^0$ of conditional events, denoted as $E|H$, is a function $\mu : \mathcal{G} \times \mathcal{B}^0 \rightarrow [0, 1]$ satisfying the following axioms:*

(i) $\mu(H \mid H) = 1$, for all $H \in \mathcal{B}^0$
(ii) $\mu(\cdot \mid H)$ is a (finitely additive) probability on $\mathcal{G}$ for any given $H \in \mathcal{B}^0$
(iii) $\mu(E \cap A \mid H) = \mu(E \mid H) \cdot \mu(A \mid E \cap H)$, for all $A \in \mathcal{G}$ and $E, H, E \cap H \in \mathcal{B}^0$.

In this paper we follow the above fuzzy logic approach to define a logic to reason about conditional probability in the sense of Definition 1 [1]. Thus, over the fuzzy logic $L\Pi\frac{1}{2}$ we directly introduce a modal operator P as primitive, and apply it to *conditional events* of the form $\varphi|\chi$. Unconditional probability, then, arises as non-primitive whenever the conditioning event is a (classical) tautology. The obvious reading of a statement like $P(\varphi \mid \chi)$ is "the conditional event "φ given χ" is probable". Similarly to the case mentioned above, the truth-value of $P(\varphi \mid \chi)$ will be given by a conditional probability $\mu(\varphi \mid \chi)$. It is worth mentioning a very related approach by Flaminio and Montagna [8] which deals with conditional probability in the frame of the fuzzy logic $L\Pi\frac{1}{2}$, but differs from ours in that they use non-standard probabilities.

The paper is structured as follows. After this introduction, in Section 2 we overview the basic facts about the fuzzy logic $L\Pi\frac{1}{2}$. In Section 3 we define our conditional probability logic FCP($L\Pi$) as a modal fuzzy logic over $L\Pi\frac{1}{2}$ and prove soundness and completeness results with respect to the intended probabilistic semantics. Then, in Section 4 we show how the problem of coherent conditional probability assessments can be cast as a problem of determining the logical consistency of a given theory in our logic. We end with some conclusions.

2   Logical Background: The $L\Pi\frac{1}{2}$ Logic

The language of the $L\Pi$ logic is built in the usual way from a countable set of propositional variables, three binary connectives $\to_L$ (Łukasiewicz implication), $\odot$ (Product conjunction) and $\to_\Pi$ (Product implication), and the truth constant $\bar{0}$. A truth-evaluation is a mapping e that assigns to every propositional variable a real number from the unit interval $[0, 1]$ and extends to all formulas as follows:

$$
\begin{aligned}
e(\bar{0}) \quad &= 0, \\
e(\varphi \to_L \psi) &= \min(1 - e(\varphi) + e(\psi), 1), \\
e(\varphi \odot \psi) \quad &= e(\varphi) \cdot e(\psi), \\
e(\varphi \to_\Pi \psi) &= \begin{cases} 1, & \text{if } e(\varphi) \le e(\psi) \\ e(\psi)/e(\varphi), & \text{otherwise} \end{cases}.
\end{aligned}
$$

The truth constant $\bar{1}$ is defined as $\varphi \to_L \varphi$. In this way we have $e(\bar{1}) = 1$ for any truth-evaluation e. Moreover, many other connectives can be defined from those introduced above:

$$
\begin{array}{ll}
\neg_L\varphi \text{ is } \varphi \to_L \bar{0}, & \neg_\Pi\varphi \text{ is } \varphi \to_\Pi \bar{0}, \\
\varphi \wedge \psi \text{ is } \varphi \& (\varphi \to_L \psi), & \varphi \vee \psi \text{ is } \neg_L(\neg_L\varphi \wedge \neg_L\psi), \\
\varphi \oplus \psi \text{ is } \neg_L\varphi \to_L \psi, & \varphi \& \psi \text{ is } \neg_L(\neg_L\varphi \oplus \neg_L\psi), \\
\varphi \ominus \psi \text{ is } \varphi \& \neg_L\psi, & \varphi \equiv \psi \text{ is } (\varphi \to_L \psi) \& (\psi \to_L \varphi), \\
\Delta\varphi \text{ is } \neg_\Pi\neg_L\varphi, & \nabla\varphi \text{ is } \neg_\Pi\neg_\Pi\varphi,
\end{array}
$$

---

[1] Notice that somewhat similar definitions of conditional probability can be found in the literature. For instance, in [15] $\mathcal{B}^0$ is further required to be closed under supersets and $\mathcal{G} \times \mathcal{B}^0$ is called a Popper algebra. See also [4] for a discussion concerning weaker notions of conditional probability and their unpleasant consequences.

with the following interpretations:

$$e(\neg_L \varphi) = 1 - e(\varphi), \qquad\qquad e(\neg_\Pi \varphi) = \begin{cases} 1, \text{ if } e(\varphi) = 0 \\ 0, \text{ otherwise} \end{cases},$$

$$e(\varphi \wedge \psi) = \min(e(\varphi), e(\psi)), \qquad e(\varphi \vee \psi) = \max(e(\varphi), e(\psi)),$$

$$e(\varphi \oplus \psi) = \min(1, e(\varphi) + e(\psi)), \qquad e(\varphi \& \psi) = \max(0, e(\varphi) + e(\psi) - 1),$$

$$e(\varphi \ominus \psi) = \max(0, e(\varphi) - e(\psi)), \qquad e(\varphi \equiv \psi) = 1 - |e(\varphi) - e(\psi)|,$$

$$e(\Delta \varphi) = \begin{cases} 1, \text{ if } e(\varphi) = 1 \\ 0, \text{ otherwise} \end{cases}, \qquad e(\nabla \varphi) = \begin{cases} 1, \text{ if } e(\varphi) > 0 \\ 0, \text{ otherwise} \end{cases}.$$

The logic $L\Pi$ is defined Hilbert-style as the logical system whose axioms and rules are the following[2]:

(i)   Axioms of Łukasiewicz Logic:
   (Ł1) $\varphi \rightarrow_L (\psi \rightarrow_L \varphi)$
   (Ł2) $(\varphi \rightarrow_L \psi) \rightarrow_L ((\psi \rightarrow_L \chi) \rightarrow_L (\varphi \rightarrow_L \chi))$
   (Ł3) $(\neg_L \varphi \rightarrow_L \neg_L \psi) \rightarrow_L (\psi \rightarrow_L \varphi)$
   (Ł4) $((\varphi \rightarrow_L \psi) \rightarrow_L \psi) \rightarrow_L ((\psi \rightarrow_L \varphi) \rightarrow_L \varphi)$

(ii)   Axioms of Product Logic[3]:
   (A1) $(\varphi \rightarrow_\Pi \psi) \rightarrow_\Pi ((\psi \rightarrow_\Pi \chi) \rightarrow_\Pi (\varphi \rightarrow_\Pi \chi))$
   (A2) $(\varphi \odot \psi) \rightarrow_\Pi \varphi$
   (A3) $(\varphi \odot \psi) \rightarrow_\Pi (\psi \odot \varphi)$
   (A4) $(\varphi \odot (\varphi \rightarrow_\Pi \psi)) \rightarrow_\Pi (\psi \odot (\psi \rightarrow_\Pi \varphi))$
   (A5a) $(\varphi \rightarrow_\Pi (\psi \rightarrow_\Pi \chi)) \rightarrow_\Pi ((\varphi \odot \psi) \rightarrow_\Pi \chi)$
   (A5b) $((\varphi \odot \psi) \rightarrow_\Pi \chi) \rightarrow_\Pi (\varphi \rightarrow_\Pi (\psi \rightarrow_\Pi \chi))$
   (A6) $((\varphi \rightarrow_\Pi \psi) \rightarrow_\Pi \chi) \rightarrow_\Pi (((\psi \rightarrow_\Pi \varphi) \rightarrow_\Pi \chi) \rightarrow_\Pi \chi)$
   (Π1) $\neg_\Pi \neg_\Pi \chi \rightarrow_\Pi (((\varphi \odot \chi) \rightarrow_\Pi (\psi \odot \chi)) \rightarrow_\Pi (\varphi \rightarrow_\Pi \psi))$
   (Π2) $\varphi \wedge \neg_\Pi \varphi \rightarrow_\Pi \bar{0}$

(iii) The following additional axioms relating Łukasiewicz and Product logic connectives:
   ($\neg$) $\neg_\Pi \varphi \rightarrow_L \neg_L \varphi$
   (Δ) $\Delta(\varphi \rightarrow_L \psi) \equiv \Delta(\varphi \rightarrow_\Pi \psi)$
   ($L\Pi$) $\varphi \odot (\psi \ominus \chi) \equiv (\varphi \odot \psi) \ominus (\varphi \odot \chi)$

(iv)   Deduction rules of $L\Pi$ are modus ponens for $\rightarrow_L$ (modus ponens for $\rightarrow_\Pi$ is derivable), and necessitation for Δ: from φ derive $\Delta \varphi$.

The logic $L\Pi\frac{1}{2}$ is the logic obtained from $L\Pi$ by expanding the language with a propositional variable $\overline{\frac{1}{2}}$ and adding the axiom:

$$(L\Pi\tfrac{1}{2}) \; \overline{\tfrac{1}{2}} \equiv \neg_L \overline{\tfrac{1}{2}}$$

Obviously, a truth-evaluation e for $L\Pi$ is easily extended to an evaluation for $L\Pi\frac{1}{2}$ by further requiring $e(\overline{\frac{1}{2}}) = \frac{1}{2}$.

---

[2] This definition, proposed in [3], is actually a simplified version of the original definition of $L\Pi$ given in [5].

[3] Actually Product logic axioms also include axiom A7 $[\bar{0} \rightarrow_\Pi \varphi]$ which is redundant in $L\Pi$.

From the above axiom systems, the notion of proof from a theory (a set of formulas) in both logics, denoted $\vdash_{L\Pi}$ and $\vdash_{L\Pi 1/2}$ respectively, is defined as usual. Strong completeness of both logics for finite theories with respect to the given semantics has been proved in [5]. In what follows we will restrict ourselves to the logic $L\Pi \frac{1}{2}$.

Theorem 1. *For any finite set of formulas T and any formula φ of $L\Pi \frac{1}{2}$, we have $T \vdash_{L\Pi 1/2} \varphi$ iff $e(\varphi) = 1$ for any truth-evaluation e which is a model[4] of T.*

As it is also shown in [5], for each rational $r \in [0,1]$ a formula $\bar{r}$ is definable in $L\Pi \frac{1}{2}$ from the truth constant $\frac{1}{2}$ and the connectives, so that $e(\bar{r}) = r$ for each evaluation e. Therefore, in the language of $L\Pi \frac{1}{2}$ we have a truth constant for each rational in $[0, 1]$, and due to completeness of $L\Pi \frac{1}{2}$, the following book-keeping axioms for rational truth constants are provable:

$(RL\Pi 1)$ $\neg_L \bar{r} \equiv \overline{1-r}$
$(RL\Pi 2)$ $\bar{r} \to_L \bar{s} \equiv \overline{\min(1, 1-r+s)}$
$(RL\Pi 3)$ $\bar{r} \odot \bar{s} \equiv \overline{r \cdot s}$
$(RL\Pi 4)$ $\bar{r} \to_\Pi \bar{s} \equiv \overline{r \Rightarrow_P s}$

where $r \Rightarrow_P s = 1$ if $r \leq s$, $r \Rightarrow_P s = s/r$ otherwise.

3   A Logic of Conditional Probability

In this section we define a fuzzy modal logic, built up over the many-valued logic $L\Pi \frac{1}{2}$, that we shall call FCP($L\Pi$) —FCP for Fuzzy Conditional Probability—, to reason about coherent conditional probability of crisp propositions.

The language of FCP($L\Pi$) is defined in two steps:

Non-modal formulas: they are built from a set V of propositional variables $\{p_1, p_2, \ldots p_n, \ldots\}$ using the classical binary connectives $\wedge$ and $\neg$. Other connectives like $\vee$, $\to$ and $\leftrightarrow$ are defined from $\wedge$ and $\neg$ in the usual way. Non-modal formulas (we will also refer to them as Boolean propositions) will be denoted by lower case Greek letters φ, ψ, etc. The set of non-modal formulas will be denoted by $\mathcal{L}$.

Modal formulas: they are built from elementary modal formulas of the form $P(\varphi \mid \chi)$, where φ and χ are non-modal formulas, using the connectives of $L\Pi$ ($\to_L$, $\odot$, $\to_\Pi$) and the truth constants $\bar{r}$, for each rational $r \in [0,1]$. We shall denote them by upper case Greek letters Φ, Ψ, etc. Notice that we do not allow nested modalities.

Definition 2. *The axioms of the logic FCP($L\Pi$) are the following:*

(i)   *Axioms of Classical propositional Logic for non-modal formulas*
(ii)   *Axioms of $L\Pi \frac{1}{2}$ for modal formulas*

---

[4] We say that an evaluation e is a *model* of a theory T whenever $e(\psi) = 1$ for each $\psi \in T$.

(iii) Probabilistic modal axioms:

$\quad$ (FCP1) $\quad P(\varphi \to \psi \mid \chi) \to_L (P(\varphi \mid \chi) \to_L P(\psi \mid \chi))$

$\quad$ (FCP2) $\quad P(\neg\varphi \mid \chi) \equiv \neg_L P(\varphi \mid \chi)$

$\quad$ (FCP3) $\quad P(\varphi \lor \psi \mid \chi) \equiv ((P(\varphi \mid \chi) \to_L P(\varphi \land \psi \mid \chi)) \to_L P(\psi \mid \chi)$

$\quad$ (FCP4) $\quad P(\varphi \land \psi \mid \chi) \equiv P(\psi \mid \varphi \land \chi) \odot P(\varphi \mid \chi)$

$\quad$ (FCP5) $\quad P(\chi \mid \chi)$

Deduction rules of FCP(LΠ) are those of LΠ (i.e. modus ponens *and* necessitation *for* Δ*), plus:*

(iv) necessitation *for P: from* φ *derive* $P(\varphi \mid \chi)$

(v) substitution of equivalents *for the conditioning event: from* $\chi \leftrightarrow \chi'$*, derive* $P(\varphi \mid \chi) \equiv P(\varphi \mid \chi')$

The notion of proof is defined as usual. We will denote that in FCP(LΠ) a formula Φ follows from a theory (set of formulas) T by $T \vdash_{FCP} \Phi$. The only remark is that the rule of necessitation for $P(\cdot \mid \chi)$ can only be applied to Boolean theorems.

$\quad$ The semantics for FCP(LΠ) is given by *conditional probability Kripke structures* $K = \langle W, \mathcal{U}, e, \mu \rangle$, where:

– W is a non-empty set of possible worlds.

– $e : V \times W \to \{0, 1\}$ provides for each world a *Boolean* (two-valued) evaluation of the propositional variables, that is, $e(p, w) \in \{0, 1\}$ for each propositional variable $p \in V$ and each world $w \in W$. A truth-evaluation $e(\cdot, w)$ is extended to Boolean propositions as usual. For a Boolean formula φ, we will write $[\varphi]_W = \{w \in W \mid e(\varphi, w) = 1\}$.

– $\mu : \mathcal{U} \times \mathcal{U}^0 \to [0, 1]$ is a conditional probability over a Boolean algebra $\mathcal{U}$ of subsets of W[5] where $\mathcal{U}^0 = \mathcal{U} \backslash \{\emptyset\}$, and such that $([\varphi]_W, [\chi]_W)$ is μ-measurable for any non-modal φ and χ (with $[\chi]_W \neq \emptyset$).

– $e(\cdot, w)$ is extended to elementary modal formulas by defining

$$ e(P(\varphi \mid \chi), w) = \mu([\varphi]_W \mid [\chi]_W)^6, $$

and to arbitrary modal formulas according to $L\Pi\frac{1}{2}$ semantics, that is:

$$ e(\bar{r}, w) = r, $$
$$ e(\Phi \to_L \Psi, w) = \min(1 - e(\Phi, w) + e(\Psi, w), 1), $$
$$ e(\Phi \odot \Psi, w) = e(\Phi, w) \cdot e(\Psi, w), $$
$$ e(\Phi \to_\Pi \Psi, w) = \begin{cases} 1, & \text{if } e(\Phi, w) \leq e(\Psi, w) \\ e(\Psi, w)/e(\Phi, w), & \text{otherwise} \end{cases}. $$

Notice that if Φ is a modal formula the truth-evaluations $e(\Phi, w)$ depend only on the conditional probability measure μ and not on the particular world w.

---

[5] Notice that in our definition the factors of the Cartesian product are the same Boolean algebra. This is clearly a special case of what stated in Definition 1.

[6] When $[\chi]_W = \emptyset$, we define $e(P(\varphi \mid \chi), w) = 1$.

The truth-degree of a formula Φ in a conditional probability Kripke structure $K = \langle W, \mathcal{U}, e, \mu \rangle$, written $\|\Phi\|^K$, is defined as

$$\|\Phi\|^K = \inf_{w \in W} e(\Phi, w).$$

When $\|\Phi\|^K = 1$ we will say that Φ is valid in K or that K is a model for Φ, and it will be also written $K \models \Phi$. Let T be a set of formulas. Then we say that K is a model of T if $K \models \Phi$ for all $\Phi \in T$. Now let $\mathcal{M}$ be a class of conditional probability Kripke structures. Then we define the truth-degree $\|\Phi\|_T^{\mathcal{M}}$ of a formula in a theory T relative to the class $\mathcal{M}$ as

$$\|\Phi\|_T^{\mathcal{M}} = \inf\{\|\Phi\|^K \mid K \in \mathcal{M}, \ K \text{ being a model of } T\} \ .$$

The notion of logical entailment relative to the class $\mathcal{M}$, written $\models_{\mathcal{M}}$, is then defined as follows:

$$T \models_{\mathcal{M}} \Phi \text{ iff } \|\Phi\|_T^{\mathcal{M}} = 1 \ .$$

That is, Φ logically follows from a set of formulas T if every structure of $\mathcal{M}$ which is a model of T also is a model of Φ. If $\mathcal{M}$ denotes the whole class of conditional probability Kripke structures we shall write $T \models_{FCP} \Phi$ and $\|\Phi\|_T^{FCP}$.

It is easy to check that axioms FCP1-FCP5 are valid formulas in the class of all conditional probability Kripke structures. Moreover, the inference rule of substitution of equivalents preserves truth in a model, while the necessitation rule for P preserves validity in a model. Therefore we have the following soundness result.

Lemma 1. (Soundness) *The logic FCP(LΠ) is sound with respect to the class of conditional probability Kripke structures.*

For any $\varphi, \psi \in \mathcal{L}$, define $\varphi \sim \psi$ iff $\vdash \varphi \leftrightarrow \psi$ in classical logic. The relation $\sim$ is an equivalence relation in the crisp language $\mathcal{L}$ and $[\varphi]$ will denote the equivalence class of φ, containing the propositions provably equivalent to φ. Obviously, the quotient set $\mathcal{L}/_\sim$ of classes of provably equivalent non-modal formulas in FCP($L\Pi$) forms a Boolean algebra which is isomorphic to a corresponding Boolean subalgebra $\mathbf{B}(\Omega)$ of the power set of the set Ω of Boolean interpretations of the crisp language $\mathcal{L}$[7]. For each $\varphi \in \mathcal{L}$, we shall identify the equivalence class $[\varphi]$ with the set $\{\omega \in \Omega \mid \omega(\varphi) = 1\} \in \mathbf{B}(\Omega)$ of interpretations that make φ true. We shall denote by $\mathcal{CP}(\mathcal{L})$ the set of conditional probabilities over $\mathcal{L}/_{\sim_{FCP}} \times (\mathcal{L}/_{\sim_{FCP}} \setminus [\bot])$ or equivalently on $\mathbf{B}(\Omega) \times \mathbf{B}(\Omega)^0$.

Notice that each conditional probability $\mu \in \mathcal{CP}(\mathcal{L})$ induces a conditional probability Kripke structure $\langle \Omega, \mathbf{B}(\Omega), e_\mu, \mu \rangle$ where $e_\mu(p, \omega) = \omega(p) \in \{0, 1\}$ for each $\omega \in \Omega$ and each propositional variable p. We shall denote by $\mathcal{CPS}$ the

---

[7] Actually, $\mathbf{B}(\Omega) = \{\{\omega \in \Omega \mid \omega(\varphi) = 1\} \mid \varphi \in \mathcal{L}\}$. Needless to say, if the language has only finitely many propositional variables then the algebra $\mathbf{B}(\Omega)$ is just the whole power set of Ω, otherwise it is a strict subalgebra.

class of Kripke structures induced by conditional probabilities $\mu \in \mathcal{CP}(\mathcal{L})$, i.e. $\mathcal{CPS} = \{\langle \Omega, \mathbf{B}(\Omega), e_\mu, \mu \rangle \mid \mu \in \mathcal{CP}(\mathcal{L})\}$. Abusing the language, we will say that a conditional probability $\mu \in \mathcal{CP}(\mathcal{L})$ is a *model* of a modal theory T whenever the induced Kripke structure $\Omega_\mu = \langle \Omega, \mathbf{B}(\Omega), e_\mu, \mu \rangle$ is a model of T. Besides, we shall often write $\mu(\varphi \mid \chi)$ actually meaning $\mu([\varphi] \mid [\chi])$.

Actually, for our purposes, we can restrict ourselves to the class of conditional probability Kripke structures $\mathcal{CPS}$. In fact, it is not difficult to prove the following lemma.

Lemma 2. *For each conditional probability Kripke structure $K = \langle W, \mathcal{U}, e, \mu \rangle$ there is a conditional probability $\mu^* : \mathbf{B}(\Omega) \times \mathbf{B}(\Omega)^0 \to [0,1]$ such that $\|P(\varphi \mid \chi)\|^K = \mu^*(\varphi \mid \chi)$ for all $\varphi, \chi \in \mathcal{L}$ such that $[\chi] \neq \emptyset$. Therefore, it also holds that $\|\Phi\|_T = \|\Phi\|_T^{\mathcal{CPS}}$ for any modal formula Φ and any modal theory T.*

As a consequence we have the following simple corollary.

Corollary 1. *For any modal theory T over FCP(LΠ) and non-modal formulas φ and χ (with $[\chi] \neq \emptyset$) the following conditions hold:*

(i) $T \models_{FCP} \bar{r} \to P(\varphi \mid \chi)$ *iff* $\mu(\varphi \mid \chi) \geq r$ *for each* $\mu \in \mathcal{CP}(\mathcal{L})$ *model of T.*
(ii) $T \models_{FCP} P(\varphi \mid \chi) \to \bar{r}$ *iff* $\mu(\varphi \mid \chi) \leq r$ *for each* $\mu \in \mathcal{CP}(\mathcal{L})$ *model of T.*

Now, we show that FCP(LΠ) is strongly complete for finite modal theories with respect to the intended probabilistic semantics.

Theorem 2. (Strong finite probabilistic completeness of FCP(LΠ)) *Let T be a finite modal theory over FCP(LΠ) and Φ a modal formula. Then $T \vdash_{FCP} \Phi$ iff $e_\mu(\Phi) = 1$ for each conditional probability model μ of T.*

Proof. The proof is an adaptation of the proof in [11], which in turn is based on [13,12] where the underlying logics considered were Łukasiewicz logic and Rational Pavelka logic rather than $LΠ\frac{1}{2}$.

By soundness we have that $T \vdash_{FCP(LΠ)} \Phi$ implies $T \models_{FCP(LΠ)} \Phi$. We have to prove the converse. In order to do so, the basic idea consists in transforming modal theories over FCP(LΠ) into theories over $LΠ\frac{1}{2}$.

Define a theory, called $\mathcal{F}$, as follows:

1. take as propositional variables of the theory variables of the form $f_{\varphi|\chi}$, where φ and χ are classical propositions from $\mathcal{L}$.
2. take as axioms of the theory the following ones, for each φ, ψ and χ:
   ($\mathcal{F}1$) $f_{\varphi|\chi}$, for φ being a classical tautology,
   ($\mathcal{F}2$) $f_{\varphi|\chi} \equiv f_{\varphi|\chi'}$, for any χ, χ' such that $\chi \leftrightarrow \chi'$ is a tautology,
   ($\mathcal{F}3$) $f_{\varphi \to \psi|\chi} \to_L (f_{\varphi|\chi} \to_L f_{\psi|\chi})$,
   ($\mathcal{F}4$) $f_{\neg\varphi|\chi} \equiv \neg_L f_{\varphi|\chi}$,
   ($\mathcal{F}5$) $f_{\varphi\vee\psi|\chi} \equiv [(f_{\varphi|\chi} \to_L f_{\varphi\wedge\psi|\chi}) \to_L f_{\psi|\chi}]$,
   ($\mathcal{F}6$) $f_{\varphi\wedge\psi|\chi} \equiv f_{\psi|\varphi\wedge\chi} \odot f_{\varphi|\chi}$,
   ($\mathcal{F}7$) $f_{\varphi|\varphi}$.

Then define a mapping $*$ from modal formulas to $LΠ\frac{1}{2}$-formulas as follows:

1. $(P(\varphi \mid \chi))^* = f_{\varphi|\chi}$
2. $\bar{r}^* = \bar{r}$
3. $(\Phi \circ \Psi)^* = \Phi^* \circ \Psi^*$, for $\circ \in \{\rightarrow_L, \odot, \rightarrow_\Pi\}$

Let us denote by T^* the set of all formulas translated from T. First, by the construction of $\mathcal{F}$, one can easily check that for any Φ,

$$T \vdash_{FCP(L\Pi)} \Phi \text{ iff } T^* \cup \mathcal{F} \vdash_{L\Pi\frac{1}{2}} \Phi^*. \tag{1}$$

Notice that the use in a proof from $T^* \cup \mathcal{F}$ of instances of $(\mathcal{F}1)$ and $(\mathcal{F}2)$ corresponds to the use of the inference rules of necessitation for P and substitution of equivalents in $FCP(L\Pi)$, while instances of $(\mathcal{F}3) - (\mathcal{F}7)$ obviously correspond to axioms (FCP1) - (FCP5) respectively.

Now, we prove that the semantical analogue of (1) also holds, that is,

$$T \models_{FCP(L\Pi)} \Phi \text{ iff } T^* \cup \mathcal{F} \models_{L\Pi\frac{1}{2}} \Phi^*. \tag{2}$$

First, we show that each $L\Pi\frac{1}{2}$-evaluation e which is model of $T^* \cup \mathcal{F}$ determines a conditional probabilistic Kripke model K_e of T such that $e(\Phi^*) = \|\Phi\|_e^K$ for any modal formula Φ. Actually, we can define the conditional probability μ_e on $\mathbf{B}(\Omega) \times \mathbf{B}(\Omega)^0$ as follows:

$$\mu_e([\varphi] \mid [\chi]) = e(f_{\varphi|\chi}).$$

So defined μ_e is indeed a conditional probability, but this is clear since by hypothesis e is a model of $\mathcal{F}$. Then, it is also clear that in the model $K_e = \Omega_{\mu_e}$ the truth-degree of modal formulas Φ coincides with the truth-evaluations $e(\Phi^*)$ since they only depend on the values of μ_e and e over the elementary modal formulas $P(\varphi \mid \chi)$ and the atoms $f_{\varphi|\chi}$ respectively.

Conversely, we have now to prove that each conditional probability Kripke structure $K = (W, \mathcal{U}, e, \mu)$ determines a $L\Pi\frac{1}{2}$-evaluation e_K model of $\mathcal{F}$ such that $e_K(\Phi^*) = \|\Phi\|^K$ for any modal formula Φ. Then, we only need to set

$$e_K(f_{\varphi|\chi}) = \begin{cases} \mu([\varphi]_W \mid [\chi]_W), & \text{if } [\chi]_W \neq \emptyset \\ 1, & \text{if } [\chi]_W = \emptyset \end{cases}.$$

It is easy to see then that e_K is a model of axioms $\mathcal{F}1 - \mathcal{F}7$, and moreover that for any modal formula Φ, we have $e_K(\Phi^*) = \|\Phi\|^K$. Hence we have proved the equivalence (2).

From (1) and (2), to prove the theorem it remains to show that

$$T^* \cup \mathcal{F} \vdash_{L\Pi\frac{1}{2}} \Phi^* \text{ iff } T^* \cup \mathcal{F} \models_{L\Pi\frac{1}{2}} \Phi^*.$$

Note that $L\Pi\frac{1}{2}$ is strongly complete but only for finite theories. We have that the initial modal theory T is finite, so is T^*. However $\mathcal{F}$ contains infinitely many instances of axioms $\mathcal{F}1 - \mathcal{F}7$. Nonetheless one can prove that such infinitely many instances can be replaced by only finitely many instances, by using propositional normal forms, again following the lines of [12, 8.4.12].

Take n propositional variables $p_1, \ldots, p_n$ containing at least all variables in T. For any formula φ built from these propositional variables, take the corresponding disjunctive normal form $(\varphi)_{dnf}$. Notice that there are 2^n different normal forms. Then, when translating a modal formula Φ into Φ^*, we replace each atom $f_{\varphi|\chi}$ by $f_{(\varphi)_{dnf}|(\chi)_{dnf}}$ to obtain its normal translation Φ^*_{dnf}. The theory T^*_{dnf} is the (finite) set of all Ψ^*_{dnf}, where $\Psi \in T$. The theory $\mathcal{F}_{dnf}$ is the *finite* set of instances of axioms $\mathcal{F}1 - \mathcal{F}7$ for disjunctive normal forms of Boolean formulas built from the propositional variables $p_1, \ldots, p_n$. We can now prove the following lemma.

Lemma 3. *(i)* $T^* \cup \mathcal{F} \vdash_{L\Pi\frac{1}{2}} \Phi^*$ *iff* $T^*_{dnf} \cup \mathcal{F}_{dnf} \vdash_{L\Pi\frac{1}{2}} \Phi^*_{dnf}$.
(ii) $T^* \cup \mathcal{F} \models_{L\Pi\frac{1}{2}} \Phi^*$ *iff* $T^*_{dnf} \cup \mathcal{F}_{dnf} \models_{L\Pi\frac{1}{2}} \Phi^*_{dnf}$.

The proof of is similar to [12, 8.4.13]. Finally, we obtain the following chain of equivalences:

$$
\begin{array}{lll}
T \vdash_{FCP} \Phi & \text{iff } T^* \cup \mathcal{F} \vdash_{L\Pi} \Phi^* & \text{by (i) above} \\
& \text{iff } T^*_{dnf} \cup \mathcal{F}_{dnf} \vdash_{L\Pi\frac{1}{2}} \Phi^*_{dnf} & \text{by (1) of Lemma 3} \\
& \text{iff } T^*_{dnf} \cup \mathcal{F}_{dnf} \models_{L\Pi\frac{1}{2}} \Phi^*_{dnf} & \text{by finite strong completeness of } L\Pi\frac{1}{2} \\
& \text{iff } T^* \cup \mathcal{F} \models_{L\Pi\frac{1}{2}} \Phi^* & \text{by (ii) of Lemma 3} \\
& \text{iff } T \models_{FCP} \Phi & \text{by (2) above}
\end{array}
$$

This completes the proof of theorem.

The following direct corollary exemplifies some kinds of deductions that are usually of interest.

Corollary 2. *Let T be a finite modal theory over $FCP(L\Pi)$ and let φ and χ be non-modal formulas, with $[\chi] \neq \emptyset$. Then:*

(i) $T \vdash_{FCP} \bar{r} \rightarrow P(\varphi \mid \chi)$ *iff $\mu(\varphi \mid \chi) \geq r$, for each conditional probability model μ of T.*

(ii) $T \vdash_{FCP} P(\varphi \mid \chi) \rightarrow \bar{r}$ *iff $\mu(\varphi \mid \chi) \leq r$, for each conditional probability model μ of T.*

It is worth pointing out that the logic $FCP(L\Pi)$ is actually very powerful from a knowledge representation point of view. Indeed, it allows to express several kinds of statements about conditional probability, such as purely comparative statements like "the conditional event $\varphi|\chi$ is at least as probable as the conditional event $\psi|\delta$" as

$$P(\psi \mid \delta) \rightarrow_L P(\varphi \mid \chi),$$

or numerical probability statements like

- "the probability of $\varphi|\chi$ is 0.8" as $P(\varphi \mid \chi) \equiv \overline{0.8}$,
- "the probability of $\varphi|\chi$ is at least 0.8" as $\overline{0.8} \rightarrow_L P(\varphi \mid \chi)$,
- "the probability of $\varphi|\chi$ is at most 0.8" as $P(\varphi \mid \chi) \rightarrow_L \overline{0.8}$,
- "$\varphi|\chi$ has positive probability" as $\neg_\Pi \neg_\Pi P(\varphi \mid \chi)$,

or even statements about *independence*, like "φ and ψ are independent given χ" as

$$P(\varphi \mid \chi \wedge \psi) \equiv P(\varphi \mid \chi).$$

4   Applications to the Coherence Problem

Another well-known solution to overcome the difficulties concerning conditional probability when dealing with zero probabilities consists in using non-standard probabilities. In this approach only the impossible event can take on probability 0, but non-impossible events can have an infinitesimal probability. Then the non-standard conditional probability $Pr^*(\varphi \mid \psi)$ may be expressed as $Pr^*(\varphi \wedge \psi)/Pr^*(\psi)$, which can be taken then as the truth-value of the formula

$$P(\psi) \to_\Pi P(\varphi \wedge \psi),$$

where P is a (unary) modal operator standing for (unconditional) non-standard probability. This is the previously mentioned approach[8] followed by Flaminio and Montagna in [8], where the authors develop the logic $FP(S\!L\Pi)$ in which conditional probability can be treated along with both standard and non-standard probability. Standard probability Pr is recovered by taking the *standard part* of Pr^*. This is modelled in the logic by means of a unary connective S, so that the truth-value of $S(P\varphi)$ is the standard probability of φ. Furthermore, they show that the notion of coherence of a probabilistic assessment to a set of conditional events is tantamount to the consistency of a suitable defined theory over $FP(S\!L\Pi)$.

Definition 3 ([4]). *A probabilistic assessment* $\{Pr(\varphi_i \mid \chi_i) = \alpha_i\}_{i=1,n}$ *over a set of conditional events* $\varphi_i \mid \chi_i$ *(with* χ_i *not being a contradiction) is coherent if there is a conditional probability* μ, *in the sense of Definition 1, such that* $Pr(\varphi_i \mid \chi_i) = \mu(\varphi_i \mid \chi_i)$ *for all* $i = 1, \ldots, n$.

Remark that the above notion of *coherence* can be alternatively found in the literature in a different form, like in [2], in terms of a betting scheme.

Theorem 3 ([8]). *Let* $\kappa = \{Pr(\varphi_i \mid \chi_i) = \alpha_i : i = 1, \ldots, n\}$ *be a rational probabilistic assignment. Let* $\mathcal{B}$ *the Boolean algebra generated by* $\{\varphi_i, \chi_i \mid i = 1, \ldots, n\}$ *and let* Ω *and* $\emptyset$ *be its top element and its bottom element respectively. Then* κ *is coherent iff the theory* T_κ^* *consisting of the axioms of the form* $\neg_\Pi \neg_\Pi Pr(\psi)$ *for* $\psi \in \mathcal{B}\backslash\{\emptyset\}$, *plus the axioms* $S(P(\chi_i) \to_\Pi P(\varphi_i \wedge \chi_i)) \equiv \overline{\alpha_i}$ $(i = 1, \ldots, n)$ *is consistent in* $FP(S\!L\Pi)$, *i.e.* $T_\kappa^* \not\vdash_{FP(S\!L\Pi)} \bar{0}$.

The proof of this theorem is based on two characterizations of coherence, given in [4] and [17], using non-standard probabilities, and it is quite complicated. However in $FCP(L\Pi)$, contrary to $FP(S\!L\Pi)$, conditional probability is a primitive notion, then it can be easily shown that in the logic $FCP(L\Pi)$ an analogous theorem can be proved in a simpler way.

Theorem 4. *Let* $\kappa = \{Pr(\varphi_i \mid \chi_i) = \alpha_i : i = 1, \ldots, n\}$ *be a rational probabilistic assessment. Then* κ *is coherent iff the theory* $T_\kappa = \{P(\varphi_i \mid \chi_i) \equiv \overline{\alpha_i} : i = 1, \ldots, n\}$ *is consistent in* $FCP(L\Pi)$, *i.e.* $T_\kappa \not\vdash_{FCP(L\Pi)} \bar{0}$.

---

[8] A related approach due to Rašković et al. [21] deals with conditional probability by defining graded (two-valued) operators over the unit interval of a recursive non-archimedean field containing all rationals.

Proof. Remember that we are allowed to restrict ourselves to the subclass $\mathcal{CPS}$ of conditional probability structures. Now, suppose that T_κ is consistent. By strong completeness, there exists a model $\langle \Omega, \mathbf{B}(\Omega), e_\mu, \mu \rangle$ of T_κ, hence satisfying $\mu(\varphi_i \mid \chi_i) = \alpha_i$: therefore κ is coherent. Conversely, suppose κ is a coherent assessment. Then, there is a conditional probability μ which extends κ. Then the induced Kripke structure $\langle \Omega, \mathbf{B}(\Omega), e_\mu, \mu \rangle$ is a model of T_κ.

5   Conclusions

In this paper, we have been concerned with defining the modal logic $FCP(L\Pi)$ to reason about coherent conditional probability exploiting a previous fuzzy logic approach which deals with unconditional probabilities [11]. Conditional probability has been taken as a primitive notion, in order to overcome difficulties related to conditioning events with zero probabilities. $FCP(L\Pi)$ has been shown to be strongly complete with respect to the class of conditional probability Kripke structures when dealing with finite theories. Furthermore, we have proved that testing consistency of a suitably defined modal theory over $FCP(L\Pi)$ is tantamount to testing the coherence of an assessment to an arbitrary set of conditional events, as defined in [4].

To conclude, we would like to point out some possible directions of our future work. First, it will be interesting to study whether we could use a logic weaker than $L\Pi\frac{1}{2}$, since in fact we do not need in the probabilistic modal axioms to explicitly deal with the Product implication connective $\rightarrow_\Pi$. Thus, it seems it would be enough to use a logic including only the connectives $\rightarrow_L$ and $\odot$. Second, it will be worth studying theories also including non-modal formulas over the framework defined. Indeed, this would allow us to treat deduction for Boolean propositions as well as a logical representation of relationships between events, like, for instance when two events are incompatible or one follows from another. Clearly such an extension would enhance the expressive power of $FCP(L\Pi)$. Then, from a semantical point of view, we would be very close to the so-called *model-theoretic probabilistic logic* in the sense of Biazzo et al's approach [2] and the links established there to probabilistic reasoning under coherence and default reasoning (see also [20] for a another recent probability logic approach to model defaults). Actually, $FCP(L\Pi)$ can provide a (syntactical) deductive system for such a rich framework. Exploring all these connections will be an extremely interesting matter of research in the immediate future.

Acknowledgments. Marchioni recognizes support of the grant No. AP2002-1571 of the Ministerio de Educación, Cultura y Deporte of Spain and Godo recognizes partial support of the Spanish project LOGFAC, TIC2001-1577-C03-01.

References

1. BACCHUS, F. *Representing and Reasoning with Probabilistic Knowledge.* MIT-Press, Cambridge Massachusetts, 1990.

2. BIAZZO V., GILIO A., LUKASIEWICZ T., AND SANFILIPPO G. Probabilistic logic under coherence, model-theoretic probabilistic logic, and default reasoning. In *Proc. of ECSQARU-2001*, 290–302, 2001.
3. CINTULA P. The $L\Pi$ and $L\Pi\frac{1}{2}$ propositional and predicate logics. *Fuzzy Sets and Systems* 124, 289–302, 2001.
4. COLETTI, G. AND SCOZZAFAVA R. *Probabilistic Logic in a Coherent Setting*. Kluwer Academic Publisher, Dordrecht, The Netherlands, 2002.
5. ESTEVA F., GODO L. AND MONTAGNA F. The $L\Pi$ and $L\Pi\frac{1}{2}$ logics: two complete fuzzy logics joining Lukasiewicz and Product logic. *Archive for Mathematical Logic* 40, 39–67, 2001.
6. FAGIN R., HALPERN J.Y. AND MEGIDDO N. A logic for reasoning about probabilities. *Information and Computation* 87 (1/2), 78–128, 1990.
7. FATTAROSI-BARNABA M. AND AMATI G. Modal operators with probabilistic interpretations I. *Studia Logica* 48, 383–393, 1989.
8. FLAMINIO T. AND MONTAGNA F. A logical and algebraic treatment of conditional probability. To appear in *Proc. of IPMU'04*, Perugia, Italy, 2004.
9. GAIFMAN H. AND SNIR M. Probabilities over rich languages, testing and randomness *The Journal of Symbolic Logic* 47, No. 3, 495–548, 1982.
10. GERLA, G. Inferences in probability logic. *Artificial Intelligence* 70, 33–52, 1994.
11. GODO L., ESTEVA F. AND HÁJEK P. Reasoning about probability using fuzzy logic. *Neural Network World* 10, No. 5, 811–824, 2000.
12. HÁJEK P. *Metamathematics of Fuzzy Logic*. Kluwer 1998.
13. HÁJEK P., GODO L. AND ESTEVA F. Fuzzy logic and probability. In *Proc. of UAI'95*, Morgan Kaufmann, 237–244, 1995.
14. HALPERN J. Y. An analysis of first-order logics of probability. In *Proceedings of the International Joint Conference on Artificial Intelligence (IJCAI'89)*, 1375–1381, 1989.
15. HALPERN J. Y. *Reasoning about Uncertainty*. The MIT Press, Cambridge Massachusetts, 2003.
16. KEISLER J. Probability quantifiers. In *Model-theoretic Logics*, J. Barwise and S. Feferman (eds.), Springer-Verlag, New York, 539–556, 1985.
17. KRAUSS P. H. Representation of conditional probability measures on Boolean algebras. In *Acta Mathematica Academiae Scientiarum Hungaricae*, Tomus 19 (3-4), 229–241, 1969.
18. NILSSON N. J. Probabilistic logic *Artificial Intelligence* 28, No. 1, 71–87, 1986.
19. OGNJANOVIĆ Z., RAŠKOVIĆ M. Some probability logics with new types of probability operators. *Journal of Logic and Computation*, Vol. 9, Issue 2, 181–195, 1999.
20. RAŠKOVIĆ M., OGNJANOVIĆ Z. AND MARKOVIĆ Z. A probabilistic approach to default reasoning. In *Proc. of NMR 2004*, Whistler (Canada), 335–341, 2004.
21. RAŠKOVIĆ M., OGNJANOVIĆ Z. AND MARKOVIĆ Z. A logic with conditional probabilities. In *Proc. of JELIA'2004*, in this volume.
22. SCOTT D. AND KRAUSS P. Assigning probabilities to logical formulas In *Aspects of Inductive Logic*, J. Hintikka and P. Suppes (eds.), North-Holland, Amsterdam, 219–264, 1966
23. VAN DER HOEK, W. Some considerations on the logic PFD. *Journal of Applied Non-Classical Logics* Vol. 7, Issue 3, 287–307, 1997.
24. WILSON N. AND MORAL S. A logical view of probability In *Proc. of the 11th European Conference on Artificial Intelligence (ECAI'94)*, 386–390, 1994.

A Logic with Conditional Probabilities

Miodrag Rašković[1], Zoran Ognjanović[2], and Zoran Marković[2]

[1] Učiteljski fakultet
Narodnog fronta 43, 11000 Beograd, Srbija i Crna Gora
miodragr@mi.sanu.ac.yu
[2] Matematički Institut
Kneza Mihaila 35, 11000 Beograd, Srbija i Crna Gora
zorano@mi.sanu.ac.yu, zoranm@mi.sanu.ac.yu

Abstract. The paper presents a logic which enriches propositional calculus with three classes of probabilistic operators which are applied to propositional formulas: $P_{\geq s}(\alpha)$, $CP_{=s}(\alpha, \beta)$ and $CP_{\geq s}(\alpha, \beta)$, with the intended meaning "the probability of α is at least s", "the conditional probability of α given β is s", and "the conditional probability of α given β is at least s", respectively. Possible-world semantics with a probability measure on sets of worlds is defined and the corresponding strong completeness theorem is proved for a rather simple set of axioms. This is achieved at the price of allowing infinitary rules of inference. One of these rules enables us to syntactically define the range of the probability function. This range is chosen to be the unit interval of a recursive nonarchimedean field, making it possible to define another probabilistic operator $CP_{\approx 1}(\alpha, \beta)$ with the intended meaning "probabilities of $\alpha \wedge \beta$ and β are almost the same". This last operator may be used to model default reasoning.

1 Introduction

The problem of reasoning with uncertain knowledge is an ancient problem dating, at least, from Leibnitz and Boole. In the last decades an approach was developed, connected with computer science and artificial intelligence, which starts with propositional calculus and adds "probability operators" that behave like modal operators. Consequently, the semantics consists in special types of Kripke models (possible worlds) with addition of probability measure defined over the worlds [6,7]. The main problem with that approach is providing an axiom system which would be strongly complete. This results from the inherent non-compactness of such systems. Namely, in such languages it is possible to define an inconsistent infinite set of formulas, every finite subset of which is consistent (e.g., $\{\neg P_{=0}\alpha\} \cup \{P_{<1/n}\alpha : n$ is a positive integer$\}$). Building on our previous work [14,15,16, 17], we define a system which we show to be sound and strongly complete, using infinitary rules of inference (i.e., rules where a conclusion has a countable set of premises). Thus, all formulas, axioms and theorems are finite, but the proofs might be countably infinite. Since we already have infinitary rules, we also introduce another infinitary rule which enables us to syntactically define

J.J. Alferes and J. Leite (Eds.): JELIA 2004, LNAI 3229, pp. 226–238, 2004.
© Springer-Verlag Berlin Heidelberg 2004

the range of the probability function which will appear in the interpretation. We choose here this range to be the unit interval of a recursive nonarchimedean field containing all rational numbers (an example of such field would be the Hardy field $Q[\epsilon]$, where ϵ is an infinitesimal). A similar rule was given in [2] but restricted to rationals only. In this paper we introduce, in addition to the usual probabilistic operators $P_{\geq s}\alpha$ (with the intended meaning "the probability of α is at least s"), also the conditional probability operators: $CP_{=s}(\alpha, \beta)$, $CP_{\geq s}(\alpha, \beta)$ with the intended meaning "the conditional probability of α given β is s", "at least s", respectively. Since we specify, already in the syntax, that the range of probability is nonarchimedean, it is possible also to introduce the conditional probability operator $CP_{\approx 1}(\alpha, \beta)$ with the intended meaning "the probabilities of $\alpha \wedge \beta$ and β are almost the same". It turns out that this formula may be used to model defaults. In a companion paper [18] it is shown that, if we restrict attention only to formulas of this type, the resulting system coincides with the system P of [12] when we work only with the finite sets of assumptions. If we allow inference from an infinite set of "defaults" our system is somewhat stronger. The main advantage, however, is that we can use the full probability logic and thus express explicitly properties that cannot be formulated in the language of defaults.

There are not too many papers discussing conditional probabilities from the logical point. We are aware of only one paper [7] in which conditional probability is defined syntactically. However, a complicated machinery of real closed fields was needed to obtain a corresponding sound and complete axiomatization. In our approach, since the parts of field theory are moved to the meta theory, the axioms are rather simple. Also, we are able to prove the extended completeness theorem ('every consistent set of formulas has a model') which is impossible for the system in [7], although at a price of introducing infinitary deduction rules. One should add that systems with infinitary rules of inference may be decidable which remains to be determined for the present system. Conditional probability is also analyzed in [4] but only on the semantical level along the ideas proposed by de Finetti. In [1,9,8,13] conditional probabilities are used in the field of nonmonotonic reasoning, but without any axiomatization.

The rest of the paper is organized as follows. In Section 2 syntax of the logic is given. Section 3 describes the class $LPP^S_{Meas,Neat}$ of measurable models, while in Section 4 a corresponding sound and complete axiomatic system is introduced. A proof of the completeness theorem is presented in Section 5. In Section 6 we describe how our system can be used to model default reasoning and analyze some properties of the corresponding default consequence relation. We conclude in Section 7.

2   Syntax

Let S be the unit interval of a recursive nonarchimedean field containing all rational numbers. An example of such field is the Hardy field $Q[\epsilon]$. $Q[\epsilon]$ contains all rational functions of a fixed infinitesimal ϵ which belongs to a nonstandard elementary extension R^* of the standard real numbers [10,19]. We use ϵ_1, ϵ_2, ...to denote infinitesimals from S.

Let $\{s_0, s_1, \ldots\}$ be an enumeration of S. The language of the logic consists of: a denumerable set $\mathrm{Var} = \{p, q, r, \ldots\}$ of propositional letters, classical connectives $\neg$, and $\wedge$, a list of unary probabilistic operators $(P_{\geq s})_{s \in S}$, a list of binary probabilistic operators $(CP_{\geq s})_{s \in S}$, a list of binary probabilistic operators $(CP_{=s})_{s \in S}$ and a binary probabilistic operator $CP_{\approx 1}$.

The set For_C of classical propositional formulas is the smallest set X containing Var and closed under the formation rules: if α and β belong to X, then $\neg \alpha$ and $(\alpha \wedge \beta)$, are in X. Elements of For_C will be denoted by α, β, ... The set For_P^S of probabilistic propositional formulas is the smallest set Y containing all formulas of the forms: $P_{\geq s}\alpha$ for $\alpha \in For_C$, $s \in S$, $CP_{=s}(\alpha, \beta)$ for $\alpha, \beta \in For_C$, $s \in S$, $CP_{\geq s}(\alpha, \beta)$ for $\alpha, \beta \in For_C$, $s \in S$ and $CP_{\approx 1}(\alpha, \beta)$ for $\alpha, \beta \in For_C$, and closed under the formation rules: if A and B belong to Y, then $\neg A$, and $(A \wedge B)$ are in Y. Formulas from For_P^S will be denoted by A, B, ... Note that we use the prefix notation $CP_{\geq s}(\alpha, \beta)$ (and similarly for $CP_{=s}(\alpha, \beta)$ and $CP_{\approx 1}(\alpha, \beta)$) rather than the corresponding infix notation $\alpha CP_{\geq s}\beta$ ($\alpha CP_{=s}\beta$, $\alpha CP_{\approx 1}\beta$).

As it can be seen, neither mixing of pure propositional formulas and probability formulas, nor nested probabilistic operators are allowed. For example, $\alpha \wedge P_{\geq s}\beta$ and $P_{\geq s}P_{\geq r}\alpha$ are not well defined formulas.

The other classical connectives ($\vee$, $\rightarrow$, $\leftrightarrow$) can be defined as usual, while we denote $\neg P_{\geq s}\alpha$ by $P_{<s}\alpha$ $P_{\geq 1-s}\neg\alpha$ by $P_{\leq s}\alpha$, $\neg P_{\leq s}\alpha$ by $P_{>s}\alpha$, $P_{\geq s}\alpha \wedge \neg P_{>s}\alpha$ by $P_{=s}\alpha$, $\neg P_{=s}\alpha$ by $P_{\neq s}\alpha$, $\neg CP_{\geq s}(\alpha, \beta)$ by $CP_{<s}(\alpha, \beta)$, $CP_{<s}(\alpha, \beta) \vee CP_{=s}(\alpha, \beta)$ by $CP_{\leq s}(\alpha, \beta)$, and $CP_{\geq s}(\alpha, \beta) \wedge \neg CP_{=s}(\alpha, \beta)$ by $CP_{>s}(\alpha, \beta)$.

Let $For^S = For_C \cup For_P^S$. φ, ψ, ... will be used to denote formulas from the set For^S. For $\alpha \in For_C$, and $A \in For_P^S$, we abbreviate both $\neg(\alpha \rightarrow \alpha)$ and $\neg(A \rightarrow A)$ by $\bot$ letting the context determine the meaning.

3   Semantics

The semantics for For^S will be based on the possible-world approach.

Definition 1. *An LPP^S-model is a structure $\langle W, H, \mu, v \rangle$ where:*

- *W is a nonempty set of elements called worlds,*
- *H is an algebra of subsets of W,*
- *$\mu : H \rightarrow S$ is a finitely additive probability measure, and*
- *$v : W \times \mathrm{Var} \rightarrow \{true, false\}$ is a valuation which associates with every world $w \in W$ a truth assignment $v(w)$ on the propositional letters.*

The valuation v is extended to a truth assignment on all classical propositional formula. Let M be an LPP^S model and $\alpha \in For_C$. The set $\{w : v(w)(\alpha) = true\}$ is denoted by $[\alpha]_M$.

Definition 2. *An LPP^S-model M is measurable if $[\alpha]_M$ is measurable for every formula $\alpha \in For_C$ (i.e., $[\alpha]_M \in H$). An LPP^S-model M is neat if only the empty* *set has the zero probability. $LPP^S_{Meas,Neat}$ denotes the the class of all neat and measurable LPP^S-models.*

The neatness-condition is introduced in order to make our models a subclass of R^*-probabilistic models [11,12]. This facilitates the explanation of a possible application of our system to default reasoning (see Section 6). All the results presented in Section 5 can be also proved for the class of measurable LPP^S-models.

Definition 3. *The satisfiability relation $\models \subset LPP^S_{Meas,Neat} \times For^S$ is defined by the following conditions for every $LPP^S_{Meas,Neat}$-model M:*

1. *if $\alpha \in For_C$, $M \models \alpha$ if $(\forall w \in W) v(w)(\alpha) = true$,*
2. *$M \models P_{\geq s}\alpha$ if $\mu([\alpha]_M) \geq s$,*
3. *$M \models CP_{\geq s}(\alpha, \beta)$ if either $\mu([\beta]_M) = 0$ or $\mu([\beta]_M) > 0$ and $\frac{\mu([\alpha \wedge \beta]_M)}{\mu([\beta]_M)} \geq s$,*
4. *$M \models CP_{=s}(\alpha, \beta)$ if either $\mu([\beta]_M) = 0$ and $s = 1$ or $\mu([\beta]_M) > 0$ and $\frac{\mu([\alpha \wedge \beta]_M)}{\mu([\beta]_M)} = s$,*
5. *$M \models CP_{\approx 1}(\alpha, \beta)$ if either $\mu([\beta]_M) = 0$ or $\mu([\beta]_M) > 0$ and for every positive integer n, $\frac{\mu([\alpha \wedge \beta]_M)}{\mu([\beta]_M)} \geq 1 - \frac{1}{n}$.*
6. *if $A \in For^S_P$, $M \models \neg A$ if $M \not\models A$,*
7. *if $A, B \in For^S_P$, $M \models A \wedge B$ if $M \models A$ and $M \models B$.*

Note that the condition 5 is equivalent to saying that the conditional probability equals $1 - \epsilon_i$ for some infinitesimal $\epsilon_i \in S$.

A formula $\varphi \in For^S$ is satisfiable if there is an $LPP^S_{Meas,Neat}$-model M such that $M \models \varphi$; φ is valid if for every $LPP^S_{Meas,Neat}$-model M, $M \models \varphi$; a set of formulas is satisfiable if there is a model in which every formula from the set is satisfiable. A formula $\varphi \in For^S$ is a semantical consequence of a set of formulas T ($T \models \varphi$) if φ holds in every $LP_{Meas,Neat}$-model in which all formulas from T are satisfied.

4   Axiomatization

The set of all valid formulas can be characterized by the following set of axiom schemata:

1. all For_C-instances of classical propositional tautologies
2. all For^S_P-instances of classical propositional tautologies
3. $P_{\geq 0}\alpha$
4. $P_{\leq s}\alpha \rightarrow P_{<r}\alpha$, $r > s$
5. $P_{<s}\alpha \rightarrow P_{\leq s}\alpha$
6. $P_{\geq 1}(\alpha \leftrightarrow \beta) \rightarrow (P_{=s}\alpha \rightarrow P_{=s}\beta)$
7. $(P_{=s}\alpha \wedge P_{=r}\beta \wedge P_{\geq 1}\neg(\alpha \wedge \beta)) \rightarrow P_{=\min(1,s+r)}(\alpha \vee \beta)$
8. $CP_{=r}(\alpha, \beta) \rightarrow \neg CP_{=t}(\alpha, \beta)$, $r \neq t$
9. $P_{=0}\beta \rightarrow CP_{=1}(\alpha, \beta)$

10. $(P_{=r}\beta \wedge P_{=s}(\alpha \wedge \beta)) \to CP_{=s/r}(\alpha, \beta)$, $r \neq 0$
11. $CP_{=r}(\alpha, \beta) \to \neg CP_{\geq t}(\alpha, \beta)$, $r < t$
12. $CP_{=r}(\alpha, \beta) \to CP_{\geq t}(\alpha, \beta)$, $r \geq t$
13. $CP_{=r}(\alpha, \beta) \to (P_{=tr}(\alpha \wedge \beta) \leftrightarrow P_{=t}\beta)$, $t \neq 0$
14. $CP_{\approx 1}(\alpha, \beta) \to CP_{\geq r}(\alpha, \beta)$, for every rational $r \in [0, 1)$
15. $CP_{=1}(\alpha, \beta) \to CP_{\approx 1}(\alpha, \beta)$

and inference rules:

1. From φ and $\varphi \to \psi$ infer ψ.
2. If $\alpha \in For_C$, from α infer $P_{\geq 1}\alpha$.
3. From $A \to P_{\neq s}\alpha$, for every $s \in S$, infer $A \to \bot$.
4. From $A \to (P_{=tr}(\alpha \wedge \beta) \leftrightarrow P_{=r}\beta)$, for every $r \in S \setminus \{0\}$, infer $A \to CP_{=t}(\alpha, \beta)$.
5. From $A \to CP_{>r}(\alpha \wedge \beta)$, for every rational $r \neq 1$, infer $A \to CP_{\approx 1}(\alpha, \beta)$.

We denote this axiomatic system by Ax_{LPPS}. Let us briefly discuss it. Axiom 3 says that every formula is satisfied in a set of worlds of the probability at least 0. By substituting $\neg\alpha$ for α in Axiom 3, the formula $P_{\leq 1}\alpha$ ($= P_{\geq 0}\neg\alpha$) is obtained. This formula means that every formula is satisfied in a set of worlds of the probability at most 1. Let us denote it by 3'. Axiom 6 means that the equivalent formulas must have the same probability. Axiom 7 corresponds to the property of the finite additivity of probability. It says that, if the sets of worlds that satisfy α and β are disjoint, then the probability of the set of worlds that satisfy $\alpha \vee \beta$ is the sum of the probabilities of the former two sets. Axiom 13 and Rule 4 express the standard definition of conditional probability, while the axioms 14 and 15 and Rule 5 describe the relationship between the standard conditional probability and the conditional probability infinitesimally close to 1. From Axiom 3' and Rule 2 we obtain another inference rule: from α infer $P_{=1}\alpha$. The rules 3 – 5 are infinitary. Rule 3 guarantees that the probability of a formula belongs to the set S. Rule 4 corresponds to the standard meaning of the conditional probability, and Rule 5 syntactically defines the notion "infinitesimally close to 1". We should point out that, although infinitary rules might seem undesirable, especially to a computer scientist, similar types of logics with infinitary rules were proved to be decidable [16]. On the other hand, since the compactness theorem does not hold for our logic (there exists a countably infinite set of formulas that is unsatisfiable although every finite subset is satisfiable: for instance, consider $\{\neg P_{=0}\alpha\} \cup \{P_{<\epsilon^n}\alpha : n$ is a positive integer$\}$) involving infinitary rules in the axiomatic system is the only way to obtain the extended completeness.

A formula φ is deducible from a set T of formulas (denoted $T \vdash_{Ax_{LPPS}} \alpha$) if there is an at most denumerable sequence (called proof) of formulas $\varphi_0, \varphi_1, \ldots, \varphi$, such that every φ_i is an axiom or a formula from the set T, or it is derived from the preceding formulas by an inference rule. A formula φ is a theorem ($\vdash \varphi$) if it is deducible from the empty set. A set T of formulas is consistent if there are at least a formula from For_C, and at least a formula from For_P^S that are not deducible from T. A consistent set T of formulas is said to be maximal consistent if the following holds:

– for every $\alpha \in For_C$, if $T \vdash \alpha$, then $\alpha \in T$ and $P_{\geq 1}\alpha \in T$, and
– for every $A \in For_P^S$, either $A \in T$ or $\neg A \in T$.

A set T is deductively closed if for every $\varphi \in For^S$, if $T \vdash \varphi$, then $\varphi \in T$.

5   Soundness and Completeness

Soundness of our system follows from the soundness of propositional classical logics, and from the properties of probabilistic measures. The arguments are of the type presented in the proof of Theorem 13 in [14].

In the proof of the completeness theorem the following strategy is applied. We start with a form of the deduction theorem, and some other useful statements. In the next step we show how to extend a consistent set T of formulas to a maximal consistent set T^*. Finally, a canonical $LPP_{Meas,Neat}^S$-model M is constructed out of the formulas from the set T^* such that $M \models \varphi$ iff $\varphi \in T^*$.

Theorem 4 (Deduction theorem). *If T is a set of formulas and $T \cup \{\varphi\} \vdash \psi$, then $T \vdash \varphi \rightarrow \psi$, where either $\varphi, \psi \in For_C$ or $\varphi, \psi \in For_P^S$.*

Proof. We use the transfinite induction on the length of the proof of ψ from $T \cup \{\varphi\}$. Let us first consider the case where $\psi = P_{\geq 1}\alpha$ is obtained from $T \cup \{\varphi\}$ by an application of Rule 2, and $\varphi \in For_P^S$. In that case:

$T, \varphi \vdash \alpha$
$T, \varphi \vdash P_{\geq 1}\alpha$ by Rule 2

However, since $\alpha \in For_C$, and $\varphi \in For_P^S$, φ does not affect the proof of α from $T \cup \{\varphi\}$, and we have:

$T \vdash \alpha$
$T \vdash P_{\geq 1}\alpha$ by Rule 2
$T \vdash P_{\geq 1}\alpha \rightarrow (\varphi \rightarrow P_{\geq 1}\alpha)$
$T \vdash \varphi \rightarrow P_{\geq 1}\alpha$ by Rule 1.

Next, assume that $\psi = C \rightarrow \bot$ is obtained from $T \cup \{\varphi\}$ by an application of Rule 3, and $\varphi \in For_P^S$. Then:

$T, \varphi \vdash C \rightarrow P_{\neq s}\delta$, for every $s \in S$
$T \vdash \varphi \rightarrow (C \rightarrow P_{\neq s}\delta)$, for every $s \in S$, by the induction hypothesis
$T \vdash (\varphi \wedge C) \rightarrow P_{\neq s}\delta$, for every $s \in S$
$T \vdash (\varphi \wedge C) \rightarrow \bot$, by Rule 3
$T \vdash \varphi \rightarrow \psi$.

The other cases follow similarly.   □

Theorem 5. *Let $\alpha, \beta \in For_C$. Then:*

1. $\vdash P_{\geq r}\alpha \rightarrow P_{\geq s}\alpha$, $r > s$
2. $\vdash P_{\leq r}\alpha \rightarrow P_{\leq s}\alpha$, $r < s$
3. $\vdash P_{=r}\alpha \rightarrow \neg P_{=s}\alpha$, $r \neq s$

Proof. (1 – 2) Let us call the property expressed by these two formulas the monotonicity of the probability. The formulas follow from the axioms 4 and 5. (3) Note that $\vdash P_{=r}\alpha$ denotes $P_{\geq r}\alpha \wedge P_{\leq r}\alpha$. From Axiom 4, for every $s > r$ we have $\vdash P_{\leq r}\alpha \to P_{<s}\alpha$, i.e., $\vdash P_{\leq r}\alpha \to \neg P_{\geq s}\alpha$. Similarly, by Axiom 4', for every $s < r$, we have $\vdash P_{\geq r}\alpha \to \neg P_{\leq s}\alpha$. It follows that $\vdash (P_{\leq r}\alpha \wedge P_{\geq r}\alpha) \to (\neg P_{\leq s}\alpha \vee \neg P_{\geq s}\alpha)$, and that $\vdash P_{=r}\alpha \to \neg P_{=s}\alpha$ for every $s \neq r$.   □

Theorem 6. *Every consistent set can be extended to a maximal consistent set.*

Proof. Let T be a consistent set, $Cn_C(T)$ the set of all classical formulas that are consequences of T, A_0, A_1, ... an enumeration of all formulas from For_P^S and α_0, α_1, ... an enumeration of all formulas from For_C. We define a sequence of sets T_i, $i = 0, 1, 2, \ldots$ such that:

1. $T_0 = T \cup Cn_C(T) \cup \{P_{\geq 1}\alpha : \alpha \in Cn_C(T)\}$
2. for every $i \geq 0$, if $T_{2i} \cup \{A_i\}$ is consistent, then $T_{2i+1} = T_{2i} \cup \{A_i\}$; otherwise, if A_i is of the form $A \to CP_{=s}(\alpha, \beta)$, then $T_{2i+1} = T_{2i} \cup \{\neg A_i, A \to \neg(P_{=st}(\alpha \wedge \beta) \leftrightarrow P_{=t}\beta)\}$, for some $t > 0$; otherwise, if A_i is of the form $A \to CP_{\approx 1}(\alpha, \beta)$, then $T_{2i+1} = T_{2i} \cup \{\neg A_i, A \to \neg CP_{>r}(\alpha, \beta)\}$, for some rational number $r \in [0, 1)$; otherwise, $T_{2i+1} = T_{2i} \cup \{\neg A_i\}$,
3. for every $i \geq 0$, $T_{2i+2} = T_{2i+1} \cup \{P_{=r}\alpha_i\}$, for some $r \in S$, so that T_{2i+2} is consistent,
4. for every $i \geq 0$, if T_i is enlarged by a formula of the form $P_{=0}\alpha$, add $\neg\alpha$ to $T_i \cup \{P_{=0}\alpha\}$ as well.

We have to show that every T_i is a consistent set. T_0 is consistent because it is a set of consequences of a consistent set. Suppose that T_{2i+1} is obtained by the step 2 of the above construction and that neither $T_{2i} \cup \{A_i\}$, nor $T_{2i} \cup \{\neg A_i\}$ are consistent. It follows by the deduction theorem that $T_{2i} \vdash A_i \wedge \neg A_i$, which is a contradiction. Next, suppose that A_i is of the form $A \to CP_{=s}(\alpha, \beta)$, and that neither $T_{2i} \cup \{A \to CP_{=s}(\alpha, \beta)\}$ nor $T_{2i} \cup \{\neg(A \to CP_{=s}(\alpha, \beta)), A \to \neg(P_{=st}(\alpha \wedge \beta) \leftrightarrow P_{=t}\beta)\}$, for every $t > 0$, are consistent. It means that:

1. $T_{2i}, \neg(A \to CP_{=s}(\alpha, \beta)), A \to \neg(P_{=st}(\alpha \wedge \beta) \leftrightarrow P_{=t}\beta) \vdash \bot$, for every $t > 0$,
2. $T_{2i}, \neg(A \to CP_{=s}(\alpha, \beta)) \vdash (A \to \neg(P_{=st}(\alpha \wedge \beta) \leftrightarrow P_{=t}\beta)) \to \bot$, for every $t > 0$, by Deduction theorem,
3. $T_{2i}, \neg(A \to CP_{=s}(\alpha, \beta)) \vdash \neg(A \to \neg(P_{=st}(\alpha \wedge \beta) \leftrightarrow P_{=t}\beta))$, for every $t > 0$,
4. $T_{2i}, \neg(A \to CP_{=s}(\alpha, \beta)) \vdash A \to (P_{=st}(\alpha \wedge \beta) \leftrightarrow P_{=t}\beta)$, for every $t > 0$, by the classical tautology $\neg(\alpha \to \beta) \to (\alpha \to \neg\beta)$,
5. $T_{2i}, \neg(A \to CP_{=s}(\alpha, \beta)) \vdash A \to CP_{=s}(\alpha, \beta)$, by Rule 4,
6. $T_{2i} \vdash \neg(A \to CP_{=s}(\alpha, \beta)) \to (A \to CP_{=s}(\alpha, \beta))$, by Deduction theorem,
7. $T_{2i} \vdash A \to CP_{=s}(\alpha, \beta)$, by classical reasoning

which contradicts consistency of T_{2i}. The case when $A_i = A \to CP_{\approx 1}(\alpha, \beta)$ follows similarly, using Rule 5. Consider the step 3 of the construction, and suppose that for every $r \in S$, $T_{2i+1} \cup \{P_{=r}\alpha_i\}$ is not consistent. Let $T_{2i+1} = T_0 \cup T_{2i+1}^+$, where T_{2i+1}^+ denotes the set of all formulas $B \in For_P^S$ that are added to T_0 in the previous steps of the construction. Then:

1. $T_0, T_{2i+1}^+, P_{=s}\alpha_i \vdash \bot$, for every $s \in S$, by the hypothesis
2. $T_0, T_{2i+1}^+ \vdash \neg P_{=s}\alpha_i$, for every $s \in S$, by Deduction theorem
3. $T_0 \vdash (\bigwedge_{B \in T_{2i+1}^+} B) \to \neg P_{=s}\alpha_i$, for every $s \in S$, by Deduction theorem
4. $T_0 \vdash (\bigwedge_{B \in T_{2i+1}^+} B) \to \bot$, by Rule 3
5. $T_{2i+1} \vdash \bot$,

which contradicts consistency of T_{2i+1}. Finally, consider the step 4 of the construction, and suppose that for some $\alpha \in For_C$, $T_i \cup \{P_{=0}\alpha, \neg\alpha\} \vdash \bot$. By Deduction theorem, we have that $T_i \cup \{P_{=0}\alpha\} \vdash \alpha$. Since $\alpha \in For_C$, α is a consequence of $Cn_C(T)$, the set of all classical formulas that are consequences of T, and $\alpha \in Cn_C(T)$. Then, by the construction, we have that $P_{\geq 1}\alpha \in T_0$ which leads to inconsistency of $T_i \cup \{P_{=0}\alpha\}$ since:

1. $T_i, P_{=0}\alpha \vdash P_{\leq 1}\alpha$ by Axiom 3'
2. $T_i, P_{=0}\alpha \vdash P_{\geq 1}\alpha$ since $P_{\geq 1}\alpha \in T_0 \subset T_i$
3. $T_i, P_{=0}\alpha \vdash P_{=1}\alpha$
4. $T_i \vdash P_{=0}\alpha \to P_{=1}\alpha$ by Deduction theorem
5. $T_i \vdash P_{=0}\alpha \to \neg P_{=1}\alpha$ by Theorem 5.3
6. $T_i, P_{=0}\alpha \vdash \bot$

Let $T^* = \cup_i T_i$. We have to prove that T^* is a maximal consistent set.

First, note that if $P_{=s}\alpha \in T^*$, then for every $B \in For_P^S$, $B \to P_{=s}\alpha \in T^*$. Suppose that it is not the case. Then, according to the above construction, for some $B \in For_P^S$, and some j, $P_{=s}\alpha$ and $\neg(B \to P_{=s}\alpha)$ (i.e., $B \wedge \neg P_{=s}\alpha$) belongs to T_j. It means that $T_j \vdash P_{=s}\alpha \wedge \neg P_{=s}\alpha$, a contradiction. We continue by showing that T^* is a deductively closed set which does not contain all formulas, and, as a consequence, that T^* is consistent. If a formula $\alpha \in For_C$, by the construction of T_0, α and $\neg\alpha$ cannot be simultaneously in T_0. For a formula $A \in For_P^S$ the set T^* does not contain both $A = A_i$ and $\neg A = A_j$, because $T_{\max(2i,2j)+1}$ is a consistent set.

If a formula $\alpha \in For_C$ and $T^* \vdash \alpha$, then by the construction of T_0, $\alpha \in T^*$ and $P_{\geq 1}\alpha \in T^*$. Let $A \in For_P^S$. It can be proved by the induction on the length of the inference that if $T^* \vdash A$, then $A \in T^*$. Note that if $A = A_j$ and $T_i \vdash A$, it must be $A \in T^*$ because $T_{\max(i,2j)+1}$ is consistent. Suppose that the sequence $\varphi_1, \varphi_2, \ldots, A$ forms the proof of A from T^*. If the sequence is finite, there must be a set T_i such that $T_i \vdash A$, and $A \in T^*$. Thus, suppose that the sequence is countably infinite. We can show that for every i, if φ_i is obtained by an application of an inference rule, and all the premises belong to T^*, then it must be $\varphi_i \in T^*$. If the rule is a finitary one, then there must be a set T_j which contains all the premises and $T_j \vdash \varphi_i$. Reasoning as above, we conclude $\varphi_i \in T^*$. Next, we consider infinitary rules. Let $\varphi_i = B \to \bot$ be obtained from the set of premises $\{\varphi_i^k = B \to \neg P_{=s_k}\gamma : s_k \in S\}$ by Rule 3. By the induction hypothesis, $\varphi_i^k \in T^*$ for every k. If $\varphi_i \notin T^*$, by the step 3 of the construction, there are some l and $s_l \in S$ such that $P_{=s_l}\gamma \in T_l$. Reasoning as above, we conclude that $B \to P_{=s_l}\gamma \in T^*$. Thus, there must be some j such that $B \to \neg P_{=s_l}\gamma$, $B \to P_{=s_l}\gamma \in T_j$, $T_j \vdash B \to \neg P_{=s_l}\gamma$, $T_j \vdash B \to P_{=s_l}\gamma$, and $T_j \vdash B \to \bot$, which means that $B \to \perp \in T^*$, a contradiction. Let $\varphi_i = B \to CP_{\approx 1}(\gamma, \delta)$ be obtained from the set of premises $\{\varphi_i^k = B \to CP_{>s_k}(\gamma, \delta) : s_k \in S \cap Q \cap [0, 1)\}$ by Rule 5. By the induction hypothesis, $\varphi_i^k \in T^*$ for every k. If $\varphi_i \notin T^*$, by the step 2 of the construction, there are some l and $s_l \in S \cap Q \cap [0, 1)$ such that $B \to \neg CP_{>s_l}(\gamma, \delta) \in T^*$. Thus, there is some j such that $\{B \to CP_{>s_l}(\gamma, \delta), B \to \neg CP_{>s_l}(\gamma, \delta)\} \subset T_j$, $T_j \vdash B \to CP_{>s_l}(\gamma, \delta)$, $T_j \vdash B \to \neg CP_{>s_l}(\gamma, \delta)$, $T_j \vdash B \to \perp$, $T_j \vdash B \to CP_{\approx 1}(\gamma, \delta)$, and $B \to CP_{\approx 1}(\gamma, \delta) \in T^*$, a contradiction. Finally, the case $\varphi_i = B \to CP_{=s}(\gamma, \delta)$ follows similarly.

Hence, from $T^* \vdash \varphi$, we have $\varphi \in T^*$. Since T^* is consistent, according to the above definition of a maximal set, the construction guarantees that T^* is maximal. $\square$

Being a maximal consistent set, T^* has all the expected properties summarized in the next statement.

Theorem 7. *Let T^* be defined as above. Then, the following holds for every φ, $\psi \in For^S$, and all $\alpha, \beta \in For_C$.*

1. *T^* contains all theorems.*
2. *If $\varphi \in T^*$, then $\neg \varphi \notin T^*$.*
3. *$\varphi \land \psi \in T^*$ iff $\varphi \in T^*$ and $\psi \in T^*$.*
4. *If $\varphi, \varphi \to \psi \in T^*$, then $\psi \in T^*$.*
5. *There is exactly one $s \in S$ such that $P_{=s}\alpha \in T^*$.*
6. *If $P_{\geq s}\alpha \in T^*$, there is some $r \in S$ such that $r \geq s$ and $P_{=r}\alpha \in T^*$.*
7. *If $P_{\leq s}\alpha \in T^*$, there is some $r \in S$ such that $r \leq s$ and $P_{=r}\alpha \in T^*$.*
8. *There is exactly one $s \in S$ such that $CP_{=s}(\alpha, \beta) \in T^*$.*
9. *If $CP_{\geq s}\alpha \in T^*$, there is some $r \in S$ such that $r \geq s$ and $CP_{=r}(\alpha, \beta) \in T^*$.*

Proof. (1 - 4) The proof is standard and left to the reader.
(5) First, note that, according to Theorem 5.3, if $P_{=s}\alpha \in T^*$, then for every $r \neq s$, $P_{=r}\alpha \notin T^*$. On the other hand, suppose that for every $s \in S$, $\neg P_{=s}\alpha \in T^*$. It follows that $T^* \vdash \neg P_{=s}\alpha$ for every $s \in S$, and by Rule 3, $T^* \vdash \perp$ which contradicts consistency of T^*. Thus, for every $\alpha \in For_C$, there is exactly one $s \in S$ such that $P_{=s}\alpha \in T^*$.
(6) Since $P_{\geq s}\alpha \in T^*$, we have that $\neg P_{<s}\alpha \in T^*$. By the step (5), for every $\alpha \in For_C$ there is some $r \in S$ such that $P_{=r}\alpha \in T^*$. It means that $P_{\geq r}\alpha \in T^*$, and $P_{\leq r}\alpha \in T^*$. If $r < s$, then by Axiom 4 from $P_{\leq r}\alpha \in T^*$ it follows that $P_{<s}\alpha \in T^*$ (i.e., $\neg P_{\geq s}\alpha \in T^*$), a contradiction. Thus, it must be $r \geq s$.
(7) Similarly as the statement 7.6.
(8) According to Axiom 8 there cannot be two different $r, s \in S$ such that $CP_{=r}(\alpha, \beta) \in T^*$ and $CP_{=s}(\alpha, \beta) \in T^*$. From the statement 7.6 we have that for exactly one r and exactly one t, $P_{=r}\beta \in T^*$ and $P_{=t}(\alpha \land \beta) \in T^*$. If $r = 0$, then $CP_{=1}(\alpha, \beta) \in T^*$, by Axiom 9. Let $r \neq 0$, and $s = \frac{t}{r}$. Using Axiom 10 we have that $CP_{=s}(\alpha, \beta) \in T^*$. Thus, for all $\alpha, \beta \in For_C$, there is exactly one $s \in S$ such that $CP_{=s}(\alpha, \beta) \in T^*$.
(9) Let $CP_{\geq s}\alpha \in T^*$. From the statement 7.8 there is exactly one $r \in S$ such that $CP_{=r}(\alpha, \beta) \in T^*$. It follows from Axiom 11 that r cannot be less than s. Thus, it must be $r \geq s$. $\square$

Using a maximal consistent set T^*, we can define a tuple $M = \langle W, \{[\alpha]_M : \alpha \in For_C\}, \mu, v \rangle$, where:

- $W = \{w \models Cn_C(T)\}$ contains all the classical propositional interpretations that satisfy the set $Cn_C(T)$ of all classical consequences of the set T,
- $[\alpha]_M = \{w \in W : w \models \alpha\}$,
- for every world w and every propositional letter $p \in Var$, $v(w)(p) = true$ iff $w \models p$, and
- μ is defined on $\{[\alpha]_M : \alpha \in For_C\}$ by $\mu([\alpha]_M) = s$ iff $P_{=s}\alpha \in T^*$.

The next theorem states that M is an $LPP^S_{Meas,Neat}$-model.

Theorem 8. Let $M = \langle W, \{[\alpha]_M : \alpha \in For_C\}, \mu, v \rangle$ be defined as above. Then, the following hold:

1. μ is a well-defined function.
2. $\{[\alpha]_M : \alpha \in For_C\}$ is an algebra of subsets of W.
3. μ is a finitely additive probability measure.
4. for every $\alpha \in For_C$, $\mu([\alpha]_M) = 0$ iff $[\alpha]_M = \emptyset$.

Proof. (1) It follows from Theorem 7.5 that for every $\alpha \in For_C$ there is exactly one $s \in S$ such that $\mu([\alpha]_M) = s$. On the other hand, let $[\alpha]_M = [\beta]_M$ for some $\alpha, \beta \in For_C$. It means that for every $w \in W$, $w \models \alpha \leftrightarrow \beta$. From the completeness of the propositional logic we have that $\alpha \leftrightarrow \beta \in Cn_C(T)$. Using the above construction, $P_{\geq 1}(\alpha \leftrightarrow \beta) \in T^*$. Axiom 6 guarantees that $P_{=s}\alpha \in T^*$ iff $P_{=s}\beta \in T^*$. Thus, $[\alpha]_M = [\beta]_M$ implies that $\mu([\alpha]_M) = \mu([\beta]_M)$.
(2) For an arbitrary $\beta \in For_C$, $W = [\beta \vee \neg\beta]_M$, and $W \in \{[\alpha]_M : \alpha \in For_C\}$. If $[\beta]_M \in \{[\alpha]_M : \alpha \in For_C\}$, then the complement of $[\beta]_M$ is $[\neg\beta]_M$, and it belongs to $\{[\alpha]_M : \alpha \in For_C\}$. If $[\beta_1]_M, \ldots, [\beta_k]_M \in \{[\alpha]_M : \alpha \in For_C\}$, then the union $[\beta_1]_M \cup \ldots \cup [\beta_k]_M \in \{[\alpha]_M : \alpha \in For_C\}$ because $[\beta_1]_M \cup \ldots \cup [\beta_k]_M = [\beta_1 \vee \ldots \vee \beta_k]_M$. Thus, $\{[\alpha]_M : \alpha \in For_C\}$ is an algebra of subsets of W.
(3) From the axioms 3 and 3' it follows that $\mu : \{[\alpha]_M : \alpha \in For_C\} \to [0,1]$. Let $\alpha \in For_C$. Then, $W = [\alpha \vee \neg\alpha]_M$, $\alpha \vee \neg\alpha \in T^*$, and $P_{\geq 1}(\alpha \vee \neg\alpha) \in T^*$. It means that $\mu(W) = 1$. Let $\alpha, \beta \in For_C$, $[\alpha]_M \cap [\beta]_M = \emptyset$, $\mu([\alpha]_M) = s$, and $\mu([\beta]_M) = r$. Since, $[\alpha]_M \cap [\beta]_M = \emptyset$, we have that $[\neg(\alpha \wedge \beta)]_M = W$, and $\mu([\neg(\alpha \wedge \beta)]_M) = 1$. From the assumptions we have that $P_{=s}\alpha$, $P_{=r}\beta$, $P_{\geq 1}\neg(\alpha \wedge \beta) \in T^*$. Using Axiom 7 it follows that $P_{=r+s}(\alpha \vee \beta) \in T^*$, i.e., $\mu([\alpha \vee \beta]_M) = r + s$.
(4) It follows from the step 4 of the construction from Theorem 6.   □

Theorem 9 (Extended completeness theorem). *A set T of formulas is consistent if and only if T has an $LPP^S_{Meas,Neat}$-model.*

Proof. The ($\Leftarrow$)-direction follows from the soundness of the above axiomatic system. In order to prove the ($\Rightarrow$)-direction we construct the $LPP^S_{Meas,Neat}$-model M as above, and show that for every $\varphi \in For^S$, $M \models \varphi$ iff $\varphi \in T^*$.

Let $\varphi \in For_C$. If $\varphi \in T^*$, then certainly $\varphi \in Cn_C(T)$, and for every $w \in W$, $w \models \varphi$, i.e., $M \models \varphi$. If $M \models \varphi$, then by the completeness of classical propositional logic $\varphi \in Cn_C(T)$, and $\varphi \in T^*$.

Let $\varphi = P_{\geq s}\alpha$. If $P_{\geq s}\alpha \in T^*$, then, by Theorem 7.6, there is some $r \geq s$ such that $P_{=r}\alpha \in T^*$, i.e., such that $\mu([\alpha]_M) = r \geq s$. Thus, $M \models P_{\geq s}\alpha$. On the other hand suppose that $M \models P_{\geq s}\alpha$, i.e., that $\mu([\alpha]_M) = r \geq s$, and $P_{=r}\alpha \in T^*$. It means that $P_{\geq r}\alpha \in T^*$, and by Theorem 5.1 it follows that $P_{\geq s}\alpha \in T^*$.

Let $\varphi = \neg A$, $A \in For_P^S$. $M \models \neg A$ iff $M \models A$ does not hold iff $A \notin T^*$ iff $\neg A \in T^*$. Let $\varphi = A \wedge B$, A, $B \in For_P^S$. $M \models A \wedge B$ iff $M \models A$ and $M \models B$ iff $A \in T^*$ and $B \in T^*$ iff $A \wedge B \in T^*$.

Let $\varphi = CP_{=s}(\alpha, \beta)$. Suppose that $CP_{=s}(\alpha, \beta) \in T^*$. If $P_{=0}\beta \in T^*$, from Axiom 9 and Lemma 7.8 it must be $CP_{=1}(\alpha, \beta) \in T^*$, and $s = 1$. Since $\mu([\beta]_M) = 0$, we have $M \models CP_{=1}(\alpha, \beta)$. Otherwise, let $P_{=t}\beta \in T^*$, $t \neq 0$. It follows from Axiom 13 that $P_{=st}(\alpha \wedge \beta) \in T^*$, $\mu([\beta]_M) = t \neq 0$, $\mu([\alpha \wedge \beta]_M) = st$, $M \models CP_{=s}(\alpha, \beta)$. Next, suppose that $M \models CP_{=s}(\alpha, \beta)$. If $M \models P_{=0}\beta$, then $s = 1$ and $P_{=0}\beta \in T^*$. From Axiom 9 we have that $CP_{=1}(\alpha, \beta) \in T^*$. Otherwise, let $M \models P_{=t}\beta$, $t \neq 0$, and $CP_{=s}(\alpha, \beta) \notin T^*$. Then, by the step 2 of the construction of T^*, there is some r such that $\neg(P_{=sr}(\alpha \wedge \beta) \leftrightarrow P_{=r}\beta) \in T^*$, for some $r > 0$. It means that $(P_{=sr}(\alpha \wedge \beta) \wedge \neg P_{=r}\beta) \in T^*$ or $(\neg P_{=sr}(\alpha \wedge \beta) \wedge P_{=r}\beta) \in T^*$, ie. $P_{=sr}(\alpha \wedge \beta) \in T^*$ and $\neg P_{=r}\beta \in T^*$ or $\neg P_{=sr}(\alpha \wedge \beta) \in T^*$ and $P_{=r}\beta \in T^*$, ie. $M \models P_{=sr}(\alpha \wedge \beta)$ and $M \models \neg P_{=r}\beta$ or $M \models \neg P_{=sr}(\alpha \wedge \beta)$ and $M \models P_{=r}\beta$. In the former case, $M \models P_{=sr}(\alpha \wedge \beta)$ and $M \models \neg P_{=r}\beta$, we have that $\mu([\alpha \wedge \beta]_M) = sr$ and $\mu([\beta]_M) = t$, $t \notin \{0, r\}$. It follows that $\frac{\mu([\alpha \wedge \beta]_M)}{\mu([\beta]_M)} \neq s$, a contradiction since $M \models CP_{=s}(\alpha, \beta)$. In the later case, $M \models \neg P_{=sr}(\alpha \wedge \beta)$ and $M \models P_{=r}\beta$, we have that $r = t \neq 0$, $\mu([\alpha \wedge \beta]_M) \neq st$ and $\mu([\beta]_M) = t$. It follows that $\frac{\mu([\alpha \wedge \beta]_M)}{\mu([\beta]_M)} \neq s$, a contradiction since $M \models CP_{=s}(\alpha, \beta)$. Thus, $CP_{=s}(\alpha, \beta) \in T^*$.

Let $\varphi = CP_{\geq s}(\alpha, \beta)$. Suppose that $CP_{\geq s}(\alpha, \beta) \in T^*$. From Lemma 7.8 and Lemma 7.9, there is exactly one $r \geq s$ such that $CP_{=r}(\alpha, \beta) \in T^*$, and $M \models CP_{=r}(\alpha, \beta)$. It follows that $M \models CP_{\geq s}(\alpha, \beta)$. Next, suppose that $M \models CP_{\geq s}(\alpha, \beta)$. If $\mu([\beta]_M) = 0$, we have that $M \models CP_{=1}(\alpha, \beta)$, and $CP_{=1}(\alpha, \beta) \in T^*$. It follows from Axiom 12 that $CP_{\geq s}(\alpha, \beta) \in T^*$. Otherwise, let $\mu([\beta]_M) \neq 0$. From Lemma 7.5 there is exactly one r such that $P_{=r}(\alpha \wedge \beta) \in T^*$, and exactly one $t \neq 0$ such that $P_{=t}\beta \in T^*$. It means that $\mu([\alpha \wedge \beta]_M) = r$ and $\mu([\beta]_M) = t$, $M \models CP_{=r/t}(\alpha, \beta)$, and $CP_{=r/t}(\alpha, \beta) \in T^*$. Since $M \models CP_{\geq s}(\alpha, \beta)$, it must be $s \leq \frac{r}{t}$. It follows from Axiom 12 that $CP_{\geq s}(\alpha, \beta) \in T^*$.

Finally, let $\varphi = CP_{\approx 1}(\alpha, \beta)$. Suppose that $CP_{\approx 1}(\alpha, \beta) \in T^*$. If $\mu([\beta]_M) = 0$, it follows that $M \models CP_{\approx 1}(\alpha, \beta)$. Next, suppose that $\mu([\beta]_M) \neq 0$. From Axiom 14, we have that for every rational $r \in [0, 1)$ $CP_{\geq r}(\alpha, \beta) \in T^*$, and $CP_{=r}(\alpha, \beta) \notin T^*$. It means that for every rational $r \in [0, 1)$, $M \models CP_{\geq r}(\alpha, \beta)$, and $M \not\models CP_{=r}(\alpha, \beta)$, i.e. that for every positive integer n, $\frac{\mu([\alpha \wedge \beta]_M)}{\mu([\beta]_M)} \geq 1 - \frac{1}{n}$. It follows that $M \models CP_{\approx 1}(\alpha, \beta)$. Let $CP_{\approx 1}(\alpha, \beta) \notin T^*$. If $\mu([\beta]_M) = 0$, then $M \models CP_{=1}(\alpha, \beta)$, $CP_{=1}(\alpha, \beta) \in T^*$, and using Axiom 15 $CP_{\approx 1}(\alpha, \beta) \in T^*$, a contradiction. Thus, let $\mu([\beta]_M) \neq 0$. By the step 2 of the construction of T^*, there is some rational number $r \in [0, 1)$ such that $\neg CP_{>r}(\alpha, \beta) \in T^*$. It means that there is some rational number $r \in [0, 1)$ such that $M \not\models CP_{\geq r}(\alpha, \beta)$, and it does not hold that for every positive integer n, $\frac{\mu([\alpha \wedge \beta]_M)}{\mu([\beta]_M)} \geq 1 - \frac{1}{n}$. Thus, we have that $M \not\models CP_{\approx 1}(\alpha, \beta)$. $\qquad\square$

6 Modeling Default Reasoning

In [11,12] a set of properties which form a core of default reasoning, the corresponding formal system P and a family of nonstandard (R^*) probabilistic models characterizing the default consequence relation defined by the system P, are proposed (where R^* denotes a nonstandard elementary extension of the standard real numbers). Those models are very similar to our $LPP^S_{Meas,Neat}$-models. The only difference is that probabilities from R^*-probabilistic models are R^*-valued, while in our approach the range of probabilities is a countable subset S of the unit interval of R^*. Using that restriction of the range of probabilities, in the companion paper [18] we describe in details how our system can be used to model default reasoning. In this section we just list the main results from [18]. We use $CP_{\approx 1}(\beta,\alpha)$ to syntactically describe the behavior of the default 'if α, then generally β' (denoted by $\alpha \rightarrowtail \beta$). It is shown that:

- If we consider the language of defaults and finite default bases, the entailment coincides with the one in the system P.
- If we consider the language of defaults and arbitrary default bases, more conclusions can be obtained in our system than in the system P. For example, in our system we can go beyond the system P, when we consider the infinite default base $\Delta = \{p_i \rightarrowtail p_{i+1}, p_{i+1} \rightarrowtail \neg p_i\}$, $i = 0, 1, \ldots$ Namely, p_0 is P-consistent [12], while we obtain $\Delta \vdash_{Ax_{LPPS}} CP_{\approx 1}(\bot, p_0)$.
- When we consider our full language, we can express probabilities of formulas, negations of defaults, combinations of defaults with the other (probabilistic) formulas etc. For example, the translation of rational monotonicity, $((\alpha \rightarrowtail \beta) \wedge \neg(\alpha \rightarrowtail \neg\gamma)) \to ((\alpha \wedge \gamma) \rightarrowtail \beta)$, which is an important default-reasoning principle is $LPP^S_{Meas,Neat}$-valid, while it cannot be even formulated in the framework of the pure language of defaults.
- Our system is not sensitive to the syntactical form which represents the available knowledge (for example, duplications of rules in the knowledge base).

Finally, although the ideas of using probabilities and infinitesimals in default reasoning are not new (see, for example [1,3,9,12,20]), the above facts show that our approach does not coincide with any of those systems.

7 Conclusion

In this paper we consider a language, a class of probabilistic models and a sound and complete axiomatic system (at a price of introducing infinitary deduction rules). In the formalization most parts of field theory are moved to the meta theory, so the axioms are rather simple. There are many possible directions for further investigations. First of all, in this paper there is a constraint that probabilistic operators may be applied to classical propositional formulas only. It is enough to reason about probabilities of events described by (classical propositional) formulas, but we cannot speak about higher order probabilities (probabilities of

238   M. Rašković, Z. Ognjanović, and Z. Marković

probabilities). The ideas from [16] may help us in obtaining an axiomatization of the logic with higher order conditional probabilities as well as of the corresponding first order logic. Also, the question of decidability of our logic naturally arises. In [7] decidability of a similar logic was proven. For the present approach the problem is still open since we do not consider real-valued probabilities, but the range of probability is the unit interval of a recursive nonarchimedean field.

References

1. E. W. Adams. *The logic of Conditional*. Dordrecht: Reidel. 1975.
2. N. Alechina. Logic with probabilistic operators. In *Proc. of the ACCOLADE '94*, 121 – 138. 1995.
3. S. Benferhat, A. Saffiotti, and P. Smets. Belief functions and default reasoning. *Artificial Intelligence* (122):1 – 69. 2000.
4. G. Coletti, and R. Scozzafava. *Probabilistic logic in a coherent setting*. Kluwer Academic Press, Dordrecht, The Netherlands. 2002.
5. R. Đorđević, M. Rašković, and Z. Ognjanović. Completeness theorem for propositional probabilistic models whose measures have only finite ranges. *Archive for Mathematical Logic* 43, 557 – 563. 2004.
6. R. Fagin, and J. Halpern. Reasoning about knowledge and probability. *Journal of the ACM* 41(2):340 – 367. 1994.
7. R. Fagin, J. Halpern, and N. Megiddo. A logic for reasoning about probabilities. *Information and Computation* 87(1-2):78 – 128. 1990.
8. A. Gilio. Probabilistic reasoning under coherence in System P. *Annals of Mathematics and Artificial Intelligence* 34, 5 – 34. 2002.
9. M. Goldszmidt, and J. Pearl. Qualitative probabilities for default reasoning, belief revision and causal modeling. *Artificial Intelligence* 84(1-2):57 – 112. 1996.
10. J. Keisler. *Elementary calculus. An infinitesimal approach. 2nd ed.* Boston, Massachusetts: Prindle, Weber & Schmidt. 1986.
11. S. Kraus, D. Lehmann, and M. Magidor. Nonmonotonic reasoning, preferential models and cumulative logics. *Artificial Intelligence* 44:167 – 207. 1990.
12. D. Lehmann, and M. Magidor. What does a conditional knowledge base entail? *Artificial Intelligence* 55:1 – 60. 1992.
13. T. Lukasiewicz. Probabilistic Default Reasoning with Conditional Constraints. *Annals of Mathematics and Artificial Intelligence* 34, 35 – 88. 2002.
14. Z. Marković, Z. Ognjanović, and M. Rašković. A probabilistic extension of intuitionistic logic. *Mathematical Logic Quarterly* 49:415 – 424. 2003.
15. Z. Ognjanović, and M. Rašković. Some probability logics with new types of probability operators. *Journal of Logic and Computation* 9(2):181 – 195. 1999.
16. Z. Ognjanović, and M. Rašković. Some first-order probability logics. *Theoretical Computer Science* 247(1-2):191 – 212. 2000.
17. M. Rašković. Classical logic with some probability operators. *Publications de l'Institut Mathématique, Nouvelle Série, Beograd* (53(67)):1 – 3. 1993.
18. M. Rašković, Z. Ognjanović, and Z. Marković. A Probabilistic Approach to Default Reasoning. In *Proc. of the NMR '04*, 335 – 341. 2004.
19. Robinson, A. *Non-standard analysis*. Amsterdam: North-Holland. 1966.
20. Satoh, K. A probabilistic interpretation for lazy nonmonotonic reasoning. In *Proc. of the Eighth American Conference on Artificial Intelligence*, 659 – 664. 1990.

Reasoning About Quantum Systems

P. Mateus and A. Sernadas

CLC, Department of Mathematics, IST,
Av. Rovisco Pais, 1000-149 Lisbon, Portugal

Abstract. A new logic is proposed for reasoning about quantum systems. The logic embodies the postulates of quantum physics and it was designed from the semantics upwards by identifying quantum models with superpositions of classical models. This novel approach to quantum logic is completely different from the traditional approach of Birkhoff and von Neumann. It has the advantage of making quantum logic an extension of classical logic. The key new ingredient of the language of the proposed logic is a rather general modal operator. The logic incorporates probabilistic reasoning (in the style of Nilsson) in order to deal with uncertainty on the outcome of measurements. The logic also incorporates dynamic reasoning (in the style of Hoare) in order to cope with the evolution of quantum systems. A Hilbert calculus for the logic is sketched. A quantum key distribution protocol is specified and analyzed.

1 Motivation and Related Work

A new logic is proposed for modeling and reasoning about quantum systems, embodying all that is stated in the postulates of quantum physics (as presented, for instance, in [1]). The logic was designed from the semantics upwards starting with the key idea of adopting superpositions of classical models as the models of the quantum logic.

This novel approach to quantum logic semantics is completely different from the traditional approach [2,3] to the problem, as initially proposed by Birkhoff and von Neumann [4] focusing on the lattice of closed subspaces of a Hilbert space. Our semantics has the advantage of closely guiding the design of the language around the underlying concepts of quantum physics while keeping the classical connectives and was inspired by the possible worlds approach originally proposed by Kripke [5] for modal logic. It is also akin to the society semantics introduced in [6] for many-valued logic and to the possible translations semantics proposed in [7] for paraconsistent logic. The possible worlds approach was also used in [8,9,10,11,12] for probabilistic logic. Our semantics to quantum logic, although inspired by modal logic, is also completely different from the alternative Kripke semantics given to traditional quantum logics (as first proposed in [13]) still closely related to the lattice-oriented operations.

Contrarily to traditional quantum logics that replace the classical connectives by new connectives inspired by the lattice-oriented operations, by adopting superpositions of classical models as the models of the quantum logic we are led

J.J. Alferes and J. Leite (Eds.): JELIA 2004, LNAI 3229, pp. 239–251, 2004.

to a natural extension of the classical language containing the classical connectives (like modal languages are extensions of the classical language). The key new ingredient of our quantum language is a rather general modal operator.

The proposed logic also incorporates probabilistic reasoning (in the style of Nilsson's calculus [8,9]) since the postulates of quantum physics impose uncertainty on the outcome of measurements. From a quantum state (superposition of classical valuations living in a suitable Hilbert space) it is straightforward to generate a probability space of classical valuations in order to provide the semantics for reasoning about the probabilistic measurements made on that state. Our logic also incorporates dynamic reasoning (in the style of Hoare's calculus [14]) in order to cope with the evolution of quantum systems. Two types of quantum state transitions are considered: unitary transformations and projections. A Hilbert calculus for the logic is sketched having in mind a completeness result obtained elsewhere. As an illustration of the power of the proposed logic, a quantum key distribution protocol is specified and analyzed.

In Section 2, we briefly present the relevant mathematical structures based on the postulates of quantum physics. In Section 3, we present EQPL (exogenous quantum propositional logic) for reasoning about a quantum system in a given quantum state. In Section 4, we extend EQPL to DEQPL (dynamic exogenous quantum propositional logic) for reasoning also about quantum state transitions. Finally, in Section 5, we present and analyze a quantum key distribution protocol.

2   Basic Concepts

In order to materialize the key idea of adopting superpositions of classical models as the models of the envisaged quantum logic, we need to recall the postulates of quantum physics (that we do following closely [1]) and to set up some important mathematical structures.

Postulate 1. Associated to any isolated quantum system is a Hilbert space[1]. The state of the system is completely described by a unit vector $|w\rangle$ in the Hilbert space.

For example, a quantum bit or *qubit* is associated to a Hilbert space of dimension two: a state of a qubit is a vector $\alpha_0|0\rangle + \alpha_1|1\rangle$ where $\alpha_0, \alpha_1 \in \mathbb{C}$ and $|\alpha_0|^2 + |\alpha_1|^2 = 1$. That is, the quantum state is a *superposition* of the two classical states $|0\rangle$ and $|1\rangle$ of a classical bit. Therefore, from a logical point of view, representing the qubit by a propositional constant, a *quantum valuation* is a superposition of the two classical valuations.

---

[1] Recall that a Hilbert space is a complex vector space with inner product which is complete for the induced norm. It is customary to present its elements using the *ket* Dirac notation $|w\rangle$.

Postulate 2. The Hilbert space associated to a quantum system composed of n independent component systems is the tensor product[2] of the component Hilbert spaces.

For instance, a system composed of two independent qubits is associated to a Hilbert space of dimension four: a state of such a system is a vector $\alpha_{00}|00\rangle + \alpha_{01}|01\rangle + \alpha_{10}|10\rangle + \alpha_{11}|11\rangle$ where $\alpha_{00}, \alpha_{10}, \alpha_{01}, \alpha_{11} \in \mathbb{C}$ and $|\alpha_{00}|^2 + |\alpha_{01}|^2 + |\alpha_{10}|^2 + |\alpha_{11}|^2 = 1$. Again, representing the two qubits by two propositional constants, a *quantum valuation* is a superposition of the four classical valuations. And, so, the Hilbert space of the system composed of two independent qubits is indeed the tensor product of the two Hilbert spaces, each corresponding to a qubit.

The systems we envisage to reason about are composed by a denumerable set of possibly interdependent qubits and, therefore, we fix once and for all the following set of propositional constants $\{\mathbf{p}_k : k \in \mathbb{N}\}$, once for each qubit. In this context, a classical valuation is a map $v : \{\mathbf{p}_k : k \in \mathbb{N}\} \to \{0,1\}$. We now face the problem of setting up the suitable Hilbert space where the superpositions of such classical valuations will live.

Given a nonempty set V of classical valuations, $\mathcal{H}(V)$ is the following inner product space over $\mathbb{C}$:

- each element is a map $|w\rangle : V \to \mathbb{C}$ such that:
  - $\mathrm{supp}(|w\rangle) = \{v : |w\rangle(v) \neq 0\}$ is countable;
  - $\displaystyle\sum_{v \in \mathrm{supp}(|w\rangle)} \||w\rangle(v)\|^2 < \infty$.
- $|w_1\rangle + |w_2\rangle = \lambda v.\, |w_1\rangle(v) + |w_2\rangle(v)$.
- $\alpha|w\rangle = \lambda v.\, \alpha|w\rangle(v)$.
- $\langle w_1|w_2\rangle = \displaystyle\sum_{v \in V} |w_1\rangle(v)\overline{|w_2\rangle(v)}$.

As usual, the inner product induces the norm $\||w\rangle\| = \sqrt{\langle w|w\rangle}$ and, so, the distance $d(|w_1\rangle, |w_2\rangle) = \||w_1\rangle - |w_2\rangle\|$. Since $\mathcal{H}(V)$ is complete for this distance, $\mathcal{H}(V)$ is a Hilbert space . Clearly, $\{|v\rangle : v \in V\}$ is an orthonormal basis of $\mathcal{H}(V)$ where $|v\rangle(v) = 1$ and $|v\rangle(v') = 0$ for every $v' \neq v$.

A quantum structure $\mathbf{w}$ is a pair $\langle V, |w\rangle\rangle$ where: V is a nonempty set of classical valuations; and $|w\rangle \in \mathcal{H}(V)$ such that $\||w\rangle\| = 1$. This structure provides the means for reasoning about a quantum system composed of a denumerable set of qubits (one for each $\mathbf{p}_k$) such that by observing it we get a classical valuation in V. The current state of the system is the unit vector $|w\rangle$ (a unit superposition of the observable classical valuations).

---

[2] Recall that the tensor product of Hilbert spaces $\mathcal{H}_1$ and $\mathcal{H}_2$ is the Hilbert space composed by the pairs $|w_1\rangle \otimes |w_2\rangle$ such that the following equalities hold for all $\alpha \in \mathbb{C}, |w_1\rangle, |w_1'\rangle \in \mathcal{H}_1$ and $|w_2\rangle, |w_2'\rangle \in \mathcal{H}_2$: $(\alpha(|w_1\rangle \otimes |w_2\rangle)) = ((\alpha|w_1\rangle) \otimes |w_2\rangle) = (|w_1\rangle \otimes (\alpha|w_2\rangle)); ((|w_1\rangle + |w_1'\rangle) \otimes |w_2\rangle) = ((|w_1\rangle \otimes |w_2\rangle) + (|w_1'\rangle \otimes |w_2\rangle)); (|w_1\rangle \otimes (|w_2\rangle + |w_2'\rangle)) = ((|w_1\rangle \otimes |w_2\rangle) + (|w_1\rangle \otimes |w_2'\rangle)).$

Since we start with the whole system composed of a denumerable set of qubits, we have to use Postulate 2 in the reverse direction: how can we identify an independent subsystem?

Given a set S of propositional constants (qubits), we denote by $V_{[S]}$ the set $\{v|_S : v \in V\}$ and by $V_{]S[}$ the set $\{v|_{S^c} : v \in V\}$. Clearly, $\mathcal{H}(V) = \mathcal{H}(V_{[S]}) \otimes \mathcal{H}(V_{]S[})$ where V is the set of all classical valuations. But, $\mathcal{H}(V) \subseteq \mathcal{H}(V_{[S]}) \otimes \mathcal{H}(V_{]S[})$ where equality does not hold in general. When it does, we say that the quantum system is composed of two independent subsystems (one with the qubits in S and the other with rest of the qubits). Furthermore, given a unit $|w\rangle \in \mathcal{H}(V)$, if there are unit $|w'\rangle \in \mathcal{H}(V_{[S]})$ and unit $|w''\rangle \in \mathcal{H}(V_{]S[})$ such that $|w\rangle = |w'\rangle \otimes |w''\rangle$ then we say that, in state $|w\rangle$, the qubits in S are not entangled with the qubits not in S and, therefore, that the qubits in S are independent of the other qubits at that state $|w\rangle$.

The two remaining postulates of quantum physics state how the state of the quantum system is changed: either when it is observed or when it evolves by itself without interference.

Postulate 3. Each type of projective measurement or observation that can be made over a quantum system is associated to a Hermitian operator[3] M over its Hilbert space. The possible outcomes of the measurement are the eigenvalues of M. Upon making an observation with M of the system in state $|w\rangle$, the probability of getting an eigenvalue m is given by $\langle w|P_m|w\rangle$ where P_m is the projector onto the eigenspace of M with eigenvalue m. When the outcome m occurs, the quantum system evolves to the state given by $\frac{P_m|w\rangle}{\sqrt{\langle w|P_m|w\rangle}}$.

For the applications we have in mind in quantum computation and information, the most relevant type of measurement is the one corresponding to the identity operator. In this case, the possible outcomes are the classical valuations in V and each v is observed at state $|w\rangle$ with probability $|\langle v|w\rangle|^2$. More precisely, a measurement induces a probability space over the possible outcomes as we proceed to explain after introducing the notion of Nilsson structure[4] that we shall use for providing the semantics of the probabilistic component of the quantum logic.

A *Nilsson structure* $\mathbf{V}$ is a tuple $\langle V, \mathcal{B}, \nu \rangle$ where: V is a non empty set of classical valuations; $\mathcal{B}$ is a σ-algebra over V (that is, $\mathcal{B} \subseteq \wp V$ and $\mathcal{B}$ is closed under complements and countable unions) such that $\{v \in V : v \Vdash \mathbf{p}_k\} \in \mathcal{B}$ for each $k \in \mathbb{N}$; and ν is a map from $\mathcal{B}$ to $[0,1]$ such that $\nu(V) = 1$ and $\nu(\bigcup_{j \in \mathbb{N}} B_j) = \sum_{j \in \mathbb{N}} \nu(B_j)$ whenever $B_{j_1} \cap B_{j_2} = \emptyset$ for every $j_1 \neq j_2 \in \mathbb{N}$. In short, a Nilsson structure is a probability space where outcomes are classical valuations and the extent of every propositional constant is among the events. Such structures provide the semantic basis for several probabilistic logics used for reasoning with uncertainty [8,12,9].

---

[3] Recall that a Hermitian operator H is an operator such that $H = H^*$ where H^* is the adjoint operator of H, that is, the unique operator such that $\langle \psi_1|H\psi_2\rangle = \langle H^*\psi_1|\psi_2\rangle$.

[4] We propose this terminology in recognition of the significance of [8] for the development of probabilistic logic.

As we saw, according to Postulate 3, the stochastic result of observing the system at state $|w\rangle$ is fully described by the Nilsson structure $\mathcal{N}(\mathbf{w}) = \langle V, \wp V, \nu_{|w\rangle}\rangle$ where, for each $U \subseteq V$, $\nu_{|w\rangle}(U) = \sum_{u \in U} |\langle u|w\rangle|^2$.

Postulate 4. Barring measurements, the evolution of a quantum system is described by unitary transformations[5].

Taking into account the applications we have in mind, we can restrict our attention to finite unitary transformations (a transformation is said to be finite if only changes a finite number of components of the argument vector).

It was established in [15] that a finite unitary transformation can be approximated by composing eight basic transformations: identity, Hadamard, phase, $\frac{\pi}{8}$, Pauli X, Y, Z and controlled not. This result helps in choosing the language for denoting such transformations as we shall in Section 4, where we shall provide further information about the basic transformations.

3   Reasoning About a Quantum State

The envisaged quantum logic should first provide the means for reasoning about a given state of a quantum system composed of a denumerable set of qubits (one for each propositional constant $\mathbf{p}_k$) and where the relevant projective observation values are classical valuations. Given the stochastic nature of the outcomes of measurements the logic should incorporate probabilistic reasoning. Therefore, we extended the classical language first with the means for writing probabilistic assertions (loosely inspired by [8,9,10,11,12]) and later with the means for making assertions about superpositions of classical valuations.

This design effort resulted in the (denumerable) quantum language composed of formulae of the form[6]

$$\gamma = \omega_k \curlyvee \varphi \curlyvee (t \leq t) \curlyvee ([S] \diamond \overrightarrow{\psi : u}) \curlyvee (\boxminus \gamma) \curlyvee (\gamma \sqsupset \gamma)$$

where φ is a classical formula, t is a real term, u is a complex term, S is a non empty recursive set of propositional constants (qubits), and ψ is a classical formula over S. A classical formula φ is of the form

$$\varphi = \xi_k \curlyvee \mathbf{p}_k \curlyvee (\neg \varphi) \curlyvee (\varphi \Rightarrow \varphi).$$

The set of real terms and the set of complex terms are jointly defined as follows

$$\begin{cases} t = \theta_k \curlyvee r \curlyvee (\int \varphi) \curlyvee (\int \varphi \,|\, \varphi) \curlyvee (t + t) \curlyvee (t\,t) \curlyvee \mathrm{Re}(u) \curlyvee \mathrm{Im}(u) \curlyvee \arg(u) \curlyvee |u| \\ u = \upsilon_k \curlyvee (t + it) \curlyvee t e^{it} \curlyvee \overline{u} \curlyvee (u + u) \curlyvee (u\,u) \end{cases}$$

---

[5] Recall that a unitary transformation (or operator) on a Hilbert space $\mathcal{H}$ is a linear map $U : \mathcal{H} \to \mathcal{H}$ such that $U \circ U^* = I$. It is easy to see that unitary transformations are closed under composition and inverse.

[6] When defining languages, we use the abstract Backus Naur notation [16], but adopting $\curlyvee$ instead of the traditional $|$ in order to avoid confusions with the object language. We also extend the Backus-Naur notation: we write $\overrightarrow{\delta}$ for a finite sequence of elements of the form δ.

where r is a computable real number. The ξ's, ω's, θ's and v's are schema variables (to be used in rules) that can be the target of substitutions respecting the syntactic categories. An expression is said to be ground if it does not contain any such variable.

The denotation at $\mathbf{w}$ of ground terms is mostly straightforward, but it is worthwhile to mention how the probability terms are interpreted on a given quantum structure $\mathbf{w}$.

Recall the Nilsson structure induced by $\mathbf{w}$ defined in Section 2: $\mathcal{N}(\mathbf{w}) = \langle V, \wp V, \nu_{\mathbf{w}} \rangle$ where, for each $U \subseteq V$, $\nu_{\mathbf{w}}(U) = \sum_{u \in U} |\langle u | w \rangle|^2$.

Clearly, for each ground classical formula φ, its extent at $\mathbf{w}$, $[\varphi]_{\mathbf{w}} = \{v \in V : v \Vdash \varphi\}$, is in $\wp V$. So, we are ready to define the denotation at $\mathbf{w}$ of the probabilistic ground terms:

- $[\![(\int \varphi)]\!]_{\mathbf{w}} = \nu_{\mathbf{w}}([\varphi]_{\mathbf{w}})$;
- $[\![(\int \varphi_2 \,|\, \varphi_1)]\!]_{\mathbf{w}} = \begin{cases} \frac{\nu_{\mathbf{w}}([\varphi_1]_{\mathbf{w}} \cap [\varphi_2]_{\mathbf{w}})}{\nu_{\mathbf{w}}([\varphi_1]_V)} & \text{if } \nu_{\mathbf{w}}([\varphi_1]_{\mathbf{w}}) \neq 0 \\ 1 & \text{otherwise} \end{cases}$.

Intuitively, $(\int \varphi)$ gives the probability of getting an outcome (classical valuation) where φ holds, when we observe the quantum system. And $(\int \varphi_2 \,|\, \varphi_1)$ gives the probability of getting an outcome (classical valuation) where φ_2 holds given that φ_1 holds, when we observe the quantum system[7].

The satisfaction of formulae by $\mathbf{w}$ and ground substitution ρ is as follows:

- $\mathbf{w}\rho \Vdash \omega_j$ iff $\mathbf{w}\rho \Vdash \omega_j\rho$;
- $\mathbf{w}\rho \Vdash \varphi$ iff $v \Vdash \varphi\rho$ for every $v \in V$;
- $\mathbf{w}\rho \Vdash (t_1 \leq t_2)$ iff $[\![t_1\rho]\!]_{\mathbf{w}} \leq [\![t_2\rho]\!]_{\mathbf{w}}$;
- $\mathbf{w}\rho \Vdash ([S] \Diamond \psi_1 : u_1, \ldots, \psi_n : u_n)$ iff there are unit $|w'\rangle \in \mathcal{H}(V_{[S]})$ and unit $|w''\rangle \in \mathcal{H}(V_{|S|})$ such that $|w\rangle = |w'\rangle \otimes |w''\rangle$ and there are distinct $v_1, \ldots, v_n \in \text{supp}(|w'\rangle)$ such that $v_k \Vdash \psi_k\rho$ and $|w'\rangle(v_k) = [\![u_k\rho]\!]_{\mathbf{w}}$ for $k = 1, \ldots, n$ (generalized quantum possibility);
- $\mathbf{w}\rho \Vdash (\boxminus \alpha)$ iff $\mathbf{w}\rho \not\Vdash \alpha$ (quantum negation);
- $\mathbf{w}\rho \Vdash (\alpha_1 \sqsupset \alpha_2)$ iff $\mathbf{w}\rho \not\Vdash \alpha_1$ or $\mathbf{w}\rho \Vdash \alpha_2$ (quantum implication).

The notion of quantum entailment is introduced as expected: $\Gamma \vDash \delta$ iff, for every quantum structure $\mathbf{w}$ and ground substitution ρ, $\mathbf{w}\rho \Vdash \delta$ whenever $\mathbf{w}\rho \Vdash \gamma$ for each $\gamma \in \Gamma$.

As usual, other (classical and quantum) connectives can be used as abbreviations. Furthermore, we write $(t_1 = t_2)$ for $((t_1 \leq t_2) \sqcap (t_2 \leq t_1))$. The following abbreviations are useful for expressing some important derived concepts:

- $(\Diamond \varphi_1 : u_1, \ldots, \varphi_n : u_n)$ for $([\{\mathbf{p}_k : k \in \mathbb{N}\}] \Diamond \varphi_1 : u_1, \ldots, \varphi_n : u_n)$;
- $[S]$ for $([S] :)$ — qubits in S are not entangled with those outside S;
- $(\Diamond \varphi)$ for $((\int \varphi) > 0)$ and $(\Box \varphi)$ for $((\int \varphi) = 1)$;

---

[7] By convention, we imposed this to be one when $(\int \varphi_1)$ is zero.

– $(\bigwedge_F A)$ for $((\bigwedge_{p_k \in A} \mathbf{p}_k) \wedge (\bigwedge_{p_k \in (F \setminus A)} (\neg \mathbf{p}_k)))$ whenever F is a finite set of propositional constants and $A \subseteq F$.

Note that the quantum connectives are still classical but should not be confused with the connectives of classical logic. Indeed, consider the following quantum formulae where φ is a classical formula: (i) $(\varphi \vee (\neg \varphi))$; (ii) $(\varphi \sqcup (\boxminus \varphi))$; and (iii) $(\varphi \sqcup (\neg \varphi))$. Clearly, (i) and (ii) hold in every quantum system for every ground substitution, while (iii) does not hold in general.

The generalized quantum modality is quite powerful and is better understood in the context of a concrete example. Consider the following specification of a state of the quantum system composed of two entangled pairs of qubits where each pair of qubits is at state $\frac{1}{\sqrt{2}}|00\rangle + \frac{1}{\sqrt{2}}|11\rangle$:

– $([\mathbf{p}_0, \mathbf{p}_1] \Diamond (\mathbf{p}_0 \wedge \mathbf{p}_1) : \frac{1}{\sqrt{2}}, ((\neg \mathbf{p}_0) \wedge (\neg \mathbf{p}_1)) : \frac{1}{\sqrt{2}})$;
– $([\mathbf{p}_2, \mathbf{p}_3] \Diamond (\mathbf{p}_2 \wedge \mathbf{p}_3) : \frac{1}{\sqrt{2}}, ((\neg \mathbf{p}_2) \wedge (\neg \mathbf{p}_3)) : \frac{1}{\sqrt{2}})$.

The specified state of the quantum system composed of the four qubits is $\frac{1}{2}|0000\rangle + \frac{1}{2}|0011\rangle + \frac{1}{2}|1100\rangle + \frac{1}{2}|1111\rangle$. This state will be a relevant state of the quantum system discussed in Section 5 for modeling a quantum key distribution protocol. This specification entails the following formulae:

– $([\mathbf{p}_0, \mathbf{p}_1] \sqcap [\mathbf{p}_2, \mathbf{p}_3])$;
– $(\int \mathbf{p}_0) = \frac{1}{2}$;
– $(\int (\mathbf{p}_0 \Leftrightarrow \mathbf{p}_1)) = 1$;
– $(\int (\mathbf{p}_0 \Leftrightarrow \mathbf{p}_2)) = \frac{1}{2}$.

Our ultimate goal was to develop a deduction calculus complete in some useful sense with respect to the above semantics. However, when using only finitary rules, strong completeness is out of question because of quantum entailment is not compact[8].

Despite this negative result, we are able to define a weak complete Hilbert calculus (with respect to an arithmetic oracle)[9]. Here are the interesting axioms for the quantum modality:

SUPP $\vdash (\boxminus ([S] \Diamond \psi : 0))$;

PROJ $\vdash (([S] \Diamond \psi_1 : u_1, \ldots, \psi_n : u_n) \sqsupset ([S] \Diamond \psi_k : e^{it} u_k))$ for $k = 1, \ldots, n$;

NORM $\vdash (([S] \Diamond (\psi \vee \psi') : u) \equiv (([S] \Diamond \psi : u) \sqcup ([S] \Diamond \psi' : u)))$;

RPROB $\vdash (([S] \Diamond \psi_1 : u_1, \ldots, \psi_n : u_n) \sqsupset$
$((|u_1|^2 + \cdots + |u_n|^2) \leq (\int (\psi_1 \vee \ldots \vee \psi_n))))$;

LPROB $\vdash (([F] \Diamond (\bigwedge_F A) : u) \sqsupset ((\int (\bigwedge_F A)) \leq |u|^2))$;

QMON $\vdash ((\psi_1 \Rightarrow \psi_2) \sqsupset ([S] \Diamond \psi_1 : u) \leq ([S] \Diamond \psi_2 : u)))$.

---

[8] Take $\Gamma = \{((r' \leq (\int \mathbf{p}_1)) \sqcap ((\int \mathbf{p}_1) \leq r'')) : r' < \frac{1}{2} < r''\}$ and $\delta = ((\int \mathbf{p}_1) = \frac{1}{2})$. So, $\Gamma \vDash \delta$, but, clearly, there is no finite $\Gamma_0 \subset \Gamma$ such that $\Gamma_0 \vDash \delta$.

[9] The proof will be presented elsewhere given its size and complexity.

Concerning probabilistic reasoning, the key axioms are as follows:

PM $\vdash ((\int \mathbf{t}) = 1);$

FA $\vdash ((((\int(\neg(\xi_1 \wedge \xi_2))) = 1) \sqsupset ((\int(\xi_1 \vee \xi_2)) = ((\int \xi_1) + (\int \xi_2)))));$

CP $\vdash (((\int \xi_2 \,|\, \xi_1)(\int \xi_1)) = (\int(\xi_1 \wedge \xi_2)));$

UCP $\vdash (((\int \xi_1) = 0) \sqsupset ((\int \xi_2 \,|\, \xi_1) = 1));$

PMON $\vdash ((\xi_1 \Rightarrow \xi_2) \sqsupset ((\int \xi_1) \leq (\int \xi_2))).$

By restricting the quantum language to the probabilistic connectives, we obtain a logic for reasoning with uncertainty. The resulting logic has such nice properties that it is worthwhile to study it by itself.

4   Reasoning About Quantum Evolution

For reasoning about changes in the state of a quantum system (including transitions resulting from projective observations of a single qubit), we need to enrich the language. First, we need transition terms for denoting all such state transitions, of the form

$$Z = \tau_k \,\Upsilon\, U \,\Upsilon\, P \,\Upsilon\, (Z \circ Z)$$

where U is a unitary operator term of the form

$$U = \mathbf{I} \,\Upsilon\, \mathbf{H}_k \,\Upsilon\, \mathbf{S}_k \,\Upsilon\, \left(\frac{\pi}{8}\right)_k \,\Upsilon\, \mathbf{X}_k \,\Upsilon\, \mathbf{Y}_k \,\Upsilon\, \mathbf{Z}_k \,\Upsilon\, \mathbf{cN}_{k_2}^{k_1} \,\Upsilon\, U^{-1} \,\Upsilon\, (U \circ U)$$

and P is a qubit projective observation transition term of the form

$$P = \mathbf{P}_k^{c|0\rangle + c|1\rangle}$$

where c is a complex number of the form $r + ir$ where r is, as before, a computable real number. The eight symbols in U denote the eight basic unitary operators (identity, Hadamard, phase, $\pi/8$, Pauli X, Y, Z, and control not, respectively). As mentioned already at the end of Section 2, any finite, unitary operator can be approximated as close as desired by a finite composition of these basic operators [15]. We also need transition formulae of the form[10]

$$H = \{\gamma\} \, Z \, \{\gamma\} \,\Upsilon\, \{\gamma\} \, \Omega Z$$

where γ is a quantum formula as defined in the Section 3.

The denotation $[\![Z]\!]$ of a transition term Z is a partial map from the unit circle of $\mathcal{H}(\mathcal{V})$ to itself (recall that $\mathcal{V}$ is the set of all classical valuations). In the case of every unitary operator term this map is total. Partiality only arises for observation transitions (as illustrated below).

---

[10] Adapting from the Hoare (pre and post condition) triplets in the logic of imperative programs [14].

Observe that, given $V \subseteq \mathcal{V}$, it may happen that $[\![Z]\!]|w\rangle \notin \mathcal{H}(V)$ even when $|w\rangle \in \mathcal{H}(V)$ and $[\![Z]\!]$ is defined on $|w\rangle$. We must keep this in mind when defining the satisfaction of transition formulae[11]:

- $V\rho \Vdash \{\gamma_1\} Z \{\gamma_2\}$ iff, for any $|w\rangle \in \mathcal{H}(V)$, if $\langle V, |w\rangle\rangle\rho \Vdash \gamma_1$ then $\langle V, [\![Z]\!]|w\rangle\rangle\rho \Vdash \gamma_2$ whenever $[\![Z]\!]|w\rangle{\downarrow}$ and $[\![Z]\!]|w\rangle \in \mathcal{H}(V)$;
- $V\rho \Vdash \{\gamma\} \Omega Z$ iff, for any $|w\rangle \in \mathcal{H}(V)$, if $\langle V, |w\rangle\rangle\rho \Vdash \gamma$ then $[\![Z]\!]|w\rangle{\downarrow}$ and $[\![Z]\!]|w\rangle \in \mathcal{H}(V)$.

That is, $\{\gamma_1\} Z \{\gamma_2\}$ means that if the quantum system evolves by Z from a state where γ_1 holds to a legitimate state (that is, in $\mathcal{H}(V)$) then γ_2 holds at the resulting state. If the resulting state is not legitimate the transition formula is vacuously satisfied. And $\{\gamma\} \Omega Z$ means that the quantum system reaches a legitimate state when it evolves by Z from a state where γ holds.

It is worthwhile to spell out in detail the semantics of the basic unitary operators. To this end, we need the notion of the dual of a valuation on a qubit: $\overline{v}^k$ is the valuation that agrees with v on all propositional symbols barring $\mathbf{p}_k$ and gives the other Boolean value to $\mathbf{p}_k$. For instance:

- $[\![\mathbf{H}_k]\!]|w\rangle(v) = \begin{cases} \frac{1}{\sqrt{2}}(|w\rangle(v) + |w\rangle(\overline{v}^k)) & \text{if } v \not\Vdash \mathbf{p}_k \\ \frac{1}{\sqrt{2}}(|w\rangle(\overline{v}^k) - |w\rangle(v)) & \text{otherwise} \end{cases}$;

- $[\![\mathbf{S}_k]\!]|w\rangle(v) = \begin{cases} |w\rangle(v) & \text{if } v \not\Vdash \mathbf{p}_k \\ i|w\rangle(v) & \text{otherwise} \end{cases}$;

- $[\![\mathbf{cN}_{k_2}^{k_1}]\!]|w\rangle(v) = \begin{cases} |w\rangle(v) & \text{if } v \not\Vdash \mathbf{p}_{k_1} \\ |w\rangle(\overline{v}^{k_2}) & \text{otherwise} \end{cases}$.

Before describing the semantics of the projective observation operators, we need some notation. Given a set S of propositional constants (qubits), we denote by $I_{[S]}$ the identity operator on $\mathcal{H}(\mathcal{V}_{[S]})$ and by $I_{]S[}$ the identity operator on $\mathcal{H}(\mathcal{V}_{]S[})$. Given $|b\rangle = \alpha_0|\mathbf{0}\rangle + \alpha_1|\mathbf{1}\rangle$ in $\mathcal{H}(2)$ we also need to use the projector along $|b\rangle$, that is, the operator $|b\rangle\langle b|$ on $\mathcal{H}(2)$ defined by the following matrix:

$$\begin{pmatrix} \alpha_0\overline{\alpha_0} & \alpha_0\overline{\alpha_1} \\ \alpha_1\overline{\alpha_0} & \alpha_1\overline{\alpha_1} \end{pmatrix} .$$

Letting $P_k^{|b\rangle}$ be the projector along $|b\rangle$ for qubit k in $\mathcal{H}(\mathcal{V})$ that is given by $I_{[\{\mathbf{p}_0,\dots,\mathbf{p}_{k-1}\}]} \otimes |b\rangle\langle b| \otimes I_{]\{\mathbf{p}_0,\dots,\mathbf{p}_k\}[}$, the semantics of the projective observation transition terms is as follows:

- $[\![\mathbf{P}_k^{c_0|\mathbf{0}\rangle+c_1|\mathbf{1}\rangle}]\!]|w\rangle = \dfrac{P_k^{c_0|\mathbf{0}\rangle+c_1|\mathbf{1}\rangle}|w\rangle}{\|P_k^{c_0|\mathbf{0}\rangle+c_1|\mathbf{1}\rangle}|w\rangle\|}.$

Observe that $[\![\mathbf{P}_k^{c_0|\mathbf{0}\rangle+c_1|\mathbf{1}\rangle}]\!]$ is undefined at $|w\rangle$ if $\|P_k^{c_0|\mathbf{0}\rangle+c_1|\mathbf{1}\rangle}|w\rangle\| = 0$. In particular, $[\![\mathbf{P}_k^{|\mathbf{0}\rangle}]\!]$ is undefined at $|w\rangle$ whenever $|w\rangle \Vdash ((\int(\neg \mathbf{p}_k)) = 0)$. In fact, it

---

[11] As usual when dealing with partial maps, we write $[\![Z]\!]|w\rangle{\downarrow}$ for asserting that $[\![Z]\!]$ is defined on $|w\rangle$.

is not possible to observe 0 on $\mathbf{p}_k$ when all valuations in the support of the state of the system satisfy $\mathbf{p}_k$.

The projective observation transition terms play the role of qubit assignments in quantum computation since they impose the superposition of the the target qubit in the resulting state. But, contrarily to classical computation, an assignment to qubit $\mathbf{p}_k$ may also affect other qubits (those that were entangled with $\mathbf{p}_k$), this is a core property of quantum systems where the EPR quantum key distribution protocol relies on.

As an illustration, consider the transition formula

$$\{([\mathbf{p}_0, \mathbf{p}_1] \Diamond (\mathbf{p}_0 \wedge \mathbf{p}_1) : \tfrac{1}{\sqrt{2}}, ((\neg \mathbf{p}_0) \wedge (\neg \mathbf{p}_1)) : \tfrac{1}{\sqrt{2}})\}$$

$$\mathbf{P}_{\mathbf{p}_0}^{|1\rangle}$$

$$\{([\mathbf{p}_1] \Diamond \mathbf{p}_1 : 1)\}$$

This formula states, among other things, that if the qubits are entangled then after observing $\mathbf{p}_0$ taking value one we end up in a state where the other qubit also takes value one.

Given a weak complete axiomatization of EQPL (the logic defined in Section 3), it is straightforward to set up a weak complete axiomatization of DEQPL as defined in this section.

5   Quantum Key Distribution

For illustrating the power of the proposed quantum logic, we specify and reason about the EPR quantum key distribution protocol [17]. This protocol is used for sharing a private classical key (that is, a sequence of n bits) via a public quantum channel (composed of $4n$ qubits).

The quantum system is composed of $12n$ qubits: $2n$ pairs of public channel qubits — $\langle \mathbf{x}_1, \mathbf{x}_2 \rangle, \ldots, \langle \mathbf{x}_{4n-1}, \mathbf{x}_{4n} \rangle$; $4n$ private qubits owned by Alice — $\mathbf{aw}_1, \ldots, \mathbf{aw}_{2n}$ for storing channel qubits, $\mathbf{at}_1, \ldots, \mathbf{at}_n$ to be used in a test, and $\mathbf{ak}_1, \ldots, \mathbf{ak}_n$ to be used to generate the key; and, analogously, $4n$ private qubits owned by Bob — $\mathbf{bw}_1, \ldots, \mathbf{bw}_{2n}, \mathbf{bt}_1, \ldots, \mathbf{bt}_n, \mathbf{bk}_1, \ldots, \mathbf{bk}_n$. The protocol runs as follows:

1. A third trusted party sets up each pair of channel qubits at state $\tfrac{1}{\sqrt{2}}|00\rangle + \tfrac{1}{\sqrt{2}}|11\rangle$.
2. Alice fetches the odd channel qubits and Bob fetches the even channel qubits. Since copying qubits is physically impossible, this is achieved by swapping.
3. Alice and Bob agree on a partition $\langle \{j_1, \ldots, j_n\}, \{j'_1, \ldots, j'_n\} \rangle$ of $\{1, \ldots, 2n\}$. Alice transfers (by swapping) $\mathbf{aw}_{j_k}$ to $\mathbf{at}_k$ and $\mathbf{aw}_{j'_k}$ to $\mathbf{ak}_k$. Bob does the same on his qubits.
4. Alice tests if the qubits $\mathbf{at}$ and $\mathbf{bt}$ are still entangled. If this fidelity test fails, she assumes Eve has been eavesdropping and resets the protocol. Otherwise, she projectively measures the $\mathbf{ak}$ qubits (one by one) and obtains the private classical key shared with Bob. Bob does the same with his qubits in order to obtain the key.

For the sake of economy of presentation, we analyze the protocol for $n = 1$. Barring the test of fidelity, this choice is made without loss of generality. But, in practice, n should be large in order to lower the probability of Eve guessing the key, and, for testing if Eve was eavesdropping while the protocol was running, it is also essential to work with large n (given the statistical nature of the fidelity test). Anyway, it is straightforward to describe and analyze the protocol in the proposed quantum logic for arbitrary n (including proving the soundness of the fidelity test).

Initially all qubits are set to $|0\rangle$ and they constitute an independent closed quantum system. Therefore, the initial state of the protocol fulfills $IC = (((\neg \mathbf{x_1}) \wedge (\neg \mathbf{x_2}) \wedge \ldots \wedge (\neg \mathbf{bk_1})) \sqcap [\mathbf{x_1}, \mathbf{x_2}, ..., \mathbf{bk_1}])$. Each step of the protocol corresponds to a quantum transition on these twelve qubits.

1. Set up each pair of channel qubits at state $\frac{1}{\sqrt{2}}|00\rangle + \frac{1}{\sqrt{2}}|11\rangle$ by applying the following composition: $Z_1 = ((\mathbf{cN_{x_4}^{x_3}} \circ \mathbf{H_{x_3}}) \circ (\mathbf{cN_{x_2}^{x_1}} \circ \mathbf{H_{x_1}}))$.

2. Swap the odd channel qubits with the storing channel qubits of Alice by applying the following composition: $((\mathbf{cN_{aw_2}^{x_3}} \circ \mathbf{cN_{x_3}^{aw_2}} \circ \mathbf{cN_{aw_2}^{x_3}}) \circ (\mathbf{cN_{aw_1}^{x_1}} \circ \mathbf{cN_{x_1}^{aw_1}} \circ \mathbf{cN_{aw_1}^{x_1}}))$. Analogously, swap the even channel qubits with the storing channel qubits of Bob by applying the following composition: $((\mathbf{cN_{bw_2}^{x_4}} \circ \mathbf{cN_{x_4}^{bw_2}} \circ \mathbf{cN_{bw_2}^{x_4}}) \circ (\mathbf{cN_{bw_1}^{x_2}} \circ \mathbf{cN_{x_2}^{bw_1}} \circ \mathbf{cN_{bw_1}^{x_2}}))$. Obtain the whole transition by composing the previous two transitions: $Z_2 = ((\mathbf{cN_{bw_1}^{x_3}} \circ \mathbf{cN_{x_3}^{bw_1}} \circ \mathbf{cN_{bw_1}^{x_3}}) \circ \ldots \circ (\mathbf{cN_{aw_1}^{x_1}} \circ \mathbf{cN_{x_1}^{aw_1}} \circ \mathbf{cN_{aw_1}^{x_1}}))$.

3. Assume that Alice and Bob agree on the partition $\langle \{2\}, \{1\} \rangle$ of $\{1, 2\}$. Swap $\mathbf{aw_2}$ with $\mathbf{at_1}$ and $\mathbf{aw_1}$ with $\mathbf{ak_1}$ by applying the following composition: $((\mathbf{cN_{ak_1}^{aw_1}} \circ \mathbf{cN_{aw_1}^{ak_1}} \circ \mathbf{cN_{ak_1}^{aw_1}}) \circ (\mathbf{cN_{at_1}^{aw_2}} \circ \mathbf{cN_{aw_2}^{at_1}} \circ \mathbf{cN_{at_1}^{aw_2}}))$. Analogously, swap $\mathbf{bw_2}$ with $\mathbf{bt_1}$ and $\mathbf{bw_1}$ with $\mathbf{bk_1}$ by applying the following composition: $((\mathbf{cN_{bk_1}^{bw_1}} \circ \mathbf{cN_{bw_1}^{bk_1}} \circ \mathbf{cN_{bk_1}^{bw_1}}) \circ (\mathbf{cN_{bt_1}^{bw_2}} \circ \mathbf{cN_{bw_2}^{bt_1}} \circ \mathbf{cN_{bt_1}^{bw_2}}))$. Obtain the whole transition by composing the previous two transitions: $Z_3 = ((\mathbf{cN_{bk_1}^{bw_1}} \circ \mathbf{cN_{bw_1}^{bk_1}} \circ \mathbf{cN_{bk_1}^{bw_1}}) \circ \cdots \circ (\mathbf{cN_{at_1}^{aw_2}} \circ \mathbf{cN_{aw_2}^{at_1}} \circ \mathbf{cN_{at_1}^{aw_2}}))$.

4. The fidelity test corresponds to verifying if the qubits associated to $\mathbf{at_1}$ and $\mathbf{bt_1}$ are entangled. This test amounts to checking whether $((\int \mathbf{at_1}) = \frac{1}{2})$ and $((\int(\mathbf{at_1} \Leftrightarrow \mathbf{bt_1})) = 1)$[12] hold. Finally, Alice and Bob obtain the shared key by measuring $\mathbf{ak_1}$ and $\mathbf{bk_1}$ via the following projectors: $\mathbf{P_{ak_1}^{|0\rangle}}$, $\mathbf{P_{ak_1}^{|1\rangle}}$, $\mathbf{P_{bk_1}^{|0\rangle}}$ and $\mathbf{P_{bk_1}^{|1\rangle}}$.

In what concerns the analysis of the protocol, barring the soundness of the fidelity test, there are only two properties to be checked: correctness and perfect security. The protocol is said to be correct if Alice and Bob end up with the same key. The protocol is said to be perfectly secure if: (i) the key is generated with uniform distribution and (ii) the probability of Eve eavesdropping a key

---

[12] In practice, these probabilities are estimated using several projections, but the details of this procedure are out of the scope of this paper. Clearly, here it is essential to have a large n.

of size n without being detected is $O(2^{-n})$. We do not consider (ii) since that depends on proving the soundness of the fidelity test.

Verifying correctness corresponds to checking whether the following formulae are valid:

- $\{IC\}\,\Omega\,(\mathbf{P}_{\mathbf{bk}_1}^{|0\rangle} \circ \mathbf{P}_{\mathbf{ak}_1}^{|0\rangle} \circ Z_3 \circ Z_2 \circ Z_1)$;
- $\{IC\}\,\Omega\,(\mathbf{P}_{\mathbf{bk}_1}^{|1\rangle} \circ \mathbf{P}_{\mathbf{ak}_1}^{|1\rangle} \circ Z_3 \circ Z_2 \circ Z_1)$;
- $\{IC\}\,(\mathbf{P}_{\mathbf{bk}_1}^{|0\rangle} \circ \mathbf{P}_{\mathbf{ak}_1}^{|1\rangle} \circ Z_3 \circ Z_2 \circ Z_1)\,\{\mathbf{fff}\}$;
- $\{IC\}\,(\mathbf{P}_{\mathbf{bk}_1}^{|1\rangle} \circ \mathbf{P}_{\mathbf{ak}_1}^{|0\rangle} \circ Z_3 \circ Z_2 \circ Z_1)\,\{\mathbf{fff}\}$.

The first two formulae assert that the quantum state reached when Alice and Bob obtain the same key is legitimate. The other formulae assert that if Bob and Alice obtain different keys then falsum holds. We sketch how to obtain the validity of the third formula. First, it is easy to see that $\{IC\}\,(Z_3 \circ Z_2 \circ Z_1)\,\{\delta\}$ holds, where $\delta \equiv ([\mathbf{ak}_1, \mathbf{bk}_1]\,\Diamond(\mathbf{ak}_1 \wedge \mathbf{bk}_1) : \frac{1}{\sqrt{2}}, ((\neg\,\mathbf{ak}_1) \wedge (\neg\,\mathbf{bk}_1)) : \frac{1}{\sqrt{2}})$. This happens, because Z_1 entangles $\mathbf{x}_1$ with $\mathbf{x}_2$, Z_2 swaps them with $\mathbf{aw}_1$ and $\mathbf{bw}_1$ and, finally, Z_3 swaps $\mathbf{aw}_1$ with $\mathbf{ak}_1$ and $\mathbf{bw}_1$ with $\mathbf{bk}_1$. Furthermore, by noticing that $\{\delta\}\,\mathbf{P}_{\mathbf{ak}_1}^{|1\rangle}\,\{\mathbf{ak}_1 \wedge \mathbf{bk}_1\}$ and $\{\mathbf{ak}_1 \wedge \mathbf{bk}_1\}\,\mathbf{P}_{\mathbf{bk}_1}^{|0\rangle}\,\{\mathbf{fff}\}$ we reach the desired conclusion.

Finally, note that verifying whether the key is generated with uniform distribution corresponds to checking if $\{IC\}\,(Z_3 \circ Z_2 \circ Z_1)\,\{\delta'\}$ holds where

$$\delta' \equiv ((\textstyle\int \mathbf{ak}_1) = \tfrac{1}{2}) \sqcap ((\textstyle\int(\neg\,\mathbf{ak}_1)) = \tfrac{1}{2}).$$

This validity is straightforward, since $\{IC\}\,(Z_3 \circ Z_2 \circ Z_1)\,\{\delta\}$ and $(\delta \sqsupseteq \delta')$.

6   Concluding Remarks

The key idea of identifying quantum models with superpositions of classical valuations provided us with a working semantics for a powerful quantum logic extending classical and probabilistic logic (like modal logic extends classical logic).

The resulting logic is promising and interesting in itself, but further work is necessary, namely towards a clarification of the relationship to the traditional quantum logics. In this respect it should be stressed that our quantum logic has classical implication capable of internalizing the notion of quantum entailment (both MP and MTD hold), contrarily to traditional quantum logics where the notion of implication is a big problem.

Assessing the effective role of the chosen basis for $\mathcal{H}(V)$ is also an interesting line of research. Indeed, the definition of EQPL satisfaction strongly relies upon using the orthonormal basis $\{|v\rangle : v \in V\}$. One wonders if we can relax the semantics, while preserving the intended entailment, in order to be able to deal with classical formulae when we do not know V but we are just given a Hilbert space isomorphic to $\mathcal{H}(V)$.

Acknowledgments. The authors wish to express their deep gratitude to the regular participants in the QCI Seminar who suffered early presentations of this work and gave very useful feedback that helped us to get over initial difficulties and misunderstandings of quantum physics.

This work was partially supported by FCT and FEDER through POCTI, namely via FibLog 2001/MAT/37239 Project and within the recent QuantLog initiative of CLC.

References

1. Nielsen, M.A., Chuang, I.L.: Quantum Computation and Quantum Information. Cambridge University Press (2000)
2. Foulis, D.J.: A half-century of quantum logic. What have we learned? In: Quantum Structures and the Nature of Reality. Volume 7 of Einstein Meets Magritte. Kluwer Acad. Publ. (1999) 1–36
3. Chiara, M.L.D., Giuntini, R., Greechie, R.: Reasoning in Quantum Theory. Kluwer Academic Publishers (2004)
4. Birkhoff, G., von Neumann, J.: The logic of quantum mechanics. Annals of Mathematics **37** (1936) 823–843
5. Kripke, S.A.: Semantical analysis of modal logic. I. Normal modal propositional calculi. Zeitschrift für Mathematische Logik und Grundlagen der Mathematik **9** (1963) 67–96
6. Carnielli, W.A., Lima-Marques, M.: Society semantics and multiple-valued logics. In: Advances in Contemporary Logic and Computer Science (Salvador, 1996). Volume 235 of Contemporary Mathematics. AMS (1999) 33–52
7. Carnielli, W.A.: Possible-translations semantics for paraconsistent logics. In: Frontiers of Paraconsistent Logic (Ghent, 1997). Volume 8 of Studies in Logic and Computation. Research Studies Press (2000) 149–163
8. Nilsson, N.J.: Probabilistic logic. Artificial Intelligence **28** (1986) 71–87
9. Nilsson, N.J.: Probabilistic logic revisited. Artificial Intelligence **59** (1993) 39–42
10. Bacchus, F.: Representing and Reasoning with Probabilistic Knowledge. MIT Press Series in Artificial Intelligence. MIT Press (1990)
11. Bacchus, F.: On probability distributions over possible worlds. In: Uncertainty in Artificial Intelligence, 4. Volume 9 of Machine Intelligence and Pattern Recognition. North-Holland (1990) 217–226
12. Fagin, R., Halpern, J.Y., Megiddo, N.: A logic for reasoning about probabilities. Information and Computation **87** (1990) 78–128
13. Dishkant, H.: Semantics of the minimal logic of quantum mechanics. Studia Logica **30** (1972) 23–32
14. Hoare, C.: An axiomatic basis for computer programming. Communications of the ACM **12** (1969) 576–583
15. DiVincenzo, D.P.: Two-bit gates are universal for quantum computation. Physics Reviews A **51** (1995) 1015–1022
16. Naur, P.: Revised report on the algorithmic language Algol 60. The Computer Journal **5** (1963) 349–367
17. Bennett, C.H., Brassard, G.: Quantum cryptography: Public key distribution and coin tossing. In: Proceedings of the IEEE International Conference on Computers, Systems and Signal Processing, IEEE (1984) 175–179

Sorted Multi-adjoint Logic Programs: Termination Results and Applications

C.V. Damásio[1], J. Medina[2], and M. Ojeda-Aciego[2]

[1] Centro Inteligência Artificial. Universidade Nova de Lisboa. cd@di.fct.unl.pt[*]
[2] Dept. Matemática Aplicada. Univ. de Málaga. {jmedina,aciego}@ctima.uma.es[**]

Abstract. A general framework of logic programming allowing for the combination of several adjoint lattices of truth-values is presented. The main contribution is a new sufficient condition which guarantees termination of all queries for the fixpoint semantics for an interesting class of programs. Several extensions of these conditions are presented and related to some well-known formalisms for probabilistic logic programming.

1 Introduction

In the recent years there has been an increasing interest in models of reasoning under "imperfect" information. As a result, a number of approaches have been proposed for the so-called inexact or fuzzy or approximate reasoning, involving either fuzzy or annotated or similarity-based or probabilistic logic programming. Several proposals have appeared in the literature for dealing with probabilistic information, namely Hybrid Probabilistic Logic Programs [6], Probabilistic Deductive Databases [8], and Probabilistic Logic Programs with conditional constraints [9].

Residuated and monotonic logic programs [2] and multi-adjoint logic programs [10] were introduced as general frameworks which abstract the particular details of the different approaches cited above and focus only on the computational mechanism of inference. This higher level of abstraction makes possible the development of general results about the behaviour of several of the previously cited approaches.

The main aim of this paper is to focus on some termination properties of the fixed point semantics of a sorted version of multi-adjoint logic programming. In this sorted approach each sort identifies an underlying lattice of truth-values (weights) which must satisfy the adjoint conditions. Although we restrict to the ground case, we allow infinite programs, and thus there is not loss of generality.

The major contribution of this paper is the termination theorems for a general class of sorted multi-adjoint logic programs, complementing results in the literature and enhancing previous results in [1]. Then, we illustrate the application of the termination theorems

---

[*] Partially supported by Acção Integrada Luso-Espanhola E-42/02, by FSE/FEDER project TARDE (POSI/EEI/12097/2001), by European Commission and by the Swiss Federal Office for Education and Science within the 6th Framework Programme project REWERSE number 506779 (cf. http://rewerse.net).
[**] Partially supported by Acción Integrada HP2001-0078, and Spanish MCYT project number TIC2003-09001-C02-01.

to obtain known termination results for some of the previously stated approaches and languages.

The structure of the paper is as follows. In Section 2, we introduce the preliminary concepts necessary for the definition of the syntax and semantics of sorted multi-adjoint logic programs, presented in Section 3. In Section 4, we state the basic results regarding the termination properties of our semantics, which are applied later in probabilistic settings in Section 5. The paper finishes with some conclusions and pointers to future work.

2   Preliminary Definitions

We will make extensive use of the constructions and terminology of universal algebra, in order to define formally the syntax and the semantics of the languages we will deal with. A minimal set of concepts from universal algebra, which will be used in the sequel in the style of [3], is introduced below.

2.1   Some Definitions from Universal Algebra

The notions of signature and Σ-algebra will allow the interpretation of the function and constant symbols in the language, as well as for specifying the syntax.

Definition 1. *A signature is a pair $\Sigma = \langle S, F \rangle$ where S is a set of elements, designated sorts, and F is a collection of pairs $\langle f, s_1 \times \cdots \times s_k \to s \rangle$ denoting functions, such that $s, s_1, \ldots, s_k$ are sorts and no symbol f occurs in two different pairs. The number k is the arity of f; if k is 0 then f is a constant symbol. To simplify notation, we write $f : \tau$ to denote a pair $\langle f, \tau \rangle$ belonging to F.*

Definition 2. *Let $\Sigma = \langle S, F \rangle$ be a signature, a Σ-algebra is a pair $\langle \{A^s\}_{s \in S}, I \rangle$ satisfying the two following conditions:*

1. *Each A^s is a nonempty set called the carrier of sort s,*
2. *and I is a function which assigns a map $I(f) : A^{s_1} \times \cdots \times A^{s_k} \to A^s$ to each $f : s_1 \times \cdots \times s_k \to s \in F$, where $k > 0$, and an element $I(c) \in A^s$ to each constant symbol $c : s$ in F.*

2.2   Multi-adjoint Lattices and Multi-adjoint Algebras

The main concept we will need in this section is that of *adjoint pair*.

Definition 3. *Let $\langle P, \preceq \rangle$ be a partially ordered set and let $(\leftarrow, \&)$ be a pair of binary operations in P such that:*

(a1) *Operation $\&$ is increasing in both arguments*
(a2) *Operation $\leftarrow$ is increasing in the first argument and decreasing in the second argument.*
(a3) *For any $x, y, z \in P$, we have that $x \preceq (y \leftarrow z)$ iff $(x \& z) \preceq y$*

Then $(\leftarrow, \&)$ *is said to form an* adjoint pair *in* $\langle P, \preceq \rangle$.

Extending the results in [2,3,13] to a more general setting, in which different implications (Lukasiewicz, Gödel, product) and thus, several modus ponens-like inference rules are used, naturally leads to considering several *adjoint pairs* in the lattice.

Definition 4. *A multi-adjoint lattice* $\mathcal{L}$ *is a tuple* $(L, \preceq, \leftarrow_1, \&_1, \dots, \leftarrow_n, \&_n)$ *satisfying the following conditions:*

(11) $\langle L, \preceq \rangle$ *is a bounded lattice, i.e. it has bottom* $(\bot)$ *and top* $(\top)$ *elements;*
(12) $(\leftarrow_i, \&_i)$ *is an adjoint pair in* $\langle L, \preceq \rangle$ *for all* i;
(13) $\top \&_i \vartheta = \vartheta \&_i \top = \vartheta$ *for all* $\vartheta \in L$ *for all* i.

Remark 1. Note that residuated lattices are a special case of multi-adjoint lattice, in which the underlying poset has a lattice structure, has monoidal structure wrt $\&$ and $\top$, and only one adjoint pair is present.

From the point of view of expressiveness, it is interesting to allow extra operators to be involved with the operators in the multi-adjoint lattice. The structure which captures this possibility is that of a multi-adjoint algebra.

Definition 5. *A Σ-algebra $\mathfrak{L}$ is a* multi-adjoint Σ-algebra *whenever:*

- *The carrier L^s of each sort is a lattice under a partial order $\preceq^s$.*
- *Each sort s contains operators $\leftarrow_i^s$: $s \times s \to s$ and $\&_i^s$: $s \times s \to s$ for $i = 1, \dots, n^s$ (and possibly some extra operators) such that the tuple $\mathcal{L}^s$*

$$(L^s, \preceq^s, I(\leftarrow_1^s), I(\&_1^s), \dots, I(\leftarrow_n^s), I(\&_n^s))$$

is a multi-adjoint lattice.

Multi-adjoint Σ-algebras can be found underlying the probabilistic deductive databases framework of [8] where our sorts correspond to ways of combining belief and doubt probability intervals. Our framework is richer since we do not restrain ourselves to a single and particular carrier set and allow more operators.

In practice, we will usually have to assume some properties on the extra operators considered. These extra operators will be assumed to be either aggregators, or conjunctors or disjunctors, all of which are monotone functions (the latter, in addition, are required to generalize their Boolean counterparts).

3   Syntax and Semantics of Sorted Multi-adjoint Logic Programs

Sorted multi-adjoint logic programs are constructed from the abstract syntax induced by a multi-adjoint Σ-algebra. Specifically, given an infinite set of sorted propositional symbols Π, we will consider the corresponding term Σ-algebra of formulas[1] $\mathfrak{F} = Terms(\Sigma, \Pi)$. In addition, we will consider a multi-adjoint Σ-algebra $\mathfrak{L}$, whose extra operators can be arbitrary monotone operators, to host the manipulation of the truth-values of the formulas in our programs.

---

[1] Shortly, this corresponds to the algebra freely generated from Π and the set of function symbols in $\mathfrak{L}$, respecting sort assignments.

Remark 2. As we are working with two Σ-algebras, in order to discharge the notation, we introduce a special notation to clarify which algebra a function symbol belongs to. Let σ be a function symbol in Σ, its interpretation under $\mathfrak{L}$ is denoted $\dot{\sigma}$ (a dot on the operator), whereas σ itself will denote its interpretation under $\mathfrak{F}$ when there is no risk of confusion.

3.1 Syntax of Sorted Multi-adjoint Logic Programs

The definition of sorted multi-adjoint logic program is given, as usual, as a set of rules and facts. The particular syntax of these rules and facts is given below:

Definition 6. *A* sorted multi-adjoint logic program *is a set* $\mathbb{P}$ *of rules* $\langle A \leftarrow_i^s B, \vartheta \rangle$ *such that:*

1. *The rule* $(A \leftarrow_i^s B)$ *is a formula (an algebraic term) of* $\mathfrak{F}$;
2. *The weight* ϑ *is an element (a truth-value) of* $\mathcal{L}^s$;
3. *The head of the rule* A *is a propositional symbol of* Π *of sort s.*
4. *The body* B *is a formula of* $\mathfrak{F}$ *with sort s, built from sorted propositional symbols* $B_1, \dots, B_n$ $(n \geq 0)$ *by the use of function symbols in* Σ.

Facts are rules with body $\top^s$, the top element of lattice $\mathcal{L}^s$. A *query* (or *goal*) is a propositional symbol intended as a question $?A$ prompting the system. In order to simplify notation, we alternatively represent a rule $\langle A \leftarrow_i^s B, \vartheta \rangle$ by $A \xleftarrow{\vartheta}_i^s B$.

Sometimes, we will represent bodies of formulas as $@[B_1, \dots, B_n]$, where[2] the B_is are the propositional variables occurring in the body and $@$ is the aggregator obtained as a composition.

3.2 Semantics of Sorted Multi-adjoint Logic Programs

Definition 7. *An* interpretation *is a mapping* $I: \Pi \to \bigcup_s L^s$ *such that for every propositional symbol* p *of sort s then* $I(p) \in L^s$. *The set of all interpretations of the sorted propositions defined by the* Σ-algebra $\mathfrak{F}$ *in the* Σ-algebra $\mathfrak{L}$ *is denoted* $\mathcal{I}_{\mathfrak{L}}$.

Note that by the unique homomorphic extension theorem, each of these interpretations can be uniquely extended to the whole set of formulas $\mathfrak{F}$.

The orderings $\preceq^s$ of the truth-values L^s can be easily extended to the set of interpretations as follows:

Definition 8. *Consider* $I_1, I_2 \in \mathcal{I}_{\mathfrak{L}}$. *Then,* $\langle \mathcal{I}_{\mathfrak{L}}, \sqsubseteq \rangle$ *is a lattice where* $I_1 \sqsubseteq I_2$ *iff* $I_1(p) \preceq^s I_2(p)$ *for all* $p \in \Pi^s$. *The least interpretation* $\triangle$ *maps every propositional symbol of sort s to the least element* $\bot^s \in \mathcal{L}^s$.

A rule of a sorted multi-adjoint logic program is satisfied whenever the truth-value of the rule is greater or equal than the weight associated with the rule. Formally:

---

[2] Note the use of square brackets in this context.

Definition 9. *Given an interpretation $I \in \mathcal{I}_\mathfrak{L}$, a weighted rule $\langle A \leftarrow^s_i B, \vartheta \rangle$ is satisfied by I iff $\vartheta \preceq^s \hat{I}(A \leftarrow^s_i B)$. An interpretation $I \in \mathcal{I}_\mathfrak{L}$ is a model of a sorted multi-adjoint logic program $\mathbb{P}$ iff all weighted rules in $\mathbb{P}$ are satisfied by I.*

Definition 10. *An element $\lambda \in \mathcal{L}^s$ is a correct answer for a program $\mathbb{P}$ and a query $?A$ of sort s if for an arbitrary interpretation I which is a model of $\mathbb{P}$ we have $\lambda \preceq^s I(A)$.*

The immediate consequences operator, given by van Emden and Kowalski, can be easily generalised to the framework of sorted multi-adjoint logic programs.

Definition 11. *Let $\mathbb{P}$ be a sorted multi-adjoint logic program. The immediate consequences operator $T_\mathbb{P}$ maps interpretations to interpretations, and for an interpretation I and an arbitrary propositional symbol A of sort s is defined by*

$$T_\mathbb{P}(I)(A) = \bigsqcup_s \{\vartheta \mathrel{\&}^s_i \hat{I}(B) \mid \langle A \leftarrow^s_i B, \vartheta \rangle \in \mathbb{P}\}$$

where $\bigsqcup_s$ is the least upper bound in the lattice $\mathcal{L}^s$.

The semantics of a sorted multi-adjoint logic program can be characterised, as usual, by the post-fixpoints of $T_\mathbb{P}$; that is, an interpretation I is a model of a sorted multi-adjoint logic program $\mathbb{P}$ iff $T_\mathbb{P}(I) \sqsubseteq I$. The single-sorted $T_\mathbb{P}$ operator is proved to be monotonic and continuous under very general hypotheses, see [10], and it is remarkable that these results are true even for non-commutative and non-associative conjunctors. In particular, by continuity, the least model can be reached in at most countably many iterations of $T_\mathbb{P}$ on the least interpretation. These results immediately extend to the sorted case.

4 Termination Results

In this section we focus on the termination properties of the $T_\mathbb{P}$ operator. In what follows we assume that every function symbol is interpreted as a computable function. If only monotone and continuous operators are present in the underlying sorted multi-adjoint Σ-algebra $\mathfrak{L}$ then the immediate consequences operator reaches the least fixpoint at most after ω iterations. It is not difficult to show examples in which exactly ω iterations may be necessary to reach the least fixpoint.

The termination property we investigate is stated in the following definition, and corresponds to the notion of fixpoint-reachability of Kifer and Subrahmanian [7]:

Definition 12. *Let $\mathbb{P}$ be a sorted multi-adjoint logic program with respect to a multi-adjoint Σ-algebra $\mathfrak{L}$ and a sorted set of propositional symbols Π. We say that $T_\mathbb{P}$ terminates for every query iff for every propositional symbol A there is a finite n such that $T_\mathbb{P}{}^n(\triangle)(A)$ is identical to $lfp(T_\mathbb{P})(A)$.*

In [1] several results were presented in order to provide sufficient conditions guaranteeing that every query can be answered after a finite number of iterations. In particular, this means that for finite programs the least fixpoint of $T_\mathbb{P}$ can also be reached after a *finite* number of iterations, ensuring computability of the semantics. Moreover, a general termination theorem for a wide class of sorted multi-adjoint logic programs, designated programs with finite dependencies, was anticipated.

The notion of dependency graph for sorted multi-adjoint logic programs captures (recursively) the propositional symbols which are necessary to compute the value of a given propositional symbol. The *dependency graph* of $\mathbb{P}$ has a vertex for each propositional symbol in Π, and there is an arc from a propositional symbol A to a propositional symbol B iff A is the head of a rule with body containing an occurrence of B. The dependency graph for a propositional symbol A is the subgraph of the dependency graph containing all the nodes accessible from A and corresponding edges.

Definition 13. *A sorted multi-adjoint logic program $\mathbb{P}$ has* finite dependencies *iff for every propositional symbol A the number of edges in the dependency graph for A is finite.*

The fact that a propositional symbol has finite dependencies gives us some guarantees that we can finitely evaluate its value. However, this is not sufficient since a propositional symbol may depend directly or indirectly on itself, and the $T_\mathbb{P}$ operator might after all produce infinite ascending chains of values for this symbol. The following definition identifies an important class of sorted multi-adjoint logic programs where we can show that these infinite ascending chains cannot occur, and thus ensuring termination.

Definition 14. *A multi-adjoint Σ-algebra is said to be* local *when the following conditions are satisfied:*

- *For every pair of sorts s_1 and s_2 there is a unary monotone casting function symbol $c_{s_1 s_2} : s_2 \to s_1$ in Σ.*
- *All other function symbols have types of the form $f : s \times \cdots \times s \to s$, i.e. are closed operations in each sort, satisfying the following boundary conditions for every $v \in \mathcal{L}^s$:*

$$I(f)(v, \top^s, \ldots, \top^s) \preceq^s v$$
$$I(f)(\top^s, v, \top^s, \ldots, \top^s) \preceq^s v$$
$$\vdots$$
$$I(f)(\top^s, \ldots, \top^s, v) \preceq^s v$$

where $\top^s$ is the top element of $\mathcal{L}^s$. In particular, if f is a unary function symbol then $I(f)(v) \preceq^s v$.
- *The following property is obeyed:*

$$\left(c_{ss_1} \circ c_{s_1 s_2} \circ \ldots \circ c_{s_n s} \right)(v) \preceq^s v$$

for every $v \in \mathcal{L}^s$ and finite composition of casting functions with overall sort $s \to s$.

In local sorted multi-adjoint Σ-algebras the non-casting function symbols are restricted to operations in a unique sort. In order to combine values from different sorts, one is deemed to use explicitly the casting functions in the appropriate places. Furthermore, the connectives are not assumed to be continuous. Even in this case, we are able to state a main termination result about sorted multi-adjoint logic programs:

Theorem 1. *Let* $\mathbb{P}$ *be a sorted multi-adjoint logic program with respect to a local multi-adjoint* Σ-*algebra* $\mathfrak{L}$ *and the set of sorted propositional symbols* Π, *and having finite dependencies.*

If for every iteration n *and propositional symbol* A *of sort* s *the set of relevant values for* A *with respect to* $T_{\mathbb{P}}^n(\triangle)$ *is a singleton, then* $T_{\mathbb{P}}$ *terminates for every query.*

The idea underlying the proof is to use the set of *relevant values* for a propositional symbol A to collect the maximal values contributing to the computation of A in an iteration of the $T_{\mathbb{P}}$ operator, whereas the non-maximal values are irrelevant for determining the new value for A by $T_{\mathbb{P}}$. This is formalized in the following definition:

Definition 15. *Let* $\mathbb{P}$ *be a multi-adjoint program, and* $A \in \Pi^s$.

- *The set* $R_{\mathbb{P}}^I(A)$ *of* relevant values *for* A *with respect to interpretation* I *is the set of maximal values of the set* $\{\vartheta \mathbin{\overset{\bullet}{\&}}{}_i^s \hat{I}(\mathcal{B}) \mid \langle A \leftarrow_i^s \mathcal{B}, \vartheta \rangle \in \mathbb{P}\}$
- *The* culprit set *for* A *with respect to* I *is the set of rules* $\langle A \leftarrow_i^s \mathcal{B}, \vartheta \rangle$ *of* $\mathbb{P}$ *such that* $\vartheta \mathbin{\overset{\bullet}{\&}}{}_i^s \hat{I}(\mathcal{B})$ *belongs to* $R_{\mathbb{P}}^I(A)$. *Rules in a culprit set are called* culprits.
- *The* culprit collection *for* $T_{\mathbb{P}}^n(\triangle)(A)$ *is defined as the set of culprits used in the tree of recursive calls of* $T_{\mathbb{P}}$ *in the computation.*

The proof of the theorem is based on the bounded growth of the culprit collection for $T_{\mathbb{P}}^n(\triangle)(A)$. By induction on n, it will be proved that if we assume $T_{\mathbb{P}}^{n+1}(\triangle)(A) \succ^s T_{\mathbb{P}}^n(\triangle)(A)$ for $A \in \Pi$, then the culprit collection for $T_{\mathbb{P}}^{n+1}(\triangle)(A)$ has cardinality at least $n + 1$. Since the number of rules in the dependency graph for A is finite then the $T_{\mathbb{P}}$ operator must terminate after a finite number of steps, by using all the rules relevant for the computation of A.

As we shall see, Theorem 1 can be used to obtain the Probabilistic Deductive Databases termination theorem [8], since the connectives allowed in rule bodies obey to the boundary conditions. However, the theorem cannot be applied to show termination results of Hybrid Probabilistic Logic Programs (HPLPs) appearing in [5] because operators employed to capture disjunctive probabilistic strategies do not obey to the boundary conditions. For obtaining the termination theorem for HPLPs we require the notion of *range dependency graph*:

Definition 16. *The* range dependency graph *of a sorted multi-adjoint logic program* $\mathbb{P}$ *has a vertex for each propositional symbol in* Π. *There is an arc from a propositional symbol* A *to a propositional symbol* B *iff* A *is the head of a rule with body containing an occurrence of* B *which does not appear in a sub-term with main function symbol having finite image.*

The rationale is to not include arcs of the dependency graph referring to propositional symbols which can only contribute directly or indirectly with finitely many values to the evaluation of the body. For instance, consider the rule $A \leftarrow f(g(A, B), B) \otimes g(f(C)) \otimes D \otimes g(E)$, where f is mapped to a function with infinite range and g corresponds to a function with finite range (i.e. g has finite image). According to the previous definition, we will introduce an arc from A to B and from A to D. The propositional symbol A occurs in the sub-term $g(A, B)$, with finite image, and the same happens with $g(f(C))$

and $g(E)$, and therefore they are excluded from the range dependency graph. The arc to B is introduced because of the second occurrence of B in $f(g(A, B), B)$. The notion of finite dependencies immediately extends to range dependency graphs, but one has to explicitly enforce that for each propositional symbol there are only finitely many rules for it in the program.

Theorem 2. *If $\mathbb{P}$ is a sorted multi-adjoint logic program with acyclic range dependency graph having finite dependencies, then $T_{\mathbb{P}}$ terminates for every query.*

Proof (Sketch). Consider an arbitrary propositional symbol A and the corresponding range dependency subgraph for A. We know that it is both finite and acyclic. It is possible to show that in these conditions only a finite number of values can be produced by the $T_{\mathbb{P}}$ operator, and therefore no infinite ascending chains for the values of A can be generated. This is enough to show the result (see for instance [1]).   □

Corollary 1. *If $\mathbb{P}$ is a sorted multi-adjoint logic program such that all function symbols in the underlying Σ-algebra have finite images, then $T_{\mathbb{P}}$ terminates for every query.*

The proof is immediate since in this case the range dependency graph is empty.

Mark that the conditions of the theorem do not imply that program $\mathbb{P}$ is acyclic. Cyclic dependencies through propositions in finitely ranged function symbols can occur, since these are discarded from the range dependency graph of $\mathbb{P}$. This is enough to show the results for Hybrid Probabilistic Logic Programs.

In order to remove the acyclicity condition from Theorem 2, boundary conditions are again necessary obtaining a new result combining Theorems 1 and 2. Specifically, the termination result can also be obtained if the local multi-adjoint Σ-algebra also contains function symbols $g : s_1 \times \cdots \times s_l \to s_k$ such that their interpretations are isotonic functions with finite range. We call this kind of algebra a *local multi-adjoint Σ-algebra with finite operators.*

Theorem 3. *Let $\mathbb{P}$ be a sorted multi-adjoint logic program with respect to a local multi-adjoint Σ-algebra with finite operators $\mathfrak{L}$ and the set of sorted propositional symbols Π, and having finite dependencies.*

If for all iteration n and propositional symbol A of sort s the set of relevant values for A wrt $T_{\mathbb{P}}^n(\triangle)$ is a singleton, then $T_{\mathbb{P}}$ terminates for every query.

The intuition underlying the proof of this theorem is simply to apply a cardinality argument. However, the formal presentation of the proof requires introducing some technicalities which offer enough control on the increase of the computation tree for a given query.

On the one hand, one needs to handle the number of applications of rules; this is done by using the concept of *culprit collection*, as in Theorem 1. On the other hand, one needs to consider the applications of the finite operators, which are not adequately considered by the culprit collections. With this aim, given a propositional symbol A, let us consider the subset of rules of the program associated to its dependency graph[3], and

---

[3] Mark we are using again the dependency graph, not the range dependency graph.

denote it by $\mathbb{P}^A$. This set is finite, for the program has finite dependencies, so we can write:

$$\mathbb{P}^A = \{\langle H_i \leftarrow \mathcal{B}_i, \vartheta_i\rangle \mid i \in \{1, \ldots, s\}\}$$

In addition, let us write each body of the rules above as follows:

$$\mathcal{B}_i = @_i[g_1^i(\mathcal{D}_1^i), \ldots, g_{k_i}^i(\mathcal{D}_{k_i}^i), C_1^i, \ldots, C_{m_i}^i]$$

where $g_j^i(\mathcal{D}_j^i)$ represents the subtrees corresponding to the outermost occurrences of finite operators, the C_j^i are the propositional symbols which are not in the scope of finite operator, and $@_i$ is the operator obtained after composing all the operators in the body not in the scope of any finite operator.

Now, consider $G(\mathbb{P}^A) = \{g_1^1, \ldots, g_{k_1}^1, \ldots, g_1^s, \ldots, g_{k_s}^s\}$, which is a finite multiset, and let us define the following counting sets for the contribution of the finite operators to the overall computation.

Definition 17. *The counting sets for* $\mathbb{P}$ *and* A *for all* $n \in \mathbb{N}$, *denoted* Ξ_n^A, *are defined as follows:*

$$\Xi_n^A = \{k < n \mid \text{ there is } g_j^i \in G(\mathbb{P}^A) \text{ s.t. } g_j^i(T_{\mathbb{P}}^n(\triangle)(\mathcal{D}_j^i)) > g_j^i(T_{\mathbb{P}}^{n-1}(\triangle)(\mathcal{D}_j^i))\}$$

With this definition we can state the main lemma needed in the proof of Thm 3.

Lemma 1. *Under the hypotheses of Theorem 3, if* $T_{\mathbb{P}}^{n+1}(\triangle)(A) > T_{\mathbb{P}}^n(\triangle)(A)$ *then either* $|\Xi_{n+1}^A| > |\Xi_n^A|$ *or the culprit collection for* $T_{\mathbb{P}}^{n+1}(\triangle)(A)$ *is greater than that for* $T_{\mathbb{P}}^n(\triangle)(A)$.

Proof (of Theorem 3). The previous lemma is the key to the proof:

– Firstly, since the program has finite dependencies there cannot be infinitely many rules in the culprit collections for A.
– On the other hand, the sequence of cardinals $|\Xi_n^A|$ is upper bounded (since the range of each function g_j^i is finite and $G(\mathbb{P}(A))$ is also finite).

As a result we obtain that $T_{\mathbb{P}}$ terminates for every query.   □

In the next section we apply the above results to show the termination theorems for important probabilistic based logic programming frameworks.

5   Termination of Probabilistic Logic Programs

The representation of probabilistic information in rule-based systems has attracted a large interest of the logic programming community, fostered by knowledge representation problems in advanced applications, namely for deductive databases. Several proposals have appeared in the literature for dealing with probabilistic information, namely Hybrid Probabilistic Logic Programs [6], Probabilistic Deductive Databases [8], and Probabilistic Logic Programs with conditional constraints [9]. Both Hybrid Probabilistic Logic Programs, Probabilistic Deductive Databases, and Ordinary Probabilistic Logic

Programs can be captured by Residuated Monotonic Logic Programs, as shown in [4]. We illustrate here the application of the theorems of the previous section to obtain known termination results for these languages. Notice that these results are obtained from the abstract properties of the underlying algebras and transformed programs. In this way we simplify and synthesize the techniques used to show these results, which can be applied in other settings as well.

5.1 Termination of Ordinary Probabilistic Logic Programs

Lukasiewicz [9] introduces a new approach to probabilistic logic programming in which probabilities are defined over a set of possible worlds and in which classical program clauses are extended by a subinterval of $[0, 1]$ that describes a range for the conditional probability of the head of a clause given its body. In its most general form, probabilistic logic programs of [9] are sets of conditional constraints $(H \mid B)[c_1, c_2]$ where H is a conjunction of atoms and B is either a conjunction of atoms or $\top$, and $c_1 \leq c_2$ are rational numbers in the interval $[0, 1]$. These conditional constraints express that the conditional probability of H given B is between c_1 and c_2 or that the probability of the antecedent is 0. A semantics and complexity of reasoning are exhaustively studied, and in most cases is intractable and not truth-functional. However, for a special kind of probabilistic logic programs the author provides relationships to "classical" logic programming. Ordinary probabilistic logic programs are probabilistic logic programs where the conditional constraints have the restricted form

$$(A \mid B_1 \wedge \ldots \wedge B_n)[c, 1] \text{ or } (A \mid \top)[c, 1] \tag{1}$$

Under positively correlated probabilistic interpretations (PCP-interpretations), reasoning becomes tractable and truth-functional. Ordinary conditional constraints (1) of ordinary probabilistic logic programs under PCP-interpretation can be immediately translated to a sorted multi-adjoint logic programming rule

$$A \xleftarrow{c} \min\left(B_1, \ldots, \min(B_{n-1}, B_n)\right)$$

over the multi-adjoint Σ-algebra containing a single sort u signature with carrier $[0, 1]$, with the usual ordering on real numbers. A constant symbol for every element of $[0, 1]$ is necessary, as well as the minimum function (denoted by $\min^u$) and the product of two reals (denoted by $\times^u$), and Goguen implication $\leftarrow^u$. The structure $< [0, 1], \leq, \leftarrow^u, \times^u >$ is a well-known adjoint lattice, where Goguen implication is the residuum of product t-norm. The function symbols $\leftarrow$, $\min$ are interpreted by $\leftarrow^u$ and $\min^u$, respectively. The previous rule can also be represented as:

$$A \xleftarrow{1} c \times \min\left(B_1, \ldots, \min(B_{n-1}, B_n)\right)$$

Clearly, as remarked in [9], the resulting rule is equivalent to a rule of van Emden's Quantitative Deduction [12]. It is pretty clear that in these circumstances all the conditions of Theorem 1 are fulfilled for ground programs of the above form having finite dependencies, and we can guarantee termination of $T_{\mathbb{P}}$ for every query. This is the case because we are using solely t-norms in the body, which by definition obey to the boundary condition, over the unit interval $[0, 1]$. Since the unit interval is totally ordered and we have a finite number of rules for every propositional symbol, we can guarantee that the set of relevant values for $T_P{}^n(\Delta)$ is a singleton. Thus, we obtain a termination result for Ordinary Probabilistic Logic Programs and Quantitative Deduction, extending the one appearing in [12].

In general, if we have combinations of t-norms in the bodies of rules, over totally ordered domains, we can guarantee termination for programs with finite dependencies. This extends the previous results by Paulík [11]. The same applies if we reverse the ordering in the unit interval, and use t-conorms in the bodies. This is necessary to understand the termination result for Probabilistic Deductive Databases, presented in the next section.

5.2 Termination of Probabilistic Deductive Databases

A definition of a theory of probabilistic deductive databases is described in Lakshmanan and Sadri's work [8] where belief and doubt can both be expressed explicitly with equal status. Probabilistic programs (p-programs) are finite sets of triples of the form:

$$\left(A \xleftarrow{c} B_1, \ldots, B_n; \mu_r, \mu_p\right)$$

As usual, $A, B_1, \ldots, B_n$ are atoms, which may not contain complex terms, c is a confidence level, and μ_r (μ_p) is the conjunctive (disjunctive) mode associated with the rule. For a given ground atom A, the disjunctive mode associated with all the rules for A must be the same. The authors present a termination result assuming that it is used solely positive correlation as disjunctive mode for combining several rules in the program, and arbitrary conjunctive modes. The truth-values of p-programs are confidence levels of the form $\langle[\alpha, \beta], [\gamma, \delta]\rangle$, where α, β, γ, and δ are real numbers in the unit interval[4]. The values α and β are, respectively, the expert's lower and upper bounds of belief, while γ and δ are the bounds for the expert's doubt. The fixpoint semantics of p-programs relies on truth-ordering of confidence levels. Suppose $c_1 = \langle[\alpha_1, \beta_1], [\gamma_1, \delta_1]\rangle$ and $c_2 = \langle[\alpha_2, \beta_2], [\gamma_2, \delta_2]\rangle$ are confidence levels, then we say that:

$$c_1 \leq_t c_2 \text{ iff } \alpha_1 \leq \alpha_2, \beta_1 \leq \beta_2 \text{ and } \gamma_1 \geq \gamma_2, \delta_1 \geq \delta_2,$$

with corresponding least upper bound operation $c_1 \oplus_t c_2$ defined as

$$\langle[\max\{\alpha_1, \alpha_2\}, \max\{\beta_1, \beta_2\}], [\min\{\gamma_1, \gamma_2\}, \min\{\delta_1, \delta_2\}]\rangle$$

and greatest lower bound $c_1 \otimes_t c_2$ as:

$$\langle[\min\{\alpha_1, \alpha_2\}, \min\{\beta_1, \beta_2\}], [\max\{\gamma_1, \gamma_2\}, \max\{\delta_1, \delta_2\}]\rangle$$

The least upper bound of truth-ordering corresponds to the disjunctive mode designated "positive correlation", which is used to combine the contributions from several rules for

---

[4] Even though the authors say that they usually assume that $\alpha \leq \beta$ and $\gamma \leq \delta$, this cannot be enforced otherwise they cannot specify properly the notion of trilattice. So, we also not assume these constraints.

a given propositional symbol. We restrict attention to this disjunctive mode, since the termination results presented in [8] assume all the rules adopt this mode. Conjunctive modes are used to combine propositional symbols in the body, and $\otimes_t$ corresponds to the *positive correlation* conjunctive mode. Another conjunctive mode is *independence* with $c_1 \wedge_{ind} c_2$ defined as

$$\langle [\alpha_1 \times \alpha_2, \beta_1 \times \beta_2], [1 - (1 - \gamma_1) \times (1 - \gamma_2), 1 - (1 - \delta_1) \times (1 - \delta_2)] \rangle$$

The attentive reader will surely notice that all these operations work independently in each component of the confidence level. Furthermore, the *independence* conjunctive mode combines the α's and β's with a t-norm (product), and the γ and δ parts are combined with a t-conorm. This is a property enjoyed by all conjunctive modes specified in [8]. In order to show the termination result we require two sorts, both with carrier $[0, 1]$, the first one denoted by m and ordered by $\leq$, while the other is denoted by M and ordered by $\geq$ (this means that for this sort the bottom element is 1 and the top one is 0, least upper bound is min). The program transformation translates each ground atom P in a p-program into four propositional symbols P^α, P^β, P^γ and P^δ, representing each component of the confidence level associated with P. The translation generates four rules, in the resulting sorted multi-adjoint logic programming, from each rule in the p-program. We illustrate this with an example, where the conjunctive mode use is independence (remember that the disjunctive mode is fixed). A p-program rule of the form

$$(A \xleftarrow{\langle [a,b],[c,d] \rangle} B_1, \dots, B_n \; ; \; ind, pc)$$

is encoded as the following four rules:

$$A^\alpha \xleftarrow{a}_m B_1^\alpha \times \dots \times B_n^\alpha \qquad A^\beta \xleftarrow{b}_m B_1^\beta \times \dots \times B_n^\beta$$
$$A^\gamma \xleftarrow{c}_M B_1^\gamma \oplus \dots \oplus B_n^\gamma \qquad A^\delta \xleftarrow{d}_M B_1^\delta \oplus \dots \oplus B_n^\delta$$

The operation $\oplus$ denotes the t-conorm function defined by $v \oplus w = 1 - (1 - v) \times (1 - w)$. Other conjunctive modes can be encoded similarly. The termination of these programs is now immediate. First, the rules for α propositional symbols only involve α propositional symbols in the body. The same applies to the other β, γ and δ rules. The underlying carriers are totally ordered, and the functions symbols in the body obey to the boundary condition since they are either t-norms (for α and β rules) or t-conorms (for γ and δ rules). Thus, from the discussion on the previous section, Theorem 1 is applicable and the result immediately follows for programs with finite dependencies. This is a result shown based solely on general properties of the underlying lattices, not resorting to specific procedural concepts as in [8]. Furthermore, since the grounding of p-programs always results in a finite program, there is no lack of generality by assuming finite dependencies. The use of other disjunctive modes introduce operators in the bodies which no longer obey to the boundary condition. For this case, Lakshmanan and Sadri do not provide any termination result, which is not strange since this violates the general conditions of applicability of Theorem 1.

5.3 Termination of Hybrid Probabilistic Logic Programs

Hybrid Probabilistic Logic Programs [6] have been proposed for constructing rule systems which allow the user to reason with and combine probabilistic information under different probabilistic strategies. The conjunctive (disjunctive) probabilistic strategies are pairwise combinations of t-norms (t-conorms, respectively) over pairs of real numbers in the unit interval $[0, 1]$, i.e. intervals. In order to obtain a residuated lattice, the carrier $\mathcal{INT}$ is the set of pairs $[a, b]$ where a and b are real numbers in the unit interval[5].

The termination results presented in [5] assume finite ground programs. From a difficult analysis of the complex fixpoint construction one can see that only a finite number of different intervals can be generated in the case of finite ground programs. We show how this result can be obtained from Theorem 2 almost directly, given the embedding of Hybrid Probabilistic Logic Programs into Residuated ones presented in [3]. This embedding generates rules of the following kind

$$1. \ F \xleftarrow{[a,b]} s_{\mu_1}\left(\overline{\overline{F_1}}\right) \sqcap \ldots \sqcap s_{\mu_k}\left(\overline{\overline{F_k}}\right) \qquad 3. \ F \xleftarrow{[0,b]} s_{\mu_1}\left(\overline{\overline{E_1}}\right) \sqcap \ldots \sqcap s_{\mu_m}\left(\overline{\overline{E_m}}\right)$$

$$2. \ F \xleftarrow{[a,1]} s_{\mu_1}\left(\overline{\overline{E_1}}\right) \sqcap \ldots \sqcap s_{\mu_m}\left(\overline{\overline{E_m}}\right) \qquad 4. \ F \xleftarrow{[1,0]} c_{\rho}\left(\overline{\overline{G}}, \overline{\overline{H}}\right)$$

resorting to the auxiliary double bar function $\overline{\overline{}}$ from $\mathcal{INT}$ to $\mathcal{INT}$ and the functions $s_\mu : \mathcal{INT} \to \mathcal{INT}$, with μ in $\mathcal{INT}$. For our analysis, it is only important to know that all these functions have finite image, and thus when constructing the range dependency graph no arc will be introduced for rules of the first three types.

The next important detail is that the rules of the fourth type, which use either conjunctive or disjunctive strategies c_ρ, do not introduce any cyclic dependencies and the dependencies are finite. This is the case, because F, G and H are propositional symbols which represent ground hybrid basic formulas (see [6,3] for details), such that $F = G \oplus_\rho H$, i.e. the propositional symbol F represents a more complex formula obtained from the conjunctive or disjunctive combination of the simpler formulas G and H. Therefore, it is not possible to have a dependency from a simpler formula to a more complex one. By application of Theorem 2 it immediately follows that $T_\mathbb{P}$ terminates for every finite ground program, as we intended to show. Just as a side remark, Theorem 3 can also be applied if in the program only occurs conjunctive basic formulas, without requiring any reasoning about the shape of the transformed program and its dependencies.

6   Conclusions

A sorted version of multi-adjoint logic programming has been introduced, together with several general sufficient results about the termination of its fix-point semantics. Later, these results are instantiated in order to prove termination theorems for some probabilistic approaches to logic programming. Notice that these results are obtained solely from the abstract properties of the underlying algebras and transformed programs. In this way we

---

[5] We do not impose that $a \leq b$.

simplify and synthesize the techniques used to show these results, which can be applied in other settings as well.

References

1. C.V. Damásio, J. Medina and M. Ojeda-Aciego. Termination results for sorted multi-adjoint logic programming. In *Information Processing and Management of Uncertainty for Knowledge-Based Systems*, IPMU'04. Accepted.
2. C. V. Damásio and L. M. Pereira. Monotonic and residuated logic programs. Lect. Notes in Artificial Intelligence 2143, pp. 748–759, 2001.
3. C. V. Damásio and L. M. Pereira. Hybrid probabilistic logic programs as residuated logic programs. *Studia Logica*, 72(1):113–138, 2002.
4. C. V. Damásio and L. M. Pereira. Sorted monotonic logic programs and their embeddings. In *Information Processing and Management of Uncertainty for Knowledge-Based Systems*, IPMU'04. Accepted.
5. M. Dekhtyar, A. Dekhtyar and V.S. Subrahmanian. Hybrid Probabilistic Programs: Algorithms and Complexity. Proc. of Uncertainty in AI'99 conference, 1999
6. A. Dekhtyar and V.S. Subrahmanian. Hybrid Probabilistic Programs, *Journal of Logic Programming* 43(3):187–250, 2000
7. M. Kifer and V. S. Subrahmanian, Theory of generalized annotated logic programming and its applications. *J. of Logic Programming* 12(4):335–367, 1992
8. L. Lakhsmanan and F. Sadri, On a theory of probabilistic deductive databases. *Theory and Practice of Logic Programming* 1(1):5–42, 2001
9. T. Lukasiewicz. Probabilistic logic programming with conditional constraints. *ACM Trans. Comput. Log.* 2(3): 289-339 (2001).
10. J. Medina, M. Ojeda-Aciego, and P. Vojtáš. Multi-adjoint logic programming with continuous semantics. Lect. Notes in Artificial Intelligence 2173, pp. 351–364, 2001.
11. L. Paulík. Best possible answer is computable for fuzzy SLD-resolution. Lecture Notes on Logic 6, pp. 257–266, 1996.
12. M. H. van Emden. Quantitative deduction and its fixpoint theory. *Journal of Logic Programming*, 4(1):37–53, 1986.
13. P. Vojtáš. Fuzzy logic programming. *Fuzzy Sets and Systems*, 124(3):361–370, 2001.

The Modal Logic Programming System MProlog

Linh Anh Nguyen

Institute of Informatics, University of Warsaw
ul. Banacha 2, 02-097 Warsaw, Poland
nguyen@mimuw.edu.pl

Abstract. We present the design of our implemented modal logic programming system MProlog. This system is written in Prolog as a module for Prolog. Codes, libraries, and most features of Prolog can be used in MProlog programs. The system contains a number of built-in SLD-resolution calculi for modal logics, including calculi for useful multimodal logics of belief. It is a tool to experiment with applications of modal logic programming to AI.

1   Introduction

Modal logics can be used to reason about knowledge, belief, actions, etc. Many authors have proposed modal extensions for logic programming [4,2,1,5,12,3,9, 10]. There are two approaches: the direct approach and the translational approach. The first approach directly uses modalities, while the second one translates modal logic programs to classical logic programs. The works by Akama [1], Debart et al [5], and Nonnengart [12] use the translational approach, while the works by Fariñas del Cerro [4], Balbiani et al [2], Baldoni et al [3], and our works [9,10] use the direct approach.

In modal logic programming, it seems more intuitive and convenient to use modalities in a direct way[1] (e.g., in the debugging and interactive modes of programming). In the direct approach, the work by Balbiani et al [2] disallows $\Box$ in bodies of program clauses and goals, and the work by Baldoni et al [3] disallows $\Diamond$ in programs and goals. In the Molog system implemented by the group of Fariñas del Cerro [4], universal modal operators in bodies of program clauses and goals are also translated away.

In [9], we developed a fixpoint semantics, the least model semantics, and an SLD-resolution calculus in a direct way for modal logic programs in all of the basic serial[2] monomodal logics. There are two important properties of our approach in [9]: no special restriction on occurrences of $\Box$ and $\Diamond$ is required (programs and goals are of a normal form but the language is as expressive as the general modal Horn fragment) and the semantics are formulated closely to the style of classical logic programming (as in Lloyd's book [8]). In [10], we generalized the methods and extended the results of [9] for multimodal logic programming, giving a general framework for developing semantics of multimodal logic programs

---

[1] Somehow one still has to use skolemization or a labeling technique for $\Diamond$.
[2] A monomodal logic is serial if it contains the axiom $\Box\varphi \rightarrow \Diamond\varphi$.

J.J. Alferes and J. Leite (Eds.): JELIA 2004, LNAI 3229, pp. 266–278, 2004.

and presenting sound and complete SLD-resolution calculi for a number of useful multimodal logics of belief, which will be considered in this work.

Despite that the theory of modal logic programming has been studied in a considerable number of works, it has not received much attention in practice. But if we want to use modal logics for practical applications, then modal logic programming deserves for further investigations, especially in practical issues.

As far as we know, amongst the works by other authors that use the direct approach for modal logic programming, only the Molog system proposed by Fariñas del Cerro [4] has been implemented. The current version of this system has, however, some drawbacks in design. It only says yes or no without giving computed answers. Molog uses a special predicate, named *prolog*, to call formulas of Prolog, which is undesirable when the amount of Prolog code is not small. Molog uses <-- instead of :-, and & instead of ',', which means that Prolog program files cannot be included in Molog programs.

In this work, we present the design of our implemented modal logic programming system MProlog [11], whose theoretical foundations are our work [9,10]. Our system is written in Prolog as a module for Prolog. Codes, libraries, and most features of Prolog can be used in MProlog programs in a pure way. The system contains a number of built-in SLD-resolution calculi for modal logics, including calculi for multimodal logics intended for reasoning about multi-degree belief, for use in distributed systems of belief, or for reasoning about epistemic states of agents in multi-agent systems.

Due to the lack of space, we will not discuss implementation details. The design of MProlog presented here together with comments given in code files [11] is sufficient to understand the implementation of the system. We assume that the reader is familiar with the classical SLD-resolution calculus and Prolog.

2 Preliminaries

2.1 Syntax and Semantics of Quantified Multimodal Logics

A language for quantified multimodal logics is an extension of the language of classical predicate logic with modal operators $\Box_i$ and $\Diamond_i$, for $1 \leq i \leq m$ (where m is fixed). If $m = 1$ then we ignore the subscript i and write $\Box$ and $\Diamond$. The operators $\Box_i$ are called *universal modal operators*, while $\Diamond_i$ are called *existential modal operators*. Terms and formulas are defined in the usual way, with an emphasis that if φ is a formula then $\Box_i \varphi$ and $\Diamond_i \varphi$ are also formulas.

A *Kripke frame* is a tuple $\langle W, \tau, R_1, \ldots, R_m \rangle$, where W is a nonempty set of possible worlds, $\tau \in W$ is the *actual world*, and R_i is a binary relation on W, called the *accessibility relation* for the modal operators $\Box_i$, $\Diamond_i$. If $R_i(w, u)$ holds then we say that the world u is accessible from the world w via R_i.

A *fixed-domain Kripke model with rigid terms*, hereafter simply called a Kripke model or just a model, is a tuple $M = \langle D, W, \tau, R_1, \ldots, R_m, \pi \rangle$, where D is a set called the *domain*, $\langle W, \tau, R_1, \ldots, R_m \rangle$ is a Kripke frame, and π is an interpretation of constant symbols, function symbols and predicate symbols. For a constant symbol a, $\pi(a)$ is an element of D. For an n-ary function symbol f,

$\pi(f)$ is a function from D^n to D. For an n-ary predicate symbol p and a world $w \in W$, $\pi(w)(p)$ is an n-ary relation on D.

A *variable assignment* V w.r.t. a Kripke model M is a function that maps each variable to an element of the domain of M. The value of $t^M[V]$ for a term t is defined as usual.

Given some Kripke model $M = \langle D, W, \tau, R_1, \ldots, R_m, \pi \rangle$, some variable assignment V, and some world $w \in W$, the *satisfaction relation* $M, V, w \vDash \psi$ for a formula ψ is defined as follows:

$$M, V, w \vDash p(t_1, \ldots, t_n) \text{ iff } (t_1^M[V], \ldots, t_n^M[V]) \in \pi(w)(p);$$
$$M, V, w \vDash \Box_i \varphi \qquad \text{iff for all } v \in W \text{ such that } R_i(w, v), M, V, v \vDash \varphi;$$
$$M, V, w \vDash \forall x.\varphi \qquad \text{iff for all } a \in D, (M, V', w \vDash \varphi),$$
$$\text{where } V'(x) = a \text{ and } V'(y) = V(y) \text{ for } y \neq x;$$

and as usual for other cases (treating $\Diamond_i \varphi$ as $\neg \Box_i \neg \varphi$, and $\exists x.\varphi$ as $\neg \forall x. \neg \varphi$). We say that M satisfies φ, or φ is true in M, and write $M \vDash \varphi$, if $M, V, \tau \vDash \varphi$ for every V. For a set Γ of formulas, we call M a model of Γ and write $M \vDash \Gamma$ if $M \vDash \varphi$ for every $\varphi \in \Gamma$.

2.2   Modal Logics of Belief

If as the class of admissible interpretations we take the class of all Kripke models (with no restrictions on the accessibility relations) then we obtain a quantified multimodal logic which has a standard Hilbert-style axiomatization denoted by $K_{(m)}$. Normal modal logics are extensions of $K_{(m)}$ using additional axioms. A modal logic L is *serial* if it contains the axiom $\Box_i \varphi \rightarrow \neg \Box_i \neg \varphi$ (for all $1 \leq i \leq m$). To reflect properties of belief, one can extend $K_{(m)}$ with some of the following axioms (see [10] for the corresponding restrictions on the accessibility relations and [6,7] for further readings on first-order modal logics):

Name	Schema	Meaning
(D)	$\Box_i \varphi \rightarrow \neg \Box_i \neg \varphi$	belief is consistent
(I)	$\Box_i \varphi \rightarrow \Box_j \varphi$ if $i > j$	subscript indicates degree of belief
(4)	$\Box_i \varphi \rightarrow \Box_i \Box_i \varphi$	belief satisfies positive introspection
(4_s)	$\Box_i \varphi \rightarrow \Box_j \Box_i \varphi$	belief satisfies strong positive introspection
(5)	$\neg \Box_i \varphi \rightarrow \Box_i \neg \Box_i \varphi$	belief satisfies negative introspection
(5_s)	$\neg \Box_i \varphi \rightarrow \Box_j \neg \Box_i \varphi$	belief satisfies strong negative introspection

By adding appropriate combinations of these axioms to $K_{(m)}$, we obtain the modal logics $KDI4$, $KDI4_s$, $KDI45$, $KDI4_s5$ for reasoning about multi-degree belief, the modal logic $KD4_s5_s$ for use in distributed systems of belief, and the modal logic $KD45_{(m)}$ for reasoning about epistemic states of agents in multi-agent systems. (We use a subscript in $KD45_{(m)}$ to distinguish it from the monomodal logic $KD45$.) In the mentioned modal logics of multi-degree belief, the axiom (I) gives $\Box_i \varphi$ the meaning "φ is believed up to degree i"; while in the logics $KD4_s5_s$ and $KD45_{(m)}$, the formula $\Box_i \varphi$ means "the agent i believes in φ". For reasoning about belief and common belief of groups of agents, there is a multimodal logic denoted by $KD4I_g5_a$ which combines features of $KD45_{(m)}$ and $KDI4$. For further descriptions of the mentioned logics, see [10].

2.3   Modal Logic Programs

In this subsection, we define a modal logic programming language called MProlog, which is a purely logical formalism. Its implementation as an extension of Prolog has a specific syntax and will be studied in Section 4.

A *modality* is a (possibly empty) sequence of modal operators. A *universal modality* is a modality which contains only universal modal operators. We use $\triangle$ to denote a modality and $\boxdot$ to denote a universal modality. Similarly as in classical logic programming, we use a clausal form $\boxdot(\varphi \leftarrow \psi_1, \ldots, \psi_n)$ to denote the formula $\forall(\boxdot(\varphi \vee \neg\psi_1 \ldots \vee \neg\psi_n))$. We use E to denote a classical atom and $A, B_1, \ldots, B_n$ to denote formulas of the form E, $\Box_i E$, or $\Diamond_i E$.

A *program clause* is a formula of the form $\boxdot(A \leftarrow B_1, \ldots, B_n)$, where $\boxdot$ is a universal modality and $n \geq 0$. $\boxdot$ is called the *modal context*, A the *head*, and $B_1, \ldots, B_n$ the *body* of the program clause.

An *MProlog program* is a finite set of program clauses. An *MProlog goal atom* is a formula of the form $\boxdot E$ or $\boxdot \Diamond_i E$, where $\boxdot$ is a universal modality. An *MProlog goal* is a formula written in the clausal form $\leftarrow \alpha_1, \ldots, \alpha_k$, where each α_i is an MProlog goal atom.

It is shown in [10] that MProlog has the same expressiveness power as the general Horn fragment in normal modal logics. For a specific logic L, we may adopt some restrictions on modal contexts of MProlog program clauses and MProlog goals and call the obtained language L-*MProlog*. Such restrictions either follow from equivalencies in L or are acceptable from the practical of view, and furthermore, they do not reduce expressiveness of the language.

For example, in $KDI4_s5$ we have the equivalence $\nabla\nabla'\varphi \equiv \nabla'\varphi$, where ∇ and ∇' are modal operators. Hence we can assume that the modal context of an $KDI4_s5$-*MProlog program clause* has length 1 or 0, and an $KDI4_s5$-*MProlog goal* has goal atoms of the form E, $\Box_i E$, or $\Diamond_i E$ with E being a classical atom. See [10] for restrictions of L-MProlog in the other modal logics of belief.

3   A Framework of SLD-Resolution for MProlog

In [10], we give a general framework for developing fixpoint semantics, least model semantics, and SLD-resolution calculi for L-MProlog, where L is a serial modal logic whose frame restrictions, except seriality, are Horn clauses (in particular, L can be any one of the modal logics of belief considered in this paper). In this section, we outline the fragment involving SLD-resolution of that framework. For fixpoint semantics, the reader is referred to [10].

A modal operator is now $\Box_i$, $\Diamond_j$, or $\langle S \rangle_k$, where $\langle S \rangle_k$ is a $\Diamond_k$ labeled by S which is either a classical atom or a variable for classical atoms (called an *atom variable*). For further information on labeled modal operators, see [10].

We use ∇ and ∇' to denote modal operators, $\triangle$ to denote a modality (which now may contain labeled modal operators). A *modal atom* is a formula of the form $\triangle E$. A *simple modal atom* is a formula of the form E or ∇E. We use A, B to denote simple modal atoms, and α, β to denote modal atoms.

There may exist a compact form for modalities in L. For each specific modal logic L, we define the *L-normal form of modalities*. For example, a modality is in $KDI4_s5$-normal form if its length is 0 or 1. It is possible that no restriction is adopted for L-normal form of modalities. A modality is in *L-normal labeled form* if it is in L-normal form and does not contain unlabeled existential modal operators $\Diamond_i$. A modal atom $\triangle E$ is in L-normal (labeled) form if $\triangle$ is in L-normal (labeled) form. Given a ground modal atom not in L-normal form, the NF_L *operator* converts it to L-normal form.

Given a modal atom α, one can derive other modal atoms from α using axioms of L. The corresponding operator is called the Sat_L operator. The "direct consequences" operator $T_{L,P}$ is defined using Sat_L and NF_L. An SLD-resolution calculus can be viewed as a reversed analogue of a direct consequences operator. Hence, to define an SLD-resolution calculus for L-MProlog we need reversed analogues of the operators Sat_L and NF_L. These operators are called the $rSat_L$ *operator* and the rNF_L *operator*, respectively. See [10,9] for formal definitions of the operators Sat_L, NF_L, $rSat_L$, and rNF_L.

The $rSat_L/rNF_L$ operators are each specified by a finite set of rules of the form $\alpha \leftarrow \beta$, where α and β are (schemata of) modal atoms. The rules are used as meta-clauses (i.e. schemata of clauses) in SLD-derivations. Such rules can be accompanied by conditions which specify when the rule can be used.

As an example, for $L = KDI4_s5$, the rNF_L operator is specified by the only rule $\nabla E \leftarrow \langle X \rangle_i \nabla E$, and the $rSat_L$ operator is specified by three rules: (a) $\nabla \nabla' E \leftarrow \nabla' E$, (b) $\Diamond_i E \leftarrow \Diamond_j E$ if $i > j$, (c) $\Diamond_i E \leftarrow \langle X \rangle_i E$; where X is a fresh[3] atom variable. We will use these rules for the example in the next page.

Resolvents of a goal $\leftarrow \alpha_1, \ldots, \alpha_k$ and an $rSat_L/rNF_L$ rule $\alpha \leftarrow \beta$ are defined in the usual way. For example, resolving $\leftarrow \Box_1 \Diamond_2 p(x)$ with the rule $\nabla \nabla' E \leftarrow \nabla' E$ results in $\leftarrow \Diamond_2 p(x)$, since ∇ is instantiated to $\Box_1$, and ∇' is instantiated to $\Diamond_2$.

For each specific modal logic L, we define a pre-order $\preceq_L$ to compare modal operators. For example, for $L = KDI4_s5$, the pre-order $\preceq_L$ is the least reflexive and transitive binary relation between modal operators such that: $\Diamond_i \preceq_L \langle S \rangle_i \preceq_L \Box_i$, and if $i < j$ then $\Box_i \preceq_L \Box_j$ and $\Diamond_j \preceq_L \Diamond_i$. If $\nabla \preceq_L \nabla'$ then we say that ∇ is an *L-instance* of ∇'. We say that an atom $\triangle E$ is an *L-instance* of $\triangle' E'$ if $\triangle$ and $\triangle'$ have the same length k and there exists a substitution θ such that $E = E'\theta$ and for any $1 \leq i \leq k$, the modal operator in position i of $\triangle$ is an L-instance of the modal operator in position i of $\triangle'\theta$.

The *forward labeled form* of an atom α is the atom α' such that if α is of the form $\triangle \Diamond_i E$ then $\alpha' = \triangle \langle E \rangle_i E$, else $\alpha' = \alpha$. For example, the forward labeled form of $\Diamond_1 s(a)$ is $\langle s(a) \rangle_1 s(a)$.

If $\boxdot$ and $\boxdot'$ are universal modalities, and furthermore, $\boxdot$ is a modal context of an L-MProlog program clause, then we say that $\boxdot'$ is an *L-context instance* of $\boxdot$ if $\boxdot \varphi \rightarrow \boxdot' \varphi$ is a theorem in L for an arbitrary φ. For example, $\Box_1$ is a $KDI4_s5$-context instance of $\Box_2$.

---

[3] This means that *standardizing* is also needed for atom variables.

Let $G = \leftarrow \alpha_1, \ldots, \alpha_i, \ldots, \alpha_k$ be a goal and $\varphi = \boxdot(A \leftarrow B_1, \ldots, B_n)$ a program clause. Then G' is *derived* from G and φ in L using mgu θ, and called an *L-resolvent* of G and φ, if the following conditions hold:

- $\alpha_i = \triangle' A'$, with $\triangle'$ in L-normal labeled form, is called the *selected atom*.
- $\triangle'$ is an L-instance of $\boxdot'$ which is an L-context instance of $\boxdot$.
- θ is an mgu such that: $A'\theta$ has the same classical atom as $A\theta$, and $A'\theta$ is an L-instance of the forward labeled form of $A\theta$.
- G' is the goal $\leftarrow (\alpha_1, \ldots, \alpha_{i-1}, \triangle'B_1, \ldots, \triangle'B_n, \alpha_{i+1}, \ldots, \alpha_k)\theta$.

For example, the unique $KDI4_s5$-resolvent of $\leftarrow \Box_1 p(x)$ and $\Box_2(p(x) \leftarrow \Diamond_2 q(x))$ is $\leftarrow \Box_1 \Diamond_2 q(x)$ (here, $\boxdot = \Box_2$ and $\triangle' = \boxdot' = \Box_1$). As another example, the unique $KDI4_s5$-resolvent of $\leftarrow \langle Y \rangle_1 \langle X \rangle_1 r(x), \langle X \rangle_1 s(x)$ and $\Box_1(\Box_1 r(x) \leftarrow s(x))$ is $\leftarrow \langle Y \rangle_1 s(x), \langle X \rangle_1 s(x)$ (here, $\boxdot = \Box_1$ and $\triangle' = \boxdot' = \langle Y \rangle_1$).

SLD-derivation is defined using two kinds of steps: a) resolving a goal with a program clause, b) resolving a goal with an $rSat_L/rNF_L$ rule. SLD-refutation and computed answer are defined in the usual way.

Using the framework, in [10] we have given sound and complete SLD-resolution calculi for L-MProlog for all the modal logics of belief considered in this work.

As an example, consider the goal $G = \leftarrow \Box_1 p(x)$ and the program P:

$$\varphi_1 = \Box_2(p(x) \leftarrow \Diamond_2 q(x))$$
$$\varphi_2 = \Box_1(q(x) \leftarrow r(x), s(x))$$
$$\varphi_3 = \Box_1(\Box_1 r(x) \leftarrow s(x))$$
$$\varphi_4 = \Diamond_1 s(a) \leftarrow$$

Here is an SLD-refutation of $P \cup \{G\}$ in $L = KDI4_s5$:

Goals	Input clauses/rules	MGUs
$\leftarrow \Box_1 p(x)$		
$\leftarrow \Box_1 \Diamond_2 q(x)$	φ_1	$\{x_1/x\}$
$\leftarrow \Diamond_2 q(x)$	$rSat_L(a)$	
$\leftarrow \Diamond_1 q(x)$	$rSat_L(b)$	
$\leftarrow \langle X \rangle_1 q(x)$	$rSat_L(c)$	
$\leftarrow \langle X \rangle_1 r(x), \langle X \rangle_1 s(x)$	φ_2	$\{x_5/x\}$
$\leftarrow \langle Y \rangle_1 \langle X \rangle_1 r(x), \langle X \rangle_1 s(x)$	rNF_L	
$\leftarrow \langle Y \rangle_1 s(x), \langle X \rangle_1 s(x)$	φ_3	$\{x_7/x\}$
$\leftarrow \langle X \rangle_1 s(a)$	φ_4	$\{x/a, Y/s(a)\}$
empty clause	φ_4	$\{X/s(a)\}$

4   Design of MProlog

Starting from the purely logical formalism of MProlog, we have built a real system for it [11]. The implemented system adds extra features to the purely logical formalism in order to increase usefulness of the language. It is written in Prolog and can run in SICStus Prolog and SWI-Prolog. From now on we use MProlog to refer to the implemented system.

MProlog is designed as an extension of Prolog. This means that we can use Prolog codes, libraries and most features of Prolog in MProlog programs. This gives MProlog capabilities for real applications. MProlog is implemented as a module for Prolog and does not have its own running environment. It provides instead a list of built-in predicates to be used in Prolog.

4.1   Syntax of MProlog Programs

In MProlog, there are three kinds of predicates: classical predicates, modal predicates, and classical predicates which are defined using modal formulas. Predicates of the last kind are called *dum* predicates. The semantics of classical predicates and *dum* predicates does not depend on worlds in Kripke models. If E is a classical atom of a classical predicate or a *dum* predicate then $\triangle E \equiv E$ for every modality $\triangle$. An MProlog program consists of *modal fragments* and *classical fragments* (in an arbitrary number and order). Predicates defined in classical fragments are *classical predicates*. *Dum predicates* are declared in an MProlog program as follows

:- *dum_pred* $Pred_1$, . . . , $Pred_n$.

where each $Pred_i$ is a pair $Name_i/Arity_i$. *Dum* predicates are defined in modal fragments by clauses of the form E :- *Body*, where E is a classical atom. A predicate defined in a modal fragment and not declared earlier as a *dum* predicate is a *modal predicate*.

From now on, by a *calculus* we mean an SLD-resolution calculus for MProlog. An MProlog program may use different calculi, as explained in Section 5. In an MProlog program, a modal fragment starts with a declaration of the form:

:- *calculus* Cal_1, . . . , Cal_n.

where Cal_1, . . . , Cal_n are names of calculi. These calculi are called the *calculi of the fragment*. If an MProlog program is loaded by *mconsult(File,Cal)* then the program in *File* is treated as if it begins with

:- *calculus Cal*.

A modal fragment ends either by a declaration of another modal fragment, or by the end of the program, or by one of the two following declarations:

:- *calculus classical*.

:- *end*.

In MProlog, modalities are represented as lists, e.g., as follows:

$\Box\Diamond q(x,y)$	$[b,d] : q(X,Y)$
$\Box_i\langle X\rangle_3\Diamond_j q(a)$	$[bel(I), pos(3,X), pos(J)] : q(a)$
$\Box_x god\_exists \leftarrow christian(x)$	$[bel(X)] : god\_exists :- christian(X)$

Here, b stands for "box", d for "diamond", *bel* for "believes", and *pos* for "possible". We use $\triangle : \varphi$ to represent $\triangle\varphi$. Notations of modal operators depend on how the base SLD-resolution calculus is defined. As another example, for MProlog-$\Box$ [10], which disallows existential modal operators in program clauses and goals, we represent $\Box_{i_1} \ldots \Box_{i_k}$ as $[I1, \ldots, Ik]$ (see *belief_box.cal* of [11]).

Syntactically, an MProlog program is a Prolog program. Modal fragments in an MProlog program may contain directives and clauses. Each clause in a modal fragment is of one of the following forms:

> *Context : (Head :- Body).*
>
> *Head :- Body.*

where *Context* is a list representing a modality, *Head* is of the form E or $M : E$, where E is a classical atom (in the sense of Prolog) and M is a list containing one modal operator. All clauses in a modal fragment are *declared* to all of the calculi of the fragment.

4.2   Syntax of SLD-Resolution Calculi for MProlog

SLD-resolution calculi for MProlog are specified using the framework given in Section 3 and written in Prolog. An SLD-resolution calculus for L contains $rSat_L/rNF_L$ rules, definitions of auxiliary predicates, and definitions for the following required predicates:

1. *universal_modal_operator(Calculus, Operator)*
2. *dual_modal_operator(Calculus, Operator, DualOperator)*
3. *box_lifting_form(Calculus, ModalOperator, BoxLiftingForm)*
   which returns true iff *BoxLiftingForm* is the universal modal operator of the same modal index as *ModalOperator* in the calculus *Calculus*
4. *forward_labeled_form(Calculus, SimpleModalAtom, ForwardLabeledF)*
5. *normal_labeled_form(Calculus, Modality)*
6. *operator_instance(Calculus, Instance, ModalOperator)*
7. *context_instance(Calculus, UniversalModality, ModalContext)*

If the option *check_in_two_steps* of the defined calculus is set to *true*, then instead of the last three predicates of the above list, the calculus must implement two predicates with name prefixed by *pre_check_* or *post_check_* for each of the replaced predicates.

Let us discuss the usefulness of the *check_in_two_steps* option. Suppose that we want to reason about multi-degree belief. We represent, e.g., $\Box_i(p(x) \leftarrow q(x))$ by [bel(I)]: (p(X) :- q(X)). Thus we use variables like I for degrees of belief. Sometimes it is better to delay instantiating such variables to concrete values in order to eliminate branching. If we want to allow users to have ability to turn on/off this option of delaying, then the defined calculus should be designed with the *check_in_two_steps* option turned on. The intention of *pre_check* predicates is to check the involved condition as much as possible without generating branch points and to pass unchecked fragments of the condition to *post_check* predicates, which will be fired latter. In Section 5, we will describe the functioning of those predicates in the MProlog interpreter.

A *resolution cycle* is a derivation consisting of a sequence of applications of $rSat_L/rNF_L$ rules and an application of a program clause. To create an ability to reduce nondeterminism, we provide 4 categories (kinds) of rules: *pre_rSat*, *rSat*, *post_rSat*, and *rNF*. Informally, operators *pre_rSat* and *post_rSat* are deterministic, while operators *rSat* and *rNF* are nondeterministic. This means that when the system tries to resolve a modal atom using an operator of the category *pre_rSat* or *post_rSat*, the first applicable rule of the category will be used, and when the system wants to use *rSat* (resp. *rNF*), different sequences of *rSat* rules (resp. *rNF* rules) will be tried. Lengths of such sequences of *rSat* rules (resp. *rNF* rules) are restricted by the option *limit_rSat* (resp. *limit_rNF*) of the calculus.

Rules of the mentioned categories are of one of the following forms:

AtomIn :- PreCondition, AtomOut, PostComputation.

RuleName :: (AtomIn :- PreCondition, AtomOut, PostComputation).

AtomIn and *AtomOut* are atoms of the form $M : E$, where M (standing for a modality) and E (standing for a classical atom) may be variables in Prolog, and M may be also a list. *RuleName* is a name in Prolog. *PreCondition* and *PostComputation* are (possibly empty) sequences of formulas in Prolog separated by ','. *AtomOut* is called the *atom out* of the rule. It is the first outer (w.r.t. ',') atom of the form $M : E$ of the body of the rule. Names of rules are unique. If a rule is declared without a name, it will be given a unique name by the system. We give below an example rule, a version of : $\Diamond_i E \leftarrow \Diamond_j E$ if $i > j$.

```
rSatKDI4s5 :: ( [pos(I)]:E :-
    get_calling_history(rSat, Cal, _, RNames),
    \+ memberchk(rSatKDI4s5, RNames), % not called before
    pre_compare_deg(Cal, I > J), [pos(J)]:E, post_compare_deg(Cal, I > J)).
```

As shown in the above example, designers of calculi have access to the history of rules called in the current resolution cycle. Such a history for a given category of rules is obtained by

get_calling_history(RuleCategory, Calculus, CalledAtom, RuleNames)

where the last three arguments are outputs. *RuleNames* is the list of names of rules of the category *RuleCategory* which have been applied, in the reverse order, in the current resolution cycle for the beginning atom *CalledAtom* .

Syntactically, rules are clauses in Prolog. They are *defined* as usual clauses. Rules are *declared* to calculi either by a *section of rules* or by a directive. A section of rules is a list of (definitions of) rules bounded by directives. A directive opening a section of rules is of the following form:

:- RuleCategory Cal$_1$, . . . , Cal$_n$.

where *RuleCategory* is one of *pre_rSat, rSat, post_rSat, rNF*; and $Cal_1, \ldots, Cal_n$ are names of calculi, to which the rules in the section are declared. A section of rules is closed by any directive in Prolog or by the end of the main file. Rules of the same category can also be declared to a calculus using a directive of the following form:

:- set_list_of_mrules(Calculus, RuleCategory, ListOfRuleNames).

Some options are automatically created with default values for each loaded calculus. A definition of a calculus can change values of those options using *set_option(Option, Calculus, Value)* and set new options for itself (e.g., a numeric option like *max_modal_index* is needed for modal logics of multi-degree belief).

4.3   Options and Built-In Predicates of MProlog

Before listing built-in predicates of MProlog, we give a list of options of MProlog, which may affect the way the system interprets MProlog programs. There are two kinds of options: options for calculi, and options for the system. Setting values of options is done by the following predicates:

  set_option(OptionName, Calculus, Value)

  set_option(OptionName, Value)

There are the following built-in options for calculi: *limit_modality_length* (default: 4), *limit_rSat* (default: 3), *limit_rNF* (default: 1), *use_calling_history* (default: false), *check_in_two_steps* (default: false). The *limit_modality_length* option is used to restrict lengths of modalities that may appear in derivations. The options *limit_rSat* and *limit_rNF* have been described in the previous subsection. For some built-in calculi, those numeric limits are firmly set, as they follow from the nature of the base modal logic. In general, they are used to restrict the search space and may affect completeness of the calculus. The boolean option *use_calling_history* should be turned on if rules of the calculus use the history of rules called in the current resolution cycle. The boolean option *check_in_two_steps* has been discussed in the previous subsection.

The boolean option *loop_checking* is a useful option of the system. If it is turned on, the MProlog interpreter will check whether the current modal atom to be resolved has already appeared in the current derivation in order to prevent infinite loops. There are also other options of the system: *loop_checking_stack_size* (default: 300), *random_selection_of_rules* (default: false), *debug* (default: false), *current_calculus* (default: classical), and *priority_list_of_calculi* (default not set).

There are three groups of built-in predicates which are useful for users: main predicates (for consulting, calling, and tracing), predicates for getting and displaying the status of the system, and predicates for dynamic modification of programs. We list here only main predicates of the system[4]:

  consult_calculi(Files),

  mconsult(ProgramFile, Calculus),   *mconsult(ProgramFile),*

  mcall(Goal, Calculus),   *mcall(Goal),*

  mtrace,   *nomtrace.*

Our MProlog module can be loaded by consulting the file "mprolog.pl" of the package. The user can then load SLD-resolution calculi for modal logics using the predicate *consult_calculi*, whose argument may be a file name or a list of file names. The user can consult MProlog programs using the predicate *mconsult/2* (see Section 4.1 for the meaning of the second argument). *mconsult(ProgramFile)* is treated as *mconsult(ProgramFile, classical)*. Goals involved with modal logics can be asked using the predicate *mcall/2*, where the second argument indicates the calculus in which the goal is asked. If a default calculus is set using the *current_calculus* option, then *mcall/1* can be used instead of *mcall/2*. The predicates *mtrace* and *nomtrace* are used to turn on and off the trace mode for MProlog (which concentrates on modal formulas and is not the trace mode of Prolog).

---

[4] See [11] for predicates of the remaining groups.

5   The MProlog Interpreter

The MProlog interpreter is realized by the predicate *mcall(Goal, Calculus)*, which initiates some variables and then calls *mcall_ (Goal, Calculus)*. In this section, we describe in detail the latter predicate, ignoring some aspects like loop checking, updating the history of called rules, or effects of options.

The predicate of the argument *Goal* belongs to one of the following groups: control predicates[5] (\+, ';', ',', ->, if/3), classical predicates, *dum* predicates, and modal predicates.

If *Goal* is an atom of a classical predicate, then *mcall_ (Goal,_)* is defined as *Goal* itself. Formulas *PreCondition* and *PostComputation* from a rule *Head :- PreCondition, AtomOut, PostComputation* are treated as atoms of classical predicates, despite that they may be complicated formulas.

Because *dum* predicates can be defined in different calculi and their semantics does not depend on worlds in Kripke models, they can be used to mix different calculi. If *Goal* is an atom of a *dum* predicate then to resolve *mcall_ (Goal, Calculus)*, the interpreter will try to resolve *Goal* first in *Calculus* and then in different calculi as well. The list of those latter calculi is determined by the value of the *priority_list_of_calculi* option if it is set, and by the list of all calculi otherwise; both cases exclude *Calculus* (the argument). Resolving *Goal* of a *dum* predicate in a calculus *Cal* is done as follows: select a modal clause *Head :- Body* of *Cal*, unify *Goal* with *Head*, and then call *mcall_ (Body, Cal)*.

For the case of modal atoms, we first discuss some auxiliary predicates.

Resolving a modal atom *Goal* with a rule
        Head :- PreCondition, AtomOut, PostComputation
is done by unifying *Goal* with *Head*, executing *PreCondition*, and returning *AtomOut* and *PostComputation* as outputs. This task is done by the predicate
        solve_using_mrule(Cal, Cat, RName, AtomIn, AtomOut, PostComputation)
with *AtomIn = Goal* and *Cal, Cat, RName* being respectively the calculus, the category, and the name of the rule.

Resolving a modal atom *Goal* using a sequence of rules is done by calling the above described predicate *solve_using_mrule* for each rule of the sequence, where *AtomIn* of the first call of *solve_using_mrule* is *Goal*, and *AtomIn* of each one of the next calls is *AtomOut* of the previous call. As outputs, it returns *AtomOut* of the last call of *solve_using_mrule* and the composition (using ',' and the reverse order) of the obtained *PostComputation* formulas. If the sequence of rules is empty then the outputs are *Goal* and *true*.

To resolve a modal atom *Goal* using rules of a calculus *Cal* that belong to a category *Cat*, the interpreter searches for a sequence of rules to be used using the following strategy: if the rule category is *pre_rSat* or *post_rSat* then the sequence consists of only the first applicable rule – if there exists, or is empty – otherwise; if the rule category is *rSat* or *rNF* then different sequences of rules will be tried, where short sequences have higher priorities. Having a sequence of rules, the interpreter applies it to *Goal* as described in the previous paragraph. The task

---

[5] From now on, we distinguish control predicates from classical predicates.

is done by the predicate

  solve_using_mrules(Cal, Cat, Goal, AtomOut, PostComputation),

where *AtomOut* and *PostComputation* are outputs.

Resolving a modal atom *Goal* with a modal clause in *Calculus* is done according to the framework of SLD-resolution for MProlog, using the required predicates of *Calculus* in an appropriate way. The task is done by the predicate

  solve_using_mclauses(Calculus, Goal).

Now return to the problem of resolving *mcall_ (Goal, Calculus)* for the case when *Goal* is a modal atom. It is done by executing the following statements

  solve_using_mrules(Calculus, pre_rSat, Goal, A2, F2),
  solve_using_mrules(Calculus, rSat, A2, A3, F3),
  solve_using_mrules(Calculus, post_rSat, A3, A4, F4),
  solve_using_mrules(Calculus, rNF, A4, A5, F5),
  solve_using_mclauses(Calculus, A5),
  F5, F4, F3, F2.

It remains to discuss the interpretation of the control predicates. In the current version of MProlog, we just adopt the following solution, which does not have a logical basis:

```
mcall_(M:(F1,F2), Cal) :- !, mcall_(M:F1, Cal), mcall_(M:F2, Cal).
mcall_(M:(F1;F2), Cal) :- !, mcall_(M:F1, Cal); mcall_(M:F2, Cal).
mcall_(M:(\+ F), Cal) :- !,
    make_dual_modality(Cal, M, M2), \+ mcall_(M2:F, Cal).
mcall_(M:(F1 -> F2), Cal) :- mcall_(M:F1, Cal)->mcall_(M:F2, Cal).
mcall_(M:if(F1, F2, F3), Cal) :- !,
    call(F1) -> mcall_(M:F2, Cal); mcall_(M:F3, Cal).
```

The interpretation for the case of $M : (F1, F2)$ is sound and complete if M is a modality in labeled form (i.e. M does not contain unlabeled existential modal operators). The interpretation for the case of $M : (F1; F2)$ is also sound.

6   Conclusions

This work presents a new design for modal logic programming. We have designed MProlog to obtain high usefulness, effectiveness, and flexibility. For usefulness: codes, libraries, and most features of Prolog can be used in MProlog programs; for effectiveness: classical fragments are interpreted by Prolog itself, and a number of options can be used for MProlog to restrict the search space; for flexibility: there are three kinds of predicates (classical, modal, *dum*) and we can use and mix different calculi in an MProlog program.

MProlog has a very different theoretical foundation than the existing Molog system. In MProlog, a labeling technique is used for existential modal operators instead of skolemization. We also provide and use new technicalities like normal forms of modalities or pre-orders between modal operators. MProlog also eliminates drawbacks of Molog (e.g., MProlog gives computed answers).

We have implemented SLD-resolution calculi for a number of useful modal logics [11], including all of the multimodal logics of belief considered in this work.

The multimodal logics of belief $KDI4_s$, $KDI4_s5$, $KDI45$, $KD4_s5_s$, $KD4I_g5_a$ were first introduced and studied by us for modal logic programming [10]. Some of the implemented SLD-resolution calculi, e.g. the ones for KD, $KD45$, $S5$, $KDI4_s5$, $KD4_s5_s$, $KD45_{(m)}$, are very efficient[6].

Our system is a tool for experimenting with applications of modal logic programming to AI. See [11] for an interesting formulation of the wise men puzzle in MProlog. Our system is also a tool for developing and experimenting with new SLD-resolution calculi for modal logic programming.

Acknowledgements. I would like to thank professors Andreas Herzig and Luis Fariñas del Cerro for a discussion on this paper. I would like also to thank Dr. Rajeev Goré and the anonymous reviewers for many helpful comments and suggestions.

References

1. Akama, S.: A Meta-Logical Foundation of Modal Logic Programming. 1-20-1, Higashi-Yurigaoka, Asao-ku, Kawasaki-shi, 215, Japan, December 1989.
2. Balbiani, P., Fariñas del Cerro, L., Herzig, A.: Declarative Semantics for Modal Logic Programs, *Proceedings of the 1988 International Conference on Fifth Generation Computer Systems*, ICOT, 1988, 507–514.
3. Baldoni, M., Giordano, L., Martelli, A.: A Framework for a Modal Logic Programming, *Joint International Conference and Symposium on Logic Programming*, MIT Press, 1996, 52–66.
4. Fariñas del Cerro, L.: MOLOG: A System that Extends PROLOG with Modal Logic, *New Generation Computing*, **4**, 1986, 35–50.
5. Debart, F., Enjalbert, P., Lescot, M.: Multimodal Logic Programming Using Equational and Order-Sorted Logic, *Theoretical Computer Science*, **105**, 1992, 141–166.
6. Fitting, M., Mendelsohn, R. L.: *First-Order Modal Logic*, Kluwer Academic Publishers, 1999.
7. Garson, J.: Quantification in Modal Logic, in: *Handbook of Philosophical Logic, Volume II* (F. Guenthner, D. Gabbay, Eds.), 1999, 249–307.
8. Lloyd, J.: *Foundations of Logic Programming, 2nd Edition*, Springer-Verlag, 1987.
9. Nguyen, L. A.: A Fixpoint Semantics and an SLD-Resolution Calculus for Modal Logic Programs, *Fundamenta Informaticae*, **55**(1), 2003, 63–100.
10. Nguyen, L. A.: Multimodal Logic Programming and Its Applications to Modal Deductive Databases, *manuscript (served as a technical report), available on Internet at http://www.mimuw.edu.pl/~nguyen/papers.html*, 2003.
11. Nguyen, L. A.: Source Files, Calculi, and Examples of MProlog, *available on Internet at http://www.mimuw.edu.pl/~nguyen/mprolog*, 2004.
12. Nonnengart, A.: How to Use Modalities and Sorts in Prolog, *Proceedings of JELIA'94, LNCS 838* (C. MacNish, D. Pearce, L. M. Pereira, Eds.), Springer, 1994, 365–378.

---

[6] For the mentioned logics, the *rSat* operator is either deterministic (for KD, $KD45$, and $KD4_s5_s$) or nondeterministic but with a low branching factor (2 for $KD45_{(m)}$, 3 for $S5$, and m for $KDI4_s5$).

Soundness and Completeness of an "Efficient" Negation for Prolog*

Juan José Moreno-Navarro and Susana Muñoz-Hernández

Universidad Politécnica de Madrid Dpto. LSIIS – Facultad de Informática.
Campus de Montegancedo s/n, 28660, Madrid, Spain.
{jjmoreno,susana}@fi.upm.es, voice: +34-91-336-7455, fax: +34-91-336-6595.

Abstract. The role for logic in knowledge and artificial intelligence (AI) representation and reasoning is an interesting and active area of research. In this framework, negation plays an essential role. On the other hand, Logic Programming (LP), and Prolog as its most representative programming language, has been extensively used for the implementation of logic-based systems. However, up to now we cannot find a Prolog implementation that supports an adequate negation subsystem what precludes important uses in AI applications. By *adequate* we mean correct and complete as well as efficiently implemented. In fact, there is no single method with this characteristic (for instance, negation as failure is incomplete, while constructive negation is hard to implement and until our work there were no running implementation of it). In previous work, we presented a novel method for incorporating negation into a Prolog compiler which takes a number of existing methods (some modified and improved by us) and uses them in a combined fashion. The method makes use of information provided by a global analysis of the source code. However, the correctness of the system was only informally sketched. In this paper, we present a general framework that can be used either to define strategies by combination of negation techniques as well as proving correctness and completeness of the resulting system. From this framework it is possible to define new strategies and, in particular, we describe the strategy that we have implemented, proving its soundness and completeness.

Keywords: Negation in Prolog, LP and nonmonotonic reasoning, Constructive Negation.

1 Introduction

One of the main advantages of Prolog is that it can be used for the specification of AI and knowledge representation systems. These specifications can be executed using the inference engine of Prolog but some reasoning about them can be implemented in Prolog itself. However, expresiveness of Prolog is limited by the lack of negation capabilities, what prevents important uses. Originally this decision was taking by Kowalski and Colmerauer because of the difficulties for providing adequate semantics as well as for developing an efficient implementation. While the first problem (semantics) can be considered sufficiently understood and addressed by many researchers (although

---

* This research was partly supported by the Spanish MCYT projectTIC2003-01036.

J.J. Alferes and J. Leite (Eds.): JELIA 2004, LNAI 3229, pp. 279–293, 2004.

there is already room for significant improvements), the second one (implementation) is poorly developed. In fact, there is no method in the literature that shares correctness and completeness results with a reasonable efficient implementable procedure. We will ellaborate more this later. As a result, there is no available Prolog (understood as left-to-right, depth-first implementation of Logic Programming) with an adequate negation subsystem. This means that Prolog cannot be used in full for certain logic-based approaches to AI, specially those including nonmonotonic reasoning. Consequently, many potential Prolog applications demand for extensions to incorporate negative information and the execution of negative goals. Notice that these applications are already developed in Prolog using libraries to access databases, web services, constraints, etc. Therefore, the recoding of them in a new system is not feasible.

As we have mentioned, the collection of methods to handle negation in Prolog compilers is relatively short: Negation as failure is present in most Prolog compiler, but it is unsound. It has been refined into the delay technique of the language Gödel[9], or Nu-Prolog[15] but because of the risk of floundering it is incomplete. Intensional negation [1,2,3] is a very promising method but the generation of universally quantified goals has prevented any (efficient or not) concrete implementation until our work [11]. It is sound and complete but the execution of forall goals, although possible, introduces serious inneficiencies. Constructive negation [4,5,20,8] is also sound and complete. The name *constructive negation* has also been used as a generic name for systems handling nonground literals: Chan's *constructive negation*, fail substitutions, fail answers, *negation as instantiation*[16], etc. From a theoretical viewpoint Chan's approach is sufficient but it is quite difficult to implement and expensive in terms of execution resources as we have reported in our recent implementation [12].

The authors have been involved in a project [13,14] to incorporate negation into a real Prolog system. We are proud to have developed a real system for negation in Prolog, an open problem for more than 25 years. However, the claims about its soundness and completeness were never formally stated.

In this paper we provide a formal generalization of the concept of strategy that is amenable for defining our proposal as well as variations of it. The former can be done either by combining our techniques in a different way or by including new techniques. Furthermore, the framework can be used to reason about the soundness and completeness of the combination of techniques. In particular, we prove these results for the strategy we have implemented.

Notice that the goal of the paper is not the presentation of the system, that have been done in previous papers, but the formal results instead. In order to provide this we rely on the soundness and completeness results of the combined techniques. In order to make the paper self-contained we recall on these results, although most of them come from different authors (and those that have been developed by ourselves have been previously published). One of the objectives of the paper is to reformulate all these results in an uniform way, in order to combine them into the soundness and completeness of our proposal. In this sense, the key idea of the paper is the formal description of what a strategy is. The definition is given in such a way that the formal results can be obtained from the combination of techniques.

The rest of the paper is organized as follows. Section 2 introduces basic syntactic and semantic concepts needed to understand our method. We introduce the main negation techniques that we are going to deal with in Section 3, discussing their soundness and completeness results (refereing the source of them) as well as implementation issues. Section 4 contains the main contributions of the paper, namely to provide a formal framework definition and the results of soundness and completeness for the negation system. Finally, we conclude and discuss some future work (Section 5).

2 Syntax and Semantics

In this section the syntax of (constraint) normal logic programs and the intended notion of correctness are introduced. Programs will be constructed from a signature $\Sigma = \langle FS_\Sigma, PS_\Sigma \rangle$ of function and predicate symbols. Provided a numerable set of variables V the set $Term(FS_\Sigma, V)$ of terms is constructed in the usual way.

A (constrained) normal Horn clause is a formula $h(\overline{x}) : -(\neg)b_1(\overline{y} \cdot \overline{z}), \ldots, (\neg)b_n(\overline{y} \cdot \overline{z}) [\![c(\overline{x} \cdot \overline{y})$ where $\overline{x}$, $\overline{y}$ and $\overline{z}$ are tuples from disjoint sets of variables[1]. The variables in $\overline{z}$ are called the *free* variables in the clause. The symbols "," and "$[\![$" act here as aliases of logical conjunction. The atom to the left of the symbol ": $-$" is called the *head* or *left hand side* (lhs) of the clause. In general, normal Horn clauses of the form $h(\overline{x}) : -B(\overline{y} \cdot \overline{z}) [\![c(\overline{x} \cdot \overline{y})$ where the body B can have arbitrary disjunctions, denoted by ";", and conjunctions of atoms will be allowed as they can be easily translated into "traditional" ones. A normal Prolog program (in Σ) is a set of clauses indexed by $p \in PS_\Sigma$:

$$p(\overline{x}) : -B_1(\overline{y}_1 \cdot \overline{z}_1) [\![c_1(\overline{x} \cdot \overline{y}_1)$$

$$\vdots$$

$$p(\overline{x}) : -B_m(\overline{y}_m \cdot \overline{z}_m) [\![c_m(\overline{x} \cdot \overline{y}_m)$$

The set of defining clauses for predicate symbol p in program P is denoted $def_P(p)$. Without loss of generality we have assumed that the left hand sides in $def_P(p)$ are syntactically identical. Actual Prolog programs, however, will be written using a more traditional syntax.

Assuming the normal form, let $def_P(p) = \{p(\overline{x}) : -B_i(\overline{y}_i \cdot \overline{z}_i) [\![c_i(\overline{x} \cdot \overline{y}_i) | i \in 1 \ldots m\}$. The *completed definition* of p, $cdef_P(p)$ is defined as the formula

$$\forall \overline{x}. \left[p(\overline{x}) \iff \bigvee_{i=1}^{m} \exists \overline{y}_i. \ c_i(\overline{x} \cdot \overline{y}_i) \wedge \exists \overline{z}_i . B_i(\overline{y}_i \cdot \overline{z}_i) \right]$$

The *Clark's completion* of the program is the conjunction of the completed definitions for all the predicate symbols in the program along with the formulas that establish the standard interpretation for the equality symbol, the so called *Clark's Equality Theory* or *CET*. The completion of program P will be denoted as $Comp(P)$. Throughout the paper, the standard meaning of logic programs will be given by the three-valued interpretation $\models_3$ of their completion – i.e. its minimum 3-valued model, as defined in [10]. These 3 values will be denoted as $\underline{t}$ (or success), $\underline{f}$ (or fail) and $\underline{u}$ (or unknown).

---

[1] The notation $p(\overline{x})$ expresses that $Vars(p(\overline{x})) \in \overline{x}$, note that it is identical to $p(x_1, \ldots, x_n)$

3   Preliminaries: Negation in Prolog

In this section we present briefly the negation techniques in Prolog from the literature which we have integrated into a uniform framework. We also indicate their associated soundness and completeness theorems (pointing to the adequate reference when it is necessary) in an uniform manner. We do not prove the adapted version of the theorems, although in many cases it is trivial. The techniques and the proposed combination share the following characteristics:

– They can be modelled in the previously defined semantics: Clark's completion and Kunen's 3-valued semantics [10]. These semantics will be the basis for soundness and completeness results.
– They must be "constructive", i.e., program execution should produce adequate goal variable values for making a negated goal false.

The following techniques meet the previous requirements. We briefly present the technique, discuss theoretical results, our contributions (if any) as well as the existing implementations:

3.1   Negation as Failure

Negation as failure was originally proposed by Clark [6]. The operational semantics associated with the technique is SLDNF. Clark proved soundness with respect to 2-valued semantics while Shephersond [19] extended it to 3-valued semantics. From his theorems we can infer the following corollary:

Corollary 1 (Soundness and Completeness of ground naf).
Given a program P and a ground goal G

$$Comp(P) \models_3 G \quad \textit{iff } G \textit{ has an empty computed answer substitution}$$
$$Comp(P) \models_3 \neg G \quad \textit{iff } G \textit{ finitely fails}$$

Negation as failure is present in most Prolog compilers (Sicstus, Bin Prolog, Quintus, Ciao, etc.) usually implemented as:

```
naf(P) :- P, !, fail.
naf (P).
```

what unfortunately is an unsound approach, because it can only be used for computations that do not bind any variable involved into the negated goal. Apart from this incomplete behaviour, another drawback is that it cannot produce answer substitution to negated queries and therefore they can only be used as tests. In practice, this is implemented by using it only for ground goals. For our purposes, the built-in version of naf can be used as it is.

3.2 Delay Technique

This approach is a variation of the previous one which applies negation as failure (SLDNF resolution) when, dynamically, it is detected that the variables of the negated goal are sufficiently instantiated (by using some kind of when, or delay directive). It is well known that this approach has the risk of floundering, and floundering is an undecidible property. This technique is sound when it can be applied, but it is incomplete. This technique is implemented in (Gödel [9] and Nu-Prolog [15]) as its unique negation mechanism and without the help of a program analizer. The implementation we use is *when(ground(Goal), naf(Goal)*. The preprocessor can reorder the subgoals of the clause, that contains the negation in the body, to avoid the delay call. This means that negation as failure can be used after the subgoals have been reordered.

3.3 Intensional Negation

Intensional negation [1,2], is a novel approach to obtain the program completion by transforming the original program into a new one that introduces the "only if" part of the predicate definitions (i.e., interpreting implications as equivalences). It was extended to CLP in [3]. In both cases, completeness is stated under SLD-$\forall$, an extension of SLD to cope with universally quantified goals. In [11] we developed a logic programming definition of universal quantification in such a way that SLD suffices as operational semantics. However, the evaluation of universally quantified goals is hard to compute.

Formally, the intensional negation consists in including for every $p \in PS_\Sigma$ a new symbol $neg(p)$ such that:

Definition 1 (Intensional Negation of a Program).
Given a program P, its intensional negation *is a program P' such that for every p in PS_Σ the following holds $\forall \overline{x}. [Comp(P) \models_3 p(\overline{x}) \iff Comp(P') \models_3 \neg(neg(p)(\overline{x}))]$*

The idea of the transformation to be defined below is to obtain a program whose completion corresponds to the negation of the original program, in particular to a representation of the completion where negative literals have been eliminated. We call this transformation *Negate*.

Definition 2 (Constructive Intensional Negation of a predicate.).
Let p be a predicate of a program P and let def $_P(p) = \forall \overline{x}. [p(\overline{x}) \iff D]$ be its completed definition. The constructive intensional negation *of p, Negate(p), is the formula obtained after the successive application of the following transformation steps:*

1. *For every completed definition of a predicate p in PS_Σ, $\forall \overline{x}. [p(\overline{x}) \iff D]$, add the completed definition of its negated predicate, $\forall \overline{x}. [neg\_p(\overline{x}) \iff \neg D]$.*
2. *Move negations to the subgoals that are not constraints using the property of a set of exhaustive and nonoverlapping first-order formulas (constraints)*
3. *If negation is applied to an existential quantification, replace $\neg \exists \overline{z}.C$ by $\forall \overline{z}.\neg C$.*

4. *Replace* $\neg C$ *by its* negated normal form[2] $NNF(\neg C)$.
5. *Replace* $\neg \underline{t}$ *by* $\underline{f}$, $\neg \underline{f}$ *by* $\underline{t}$, *for every predicate symbol* p, $\neg p(\bar{t})$ *by* $neg\_p(\bar{t})$.

Definition 3 (Constructive Intensional Negation).

For every predicate p *in the original program, assuming* $def_P(p) = \{p(\bar{x}) : -B_i(\bar{y}_i \cdot \bar{z}_i) [\!] c_i(\bar{x} \cdot \bar{y}_i) | i \in 1\ldots m\}$ *a nonoverlapping and exhaustive definition, the following clauses will be added to the negated program:*

- *If the set of constraints* $\{\exists \bar{y}_i.c_i(\bar{x}.\bar{y}_i)\}$ *is not exhaustive,* $neg\_p(\bar{x})$:
  $-[\!] \bigwedge_1^m \neg \exists \bar{y}_i.c_i(\bar{x}.\bar{y}_i)$
- *If* $\bar{z}_j$ *is empty, the clause* $neg\_p(\bar{x}) : -negate\_rhs(B_j(\bar{y}_j)) [\!] c_j(\bar{x}.\bar{y}_j)$
- *If* $\bar{z}_j$ *is not empty, the clauses* $neg\_p(\bar{x}) : -forall(\bar{z}_j, p\_j(\bar{y}_j \cdot \bar{z}_j)) [\!] c_j(\bar{x}.\bar{y}_j)$
  $p\_j(\bar{y}_j \cdot \bar{z}_j) : -negate\_rhs(B_j(\bar{y}_j \cdot \bar{z}_j))$

We can see that negating a clause with free variables introduces "universally quantified" goals by means of a new predicate *forall*/2 that is discussed in [11] (where the reader can find soundness and completeness results, and implementation issues). In the absence of free variables the transformation is trivially correct, as the completion of the negated predicate corresponds to the negation-free normal form described above. The main result of the transformation is the following:

Theorem 1. *The result of applying the* Constructive Intensional Negation *transformation to a (nonoverlapping)[3] program P is an intensional negation (see def. 1).*

In order to obtain the new clauses of the program, we have to use the preprocessor to output the transformed program from the input program at compilation time. It is a simple implementation as we don't need to modify the execution mechanism.

3.4 Constructive Negation

This technique was proposed by Chan [4,5] and it is widely accepted as the "most promising" method for handling negation through SLD-CNF resolution. It is based on the negation of the frontier of the goal (a complete subderivation of the derivation tree of a goal) that we want to negate.

Stuckey in [20] established the main theoretical results, extending Chan's approach to CLP($\mathcal{X}$). The results assume a structure $\mathcal{A}$ for the constraint system $\mathcal{X}$ that must be *admissible* and a computation rule R that must be fair consistent. In the case of Prolog, the structure $\mathcal{A}$ is the Herbrand universe (that obviously satisfies the admissibility conditions).

Definition 4 (Constructive Negation).

If P is a normal program and $\{G_1, ..., G_n\}$ is a frontier for G then cneg *is a predicate that verifies* $Comp(P) \models_3 cneg(G) \iff \neg((\exists \bar{y}_1 G_1) \vee ... \vee (\exists \bar{y}_n G_n))$ *where $\bar{y}_i$ is the set of variables in G_i not in G.*

---

[2] The *negated normal form* of C, is obtained by successive application of the De Morgan laws until negations only affect atomic subformulas of C.

[3] There is a simple transformation to get a nonoverlapping program from any general program.

The corresponding (adapted) soundness result follows.

Theorem 2 (Soundness of Constructive Negation).
If P is a normal program:

- *If G has a totally successful derivation tree then* $Comp(P) \models_3 \overline{\forall} G$
- *If G has a finitely failed derivation tree then* $Comp(P) \models_3 \neg \overline{\exists} G$

A result on the completeness of constructive negation was given by [17] for a very restricted class of programs. [18] and [7] got similar completeness results for the particular case of the Herbrand Universe. The result here is adapted from [20]

Theorem 3 (Completeness of Constructive Negation).
Let P be a normal program and G a goal.

- *If* $Comp(P) \models_3 \overline{\forall} G$ *then the derivation tree for G is totally successful.*
- *If* $Comp(P) \models_3 \neg \overline{\exists} G$ *then the derivation tree for G is finitely failed.*

To our knowledge, the only reported implementation of Constructive Negation was announced in earlier versions of the Eclipse System, but it has been removed from recent releases, probably due to some problems related to floundering. By its own nature, constructive negation is quite inefficient and, at the same time, extremely difficult to implement. We have recently provided a full Prolog implementation, reported in [12] which has been included in our system by the predicate cneg(Goal).

Finite constructive negation. There is a variant, finite constructive negation cnegf(Goal), for goals with a finite number of solutions. It is a limited version of full constructive negation. While it is easier to understand and implement (see [13] to find our approach) it is also considerably more efficient than the general technique. However it can only be used if we know that there is a finite number of solutions of the positive goal. This can be ascertained by approximations or preprocessor analysis to get this information statically. The implementation is easier and faster, because the built-in setof can be used. Formally, it is a particular case of constructive negation where the frontier of maximum depth is used. The following result establishes this property.

Theorem 4 (Finite Constructive Negation is well defined).
Let P be a normal program and G a goal such that the derivation tree for G has a finite number of finite branches.
Then, it is possible to use as the frontier in the constructive negation algorithm the whole derivation.

Therefore, soundness and completeness of finite constructive negation are corollaries of theorems 2 and 3.

4   Combining Techniques

This section provides the general framework that we use to define strategies of combination of negation techniques. From this framework it is possible to define new strategies, and prove soundness and completeness. In particular, we define the strategy that we have chosen although our soundness and completeness results are applicable to a wider range of strategies than the particular one we propose.

4.1   Definitions

We start with a general definition for the use of a particular negation technique, called TAS (*Technique application scheme*), including applicability checking, as well as the new code proposed for evaluation. The formalization covers when the technique is going to be applied in the form of a test. The arguments include the program, the goal and the selected negated atom. The result of an application is a new goal (usually by replacing the selected atom by a goal), with an implicit operational semantics for them. Notice that it easily describes the techniques we have discussed.

Definition 5 (Technique Application Scheme - TAS). *A technique application scheme (TAS) is a pair* $(check, change\_goal)$ *where*

- *$check : \mathbb{N} \times Goal \times Program \rightarrow Bool$ is a predicate where the second argument is a conjunction of n subgoals $Goal \equiv (B_1, ..., B_n)$, the first argument identifies one of these subgoals, B_i, (i belongs to $\{1..n\}$) that is a negation of the form $neg(\overline{B})$ ($B_i \equiv \neg(\overline{B})$) and the third argument is a program. This predicate imposes a set of conditions to the goal,*
- *$change\_goal : \mathbb{N} \times Goal \times Program \rightarrow Goal$ is a function that receives (i, G, P) and modifies the input goal, G, (depending on one of its subgoals, identified by the first argument, that is a negation of the form $\neg(\overline{B})$).*

A *TAS* establishes (by *check*) the sufficient condition for using a negation technique to negate a goal into a program. We apply the technique by generating a new goal (by *change_goal*) where the negation technique is explicit. It is supposed that newly introduced goals are computed according to a fixed operational semantics for each case (technique). The relationship between the goals is established by the name of the goal.

To define interesting TASs, we specify a collection of predicates and functions that will be used throughout the section.

- **Predicate detected_ground:**
  If $detected\_ground(i, (B_1, ..., B_i, ..., B_n), P)$ holds then for all substitutions σ of the variables of $G \equiv (B_1, ..., B_n)$ such that $(B_1, ..., B_{i-1}) \vdash_{SLD,P,\sigma}$, it is satisfied that $B_i\sigma$ is ground[4]

---

[4] In fact, *detected_ground* just specifies a property to be satisfied by a concrete Boolean function. In the rest of the section, this is the property we need to prove our results. The concrete definition of *detected_ground* will depend on the accuracy of the groundness analysis and it will penalize the efficiency of the implementation, but it does not affect either the soundness or the completeness of strategies.

- **Function to_naf**:
  $to\_naf(i, (B_1, ..., \neg(B), ..., B_n), P) = (B_1, ..., B_{i-1}, naf(B), B_{i+1}, ..., B_n)$ and
  $naf(B)$ is evaluated by $\vdash_{SLDNF,P}$
- **Function secure_to_naf**:
  $secure\_to\_naf(i, (B_1, ..., \neg(B), ..., B_n, P) = (B_1, ..., B_{i-1},$
  $(ground(B) \to naf(B); \neg(B)), B_{i+1}, ..., B_n)$ and $naf(B)$ is evaluated by
  $\vdash_{SLDNF,P}$
- **Predicate true**:
  This boolean function always returns $\underline{t}$, i.e. $true(i, G, P)$ holds for every i, G, P

Now, we are in a position to define the static application of negation as failure as the
following TAS:

$$static\_ground \equiv (detected\_ground, to\_naf)$$

Let us show a couple of examples of the evaluation of the elements of this TAS.
Suppose that P contains the definition of the well-known predicate $member/2$ and another predicate $p/1$. The goal $detected\_ground(2, (member(X, [1, 2]), neg(p(X))), P)$
could yield the result true, because the second subgoal of G, in this case $neg(p(X))$,
will be completely instantiated when it is selected by the SLD selection rule and the
function

$$to\_naf(2, (member(X, [1, 2]), neg(p(X))), P) = (member(X, [1, 2]), naf(p(X)))$$

Alternatively, the dynamic application of negation as failure can be modeled using
the following predicate:

$$dynamic\_ground \equiv (true, secure\_to\_naf)$$

To complete the techniques we are using in our work, we define some additional TASs. Again, some auxiliary predicates and functions are needed. Assume
$G \equiv (B_1, ..., B_i, ..., B_n)$ is the goal in a program P and $B_i \equiv \neg(\overline{B})$,

- **Predicate can_be_ordered**:
  $can\_be\_ordered(i, (B_1, ..., \neg(B), ..., B_n), P)$ holds iff there exists a permutation G'
  of the subgoals of G (where the subgoal $neg(B)$ of G is placed in the position j of
  G') such that $detected\_ground(j, G', P)$ holds.
- **Function reorder**:
  $reorder(i, (B_1, ..., \neg(B), ..., B_n), P) \qquad = \qquad G'' \qquad$ when
  $can\_be\_ordered(i, (B_1, ..., \neg(B), ..., B_n), P)$ is true with permutation G',
  where j is the position of $\neg(B)$ and G'' is G' with the atom $naf(B)$ in the jth
  place. Again, $naf(B)$ is evaluated by $\vdash_{SLDNF,P}$.
- **Predicate finiteness**:
  $finiteness(i, G, P)$ holds iff there exists a finite positive number of substitutions
  $\sigma_1, ... \sigma_n$ such that $G \vdash_{SLD,P,\sigma_k}, k \in \{1..n\}$, any σ_k can be ϵ and there is no substitution θ different from all σ_k such that $G \vdash_{SLD,P,\theta}$.
- **Function to_cnegf**:
  $to\_cnegf(i, (B_1, ..., \neg(B_i), ..., B_n), P) = (B_1, ..., B_{i-1}, cnegf(B_i), B_{i+1}, ..., B_n)$
  and the new subgoal $cnegf(B_i)$ is evaluated by $\vdash_{SLD\_CNF,P}$ using the maximum
  depth frontier selection.

- **Function to_intneg**:
  $to\_intneg(i, (B_1, ..., \neg(B_i), ..., B_n), P) = (B_1, ..., B_{i-1}, intneg(B_i), B_{i+1}, ..., B_n)$
  where $intneg(\overline{B})$ is evaluated by $\vdash_{SLD, Negate(P)}$[5]
- **Predicate no_forall**:
  $no\_forall(i, (B_1, ..., \neg(p(\overline{X})), ..., B_n), P)$ holds iff there are no free variables in the completed definition $cdef_P(p)$.
- **Function to_cneg**:
  $to\_cneg(i, (B_1, ..., \neg(B_i), ..., B_n), P) = (B_1, ..., cneg(B_i), ..., B_n)$, where $cneg(\overline{B})$ is evaluated by $\vdash_{SLD\_CNF, P}$.

Thanks to these auxiliary definitions, we can provide TAS definitions for all the negation techniques that we have studied. Furthermore, we claim that many other techniques can be modeled similarly:

- *Atom reordering and negation as failure*:
$$static\_reordering \equiv (can\_be\_ordered, reorder)$$
- *Finite version for constructive negation*:
$$finite\_cneg \equiv (finiteness, to\_cnegf)$$
- *Intensional negation*:
$$unconditional\_intneg \equiv (true, to\_intneg)$$
- *Intensional negation when there are no free variables*:
$$no\_forall\_intneg \equiv (no\_forall, to\_intneg)$$
- *General constructive negation*:
$$unconditional\_cneg \equiv (true, to\_cneg)$$
- Just to give an example of a correct TAS, which will not be useful, we can define
$$unconditional\_naf \equiv (true, to\_naf)$$

The characterization of TASs that can be used in a strategy definition is an interesting task. The following definition indicates the conditions that the $(check, change\_goal)$ must satisfy.

Definition 6 (Admissible TAS).
We say that a TAS is admissible *when the operational semantics associated with the modified goal by change_goal is sound and complete with respect to the conditions imposed by check.*

Now, we can check the admissibility property of the previously defined techniques:

Proposition 1. *The TASs static_ground, dynamic_ground, static_reordering, finite_cneg, unconditional_intneg, no_forall_intneg and unconditional_cneg are* admissible.

---

[5] Note the abuse of the notation, where we use $intneg(p(\overline{X}))$ with the meaning of $intneg(p)(\overline{X})$ (or $neg\_p(\overline{X})$)

Proof. It comes from the respective soundness and completeness results of the operational semantics associated with each modified goal (corollary 1, theorems 1 .. 3).

- *static_ground, dynamic_ground* and *static_reordering* are complete and sound from corollary 1.
- *finite_cneg* is complete and sound (see section 3.4),
- *unconditional_intneg* is complete and sound from theorem 1,
- *no_forall_intneg* is complete and sound from theorem 1 with SLD (without universal quantifications),
- *unconditional_cneg* is complete and sound from theorems 2 and 3.

It is easy to see that the TAS *unconditional_naf* is not admissible.

The previous TASs are not the only ones that are admissible, and the definition can cover other techniques that we have not considered in our work (i.e. dynamic finite constructive negation, Drabent's approach, etc.).

An admissible TAS by itself only defines the applicability of a technique. However, we are interested in strategies, i.e. the combination of several TASs. More properly, a strategy is the sequential application of several TASs as stated in the following definition:

Definition 7 (Strategy (ST)).
A strategy (ST) is a sequence of technique application schemes.

The definition allows for several different strategies. Let us enumerate some of them:

- *Try naf and then constructive negation*:

$$naf\_then\_cneg\_st \equiv \langle static\_ground, dynamic\_ground, unconditional\_cneg \rangle$$

- *Pure general constructive negation*:

$$cneg\_st \equiv \langle unconditional\_cneg \rangle$$

- *Pure intensional negation*:

$$intneg\_st \equiv \langle unconditional\_intneg \rangle$$

- *Try naf and then intensional negation*:

$$naf\_then\_intneg\_st \equiv \langle static\_ground, unconditional\_intneg \rangle$$

- Of course, we can define useless strategies:

$$nonsense\_st \equiv \langle unconditional\_intneg \rangle$$

- The main strategy we are proposing thorough our work is as follows

$$MM\_st \equiv \langle\ static\_ground,$$
$$static\_reordering,$$
$$no\_forall\_intneg,$$
$$finite\_cneg,$$
$$unconditional\_cneg \rangle$$

A strategy defines the way to compute a goal. More formally, a strategy establishes a concrete operational semantics for a Prolog program and goal, possibly including negated atoms:

Definition 8 (Operational semantics induced by a strategy.).
Operational semantics $\vdash^{ST}$ induced by an strategy *is defined as follows: Let P be a program, $G \equiv B_1, ..., B_i, ..., B_n$ be a goal and B_i the subgoal selected by the selection rule.*

- *If $B_i \neq \neg(\overline{B})$ and $G \vdash_{SLD,P,\sigma} G'$ then $G \vdash_{P,\sigma}^{ST} G'$.*
- *Otherwise, when $B_i = \neg(B')$, let $ST = \langle tas_1, ..., tas_j, ..., tas_n \rangle$,
  $tas_j \equiv (check_j, change\_goal_j)$ such that:*

  - *$check_k(i, G, P)$, $k < j$ are false,*
  - *$check_j(i, G, P)$ is true,*
  - *$\vdash_{\mathcal{O},P'}$ is the operational semantics associated with the modified goal (where $\mathcal{O}$ will be SLDNF, SLD_CNF or SLD and $P' = P$, except when intensional negation that $P' = Negate(P)$ is used),*
  - *$G^\dagger = change\_goal_j(i, G, P)$ is the modified goal and there exists a substitution σ such that $G^\dagger \vdash_{\mathcal{O},P',\sigma}^* G'$*

  then $G \vdash_{P,\sigma}^{ST} G'$.

The operational semantics induced by a strategy mimics the way the system can be implemented. Furthermore, it is the basis for the formal results. As above, we need to characterize the strategies that are candidates to be used in practice. We also call them *admissible*:

Definition 9 (Admissible ST).
A strategy $ST = \langle tas_1, ..., tas_n \rangle$ is admissible if

- *each tas_i, $i \in \{1..n\}$, is admissible,*
- *$tas_n \equiv (true, change\_goal)$, and*
- *the operational semantics associated with the modified goal by $change\_goal$ is unconditionally sound and complete.*

It is easy to check that all the interesting strategies described above are admissible strategies:

Proposition 2. *The STs $naf\_then\_cneg\_st$, $cneg\_st$, $intneg\_st$, $naf\_then\_intneg\_st$ and MM_st are admissible.*

Proof. The result comes form proposition 1 and soundness and completeness of intensional negation (theorem 1) and constructive negation (theorems 2 and 3).

4.2   Soundness and Completeness Results

Now we can proceed with the main formal results of the paper. First of all we prove that the admissible strategies are exactly the strategies that can be used in practice, i.e. they are sound and complete.

Theorem 5 (Soundness of $\vdash^{ST}_{P,\sigma}$).
The operational semantics of $\vdash^{ST}_{P,\sigma}$ when ST is an admissible strategy is sound:

$$G \vdash^{ST}_{P,\sigma} G' \quad implies \quad Comp(P) \models_3 (G' \to G)\sigma.$$

Proof. It can be deduced form the soundness results of every different technique. When $\vdash^{ST}_{P,\sigma}$ performs a SLD step, the result is obvious because $G \vdash^{*}_{P,\sigma} G'$ implies $P \models (G' \to G)\sigma$, which implies $Comp(P) \models_3 (G' \to G)\sigma$.

If $G \vdash^{ST}_{P,\sigma} G'$, $G \equiv B_1, ..., B_i, ..., B_n$, $ST = \langle tas_1, ..., tas_j, ..., tas_n \rangle$ an admissible strategy for all $i \in \{1..m\}$ there exists a TAS $tas_j \in ST$, such that, all $check_k(i, G, P)$, $k < j$ are false, $check_j(i, G, P)$ is true and $change\_goal_j(i, G, P) = G^\dagger$. Now $G^\dagger$ is reduce by $\vdash^{ST}_{P,\sigma}$ to G' By definition 6 the step is sound with respect the condition of $check_j$ that is true, so $Comp(P) \models_3 (G' \to G)\sigma$.

Now we are in a position to prove the general result:

Theorem 6 (Soundness of an admissible strategy).
An admissible strategy ST is sound:

$$G \vdash^{*\,ST}_{P,\sigma} \quad then \quad Comp(P) \models_3 G\sigma.$$

Proof. We can proceed by induction on the number of $\vdash^{ST}$ steps and the previous theorem.

The completeness theorem relies again on the admissibility of the strategy that provides the adequate completeness results:

Theorem 7 (Completeness of an admissible strategy).
An admissible strategy ST is complete:

- *$Comp(P) \models_3 \forall G$, then the derivation tree under $\vdash^{ST}_{P,\sigma}$ is totally successfull.*
- *$Comp(P) \models_3 \neg \exists G$, then the derivation tree under $\vdash^{ST}_{P,\sigma}$ finitely fails.*

Proof. If $Comp(P) \models_3 \forall G$, $G \equiv B_1, ..., B_i, ..., B_n$, $ST = \langle tas_1, ..., tas_j, ..., tas_n \rangle$ an admissible strategy then for all $i \in \{1..m\}$ there exists a TAS $tas_j \in ST$, such that, all $check_k(i, G, P)$, $k < j$ are false, $check_j(i, G, P)$ is true, $change\_goal_j(i, G, P) = G^\dagger$ and $\mathcal{O}$ is the operational semantics associated with $G^\dagger$.

By definition 6, $G^\dagger$ is complete with respect the condition of $check_j$ that is true, so there exists a substitution σ such that $G \vdash_{\mathcal{O},P,\sigma}$ and by definition 8 $G \vdash^{ST}_{P,\sigma}$.

Similarly, the second case can be proved.

As a corollary of the previous result we can establish the soundness and completeness of our strategy.

Corollary 2 (Soundness and Completeness of our strategy).
MM_st is sound and complete.

Proof. *Obvious from theorems 6 and 7 and proposition 2.*

5   Conclusion and Future Work

As we have discussed, up to now it is not possible to find a negation technique for Prolog that is efficient, sound and complete at the same time. Some approaches (such as naf) are very efficient and simple to implement but incomplete. Other approaches are complete and sound but with an implementation so complicated that the efficiency of the program turns out unacceptable for simple uses, present in many programs. Furthermore, it is difficult to find papers reporting concrete implementations of negation. Therefore, to overcome these problems we propose the combination of techniques to open new possibilities on negation implementation in Prolog.

Let us briely explain, the quotes on the word "efficient" in the title. Talking about efficiency, when we are dealing with negation techniques, is relative. Indeed, when working with negation as failure, any technique must check that "all" branches of the search space are failing and, so on, the *complexity* of the process is exponential in all the mentioned techniques. The variation from one technique to the other is: i) the order of traversing the resolution tree (depth first in naf, finite constructive negation, or breath first in constructive negation), ii) what to do with tree nodes (nothing in the case of naf, collecting substitutions in the case of constructive negation), and iii) how the tree is constructed (a part of it is "constructed in the code" for intensional negation). Therefore, the difference from one technique to another is in the coefficient that is applied to the exponential function. As we work in this exponential terms, execution time can be sometimes impracticable. So the concern for improving efficiency of the negation is pretty important.

Based on experimental results, we define our pragmatical strategy that performs reasonable well (see [14] where execution times are reported). However, we only provided an intuitive approach for correctness. Nevertheless, a more formal approach proving soundness and completeness results was needed in order to ensure the appropiate behaviour of the running system. Furthermore, as the strategy can be modified, improved, or enlarged with other methods for efficiency reasons, we needed a more general framework for reasoning about soundness and completeness properties of every concrete combination of techniques. These are the main contributions of the paper.

The ideas we have shown can be applied to other semantics and we plan to develop future work in well-founded semantics. We are also studing other negation techniques (as the one of Drabent [7]) and it is our intention to get implementations of negation algorithms and with them design comparison of different strategies we can select the strategy with the best efficiency results. Our framework will provide correctness results for free.

References

1. R. Barbuti, D. Mancarella, D. Pedreschi, and F. Turini. Intensional negation of logic programs. *Lecture notes on Computer Science*, 250:96–110, 1987.
2. R. Barbuti, D. Mancarella, D. Pedreschi, and F. Turini. A transformational approach to negation in logic programming. *JLP*, 8(3):201–228, 1990.
3. P. Bruscoli, F. Levi, G. Levi, and M.C. Meo. Compilative constructive negation in constraint logic programs. In Sophie Tyson, editor, *Proc. of the Nineteenth International Colloquium on Trees in Algebra and Programming, CAAP '94*, volume 787 of *LNCS*, pages 52–67, Berlin, 1994. Springer-Verlag.
4. D. Chan. Constructive negation based on the completed database. In *Proc. Int. Conference on LP'88*, pages 111–125. The MIT Press, 1988.
5. D. Chan. An extension of constructive negation and its application in coroutining. In *Proc. NACLP'89*, pages 477–493. The MIT Press, 1989.
6. K. L. Clark. Negation as failure. In H. Gallaire and J. Minker, editors, *Logic and Data Bases*, pages 293–322, New York, NY, 1978. Plenum Press.
7. W. Drabent. What is a failure? An approach to constructive negation. *Acta Informatica.*, 33:27–59, 1995.
8. F. Fages. Constructive negation by pruning. *Journal of Logic Programming*, 32(2), 1997.
9. P.M. Hill and J.W. Lloyd. *The Gödel Programming Language*. The MIT Press, 1994.
10. K. Kunen. Negation in logic programming. *JLP*, 4:289–308, 1987.
11. S. Muñoz, J. Mariño, and J. J. Moreno-Navarro. Constructive intensional negation. In *FLOPS'04*, LNCS, 2004.
12. S. Muñoz and J. J. Moreno-Navarro. Implementation results in classical constructive negation. In V. Lifschizt B. Demoen, editor, *ICLP'04*, LNCS. Springer Verlag, 2004. to appear.
13. S. Muñoz-Hernández and J.J. Moreno-Navarro. How to incorporate negation in a Prolog compiler. In V. Santos Costa E. Pontelli, editor, *2nd International Workshop PADL'2000*, volume 1753 of *LNCS*, pages 124–140, Boston, MA (USA), 2000. Springer.
14. S. Muñoz-Hernández, J.J. Moreno-Navarro, and M. Hermenegildo. Efficient negation using abstract interpretation. In R. Nieuwenhuis and A. Voronkov, editors, *Logic for Programming, Artificial Intelligence and Reasoning*, La Habana (Cuba), 2001.
15. L. Naish. Negation and quantifiers in NU-Prolog. In *Proc. 3rd ICLP*, 1986.
16. A. Di Pierro, M. Martelli, and C. Palamidessi. Negation as instantiation. *Information and Computation*, 120(2):263–278, 1995.
17. T. C. Przymusinski. On constructive negation in logic programming. In *North American Conference on Logic Programming*, October 1989.
18. T. Sato and F. Motoyoshi. A complete top-down interpreter for first order programs. In *International Logic Programming Symposium*, pages 35–53, 1991.
19. J. C. Shepherdson. Negation as failure ii. *JLP*, pages 185–202, 1985.
20. P. Stuckey. Negation and constraint logic programming. In *Information and Computation*, volume 118(1), pages 12–33, 1995.

Logic Programs with Functions
and Default Values

Pedro Cabalar and David Lorenzo

Dept. of Computer Science,
University of Corunna,
E-15071, A Coruña, Spain.
{cabalar,lorenzo}@dc.fi.udc.es

Abstract. In this work we reconsider the replacement of predicate-like notation by functional terms, using a similar syntax to Functional Logic Programming, but under a completely different semantic perspective. Our starting point comes from the use of logic programs for Knowledge Representation and Nonmonotonic Reasoning, especially under three well-known semantics for default negation: Clark's completion, stable models and well-founded semantics. The motivation for introducing functions in this setting arises from the frequent occurrence of functional dependences in the representation of many domains. The use of functions allows us to avoid explicit axiomatization and provides a more compact representation by nesting functional terms. From a representational point of view, the most interesting introduced feature is the possibility of replacing default negation by the concept of default value of a function. In the paper, we explore this idea of functions with default values, providing adapted versions of the three mentioned semantics for the functional case, and equivalent translations into logic programs.

1 Introduction

One of the uses of Logic Programming (LP) that is probably attracting more research interest is its application for practical knowledge representation, and particularly, for solving problems related to the area of Nonmonotonic Reasoning (NMR). This application became possible thanks to the availability of several semantics for LP (like *Clark's completion* [1], *stable models* [3] or *well-founded semantics* [11]) that allowed ignoring the operational aspects of Prolog, focusing instead on the use of default negation as a declarative tool for NMR. As a consequence of this application, a considerable number of extensions of the LP paradigm have emerged to cope with different knowledge representation issues.

In this work we consider one more possible extension of the LP paradigm consisting in the use of functions instead of relation symbols, with a syntax much in the style of the field of *Functional Logic Programming* [5] (FLP) but under a more semantic perspective, stressing its use for default reasoning. In this way, for instance, rather than being concerned on the operational behavior of unification in FLP (usually related to the rewriting technique of *narrowing* [9]) we will omit

J.J. Alferes and J. Leite (Eds.): JELIA 2004, LNAI 3229, pp. 294–306, 2004.

the use of functors (like the list constructors) from the very beginning, so that we handle a finite Herbrand base.

When representing many domains in NMR we face the typical situation where some relational symbol, for instance $father(x, y)$ actually represents a function $father(x) = y$. In this case, the program must be extended with several rules for explicitly asserting the uniqueness of value y in $father(x, y)$. Functions avoid this explicit axiomatization and, thanks to the possibility of nesting functional terms, allow removing a considerable number of unnecessary variables. Apart from a more comfortable representation, the most important feature we consider in this paper is perhaps the generalization of default negation to the notion of *default value* of each function. This concept is described under the three above-mentioned semantics.

The paper is organized as follows. Section 2 contains a brief review of LP definitions, in order to make the paper self-contained. In the next section, we begin considering ground functional logic programs, where we handle 0-ary functions with default values and we describe the three adapted semantics, providing their translations into standard LP too. After that, we comment on some aspects about expressiveness, showing that functional logic programs generalize normal and extended logic programming. The next section briefly describes non-ground programs with nested functions. Finally, Section 6 outlines some connections to related work and contains the conclusions of the paper.

2   Review of Logic Programming

Given a finite set of atoms $\mathcal{H}$ called the *Herbrand Base*, we define a *program literal* as an atom $p \in \mathcal{H}$ or its default negation *not p* (being the latter also called *default literal*). By *normal logic program* (or just *program* for short) we mean a set of rules like:

$$H \leftarrow B_1, \ldots, B_n$$

where H is an atom called the *head* of the rule, and the $B_i's$ are program literals. We will write B as an abbreviation of $B_1, \ldots, B_n$ and call it the *body* of the rule. We will also allow a special atom $\perp \notin \mathcal{H}$ as rule head, standing for inconsistency and used for rejecting undesired models. When $n = 0$ we say that the rule is a *fact* and directly write H, omitting the arrow. A program P is said to be *positive* iff it contains no default negation.

A *propositional interpretation* I is any subset of $\mathcal{H}$. We use symbol $\models$ to represent classical propositional satisfaction, provided that $\leftarrow$, comma and *not* are understood as classical implication, conjunction and negation, respectively. Using this reading, the concept of (classical) *model* of a program is defined in the usual way. We also define the *direct consequences* operator T_P on interpretations, as follows: $T_P(I) \overset{\text{def}}{=} \{H \mid (H \leftarrow B) \in P \text{ and } I \models B\}$. A well-known result [10] establishes that any positive program P has a least model, we will denote as $least(P)$. Furthermore, for positive programs, T_P is monotonic and its least fixpoint (computable by iteration on $\emptyset$) coincides with $least(P)$.

A *supported model* I of a program P is any fixpoint of T_P, that is, any $I = T_P(I)$. Supported models can also be computed as classical models of a propositional theory called *Clark's completion* [1] which can be easily obtained from P (we omit its description for brevity sake).

The *reduct* of a program P with respect to interpretation I, written P^I corresponds to: (1) removing from P all rules with a program literal *not* p such that $p \in I$; and (2) removing all the default negated literals from the remaining rules. Therefore, P^I is a positive program and has a least model $least(P^I)$. We represent this model as $\Gamma_P(I)$ or simply $\Gamma(I)$ when there is no ambiguity. A *stable model* I of a program P is any fixpoint of Γ, that is: $I = \Gamma(I)$. Furthermore, operator Γ^2 (i.e., Γ applied twice) is monotonic and has a greatest and a least fixpoint, $gfp(\Gamma^2)$ and $lfp(\Gamma^2)$ respectively. The *well-founded model* (WFM) of a program P is a pair of interpretations (I, J) where $I = lfp(\Gamma^2)$ and $J = gfp(\Gamma^2)$. As $I \subseteq J$, we can see the WFM as a three-valued interpretation where atoms in I are *true* (or *founded*), atoms in $J - I$ *undefined*, and atoms not in J are *false* (or *unfounded*).

We will also consider *Extended Logic Programming* (ELP), that is, programs dealing with *explicit negation* '¬'. For simplicity sake, however, we understand ELP as a particular case of normal programs where the Herbrand Base contains an atom "¬p" per each atom p without explicit negation. Given an atom $A \in \mathcal{H}$, we write $\overline{A}$ to denote its complementary atom, that is $\overline{p} = \neg p$ and $\overline{\neg p} = p$. Under this setting, an interpretation I is said to be *consistent* iff it contains no pair of atoms p and $\neg p$. Consistent stable models for ELP receive the name of *answer sets*.

In the case of WFS for ELP, some counterintuitive results have led to the need for a variation called WFSX (*WFS with eXplicit negation*) [8]. This semantics guarantees the so-called *coherence principle*: if an atom $A \in \mathcal{H}$ is founded in the WFM, its complementary atom $\overline{A}$ must be unfounded. In other words, explicit negation $\neg p$ must imply default negation *not* p. The definition of WFSX relies on the idea of seminormal programs. For any ELP rule $r = (H \leftarrow B)$, its *seminormal* version r_s is defined as $(H \leftarrow B, not\ \overline{H})$. Similarly, given program P, its seminormal version P_s consists of a rule r_s per each rule r in P. We write $\Gamma_s(I)$ to stand for $least(P_s^I)$, and say that Γ_s is not defined for an inconsistent I. When defined, operator $\Gamma\Gamma_s$ is monotonic. The *WFM* of a program P (under WFSX) is a pair of interpretations (I, J) such that $I = lfp(\Gamma\Gamma_s)$ and $J = \Gamma_s(I)$, provided that $lfp(\Gamma\Gamma_s)$ is defined (otherwise, the program is said to be *inconsistent*). It has been shown [8] that the WFM under WFSX satisfies the coherence principle.

3   Functional Logic Programs

For describing the syntax of Functional Logic Programs, we begin considering a finite set of ground terms $\mathcal{F}$, that we can consider as 0-ary *function names*, together with a finite set of *constant values* $\mathcal{V}$. We will use letters $f, g, \ldots$ to stand for elements of $\mathcal{F}$ and $v, w, \ldots$ for constant values. The *definition* of each function $f \in \mathcal{F}$ is a sentence like:

$$f : R \quad [= d]$$

where $R \subseteq \mathcal{V}$ is called the *range* of f, and the declaration '$= d$' is optional, representing a *default value* $d \in R$. We will use the notation, $range(f) = R$ and, when defined, $default(f) = d$. As usual, range *boolean* stands for the set $\{\text{true}, \text{false}\}$. A *functional literal* (*F-literal* for short) is any expression like $f = v$, satisfying $v \in range(f)$. For simplicity sake, when $range(f) = boolean$ we may omit the '$= v$' and use a standard logical literal instead, so that:

$$f \stackrel{\text{def}}{=} f = \text{true} \qquad\qquad \neg f \stackrel{\text{def}}{=} f = \text{false}$$

A *functional logic program* (*F-program* for short) is a finite set of rules like:

$$H \leftarrow B_1, \ldots, B_n$$

where H and all the $B'_i s$ are now F-literals. Again, H is called the *head* and can also be the special symbol $\bot$ that denotes inconsistency, whereas $B_1, \ldots, B_m$ are the *body*, which will be abbreviated as B. When convenient, B can also be seen as a set of F-literals. In order to describe the correspondence with normal logic programs, we will always bear in mind the translation of each F-literal L with shape $f = v$ into a ground atom L' of shape $holds(f, v)$. We generalize the use of the prime operator for any construction (expressions, rules, sets, etc) having the expected meaning: it replaces each occurring F-literal L by atom L'. A first important observation in this sense is that given the F-program P, the corresponding normal program P' is *positive* (that is, it contains no default negation).

3.1   Semantics: Stable and Supported Models

An *F-interpretation* I is defined as a (possibly partial) function $I : \mathcal{F} \to \mathcal{V}$ where $I(f)$ can be undefined only if f has no default value and, otherwise, $I(f) \in range(f)$. We alternatively represent an F-interpretation as a consistent set of F-literals, where by *consistent* we mean containing no pair of literals $f = v$ and $f = w$ with $v \neq w$, or the symbol $\bot$. A useful definition is the idea of *default portion* of an F-interpretation I:

$$default(I) \stackrel{\text{def}}{=} \{(f = d) \in I \mid d = default(f)\}$$

that is, the F-literals in I that correspond to assignments of default values.

An F-interpretation I *satisfies* a rule $H \leftarrow B$ iff $H \in I$ whenever $B \subseteq I$. An *F-model* of an F-program P is any F-interpretation I satisfying all the rules of P. An F-program P is said to be *consistent* iff it has some model.

As we did with T_P for normal logic programs, we can easily define an analogous *direct consequences* operator, $t_P(I)$, for F-programs as follows:

$$t_P(I) = \{H \mid (H \leftarrow B) \in P \text{ and } B \subseteq I\}$$

Note that $t_P(I)$ is just a set of F-literals which could be inconsistent or partial, even for functions with default values. In this way, we actually have the straightforward correspondence: $T_{P'}(I') = (t_P(I))'$. Therefore, T_P properties are also applicable for t_P:

Proposition 1. *Any (consistent) F-program P has a least F-model, written F-least(P).*

In the same way, for any program P, operator t_P is monotonic and has a least fixpoint which can be computed by iteration on the least set of F-literals $\emptyset$. Again, by adapting T_P results, we get:

Proposition 2. *If F-program P is consistent, its least F-model corresponds to the least fixpoint of t_P.*

Now, we can extend the idea of stable and supported models for F-programs.

Definition 1 (Functional supported model). *A functional supported model of an F-program P is any F-interpretation I satisfying: $I = t_P(I) \cup default(I)$.*

Definition 2 (Functional stable model). *A functional stable model of a program P is any F-interpretation I satisfying $I = \gamma(I)$, where:*
$$\gamma(I) \stackrel{\text{def}}{=} \text{F-least}(P \cup default(I))$$

3.2   Translation into Normal Logic Programs

When we interpret the previous definitions for stable and supported models of F-programs, it is interesting to note that, in both cases, we deal with a positive program that is "completed" somehow with the default information in I. We will see that this effect can be captured inside normal logic programs by the addition of the axiom rule schemata:

$$\bot \leftarrow holds(f, v), holds(f, w) \tag{1}$$
$$holds(f, d) \leftarrow not\ holds(f, v_1), \ldots, not\ holds(f, v_n) \tag{2}$$

for all function f, values $v, w \in range(f)$ with $v \neq w$, and $d = default(f)$, $\{v_1, \ldots, v_n\} = range(f) - \{d\}$. Axiom (1) simply gets rid of models where a function takes two different values. Axiom (2) allows assuming the default value d for any function f, whenever the function does not take any of the rest of possible values. Any propositional interpretation I' that classically satisfies (1) and (2) can be seen as an F-interpretation I, since it will not contain an inconsistent pair of literals (due to (1)) and will not be partial for functions with default value (due to (2)). This is important because, since any stable (or supported) model is also a classical model of P', axioms (1) and (2) will guarantee that it has an associated F-interpretation.

Theorem 1. *An F-interpretation I is a functional supported model of P iff I' is a supported model of $P^* = P' \cup (1) \cup (2)$.*

Proof. First, note that $T_{P^*}(I')$ contains $T_{P'}(I')$, which corresponds to the translation of $t_P(I)$, as we had seen. The remaining atoms in $T_{P^*}(I')$ come from those heads of axioms (1) and (2) for the cases in which their body is true in I'. Clearly, by consistence of I as an F-interpretation, the body of (1) cannot be true in I'. As for (2), we must collect the set of $holds(f, d)$ for which no other value for f is included in I'. As I' cannot be partial for f, this is equivalent to collect all the $holds(f, d)$ such that $holds(f, d) \in I'$. But this is exactly the translation into atoms of the set $default(I)$. □

The proof suggests that, for the case of supported models, we can replace axiom (2) by the simpler expression:

$$holds(f, d) \leftarrow holds(f, d) \tag{3}$$

For the case of stable models, we first prove that there exists a one-to-one correspondence between operators γ for F-program P and Γ for P^*.

Theorem 2. *Let I, J be a pair of sets of F-literals and P an F-program. Then $J = \gamma(I)$ for P iff $J' = \Gamma(I')$ for P^*.*

Proof. As a proof sketch, we outline a quite obvious correspondence between the reduct $(P^*)^{I'}$ and the F-program $P \cup default(I)$. Consider rule (2) for each function f with $default(f) = d$. If $holds(f, d) \notin I'$, since I' is not partial for f, there must exist some $holds(f, v_i) \in I'$ with $v_i \neq d$, and so, the whole rule (2) will be deleted when computing the reduct. On the other hand, if $holds(f, d) \in I'$, since I' is consistent, no other different $holds(f, v_i)$ belongs to I, and so we can delete all the default literals in (2), what simply amounts to the fact $holds(f, d)$ in the reduct. As a result, the reduct $(P^*)^{I'}$ is exactly the same program than $(P \cup default(I))' \cup (1)$. Finally, note that computing the least model of $(P^*)^{I'}$ is completely analogous to computing the least functional model of $P \cup default(I)$ (for instance, using the direct consequences operator in both cases), where axiom (1) just rules out inconsistent results in the logic program. □

Corollary 1. *An F-interpretation I is a functional stable model of P iff I' is a stable model of P^*.*

3.3   Well-Founded Semantics

The third type of semantics we will consider is the generalization of WFS for the case of F-programs. As we saw in Section 2, the main difference of WFS with respect to the two previous semantics is that, instead of considering multiple models for a program, we get a single model which may leave some atoms undefined. When we move to the functional case, the well-founded model would now have the shape of a pair of sets of F-literals (I, J), $I \subseteq J$. This means, in principle, that each F-literal $f = v$ could be founded, unfounded or undefined regardless the rest of values for function f. However, it is clear that, as happened with WFS for ELP, we must impose the restriction of consistency[1] for the set of founded literals I.

---

[1] Note that, on the other hand, the possibility of an "inconsistent" set of non-unfounded literals J must be allowed, since we could simultaneously have different undefined values for a same function.

Since ELP can be seen as a particular case of F-programs (where all ranges are fixed to *boolean*), it is easy to find similar examples of possible counterintuitive behavior due to the non-satisfaction of the coherence principle. For instance, assume we try to define WFS for any F-program P by correspondence with the standard WFS for P^*.

Example 1. Let P_1 be the F-program $\{(a \leftarrow \neg a), (b \leftarrow a), (c \leftarrow b), \neg b\}$ where $a, b, c : boolean = \texttt{false}$.

The WFM of P_1^* leaves both values of a undefined due to cycle $(a \leftarrow not\ a)$ and, as a consequence, this undefinedness is propagated to literals $b = \texttt{true}$ and $c = \texttt{true}$ through rules $(b \leftarrow a)$ and $(c \leftarrow b)$. This result, however, seems counterintuitive in the presence of fact $\neg b$ which makes $b = \texttt{false}$ founded. As a result, we should expect that condition of rule $(c \leftarrow b)$ became *unfounded*, leaving c false by default.

The generalization of Alferes and Pereira's coherence principle for the case of arbitrary function ranges would be:

Definition 3 (Coherence). *A pair* (I, J) *of sets of literals with* $I \subseteq J$ *and* I *consistent is said to be* coherent *iff for each* $(f = v) \in I$, *we have that* $(f = w) \notin J$ *for all* $w \in range(f) - \{v\}$.

In other words, a coherent pair (I, J) satisfies that, if a function value is founded, then the rest of values for that function are unfounded. As shown with Example 1, using the WFM of P^* as a guide for defining a functional WFS is not adequate for dealing with coherence. Instead, we could think about using a translation of P into ELP interpreted under WFSX.

Definition 4. *Given F-program* P *we define the extended logic program* P^e *as the set of rules in* P' *together with the axiom rule schemata:*

$$\neg holds(f, v) \leftarrow holds(f, w) \tag{4}$$

$$holds(f, d) \leftarrow not\ \neg holds(f, d) \tag{5}$$

where $v, w \in range(f)$ *with* $v \neq w$, *and* $d = default(f)$.

That is, P^e corresponds to P^* where axioms (1) and (2) are now replaced by (4) and (5). It is not difficult to see that these two new axioms are an alternative way of representing (2), provided that (1) is not needed when we deal with explicit negation. An important remark at this point is that program P^e actually handles an extended Herbrand Base $\mathcal{H}$, containing atoms of shape $holds(f, v)$ or $\neg holds(f, v)$. Therefore, when translating an F-interpretation I into a propositional interpretation, we must also describe the truth values for atoms like $\neg holds(f, v)$. Although this information is not explicitly included in I', axiom (4) allows us to consider it as implicit in the following way. For all function f and value v: $\neg holds(f, v) \in I'$ iff exists some $holds(f, w) \in I'$ with $w \neq v$.

Bearing in mind this new translation, we proceed now to define the adapted WFS for the functional case. For any F-program P and any consistent set of literals I, the program $P_s(I)$ (the s stands for "seminormal," by analogy with WFSX) is defined as follows:

$$P_s(I) \stackrel{\text{def}}{=} \{(f = v \leftarrow B) \in P \mid \text{such that no } f = w \in I, \text{ with } v \neq w\}$$

that is, we get those rules of P where the head literal is not contradictory with respect to another literal in I. We write γ_s to stand for γ with respect to program $P_s(I)$, that is: $\gamma_s(I) \stackrel{\text{def}}{=} least(P_s(I) \cup default(I))$. As the definition of $P_s(I)$ requires I to be consistent, γ_s is not defined for an inconsistent I. The following result relating operators γ_s and Γ_s will allow us to inherit properties from WFSX for the case of F-programs:

Theorem 3. *Let I, J be a pair of sets of F-literals (with I consistent) and P an F-program. Then $J = \gamma_s(I)$ for P iff $J' = \Gamma_s(I')$ for P^e.*

Proof. The seminormal program P_s^e contains a rule r_s':

$$holds(f, v) \leftarrow B', not \, \neg holds(f, v) \tag{6}$$

per each rule $r = (f = v \leftarrow B)$ in P, plus the seminormal version of rule schemata (4):

$$\neg holds(f, v) \leftarrow holds(f, w), not \, holds(f, v) \tag{7}$$

and rule schemata (5) (which is already, in fact, a seminormal rule). Now note that the reduct $(P_s^e)^{I'}$ will contain a rule $holds(f, v) \leftarrow B'$ per each r_s' satisfying $\neg holds(f, v) \notin I'$. As we saw for explicitly negated atoms in I', this means that there is no other $w \neq v$ such that $holds(f, w) \in I'$. So, we take rules whose head is consistent in I', what corresponds exactly to $P_s(I)$ in the functional case. $\square$

Consider now the composed operator $\gamma\gamma_s$. The last theorem, together with Theorem 2, allows us to import the next property from operator $\Gamma\Gamma_s$:

Corollary 2. *When defined, operator $\gamma\gamma_s$ is monotonic.*

Thus, we can compute a least fixpoint of $\gamma\gamma_s$, written $lfp(\gamma\gamma_s)$, by iteration on the least consistent set of literals $\emptyset$, provided that this iteration keeps consistence in each step.

Definition 5 (Functional Well-Founded Model). *For any F-program P, if $lfp(\gamma\gamma_s)$ is defined, then the well-founded model (WFM) of P is a pair of sets of F-literals (I, J) where: $I \stackrel{\text{def}}{=} lfp(\gamma\gamma_s)$ and $J \stackrel{\text{def}}{=} \gamma_s(I)$. When $lfp(\gamma\gamma_s)$ is not defined, we say that P is inconsistent.*

As this definition is completely analogous to the WFM under WFSX, Theorem 3 also allows us to derive the following results:

Corollary 3. *The pair (I, J) is the WFM of a program P iff (I', J') is the WFM of P^e under WFSX.*

Corollary 4. *The WFM (I, J) of a F-program P is coherent.*

4   Expressiveness of Functional Programs

The correspondence in the shape of F-programs with positive logic programs may incorrectly lead us to think that the expressive power of the current proposal is lower than full logic programming with default negation. In this section we show that this impression is wrong – the use of default values constitutes an alternative to default negation. To this aim, we show now how to make the converse translation, that is, from a normal logic program to an F-program. Assume we have a (ground) normal logic program P with Herbrand Base $\mathcal{H}$. We can define its corresponding F-program P_F by declaring each ground atom $p \in \mathcal{H}$ as a 0-ary boolean function $p : boolean = \texttt{false}$, (i.e., false by default) and replacing each default literal $(not\ p)$ in P by the F-literal $\neg p$ (that is, $p = \texttt{false}$).

Theorem 4. *An interpretation I is a supported (resp. stable) model of a normal logic program P iff the F-interpretation $I_F = \{p = \texttt{true} \mid p \in I\} \cup \{p = \texttt{false} \mid p \in \mathcal{H} - I\}$ is a functional supported (resp. stable) model of the corresponding F-program P_F.*

Proof. For supported models, first note that $I \models B$ for any rule body B of P iff $B_F \subseteq I_F$ for the corresponding body B_F in P_F. As a result

$$p \in T_P(I) \quad \text{iff} \quad (p = \texttt{true}) \in t_{P_F}(I_F) \tag{8}$$

Now, for the left to right direction, assume that I_F is a functional supported model of P_F. Then, by (8) and construction of I_F it is clear that I is supported model of P. For the other direction, assume that I is a supported model of P. This means that $p \in I$ iff $p \in T_P(I)$ and thus, by (8) and construction of I_F, $(p = \texttt{true}) \in I_F$ iff $(p = \texttt{true}) \in t_{P_F}(I_F)$. On the other hand, if $(p = \texttt{false}) \in I_F$ then $(p = \texttt{false}) \in default(I_F)$. As no $\texttt{false}$ value is in the head of P_F, we get that $t_{P_F}(I_F) \cup default(I_F) = I_F$.

For the case of stable models, we just provide a proof sketch. It is not difficult to see that, informally speaking, the addition of facts in $default(I_F)$ to P_F yields the same effects than the program modulo P^I: in other words, F-programs $P_F \cup default(I_F)$ and P_F^I are equivalent. As a result: $p \in \Gamma(I)$ iff $(p = \texttt{true}) \in \gamma(I_F)$. The rest of the proof is straightforward. $\qquad\qquad\qquad\qquad\square$

Notice how, under this translation, explicit negation behaves as default negation when we have default value $\texttt{false}$. In the case of extended logic programs, the translation is slightly more complicated, since we need handling simultaneously default and explicit negation for each symbol p. This can be accomplished by the inclusion of extra atoms for representing default negation. Given an extended logic program P, we define the corresponding F-program P_k as follows:

1. we declare all atoms $p \in \mathcal{H}$ as $p : boolean$ (i.e., *without* default value),
2. we add a new special function $know : \mathcal{H} \times boolean \longrightarrow boolean = \texttt{false}$,
3. we add the rule schemata: $(know(p, \texttt{true}) \leftarrow p)$, $(know(p, \texttt{false}) \leftarrow \neg p)$,
4. and, finally, for any $p \in \mathcal{H}$, we make the following replacements for extended default literals:

$$not\ p \overset{\text{def}}{=} \neg know(p, \texttt{true}) \qquad\qquad not\ \neg p \overset{\text{def}}{=} \neg know(p, \texttt{false})$$

Function $know(p,v)$ is used to assert that we know that atom p takes value $v \in \{\mathtt{true}, \mathtt{false}\}$. Note that $know(p,v)$ is false by default, and so, the literal $\neg know(p,v)$ will work as default negation. Given a propositional interpretation I, let I_k denote the set of F-literals:

$$\{(know(p, \mathtt{true}) = \mathtt{true}) \mid p \in I \} \cup \{know(p, \mathtt{false}) = \mathtt{true} \mid \overline{p} \in I\}$$
$$\cup\{(know(p, \mathtt{true}) = \mathtt{false}) \mid p \notin I \} \cup \{know(p, \mathtt{false}) = \mathtt{false} \mid \overline{p} \notin I\}$$

Conjecture 1. A pair of interpretations (I, J), with $I \subseteq J$, are the WFM of an extended logic program P under WFSX iff the pair of F-interpretations (I_k, J_k) are the WFM of the F-program P_k. $\qquad\square$

5 Non-ground Programs and Nested Functions

When we consider the use of variables, we will naturally require function arities greater than zero. Although, in principle, the same function name and arity could be used for an arbitrary set of ground functional terms, it will usually be more convenient to define a function domain, that specifies the types of all the possible arguments. The *definition* of a function is now a sentence like:

$$f : D_1 \times D_2 \times \cdots \times D_n \longrightarrow R \quad [= d]$$

where the new $D_1 \times D_2 \times \cdots \times D_n$, with $n \geq 0$, is called the *domain* of f, written $domain(f)$, and being each D_i a finite set of constant values. Under this extension, a (ground) literal would simply have the shape $f(\hat{w}) = v$ where $v \in range(f)$ and $\hat{w}$ is a tuple of values $\hat{w} \in domain(f)$.

Consider the following program P_2 with the function definitions:

$$sex : person \longrightarrow \{\mathtt{male}, \mathtt{female}\}$$
$$parent : person \times person \longrightarrow boolean = \mathtt{false}$$
$$offspring : person \times person \longrightarrow boolean = \mathtt{false}$$
$$father, mother, grandpa, grandma : person \longrightarrow person$$
$$likes : person \times person \cup object \longrightarrow boolean$$
$$nationality : person \longrightarrow \{\mathtt{fr}, \mathtt{es}, \mathtt{pt}, \mathtt{at}, \mathtt{uk}, \dots \} = \mathtt{pt}$$
$$birth : person \longrightarrow [1900, 2100]$$
$$older : person \times person \longrightarrow boolean$$

for some finite ranges *person, object*, and the set of rules (we omit the irrelevant facts database):

$$father(X) = Y \leftarrow parent(Y, X), sex(Y) = \mathtt{male} \qquad (9)$$
$$mother(X) = Y \leftarrow parent(Y, X), sex(Y) = \mathtt{female} \qquad (10)$$
$$offspring(X, Y) \leftarrow parent(X, Y) \qquad (11)$$
$$offspring(X, Y) \leftarrow parent(X, Z), Z \neq Y, \; offspring(Z, Y) \qquad (12)$$
$$grandpa(X, Y) \leftarrow parent(Z, Y), father(Z) = X \qquad (13)$$

$$likes(X,Y) \leftarrow mother(X) = Y \tag{14}$$
$$\neg likes(X,Y) \leftarrow mother(X) = M, mother(Y) = M,$$
$$father(X) = F, father(Y) = G,$$
$$nationality(A) = R, nationality(Y) = S, R \neq S \tag{15}$$
$$older(X,Y) \leftarrow birth(X) = A, birth(Y) = B, A < B \tag{16}$$
$$older(X,Y) \leftarrow offspring(X,Y) \tag{17}$$
$$\perp \leftarrow older(X,Y), older(Y,X), X \neq Y \tag{18}$$

Notice how boolean function *parent* has been declared false by default in order to avoid specifying those pairs of persons for which one is not parent of the other (what actually constitute most of the possible combinations). On the other hand, *likes* is unknown by default, since in some cases we know it is true, in some cases we know it is false, but in most cases we just do not have any information. For instance, rule (14) says that any person likes his/her mother, whereas rule (15) says that X dislikes Y if they have the same mother, but their fathers are of different nationality. Using a default Portuguese nationality (pt) can be useful when dealing with inhabitants of Lisbon, for instance. Relation *older* is partial, since it may be the case that we ignore the birth date of some ancestors.

As for the rules shape, variables are understood as abbreviations of all possible values and, as it can be observed, we allow arbitrary expressions relating variables (with arithmetic and relational operators) so that they describe the final combinations that generate a ground instance.

For simplicity sake, until now we have restricted the study to 0-ary functions, what has just meant a slight change in the shape of program literals. However, one of the most interesting advantages of functional terms is the possibility of constructing nested expressions. Consider, for instance, rule (13). Clearly, variable X is exclusively used for representing the value of $father(Z)$. Thus, it seems natural to replace this auxiliary variable by the functional term $father(Z)$, writing instead:

$$grandpa(father(Z),Y) \leftarrow parent(Z,Y)$$

Similar steps could be applied to rules (14) and (16), respectively leading to:

$$likes(X, mother(X))$$
$$older(X,Y) \leftarrow birth(X) < birth(Y)$$

However, the most interesting example would be rule (15) where we can save many unnecessary variables:

$$\neg likes(X,Y) \leftarrow mother(X) = mother(Y),$$
$$nationality(father(X)) \neq nationality(father(Y)) \tag{19}$$

Allowing this nested use of functions does not introduce any special difficulty, since a nested rule can always be easily unfolded back into the non-nested version by a successive introduction auxiliary variables[2]. Instead, without entering into a more formal description, consider for instance the unfolding of a rule like (19). We can go replacing each inner subexpression by a fresh variable, generating the sequence of transformations:

$$\neg likes(X, Y) \leftarrow mother(X) = mother(Y),$$
$$nationality(father(X)) \neq nationality(father(Y))$$
$$\neg likes(X, Y) \leftarrow V_1 = V_2,$$
$$nationality(father(X)) \neq nationality(father(Y)),$$
$$mother(X) = V_1, mother(Y) = V_2$$
$$\neg likes(X, Y) \leftarrow V_1 = V_2,$$
$$nationality(V_3) \neq nationality(V_4)$$
$$mother(X) = V_1, mother(Y) = V_2,$$
$$father(X) = V_3, father(Y) = V_4$$
$$\neg likes(X, Y) \leftarrow V_1 = V_2,$$
$$V_5 \neq V_6,$$
$$mother(X) = V_1, mother(Y) = V_2,$$
$$father(X) = V_3, father(Y) = V_4$$
$$nationality(V_3) = V_5, nationality(V_4) = V_6$$

that ends up with a rule equivalent to (15).

6   Conclusion and Related Work

We have presented an extension of logic programs with functional terms for their use in Knowledge Representation and Nonmonotonic Reasoning. This extension provides a common framework for default reasoning with functions, declaring the concept of default values of functions under three different semantics adapted from Clark's completion, stable models and WFS.

There exist many connections to related work that deserve to be formally studied in future work. The closer approach inside Nonmonotonic Reasoning is probably the formalism of *Causal Theories* [4] inspired by the causal logic in [6]. Our description of the supported models semantics for functional programs has a close relation to the idea of *causally explained models* previously introduced in that approach[3]. Furthermore, the use of *multi-valued* symbols does not suppose a real novelty in Causal Theories and, in fact, the definition of default values is something usually done by the addition of expressions like rule (3). The only part

---

[2] Another alternative would also be to describe the semantics taking into account these nested expressions from the very beginning, but we have preferred a more incremental presentation in this paper.

[3] As pointed out by a referee, causally explained models are more restrictive in the sense that they are always *total*, that is, for any atom p, either literal p or literal $\neg p$ belongs to the model.

of our proposal (for supported models) that would mean a real contribution in this sense is the possibility of nesting functional terms as described in Section 5, which is directly applicable to Causal Theories too.

As for the relation to Functional LP, much work remain to be done yet. For instance, the use of default rules for FLP has already been studied in [7], although mostly analyzed from an operational perspective with respect to narrowing. It would be very interesting to establish a formal relationship between that work and some or all the semantics we propose in this paper (perhaps, due to the kind of programming paradigm, especially with WFS).

Other topics for future work include the extension of this framework for its use for Reasoning about Actions and Change. We expect that the definition of functions will allow efficiency improvements by restricting the grounding process, as happens for instance, with the functional extension [2] of the classical planning language STRIPS.

References

1. K. L. Clark. Negation as failure. In H. Gallaire and J. Minker, editors, *Logic and Databases*, pages 241–327. Plenum, 1978.
2. H. Geffner. Functional STRIPS: a more flexible language for planning and problem solving. In *Logic-Based Artificial Intelligence*. Kluwer, 2000.
3. M. Gelfond and V. Lifschitz. The stable models semantics for logic programming. In *Proc. of the 5th Intl. Conf. on Logic Programming*, pages 1070–1080, 1988.
4. E. Giunchiglia, J. Lee, V. Lifschitz, N. McCain, and H. Turner. Nonmonotonic causal theories. *Artificial Intelligence Journal*, 153:49–104, 2004.
5. M. Hanus. The integration of functions into logic programming: from theory to practice. *Journal of Logic Programming*, 19,20:583–628, 1994.
6. N. McCain and H. Turner. Causal theories of action and change. In *Proc. of the AAAI-97*, pages 460–465, 1997.
7. J. J. Moreno-Navarro. Extending constructive negation for partial functions in lazy functional-logic languages. In *Extensions of Logic Programming*, pages 213–227, 1996.
8. L. M. Pereira and J. J. Alferes. Well founded semantics for logic programs with explicit negation. In *Proceedings of ECAI'92*, pages 102–106, Montreal, Canada, 1992. John Wiley & Sons.
9. J. R. Slagle. Automated theorem-proving for theories with simplifiers, commutativity and associativity. *Journal of the ACM*, 21(4):622–642, 1974.
10. M. H. van Emden and R. A. Kowalski. The semantics of predicate logic as a programming language. *Journal of the ACM*, 23:733–742, 1976.
11. A. van Gelder, K. A. Ross, and J. S. Schlipf. The well-founded semantics for general logic programs. *Journal of the ACM*, 38(3):620–650, 1991.

Parallel Encodings of Classical Planning as Satisfiability

Jussi Rintanen[1], Keijo Heljanko[2], and Ilkka Niemelä[2]

[1] Albert-Ludwigs-Universität Freiburg
Institut für Informatik, Georges-Köhler-Allee
79110 Freiburg im Breisgau
Germany
[2] Helsinki University of Technology
Laboratory for Theoretical Computer Science
P. O. Box 5400, FI-02015 HUT
Finland

Abstract. We consider a number of semantics for plans with parallel operator application. The standard semantics used most often in earlier work requires that parallel operators are independent and can therefore be executed in any order. We consider a more relaxed definition of parallel plans, first proposed by Dimopoulos et al., as well as normal forms for parallel plans that require every operator to be executed as early as possible. We formalize the semantics of parallel plans emerging in this setting, and propose effective translations of these semantics into the propositional logic. And finally we show that one of the semantics yields an approach to classical planning that is sometimes much more efficient than the existing SAT-based planners.

1 Introduction

Satisfiability planning [6] is a leading approach to solving difficult planning problems. An important factor in its efficiency is the notion of parallel plans [6,2]. The standard parallel encoding, the *state-based encoding* [6], allows the simultaneous execution of a set of operators as long as the operators are mutually non-interfering. This condition guarantees that any total ordering on the simultaneous operators is a valid execution and in all cases leads to the same state. We call this semantics of parallelism *the step semantics*. Two benefits of this form of parallelism in planning as satisfiability are that, first, it is unnecessary to consider all possible orderings of a set of non-interfering operators, and second, less clauses and propositional variables are needed as the values of the state variables in the intermediate states need not be represented.

In this paper we formalize two more refined parallel semantics for AI planning and present efficient encodings of them in the propositional logic. Both of the semantics are known from earlier research but the first, *process semantics*, has not been considered in connection with planning, and the second, *1-linearization semantics*, has not been given efficient encodings in SAT/CSP before. With our new encoding this semantics dramatically outperforms the other semantics and encodings given earlier. Our main innovations here are the definition of *disabling graphs* and the use of the strong components (or strongly connected components SCCs) of these graphs to derive very efficient encodings.

J.J. Alferes and J. Leite (Eds.): JELIA 2004, LNAI 3229, pp. 307–319, 2004.

The two semantics considered in this paper are orthogonal refinements of the step semantics. The process semantics is stricter than the step semantics in that it requires all actions to be taken as early as possible. Process semantics was first introduced for Petri nets; for an overview see [1]. Heljanko [5] has applied this semantics to the deadlock detection of 1-safe Petri nets and has shown that it leads to big efficiency gains on many types of problems in bounded model-checking.

The idea of the 1-linearization semantics was proposed by Dimopoulos et al. [4]. They pointed out that it is not necessary to require that all parallel operators are non-interfering as long as the parallel operators can be executed in at least one order. They also showed how blocks worlds problems can be modified to satisfy this condition and that the reduction in the number of time points improves runtimes. Until now the application of 1-linearization in satisfiability planning had been hampered by the cubic size of the obvious encodings. We give more compact encodings for this semantics and show that this often leads to dramatic improvements in planning efficiency. Before the developments reported in this paper, this semantics had never been used in an automated planner that is based on a declarative language like the propositional logic.

The structure of this paper is as follows. In Section 4 we discuss the standard step semantics of parallel plans and its encoding in the propositional logic. Section 5 introduces the underlying ideas of the process semantics and discusses its representation in the propositional logic. In Section 6 we present the 1-linearization refinement to step semantics and its encoding. Section 7 evaluates the advantages of the different semantics in terms of some planning problems. Section 8 discusses related work.

2   Notation

We consider planning in a setting where the states of the world are represented in terms of a set P of Boolean state variables that take the value *true* or *false*. Each *state* is a valuation of P, that is, an assignment $s : P \to \{T, F\}$. We use *operators* for expressing how the state of the world can be changed.

Definition 1. *An* operator *on a set of state variables P is a triple $\langle p, e, c \rangle$ where*

1. *p is a propositional formula on P (the precondition),*
2. *e is a set of literals on P (unconditional effects), and*
3. *c is a set of pairs $f \rhd d$ (conditional effects) where f is a propositional formula on P and d is a set of literals on P.*

For an operator $\langle p, e, c \rangle$ its *active effects* in state s are

$$e \cup \bigcup \{d | f \rhd d \in c, s \models f\}.$$

The operator is *applicable* in s if $s \models p$ and its set of active effects in s is consistent (does not contain both p and $\neg p$ for any $p \in P$.) If this is the case, then we define $\text{app}_o(s) = s'$ as the unique state that is obtained from s by making the active effects of o true and retaining the truth-values of the state variables not occurring in the active effects. For sequences $o_1; o_2; \ldots; o_n$ of operators we define $\text{app}_{o_1;o_2;\ldots;o_n}(s)$ as

$app_{o_n}(\cdots app_{o_2}(app_{o_1}(s))\cdots)$. For sets S of operators and states s we define $app_S(s)$: the result of simultaneously applying all operators $o \in S$. We require that $app_o(s)$ is defined for every $o \in S$ and that the set of active effects of all operators in S is consistent. Different semantics of parallelism impose further restrictions on sets S.

Let $\pi = \langle P, I, O, G \rangle$ be a *problem instance*, consisting of a set P of state variables, a state I on P (the initial state), a set O of operators on P, and a formula G on P (the goal formula). A (sequential) *plan* for π is a sequence $\sigma = o_1; \ldots; o_n$ of operators from O such that $app_\sigma(I) \models G$, that is, applying the operators in the given order starting in the initial state is defined (precondition of every operator is true when the operator is applied) and produces a state that satisfies the goal formula.

In the rest of this paper we also consider plans that are sequences of *sets of operators*, so that at each execution step all operators in the set are simultaneously applied. The different semantics discussed in the next sections impose further constraints on these sets.

3 Planning as Satisfiability

Planning can be performed by propositional satisfiability testing as follows. Produce formulae $\phi_0, \phi_1, \phi_2, \ldots$ such that ϕ_i is satisfiable if there is a plan of length i. The formulae are tested for satisfiability in the order of increasing plan length, and from the first satisfying assignment that is found a plan is constructed. Length i of a plan means that there are i time points in which a *set* of operators is applied simultaneously. There are alternative semantics for this kind of parallel plans and their encodings in the propositional logic differ only in axioms restricting simultaneous application of operators. Next we describe the part of the encodings shared by all the semantics.

The state variables in a problem instance are $P = \{a^1, \ldots, a^n\}$ and the operators are $O = \{o^1, \ldots, o^m\}$. For a state variable a we have the propositional variable a_t that expresses the truth-value of a at time point t. Similarly, for an operator o we have o_t for expressing whether o is applied at t. For formulae ϕ we denote the formula with all propositional variables subscripted with the index to a time point t by ϕ_t.

A formula is generated to answer the following question. Is there an execution of a sequence of sets of operators taking l time points that reaches a state satisfying G from the initial state I? The formula is conjunction of I_0 (formula describing the initial state with propositions marked with time point 0), G_l, and the formulae described below, instantiated with all $t \in \{0, \ldots, l-1\}$.

First, for every $o = \langle p, e, c \rangle \in O$ there are the following axioms. The precondition p has to be true when the operator is applied.

$$o_t \rightarrow p_t \tag{1}$$

If o is applied, then its (unconditional) effects e are true at the next time point.

$$o_t \rightarrow e_{t+1} \tag{2}$$

Here we view the set e of literals as a conjunction of literals. For every $f \rhd d \in c$ the effects d will be true if the antecedent f is true at the preceding time point.

$$(o_t \wedge f_t) \rightarrow d_{t+1} \tag{3}$$

Second, the value of a state variable does not change if no operator that changes it is applied. Hence for every state variable a we have two formulae, one expressing the conditions for the change of a to false from true, and another from true to false. The formulae are analogous, and here we only give the one for change from true to false:

$$(a_t \wedge \neg a_{t+1}) \rightarrow ((o_t^1 \wedge \phi_t^1) \vee \cdots \vee (o_t^m \wedge \phi_t^m)) \tag{4}$$

where ϕ^i expresses the condition under which operator o^i changes a from true to false. So let $o^i = \langle p, e, c \rangle$. If a is a negative effect in e then simply $\phi^i = \top$. Otherwise, the change takes place if one of the conditional effects is active. Let $f^1 \rhd d^1, \ldots, f^k \rhd d^k$ be the conditional effects with a as a negative effect in d^j. Here $k \geq 0$. Then $\phi^i = f^1 \vee \ldots \vee f^k$. The empty disjunction with $k = 0$ is the constant false $\bot$.

Finally, we need axioms for restricting the parallel application of operators: we will describe them in the next sections for each semantics. The resulting set of formulae is satisfiable if and only if there is an operator sequence taking l time points that reaches a goal state from the initial state.

In addition to the above axioms, which are necessary to guarantee that the set of satisfying assignments exactly corresponds to the set of plans with l time points, it is often useful to add further constraints that do not affect the set of satisfying assignments but instead help in pruning the set of incomplete solutions need to be looked at, and thereby speed up plan search. The most important type of such constraints for many planning problems is invariants, which are formulae that are true in all states reachable from the initial state. Typically, one uses only a restricted class of invariants that are efficient (polynomial time) to identify. There are efficient algorithms for finding many invariants that are 2-literal clauses [8,2]. In the experiments in Section 7 we use formulae $l_t \vee l'_t$ for invariants $l \vee l'$ as produced by the algorithm by Rintanen [8].

4   Step Semantics

In this section we formally present a semantics that generalizes the semantics used in most works on parallel plans, for example Kautz and Selman [6]. Practical implementations of satisfiability planning approximate this semantics as described in Section 4.1.

For defining parallel plans under step semantics, we need to define when operators interfere in a way that makes their simultaneous application unwanted.

Definition 2 (Interference). *Operators* $o_1 = \langle p_1, e_1, c_1 \rangle$ *and* $o_2 = \langle p_2, e_2, c_2 \rangle$ *interfere in state* s *if*

1. $s \models p_1 \wedge p_2$,
2. *the set* $e_1 \cup \bigcup \{d | f \rhd d \in c_1, s \models f\} \cup e_2 \cup \bigcup \{d | f \rhd d \in c_2, s \models f\}$ *is consistent, and*
3. *the operators are not applicable in both orders or applying them in different orders leads to different results, that is, at least one of the following holds:*
    a) $app_{o_1}(s) \not\models p_2$,
    b) $app_{o_2}(s) \not\models p_1$, *or*
    c) *active effects of* o_2 *are different in* s *and in* $app_{o_1}(s)$ *or active effects of* o_1 *are different in* s *and in* $app_{o_2}(s)$.

The first two conditions are the *applicability conditions* for parallel operators: preconditions have to be satisfied and the effects may not contradict each other. The third condition says that interference is the impossibility to interpret parallel application as application in any order, o_1 followed by o_2, or o_2 followed by o_1, leading to the same state in both cases: one execution order is impossible or the resulting states may be different.

The conditions guarantee that two operators may be exchanged in any total ordering of a set of pairwise non-interfering operators without changing the state that is reached.

Definition 3 (Step plans). *For a set of operators O and an initial state I, a plan is a sequence $T = S_1, \ldots, S_l$ of sets of operators such that there is a sequence of states $s_0, \ldots, s_l$ (the execution of T) such that*

1. $s_0 = I$,
2. $s_{i-1} \models p$ *for all $i \in \{1, \ldots, l\}$ and $\langle p, e, c \rangle \in S_i$,*
3. $\bigcup_{\langle p,e,c \rangle \in S_i} (e \cup \bigcup \{d | f \rhd d \in c, s_{i-1} \models f\})$ *is consistent for every $i \in \{1, \ldots, l\}$,*
4. $s_i = app_{S_i}(s_{i-1})$ *for all $i \in \{1, \ldots, l\}$, and*
5. *for all $i \in \{1, \ldots, l\}$ and $o, o' \in S_i$ and $S \subseteq S_i \setminus \{o, o'\}$, o and o' are applicable in $app_S(s_{i-1})$ and do not interfere in $app_S(s_{i-1})$.*

Example 1. Consider $S_1 = \{o_1, o_2, o_3\}$ where $o_1 = \langle p \vee \neg p, \{q\}, \emptyset \rangle$, $o_2 = \langle p \vee \neg p, \emptyset, \{q \rhd p\} \rangle$, and $o_3 = \langle p \vee \neg p, \emptyset, \{p \rhd r\} \rangle$. S_1 cannot be the first step of a step plan starting from an initial state I in which p, q and r are false because the fifth condition of step plans is not satisfied: there is $S = \{o_1\} \subseteq S_1$ such that o_2 and o_3 interfere in $app_S(I)$, because applying o_3 in $app_S(I)$ has no effect but applying o_3 in $app_{o_2}(app_S(I))$ makes r true.

Lemma 1. *Let $T = S_1, \ldots, S_k, \ldots, S_l$ be a step plan. Let $T' = S_1, \ldots, S_k^0, S_k^1, \ldots, S_l$ be the step plan obtained from T by splitting the step S_k into two steps S_k^0 and S_k^1 such that $S_k = S_k^0 \cup S_k^1$ and $S_k^0 \cap S_k^1 = \emptyset$.*

If $s_0, \ldots, s_k, \ldots, s_l$ is the execution of T then $s_0, \ldots, s_k', s_k, \ldots, s_l$ for some s_k' is the execution of T'.

Proof. So $s_k' = app_{S_k^0}(s_{k-1})$ and $s_k = app_{S_k}(s_{k-1})$ and we have to prove that $app_{S_k^1}(s_k') = s_k$ and operators in S_k^1 are applicable in s_k'. For the first we will show that the active effects of every operator in S_k^1 are the same in s_{k-1} and in s_k', and hence the changes from s_{k-1} to s_k are the same in both plans. Let $o^1, \ldots, o^z$ be the operators in S_k^0 and let $T_i = \{o^1, \ldots, o^i\}$ for every $i \in \{0, \ldots, z\}$. We show by induction that the active effects of every operator in S_k^1 are the same in s_{k-1} and $app_{T_i}(s_{k-1})$ and that every operator in S_k^1 is applicable in $app_{T_i}(s_{k-1})$, from which the claim follows as $s_k' = app_{T_z}(s_{k-1})$.

Base case $i = 0$: Immediate because $T_0 = \emptyset$.

Inductive case $i \geq 1$: By the induction hypothesis the active effects of every operator $o \in S_k^1$ are the same in s_{k-1} and in $app_{T_{i-1}}(s_{k-1})$ and o is applicable in $app_{T_{i-1}}(s_{k-1})$. In $app_{T_i}(s_{k-1})$ additionally the operator o^i has been applied. We have to show that this operator application does not affect the set of active effects of o nor does it disable o. By the definition of step plans, the operators o and o^i do not interfere in $\mathrm{app}_{T_{i-1}}(s_{k-1})$, and hence the active effects of o are the same in $\mathrm{app}_{T_{i-1}}(s_{k-1})$ and in $\mathrm{app}_{T_{i-1}\cup\{o^i\}}(s_{k-1})$ and o^i does not disable o. This completes the induction and the proof.

Theorem 1. *Let* $T = S_1, \ldots, S_k, \ldots, S_l$ *be a step plan. Then any* $\sigma = o_1^1; \ldots; o_{n_1}^1; o_2^2;$ $\ldots; o_{n_2}^2; \ldots; o_1^l; \ldots; o_{n_l}^l$ *such that for every* $i \in \{1, \ldots, l\}$ *the sequence* $o_1^i; \ldots; o_{n_i}^i$ *is a total ordering of* S_i, *is a plan, and its execution leads to the same final state as that of* T.

Proof. First all empty steps are removed from the step plan. By Lemma 1 non-singleton steps can be split repeatedly to smaller non-empty steps until every step is singleton and the desired ordering is obtained. The resulting plan is a sequential plan.

4.1 Encoding in the Propositional Logic

Definition 3 provides a notion of step plans that attempts to maximize parallelism. Most works on satisfiability planning [6] use a simple syntactic condition for guaranteeing non-interference, approximating Condition 3 in Definition 2. For example, the simultaneous application of two operators is forbidden always when a state variable affected by one operator occurs in the precondition or in the antecedents of conditional effects of the other. In our experiments in Section 7 we include the formula $\neg o_t \vee \neg o'_t$ for any such pair of operators o and o' with mutually non-contradicting effects and mutually non-contradicting preconditions to guarantee that we get step plans. There are $O(m^2)$ such constraints for m operators.

5   Process Semantics

The idea of process semantics is that we only consider those step plans that fulfill the following condition. There is no operator o applied at time $t + 1$ with $t \geq 0$ such that the sequence of sets of operators obtained by moving o from time $t + 1$ to time t would be a step plan according to Definition 3.

The important property of process semantics is that even though the additional condition reduces the number of acceptable plans, whenever there is a plan with t time steps under step semantics, there is also a plan with t time steps under process semantics. A plan satisfying the process condition is obtained from a step plan by repeatedly moving operators violating the condition one time point earlier. As a result of this procedure a step plan satisfying the process condition is obtained which is greedy in the sense that it applies each operator of the original step plan as early as possible.

As an example consider a set S in which no two operators interfere nor have contradicting effects and are applicable in state s. If we have time points 0 and 1, we can apply each operator alternatively at 0 or at 1. The resulting state at time point 2 will be the same in all cases. So, under step semantics the number of equivalent plans on two time points is $2^{|S|}$. Process semantics says that no operator that is applicable at 0 may be applied later than at 0. Under process semantics there is only one plan instead of $2^{|S|}$.

5.1 Encoding in the Propositional Logic

The encoding of process semantics extends the encoding of step semantics, so we take all axioms for the latter and have further axioms specific to process semantics.

The axioms for process semantics deny the application of an operator o at time $t + 1$ if it can be shown that moving o to time t would also be a valid step plan according to Definition 3. The idea is that if an operator o is delayed to be applied at time $t + 1$ then there must be some operator o' applied at time t which is the reason why o cannot be moved to time t. More precisely, (i) o' may have enabled o, (ii) o' may have conflicting effects with o, or (iii) moving o to time t might make it interfere with o' according to Condition 5 of Definition 3.

We cautiously approximate the process semantics using simple syntactic conditions to compute for each operator o the set of operators $\{o^1, \ldots, o^n\}$ which are the potential reasons why o cannot be moved one time point earlier. Then we have the following axioms guaranteeing that the application of o is delayed only when there is a reason for this.

$$o_{t+1} \rightarrow (o_t^1 \vee o_t^2 \vee \cdots \vee o_t^n)$$

These disjunctions may be long and it may be useful to use only the shortest of these constraints, as they are most likely to help speed up plan search. In the experiments reported later, we used only constraints with 6 literals or less. We tried the full set of process axioms, but the high number of long disjunctions led to poor performance.

6   1-Linearization Semantics

Dimopoulos et al. [4] adapted the idea of satisfiability planning to answer set programming and presented an interesting idea. The requirement that parallel operators are executable in any order can be relaxed, only requiring that *one* ordering is executable. They called this idea *post-serializability* and showed how to transform operators for blocks world problems to make them post-serializable. The resulting nonmonotonic logic programs were shown to be more efficient due to a shorter parallel plan length. Rintanen [8] implemented this idea in a constraint-based planner and Cayrol et al. [3] in the GraphPlan framework.

We will present a semantics and general-purpose domain-independent translations of this more relaxed semantics into the propositional logic. Our approach does not require transforming the problem. Instead, we synthesize constraints that guarantee that the operators applied simultaneously can be ordered to an executable plan.

Definition 4 (1-linearization plans). *For a set of operators O and an initial state I, a 1-linearization plan is a sequence $T = S_1, \ldots, S_l$ of sets of operators such that there is a sequence of states $s_0, \ldots, s_l$ (the execution of T) such that*

1. $s_0 = I$,
2. $s_{i-1} \models p$ *for all $i \in \{1, \ldots, l\}$ and $\langle p, e, c \rangle \in S_i$,*
3. *the set $\bigcup_{\langle p,e,c \rangle \in S_i} (e \cup \bigcup \{d | f \rhd d \in c, s_{i-1} \models f\})$ is consistent for every $i \in \{1, \ldots, l\}$,*
4. $s_i = app_{S_i}(s_{i-1})$ *for all $i \in \{1, \ldots, l\}$, and*

5. *for every $i \in \{1, \ldots, l\}$ there is a total ordering $o_1 < o_2 < \ldots < o_n$ of S_i such that for all operators $o_j = \langle p_j, e_j, c_j \rangle \in S_i$*
   a) *$app_{o_1;o_2;\ldots;o_{j-1}}(s_{i-1}) \models p_j$, and*
   b) *for all $f \rhd d \in c_j$, $s_{i-1} \models f$ if and only if $app_{o_1;o_2;\ldots;o_{j-1}}(s_{i-1}) \models f$.*

The difference to step semantics is that we have replaced the non-interference condition with a weaker condition. From an implementations point of view, the main difficulty here is finding appropriate total orderings $<$.

Theorem 2. *(i) Each step plan is a 1-linearization plan and (ii) for every 1-linearization plan T there is a step plan whose execution leads to the same final state as that of T.*

Proof. (Sketch) (i) Consider a step plan $T = S_1, \ldots, S_l$. By Theorem 1 for every $i \in \{1, \ldots, l\}$ any total ordering of the operators in S_i can be used to satisfy Condition 5 in Definition 4. Hence, T is a 1-linearization plan. (ii) For a 1-linearization plan $T = S_1, \ldots, S_l$, a step plan whose execution leads to the same final state as that of T can be obtained as follows: $\{o_1^1\}, \ldots, \{o_{n_1}^1\}, \ldots, \{o_1^l\}, \ldots, \{o_{n_l}^l\}$ where for every $i \in \{1, \ldots, l\}$, the sequence $\{o_1^i\}, \ldots, \{o_{n_i}^i\}$ is a total ordering of S_i given by Condition 5 of Definition 4.

6.1   Encoding in the Propositional Logic

Given the precondition and effect axioms (1), (2) and (3), we have to guarantee that there is a total ordering of the operators so that no operator application disables the operators that will be applied later, and no operator application changes the set of active (conditional) effects of later operators. The encodings we give are stricter than our formal definition of 1-linearization semantics and do not always allow all the parallelism that is possible. Next we define the notion of *disabling graphs* in order to provide compact and effective encodings of 1-linearization semantics in the propositional logic.

The motivation for using disabling graphs is the following. Define a *circularly disabled set* as a set of operators that is applicable in some state without the effects contradicting each other and that cannot be totally ordered into a sequential plan so that no operator disables or changes the active effects of a later operator. Now any set-inclusion minimal circularly disabled set is a subset of an SCC of the disabling graph. We may allow the simultaneous application of a set of operators from the same SCC if the subgraph of the disabling graph induced by those operators does not contain a cycle.[1]

Definition 5 (Disabling graph). *A graph $\langle O, E \rangle$ is a disabling graph of a set of operators O where $E \subseteq O \times O$ is the set of directed edges so that $\langle o_1, o_2 \rangle \in E$ if for $o_1 = \langle p_1, e_1, c_1 \rangle$ and $o_2 = \langle p_2, e_2, c_2 \rangle$ there is a state s[2] such that*

1. *$s \models p_1 \wedge p_2$, and*

---

[1] In step semantics simultaneous application is allowed if the subgraph does not have *any* edges.
[2] Clearly, this could be restricted to states that are reachable from the initial state, but testing reachability is PSPACE-hard. Instead, one can use some subclass of invariants computable in polynomial time to ignore some of the unreachable states, like we have done in our implementation of disabling graphs.

2. $F_1 \cup F_2$ *is consistent where* $F_1 = e_1 \cup \bigcup\{d|f \rhd d \in c_1, s \models f\}$ *and* $F_2 = e_2 \cup \bigcup\{d|f \rhd d \in c_2, s \models f\}$, *and*
3. *applying* o_1 *may make* o_2 *inapplicable or may change the active effects of* o_2:
   a) $app_{o_1}(s) \not\models p_2$, *or*
   b) *there is* $f \rhd d \in c_2$ *such that either* $s \models f$ *and* $app_{o_1}(s) \not\models f$, *or* $s \not\models f$ *and* $app_{o_1}(s) \models f$.

For a given set of operators there are typically several disabling graphs because the graph obtained by adding an edge to a disabling graph is also a disabling graph. In the experiments in Section 7 we use disabling graphs that are not necessarily minimal but can be computed in polynomial time. For STRIPS operators they are minimal.

Our disabling graphs are related to the definition of preconditions-effects graphs of Dimopoulos et al. [4], but they often have many less edges and much smaller SCCs. For example, in the well-known logistics problems all the strong components have 1 or $n + 1$ operators, where n is the number of airplanes[3]. This means that encoding the constraints that guarantee that simultaneous operators indeed can be linearized will be rather efficient, as only cycles of rather small length have to be considered. Notice that operators in different strong components cannot be part of the same cycle; therefore constraints on their simultaneous application are not needed. Hence when every strong component has cardinality 1, no constraints whatsoever are needed.

Next we discuss two ways of synthesizing constraints that guarantee that simultaneous operators can be ordered to a valid totally ordered plan.

6.2 General $O(n^3)$ Encoding

We can exactly test that the intersection of one SCC and a set of simultaneous operators do not form a cycle. The next encoding allows the maximum parallelism with respect to a given disabling graph, but it is expensive in terms of formula size.

Let o^i and $o^{i'}$ belong to the same SCC of the disabling graph and let there be an edge from o^i to $o^{i'}$. We use auxiliary propositions $c^{i,j}$ for all operators with indices i and j, indicating that there is a set of applied operators $o^i, o^1, o^2, \ldots, o^n, o^j$ such that every operator disables or changes the effects of its immediate successor in the sequence. Then we have the formulae $(o^i_t \land c^{i',j}_t) \rightarrow c^{i,j}_t$ for all i, i' and j such that $i \neq i' \neq j \neq i$. Further we have formulae $\neg(o^i_t \land c^{i',i}_t)$ for preventing the completion of a cycle.

The size of the encoding is cubic and the number of new propositional variables is quadratic in the number of operators in an SCC. Some problems have SCCs of dozens or hundreds of operators, and this $O(n^3)$ means that there are thousands or millions of formulae, which often makes this encoding impractical.

6.3 Fixed Ordering

The simplest and possibly the most effective encoding does not allow all the parallelism that allowed by the preceding encoding, but it leads to small formulae. With this encoding

---

[3] The refinement to disabling graphs involving invariants in the preceding footnote makes all SCCs for Logistics singleton sets.

the number of constraints on parallel application *is smaller* than with the less permissive step semantics, as the set of constraints on parallelism is a subset of the constraints for step semantics. One therefore receives two benefits simultaneously: possibly much shorter parallel plans and formulae with a smaller size / time points ratio.

The idea is to impose beforehand an (arbitrary) ordering on the operators $o^1, \ldots, o^n$ in an SCC and to disallow parallel application of two operators o^i and o^j such that o^i may disable or change the effects of o^j only if $i < j$. Hence, in comparison to step semantics, part of the parallelism axioms on operators within one SCC are left out. In comparison to step semantics, the total reduction in the number of constraints can be significant because none of the inter-SCC parallelism constraints are needed.

This is the encoding we have very successfully applied to a wide range of planning problems, as discussed in the next section. Selecting the ordering carefully may increase parallelism. In our experiments we order the operators in the order they happen to come out of our PDDL front-end. Better orderings could be produced by heuristic methods.

7 Experiments

We evaluate the different semantics on a number of benchmarks from the AIPS planning competitions. In addition to the Logistics, Depots and Satellite benchmarks reported here, we also test Driver, Zeno, Freecell, Schedule and Mystery, but do not report runtimes because of lack of space. On Freecell and Schedule 1-linearization does not decrease plan length and runtimes are comparable to step semantics. Process semantics fares worse than step semantics on Schedule. Mystery is trivial for 1-linearization semantics. Runtime differences with Driver and Zeno are like with Logistics.

In Tables 1 and 2 we present the name of the problem instance and the runtimes for the formulae corresponding to the highest number(s) of time points without a plan (truth value F) and the first satisfiable formula corresponding to a plan (truth value T). Runtimes for 1-linearization semantics are reported on their own lines because its shortest plan lengths differ from the other semantics.

For the experiments we use a 3.6 GHz Intel Xeon processor with 512 KB internal cache and the Siege SAT solver version 3 by Ryan of the Simon Fraser University. Because Siege uses randomization, the runtimes for a given formula vary across executions. We run Siege 40 times on each formula and report the average. When only some of the runs finish within a time limit of 3 to 4 minutes (we terminate every 60 seconds those processes that have consumed over 180 seconds of CPU) we report the average time t of the finished runs as $> n$. This roughly means that the average runtime on Siege exceeds n seconds. A dash $-$ indicates that none of the runs finished.

The best runtimes are usually obtained with the 1-linearization semantics. It is often one or two orders of magnitude faster. This usually goes back to the shorter plan length: formulae are smaller and easier to evaluate.

Contrary to our expectations, process semantics usually does not provide an advantage over step semantics although there are often far fewer potential plans to consider. When showing the inexistence of plans of certain length, the additional constraints could provide a big advantage, similarly to symmetry-breaking constraints. In a few cases, like

Table 1. Runtimes of Satellite and Logistics problems in seconds

instance	len	val	1-lin	step	proc
satell-15	4	F	8.86		
satell-15	5	T	1.65		
satell-15	7	F		24.15	21.91
satell-15	8	T		3.61	3.50
satell-16	3	F	2.27		
satell-16	4	T	3.91		
satell-16	5	F		9.17	8.24
satell-16	6	?		-	-
satell-16	7	T		6.57	6.85
satell-17	3	F	0.22		
satell-17	4	T	2.48		
satell-17	5	F		1.12	1.31
satell-17	6	T		1.86	1.96
satell-18	4	F	0.06		
satell-18	5	T	0.23		
satell-18	7	F		0.24	0.27
satell-18	8	T		0.48	0.57
satell-19	6	F	46.26		
satell-19	7	T	25.78		
satell-19	10	F		> 225.50	-
satell-19	11	?		-	-
satell-19	12	T		> 170.69	-

instance	len	val	1-lin	step	proc
log-23-0	8	F	0.56		
log-23-0	9	T	2.93		
log-23-0	14	F		37.69	27.86
log-23-0	15	?		-	-
log-23-0	16	T		> 139.10	> 132.64
log-23-1	8	F	1.70		
log-23-1	9	T	0.57		
log-23-1	14	F		48.34	44.12
log-23-1	15	T		> 66.07	> 76.50
log-24-0	8	F	0.40		
log-24-0	9	T	3.33		
log-24-0	14	F		35.93	13.77
log-24-0	15	?		-	-
log-24-0	16	T		> 108.92	> 99.44
log-24-1	9	F	9.66		
log-24-1	10	T	2.61		
log-24-1	15	F		> 101.29	> 112.07
log-24-1	16	?		-	-
log-24-1	17	T		> 131.52	> 119.01

the last or second to last unsatisfiable formula for log-24-0, process constraints do halve the runtimes. The reason for the ineffectiveness of process semantics may lie in these benchmarks: many operators may prevent earlier application of an operator, and this results in long clauses that figure only very late in the search.

8   Related Work

The BLACKBOX planner of Kautz and Selman [7] is the best-known planner that implements the satisfiability planning paradigm. Its GraphPlan-based encoding is similar to our step semantics encoding, but less compact for example because of its use of GraphPlan's NO-OPs. Comparison of sizes and evaluation times (Siege V3) between our step semantics encoding and BLACKBOX's encoding is given in Table 3.

Corresponding 1-linearization encodings are, per time point, between 94 per cent (depot-11) and 69 per cent (logistics-23-1) of the step encoding sizes.

The above data suggest that the efficiency of BLACKBOX encodings is either roughly comparable or lower than our basic encoding for step semantics, and hence sometimes much lower than our 1-linearization encoding.

Table 2. Runtimes of Depot problems in seconds

instance	len	val	1-lin	step	proc
depot-10	7	F	0.01		
depot-10	8	T	0.02		
depot-10	9	F		0.28	0.30
depot-10	10	T		0.29	0.34
depot-11	13	F	0.04		
depot-11	14	T	0.44		
depot-11	17	F		69.56	70.29
depot-11	18	?		-	-
depot-11	19	?		-	-
depot-11	20	T		> 154.43	> 157.28
depot-12	19	F	0.24		
depot-12	20	T	> 143.73		
depot-12	21	F		142.12	> 140.75
depot-12	22	?		-	-
depot-13	7	F	0.01		
depot-13	8	T	0.01		
depot-13	8	F		0.01	0.01
depot-13	9	T		0.04	0.05
depot-14	9	F	0.05		
depot-14	10	T	0.11		
depot-14	11	F		1.25	1.28
depot-14	12	T		2.97	2.89

Table 3. Sizes and runtimes of our step encoding and BLACKBOX's GraphPlan-based encoding

instance	len	val	size in MB		runtime in secs	
			step	BB	step	BB
depot-11-8765	17	F	6.9	57.0	69.56	331.60
depot-11-8765	20	T	8.3	85.6	207.88	> 1200
logistics-23-1	14	F	4.8	20.9	48.34	71.97
logistics-23-1	15	T	5.2	25.6	99.31	115.16
driver-4-4-8	10	F	5.5	35.0	1.26	0.53
driver-4-4-8	11	T	6.1	53.2	5.56	21.00

9 Conclusions

We have given translations of semantics for parallel planning into SAT and shown that one of them, for 1-linearization semantics, is very efficient, often being one or two orders of magnitude faster than previous encodings. This semantics is superior because with our encoding the number of time steps and parallelism constraints is small. Interestingly, the process semantics, a refinement of the standard step semantics that imposes a further condition on plans, usually did not improve planning efficiency in our tests.

The 1-linearization encoding combined with novel strategies for finding satisfiable formulae that correspond to plans [9] sometimes lead to a substantial improvement in efficiency for satisfiability planning.

Acknowledgments. We thank Lawrence Ryan for his assistance with Siege. Part of the authors gratefully acknowledge the financial support of the Academy of Finland (project 53695 and grant for research work abroad), FET project ADVANCE contract No IST-1999-29082, and EPSRC grant 93346/01.

References

1. Best, E., Devillers, R.: Sequential and concurrent behavior in Petri net theory. Theoretical Computer Science **55** (1987) 87–136
2. Blum, A.L., Furst, M.L.: Fast planning through planning graph analysis. Artificial Intelligence **90** (1997) 281–300
3. Cayrol, M., Régnier, P., Vidal, V.: Least commitment in Graphplan. Artificial Intelligence **130** (2001) 85–118
4. Dimopoulos, Y., Nebel, B., Koehler, J.: Encoding planning problems in nonmonotonic logic programs. In Steel, S., Alami, R., eds.: Recent Advances in AI Planning. Fourth European Conference on Planning (ECP'97). Number 1348 in Lecture Notes in Computer Science, Springer-Verlag (1997) 169–181
5. Heljanko, K.: Bounded reachability checking with process semantics. In: Proceedings of the 12th International Conference on Concurrency Theory (Concur'2001). Volume 2154 of Lecture Notes in Computer Science., Springer-Verlag (2001) 218–232
6. Kautz, H., Selman, B.: Pushing the envelope: planning, propositional logic, and stochastic search. In: Proceedings of the Thirteenth National Conference on Artificial Intelligence and the Eighth Innovative Applications of Artificial Intelligence Conference, Menlo Park, California, AAAI Press (1996) 1194–1201
7. Kautz, H., Selman, B.: Unifying SAT-based and graph-based planning. In Dean, T., ed.: Proceedings of the 16th International Joint Conference on Artificial Intelligence, Morgan Kaufmann Publishers (1999) 318–325
8. Rintanen, J.: A planning algorithm not based on directional search. In Cohn, A.G., Schubert, L.K., Shapiro, S.C., eds.: Principles of Knowledge Representation and Reasoning: Proceedings of the Sixth International Conference (KR '98), Morgan Kaufmann Publishers (1998) 617–624
9. Rintanen, J.: Evaluation strategies for planning as satisfiability. In Saitta, L., ed.: Proceedings of the 16th European Conference on Artificial Intelligence, IOS Press (2004) to appear.

Relational Markov Games

Alberto Finzi and Thomas Lukasiewicz*

Dipartimento di Informatica e Sistemistica, Università di Roma "La Sapienza"
Via Salaria 113, I-00198 Rome, Italy
{finzi, lukasiewicz}@dis.uniroma1.it

Abstract. Towards a compact and elaboration-tolerant first-order representation of Markov games, we introduce *relational Markov games*, which combine standard Markov games with first-order action descriptions in a stochastic variant of the situation calculus. We focus on the zero-sum two-agent case, where we have two agents with diametrically opposed goals. We also present a symbolic value iteration algorithm for computing Nash policy pairs in this framework.

1 Introduction

During the recent decade, the development of controllers for autonomous agents has become increasingly important in AI. One way of designing such controllers is the planning approach, where goals or reward functions are specified, and the agent is given a planning ability to achieve a goal or to maximize a reward function. In particular, decision-theoretic planning in fully observable Markov decision processes (MDPs) [13] and the more general partially observable Markov decision processes (POMDPs) [8] has attained much attention in recent research on such issues in AI.

Recent work [2,18,6,7] also proposes first-order and relational extensions to MDPs. The main aims behind such extensions are essentially (i) to compactly represent MDPs without explicitly referring to atomic or propositional states and state transitions, (ii) to exploit such compact representations for efficiently solving large-scale problems, and (iii) to allow for reusing plans in similar environments with few or no replanning.

Along another line, MDPs have also been generalized to multi-agent systems. Here, the optimal actions of each agent may depend on the actions of all the other agents. One such generalization are multi-agent MDPs [1], which are similar to MDPs except that actions (and decisions) are distributed among multiple agents. The agents are cooperative in the sense that they all share the same reward, and thus the main aspect is how to coordinate the activities of different agents. Another such generalization are Markov games [16,9], also called stochastic games [11], which generalize MDPs as well as matrix games from game theory. Here, actions (and decisions) are also distributed among multiple agents, but the agents are not necessarily cooperative anymore. The agents may have different rewards, and in the case of zero-sum Markov games between two agents, even diametrically opposed rewards. Hence, rather than aiming at acting optimally in a team of cooperative agents, as in multi-agent MDPs, we now aim at acting

---

* Alternate address: Institut für Informationssysteme, Technische Universität Wien, Favoritenstraße 9-11, A-1040 Vienna, Austria; lukasiewicz@kr.tuwien.ac.at.

J.J. Alferes and J. Leite (Eds.): JELIA 2004, LNAI 3229, pp. 320–333, 2004.
© Springer-Verlag Berlin Heidelberg 2004

optimally among possibly competing agents. For example, in robotic soccer, we have two competing teams of agents, where each team consists of cooperative agents [4].

Even though there exists already extensive work on ordinary Markov games, to the best of our knowledge, there has been no work on relational Markov games so far. In this paper, we are trying to fill this gap. We present relational Markov games, where first-order action descriptions in a stochastic variant of the situation calculus are combined with ordinary Markov games. The main contributions can be summarized as follows:

- We introduce relational Markov games, where a stochastic variant of the situation calculus is used for first-order action descriptions. For ease of presentation, we concentrate on the zero-sum two-agent case, but the representation can be easily extended to the general-sum k-agent case where $k \geq 2$.
- As a semantics of relational Markov games, we provide a mapping to ordinary Markov games. In particular, we then show that every ordinary Markov game G can be represented as a relational Markov game G' such that G is the ordinary Markov game semantics of G'.
- We present a symbolic value iteration algorithm for relational Markov games. We show that it provably converges and that it computes the quality and the value function of the encoded ordinary Markov game, which can be used to compute a Nash policy pair for relational Markov games.
- We then introduce acyclic relational Markov games. We show that for them, the logical inference in the symbolic value iteration can be reduced to deciding whether an acyclic logic program (with integrity constraints) has an answer set. Furthermore, in the propositional case, every value iteration step can be done in polynomial time.

2 Preliminaries

We recall the basic concepts of the situation calculus and of matrix and Markov games.

Situation Calculus. The situation calculus [10,15] is a first-order language for representing dynamic domains. Its main ingredients are *actions*, *situations*, and *fluents*. An *action* is a first-order term of the form $a(\boldsymbol{u})$, where a is an action function symbol and $\boldsymbol{u}$ are its arguments. E.g., $moveTo(pos)$ may represent the action of moving to position pos. A *situation* is a first-order term encoding a sequence of actions. It is either a constant symbol or of the form $do(a, s)$, where a is an action and s is a situation. The constant symbol S_0 is the *initial situation* and represents the empty sequence, while $do(a, s)$ encodes the sequence obtained from executing a after the sequence of s. E.g., $do(moveTo(pos2), do(moveTo(pos1), S_0))$ represents the sequence of actions $moveTo(pos1)$, $moveTo(pos2)$. A *fluent* represents a world or agent property that may change when executing an action. It is a predicate symbol whose most right argument is a situation. E.g., $at(pos, s)$ may express that an agent is at position pos in situation s. A dynamic domain is encoded as a *basic action theory* $AT = (\Sigma, \mathcal{D}_{S_0}, \mathcal{D}_{ssa}, \mathcal{D}_{una}, \mathcal{D}_{ap})$:

- Σ is the set of foundational axioms for situations;
- $\mathcal{D}_{una}$ is the set of *unique name axioms for actions*, saying that different action terms stand for different actions;

- $\mathcal{D}_{S_0}$ is a set of first-order formulas describing the *initial state of the domain* (represented by S_0). E.g., $at(a, 1, 2, S_0) \wedge at(o, 3, 4, S_0)$ may express that agent a (resp., o) is initially at position $(1, 2)$ (resp., $(3, 4)$);
- $\mathcal{D}_{ssa}$ is the set of *successor state axioms* [14,15]. For each fluent $F(x, s)$, it contains an axiom of the form $F(x, do(a, s)) \equiv \Phi_F(x, a, s)$, where $\Phi_F(x, a, s)$ is a formula with free variables among x, a, s. These axioms specify the truth of the fluent F in the next situation $do(a, s)$ in terms of the current situation s, and are a solution to the frame problem (for deterministic actions). E.g.,

$$at(o, x, y, do(a, s)) \equiv a = moveTo(o, x, y) \vee \\ at(o, x, y, s) \wedge \neg(\exists x', y')a = moveTo(o, x', y') \tag{1}$$

may express that o is at (x, y) in $do(a, s)$ iff it is either moved there in s, or already there and not moved away in s;
- $\mathcal{D}_{ap}$ is the set of *action precondition axioms*. For each action a, it contains an axiom of the form $Poss(a(x), s) \equiv \Pi(x, s)$, which characterizes the preconditions of action a. E.g., $Poss(moveTo(o, x, y), s) \equiv \neg(\exists o')at(o', x, y, s)$ may express that it is possible to move the object o to (x, y) in s iff no other object o' is at (x, y) in s.

The *regression* of a formula ϕ through an action a, denoted $Regr(\phi)$, is a formula ϕ' that holds before the execution of a, given that ϕ holds after the execution of a. The regression of a formula ϕ whose situations are all of the form $do(a, s)$ is defined by induction using the successor state axioms $F(x, do(a, s)) \equiv \Phi_F(x, a, s)$ as follows: $Regr(F(x, do(a, s))) = \Phi_F(x, a, s)$, $Regr(\neg\phi) = \neg Regr(\phi)$, $Regr(\phi_1 \wedge \phi_2) = Regr(\phi_1) \wedge Regr(\phi_2)$, and $Regr((\exists x)\phi) = (\exists x)Regr(\phi)$.

Matrix Games. We now briefly recall two-player matrix games from game theory [17]. Intuitively, they describe the possible actions of two agents and the rewards that they receive when they simultaneously execute one action each. For example, in the matrix game *two-finger Morra*, two players E and O simultaneously show one or two fingers. Let f be the total numbers of fingers shown. If f is odd, then O gets f dollars from E, and if f is even, then E gets f dollars from O.

Formally, a *two-player matrix game* $G = (A, O, R_a, R_o)$ consists of two nonempty finite sets of *actions* A and O for two agents a and o, respectively, and two *reward functions* $R_a, R_o : A \times O \to \mathbf{R}$ for a and o, respectively. The game G is *zero-sum* iff $R_a = -R_o$; we then often omit R_o.

A pure (resp., mixed) strategy specifies which action an agent should execute (resp., which actions an agent should execute with which probability). Formally, a *pure strategy* for agent a (resp., o) is any action from A (resp., O). If a and o play the pure strategies $a \in A$ and $o \in O$, respectively, then they receive the *rewards* $R_a(a, o)$ and $R_o(a, o)$, respectively. A *mixed strategy* for agent a (resp., o) is any probability distribution over A (resp., O). If a and o play the mixed strategies π_a and π_o, respectively, then the *expected reward* to agent $k \in \{a, o\}$ is $R_k(\pi_a, \pi_o) = \mathbf{E}[R_k(a, o)|\pi_a, \pi_o] = \sum_{a \in A, o \in O} \pi_a(a) \cdot \pi_o(o) \cdot R_k(a, o)$.

One is especially interested in *Nash equilibria*, which are pairs of mixed strategies (π_a, π_o), where no agent has the incentive to deviate from its half of the pair, once the other agent plays the other half. Formally, (π_a, π_o) is a *Nash equilibrium* (or *Nash pair*) for G iff (i) for any mixed strategy π'_a, it holds $R_a(\pi'_a, \pi_o) \leq R_a(\pi_a, \pi_o)$, and (ii) for any mixed strategy π'_o, it holds $R_o(\pi_a, \pi'_o) \leq R_o(\pi_a, \pi_o)$. Every two-player matrix game G has at least one Nash pair among its mixed (but not necessarily pure) strategy pairs, and many have multiple Nash pairs, which can be computed by linear complementary (resp., linear) programming in the general (resp., zero-sum) case.

In particular, in the zero-sum case, if (π_a, π_o) and (π'_a, π'_o) are Nash pairs, then $R_a(\pi_a, \pi_o) = R_a(\pi'_a, \pi'_o)$, and also (π_a, π'_o) and (π'_a, π_o) are Nash pairs. That is, the expected reward to the agents is the same under any Nash pair, and Nash pairs can be freely "mixed" to form new Nash pairs. Here, a's expected reward under a Nash pair is

$$\max_{\pi \in PD(A)} \min_{o \in O} \sum_{a \in A} \pi(a) \cdot R_a(a, o). \tag{2}$$

Hence, a's expected reward under a Nash pair is the optimal value of the linear program in (3) over the variables $(\pi_a)_{a \in A}$ and v. Furthermore, a's strategies in Nash pairs are the optimal solutions of the linear program in (3):

$$\begin{aligned}
\max\ v \quad &\text{subject to} \\
\sum_{a \in A} \pi_a \cdot R_a(a, o) \geq\ &v \quad \text{(for all } o \in O) \\
\pi_a \geq\ &0 \quad \text{(for all } a \in A) \\
\sum_{a \in A} \pi_a =\ &1.
\end{aligned} \tag{3}$$

Markov Games. Markov games [16,9], also called stochastic games [11], generalize both matrix games and (fully observable) Markov decision processes (MDPs) [13].

Roughly, a Markov game consists of a set of states S, a matrix game for every state $s \in S$, and a probabilistic transition function that associates with every state $s \in S$ and every combination of actions, one for each agent, a probability distribution on future states $s' \in S$. We only consider the two-player case here. Formally, a *two-player Markov game* $G = (S, A, O, P, R_a, R_o)$ consists of a nonempty set of states S, two finite nonempty sets of actions A and O for two agents a and o, respectively, a transition function $P \colon S \times A \times O \to PD(S)$, where $PD(S)$ denotes the set of all probability functions over S, and two *reward functions* $R_a, R_o \colon S \times A \times O \to \mathbf{R}$ for a and o, respectively. G is *zero-sum* iff $R_a = -R_o$; we then often omit R_o.

Pure (resp., mixed) matrix-game strategies now generalize to pure (resp., mixed) policies, which associate with every state $s \in S$ a pure (resp., mixed) matrix-game strategy. Formally, a *pure policy* α (resp., ω) for agent a (resp., o) assigns to each state $s \in S$ an action from A (resp., O). The *reward* to agent $k \in \{a, o\}$ under a start state $s \in S$ and the pure policies α and ω, denoted $G_k(s, \alpha, \omega)$, is defined as $R_k(s, \alpha(s), \omega(s)) + \gamma \cdot \sum_{s' \in S} P(s'|s, \alpha(s), \omega(s)) \cdot G_k(s', \alpha, \omega)$, where $G_k(s', \alpha, \omega)$ is the reward to k under the state s' and the pure policies α and ω, and $\gamma \in [0, 1)$ is the *discount factor*. A *mixed policy* π_a (resp., π_o) for a (resp., o) assigns to every state $s \in S$ a probability distribution over A (resp., O). The *expected reward* to agent k under a start state s and the mixed policies π_a and π_o, denoted $G_k(s, \pi_a, \pi_o)$, is defined as $\mathbf{E}[R_k(s, a, o) + \gamma \cdot \sum_{s' \in S} P(s' \mid s, a, o) \cdot G_k(s', \pi_a, \pi_o) \mid \pi_a(s), \pi_o(s)]$.

The notion of a Nash equilibrium is then generalized from matrix games to Markov games as follows. A pair of mixed policies (π_a, π_o) is a *Nash equilibrium* (or *Nash pair*) for G iff (i) for any start state s and any π'_a, it holds $G_a(s, \pi'_a, \pi_o) \leq G_a(s, \pi_a, \pi_o)$, and

(ii) for any start state s and any π_o', it holds $G_o(s, \pi_a, \pi_o') \leq G_o(s, \pi_a, \pi_o)$. Every two-player Markov game G has at least one Nash pair among its mixed (but not necessarily pure) policy pairs, and it may have exponentially many Nash pairs.

In the zero-sum case, Nash pairs can be computed by value iteration as follows. The *quality* of agent a's action a against agent o's action o in state $s \in S$ is defined by:

$$Q(s, a, o) = R_a(s, a, o) + \gamma \cdot \sum_{s' \in S} P(s' \,|\, s, a, o) \cdot V(s'), \tag{4}$$

where the *value* of state $s \in S$, denoted $V(s)$, is defined by:

$$V(s) = \max_{\pi \in PD(A)} \min_{o \in O} \sum_{a \in A} \pi(a) \cdot Q(s, a, o). \tag{5}$$

Informally, $Q(s, a, o)$ is the immediate reward of actions a and o in s plus the discounted expected value of all succeeding states, while $V(s)$ is the expected reward under a Nash pair for the quality matrix game at s. The functions V and Q can be approximately computed as follows. We initially set $Q^0 = R_a$. For $n \geq 0$, we then compute V^n as V from Eq. (5) using Q^n as Q. For $n > 0$, we compute Q^n as Q from Eq. (4) using V^{n-1} as V. The iteration is repeated until the difference between V^n and V^{n+1} is smaller than a given error threshold ε. This procedure provably converges [11]. Given the quality function Q, for every $s \in S$, let $(\pi_a(s), \pi_o(s))$ be a Nash pair for the matrix game $(A, O, (Q(s, a, o))_{a \in A, o \in O})$. Then, (π_a, π_o) is a Nash pair for Markov game G.

3 Relational Markov Games

In this section, we introduce relational Markov games for the zero-sum two-agent case. After defining state and action partitions, we define the syntax of relational Markov games and their semantics in ordinary Markov games.

Preliminaries. The execution of an action often affects only few properties of the world and thus has the same effect in many different states of the world. For every action, these states can be grouped together into equivalence classes, which thus form a partition of the set of all states. Similarly, two action terms with different arguments may behave in the same way in all states, and thus also actions with their arguments can be grouped together into equivalence classes.

Formally, a *fluent formula* over x, s is a formula $\phi(x, s)$ in which all predicate symbols are fluents, and the only free variables are the non-situation variables x and the situation variable s. A *state partition* over x, s is a nonempty set of fluent formulas $P(x, s) = \{\phi_i(x, s) \,|\, i \in \{1, \ldots, m\}\}$ such that (i) $\forall x, s\, (\phi_i(x, s) \Rightarrow \neg \phi_j(x, s))$ is valid for all $i, j \in \{1, \ldots, m\}$ with $j > i$, (ii) $\forall x, s\, \bigvee_{i=1}^{m} \phi_i(x, s)$ is valid, and (iii) every $\exists x, s\, \phi_i(x, s)$ is satisfiable.

An *action formula* for the action $a(x)$ is a formula $\alpha(x)$ that has the non-situation variables x as the only free variables. An *action partition* for $a(x)$ is a nonempty set of action formulas $P(x) = \{\alpha_i(x) \,|\, i \in \{1, \ldots, m\}\}$ such that (i) $\forall x\, (\alpha_i(x) \Rightarrow \neg \alpha_j(x))$ is valid for all $i, j \in \{1, \ldots, m\}$ with $j > i$, (ii) $\forall x\, \bigvee_{i=1}^{n} \alpha_i(x)$ is valid, and (iii) every $\exists x\, \alpha_i(x)$ is satisfiable. We often identify the members of $P(x)$ with the action terms that they represent.

Syntax. A *relational Markov game* $G = (T, A, O, P, R)$ consists of a basic action theory T in the situation calculus, two finite nonempty sets of actions A and O for two agents a and o, respectively, a set of axioms P defining stochastic actions, and a set of axioms R defining the reward to agent a. We assume the *zero-sum* case, and so the reward to o is the negation of the reward to a. Every action $a(x) \in A \cup O$ has an associated action partition $P_a(x)$. We represent stochastic actions by a finite set of deterministic actions as in [3]. When a stochastic action is executed, then "nature" chooses and executes with a certain probability exactly one of the associated deterministic actions.

Formally, we assume that every pair of actions $a(x) \in A$ and $o(y) \in O$ is stochastic, and has an associated state partition $P_{a,o}(z, s)$, where $z = xy$. We then use

$$stochastic(\alpha(x), \omega(y), \phi(z, s), n(z))$$

in P to associate the stochastic pair of actions $\alpha(x) \in P_a(x)$ and $\omega(y) \in P_o(y)$ with the deterministic action $n(z)$ in the context of the class of states encoded by $\phi(z, s) \in P_{a,o}(z, s)$. Furthermore, we use

$$prob(\alpha(x), \omega(y), \phi(z, s), n(z)) = p$$

to encode that "nature" chooses $n(z)$ with probability p. Here, we also assume that the pair of actions $a(x) \in A$ and $o(y) \in O$ has the same preconditions as every $n(z)$.

Hence, a stochastic pair of actions $a(x)$ and $o(y)$ can be indirectly represented by providing a successor state axiom for each associated nature choice $n(z)$. Thus, T is extended to a probabilistic setting in a minimal way. For example, consider the stochastic pair of actions $moveS(obj, x, y) \in A$ and $moveS(obj, x', y') \in O$, where agents a and o simultaneously try to move the object obj to the positions (x, y) and (x', y'), respectively. Depending on the context, this may correspond to actually moving obj to either (x, y) or (x', y'), which is represented by $stochastic(moveS(obj, x, y)$, $moveS(obj, x', y'), s = s_1, moveTo(obj, x, y))$ and $stochastic(moveS(obj, x, y)$, $moveS(obj, x', y'), s=s_2, moveTo(obj, x', y'))$ along with the associated probabilities, for example, 0.1 and 0.9, respectively. We specify $moveS$ by defining preconditions for $moveTo(a, x, y')$ and the successor state axiom (1).

Finally, R specifies a reward function, which associates with every pair of actions $\alpha(x) \in P_a(x)$ and $\omega(y) \in P_o(y)$, and every context $\phi(z, s) \in P_{a,o}(z, s)$, where $z = xy$, a reward r to agent a, expressed by:

$$reward(\alpha(x), \omega(y), \phi(z, s)) = r .$$

E.g., we may have that $reward(moveS(obj, x, y), moveS(obj, x', y'), s = s_1) = 1$ and $reward(moveS(obj, x, y), moveS(obj, x', y'), s = s_2) = -1$.

Semantics. We now define the semantics of relational Markov games $G = (T, A, O, P, R)$ by providing a mapping to ordinary zero-sum two-player Markov games.

We first define the state and the action space of this ordinary Markov game. The *unified state partition*, denoted USP, is the product of all state partitions for every pair of actions $a(x) \in A$ and $o(y) \in O$. Here, the *product* of $k \geq 1$ state partitions $P^1, \ldots, P^k$, denoted $P^1 \times \cdots \times P^k$, is defined as the set of all $\phi_1 \wedge \cdots \wedge \phi_k$ such that $\phi_i \in P^i$ for all $i \in \{1, \ldots, k\}$. We assume that every $\phi \in USP$ is satisfiable. The *unified action partition* of agents a and o, denoted UAP_a and UAP_o, is the union of all action partitions of the actions of agents a and o, respectively.

We define probabilistic transitions on state partitions using the concept of regression from the situation calculus. We associate with every current $\phi(z, s) \in P_{a,o}(z, s)$ a probability distribution on successor $\psi(z, s) \in P_{a,o}(z, s)$ after executing a and o. Formally, suppose $\phi(z, s) \in P_{a,o}(z, s)$, where $z = xy$, and the pair of actions $\alpha(x) \in P_a(x)$ and $\omega(y) \in P_o(y)$ is executable in $\phi(z, s)$. Then, the successor fluent formulas under $\alpha(x)$ and $\omega(y)$ in $\phi(z, s)$ are all $\psi(z, s) \in P_{a,o}(z, s)$ such that $Regr(\psi(z, do(n(z), s))) = \phi(z, s)$ and $stochastic(\alpha(x), \omega(y), \phi(z, s), n(z))$ is in P, along with the probabilities $prob(\alpha(x), \omega(y), \phi(z, s), n(z))$. We use $\widehat{P}(\cdot \,| \phi(z, s), \alpha(x), \omega(y))$ to denote this probability distribution on successor fluent formulas.

The above transitions require the closure property that pairs of actions do not lead outside their state partitions. Intuitively, pairs of actions only locally manipulate few properties of the world. This often holds. Formally, for every pair of actions $a(x) \in A$ and $o(y) \in O$, we assume that $P_{a,o}(z, s) = \{\phi_i(z, s) \,| \, i \in \{1, \dots, m\}\}$ is closed under transition to the successor state. That is, for all $z = xy$ and all situations s_1 and s_2, if $\phi_i(z, s_1) \equiv \phi_i(z, s_2)$ for all $i \in \{1, \dots, m\}$, then $\phi_i(z, do(n(z), s_1)) \equiv \phi_i(z, do(n(z), s_2))$ for all $i \in \{1, \dots, m\}$, where $n(z)$ is associated with $a(x)$ and $o(y)$ in $\phi_i(z, s)$ through P. Furthermore, we assume that the preconditions of every pair $a(x) \in A$ and $o(y) \in O$ can be evaluated on the members of $P_{a,o}(z, s)$.

Finally, we extend the probabilistic transition and the reward function to USP as follows. Let $\phi(z, s) \in P_{a,o}(z, s)$, where $z = xy$, and let the pair $\alpha(x) \in P_a(x)$ and $\omega(y) \in P_o(y)$ be executable in $\phi(z, s)$. Then, for all $\phi(z, s) \wedge \rho \in USP$, define $\widehat{P}(\cdot \,| \phi(z, s) \wedge \rho, \alpha(x), \omega(y)) = \widehat{P}(\cdot \,| \, \phi(z, s), \alpha(x), \omega(y))$. Moreover, for all $\phi(z, s) \wedge \rho \in USP$, define $\widehat{R}(\phi(z, s) \wedge \rho, \alpha(x), \omega(y)) = reward(\alpha(x), \omega(y), \phi(z, s))$.

In summary, as a semantics, every relational Markov game $G = (T, A, O, P, R)$ is associated with the ordinary zero-sum two-player Markov game $G' = (S', A', O', P', R')$, where $S' = USP$, $A' = UAP_a$, $O' = UAP_o$, $P' = \widehat{P}$, and $R' = \widehat{R}$ as above, and where we additionally assume the same action preconditions as in G.

Representation Theorem. The following result shows that every zero-sum two-player Markov game G with finite set of states can be encoded as a relational Markov game G' that has its semantics in G.

Theorem 3.1. *Let $G = (S, A, O, P, R)$ be a zero-sum two-player Markov game, where S is finite. Then, there is a relational Markov game $G' = (T', A', O', P', R')$ such that the ordinary Markov game semantics of G' is given by G.*

Proof (sketch). The sets of actions A' and O' are defined as A and O, respectively, and all have singletons as action partitions. We thus have $UAP_a = A'$ and $UAP_o = O'$, respectively. We assume only the state partition $\{s = s_i \,| \, s_i \in S\}$, which thus already coincides with USP. We then use P' to associate with every $a \in A'$, $o \in O'$, and $s = s_i$ $(s_i \in S)$ the deterministic action n_{s_j} $(s_j \in S)$, along with the probability $P(s_j|s_i, a, o)$, where n_{s_j} represents the transition to the successor fluent formula $s = s_j$. Finally, we use R' to associate with every $a \in A'$, $o \in O'$, and $s = s_i$ $(s_i \in S)$ the reward $R(s_i, a, o)$ to agent a. It is then easy to verify that the thus constructed relational Markov game $G' = (T', A', O', P', R')$ has G as associated semantics. $\square$

4   Symbolic Value Iteration

In this section, we present a symbolic value iteration algorithm for the framework of this paper, and we prove its soundness.

Algorithm and its Soundness. The quality (resp., value) function for ordinary (zero-sum two-player) Markov games in Eq. (4) (resp., (5)) is extended to relational Markov games $G = (T, A, O, P, R)$ as follows. The *quality* of action $\alpha(\boldsymbol{x}) \in P_a(\boldsymbol{x})$ against action $\omega(\boldsymbol{y}) \in P_o(\boldsymbol{y})$ in $\sigma \wedge \rho \in USP$, denoted $Q(\alpha(\boldsymbol{x}), \omega(\boldsymbol{y}), \sigma \wedge \rho)$, where $\sigma = \phi(\boldsymbol{z}, s) \in P_{a,o}(\boldsymbol{z}, s)$, $\boldsymbol{z} = \boldsymbol{x}\boldsymbol{y}$, and ρ completes σ to an element of USP, is defined as follows ($\gamma \in [0, 1)$ is the *discount factor*):

$$Q(\alpha(\boldsymbol{x}), \omega(\boldsymbol{y}), \sigma \wedge \rho) \;=\; reward(\alpha(\boldsymbol{x}), \omega(\boldsymbol{y}), \sigma) + \\ \gamma \cdot \sum_{n \in N} prob(\alpha(\boldsymbol{x}), \omega(\boldsymbol{y}), \sigma, n(\boldsymbol{z})) \cdot V(\sigma_n \wedge \rho) \,, \tag{6}$$

where $\sigma_n = \psi(\boldsymbol{z}, s) \in P_{a,o}(\boldsymbol{z}, s)$ such that $Regr(\psi(\boldsymbol{z}, do(n(\boldsymbol{z}), s))) = \sigma$, and N is the set of all deterministic actions $n(\boldsymbol{z})$ that P associates with $\alpha(\boldsymbol{x})$ and $\omega(\boldsymbol{y})$ in σ and that are executable in σ. Finally, the *value* of $\sigma \wedge \rho \in USP$, denoted $V(\sigma \wedge \rho)$, is defined by:

$$V(\sigma \wedge \rho) = \max_{\pi \in PD(UAP_a)} \min_{o \in UAP_o} \sum_{a \in UAP_a} \pi(a) \cdot Q(a, o, \sigma \wedge \rho) \tag{7}$$

The following theorem shows that Eqs. (6) and (7) correctly describe the quality and the value function of the ordinary Markov game G' that is encoded by G.

Theorem 4.1. *Let G be a relational Markov game. Then, the quality and the value function of the encoded ordinary Markov game G' are given by Eqs. (6) and (7).*

Proof (sketch). The result follows from the ordinary Markov game semantics of relational Markov games. $\square$

Like in the ordinary case, the value iteration algorithm initially sets $Q^0(\alpha(\boldsymbol{x}), \omega(\boldsymbol{y}), \sigma \wedge \rho) = reward(\alpha(\boldsymbol{x}), \omega(\boldsymbol{y}), \sigma)$ for all $\sigma \wedge \rho \in USP$ and $\sigma \in P_{a,o}(\boldsymbol{x}\boldsymbol{y}, s)$. For $n \geq 0$, it then computes V^n as V from Eq. (7) using Q^n as Q. For $n > 0$, it computes Q^n as Q from Eq. (6) using V^{n-1} as V. The iteration is repeated until the difference between V^n and V^{n+1} is smaller than a given error threshold ε.

As a corollary of Theorem 4.1, this procedure converges, since it converges in the ordinary case [11].

Corollary 4.1. *Let G be a relational Markov game. Then, the symbolic value iteration on G converges.*

Another corollary of Theorem 4.1 is that a Nash policy pair can be calculated as usual from the quality function Q.

Corollary 4.2. *Let G be a relational Markov game, and let Q be its quality function specified by Eqs. (6) and (7). For every $\rho \in USP$, let $(\pi_a(\rho), \pi_o(\rho))$ be a Nash pair for $(UAP_a, UAP_o, (Q(a, o, \rho))_{a \in UAP_a, o \in UAP_o})$. Then, (π_a, π_o) is a Nash pair for G.*

Acyclic Relational Markov Games.   The above symbolic value iteration requires inference in first-order logic (i) to decide whether the preconditions of a pair of actions are satisfied, and (ii) to compute the successor fluent formula under a pair of actions. We now show that for *acyclic relational Markov games*, the problems (i) and (ii) can be reduced to deciding whether an acyclic logic program (with integrity constraints) has an answer set. We first formally define acyclic relational Markov games.

A *literal* is an atomic formula $p(t_1, \ldots, t_k)$ or its negation. A *literal conjunction* is either $\top$ or a conjunction of literals $l_1, \ldots, l_n$ with $n > 0$. A *clause* is a formula of the form $H \Leftarrow B$, where H is either $\bot$ or an atomic formula, and B is a literal conjunction. The clause $\bot \Leftarrow B$ is also called an *integrity constraint*. A *(normal) logic program (with integrity constraints)* L is a finite set of clauses. A formula or term is *ground* iff it is variable-free. A *ground instance* of a clause C is obtained from C by uniformly replacing all variables in C by ground terms. We use $ground(L)$ to denote the set of all ground instances of clauses in L. A logic program L is *acyclic* iff there exists a mapping κ from all ground atomic formulas to the non-negative integers such that $\kappa(p) > \kappa(q)$ for all p and q where p (resp., q) occurs in the head (resp., body) of some clause in $ground(L)$. Acyclic logic programs are a special case of locally stratified logic programs; they have a natural semantics, which is given by their answer sets. Formally, an *answer set* of an acyclic logic program L is a Herbrand interpretation I such that for every ground atomic formula p, it holds that $I \models p$ iff $I \models \psi$ for some clause $p \Leftarrow \psi$ in $ground(L)$. Note that acyclic logic programs have either no or exactly one answer set, which can be computed by fixpoint iteration.

A relational Markov game $G = (T, A, O, P, R)$ is *acyclic* iff (i) for every deterministic action $n(z)$ specified by T, the set of successor state axioms and the set of action precondition axioms both form an acyclic logic program each, and (ii) every fluent (resp., action) formula in every state (resp., action) partition is a literal conjunction. The relational Markov game G is *propositional* iff (i) every successor state and action precondition axiom in T is free of non-situation variables, and (ii) every state (resp., action) partition is free of non-situation variables.

The following theorem shows that (i) deciding whether the action preconditions are satisfied and (ii) computing the successor fluent formula in Eq. (6) can be reduced to the standard task of deciding whether an acyclic logic program has an answer set.

Theorem 4.2. *Let $n(z)$ be a deterministic action with state partition $P_{a,o}(z) = \{\phi_i(z, s) \mid i \in \{1, \ldots, m\}\}$ and successor state (resp., action precondition) axioms given by the acyclic logic program $P_{ssa}(z, s)$ (resp., $P_{ap}(z, s)$), where $do(a, s)$ occurs only in clause heads in $P_{ssa}(z)$. Then, (a) $Regr(\phi_j(z, do(n(z), s))) = \phi_i(z, s)$ iff $P_{ssa}(z, s) \cup \{\phi_i(z, s)\} \cup \{\phi_j(z, do(n(z), s))\}$ has an answer set; and (b) $n(z)$ is executable in $\phi_i(z, s)$ iff $P_{ap}(z, s) \cup \{\phi_i(z, s)\}$ has an answer set.*

Proof (sketch). We basically have to show that the closed-world answer set semantics of acyclic logic programs correctly implements the open-world view of first-order statements in the situation calculus. In (a), this is the case, since $do(a, s)$ appears only in clause heads in $P_{ssa}(z, s)$. In (b), this is also the case, since we assume that action preconditions can be evaluated on $\phi_i(z, s)$ only. □

The next result shows that in the propositional acyclic case, each value iteration step can be done efficiently, that is, in polynomial time.

Theorem 4.3. *Let $G = (T, A, O, P, R)$ be an acyclic and propositional relational Markov game. Then, each step of symbolic value iteration on G can be done in polynomial time in the size of the encoded ordinary Markov game.*

Proof (sketch). It is sufficient to show that (i) deciding whether the preconditions of a pair of actions are satisfied and (ii) computing the successor fluent formula under pairs of actions can be done in polynomial time. By Theorem 4.2, (i) and (ii) can be reduced to deciding whether an acyclic logic program has an answer set, which can be done in polynomial time in the propositional case. □

5   Example

In this section, we consider a rugby example (see Fig. 1), which is a slightly modified version of the soccer example by Littman [9]. The rugby field is a 4×5 grid. There are two agents, A and B, each occupying a square, and each able to do one of the following actions on each turn: N, S, E, W, and *stand* (move up, move down, move right, move left, and no move, respectively). The ball is represented by an oval and also occupies a square. An agent is a *ball owner* iff it occupies the same square as the ball. The ball follows the moves of the ball owner, and we have a goal when the ball owner steps into the adversary goal. When the ball owner goes into the square occupied by the other agent, if the other agent stands, possession of ball changes. Therefore, a good defensive maneuver is to stand where the other agent wants to go.

This domain can be represented by the following relational Markov game $G = (T, A, O, P, R)$. To axiomatize the basic action theory T, we introduce the deterministic actions $move(\alpha, \beta, m, n)$ where $n, m \in \{N, S, E, W, stand\}$ (agents α and β execute concurrently n and m, respectively) and the fluents $at(\alpha, x, y, s)$ (agent α is at (x, y) in situation s) and $haveBall(\alpha, s)$ (agent α has the ball in situation s) defined by the following successor state axioms:

$$at(\alpha, x, y, do(a, s)) \equiv (\exists x', y', m, n).at(\alpha, x', y', s) \wedge a = move(\alpha, \beta, m, n) \wedge$$
$$(m = stand \wedge y' = y \vee m = N \wedge y' = y - 1 \vee m = S \wedge y' = y + 1) \wedge x = x' \vee$$
$$(m = E \wedge x' = x - 1 \vee m = W \wedge x' = x + 1) \wedge y' = y\,;$$

$$haveBall(\alpha, do(a, s)) \equiv (\exists \alpha').haveBall(\alpha', s) \wedge$$
$$(\alpha = \alpha' \wedge \neg cngBall(\alpha', a, s) \vee \alpha \neq \alpha' \wedge cngBall(\alpha, a, s))\,.$$

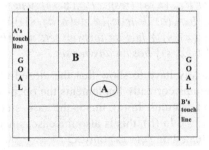

Fig. 1. Rugby Example

Here, $cngBall(\alpha, a, s)$ is true iff the ball possession changes after an action a of α in s:

$$cngBall(\alpha, a, s) \equiv (\exists \beta).\beta \neq \alpha \wedge \delta_y(\alpha, \beta, s) = 0 \wedge (a = move(\alpha, \beta, stand, R) \wedge$$
$$\delta_x(\alpha, \beta, s) = 1 \vee a = move(\alpha, \beta, stand, L) \wedge \delta_x(\alpha, \beta, s) = -1) \vee$$
$$\delta_x(\alpha, \beta, s) = 0 \wedge (a = move(\alpha, \beta, stand, N) \wedge \delta_y(\alpha, \beta, s) = 1 \wedge$$
$$a = move(\alpha, \beta, stand, S) \wedge \delta_y(\alpha, \beta, s) = -1).$$

Here, $\delta_x(\alpha, \beta, s) / \delta_y(\alpha, \beta, s)$ is the horizontal / vertical distance between α and β:

$$\delta_x(\alpha, \beta, s) = dx \equiv (\exists x, y, x', y').at(\alpha, x, y, s) \wedge at(\beta, x', y', s) \wedge dx = x - x'.$$

Once the deterministic action $move(\alpha, \beta, x, y)$ is defined in the basic action theory T, we can introduce the stochastic actions $moveTo(\alpha, x) \in A$ and $moveTo(\beta, x) \in O$. These are defined by the axioms in P. We suppose that $moveTo(\alpha, x)$ can succeed, and then the action $move(\alpha, \beta, x, k)$ is executed (for any action k performed by β), or it can fail, and then $move(\alpha, \beta, stand, k)$ is performed. We assume that the action execution of an agent can only fail iff it is the ball owner, e.g.,

$$prob(moveTo(\alpha, x_1), moveTo(\beta, x_2), s, move(\alpha, \beta, y_1, y_2)) = p \equiv$$
$$(haveBall(\alpha, s) \wedge y_2 = x_2 \wedge (y_1 = stand \wedge p = 0.2 \vee y_1 = x_1 \wedge p = 0.8)) \wedge$$
$$(\neg haveBall(\alpha, s) \wedge y_1 = x_1 \wedge (y_2 = stand \wedge p = 0.2 \vee y_2 = x_2 \wedge p = 0.8)).$$

We can now define the axioms in R. The zero-sum reward function (which here only depends on the state properties) is represented as follows:

$$reward(\alpha, s) = r \equiv (\exists \alpha', \beta, dx, dy)haveBall(\alpha', s) \wedge \delta_x(\alpha', \beta, x, y, s) = dx \wedge$$
$$\delta_y(\alpha', \beta, x, y, s) = dy \wedge r' = M \cdot dx + K \cdot |dy| \wedge (\alpha = \alpha' \wedge r = r' \vee \alpha' \neq \alpha \wedge r = -r').$$

The reward is defined relative to the ball owner, and it is given by the linear combination of the horizontal and (the absolute value of) the vertical distances. The horizontal component is emphasized by the big M ($M >> K$). Since this gives us the relative distance from the adversary, maximizing this value, the agent is both closer to the touch-line and far from the adversary. The second component ($K \cdot |dy|$) represents the secondary goal of a ball owner trying to avoid being engaged by the adversary.

In this example, we have only one state partition, which already forms the unified state partition. To formulate it, we introduce the following formulas:

$$\phi_{i,j}^1(\alpha, s) = \exists \beta.haveBall(\alpha, s) \wedge \delta_x(\alpha, \beta, s) = i \wedge \delta_y(\alpha, \beta, s) = j;$$
$$\phi_{i,j}^0(\alpha, s) = \exists \beta.\neg haveBall(\alpha, s) \wedge \delta_x(\alpha, \beta, s) = i \wedge \delta_y(\alpha, \beta, s) = j$$

with $i \in \{-5, \ldots, 5\}$ and $i \in \{-3, \ldots, 3\}$. It is easy to verify that the above formulas define a state partition. That is, $\phi_{i,j}^l(\alpha, s) \Rightarrow \neg \phi_{i',j'}^m(\alpha, s)$, for all $\langle i, j, l \rangle \neq \langle i', j', m \rangle$, and $\bigvee_{i,j,l} \phi_{i,j}^l(\alpha, s)$ are valid. This state partition also satisfies the closure property with respect to each deterministic action $move(\alpha, \beta, x, y)$.

Given this state partition, we can represent the *quality* of, e.g., action $moveTo(\alpha, N)$ against action $moveTo(\beta, stand)$ in any state $\phi_{i,j}^l(\alpha, s)$. For instance, given the state $\phi_{0,2}^1(\alpha, s)$, since α is the ball owner, associated to the actions above, we have two deterministic actions, i.e., $move(\alpha, \beta, N, stand)$ and $move(\alpha, \beta, stand, stand)$. The first action leads to the state $\phi_{0,3}^1$, while the second one is equivalent to an empty action, and thus the next state is $\phi_{0,2}^1$. The probabilities associated with the two transitions are $p = 0.8$ and $p = 0.2$, respectively, and the reward for α in $\phi_{0,x}^1$ is $|x| \cdot K$. Considering the first step of the value iteration (where V is equal to the reward R), the Q^1 value is given by $(2 + \gamma \cdot (0.8 \cdot 3 + 0.2 \cdot 2)) \cdot K$. In general, the Q^1 value of $moveTo(\alpha, N)$ against $moveTo(\beta, stand)$ can be expressed by a disjunction on the unified state partition:

$$Q^1(moveTo(\alpha, N), moveTo(\beta, stand), s) = q_1 \equiv \bigvee_{i,j,l}(\exists q_i)\phi^l_{i,j}(\alpha, s) \wedge q_1 = q_i .$$

We have this shape for Q^1, because of the closure property of the state partition. The previous formula is equivalent the following one, which is the explicit definition of Q^1:

$$Q^1(moveTo(\alpha, N), moveTo(\beta, stand), s) = q_1 \equiv$$
$$(\exists r, p_1, p_2, r_1, r_2).reward(\alpha, s) = r \wedge prob(moveTo(\alpha, N), moveTo(\beta, stand), s,$$
$$move(\alpha, \beta, stand, stand)) = p_1 \wedge reward(\alpha, do(move(\alpha, \beta, stand, stand), s)) = r_1 \wedge$$
$$prob(moveTo(\alpha, N), moveTo(\beta, stand), s, move(\alpha, \beta, N, stand)) = p_2 \wedge$$
$$reward(\alpha, do(move(\alpha, \beta, N, stand), s)) = r_2 \wedge q_1 = r + \gamma \cdot (p_1 \cdot r_1 + p_2 \cdot r_2) .$$

6   Related Work

The work closest in spirit to this paper is perhaps the important one by Boutilier et al. [2], which introduces first-order MDPs where actions are similarly described in a stochastic variant of the situation calculus, along with a symbolic value iteration algorithm for first-order MDPs. There are, however, several crucial differences. First, rather than having only a single agent, we consider the more general setting of multiple and possibly competing agents. That is, rather than combining action descriptions in the situation calculus with MDPs, we combine them with the more general Markov games. As a consequence, our value iteration procedure becomes technically more involved, since it also requires a linear programming step where Nash equilibria of matrix games are computed, which is not needed in [2]. Second, as an important technical difference, rather than dynamically partitioning the state space at every value iteration step, we assume that the state space is statically partitioned in advance, which is possible when it holds the natural property that pairs of actions do not lead outside their state partitions (see Sections 3 and 5). This avoids that the state space partitioning exponentially increases along the value iteration procedure. Furthermore, it also allows for defining probability distributions on the state space partitioning, and thus for partial observability in relational Markov games; exploring this aspect to some more depth is an interesting topic of future research. Third, [2] also does not consider any restricted classes of first-order MDPs (like our acyclic relational Markov games) where the symbolic value iteration can be done easily and/or efficiently.

Another closely related approach is Poole's independent choice logic (ICL) [12], which is based on acyclic logic programs under different "choices". Each choice along with the acyclic logic program produces a first-order model. By placing a probability distribution over the different choices, one then obtains a distribution over the set of first-order models. Like our work, Poole's one also combines a first-order logical formalism for dynamic domains with concepts from game theory. But Poole's work is a combination of his ICL with games in extensive and normal form, while our work combines action descriptions in the situation calculus with Markov games. Moreover, Poole focuses more on representational aspects and less on computing optimal policies.

There are other important works on first-order and relational MDPs [18,7,6] and an approach to integrating explicit agent programming in Golog with game-theoretic multi-agent planning in Markov games [5], which are all, however, less closely related to the approach to relational Markov games introduced in the present paper.

7   Summary and Outlook

We have introduced an approach to relational Markov games, where first-order action descriptions in a stochastic variant of the situation calculus are combined with ordinary zero-sum two-player Markov games. In particular, we have then presented a symbolic value iteration algorithm for computing Nash policy pairs in this framework.

An interesting topic of future research is to extend this approach to also allow for partial observability as well as for additional knowledge about the agents and their preferences (for example, as in *Bayesian games*).

Acknowledgments.   This work has been partially supported by the Austrian Science Fund Project Z29-N04 and a Marie Curie Individual Fellowship of the EU programme "Human Potential" under contract number HPMF-CT-2001-001286 (disclaimer: The authors are solely responsible for information communicated and the European Commission is not responsible for any views or results expressed). We thank the reviewers for their constructive comments, which helped to improve our work.

References

1. C. Boutilier. Sequential optimality and coordination in multiagent systems. In *Proceedings IJCAI-1999*, pp. 478–485.
2. C. Boutilier, R. Reiter, and B. Price. Symbolic dynamic programming for first-order MDPs. In *Proceedings IJCAI-2001*, pp. 690–700.
3. C. Boutilier, R. Reiter, M. Soutchanski, and S. Thrun. Decision-theoretic, high-level agent programming in the situation calculus. In *Proceedings AAAI-2000*, pp. 355–362.
4. M. Bowling and M. Veloso. Multiagent learning using a variable learning rate. *Artif. Intell.*, 136(2):215–250, 2002.
5. A. Finzi and T. Lukasiewicz. Game-theoretic agent programming in Golog. In *Proceedings ECAI-2004*. To appear.
6. N. H. Gardiol and L. P. Kaelbling. Envelope-based planning in relational MDPs. In *Proceedings NIPS-2003*.
7. C. Guestrin, D. Koller, C. Gearhart, and N. Kanodia. Generalizing plans to new environments in relational MDPs. In *Proceedings IJCAI-2003*, pp. 1003–1010.
8. L. P. Kaelbling, M. L. Littman, and A. R. Cassandra. Planning and acting in partially observable stochastic domains. *Artif. Intell.*, 101:99–134, 1998.
9. M. L. Littman. Markov games as a framework for multi-agent reinforcement learning. In *Proceedings ICML-1994*, pp. 157–163.
10. J. McCarthy and P. J. Hayes. Some philosophical problems from the standpoint of artificial intelligence. In *Machine Intelligence*, vol. 4, pp. 463–502. Edinburgh University Press, 1969.
11. G. Owen. *Game Theory: Second Edition*. Academic Press, 1982.
12. D. Poole. The independent choice logic for modelling multiple agents under uncertainty. *Artif. Intell.*, 94:7–56, 1997.

13. M. L. Puterman. *Markov Decision Processes: Discrete Stochastic Dynamic Programming*. Wiley, 1994.
14. R. Reiter. The frame problem in the situation calculus: A simple solution (sometimes) and a completeness result for goal regression. In *Artificial Intelligence and Mathematical Theory of Computation: Papers in Honor of John McCarthy*, pp. 359–380. Academic Press, 1991.
15. R. Reiter. *Knowledge in Action: Logical Foundations for Specifying and Implementing Dynamical Systems*. MIT Press, 2001.
16. J. van der Wal. *Stochastic Dynamic Programming*, vol. 139 of *Mathematical Centre Tracts*. Morgan Kaufmann, 1981.
17. J. von Neumann and O. Morgenstern. *The Theory of Games and Economic Behavior*. Princeton University Press, 1947.
18. S. W. Yoon, A. Fern, and B. Givan. Inductive policy selection for first-order MDPs. In *Proceedings UAI-2002*, pp. 569–576.

On the Logic of 'Being Motivated to Achieve ρ, Before δ'

Jan Broersen

Institute of Information and Computing Sciences
Utrecht University,
P.O. Box 80.089, 3508 TB Utrecht, The Netherlands
broersen@cs.uu.nl

Abstract. This paper studies the logic of modalities for motivational attitudes (desires, obligations, wishes, wants, intentions, etc.) that come with a deadline condition. For instance, an agent may want to get home before it starts raining. We use a 'reduction approach' from deontic logic to characterize two separate semantic definitions for these motivational modalities in CTL. The main advantage of applying reductions is that the formal reasoning can be performed entirely in CTL. We claim that the reduction approach applies to any motivational modality.

1 Introduction

High-level logical specification languages for the specification and verification of intelligent agent systems typically combine (modal) logics for informational attitudes (knowledge, belief, observations, communications), motivational attitudes (desires, obligations, wishes, wants, intentions, preferences), capacities (ability, controllability) and dynamics (action composition, time). Examples are the BDI logics [16,17], KARO [14], and the work by Cohen and Levesque [7]. A much regreted disadvantage of combining that many modalities in one logical system, is the high complexity of the resulting system, both computationally and conceptually. In this paper we focus on the interaction between time and motivational attitudes, and show that, under some restrictions, we can reduce a combined logic for time and motivational attitudes, to the temporal component only. This has clear advantages in terms of complexity and availability of proof systems and other logic tools.

We are interested in logic operators of the form $M(\rho \leq \delta)$, for being motivated to meet a condition ρ before a condition δ becomes true. Note first that this is an 'achievement motivation', where the objective is to achieve something that is not already true (necessarily), as opposed to 'maintenance motivations', where the objective is to maintain something that *is* already true. We do not consider maintenance motivations in this paper. Second, the motivations as represented by these operators are 'temporally constrained'; *if* δ occurs at some point, the agent wants that the condition ρ has been satisfied before that at least once. We think of the operator M for motivations as either an 'external' motivation, i.e.,

J.J. Alferes and J. Leite (Eds.): JELIA 2004, LNAI 3229, pp. 334–346, 2004.

an *obligation*, or an 'internal' motivation, i.e., a *desire, wish* or *want*. For now, we also rely on in informal understanding of the branching time temporal logic CTL [5,10,6] to discuss our motivations to study operators of the form $M(\rho \leq \delta)$. In CTL, the symbols E and A denote an existential and a universal quantifier respectively, ranging over possible future courses (branches) of time. Within the scope of these quantifiers, CTL uses the linear time operators (LTL [10]) $\varphi U \psi$ (strong Until, i.e., ψ will occur, and φ holds up until then), $\varphi U_w \psi$ (weak Until, i.e., if ψ will occur, then φ holds up until then), $X\varphi$ (next, i.e., φ holds at the next time point) to talk about individual future courses of time (from now on simply called 'possible futures').

There are several reasons to study motivational attitudes that are temporally constrained. First we give a reason for considering the temporal structure of motivations as such: if we cannot express the temporal structure of motivational content, we may be tempted to write down conflicting formulas where actually there is no conflict involved. An example is the following. An agent can have a desire to smoke (because it is pleasant), and at the same time a desire to quit smoking (because it is unhealthy). If we cannot express the temporal structure of motivational content, we may be tempted to represent this as $M\,smoke\_cigarette$ and $M\neg smoke\_cigarette$, which, in most logics for the motivational modality M, leads to unintended conflicts[1]. However, if we add temporal expressiveness to the language, we may recognize that there is actually no conflict, because the agent wants a cigarette *next*, i.e., $MX\,smoke\_cigarette$, but also wants to quit smoking *at some time in the future*, i.e., $MFG\neg smoke\_cigarette$. These formulas can be consistently dealt with under any logic for the motivational modality M.

The smoking example also, more specifically, points to a motivation to study 'temporally constrained' modalities of the form $M(\rho \leq \delta)$, where the motivation for ρ is limited to the time frame *before* the deadline condition δ occurs for the first time. A puzzling aspect of an achievement motivation like 'wanting to quit at some time in the future', as represented by the formula $MFG\neg smoke\_cigarette$, is that it gives us no clue as to under which circumstances it can be said that an agent actually fails to meet it. The point is that the formulation 'at some point in the future' does not mean 'as soon as possible', or 'within an agent's lifetime'. It simply means that *any* future point is as good as any other future point. For actual motivations of actual agents, it seems that this is almost never the case. If any future point would be as good as any other future point, an agent can procrastinate forever, without ever falling in danger of not being able to satisfy the motivation. For achievement motivations of the form $M(\rho \leq \delta)$, this problem does not occur. The δ functions as a deadline for the fulfilment of the motivation to achieve ρ. To put it bluntly: it does not mean much to specify that agent a has an achievement motivation for ρ if somehow this motivation is not 'concretized' by some sort of deadline. To come back to the smoking example: it does not mean much to say that you want to quite smoking 'at some point in

---

[1] For instance, in the modal logic KD, these two formulas are inconsistent, and, in any normal modal logic, we get a motivational 'explosion': $Mp \wedge M\neg p \models Mq$.

the future'. In order to asses, in the future, whether or not you have 'complied' to your motivation, you have to stipulate a deadline.

This same point was alluded to by Both Cohen and Levesque [7] and Rao and Georgeff [16] when they formulated the principle of 'no infinite deferral'. They associate this principle with the formula $I\varphi \to AF\neg I\varphi$, where the I is a modality for 'intention'. However, in our opinion this formula expresses something different. It says that any intention will eventually be dropped at some future point. This is quite different from saying that an intention *applies* to a limited time frame, and thus, that its satisfaction cannot be deferred. The problem here is the sometimes subtle difference between 'time of reference' and 'time of validity' for temporalized modal operators. The property $I\varphi \to AF\neg I\varphi$ expresses that the intention's *time of validity* is limited to a finite future amount of time. Our modality $M(\rho \le \delta)$, on the other hand, expresses that the motivations *time of reference* is limited to the time frame before δ occurs. These 'relationships' with time are essentially different. The distinction between validity time and reference time for logics that contain a temporal modality as one of the logic components, was, for instance, formulated by Lindström and Rabinowicz [12] in the context of temporal epistemic logics. But it equally applies to temporal motivational logics. And we belief that a failure to distinguish the two concepts is the source of a lot of confusion. To come back to the formula $I\varphi \to AF\neg I\varphi$: it is as if it tries to express that the intention's *time of reference* is limited by demanding that the *evaluation time* of the intention is constrained to a finite part of the future. Maybe the intuition was: the only reason for an intention to be in force no longer (evaluation time) can be that the achievement is accomplished, which means that the intention refers (reference time) only to a limited time frame. However, intentions may be dropped for a number of reasons; accomplishment of the achievement associated with the intention being only one of them.

We want to stress that the conditions δ in the operator $M(\rho \le \delta)$ are not deadlines in the usual sense of the word. They are logical conditions that may or may not be valid at certain points in time. This is different from the everyday use of the word 'deadline', which usually refers to a certain time point relative to a time metric. In the present setting we do not have a time metric, but only logic conditions. A consequence of our abstract view is that we have to deal with the possibility that δ never occurs. Note that for a theory of deadlines that uses a time metric, this would never be a problem. In particular, the point 'two hours from now' will always occur, while meeting a condition 'δ' may be impossible.

2   Preliminaries: CTL

Well-formed formulas of the temporal language $\mathcal{L}_{\text{CTL}}$ are defined by:

$$\varphi, \psi, \ldots := p \mid \neg\varphi \mid \varphi \wedge \psi \mid E\alpha \mid A\alpha$$
$$\alpha, \beta, \ldots := \varphi U^{ee}\psi$$

where φ, ψ represent arbitrary well-formed formulas, and where the p are elements from an infinite set of propositional symbols $\mathcal{P}$. Formulas $\alpha, \beta, \ldots$ are called 'path formulas'. We use the superscript 'ee' for the until operator to denote that this is the version of 'the until' where φ is not required to hold for the present, nor for the point where ψ, i.e., the present and the point where ϕ are *both* excluded. This gives us the following informal meanings of the until operator:

$E(\varphi U^{ee}\psi)$: there is a future for which eventually, at some point m, the condition ψ will hold, while φ holds from the next moment until the moment before m

We define all other CTL-operators as abbreviations[2]. Although we do not use all of the LTL operators X, F, and G in this paper, we give their abbreviations (in combination with the path quantifiers E and A) in terms of the defined operators for the sake of completeness. We also assume the standard propositional abbreviations.

$$EX\varphi \equiv_{def} E(\bot U^{ee}\varphi) \qquad\qquad AX\varphi \equiv_{def} \neg EX\neg\varphi$$
$$EF\varphi \equiv_{def} \varphi \vee E(\top U^{ee}\varphi) \qquad AG\varphi \equiv_{def} \neg EF\neg\varphi$$
$$AF\varphi \equiv_{def} \varphi \vee A(\top U^{ee}\varphi) \qquad EG\varphi \equiv_{def} \neg AF\neg\varphi$$
$$A(\varphi U^e\psi) \equiv_{def} \varphi \wedge A(\varphi U^{ee}\psi) \qquad E(\varphi U^e\psi) \equiv_{def} \varphi \wedge E(\varphi U^{ee}\psi)$$
$$A(\varphi U\psi) \equiv_{def} A(\varphi U^e(\varphi \wedge \psi)) \qquad E(\varphi U\psi) \equiv_{def} E(\varphi U^e(\varphi \wedge \psi))$$
$$A(\varphi U_w\psi) \equiv_{def} \neg E(\neg\psi U\neg\varphi) \qquad E(\varphi U_w\psi) \equiv_{def} \neg A(\neg\psi U\neg\varphi)$$

The informal meanings of the formulas with a universal path quantifier are as follows (the informal meanings for the versions with an existential path quantifier follow trivially):

$A(\varphi U^e\psi)$: for all futures, eventually, at some point m, the condition ψ will hold, while φ holds from now until the moment before m

$A(\varphi U\psi)$: for all futures, eventually, at some point the condition ψ will hold, while φ holds from now until then

$A(\varphi U_w\psi)$: for all possible futures, if eventually ψ will hold, then φ holds from now until then, or forever otherwise

$AX\varphi$: at any next moment φ will hold

$AF\varphi$: for all futures, eventually φ will hold

$AG\varphi$: for all possible futures φ holds globally

A CTL model $\mathcal{M} = (S, \mathcal{R}, \pi)$, consists of a non-empty set S of states, an accessibility relation $\mathcal{R}$, and an interpretation function π for propositional atoms. A full path σ in M is a sequence $\sigma = s_0, s_1, s_2, \ldots$ such that for every $i \geq 0$,

---

[2] Often, the CTL-operators $EG\varphi$ and $E(\psi U\varphi)$ are taken as the basic ones, and other operators are defined in terms of them. The advantage of that approach is that we do not have to use the notion of 'full path', that is crucial for the truth condition of $A(\varphi U^{ee}\psi)$. However, that approach is not applicable here, since we cannot define the 'exclusive' versions of the operators in terms of them. And, even if we take $EG\varphi$ and $E(\psi U^{ee}\varphi)$ as basic, we can still not define the for our purposes important operator $A(\psi U^e\varphi)$ as an abbreviation.

s_i is an element of S and $s_i \mathcal{R} s_{i+1}$, and if σ is finite with s_n its final situation, then there is no situation s_{n+1} in S such that $s_n \mathcal{R} s_{n+1}$. We say that the full path σ starts at s if and only if $s_0 = s$. We denote the state s_i of a full path $\sigma = s_0, s_1, s_2, \ldots$ in $\mathcal{M}$ by σ_i. Validity $\mathcal{M}, s \models \varphi$, of a CTL-formula φ in a world s of a model $\mathcal{M} = (S, \mathcal{R}, \pi)$ is defined as:

$$\begin{aligned}
\mathcal{M}, s &\models p && \Leftrightarrow s \in \pi(p) \\
\mathcal{M}, s &\models \neg\varphi && \Leftrightarrow \text{not } \mathcal{M}, s \models \varphi \\
\mathcal{M}, s &\models \varphi \wedge \psi && \Leftrightarrow \mathcal{M}, s \models \varphi \text{ and } \mathcal{M}, s \models \psi \\
\mathcal{M}, s &\models E\alpha && \Leftrightarrow \exists\sigma \text{ in } \mathcal{M} \text{ such that } \sigma_0 = s \text{ and } \mathcal{M}, \sigma, s \models \alpha \\
\mathcal{M}, s &\models A\alpha && \Leftrightarrow \forall\sigma \text{ in } \mathcal{M} \text{ such that } \sigma_0 = s \text{ it holds that } \mathcal{M}, \sigma, s \models \alpha \\
\mathcal{M}, \sigma, s &\models \varphi U^{ee}\psi && \Leftrightarrow \exists n > 0 \text{ such that}
\end{aligned}$$
$$\begin{aligned}
&(1) \ \mathcal{M}, \sigma_n \models \psi \text{ and} \\
&(2) \ \forall i \text{ with } 0 < i < n \text{ it holds that } \mathcal{M}, \sigma_i \models \varphi
\end{aligned}$$

Validity on a CTL model $\mathcal{M}$ is defined as validity in all states of the model. If φ is valid on a CTL model $\mathcal{M}$, we say that $\mathcal{M}$ is a model for φ. General validity of a formula φ is defined as validity on all CTL models. The logic CTL is the set of all general validities of $\mathcal{L}_{CTL}$ over the class of CTL models.

3   Reduction Approaches for Deontic Logic

In deontic logic, reduction approaches have been advocated foremost by Anderson [1], Kanger [11] and Meyer [13]. The idea behind Anderson's approach is that we can identify the logic of being obliged a condition φ with the logic of it being a necessity that if φ is not satisfied, there is a violation. Anderson thus reduces the logic for the obligation operator $O\varphi$ to the standard (alethic) modality $\Box\varphi$ by defining $O\varphi \equiv_{def} \Box(\neg\varphi \to Viol)$, where $Viol$ is a new propositional constant in the language of the modality $\Box$, standing for 'violation'. It is not difficult to prove that through this reduction, we can reduce Standard Deontic Logic (SDL [20]) to alethic modal logic. Kanger was the first to not only use violation constants, but also success constants. We come back to this point in section 6.1. Finally, Meyer adapted Anderson's idea to the action setting by making the identification that an action α is obliged if alternatives to this action (being referred to by means of an 'action negation' connective) lead to a violation. Meyer thus proposed to define the deontic logic of obligations $O\alpha$, where α is an explicit action name, as a reduction to dynamic logic: $O\alpha \equiv_{def} [\overline{\alpha}]Viol$, where $\overline{\alpha}$ stands for the 'negation' of the action α, and the operator '$[\,.\,]\,.$' is the action execution modality from dynamic logic [15] (see our earlier work [3] for more on this). The idea of expressing the semantics of *deontic deadlines* by characterizing violation conditions in CTL supplemented with violation constants, was first explored in [9]. The present work adapts, extends and generalizes this idea.

The general idea behind the reduction approaches in deontic logic is thus that we try to characterize the violation conditions of obligations, in the logic we want to reduce the obligation modality to. If we have a deontic logic of general propositions, we reduce to a general modal logic of necessity supplemented with violation constants (Anderson). If we have a deontic logic of actions, we reduce to a logic of action supplemented with violation constants (Meyer). If we have a deontic logic of deadlines, we reduce to a temporal logic supplemented with violation constants (Dignum). In this paper we take a more general view on this last idea: we reduce a logic for motivational attitudes that are temporally constrained to a temporal logic supplemented with *Negative Condition* constants.

Deontic logician like to argue that deontic reasoning is inherently different from reasoning with desires, wishes, wants, etc., because it has to deal with circumstances where obligations are not satisfied. In other words: deontic logics have to be able to reason about *violations*. The reduction approaches form the most literal manifestation of this idea. However, we do not agree that deontic reasoning is inherently different from reasoning with desires, wishes, wants, etc. The only difference we see between violating an obligation and violating, for instance, a desire, is that the first violation is relative to some other agent, while the second is only relative to the agent himself. Although this difference may be of practical significance in concrete situations, we see no difference from a logical point of view. Therefore, as long as we are interested in logical properties, the reduction approaches apply to any motivational attitude. To emphasize this point, we will not talk about 'violations' but about 'negative conditions'.

4   Two Alternative Reductions for the Motivation Operator

We minimally extend the language $\mathcal{L}_{\text{CTL}}$ by extending the set of propositional atoms with a negative condition constant of the form $NegC$[3]. Furthermore, the formal interpretation of the atom $NegC$ is treated like that of all other atomic propositions. So, we can view the propositional constant $NegC$ also as a special element of $\mathcal{P}$: a 'special purpose' proposition solely used to interpret motivational formulas in a temporal setting.

Let $\mathcal{M}$ be a CTL model, s a state, and σ a full path starting at s. A straightforward modal semantics for the operator $M^1(\rho \leq \delta)$ is then defined as follows:

$$\mathcal{M}, s \models M^1(\rho \leq \delta) \Leftrightarrow \forall \sigma \text{ with } \sigma_0 = s, \forall j :$$
$$\text{if}$$
$$\mathcal{M}, \sigma_j \models \delta \text{ and } \forall 0 \leq i \leq j : \mathcal{M}, \sigma_i \models \neg\rho$$
$$\text{then}$$
$$\mathcal{M}, \sigma_j \models NegC$$

This says: if at some future point the deadline occurs, and until then the result has not yet been achieved, then we have a negative condition at that point. This semantic definition is equivalent to the following definition as a reduction to CTL:

$$M^1(\rho \leq \delta) \equiv_{def} \neg E(\neg\rho U(\delta \wedge \neg NegC))$$

---

[3] For reasoning in a multi-agent context we may provide negative condition constants of the form $NegC(a)$ where $a \in \mathcal{A}$, and $\mathcal{A}$ an infinite set of agent identifiers.

This formula simply 'negates' the situation that should be excluded when a motivational deadline is in force[4]. In natural language this *negative* situation is: 'δ becomes true at a certain point, the achievement has not been met until then, and there is *no* negative condition at δ'. Therefore this CTL formula exactly characterizes the truth condition for the above defined motivational deadline operator: the semantic conditions are true is some state if and only if the CTL formula is true in that state.

The above definition gives rise to a number of logical properties, to be presented in the next section. However, at this point we already want to mention one particular property that will lead us to a variation on the above definition. This logical property concerns the 'evaluation time' of the defined operator $M^1(\rho \leq \delta)$. It holds that:

$$\models M^1(\rho \leq \delta) \rightarrow A(M^1(\rho \leq \delta)U_w\rho)$$

To see that this holds[5], it is easiest to fall back on the semantics of the operator. The semantics says that on futures (branches of time) where δ occurs at some point t, while until then ρ has not been done once, there is a negative condition at t. Now, if we follow such a branch for some time-steps in the future, and we do not meet a ρ, then, the deadline conditions do still apply: still it holds that if δ will occur later on, we get a negative condition if we do not meet a ρ until then.

Now, a crucial observation is that even if we have passed one or more δ-states, the motivation still applies; only if we meet a ρ, the conditions are no longer guaranteed. Thus, the above notion of motivation persists, even if we have passed a deadline. This might be considered counter-intuitive, since it seems correct to assume that the deadline motivation itself is discharged by passing the deadline. Therefore, we will show how to define a version that does not have this property. However, we first want to stress that we do *not* consider the above notion of motivation to be counter-intuitive; it is simply a variant. Persistence of the motivation at the passing of a deadline is not a priori counter-intuitive. An example is the following: you want to repair the roof of your house before it will rain (or otherwise you and your interior get wet). This motivation is only discarded by the act of repairing the roof, and not by the event of raining.

So, the above defined motivations are not discarded by failing the deadline: as long as the condition ρ is not yet achieved, we have a negative condition at every point where the deadline condition δ holds. Now we are going to drop this property. Thus, we need to take care that the motivation is dropped the first time we meet the deadline condition, irrespective of whether we have achieved the goal or not. We can achieve this, by adding to the definition that only the first δ occurring, is relevant for assessing whether there is a violation.

---

[4] Alternatively this definition can be given using the weak until: $M^1(\rho \leq \delta) \equiv_{def} A((\neg\delta \vee NegC)U_w\rho)$. But for the version with the strong until it is much easier to see that it corresponds with the semantic truth conditions defined above.

[5] Alternatively we may write this as $\models M^1(\rho \leq \delta) \rightarrow \neg E(\neg\rho U \neg M^1(\rho \leq \delta))$. But in our opinion, here the version with the weak until is easier to understand.

$$\mathcal{M}, s \models M^2(\rho \leq \delta) \Leftrightarrow \forall \sigma \text{ with } \sigma_0 = s, \forall j :$$

$$\text{if}$$

$$\mathcal{M}, \sigma_j \models \neg\rho \wedge \delta \text{ and } \forall 0 \leq i < j : \mathcal{M}, \sigma_i \models \neg\rho \wedge \neg\delta$$

$$\text{then}$$

$$\mathcal{M}, \sigma_j \models NegC$$

This says: if at some future point the deadline occurs for the first time, and until then the result has not yet been achieved, then we have a negative condition at that point. For this notion of deadline it is a slightly harder to give a CTL characterization. We need to use the notion of until that talks about the states until the last state before φ (i.e., $\psi U^e \varphi$).

$$M^2(\rho \leq \delta) \equiv_{def} \neg E((\neg\rho \wedge \neg\delta)U^e(\delta \wedge \neg\rho \wedge \neg NegC))$$

The main point of this variant is thus that it has a different dynamical behavior. In particular, it is discarded by the first δ, even if the achievement has not been met. Therefore, the following holds for the evaluation time of the operator $M^2(\rho \leq \delta)$:

$$\models M^2(\rho \leq \delta) \rightarrow A(M^2(\rho \leq \delta)U_w(\rho \vee \delta))$$

It is clear that the following holds for the relation between the two variants:

$$\models M^1(\rho \leq \delta) \rightarrow M^2(\rho \leq \delta)$$

5 More Logical Properties

In the previous section we discussed logical properties concerning the validity time[6] of the defined operators. In this section, we present some more logical properties. Most properties hold for both operators defined in the previous section. Therefore, in the formulas to come, we will use the notation $M^i(\rho \leq \delta)$, to express that we talk about a property for both variants. Since the properties we present in this section are discussed elsewhere (for the case where motivations are obligations) [4], we do not spend much words on them.

The following properties can be proven, by substituting the CTL-characterization of the operators, and assessing the resulting CTL-formulas on CTL-validity:

$$\models M^i((\rho \wedge \chi) \leq \delta) \rightarrow M^i(\rho \leq \delta)$$

$$\not\models M^i(\rho \leq \delta) \wedge M^i(\chi \leq \delta) \rightarrow M^i((\rho \wedge \chi) \leq \delta)$$

$$\models M^1(\rho \leq \delta) \rightarrow M^1(\rho \leq (\delta \wedge \gamma))$$

$$\not\models M^2(\rho \leq \delta) \rightarrow M^2(\rho \leq (\delta \wedge \gamma))$$

$$\not\models M^i(\rho \leq \delta) \wedge M^i(\rho \leq \gamma) \rightarrow M^i(\rho \leq (\delta \vee \gamma))$$

---

[6] In BDI-literature, these are also called 'dynamical properties'

$$\models M^i(\rho \leq \delta) \wedge M^i(\delta \leq \gamma) \rightarrow M^i(\rho \leq \gamma)$$

$$\not\models M^i(\rho \leq \delta) \rightarrow M^i(\delta \leq \rho)$$

$$\models M^i(\gamma \leq \gamma)$$

$$\models M^i(\top \leq \delta) \qquad \not\models M^i(\bot \leq \delta) \qquad \not\models \neg M^i(\bot \leq \delta)$$

$$\models M^i(\rho \leq \bot) \qquad \not\models M^i(\rho \leq \top) \qquad \not\models \neg M^i(\rho \leq \top)$$

$$\models \neg M^i(\bot \leq \top)$$

6   Limitations and Advantages of the Present Approach

6.1   A Counter-Intuitive Logical Property

The operators defined in section 4 obey intuitive properties. However, there is also a class of properties of these operators, whose intuitiveness is disputable. For instance, we have the following property:

$$\models \rho \rightarrow M^i(\rho \leq \delta)$$

This says that the deadline motivations as defined in section 4 are implied by the actual achievement of ρ in the current state. Moreover, this property is an instance of a more general, stronger property that holds for the motivational deadline operators of section 4. The motivation is valid in any state where it is sure that the motivation will be satisfied before the deadline. In particular:

$$\models \neg E(\neg \rho U \delta) \rightarrow M^i(\rho \leq \delta)$$

This can be verified by substituting the CTL characterization of the motivation operator: $\neg E(\neg \rho U \delta) \rightarrow \neg E(\neg \rho U(\delta \wedge \neg NegC))$. We may see this as the *strengthening* of δ to $\delta \wedge \neg NegC$ in the schema $\neg E(\neg \rho U \delta)$. It is quite easy to see that this strengthening property holds. We start with the fact that validity of the schema $E(\varphi U \psi)$ is closed under *weakening* with respect to φ and with respect to ψ, that is, if at some point in a model we satisfy $E(\varphi U \psi)$, we also satisfy both $E((\varphi \vee \gamma)U\psi)$ and $E(\varphi U(\psi \vee \gamma))$. But this means[7] that the schema $\neg E(\varphi U \psi)$ is closed under strengthening with respect to ψ, which is what we needed to show (with $\neg \rho$ substituted for φ, and δ for ψ).

Now the question rises whether we cannot defend intuitiveness of this property in the same way as we can defend intuitiveness of, for instance $\models M^i(\gamma \leq \gamma)$ and $\models M^i(\top \leq \delta)$ and $\models M^i(\rho \leq \bot)$. We can argue that the situation is comparable to the axiom $O\top$ of standard deontic logic. The common denominator

---

[7] We actually use some background theory here about how logical properties of defined operators can be determined by looking at the way they are constructed from simpler operators. In particular, a negation in the definition flips closure under strengthening to closure under weakening and vice versa. This is why any modal operator $M\varphi$ is closed under weakening (strengthening) if and only if its dual $\neg M \neg \varphi$ is closed under weakening (strengthening).

of these properties is that they concern a motivation for something that actually cannot be avoided. The point is that although it seems strange that a logic validates motivations for things that cannot be avoided, it is not harmful either. No agent will ever let his decision making be influenced by motivations for things that are true inevitably and always. In other words, such motivations are void. Then, we might also argue that if ρ is unavoidable, in particular, if it is true now, the motivation $M^i(\rho \leq \delta)$ is void, because it concerns an achievement that is met anyway.

However, we consider the issue whether or not $\rho \rightarrow M^i(\rho \leq \delta)$ to be different from, for instance, the issue whether or not $M^i(\top \leq \delta)$. Whereas the second motivation is void because it concerns a tautology, i.e., something that is considered to be true inevitably and always, the first motivation results from a condition that can be considered to be only *occasionally* true.

We want to stress that in deontic logic, the approaches of Anderson and Meyer lead to similar problems. In Meyer's system we have the counter intuitive $[\overline{\alpha}]\bot \rightarrow O(\alpha)$, which says that if α is the only possible action (we cannot perform an alternative action), it is obliged to perform it. In Anderson's reduction we have the counter intuitive $\Box\varphi \rightarrow O\varphi$, which says that if a condition is a necessity, it is also obliged. It appears that these properties were not perceived as problematic in deontic logic. But, as we claimed above, in the present, temporal context, similar properties seem more problematic. Recently we presented two alternative possible remedies to this problem, in the context of deontic deadlines. In the first approach [8] we try to capture that there is violation (negative condition) if and only if the achievement is not accomplished at the deadline. In the second approach [4], we argue that the problem is caused by the fact that we model the motivation (obligation) only from the point of view of its negative (violation) conditions. We show that the undesired property is eliminated by considering success conditions also. This shows that the problem of these counter intuitive properties is not a problem of reduction approaches as such.

6.2 Commutativity Between the Temporal and the Motivational Dimension

Until now we did not say anything about whether or not the conditions ρ and δ can be temporal formulas, or even motivational operators themselves. A priori, there seems no technical reason to exclude this; any formula may represent an achievement or deadline condition. However, semantically, things get harder. What does it mean to achieve *now* that *next* ρ? What does it mean to encounter a deadline *next* δ? Let us, for the moment, assume that such expressions can be given interpretations that make sense. Then, we are in the position to discuss whether or not we can find, in this setting, a commutativity property for the interaction of time and motivation.

Commutativity properties are well-known from the interactions of time and knowledge. For instance, 'perfect recall' is expressed by the commutativity property (the modality K stands for 'Knowledge') $KX\varphi \rightarrow XK\varphi$, and 'no learning' by $XK\varphi \rightarrow KX\varphi$. Roughly, these properties express that, when time passes, no things are forgotten, and no new things are learned. Now, similar properties should hold for the interaction of time and motivations as defined in section 4. The reason is simple: within a model, the truth of negative condition constants is fixed. So, when going through a time path within a model, no new negative condition constants come into play, and no existing constants are removed. To what commutativity property does this lead? This turns out not to be entirely trivial. The point is, that we cannot express the property alluded to in the syntax we have chosen for the motivation operators. We have to slightly generalize our notation and definition. First we generalize the constants $NegC$ to general negative condition *formulas*. Second, we include these negative condition formulas in the notation for the operators: $M^i(\rho \leq \delta, NegC)$. All other details of the definitions of section 4 stay the same. With this slight adaptation of the definition and the notation, we can now formulate the commutativity property we alluded to, in the stronger temporal language of CTL*[8]:

$$M^i(X\rho \leq X\delta, XNegC) \leftrightarrow AXM^i(\rho \leq \delta, NegC)$$

This expresses that when time evolves, the temporal 'content' of deadline motivations adapts accordingly. The left to right implication expresses that at any point in time, all motivations are actualized versions of motivations that where already there in the past (compare this with 'no learning', from dynamic epistemic logic), and the right to left implication expresses that all past motivations are 'actualized'[9] to motivations for the present state (compare this with 'perfect recall', from dynamic epistemic logic). This means that the language cannot talk about the motivational and the temporal dimension independently. The motivational dimension is, as it were, 'embedded' in the temporal dimension.

The above commutativity property completely 'fixes' the relation between motivation and time. There is no room for motivational updates: new motivations are not 'learned', and all old motivations are 'recalled'. The property holds because the negative conditions are fixed within models. Therefore, this 'limitation' applies to any reduction approach to achievement motivations which are temporally constrained.

6.3   Reducing Multiple Motivational Modalities

For separate motivational attitudes (desires, obligations, preferences, etc) we can define separate propositional constants. This is a real advantage, since it reduces the complexity of the overall logical system considerably. At the same time, this does not prevent us from introducing some simple interactions between the separate motivational attitudes. For instance, if $NegD$ is the constant for

---

[8] Roughly, CTL* adds the full power of LTL (linear time temporal logic) to the path formulas of CTL. Details can be found in the literature.

[9] Note that although the motivations are certainly 'modified', we do not use the word 'update'. The point is that commutativity means that no 'new' motivations are allowed to enter the stage. The only 'dynamics' that is going on is that existing motivations are actualized.

desires, and $NegO$ the one for obligations we might define that an agent is 'prudent' simply as an axiom $NegO \rightarrow NegD$.

6.4 Other Temporal Formalisms

The choice in this paper for the temporal logic CTL is a pragmatic one. We believe the theory applies equally well, and probably better, to linear time temporal logic (LTL [10]). However, CTL has nice properties (P-complete complexity of the model checking problem for CTL, versus PSPACE-complete complexity for LTL [18]), and is popular in agent theory [17].

7 Conclusion

Given that motivations are a prerequisite for action, that action involves change, and that change presupposes time, motivational and temporal notions have very strong conceptual connections. Therefore, any contribution to the study of such connections is welcome.

In this paper we discussed intuitions concerning the notion of 'being motivated to obey a condition ρ before a condition δ occurs'. We studied this notion by defining a reduction to the logic CTL, minimally extended with 'negative condition constants'. We discussed some limitations, possible problems and possible extensions of the definitions.

It would be interesting to test the logic by means of a CTL-theorem prover. There are no such implemented theorem provers available. However, they can be written by using the results in either [2] or [19]. We plan to do this in the near future.

References

1. A.R. Anderson. A reduction of deontic logic to alethic modal logic. *Mind*, 67:100–103, 1958.
2. A. Bolotov and M. Fisher. A clausal resolution method for CTL branching-time temporal logic. *Journal of Experimental and Theoretical Artificial Intelligence*, 11(1):77–93, 1999.
3. J.M. Broersen. Action negation and alternative reductions for dynamic deontic logics. *Journal of Applied Logic*, 2(1):153–168, 2003.
4. J.M. Broersen, F. Dignum, V. Dignum, and J.-J Meyer. Designing a deontic logic of deadlines. In A. Lomuscio and D. Nute, editors, *Proceedings 7th International Workshop on Deontic Logic in Computer Science (DEON'04)*, volume 3065 of *Lecture Notes in Computer Science*, pages 43–56. Springer, 2004.
5. E.M. Clarke, E.A. Emerson, and A.P. Sistla. Automatic verification of finite-state concurrent systems using temporal logic specifications. *ACM Transactions on Programming Languages and Systems*, 8(2), 1986.
6. E.M. Clarke, O. Grumberg, and D. Long. Verification tools for finite-state concurrent systems. In *A decade of concurrency*, volume 803 of *Lecture Notes in Computer Science*, pages 124–175. Springer, 1993.

7. P.R. Cohen and H.J. Levesque. Intention is choice with commitment. *Artificial Intelligence*, 42(3):213–261, 1990.
8. F. Dignum, J. Broersen, V. Dignum, and J.-J Meyer. Meeting the deadline: Why, when and how. In *Proceedings 3th International Workshop on Formal Aspects of Agent-Based Systems (FAABS'04)*, Lecture Notes in Computer Science. Springer, 2004. to appear.
9. F. Dignum and R. Kuiper. Combining dynamic deontic logic and temporal logic for the specification of deadlines. In R. Sprague Jr., editor, *Proceedings of thirtieth HICSS*, 1997.
10. E.A. Emerson. Temporal and modal logic. In J. van Leeuwen, editor, *Handbook of Theoretical Computer Science, volume B: Formal Models and Semantics*, chapter 14, pages 996–1072. Elsevier Science, 1990.
11. S. Kanger. New foundations for ethical theory. In R. Hilpinen, editor, *Deontic Logic: Introductory and Systematic Readings*, pages 36–58. D. Reidel Publishing Company, 1971.
12. S. Lindström and W. Rabinowicz. Unlimited doxastic logic for introspective agents. *Erkenntnis*, 50:353–385, 1999.
13. J.-J.Ch. Meyer. A different approach to deontic logic: Deontic logic viewed as a variant of dynamic logic. *Notre Dame Journal of Formal Logic*, 29:109–136, 1988.
14. J.-J.Ch Meyer, W. van der Hoek, and B. van Linder. A logical approach to the dynamics of commitments. *Artificial Intelligence*, 1999.
15. V.R. Pratt. Semantical considerations on Floyd-Hoare logic. In *Proceedings 17th IEEE Symposium on the Foundations of Computer Science*, pages 109–121. IEEE Computer Society Press, 1976.
16. A.S. Rao and M.P. Georgeff. Modeling rational agents within a BDI-architecture. In J. Allen, R. Fikes, and E. Sandewall, editors, *Proceedings of the 2nd International Conference on Principles of Knowledge Representation and Reasoning (KR'91)*, pages 473–484. Morgan Kaufmann Publishers, 1991.
17. K. Schild. On the relationship between BDI-logics and standard logics of concurrency. *Autonomous agents and multi-agent systems*, 3:259–283, 2000.
18. Ph Schnoebelen. The complexity of temporal logic model checking. In P. Balbiani, N-Y. Suzuki, F. Wolter, and M. Zakharyaschev, editors, *Advances in Modal Logic*, volume 4, pages 393–436, 2003.
19. N. Shankar. Machine-assisted verification using theorem proving and model checking. In M. Broy, editor, *Mathematical Methods in Program Development*. Springer, 1997.
20. G.H. von Wright. Deontic logic. *Mind*, 60:1–15, 1951.

Representation and Complexity in Boolean Games

Paul E. Dunne and Wiebe van der Hoek

Dept. of Computer Science
University of Liverpool
Liverpool L69 7ZF, United Kingdom
{ped,wiebe}@csc.liv.ac.uk

Abstract. Boolean games are a class of two-player games which may be defined via a Boolean form over a set of atomic actions. A particular game on some form is instantiated by partitioning these actions between the players – player 0 and player 1 – each of whom has the object of employing its available actions in such a way that the game's outcome is that sought by the player concerned, i.e. player i tries to bring about the outcome i. In this paper our aim is to consider a number of issues concerning how such forms are represented within an algorithmic setting. We introduce a concept of *concise form* representation and compare its properties in relation to the more frequently used "extensive form" descriptions. Among other results we present a "normal form" theorem that gives a characterisation of winning strategies for each player. Our main interest, however, lies in classifying the computational complexity of various decision problems when the game instance is presented as a concise form. Among the problems we consider are: deciding existence of a winning strategy given control of a particular set of actions; determining whether two games are "equivalent".

1 Introduction

The combination of logic and games has a significant history: for instance, a game theoretic interpretation of quantification goes back at least to the 19th century with C.S. Peirce ([9]), but it took until the second half of the previous century, when Henkin suggested a way of using games to give a semantics for infinitary languages ([5]), that logicians used more and more game-theoretic techniques in their analysis, and that game theoretic versions for all essential logical notions (truth in a model, validity, model comparison) were subsequently developed. In addition, connections between game theory and modal logic have recently been developed.

Where the above research paradigm can be summarised as 'game theory in logic', toward the end of the last decade, an area that could be coined 'logic in game theory' received a lot of attention (we only mention [7]; the reader can find more references there); especially when this field is conceived as formalising the dynamics and the powers of coalitions in multi-agent systems, this boost in attention can be explained.

Boolean Games, as introduced by Harrenstein *et. al* ([4]) fit in this research paradigm by studying two-player games in which each player has control over a set of atomic propositions, is able to force certain states of affairs to be true, but is dependent on the other player concerning the realisation of many other situations. This seems to model

J.J. Alferes and J. Leite (Eds.): JELIA 2004, LNAI 3229, pp. 347–359, 2004.
© Springer-Verlag Berlin Heidelberg 2004

a rather general set of multi-agent scenarios, where it is quite common that each agent has its own goals, but, at the same time, only limited control over the resources (the particular propositional variables); at the same time, all two-player games in strategic form can be modelled as such.

The issues treated in [3,4], are primarily driven by semantic concerns, thus: presenting inductive definitions of two-player fully competitive games; introducing viable ideas of what it means for two games to be "strategically equivalent"; constructing sound and complete calculi to capture winning strategies; and exploring the logical and algebraic relationship between the game-theoretic formalism and propositional logic functions.

Our concerns in the present paper are two-fold: firstly, we revisit the correspondence between propositional logic functions and Boolean forms presented in [4] under which a given form g involving atomic actions A maps to a propositional function $\lceil g \rceil$ of the propositional arguments A. We establish a strong connection between the concept of winning strategy in a game and classical representation theorems for propositional functions. Among the consequences following from this connection we may,

a. Characterise all winning strategies for either player in a form g in terms of particular representations of $\lceil g \rceil$.
b. Obtain various "normal form" theorems for Boolean forms.
c. Characterise the "minimal winning control allocations" for a player,
d. Characterise precisely those forms, g, for which neither player has a winning strategy unless they have control over every atomic action.

Our second and principal interest, however, is to examine the computational complexity of a number of natural decision problems arising in the domain of Boolean game forms. In particular,

e. Given a description of a form g and an allocation of atomic actions, σ_i, to player i, does σ_i give a winning strategy for i?
f. Given descriptions of two forms g and h are these *strategically equivalent*?
g. Given a description of some form g, is there *any* subset of actions with which player i has a winning strategy in g?
h. Given g and h together with instantiations of these to games via σ for g and τ for h, are the resulting *games* – (g, σ) and (h, τ) – "equivalent"?

The computational complexity of these decision problems turns on how much freedom is permitted in representing the forms within an instance of the problem. If we insist on an "extensive form" description then all may be solved by deterministic polynomial-time methods: this bound, however, is polynomial in the size of the instance, which for extensive forms will typically be exponential in the number of atomic actions. If, on the other hand, we allow so-called "concise forms", each of the problems above is, under the standard assumptions, computationally intractable, with complexities ranging from NP–complete to completeness for a class believed to lie strictly between the second and third levels of the polynomial hierarchy.

As one point of interest we observe that the classification results for the problems described by (e)–(g) are fairly direct consequences of the characterisations given by (a) and (b). The constructions required in our analysis of the "game equivalence" problem (h) are, however, rather more intricate and we omit the details of this.

In total these results suggest a trade-off between extensive, computationally tractable descriptions that, in general, will be unrealistically large and concise descriptions for which decision methods for those questions of interest are unlikely to be viable. It may, however, be the case that this apparent dichotomy is not as clearly defined as our results imply: we show that there are natural questions which even in terms of extensive forms are computationally intractable.

The remainder of this paper is organised as follows. In the next section we review the definitions of Boolean form, game and "winning strategy" originating in [3,4]. In Section 3 we examine the relationship between forms and propositional functions from [4] and show that this can be used to characterise winning strategies as well as yielding various "normal form" representations for Boolean forms. We then introduce the ideas that form the central concern of this paper, namely the notion of concise form descriptions, and discuss the properties of these in relation to extensive forms. We continue this analytic comparison in Section 5, wherein various decision problems are defined and classified with respect to their computational complexity. The final section outlines some directions for further research.

2   Boolean Forms and Games

Definition 1. *(Harrenstein et al. [4]) Let $A = \{a_1, \ldots, a_n\}$ be a (finite) set of atomic actions and $\mathcal{G}_A$ the smallest set that satisfies both:*

a. $\{0, 1\} \subset \mathcal{G}_A$.
b. If g_0, $g_1 \in \mathcal{G}_A$ and $\alpha \in A$ then $\alpha(g_0, g_1) \in \mathcal{G}_A$.

Thus $\mathcal{G}_A$ defines the set of Boolean forms with atomic strategies A.

A Boolean form $g \in \mathcal{G}_A$ is instantiated as a Boolean game, $\langle g, \sigma \rangle$, by specifying for each player $i \in \{0, 1\}$ which subset of the actions the player has complete control over. Thus $\sigma : A \rightarrow \{0, 1\}$ describes a partition of A as $\langle \sigma_0, \sigma_1 \rangle$ with σ_i the subset of A mapped to i by σ. We refer to σ_i as the control allocation for player i.

Given some Boolean form $g \in \mathcal{G}_A$, we may think of g depicted as a *binary tree* so that: if $g \in \{0, 1\}$, then this tree is a single vertex labelled with the relevant outcome $\mathbf{0}$ or $\mathbf{1}$; if $g = \alpha(g_0, g_1)$ this tree comprises a root labelled with the action α one of whose out-going edges is directed into the root of the tree for g_0, with the other out-going edge directed into the root of the tree for g_1. An outcome of $\alpha(g_0, g_1)$ is determined by whether the action α is invoked – in which event play continues with g_0 – or abstained from – resulting in play continuing from g_1. Thus given some subset s of A, and the form g, the outcome $\mathbf{sf}(g)(s)$ (the "strategic form" of [4]) resulting from this process is inductively defined via

$$\mathbf{sf}(g)(s) := \begin{cases} 0 & \text{if } g = 0 \\ 1 & \text{if } g = 1 \\ \mathbf{sf}(g_0)(s) & \text{if } g = \alpha(g_0, g_1) \text{ and } \alpha \in s \\ \mathbf{sf}(g_1)(s) & \text{if } g = \alpha(g_0, g_1) \text{ and } \alpha \notin s \end{cases}$$

The forms g and $h \in \mathcal{G}_A$ are regarded as *strategically equivalent* ($g \equiv_{\mathbf{sf}} h$) if for every choice $s \subseteq A$ it holds that $\mathbf{sf}(g)(s) = \mathbf{sf}(h)(s)$.

We note one important feature of this model is its requirement that having committed
to playing or refraining from playing an action α the player allocated control of α does
not subsequently reverse this choice. In consequence it may be assumed in terms of the
binary tree presentation of forms that a path from the root to an outcome contains at
most one occurrence of any atomic action.

Given an instantiation of g to a game $\langle g, \sigma \rangle$ the aim of player i is to choose for each
action, α, within its control, i.e. in the set σ_i, whether or not to play α. Thus a *strategy*
for i in $\langle g, \sigma \rangle$ can be identified as the *subset* of σ_i that i plays. This gives rise to the
following definition of *winning strategy* in [4].

Definition 2. *A player* $i \in \{0, 1\}$ *has a* winning strategy *in the game* $\langle g, \sigma \rangle$ *if there
is a subset* ν *of* σ_i *such that regardless of which instantiation* τ *of* σ_{1-i} *is chosen,*
$\mathbf{sf}(g)(\nu \cup \tau) = i$.

A control allocation, σ_i, *is minimal for* i *in* g *if there is a winning strategy,* ν *for
player* i *in* $\langle g, \sigma \rangle$ *and changing the allocation of any* $\alpha \in \sigma_i$ *to* σ_{1-i}, *results in a game
where* i *no longer has a winning strategy, i.e. in the control allocation,* σ' *for which
$\sigma(\alpha) = i$ becomes* $\sigma'(\alpha) = 1 - i$, i *does not have a winning strategy in the game* $\langle g, \sigma' \rangle$.

The basic definition of Boolean form is extended by introducing a number of operations
on these.

Definition 3. *Let* $g_0, g_1, h \in \mathcal{G}_A$, *and* $\alpha \in A$. *The operations* $+$, $\cdot$, $\otimes$ *and* $^-$ *are,*

1. $\mathbf{0} + h := h$; $\mathbf{1} + h := \mathbf{1}$; $\alpha(g_0, g_1) + h := \alpha(g_0 + h, g_1 + h)$
2. $\mathbf{0} \cdot h := \mathbf{0}$; $\mathbf{1} \cdot h := h$; $\alpha(g_0, g_1) \cdot h := \alpha(g_0 \cdot h, g_1 \cdot h)$
3. $\overline{\mathbf{0}} := \mathbf{1}$; $\overline{\mathbf{1}} := \mathbf{0}$; $\overline{\alpha(g_0, g_1)} := \alpha(\overline{g_0}, \overline{g_1})$
4. $\otimes(\mathbf{0}, g, h) := h$; $\otimes(\mathbf{1}, g, h) := g$; $\otimes(\alpha(g_0, g_1), h_0, h_1) :=$
$$\alpha(\otimes(g_0, h_0, h_1), \otimes(g_1, h_0, h_1))$$

Informally we may regard the operations of Definition 3 in terms of transformations
effected on the associated binary tree form describing g. Thus, $g + h$ is the form obtained
by replacing each 0 outcome in g with a copy of h; $g \cdot h$ that resulting by replacing each
1 outcome in g with a copy of h; and $\overline{g}$ the form in which 0 outcomes are changed to
1 and *vice-versa*. The operation $\otimes$ is rather more involved, however, the form resulting
from $\otimes(g, h_0, h_1)$ is obtained by *simultaneously* replacing 0 outcomes in g with h_1 and
1 outcomes with h_0.

Finally we recall the following properties,

Fact 1. *The set of Boolean forms* $\mathcal{G}_A$ *is such that,*

1. *The relationship* $\equiv_{\mathbf{sf}}$ *is an equivalence relation.*
2. *Let* $[g]$ *denote* $\{h : g \equiv_{\mathbf{sf}} h\}$ *and* $\mathcal{G}_\equiv$ *be* $\{[g] : g \in \mathcal{G}_A\}$. *The operations of
Definition 3 may be raised to corresponding operations on equivalence classes of
forms so that,*

$$[g] + [h] = [g + h] \; ; \; [g] \cdot [h] = [g \cdot h]$$

$$\overline{[g]} = [\overline{g}] \qquad ; \; \otimes([g], [h_0], [h_1]) = [\otimes(g, h_0, h_1)]$$

3. *Each form g may be associated with a propositional function, $\lceil g \rceil$ with arguments A so that $\lceil g \rceil [s] = 0$ if and only if $\text{sf}(g)(s) = 0$ (where for a propositional function $f(X)$ and $Q \subseteq X$, $f[Q]$ denotes the value of the function f under the instantiation $x := 1$ if $x \in Q$, $x := 0$ if $x \notin Q$). For g and h forms in $\mathcal{G}_A$*

$$g \equiv_{\text{sf}} h \;\Leftrightarrow\; \lceil g \rceil \equiv \lceil h \rceil$$

3   Characterising Winning Strategies

We recall the following standard definitions concerning propositional logic functions.

Definition 4. *Let $X_n = \{x_1, \ldots, x_n\}$ be a set of n propositional variables and $f(X_n)$ some propositional logic function defined over these. A literal, y over X_n, is a term x or $\neg x$ for some $x \in X_n$. A set of literals, $S = \{y_1, \ldots, y_r\}$, is well-formed if for each x_k at most one of x_k, $\neg x_k$ occurs in S. A well-formed set S defines an implicate of $f(X_n)$ if the (partial) instantiation, α_S, of X_n by $x_k := 1$ if $\neg x_k \in S$, $x_k := 0$ if $x_k \in S$ is such that $f(\alpha) = 0$ for all α that agree with α_S. A well-formed set S is an implicant of $f(X_n)$ if the (partial) instantiation, β_S, of X_n by $x_k := 0$ if $\neg x_k \in S$, $x_k := 1$ if $x_k \in S$ is such that $f(\alpha) = 1$ for all α that agree with β_S. An implicate (resp. implicant) is a prime implicate (resp. implicant) of $f(X_n)$ if no strict subset S' of S is an implicate (implicant) of $f(X_n)$.*

We require some further notation in order to describe the main results of this section.

Definition 5. *For a form $g \in \mathcal{G}_A$,*

$$W_i(g) \triangleq \{(\sigma_i, \nu) \;:\; \nu \subseteq \sigma_i \text{ and } \forall \tau \subseteq \sigma_{1-i} \;:\; \text{sf}(g)(\nu \cup \tau) = i\}$$

$$
\begin{aligned}
M_i(g) \triangleq \{(\sigma_i, \nu) \;:\; &(\sigma_i, \nu) \in W_i(g) \text{ and} \\
&\forall \alpha \in \nu \; \exists \tau \subseteq \sigma_{1-i} \;:\; \text{sf}(g)(\nu \setminus \{\alpha\} \cup \tau) = 1 - i \text{ and} \\
&\forall \alpha \in \sigma_i \setminus \nu \; \exists \tau \subseteq \sigma_{1-i} \;:\; \text{sf}(g)(\nu \cup \{\alpha\} \cup \tau) = 1 - i\}
\end{aligned}
$$

Thus, $W_i(g)$ is the set of allocations (σ_i) paired with winning strategies for i in these (ν), while $M_i(g)$ is the subset of these in which σ_i is a minimal control allocation for i.
    Now consider the set of *play choices*, $\mathcal{P}(A)$, given by

$$\mathcal{P}(A) = \{(\nu, \pi) \;:\; \nu \subseteq A, \; \pi \subseteq A, \text{ and } \nu \cap \pi = \emptyset\}$$

and define a (bijective) mapping, *Lits*, between these and well-formed literal sets over the propositional variables $\{a_1, \ldots, a_n\}$ by

$$Lits(\,(\nu, \pi)\,) \;:=\; \bigcup_{a_i \in \nu} \{a_i\} \;\cup\; \bigcup_{a_i \in \pi} \{\neg a_i\}$$

We now obtain,

Theorem 1. *Let $\langle g, \sigma \rangle$ be a Boolean game with $g \in \mathcal{G}_A$.*

a. *Player 0 has a winning strategy in $\langle g, \sigma \rangle$ if and only if there exists $\nu \subseteq \sigma_0$ for which $Lits((\nu, \sigma_0 \setminus \nu))$ is an implicate of $\lceil g \rceil(A)$.*

b. *Player 1 has a winning strategy in $\langle g, \sigma \rangle$ if and only if there exists $\nu \subseteq \sigma_1$ for which $Lits((\nu, \sigma_1 \setminus \nu))$ is an implicant of $\lceil g \rceil (A)$.*

c. *The control allocation σ_0 is minimal for player 0 in g if and only if there exists $\nu \subseteq \sigma_0$ for which $Lits((\nu, \sigma_0 \setminus \nu))$ is a prime implicate of $\lceil g \rceil (A)$.*

d. *The control allocation σ_1 is minimal for player 1 in g if and only if there exists $\nu \subseteq \sigma_1$ for which $Lits((\nu, \sigma_1 \setminus \nu))$ is a prime implicant of $\lceil g \rceil (A)$.*

Corollary 1. *Let $\sum$ and $\prod$ denote the raised versions of the operations $+$ and $\cdot$ when applied over a collection of forms. For $(\nu, \mu) \in \mathcal{P}(A)$ the forms $c_{(\nu, \mu)}$ and $d_{(\nu, \mu)}$ are*

$$c_{(\nu, \mu)} \triangleq \sum_{\alpha \in \nu} \alpha(0, 1) + \sum_{\alpha \in \mu} \alpha(1, 0)$$

$$d_{(\nu, \mu)} \triangleq \prod_{\alpha \in \nu} \alpha(1, 0) \cdot \prod_{\alpha \in \mu} \alpha(0, 1)$$

a. *For all $g \in \mathcal{G}_A$,*

$$g \equiv_{sf} \sum_{(\sigma_1, \nu) \in W_1(g)} d_{(\nu, \sigma_1 \setminus \nu)} \equiv_{sf} \prod_{(\sigma_0, \nu) \in W_0(g)} c_{(\nu, \sigma_0 \setminus \nu)}$$

b. *For all $g \in \mathcal{G}_A$,*

$$g \equiv_{sf} \sum_{(\sigma_1, \nu) \in M_1(g)} d_{(\nu, \sigma_1 \setminus \nu)} \equiv_{sf} \prod_{(\sigma_0, \nu) \in M_0(g)} c_{(\nu, \sigma_0 \setminus \nu)}$$

Proof. Both are immediate from Theorem 1 and the fact that every propositional function $f(X_n)$ is equivalent to formulae described by the disjunction of product terms matching (prime) implicants and the conjunction of clause terms matching (prime) implicates.   □

Corollary 2. *For any set $A^{(n)} = \{a_1, \ldots, a_n\}$ of n atomic actions, there are (modulo strategic equivalence) exactly two $g \in \mathcal{G}_{A^{(n)}}$ with the property that neither player has a winning strategy in the game $\langle g, \sigma \rangle$ unless $\sigma_i = A^{(n)}$.*

Thus, with these two exceptions, in any g at least one of the players can force a win without having control over the entire action set.

Proof. We first show that there are at least two such cases.

Consider the form, $Par_n \in \mathcal{G}_{A^{(n)}}$, inductively defined as

$$Par_n := \begin{cases} a_1(0, 1) & \text{if } n = 1 \\ \otimes(Par_{n-1}, a_n(0, 1), a_n(1, 0)) & \text{if } n \geq 2 \end{cases}$$

Then, it is easy to show that $\lceil Par_n \rceil \equiv a_1 \oplus a_2 \oplus \ldots \oplus a_n$, where $\oplus$ is binary exclusive or. This function, however, cannot have its value determined by setting any *strict* subset of its arguments, i.e. i has a winning strategy only if i has control over the entire action set $A^{(n)}$. The second example class is obtained simply by considering $\overline{Par_n}$.

To see that there at most two cases, it suffices to note that if $f(A^{(n)}) \not\equiv \lceil Par_n \rceil$ and $f(A^{(n)}) \not\equiv \neg \lceil Par_n \rceil$ then there is either a prime implicate or prime implicant of f that depends on at most $n - 1$ arguments. Theorem 1(c–d) presents an appropriate winning strategy in either case.

□

4   Representation Issues – Concise Versus Extensive

Representational issues are one aspect that must be considered in assessing the computational complexity of particular decision problems on Boolean forms/games: thus one has a choice of using *extensive forms* whereby $g \in \mathcal{G}_A$ is described in terms of Definition 1(a,b) or, alternatively, in some *"concise"* form, e.g. $g \in \mathcal{G}_A$ is described by its construction in terms of the operations in Definition 3. Formally,

Definition 6. *A game* $g \in \mathcal{G}_A$, *is described in* extensive *form if it is presented as a labelled binary tree* $T(V, E)$ *each internal vertex of which is labelled with some* $a_i \in A$ *and whose leaves are labelled with an outcome from the set* $\{0, 1\}$. *The size of an extensive form representation* T *of* g, *denoted* $S^{ext}(g, T)$ *is the total number of internal vertices in* T, *i.e. the number of occurrences of atomic strategy labels.*

A game $g \in \mathcal{G}_A$ *is described in* concise *form if given as a well-formed expression in the language* $\mathcal{L}_A$ *defined as follows:*

a. $\{0, 1\} \subset \mathcal{L}_A$.
b. *For each* $\alpha \in A$ *and* F_0, $F_1 \in \mathcal{L}_A$, $\alpha(F_0, F_1) \in \mathcal{L}_A$.
c. *For each* $\theta \in \{+, \cdot\}$, *and* F, $G \in \mathcal{L}_A$, $F \theta G \in \mathcal{L}_A$.
d. *For each* F, G, $H \in \mathcal{L}_A$, $\otimes(F, G, H) \in \mathcal{L}_A$.
e. *For each* $F \in \mathcal{L}_A$, $\overline{F} \in \mathcal{L}_A$
f. *For each* $F \in \mathcal{L}_A$, $(F) \in \mathcal{L}_A$ *(bracketing).*
g. $F \in \mathcal{L}_A$ *if and only if* F *is formed by a finite number of applications of the rules* (a)–(f).

The size *of a concise representation,* F *of* g, *denoted* $S^{con}(F, g)$ *is the total number of applications of rule (b) used to form* F.

It will be useful, subsequently, to consider the following measures in capturing ideas of representational complexity.

Definition 7. *For* $g \in \mathcal{G}_A$, *the* extensive complexity *of (the class)* $[g]$ *is,*

$$S^{ext}([g]) := \min \{S^{ext}(h, T) : T \text{ is an extensive representation of } h \text{ with } g \equiv_{sf} h\}$$

Similarly, the concise complexity *of (the class)* $[g]$, *is*

$$S^{con}([g]) := \min \{S^{con}(h, F) : F \text{ is a concise representation of } h \text{ with } g \equiv_{sf} h\}$$

A significant difference between extensive and concise descriptions of $g \in \mathcal{G}_A$ is that the latter may be exponentially shorter (in terms of $n = |A|$) than the former, even for quite "basic" game forms. Thus we have the following result concerning these measures,

Proposition 1.

a. *For all* $g \in \mathcal{G}_A$, $S^{con}([g]) \leq S^{ext}([g]) \leq 2^{|A|} - 1$.
b. *For each* $n \geq 1$, *let* $A^{(n)}$ *denote the set of atomic strategies* $\{a_1, a_2, \ldots, a_n\}$. *There is a sequence* $\{g^{(n)}\}$ *of forms with* $g^{(n)} \in \mathcal{G}_{A^{(n)}}$ *for which:*

$$S^{ext}([g^{(n)}]) = 2^n - 1 \quad ; \quad S^{con}([g^{(n)}]) = O(n)$$

Proof. (*outline*)

a. The upper bound $S^{con}([g]) \leq S^{ext}([g])$ is obvious. For $S^{ext}([g]) \leq 2^{|A|} - 1$ it suffices to observe that in any extensive representation of h for which $g \equiv_{sf} h$ no atomic strategy $\alpha \in A$ need occur more than once on any path leading from the root to a leaf. Thus each path contains at most $|A|$ distinct labels. Since the representation is a binary tree the upper bound is immediate.

b. Use the form Par_n of Corollary 2 whose concise form complexity is $2n - 1$[1]. It may be shown that a minimal extensive form representation of Par_n must be a complete binary tree of depth n.   □

We can, in fact, obtain a rather stronger version of Proposition 1(a), by considering another idea from the study of propositional logic functions, namely:

Definition 8. *A set C of implicates (implicants) is a covering set for $f(X_n)$ if for any instantiation α under which $f(\alpha)$ takes the value 0 (1) there is at least one $S \in C$ that evaluates to 0 (1) under α. For a propositional function $f(X_n)$ we denote by $R_i(f)$ the sizes of the smallest covering set of implicates (when $i = 0$) and implicants ($i = 1$).*

From this,

Proposition 2. *For all $g \in \mathcal{G}_A$,*

a. $S^{ext}([g]) \geq R_0(\lceil g \rceil) + R_1(\lceil g \rceil) - 1$.
b. $S^{con}([g]) \leq |A| \min\{R_0(\lceil g \rceil), R_1(\lceil g \rceil)\}$.

Proof. (*outline*)

a. Suppose T is a minimal size extensive representation of $g \in \mathcal{G}_A$. It must be the case that for $i \in \{0, 1\}$, T has at least $R_i(\lceil g \rceil)$ leaves labelled with the outcome i. For if this failed to be the case for $i = 0$ say, then from Theorem 1(a) we could construct a covering set of implicates for $\lceil g \rceil$ via the choice of actions on each path from the root of T to an outcome 0: this covering set, however, would contain fewer than $R_0(\lceil g \rceil)$ implicates. We deduce that T has at least $R_0(\lceil g \rceil) + R_1(\lceil g \rceil)$ *leaves* and hence, $R_0(\lceil g \rceil) + R_1(\lceil g \rceil) - 1$ internal vertices.

b. Consequence of Corollary 1.   □

We note that Proposition 2(a) implies the first part of Propostion 1(b) since $R_0(\lceil Par_n \rceil) = R_1(\lceil Par_n \rceil) = 2^{n-1}$.

5 Decision Problems for Boolean Games

Given a description of some Boolean game (g, σ), probably the most basic question one would be concerned with is whether one or other of the players can force a win with their allotted set of actions, σ_i. Similarly, if one is just presented with the form $g \in \mathcal{G}_A$,

---

[1] A similar result can be shown even if the concise form representation may only use the operations $\{+, \cdot, -\}$. The gap between $S^{ext}(g^{(n)})$ and $S^{con}_{\{+, \cdot, -\}}(g^{(n)})$, however, is not fully exponential in this case: $S^{con}_{\{+, \cdot, -\}}(g^{(n)}) = \Theta(n^2)$.

a player may wish to discover which subset of A it would be beneficial to gain control of, since it would admit a winning strategy in g. We note that our notion of "winning strategy" for i using a set of actions σ_i has one consequence: if σ_i admits a winning strategy for i in g, then any superset of σ_i also admits a winning strategy for i. From this observation it follows that in order to decide if i has *any* winning strategy in g it suffices to determine if setting $\sigma_i = A$, that is giving i control of *every* atomic action, admits such.

As well as these questions concerning two different aspects of whether one player has the capability to win a game, another set of questions arises in determining various concepts of games being "equivalent". At one level, we have the idea of *strategic* equivalence: thus deciding of given forms g and h in $\mathcal{G}_A$ whether these are strategically equivalent. The concept of strategic equivalence, however, is in some ways rather too precise: there may be forms g and h which, while not strategically equivalent, we may wish to regard as "equivalent" under certain conditions, for example if it were the case that particular *instantiations* of g and h as *games* were "equivalent" in some sense. Thus, Harrenstein (personal communication), has suggested a concept of two Boolean games – $\langle g, \sigma \rangle$ and $\langle h, \tau \rangle$ – being *equivalent* based on the players being able to bring about "similar" outcomes: the formal definition being presented in terms of a "forcing relationship" similar in spirit to those introduced in [2,8]. We may very informally describe this notion as follows,

Definition 9. *Given a game $\langle g, \sigma \rangle$, a subset s of the action set A and a possible outcome, X, from the set $\{\{0\}, \{1\}, \{0,1\}\}$, the relationship $s \; \rho^i_{\langle g,\sigma \rangle} \; X$ holds whenever: there is a choice (s') for player i that is consistent with the profile s and such that no matter what choice of actions (s'') is made by the other player, the outcome of the g will be in X. The notation $\rho^i_{\langle g,\sigma \rangle} \; X$ indicates that $s \; \rho^i_{\langle g,\sigma \rangle} \; X$ for every choice of $s \subseteq A$.*

We write $\langle g, \sigma \rangle \equiv_\mathbf{H} \langle h, \tau \rangle$ if and only if: for each player i and possible outcome X, $\rho^i_{\langle g,\sigma \rangle} X \Leftrightarrow \rho_{\langle h,\tau \rangle} X$.

We have given a rather informally phrased definition of the "game equivalence" concept engendered via $\equiv_\mathbf{H}$, since the definition we employ is given in,

Definition 10. *Let $\langle g, \sigma \rangle$ and $\langle h, \tau \rangle$ be Boolean games with $g \in \mathcal{G}_A$ and $h \in \mathcal{G}_B$, noting that we do* not *require $A = B$ or even $A \cap B \neq \emptyset$. We say that $\langle g, \sigma \rangle$ and $\langle h, \tau \rangle$ are equivalent games, written $\langle g, \sigma \rangle \equiv_\mathbf{g} \langle h, \tau \rangle$, if the following condition is satisfied:*

For each $i \in \{0,1\}$, player i has a winning strategy in $\langle g, \sigma \rangle$ if and only if player i has a winning strategy in $\langle h, \tau \rangle$.

Thus, we interpret $\langle g, \sigma \rangle \equiv_\mathbf{g} \langle h, \tau \rangle$ as indicating that i's capabilities in $\langle g, \sigma \rangle$ are *identical to* its capabilities in $\langle h, \tau \rangle$: if i can force a win in one game then it can force a win in the other; if *neither* player can force a win in one game then neither player can force a win in the other. The following properties of $\equiv_\mathbf{g}$ with respect to $\equiv_\mathbf{H}$ may be shown

Lemma 1. *For a control allocation mapping, σ, let $\bar{\sigma}$ denote the control allocation in which $\bar{\sigma}_0 := \sigma_1$ and $\bar{\sigma}_1 := \sigma_0$, i.e. $\bar{\sigma}$ swops the control allocations around. For games $\langle g, \sigma \rangle$ and $\langle h, \tau \rangle$, it holds: $\langle g, \sigma \rangle \equiv_\mathbf{H} \langle h, \tau \rangle$ if and only if both $\langle g, \sigma \rangle \equiv_\mathbf{g} \langle h, \tau \rangle$ and $\langle g, \bar{\sigma} \rangle \equiv_\mathbf{g} \langle h, \bar{\tau} \rangle$.*

The relationship between $\equiv_\mathbf{H}$ and $\equiv_\mathbf{g}$ described in Lemma 1 merits some comment. Certainly it is clear that $\equiv_\mathbf{g}$ does not capture the entire class of equivalent games within the sense of being able to "enforce similar outcomes" defined in $\equiv_H$. There is, however, a simple mechanism by which those missed can be recovered, i.e. by requiring the additional condition $\langle g, \bar{\sigma} \rangle \equiv_g \langle h, \bar{\tau} \rangle$ to hold. We have interpreted $\langle g, \sigma \rangle \equiv_g \langle h, \tau \rangle$ as "player i can force a win in $\langle g, \sigma \rangle$ if and only if player i can force a win in $\langle h, \tau \rangle$". In this light, $\langle g, \bar{\sigma} \rangle \equiv_g \langle h, \bar{\tau} \rangle$ indicates "player i can force *their opponent* to win in $\langle g, \sigma \rangle$ if and only if player i can force their opponent to win in $\langle h, \tau \rangle$". In passing we observe that while "forcing one's opponent to win" may seem rather eccentric, examples of problems involving such strategies are well-known, e.g. "self-mate" puzzles in Chess. In total the view of game equivalence engendered by the "traditional" notion of state-to-outcome-set relationship, is identical to an arguably rather more intuitive notion of equivalence, namely: for each possible choice of i and j, player i can force a win for player j in $\langle g, \sigma \rangle$ if and only if player i can force a win for player j in $\langle h, \tau \rangle$.

The formal definition of the decision problems examined in the remainder of this section is given below.

- Winning Strategy (ws)
  Instance: a game $\langle g, \sigma \rangle$; set A of atomic strategies, a player $i \in \{0, 1\}$.
  Question: Does i have a winning strategy in the game (g, σ)?
- Equivalence (EQUIV)
  Instance: forms $g, h \in \mathcal{G}_A$.
  Question: Is it the case that $g \equiv_{sf} h$, i.e. are g and h *strategically equivalent*?
- Win Existence (WE)
  Instance: a form $g \in \mathcal{G}_A$ and a player $i \in \{0, 1\}$.
  Question: Is there *some* set of actions with which i has a winning strategy?
- Game Equivalence (GE)
  Instance: two games $\langle g, \sigma \rangle$, $\langle h, \tau \rangle$ with $g \in \mathcal{G}_A, h \in \mathcal{G}_B$.
  Question: Is it the case that $\langle g, \sigma \rangle \equiv_g \langle h, \tau \rangle$, i.e. are $\langle g, \sigma \rangle$ and $\langle h, \tau \rangle$ equivalent *games*?

We note that our definitions have not specified any restrictions on how a given form is described within an instance of these decision problems. We have, as noted in our discussion opening Section 4 above, (at least) two choices: allow $g \in \mathcal{G}_A$ to be described using an equivalent *concise form*, F_g; or insist that g is presented as an *extensive form*, T_g. One difference that we have already highlighted is that the space required for some descriptions F_g may be significantly less than that required for the minimum extensive form descriptions of g. While this fact appears to present a powerful argument in favour of employing concise form descriptions, our first set of results indicate some drawbacks.

If Q is a decision problem part of the instance for which is a Boolean form, we shall use the notation Q^c to describe the case which permits *concise* representations and Q^e for that which insists on *extensive* form descriptions.

Theorem 2.

a. WS^c *is* Σ_2^p-*complete.*
b. EQUIV^c *is* co-NP-*complete.*

Proof. (*Outline*)For (a), that $\text{WS}^c \in \Sigma_2^p$ follows directly from Definition 2 and the fact that $\mathbf{sf}(g)(\pi) = i$ can be tested in time polynomial in $S^{con}(F_g, g)$. The proof of

Σ_2^p–hardness uses a reduction from QSAT_2^Σ, instances of which comprise a propositional formula $\varphi(X_n, Y_n)$, these being accepted if there is some instantiation, α_X of X_n, under which every instantiation β_Y of Y_n renders $\varphi(\alpha_X, \beta_Y)$ false. An instance $\varphi(X_n, Y_n)$ can be translated into a Boolean form F_φ with atomic actions $A = X_n \cup Y_n$. Player 0 has a winning strategy with $\sigma_0 = X_n$ in F_φ if and only if $\varphi(X_n, Y_n)$ is a positive instance of QSAT_2^Σ.

For (b) given G and H, concise representations of forms g, $h \in \mathcal{G}_A$, we note that $g \equiv_{\text{sf}} h$ if and only if $G \cdot \overline{H} + \overline{G} \cdot H \equiv_{\text{sf}} 0$ Thus, a CO-NP algorithm to decide $g \equiv_{\text{sf}} h$ simply tests $\forall \sigma$ $\text{sf}(g \cdot \overline{h} + \overline{g} \cdot h)(\sigma) = 0$ employing the forms G and H. That EQUIV^c is CO-NP–hard is an easy reduction from UNSAT: given $\varphi(X_n)$ an instance of UNSAT, construct the form F_φ (with action set X_n) by similar methods to those used in the proof of (a). For the instance $\langle F_\varphi, 0 \rangle$ we have $F_\varphi \equiv_{\text{sf}} 0$ if and only if $\varphi(X_n)$ is unsatisfiable.   □

Corollary 3. WE^c *is* NP–*complete*.

Proof. Given $\langle F_g, i \rangle$ with F_g a concise representation of $g \in \mathcal{G}_A$ use an NP computation to test if $\sigma_i = A$ admits a winning strategy for i: since $\sigma_{1-i} = \emptyset$ this only requires finding a single $\nu \subseteq A$ for which $\text{sf}(g)(\nu) = i$. The proof of NP–hardness follows from Theorem 2(b) and the observation that i has some choice yielding a winning strategy in g if and only if $g \not\equiv_{\text{sf}} 1 - i$.   □

While it may seem odd that deciding if there is *some* winning strategy for i in g is more tractable than deciding if a *specific* profile gives a winning strategy, the apparent discrepancy is easily resolved: i has *some* profile that admits a winning strategy if and only if giving i control of the set of *all* actions admits a winning strategy. Thus testing $\langle \langle g, \sigma \rangle, A, i \rangle$ as a positive instance of WS^c can be done in NP in those cases where $|\sigma_{1-i}| = O(\log |A|)$ since there are only polynomially many possible choices of $\tau \subseteq \sigma_{1-i}$ to test against.

Our final problem – Game Equivalence – turns out to be complete for a complexity class believed strictly to contain $\Sigma_2^p \cup \Pi_2^p$, namely the complement of the class D_2^p formed by those languages expressible as the intersection of a language $L_1 \in \Sigma_2^p$ with a language $L_2 \in \Pi_2^p$. We note that "natural" complete problems for this class are extremely rare.[2]

Theorem 3. GE^c *is* $\text{co} - \text{D}_2^p$–*complete*.

Proof. Omitted.   □

In total Theorems 2, 3 and Corollary 3 indicate that the four decision problems considered are unlikely to admit efficient algorithmic solutions when a concise representation of forms is allowed. In contrast,

Theorem 4. *The decision problems* WS^e, EQUIV^e, WE^e, *and* GE^e *are all in* P.

Proof. (*Outline*) All follow easily from the fact that $\text{WS}^e \in$ P: for EQUIV^e constructing an extensive form equivalent to $\overline{f} \cdot g + f \cdot \overline{g}$ can be done in time polynomial in the size

---

[2] i.e. other than those comprising pairs of the form $\langle x, y \rangle$ with x in some Σ_2^p-complete language L_1 and y in some Π_2^p-complete language L_2. The only exception we know of is the problem *Incomplete Game* of [10] from which our notation D_2^p for this class is taken.

of the extensive representations; after simplifying to ensure no path repeats any action, it suffices to verify that only the outcome 0 can be achieved. For WE^e we simply have to test that $\sigma_i := A$ admits a winning strategy for i. Similar arguments give $GE^e \in P$. □

In combination, Theorems 2, 3, and 4, might seem to offer a choice between efficient in length but computationally intractable concise forms and infeasible length though computationally malleable extensive forms. We can, however, identify a number of problems whose solution is hard even measured in terms of extensive representations. For example, we may interpret the problem of identifying a *minimal* size extensive form in terms of the following "high-level" algorithmic process given T_g: identify an action $\beta \in A$ and forms h_0, h_1 in $\mathcal{G}_{A \setminus \{\beta\}}$ for which $\beta(h_0, h_1) \equiv_{sf} g$ and for which $1 + S^{ext}([h_0]) + S^{ext}([h_1])$ is minimised. One key feature of such an approach is its requirement to find a suitable choice of β. Thus, for extensive forms we have the following decision problem:

Optimal Branching Action OBA

Instance: T_g extensive form description of $g \in \mathcal{G}_A$.
Question: Is there an action β and extensive forms T_{h_0}, T_{h_1} for which $\beta(h_0, h_1) \equiv_{sf} g$ and $1 + S^{ext}(T_{h_0}, h_0) + S^{ext}(T_{h_1}, h_1) < S^{ext}(T_g, g)$?

Informally, OBA asks of a given extensive form whether it is possible to construct a *smaller* equivalent form. An immediate consequence of [6] is that OBA is NP–hard.

6 Conclusions and Further Work

Our principal goal in this paper has been to examine the computational complexity of a number of natural decision problems arising in the context of the Boolean game formalism from [3,4]. Building from the correspondence between the underlying forms of such games and propositional functions we can characterise winning strategies and their structure for any game. Using the operational description developed in [4] allows a precise formulation for the concept of "concise form" to be defined in contrast to the usual idea of "extensive form". We have indicated both advantages and drawbacks with both approaches so that the apparent computational tractability of extensive forms is paid for in terms of potentially exponentially large (in the number of atomic actions) descriptions; on the other hand, while the concise forms may admit rather terser descriptions of a given game all four of the basic decision questions raised are unlikely to admit feasible algorithmic solutions.

We conclude by, briefly, summarising some potential developments of the ideas discussed above. We have already noted that our concept of "game equivalence" – $\equiv_g$ is defined independently of ideas involving the "forcing relations" of [2,8] and have observed in Lemma 1 that it describes a proper subset of games equivalent under $\equiv_H$. A natural open question is to determine the computational complexity of deciding if $\langle g, \sigma \rangle \equiv_H \langle h, \tau \rangle$: noting the correspondence presented in Lemma 1, it is certainly the case that this is within the class $P^{\Sigma_2^p[4]}$ of languages decidable by (deterministic) polynomial-time algorithms that may make up to 4 calls on a Σ_2^p oracle. We are unaware of natural complete problems for $P^{\Sigma_2^p[4]}$ and thus, it would be of some interest to determine whether deciding $\langle g, \sigma \rangle \equiv_H \langle h, \tau \rangle$ is $P^{\Sigma_2^p[4]}$–complete

One final issue concerns the algebraic relationship between forms and propositional functions. Our analysis in Section 3 could be viewed as relating winning strategies in g to terms occurring in a "standard" representation of $\lceil g \rceil$ over the complete logical basis $\{\wedge, \vee, \neg\}$. An alternative complete logical basis is given by $\{\wedge, \oplus, \top\}$ ($\top$ being the nullary function evaluating to true) within which a normal form theorem holds, i.e. the ringsum expansion of Zhegalkin [11], see, e.g. [1, p. 14]: it is unclear, but may be of some interest, to what extent terms within this descriptive form correspond to properties of winning strategies.

References

1. P. E. Dunne. The Complexity of Boolean Networks. Academic Press, London, 1988
2. V. Goranko. The Basic Algebra of Game Equivalences. In *ESSLLI Workshop on Logic and Games* (ed: M. Pauly and G. Sandhu), 2001
3. P. Harrenstein. Logic in Conflict – Logical Exploration in Strategic Equilibrium. Ph.D. dissertation, Dept. of Computer Science, Univ. of Utrecht, 2004 (submitted)
4. B. P. Harrenstein, W. van der Hoek, J. -J. Meyer, and C. Witteveen. Boolean Games. In *Proc. 8th Conf. on Theoretical Aspects of Rationality and Knowledge (TARK 2001)*, (ed: J. van Benthem), Morgan–Kaufmann, San Francisco, pages 287–298, 2001
5. L. Henkin. Some remarks on infinitely long formulas. In *Infinistic Methods*, pages 167–183. Pergamon Press, Oxford, 1961.
6. L. Hyafil and R. Rivest. Constructing Optimal Binary Decision Trees is NP–complete. *Inf. Proc. Letters*, 5, pp. 15–17, 1976
7. Logic and games. Special issue of *Journal of Logic, Language and Information*, 2002.
8. M. Pauly. Logic for Social Software. Ph.D. dissertation, Institute for Logic, Language and Information, Amsterdam, 2001
9. C. S. Peirce. *Reasoning and the Logic of Things: The Cambridge Conferences Lectures of 1898*. Harvard University Press, 1992.
10. M. Wooldridge and P. E. Dunne. On the Computational Complexity of Qualitative Coalitional Games. Technical Report, ULCS-04-007, Dept. of Computer Science, Univ. of Liverpool, 2004, (to appear: *Artificial Intelligence*)
11. I. I. Zhegalkin. The technique of calculation of statements in symbolic logic. *Matem. Sbornik*, 34, pp. 9–28, 1927 (in Russian)

Complexity in Value-Based Argument Systems

Paul E. Dunne and Trevor Bench-Capon

Dept. of Computer Science
University of Liverpool
Liverpool L69 7ZF, United Kingdom
{ped,tbc}@csc.liv.ac.uk

Abstract. We consider a number of decision problems formulated in *value-based argumentation frameworks* (VAFs), a development of Dung's argument systems in which arguments have associated abstract values which are considered relative to the orderings induced by the opinions of specific audiences. In the context of a single fixed audience, it is known that those decision questions which are typically computationally hard in the standard setting admit efficient solution methods in the value-based setting. In this paper we show that, in spite of this positive property, there still remain a number of natural questions that arise solely in value-based schemes for which there are unlikely to be efficient decision processes.

1   Introduction

Argument systems as a model of defeasible reasoning date from the seminal paper of Dung [11], and have subsequently proved useful both to theorists who can use them as an abstract framework for the study and comparison of non-monotonic logics, e.g. [5, 7,8,9], and for those who wish to explore more concrete contexts where defeasibility is central e.g., for the legal domain, [2], [18], and [15].

In many domains, especially those relating to practical reasoning, such as law, politics and ethics, however, it is not possible to demonstrate the acceptability of an argument absolutely. Which arguments are found persuasive depends on the opinions, values and, perhaps, even the prejudices of the audience to which they are addressed. The point is made by Perelman [17] thus:

> If men oppose each other concerning a decision to be taken, it is not because they commit some error of logic or calculation. They discuss *apropos* the applicable rule, the ends to be considered, the meaning to be given to values, the interpretation and characterisation of facts.

What this means is that because people may differ as to what they hold to be important or worth attempting to achieve, they may differ in their evaluations of the strengths of the arguments about the choices that should be made. For example: it is an argument in favour of raising income tax that it promotes equality, and for decreasing income tax that it promotes enterprise. Most people would acknowledge that both arguments are valid, but which they will choose to follow depends on the importance they ascribe to equality as against enterprise in the given situation. Thus which of the arguments is found persuasive by a given audience will depend on the ordering of these two values

J.J. Alferes and J. Leite (Eds.): JELIA 2004, LNAI 3229, pp. 360–371, 2004.

by that audience. So if I claim that income tax should be raised to promote equality, I can defend my claim against the attack that so doing would discourage enterprise not by attacking this counter argument but by declaring my preference for equality over enterprise. Whether this defence will be persuasive will depend on whether the audience shares my preference. A similar viewpoint has been proposed in philosophical studies of rational and persuasive argument, e.g from [19, p. xv]

> Assume universally valid and accepted standards of rationality. Assume perfectly rational agents operating with perfect information, and you will find that rational disagreement will still occur; because, for example, the rational agents are likely to have different and inconsistent values and interests, each of which may be rationally acceptable.

In order to reason about arguments dependent on values and to accommodate the notion of audiences with different values, Dung's original framework was extended in [3] and [4] to give what are termed there Value Based Argumentation Frameworks (VAFs). In those papers a number of properties of VAFs are demonstrated. In this paper we will consider some questions relating to the computational complexity of these frameworks.

Section 2 will provide the definitions of Argumentation Systems and Value Based Argumentation Frameworks, and of the decision problems we will address. Section 3 will present the proofs of our results, and section 4 will offer some discussion and concluding remarks.

2   Basic Definitions

The basic definition below of an Argument System is derived from that given in [11].

Definition 1. *An* argument system *is a pair* $\mathcal{H} = \langle \mathcal{X}, \mathcal{A} \rangle$, *in which* $\mathcal{X}$ *is a finite set of* arguments *and* $\mathcal{A} \subset \mathcal{X} \times \mathcal{X}$ *is the* attack relationship *for* $\mathcal{H}$. *A pair* $\langle x, y \rangle \in \mathcal{A}$ *is referred to as 'y is attacked by x' or 'x attacks y'. For R, S subsets of arguments in the system* $\mathcal{H}(\langle \mathcal{X}, \mathcal{A} \rangle)$, *we say that*

a. $s \in S$ *is attacked by R if there is some* $r \in R$ *such that* $\langle r, s \rangle \in \mathcal{A}$.
b. $x \in \mathcal{X}$ *is* acceptable with respect to S *if for every* $y \in \mathcal{X}$ *that attacks x there is some* $z \in S$ *that attacks y.*
c. *S is* conflict-free *if no argument in S is attacked by any other argument in S.*
d. *A conflict-free set S is* admissible *if every argument in S is acceptable with respect to S.*
e. *S is a* preferred extension *if it is a maximal (with respect to* $\subseteq$) *admissible set.*
f. *S is a* stable extension *if S is conflict free and every argument* $y \notin S$ *is attacked by S.*
g. $\mathcal{H}$ *is* coherent *if every preferred extension in* $\mathcal{H}$ *is also a stable extension.*

An argument x is credulously accepted *if there is some preferred extension containing it; x is* sceptically accepted *if it is a member of every preferred extension.*

Abstracting away concerns regarding the internal structure and representation of arguments affords a formalism which focuses on the relationship between individual arguments as a means of defining divers ideas of acceptance. In particular preferred extensions are of interest as these represent maximal coherent positions that can be defended against all attackers.

While this approach offers a powerful tool for the abstract analysis of defeasible reasoning, there are, however, several potential problems. While every argument system has *some* preferred extension, this may simply be the empty set of arguments and although the use of *stable* extensions avoids such difficulties these in turn have the drawback that there are systems which contain no stable extension. An additional concern is the computational complexity of a number of the associated decision problems that has been shown to range from NP–complete to Π_2^p–complete. A summary of these is given in Table 1 below. The classification of problems (3–5) follows from [10]; that of (6) and (7) has recently been demonstrated in [12]. Related problems arise with proof-theoretic mechanisms for establishing credulous acceptance, e.g. for the TPI-dispute mechanism proposed in [20], Dunne and Bench-Capon [13] show that this defines a weak propositional proof system under which proofs that arguments are not credulously accepted require exponentially many steps.

While the issues discussed above concern algorithmic and combinatorial properties of the standard argument system framework, there is also one interpretative issue of some importance. A typical argument system may contain many distinct preferred extensions and, in some cases, two different preferred extensions may define a partition of the argument set. Thus a single argument system can give rise to a number of disjoint internally consistent admissible argument sets. The abstract level at which Dung's formalism operates avoids any mechanism for distinguishing notions of the relative merit of such mutually incompatible outcomes. Thus the situation arises in which we appear to have several coherent positions that could be adopted, and no well motivated way of choosing between them.

Recognising the benefits of Dung's approach, a number of extensions have been mooted in order to ameliorate the various interpretative and computational difficulties outlined above. Among such are the *preference-based argumentation frameworks* (PAFs) of Amgoud and Cayrol [1] and, the formalism with which the present article is concerned, the *value-based argumentation frameworks* (VAFs) of Bench-Capon [3,4]. It is important to note that while there are some superficial similarities, these two mechanisms are, in

Table 1. Decision Problems in Argument Systems

	Problem	Decision Question	Complexity
1	ADM$(\mathcal{H}, S)$	Is S admissible?	P
2	STAB$(\mathcal{H}, S)$	Is S stable?	P
3	PREF-EXT$(\mathcal{H}, S)$	Is S preferred?	CO-NP-complete.
4	CA$(\mathcal{H}, x)$	Is x in a *preferred S*?	NP-complete
5	STAB-EXIST$(\mathcal{H})$	Has $\mathcal{H}$ a stable extension?	NP-complete
6	SA$(\mathcal{H}, x)$	Is x in *every* preferred S?	$\Pi_2^{(p)}$-complete
7	COHERENT$(\mathcal{H})$	Preferred≡stable?	$\Pi_2^{(p)}$-complete

fact, quite distinct. We shall defer a more detailed comparison until the concluding section, since this distinction can be rather more readily discerned and appreciated in the light of our subsequent technical results.

As we have indicated, [3,4] extend Dung's framework to provide a semantics for distinguishing and choosing between consistent but incompatible belief sets through the use of *argument values*. Thus arguments are seen as grounded on one of a finite number of abstract values and the interpretation of which of a set of arguments to "accept" is treated in terms of preference orderings of the underlying value set according to the views held by a particular *audience*. Thus while in the standard Argumentation system the choice between preferred extensions is arbitrary, in a VAF we are able to motivate such choices by reference to the values of the audience. The formal definition of such *value-based argumentation frameworks* is given below.

Definition 2. *A* value-based argumentation framework *(VAF), is defined by a triple* $\langle \mathcal{H}(\mathcal{X}, \mathcal{A}), \mathcal{V}, \eta \rangle$, *where* $\mathcal{H}(\mathcal{X}, \mathcal{A})$ *is an argument system,* $\mathcal{V} = \{v_1, v_2, \ldots, v_k\}$ *a set of* k *values, and* $\eta : \mathcal{X} \to \mathcal{V}$ *a mapping that associates a value* $\eta(x) \in \mathcal{V}$ *with each argument* $x \in \mathcal{X}$. *An audience,* α, *for a VAF* $\langle \mathcal{H}, \mathcal{V}, \eta \rangle$, *is a total ordering of the values* $\mathcal{V}$. *We say that* v_i *is preferred to* v_j *in the audience* α, *denoted* $v_i \succ_\alpha v_j$, *if* v_i *is ranked higher than* v_j *in the total ordering defined by* α.

Using VAFs, ideas analogous to those of admissible argument in standard argument systems are defined in the following way. Note that all these notions are now relative to some audience.

Definition 3. *Let* $\langle \mathcal{H}(\mathcal{X}, \mathcal{A}), \mathcal{V}, \eta \rangle$ *be a VAF and* α *an audience.*

a. *For arguments x, y in* $\mathcal{X}$, *x is a* successful attack *on y (or x defeats y) with respect to the audience* α *if:* $\langle x, y \rangle \in \mathcal{A}$ *and it is not the case that* $\eta(y) \succ_\alpha \eta(x)$.
b. *An argument x is* acceptable *to the subset S with respect to an audience* α *if: for every* $y \in \mathcal{X}$ *that successfully attacks x with respect to* α, *there is some* $z \in S$ *that successfully atttacks y with respect to* α.
c. *A subset R of* $\mathcal{X}$ *is* conflict-free *with respect to the audience* α *if: for each* $\langle x, y \rangle \in R \times R$, *either* $\langle x, y \rangle \notin \mathcal{A}$ *or* $\eta(y) \succ_\alpha \eta(x)$.
d. *A subset R of* $\mathcal{X}$ *is* admissible *with respect to the audience* α *if: R is conflict free with respect to* α *and every* $x \in R$ *is acceptable to R with respect to* α.
e. *A subset R is a* preferred extension *for the audience* α *if it is a maximal admissible set with respect to* α.
f. *A subset R is a* stable extension *for the audience* α *if R is admissible with respect to* α *and for all* $y \notin R$ *there is some* $x \in R$ *which successfully attacks y.*

A standard consistency requirement which we assume of the VAFs considered is that every directed cycle of arguments in these contains *at least two* differently valued arguments. We do not believe that this condition is overly restricting, since the existence of such cycles in VAFs can be seen as indicating a flaw in the formulation of the framework. While in standard argumentation frameworks cycles arise naturally, especially if we are dealing with uncertain or incomplete information, in VAFs odd length cycles in a single value represent paradoxes and even length cycles in a single value can be reduced to a self-defeating argument. Given the absence of cycles in a single value the following important property of VAFs and audiences was demonstrated in [3].

Fact 1. *For every audience,* α*,* $\langle \mathcal{H}(\langle \mathcal{X}, \mathcal{A} \rangle), \mathcal{V}, \eta \rangle$ *has a unique non-empty preferred extension,* $P(\mathcal{H}, \eta, \alpha)$ *which can be constructed by an algorithm that takes* $O(|\mathcal{X}| + |\mathcal{A}|)$ *steps. Furthermore* $P(\mathcal{H}, \eta, \alpha)$ *is a stable extension with respect to* α*.*

From Fact 1 it follows that, when attention is focused on one specific audience, the decision questions analogous to those described in Table 1 become much easier. There are, however, a number of new issues that arise in the value-based framework from the fact that that the relative ordering of different values promoted by distinct audiences results in arguments falling into one of three categories.

C1. Arguments, x, that are in the preferred extension $P(\mathcal{H}, \eta, \alpha)$ for some audiences but not all. Such arguments being called *subjectively acceptable*.
C2. Arguments, x, that are in the preferred extension $P(\mathcal{H}, \eta, \alpha)$ for *every* audience. Such arguments being called *objectively acceptable*.
C3. Arguments, x, that do not belong to the preferred extension $P(\mathcal{H}, \eta, \alpha)$ for *any* choice of audience. Such arguments being called *indefensible*.

To show the advantages of taking values into account, consider the following ethical debate, discussed in, e.g. [6]. Hal, a diabetic, loses his insulin and can save his life only by breaking into the house of another diabetic, Carla, and using her insulin. We may consider the following arguments:

A. Hal should not take Carla's insulin as he may be endangering her life.
B. Hal can take the insulin as otherwise he will die, whereas there is only a potential threat to Carla.
C. Hal must not take Carla's insulin because it is Carla's property.
D. Hal must replace Carla's insulin once the emergency is over.

Now B attacks A, since the permission licensed by the actual threat overrides the obligation arising from the potential threat. A does not attack B, since the immediate threat represents an exception to the general rule which A instantiates. C attacks B, construing property rights as strict obligations whereas possible endangerment is a defeasible obligation. D attacks C. since it provides a way for the insulin to be taken whilst property rights are respected. Further, Christie argues in [6] that B attacks D, since even if Hal were unable to replace the insulin he would still be correct to act so as to save his life, and therefore he can be under no strict obligation to replace the insulin. The resulting argumentation system can be depicted as a directed graph as shown in Figure 1.

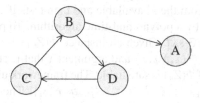

Fig. 1. VAF Example Argument System

Considered as a standard Argumentation System there is no non-empty preferred extension, and it seems we have no coherent position, which is why it is seen and discussed as an ethical dilemma. If, however, we consider it as a VAF, we can see that arguments A and B rely on the importance of preserving life, whereas C and D depend on respect for property. We will now have two preferred extensions, depending on whether life or property is preferred. If we prefer life, we will accept $\{B, C\}$: whilst we respect Carla's property rights, we regard Hal's need as paramount. In contrast if we prefer property to life, the preferred extension is $\{B, D\}$: the property claim can be discharged if restitution is made. Thus B is objectively acceptable, C and D are subjectively acceptable and A is indefensible. This small example shows how we can use explicit value preferences to cut through what would otherwise be an irresolvable dilemma.

Our initial concern, in this article, is to consider the following questions specific to the value-based setting

Definition 4. *The decision problem* Subjective Acceptance *(SBA) takes as an instance a VAF $\langle \mathcal{H}, \mathcal{V}, \eta \rangle$ and an argument x in this. The instance is accepted if there is at least one audience, α, for which $x \in P(\mathcal{H}, \eta, \alpha)$. The decision problem* Objective Acceptance *(OBA) takes as an instance a VAF $\langle \mathcal{H}, \mathcal{V}, \eta \rangle$ and an argument x in this. The instance is accepted if $x \in P(\mathcal{H}, \eta, \alpha)$ for every audience α.*

The status of these problems was left unresolved in the original study presented in [3].

The remainder of this paper is structured as follows. In the next section we consider the decision problems SBA and OBA defined above and classify their complexity as, respectively, NP–complete and CO-NP–complete. We then consider decision problems motivated by approaches to determining subjective acceptance by attempting to identify which pair-wise orderings are "critical" in the sense that a given ordering will admit an audience for which an argument is subjectively accepted, whereas reversing this order will yield a context within which the argument of interest is never accepted. We show that the decision problem formulated with respect to this question is D^p-complete and hence within a class that is "harder" than either NP or CO-NP. Discussion and conclusions are the subject of the final section.

3   Complexity of Decision Problems for VAFs

Theorem 1. SBA *is NP–complete.*

Proof. For membership in NP simply use the algorithm which non-deterministically chooses an audience α from the $k!$ available and then tests if $x \in P(\mathcal{H}, \eta, \alpha)$, the latter test being accomplished by a polynomial-time algorithm. To prove that SBA is NP–hard we use a reduction from 3-SAT. Given an instance $\Phi(Z_n) = \wedge_{i=1}^{m}(y_{i,1} \vee y_{i,2} \vee y_{i,3})$ of this we construct a VAF $\langle \mathcal{H}_\Phi, \mathcal{V}_\Phi, \eta \rangle$ and argument x that is subjectively acceptable in $\langle \mathcal{H}_\Phi, \mathcal{V}_\Phi, \eta \rangle$ if and only if $\Phi(Z_n)$ is satisfiable. The framework uses $4n + m + 1$ arguments which we denote $\{\Phi, C_1, \ldots, C_m\} \cup \cup_{i=1}^{n}\{p_i, q_i, r_i, s_i\}$. The relationship $\mathcal{A}$ contains attacks $\langle C_j, \Phi \rangle$ for each $1 \leq j \leq m$ and attacks $\{\langle p_i, q_i \rangle, \langle q_i, r_i \rangle, \langle r_i, s_i \rangle, \langle s_i, p_i \rangle\}$ for each $1 \leq i \leq n$. The remaining attacks in $\mathcal{A}$ are as follows. For each clause $y_{i,1} \vee y_{i,2} \vee y_{i,3}$

of $\Phi(Z_n)$ if $y_{i,j}$ is the literal z_k, the attack $\langle p_k, C_i \rangle$ is included in $\mathcal{A}$; if $y_{i,j}$ is the literal $\neg z_k$, then the attack $\langle q_k, C_i \rangle$ is added. The final part of the construction is to describe the value set $\mathcal{V}_\Phi$ and association of arguments with values prescribed by η. The set $\mathcal{V}_\Phi$ contains $2n + 1$ values $\{con\} \cup \cup_{i=1}^n \{pos_i, neg_i\}$ and the mapping η assigns the value con to Φ and each argument in $\{C_1, \ldots, C_m\}$. Finally the arguments $\{p_i, r_i\}$ are mapped to the value pos_i and the arguments $\{q_i, s_i\}$ to the value neg_i. To complete the instance we set x to be Φ. We note that the constructed system satisfies the requirement that all cycles contain at least two distinct values.

We claim that Φ is subjectively accepted in the VAF $\langle \mathcal{H}_\Phi, \mathcal{V}_\Phi, \eta \rangle$ if and only if $\Phi(Z_n)$ is satisfiable. Suppose first that $\Phi(Z_n)$ is satisfied by an instantiation $\langle a_1, a_2, \ldots, a_n \rangle$ of Z_n. Consider any audience α for which $pos_i \succ_\alpha neg_i$ if $a_i = \top$, $neg_i \succ_\alpha pos_i$ if $a_i = \bot$, and $v \succ_\alpha con$ for all $v \in \mathcal{V}_\Phi/\{con\}$. Since $\Phi(Z_n)$ is satisfied, for each C_i there is some literal $y_{i,j}$ that is assigned $\top$ in the instantiation $\langle a_1, \ldots, a_n \rangle$. Consider the arguments $\{p_k, q_k, r_k, s_k\}$ for which $y_{i,j} \in \{z_k, \neg z_k\}$. If $y_{i,j} = z_k$ then p_k is acceptable in $\{p_k, r_k\}$ and, in addition, p_k successfully attacks C_i; if $y_{i,j} = \neg z_k$ then q_k is acceptable in $\{q_k, s_k\}$ and, again, successfully attacks C_i. Thus every argument C_i is successfully attacked by an argument p_k or q_k and thence Φ together with these form an admissible set. Thus we have an audience with respect to which Φ is subjectively accepted.

On the other hand, suppose α is an audience for which $\Phi \in P(\mathcal{H}_\Phi, \eta, \alpha)$. It cannot be the case that $C_i \in P(\mathcal{H}_\Phi, \eta, \alpha)$ since $\eta(\Phi) = \eta(C_i) = con$ and so the presence of any C_i would suffice to eliminate Φ. The audience α must therefore be such that every C_i is successfully attacked by one of its three possible attackers. Let $\langle t_1, t_2, \ldots, t_m \rangle$ be the choices which give successful attacks on $\langle C_1, \ldots, C_m \rangle$. First observe that we cannot have $t_i = p_k$ and $t_j = q_k$ for any $1 \leq k \leq n$ and distinct C_i and C_j: under α either $\eta(p_k) \succ_\alpha \eta(q_k)$ and so q_k would not succeed in its attack or $\eta(q_k) \succ_\alpha \eta(p_k)$ with the attack by p_k failing. It follows that the instantiation of Z_n by $z_i = \top$ if $p_i \in \langle t_1, t_2, \ldots, t_m \rangle$, $z_i = \bot$ if $q_i \in \langle t_1, t_2, \ldots, t_m \rangle$ is well-defined and yields a true literal in every clause, i.e. results in a satisfying instantiation of $\Phi(Z_n)$. This suffices to complete the proof.

The structure introduced in the proof of Theorem 1 provides the basis for developing a number of our subsequent results. Thus,

Theorem 2. OBA *is* CO-NP–*complete.*

Proof. Membership is CO-NP follows by the algorithm which tests that all $k!$ audiences accept x. For CO-NP–hardness, we employ a reduction from 3-UNSAT, the problem of deciding if a 3-CNF formula $\Phi(Z_n) = \wedge_{i=1}^m (y_{i,1} \vee y_{i,2} \vee y_{i,3})$ is unsatisfiable. The reduction constructs an identical VAF to that of the previous theorem, but with one additional argument, $\{test\}$, having $\eta(test) = con$ and whose sole attacker is the argument Φ. We claim that $test$ is objectively acceptable if and only if Φ is unsatisfiable. From the proof of Theorem 1, $test$ will fail to be acceptable with respect to any audience α for which Φ is admissible. Such an audience exists if and only if $\Phi(Z_n)$ is satisfiable. We therefore deduce that $test$ is objectively accepted if and only if $\Phi(Z_n)$ is unsatisfiable.

In applying the value-based framework to promote a particular argument an important consideration is the relationship between the value of the argument defended to that of the other values employed in the system. Thus the existence of an audience that provides subjective acceptance may depend on the specific ordering of a subset of the values. Thus, an audience granting subjective acceptance of some x exists if $v_i \succ v_j$, but should an audience prescribe $v_j \succ v_i$ then x cannot be defended. For example in law we find that values are ranked differently in different jurisdictions. Can we determine which difference affect the status of a given argument? Such scenarios motivate the concept of a *critical pair*.

Definition 5. *Let* $\langle \mathcal{H}(\mathcal{X}, \mathcal{A}), \mathcal{V}, \eta \rangle$ *be a VAF, and* $\langle v, v' \rangle$ *be an ordered pair of distinct values from* $\mathcal{V}$. *The pair* $\langle v, v' \rangle$ *is* critical *with respect to an argument* $x \in \mathcal{X}$ *if there is an audience* α *for which* $v \succ_\alpha v'$ *and* $x \in P(\mathcal{H}, \eta, \alpha)$, *but for every audience* β *for which* $v' \succ_\beta v$ *it holds that* $x \notin P(\mathcal{H}, \eta, \beta)$.

We can, of course, generalise the notion of critical pair from Definition 5 to encompass relationships involving three or more values.

Definition 6. *Let* $\langle \mathcal{H}(\mathcal{X}, \mathcal{A}), \mathcal{V}, \eta \rangle$ *be a VAF,* $\mathcal{W} \subseteq \mathcal{V}$ *and* $\mathcal{C} = \{c_1, c_2, \ldots, c_r\}$ *a finite set of* constraints *on* $\mathcal{W}$ *each of which is of the form* $w \succ w'$ *for* $\{w, w'\} \subset \mathcal{W}$. *The structure* $\langle \mathcal{W}, \mathcal{C} \rangle$ *is a* critical set *for an argument* $x \in \mathcal{X}$ *if there is an audience* α *under which* $w \succ_\alpha w'$ *for each* $c_i \in \mathcal{C}$ *and with* $x \in P(\mathcal{H}, \eta, \alpha)$, *but for any audience* β *in which at least one constraint of* $\mathcal{C}$ *is broken it holds that* $x \notin P(\mathcal{H}, \eta, \beta)$.

From these we define the following decision problems.

Definition 7. *The decision problem* Critical Pair *(CP) takes as an instance a triple of the form* $\langle \langle \mathcal{H}, \mathcal{V}, \eta \rangle, \langle v, v' \rangle, x \rangle$ *comprising a VAF, ordered pair of values* $\langle v, v' \rangle$ *within this, and argument* x. *An instance is accepted if* $\langle v, v' \rangle$ *is critical with respect to* x. *The decision problem* Critical Set *(CS) takes as its instance a quadruple* $\langle \langle \mathcal{H}, \mathcal{V}, \eta \rangle, \mathcal{W}, \mathcal{C}, x \rangle$ *of VAF, subset of values, set of constraints, and argument. The instance is accepted if* $\langle \mathcal{W}, \mathcal{C} \rangle$ *defines a critical set for* x.

Noting that the problem CP is a restricted case of CS, we can establish a lower bound on the complexity of the latter by considering the complexity of CP only. Under the standard complexity-theoretic assumptions this problem turns out to be "more difficult" than Subjective Acceptance and Objective Acceptance. Formally we show that it is D^p–complete, the class D^p comprising those languages L formed by the intersection of some NP language L_1 with some CO-NP language L_2, i.e. $L \in \mathrm{D}^p$ if $L = L_1 \cap L_2$, $L_1 \in$ NP, and $L_2 \in$ CO-NP. The class D^p was introduced in [16] where the problem SAT-UNSAT – instances of pairs of formulae $\langle \Phi_1, \Phi_2 \rangle$ for which Φ_1 is satisfiable and Φ_2 unsatisfiable – was shown to be D^p–complete.

Theorem 3. CP *is* D^p*–complete.*

Proof. For membership in D^p, define the language L_1 to be

$$\{\langle \langle \mathcal{H}, \mathcal{V}, \eta \rangle, \langle v, v' \rangle, x \rangle \ : \ \exists \alpha \text{ with } v \succ_\alpha v' \text{ and } x \in P(\mathcal{H}, \eta, \alpha)\}$$

Similarly, define L_2 as

$$\{\langle \langle \mathcal{H}, \mathcal{V}, \eta \rangle, \langle v, v' \rangle, x \rangle \ : \ \forall \alpha \text{ with } v' \succ_\alpha v, x \notin P(\mathcal{H}, \eta, \alpha)\}$$

Then $\langle\langle\mathcal{H}, \mathcal{V}, \eta\rangle, \langle v, v'\rangle, x\rangle$ is accepted as an instance of CP if and only if it belongs to the set $L_1 \cap L_2$. Since it is immediate that $L_1 \in$ NP and $L_2 \in$ CO-NP this suffices to give CP $\in$ D^p. To prove that CP is D^p–hard, we first show that the problem *Critical Variable* (CV) is D^p–hard: instances of this comprise a CNF formula $\Phi(Z_n)$ and a variable $z \in Z_n$ with instances accepted if there is a satisfying instantiation in which $z = \top$ but no satisfying instantiation in which $z = \bot$. To see that CV is D^p–hard we use a reduction from the D^p–complete problem SAT-UNSAT. Given an instance $\langle\Phi_1(Z_n), \Phi_2(Z_n)\rangle$ of this, the instance $\langle\Psi, z\rangle$ of CV is simply $\langle(\neg z \vee \Phi_1) \wedge (z \vee \Phi_2), z\rangle$ where z is a new variable. We note that for Φ in CNF, $z \vee \Phi$ translates to the CNF formula in which every clause C of Φ is replaced by the clause $z \vee C$. It is easy to see that $\langle(\neg z \vee \Phi_1) \wedge (z \vee \Phi_2), z\rangle$ is a positive instance of CV if and only if $\langle\Phi_1(Z_n), \Phi_2(Z_n)\rangle$ is a positive instance of SAT-UNSAT: if Φ_1 is satisfiable then $(\neg z \vee \Phi_1) \wedge (z \vee \Phi_2)$ has a satisfying instantiation with $z = \top$ since it reduces to Φ_1; if Φ_2 is unsatisfiable then there is no satisfying instantiation with $z = \bot$ since the formula now reduces to Φ_2, hence if $\langle\Phi_1, \Phi_2\rangle$ accepted as an instance of SAT-UNSAT then $\langle(\neg z \vee \Phi_1) \wedge (z \vee \Phi_2), z\rangle$ is accepted as an instance of CV. Similarly, if $\langle(\neg z \vee \Phi_1) \wedge (z \vee \Phi_2), z\rangle$ is a positive instance of CV then $(\neg z \vee \Phi_1) \wedge (z \vee \Phi_2)$ is satisfiable when $z = \top$, i.e. Φ_1 is satisfiable, and $(\neg z \vee \Phi_1) \wedge (z \vee \Phi_2)$ is unsatisfiable when $z = \bot$, i.e. Φ_2 is unsatisfiable.

The proof that CP is D^p–hard now follows easily, using the reduction of Theorem 1: given an instance $\langle\Phi(Z_n), z\rangle$ of CV form the VAF $\langle\mathcal{H}_\Phi, \mathcal{V}_\Phi, \eta\rangle$ described in the proof of Theorem 1 (where we note that this trivially extends to arbitrary CNF formulae). Set the value pair in the instance of CP to be $\langle pos_z, neg_z\rangle$ and the argument x to be Φ. Consider the resulting instance $\langle\langle\mathcal{H}_\Phi, \mathcal{V}_\Phi, \eta\rangle, \langle pos_z, neg_z\rangle, \Phi\rangle$. If it is a positive instance of CP then there is an audience α within which $\Phi \in P(\mathcal{H}_\Phi, \eta, \alpha)$ and $pos_z \succ_\alpha neg_z$: it has already been seen that this indicates $\Phi(Z_n)$ has a satisfying instantiation with $z = \top$. Similarly, if it is a positive instance of CP, then $\Phi \notin P(\mathcal{H}_\Phi, \eta, \alpha)$ for any audience within which $neg_z \succ_\alpha pos_z$ so that, from our earlier analysis, $\Phi(Z_n)$ has no satisfying instantiation with $z = \bot$. On the other hand should $\langle\Phi(Z_n), z\rangle$ be a positive instance of CV then the argument of Theorem 1 yields an audience α with $pos_z \succ_\alpha neg_z$ for which $\Phi \in P(\mathcal{H}_\Phi, \eta, \alpha)$ from a satisfying instantiation of $\Phi(Z_n)$ with $z = \top$ while the unsatisfiability of $\Phi(Z_n)$ when $z = \bot$ indicates that no audience α having $neg_z \succ_\alpha pos_z$ will result in $\Phi \in P(\mathcal{H}_\Phi, \eta, \alpha)$. We deduce that $\langle\Phi(Z_n), z\rangle$ is a positive instance of CV if and only if $\langle\langle\mathcal{H}_\Phi, \mathcal{V}_\Phi, \eta\rangle, \langle pos_z, neg_z\rangle, \Phi\rangle$ is a positive instance of CP, thereby establishing that CP is D^p–complete.

4   Discussion

Preferences and Values

We referred earlier to the preference-based formalism (PAFs) of Amgoud and Cayrol [1] as another approach to developing Dung's abstract framework in order to enrich the idea of one argument "defeating" another. Formally, [1] defines a PAF as a pair $\langle\mathcal{H}(\mathcal{X}, \mathcal{A}), Pref\rangle$ wherein $\mathcal{H}(\mathcal{X}, \mathcal{A})$ is a standard argument system and $Pref$ a binary preorder (i.e. reflexive and transitive) relation on the argument set $\mathcal{X}$. The property that "x *successfully attacks* y"[1], then holds if $\langle x, y\rangle \in \mathcal{A}$ *and* $\neg(\langle y, x\rangle \in Pref)$, that is: a (po-

---

[1] [1] employs the term "defeats" rather than "attacks"

tential) attack exists ($\langle x, y \rangle \in \mathcal{A}$) and it is not the case that the *argument y* is preferred to the *argument x*, i.e. $\neg(\langle y, x \rangle \in Pref)$. Compare this with the VAF notion of "successful attack": $\langle x, y \rangle \in \mathcal{A}$ and $\neg(\eta(y) \succ_\alpha \eta(x))$, i.e. a (potential) attack exists (as before) and *with respect to the audience α* it is not the case that *the value promoted by y* is preferred to the *value promoted by x*. Now, despite the superficial "syntactic" similarity that is present, these two approaches have significant differences. Certainly it is the case that one could describe a particular VAF instantiation by a PAF: the consequent *Pref* relationship, however, would relate only to a fixed audience α. Similarly one could model a given PAF by a VAF simply by assuming that the number of distinct values is $|\mathcal{X}|$ and considering an audience defined in a manner consistent with the preference relationship, i.e. so that $\eta(x) \succ_\alpha \eta(y)$ if $\langle x, y \rangle \in Pref$.

Of course, the fact that one may mutually relate the formal models of both systems, is very far from providing a credible case for the redundancy of either. If we consider the basic schemata of standard argument systems, PAFs and VAFs, in very informal terms one might view Dung's systems as VAFs in which a single value is present and PAFs as one in which $|\mathcal{X}|$ values are related (within *Pref*) to the views of a single audience. It has been observed in [3,4] that typically the number of values is "small" by comparison with the number of arguments and thus the interpretation of PAFs within a value context as we have outlined does not reflect this. We also observe that the problems of subjective and objective acceptance in VAFs, arising as they do from questions concerning properties of *audiences* with respect to a set of values, do not have "sensible" counterparts in the PAF context. For example, were one to consider "preference-based subjective acceptance" in PAFs as "does there exists a preference relation on $\mathcal{X}$ under which a given argument x is accepted?", then it is bordering on the facile to observe that this question is of minimal interest: every instance returns the answer true by virtue of any preference relation under which x is a maximal element. We have seen that this is far from being the case as regards "value-based subjective acceptance", cf. Theorem 1. This is because, in VAFS, the strengths of arguments are not independent of one another. Thus raising the priority of one argument will raise the priority of all other arguments associated with the same value. In particular, if an argument is attacked by an argument associated with the same value, that attack will succeed, if the attacker, is not itself defeated, whatever the relative rank of the associated value.

In total these two formalisms although deriving from similar motivating factors – extending the concept of "acceptability" to take into account subjective relationships – take quite distinct approaches: PAFs by "embedding" a *single* preferrence relation within an argument framework; VAFs by an abstract association of values with arguments with the ordering of these being a feature "external" to the framework itself.

Summary and Further Work

The above results show that the identification of an argument as subjectively or objectively acceptable is just as hard as the corresponding problems of credulous and sceptical acceptance in standard *coherent* Argumentation Systems, cf. [12, p. 202]. Moreover Theorem 3 demonstrates that the effort required to identify the points of disagreement on which the acceptance or rejection of an argument turns is likely to be not well spent.

This does not, however, vitiate the intent underlying the use of VAFs. The situations in which VAFs are intended to be deployed are specific rather than entirely general: a particular legal case, a particular political decision. In such concrete situations, even where the values are many the audiences are few, and thus the relevant status of an argument can be determined by reference to the particular audiences engaged in the debate. Where the ordering of preferences of the audiences involved is not given in advance - as in the dialogue situations envisaged in [3] - a major thrust of the dialogue is to clarify the order of preferences of the participants. Since the motivation of VAFs is to resolve disagreements among particular parties with different value preferences, we can, for the purpose of any given dispute, rely on there being only a small set of audiences that need to be considered.

It could be claimed, with some justification, that the emphases in developing practical exploitation of the VAF formalism should be directed towards such studies. Thus one can consider algorithmic approaches by which a defender of a particular argument can determine in the light of information discovered concerning individual preferences whether there is a possible defence under which the argument in question is acceptable to all of the participating audiences. In principle such methods ought not to require an exhaustive enumeration of *all* possible value orderings since almost all of these will be irrelevant. An important related issue concerns *processes* for uncovering value preferences. Given that the question of whether a particular argument is accepted by a given audience can be decided by efficient methods, it may be possible to determine the exact value preferences of a participant from the answers given to questions concerning whether particular arguments are accepted or not, e.g. if x and y are different arguments with $\eta(x) \neq \eta(y)$ and $\langle x, y \rangle \in \mathcal{A}$, then should some participant answer that *both* x and y are acceptable, it must be the case that the ordering $\eta(y) \succ \eta(x)$ pertains. This prompts the algorithmic question, given a VAF and an *unknown* value ordering, of identifying a suitable set of queries regarding acceptance the answers to which allow the specific audience to be fully determined. It is interesting to note that the preliminary study of these issues reported in [14] indicates that the problem of constructing an audience with respect which a specific set of arguments is a *preferred extension* admits an efficient algoirthmic solution.

As one final issue there is the development of dialogue and reasoning processes specifically intended for VAFs. Although, [3] presents a reasoning semantics for subjective acceptance with respect to a particular audience, akin to the formal basis for TPI-disputes in standard frameworks described in [13], there are several directions in which this may need further refinement. Thus, sound and complete dialogue mechanisms for deciding subjective and objective acceptance in general would be of interest. In view of Theorem 2 it is likely to be the case that "reasonable" sound and complete schemes determining objective acceptance engender exponential length reasoning processes in some cases, cf. [13], however, when the notion of "objective acceptance" is qualified to refer to relevant audiences only (so that the context of Theorem 2 does not apply) it may be the case that such reasoning processes are feasible within appropriate VAF settings.

References

1. L. Amgoud and C. Cayrol. 'A reasoning model based on the production of acceptable arguments', *Annals of Math. and Artificial Intelligence*, **34**, 197–215, (2002)
2. T. J. M. Bench-Capon. 'Representation of Case Law as an Argumentation Framework' in *Legal Knowledge and Information Systems*, eds., T. Bench-Capon, A. Daskalopoulu and R. Winkels, IOS Press: Amsterdam. 103-112 (2002)
3. T. J. M. Bench-Capon. 'Agreeing to differ: modelling persuasive dialogue between parties with different values', *Informal Logic*, **22** 3 (2003).
4. T. J. M. Bench-Capon. 'Persuasion in Practical Argument Using Value Based Argumentation Frameworks', *Journal of Logic and Computation*, **13** 3 429-48 (2003).
5. A. Bondarenko, P. M. Dung, R. A. Kowalski, and F. Toni. 'An abstract, argumentation-theoretic approach to default reasoning', *Artificial Intelligence*, **93**(1–2), 63–101, (1997).
6. G. Christie. *The Notion of an Ideal Audience in Legal Argument*, Kluwer Academic, Dordrecht, (2000).
7. Y. Dimopoulos, B. Nebel, and F. Toni. 'Preferred arguments are harder to compute than stable extensions', in *Proceedings of the 16th International Joint Conference on Artificial Intelligence (IJCAI-99-Vol1)*, ed., T. Dean, pp. 36–43, San Francisco, (1999). Morgan Kaufmann Publishers.
8. Y. Dimopoulos, B. Nebel, and F. Toni. 'Finding admissible and preferred arguments can be very hard', in *KR2000: Principles of Knowledge Representation and Reasoning*, eds., A. G. Cohn, F. Giunchiglia, and B. Selman, pp. 53–61, San Francisco, (2000). Morgan Kaufmann.
9. Y. Dimopoulos, B. Nebel, and F. Toni. 'On the compuational complexity of assumption-based argumentation by default reasoning', *Artificial Intelligence*, **141**, 57–78, (2002).
10. Y. Dimopoulos and A. Torres. 'Graph theoretical structures in logic programs and default theories', *Theoretical Computer Science*, **170**, 209–244, (1996).
11. P. M. Dung. 'On the acceptability of arguments and its fundamental role in nonmonotonic reasoning, logic programming, and N-person games', *Artificial Intelligence*, **77**, 321–357, (1995).
12. P.E. Dunne and T.J.M. Bench-Capon. 'Coherence in finite argument systems', *Artificial Intelligence*, **141**, 187–203, (2002).
13. P.E. Dunne and T.J.M. Bench-Capon. 'Two party immediate response disputes: properties and efficiency', *Artificial Intelligence*, **149**, 221–250, (2003).
14. P.E. Dunne and T.J.M. Bench-Capon. 'Identifying Audience Preferences in Legal and Social Domains', Technical Report, ULCS-04-010, Dept. of Computer Science, Univ. of Liverpool, 2004 (to appear, Proc. DEXA'04, Zaragoza, August 2004)
15. H. Jakobovits and D. Vermeir. 'Dialectic semantics for argumentation frameworks', in *Proceedings of the Seventh International Conference on Artificial Intelligence and Law (ICAIL-99)*, ACM SIGART, pp. 53–62, N.Y., (June 1999). ACM Press.
16. C. H. Papadimitriou and M. Yannakakis. 'The complexity of facets (and some facets of complexity)', in *Proceedings of the Fourteenth ACM Symposium on the Theory of Computing (STOC-82)*, pp. 255–260, San Francisco, CA, (1982).
17. C. Perelman. *Justice, Law and Argument*, Reidel: Dordrecht, 1980.
18. H. Prakken. *Logical Tools for Modelling Legal Argument*, Kluwer Academic Publishers, 1997.
19. J.R. Searle. *Rationality in Action*. MIT Press, Cambridge Mass., 2001
20. G. Vreeswijk and H. Prakken. 'Credulous and sceptical argument games for preferred semantics.', in *Proceedings of JELIA'2000, The 7th European Workshop on Logic for Artificial Intelligence.*, pp. 224–238, Berlin, (2000). Springer LNAI 1919, Springer Verlag.

A Polynomial Translation from the Two-Variable Guarded Fragment with Number Restrictions to the Guarded Fragment

Yevgeny Kazakov

MPI für Informatik, D-66123 Saarbrücken, Germany
ykazakov@mpi-sb.mpg.de

Abstract. We consider a two-variable guarded fragment with number restrictions for binary relations and give a satisfiability preserving transformation of formulas in this fragment to the three-variable guarded fragment. The translation can be computed in polynomial time and produces a formula that is linear in the size of the initial formula even for the binary coding of number restrictions. This allows one to reduce reasoning problems for many description logics to the satisfiability problem for the guarded fragment.

1 Introduction and Motivation

The guarded fragment $\mathcal{GF}$ has been introduced by Andréka, van Benthem & Németi (1998) as a first-order counterpart of modal and description logics. Its basic principle is to restrict the usage of quantifiers to the following bounded forms: $\forall \overline{x}.(G \rightarrow F)$ or $\exists \overline{x}.(G \wedge F)$, where G is an atom-*"guard"* that contains all free variables of F. The guarded fragment inherits many nice computational properties from modal logics, the most important of them are the (generalized) tree-model property and the decidability.

Although the guarded fragment covers a considerable part of logical formalisms, some decidable extensions of modal logics, in particular by functionality and transitivity, remain outside of the guarded fragment. Grädel (1999*b*) has shown that already the three-variable guarded fragment $\mathcal{GF}^3$ with one functional relation becomes undecidable. In this paper we study an extension of the two-variable guarded fragment $\mathcal{GF}^2$ by number restrictions, which we denote by $\mathcal{GF}^2\mathcal{N}$. Number restrictions generalize functionality restrictions. They are often used for representing configuration constraints, like, for example:

$$\texttt{Client}(x) \equiv \texttt{Computer}(x) \wedge \exists^{\geq 1} y.\texttt{Connection}(x, y),$$
$$\texttt{Server}(y) \equiv \texttt{Computer}(y) \wedge \exists^{<100} x.\texttt{Connection}(x, y).$$

$\mathcal{GF}^2\mathcal{N}$ relates to many known description logics, the most expressive of which is $\mathcal{ALCQIb}$. Cardinality and qualifying number restrictions are hard to handle, especially for big numbers, because not many efficient optimization techniques are known for them (the notable exceptions are algebraic methods developed by Haarslev, Timmann & Möller 2001, Haarslev & Möller 2001). This contrasts

J.J. Alferes and J. Leite (Eds.): JELIA 2004, LNAI 3229, pp. 372–384, 2004.

to the fact that $\mathcal{ALCQI}$ and even $\mathcal{ALCQIb}$ has the same complexity as $\mathcal{ALC}$, namely EXPTIME (Tobies 2001). In this paper we propose a translation which allows one to reason about number restrictions through the guarded fragment.

The contribution of this paper can be summarized as follows. First, we show that reasoning in $\mathcal{ALCQIb}$ knowledge bases can be polynomially reduced to satisfiability of $\mathcal{GF}^2\mathcal{N}$-formulas. Second, we give a satisfiability preserving translation from $\mathcal{GF}^2\mathcal{N}$ to $\mathcal{GF}^3$. The translation is computable in polynomial time and produces a guarded formula of linear size, even if number restrictions are coded in binary. This result has both theoretical and practical implications. From the theoretical side, we obtain a neat complexity result for satisfiability of $\mathcal{GF}^2\mathcal{N}$-formulas. Complexity results for $\mathcal{GF}^3$, imply that satisfiability of $F \in \mathcal{GF}^2\mathcal{N}$ can be decided in time $2^{O(|F|)}$. On the practical side, our translation provides a bridge between the fragment $\mathcal{GF}^2\mathcal{N}$ and the formalism for which optimization techniques are relatively well-studied. This makes it possible to use any decision procedure for the guarded fragment (Ganzinger & de Nivelle 1999, Hladik 2002), for deciding $\mathcal{GF}^2\mathcal{N}$ and reasoning in description logics.

2   The Guarded Fragment and Number Restrictions

Throughout this paper we assume a standard logical notation for first-order logic with equality and description logics, and the correspondence between the syntax of description logics and the first-order syntax (that is, role names correspond to binary predicates, $\sqcap$ to conjunction, etc.). For an interpretation $\mathcal{I} = (D, \cdot^{\mathcal{I}})$, we denote by $\mathcal{I}|_S$ the interpretation induced by a subset $S \subseteq D$ of domain elements. We say that a formula F' is *conservative over* F if (*i*) every model of F can be expanded (by interpreting new predicate symbols) to a model of F' and (*ii*) F is a logical consequence of F'. A transformation $F \implies F'$ is called *conservative* if F' is conservative over F. The *size* $|F|$ ($|C|$, $|T|$) of a formula F (a concept C or a TBox T) is its length when an appropriate coding of numbers (binary or unary) is assumed. The *width* $wd(F)$ of a *formula* F is the maximal number of free variables in subformulas of F.

The *guarded fragment* (with equality) can be defined by the grammar:

$$\mathcal{GF} ::= \mathsf{A} \mid \neg\mathsf{F}_1 \mid \mathsf{F}_1 \vee \mathsf{F}_2 \mid \mathsf{F}_1 \wedge \mathsf{F}_2 \mid \forall\overline{x}.(\mathsf{G}\rightarrow\mathsf{F}_1) \mid \exists\overline{x}.(\mathsf{G}\wedge\mathsf{F}_1). \qquad (1)$$

where A is an atom, $\mathsf{F}_i, i = 1,2$ are guarded formulas, and G is an atom called *the guard* containing all free variables of F_1. We assume that for $\mathsf{F}(x) \in \mathcal{GF}$, the formula $\forall x.\mathsf{F}(x)$ is also guarded, since it can be equivalently written in the form $\forall x.[(x \simeq x)\rightarrow\mathsf{F}(x)] \in \mathcal{GF}$. As usual we assume that implication and equivalence are expressible by means of the other boolean connectives. The bounded-variable variant $\mathcal{GF}^k$ of the guarded fragment is the set the guarded formulas that use at most k variable names. Note that for every $F \in \mathcal{GF}^k$, $wd(F) \leq k$.

2.1   The Two-Variable Guarded Fragment with Number Restrictions

In this paper we consider an extension of the two-variable guarded fragment $\mathcal{GF}^2$ with expressions of the form $\exists^{\geq n}y.e(x,y)$ and $\exists^{<n}y.e(x,y)$, where n is a natural

number and e is a binary atom. These expressions are called *"at-most"* and *"at-least"* *number restrictions* respectively. The semantics of number restrictions can be first-order defined as follows: $\exists^{<n}y.e(x,y) \equiv \neg[\exists^{\geq n}y.e(x,y)]$ where

$$\exists^{\geq n}y.e(x,y) \equiv \exists y_1 y_2 \ldots y_n.[\bigwedge_{1 \leq i \leq n} e(x,y_i) \wedge \bigwedge_{1 \leq i < j \leq n} y_i \not\approx y_j].$$

The meaning of "at-most" and "at-least" number restrictions is that they require or respectively restrict the number of different elements in a model that can be connected by a binary relation with a given element.

The *two-variable guarded fragment with number restrictions* is defined by:

$$\mathcal{GF}^2\mathcal{N} ::= \mathsf{A} \mid \exists^{\bowtie n}y.e(x,y) \mid \neg\mathsf{F}_1 \mid \mathsf{F}_1 \bowtie \mathsf{F}_2 \mid \forall\overline{x}.(\mathsf{G} \to \mathsf{F}_1) \mid \exists\overline{x}.(\mathsf{G} \wedge \mathsf{F}_1), \qquad (2)$$

where $\exists^{\bowtie n}y.e(x,y)$ are number restrictions, $\bowtie$ stands for conjunction or disjunction and only variables from $\{x,y\}$ can be used in formulas. In the sequel we will work with conjunctions of number restrictions of the form:

$$\mathcal{N}(x) \equiv \bigwedge_{l \in L} \exists^{\geq n_l}y.e_l(x,y) \wedge \bigwedge_{m \in M} \exists^{<n_m}y.e_m(x,y). \qquad (3)$$

where L and M are disjoint finite sets of indexes, n_l, n_m are natural numbers and e_l, e_m are binary predicate symbols for $l \in L$, $m \in M$.

2.2   A Relationship Between $\mathcal{GF}^2\mathcal{N}$ and $\mathcal{ALCQIb}$

The fragment $\mathcal{GF}^2\mathcal{N}$ is closely related to the description logic $\mathcal{ALCQIb}$ introduced by Tobies (2001). $\mathcal{ALCQIb}$ extends the description logic $\mathcal{ALCQI}$ with the "safe" boolean combinations of roles. The unrestricted boolean combinations of roles are defined from the atomic roles and their inverses by the grammar:[1]

$$\mathcal{R}_B ::= R_a \mid R_a^{-1} \mid \neg R_a \mid \neg R_a^{-1} \mid R_B^1 \sqcap R_B^2 \mid R_B^1 \sqcup R_B^2,$$

whereas the "safe" boolean combinations of roles are restricted to:[2]

$$\mathcal{R}_b ::= R_a \mid R_a^{-1} \mid R_b^1 \sqcap R_b^1 \mid R_b^1 \sqcup R_b^2 \quad \text{where } R_b^1, R_b^2 \in \mathcal{R}_b, \, R_B^1, R_B^2 \in \mathcal{R}_B.$$

The set of $\mathcal{ALCQIb}$-concepts is defined in the same way as in $\mathcal{ALCQI}$, except that now any "safe" role expression R can be used as a role filler:

$$\mathcal{C} ::= \mathsf{A} \mid \neg C_1 \mid C_1 \sqcap C_2 \mid \exists^{\geq n}R.C_1, \qquad (4)$$

where A is an atomic concept, $C_1, C_2 \in \mathcal{C}$, $R \in R_b$ and n is a natural number.

Tobies (2001) has demonstrated that concept satisfiability w.r.t. general $\mathcal{ALCQIb}$ TBoxes is EXPTIME-complete, even if the numbers in qualifying number restrictions are coded in binary. The result has been obtained by a reduction to the emptiness problem for looping tree automata. Given a TBox T and a concept C, an automaton L can be constructed such that L accepts a tree *iff* C has a T-model. The emptiness of L can be verified in polynomial time in the size of $|L|$, which gives an algorithm for checking T-satisfiability of C (see Fig. 1). However

---

[1] For convenience, we define boolean combinations that are in negation normal form.

[2] In the original definition (Tobies 2001), a boolean combination of roles is "safe" if its disjunction normal form contains a positive conjunct in every disjunct.

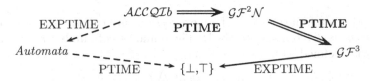

Fig. 1. The outline of decision procedures for $\mathcal{ALCQI}b$ and $\mathcal{GF}^2\mathcal{N}$: the dashed arrows represent an automata-based approach; the solid arrows represent a decision procedure through the guarded fragment. We give the translations shown by the double arrows

L can be exponentially large in $|C|+|T|$ in worst case and this blow-up cannot be avoided, since the problem is EXPTIME-hard. Moreover, the translation can be exponential in many trivial cases, say, when T contains lots of definitions that are not relevant to C, which is often the case in real knowledge bases. Therefore, a straightforward implementation of the automata-based decision procedure seems to be not very useful in practice. In this paper we propose an alternative decision procedure through the guarded fragment (see Fig. 1). This approach might be more efficient yet having the optimal complexity. As a first step of our procedure we establish a correspondence between $\mathcal{ALCQI}b$-knowledge bases and $\mathcal{GF}^2\mathcal{N}$.

Lemma 1. *For every $\mathcal{ALCQI}b$ TBox T one can construct in polynomial time a formula $F \in \mathcal{GF}^2\mathcal{N}$ that is conservative over T such that $|F| = O(|T|)$.*

Proof. Without loss of generality, we may assume that T contains only simple definitions, that is, definitions corresponding to one case in (4). Moreover, we introduce auxiliary role names $\mathsf{R_b}$ for every compound subrole $R_b \in \mathcal{R}_b$ that occurs in T. We extend T with definitions for $\mathsf{R_b}$ and use them in complex expressions instead of R_b. We also introduce additional binary predicate symbol $\mathsf{R_C}$ for every definition of qualifying number restrictions $\mathsf{C} \doteq \exists^{\geq n}\mathsf{R.C_1}$. The definitions from T and their first-order translations are given on Fig. 2. It is easy to see that the translation maps TBox T to a conjunction of formulas from $\mathcal{GF}^2\mathcal{N}$.   □

Corollary 1. *The problem of concept satisfiability w.r.t. $\mathcal{ALCQI}b$ TBox-es is polynomially reducible to satisfiability of $\mathcal{GF}^2\mathcal{N}$-formulas.*

$\mathsf{C} \doteq \mathsf{A}$	$\Rightarrow \forall x.[\mathsf{C}(x) \leftrightarrow \mathsf{A}(x)]$	$R_b \doteq R_a$	$\Rightarrow \forall xy.[\mathsf{R_b}(x,y) \leftrightarrow \mathsf{R_a}(x,y)]$
$\mathsf{C} \doteq \neg \mathsf{C_1}$	$\Rightarrow \forall x.[\mathsf{C}(x) \leftrightarrow \neg \mathsf{C_1}(x)]$	$R_b \doteq R_a^{-1}$	$\Rightarrow \forall xy.[\mathsf{R_b}(x,y) \leftrightarrow \mathsf{R_a}(y,x)]$
$\mathsf{C} \doteq \mathsf{C_1} \sqcap \mathsf{C_2}$	$\Rightarrow \forall x.(\mathsf{C}(x) \leftrightarrow [\mathsf{C_1}(x) \wedge \mathsf{C_2}(x)])$		

$\mathsf{C} \doteq \exists^{\geq n}\mathsf{R.C_1}$	$\Rightarrow \forall x.(\mathsf{C}(x) \rightarrow \exists^{\geq n}y.\mathsf{R_C}(x,y)) \wedge \forall xy.(\mathsf{R_C}(x,y) \rightarrow [\mathsf{R_C}(x,y) \wedge \mathsf{C_1}(y)]) \wedge$
	$\wedge \forall x.(\exists^{\geq n}y.\mathsf{R_C}(x,y) \rightarrow \mathsf{C}(x)) \wedge \forall xy.(\mathsf{R}(x,y) \rightarrow [\mathsf{C_1}(y) \rightarrow \mathsf{R_C}(x,y)])$
$R_b \doteq R_b^1 \sqcap R_B^1$	$\Rightarrow \forall xy.(\mathsf{R_b}(x,y) \rightarrow [R_b^1(x,y) \wedge R_B^1(x,y)]) \wedge$
	$\wedge \forall xy.(\mathsf{R}_b^1(x,y) \rightarrow [\mathsf{R_b}(x,y) \vee \neg R_B^1(x,y)])$
$R_b \doteq R_b^1 \sqcup R_b^2$	$\Rightarrow \forall xy.(\mathsf{R_b}(x,y) \rightarrow [\mathsf{R}_b^1(x,y) \vee \mathsf{R}_b^2(x,y)]) \wedge$
	$\wedge \forall xy.[\mathsf{R}_b^1(x,y) \rightarrow \mathsf{R_b}(x,y)] \wedge \forall xy.[\mathsf{R}_b^2(x,y) \rightarrow \mathsf{R_b}(x,y)]$

Fig. 2. A translation of $\mathcal{ALCQI}b$ TBox-es to $\mathcal{GF}^2\mathcal{N}$

It is not clear whether the expressive power of $\mathcal{ALCQI}b$ reaches $\mathcal{GF}^2\mathcal{N}$, since $\mathcal{ALCQI}b$ does not have a built-in equality. However, we conjecture, that $\mathcal{GF}^2\mathcal{N}$ without equality has the same expressive power as $\mathcal{ALCQI}b$.

Remark 1. In some papers on the guarded fragment, e.g. in (Grädel 1999*b*), atoms are allowed to contain individual constants. In this paper, however, we do not assume this. Reasoning with individual constants in the presence of number restrictions becomes much harder, since so-called *cardinality restrictions* can be expressed using them: The formula $\forall x.[a(x) \to e(c,x)] \wedge \forall x.\exists^{<n+1}y.e(x,y)$ has only models where a is satisfied in at most n elements. The extension of $\mathcal{ALCQI}$ with cardinality restrictions becomes NEXPTIME-complete already for the unary coding of numbers and the exact complexity for binary coding is still an open problem (for details see Tobies 2001).   ◇

2.3   A Normal Form for Formulas in $\mathcal{GF}^2\mathcal{N}$

To prove properties for guarded formulas it is convenient to have them in a simple normal form. We show that $\mathcal{GF}^2\mathcal{N}$-formulas have a Scott-like normal form that is similar to the one found by Grädel (1999*b*) for $\mathcal{GF}$.

Lemma 2. *For every formula $F \in \mathcal{GF}^2\mathcal{N}$ there is a formula F' of the form:*

$$\bigwedge_{i \in I} \forall xy.[g_i(x,y) \to \varphi_i(x,y)] \wedge \forall x.\mathcal{N}(x) \tag{5}$$

where $g_i(x,y)$ are atoms, $i \in I$, $\varphi_i(x,y)$ are quantifier-free formulas and $\mathcal{N}(x)$ are number restrictions of the form (3), such that: (i) F' is conservative over F, (ii) $|F'| = O(|F|)$ and F' is computable in polynomial time from F.

Proof. Given a guarded formula $F \in \mathcal{GF}^2\mathcal{N}$, first, we put F into *negation normal form (NNF)* by pushing all negations inside to atoms using the usual *de Morgan*'s laws. The resulting formula $[F]^{nnf}$ belongs to the following fragment:

$$[\mathcal{GF}^2\mathcal{N}]^{nnf} ::= (\neg)\mathtt{A} \mid \exists^{\bowtie n}y.e(x,y) \mid \mathtt{F}_1 \mathbin{\text{⋈}} \mathtt{F}_2 \mid \forall \overline{x}.(\mathtt{G} \to \mathtt{F}_1) \mid \exists \overline{x}.(\mathtt{G} \wedge \mathtt{F}_1).$$

we extend this fragment by dropping the restrictions for the existential part:

$$[\mathcal{GF}^2\mathcal{N}]^{nnf}_w ::= (\neg)\mathtt{A} \mid \exists^{\bowtie n}y.e(x,y) \mid \mathtt{F}_1 \mathbin{\text{⋈}} \mathtt{F}_2 \mid \forall \overline{x}.(\mathtt{G} \to \mathtt{F}_1) \mid \exists \mathbf{y}.\mathtt{F}_1.$$

thus, the existential closure $F^n := \exists \overline{x}.[F]^{nnf} \in [\mathcal{GF}^2\mathcal{N}]^{nnf}_w$. Note that F^n is conservative over F. After that, we apply a so-called *structural transformation* for the sentence F^n by introducing *definitions* for its subformulas. We assume that to every subformula $\mathtt{F}$ of F^n corresponding to a case in the recursive definition, a unique predicate $P_\mathtt{F} = p_\mathtt{F}(\overline{x})$ is assigned, where $\overline{x} = \mathrm{free}[\mathtt{F}] \subseteq \{x,y\}$. If $\mathtt{F}$ is a number restriction $\exists^{\bowtie n}y.e(x,y)$, then we also introduce an auxiliary binary predicate $e_\mathtt{F}(x,y)$. The result of the structural transformation for F^n is the formula $P_{F^n} \wedge [F^n]^{st}$, where $[\mathtt{F}]^{st}$ is defined recursively for $\mathtt{F} \in [\mathcal{GF}]^{nnf}_w$ as follows:

$$[\mathbf{F}]^{st} := \quad [(\neg)\mathbf{A}]^{st} : \forall \overline{x}.(P_{\mathbf{F}} \rightarrow (\neg)\mathbf{A}) \qquad \qquad |$$
$$[\exists^{\geq n} y.e(x,y)]^{st} : \forall x.\exists^{\geq n} y.e_{\mathbf{F}}(x,y) \wedge \forall xy.[e_{\mathbf{F}}(x,y) \rightarrow (p_{\mathbf{F}}(x) \rightarrow e(x,y))] \mid$$
$$[\exists^{<n} y.e(x,y)]^{st} : \forall xy.[e(x,y) \rightarrow (p_{\mathbf{F}}(x) \rightarrow e_{\mathbf{F}}(x,y))] \wedge \forall x.\exists^{<n} y.e_{\mathbf{F}}(x,y) \mid$$
$$[\mathbf{F}_1 \bowtie \mathbf{F}_2]^{st} : \forall \overline{x}.(P_{\mathbf{F}} \rightarrow [P_{\mathbf{F}_1} \bowtie P_{\mathbf{F}_2}]) \wedge [\mathbf{F}_1]^{st} \wedge [\mathbf{F}_2]^{st} \qquad \qquad |$$
$$[\forall \overline{y}.(\mathbf{G} \rightarrow \mathbf{F}_1)]^{st} : \forall \overline{xy}.(\mathbf{G} \rightarrow [P_{\mathbf{F}} \rightarrow P_{\mathbf{F}_1}]) \wedge [\mathbf{F}_1]^{st} \qquad \qquad |$$
$$[\exists y.\mathbf{F}_1]^{st} : \forall \overline{x}.(P_{\mathbf{F}} \rightarrow \exists y.P_{\mathbf{F}_1}) \wedge [\mathbf{F}_1]^{st}.$$

The function $[\mathbf{F}]^{st}$ is defined recursively over the definition of $[\mathcal{GF}^2\mathcal{N}]_w^{nnf}$. On each step, subformulas of $\mathbf{F}$ are replaced by fresh atoms. These atoms are defined in separate conjuncts by means of subformulas that they replace. It is easy to see that the result of the transformation can be captured by a formula F' of the form (5) that is conservative over F^n. The formula F' has the size $O(|F^n|) = O(|F|)$ and the translation can be computed in polynomial time. □

2.4 The Tree-Model Property for $\mathcal{GF}^2\mathcal{N}$

As Vardi (1996) has argued, the tree-model property is the main reason why modal logics are decidable. The existence of tree-models for satisfiable formulas is a basis of all tableau and automata-based decision procedures for modal and description logics. In many cases the tree-model property allows to establish a finite model property and even to extract bounds on the sizes of models for satisfiable formulas, which gives rise to model-enumeration techniques.

Definition 1. *An interpretation* $\mathcal{M} = (D, \cdot^{\mathcal{T}})$ *has a tree width k if k is the minimal natural number such that there exists a tree $T = (V, E)$ (a connected acyclic graph) and a function $\pi : V \rightarrow 2^D$ with $|\pi(v)| \leq k + 1$ for every $v \in V$, such that the following conditions hold:*
   (i) $\mathcal{M} \models a(d_1, ..., d_n)$ *implies* $\{d_1, ..., d_n\} \subseteq \pi(v)$ *for some $v \in V$; and*
   (ii) *The set* $\mathcal{O}(d) := \{v \in V \mid d \in \pi(v)\}$ *induces a connected subtree in T.* ◇

Grädel (1999a) has shown that every satisfiable guarded formula with width k has a model of the tree width $k - 1$. In particular, every satisfiable formula from $\mathcal{GF}^2$ has a tree-model (a model with the tree width $= 1$). We are going to extend this results to $\mathcal{GF}^2\mathcal{N}$ by taking into account number restrictions. For convenience, we use the following (equivalent) definition of a tree model:

Definition 2. *An interpretation* $\mathcal{T} = (V, \cdot^{\mathcal{T}})$ *is called a tree if there is a tree $T = (V, E)$, such that $\mathcal{T} \models a(v_1, ..., v_n)$ implies $\{v_1, \ldots, v_n\} \subseteq \{v_1', v_2'\}$ for some edge $e = (v_1', v_2') \in E$.* ◇

A correspondence between these two definitions can be established by assigning $\pi(v)$ to be the set $\{v, v_{-1}\} \subseteq V$, where v_{-1} is a parent of v in T (we assume that the root of T is a parent of itself). For proving the tree-model property for $\mathcal{GF}^2\mathcal{N}$ we show how a tree-model can be extracted from any model of a $\mathcal{GF}^2\mathcal{N}$-formula. Surprisingly, a tree-model satisfying number restrictions can be extracted from interpretations that satisfy weaker conditions than number restrictions themselves.

Definition 3. *A counting pattern for a model $\mathcal{M} = (D, \cdot^{\mathcal{M}})$ and number restrictions $\mathcal{N}(x)$ is a pair $\mathcal{P} = (R, w)$, where $R \subseteq D \times D$ is a reachability relation and $w : R \rightarrow 2^R$ is a witnessing function such that: **(i)** $(d_r, d_r) \in R$ for some $d_r \in D$ and **(ii)** for any $(d_{-1}, d_0) \in R$, $w[(d_{-1}, d_0)] = \{(d_0, d_1), (d_0, d_2), \dots, (d_0, d_b)\}$ for some $d_1, \dots, d_b \in D \setminus \{d_{-1}, d_0\}$ such that $\mathcal{M}|_{\{d_{-1}, d_0, \dots, d_b\}} \models \mathcal{N}(d_0)$.* ◇

Example 1. The fragment $\mathcal{GF}^2\mathcal{N}$ does not have the finite model property. To demonstrate this, consider the formula $Binary\,Tree \equiv \forall x.\mathcal{N}_{bt}(x)$, where $\mathcal{N}_{bt}(x) \equiv [\exists^{\geq 2} y.s(x, y) \wedge \exists^{<2} y.s(y, x)]$. It is easy to see that the formula $Binary\,Tree$ is satisfiable in a tree-model $\mathcal{T}$ (see Fig 3), but has no finite models. However, there is a finite interpretation $\mathcal{M} = (D = \{a, b, c, d, e\}, \cdot^{\mathcal{M}})$ given on Fig. 3 that has a counting pattern for $\mathcal{N}_{bt}(x)$. The counting pattern $\mathcal{P}_{bt} = (R, w)$ for $\mathcal{N}_{bt}(x)$ in $\mathcal{M}$ can be defined by taking $R = D \times D$ and setting the witnessing function $w[(d_{-1}, d_0)]$ to return the remaining edges incident to the node d_0. For instance, $w[(e, a)] := \{(a, b), (a, c)\}$, $w[(d, b)] := \{(b, c)\}$. ◇

It will be shown below, that every model of number restrictions has a counting pattern. However, the converse does not hold: the interpretation $\mathcal{M}$ from Fig. 3 does not satisfy $\forall x.\mathcal{N}_{bt}(x)$, but has a counting pattern for $\mathcal{N}_{bt}(x)$. Yet, we show that a tree-model satisfying number restrictions $\mathcal{N}(x)$ can be *extracted* from any model having a counting pattern for $\mathcal{N}(x)$.

Lemma 3. *Let $\mathcal{N}(x)$ be number restrictions of the form (3), and $\mathcal{M} = (D, \cdot^{\mathcal{M}})$ be a model of $\forall x.\mathcal{N}(x)$. Then $\mathcal{M}$ has a counting pattern for $\mathcal{N}(x)$.*

Proof. The intended counting pattern $\mathcal{P} = (R, w)$ can be defined as follows. Let $R = D \times D$. This guarantees that condition **(i)** in Definition 3 holds since D is a non-empty set. Note that for every vector $(d_{-1}, d_0) \in R$ one can find a finite set of elements $d_1, d_2, \dots, d_b$ such that $\mathcal{M}|_{\{d_{-1}, d_0, d_1, \dots, d_b\}} \models \mathcal{N}(d_0)$, since $\mathcal{M} \models \mathcal{N}(d_0)$ and number restrictions require only finitely many witnesses. This suggests us to define a witnessing function by $w[(d_{-1}, d_0)] := \{(d_0, d_1), (d_0, d_2), \dots, (d_0, d_b)\}$. This definition guarantees the remaining property **(ii)** of Definition 3. □

Lemma 4. *Let $F \equiv F_g \wedge \forall x.\mathcal{N}(x)$ be a $\mathcal{GF}^2\mathcal{N}$-formula in a normal form (5). Let $\mathcal{M}$ be a model of F_g that has a counting pattern for the number restrictions $\mathcal{N}(x)$. Then F has a tree-model.*

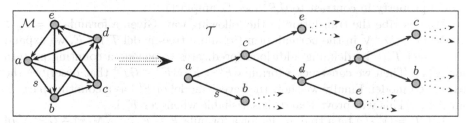

Fig. 3. Tree decomposition of an interpretation having a counting pattern

Proof. Given a model $\mathcal{M}$ for F_g and a counting pattern $\mathcal{P} = (R, w)$ for $\mathcal{N}(x)$ in $\mathcal{M}$, we construct a tree-model $\mathcal{T} = (V, \cdot^{\mathcal{T}})$ for F based on a tree $T = (V, E)$. The model $\mathcal{T}$ is constructed inductively together with a function $\pi : V \to D$ that represents a *bisimulation relation* between $\mathcal{M}$ and $\mathcal{T}$, such that for every node $v_0 \in V$ and its parent v_{-1}, the substructures $\mathcal{M}|_{\{v_{-1}, v_0\}}$ and $\mathcal{T}|_{\{\pi(v_{-1}), \pi(v_0)\}}$ are isomorphic and $(\pi(v_{-1}), \pi(v_0)) \in R$.

First, we create a root $v_r \in V$ of a tree T and set $\pi(v_r) := d_r$, where $d_r \in D$ is given in Definition 3, so $(\pi(v_r), \pi(v_r)) \in R$. For every leaf v_0 of a tree T constructed so far and its parent v_{-1}, consider $(d_{-1}, d_0) = (\pi(v_{-1}), \pi(v_0)) \in R$ (by induction hypothesis), and let $d_1, \ldots, d_b \in D$ be such that $R(d_{-1}, d_0) = \{(d_0, d_1), (d_0, d_2), \ldots, (d_0, d_b)\}$. For every d_i with $1 \le i \le b$ we create a child v_i of v_0 in T, set $\pi(v_i) := d_i$, and extend the interpretation $\mathcal{T}$ in such a way that the substructure $\mathcal{T}|_{\{v_0, v_i\}}$ is isomorphic to the substructure $\mathcal{M}|_{\{d_0, d_i\}}$ for $1 \le i \le b$. This can be always done in a consistent way. Note that $\mathcal{T} \vDash \mathcal{N}(v_0)$ because $\mathcal{M}|_{\{d_{-1}, d_0, d_1, \ldots, d_b\}} \vDash \mathcal{N}(d_0)$ and π is a bijection between the sets $\{v_{-1}, v_0, \ldots, v_b\}$ and $\{d_{-1}, d_0, \ldots, d_b\}$. The constructed interpretation $\mathcal{T}$ is a tree. It is a model of F_g since every edge of a tree is isomorphic to a substructure of the model $\mathcal{M}$ and since F_g is a guarded formula. Therefore $\mathcal{T} \vDash F$. $\square$

The process described in the proof of Lemma 4 is known as a *tree decomposition* of a structure (Grädel 1999a). Figure 3 demonstrates the construction given in the proof of Lemma 4 for the interpretation $\mathcal{M}$ from Example 1. Now the tree-model property for $\mathcal{GF}^2\mathcal{N}$ is an easy consequence of Lemma 4:

Theorem 1. *Every satisfiable formula $F \in \mathcal{GF}^2\mathcal{N}$ has a tree-model.*

Proof. By Lemma 2, we may assume that F is of the form (5). Let $\mathcal{M}$ be a model for $F = F_g \wedge \forall x.\mathcal{N}(x)$. By Lemma 3, $\mathcal{M}$ has a counting pattern for $\mathcal{N}(x)$. Therefore, by Lemma 4, F has a tree-model. $\square$

3   The Translation

In this section we give a polynomial-time translation mapping any formula $F \in \mathcal{GF}^2\mathcal{N}$ of the form (5) to a formula $F' \in \mathcal{GF}^3$ such that (i) every tree-model of F can be expanded to a model of F', (ii) for every model of F' one can construct a tree-model of F and (iii) $|F'| = O(|F|)$. Note that it is not possible to give a conservative translation from $\mathcal{GF}^2\mathcal{N}$ to $\mathcal{GF}^3$, since $\mathcal{GF}^2\mathcal{N}$ does not have a finite model property in contrast to $\mathcal{GF}^3$ (see Example 1).

We describe the translation in the following way. Given a formula $F = F_g \wedge \forall x.\mathcal{N}(x) \in \mathcal{GF}^2\mathcal{N}$ in the normal form (5) and a tree-model $\mathcal{T}$ for F, we expand the model $\mathcal{T}$ to by defining additional predicates to encode a counting pattern for $\mathcal{N}(x)$. Then we construct a formula $F' = F_g \wedge F'' \in \mathcal{GF}^3$ that describes the expanded model. Finally we show that every model of F' has a counting pattern for $\mathcal{N}(x)$. This will prove that F is satisfiable whenever F' is.

Let $\mathcal{T} = (V, \cdot^{\mathcal{T}})$ be a tree-model for a formula $F \equiv F_g \wedge \forall x.\mathcal{N}(x) \in \mathcal{GF}^2\mathcal{N}$ of the form (5). We introduce a new binary predicate R to encode the reachability relation of a counting pattern $\mathcal{P} = (R, w)$. R is interpreted in $\mathcal{T}$ by setting $\mathcal{T} \vDash R(v_1, v_2)$ *iff* either $v_1 = v_2$ or v_2 is a child of the node v_1.

To encode the number restrictions, for every node $v \in V$ consider an ordered set $\mathcal{O}(v) = [(v_{-1},) v_0, v_1, ..., v_{b_v}]$ of *neighbors* of v in $\mathcal{T}$: The first element in $\mathcal{O}(v)$ should be the parent v_{-1} of v, which is followed by the node v itself: $v_0 := v$ (we assume that $v_{-1} = v_0$ for the root node). After that, all children of v are listed in some order $v_1, ..., v_{b_v}$: see Fig. 4. The order on the set of neighbors is used to count the number of edges satis-

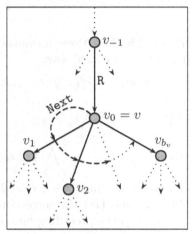

fying the counting relations. We encode this order using a special ternary predicate symbol Next (this will be the only ternary relation that is used in our construction). The intended interpretation of Next is given by $\mathcal{T} \vDash \text{Next}(v, v', v'')$ *iff* $v' = v_i$ and $v'' = v_{i+1}$ for some $v_i, v_{i+1} \in \mathcal{O}(v)$ with $0 \le i \le b_v$. In other words, $\text{Next}(x, y, z)$ holds if and only if z is the child of x that comes directly after y.

For every index $c \in L \cup M$, $v \in V$ and $v_i \in \mathcal{O}(v)$, $1 \le i \le b_v$, we define the number $n_{c,i} := \#\{v_j \in \mathcal{O}(v) \mid j \le i \ \& \ \mathcal{T} \vDash e_c(v, v_j)\}$, that is the number of times the relation e_c has been realized up to v_i. Note that for every $l \in L$ there exists i with $0 \le i \le b_v$ such that

Fig. 4. The counting order of the neighbors of a node

$n_{l,i} \ge n_l$, and for every $m \in M$ and every j with $0 \le j \le b_v$, $n_{m,j} < n_m$ since $\mathcal{T} \vDash \mathcal{N}(v)$.

Moreover, the following property can be assumed for the set $\mathcal{O}(v)$. We say that a child v_i with $1 \le i \le b_v$ of the node v is *essential*, if whenever $n_{l,i} \le n_l$ for some $l \in L$, then there exists an $l' \in L$ such that $\mathcal{T} \vDash e_{l'}(v_0, v_i)$ and $n_{l',i} \le n_{l'}$. In other words, if some "at-least" number restrictions are not yet realized up to v_i, then the node v_i should contribute in one of them. By reordering the children of v in $\mathcal{O}(v)$, if needed, one can always fulfill this condition.

For encoding the numbers $n_{c,i}$ for an index $c \in L \cup M$, we introduce additional binary predicate symbols $e_c^0, e_c^1, ..., e_c^{k_c}$, where $k_c := \lceil \log n_c \rceil$. In fact, we will encode not the numbers $n_{c,i}$ themselves, but $n'_{c,i} := min(2^{k_c} - 1, n_{c,i})$, since we do not need to count beyond n_c to check number restrictions. Every number $n'_{c,i}$ in binary coding is a *bit vector* of the size k_c. We represent this bit vector using the values of the predicates $e_c^0, e_c^1, ..., e_c^{k_c}$ on the edge (v, v_i), in such a way that $\mathcal{T} \vDash$ "$\bar{e}_c(v, v_i) = n'_{c,i}$". Formally, for every $c \in L \cup M$ and $v_1, v_2 \in V$ let

$$\bar{e}_c^{\mathcal{I}}(v_1, v_2) := \sum_{i=1}^{k_c} e_c^{i\,\mathcal{I}}(v_1, v_2) \cdot 2^i, \text{ where } e^{\mathcal{I}}(v_1, v_2) := \begin{cases} 1 & \text{if } \mathcal{T} \vDash e(v_1, v_2), \\ 0 & \text{if } \mathcal{T} \vDash \neg e(v_1, v_2). \end{cases}$$

Arithmetical expressions involving $\bar{e}_c(x, y)$ and $e_c(x, y)$ are evaluated in interpretations as usual. For instance, given an interpretation $\mathcal{I} = (D, \cdot^{\mathcal{I}})$ and a valuation of variables δ, the proposition "$\bar{e}_c(x, y) \ge e_c(x, y) + 1$" is evaluated to **true** *iff* "$\bar{e}_c^{\mathcal{I}}(\delta(x), \delta(y)) \ge e_c^{\mathcal{I}}(\delta(x), \delta(y)) + 1$".

Lemma 5. *For every index $c \in L \cup M$ there exist quantifier-free formulas of size linear in k_c that express the following relations:*

$$\begin{aligned}
Init_c(x,y) &\equiv \text{``}\overline{e}_c(x,y) = e_c(x,y)\text{''}, \\
Full_c(x,y) &\equiv \text{``}\overline{e}_c(x,y) = 2^{k_c} - 1\text{''}, \\
Copy_c(x,y,z) &\equiv \text{``}\overline{e}_c(x,z) = \overline{e}_c(x,y)\text{''}, \\
Incr_c(x,y,z) &\equiv \text{``}\overline{e}_c(x,z) = \overline{e}_c(x,y) + 1 \bmod 2^{k_c}\text{''}, \\
Less_c(x,y) &\equiv \text{``}\overline{e}_c(x,y) < n_c\text{''}.
\end{aligned}$$

Proof. The first three formulas can be defined in the straightforward way:

$$Init_c(x,y) \equiv [e_c^0(x,y) \leftrightarrow e_c(x,y)] \wedge \bigwedge_{1 \le i \le k_c} \neg e_c^i(x,y),$$

$$Full_c(x,y) \equiv \bigwedge_{i \le k_c} e_c^i(x,y),$$

$$Copy_c(x,y,z) \equiv \bigwedge_{i \le k_c} [e_c^i(x,y) \leftrightarrow e_c^i(x,z)]$$

		k_c					i			0
n	:	*	*	$\cdots$	*	0	1	1	$\cdots$	1
		‖	‖			‖				‖
$n{+}1$:		*	*	$\cdots$	*	1	0	0	$\cdots$	0

		k_c					j			0
n	:	*	*	$\cdots$	*	0	*	*	$\cdots$	*
	$\wedge$		‖	‖		‖				
m	:	*	*	$\cdots$	*	1	*	*	$\cdots$	*

Fig. 5. The arithmetical properties of bit vectors

The relation "$m = n + 1 \bmod 2^k$" holds *iff* (*i*) the lowest bits of n and m are different and (*ii*) the correspondent bits of any other position of n and m are different *iff* the preceding bits of n and m are 1 and 0 respectively (see Fig. 5):

$$Incr_c(x,y,z) \equiv \quad [e_c^0(x,y) \leftrightarrow \neg e_c^0(x,z)] \wedge$$
$$\bigwedge_{0 < i \le k_c} ([e_c^i(x,y) \leftrightarrow \neg e_c^i(x,z)] \leftrightarrow [e_c^{i-1}(x,y) \wedge \neg e_c^{i-1}(x,z)]).$$

The relation "$m^k...m^1m^0 > n^k...n^1n^0$" between binary numbers holds if either "$m^k > n^k$", or, "$m^k = n^k$" and "$m^{k-1}...m^1m^0 > n^{k-1}...n^1n^0$":

$$\begin{aligned}
Less_c(x,y) &\equiv Less_{c,k_c}(x,y), \text{ where} \\
Less_{c,i}(x,y) &\equiv [\text{``}n_c^i = 1\text{''} \wedge \neg e_c^i(x,y)] \vee \\
&\quad ([\text{``}n_c^i = 1\text{''} \leftrightarrow e_c^i(x,y)] \wedge Less_{c,i-1}(x,y)), \quad 0 < i < k_c, \\
Less_{c,0}(x,y) &\equiv [\text{``}n_c^0 = 1\text{''} \wedge \neg e_c^0(x,y)].
\end{aligned}$$

where the expressions "$n_c^i = 1$" stand for the respective boolean constants. It is easy to see that the length of every formula above is linear in k_c. More precisely, every predicate e_c^i, $1 \le i \le k_c$ is used in every definition at most 4 times. $\square$

Using the formulas defined in Lemma 5, we introduce additional quantifier-free formulas, that are linear in the size of the input formula F:

$$Init(x,y) \equiv \bigwedge_{l \in L} Init_l(x,y) \wedge \bigwedge_{m \in M} Init_m(x,y),$$

$$\begin{aligned}
Count_c(x,y,z) \equiv &[(\neg Full(x,y) \wedge e_c(x,z)) \rightarrow Incr_c(x,y,z)] \wedge \\
&[(Full(x,y) \vee \neg e_c(x,y)) \rightarrow Copy_c(x,y,z)],
\end{aligned}$$

$$Count(x,y,z) \equiv \bigwedge_{l \in L} Count_l(x,y,z) \wedge \bigwedge_{m \in M} Count_m(x,y,z),$$

$$AtMost(x, y) \equiv \bigwedge_{m \in M} Less_m(x, y),$$

$$Require(x, y) \equiv [\bigvee_{l \in L} Less_l(x, y)],$$

$$Child(x, y) \equiv R(x, y) \wedge R(y, y) \wedge Init(y, x) \wedge Count(y, x, y),$$

$$Fair(x, y, z) \equiv \bigvee_{l \in L} [Less_l(x, y) \wedge e_l(x, z)],$$

The formula $Init(x, y)$ is used in our encoding of number restrictions for initializing the counters on the edge (x, y). The formula $Count(x, y, z)$ increments every counter between the edges (x, y) and (x, z), if the correspondent binary relation shows up on the edge (x, z) and if the limit of the counter is not yet reached. Otherwise, the current value of the counter on (x, y) is copied to (x, z). The formula $AtMost(x, y)$ ensures that the values of the counters corresponding "at-most" restrictions do not go beyond the maximal allowed limits. Dually, the formula $Require(x, y)$ expresses that the "at-least" restrictions are not yet fulfilled. This should require a Next child of x to be created. The child of a node x is created using the formula $Child(x, y)$. It expresses initialization operations for the node y: the predicate R should be defined; the counters for the node y should be initialized on the edge (y, x) and computed for the edge (y, y). The formula $Fair(x, y, z)$ is responsible for termination of the process of creating the required children of a node. It says, essentially, that at least one of the relations required on (x, y) should be realized on the next edge (x, z). This guaranties that all "at-least" restrictions will be eventually fulfilled for a node if the process of creating new children can be continued consistently.

The result of the translation is define by $F' \equiv F_g \wedge \Phi_1 \wedge \Phi_2 \wedge \Phi_3 \in \mathcal{GF}^3$, where

$$\Phi_1 \equiv \exists x.[R(x, x) \wedge Init(x, x)],$$
$$\Phi_2 \equiv \forall xy.[R(x, y) \rightarrow (AtMost(x, y) \wedge [Require(x, y) \rightarrow \exists z.\text{Next}(x, y, z)])]^3, \quad (6)$$
$$\Phi_3 \equiv \forall xyz.(\text{Next}(x, y, z) \rightarrow [Child(x, z) \wedge Fair(x, y, z) \wedge Count(x, y, z)]).$$

The following lemma is immediate from our construction:

Lemma 6. *Every tree-model of F can be expanded to a model of F'.*

Proof. Given a tree-model $\mathcal{T} = (V, \cdot^{\mathcal{T}})$ for F, we interpret the new predicates R, Next and e_c^i for $c \in L \cup M$ as given in the construction above. It is a routine to check that all formulas Φ_1, Φ_2 and Φ_3 are true in $\mathcal{T}$. For example, the implication $\forall xyz.[\text{Next}(x, y, z) \rightarrow Fair(x, y, z)]$ holds in $\mathcal{T}$ since every child node of every $v \in V$ is essential in $\mathcal{O}(v)$. $\square$

Now we show that a witness for number restrictions $\mathcal{N}(x)$ can be extracted from a model of F':

Lemma 7. *Every model of F' has a counting pattern for $\mathcal{N}(x)$.*

Proof. Given a model $\mathcal{M}' = (D', \cdot^{\mathcal{M}'})$ of F', we construct a counting pattern $\mathcal{P} = (R, w)$ in the following way. We define the reachability relation by $R := \{(d_1, d_2) \in D' \times D' \mid \mathcal{M}' \vDash \mathtt{R}(d_1, d_2)\}$. For every pair $(d_{-1}, d_0) \in R$, let $w[(d_{-1}, d_0)] := \{(d_0, d_1), \ldots, (d_0, d_b)\}$ be such that (i) $\mathcal{M}' \vDash \mathtt{Next}(d_0, d_i, d_{i+1})$ for $0 \leq i < b$ and (ii) $\mathcal{M}' \vDash \mathtt{Next}(d_0, d_b, d)$ for no $d \in D'$. Such a (finite) set always can be found since for any $d_0, d_i, d_{i+1} \in D'$ with $\mathcal{M}' \vDash \mathtt{Next}(d_0, d_i, d_{i+1})$, we have $\mathcal{M}' \vDash$ " $\sum_{l \in L} \bar{e}_l(d_0, d_i) \leq \sum_{l \in L} \bar{e}_l(d_0, d_{i+1})$ " because $\mathcal{M}' \vDash Fair(d_0, d_i, d_{i+1}) \wedge Count(d_0, d_i, d_{i+1})$. Therefore, there cannot be infinitely many d_i connected in a $\mathtt{Next}$-chain. So the witnessing function w is well-defined.

Now we show that $\mathcal{P}$ is a counting pattern for the number restrictions $\mathcal{N}(x)$. The condition (i) from Definition 3 holds since $\mathcal{M}' \vDash \Phi_1$, so there exists $d \in D'$ such that $\mathcal{M}' \vDash \mathtt{R}(d, d)$. To show that the condition (ii) also holds, consider the elements $d_{-1}, d_0, d_1, \ldots, d_b \in D'$ such that $w[(d_{-1}, d_0)] = \{(d_0, d_1), \ldots, (d_0, d_b)\}$. Let $n_{c,i} := \#\{d_j \mid j \leq i \ \& \ \mathcal{M}' \vDash e_c(d_0, d_j)\}$ and $n'_{c,i} := min(2^{k_c} - 1, n_{c,i})$ for $c \in L \cup M$ and $-1 \leq i \leq b$, be similar counters as were introduced for a tree-model. By induction on i with $-1 \leq i \leq b$ it is possible to show that $\mathcal{M}' \vDash$ " $\bar{e}_c(d_0, d_i) = n'_{c,i}$ " for every $c \in L \cup M$, because $\mathcal{M}' \vDash Child(d_{-1}, d_0)$ and $\mathcal{M}' \vDash Count(d_0, d_i, d_{i+1})$ for i with $0 \leq i < d$. Moreover, $\mathcal{M}' \vDash$ " $\bar{e}_l(d_0, d_b) \geq n_l$ " and $\mathcal{M}' \vDash$ " $\bar{e}_m(d_0, d_b) < n_m$ " for every $l \in L$ and $m \in M$, since $\mathcal{M}' \vDash AtMost(d_0, d_b) \wedge \neg Require(d_0, d_b)$ (there is no $\mathtt{Next}$-successor of d_b). As a conclusion, we have $\mathcal{M}'|_{\{d_{-1}, d_0, \ldots, d_b\}} \vDash \mathcal{N}(b_0)$, which implies the condition (ii) for a counting pattern. So, $\mathcal{P}$ is indeed a counting pattern for the number restrictions $\mathcal{N}(x)$. $\square$

Corollary 2. *F' is satisfiable iff F is satisfiable.*

Proof. The "*if*" part follows directly from Theorem 1 and Lemma 6. To prove the converse, assume that $\mathcal{M}'$ is a model of F'. In particular, $\mathcal{M}'$ is a model of F_g. By Lemma 7, $\mathcal{M}'$ has a counting pattern for $\mathcal{N}(x)$. Therefore, by Lemma 4 there is a tree-model $\mathcal{T}$ for $F \equiv F_g \wedge \forall x.\mathcal{N}(x)$. $\square$

The results obtained in this section can be summarized in our main theorem:

Theorem 2. *For any formula $F \in \mathcal{GF}^2\mathcal{N}$ there exists a formula $F' \in \mathcal{GF}^3$ such that (i) F is satisfiable iff F' is satisfiable, (ii) $|F'| = O(|F|)$ and F' can be computed in polynomial time from F.*

Proof. Let $F \in \mathcal{GF}^2\mathcal{N}$. By Lemma 2, one can find $F^n \equiv F_g \wedge \forall x.\mathcal{N}(x)$ in the normal form (5) that is equisatisfiable with F. Taking $F' \equiv F_g \wedge \Phi_1 \wedge \Phi_2 \wedge \Phi_3$ as defined in (6), by Corollary 2, F' is equisatisfiable with F^n, and thus with F. F' has a linear size and can be computed in polynomial time in $|F|$. $\square$

Corollary 3. *There is a decision procedure for $\mathcal{GF}^2\mathcal{N}$ that can be implemented in time $2^{O|F|}$, where $|F|$ is the size of a formula $F \in \mathcal{GF}^2\mathcal{N}$.*

Proof. A decision procedure for $F \in \mathcal{GF}^3$ can be implemented in time $2^{O|F|}$. (see Grädel 1999*b*, Hladik 2002, Ganzinger & de Nivelle 1999)[4]. $\square$

---

[4] Most decision procedures are given here for the full guarded fragment, but is easy to see that their specializations for the bounded-variable case run in EXPTIME.

4   Conclusions and the Future Work

We have described a procedure, that allows one to translate every formula from
$\mathcal{GF}^2\mathcal{N}$ to an equisatisfiable formula from $\mathcal{GF}^3$. The procedure is quite intriguing,
since it runs in polynomial time and has only linear overhead in the size of the
produced formula. However, only experimental evaluation can judge the practical
usefulness of the procedure. For the future work we try to find a translation
from $\mathcal{GF}^2\mathcal{N}$ to smaller fragments, in particular to $\mathcal{GF}^2$, or to the description
logic $\mathcal{ALCI}$, so that existing systems for description logics can be employed.
This idea is related to the work of Hladik & Sattler (2003). We believe that
a translation to simpler formalisms can be found by exploiting the automata
translation proposed by Tobies (2001).

References

Andréka, H., van Benthem, J. & Németi, I. (1998), 'Modal languages and bounded
    fragments of predicate logic', *Journal of Philosophical Logic* **27**, 217–274.
Ganzinger, H. & de Nivelle, H. (1999), A superposition decision procedure for the
    guarded fragment with equality, in 'Proc. 14th IEEE Symposium on Logic in
    Computer Science', IEEE Computer Society Press, pp. 295–305.
Grädel, E. (1999a), Decision procedures for guarded logics, in 'Automated Deduction -
    CADE16. Proceedings of 16th International Conference on Automated Deduction,
    Trento, 1999', Vol. 1632 of *LNCS*, Springer-Verlag.
Grädel, E. (1999b), 'On the restraining power of guards', *Journal of Symbolic Logic*
    64(4), 1719–1742.
Haarslev, V. & Möller, R. (2001), Optimizing reasoning in description logics with qual-
    ified number restrictions, in 'Proceedings of the International Workshop on De-
    scription Logics (DL-2001)', Stanford, USA, pp. 142–151.
Haarslev, V., Timmann, M. & Möller, R. (2001), Combining tableau and algebraic
    methods for reasoning with qualified number restrictions in description logics, in
    'Proceedings of the International Workshop on Methods for Modalities 2 (M4M-
    2)', Amsterdam, Netherlands.
Hladik, J. (2002), Implementation and optimisation of a tableau algorithm for the
    guarded fragment, in U. Egly & C. G. Fermüller, eds, 'Proceedings of the Interna-
    tional Conference on Automated Reasoning with Tableaux and Related Methods
    (Tableaux 2002)', Vol. 2381 of *Lecture Notes in Artificial Intelligence*, Springer-
    Verlag.
Hladik, J. & Sattler, U. (2003), A translation of looping alternating automata to
    description logics, in 'Proc. of the 19th Conference on Automated Deduction
    (CADE-19)', Vol. 2741 of *Lecture Notes in Artificial Intelligence*, Springer Ver-
    lag.
Tobies, S. (2001), Complexity Results and Practical Algorithms for Logics in Knowl-
    edge Representation, PhD thesis, RWTH Aachen, Germany.
Vardi, M. (1996), Why is modal logic so robustly decidable?, in N. Immerman & P. G.
    Kolaitis, eds, 'Descriptive Complexity and Finite Models', Vol. 31 of *DIMACS Se-
    ries in Discrete Mathematics and Theoretical Computer Science*, American Math-
    ematical Society, Princeton University, pp. 149–184.

Transforming Fuzzy Description Logics into Classical Description Logics

Umberto Straccia

ISTI-CNR, Via G. Moruzzi 1, I-56124 Pisa, ITALY
straccia@isti.cnr.it

Abstract. In this paper we consider Description Logics (DLs), which are logics for managing structured knowledge, with a well-known fuzzy extension to deal with vague information. While for fuzzy DLs ad-hoc, tableaux-like reasoning procedures have been given in the literature, the topic of this paper is to present a reasoning preserving transformation of fuzzy DLs into classical DLs. This has the considerable practical consequence that reasoning in fuzzy DLs is feasible using already existing DL systems.

1 Introduction

In the last decade a substantial amount of work has been carried out in the context of *Description Logics* (DLs) [1]. DLs are a logical reconstruction of the so-called frame-based knowledge representation languages, with the aim of providing a simple well-established Tarski-style declarative semantics to capture the meaning of the most popular features of structured representation of knowledge. Nowadays, a whole family of knowledge representation systems has been build using DLs, which differ with respect to their expressiveness and their complexity, and they have been used for building a variety of applications (see the DL community home page http://dl.kr.org/).

Despite their growing popularity, relative little work has been carried out [1] in extending them to the management of uncertain information. This is a well-known and important issue whenever the real world information to be represented is of imperfect nature. In DLs, the problem has attracted the attention of some researchers and some frameworks have been proposed, which differ in the underlying notion of uncertainty, e.g. probability theory [10,11,15,18,25], possibility theory [13], metric spaces [22], fuzzy theory [7,12,27,29,30] and multi-valued theory [27,28].

In this paper we consider the fuzzy extension of DLs towards the management of vague knowledge [27]. The choice of fuzzy set theory [31] as a way of endowing a DL with the capability to deal with imprecision is motivated as fuzzy logics capture the notion of imprecise concept, i.e. a concept for which a clear and precise definition is not possible. Therefore, fuzzy DLs allow to express that a

---

[1] Comparing with other formalisms -notably logic programming (see, e.g. [17,20], for an overview).

J.J. Alferes and J. Leite (Eds.): JELIA 2004, LNAI 3229, pp. 385–399, 2004.

sentence, like "it is Cold", is not just true or false like in classical DLs, but has a degree of truth, which is taken from the real unit interval $[0, 1]$. The truth degree dictates to which extent a sentence is true.

The fuzzy DL we consider ([27]) has been applied in the context of *Logic-based Multimedia Information Retrieval* (LMIR) [23,26] in which multimedia documents are "semantically annotated" (more generally, the logic is applicable to the context of the *Semantic Web* [5] as well, where DLs already play an important role [14]). LMIR points out the necessity of extending DLs with capabilities which allow the treatment of the inherent imprecision in multimedia object content representation and retrieval. In fact, classical DLs are insufficient for describing *real* multimedia retrieval situations, as the retrieval is usually not only a yes-no question: (*i*) the representations of multimedia objects' content and queries which the system (and the logic) have access to are inherently imperfect; and (*ii*) the relevance of a multimedia object to a query can thus be established only up to a limited degree (an explanatory example will be provided later one in the paper).

However, from a computational point of view, the reasoning procedures in [27], which are at the core of the LMIR model and system described in [23], are based on an *ad-hoc* tableaux calculus, similar to the ones presented for almost all DLs. Unfortunately, a drawback of the tableaux calculus in [27] is that any system, which would like to implement this fuzzy logic, has to be worked out from scratch (as we did in [23]) and requires a notable effort to become truly efficient (which was not the case for [23]).

The contribution of this paper is as follows. Primarily, we present a reasoning preserving transformation of fuzzy DLs into classical DLs. This has the considerable practical consequence that reasoning in fuzzy DLs is feasible using already existing DL systems and may take advantage of their efficiency. Secondarily, we allow the representation of so-called general terminological axioms, while in [23, 27], the axioms were very limited in the form. To best of our knowledge, no algorithm has yet been worked out for general axioms in fuzzy DLs. Overall, our approach may be extended to more expressive DLs than the one we present here as well and turns out to be very useful for our LMIR model and system.

We proceed as follows. In the next section, we recall some minimal notions about DLs. In Section 3 we recall fuzzy DLs and show their application to LMIR. Section 4 is the main part of this paper, where we present our reduction of fuzzy DLs into classical DLs, while Section 5 concludes.

2   A Quick Look to DLs

Instrumental to our purpose, the specific DL we extend with "fuzzy" capabilities is $\mathcal{ALC}$ with role hierarchies, i.e. $\mathcal{ALCH}$, a significant representative of DLs (see, e.g. [1]). $\mathcal{ALCH}$ is sufficiently expressive to illustrate the main concepts introduced in this paper. More expressive DLs will be the subject of an extended work. Note that [23,27] considered $\mathcal{ALC}$ only. So, consider three alphabets of symbols, for *concept names* (denoted A), for *role names* (denoted R) and *indi-*

vidual names (denoted a and b) [2]. A *concept* (denoted C or D) of the language $\mathcal{ALCH}$ is built inductively from concept names A, role names R, top concept $\top$ and bottom concept $\bot$, according to the following syntax rule:

$$C, D \longrightarrow C \sqcap D| \text{ (concept conjunction)}$$
$$C \sqcup D| \text{ (concept disjunction)}$$
$$\neg C| \text{ (concept negation)}$$
$$\forall R.C| \text{ (universal quantification)}$$
$$\exists R.C \text{ (existential quantification)} .$$

A *terminology*, $\mathcal{T}$, is a finite set of concept inclusions or role inclusions, called *terminological axioms*, τ, where given two concepts C and D, and two role names R and R', a terminological axiom is an expression of the form $C \sqsubseteq D$ (D subsumes C) or of the form $R \sqsubseteq R'$ (R' subsumes R). We also write $C = D$ (concept definition) as a short hand for $C \sqsubseteq D$ and $D \sqsubseteq C$ (and similarly for role definitions). An *assertion*, α, is an expression of the form $a{:}C$ ("a is an instance of C"), or an expression $(a, b){:}R$ ("(a, b) is an instance of R"). A *Knowledge Base* (KB), $\mathcal{K} = \langle \mathcal{T}, \mathcal{A} \rangle$, is such that $\mathcal{T}$ and $\mathcal{A}$ are finite sets of terminological axioms and assertions, respectively.

An *interpretation* $\mathcal{I}$ is a pair $\mathcal{I} = (\Delta^{\mathcal{I}}, \cdot^{\mathcal{I}})$ consisting of a non empty set $\Delta^{\mathcal{I}}$ (called the *domain*) and of an *interpretation function* $\cdot^{\mathcal{I}}$ mapping individuals into elements of $\Delta^{\mathcal{I}}$ (note that usually the *unique name assumption* [3] is considered, but it does not matter us here), concepts names into subsets of $\Delta^{\mathcal{I}}$, roles names into subsets of $\Delta^{\mathcal{I}} \times \Delta^{\mathcal{I}}$ and satisfies $\top^{\mathcal{I}} = \Delta^{\mathcal{I}}$ and $\bot^{\mathcal{I}} = \emptyset$. The interpretation of complex concepts is defined inductively as usual:

$$(C \sqcap D)^{\mathcal{I}} = C^{\mathcal{I}} \cap D^{\mathcal{I}}$$
$$(C \sqcup D)^{\mathcal{I}} = C^{\mathcal{I}} \cup D^{\mathcal{I}}$$
$$(\neg C)^{\mathcal{I}} = \Delta^{\mathcal{I}} \setminus C^{\mathcal{I}}$$
$$(\forall R.C)^{\mathcal{I}} = \{d \in \Delta^{\mathcal{I}} \mid \forall d'.(d, d') \notin R^{\mathcal{I}} \text{ or } d' \in C^{\mathcal{I}}\}$$
$$(\exists R.C)^{\mathcal{I}} = \{d \in \Delta^{\mathcal{I}} \mid \exists d'.(d, d') \in R^{\mathcal{I}} \text{ and } d' \in C^{\mathcal{I}}\} .$$

A concept C is *satisfiable* iff there is an interpretation $\mathcal{I}$ such that $C^{\mathcal{I}} \neq \emptyset$. Two concepts C and D are *equivalent* (denoted $C \equiv D$) iff $C^{\mathcal{I}} = D^{\mathcal{I}}$, for all interpretations $\mathcal{I}$. An interpretation $\mathcal{I}$ *satisfies* an assertion $a{:}C$ (resp. $(a, b){:}R$) iff $a^{\mathcal{I}} \in C^{\mathcal{I}}$ (resp. $(a^{\mathcal{I}}, b^{\mathcal{I}}) \in R^{\mathcal{I}}$), while $\mathcal{I}$ *satisfies* a terminological axiom $C \sqsubseteq D$ iff $C^{\mathcal{I}} \subseteq D^{\mathcal{I}}$. The satisfiability of role inclusions $R \sqsubseteq R'$ is similar. Furthermore, an interpretation $\mathcal{I}$ *satisfies* (is a *model* of) a terminology $\mathcal{T}$ (resp. a set of assertions $\mathcal{A}$) iff $\mathcal{I}$ satisfies each element in $\mathcal{T}$ (resp. $\mathcal{A}$), while $\mathcal{I}$ *satisfies* (is a *model* of) a KB $\mathcal{K} = \langle \mathcal{T}, \mathcal{A} \rangle$ iff $\mathcal{I}$ satisfies both $\mathcal{T}$ and $\mathcal{A}$. Finally, given a KB $\mathcal{K}$ and an assertion α we say that $\mathcal{K}$ *entails* α, denoted $\mathcal{K} \models \alpha$, iff each model of $\mathcal{K}$ satisfies α.

Example 1. Consider the following simple KB, $\mathcal{K} = \langle \mathcal{T}, \mathcal{A} \rangle$, where

$$\mathcal{T} = \{\texttt{Bird} \sqsubseteq \texttt{Animal}, \texttt{Dog} \sqsubseteq \texttt{Animal}\} , \mathcal{A} = \{\texttt{snoopy:Dog}, \texttt{woodstock:Bird}\} .$$

---

[2] Metavariables may have a subscript or a superscript.
[3] $a^{\mathcal{I}} \neq b^{\mathcal{I}}$, if $a \neq b$.

Consider the query concept Animal, i.e. we are looking for animals. It can easily be shown that both Snoopy and Woodstock are animals, i.e. $\{a \mid \mathcal{K} \models a\text{:Animal}\} = \{\text{snoopy}, \text{woodstock}\}$. □

The next example is slightly more involved.

Example 2. Consider the following KB $\mathcal{K} = \langle \mathcal{T}, \mathcal{A} \rangle$, where

$$\mathcal{T} = \{A = \forall R.\neg B\} \ , \ \mathcal{A} = \{a{:}\forall R.C\} \ .$$

Consider the assertion $\alpha = a{:}A \sqcup \exists R.(B \sqcap C)$. It can be shown that $\mathcal{K} \models \alpha$ holds. In fact, consider a model $\mathcal{I}$ of $\mathcal{K}$. Then either $a^{\mathcal{I}} \in A^{\mathcal{I}}$ or $a^{\mathcal{I}} \notin A^{\mathcal{I}}$. In the former case, $\mathcal{I}$ satisfies α. In the latter case, as $\mathcal{I}$ satisfies $\mathcal{T}$, $a^{\mathcal{I}} \notin (\forall R.\neg B)^{\mathcal{I}}$, i.e. $a^{\mathcal{I}} \in (\exists R.B)^{\mathcal{I}}$ holds. But, $\mathcal{I}$ satisfies $\mathcal{A}$ as well, i.e. $a^{\mathcal{I}} \in (\forall R.C)^{\mathcal{I}}$ and, thus, $a^{\mathcal{I}} \in (\exists R.(B \sqcap C))^{\mathcal{I}}$. Therefore, $\mathcal{I}$ satisfies α, which concludes. □

Finally, note that there are efficient implemented reasoners like, for instance, RACER [4] or FACT [5], which allow to reason in quite more expressive DLs as $\mathcal{ALCH}$.

3   A Quick Look to Fuzzy DLs

We recall here the main notions related to fuzzy DLs, taken from [27]. Worth noting is that we deal with general terminological axioms of the form $C \sqsubseteq D$, while in [23,27] the terminological component is restricted in the form. For convenience, we call the fuzzy extension of $\mathcal{ALCH}$, $\mathfrak{f}\mathcal{ALCH}$. The main idea underlying $\mathfrak{f}\mathcal{ALCH}$ is that an assertion $a{:}C$, rather being interpreted as either true or false, will be mapped into a truth value $c \in [0,1]$. The intended meaning is that c indicates to which extend (how certain it is that) 'a is a C'. Similarly for role names.

Formally, a $\mathfrak{f}$*interpretation* is a pair $\mathcal{I} = (\Delta^{\mathcal{I}}, \cdot^{\mathcal{I}})$, where $\Delta^{\mathcal{I}}$ is the *domain* and $\cdot^{\mathcal{I}}$ is an *interpretation function* mapping

- individuals as for the classical case;
- a concept C into a function $C^{\mathcal{I}}: \Delta^{\mathcal{I}} \to [0,1]$; and
- a role R into a function $R^{\mathcal{I}}: \Delta^{\mathcal{I}} \times \Delta^{\mathcal{I}} \to [0,1]$.

If C is a concept then $C^{\mathcal{I}}$ will naturally be interpreted as the *membership degree function* (f_C in 'fuzzy notation') of the fuzzy concept (set) C w.r.t. $\mathcal{I}$, i.e. if $d \in \Delta^{\mathcal{I}}$ is an object of the domain $\Delta^{\mathcal{I}}$ then $C^{\mathcal{I}}(d)$ gives us the degree of being the object d an element of the fuzzy concept C under the $\mathfrak{f}$interpretation $\mathcal{I}$. Similarly for roles.

The definition of concept *equivalence* is like for $\mathcal{ALCH}$. Two concepts C and D are equivalent iff $C^{\mathcal{I}} = D^{\mathcal{I}}$, for all $\mathfrak{f}$interpretations $\mathcal{I}$. The interpretation

---

[4] http://www.cs.concordia.ca/~haarslev/racer/
[5] http://www.cs.man.ac.uk/~horrocks/FaCT/

function $\cdot^{\mathcal{I}}$ has also to satisfy the following equations: for all $d \in \Delta^{\mathcal{I}}$, $\top^{\mathcal{I}}(d) = 1$, $\bot^{\mathcal{I}}(d) = 0$ and

$$(C \sqcap D)^{\mathcal{I}}(d) = \min(C^{\mathcal{I}}(d), D^{\mathcal{I}}(d))$$
$$(C \sqcup D)^{\mathcal{I}}(d) = \max(C^{\mathcal{I}}(d), D^{\mathcal{I}}(d))$$
$$(\neg C)^{\mathcal{I}}(d) = 1 - C^{\mathcal{I}}(d)$$
$$(\forall R.C)^{\mathcal{I}}(d) = \inf_{d' \in \Delta^{\mathcal{I}}}\{\max(1 - R^{\mathcal{I}}(d, d'), C^{\mathcal{I}}(d'))\}$$
$$(\exists R.C)^{\mathcal{I}}(d) = \sup_{d' \in \Delta^{\mathcal{I}}}\{\min(R^{\mathcal{I}}(d, d'), C^{\mathcal{I}}(d'))\} \ .$$

These equations are the standard interpretation of conjunction, disjunction, negation and quantification, respectively for fuzzy sets [31] (see also [21,29]). Nonetheless, some conditions deserve an explanation. The semantics of $\exists R.C$ is the result of viewing $\exists R.C$ as the open first order formula $\exists y.R(x,y) \wedge \bar{C}(y)$ (where $\bar{C}$ is the translation of C into first-order logic) and $\exists$ is viewed as a disjunction over the elements of the domain. Similarly, the semantics of $\forall R.C$ is related to $\forall y.\neg R(x,y) \vee \bar{C}(y)$, where $\forall$ is viewed as a conjunction over the elements of the domain. As for the classical DLs, dual relationships between concepts hold: e.g. $(C \sqcap D) \equiv \neg(\neg C \sqcup \neg D)$ and $(\forall R.C) \equiv \neg(\exists R.\neg C)$, but $C \sqcap (\neg C \sqcup D) \not\equiv D$.

A $\mathfrak{f}assertion$ (denoted $\mathfrak{f}\alpha$) is an expression of the form $\langle \alpha \geq c_1 \rangle$, $\langle \alpha > c_2 \rangle$, $\langle \alpha' \leq c_2 \rangle$ or $\langle \alpha' < c_1 \rangle$, where α is an $\mathcal{ALCH}$ assertion, $c_1 \in (0, 1]$ and $c_2 \in [0, 1)$, but α' is an $\mathcal{ALCH}$ assertion of the form $a{:}C$ only. For coherence, we do not allow $\mathfrak{f}$assertions of the form $\langle (a, b){:}R \leq c \rangle$ or $\langle (a, b){:}R < c \rangle$ as they relate to 'negated roles', which is not part of classical $\mathcal{ALCH}$. From a semantics point of view, a $\mathfrak{f}$assertion $\langle \alpha \leq c \rangle$ constrains the truth value of α to be less or equal to c (similarly for $\geq, >$ and $<$). So, a $\mathfrak{f}$interpretation $\mathcal{I}$ $satisfies$ $\langle a{:}C \geq c \rangle$ (resp. $\langle (a, b){:}R \geq c \rangle$) iff $C^{\mathcal{I}}(a^{\mathcal{I}}) \geq c$ (resp. $R^{\mathcal{I}}(a^{\mathcal{I}}, b^{\mathcal{I}}) \geq c$). Similarly for $>, \leq$ and $<$. Note that, e.g. $\langle a{:}\neg C \geq c \rangle$ and $\langle a{:}C \leq 1 - c \rangle$ are satisfied by the same set of $\mathfrak{f}$interpretations.

Concerning terminological axioms, a $\mathfrak{f}\mathcal{ALCH}$ terminological axiom is, as for the classical DL $\mathcal{ALCH}$, of the form $C \sqsubseteq D$, where C and D are $\mathcal{ALCH}$ concepts, or of the form $R \sqsubseteq R'$, where R and R' are role names. From a semantics point of view, a $\mathfrak{f}$interpretation $\mathcal{I}$ $satisfies$ $C \sqsubseteq D$ iff for all $d \in \Delta^{\mathcal{I}}, C^{\mathcal{I}}(d) \leq D^{\mathcal{I}}(d)$. Similarly, $\mathfrak{f}$interpretation $\mathcal{I}$ $satisfies$ $R \sqsubseteq R'$ iff for all $\{d, d'\} \subseteq \Delta^{\mathcal{I}}, R^{\mathcal{I}}(d, d') \leq R'^{\mathcal{I}}(d, d')$.

A $\mathfrak{f}Knowledge$ $Base$ (fKB) is pair $\mathfrak{f}\mathcal{K} = \langle \mathcal{T}, \mathcal{A} \rangle$, where $\mathcal{T}$ and $\mathcal{A}$ are finite sets of terminological axioms and $\mathfrak{f}$assertions, respectively. A $\mathfrak{f}$interpretation $\mathcal{I}$ $satisfies$ (is a $model$ of) a terminology $\mathcal{T}$ (resp. a set of $\mathfrak{f}$assertions $\mathcal{A}$) iff $\mathcal{I}$ satisfies each element in $\mathcal{T}$ (resp. $\mathcal{A}$), while $\mathcal{I}$ $satisfies$ (is a $model$ of) a KB $\mathfrak{f}\mathcal{K} = \langle \mathcal{T}, \mathcal{A} \rangle$ iff $\mathcal{I}$ satisfies both $\mathcal{T}$ and $\mathcal{A}$. Given a fKB $\mathfrak{f}\mathcal{K}$, and a $\mathfrak{f}$assertion $\mathfrak{f}\alpha$, we say that $\mathfrak{f}\mathcal{K}$ $entails$ $\mathfrak{f}\alpha$, denoted $\mathfrak{f}\mathcal{K} \models \mathfrak{f}\alpha$, iff each model of $\mathfrak{f}\mathcal{K}$ satisfies $\mathfrak{f}\alpha$. For instance, if $c' > 1 - c$ then

$$\{\langle (a, b){:}R \geq c' \rangle, \langle a{:}\forall R.C \geq c \rangle\} \models \langle b{:}C \geq c \rangle \ . \tag{1}$$

Finally, given $\mathfrak{f}\mathcal{K}$ and an $\mathcal{ALCH}$ assertion α, it is of interest to compute α's best lower and upper truth value bounds. The $greatest$ $lower$ $bound$ of α w.r.t. $\mathfrak{f}\mathcal{K}$ (denoted $glb(\mathfrak{f}\mathcal{K}, \alpha)$) is $glb(\mathfrak{f}\mathcal{K}, \alpha) = \sup\{c \mid \mathfrak{f}\mathcal{K} \models \langle \alpha \geq c \rangle\}$, while the $least$ $upper$

bound of α with respect to $f\mathcal{K}$ (denoted $lub(f\mathcal{K}, \alpha)$ is $lub(f\mathcal{K}, \alpha) = \inf\{c \mid f\mathcal{K} \models \langle \alpha \leq c \rangle\}$, where $\sup \emptyset = 0$ and $\inf \emptyset = 1$. Determining the *lub* and the *glb* is called the *Best Truth Value Bound* (BTVB) problem. Note that

$$lub(\Sigma, a{:}C) = 1 - glb(\Sigma, a{:}\neg C) , \qquad (2)$$

i.e. the *lub* can be determined through the *glb* (and vice-versa). The same reduction to *glb* does not hold for $lub(\Sigma, (a, b){:}R)$ as $(a, b){:}\neg R$ is not an expression of our language. [6] Finally, note that, $\Sigma \models_{\mathcal{L}} \langle \alpha \geq n \rangle$ iff $glb(\Sigma, \alpha) \geq n$, and similarly $\Sigma \models_{\mathcal{L}} \langle \alpha \leq n \rangle$ iff $lub(\Sigma, \alpha) \leq n$ hold. Concerning roles, note that $\Sigma \models_{\mathcal{L}} \langle (a, b){:}R \geq n \rangle$ iff $\langle (a, b){:}R \geq m \rangle \in \Sigma$ with $m \geq n$. Therefore,

$$glb(\Sigma, R(a, b)) = \max\{n \mid \langle R(a, b) \geq n \rangle \in \Sigma\} . \qquad (3)$$

Concerning the entailment problem, it is quite easily verified that the entailment problem can be reduced to the unsatisfiability problem:

$$\langle \mathcal{T}, \mathcal{A} \rangle \models \langle \alpha \geq n \rangle \text{ iff } \langle \mathcal{T}, \mathcal{A} \cup \{\langle \alpha < n \rangle\} \rangle \text{ is not satisfiable } , \qquad (4)$$

$$\langle \mathcal{T}, \mathcal{A} \rangle \models \langle \alpha \leq n \rangle \text{ iff } \langle \mathcal{T}, \mathcal{A} \cup \{\langle \alpha > n \rangle\} \rangle \text{ is not satisfiable } . \qquad (5)$$

In [27] decision procedures for the satisfiability, the entailment and the BTVB problem are given for $f\mathcal{ALCH}$, but with the already discussed restrictions on the form of terminological axioms and terminologies.

Example 3. Similarly to Example 2, consider $f\mathcal{K} = \langle \mathcal{T}, \mathcal{A} \rangle$, where

$$\mathcal{T} = \{A = \forall R.\neg B\} , \mathcal{A} = \{\langle a{:}\forall R.C \geq 0.7 \rangle\} .$$

Consider the assertion $\alpha = a{:}A \sqcup \exists R.(B \sqcap C)$. It can be shown that $glb(f\mathcal{K}, \alpha) = 0.5$ and $lub(f\mathcal{K}, \alpha) = 1$ hold. In fact, for any model $\mathcal{I}$ of $f\mathcal{K}$, we have that

$$(A \sqcup \exists R.(B \sqcap C))^{\mathcal{I}}(a^{\mathcal{I}}) \geq \max(c, \min(0.7, 1 - c)) , \qquad (6)$$

for any $c \in [0, 1]$. Indeed, let $\mathcal{I}$ be a model of $f\mathcal{K}$. Assume that $(A \sqcup \exists R.(B \sqcap C))^{\mathcal{I}}(a^{\mathcal{I}}) = w$. Consider $c \in [0, 1]$. Then either $A^{\mathcal{I}}(a^{\mathcal{I}}) \geq c$ or $A^{\mathcal{I}}(a^{\mathcal{I}}) < c$. In the former case, it follows that $w \geq c$. In the latter case, as $\mathcal{I}$ satisfies $\mathcal{T}$, from $A^{\mathcal{I}}(a^{\mathcal{I}}) < c$ it follows that $(\forall R.\neg B)^{\mathcal{I}}(a^{\mathcal{I}}) < c$. But, $\forall R.\neg B \equiv \neg \exists R.B$ and, thus, $(\exists R.B)^{\mathcal{I}}(a^{\mathcal{I}}) > 1 - c$. Therefore, there is $d \in \Delta^{\mathcal{I}}$ such that $R^{\mathcal{I}}(a^{\mathcal{I}}, d) > 1 - c$ and $B^{\mathcal{I}}(d) > 1 - c$. But, $\mathcal{I}$ satisfies $\mathcal{A}$, i.e. $(\forall R.C)^{\mathcal{I}}(a^{\mathcal{I}}) \geq 0.7$. By definition, this means that $\inf_{d' \in \Delta^{\mathcal{I}}}\{\max(1 - R^{\mathcal{I}}(a^{\mathcal{I}}, d'), C^{\mathcal{I}}(d'))\} \geq 0.7$ and, in particular, for $d' = d$, $\max(1 - R^{\mathcal{I}}(a^{\mathcal{I}}, d), C^{\mathcal{I}}(d)) \geq 0.7$ holds. Therefore, $1 - R^{\mathcal{I}}(a^{\mathcal{I}}, d) < 0.7$ (i.e., $R^{\mathcal{I}}(a^{\mathcal{I}}, d) > 0.3$) implies $C^{\mathcal{I}}(d)) \geq 0.7$. As a consequence, from $R^{\mathcal{I}}(a^{\mathcal{I}}, d) > 1 - c$, for $c \leq 0.7$ it follows that $C^{\mathcal{I}}(d) \geq 0.7$ (see also Equation 1). Therefore, $(\exists R.(B \sqcap C))^{\mathcal{I}}(a^{\mathcal{I}}) \geq \min(0.7, 1 - c)$ and, thus, $w \geq \max(c, \min(0.7, 1 - c))$, which proofs (6). Finally, as for any $c \in [0, 1]$, $\max(c, \min(0.7, 1 - c)) \geq 0.5$ and there is no $c' > 0.5$ such that for all $c \in [0, 1]$, $\max(c, \min(0.7, 1 - c)) \geq c'$, by (6), $glb(f\mathcal{K}, \alpha) = 0.5$ follows. The proof of $lub(f\mathcal{K}, \alpha) = 1$ is easy. $\square$

---

[6] Of course, $lub(\Sigma, (a, b){:}R) = 1 - glb(\Sigma, (a, b){:}\neg R)$ holds, where $(\neg R)^{\mathcal{I}}(d, d') = 1 - R^{\mathcal{I}}(d, d')$.

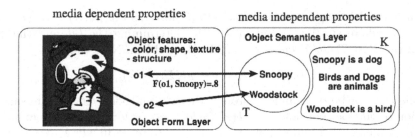

Fig. 1. LMIR model layers and objects

In the following, we show the application of f$\mathcal{ALCH}$ to LMIR, which, among others, shows how fassertions are generated automatically.

Logic-based multimedia information retrieval. Let us first roughly present (parts of) the LMIR model of [23,26]. In doing this, we rely on Figure 1. The model has two layers addressing the multidimensional aspect of multimedia objects $o \in \mathbb{O}$ (e.g. objects o1 and o2 in Figure 1): that is, their *form* and their *semantics* (or *meaning*). The form of a multimedia object is a collective name for all its *media dependent*, typically automatically extracted features, like text index term weights (object of type text), colour distribution, shape, texture, spatial relationships (object of type image), mosaiced video-frame sequences and time relationships (object of type video). On the other hand, the semantics (or meaning) of a multimedia object is a collective name for those features that pertain to the slice of the real world being *represented*, which exists independently of the existence of a object referring to it. Unlike form, the semantics of a multimedia object is thus *media independent* (typically, constructed manually perhaps with the assistance of some automatic tool).

Therefore, we have two layers, the *object form layer* and the *object semantics layer*. The former represents media dependent features of the objects, while the latter describes the semantic properties of the slice of world the objects are about. The semantic entities (e.g., Snoopy, Woodstock), which objects can be about are called *semantic index terms* ($t \in \mathbb{T}$). The mapping of objects $o \in \mathbb{O}$ to semantic entities $t \in \mathbb{T}$ (e.g., "object o1 is about Snoopy") is called *semantic annotation*. According to the fuzzy information retrieval model [6,16,19,24], semantic annotation can be formalized as a membership function $F \colon \mathbb{O} \times \mathbb{T} \to [0,1]$ describing the *correlation* between multimedia objects and semantic index terms. The value $F(o,t)$ indicates to which degree the multimedia object o deals with the semantic index term t. The meaning of a semantic index term t may in this context be represented as a fuzzy subset of multimedia objects in $\mathbb{O}$, $m(t)$, with the quantitative measure of aboutness being the values of function F for a given semantic index term t, i.e. $m(t) = \{\langle o, f_t(o)\rangle \colon o \in \mathbb{O}\}$, in which $f_t(o) = F(o,t)$. $m(t)$ is the meaning of term t. The function F acts as the membership function of $m(t)$. Depending on the context, the function F may be computed automatically (e.g., for text we may have [8], for images we may have an automated image annotation (classification) tool, as e.g. [9]). Note that the function F will be a source for fassertions of the form $\langle(\mathsf{o},\mathsf{t}){:}\mathsf{F} \geq F(o,t)\rangle$ (see [23]). In practice, the scenario depicted in Figure 1 may roughly be represented in $\mathsf{f}\mathcal{ALCH}$ with the following knowledge base $\mathsf{f}\mathcal{K} = \langle\mathcal{T},\mathcal{A}\rangle$:

$$\mathcal{T} = \{\mathtt{Bird} \sqsubseteq \mathtt{Animal},\mathtt{Dog} \sqsubseteq \mathtt{Animal},\mathtt{Object} \sqcap \mathtt{IndexTerm} \sqsubseteq \bot,\mathtt{F} = \mathtt{IsAbout}\}$$
$$\mathcal{A} = \{\langle\mathtt{snoopy{:}Dog} \geq 1\rangle, \langle\mathtt{woodstock{:}Bird} \geq 1\rangle,$$
$$\langle(\mathtt{o1},\mathtt{snoopy}){:}\mathtt{F} \geq 0.8\rangle, \langle(\mathtt{o2},\mathtt{woodstock}){:}\mathtt{F} \geq 0.7\rangle\} \ .$$

Now, consider the query concept $Q = \mathtt{Object}.\exists\mathtt{IsAbout}.\mathtt{Animal}$, i.e. retrieve all objects about animals. Then it is easily verified that we retrieve both objects, but with different *Retrieval Status Values* [2], which indicate their relatedness to the query ($\mathcal{K} \models \langle\mathtt{snoopy{:}}Q \geq 0.8\rangle$, $\mathcal{K} \models \langle\mathtt{woodstock{:}}Q \geq 0.7\rangle$).

4 Mapping $\mathsf{f}\mathcal{ALCH}$ into $\mathcal{ALCH}$

Our aim is to map $\mathsf{f}\mathcal{ALCH}$ knowledge bases into satisfiability and entailment preserving classical $\mathcal{ALCH}$ knowledge bases. An immediate consequence is then that (i) we have reasoning procedures for $\mathsf{f}\mathcal{ALCH}$ with general terminological axioms, which are still unknown; and (ii) we can rely on already implemented reasoners to reason in $\mathsf{f}\mathcal{ALCH}$.

Before we are going to formally present the mapping, we first illustrate the basic idea we rely on. Our mapping relies on ideas presented in [3,4] for so-called regular multi-valued logics.

Assume we have a fKB, $\mathsf{f}\mathcal{K} = \langle\emptyset,\mathcal{A}\rangle$, where $\mathcal{A} = \{\mathsf{f}\alpha_1,\mathsf{f}\alpha_2,\mathsf{f}\alpha_3,\mathsf{f}\alpha_4\}$ and $\mathsf{f}\alpha_1 = \langle a{:}A \geq 0.4\rangle$, $\mathsf{f}\alpha_2 = \langle a{:}A \leq 0.7\rangle$, $\mathsf{f}\alpha_3 = \langle a{:}B \leq 0.2\rangle$, $\mathsf{f}\alpha_4 = \langle b{:}B \leq 0.1\rangle$. Let us introduce some new concepts, namely $A_{\geq 0.4}$, $A_{\leq 0.7}, B_{\leq 0.2}$ and $B_{\leq 0.1}$. Informally, the concept $A_{\geq 0.4}$ represents the set of individuals, which are instance of A with degree $c \geq 0.4$, while $A_{\leq 0.7}$ represents the set of individuals, which are instance of A with degree $c \leq 0.7$. Similarly, for the other concepts. Of course, we have to consider also the relationships among the introduced concepts. For instance, we need the terminological axiom $B_{\leq 0.1} \sqsubseteq B_{\leq 0.2}$. This axiom dictates that if a truth value is ≤ 0.1 then it is also ≤ 0.2. We may represent, thus, the fassertion $\mathsf{f}\alpha_1$ with the $\mathcal{ALCH}$ assertion $a{:}A_{\geq 0.4}$, indicating that a is an instance of A with a degree ≥ 0.4. Similarly, $\mathsf{f}\alpha_2$ may be mapped into $a{:}A_{\geq 0.7}$, $\mathsf{f}\alpha_3$ may be mapped into $a{:}B_{\geq 0.2}$, while $\mathsf{f}\alpha_4$ may be mapped into $b{:}B_{\geq 0.1}$. From a semantics point of view, let us consider the so-called *canonical model* [1] $\mathcal{I}$ of the resulting classical $\mathcal{ALCH}$ KB, i.e.

$$\mathcal{I} = \{A_{\geq 0.4}(a), A_{\leq 0.7}(a), B_{\leq 0.2}(a), B_{\leq 0.1}(b), B_{\leq 0.2}(b)\} \ .$$

It is then easily verified that, from $\mathcal{I}$ a model $\mathcal{I}'$ of $\mathsf{f}\mathcal{K}$ can easily be built and, vice-versa, if $\mathcal{I}'$ is a model of $\mathsf{f}\mathcal{K}$, then a model like $\mathcal{I}$ above can be obtained as well. Therefore, our transformation of $\mathsf{f}\mathcal{K}$ into an $\mathcal{ALCH}$ KB, at least for the above case, is satisfiability preserving. This illustrates our basic idea.

Let us now proceed formally. Consider a fKB $\mathsf{f}\mathcal{K} = \langle\mathcal{T},\mathcal{A}\rangle$. Let $\mathcal{A}^{\mathsf{f}\mathcal{K}}$ and $\mathcal{R}^{\mathsf{f}\mathcal{K}}$ be the set of concept names and concept roles occurring in $\mathsf{f}\mathcal{K}$. Of course, both $|\mathcal{A}^{\mathsf{f}\mathcal{K}}|$ and $|\mathcal{R}^{\mathsf{f}\mathcal{K}}|$ are linearly bounded by $|\mathsf{f}\mathcal{K}|$. Consider

$$X^{f\mathcal{K}} = \{0, 0.5, 1\} \cup \{c \mid \langle \alpha \geq c \rangle \in \mathcal{A}\}$$
$$\cup \{c \mid \langle \alpha > c \rangle \in \mathcal{A}\}$$
$$\cup \{1 - c \mid \langle \alpha \leq c \rangle \in \mathcal{A}\}$$
$$\cup \{1 - c \mid \langle \alpha < c \rangle \in \mathcal{A}\} \tag{7}$$

from which we define

$$N^{f\mathcal{K}} = X^{f\mathcal{K}} \cup \{1 - c \mid c \in X^{f\mathcal{K}}\} \ . \tag{8}$$

Note that $|N^{f\mathcal{K}}|$ is linearly bounded by $|\mathcal{A}|$. Essentially, with $N^{f\mathcal{K}}$ we collect from $f\mathcal{K}$ all the relevant numbers we require for the transformation. Without loss of generality, we may assume that $N^{f\mathcal{K}} = \{c_1, \ldots, c_{|N^{f\mathcal{K}}|}\}$ and $c_i < c_{i+1}$, for $1 \leq i \leq |N^{f\mathcal{K}}| - 1$. Note that $c_1 = 0$ and $c_{|N^{f\mathcal{K}}|} = 1$.

For each $c \in N^{f\mathcal{K}}$, for each relation $\bowtie \in \{\geq, >, \leq, <\}$, for each $A \in \mathcal{A}^{f\mathcal{K}}$ and for each $R \in \mathcal{R}^{f\mathcal{K}}$, consider a new concept name $A_{\bowtie c}$ and new role names $R_{\geq c}$ and $R_{>c}$, but we do not consider $A_{<0}, A_{>1}$ and $R_{>1}$ (which are not needed). There are as many as $(4|N^{f\mathcal{K}}| - 2)|\mathcal{A}^{f\mathcal{K}}|$ new concept names and $(2|N^{f\mathcal{K}}| - 1)|\mathcal{R}^{f\mathcal{K}}|$ new role names. Note that we do not require new role names $R_{\leq c}$ and $R_{<c}$, as e.g. expressions of the form $\langle (a, b):R \leq c \rangle$ are not part of our language.

Let $\mathcal{T}(N^{f\mathcal{K}})$ be the following terminology relating the newly introduced concept names and role names: $\mathcal{T}(N^{f\mathcal{K}})$ is the smallest terminology such that for each $1 \leq i \leq |N^{f\mathcal{K}}| - 1$, for each $2 \leq j \leq |N^{f\mathcal{K}}|$, for each $A \in \mathcal{A}^{f\mathcal{K}}$ and for each $R \in \mathcal{R}^{f\mathcal{K}}$, $\mathcal{T}(N^{f\mathcal{K}})$ contains

$$\begin{array}{cccc}
A_{\geq c_{i+1}} \sqsubseteq A_{>c_i} & , & A_{>c_i} \sqsubseteq A_{\geq c_i} & \\
A_{<c_j} \sqsubseteq A_{\leq c_j} & , & A_{\leq c_i} \sqsubseteq A_{<c_{i+1}} & \\
A_{\geq c_j} \sqcap A_{<c_j} \sqsubseteq \bot & , & A_{>c_i} \sqcap A_{\leq c_i} \sqsubseteq \bot & \\
\top \sqsubseteq A_{\geq c_j} \sqcup A_{<c_j} \ , & & \top \sqsubseteq A_{>c_i} \sqcup A_{\leq c_i} \ . &
\end{array} \tag{9}$$

The first group reflects the $\geq, <, \leq, >$ ordering among the newly introduced concepts, while the second group identifies 'disjointness' conditions. For instance, among these terminological axioms we may have $A_{\geq 0.4} \sqcap A_{<0.4} \sqsubseteq \bot$ indicating that it cannot be that an individual a is an instance of the concept name A both with degree ≥ 0.4 and degree < 0.4. The last group establishes the complimentarily relationships among the new concepts, e.g. $A_{\geq 0.4} \sqcup A_{<0.4} \equiv \top$. Note that $\mathcal{T}(N^{f\mathcal{K}})$ contains $8|\mathcal{A}^{f\mathcal{K}}|(|N^{f\mathcal{K}}| - 1)$ terminological axioms involving the newly introduced concepts names.

The terminological axioms in $\mathcal{T}(N^{f\mathcal{K}})$ relating the newly introduced role names are quite similar to the above axioms:

$$R_{\geq c_{i+1}} \sqsubseteq R_{>c_i} \ , \ R_{>c_i} \sqsubseteq R_{\geq c_i} \ . \tag{10}$$

Note that $\mathcal{T}(N^{f\mathcal{K}})$ contains $2|\mathcal{R}^{f\mathcal{K}}|(|N^{f\mathcal{K}}| - 1)$ terminological axioms involving the newly introduced role names. Please note also that in case we would like to allow expressions of the form $\langle(a,b){:}R \leq c\rangle$ and $\langle(a,b){:}R < c\rangle$, then we need new role names $R_{\leq c}$ and $R_{<c}$ (excluding $R_{<0}$), and terminological axioms $R_{<c_j} \sqsubseteq R_{\leq c_j}$, $R_{\leq c_i} \sqsubseteq R_{<c_{i+1}}$, $R_{\geq c_j} \sqcap R_{<c_j} \sqsubseteq \perp^r$, $R_{>c_i} \sqcap R_{\leq c_i} \sqsubseteq \perp^r$, $\top^r \sqsubseteq R_{\geq c_j} \sqcup R_{<c_j}$ and $\top^r \sqsubseteq R_{>c_i} \sqcup R_{\leq c_i}$. In particular, note that 'role conjunction', 'role disjunction' and a 'bottom role' and a 'top role' are needed.

Example 4. Consider Example 3. Then $N^{\mathfrak{f}\mathcal{K}}$ is $N^{\mathfrak{f}\mathcal{K}} = \{0, 0.3, 0.5, 0.7, 1\}$, while $A^{\mathfrak{f}\mathcal{K}} = \{A, B, C\}$ and $\mathcal{R}^{\mathfrak{f}\mathcal{K}} = \{R\}$. Below, we provide an excerpt of the terminology $\mathcal{T}(N^{\mathfrak{f}\mathcal{K}})$:

$$\begin{aligned}
\mathcal{T}(N^{\mathfrak{f}\mathcal{K}}) &= \{A_{\geq 1} \sqsubseteq A_{>0.7}, A_{\geq 0.7} \sqsubseteq A_{>0.5}, \ldots\} \\
&\cup \{\ldots, A_{\geq 0.3} \sqcap A_{<0.3} \sqsubseteq \perp, \ldots\} \\
&\cup \{\ldots, \top \sqsubseteq A_{\geq 0.3} \sqcup A_{<0.3}, \ldots\} \\
&\cup \{\ldots, B_{\geq 1} \sqsubseteq B_{>0.7}, \ldots\} \\
&\cup \{\ldots, R_{\geq 1} \sqsubseteq R_{>0.7}, \ldots\} \;.
\end{aligned}$$

$\square$

This concludes the management of the newly introduced concept names and role names.

We proceed now with the mapping of the fassertions in a fKB into $\mathcal{ALCH}$ assertions. We define two mappings σ and ρ, defined as follows. Let $\mathfrak{f}\alpha$ be a fassertion. Then σ maps a fassertion into a classical $\mathcal{ALCH}$ assertion, using ρ, as follows. In the following, we assume that $c \in [0,1]$ and $\bowtie \in \{\geq, >, \leq, <\}$.

$$\sigma(\mathfrak{f}\alpha) = \begin{cases} a{:}\rho(C, \bowtie c) & \text{if } \mathfrak{f}\alpha = \langle a{:}C \bowtie c\rangle \\ (a,b){:}\rho(R, \bowtie c) & \text{if } \mathfrak{f}\alpha = \langle(a,b){:}R \bowtie c\rangle \;. \end{cases}$$

We extend σ to a set of fassertions $\mathcal{A}$ point-wise, i.e. $\sigma(\mathcal{A}) = \{\sigma(\mathfrak{f}\alpha)|\mathfrak{f}\alpha \in \mathcal{A}\}$.

The mapping ρ encodes the idea we have previously presented in a simplified example and is inductively defined on the structure of concepts and roles. For roles, we have simply

$$\rho(R, \bowtie c) = R_{\bowtie c} \;.$$

So, for instance the fassertion $\langle(a,b){:}R \geq c\rangle$ is mapped into the $\mathcal{ALCH}$ assertion $(a,b){:}R_{\geq c}$. Concerning concepts, we have the following inductive definitions: for $\top$

$$\rho(\top, \bowtie c) = \begin{cases} \top & \text{if } \bowtie c = \geq c \\ \top & \text{if } \bowtie c = > c, c < 1 \\ \perp & \text{if } \bowtie c = > 1 \\ \top & \text{if } \bowtie c = \leq 1 \\ \perp & \text{if } \bowtie c = \leq c, c < 1 \\ \perp & \text{if } \bowtie c = < c \;. \end{cases}$$

For $\perp$,

$$\rho(\perp, \bowtie c) = \begin{cases} \top & \text{if } \bowtie c = \geq 0 \\ \perp & \text{if } \bowtie c = \geq c, c > 0 \\ \perp & \text{if } \bowtie c = > c \\ \top & \text{if } \bowtie c = \leq c \\ \top & \text{if } \bowtie c = < c, c > 0 \\ \perp & \text{if } \bowtie c = < 0 \;. \end{cases}$$

For concept name A,

$$\rho(A, \bowtie c) = A_{\bowtie c} \ .$$

For concept conjunction $C \sqcap D$,

$$\rho(C \sqcap D, \bowtie c) = \begin{cases} \rho(C, \bowtie c) \sqcap \rho(D, \bowtie c) & \text{if } \bowtie \in \{\geq, >\} \\ \rho(C, \bowtie c) \sqcup \rho(D, \bowtie c) & \text{if } \bowtie \in \{\leq, <\} \ . \end{cases}$$

For concept disjunction $C \sqcup D$,

$$\rho(C \sqcup D, \bowtie c) = \begin{cases} \rho(C, \bowtie c) \sqcup \rho(D, \bowtie c) & \text{if } \bowtie \in \{\geq, >\} \\ \rho(C, \bowtie c) \sqcap \rho(D, \bowtie c) & \text{if } \bowtie \in \{\leq, <\} \ . \end{cases}$$

For concept negation $\neg C$,

$$\rho(\neg C, \bowtie c) = \rho(C, \neg\bowtie 1 - c) \ .$$

where $\neg \geq \ = \ \leq$, $\neg < \ = \ >$, $\neg \leq \ = \ \geq$ and $\neg < \ = \ >$. For instance, the fassertion $\langle a : \neg C \geq c \rangle$ is mapped into the $\mathcal{ALCH}$ assertion $a : C_{\leq 1-c}$.

For existential quantification $\exists R.C$,

$$\rho(\exists R.C, \bowtie c) = \begin{cases} \exists \rho(R, \bowtie c).\rho(C, \bowtie c) & \text{if } \bowtie \in \{\geq, >\} \\ \forall \rho(R, -\bowtie c).\rho(C, \bowtie c) & \text{if } \bowtie \in \{\leq, <\} \ . \end{cases}$$

where $- \leq \ = \ >$ and $- < \ = \ \geq$. For instance, the fassertion $\langle a : \exists R.C \geq c \rangle$ is mapped into the $\mathcal{ALCH}$ assertion $a : \exists R_{\geq c}.C_{\geq c}$, while $\langle a : \exists R.C \leq c \rangle$ is mapped into $a : \forall R_{>c}.C_{\leq c}$.

Finally, for universal quantification $\forall R.C$,

$$\rho(\forall R.C, \bowtie c) = \begin{cases} \forall \rho(R, +\bowtie 1 - c).\rho(C, \bowtie c) & \text{if } \bowtie \in \{\geq, >\} \\ \exists \rho(R, \neg\bowtie 1 - c).\rho(C, \bowtie c) & \text{if } \bowtie \in \{\leq, <\} \ . \end{cases}$$

where $+ \geq \ = \ >$ and $+ > \ = \ \geq$. For instance, the fassertion $\langle a : \forall R.C \geq 0.7 \rangle$ in Example 3 is mapped into the $\mathcal{ALCH}$ assertion $a : \forall R_{>0.3}.C_{\geq 0.7}$, while $\langle a : \forall R.C \leq c \rangle$ is mapped into $a : \exists R_{\geq 1-c}.C_{\leq c}$.

It is easily verified that for a set of fassertions $\mathcal{A}$, $|\sigma(\mathcal{A})|$ is linearly bounded by $|\mathcal{A}|$.

We conclude with the reduction of a terminological axiom τ in a terminology $\mathcal{T}$ of a fKB $f\mathcal{K} = \langle \mathcal{T}, \mathcal{A} \rangle$ into a $\mathcal{ALCH}$ terminology, $\kappa(f\mathcal{K}, \tau)$. Note that a terminological axiom in $f\mathcal{ALCH}$ is reduced into a *set* of $\mathcal{ALCH}$ terminological axioms. As for σ, we extend κ to a terminology $\mathcal{T}$ point-wise, i.e. $\kappa(f\mathcal{K}, \mathcal{T}) = \bigcup_{\tau \in \mathcal{T}} \kappa(f\mathcal{K}, \tau)$. $\kappa(f\mathcal{K}, \tau)$ is defined as follows. For a concept specialization $C \sqsubseteq D$,

$$\kappa(C \sqsubseteq D) = \bigcup_{c \in N^{f\mathcal{K}}, \bowtie \in \{\geq, >\}} \{\rho(C, \bowtie c) \sqsubseteq \rho(D, \bowtie c)\}$$
$$\bigcup_{c \in N^{f\mathcal{K}}, \bowtie \in \{\leq, <\}} \{\rho(D, \bowtie c) \sqsubseteq \rho(C, \bowtie c)\} \ .$$

For instance, by relying on the fKB $f\mathcal{K}$ in Example 3, it can be verified that $\kappa(f\mathcal{K}, \mathcal{T})$ contains the $\mathcal{ALCH}$ terminological axioms (e.g. for $c = 0.3$) $A_{\geq 0.3} \sqsubseteq \forall R_{>0.7}.B_{\leq 0.7}$ and $\exists R_{\geq 0.7}.B_{\geq 0.7} \sqsubseteq A_{\leq 0.3}$.

For a role specialization $R \sqsubseteq R'$,

$$\kappa(R \sqsubseteq R') = \bigcup_{c \in N^{fK}, \bowtie \in \{\geq, >\}} \{\rho(R, \bowtie c) \sqsubseteq \rho(R', \bowtie c)\} \ .$$

Note that $|\kappa(fK, \mathcal{T})|$ contains at most $6|\mathcal{T}||N^{fK}|$ terminological axioms.

We have now all the ingredients to complete the reduction of a fKB into an $\mathcal{ALCH}$ KB. Let $fK = \langle \mathcal{T}, \mathcal{A} \rangle$ be fKB. The *reduction* of fK into an $\mathcal{ALCH}$ KB, denoted $\mathcal{K}(fK)$, is defined as

$$\mathcal{K}(fK) = \langle \mathcal{T}(N^{fK}) \cup \kappa(fK, \mathcal{T}), \sigma(\mathcal{A}) \rangle \ .$$

Therefore, $|\mathcal{K}(fK)|$ is $O(|fK|^2)$, i.e. the transformation of a fKB into a classical KB is quadratic in complexity.

Example 5. Consider the fKB of Example 3. We have already shown an excerpt of its reduction into $\mathcal{ALCH}$ during this section. Due to space limitations, the whole reduction of fK cannot be represented in this paper. However, we have seen that $fK \models \langle \alpha \geq 0.5 \rangle$, which means that the fKB $fK' = \langle \mathcal{T}, \mathcal{A} \cup \{\langle \alpha < 0.5 \rangle\} \rangle$ is not satisfiable. Let us verify that indeed our reduction is satisfiability preserving, by verifying that $\mathcal{K}(fK')$ is not satisfiable as well. First, let us note that $\sigma(\langle \alpha < 0.5 \rangle)$ is the assertion

$$\sigma(\langle \alpha < 0.5 \rangle) = a{:}A_{<0.5} \sqcap \forall R_{\geq 0.5}.(B_{<0.5} \sqcup C_{<0.5}) \ . \tag{11}$$

We proceed similarly as for Example 3. We show that any model $\mathcal{I}$ satisfying $\mathcal{K}(fK')$, where (11) has been removed, does not satisfy (11). Therefore, there cannot be any model of $\mathcal{K}(fK')$. Indeed, as $A_{\geq 0.5} \sqcap A_{<0.5} \sqsubseteq \bot$ and $\top \sqsubseteq A_{\geq 0.5} \sqcup A_{<0.5}$ occur in the terminology of $\mathcal{K}(fK')$, we have that either $a^{\mathcal{I}}$ is an instance of $(A_{\geq 0.5})^{\mathcal{I}}$ or $a^{\mathcal{I}}$ is an instance of $(A_{<0.5})^{\mathcal{I}}$. In the former case, $\mathcal{I}$ does not satisfy (11). In the latter case, we note that $\forall R.\neg B \sqsubseteq A$ belongs to $\mathcal{T}$ and, thus, $\rho(A, < 0.5) \sqsubseteq \rho(\forall R.\neg B, < 0.5)$, i.e. $A_{<0.5} \sqsubseteq \exists R_{>0.5}.B_{>0.5}$), belongs to the terminology of $\mathcal{K}(fK')$. Therefore, as $a^{\mathcal{I}}$ is an instance of $(A_{<0.5})^{\mathcal{I}}$, $a^{\mathcal{I}}$ has an $(R_{>0.5})^{\mathcal{I}}$ successor d which is an instance of $(B_{>0.5})^{\mathcal{I}}$. But then, as $\langle a{:}\forall R.C \geq 0.7 \rangle$ occurs in fK and, thus, $a{:}\forall R_{>0.3}.C_{\geq 0.7}$ occurs in $\mathcal{K}(fK')$, and $R_{>0.5} \sqsubseteq R_{>0.3}$ is axiom of $\mathcal{K}(fK')$, it follows that d is also an instance of $(C_{\geq 0.7})^{\mathcal{I}}$. Now, it can easily verified that $a^{\mathcal{I}}$ cannot be an instance of $(\forall R_{\geq 0.5}.(B_{<0.5} \sqcup C_{<0.5}))^{\mathcal{I}}$ as $a^{\mathcal{I}}$ has an $(R_{\geq 0.5})^{\mathcal{I}}$ successor d $((R_{>0.5})^{\mathcal{I}} \sqsubseteq (R_{\geq 0.5})^{\mathcal{I}})$, which is neither an instance of $(B_{<0.5})^{\mathcal{I}}$ $((B_{<0.5})^{\mathcal{I}} \cap (B_{>0.5})^{\mathcal{I}} = \emptyset)$ nor of $(C_{<0.5})^{\mathcal{I}}$ $((C_{<0.5})^{\mathcal{I}} \cap (C_{\geq 0.7})^{\mathcal{I}} = \emptyset)$. Therefore, $\mathcal{I}$ does not satisfy (11).   □

The following satisfiability preserving reduction theorem can be shown.

Theorem 1. *Let fK be fKB. Then fK is satisfiable iff the $\mathcal{ALCH}$ KB $\mathcal{K}(fK)$ is satisfiable.*

Theorem 1, together with Equations (4) and (5), gives us also the possibility to reduce the entailment problem in $f\mathcal{ALCH}$, to an entailment problem in $\mathcal{ALCH}$.

Finally, concerning the BTVB problem, Equation (3) solves straightforwardly the case for 'role assertions'. On the other hand, for assertions of the form $a{:}C$, we have to solve the case of the glb only, as from it the lub can derived (see Equation 2). In [27] it has been shown that $glb(\mathfrak{f}\mathcal{K}, a{:}C) \in N^{\mathfrak{f}\mathcal{K}}$ and it can be verified that this holds in $\mathfrak{f}\mathcal{ALCH}$ as well. Therefore, by a binary search on $N^{\mathfrak{f}\mathcal{K}}$, the value of $glb(\mathfrak{f}\mathcal{K}, \alpha)$ can be determined in at most $\log |N^{\mathfrak{f}\mathcal{K}}|$ entailment tests in $\mathfrak{f}\mathcal{ALCH}$ and, thus, entailment tests in $\mathcal{ALCH}$. Therefore, the BTVB problem can be reduced to $\mathcal{ALCH}$ as well.

5   Conclusions

We have presented a reasoning preserving transformation of $\mathfrak{f}\mathcal{ALCH}$ into classical $\mathcal{ALCH}$, where general terminological axioms are allowed. This gives us immediately a new method to reason in $\mathfrak{f}\mathcal{ALCH}$ by means of already existing DL systems and its use in the context of logic-based multimedia information retrieval and, more generally, in the Semantic Web.

Our primary line of future work consists in exploring to which extent the translation technique can be applied to more expressive DLs than $\mathfrak{f}\mathcal{ALCH}$ and contexts where the "truth space" is more general than $[0, 1]$, as, for instance, in [28].

References

1. F. Baader, D. Calvanese, D. McGuinness, D. Nardi, and P. F. Patel-Schneider, editors. *The Description Logic Handbook: Theory, Implementation, and Applications.* Cambridge University Press, 2003.
2. R. A. Baeza-Yates, R. Baeza-Yates, and B. Ribeiro-Neto. *Modern Information Retrieval.* Addison-Wesley Longman Publishing Co., Inc., 1999.
3. B. Beckert, R. Hähnle, and F. Manyá. Transformations between signed and classical clause logic. In *ISMVL*, pages 248–255, 1999.
4. R. Bejar, R. Hahnle, and F. Manyá. A modular reduction of regular logic to classical logic. In *ISMVL*, pages 221–226, 2001.
5. T. Berners-Lee, J. Hendler, and O. Lassila. The semantic web. *The Scientific American*, 284(5):34–43, 2001.
6. G. Bordogna, P Carrara, and G. Pasi. Query term weights as constraints in fuzzy information retrieval. *Information Processing and Management*, 27(1):15–26, 1991.
7. R. M. da Silva, A. E. C. Pereira, and M. A. Netto. A system of knowledge representation based on formulae of predicate calculus whose variables are annotated by expressions of a fuzzy terminological logic. In *IPMU*, LNCS 945, Springer-Verlag, 1994.
8. S. Dill, N. Eiron, D. Gibson, D. Gruhl, R. Guha, A. Jhingran, T. Kanungo, S. Rajagopalan, A. Tomkins, J.A. Tomlin, and J.Y. Zien. SemTag: and Seeker: Bootstrapping the semantic web via automated semantic annotation. In *ACM WWW*, Budapest, Hungary, 2003.
9. Th. Gevers and A.W.M. Smeulders. Content-based image retrieval: An overview. In G. Medioni and S. B. Kang, editors, *Emerging Topics in Computer Vision*. Prentice Hall, 2004.

10. T. R. Giugno and T. Lukasiewicz. P-SHOQ(D): A probabilistic extension of SHOQ(D) for probabilistic ontologies in the semantic web. In *JELIA*, LNAI 2424, Springer-Verlag, 2002.
11. J. Heinsohn. Probabilistic description logics. In *Proc. of the 10th Conference on Uncertainty in Artificial Intelligence*, pages 311–318, 1994.
12. S. Hölldobler, T. D. Khang, and H.-P. Störr. A fuzzy description logic with hedges as concept modifiers. In Nguyen Hoang Phuong, Hung T. Nguyen, Nguyen Cat Ho, and Pratit Santiprabhob, editors, *Proceedings InTech/VJFuzzy'2002*, pages 25–34, Hanoi, Vietnam, 2002. Institute of Information Technology, Vietnam Center for Natural Science and Technology, Science and Technics Publishing House, Hanoi, Vietnam.
13. B. Hollunder. An alternative proof method for possibilistic logic and its application to terminological logics. In *10th Conference on Uncertainty in Artificial Intelligence*, pages 327–335, 1994. Morgan Kaufmann.
14. I. Horrocks, P. F. Patel-Schneider, and F. van Harmelen. From SHIQ and RDF to OWL: The making of a web ontology language. *Journal of Web Semantics*, 1(1):7–26, 2003.
15. M. Jäger. Probabilistic reasoning in terminological logics. In *Proceedings of KR-94, 5-th International Conference on Principles of Knowledge Representation and Reasoning*, pages 305–316, 1994.
16. E.E. Kerre, R.B. Zenner, and R.M. De Caluwe. The use of fuzzy set theory in information retrieval and databases: a survey. *Journal of the American Society for Information Science*, 37(5):341–345, 1986.
17. M. Kifer and V. S. Subrahmanian. Theory of generalized annotated logic programming and its applications. *Journal of Logic Programming*, 12:335–367, 1992.
18. D. Koller, A. Levy, and A. Pfeffer. P-CLASSIC: A tractable probabilistic description logic. In *Proc. of the 14th Nat. Conf. on Artificial Intelligence (AAAI-97)*, pages 390–397, 1997.
19. D. H. Kraft and D. Buel. Fuzzy sets and generalised boolean retrieval systems. *Int. J. Man-Machine Studies*, 19:45–56, 1983.
20. L. V.S. Lakshmanan and N. Shiri. A parametric approach to deductive databases with uncertainty. *IEEE Transactions on Knowledge and Data Engineering*, 13(4):554–570, 2001.
21. R. C. T. Lee. Fuzzy logic and the resolution principle. *Journal of the ACM*, 19(1):109–119, January 1972.
22. C. Lutz, F. Wolter, and M. Zakharyaschev. A tableau algorithm for reasoning about concepts and similarity. In *TABLEAUX*, LNAI 2796, Springer Verlag, 2003.
23. C. Meghini, F. Sebastiani, and U. Straccia. A model of multimedia information retrieval. *Journal of the ACM*, 48(5):909–970, 2001.
24. C.V. Negoita and P. Flondor. On fuzziness in information retrieval. *Int. J. Man-Machine Studies*, 8:711–716, 1976.
25. F. Sebastiani. A probabilistic terminological logic for modelling information retrieval. In *Proc. of SIGIR-94, 17th ACM International Conference on Research and Development in Information Retrieval*, pages 122–130, Dublin, IRL, 1994. Published by Springer Verlag, Heidelberg, FRG.
26. U. Straccia. A framework for the retrieval of multimedia objects based on four-valued fuzzy description logics. In F. Crestani and Gabriella Pasi, editors, *Soft Computing in Information Retrieval: Techniques and Applications*, pages 332–357. Physica Verlag (Springer Verlag), Heidelberg, Germany, 2000.
27. U. Straccia. Reasoning within fuzzy description logics. *Journal of Artificial Intelligence Research*, 14:137–166, 2001.

28. U. Straccia.   Uncertainty in description logics: a lattice-based approach.   In *Proc. IPMU*, 2004.
29. C. Tresp and R. Molitor. A description logic for vague knowledge. In *Proc. of the 13th European Conf. on Artificial Intelligence (ECAI-98)*, Brighton (England), August 1998.
30. J. Yen. Generalizing term subsumption languages to fuzzy logic. In *Proc. of the 12th International Joint Conference on Artificial Intelligence (IJCAI-91)*, pages 472–477, Sydney, Australia, 1991.
31. L. A. Zadeh. Fuzzy sets. *Information and Control*, 8(3):338–353, 1965.

Computing the Least Common Subsumer
w.r.t. a Background Terminology*

Franz Baader, Baris Sertkaya, and Anni-Yasmin Turhan

Theoretical Computer Science, TU Dresden, Germany

Abstract. Methods for computing the least common subsumer (lcs) are usually restricted to rather inexpressive Description Logics (DLs) whereas existing knowledge bases are written in very expressive DLs. In order to allow the user to re-use concepts defined in such terminologies and still support the definition of new concepts by computing the lcs, we extend the notion of the lcs of concept descriptions to the notion of the lcs w.r.t. a background terminology. We will both show a theoretical result on the existence of the *least* common subsumer in this setting, and describe a practical approach (based on a method from formal concept analysis) for computing *good* common subsumers, which may, however, not be the least ones.

1 Introduction

Description Logics (DLs) [3] are a class of knowledge representation formalisms in the tradition of semantic networks and frames, which can be used to represent the terminological knowledge of an application domain in a structured and formally well-understood way. DL systems provide their users with standard inference services (like subsumption and instance checking) that deduce implicit knowledge from the explicitly represented knowledge. More recently, non-standard inferences [21] were introduced to support building and maintaining large DL knowledge bases. For example, such non-standard inferences can be used to support the *bottom-up* construction of DL knowledge bases, as introduced in [4,5]: instead of directly defining a new concept, the knowledge engineer introduces several typical examples as objects, which are then automatically generalized into a concept description by the system. This description is offered to the knowledge engineer as a possible candidate for a definition of the concept. The task of computing such a concept description can be split into two subtasks: computing the most specific concepts of the given objects, and then computing the least common subsumer of these concepts. The *most specific concept* (msc) of an object o (the *least common subsumer* (lcs) of concept descriptions $C_1, \ldots, C_n$) is the most specific concept description C expressible in the given DL language that has o as an instance (that subsumes $C_1, \ldots, C_n$). The problem of computing the lcs and (to a more limited extent) the msc has already been investigated in the literature [12,13,4,5,24,23,22,2,11].

---

* This work has been supported by DFG under grants GRK 334/3 and BA 1122/4-3.

J.J. Alferes and J. Leite (Eds.): JELIA 2004, LNAI 3229, pp. 400–412, 2004.
© Springer-Verlag Berlin Heidelberg 2004

The methods for computing the least common subsumer are restricted to rather inexpressive descriptions logics not allowing for disjunction (and thus not allowing for full negation). In fact, for languages with disjunction, the lcs of a collection of concepts is just their disjunction, and nothing new can be learned from building it. In contrast, for languages without disjunction, the lcs extracts the "commonalities" of the given collection of concepts. Modern DL systems like FaCT[20] and RACER[19] are based on very expressive DLs, and there exist large knowledge bases that use this expressive power and can be processed by these systems [25,26,18]. In order to allow the user to re-use concepts defined in such existing knowledge bases and still support the user during the definition of new concepts with the bottom-up approach sketched above, we propose the following extended bottom-up approach.

Consider a *background terminology* $\mathcal{T}$ defined in an expressive DL $\mathcal{L}_2$. When defining new concepts, the user employs only a sublanguage $\mathcal{L}_1$ of $\mathcal{L}_2$, for which computing the lcs makes sense. However, in addition to primitive concepts and roles, the concept descriptions written in the DL $\mathcal{L}_1$ may also contain names of concepts defined in $\mathcal{T}$. Let us call such concept descriptions $\mathcal{L}_1(\mathcal{T})$-concept descriptions. Given $\mathcal{L}_1(\mathcal{T})$-concept descriptions $C_1, \ldots, C_n$, we are now looking for their lcs in $\mathcal{L}_1(\mathcal{T})$, i.e., the least $\mathcal{L}_1(\mathcal{T})$-concept description that subsumes $C_1, \ldots, C_n$ w.r.t. $\mathcal{T}$.

In this paper, we consider the case where $\mathcal{L}_1$ is the DL $\mathcal{ALE}$ and $\mathcal{L}_2$ is the DL $\mathcal{ALC}$. We first show the following result: If $\mathcal{T}$ is an acyclic $\mathcal{ALC}$-TBox, then the lcs w.r.t. $\mathcal{T}$ of $\mathcal{ALE}(\mathcal{T})$-concept descriptions always exists. This result (which will be shown in Section 3) is theoretical in the sense that it does not yield a practical algorithm.

In Section 4 we follow a more practical approach. Assume that $\mathcal{L}_1$ is a DL for which least common subsumers (without background TBox) always exist. Given $\mathcal{L}_1(\mathcal{T})$-concept descriptions $C_1, \ldots, C_n$, one can compute a common subsumer w.r.t. $\mathcal{T}$ by just ignoring $\mathcal{T}$, i.e., by treating the defined names in $C_1, \ldots, C_n$ as primitive and computing the lcs of $C_1, \ldots, C_n$ in $\mathcal{L}_1$. However, the common subsumer obtained this way will usually be too general. In Section 4 we sketch a practical method for computing "good" common subsumers w.r.t. background TBoxes, which may not be the *least* common subsumers, but which are better than the common subsumers computed by ignoring the TBox. As a tool, this method uses attribute exploration with background knowledge [15,16], an algorithm developed in formal concept analysis [17] for computing concept lattices.

2   Basic Definitions

In order to define concepts in a DL knowledge base, one starts with a set N_C of concept names (unary predicates) and a set N_R of role names (binary predicates), and defines more complex *concept descriptions* using the constructors provided by the concept description language of the particular system. In this paper, we consider the DL $\mathcal{ALC}$ and its sublanguages $\mathcal{ALE}$ and $\mathcal{EL}$, which allow for concept descriptions built from the indicated subsets of the constructors shown

Table 1. Syntax and semantics of concept descriptions and definitions.

Name of constructor	Syntax	Semantics	$\mathcal{ALC}$	$\mathcal{ALE}$	$\mathcal{EL}$
top-concept	$\top$	$\Delta^{\mathcal{I}}$	x	x	x
bottom-concept	$\bot$	$\emptyset$	x	x	
negation	$\neg C$	$\Delta^{\mathcal{I}} \setminus C^{\mathcal{I}}$	x		
atomic negation	$\neg A$	$\Delta^{\mathcal{I}} \setminus A^{\mathcal{I}}$	x	x	
conjunction	$C \sqcap D$	$C^{\mathcal{I}} \cap D^{\mathcal{I}}$	x	x	x
disjunction	$C \sqcup D$	$C^{\mathcal{I}} \cup D^{\mathcal{I}}$	x		
value restriction	$\forall r.C$	$\{x \in \Delta^{\mathcal{I}} \mid \forall y : (x,y) \in r^{\mathcal{I}} \rightarrow y \in C^{\mathcal{I}}\}$	x	x	
existential restriction	$\exists r.C$	$\{x \in \Delta^{\mathcal{I}} \mid \exists y : (x,y) \in r^{\mathcal{I}} \wedge y \in C^{\mathcal{I}}\}$	x	x	x
concept definition	$A \equiv C$	$A^{\mathcal{I}} = C^{\mathcal{I}}$	x	x	x

in Table 1. In this table, r stands for a role name, A for a concept name, and C, D for arbitrary concept descriptions. A *concept definition* (as shown in the last row of Table 1) assigns a concept name A to a complex description C. A finite set of such definitions is called a *TBox* iff it is acyclic (i.e., no definition refers, directly or indirectly, to the name it defines) and unambiguous (i.e., each name has at most one definition). The concept names occurring on the left-hand side of a concept definition are called *defined* concepts, and the others *primitive*.

The semantics of concept descriptions is defined in terms of an *interpretation* $\mathcal{I} = (\Delta^{\mathcal{I}}, \cdot^{\mathcal{I}})$. The domain $\Delta^{\mathcal{I}}$ of $\mathcal{I}$ is a non-empty set and the interpretation function $\cdot^{\mathcal{I}}$ maps each concept name $A \in N_C$ to a set $A^{\mathcal{I}} \subseteq \Delta^{\mathcal{I}}$ and each role name $r \in N_R$ to a binary relation $r^{\mathcal{I}} \subseteq \Delta^{\mathcal{I}} \times \Delta^{\mathcal{I}}$. The extension of $\cdot^{\mathcal{I}}$ to arbitrary concept descriptions is inductively defined, as shown in the third column of Table 1. The interpretation $\mathcal{I}$ is a model of the TBox $\mathcal{T}$ iff it satisfies all its concept definitions, i.e., $A^{\mathcal{I}} = C^{\mathcal{I}}$ holds for all $A \equiv C$ in $\mathcal{T}$.

One of the most important traditional inference services provided by DL systems is computing subconcept/superconcept relationships (so-called *subsumption* relationships). The concept description C_2 *subsumes* the concept description C_1 *w.r.t. the TBox* $\mathcal{T}$ ($C_1 \sqsubseteq_{\mathcal{T}} C_2$) iff $C_1^{\mathcal{I}} \subseteq C_2^{\mathcal{I}}$ for all models $\mathcal{I}$ of $\mathcal{T}$. Two concept descriptions C_1, C_2 are called *equivalent* iff they subsume each other w.r.t. the empty TBox.

We are now ready to define the new non-standard inference introduced in this paper. Let $\mathcal{L}_1, \mathcal{L}_2$ be DLs such that $\mathcal{L}_1$ is a sub-DL of $\mathcal{L}_2$, i.e., $\mathcal{L}_1$ allows for less constructors. For a given $\mathcal{L}_2$-TBox $\mathcal{T}$, we call $\mathcal{L}_1(\mathcal{T})$-*concept descriptions* those $\mathcal{L}_1$-concept descriptions that may contain concepts defined in $\mathcal{T}$.

Definition 1. *Given an $\mathcal{L}_2$-TBox $\mathcal{T}$ and a collection $C_1, \ldots, C_n$ of $\mathcal{L}_1(\mathcal{T})$-concept descriptions, the least common subsumer (lcs) of $C_1, \ldots, C_n$ w.r.t. $\mathcal{T}$ is the most specific $\mathcal{L}_1(\mathcal{T})$-concept description C that subsumes $C_1, \ldots, C_n$ w.r.t. $\mathcal{T}$, i.e., it is an $\mathcal{L}_1(\mathcal{T})$-concept description D such that*

1. $C_i \sqsubseteq_{\mathcal{T}} D$ *for* $i = 1, \ldots, n$; D is a common subsumer.
2. *if E is an $\mathcal{L}_1(\mathcal{T})$-concept description satisfying* $C_i \sqsubseteq_{\mathcal{T}} E$ *for* $i = 1, \ldots, n$*, then* $D \sqsubseteq_{\mathcal{T}} E$. D is least.

Depending on the DLs $\mathcal{L}_1$ and $\mathcal{L}_2$, least common subsumers of $\mathcal{L}_1(\mathcal{T})$-concept descriptions w.r.t. an $\mathcal{L}_2$-TBox $\mathcal{T}$ may exist or not. Note that the lcs only uses concept constructors from $\mathcal{L}_1$, but may also contain concept names defined in the $\mathcal{L}_2$-TBox. This is the main distinguishing feature of this new notion of a least common subsumer w.r.t. a background terminology. Let us illustrate this by a trivial example.

Example 1. Assume that $\mathcal{L}_1$ is the DL $\mathcal{ALE}$ and $\mathcal{L}_2$ is $\mathcal{ALC}$. Consider the $\mathcal{ALC}$-TBox $\mathcal{T} := \{A \equiv P \sqcup Q\}$, and assume that we want to compute the lcs of the $\mathcal{ALE}(\mathcal{T})$-concept descriptions P and Q. Obviously, A is the lcs of P and Q w.r.t. $\mathcal{T}$. If we were not allowed to use the name A defined in $\mathcal{T}$, then the only common subsumer of P and Q in $\mathcal{ALE}$ would be the top-concept $\top$.

3   An Exact Theoretical Result

In this section, we assume that $\mathcal{L}_1$ is $\mathcal{ALE}$ and $\mathcal{L}_2$ is $\mathcal{ALC}$. In addition, we assume that the sets of concept and role names available for building concept descriptions are finite.

Theorem 1. *Let $\mathcal{T}$ be an $\mathcal{ALC}$-TBox. The lcs of $\mathcal{ALE}(\mathcal{T})$-concept descriptions w.r.t. $\mathcal{T}$ always exists and can effectively be computed.*

At first sight, one might think that this result can be shown using results on the approximation of $\mathcal{ALC}$ by $\mathcal{ALE}$ [10]. In fact, given an $\mathcal{ALC}$-TBox $\mathcal{T}$ and $\mathcal{ALE}(\mathcal{T})$-concept descriptions $C_1, \ldots, C_n$, one can first *unfold* $C_1, \ldots, C_n$ into concept descriptions $C'_1, \ldots, C'_n$ by iteratively replacing defined concepts by their definitions until they contain no defined concepts. These descriptions are $\mathcal{ALC}$-concept descriptions since they may contain constructors of $\mathcal{ALC}$ that are not allowed in $\mathcal{ALE}$. One can then build the $\mathcal{ALC}$-concept description $C := C'_1 \sqcup \ldots \sqcup C'_n$, and finally approximate C from above by an $\mathcal{ALE}$-concept description E. By construction, E is a common subsumer of $C_1, \ldots, C_n$. However, E does not contain concept names defined in $\mathcal{T}$, and thus it is not necessarily the *least* $\mathcal{ALE}(\mathcal{T})$-concept descriptions subsuming $C_1, \ldots, C_n$ w.r.t. $\mathcal{T}$ (see Example 1 above). One might now assume that this can be overcome by applying known results on rewriting concept descriptions w.r.t. a terminology [6]. However, in Example 1, the concept description E obtained using the approach based on approximation sketched above is $\top$, and this concept cannot be rewritten using the TBox $\mathcal{T} := \{A \equiv P \sqcup Q\}$.

To show the theorem, we first need to show two lemmas. Given an $\mathcal{ALC}$- or $\mathcal{ALE}(\mathcal{T})$-concept description C, its role depth is the maximal nesting of value restrictions and existential restrictions. For example, the role depth of $\exists r \forall r. A$ is 2, and the role depth of $\exists r \forall r. A \sqcup \exists r \exists r \exists r B$ is 3.

Lemma 1. *For a given bound k on the role depth, there is only a finite number of inequivalent $\mathcal{ALE}$-concept descriptions of role depth at most k.*

This is a consequence of the fact that we have assumed that the sets of concept and role names are finite, and can be shown by induction on k.[1]

Given this lemma, a first attempt to show Theorem 1 could be the following. Let $C_1, \ldots, C_n$ be $\mathcal{ALE}(\mathcal{T})$-concept descriptions, and assume that the role depths of the $\mathcal{ALC}$-concept description $C_1', \ldots, C_n'$ obtained by unfolding the C_i w.r.t. $\mathcal{T}$ are bounded by k. If we could show that this implies that the role depth of any common subsumer of $C_1, \ldots, C_n$ w.r.t. $\mathcal{T}$ is also bounded by k, then we could obtain the least common subsumer by simply building the (up to equivalence) finite conjunction of all common subsumers of $C_1, \ldots, C_n$ in $\mathcal{ALE}(\mathcal{T})$. However, due to the fact that $\mathcal{ALC}$ and $\mathcal{ALE}$ can express inconsistency, this simple approach does not work. In fact, $\bot$ has role depth 0, but is subsumed by any concept description. Given this counterexample, the next conjecture could be that it is enough to prevent this pathological case, i.e., assume that at least one of the concept descriptions $C_1, \ldots, C_n$ is consistent, i.e., not subsumed by $\bot$ w.r.t. $\mathcal{T}$. For the DL $\mathcal{EL}$ in place of $\mathcal{ALE}$, this modification of the simple approach sketched above really works (see [9] for details). However, due to the presence of value restrictions it does not work for $\mathcal{ALE}$. For example, $\forall r.\bot$ is subsumed by $\forall r.F$ for arbitrary $\mathcal{ALE}(\mathcal{T})$-concept descriptions F, and thus the role depth of common subsumers cannot be bounded. However, we can show that common subsumers having a large role depth are too general anyway.

Lemma 2. *Let $C_1, \ldots, C_n$ be $\mathcal{ALE}(\mathcal{T})$-concept descriptions, and assume that the role depths of the $\mathcal{ALC}$-concept description $C_1', \ldots, C_n'$ obtained by unfolding the C_i w.r.t. $\mathcal{T}$ are bounded by k. If the $\mathcal{ALE}(\mathcal{T})$-concept description D is a common subsumer of $C_1, \ldots, C_n$ w.r.t. $\mathcal{T}$, then there is an $\mathcal{ALE}(\mathcal{T})$-concept description $D' \sqsubseteq_{\mathcal{T}} D$ of role depth at most $k+1$ that is also a common subsumer of $C_1, \ldots, C_n$ w.r.t. $\mathcal{T}$.*

Theorem 1 is now an immediate consequence of Lemma 1 and 2. In fact, to compute the lcs of $C_1, \ldots, C_n$ w.r.t. $\mathcal{T}$, it is enough to compute the (up to equivalence) finite set of all $\mathcal{ALE}(\mathcal{T})$-concept descriptions of role depth $k + 1$, check which of them are common subsumers of $C_1, \ldots, C_n$ w.r.t. $\mathcal{T}$, and then build the conjunction E of these common subsumers. Lemma 1 ensures that the conjunction is finite. By definition, E is a common subsumer of $C_1, \ldots, C_n$ w.r.t. $\mathcal{T}$, and Lemma 2 ensures that for any common subsumer D of $C_1, \ldots, C_n$ w.r.t. $\mathcal{T}$, there is a conjunct D' in E such that $D' \sqsubseteq_{\mathcal{T}} D$, and thus $E \sqsubseteq_{\mathcal{T}} D$.

Due to the space constraints, we can only *sketch* the *proof of Lemma 2*. Assume that D is an $\mathcal{ALE}(\mathcal{T})$-concept description of role depth $> k+1$ that is a common subsumer of $C_1, \ldots, C_n$ w.r.t. $\mathcal{T}$. Then there are quantifiers $Q_1, \ldots, Q_k$, $Q \in \{\forall, \exists\}$, roles $r_1, \ldots, r_k, r$, and an $\mathcal{ALE}(\mathcal{T})$-concept description F containing a value or existential restriction such that $D \sqsubseteq_{\mathcal{T}} Q_1 r_1. \cdots Q_k r_k.Qr.F$.

Case 1: $C_i \sqsubseteq_{\mathcal{T}} Q_1 r_1. \cdots Q_k r_k.\bot$ for all $i, 1 \leq i \leq n$. Then $D \sqcap Q_1 r_1. \cdots Q_k r_k.\bot$ is a common subsumer of $C_1, \ldots, C_n$ w.r.t. $\mathcal{T}$ that is subsumed by D, and can be normalized into an equivalent concept description that is

---

[1] This is a well-known result, which holds even for full first-order predicate logic formulae of bounded quantifier depth over a finite vocabulary.

smaller than D (basically, $Qr.F$ can be replaced by $\bot$). Thus, we can apply induction to obtain the result of the lemma.

Case 2: There is an $m, 1 \leq m \leq n$ such that $C_m \not\sqsubseteq_\mathcal{T} Q_1 r_1. \cdots Q_k r_k.\bot$. Using the fact that C'_m has role depth at most k, we can show[2] that this implies $C_m \not\sqsubseteq_\mathcal{T} Q_1 r_1. \cdots Q_k r_k.\exists r\top$. Thus, $C_m \sqsubseteq_\mathcal{T} D \sqsubseteq_\mathcal{T} Q_1 r_1. \cdots Q_k r_k.Qr.F$ shows that $Q = \forall$.

If F subsumes $\top$ w.r.t. $\mathcal{T}$, then we can replace $\forall r.F$ in D by $\top$, and thus obtain an equivalent smaller description. Otherwise, we can use the fact that $C_i \sqsubseteq_\mathcal{T} Q_1 r_1. \cdots Q_k r_k.\forall r.F$ and that the role depth of C'_i is at most k to show that $C_i \sqsubseteq_\mathcal{T} Q_1 r_1. \cdots Q_k r_k.\forall r.\bot$ holds for all $i, 1 \leq i \leq n$. But then $D \sqcap Q_1 r_1. \cdots Q_k r_k.\forall r.\bot$ is a common subsumer of $C_1, \ldots, C_n$ w.r.t. $\mathcal{T}$ that is subsumed by D, and can be normalized into an equivalent concept description that is smaller than D. Again, we can apply induction to obtain the result of the lemma.

4 A Practical Approximative Approach

The brute-force algorithm for computing the lcs in $\mathcal{ALE}(\mathcal{T})$ w.r.t. a background $\mathcal{ALC}$-TBox described in the previous section is not useful in practice since the number of concept descriptions that must be considered is very large (super-exponential in the role depth). In the bottom-up construction of DL knowledge bases, it is not really necessary to take the *least* common subsumer,[3] a common subsumer that is not too general can also be used. In this section, we introduce an approach for computing such "good" common subsumers w.r.t. a background TBox. In order to explain this approach, we must first recall how the lcs of $\mathcal{ALE}$-concept descriptions (without background terminology) can be computed.

The lcs of $\mathcal{ALE}$-concept descriptions. Since the lcs of n concept descriptions can be obtained by iterating the application of the binary lcs, we describe how to compute the lcs $\text{lcs}_{\mathcal{ALE}}(C, D)$ of two $\mathcal{ALE}$-concept descriptions C, D (see [5] for more details).

First, the input descriptions C, D are normalized by applying the following rules modulo associativity and commutativity of conjunction:

$$\forall r.E \sqcap \forall r.F \longrightarrow \forall r.(E \sqcap F), \qquad \forall r.E \sqcap \exists r.F \longrightarrow \forall r.E \sqcap \exists r.(E \sqcap F),$$
$$\forall r.\top \longrightarrow \top, \qquad E \sqcap \top \longrightarrow E,$$
$$A \sqcap \neg A \longrightarrow \bot \quad \text{for each } A \in N_C,$$
$$\exists r.\bot \longrightarrow \bot, \qquad E \sqcap \bot \longrightarrow \bot.$$

Due to the second rule, this normalization may lead to an exponential blow-up of the concept descriptions. In the following, we assume that the input descriptions C, D are normalized.

---

[2] By looking a the behavior of a tableau-based subsumption algorithm for $\mathcal{ALC}$.

[3] Using it may even result in over-fitting.

In order to describe the lcs algorithm, we need to introduce some notation. Let C be a normalized $\mathcal{ALE}$-concept description. Then $\mathsf{names}(C)$ ($\overline{\mathsf{names}}(C)$) denotes the set of (negated) concept names occurring in the top-level conjunction of C, $\mathsf{roles}^{\exists}(C)$ ($\mathsf{roles}^{\forall}(C)$) the set of role names occurring in an existential (value) restriction on the top-level of C, and $\mathsf{restrict}_r^{\exists}(C)$ ($\mathsf{restrict}_r^{\forall}(C)$) denotes the set of all concept descriptions occurring in an existential (value) restriction on the role r in the top-level conjunction of C.

Now, let C, D be normalized $\mathcal{ALE}$-concept descriptions. If C (D) is equivalent to $\perp$, then $\mathsf{lcs}_{\mathcal{ALE}}(C, D) = D$ ($\mathsf{lcs}_{\mathcal{ALE}}(C, D) = C$). Otherwise, we have

$$\mathsf{lcs}_{\mathcal{ALE}}(C, D) = \prod_{A \in \mathsf{names}(C) \cap \mathsf{names}(D)} A \ \sqcap \prod_{\neg B \in \overline{\mathsf{names}}(C) \cap \overline{\mathsf{names}}(D)} \neg B \ \sqcap$$

$$\prod_{r \in \mathsf{roles}^{\exists}(C) \cap \mathsf{roles}^{\exists}(D)} \prod_{E \in \mathsf{restrict}_r^{\exists}(C), F \in \mathsf{restrict}_r^{\exists}(D)} \exists r.\mathsf{lcs}_{\mathcal{ALE}}(E, F) \ \sqcap$$

$$\prod_{r \in \mathsf{roles}^{\forall}(C) \cap \mathsf{roles}^{\forall}(D)} \prod_{E \in \mathsf{restrict}_r^{\forall}(C), F \in \mathsf{restrict}_r^{\forall}(D)} \forall r.\mathsf{lcs}_{\mathcal{ALE}}(E, F).$$

Here, the empty conjunction stands for the top-concept $\top$. The recursive calls of $\mathsf{lcs}_{\mathcal{ALE}}$ are well-founded since the role depth decreases with each call.

A good common subsumer in $\mathcal{ALE}$ w.r.t. a background TBox. Let $\mathcal{T}$ be a background TBox in some DL $\mathcal{L}_2$ extending $\mathcal{ALE}$ such that subsumption in $\mathcal{L}_2$ w.r.t. TBoxes is decidable.[4] Let C, D be normalized $\mathcal{ALE}(\mathcal{T})$-concept descriptions. If we ignore the TBox, then we can simply apply the above algorithm for $\mathcal{ALE}$-concept descriptions without background terminology to compute a common subsumer. However, in this context, taking

$$\prod_{A \in \mathsf{names}(C) \cap \mathsf{names}(D)} A \ \sqcap \prod_{\neg B \in \overline{\mathsf{names}}(C) \cap \overline{\mathsf{names}}(D)} \neg B$$

is not the best we can do. In fact, some of these concept names may be constrained by the TBox, and thus there may be relationships between them that we ignore by simply using the intersection. Instead, we propose to take the smallest (w.r.t. subsumption w.r.t. $\mathcal{T}$) conjunction of concept names and negated concept names that subsumes (w.r.t. $\mathcal{T}$) both

$$\prod_{A \in \mathsf{names}(C)} A \ \sqcap \prod_{\neg B \in \overline{\mathsf{names}}(C)} \neg B \quad \text{and} \quad \prod_{A' \in \mathsf{names}(D)} A' \ \sqcap \prod_{\neg B' \in \overline{\mathsf{names}}(D)} \neg B'.$$

We modify the above lcs algorithm in this way, not only on the top-level of the input concepts, but also in the recursive steps. It is easy to show that the $\mathcal{ALE}(\mathcal{T})$-concept description computed by this modified algorithm still is a common subsumer of A, B w.r.t. $\mathcal{T}$. In general, this common subsumer will be more

---

[4] Note that the restriction to TBoxes consisting of acyclic and unambiguous concept definitions is not really necessary here. We can also treat sets of general concept inclusions (GCIs) in this way.

specific than the one obtained by ignoring $\mathcal{T}$, though it need not be the least common subsumer. As a simple example, consider the $\mathcal{ALC}$-TBox $\mathcal{T}$:

$$\mathsf{NoSon} \equiv \forall\mathsf{has\text{-}child.Female}, \quad \mathsf{NoDaughter} \equiv \forall\mathsf{has\text{-}child.}\neg\mathsf{Female},$$
$$\mathsf{SonRichDoctor} \equiv \forall\mathsf{has\text{-}child.}(\mathsf{Female} \sqcup (\mathsf{Doctor} \sqcap \mathsf{Rich})),$$
$$\mathsf{DaughterHappyDoctor} \equiv \forall\mathsf{has\text{-}child.}(\neg\mathsf{Female} \sqcup (\mathsf{Doctor} \sqcap \mathsf{Happy})),$$
$$\mathsf{ChildrenDoctor} \equiv \forall\mathsf{has\text{-}child.Doctor},$$

and the $\mathcal{ALE}$-concept descriptions

$$C := \exists\mathsf{has\text{-}child.}(\mathsf{NoSon} \sqcap \mathsf{DaughterHappyDoctor}),$$
$$D := \exists\mathsf{has\text{-}child.}(\mathsf{NoDaughter} \sqcap \mathsf{SonRichDoctor}).$$

By ignoring the TBox, we obtain the $\mathcal{ALE}(\mathcal{T})$-concept description $\exists\mathsf{has\text{-}child.}\top$ as common subsumer of C, D. However, if we take into account that both $\mathsf{NoSon}\sqcap$ $\mathsf{DaughterHappyDoctor}$ and $\mathsf{NoDaughter} \sqcap \mathsf{SonRichDoctor}$ are subsumed by the concept $\mathsf{ChildrenDoctor}$, then we obtain the more specific common subsumer

$$\exists\mathsf{has\text{-}child.ChildrenDoctor}.$$

Computing the subsumption lattice of conjunctions of (negated) concept names w.r.t. a TBox. In order to obtain a practical lcs algorithm realizing the approach described above, we must be able to compute in an efficient way the smallest conjunction of (negated) concept names that subsumes two such conjunctions w.r.t. $\mathcal{T}$. Since in our application scenario (bottom-up construction of DL knowledge bases w.r.t. a given background terminology), the TBox $\mathcal{T}$ is assumed to be fixed, it makes sense to precompute this information. Obviously, a naive approach that calls the subsumption algorithm for each pair of conjunctions of (negated) concept names is too expensive for TBoxes of a realistic size. Instead, we propose to use methods from formal concept analysis (FCA) [17] for this purpose. In FCA, the knowledge about an application domain is given by means of a formal context.

Definition 2. *A formal context is a triple* $\mathcal{K} = (\mathcal{O}, \mathcal{P}, \mathcal{S})$, *where* $\mathcal{O}$ *is a set of objects,* $\mathcal{P}$ *is a set of attributes (or properties), and* $\mathcal{S} \subseteq \mathcal{O} \times \mathcal{P}$ *is a relation that connects each object* o *with the attributes satisfied by* o.

Let $\mathcal{K} = (\mathcal{O}, \mathcal{P}, \mathcal{S})$ be a formal context. For a set of objects $A \subseteq \mathcal{O}$, A' is the set of attributes that are satisfied by all objects in A, i.e.,

$$A' := \{p \in \mathcal{P} \mid \forall a \in A\colon (a, p) \in \mathcal{S}\}.$$

Similarly, for a set of attributes $B \subseteq \mathcal{P}$, B' is the set of objects that satisfy all attributes in B, i.e.,

$$B' := \{o \in \mathcal{O} \mid \forall b \in B\colon (o, b) \in \mathcal{S}\}.$$

A *formal concept* is a pair (A, B) consisting of an *extent* $A \subseteq \mathcal{O}$ and an *intent* $B \subseteq \mathcal{P}$ such that $A' = B$ and $B' = A$. Such formal concepts can be hierarchically ordered by inclusion of their extents, and this order induces a complete lattice, called the *concept lattice* of the context. Given a formal context, the first step for analyzing this context is usually to compute the concept lattice.

In many applications, one has a large (or even infinite) set of objects, but only a relatively small set of attributes. Also, the context is not necessarily given explicitly as a cross table; it is rather "known" to a domain "expert". In such a situation, Ganter's *attribute exploration* algorithm [14,17] has turned out to be an efficient approach for computing an appropriate representation of the concept lattice. This algorithm is interactive in the sense that at certain stages it asks the "expert" certain questions about the context, and then continues using the answers provided by the expert. Once the representation of the concept lattice is computed, certain questions about the lattice (e.g. "What is the supremum of two given concepts?") can efficiently be answered using this representation.

Recall that we are interested in the subsumption lattice[5] of conjunctions of (negated) concept names (some of which may be defined concepts in an $\mathcal{L}_2$-TBox $\mathcal{T}$). In order to apply attribute exploration to this task, we define a formal context whose concept lattice is isomorphic to the subsumption lattice we are interested in.

For the case of conjunctions of concept names (without negated names), this problem was first addressed in [1], where the objects of the context were basically all possible counterexamples to subsumption relationships, i.e., interpretations together with an element of the interpretation domain. The resulting "semantic context" has the disadvantage that an "expert" for this context must be able to deliver such counterexample, i.e., it is not sufficient to have a simple subsumption algorithm for the DL in question. One needs one that, given a subsumption problem "$C \sqsubseteq D$?", is able to compute a counterexample if the subsumption relationship does not hold, i.e., an interpretation $\mathcal{I}$ and an element d of its domain such that $d \in C^{\mathcal{I}} \setminus D^{\mathcal{I}}$.

To overcome this problem, a new "syntactic context" was recently defined in [8]:

Definition 3. *The context* $\mathcal{K}_{\mathcal{T}} = (\mathcal{O}, \mathcal{P}, \mathcal{S})$ *is defined as follows:*

$\mathcal{O} := \{E \mid E \text{ is an } \mathcal{L}_2 \text{ concept description}\}$,
$\mathcal{P} := \{A_1, \ldots, A_n\}$ *is the set of concept names occurring in* $\mathcal{T}$,
$\mathcal{S} := \{(E, A) \mid E \sqsubseteq_{\mathcal{T}} A\}$.

The following is shown in [8]:

Theorem 2. *(1) The concept lattice of the context* $\mathcal{K}_{\mathcal{T}}$ *is isomorphic to the subsumption hierarchy of all conjunctions of subsets of* $\mathcal{P}$ *w.r.t.* $\mathcal{T}$.

---

[5] In general, the subsumption relation induces a partial order, and not a lattice structure on concepts. However, in the case of conjunctions of (negated) concept names, all infima exist, and thus also all suprema.

(2) Any decision procedure for subsumption w.r.t. TBoxes in $\mathcal{L}_2$ functions as an expert for the context $\mathcal{K}_\mathcal{T}$.

This result can easily be extended to the case of conjunctions of concept names *and negated* concept names. In fact, one can simply extend the TBox $\mathcal{T}$ by a definition for each negated concept name, and then apply the approach to this extended TBox. To be more precise, if $\{A_1, \ldots, A_n\}$ is the set of concept names occurring in $\mathcal{T}$, then we introduce new concept names $\overline{A}_1, \ldots, \overline{A}_n$, and extend $\mathcal{T}$ to a TBox $\widehat{\mathcal{T}}$ by adding the definitions $\overline{A}_1 \equiv \neg A_1, \ldots, \overline{A}_n \equiv \neg A_n$.[6]

Corollary 1. *The concept lattice of the context $\mathcal{K}_{\widehat{\mathcal{T}}}$ is isomorphic to the subsumption hierarchy of all conjunctions of concept names and negated concept names occurring in $\mathcal{T}$.*

The experimental results reported in [8] show that this approach for computing the subsumption lattice of all conjunctions of concept names gives a huge increase of efficiency compared to the semi-naive approach, which introduces a new definition for each (of the exponentially many) such conjunctions, and then applies the usual algorithm for computing the subsumption hierarchy. Nevertheless, these results also show that the approach can only be applied if the number of concept names is relatively small (less than 30).[7] For this reason, we propose to use an improved algorithm for computing concept lattices [15,16], which can employ additional background knowledge that is readily available in our context, but not used by the basic attribute exploration algorithm.

An improved approach using attribute exploration with background knowledge. When starting the exploration process, all the basic attribute exploration algorithm knows about the context is the set of its attributes. It acquires all the necessary knowledge about the context by asking the expert (which in our setting means: by calling the subsumption algorithm for $\mathcal{L}_2$). However, in our application we already have some knowledge about relationships between attributes:

1. Since $\mathcal{T}$ is assumed to be an existing terminology, we can usually assume that the subsumption hierarchy between the concept names occurring in $\mathcal{T}$ has already been computed. If $A_i \sqsubseteq_\mathcal{T} A_j$ holds, then we know on the FCA side that in the context $\mathcal{K}_{\widehat{\mathcal{T}}}$ all objects satisfying attribute A_i also satisfy attribute A_j.
2. Since $A_i \sqsubseteq_\mathcal{T} A_j$ implies $\neg A_j \sqsubseteq_\mathcal{T} \neg A_i$, we also know that all objects satisfying attribute $\overline{A}_j$ also satisfy attribute $\overline{A}_i$.

---

[6] For $\widehat{\mathcal{T}}$ to be an $\mathcal{L}_2$-TBox, we must assume that $\mathcal{L}_2$ allows for full negation.
[7] It should be noted, however, that these experiments were done almost 10 years ago on a rather slow computer, using randomly generated TBoxes and the semantic context.

3. Finally, we know that no object can simultaneously satisfy A_i and $\overline{A}_i$ and every object satisfies either A_i or $\overline{A}_i$.[8]

Attribute exploration with background knowledge [15,16] is able to use such additional information on the context to speed up the exploration process and to obtain a smaller representation of the concept lattice.

Depending on the TBox, there may exist other such relationships between attributes that can be deduced, but it should be noted that deducing them makes sense only if this can be done without too much effort: otherwise, the efficiency gained during the exploration might be outweighed by the effort of obtaining the background knowledge.

First experimental results. First experiments with prototypical implementations of attribute exploration (with and without background knowledge) and of a DL "expert" based on RACER [18] yield mixed results. First, the runtime of attribute exploration (both with and without background knowledge) strongly depends on the specific shape of the TBox, not just its size. On the one hand, the TBox used as an example in this section (which has 9 concept names, and thus leads to a context with 18 attributes, and 2^{18} different conjunctions of them) resulted in runtimes of almost 50 minutes, both with and without background knowledge. One reason for this bad behavior could be that there are almost no relationships between the concepts (with background knowledge, only one additional implication is generated). On the other hand, handcrafted TBoxes with more concepts, but also more relationships between them, could be handled within several seconds.

Second, while the use of background knowledge decreases the number of calls to the expert significantly, it does not decrease the overall runtime, and in some cases even increases it. The main reason for this unexpected behavior appears to be that the examples used until now are so small that an optimized implementation like RACER needs almost no time to answer subsumption questions. In addition, our implementation of the reasoner for the background knowledge (which is used during attribute exploration with background knowledge) is still unoptimized, and thus the overhead of using the background knowledge is large.

5   Related and Future Work

In a preliminary version of this paper [9], we have considered computing the lcs in $\mathcal{EL}$ w.r.t. a background $\mathcal{ALC}$-terminology. We have shown that the lcs w.r.t. acyclic TBoxes always exists in this setting, and have also sketched a practical approach for computing an approximation of the lcs. The present version of the paper improves on this by considering the considerably more expressive DL $\mathcal{ALE}$ in place of $\mathcal{EL}$ (which makes the proof of Theorem 1 much harder), by

---

[8] If we encode both facts in the background knowledge, then the background knowledge mentioned in point 2. is redundant. However, first tests indicate that it may nevertheless be advantageous to add it explicitly.

extending the approach for computing the subsumption lattice of all conjunctions of concept names to conjunctions of concept names and negated concept names, and by using attribute exploration with background knowledge.

It should be noted that formal concept analysis and attribute exploration have already been applied in a different context to the problem of computing the least common subsumer. In [7], the following problem is addressed: given a finite collection $\mathcal{C}$ of concept descriptions, compute the subsumption hierarchy of all least common subsumers of subsets of $\mathcal{C}$. Again, this extended subsumption hierarchy can be computed by defining a formal context whose concept lattice is isomorphic to the subsumption lattice we are interested in, and then applying attribute exploration (see [7] for details). In [8], it is shown that this approach and the one sketched above can be seen as two instances of a more abstract approach.

On the experimental side, the main topic for future research is, on the one hand, to compare the behavior of attribute exploration with background knowledge to the one without on more and larger knowledge bases. We will also evaluate the trade-off between the cost of extracting more background knowledge and the performance gain this additional knowledge yields during attribute exploration. On the other hand, we will analyze how good the "good" common subsumers computed by our approximative approach really are. On the theoretical side, we will try to find exact algorithms for computing the *least* common subsumer that are better than the brute-force algorithm sketched in the proof of Theorem 1.

References

1. F. Baader. Computing a minimal representation of the subsumption lattice of all conjunctions of concepts defined in a terminology. In G. Ellis, R. A. Levinson, A. Fall, and V. Dahl, eds., *Knowledge Retrieval, Use and Storage for Efficiency: Proc. of the 1st Int. KRUSE Symposium*, 1995.
2. F. Baader. Least common subsumers and most specific concepts in a description logic with existential restrictions and terminological cycles. In G. Gottlob and T. Walsh, eds., *Proc. of the 18th Int. Joint Conf. on AI.*, Morgan Kaufm., 2003.
3. F. Baader, D. Calvanese, D. McGuinness, D. Nardi, and P. F. Patel-Schneider, eds.' *The Description Logic Handbook: Theory, Implementation, and Applications.* Cambridge University Press, 2003.
4. F. Baader and R. Küsters. Computing the least common subsumer and the most specific concept in the presence of cyclic $\mathcal{ALN}$-concept descriptions. In *Proc. of the 22nd German Annual Conf. on AI. (KI'98),LNCS*, Springer, 1998.
5. F. Baader, R. Küsters, and R. Molitor. Computing least common subsumers in description logics with existential restrictions. In *Proc. of the 16th Int. Joint Conf. on AI. (IJCAI'99)*, 1999.
6. F. Baader, R. Küsters, and R. Molitor. Rewriting concepts using terminologies. In *Proc. of the 7th Int. Conf. on Principles of Knowledge Repr. and Reasoning (KR'2000)*, 2000.
7. F. Baader and R. Molitor. Building and structuring description logic knowledge bases using least common subsumers and concept analysis. In B. Ganter and G. Mineau, eds., *Conceptual Structures: Logical, Linguistic, and Computational Issues – Proc. of the 8th Int. Conf. on Conceptual Structures (ICCS2000)*, Springer, 2000.

8. F. Baader and B. Sertkaya. Applying formal concept analysis to description logics. In P. Eklund, ed., *Proc. of the 2nd Int. Conf. on Formal Concept Analysis (ICFCA 2004)*, LNCS, Sydney, Australia, 2004. Springer.

9. F. Baader, B. Sertkaya, and A.-Y. Turhan. Computing the least common subsumer w.r.t. a background terminology. In *Proc. of the 2004 Int. Workshop on Description Logics (DL2004)*, 2004.

10. S. Brandt, R. Küsters, and A.-Y. Turhan. Approximation and difference in description logics. In D. Fensel, F. Giunchiglia, D. McGuiness, and M.-A. Williams, eds., *Proc. of the 8th Int. Conf. on Principles of Knowledge Repr. and Reasoning (KR2002)*, San Francisco, CA, 2002. Morgan Kaufm.

11. S. Brandt, A.-Y. Turhan, and R. Küsters. Extensions of non-standard inferences for description logics with transitive roles. In M. Vardi and A. Voronkov, eds., *Proc. of the 10th Int. Conf. on Logic for Programming and Automated Reasoning (LPAR'03)*, LNAI. Springer, 2003.

12. W. Cohen and H. Hirsh. Learning the CLASSIC description logics: Theoretical and experimental results. In J. Doyle, E. Sandewall, P. Torasso, eds., *Proc. of the 4th Int. Conf. on Principles of Knowledge Repr. and Reasoning (KR'94)*, 1994.

13. M. Frazier and L. Pitt. CLASSIC learning. *Machine Learning*, 25:151–193, 1996.

14. B. Ganter. Finding all closed sets: A general approach. *Order*, 8:283–290, 1991.

15. B. Ganter. Attribute exploration with background knowledge. *Theoretical Computer Science*, 217(2):215–233, 1999.

16. B. Ganter and R. Krauße. Pseudo models and propositional Horn inference. Technical Report MATH-AL-15-1999, Inst. f. Algebra, TU Dresden, Germany, 1999.

17. B. Ganter and R. Wille. *Formal Concept Analysis: Mathematical Foundations*. Springer, Berlin, 1999.

18. V. Haarslev and R. Möller. High performance reasoning with very large knowledge bases: A practical case study. In *Proc. of the 17th Int. Joint Conf. on AI. (IJCAI 2001)*, 2001.

19. V. Haarslev and R. Möller. RACER system description. In *Proc. of the Int. Joint Conf. on Automated Reasoning (IJCAR 2001)*, 2001.

20. I. Horrocks. Using an expressive description logic: FaCT or fiction? In *Proc. of the 6th Int. Conf. on Principles of Knowledge Repr. and Reasoning (KR'98)*, 1998.

21. R. Küsters. *Non-standard Inferences in Description Logics, LNAI*. Springer, 2001.

22. R. Küsters and A. Borgida. What's in an attribute? Consequences for the least common subsumer. *J. of AI. Research*, 14:167–203, 2001.

23. R. Küsters and R. Molitor. Approximating most specific concepts in description logics with existential restrictions. In F. Baader, G. Brewka, and T. Eiter, eds., *Proc. of the Joint German/Austrian Conf. on AI. (KI 2001)*, LNAI, 2001. Springer.

24. R. Küsters and R. Molitor. Computing least common subsumers in $\mathcal{ALEN}$. In *Proc. of the 17th Int. Joint Conf. on AI. (IJCAI 2001)*, 2001.

25. A. Rector and I. Horrocks. Experience building a large, re-usable medical ontology using a description logic with transitivity and concept inclusions. In *Proc. of the Workshop on Ontological Engineering, AAAI Spring Symposium (AAAI'97)*, Stanford, CA, 1997. AAAI Press.

26. S. Schultz and U. Hahn. Knowledge engineering by large-scale knowledge reuse—experience from the medical domain. In A. G. Cohn, F. Giunchiglia, and B. Selman, eds., *Proc. of the 7th Int. Conf. on Principles of Knowledge Repr. and Reasoning (KR'2000)*, Morgan Kaufm., 2000.

Explaining Subsumption by Optimal Interpolation

Stefan Schlobach

Informatics Institute
University of Amsterdam, NL,
schlobac@science.uva.nl

Abstract. We describe ongoing research to support the construction of terminologies with Description Logics. For the *explanation of subsumption* we search for particular concepts because of their syntactic and semantic properties. More precisely, the set of explanations for a subsumption $P \sqsubseteq N$ is the set of *optimal interpolants* for P and N. We provide definitions for optimal interpolation and an algorithm based on Boolean minimisation of concept-names in a tableau proof for $\mathcal{ALC}$-satisfiability. Finally, we describe our implementation and some experiments to assess the computational scalability of our proposal.

1 Introduction

Building ontologies is a time consuming and error-prone process and one of the bottle-necks in a number of AI applications. We have recently suggested various methods to tackle this problem. First, we investigated methods to automatically learn terminologies from data [12] and, secondly, we added explanation facilities to terminological reasoning [14]. Modern Description Logic (DL) reasoning systems efficiently answer queries, e.g., whether a concept $\exists child.\top \sqcap \forall child.Doctor$ is *subsumed* by $\exists child.(Doctor \sqcup Rich)$, i.e. whether one is a subclass of the other. Unfortunately, they do not provide explanatory information. In our approach a suitable explanation for this subsumption is that the former concept is more special than a third concept $\exists child.Doctor$ which, again, is more special than the latter. Not only is this concept, which we will call an *illustration*, strongly linked by the common vocabulary to both the subsumer and the subsumed concept, it is also the simplest such illustration.

The solutions we proposed can be generalised; given two concepts C and D we need to find an *interpolant*, i.e. a concepts I such that $\models C \sqsubseteq I \sqsubseteq D$, and where I is syntactically related to both C and D. Moreover, we need interpolants which are *optimal* with respect to particular syntactic properties such as number of concept-names or size. Algorithms for interpolation for concept subsumption in $\mathcal{ALC}$ are well known (e.g. [11]) as $\mathcal{ALC}$ is a notational variant of modal **K**. In this paper we extend these algorithms in order to calculate an interpolant I with a minimal number of concept-names, i.e., where there are no interpolants built from a proper subset of the concept-names occurring in I. For this purpose we

J.J. Alferes and J. Leite (Eds.): JELIA 2004, LNAI 3229, pp. 413–425, 2004.

saturate a tableau according to the usual rules for $\mathcal{ALC}$-satisfiability. Boolean minimisation then renders *reducts*, minimal sets of concept-names preserving the existence of interpolants. Finally, given reducts we calculate optimal interpolants.

This paper focuses on the discussion of optimal interpolants which not only lie at the core of our applications but which, as the most concise extracts of a proof for subsumption, are of more general and theoretic interest. Optimal interpolants play a key role in our ongoing efforts to support knowledge engineering, and robust algorithms are essential for the evaluation in particular applications. A prototypical implementation provides first insights to the potential of our approach, in particular our ealy experiments show that the methods do not easily scale up for more complex subsumption relations. To solve this problem we discuss a number of well-studied optimization techniques with respect to optimal interpolation.

The remainder of the paper is organised as follows: in Section 2 we introduce the relevant DL notation to make the paper self-contained. In Section 3 we discuss the applications of explanation in more detail. Section 4 introduces interpolation for DL, more specifically for $\mathcal{ALC}$, with the vocabulary $\mathcal{L}$ of a concept, and formal notions of optimality. In Section 5 we provide an algorithm to calculate optimal $\mathcal{L}$-interpolants based on Boolean minimisation of concept-names w.r.t. the closure of a tableau for $\mathcal{ALC}$-satisfiability. We finish with an evaluation of the proposed methods in Section 6 and a brief discussion of related and further work.

2   Description Logics

We shall not give a formal introduction to Description Logics (DL) here, but point to the first two chapters of the DL handbook [1] for an excellent overview. Briefly, DLs are set description languages with concepts (usually we use capital letters), interpreted as subsets of a domain, and roles which are binary relations, denoted by small letters. $\mathcal{ALC}$ is a simple yet relatively expressive DL with conjunction $C \sqcap D$, disjunction $C \sqcup D$, negation $\neg C$ and universal $\forall r.C$ and existential quantification $\exists r.C$. In a terminology $\mathcal{T}$ (called TBox) the interpretations of concepts can be restricted to the *models* of $\mathcal{T}$ by *axioms* of the form $C \sqsubseteq D$ or $C \doteq D$. Based on this model-theoretic semantics, concepts can be checked for *unsatisfiability*: whether they are necessarily interpreted as the empty set.

A TBox $\mathcal{T}$ is called *coherent* if no unsatisfiable concept-name occurs in $\mathcal{T}$. Other checks include *subsumption* of two concepts C and D (a subset relation of $C^{\mathcal{I}}$ and $D^{\mathcal{I}}$ w.r.t. all models $\mathcal{I}$ of $\mathcal{T}$). Subsumption between concepts C and D w.r.t. a TBox $\mathcal{T}$ will be denoted by $\mathcal{T} \models C \sqsubseteq D$. A TBox is *unfoldable* if the left-hand side of the axioms are atomic, and if the right-hand sides (the definitions) contain no reference to the defined concept [9]. Unfolding then comes down to replacing atomic sub-concepts by their definitions. Subsumption without reference to a TBox will be denoted by *concept subsumption* and we will write $C \sqsubseteq D$.

3   Explaining Subsumption by Illustration

Recently, the DL community has shown growing interest in explanation of reasoning (e.g. [6]) to provide additional information to increase the acceptance of logical reasoning, and to give additional insights to the structure of represented knowledge. Let us consider a variant of an example introduced in [4] for the author's "explanation as proof-fragment" strategy, where a concept $C_{ex} := \exists child.\exists child.Rich \sqcap \forall child.\neg((\exists child.\neg Doctor) \sqcup (\exists child.Lawyer))$ is subsumed by $D_{ex} := \exists child.\forall child (Rich \sqcup Doctor)$. Instead of providing a concise and simplified extract of a formal proof as an explanation as done in [4] we suggest an alternative, more static approach, which we call *explaining by illustration*. Imagine the above information is given in natural language: *Suppose somebody has a rich grand-child, and each child has neither a child which is not a doctor nor a child which is a Lawyer. Then, this person must have a child, every child of which is either rich or a doctor.* A natural language explanation for this statement is: *The person described above must have a child every child of which is a doctor.* This intermediate statement can be considered an *illustration* of $\models C_{ex} \sqsubseteq D_{ex}$. It can be formalised as $I_{ex} := \exists child.\forall child.Doctor$, and it subsumes C_{ex} and is subsumed by D_{ex}. Moreover, it is constructed from vocabulary both in C_{ex} and D_{ex}, e.g., the information that the person's grandchildren might be a Lawyer is irrelevant as, just from D_{ex}, we don't know anything about grandchildren being Lawyers or not. Finally, the illustration should use a minimal number of concept-names and be of minimal size, as this increases the likelihood of it being understandable.

To explain more complex subsumption relations a single illustration might not be sufficient, and iterative explanation is needed. Here, subsumption between concepts and their illustrations could, again, be explained by new illustrations or traditional explanation of proofs which are now, though, simpler to understand.

4   Optimal Interpolation

Calculating illustrations and optimal TBox axioms are interpolation problems, more precisely, problems of finding *optimal interpolants*. Remember that an axiom $D \sqsubseteq L_D$ is correct if $\models \bigsqcup_{P \in \mathbf{P}} P \sqsubseteq L_D \sqsubseteq \bigsqcap_{N \in \mathbf{N}} \neg N$ for examples $\mathbf{P}$ and counterexamples $\mathbf{N}$ of a concept D, and that an illustration for the subsumption $\models C \sqsubseteq D$ was a concept I s.t. $\models C \sqsubseteq I \sqsubseteq D$. In both cases we have argued that common vocabulary and syntactic minimality is desirable.

An *interpolant* for concepts P (for the positive) and N (the negative examples), where $\models P \sqsubseteq N$, is a concept I which is more general than P but more special than N. Furthermore, I has to be built from the vocabulary occurring both in P and N. In the standard definition of interpolation [5] the vocabulary of a formula ϕ is defined as the set of non-logical symbols in ϕ. Because we use interpolants for learning and explanation we propose a stronger notion of vocabulary for concepts: including information about the context in which the non-logical symbols (such as concept- and role-names) occur. Formally, $\mathcal{L}(C)$ is a set of pairs $(A, +)^S$ or $(B, -)^S$ of concept-names A, B and polarity $+$ or $-$, labelled with sequences S of role-names. A concept-name A has positive (negative) polarity if it is embedded in an even (odd) number of negations. $\perp$ and $\top$ always occur without polarity (represented by pairs $(\perp, \_)$ and $(\top, \_)$). $\overline{\mathcal{L}}(C)$ denotes the set $\mathcal{L}(C)$ where the polarity of each pair is interchanged (i.e. $+$ replaced by $-$ and vice versa). Furthermore, for a set S, let S^r denote that the sequence of role-names for each element of S has been extended by r. The vocabulary $\mathcal{L}(C)$ of a concept C is then defined as follows.

Definition 1. $\mathcal{L}$ is a mapping from $\mathcal{ALC}$ to triples of concept-names, polarities and sequences of role-names defined as follows:

- $\mathcal{L}(\top) = \mathcal{L}(\perp) := \{(\top, \_)^\epsilon, (\perp, \_)^\epsilon\}$
- $\mathcal{L}(C \sqcap D) := \mathcal{L}(C) \cup \mathcal{L}(D)$
- $\mathcal{L}(A) := (A, +)^\epsilon \cup \mathcal{L}(\top)$ if A is atomic
- $\mathcal{L}(C \sqcup D) := \mathcal{L}(C) \cup \mathcal{L}(D)$
- $\mathcal{L}(\exists r.C) = \mathcal{L}(\forall r.C) := \mathcal{L}(C)^r \cup \mathcal{L}(\top)^\epsilon$
- $\mathcal{L}(\neg C) := \overline{\mathcal{L}}(C)$

Take a concept $\forall r.(D \sqcap \neg \exists s.C)$. The related language is the set $\{(C, -)^{rs},$ $(D, +)^r, (\top, \_)^\epsilon, (\top, \_)^r, (\top, \_)^{rs}, (\perp, \_)^\epsilon, (\perp, \_)^r, (\perp, \_)^{rs}\}$. Note that this definition implies that $\mathcal{L}(\perp) \in \mathcal{L}(C)$ and $\mathcal{L}(\top) \in \mathcal{L}(C)$ for every concept C.

The set of interpolants w.r.t. $\mathcal{L}$ will be denoted by $I(P, N)$. In applications where interpolants are used for explanation or learning, additional restrictions are important to identify optimal illustrations or learning targets. There are several types of syntactic restrictions, e.g., interpolants with a minimal set of concept- or role-names or of minimal size, but we will focus on concept-name optimal interpolants. To simplify the presentation we only consider concept interpolation, i.e. interpolation for concept subsumption w.r.t. empty TBoxes.

Definition 2. Let P and N be concepts, and let $\mathcal{N}(C)$ denote the set of concept-names occurring in an arbitrary concept C. A concept I is an *optimal interpolant* for P and N if $\models P \sqsubseteq I$ and $\models I \sqsubseteq N$, $\mathcal{L}(I) \subseteq \mathcal{L}(P) \cap \mathcal{L}(N)$, and if there is no interpolant I' for P and N with $\mathcal{N}(I') \subset \mathcal{N}(I)$.

Take $I_{ex} := \exists child.\forall child.Doctor$ from Section 3 which is an interpolant for $C_{ex} := \exists child.\exists child.Rich \sqcap \forall child.\neg((\exists child.\neg Doctor) \sqcup (\exists child.Lawyer))$ and $D_{ex} := \exists child.\forall child.(Rich \sqcup Doctor)$, as $\mathcal{L}(I_{ex}) = \{(Doctor, +)^{child\ child}, \dots\}$ is a subset of $\mathcal{L}(C_{ex}) \cap \mathcal{L}(D_{ex})$. Moreover, the set of concept-names in I_{ex} is $\{Doctor\}$ which is minimal, and I_{ex} is an optimal interpolant for C_{ex} and D_{ex}. Such a minimal set of concept-names will be called a *reduct*.

To define reducts we need some more notation. Let S be an arbitrary subset of the common language of two concepts P and N. The set of interpolants for P and N built from concept-names in S only will be denoted as $I_S(P, N)$. For C_{ex} and D_{ex} and a set $S = \{Doctor, Rich\}$ the set $I_{\{Doctor, Rich\}}(C_{ex}, D_{ex})$ then contains, e.g., $\exists child.\forall child.Doctor$ and $\exists child.\forall child.Doctor \sqcup Rich$. Reducts now determine smallest sets S such that $I_S(P, N) \neq \emptyset$.

Definition 3. A *reduct* for two concepts P and N is a minimal set of concept-names R to preserve existence of an interpolant, i.e. where $I_R(P, N) \neq \emptyset$ and $I_{R'}(P, N) = \emptyset$ for every $R' \subset R$.

The set $\{Doctor, Rich\}$ is not minimal, as $I_{\{Doctor\}}(C_{ex}, D_{ex}) \neq \emptyset$. On the other hand, $\{Doctor\}$ is a reduct. Also, each interpolant in $I_{\{Doctor\}}(C_{ex}, D_{ex})$ is optimal for C_{ex} and D_{ex}. This observation can be generalised:

Lemma 1. *Let R be a reduct for two concepts P and N. Every interpolant $I \in I_R(P, N)$ is optimal for P and N.*

This lemma allows to calculate reducts and interpolants separately, and is used in the algorithms in the next section.

5   Algorithms for Optimal Interpolation

Optimal interpolants will be constructed using Boolean minimisation of the concept-names needed to close an $\mathcal{ALC}$-tableau. This calculation can be split into three steps. First, we saturate a labelled tableau as described in Section 5.1. Secondly, we calculate reducts from tableau proofs using the algorithm of Fig. 2. Finally, optimal interpolants can be constructed from the tableau proofs and the reducts according to Fig. 3. Step 1 and 3 closely follow well-known procedures that can be found, e.g., in [2] (for the saturation of the tableau) and [8] (for the calculation of interpolants). New is the calculation of reducts in Section 5.2 and their application in Section 5.3 to ensure optimality of the calculated interpolants.

5.1   Saturating Labelled Tableaux

Concept subsumption $\models P \sqsubseteq N$ can be decided by a proof deriving a closed tableau starting from a tableau with one branch $\{(i : P)^p, (i : \neg N)^n\}$ (for an arbitrary individual i). The information whether a formula has its origin in P or N is needed to construct interpolants from the proof. Each formula stemming from P will be labelled with $(\cdot)^p$, each created from N with $(\cdot)^n$. A *formula* has the form $(i : C)^x$ where i is an individual, C a concept and $x \in \{p, n\}$ a label. The labelling mechanism follows [8]. A *branch* is a set of formulas and a *tableau* a set of branches. A formula can occur with different labels on the same branch. A branch is *closed* if it contains a clash, i.e. if there are formulas with contradictory atoms on the same individual. The notions of open/closed branches and tableaux are defined as usual and do not depend on the labels. Formulas are always assumed to be in *negation normal form*.

To calculate reducts and optimal interpolants for two concepts P and N we construct a proof from a tableau containing a branch $\{(i : P)^p, (i : \neg N)^n\}$ (for a new individual i) by applying the rules in Fig. 1 as long as possible. The rules are $\mathcal{ALC}$-tableau rules (adapted from those of [2]) and have to be read in the following way; suppose that there is a tableau $T = \{B, B_1, \dots, B_n\}$ with $n + 1$ branches. Application of one of the rules on B yields the tableau $T' := \{B', B_1, \dots, B_n\}$ for the ($\sqcap$) and ($\exists$) rule or $T'' := \{B', B'', B_1, \dots, B_n\}$ in case the ($\sqcup$)-rule has been applied. Application of one of the rules is called *to expand* a tableau or a branch. If no more rule can be applied, branches and tableaux are *saturated*. Finally, a *proof* is a sequence of tableaux $T_1, \dots, T_n$ where each T_{i+1} has been created by application of one of the rules in Fig. 1 on a branches $B \in T_i$ (for $i, i + 1 \in \{1, \dots, n\}$), and where T_n is saturated.

($\sqcap$): **if** $(i : C \sqcap D)^x \in B$, but not both $(i : C)^x \in B$ and $(i : D)^x \in B$
   then $B' := B \cup \{(i : C)^x, (i : D)^x\}$.
($\sqcup$): **if** $(i : C \sqcup D)^x \in B$, but neither $(i : C)^x \in B$ nor $(i : D)^x \in B$.
   then $B' := B \cup \{(i : C)^x\}$ and $B'' := B \cup \{(i : D)^x\}$.
($\exists$): **if** $(i : \exists r.C)^x \in B$, all other rules have been applied, and $\{(i : \forall r.C_1)^{x_1},$
      $\dots, (i : \forall r.C_n)^{x_n}\}$ are all universal formulas for i and r in B,
   then $B' := B \cup \{(j : C)^x, (j : C_1)^{x_1}, \dots, (j : C_n)^{x_n}\}$, where j is new in B.

Fig. 1. Tableau rules for saturating a labelled $\mathcal{ALC}$-tableau (similar to [2])

5.2 Calculating Reducts

From a proof starting with $\{\{(i : P)^p, (i : \neg N)^n\}\}$ we find reducts by calculating a *maximal reduct-function*. To define such an interpolation-preserving propositional formula we need to introduce interpolants for branches and individuals. Let B be a branch, i an individual and $\{(i : C_1)^p, \dots, (i : C_k)^p, (i : D_1)^n, \dots, (i : D_l)^n\}$ the set of formulas for i in B. An *interpolant* for B and i is an interpolant for $C_1 \sqcap \dots \sqcap C_k$ and $\neg D_1 \sqcup \dots \sqcup \neg D_l$.

The set of interpolants for B and i will be denoted by $I(i, B)$, or $I_S(i, B)$ for the interpolants built from concept-names occurring in a particular set S only. Reduct-functions are then interpolation-preserving propositional formulas.

Definition 4. Let B be a branch in a proof, i an individual and ϕ a propositional formula built from conjunction, disjunction and propositional variables. Let, furthermore, $tr(v)$ denote the (unique) set of propositional variables true in a valuation v, called the *truth-set* of v. If $I(i, B) \neq \varnothing$, ϕ is a *reduct-function* for B and i if, and only if, $I_{tr(v)}(i, B) \neq \varnothing$ for any valuation $v(\phi) = T$. Otherwise, i.e., if $I(i, B) = \varnothing$, $\bot$ is the only reduct-function.

The idea to calculate reducts is as follows: As reduct-functions determine the sets of concept-names preserving interpolation a smallest set of this kind is a reduct. If a reduct-function is maximal, i.e. implied by all reduct-function, its prime implicants determine precisely these most general, i.e. smallest sets of concept-names.[1] A maximal reduct-function is calculated from a tableau proof: all branches of the saturated tableau must close even with a reduced set of concept-names available for closure. Therefore at least one clash per branch needs to be retained and a maximal reduct-function is the disjunction of the concept-names in all clashes. For each branch in a tableau proof complex maximal reduct-functions are then constructed recursively according to Fig. 2.

Theorem 1. Let P and N be concepts and i an arbitrary individual-name. The prime implicants of $rf(i, \{(i : P)^p, (i : \neg N)^n\})$ as calculated by the algorithm described in Fig. 2 are the reducts for P and N.

---

[1] A prime implicant of ϕ is the smallest conjunction of literals implying ϕ (see, e.g., [10]). The term *prime implicant* refers both to the conjunction and to the set of conjuncts.

if $rule = (\sqcap)$ has been applied on $(i : C \sqcap D)^{label}$ and B' is the new branch
  $rf(i, B) := rf(i, B');$
if $rule = (\sqcup)$ has been applied on $(i : C \sqcup D)^{label}$ and B' and B'' are new
  $rf(i, B) := rf(i, B') \wedge rf(i, B'');$
if $rule = (\exists)$ has been applied on $(i : \exists r.C)^{label}$, B' and j are new
  $rf(i, B) := rf(i, B') \vee rf(j, B');$
if no more rule can be applied (for arbitrary x and y)
  $rf(i, B) := \top$ if there are formulas $(i : A)^x \in B, (i : \neg A)^y \in B$ s.t. $x = y;$
  $rf(i, B) := \bigvee_{(i : A)^x \in B, (i : \neg A)^y \in B} A$ otherwise; i.e. if $(x \neq y)$.

Fig. 2. $rf(i, B)$: A maximal reduct-function for a branch B and individual i

Proof. The proof consists of three parts. First, we show that $rf(i, B)$ is a reduct-function for every branch B. The proof is by induction over the tableaux in a proof, where we construct interpolants for B and i from the truth-sets of the valuation making $rf(i, B)$ true. The rules for construction of interpolants correspond to those we will later give explicitly in Fig. 3. If B is saturated there are several cases: first, if there are contradicting atoms with positive or with negative labels only, the interpolant is $\bot$ or $\top$ respectively, and the reduct-function is $\top$. If there are only clashes on atoms which occur both positively and negatively labelled in B any of the literals occurring positively is an interpolant, and the maximal reduct function is the disjunction of all the corresponding concept-names. Finally, a branch without clashes on the individual i does not have an interpolant for B and i, and $\bot$ is the only reduct-function. If the branch B is not saturated, one of the rules of Fig. 2 must have been applied, and we can construct an interpolant for B and i from the interpolants of the newly created branches. If a disjunctive rule had been applied, two new branches B' and B'' have been created, and it can easily be checked that the disjunction of an arbitrary interpolant for B' and i with an arbitrary interpolant for B'' and i is an interpolant for B and i. The conjunctive case is even more simple, as any interpolant for the new branch B' and i is also an interpolant for B and i. The only slightly more complicated case is when an existential rule has been applied on a formula in B because we need to take into account that the interpolant for the new branch and the new individual might be $\bot$. In this case, however, we can show that $\bot$ is also an interpolant for B and i, which finishes the proof.

Next, we show that $rf(i, B)$ is maximal, again by induction over the tableaux in the proof. For each branch B we show that $\phi \rightarrow rf(i, B)$ for each reduct-function ϕ of i and B. Again, if B is saturated it is easy to show that $rf(i, B)$ is maximal for each of the cases mentioned above. For a non-saturated B we again have branches B' (and possibly B''), and we can easily show that $\phi \rightarrow rf(i, B)$ whenever $\phi \rightarrow rf(i, B')$ (and possibly $\phi \rightarrow rf(i, B'')$).

Finally, we prove that the prime implicants of maximal reduct-functions for the branch $B = \{(i : P)^p, (i : \neg N)^n\}$ are the reducts for P and N. Here, we show that there is an interpolant for P and N, and that there is no interpolant for any subset of the reduct. The other direction, i.e. the fact that every reduct R is the

---

if *rule* = ($\sqcap$) has been applied on $(i : C \sqcap D)^{label}$ and B' is the new branch
 return *oi(i, B', R)*;
if *rule* = ($\sqcup$) has been applied on $(i : C \sqcup D)^{label}$ and B' and B'' are new
 if *label* = p **return** *oi(i, B', R)* $\sqcup$ *oi(i, B'', R)*;
 else if *label* = n **return** *oi(i, B', R)* $\sqcap$ *oi(i, B'', R)*;
if *rule* = ($\exists$) has been applied on $(i : \exists r.C)^{label}$, B' and j are new
 if *oi(i, B', R)* exists
  if *oi(j, B', R)* exists
   if *label* = p **if** *oi(j, B', R)*= $\bot$ **return** *oi(i, B', R)*;
      else return *oi(i, B', R)* $\sqcup$ $\exists r.oi(j, B', R)$;
   else if *label* = n **if** *oi(j, B', R)*=$\top$ **return** $\top$
       else return *oi(i, B', R)* $\sqcup$ $\forall r.oi(j, B', R)$;
  else return *oi(i, B', R)*;
 else if *oi(j, B', R)* exists
  if *label* = p **if** *oi(j, B', R)*= $\bot$ **return** $\bot$; **else return** $\exists r.oi(j, B', R)$;
  else if *label* = n **if** *oi(j, B', R)*= $\top$ **return** $\top$; **else return** $\forall r.oi(j, B', R)$;
 else return *undefined*;
if no more rule can be applied.
 if there is a clash on a concept-name $A \in R$
  if there are formulas $(i : A)^n \in B$ and $(i : \neg A)^n \in B$ **return:** $\top$
  else if there are formulas $(i : A)^p \in B$ and $(i : \neg A)^p \in B$ **return:** $\bot$
  else return: $\bigsqcup_{(i:A)^p \in B, (i:\neg A)^n \in B, A \in R} A \sqcup \bigsqcup_{(i:A)^n \in B, (i:\neg A)^p \in B, A \in R} \neg A$
 else return: *undefined*.

Fig. 3. *oi(i, B, R)*: Optimal interpolants

prime-implicant of the maximal reduct-function of B, follows immediately from
the minimality of the reducts. See [13] for the technical details of the proof.

5.3 Calculating Optimal Interpolants

Given a tableau proof and a reduct R we construct optimal interpolants for each
branch B and each individual i recursively according to the rules in Fig. 3. It is
well-known how to calculate interpolants from a tableau proof [8,11]. If a rule
had been applied on a formula $(i : C)^x$ in B for an arbitrary label x, and one or
two new branches B' (and B'') have been created, the interpolant for B and i
can be constructed from interpolants for B' (and B''). It can easily be checked
that $oi(i, \{(i : P)^p, (i : \neg N)^n\}, R)$ is an interpolant for P and N. By Lemma
1 we now immediately know that if R is a concept-reduct for P and N, this
interpolant is also optimal.

Theorem 2. *Let R be a reduct for two concepts P and N. The concept $oi(i, \{(i : P)^p, (i : \neg N)^n\}, R)$ as calculated by the algorithm defined in Fig. 3 is an optimal
interpolant for P and N.*

Proof. Lemma 1 states that the interpolants built from concept-names in reducts
are the optimal interpolants. Therefore, it suffices to show that the rules in

Fig. 3 produce interpolants. This proof follows Kracht's proof in [8], we simply construct interpolants recursively for each branch in the proof. Full details can be found in [13].

Optimal interpolants are not unique, and a certain leeway exists for choosing suitable interpolants according to a given application. The algorithm in Fig. 3 was developed with an application to learning of terminologies in mind [12] and, for this reason, calculates very general interpolants. Whenever we have a choice we construct an interpolant in the most general way. This is the case when applying a (∃)-rule as well as when calculating an interpolant for a saturated branch. Note that this choice might lead to rather complex concepts with a relatively big size. Our decision was to separate the two problems of optimal interpolation and rewriting of concepts with minimal size for conceptual clarity. If optimal interpolants are applied to explain a subsumption relation things might be different: first, the size of an explanation should be as small as possible and, secondly, we might also want to have different levels of generality, such as the most specific optimal interpolant. It is straightforward to adapt the algorithm of Fig. 3 to calculate smaller or more specific optimal interpolants and we plan to evaluate different strategies for both described applications in future research.

5.4   Complexity

Calculating interpolants for two $\mathcal{ALC}$ concepts P and N is in PSPACE as we can apply the algorithm described in Fig. 3 in a depth-first way on one branch (of maximally polynomial space) at a time. This gives a simple bottom-up procedure to calculate optimal interpolants in PSPACE: for all subsets of the concept-names occurring in P and N we check whether there are interpolants or not, starting with the smallest, systematically increasing the size. Each of these checks can be done using only polynomial space. As soon as we find the first interpolant, i.e. as soon as $oi(i, B, R)$ is defined for some subset R, we know that R is a reduct, and the interpolant must be optimal. For a lower bound consider the subsumption relation $C \sqsubseteq \bot$ which has an interpolant if, and only if, C is unsatisfiable. This means that interpolation must be at least as hard as concept satisfiability in $\mathcal{ALC}$, which is well known to be PSPACE.

Although the problem of calculating optimal interpolants is in PSPACE the algorithm described above might be infeasible in practice. To be sure that we have calculated all optimal interpolants we might have to check all elements of the power-set of the set of concept-names, i.e., we might have to saturate an exponential number of tableaux. Instead, our approach expands a single tableau once, from which we calculate the reducts and read off the optimal interpolants. Computing reducts is the computational bottle-neck of our algorithm as we calculate prime implicants on formulas which can be exponential in the size of the concepts. Given that calculating prime implicants is NP-hard, we must ensure that the size of the reduct-function is as small as possible. Our current implementation comprises simple on-the-fly elimination of redundancies, but more evolved methods need to be investigated. Our algorithms have an exponential worst case complexity in the size of the concepts P and N. As the number of variables in the reduct-function is linear in the number of concept-names in P and N we can calculate the prime implicants in exponential time branch by branch (instead of constructing the full reduct-function first). This simple method requires exponential space as we have to keep maximally $e^{\frac{n}{e}}$ prime implicants (of size smaller than n) in memory, where n is the number of concept-names in P and N and e the base of natural logarithm.

6   Evaluation

Explanation of subsumption by interpolation has to be evaluated with respect to two different problems: first, we have to find out whether the explanation is indeed human-understandable, and, secondly, we have to study whether the approach scales up to more than toy examples. In this paper we will concentrate on the latter, as there is relatively little testing data available. Before investing too much time in studies with human assessors of explanations we decided to focus on the computational properties of explanation by interpolation.

Implementation. We implemented optimal interpolation in Java as part of our Wellington [7] reasoning system. The program takes as input two $\mathcal{ALC}$ concepts C and D in KRSS representation. First we use RACER to check for subsumption between C and D. If C subsumes D (or vice versa) we fully expand a tableau as described in the previous section, calculate the minimization function and the reducts, and finally read the optimal interpolants from the closed branches.

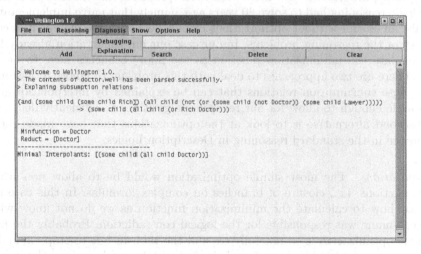

The Experiments. There is, to the best of our knowledge, no collection of subsuming concepts available to test our algorithms. To evaluate the run-times of our algorithm we therefore transformed formulas from a test-set for modal logic theorem provers provided at [3] into suitable $\mathcal{ALC}$ subsumption relations. The test-set contains 131 unsatisfiable concepts for several modal logics. For our experiments we chose 72 concepts which were unsatisfiable in modal logic K. These formulas are mostly of the form $\neg(\phi \rightarrow \psi)$ where ϕ and ψ are complex formulas (often also containing implications). To create a test-set for $\mathcal{ALC}$ subsumption we simply picked an implication and translated $\neg(\phi \rightarrow \psi)$ to $\phi^t \sqsubseteq \psi^t$, where $(\cdot)^t$ is the standard translation from K to $\mathcal{ALC}$. The transformation is very simplistic, as there is usually a number of implications in the modal formula, and we simply picked one at random.

This test-set is not useful to evaluate the explanatory quality of the interpolants because the formulas have been created to be most compact representations for computationally difficult problems in modal reasoning. In this case, explanation by interpolation is little helpful as its main purpose is to reduce syntactic overhead. But the test-set can help to get a better understanding of the computational properties of the method.

Results. Even though the test set is considered to be trivial for current specialized DL-reasoners it creates difficulties for our naive algorithm for optimal interpolation. More concretely, from the 72 subsumption relations we fail to find optimal interpolants for more than a dozen. The reason for this is obvious: remember that we had to expand the full tableau to calculate the minimization function. This means that we always expand exponentially many branches in the number of disjunctions of implications, which does not scale up even for relatively trivial concepts.

Interpreting the Results. Our method faces the problems that modal and description logic reasoning had to solve 20 years ago, namely that naive implementation of tableau calculi without optimizations cannot deal with the exponential complexity of the reasoning problems. In our case our implementation already fails to calculate the minimization function as too many branches have to be visited. There are two approaches to deal with this problem: to ignore it, assuming that those subsumption relations that can be explained by interpolation must be simple enough to allow for our reasoning algorithms to efficiently deal with. The second alternative is to look at the optimizations that have made such a difference in the standard reasoning in Description Logics.

Optimizations. The most simple optimization would be to allow non-atomic contradictions, i.e., closure of branches on complex formulas. In this case it is unclear how to calculate the minimization function as we do not know which concept-name was responsible for the logical contradiction. Probably the most obvious optimization is to not fully expand the tableau but to stop expanding once a contradiction has been found. Unfortunately, we loose completeness in both cases. This means that we do not calculate reducts, and therefore optimal interpolants, any more. A simple example is $(B \sqcap A) \sqcup A \sqsubseteq A \sqcup B$. If branch 1 is closed with B we calculate a reduct $A \wedge B$ and an interpolant $A \sqcup B$, which is not minimal as A is already an interpolant.

As a result, we would claim that our proposed way of calculating optimal interpolants is inherently intractable. If this is considered a problem, i.e., if we want to explain more complex subsumption relations we will have to accept the fact that we can approximate reducts, but not find all reducts for certain. In that case reasoning becomes immediately much more efficient, e.g., we could easily solve all of the 72 problems of our test-suite when we stopped expanding the branches as soon as we found a contradiction.

Let us discuss some of the more sophisticated optimization techniques as they are discussed, for example, in Chapter 9 of [1]. Due to lack of space we cannot introduce the techniques in more detail. One of the most important optimizations is to *pre-process* the concepts prior to running the tableau engine. For explanation this would not work because preprocessing, such as normalization, destroys the structure of the subsumption relation. This, however, is what makes the optimal interpolant an explanation, namely that it is a simplified version of the original concepts (both in terms of vocabulary and of structure).

Caching, on the other hand, is a technique that can, and has been applied for optimal interpolation, as we can cache information about satisfiability, but also about the minimization function and the interpolant for a branch. We implemented *semantic branching* in our "sub-optimal" interpolation of interpolation with great computational gain. However, we will have to study more carefully whether minimization function could still be calculated from the tableau, and whether the interpolant still has a useful structure for explanation.

To integrate *local simplification* into our calculus we would need to explicitly give rules to calculate the minimization function for each simplification. Assume a simplification has been applied on two concepts $(A \sqcup B) \sqcap (A \sqcup C)$ and $\neg A$ in a branch, with concepts B and C added to create a new branch B'. In this case we would have to add A conjunctively to the minimization function for B'. We assume that *backtracking* could be implemented because the interpolant for a redundant branch will probably be redundant, but we do not have a formal proof for this claim.

What remains as a further interesting optimization is the use of *heuristics*. In our case, we could use statistical information to strike the balance of calculating a good minimization function and having an efficient algorithm. We could, for example, expand branches as long as we find a contradiction on a concept-name which has already been frequently responsible for the closure of other branches.

7   Conclusions

We introduce an algorithm to find interpolants with a minimal number of concept-names for two concepts in the description logic $\mathcal{ALC}$, with a rigid definition of the common vocabulary. The principal novelty is that we minimise the number of concept-names in order to find most simple interpolants. These optimal interpolants are used in applications as divers as explanation and learning of terminologies.

We presented a prototypical implementation of the algorithms, in order to evaluate explanation by interpolation. In the absence of real-life data we focused on the assessment of the computational properties of the described methods, and we discussed a number of optimizations to deal with the inherent non-tractability.

For future research we plan to extend the algorithms to more expressive languages, and to apply optimal interpolation in the automatic construction of ontologies from assertions as described in [12]. An open problem is how to calculate interpolants of minimal size, as redundancy elimination will be crucial for optimal interpolants to be useful in newly learned terminologies or as illustrations.

Acknowledgment. This research was supported by the Netherlands Organization for Scientific Research (NWO) under project number 220-80-001. Thanks to the anonymous referees for some valuable comments.

References

1. F. Baader, D. Calvanese, D. McGuinness, D. Nardi, and P. Patel-Schneider, editors. *The Description Logic Handbook.* Cambridge University Press, 2003.
2. F. Baader and U. Sattler. An overview of tableau algorithms for description logics. *Studia Logica*, 69:5–40, 2001.
3. B. Beckert and R. Goré. Modleantap and modleantest.pl, 1998. http://i12www.ira.uka.de/modlean.
4. A. Borgida, E. Franconi, I. Horrocks, D. McGuinness, and P. Patel-Schneider. Explaining $\mathcal{ALC}$ subsumption. In *DL-99*, pages 37–40, 1999.
5. W. Craig. Three uses of the Herbrand-Gentzen theorem in relating model theory and proof theory. *Journal of Symbolic Logic*, 22:269–285, 1957.
6. Minutes of the DL Implementation Group Workshop. http://dl.kr.org/dig/minutes-012002.html, visited on January 9, 2003.
7. U. Endriss. Reasoning in description logics with WELLINGTON 1. 0. In *Proceedings of the Automated Reasoning Workshop 2000*, London, UK, 2000.
8. M. Kracht. *Tools and Techniques in Modal Logic.* North Holland, 1999.
9. B. Nebel. Terminological reasoning is inherently intractable. *AI*, 43:235–249, 1990.
10. W.V. Quine. The problem of simplifying truth functions. *American Math. Monthly*, 59:521–531, 1952.
11. W. Rautenberg. Modal tableau calculi and interpolation. *Journal of Philosophical Logic*, 12:403–423, 1983.
12. S. Schlobach. *Knowledge Acquisition in Hybrid Knowledge Representation Systems.* PhD thesis, University of London, 2002.
13. S. Schlobach. Optimal interpolation. Technical Report PP-2003-23, Universiteit van Amsterdam, ILLC, 2003. Beta Preprint Publication.
14. S. Schlobach and R. Cornet. Non-standard reasoning services for the debugging of description logic terminologies. In *Proceedings of the eighteenth International Joint Conference on Artificial Intelligence, IJCAI'03*. Morgan Kaufmann, 2003.

Two Approaches to Merging Knowledge Bases

James P. Delgrande[1] and Torsten Schaub[2]*

[1] School of Computing Science, Simon Fraser University , Burnaby, B.C., Canada V5A 1S6 ,
jim@cs.sfu.ca
[2] Institut für Informatik, Universität Potsdam, D–14415 Potsdam, Germany,
torsten@cs.uni-potsdam.de

Abstract. We present a framework for expressing different merging operators for belief sets. This framework is a generalisation of our earlier work concerning consistency-based belief revision and contraction. Two distinct merging operators are identified: in the first approach, belief sources are consistently combined so that the result of merging knowledge bases $K_1, \ldots, K_n$ is a maximal consistent (if possible) set of formulas comprising the joint knowledge of the knowledge bases. This approach then accords to one's intuitions as to what a "merge" operator should do. The second approach is more akin to a generalised belief revision operator: Knowledge bases $K_1, \ldots, K_n$ are "projected" onto another (in the simplest case the trivially true knowledge base). In both cases, we consider the incorporation of entailment-based and consistency-based integrity constraints. Properties of these operators are investigated, primarily by comparing their properties with postulates that have been identified previously in the literature. As well, the interrelationships between these approaches and belief revision is given.

1 Introduction

The problem of merging multiple, potentially conflicting bodies of information arises in various guises. For example, an intelligent agent may receive reports from differing sources of knowledge that must be combined. As well, an agent may receive conflicting information from sensors that needs to be reconciled. Alternately, knowledge bases or databases comprising collections of data may need to be combined into a coherent whole. Even in dealing with a single, isolated, agent the problem of merging knowledge sets may arise: consider an agent whose beliefs are modelled by various independent "states of mind", but where it is desirable in some circumstances to combine such states of mind into a coherent whole, for example, before acting in a crucial situation. In all these cases, the fundamental problem is that of combining knowledge bases that may be mutually inconsistent, or conflicting, to get a coherent merged set of beliefs.

Given this diversity of situations in which the problem may arise, it is not surprising that different approaches have arisen for combining sources of information. The major subtypes of merging that have been proposed are called (following [11]) *majority* and *arbitration* operators. In the former case, the majority opinion counts towards resolving conflicts; in the latter, informally, the idea is to try to arrive at some consensus. In this paper, we develop a specific framework for specifying merge operations. This framework

---

* Affiliated with the School of Computing Science at Simon Fraser University, Canada.

J.J. Alferes and J. Leite (Eds.): JELIA 2004, LNAI 3229, pp. 426–438, 2004.

extends our earlier work in belief revision. In both cases, the central intuition is that for belief change one begins by expressing the various knowledge bases, belief sources, etc. in distinct languages, and then (according to the belief change operation) in one way or another re-express the knowledge bases in a common language. Two approaches are presented. In the first case, the intuition is that for merging knowledge bases, the common information is in a sense "pooled". This approach then seems to conform more naturally to the commonsense notion of merging of knowledge. A key property of this approach is that knowledge common to the knowledge bases is contained in the merged knowledge base. Thus if one knowledge base contained $p \wedge q$ and another $\neg p \wedge \neg q$, then $(p \wedge q) \vee (\neg p \wedge \neg q)$ would be in the merged knowledge base. Hence in this approach to merging, an intuition underlying the merging operation is that one of the knowledge bases contains correct information, but it is not known which.

In the second approach, knowledge bases are projected onto a separate knowledge base (which in the simplest case would consist solely of the trivially true knowledge base). That is, the knowledge bases we wish to merge are used to augment the knowledge of a "target" body of knowledge. This second approach then appears to be a natural extension of belief *revision*. In this approach, knowledge common to the knowledge bases may not be contained in the merged knowledge base. Thus if two knowledge bases contained $p \wedge q$ and $\neg p \wedge \neg q$, respectively, then $(p \wedge q) \vee (\neg p \wedge \neg q)$ may not be in the merged knowledge base; thus for example $p \wedge \neg q$ may be consistent with the merged knowledge base. Hence here, an intuition underlying the merging operation is that perhaps some "common ground" is found between the merged knowledge bases.

In both approaches, we address the incorporation of entailment-based and consistency-based integrity constraints with the merge operator. Both approaches have reasonable properties, compared with postulate sets that have appeared in the literature. As well, the second type of approach has not, to our knowledge, been investigated previously. The next section describes related work while Section 3 develops our approaches. We conclude with a discussion. Proofs are omitted due to space limitations.

2   Background

2.1   Consistency-Based Belief Revision

This subsection summarises our earlier work in [5]. Throughout this paper, we deal with propositional languages and use the logical symbols $\top$, $\bot$, $\neg$, $\vee$, $\wedge$, $\supset$, and $\equiv$ to construct formulas in the standard way. We write $\mathcal{L}_{\mathcal{P}}$ to denote a language over an alphabet $\mathcal{P}$ of *propositional letters* or *atomic propositions*. Formulas are denoted by the Greek letters α, β, α_1, ... *Knowledge bases* are identified with deductively-closed sets of formulas, or *belief sets*, and are denoted K, K_1, ...[1] Thus $K = \mathit{Cn}(K)$, where $\mathit{Cn}(\cdot)$ is the deductive closure in classical propositional logic of the formula or set of formulas given as argument. Given an alphabet $\mathcal{P}$, we define a disjoint alphabet $\mathcal{P}'$ as $\mathcal{P}' = \{p' \mid p \in \mathcal{P}\}$. For $\alpha \in \mathcal{L}_{\mathcal{P}}$, α' is the result of replacing in α each proposition

---

[1] We note that while we deal solely with belief sets in this paper, our definitions work for arbitrary sets of formulas, and provide the basis for a finite representation of these operators.

$p \in \mathcal{P}$ by the corresponding proposition $p' \in \mathcal{P}'$ (so implicitly there is an isomorphism between $\mathcal{P}$ and $\mathcal{P}'$). This is defined analogously for sets of formulas.

A *belief change scenario* in $\mathcal{L}_\mathcal{P}$ is a triple $B = (K, R, C)$ where K, R, and C are sets of formulas in $\mathcal{L}_\mathcal{P}$. Informally, K is a belief set that is to be modified so that the formulas in R are contained in the result, and the formulas in C are not. For an approach to revision we have $|R| = 1$ and $C = \emptyset$, and for an approach to contraction we have $R = \emptyset$ and $|C| = 1$. An extension determined by a belief change scenario, called a *belief change extension*, is defined as follows.

Definition 1. *Let $B = (K, R, C)$ be a belief change scenario in $\mathcal{L}_\mathcal{P}$.*
Define EQ as a maximal set of equivalences $EQ \subseteq \{p \equiv p' \mid p \in \mathcal{P}\}$ such that

$$Cn(K' \cup R \cup EQ) \cap (C \cup \{\bot\}) = \emptyset.$$

Then $Cn(K' \cup R \cup EQ) \cap \mathcal{L}_\mathcal{P}$ is a (consistent) belief change extension of B.

If there is no such set EQ then B is inconsistent and $\mathcal{L}_\mathcal{P}$ is defined to be the sole (inconsistent) belief change extension *of B.*

Note that in the definition, "maximal" is with respect to set containment (rather than set cardinality). The exclusive use of "$\{\bot\}$" in the definition is to take care of consistency if $C = \emptyset$. Clearly a consistent belief change extension of B is a modification of K which contains every formula in R, and which contains no formula in C. We say that EQ *determines* the respective consistent belief change extension of B. For a given belief change scenario there may be more than one consistent belief change extension. We will make use of the notion of a *selection function* c that for any set $I \neq \emptyset$ has as value some element of I. In defining revision, we will use a selection function to select a specific consistent belief change extension. [2]

Definition 1 provides a very general framework for specifying belief change. We can restrict the definition to obtain specific functions for belief revision and contraction; here we just deal with revision.

Definition 2 (Revision). *Let K be a belief set and α a formula, and let $(E_i)_{i \in I}$ be the family of all belief change extensions of $(K, \{\alpha\}, \emptyset)$. Then, we define*

1. $K \dot{+}_c \alpha = E_i$ as a choice revision *of K by α with respect to some selection function c with $c(I) = i$.*

2. $K \dot{+} \alpha = \bigcap_{i \in I} E_i$ as the (skeptical) revision *of K by α.*

With respect to the AGM postulates [7], we obtain that the basic postulates are satisfied, along with supplementary postulate $(K\dot{+}7)$ for both choice and skeptical revision.

For instance, (skeptically) revising $Cn(p \wedge q)$ by $\neg q$ results in $Cn(p \wedge \neg q)$. This belief change extension is determined by $\{p \equiv p'\}$ from the renamed belief set $\{p' \wedge q'\}$ and the revision formula $\neg q$. As a second example, we get $\{\neg p \equiv q\} \dot{+} \neg q = Cn(p \wedge \neg q)$ by $\{p \equiv p', q \equiv q'\}$ from $\neg p' \equiv q'$ and $\neg q$. For a third example, observe that both $\{p \vee q\} \dot{+} (\neg p \vee \neg q)$ as well as $\{p \wedge q\} \dot{+} (\neg p \vee \neg q)$ result in $Cn(p \equiv \neg q)$, although the former is determined by $\{p \equiv p', q \equiv q'\}$, while the latter relies on two such sets, viz. $\{p \equiv p'\}$ and $\{q \equiv q'\}$.

---

[2] This use of selection functions is slightly different from that in the AGM approach.

Definition 1 also leads to a natural and general treatment of both consistency-based and entailment-based integrity constraints; see [5] for details.

2.2 Belief Merging

Konieczny and Pino Peréz [9] consider the problem of merging possibly contradictory belief bases. To this end, they consider finite multisets of the form $\Psi = \{K_1, \ldots, K_n\}$ and assume that all belief sets K_i are consistent, finitely representable, and therefore representable by a formula. K^{+n} is the multiset consisting of n copies of K. Multiset union is denoted $\sqcup$, wherein for example $\{\phi\} \sqcup \{\phi\} = \{\phi, \phi\}$. Following [9], we use[3] $\Delta^\mu(\Psi)$ to denote the result of merging the multi-set Ψ of belief bases given the entailment-based integrity constraint expressed by μ. They provide the following set of postulates:

Definition 3 ([9]). *Let Ψ be a multiset of sets of formulas, and ϕ, μ formulas (all possibly subscripted or primed). Δ is an IC merging operator iff it satisfies the following postulates.*

$(IC0)$ $\Delta^\mu(\Psi) \vdash \mu$.
$(IC1)$ *If* $\mu \nvdash \bot$ *then* $\Delta^\mu(\Psi) \nvdash \bot$.
$(IC2)$ *If* $\bigwedge \Psi \nvdash \neg\mu$ *then* $\Delta^\mu(\Psi) \equiv \bigwedge \Psi \wedge \mu$.
$(IC3)$ *If* $\Psi_1 \equiv \Psi_2$ *and* $\mu_1 \equiv \mu_2$ *then* $\Delta^{\mu_1}(\Psi_1) \equiv \Delta^{\mu_2}(\Psi_2)$.
$(IC4)$ *If* $\phi \vdash \mu$ *and* $\phi' \vdash \mu$ *then:* $\Delta^\mu(\phi \sqcup \phi') \wedge \phi \nvdash \bot$ *implies* $\Delta^\mu(\phi \sqcup \phi') \wedge \phi' \nvdash \bot$.
$(IC5)$ $\Delta^\mu(\Psi_1) \wedge \Delta^\mu(\Psi_2) \vdash \Delta^\mu(\Psi_1 \sqcup \Psi_2)$.
$(IC6)$ *If* $\Delta^\mu(\Psi_1) \wedge \Delta^\mu(\Psi_2) \nvdash \bot$ *then* $\Delta^\mu(\Psi_1 \sqcup \Psi_2) \vdash \Delta^\mu(\Psi_1) \wedge \Delta^\mu(\Psi_2)$.
$(IC7)$ $\Delta^{\mu_1}(\Psi) \wedge \mu_2 \vdash \Delta^{\mu_1 \wedge \mu_2}(\Psi)$.
$(IC8)$ *If* $\Delta^{\mu_1}(\Psi) \wedge \mu_2 \nvdash \bot$ *then* $\Delta^{\mu_1 \wedge \mu_2}(\Psi) \vdash \Delta^{\mu_1}(\Psi) \wedge \mu_2$.

The intent is that $\Delta^\mu(\Psi)$ is the belief base closest to the belief multiset Ψ. Of the postulates, $(IC2)$ states that the result of merging is simply the conjunction of the belief bases and integrity constraints, when consistent. $(IC4)$ is a *fairness* postulate, that when two belief bases disagree, merging doesn't give preference to one of them. $(IC5)$ states that a model of two mergings is in the union of their merging. With $(IC5)$ we get that if two mergings are consistent then their merging is implied by their conjunction. Note that merging operators are trivially commutative. $(IC7)$ and $(IC8)$ correspond to the extended AGM postulates $(K \dot{+} 7)$ and $(K \dot{+} 8)$ for revision, but with respect to the integrity constraints. Postulates $(IC1)$–$(IC6)$, with tautologous integrity constraints, correspond to basic merging, without integrity constraints, in [11].

A majority operator is characterised in addition by the postulate:

(Maj) $\exists n \Delta^\mu(\Psi_1 \sqcup \Psi_2^{+n}) \vdash \Delta^\mu(\Psi_2)$

Thus, given enough repetitions of a belief base Ψ_2, this belief base will eventually come to dominate the merge operation.

An arbitration operator is characterised by the original postulates together with the following postulate; see [9] for an explanation.

---
[3] [11] write $\Delta_\mu(\Psi)$ where we have $\Delta^\mu(\Psi)$.

(*Arb*) Let μ_1 and μ_2 be logically independent. If $\Delta^{\mu_1}(\phi_1) \equiv \Delta^{\mu_2}(\phi_2)$ and $\Delta^{\mu_1 \equiv \mu_2}(\phi_1 \sqcup \phi_2) \equiv (\mu_1 \equiv \mu_2)$ then $\Delta^{\mu_1 \vee \mu_2}(\phi_1 \sqcup \phi_2) \equiv \Delta^{\mu_1}(\phi_1)$.

[11] characterises these approaches as trying to minimize global dissatisfaction vs. trying to minimize local dissatisfaction respectively. Examples are given of a merging operator using Dalal's notion of distance [4].

Liberatore and Schaerf [13] consider merging two belief bases and propose the following postulate set to characterise a merge operator that they call an *arbitration* operator and that [9] call a *commutative revision operator*. Like [9] they restrict their attention to propositional languages over a finite set of atoms.

($LS1$) $\vdash \alpha \bigtriangleup \beta \equiv \beta \bigtriangleup \alpha$.
($LS2$) $\vdash \alpha \wedge \beta \supset \alpha \bigtriangleup \beta$.
($LS3$) If $\alpha \wedge \beta$ is satisfiable then $\vdash \alpha \bigtriangleup \beta \supset \alpha \wedge \beta$.
($LS4$) $\alpha \bigtriangleup \beta$ is unsatisfiable iff α is unsatisfiable and β is unsatisfiable.
($LS5$) If $\vdash \alpha_1 \equiv \alpha_2$ and $\vdash \beta_1 \equiv \beta_2$ then $\vdash \alpha_1 \bigtriangleup \beta_1 \equiv \alpha_2 \bigtriangleup \beta_2$.
($LS6$) $\alpha \bigtriangleup (\beta_1 \vee \beta_2) = \begin{cases} \alpha \bigtriangleup \beta_1 & \text{or} \\ \alpha \bigtriangleup \beta_2 & \text{or} \\ (\alpha \bigtriangleup \beta_1) \vee (\alpha \bigtriangleup \beta_2) \end{cases}$
($LS7$) $\vdash (\alpha \bigtriangleup \beta) \supset (\alpha \vee \beta)$.
($LS8$) If α is satisfiable then $\alpha \wedge (\alpha \bigtriangleup \beta)$ is satisfiable.

Earlier work on merging operators includes [1] and [17]. The former proposes various theory merging operators based on the selection of maximum consistent subsets in the union of the belief bases; see [10] for a pertinent discussion. The latter proposes an "arbitration" operator that satisfies a subset of the Liberatore and Schaerf postulates; see [12] for a discussion. [14] first identified and addressed the majority merge operator. [8] gives a framework for defining merging operators, where a family of merging operators is parameterised by a distance between interpretations and aggregating functions. The authors suggest that most, if not all, model-based merging operators can be captured in their approach, along with a selection of syntax-based operators. More or less concurrently, [15] proposed a general approach to formulating merging functions, based on ordinal conditional functions [19]. Roughly, epistemic states are associated with a mapping from possible worlds onto the set of ordinal numbers. Various merging operators then can be defined by considering the ways in which the "Cartesian product" of two epistemic states can be resolved into an ordinal conditional function. [3] also considers the problem of an agent merging information from different sources, via what is called *social contraction*. In a manner analogous to the Levi Identity for belief revision, information from the various sources is weakened to the extent that it can be consistently added to the agent's belief base. Last, much work has been carried out in merging possibilistic knowledge bases; see for example [2].

3   Consistency-Based Approaches to Belief Set Merging

In this section we modify the framework given by Definition 1 to deal with belief set *merging*, in which multiple sources of information (knowledge bases, etc.) are coalesced into a single belief set. We detail two different approaches to belief set merging, expressible in the general approach.

In the first case, the intuition is that for merging belief sets, the common information is in a sense "pooled". This approach then seems to conform to the commonsense notion of merging of knowledge, in which sets of knowledge are joined to produce a single knowledge set retaining as much as possible of the contents of the original knowledge sets. In the second approach, knowledge sources are projected onto a separate knowledge source (which in the simplest case could consist solely of $\top$). That is, the sources we wish to merge are used to augment the knowledge of another source.

3.1   Multi Belief Change Scenarios

A *multi belief change scenario* in $\mathcal{L}_\mathcal{P}$ is a triple $B = (\mathcal{K}, R, C)$ where $\mathcal{K}$ is a family $(K_j)_{j \in J}$ of sets of formulas in $\mathcal{L}_\mathcal{P}$, and R and C are sets of formulas in $\mathcal{L}_\mathcal{P}$. Informally, $\mathcal{K}$ is a collection of belief sets that are to be merged so that the formulas in R are contained in the result, and the formulas in C are not. So this is the same as a belief change scenario as defined in Section 2, except that the single set of formulas K is extended to several of sets of formulas. R and C will be used to express entailment-based and consistency-based integrity constraints, respectively. That is, the formulas in R will all be true in the result of a merging, whereas the negations of formulas in C will not be contained in the result. While R is intended to represent a set of entailment-based integrity constraints [16], it could just as easily be regarded as a set of formulas for revision. Similarly, while C is intended to represent a set of (negations of) consistency-based integrity constraints [18], it could just as easily be regarded as a set of formulas for contraction. Thus the overall approaches can be considered as a framework in which merging, revising, and (multiple) contractions may be carried out in parallel while taking into account integrity constraints.

To begin with, we generalise the notation α' from Section 2 in the obvious way for integers $i > 0$ and sets of integers: for alphabet $\mathcal{P}$, we define $\mathcal{P}^i$ as $\mathcal{P}^i = \{p^i \mid p \in \mathcal{P}\}$, and α^i etc. analogous to Section 2. Similarly we define for a set or list of positive integers N that $\mathcal{P}^N = \{p^i \mid p \in \mathcal{P}, i \in N\}$. Then $\alpha^N = \{\alpha^i \mid i \in N\}$. The definition of an extension to a multi belief change scenario will depend on the specific approach to merging that is being formalised. We consider each approach in turn in the following two subsections.

3.2   Belief Set Merging

Consider the first approach, in which the contents of belief sets are to be merged.

Definition 4. *Let $B = (\mathcal{K}, R, C)$ be a multi belief change scenario in $\mathcal{L}_\mathcal{P}$, where $\mathcal{K} = (K_j)_{j \in J}$. Define EQ as a maximal set of equivalences*

$$EQ \subseteq \{p^k \equiv p^l \mid p \in \mathcal{P} \text{ and } k, l \in J\}$$

such that

$$Cn\left(\bigcup_{j \in J} K_j^j \cup R^J \cup EQ\right) \cap (C^J \cup \{\bot\}) = \emptyset$$

Then

$$\left\{ \alpha \mid \{\alpha^j \mid j \in J\} \subseteq Cn\left(\bigcup_{j \in J} K_j^j \cup R^J \cup EQ\right) \right\}$$

is a consistent symmetric belief change extension *of B.*

If there is no such set EQ then B is inconsistent *and $\mathcal{L}_P$ is defined to be the sole* (inconsistent) symmetric belief change extension *of B.*

The sets R^J ensure that the integrity constraints in R are true in each belief set, and so will be true in the result. Similarly, the formulas C^J ensure that the formulas in C will not be in the result.

Definition 5 (Merging). *Let $\mathcal{K}$ be a family of sets of formulas in $\mathcal{L}_P$ and R and C be finite sets of formulas in $\mathcal{L}_P$, and let $(E_i)_{i \in I}$ be the family of all symmetric belief change extensions of $(\mathcal{K}, R, C)$.*

Then, we define

1. $\Delta_c^{R,C}(\mathcal{K}) = E_i$ as the choice merging *of $\mathcal{K}$ with respect to integrity constraints R and C, and selection function c with $c(I) = i$.*

2. $\Delta^{R,C}(\mathcal{K}) = \bigcap_{i \in I} E_i$ as the (skeptical) merging *of $\mathcal{K}$ with respect to integrity constraints R and C.*

Of particular interest is *binary* merging, where $\mathcal{K} = \{K_1, K_2\}$. In this case, we will write the merge operator Δ as an infix operator. That is, $\Delta^{R,C}(\{K_1, K_2\})$ is written as $K_1 \Delta^{R,C} K_2$. Also, given two formulas α, β along with $R = C = \emptyset$, we just write $\alpha \Delta \beta$. For conformity with the notation used in Definition 3 [9], we write $\alpha \Delta^\mu \beta$ if $R = \{\mu\}$ and $C = \emptyset$.

Example 1. $(p \wedge q \wedge r) \Delta (p \wedge \neg q \wedge s)$ yields (informally) $(p^1 \wedge q^1 \wedge r^1) \wedge (p^2 \wedge \neg q^2 \wedge s^2)$ along with $EQ = \{p^1 \equiv p^2, r^1 \equiv r^2, s^1 \equiv s^2\}$. The result of merging is $Cn(\{p \wedge r \wedge s\})$.

Example 2. Let

$$K_1 \equiv p \wedge q \wedge r \wedge s \text{ and } K_2 \equiv \neg p \wedge \neg q \wedge \neg r \wedge \neg s.$$

We obtain that $K_1 \Delta K_2$ yields $EQ = \emptyset$ and in fact

$$K_1 \Delta K_2 = Cn(\{(p \wedge q \wedge r \wedge s) \vee (\neg p \wedge \neg q \wedge \neg r \wedge \neg s)\})$$

This example is introduced and discussed in [11]; as well it corresponds to the postulate $(LS7)$. Consider where K_1 and K_2 represent two analyst's forecasts concerning how four different stocks are going to perform. p represents the fact that the first stock will rise, etc. The result of merging is a belief set, in which it is believed that either all will rise, or that all will not rise. That is, essentially, one forecast will be believed to hold in its entirety, or the other will. As [11] points out, knowing nothing else and assuming independence of the stock's movements, this is implausible: it is possible that some stocks rise while others do not. On the other hand, if we have reason to believe that one forecast is in fact highly reliable (although we don't know which) then the result of Example 2 *is* reasonable. However this example illustrates that there are cases wherein this formulation is too strong.

We obtain the following with respect to the postulate sets described in Section 2.2.

Theorem 1. *Let Δ^μ and Δ_c^μ be defined as in Definition 5.*

Then Δ^μ and Δ_c^μ satisfy the postulates $(IC0)$, $(IC2) - (IC5)$, $(IC7) - (IC8)$, as well as the weaker version of $(IC1)$:[4]

$(IC1')$ *If $K \not\vdash \neg\mu$ for every $K \in \Psi$ and $\mu \not\vdash \bot$ then $\Delta^\mu(\Psi) \not\vdash \bot$.*

A counterexample to $(IC6)$ is given by $\Psi_1 = \{Cn(p), Cn(\neg p)\}$, $\Psi_2 = \{Cn(p)\}$. Note that $(IC6)$ holds in the binary case, though.

We do not discuss the majority or arbitration postulates here (except to note that majority is easily handled by a straightforward modification to Definition 5); this is discussed in the full paper. Note however that the present approach satisfies a non-majority postulate, viz.:

$$\Delta^\mu(\Psi_1 \sqcup \Psi_2^n) = \Delta^\mu(\Psi_1 \sqcup \Psi_2).$$

This postulate is identified in [11], a weaker version of which is used to define their arbitration operator.

Theorem 2. *Let Δ and Δ_c be defined as in Definition 5.*

Then Δ and Δ_c satisfy the following postulates.

1. $(LS1)$, $(LS2)$, $(LS3)$, $(LS5)$, $(LS7)$

as well as the following weaker versions of the remaining postulates:

2. $(LS4)'$ $\alpha \bigtriangleup \beta$ *is satisfiable iff α is satisfiable and β is satisfiable.*
   $(LS6)'$ $(\alpha \bigtriangleup \beta_1) \wedge \beta_2$ *implies $\alpha \bigtriangleup (\beta_1 \wedge \beta_2)$.*
   $(LS8)'$ *If α is satisfiable and β is satisfiable then $\alpha \wedge (\alpha \bigtriangleup \beta)$ is satisfiable.*
3. $(LS6c)'$ *For any selection function c there is a selection function c' such that*
   $\alpha \bigtriangleup_c \beta_1$ *implies* $\alpha \bigtriangleup_{c'} (\beta_1 \vee \beta_2)$ *or* $\alpha \bigtriangleup_c \beta_2$ *implies* $\alpha \bigtriangleup_{c'} (\beta_1 \vee \beta_2)$.

Example 3. A counterexample to $(LS6)$ is given by the following.

$$\alpha \equiv (p \wedge q \wedge r \wedge s), \qquad \beta_1 \equiv (\neg p \wedge \neg q) \vee \neg r, \qquad \beta_2 \equiv \neg q \vee \neg s.$$

We get that:

$$\alpha \bigtriangleup (\beta_1 \vee \beta_2) \equiv (p \wedge q \wedge r) \vee (p \wedge q \wedge s) \vee (p \wedge r \wedge s),$$
$$\alpha \bigtriangleup \beta_1 \equiv (p \wedge q \wedge s) \vee (r \wedge s),$$
$$\alpha \bigtriangleup \beta_2 \equiv (p \wedge q \wedge r) \vee (p \wedge r \wedge s).$$

While the merging operator is commutative by definition, it is not associative; for example $(((p \vee q) \bigtriangleup \neg p) \bigtriangleup p) \neq (p \vee q) \bigtriangleup (\neg p \bigtriangleup p)$. Lastly, we have the following result showing that in this approach, merging two belief sets is expressible in terms of our approach to revision, and vice versa:

Theorem 3. *Let $\dot{+}$ and $\bigtriangleup$ be given as in Definitions 2 and 5 (respectively). Then,*

1. $\alpha \bigtriangleup \beta = \alpha \dot{+} \beta \cap \beta \dot{+} \alpha$.
2. $\alpha \dot{+} \beta = \alpha \bigtriangleup^\beta \top$.

---

[4] It is straightforward to obtain $(IC1)$ by essentially ignoring inconsistent belief sets. We remain with the present postulate since it reflects the most natural formulation of merging in our framework.

3.3 Belief Set Projection

In our second approach, the contents of several belief sets are "projected" onto another.[5] Again, the formulation is straightforward within the framework of belief change scenarios. For belief sets $K_1, \ldots, K_n$, we express each in a distinct language, but project these belief sets onto a distinguished belief set in which R is believed. (In the simplest case we would have $R \equiv \top$.)

In the following R, and C again represent a set of entailment-based and consistency-based integrity constraints, respectively.

Definition 6. *Let* $B = (\mathcal{K}, R, C)$ *be a multi belief change scenario in* $\mathcal{L}_\mathcal{P}$, *where* $\mathcal{K} = (K_j)_{j \in J}$. *Define EQ as a maximal set of equivalences*

$$EQ \subseteq \{p^j \equiv p \mid p \in \mathcal{P} \text{ and } j \in J\}$$

such that

$$Cn\left(\bigcup_{j \in J} K_j^j \cup R \cup EQ\right) \cap (C \cup \{\bot\}) = \emptyset$$

Then

$$Cn\left(\bigcup_{j \in J} K_j^j \cup R \cup EQ\right) \cap \mathcal{L}_\mathcal{P}$$

is a consistent projected belief change extension *of* B.

If there is no such set EQ then B is inconsistent *and $\mathcal{L}_\mathcal{P}$ is defined to be the sole* (inconsistent) projected belief change extension *of B.*

There is an interesting similarity between revision and projection. Revision in some sense "projects" the belief set onto the formula that we revise with. Similarly, the actual projection operation "projects" the belief sets onto whatever is contained in R.

Definition 7 (Merging via Projection). *Let $\mathcal{K}$ be a family of sets of formulas in $\mathcal{L}_\mathcal{P}$ and R and C be finite sets of formulas in $\mathcal{L}_\mathcal{P}$, and let $(E_i)_{i \in I}$ be the family of all projected belief change extensions of $(\mathcal{K}, R, C)$.*

Then, we define

1. $\nabla_c^{R,C}(\mathcal{K}) = E_i$ *as the* choice merging *of $\mathcal{K}$ with respect to integrity constraints R and C, and selection function c with $c(I) = i$.*

2. $\nabla^{R,C}(\mathcal{K}) = \bigcap_{i \in I} E_i$ *as the* (skeptical) merging *of $\mathcal{K}$ with respect to integrity constraints R and C.*

As above, for two formulas α and β, we just write $\alpha \nabla \beta$, if $R = C = \emptyset$ and we write $\alpha \nabla^\mu \beta$ if $R = \{\mu\}$ and $C = \emptyset$.

Example 4. We have that $(p \wedge q \wedge r) \nabla (p \wedge \neg q)$ yields two EQ sets:

$$EQ_1 = \{p^1 \equiv p, \ p^2 \equiv p, \ q^1 \equiv q, \ r^1 \equiv r, \ r^2 \equiv r\} \quad \text{and}$$
$$EQ_2 = \{p^1 \equiv p, \ p^2 \equiv p, \ q^2 \equiv q, \ r^1 \equiv r, \ r^2 \equiv r\}.$$

The result of merging is $p \wedge r \wedge s$.

---

[5] We thank Jérôme Lang for pointing out this alternative to us.

Example 5. Consider the example from [11]:

$$K_1 \equiv p \wedge q \wedge r \wedge s \text{ and } K_2 \equiv \neg p \wedge \neg q \wedge \neg r \wedge \neg s.$$

In forming a set of equivalences, EQ, we can have precisely one of $p^1 \equiv p$ or $p^2 \equiv p$ in EQ, and similarly for the other atomic sentences. Each such set of equivalences then represents one way each forecaster's prediction for a specific stock can be taken into account. Taken all together then we have 2^4 sets of equivalences, and in the end we obtain that

$$K_1 \nabla K_2 = Cn(\top).$$

We feel that this is a plausible outcome in the interpretation involving the forecasted movement of independent stocks. Note that if the example were extended so that multiple possibilities for stock movement were allowed, then we would obtain in the projection the various compromise positions for the two belief sets. Thus for example if a stock could either remain the same, or go up or down a little or a lot, and one forecaster predicted that stocks a and b would go up a lot, and another predicted that they would both go down a lot, then the projection would have both stocks moving a lot, although it would be unclear as to whether the movement would be up or down.

We obtain the following.

Theorem 4. *Let ∇ and ∇_c be defined as in Definition 7.*

Then ∇ and ∇_c satisfy the postulates $(IC0)$, $(IC2)$, $(IC3)$, $(IC5)$, $(IC7)$, $(IC8)$, as well as versions of $(IC1)$, $(IC4)$:

$(IC1')$ *If $\bigwedge \Psi \nvdash \neg\mu$ and $\mu \nvdash \bot$ then $\nabla^\mu(\Psi) \nvdash \bot$.*[6]
$(IC4')$ *If $\phi_1 \nvdash \bot$, $\phi_2 \nvdash \bot$ and $\phi_1 \vdash \mu$ and $\phi_2 \vdash \mu$ then: $\nabla^\mu(\phi_1 \sqcup \phi_2) \wedge \phi_1 \nvdash \bot$.*

Theorem 5. *Let ∇ and ∇_c be defined as in Definition 7.*

Then, ∇ and ∇_c satisfy the postulates $(LS1)$–$(LS3)$, $(LS5)$, along with:

$(LS4)'$ *$\alpha \nabla \beta$ is satisfiable iff α is satisfiable and β is satisfiable.*
$(LS8)'$ *If α is satisfiable and β is satisfiable then $\alpha \wedge (\alpha \nabla \beta)$ is satisfiable.*

As well, versions for ∇_c for $(LS4)'$ and $(LS8)'$ also hold.

Postulate $(LS6)$ does not hold here; Example 3 provides a counterexample. As well, the weaker postulate $(LS6)'$ does not hold. Recall that $(LS6)'$ is $(\alpha \nabla \beta_1) \wedge \beta_2$ implies $\alpha \nabla (\beta_1 \wedge \beta_2)$. However, consider the counterexample, derived from the stock-moving example (2):

$$[(p \wedge q) \nabla (\neg p \wedge \neg q)] \wedge (p \wedge \neg q)$$

does not imply

$$(p \wedge q) \nabla [(\neg p \wedge \neg q) \wedge (p \wedge \neg q)].$$

---

[6] It is straightforward to obtain $(IC1)$ by essentially ignoring inconsistent belief sets. We remain with the present postulate since it reflects the most natural formulation of project in our framework.

Further, postulate ($LS7$) does not hold here, as Example 5 illustrates, nor is the projection operator associative.

Last we have the following results relating projection with merging and revision, respectively:

Theorem 6. *Let $\mathcal{K}$, $\Delta^{R,C}$ and $\nabla^{R,C}$ be given as in Definitions 5 and 7 (respectively).*

$$\nabla^{R,C}(\mathcal{K}) \subseteq \Delta^{R,C}(\mathcal{K}).$$

That is, in binary terms, $\alpha \nabla^{R,C} \beta \subseteq \alpha \Delta^{R,C} \beta$.

As well, we have the following analogue to Theorem 3:

Theorem 7. *Let $\dot{+}$ and ∇ be given as in Definitions 2 and 7 (respectively).*
Then, $\alpha \dot{+} \beta = \alpha \nabla^{\beta} \top$.

4   Complexity

In [6], we analysed the computational complexity of reasoning from belief change scenarios. Specifically, we addressed the following basic reasoning tasks:

Theorem 8 ([6]).

1. *Deciding whether a belief change scenario B has a consistent belief change extension is NP-complete;*
2. *Given a belief change scenario B and formula ϕ, deciding whether ϕ is contained in at least one consistent belief change extension of B is Σ_P^2-complete; and*
3. *Given a belief change scenario B and formula ϕ, deciding whether ϕ is contained in all consistent belief change extensions of B is Π_P^2-complete.*

Clearly, the variants of these decision problems for merging and projection fall in the same complexity class and in fact follow as corollaries of the above result. This then illustrates an advantage of formulating belief change operations within a uniform framework: essentially, properties of the basic framework can be investigated in a general form; properties of specific operators (or combinations of operators) are then easily derivable as secondary results.

5   Discussion

We have presented two approaches for merging belief sets, expressed in a general, consistency-based framework for belief change [5]. In the first approach, the intuition is that for merging belief sets, common information is in a sense "pooled". This approach then seems to conform to the commonsense notion of merging of knowledge, in which belief sets are joined to produce a single belief set retaining as much as possible of the contents of the original belief sets. A characteristic of this operation is that sentences common to the original belief sets are in the merged belief set. In the second approach, belief sets are projected onto another belief set. That is, the sets we wish to merge are used to augment the knowledge of another (possibly empty) belief set. This second approach appears to differ from others that have appeared in the literature. It is strictly weaker than the first; however this weakness is not a disadvantage, since, among other things, it avoids the possible difficulty illustrated in Example (2). This second approach has something of the flavour of both belief revision and update. With respect to belief revision, projection can be viewed as a process whereby several belief sets are simultaneously revised with respect to another. With respect to belief update, semantically, individual models of a belief set are independently updated. Hence projection is like update, but where the "granularity" of the operation at the level of belief sets rather than models. Thus projection can be regarded as an operator lying intermediate between belief revision and update.

In the full paper we consider merging and projection with respect to a denumerable number of belief sets. As well, we show how these operations (in the finite case) can be equivalently expressed as functions with domain and range effectively being knowledge bases, that is, arbitrary subsets of $\mathcal{L}$, while retaining syntax-independence. Last, we provide abstract algorithms for computing these operators.

Acknowledgements. We would like to express our great thanks to Jérôme Lang for many helpful suggestions and fruitful discussions on earlier drafts of this paper. We also thank the referees for their detailed and helpful comments.

References

1. C. Baral, S. Kraus, J. Minker, and V. Subrahmanian. Combining multiple knowledge bases consisting of first order theories. *Computational Intelligence*, 8(1):45–71, 1992.
2. S. Benferhat, D. Dubois, S. Kaci, and H. Prade. Possibilistic merging and distance-based fusion of propositional information. *Annals of Mathematics and Artificial Intelligence*, 34(1-3):217–252, 2003.
3. R. Booth. Social contraction and belief negotiation. In D. Fensel, F. Giunchiglia, D. McGuiness, and M. Williams, editors, *Proceedings of the Eighth International Conference on the Principles of Knowledge Representation and Reasoning*, pages 375–384, San Francisco, 2002. Morgan Kaufmann.
4. M. Dalal. Investigations into theory of knowledge base revision. In *Proceedings of the AAAI National Conference on Artificial Intelligence*, pages 449–479, St. Paul, Minnesota, 1988.
5. J. Delgrande and T. Schaub. A consistency-based approach for belief change. *Artificial Intelligence*, 151(1-2):1–41, 2003.
6. J.P. Delgrande, T. Schaub, H. Tompits, and S. Woltran. On computing solutions to belief change scenarios. In S. Benferhat and P. Besnard, editors, *Proceedings of the Sixth European Conference on Symbolic and Quantitative Approaches to Reasoning with Uncertainty (ECSQARU-2001)*, volume 2143 of *Lecture Notes in Artificial Intelligence*, pages 510–521, Toulouse, Fr., 2001. Springer Verlag.
7. P. Gärdenfors. *Knowledge in Flux: Modelling the Dynamics of Epistemic States*. The MIT Press, Cambridge, MA, 1988.
8. S. Konieczny, J. Lang, and P. Marquis. Distance-based merging: a general framework and some complexity results. In D. Fensel, F. Giunchiglia, D. McGuiness, and M. Williams, editors, *Proceedings of the Eighth International Conference on the Principles of Knowledge Representation and Reasoning*, pages 97–108, San Francisco, 2002. Morgan Kaufmann.
9. S. Konieczny and R. Pino Pérez. Merging information under constraints: A logical framework. *Journal of Logic and Computation*, 12(5):773–808, 2002.

10. Sébastian Konieczny. On the difference between merging knowledge bases and combining them. In A. G. Cohn, F. Giunchiglia, and B. Selman, editors, *KR2000: Principles of Knowledge Representation and Reasoning*, pages 135–144, San Francisco, 2000. Morgan Kaufmann.
11. Sébastian Konieczny and Ramón Pino Pérez. On the logic of merging. In A. G. Cohn, L. Schubert, and S. C. Shapiro, editors, *KR'98: Principles of Knowledge Representation and Reasoning*, pages 488–498. Morgan Kaufmann, San Francisco, California, 1998.
12. P. Liberatore and M. Schaerf. Reducing belief revision to circumscription (and vice versa). *Artificial Intelligence*, 93(1–2):261–296, 1997.
13. P. Liberatore and M. Schaerf. Arbitration (or how to merge knowledge bases). *IEEE Transactions on Knowledge and Data Engineering*, 10(1):76–90, 1998.
14. J. Lin and A. Mendelzon. Knowledge base merging by majority. In *Dynamic Worlds: From the Frame Problem to Knowledge Management*. Kluwer, 1999.
15. T. Meyer. On the semantics of combination operations. *Journal of Applied NonClassical Logics*, 11(1-2):59–84, 2001.
16. R. Reiter. Towards a logical reconstruction of relational database theory. In M.L. Brodie, J. Mylopoulos, and J.W. Schmidt, editors, *On Conceptual Modelling*, pages 191–233. Springer-Verlag, 1984.
17. P. Revesz. On the semantics of theory change: Arbitration between old and new information. In C. Beeri, editor, *Proceedings of the Twelfth ACM Symposium on Principles of Database Systems*, pages 71–82, Washington D.C., 1993.
18. F. Sadri and R. Kowalski. A theorem-proving approach to database integrity. In J. Minker, editor, *Foundations of Deductive Databases and Logic Programming*, chapter 9, pages 313–362. Morgan Kaufmann Publishers, 1987.
19. W. Spohn. Ordinal conditional functions: A dynamic theory of epistemic states. In W.L. Harper and B. Skyrms, editors, *Causation in Decision, Belief Change, and Statistics*, volume II, pages 105–134. Kluwer Academic Publishers, 1988.

An Algebraic Approach to Belief Contraction and Nonmonotonic Entailment

Lee Flax

Macquarie University, Sydney NSW 2109, Australia
flax@ics.mq.edu.au

Abstract. The approach of Alchourrón, Gärdenfors and Makinson to belief contraction is treated algebraically. This is then used to give an algebraic treatment of nonmonotonic entailment in the context of a belief set. The algebra used is a preboolean algebra whose elements are sets of sentences and whose order relation is *restricted entailment*. Under plausible assumptions restricted entailment is computable; so I have proposed elsewhere [4] that restricted entailment be taken as the deductive process of an agent. It can also be shown (not here) that ordinary entailment can be retrieved from the family of entailments with finite restrictions. Nonmonotonic closure satisfies inclusion, supraclassicality and distribution, but satisfaction of idempotency and cumulativity depend on certain conditions being fulfilled. Casting the notions of belief contraction and nonmonotonic entailment in algebraic formalism facilitates the understanding and analysis of these ideas.

1 Introduction

This paper is about an algebraic approach to belief revision (in the form of belief contraction) and nonmonotonic entailment. An advantage of the algebraic approach is that defined notions are made explicit in algebraic notation and so their structure can be examined and insight gained. The algebra is a preboolean algebra and is based on the notion of *restricted entailment*, which is taken to be the order relation of the algebra. A restricted entailment is like ordinary entailment except that model checking is restricted to a subset of semantic structures, called a *restriction*, rather than all structures.

I have proposed elsewhere [4] that a restricted entailment be taken as the deductive component for a reasoning agent. It is therefore important that restricted entailment be computable. (Ordinary entailment is not computable.) Computability of restricted entailment depends in part on the nature of the restriction. These matters are briefly discussed in the Conclusion.

The approach that I use for knowledge representation and update is based on the AGM approach to belief contraction as expounded by Gärdenfors [5] and Gärdenfors and Rott [6]. I have developed a set of algebraic axioms characterising belief contraction that are equivalent to the AGM ones. Nonmonotonic reasoning in the context of a belief set is developed algebraically using belief contraction

J.J. Alferes and J. Leite (Eds.): JELIA 2004, LNAI 3229, pp. 439–451, 2004.

(see section 5). Analogously to the situation for restricted entailment, one can define a notion of *restricted nonmonotonic entailment*.

The next section, section 2, deals with preliminary matters. It reviews the syntax we use for first-order languages and defines the FOE extension of a first-order language. This is used to define *separators* which, in turn, are used to define the operators in a preboolean algebra PSEN. (The algebra is preboolean because it is not quite boolean: two elements of the algebra which are each less than the other with respect to the algebra's partial order are equivalent rather than being equal.) The algebra PSEN is used in our treatment of belief contraction and nonmonotonic entailment. Restricted entailment is also defined in section 2 and the complete lattice structure of the family of restricted entailments described. Section 3 introduces the algebra PSEN and gives some of its properties. Sections 4 and 5 deal with belief contraction and nonmonotonic entailment in the context of a belief set. The final section briefly discusses computability.

2   Preliminaries

We work in a standard first-order language whose *vocabulary* consists of a countable number of constant symbols, a countable number of function symbols of any finite arity and a countable number of relation symbols of any finite arity. A *structure*, $\mathcal{S}$, is a function having a *domain of interpretation*, dom($\mathcal{S}$), which is a set. It maps constants to elements in dom($\mathcal{S}$), function symbols to functions defined on dom($\mathcal{S}$) and relation symbols to relations on dom($\mathcal{S}$). The language also has a countable number of *individual variables*; the *connectives* $\neg$, $\vee$, $\wedge$ and $\rightarrow$; and the *quantifiers* $\forall$ and $\exists$. The *terms* of the language are defined in the usual way, as are the *formulas*. Given any formula, an individual variable is *free* in that formula if the variable is not in the scope of any quantifier in the formula. A *sentence* is a formula with no free variables. Meaning is given to sentences by defining, in the usual way, the *satisfaction relation* between structures and sentences. If the structure $\mathcal{S}$ satisfies the sentence φ, it is written thus: $\mathcal{S} \vDash \varphi$. The *set of models* of a set of sentences X is denoted mod$X$. A structure belongs to mod$X$ if and only if it satisfies every sentence in X.

In order to avoid difficulties with set-theoretical foundations we work entirely in a universe of sets [2]; all collections of objects are sets and all set-theoretical constructions yield sets.

Given a language, the set of all structures defined on the vocabulary is denoted STRUC. The set of all subsets of STRUC is denoted PSTRUC. The relation of *elementary equivalence* between stuctures is defined as follows [3]: two structures $\mathcal{S}$ and $\mathcal{S}'$ are elementarily equivalent, denoted $\mathcal{S} \equiv \mathcal{S}'$, if and only if they satisfy the same sentences. Elementary equivalence is an equivalence relation on the set of structures.

The results of this paper are fundamentally based upon two ideas which need to be explained: one is the notion of a *separator* and the other is *restricted entailment*. To be able to define separators we need to be able to talk about certain infinitely long sentences made up of first-order sentences. To do this we define an extension of the first-order language $\mathcal{F}$, called the FOE extension of $\mathcal{F}$. These languages are well-known; see [8, page 23].

FOE Extension

Given a first-order language $\mathcal{F}$, a language, $\mathcal{L}$, is *the* FOE *extension of* $\mathcal{F}$ if it has the same individual variables, constants, function symbols and relation symbols as $\mathcal{F}$, and the following constitute the formulas of $\mathcal{L}$:

- Any formula of $\mathcal{F}$ is a formula of $\mathcal{L}$.
- (**Conjunctive FOE formula**) For any set X of formulas of $\mathcal{F}$, $\bigwedge X$ is a formula of $\mathcal{L}$.
- (**Disjunctive FOE formula**) For any set Y of conjunctive FOE formulas, $\bigvee Y$ is a formula of $\mathcal{L}$.

Note that there is a one-to-one correspondence between the structures of $\mathcal{F}$ and $\mathcal{L}$ because they have the same vocabularies. Also, the semantics of conjunctive and disjunctive FOE formulas in $\mathcal{L}$ is a straightforward extrapolation of the rules for first-order conjunction and disjunction.

Separators

Two sets of structures, A and B, are said to be *elementarily disjoint* if and only if no member of A is elementarily equivalent to any member of B. The separator for elementarily disjoint sets of structures A and B is an infinitely long sentence, denoted $\sigma_{A,B}$, with the property that for every $\mathcal{S} \in A$, $\mathcal{S} \nvDash \sigma_{A,B}$ and for every $\mathcal{S} \in B$, $\mathcal{S} \vDash \sigma_{A,B}$.

The construction of $\sigma_{A,B}$ is as follows. First enumerate the sentences of $\mathcal{F}$. Call this enumeration the *standard* enumeration of $\mathcal{F}$. Let A and B be elementarily disjoint. For each $(\mathcal{S}, \mathcal{S}') \in A \times B$, let $\sigma_{\mathcal{S}, \mathcal{S}'}$ be the first sentence in the standard enumeration of $\mathcal{F}$ which satisfies $\mathcal{S} \nvDash \sigma_{\mathcal{S}, \mathcal{S}'}$ and $\mathcal{S}' \vDash \sigma_{\mathcal{S}, \mathcal{S}'}$. Now define $\sigma_{A,B}$ to be the following sentence in the FOE extension of $\mathcal{F}$:
$$\sigma_{A,B} = \bigvee_{\mathcal{S}' \in B} (\bigwedge_{\mathcal{S} \in A} \sigma_{\mathcal{S}, \mathcal{S}'}).$$

Note that given $(\mathcal{S}, \mathcal{S}') \in A \times B$, $\sigma_{\mathcal{S}, \mathcal{S}'}$ is unique. So given A and B, $\sigma_{A,B}$ is unique.

It is not difficult to check that the property mentioned above holds: for every $\mathcal{S} \in A$, $\mathcal{S} \nvDash \sigma_{A,B}$ and for every $\mathcal{S} \in B$, $\mathcal{S} \vDash \sigma_{A,B}$.

Two distinguished separators are given special denotations: $\sigma_{\emptyset, \text{STRUC}}$ is denoted $\top$ and $\sigma_{\text{STRUC}, \emptyset}$ is denoted $\bot$.

Restricted Entailment

Let $\mathcal{L}$ be a language, then $\mathsf{SEN}^{\mathcal{L}}$ denotes the set of sentences of $\mathcal{L}$, and $\mathsf{PSEN}^{\mathcal{L}}$ the set of subsets of $\mathsf{SEN}^{\mathcal{L}}$.

Definition 1. *Let $\mathcal{L}$ be a language, let X and Y be members of* $\mathsf{PSEN}^{\mathcal{L}}$ *and let* $R \subseteq \mathsf{STRUC}$.

1. The set of models of X restricted to R, *denoted* $\mathsf{mod}_R(X)$, *is* $\mathsf{mod}_R(X) = \{\mathcal{S} \in R : \mathcal{S} \vDash X\}$.
2. X entails Y with restriction R *iff* $\mathsf{mod}_R X \subseteq \mathsf{mod}_R Y$; *this is written as* $X \vDash_R Y$.
3. $\mathsf{Cn}_R(X) = \{\varphi \in \mathsf{SEN}^{\mathcal{L}} : \mathsf{mod}_R X \subseteq \mathsf{mod}_R \varphi\}$. *The operator* Cn_R *is called a* restricted consequence *or* restricted closure *operator.*
4. $X \sim_R Y$ *iff* $X \vDash_R Y$ *and* $Y \vDash_R X$. X *is said to be* logically equivalent to Y *with restriction* R *if* $X \sim_R Y$.

Any restricted entailment $\vDash_R$ is a set of ordered pairs: $(X, Y) \in \vDash_R$ if and only if $X \vDash_R Y$. Let ENT denote the set of restricted entailments, that is $\mathsf{ENT} = \{\vDash_R : R \subseteq \mathsf{STRUC}\}$. The following observation is true. $(\mathsf{ENT}, \subseteq)$ is a partially ordered set where the elements of ENT are partially ordered by set inclusion. In fact it is not hard to see that if $I \subseteq J \subseteq \mathsf{STRUC}$, then $\vDash_J \subseteq \vDash_I$. (The direction of inclusion is reversed in the conclusion.)

Lower and upper bounds of subsets of ENT can now be defined. Let $E \subseteq \mathsf{ENT}$.

- An element $\vDash_H$ of ENT is a *lower bound* of E if $\vDash_H \subseteq \vDash_I$ for each $\vDash_I \in E$.
- An element $\vDash_G$ of ENT is the *greatest lower bound* of $E \subseteq \mathsf{ENT}$ if $\vDash_G$ is a lower bound of E and it is a superset of, or equal to any other lower bound of E. The greatest lower bound of E, if it exists, is denoted $\bigwedge E$.
- The *least upper bound* of E is defined dually, and if it exists it is denoted $\bigvee E$.

The following theorem states that any set of restricted entailments has a greatest lower and a least upper bound and shows how to calculate them. In the theorem P is a set of subsets of STRUC. The symbol $[P]$ in the second part of the theorem means the following: $[P] = \{[I] : I \in P\}$, where $[I]$ is defined to be $\{\mathcal{S} \in \mathsf{STRUC} : \exists \mathcal{S}' \in I \ \& \ \mathcal{S} \equiv \mathcal{S}'\}$.

Theorem 2. *Let* $P \subseteq \mathsf{PSTRUC}$, *then*

1. $\bigwedge_{I \in P} \vDash_I = \vDash_{\cup P}$.
2. $\bigvee_{I \in P} \vDash_I = \vDash_{\cap [P]}$.

In the light of the above theorem $(\mathsf{ENT}, \subseteq)$ is a complete lattice. A little thought shows that the lattice has a unit, $\vDash_\emptyset$, and a zero, $\vDash_{\mathsf{STRUC}}$. It can also be shown (not here) that ordinary entailment is the least upper bound of all restricted entailments having finite restriction sets.

Preliminaries have now been covered enabling definition of the algebra PSEN in the next section. This algebra provides the basis for the elaboration of belief contraction and nonmonotonic entailment in following sections.

3   The Preboolean Algebra $\mathsf{PSEN}^{\mathcal{L}}$

Here I define a preboolean algebra associated with an FOE language. The elements of the algebra are *sets of sentences* and the lattice preorder of the algebra is *restricted entailment*. This prelattice is shown to be a complete preboolean algebra. So it turns out that each FOE language has a complete preboolean algebra associated with it. For the FOE language $\mathcal{L}$ the preboolean algebra is denoted PSEN$^{\mathcal{L}}$. The superscript will generally be dropped from the notation. In later sections PSEN is used to give an account of belief contraction and nonmonotonic entailment.

In what follows definitions of operators and relations are given in restricted form. Using separators, lattice operations as well as an inverse are defined for PSEN.

Restricted entailment is a reflexive and transitive relation. It also induces an equivalence relation. Let $\mathcal{L}$ be a language and $R \subseteq$ STRUC. The relation $\sim_R$ (see definition 1) between members of PSEN is an equivalence relation. For this reason restricted entailment is not antisymmetric but rather *antisymmetric up to equivalence*.

The relation $\vDash_R$ will be a lattice preorder on PSEN if every pair of elements of PSEN has a greatest lower bound (or *meet*) and a least upper bound (or *join*) with respect to $\vDash_R$. These bounds can be constructed using separators associated with pairs of elements of PSEN. The important point about a separator is that it is defined with respect to pairs of sets of structures which are *assumed to be elementarily disjoint*. So appropriate sets of structures are chosen to be elementarily disjoint in proposition 3 where the algebraic operations on PSEN are constructed. A property called *relative fullness* is used which guarantees elementary disjointness of the sets of structures used.

Relative fullness is defined as follows. Let $\mathcal{L}$ be a language and let $I \subseteq R \subseteq$ STRUC. Then I is *full relative to* R if and only if given members $\mathcal{S}$ and $\mathcal{S}'$ of R, if $\mathcal{S} \in I$ and $\mathcal{S}$ is elementarily equivalent to $\mathcal{S}'$ then $\mathcal{S}' \in I$. It is straightforward to show that relative fullness is preserved under arbitrary intersections, arbitrary unions and the taking of complements; and if X is a set of sentences then a restricted set of models of X is relatively full. Also, it is not difficult to prove the following criterion for elementary disjointness: suppose A and B are full relative to R, and A and B are disjoint, then A and B are elementarily disjoint.

As a byproduct of the next proposition some algebraic operations on sets of sentences of an FOE $\mathcal{L}$ are defined. The results of these operations are specific sentences in $\mathcal{L}$. The notion of a separator is used to make the definitions in a uniform way. Recall that the separator of A and B is $\sigma_{A,B}$, where A and B are elementarily disjoint subsets of STRUC. The results in the proposition are based on a restricted entailment $\vDash_R$ which is regarded as a preorder, where $R \subseteq$ STRUC. For the sake of precision, even though it leads to cluttered notation, all appropriate operators and relations are subscripted by R. As an aid to understanding the operations defined below, note that the roles played by $\wedge^\circ$ and $\vee^\circ$ are analogous to set theoretical intersection and union, and $\vDash_R$ is analogous to set inclusion. The operations are meet and join in a lattice with a partial order relation.

Proposition 3. *Let $\mathcal{L}$ be an FOE and $R \subseteq$ STRUC, let Q be an infinite index set and let X, Y and W_q ($q \in Q$) be members of* PSEN.

1. *Let* $B = \mathrm{mod}_R(X) \cap \mathrm{mod}_R(Y)$ *and* $A = R - B$ *(the set-theoretic difference), then* $\sigma_{A,B}$ *is a lower bound of* X *and* Y *with respect to* $\models_R$ *greater than any other lower bound of* X *and* Y. *Denote* $\sigma_{A,B}$ *by* $X \wedge^\circ_R Y$.

2. *Let* $B = \mathrm{mod}_R(X) \cup \mathrm{mod}_R(Y)$ *and* $A = R - B$, *then* $\sigma_{A,B}$ *is an upper bound of* X *and* Y *with respect to* $\models_R$ *less than any other upper bound of* X *and* Y. *Denote* $\sigma_{A,B}$ *by* $X \vee^\circ_R Y$.

3. *Let* $B = \bigcap_{q \in Q} \mathrm{mod}_R(W_q)$ *and* $A = R - B$, *then* $\sigma_{A,B}$ *is a lower bound of* W_q $(q \in Q)$ *with respect to* $\models_R$ *greater than any other lower bound of* W_q $(q \in Q)$. *Denote* $\sigma_{A,B}$ *by* $\bigwedge^\circ_R \{W_q : q \in Q\}$.

4. *Let* $B = \bigcup_{q \in Q} \mathrm{mod}_R(W_q)$ *and* $A = R - B$, *then* $\sigma_{A,B}$ *is an upper bound of* W_q $(q \in Q)$ *with respect to* $\models_R$ *less than any other upper bound of* W_q $(q \in Q)$. *Denote* $\sigma_{A,B}$ *by* $\bigvee^\circ_R \{W_q : q \in Q\}$.

5. $X \models_R \top$ *and* $\bot \models_R X$.

6. *Let* $A = \mathrm{mod}_R(X)$ *and* $B = R - A$, *then* $\sigma_{A,B}$ *is denoted* $-_R X$ *and the following hold.*

   a) *The sentence* $-_R X$ *satisfies* $-_R X \wedge^\circ_R X \sim_R \bot$ *and is greater with respect to* $\models_R$ *than any set of sentences* Z *satisfying* $Z \wedge^\circ_R X \sim_R \bot$.

   b) *The sentence* $-_R X$ *satisfies* $-_R X \vee^\circ_R X \sim_R \top$ *and is less with respect to* $\models_R$ *than any set of sentences* Z *satisfying* $Z \vee^\circ_R X \sim_R \top$.

Proof. Straightforward. The first part of the proposition will be proved; the rest of the proof follows a similar pattern. As was pointed out after the definition of relative fullness above, $B = \mathrm{mod}_R(X) \cap \mathrm{mod}_R(Y)$ is full relative to R and so is $A = R - (\mathrm{mod}_R(X) \cap \mathrm{mod}_R(Y))$. Both A and B are therefore elementarily disjoint sets of structures and so $\sigma_{A,B}$ is the separator of A and B. Now $\sigma_{A,B}$ is a lower bound of X and Y (with respect to $\models_R$) because $\mathrm{mod}_R(\sigma_{A,B}) = B = \mathrm{mod}_R(X) \cap \mathrm{mod}_R(Y)$. Let Z be another lower bound of X and Y; we must show $Z \models_R \sigma_{A,B}$. But this follows because $\mathrm{mod}_R(Z) \subseteq \mathrm{mod}_R(X) \cap \mathrm{mod}_R(Y) = B = \mathrm{mod}_R(\sigma_{A,B})$.

It is not difficult to show that PSEN is a complete, distributive prelattice.

Theorem 4. (PSEN, $\models_R$, $-_R$, $\wedge^\circ_R$, $\vee^\circ_R$) *is a distributive prelattice with order* $\models_R$ *and operators* $-_R$, $\wedge^\circ_R$ *and* $\vee^\circ_R$ *which are unique up to equivalence,* $\sim_R$. PSEN *also has infinitary meet and join operators* $\bigwedge^\circ_R$ *and* $\bigvee^\circ_R$ *which are unique up to equivalence.*

Corollary 5. (PSEN, $\models_R$, $-_R$, $\wedge^\circ_R$, $\vee^\circ_R$, $\bigwedge^\circ_R$, $\bigvee^\circ_R$) *is a complete preboolean algebra with preorder* $\models_R$ *and distinguished elements and operators which are unique up to equivalence,* $\sim_R$, *as follows. Zero:* $\bot$; *unit:* $\top$; *inverse:* $-_R$; *binary meet:* $\wedge^\circ_R$; *binary join:* $\vee^\circ_R$; *infinitary meet:* $\bigwedge^\circ_R$; *and infinitary join:* $\bigvee^\circ_R$.

De Morgan's laws hold for PSEN and the following restricted generalisations of well-known results are true.

$X \models_R Y$ iff $X \vee^\circ_R Y \sim_R Y$.
$X \models_R Y$ iff $X \wedge^\circ_R Y \sim_R X$.
$X \models_R Y$ iff $X \wedge^\circ_R -_R Y \sim_R \bot$.
$X \models_R Y$ iff $-_R Y \models_R -_R X$.

4   Belief Contraction Using PSEN

We will not give a detailed summary of belief revision here. Instead we highlight some basic aspects of belief revision and describe our algebraic treatment of it. We have adopted the AGM approach to belief revision as expounded by Gärdenfors [5] and Gärdenfors and Rott [6].

We suppose a reasoning agent possesses a set of beliefs which it is capable of modifying as time progesses. Following the lead of AGM, we identify the agent's set of beliefs with a *belief set* which is a set of sentences closed under consequence. According to AGM there are three kinds of operation which can be applied to the belief set to modify it in a rational way: expansion, revision and contraction.

It turns out that revision can be recovered from contraction via the *Levi identity* (see [5]) and so we work only with contraction here. Contraction can be described as follows. Given a belief set K and a sentence φ, we *contract K by φ* when we remove from K, in a *rational* way, anything that entails φ. A method of contraction is rational if it satisfies the AGM postulates for contraction (see below).

In this paper we refer to AGM contraction as expounded in [5] as *classical AGM contraction*; all operations in classical AGM contraction are performed in the context of a first-order language. The postulates for classical AGM contraction are given in definition 8, part 3. In contrast, (non-classical) AGM contraction is defined in definition 8, part 2. It generalises classical AGM contraction in that it contracts by a *set* of sentences, rather than by a single sentence. Others have defined contraction by sets of sentences in the classical setting, for example Hansson [7]. It is called multiple contraction.

The approach we use to contraction, in contrast to the classical AGM approach, involves an FOE $\mathcal{L}$ and the preboolean algebra PSEN. Our contraction construction is based upon an algebraic expression involving a *rejector*. The basic property of a rejector for a belief set K and a sentence φ is that it entails $\neg\varphi$. The definition is actually made in terms of a *rejection function*. The name, rejection function, comes from Britz [1].

For ease of reference we call our algebraic definitions of contraction *algebraic contraction*. We show that algebraic contraction and AGM contraction are interdefinable and that classical AGM contraction can be retrieved from algebraic contraction.

From now on the following convention will be adopted.

Convention 6. *A phrase such as "... let operations and relations be restricted to R ... " will mean that any operation or relation of the algebra* PSEN *will be understood to be restricted to $R \subseteq$* STRUC.

So under the convention, for example, $\vDash$ without a subscript should be read as $\vDash_R$; the subscript is understood to be there by convention.

The argument in this chapter is made easier by couching the algebraic definitions of rejection and contraction in terms of partial functions, that is functions which may not be defined for some elements in their domains.

The following gives the definition of algebraic contraction.

Definition 7. *Let $\mathcal{L}$ be the FOE of $\mathcal{F}$, let operations and relations be restricted to R (see convention 6 above) and let X and Y be members of PSEN.*

1. *A partial function M : PSEN $\times$ PSEN $\to$ PSEN, where the value of M at (K, X) is denoted $M_{K,X}$, is a rejection function if it satisfies BA-1 to BA-6 below.*
   BA-1 *If $X \sim \top$ or $K \not\vDash X$, then $M_{K,X} \sim \bot$; provided $M_{K,X}$ is defined.*
   BA-2 *If $M_{K,X} \sim \bot$, then $X \sim \top$ or $K \not\vDash X$; provided $M_{K,X}$ is defined.*
   BA-3 *$M_{K,X} \vDash -X$; provided $M_{K,X}$ is defined.*
   BA-4 *If $X \sim Y$, then $M_{K,X} \sim M_{K,Y}$; provided that if one of $M_{K,X}$ or $M_{K,Y}$ is defined then so is the other.*
   BA-5 *$M_{K, \bigwedge^\circ \{X_q : q \in Q\}} \vDash \bigvee^\circ \{M_{K,X_q} : q \in Q\}$, where Q is an index set and for each $q \in Q$, $X_q \in$ PSEN; provided $M_{K, \bigwedge^\circ \{X_q : q \in Q\}}$ and M_{K,X_q} for $q \in Q$ are all defined.*
   BA-6 *If $M_{K, \bigwedge^\circ \{X_q : q \in Q\}} \not\vDash X_n$, then $M_{K,X_n} \vDash M_{K, \bigwedge^\circ \{X_q : q \in Q\}}$, where Q is an index set, $n \in Q$ and for each $q \in Q$, $X_q \in$ PSEN; provided $M_{K, \bigwedge^\circ \{X_q : q \in Q\}}$ and M_{K,X_q} for $q \in Q$ are all defined.*
2. *Let M be a rejection function, $K \in$ PSEN and $X \in$ PSEN. The partial function $\mathrm{con}(\mathcal{L}, -, M, -)$: PSEN $\times$ PSEN $\to$ PSEN, is defined by $\mathrm{con}(\mathcal{L}, -, M, -) : (K, X) \mapsto \mathrm{Cn}^{\mathcal{L}}(K \vee^\circ M_{K,X})$. The value of $\mathrm{con}(\mathcal{L}, -, M, -)$ at (K, X) is denoted $\mathrm{con}(\mathcal{L}, K, M, X)$ and is called the algebraic contraction of K by X under M. It is assumed that $\mathrm{con}(\mathcal{L}, K, M, X)$ is defined if and only if $M_{K,X}$ is defined. If there is no danger of confusion, for example when $\mathcal{L}$, K and M have been declared and are kept fixed, then $\mathrm{con}(\mathcal{L}, K, M, X)$ will be written as $\mathrm{con}(X)$.*
3. *If K, X and $M_{K,X}$ are all members of PSEN$^{\mathcal{F}}$, then $\mathrm{con}(\mathcal{L}, K, M, X) \cap$ SEN$^{\mathcal{F}}$ is denoted $\mathrm{con}(\mathcal{F}, K, M, X)$.*

The above definition of a rejection function is not vacuous. In fact, as can be easily checked, for any $X \in$ PSEN there is a *canonical* definition of $M_{K,X}$, namely $-X$.

Gärdenfors [5] defines contraction in terms of an *unrestricted* belief set and a sentence: the sentence (and anything entailing it) is removed from the belief set. (Recall that an unrestricted belief set X is one which satisfies $\mathrm{Cn}X = X$; the restriction $R =$ STRUC.) He gives eight postulates that a belief set should satisfy to be a contraction. The postulates are given below for contraction of a belief set by a *set* of sentences X satisfying a *restricted closure*: $\mathrm{Cn}_R X = X$. When X is a singleton set, that is it consists of a single sentence, and there is no restriction ($R =$ STRUC) then the postulates revert to those given by Gärdenfors. The notation used in definition 8 parts 1 and 2 is based on Gärdenfors [5].

Definition 8.

1. *Let K be a belief set in a language $\mathcal{L}$ and let operations and relations be restricted to R. In the style of notation used in Gärdenfors [5], the expansion of K by X is $K_X^+ = \mathrm{Cn}^{\mathcal{L}}(K \wedge^\circ X)$. The last expression equals $\mathrm{Cn}^{\mathcal{L}}(K \cup X)$.*

2. Let K be a belief set in a language $\mathcal{L}$ and let operations and relations be restricted to R. A partial function $K^- :$ PSEN $\to$ PSEN, where the value of K^- at X is denoted K_X^-, is called an AGM contraction function if it satisfies the following.

K-1 K_X^- is a belief set; provided K_X^- is defined.

K-2 $K_X^- \subseteq K$; provided K_X^- is defined.

K-3   If $X \nsubseteq K$, then $K_X^- = K$; provided K_X^- is defined.

K-4   If $X \nsim \top$, then $X \nsubseteq K_X^-$; provided K_X^- is defined.

K-5   If $X \subseteq K$, then $K \subseteq (K_X^-)_X^+$; provided K_X^- is defined.

K-6   If $X \sim Y$, then $K_X^- = K_Y^-$; provided that if one of K_X^- or K_Y^- is defined then so is the other.

K-7 $\bigcap_{q \in Q} K_{X_q}^- \subseteq K_{\bigwedge° \{X_q : q \in Q\}}^-$, where Q is an index set and for each $q \in Q$, $X_q \in$ PSEN; provided $K_{X_q}^-$ for $q \in Q$ and $K_{\bigwedge° \{X_q : q \in Q\}}^-$ are all defined.

K-8   If $X_n \nsubseteq K_{\bigwedge° \{X_q : q \in Q\}}^-$, then $K_{\bigwedge° \{X_q : q \in Q\}}^- \subseteq K_{X_n}^-$, where Q is an index set, $n \in Q$ and for each $q \in Q$, $X_q \in$ PSEN; provided $K_{X_q}^-$ for $q \in Q$ and $K_{\bigwedge° \{X_q : q \in Q\}}^-$ are all defined.

3. An AGM contraction function K^- is said to be classical if the language is first-order, there is no restriction on operations and relations $(R =$ STRUC), the function K^- is a total function on its domain, the sets X and Y are singletons, $\{\varphi\}$ and $\{\psi\}$ say, and K-7 and K-8 are replaced by K-7' and K-8':

K-7' $K_\varphi^- \cap K_\psi^- \subseteq K_{\varphi \wedge \psi}^-$.

K-8'   If $\varphi \notin K_{\varphi \wedge \psi}^-$, then $K_{\varphi \wedge \psi}^- \subseteq K_\varphi^-$.

Note that notation is simplified by writing K_φ^-, for example, instead of $K_{\{\varphi\}}^-$. The postulates just given for a classical AGM contraction are the same as those in [5].

Algebraic contraction and AGM contraction are interdefinable.

Theorem 9. Let $\mathcal{L}$ be an FOE, let K be a belief set in $\mathcal{L}$, let operations and relations be restricted to R, and let X be a member of PSEN. The following are true.

1. Let M be a rejection function. The function con $=$ con$(\mathcal{L}, K, M, -)$ is an AGM contraction function in $\mathcal{L}$ which satisfies $M_{K,X} \sim^{\mathcal{L}}$ (con$(\mathcal{L}, K, M, X) \wedge° -K)$.

2. Any AGM contraction function K^- in $\mathcal{L}$ gives rise to a rejection function M in $\mathcal{L}$ defined by $M_{K,X} = K_X^- \wedge° -K$ and satisfying con$(\mathcal{L}, K, M, X) = K_X^-$.

5   Nonmonotonic Entailment

In this section we describe a certain well-known connection between belief revision and nonmonotonic entailment, which we call *classical nonmonotonic entailment*. Then we show that our algebraic approach can be used to describe classical nonmonotonic entailment. We mention that Shoham [10] defines nonmonotonic entailment in terms of entailment involving preferred models for given pairs of sentences. This turns out to be different from restricted entailment: it can be shown that restricted entailment is monotonic, whereas Shoham's preferential entailment is nonmonotonic.

The connection mentioned above is made by identifying a classical nonmonotonic entailment depending on a fixed background belief set, K, with an expression involving a certain contraction of K. This allows nonmonotonic entailment to be given an algebraic expression involving ordinary entailment.

There is a nonmonotonic consequence operator, C, corresponding to nonmonotonic entailment. We characterise it and give necessary and sufficient conditions for the equality $CX = CnX$ to hold, where X is a set of sentences. We also mention that C satisfies some properties mentioned in [9]: inclusion, supraclassicality and distribution. Idempotence and cumulativity are not automatically satisfied by C but are equivalent to certain conditions on rejection functions.

If φ and ψ are sentences and K is a fixed background belief set, then the nonmonotonic entailment of ψ by φ depending on K is denoted $\varphi \mathrel{\vdash\mkern-9mu\sim}^K \psi$. A revision of K by φ is denoted $K^\star_\varphi$. According to the approach used here (see [6]) the nonmonotonic entailment $\varphi \mathrel{\vdash\mkern-9mu\sim}^K \psi$ is identified with the expression $\psi \in K^\star_\varphi$. However the revision $K^\star_\varphi$ can be translated into an expression involving a contraction followed by an expansion by using the *Levi identity* (see [5]): $K^\star_\varphi = (K^-_{\neg\varphi})^+_\varphi$. So $\varphi \mathrel{\vdash\mkern-9mu\sim}^K \psi$ is identified with $\psi \in (K^-_{\neg\varphi})^+_\varphi$.

Now, because $(K^-_{\neg\varphi})^+_\varphi$ is a belief set (that is it is closed under consequence), $\psi \in (K^-_{\neg\varphi})^+_\varphi$ if and only if $(K^-_{\neg\varphi})^+_\varphi \vDash \psi$. This can be converted into an expression in the preboolean algebra PSEN to give the following result which translates a nonmonotonic entailment into an ordinary entailment.

Proposition 10. *Suppose the classical AGM contraction* $K^- : \mathrm{SEN}^\mathcal{F} \to \mathrm{PSEN}^\mathcal{F}$ *is given and, according to theorem 9, let* $M_{K,-} : \mathrm{SEN}^\mathcal{F} \to \mathrm{PSEN}$ *be the induced rejection function, then the following statements are equivalent.*

1. $\varphi \mathrel{\vdash\mkern-9mu\sim}^K \psi$.
2. $K^-_{\neg\varphi} \wedge^\circ \varphi \vDash \psi$.
3. $(K \wedge^\circ \varphi) \vee^\circ M_{K,-\varphi} \vDash \psi$.

Corollary 11.

1. *If* $K \nvDash \neg\varphi$, *then* $\varphi \mathrel{\vdash\mkern-9mu\sim}^K \psi$ *iff* $K \wedge^\circ \varphi \vDash \psi$.
2. *If* $K \vDash \neg\varphi$, *then* $\varphi \mathrel{\vdash\mkern-9mu\sim}^K \psi$ *iff* $M_{K,-\varphi} \vDash \psi$.

We now extend the definition of $\mathrel{\vdash\mkern-9mu\sim}^K$ to hold between sets of sentences in an FOE, $\mathcal{L}$. The role played above by a sentence, φ, is now taken by a set of sentences, X, and also because of the fact that $\neg\varphi \sim -\varphi$ in $\mathrm{PSEN}^\mathcal{F}$, the analogy is extended and $-X$ is substituted for $\neg\varphi$.

Definition 12. *Let* $\mathcal{L}$ *be an* FOE, *let* X *and* Y *be elements of* PSEN *and let* $K^- : \mathrm{PSEN} \to \mathrm{PSEN}$ *be any AGM contraction, then* $X \mathrel{\vdash\mkern-9mu\sim}^K Y$ *iff* $(K^-_{-X} \wedge^\circ X) \vDash Y$. *If there is no danger of confusion the superscript* K *in* $\mathrel{\vdash\mkern-9mu\sim}^K$ *will be dropped thus:* $X \mathrel{\vdash\mkern-9mu\sim} Y$.

The following results are analogous to 10 and 11. (The equivalence of the first two statements in 13 is really a restatement of definition 12.)

Proposition 13. *Let $\mathcal{L}$ be an FOE and let operations and relations be restricted to R. Suppose the AGM contraction K^- : PSEN $\to$ PSEN is given and, according to theorem 9, let $M_{K,-}$: PSEN $\to$ PSEN be the induced rejection function, then the following statements are equivalent.*

1. $X \mathrel{\vrule height 1.5ex depth 0pt width 0pt}\hspace{-0.5em}\sim^K Y$.
2. $K^-_{-X} \wedge^\circ X \vDash Y$.
3. $(K \wedge^\circ X) \vee^\circ M_{K,-X} \vDash Y$.

Corollary 14.

1. *If $K \nvDash -X$, then $X \mathrel{\vrule height 1.5ex depth 0pt width 0pt}\hspace{-0.5em}\sim^K Y$ iff $K \wedge^\circ X \vDash Y$.*
2. *If $K \vDash -X$, then $X \mathrel{\vrule height 1.5ex depth 0pt width 0pt}\hspace{-0.5em}\sim^K Y$ iff $M_{K,-X} \vDash Y$.*

According to what we have said in the introduction, we identify an agent's deductive process with a restricted entailment. We do the same with an agent's nonmonotonic deductive process and define *restricted nonmonotonic entailment*. In view of the equivalence of parts 1 and 3 of proposition 13, restricted nonmonotonic entailment is defined as follows.

Definition 15. *Let $\mathcal{L}$ be an FOE, let $R \subseteq$ STRUC, let X and Y be elements of PSEN, let $K \in$ PSEN satisfy $\mathsf{Cn}_R K = K$ and let $M_{K,-}$: PSEN $\to$ PSEN be a rejection function which is total on its domain. The* nonmonotonic entailment restricted to R *is defined by $X \mathrel{\vrule height 1.5ex depth 0pt width 0pt}\hspace{-0.5em}\sim^K_R Y$ iff $(K \wedge^\circ_R X) \vee^\circ_R M_{K,-RX} \vDash_R Y$.*

There is no loss of generality in making the definition in terms of a rejection function because if an AGM contraction function K^- is given then setting $M_{K,-} = K^- \wedge^\circ -K$ defines a rejection function for which $K \vee^\circ M_{K,-} \sim K^-$ (this follows from theorem 9).

For the rest of this chapter convention 6 is adopted so the restriction for operations and relations will be understood implicitly.

To justify calling $X \mathrel{\vrule height 1.5ex depth 0pt width 0pt}\hspace{-0.5em}\sim^K Y$ a nonmonotonic entailment it should satisfy some properties of nonmonotonic entailments. Propositions 20, 21 and 22 examine this. The definitions come from Makinson [9], where they are made in terms of the consequence operator, denoted C, corresponding to the nonmonotonic entailment $\mathrel{\vrule height 1.5ex depth 0pt width 0pt}\hspace{-0.5em}\sim^K$. The operator C is defined next.

Definition 16. *Let $\mathcal{L}$ be an FOE, let operations and relations be restricted to R, let $\varphi \in$ SEN$^{\mathcal{L}}$, $X \in$ PSEN and $M_{K,-}$: PSEN $\to$ PSEN be a rejection function which is a total function, then $\mathsf{C}X = \{\varphi \in$ SEN$^{\mathcal{L}} : X \mathrel{\vrule height 1.5ex depth 0pt width 0pt}\hspace{-0.5em}\sim^K \varphi\}$.*

Using the definition of $\mathrel{\vrule height 1.5ex depth 0pt width 0pt}\hspace{-0.5em}\sim^K$ the following observations can be made about the structure of the nonmonotonic consequence operator C. It is interesting to note that the first two parts of the proposition below express C in terms of Cn.

Proposition 17. *Let $\mathcal{L}$ be an FOE, let operations and relations be restricted to R and let X and Y be members of PSEN. The following are true.*

1. $CX = Cn(K^-_{-X} \wedge^\circ X)$.
2. $CX = Cn((K \wedge^\circ X) \vee^\circ M_{K,-X})$.
3. $X \mathrel{\vdash\!\sim}^K Y$ *iff* $Y \subseteq CX$.

The following simplifies the definition of C.

Corollary 18. *Under the same assumptions as above, the following are true.*

1. *If $K \not\models -X$, then $CX \sim K \wedge^\circ X$.*
2. *If $K \models -X$, then $CX \sim M_{K,-X}$.*

We can now ask the question, "When does $CX = CnX$?". A partial answer is, "When $M_{K,-X} \sim X$". That is, when $M_{K,-X}$ is the canonical rejection function, X (see the sentence following definition 7). Necessary and sufficient conditions for $CX = CnX$ to hold are given in the next proposition.

Proposition 19. *Let $\mathcal{L}$ be an FOE, let operations and relations be restricted to R, let X be a member of PSEN and let C be induced by $\mathrel{\vdash\!\sim}^K$. The following are true.*

1. *If $M_{K,-X} \sim X$ or $X \models K$, then $CX = CnX$.*
2. *If $CX = CnX$, then $\begin{cases} M_{K,-X} \sim X \text{ if } K \models -X, \\ X \models K \quad\quad\ \text{ if } K \not\models -X. \end{cases}$*

The next few propositions have to do with some important properties of the nonmonotonic consequence operator C. They are described in Makinson [9]. Proposition 20 states that C satisfies inclusion, supraclassicality and distribution. Proposition 21 gives a necessary and sufficient condition for C to satisfy idempotence and 22 does the same for cumulativity.

Proposition 20. *Let operations and relations be restricted to R, let the nonmonotonic consequence operator C be induced by $\mathrel{\vdash\!\sim}^K$ and let X and Y be members of PSEN, where $\mathcal{L}$ is an FOE, then C satisfies the following.*

Inclusion: $X \subseteq CX$.
Supraclassicality: $CnX \subseteq CX$.
Distribution: $CX \cap CY \subseteq C(CnX \cap CnY)$.

The next proposition examines idempotence of C.

Proposition 21. *Let $\mathcal{L}$ be an FOE, let operations and relations be restricted to R, let C be the nonmonotonic consequence induced by $\mathrel{\vdash\!\sim}^K$, and let $X \in$ PSEN. The following are equivalent.*

1. *C is idempotent: $CX = CCX$.*
2. *If $K \models -X$, then $M_{K,-X} \models M_{K,-CX}$.*

The next proposition examines the cumulativity of C.

Proposition 22. *Let $\mathcal{L}$ be an* FOE, *let operations and relations be restricted to R, and let* C *be the nonmonotonic consequence induced by* $\vdash^K$. *Let X and Y be members of* PSEN. *The following are equivalent.*

1. C *is cumulative:* $X \subseteq Y \subseteq CX$ *implies* $CX = CY$.
2. *If* $X \subseteq Y \subseteq CX$ *and* $K \vDash -X$, *then* $M_{K,-X} \vDash M_{K,-Y}$.

6   Conclusion

An important feature of the approach adopted here has been the fact that difficult formalisms involved in belief contraction and nonmonotonic entailment have been made amenable to algebraic examination and analysis. Also one would like all constructions to be computable. It turns out that under some plausible assumptions restricted operators and relations of PSEN are computable.

If we assume that all structures have finite domains, all structures are computable, R is finite and X and Y are finite sets of first-order sentences, then $X \wedge^{\circ}_R Y$, $X \vee^{\circ}_R Y$ and $-_R X$ are computable. If $\vDash_R$ is restricted to be a relation between finite sets of first-order sentences, then $\vDash_R$ is decidable.

The computability of algebraic belief contraction and nonmonotonic entailment depends on the computability of $M_{K,X}$, and it is here that more work needs to be done. Assuming computable $\mathsf{mod}_R(M_{H,X})$ and $\mathsf{mod}_R(M_{H,-_R X})$ (finite $M_{K,X}$ will ensure this), and finite X and Y one then has that $\mathsf{con}(\mathcal{L}, \mathsf{Cn}_R H, M, X)$ is computable and $X \vdash^{\mathsf{Cn}_R H} Y$ is decidable.

References

1. K. Britz. A power algebra for theory change. *Journal of Logic, Language, and Information*, 8:429–443, 1999.
2. Peter J. Cameron. *Sets, Logic and Categories*. Springer, 1999.
3. H-D Ebbinghaus, J Flum, and W Thomas. *Mathematical Logic*. Springer, 1984.
4. Lee Flax. A proposal for reasoning in agents: Restricted entailment. In João A. Leite, Andrea Omicini, Leon Sterling, and Paolo Torroni, editors, *Declarative Agent Languages and Technologies*, July 2003. First International Workshop, DALT 2003, Melboune, Victoria, July 15, 2003, Workshop Notes.
5. Peter Gärdenfors. *Knowledge in Flux*. MIT Press, 1988.
6. Peter Gärdenfors and Hans Rott. Belief revision. In Dov M. Gabbay, C. J. Hogger, and J.A. Robinson, editors, *Handbook of Logic in Artificial Intelligence and Logic Programming*, volume 4, pages 35–132. Oxford University Press, 1995.
7. Sven Ove Hansson. *A Textbook of Belief Dynamics*. Kluwer Academic Publishers, 1999.
8. Wilfred Hodges. *A Shorter Model Theory*. Cambridge University Press, 1997.
9. David Makinson. General patterns in nonmonotonic reasoning. In Dov M. Gabbay, C. J. Hogger, and J.A. Robinson, editors, *Handbook of Logic in Artificial Intelligence and Logic Programming*, volume 3, pages 35–110. Oxford University Press, 1994.
10. Yoav Shoham. *Reasoning about Change:Time and Causation from the Standpoint of Artificial Intelligence*. MIT Press, 1987.

Logical Connectives for Nonmonotonicity: A Choice Function-Based Approach

Jérôme Mengin

IRIT, Université Paul Sabatier, 118, route de Narbonne, 31062 Toulouse, France
mengin@irit.fr

Abstract. Several semantics for logics that model defeasible inference are based on the idea that not all models of a set F of classical formulas should be considered, but only some of them, the preferred ones. Recently, Daniel Lehmann proved that a very general family of nonmonotonic inference relations can be obtained by using choice functions, that pick some of the models of a given set of logical formulas. However, in this setting the choice function is fixed. This paper describes a semantics where the choice function is defined by formulas: instead of associating a set of models with each formula of the language, we associate a choice function which picks some models. The choice functions are defined for atomic formulas first, and then inductively for every formula, using for each connective a corresponding operator for combining choice functions. We show that this approach generalises classical logic: the choice function associated to a classical formula φ is the function that picks, from a set of models M, the elements of M that satisfy φ in the classical sense. We then describe operations on choice functions that correspond to connectives meaning for example: "p if it is consistent" or "p prior to q".

1 Introduction

The formalisation of defeasible reasoning in a logical setting motivated researchers in Artificial Intelligence to study deduction relations that are nonmonotonic: it often happens, when information about the world is incomplete, that one can draw conclusions that are not valid when more information is available. Several paths have been pursued in order to modify classical (monotonic) logic in order to obtain such inference relations. One approach is to add special inference rules, usually called "defaults", as in e.g. [1,2]; these defaults are therefore not distinguished formulas of the so-built logic. The application of such rules usually needs some condition to be checked which is not monotonic.

Another approach has been to ask what properties are desirable for these inference relations, as in e.g. [3,4], and to build the entire consequence relation as the smallest that verify these properties and validates some problem-specific deductions. In this approach again, the domain-specific deductions are not really formulas.

In the semantical approach, one studies which models of a set of formulas characterise the incompleteness of the information. One of the most successful

J.J. Alferes and J. Leite (Eds.): JELIA 2004, LNAI 3229, pp. 452–461, 2004.
© Springer-Verlag Berlin Heidelberg 2004

works in this branch was the semantical view of circumscription: a domain-specific partial ordering is assumed on the interpretations of the language, describing relative likelihoods of the situations these interpretations describe, see e.g. [5]; then, given a set of formulas Δ describing a particular situation, the interpretations describing the most likely situations are selected among all the interpretations which satisfy Δ. This approach has been generalised by Shoham [6], and recently further by Lehmann [7]: he proves that an interesting family of nonmonotonic deduction relations can be obtained by considering what the "social choice" research community calls "choice functions"; more precisely, to every such consequence relation corresponds one choice function which picks the preferred models of a set of formulas among all models of this set. With the semantical approach, the domain-related ordering on the interpretations is not described by formulas of the logical language.

The aim of the work presented in this paper is to provide a declarative way to encode what makes defeasible reasoning nonmonotonic: these pieces of knowledge which are not certain, but rather suggest how lack of information can be overcome to reach interesting conclusions. The starting point is Lehmann's idea of using choice functions. But where Lehmann consider that a choice function is fixed and generates an inference relation, we will consider that it is the formulas describing a situation which define the choice function. We will show that various logical connectives, classical or related to nonmonotonicity, can be defined by usual operations on choice functions, like intersection, union, composition. Several works have proposed to use choice functions to define various operators related to nonmonotonic reasoning. However, this paper describes how choice functions could be used as a uniform tool to interpret every formula of a logic for defeasible reasoning. This uniformity of treatment for classical and "defeasible formulas" should prove useful to study for example normal forms for formulas representing pieces of defeasible knowledge, or to gain a deeper understanding of nonmonotonic theorem proving.

The paper is organised as follows: Section 2 describes how to associate choice functions to formulas, and how to define connectives corresponding to notions widely used in the study of defeasible reasoning. Section 3 explains how our framework relates to other works. The paper ends with a conclusion and some ideas for further research.

2   Choice Functions as Interpretations

2.1   The Classical, Monotonic Semantics

Consider some classical propositional language $\mathcal{L}$, and a consequence relation $\vdash$ on $2^{\mathcal{L}} \times \mathcal{L}$, where $\Delta \vdash \varphi$ should be interpreted by "φ can be deduced from Δ". Let $\mathsf{Cn}_{\vdash}$ be the associated consequence operation: $\mathsf{Cn}_{\vdash}(\Delta) = \{\varphi \in \mathcal{L} \mid \Delta \vdash \varphi\}$. Such a consequence relation can be defined by means of a set $\mathcal{M}$ of objects, called interpretations, that are related to the formulas of $\mathcal{L}$ by means of a satisfaction relation $\models \subseteq \mathcal{M} \times \mathcal{L}$; when $m \models \varphi$ we say that m satisfies φ, and that m is a model of φ. The consequence relation is then defined by saying that $\Delta \vdash \varphi$ if and only if every interpretation that satisfies all formulas of Δ also satisfies φ:

$$\mathsf{Cn}_\vdash(\Delta) = \overline{|\Delta|}$$

where

$|\Delta|$ denotes the set of models of Δ, the interpretations that satisfy all formulas of Δ; and

$\overline{M}$ denotes the set of formulas satisfied by a set of interpretations M.

Tarski proved that a consequence relation on $\mathcal{L}$ can be defined in this way if and only if it verifies the following three properties, for any subsets Δ and Γ of $\mathcal{L}$:

Inclusion $\Delta \subseteq \mathsf{Cn}_\vdash(\Delta)$;
Idempotence $\mathsf{Cn}_\vdash(\mathsf{Cn}_\vdash(\Delta)) = \mathsf{Cn}_\vdash(\Delta)$;
Monotoniciy if $\Delta \subseteq \Gamma$ then $\mathsf{Cn}_\vdash(\Delta) \subseteq \mathsf{Cn}_\vdash(\Gamma)$.

Monotonicity is the property that is considered to be inappropriate in the case of defeasible reasoning. A number of proposals have been made to replace Monotonicity by one or more weaker properties. In the semantical approach, Monotonicity can be avoided by considering that a subset of the models of Δ, the preferred models of Δ, defines the consequences of Δ. [7] discusses *choice functions* $f : 2^{\mathcal{M}} \to 2^{\mathcal{M}}$, such that $f(M) \subseteq M$ for every $M \subseteq \mathcal{M}$. The consequences of a set Δ of formulas are then defined by:

$$\mathsf{Cn}_f(\Delta) = \overline{f(|\Delta|)}$$

There are number of ways of defining a choice function f corresponding to some particular domain-specific information. In circumscription for example an ordering $\leq$ is defined on $\mathcal{M}$, and f is defined by $f(M) = \min_{\leq}(M)$ for every $M \subseteq \mathcal{M}$.

2.2   Choice Functions Associated to Formulas Can Define a Consequence Relation

Suppose now that we want to be able to define the choice function in the logical language. This requires that a choice function can be associated to some formulas of a, probably extended, logical language. We will describe how choice functions can in fact be associated to every formula of the language. To be more precise, we will define a mapping $\|.\|$ that associates a choice function to every formula of an extended language $\mathcal{L}'$: for every $\varphi \in \mathcal{L}'$, $\|\varphi\|$ is a function: $2^{\mathcal{M}} \to 2^{\mathcal{M}}$ such that for every $M \subseteq \mathcal{M}$, $\|\varphi\|(M) \subseteq M$.

The intuition is the following: if M is a set of interpretations that correspond to some partial knowledge one has about a situation, and if φ encodes some extra information about this situation, then some elements of M will be selected: the ones in $\|\varphi\|(M)$. The set of interpretations M itself is the result of selecting some of the models in $\mathcal{M}$ according to the partial knowledge one has about the situation: if ψ is a formula representing this partial knowledge, then $M = \|\psi\|(\mathcal{M})$. We will see later that in some cases $\|\phi\|(\|\psi\|(\mathcal{M})) = \|\psi\|(\|\phi\|(\mathcal{M}))$, but not always.

We can start to define a consequence relation: we will say that ψ is a nonmonotonic consequence, or NM-consequence for short, of φ, if $\|\varphi\|(M) \subseteq \|\psi\|(M)$; we will then write $\varphi \mathrel{|\sim} \psi$. We will say that two formulas φ and ψ are *equivalent* if $\|\varphi\| = \|\psi\|$; we will then write $\varphi \equiv \psi$. Note that we can have $\varphi \mathrel{|\sim} \psi$ and $\psi \mathrel{|\sim} \varphi$ without $\varphi \equiv \psi$. We postpone the definition of an associated nonmonotonic consequence operator, since we have not yet defined the choice function associated to a set of formulas. However, the NM-consequence relation just defined verifies a simple form of Inclusion: $\varphi \mathrel{|\sim} \varphi$ for every formula $\varphi \in \mathcal{L}'$.

2.3 Choice Functions for "Classical" Formulas

Let us first note that this association of a choice function to every formula is only a small generalisation of Tarski's notion of consequence. In fact, in the classical setting, each formula $\varphi \in \mathcal{L}$ can be seen as filtering out some interpretations: the meaning of a classical formula φ is that only the interpretations that represents situations coherent with the piece of knowledge encoded in φ are kept. There is a natural choice function associated to such a classical formula: $\|\varphi\|(M) = |\varphi| \cap M$.

This choice function associated to every formula of $\mathcal{L}$ can be defined inductively as follows:

1. to every propositional symbol p is associated the choice function $\|p\|$ defined by $\|p\|(M) = |p| \cap M$;
2. the choice functions associated to formulas built using the classical connectives $\wedge$, $\vee$ and $\neg$ are defined by:

$$\|\varphi \wedge \psi\|(M) = \|\varphi\|(M) \cap \|\psi\|(M)$$
$$\|\varphi \vee \psi\|(M) = \|\varphi\|(M) \cup \|\psi\|(M)$$
$$\|\neg\varphi\|(M) = M \setminus \|\varphi\|(M)$$

We will use in the sequel a connective for implication, which we define by writing that $\varphi \to \psi \equiv \neg\varphi \vee \psi$.

A formula that is always true can be defined by: $\|\top\|(M) = M$ for every M, whereas a formula that is always false can be defined by $\|\bot\|(M) = \emptyset$ for every M.

With the definitions given so far, the usual properties inherited from the Boolean algebra on the sets of interpretations are still valid; for example, $\neg(\varphi \wedge \psi) \equiv \neg\varphi \vee \neg\psi$. Moreover, $\mathrel{|\sim}$ coincides with $\vdash$ on $\mathcal{L}$: if φ and ψ are two formulas of $\mathcal{L}$, then $\varphi \vdash \psi$ if and only if $\varphi \mathrel{|\sim} \psi$.

2.4 Defaults

Of course, our aim in using choice functions is to be able to define formulas that will represent nonmonotonic choice functions. Let us start with a formula declaring that some piece of knowledge is to be considered "by default", when nothing says that it is false; the general idea of a default is that it should be used if it is consistent. Let φ be some formula that encodes this piece of knowledge. We define a unary connective δ, such that the intended meaning of $\delta\varphi$ is that φ should be used if it consistent, by extending the inductive definition of choice function associated to classical formulas to formulas that contain this connective:

$$\|\delta\varphi\|(M) = \begin{cases} \|\varphi\|(M) \text{ if } \|\varphi\|(M) \neq \emptyset \\ M \text{ if } \|\varphi\|(M) = \emptyset \end{cases}$$

The intuition behind this definition is that if the interpretations in M are those that are coherent with what is already known about the "current" situation, the fact that $\|\varphi\|(M) = \emptyset$ means that the information encoded in φ is incoherent with what is already known: in this case φ should not be used. Otherwise, if $\|\varphi\|(M) \neq \emptyset$, then φ can be used to pick some interpretations in M.

A property of this new connective is:

$$\varphi \wedge \delta\varphi \equiv \varphi$$

Another interesting property of δ is that it is idempotent: for every formula $\varphi \in \mathcal{L}'$,

$$\delta\delta\varphi \equiv \delta\varphi$$

Note that one can deduce defaults: for example, $\varphi \mathrel{|\!\sim} \delta\varphi$.

2.5   Sequences

In general one deals with more than one formula, especially when defaults are involved, since, in the usual interpretation, a set of defaults is not equivalent to the conjunction of its elements. One prominent intuition in default reasoning is the notion of priority: if one has several pieces of defaults knowledge K_1, $\ldots K_n$ such that K_1 is "stronger" that K_2 in some sense, itself stronger than K_3, and so on, then one should try to use K_1 first, then try K_2 if it is consistent with the result of trying K_1. So K_1 is applied or not, then comes K_2. This notion of sequence can be naturally modelled in the choice function framework by considering function composition. Let $\triangleright$ be a connective that will be used to construct formulas corresponding to sequences of pieces of knowledge, we define $\triangleright$ by:

$$\|\varphi \triangleright \psi\| = \|\psi\| \circ \|\varphi\|$$

where $\circ$ denotes function composition: $\|\varphi \triangleright \psi\|(M) = \|\psi\|(\|\varphi\|(M))$. The intuition is that if M is the set of interpretations coherent with what is already known about the current situation, adding the information encoded in $\varphi \triangleright \psi$ is modelled by first picking the interpretations of M according to φ, then picking according to ψ among those already picked according to φ.

An interesting property of this new connective is the following:

$$\varphi \equiv \psi \text{ iff } \vartheta \triangleright \varphi \equiv \vartheta \triangleright \psi \text{ for all } \vartheta$$

If φ and ψ are classical formulas, so that $\|\varphi\| (M) = |\varphi| \cap M$ and $\|\psi\| (M) = |\psi| \cap M$, then:

$$\varphi \triangleright \delta\varphi \equiv \delta\varphi \triangleright \varphi \equiv \varphi \triangleright \delta\neg\varphi \equiv \varphi$$

$$\varphi \triangleright \psi \equiv \varphi \wedge \psi$$

The latter equivalence captures the intuition that in classical logic, the ordering of the formulas does not matter.

Let us close this section by showing how a classical example of defeasible reasoning can be encoded with these new connectives.

Example 1. The classical "penguins cannot fly although they are birds, and generally birds can fly" example: let p, b, f be propositional symbol representing the facts "being a penguin", "being a bird" and "being able to fly". We also introduce a symbol n for describing "normal" birds, that is, birds that can fly. We can then define the formula φ:

$$\varphi = ((p \rightarrow (b \wedge \neg f \wedge \neg n)) \wedge ((b \wedge n) \rightarrow f))$$

To declare that n is true unless something proves it is false, we will consider the formula $\varphi \triangleright \delta n$. We can add some extra formula at the beginning of this sequence, to encode what is a particular animal, a bird or a penguin.

$\|b \triangleright \varphi \triangleright \delta n\| (M) = \|\delta n\| (|b| \cap |\varphi|)$. Since $\|n\| (|b| \cap |\varphi|) = |n| \cap (|b| \cap |\varphi|) \neq \emptyset$, $\|b \triangleright \varphi \triangleright \delta n\| (M) = |n| \cap (|b| \cap |\varphi|) = |b \wedge f \wedge n \wedge \neg p| \subseteq |f| = \|f\| (M)$: hence $b \triangleright \varphi \triangleright \delta n \mid\sim f$.

On the other hand, $\|p \triangleright \varphi \triangleright \delta n\| (M) = \|\delta n\| (|p| \cap |\varphi|)$. Since $\|n\| (|p| \cap |\varphi|) = |n| \cap (|p| \cap |\varphi|) = \emptyset$, $\|p \triangleright \varphi \triangleright \delta n\| (M) = |p| \cap |\varphi| = |b \wedge \neg f \wedge \neg n \wedge p| \subseteq |\neg f| = \|\neg f\| (M)$: hence $p \triangleright \varphi \triangleright \delta n \mid\sim \neg f$.

2.6   Sets of Formulas

In classical logic, a set of formulas usually stands for the conjunction of its elements. The situation is completely different when one has a set of pieces of default knowledge: usually their conjunction is inconsistent. It is precisely an aim of logics of defeasible reasoning to accommodate these pieces of default knowledge in a way that inconsistency is avoided. Let us start by considering two defaults represented by formulas $\delta(p \wedge q)$ and $\delta(p \wedge \neg q)$, where p and q are two propositional symbols: clearly these two defaults contain information which, if used in a classical way, would be inconsistent. There are two ways to use them (supposing that no other information about the current situation is inconsistent with any one of them taken alone): either one first uses $\delta(p \wedge q)$, after which $\delta(p \wedge \neg q)$ cannot be used; or one uses $\delta(p \wedge \neg q)$, after which $\delta(p \wedge q)$ cannot be used. This corresponds to the two formulas: $\delta(p \wedge q) \triangleright \delta(p \wedge \neg q)$ and $\delta(p \wedge \neg q) \triangleright \delta(p \wedge q)$. Assuming that $|p \wedge q| \cap M \neq \emptyset$ and $|p \wedge \neg q| \cap M \neq \emptyset$, $\|\delta(p \wedge q) \triangleright \delta(p \wedge \neg q)\| (M) = |p| \cap |q| \cap M$, whereas $\|\delta(p \wedge \neg q) \triangleright \delta(p \wedge q)\| (M) = |p| \cap |\neg q| \cap M$, so that $\|(\delta(p \wedge q) \triangleright \delta(p \wedge \neg q)) \vee (\delta(p \wedge \neg q) \triangleright \delta(p \wedge q))\| (M) = |p| \cap M$: the selection function associated to the formula $(\delta(p \wedge q) \triangleright \delta(p \wedge \neg q)) \vee (\delta(p \wedge$

$\neg q) \rhd \delta(p \wedge q))$ selects from M those interpretations in which p is true. This is what one can expect from the two defaults when no ordering is given among them. So, if we let the "," be a binary connective, we can define

$$\|\varphi, \psi\| = (\|\varphi\| \circ \|\psi\|) \cup (\|\psi\| \circ \|\varphi\|)$$

(where $(f \cup g)(M) = f(M) \cup g(M)$), so that $\varphi, \psi \equiv (\varphi \rhd \psi) \vee (\psi \rhd \varphi)$. One can easily check that this new connective is commutative: $\varphi, \psi \equiv \psi, \varphi$.

However, the "," is not in general associative: it may be the case that $\varphi, (\psi, \vartheta) \not\equiv (\varphi, \psi), \vartheta$. Thus, in order to define sets of more that two formulas, one has two generalise the definition. We describe how to do it with countably infinite sets of formulas at the end of this section.

Looking back at classical formulas, let us see what effects the new connectives have on them: suppose φ and ψ are two classical formulas, such that $\|\varphi\| (M) = |\varphi| \cap M$ and $\|\psi\| (M) = |\psi| \cap M$. Then $\varphi \rhd \psi \equiv \varphi \wedge \psi \equiv \varphi, \psi$: our definitions is thus a sound generalisation of the notion of a set of classical formulas.

Let us close this section by considering the possibility of defining *countably infinite* "sets", that is, infinite formulas built using the , connective. The choice function corresponding to an infinite sequence $\varphi_1 \rhd \varphi_2 \rhd \ldots \rhd \varphi_i \rhd \ldots$ can be defined as follows: to every finite prefix of the sequence $\varphi_1 \rhd \varphi_2 \rhd \ldots \rhd \varphi_i$ corresponds a choice function f_i defined in the usual manner: $f_i = \|\varphi_i\| \circ \ldots \circ \|\varphi_2\| \circ \|\varphi_1\|$. Note that $f_{i+1}(M) \subseteq f_i(M)$ for every $M \subseteq \mathcal{M}$: $(f_i)_{1 \leq i}$ is a decreasing sequence of functions. We can define its limit f by: $f(M) \cap_{1 \leq i} f_i(M)$. This is the choice function that we associate with the infinite formula $\varphi_1 \rhd \varphi_2 \rhd \ldots \rhd \varphi_i \rhd \ldots$. Now that we have defined choice functions associated with this type of formulas, we can extend the definition of the choice function associated to the , connective to infinite sets: one just considers the union of the choice functions associated with all the possible orderings of the elements of the set.

We are now able to define a nonmonotonic consequence operator:

$$\mathsf{Cn}_{\vdash}(\Delta) = \{\varphi \in \mathcal{L}' \mid \Delta \mid\!\sim \varphi\}$$

3   Related Works

3.1   Default Logic

In this section, we formally prove that our connective for defining defaults truly corresponds to the notion of default as defined in a simple version of default logic, called *prerequisite-free normal default logic* (see e.g.[2]). We consider that a default theory is a pair (W, D) of sets of classical formulas: the formulas in W represent information that is certain, whereas the formulas in D represent default knowledge. In this simple setting, an extension of the default theory (W, D) is $\mathsf{Cn}_{\vdash}(W \cup U)$ for some $U \subseteq D$ maximal such that $W \cup U \not\vdash \bot$. Let $\mathcal{U}$ be the set of those subsets of U maximal among the subsets of D consistent with W.

We will prove that a classical formula φ is in every extension of a finite default theory (W, D) if and only if $w \rhd d \mid\!\sim \varphi$, where $w = \wedge_{\psi \in W} \psi$ and $d = ,_{\psi \in D} \delta \psi$. Let

$d_1, \ldots d_n$ be a sequence of all the elements of U, and let $\varphi_i = w \triangleright \delta d_1 \triangleright \ldots \triangleright \delta d_i$ for every $1 \leq i \leq n$; then

$$\|\varphi_i \triangleright \delta d_{i+1}\| (M) = \begin{cases} |d_{i+1}| \cap \|\varphi_i\| (M) \text{ if } \neq \emptyset \\ \|\varphi_i\| (M) \text{ otherwise} \end{cases}$$

So $\|\varphi_n\| (M) = M \cap w \cap |d_{i_1}| \cap \ldots \cap |d_{i_k}|$, where $d_{i_1}, \ldots, d_{i_k}$ is a sub-sequence of $d_1, \ldots d_n$ such that $\{d_{i_1}, \ldots, d_{i_k}\}$ is maximally consistent with W. Therefore, $\|w \triangleright d\| (M) = M \cap |w| \cap \bigcup_{U \in \mathcal{U}} \bigcap_{d \in U} |d|$, where $\mathcal{U}$ is the set of the parts of D which are maximally consistent with W. Now, let φ be another classical formula, φ is in the intersection of the extensions if and only if for every $U \in \mathcal{U}$, $|w| \cap \bigcap_{d \in U} |d| \subseteq \varphi$, thus if and only if $|w| \cap \bigcup_{U \in \mathcal{U}} \bigcap_{d \in U} |d| \subseteq |\varphi|$. This holds if and only if $M \cap |w| \cap \bigcup_{U \in \mathcal{U}} \bigcap_{d \in U} |d| \subseteq M \cap |\varphi|$ for every $M \subseteq \mathcal{M}$.

3.2 Lehmann's Choice Functions

Lehmann identified three properties for $\mathsf{Cn}_{\mid\sim}$ that make it possible to obtain a similar representation result to that of Tarski, but for nonmonotonic consequence operations. The properties are as follows, where Δ, Γ and Ω are subsets of $\mathcal{L}$:

Cautious Monotonicity if $\Delta \subseteq \Gamma \subseteq \mathsf{Cn}_{\mid\sim} (\Delta)$ then $\mathsf{Cn}_{\mid\sim} (\Delta) \subseteq \mathsf{Cn}_{\mid\sim} (\Gamma)$;
Conditional Monotonicity $\mathsf{Cn}_{\mid\sim} (\Delta \cup \Gamma) \subseteq \mathsf{Cn}_{\mid\sim} (\mathsf{Cn}_{\mid\sim} (\Delta) \cup \Gamma)$;
Treshold Motononicity if $\mathsf{Cn}_{\mid\sim} (\Delta) \subseteq \Gamma \subseteq \Omega$ then $\mathsf{Cn}_{\mid\sim} (\Gamma) \subseteq \mathsf{Cn}_{\mid\sim} (\Omega)$.

Lehmann gives a semantics to consequence relations, defined over a classical language $\mathcal{L}$, that verify these properties using one choice function over the set $\mathcal{M}$ of interpretations of $\mathcal{L}$. The main result in [7] is that a consequence operation $\mathsf{Cn}_{\mid\sim}$ on $\mathcal{L}$ verifies Inclusion, Idempotence, and Cautious, Conditional and Threshold Monotonicity if and only if there exists a set of interpretations $\mathcal{M}$, a satisfaction relation $\models \subseteq \mathcal{M} \times \mathcal{L}$ and a choice function f such that:

- $\Delta \mid\sim \varphi$ if and only if φ is satisfied by every $m \in f(|\Delta|)$, where $|\Delta|$ is the set of interpretations of $\mathcal{M}$ that satisfy all formulas of Δ; and
- f verifies the properties of Contraction, Coherence, Local Monotonicity and Definability Preservation described below.

The properties of f are, for every $M, N \subseteq \mathcal{M}$ and $\Delta \subseteq \mathcal{L}$:

Contraction $f(M) \subseteq M$;
Coherence if $M \subseteq N$ then $M \cap f(N) \subseteq f(M)$;
Local Monotonicity if $f(N) \subseteq M \subseteq N$ then $f(M) \subseteq f(N)$.
Definability Preservation $f(|\Delta|) = \left| \overline{f(|\Delta|)} \right|$, where $\overline{M}$ is, for any $M \subseteq \mathcal{M}$, the set of formulas of $\mathcal{L}$ satisfied by M.

The property of Contraction is one that we have assumed all along (we called *choice function* a function that verifies it). However, we have not imposed the other three conditions. There is one technical reason for that: it is shown in [8] that Coherence and Local Monotonicity are not stable by function intersection and composition. To be more precise, it may be the case that $f \cap g$ or $f \circ g$ do not verify these properties although f and g verify them. Whether the class of choice functions used in the preceding sections is stable for all the operations defining all the connectives remains to be investigated.

3.3 [9]'s Forgotten Connective

In [9], it is also advocated that, in order not to confuse it with conjunction, the comma separating the elements of a set of defaults should be interpreted as a particular connective. To be more precise, if φ, $\varphi_1 \ldots \varphi_n$ are classical formulas, then the models of the formula $\varphi_1, \ldots, \varphi_n$ with respect to φ are the models of φ that satisfy at least one maximal (for set inclusion) subset of the set (in the set-theoretic sense!) of the φ_is. More precisely, their definition is as follows:

$$m \models \varphi_1, \ldots, \varphi_n \text{ iff for every m' } \in \mathcal{M}, \{i \mid m \models \varphi_i\} \not\subset \{i \mid m' \models \varphi_i\}$$

Thus, in their definition, the "," embodies both the accumulation of pieces of knowledge, and their defeasible nature. The result of section 3.1 shows that the formula $\varphi_1, \ldots, \varphi_n$ in their setting corresponds to the formula $\delta\varphi_1, \ldots, \delta\varphi_n$ in ours.

4   Conclusions and Perspectives

By associating choice functions to every formula, we have been able to define three connectives that are specific to the modelling of defeasible reasoning: one permits to represent that a piece of information should be used by default. Another one can be used to represent sequences of formulas. It really makes sense in the presence of defaults: a sequence of classical formulas as we defined it is equivalent to the conjunction of these classical formulas. And finally, we were able to define a set of formulas as being the disjunction of all possible sequences of its elements; this notion coincides with the usual interpretation of a set of formula as being the conjunction of its elements when the formulas are classical ones. When the formulas are defaults, this corresponds to the disjunction of all possible arrangements of the defaults, which is logically equivalent to the intersection of the extensions of the corresponding default theory, or to a form of simultaneous formulas circumscription.

In our opinion, the most striking feature of this way of interpreting formulas is that the interpretation of a formula is entirely defined from the interpretations of its sub-formulas. This property of Tarski's semantics for classical logic is the basis for most automated deduction methods. It can seem somewhat strange to have a semantics with this feature for a logic for defeasible reasoning, since the use or not of a default does not depend on the default alone, but on the rest of the formulas as well. In fact, the choice function which interprets a default says, in a rather concise way, how the default should behave in every possible situation.

Note that, although we assumed the existence of a set of "classical" interpretations throughout for simplicity, the set $\mathcal{M}$ could be a set of more complex objects, like Kripke structures or possibility distributions.

The results presented here seem to raise more questions than they answer. As we mentioned in the preceding section, we have not investigated the properties of the choice functions used, nor that of the corresponding consequence relation. However, these properties, would certainly clarify how the non classical connectives that we have defined are different from the classical connectives.

It is possible to imagine other non classical connectives. For example, ideas similar to that used in the definition of δ could be used to define a connective enabling to represent pieces of knowledge like "if α is consistent, then β". In fact, a number of proposals have been made to define operators related to defeasible reasoning by means of choice functions; it should be possible to turn such operators into connectives.

We have worked here in a propositional setting. It would be interesting to extend the definitions to formulas containing individual variables, and quantifiers. One should then be able to define a quantifier N to represent pieces of knowledge like "normally individuals verify p", using a formula like $Nxp(x)$.

Acknowledgements. I am indebted to the referees for their helpful comments. They also provided valuable references and suggestions for further research; they could not all be taken into account here, but will be investigated in future research.

References

1. Reiter, R.: A Logic for Default Reasoning. Artificial Intelligence **13** (1980) 81–132
2. Poole, D.L.: A Logical Framework for Default Reasoning. Artificial Intelligence **36** (1988) 27–47
3. Kraus, S., Lehmann, D., Magidor, M.: Nonmonotonic reasoning, preferential models and cumulative logics. Artificial Intelligence **44** (1990) 167–207
4. Lehmann, D., Magidor, M.: What does a conditional knowledge base entail? Artificial Intelligence **55** (1991) 1–60
5. McCarthy, J.M.: Circumscription - a form of Nonmonotonic Reasoning. Artificial Intelligence **13** (1980) 27–39
6. Shoham, Y.: Nonmonotonic logics: meaning and utility. In MacDermott, D., ed.: Proceedings of the 10th International Joint Conference on Artificial Intelligence, Morgan Kaufmann (1987) 388–393
7. Lehmann, D.: Nonmonotonic logics and semantics. Journal of Logic and Computation **11** (2001) 229–256
8. Aizerman, M., Aleskerov, F.: Theory of choice. North-Holland (1995)
9. Konieczny, S., Lang, J., Marquis, P.: Raisonnement en présence d'incohérences: le connecteur oublié. In: Actes du Congrès RFIA 2004 (Toulouse, France). (2004)

On Sceptical Versus Credulous Acceptance for Abstract Argument Systems

Sylvie Doutre[1] and Jérôme Mengin[2]

[1] Department of Computer Science, The University of Liverpool, Liverpool, UK
s.doutre@csc.liv.ac.uk
[2] IRIT, Université Paul Sabatier, 118 rte de Narbonne, 31062 Toulouse, France
mengin@irit.fr

Abstract. At a high level of abstraction, many systems of argumentation can be represented by a set of abstract arguments, and a binary relation between these abstract arguments describing how they contradict each other. Acceptable sets of arguments, called *extensions*, can be defined as sets of arguments that do not contradict one another, and attack all their attackers. We are interested in this paper in answering the question: is a given argument in all extensions of an argumentation system? In fact, what is likely to be useful in AI systems is not a simple yes/no answer, but some kind of well-argued answer, called a proof: if an argument is in every extension, why is it so? Several authors have described proofs that explain why a given argument is in at least one extension. In this paper, we show that a proof that an argument is in every extension can be a proof that some *meta*-argument is in at least one extension of a *meta*-argumentation system: this meta-argumentation system describes relationships between sets of arguments of the initial system.

1 Introduction

At a high level of abstraction, many systems of argumentation can be represented by a set of abstract arguments (whose internal structure is not necessarily known), and a binary relation between abstract arguments describing how arguments contradict each other. In particular, several problems related to defeasible reasoning or logic programming can be studied in such an abstract argumentation framework (see e.g. [1]).

Given that some arguments contradict others, and considering that in general contradiction is not desirable, one of the most important questions concerning abstract argumentation systems is to define which arguments are acceptable. The most widespread definition of acceptability associated with non-monotonic logics or logic programs considers that the acceptable sets are the *stable extensions*, which correspond to kernels of the contradiction graph [2,3,4]. However, this stable *semantics* has some features that can be undesirable in some contexts: notably, it can happen that no set of arguments is stable. Under another semantics introduced in [5], acceptable sets of arguments are called *preferred*

J.J. Alferes and J. Leite (Eds.): JELIA 2004, LNAI 3229, pp. 462–473, 2004.

extensions. The preferred semantics captures well some of the intuitions behind the stable semantics, and avoids several of its drawbacks.

The next questions to address are then of the form: is a given argument in some/all extensions of an argumentation system? These questions are important since, in practical situations, an argument which would belong to at least one extension would be cautiously accepted, whereas an argument which would belong to every extension would be strongly accepted. Many works have addressed the first question [10,9], but the second one has received less attention.

In fact, what is likely to be useful in AI systems is not a simple yes/no answer, but some kind of well-argued answer: if an argument is acceptable, why is it so? In the world of mathematics, a well-argued answer is called a proof. In classical, monotonic logic, a proof is represented by a sequence of formulas, such that the sequence describes stepwise progress towards the conclusion.

In the case of abstract argumentation systems, proofs of acceptability usually have the form of a game between two players: one tries to establish the acceptability of an argument, the other tries to establish the opposite by putting forward arguments that contradict those of the former; the player that tries to establish the validity of an argument can defeat its opponent by providing arguments that contradict its opponent's ones. Several proof theories of this type have been proposed for acceptability problems under various semantics [6,7,8,9, 10]. They usually consider the credulous acceptance problem, where one tries to establish that an argument is in at least one extension of the theory; or some particular cases of the more difficult sceptical acceptance problem, where one tries to establish that an argument is in every extension of the theory.

We address here the problem of proving that an argument is in every preferred extension of some argumentation system. We formally establish a close connection between this problem and proofs of credulous acceptance in a *meta-argumentation* system describing relationships between sets of arguments of the initial system.

The paper is organized as follows: Dung's abstract argumentation framework is briefly presented in the next section. The meta-argumentation system is introduced in Section 3. Section 4 describes a general proof theory for sceptical acceptance using this meta-argumentation system. We finish the paper with some concluding remarks. Note that this article is a revised version of [11].

2   Preferred Extensions of Abstract Argumentation Systems

This section is a short presentation of Dung's abstract argumentation framework and of the preferred semantics. More details, in particular other semantics, can be found in e.g. [5,1,12].

Definition 1. *[5] An* argument system *is a pair* (A, R) *where A is a set whose elements are called* arguments *and R is a binary relation over A ($R \subseteq A \times A$). Given two arguments x and y, $(x, y) \in R$ or equivalently xRy means that x*

attacks y (x is said to be an attacker of y). Moreover, an argument x R-attacks a set S of arguments if there exists $y \in S$ such that xRy. A set S of arguments R-attacks an argument $x \in A$ if there exists $y \in S$ such that yRx. Finally, a set S of arguments R-attacks a set S' of arguments if there exists $x \in S$ such that x R-attacks S'.

In the following definitions and notations, we assume that an argument system (A, R) is given.

An argument system can be simply represented as a directed graph whose vertices are the arguments and edges correspond to the elements of R.

Notation 1. For every set $S \subseteq A$, $R^+(S) = \{x \in A \mid S$ R-attacks $x\}$, $R^-(S) = \{x \in A \mid x$ R-attacks $S\}$ and $R^{\pm}(S) = R^+(S) \cup R^-(S)$. Moreover, $\text{Refl}(A, R) = \{x \in A \mid xRx\}$ is the set of arguments that attack themselves.

Definition 2. A set $S \subseteq A$ is conflict-free if and only if there are no arguments x and y in S such that x attacks y. An argument $x \in A$ is defended by a set $S \subseteq A$ (or S defends x) iff for each argument y in A that attacks x there exists an argument in S that attacks y. A set $S \subseteq A$ is admissible if and only if S is conflict-free and S defends all its elements. It is a preferred extension if and only if S is maximal for set-inclusion among the admissible sets.

The preferred semantics coincides with several important other semantics when the graph of the argumentation system has no odd cycle, and most existing semantics coincide when the graph is acyclic.

Notation 2. Given an argumentation system (A, R), $\text{Adm}(A, R)$ denotes the collection of admissible sets of (A, R).

Dung exhibits interesting properties of preferred extensions: every admissible set is contained in a preferred extension; every argument system possesses at least one preferred extension. In the rest of the paper, when no particular semantics is mentioned, it is assumed that extensions refer to the preferred extensions.

Example 1. Consider the following system:

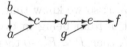

The preferred extensions are $\{a, d, g, f\}$ and $\{b, d, g, f\}$: d, g and f are in all of them; whereas a and b are in at least one preferred extensions each, but not in every preferred extension.

The crucial problem is to be able to decide which arguments are acceptable. In the case of the preferred semantics, two problems can be formally defined as follows:

Definition 3. *Let* (A, R) *be an argumentation system. Let* $x \in A$ *and* $S \subseteq A$. x *(resp. S) is* credulously accepted *(w.r.t. (A, R)) under the preferred semantics iff* x *(resp. S) is contained in at least one preferred extension of* (A, R). x *(resp. S) is* sceptically accepted *(w.r.t. (A, R)) under the preferred semantics iff* x *(resp. S) is contained in every preferred extension of* (A, R).

Note that an argument x is credulously accepted if and only if $\{x\}$ is, whereas a set of arguments S is sceptically accepted if and only if every $x \in S$ is sceptically accepted. In the next section, we relate the sceptical acceptance of an argument to the credulous acceptance of a set of arguments.

3   Sceptical Acceptance as Credulous Meta-acceptance

The credulous acceptance problem has been well-studied; several proof theories and algorithms exist to answer questions like: is a given argument in at least one extension of a given argumentation system? (See e.g. [9,10].) We are interested here in answering questions like: is a given argument in every extension of a given argumentation system?

The last question is easily (but not efficiently) answered if we can enumerate all the extensions of the system: we consider a first extension E_1 and test if $x \in E_1$. If it is, this suggests that x may indeed be in every extension (as opposed to the case where $x \notin E_1$). We then consider a second extension E_2: it may happen that $x \notin E_2$, so the existence of E_2 *a priori* casts a doubt over the fact that x is in every extension. However, if it turns out that $x \in E_2$, this reinforces the possibility that x may be in every extension. Continuing the process, each extension E starts, with its sole existence, by being an argument suggesting that x may not be in every extension, to become, if it turns out $x \in E$, an argument reinforcing the possibility that x is in every extension. Of course, enumerating all the extensions will generally not be efficient. We study in the remainder of this section how we can refine this approach, by enumerating smaller sets that can be interpreted as "meta"-arguments for or against the possibility that x is in every extension.

Since every argumentation system has at least one (preferred) extension, an argument x must be in at least one extension in order to be in all of them, so x must be in at least one admissible set. Now, suppose we have found one admissible set P that contains x; so we know that x is in at least one extension $E \supseteq P$. What could prevent x from being in every extension? If there is an extension E' such that $x \notin E'$, then $P \not\subseteq E'$, so there must be a conflict between P and E' (otherwise, since P and E' defend themselves, $P \cup E'$ would be admissible, which is not possible since E' is maximally admissible and $P \not\subseteq E'$). Thus if x is not in every extension, there must be some admissible set P' that attacks P and such that P' is not in any extension that contains x (take for instance $P' = E'$). In a sense, P can be seen as a "meta"-argument suggesting that x may well be in every extension of the system; whereas P' can be seen as a counter-argument: it suggests that, since there is an admissible set that contradicts P, there may be some maximal admissible set of arguments that does not contain x. This "meta" counter-argument is in turn contradicted if there is some admissible set of arguments P'' that contains both P' and x.

This approach can be formalised by defining a relation R_x on the admissible subsets of some argumentation system (A, R):

Definition 4. *Let (A, R) be an argumentation system. Let $X, Y \in \text{Adm}(A, R)$. Then $X R_x Y$ (or $X\ R_x$-attacks Y) if:*

1. *$x \in Y \setminus X$ and X R-attacks Y; or*
2. *$x \in X \setminus Y$ and $X \supseteq Y$.*

In case 1., Y suggests that x may be in every extension: it is at least in all the extensions that contain Y; but X suggests that there may in fact be some extensions that do not contain x: those that contain X cannot contain Y because X R-attacks Y.

In case 2., Y suggests that x may not be in every extension, since it is admissible and does not contain x; but X shows that Y can be extended to an admissible set that does contain x.

Note that X R_x-attacks Y is not equivalent to X R-attacks Y. The latter means that there is $(x, y) \in X \times Y$ such that xRy.

Example 2. Consider the element d of the argumentation system depicted on the left of Fig. 1, and the relation R_d depicted on the right of the same figure. The

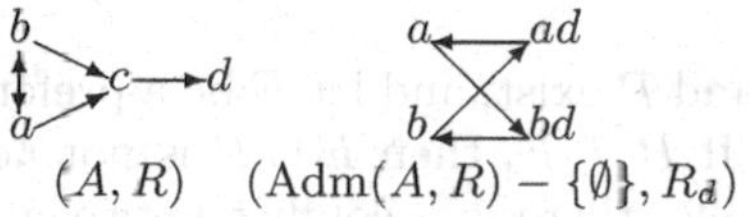

$$(A, R) \quad (\text{Adm}(A, R) - \{\emptyset\}, R_d)$$

Fig. 1. The argumentation system of Example 2.

"base" argumentation system has four non-empty admissible sets: $\{a\}$, $\{a, d\}$, $\{b\}$ and $\{b, d\}$. Since $d \in \{a, d\}$, d may be in every extensions. This may be contradicted by the fact that $\{b\}$ R_d-attacks $\{a, d\}$: this suggests that there may be an extension that does not contain d. However, $\{b, d\}$ R_d-attacks $\{b\}$: it is a larger admissible set that contains $\{b\}$ and contains d. In fact, the set $\{\{a, d\}, \{b, d\}\}$ is R_d-admissible, and d is in every extension.

Example 3. Consider the following system:

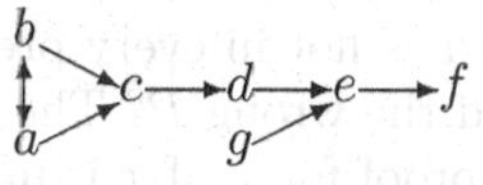

The argument d is in two admissible sets: $\{a, d\}$ and $\{b, d\}$. In fact, like on the previous example, d is in every extension. However, the set $\{\{a, d\}, \{b, d\}\}$ is not R_d-admissible, since it is R_d-attacked by e.g. $\{b, g\}$. An R_d-admissible set is $\{\{a, d, f, g\}, \{b, d, f, g\}\}$. This is somewhat surprising: the status of d only depends on the arguments a, b, c and d. However, when looking for an R_d-admissible set, we have to consider f and g as well. This is because the R_d-admissible set has to defend itself against $\{b, g\}$, although it is b, not g, that R-attacks $\{a, d\}$.

The previous example suggests that it may be sufficient to restrict R_x to some R-admissible sets only. To this end, we define the set $\mathcal{A}_x$ as follows:

Definition 5. *Let (A, R) be an argumentation system. Let $x \in A$. Then $\mathcal{A}_x = \mathcal{A}_x^{\mathrm{PRO}} \cup \mathcal{A}_x^{\mathrm{OPP}}$, where:*

$\mathcal{A}_x^{\mathrm{PRO}}$ *is the set of the R-admissible parts of A that contain x;*
$\mathcal{A}_x^{\mathrm{OPP}}$ *is the set of the R-admissible parts X of A that do not contain x and are of the form $X = \cup_{Y \in \mathcal{Y}} Y$, where the $Y \in \mathcal{Y}$ are parts of A minimal such that Y is R-admissible and R-attacks some element of $\mathcal{A}_x^{\mathrm{PRO}}$.*

We are now able to express problems of sceptical acceptance in terms of admissibility, or credulous acceptance, in the meta-graph. Our first result is that if there is a meta-admissible set in favor of a given argument x, then x is in every extension of the theory:

Proposition 1. *An argument x of an argumentation framework (A, R) is in every preferred extension of (A, R) if there exist $P \in \mathrm{Adm}(A, R)$ and $\mathcal{P} \in \mathrm{Adm}(\mathcal{A}_x, R_x)$ such that $x \in P$ and $P \in \mathcal{P}$.*

Proof. Suppose that P and $\mathcal{P}$ exist, and let E be a preferred extension of (A, R). If $P \subseteq E$, then $x \in E$. If $P \not\subseteq E$, then $E \cup P$ is not admissible, thus, since E and P are both admissible, there is a conflict between them, and E R-attacks P. Let $\mathcal{Y}$ be the set of the minimal parts of E that are admissible and attack some elements of $\mathcal{A}_x^{\mathrm{PRO}}$. Then $X = \cup_{Y \in \mathcal{Y}} Y$ is such that $x \notin X$, $X \in \mathcal{A}_x^{\mathrm{OPP}}$ (X is admissible since $X \subseteq E$ and E is admissible) and X R-attacks P, thus $X R_x P$. Since $\mathcal{P}$ is admissible in $(\mathcal{A}_x, R_x)$, there is $P' \in \mathcal{A}_x^{\mathrm{PRO}}$ such that $P' R_x X$, that is, $P' \supseteq X$. Suppose that $P' \not\subseteq E$, then E R-attacks P', but then there is some $Y \in \mathcal{Y}$ such that Y R-attacks P', thus $Y \subseteq X \subseteq P'$: this contradicts the fact that P' is R-admissible. Thus $P' \subseteq E$ and, since $x \in P'$, $x \in E$.   □

Our next result shows that the approach is complete. It guarantees that if we can find an R-admissible part $P \subseteq A$ that contains x, and an R_x-admissible part of $\mathcal{A}_x$ that contains P, then x is in every extension. However, this result alone would not guarantee the completeness of the approach: if we find P, but then cannot find $\mathcal{P}$, is it that x is not in every preferred extension of (A, R), or could it be that we just picked the wrong P? The proposition below shows that any P can be part of a meta-proof for x, if x is in every extension:

Proposition 2. *If an argument x of an argumentation framework (A, R) is in every preferred extension of (A, R), then:*

1. *for every $P \in \mathrm{Adm}(A, R)$ such that $x \in P$ there exists $\mathcal{P} \in \mathrm{Adm}(\mathcal{A}_x, \mathcal{R}_x)$ such that $P \in \mathcal{P}$;*
2. *there exist $P \in \mathrm{Adm}(A, R)$ and $\mathcal{P} \in \mathrm{Adm}(\mathcal{A}_x, \mathcal{R}_x)$ such that $x \in P$ and $P \in \mathcal{P}$.*

Proof. Let $P \in \mathrm{Adm}(A, R)$ such that $x \in P$, and let $\mathcal{P}$ be the set containing P and the preferred extensions of (A, R): $\mathcal{P}$ is without $\mathcal{R}_x$-conflict since all its elements contain x. Furthermore, suppose that $P' \in \mathcal{A}_x$ is such that $P' \mathcal{R}_x$-attacks $\mathcal{P}$: P' is contained in a preferred extension F of (A, R); and there is $E \in \mathcal{P}$ such that $P' \mathcal{R}_x E$. But then, $x \notin P'$, thus $F \mathcal{R}_x P'$. This proves that $\mathcal{P}$ is an admissible part of $(\mathcal{A}_x, \mathcal{R}_x)$. This proves part 1 of the proposition.

For part 2, we know that (A, R) has at least one preferred extension, which must contain x if x is in every preferred extension of (A, R). Let P be this preferred extension. We have proved in part 1 that there is $\mathcal{P} \in \mathrm{Adm}(\mathcal{A}_x, \mathcal{R}_x)$ such that $P \in \mathcal{P}$. □

We close this section with an example that shows why, when defining $\mathcal{A}_x^{\mathrm{OPP}}$, we cannot simply consider minimal admissible sets Y that attack elements of $\mathcal{A}_x^{\mathrm{PRO}}$, but need to consider unions of such Y's.

Example 4. Consider the following system:

It has four preferred extensions: $\{a, c, e, h\}$, $\{a, d, e, f, h\}$, $\{b, c, g\}$ and $\{b, d, f, h\}$; so h is not in the intersection of the extensions. However, let $\mathcal{P} = \{\{a, c, e, h\}, \{a, d, e, g, h\}, \{b, d, f, h\}\}$, every element of $\mathcal{P}$ is admissible and contains h; furthermore, the minimal admissible sets of arguments that attack at least one element of $\mathcal{P}$ are $\{a\}$, $\{b\}$, $\{c\}$ and $\{d\}$: each of them is contained in an element of $\mathcal{P}$. There is one admissible set of arguments that attacks some element of $\mathcal{P}$ and which is not contained in any element of $\mathcal{P}$: it is the union $\{b, c\}$ of $\{b\}$ and $\{c\}$.

4   A Proof-Theory for Sceptical Acceptance

In this section, we describe a proof theory for the problem of the sceptical acceptance of an argument, using our characterization of this problem in terms of credulous meta-acceptance.

In classical, monotonic logic, a proof is represented by a sequence of formulas, such that the sequence describes stepwise progress towards the conclusion. In the case of abstract argumentation systems, proofs of acceptability usually have the form of a game between two players, one called PRO, the other one called OPP: PRO tries to establish the acceptability of an argument, while OPP tries to establish the opposite by putting forward arguments that contradict those of PRO; PRO can defeat its opponent by providing arguments that contradict its opponent's ones. Several proof theories of this type have been proposed for acceptance problems under various semantics, [6,7,8,9,10].

Since we have characterized the sceptical acceptance problem as a credulous acceptance problem in a meta-graph, any proof theory designed for the credulous acceptance problem can be used to solve the sceptical acceptance problem. We illustrate this below with a proof theory proposed in [10].

Argument games have been formalised in [13] using sequences of *moves*, called *dialogues*. A definition of a proof theory for the credulous acceptance of an argument has been proposed in [10]. We extend this definition in order to define a proof theory for the credulous acceptance of a set of arguments.

Definition 6. *Let (A, R) be an argumentation system. A move in A is a pair $[P, X]$ where $P \in \{\text{PRO}, \text{OPP}\}$ and $X \in A$. A dialogue d in (A, R) for a finite set of arguments $S = \{a_1, a_2, \ldots, a_n\} \subseteq A$ is a countable sequence of moves of the form*

$$[\text{PRO}, a_1] \ldots [\text{PRO}, a_n][\text{OPP}, b_1][\text{PRO}, b_2][\text{OPP}, b_3] \ldots$$

$$\ldots [\text{OPP}, b_{2i-1}][\text{PRO}, b_{2i}][\text{OPP}, b_{2i+1}] \ldots$$

such that:

1. *the first n moves are played by PRO to put forward the elements of S;*
2. *the subsequent moves are played alternatively by OPP and PRO;*
3. *the ith argument put forward by OPP is $b_{2i-1} \in R^-(P_i) \setminus R^+(P_i)$, where $P_i = S \cup \{b_2, b_4, \ldots, b_{2i-2}\}$ is the set of arguments put forward by PRO so far;*
4. *the $n+i$th argument put forward by PRO is $b_{2i} \in R^-(b_{2i-1}) \setminus (P_i \cup R^{\pm}(P_i) \cup \text{Refl}(A, R))$.*

A finite dialogue is won by PRO *if OPP cannot respond to PRO's last move in accordance with rule 3 above.*

Rule 3 means that OPP can attack any argument put forward by PRO, with any argument not attacked by arguments already put forward by PRO. Rule 4 means that PRO must defend itself against OPP's last attack, with an argument that it has not already put forward, and that is not in conflict with the arguments it has already put forward. The following proposition ensures the soundness and completeness of the above proof theory for set-credulous acceptance. It is a straightforward extension of a result proved in [10] that concerns the credulous acceptance of a single argument.

Proposition 3. *Let (A, R) be an argument system such that A is finite, and let $S \subseteq A$ be a conflict-free set. If d is a dialogue for S won by PRO, then $\text{PRO}(d)$ is an admissible set containing S. If S is included in a preferred extension of (A, R) then there exists a dialogue for S won by PRO.*

The proof of the proposition relies upon the two following lemmas:

Lemma 1. *Let (A, R) be an argument system such that A is finite. Let $S \subseteq A$ be a conflict-free set. Let d be a finite dialogue about S. Then $\text{PRO}(d)$ is conflict-free.*

Proof. We prove this result by induction on the number of elements of $\mathrm{PRO}(d)$. If $\mathrm{PRO}(d)$ contains between 1 and $|S|$ elements, then these elements are all in S, and since S is conflict-free, $\mathrm{PRO}(d)$ is conflict-free. Suppose now that the property is true for any dialogue d such that $\mathrm{PRO}(d)$ contains at most $n-1$ elements, for some $n > |S|$. Let d be a dialogue such that $\mathrm{PRO}(d)$ contains n elements. Suppose first that the last move of d is played by PRO: d has the form $d = d'.[\mathrm{OPP}, x].[\mathrm{PRO}, y]$ where

- $x \in R^-(\mathrm{PRO}(d')) \setminus R^+(\mathrm{PRO}(d'))$, and
- $y \in R^-(x) \setminus (\mathrm{PRO}(d') \cup R^{\pm}(\mathrm{PRO}(d'))) \cup \mathrm{Refl}(A, R))$.

Then $\mathrm{PRO}(d) = \mathrm{PRO}(d') \cup \{y\}$ and $y \notin \mathrm{PRO}(d')$, therefore d' contains strictly less than n elements. Thus, by induction hypothesis, $\mathrm{PRO}(d')$ is conflict-free. Since $y \notin R^{\pm}(\mathrm{PRO}(d'))$, $\mathrm{PRO}(d)$ is conflict-free too. Suppose now that the last move of d is played by OPP: then d has the form $d = d'.[\mathrm{OPP}, x]$ where d' is a dialogue such that $\mathrm{PRO}(d') = \mathrm{PRO}(d)$, therefore $\mathrm{PRO}(d')$ contains n elements. We have just proved that in this case $\mathrm{PRO}(d')$ is conflict-free, hence $\mathrm{PRO}(d)$ is conflict-fee.   □

The following lemma has been proved in [10]:

Lemma 2. *Let (A, R) be an argumentation framework, and let d be a dialogue, the last move of which is played by PRO. Let S be a subset of A minimal such that S is admissible and contains $\mathrm{PRO}(d)$. If $S \neq \mathrm{PRO}(d)$, then there exists $x, y \in A$ such that the dialogue $d' = d.[\mathrm{OPP}, x].[\mathrm{PRO}, y]$ is a dialogue and S is minimal such that S is admissible and contains $\mathrm{PRO}(d')$.*

Proof (of Proposition 3). First, let d be a dialogue for S won by PRO. Clearly, $\mathrm{PRO}(d)$ contains S. According to Lemma 1, $\mathrm{PRO}(d)$ is conflict-free. Since d is won by PRO, $R^-(\mathrm{PRO}(d)) \setminus R^+(\mathrm{PRO}(d)) = \emptyset$, thus $R^-(\mathrm{PRO}(d)) \subseteq R^+(\mathrm{PRO}(d))$, that is, $\mathrm{PRO}(d)$ defends all its elements. Therefore $\mathrm{PRO}(d)$ is an admissible set containing S.

Second, let S' be a minimal subset of A such that S' is admissible and contains S. Let $S = \{a_1, \ldots, a_{|S|}\}$. Let N be the number of elements of S' (which is finite since A is assumed to be finite), let $d_1 = [\mathrm{PRO}, a_1], \ldots, [\mathrm{PRO}, a_{|S|}]$ and let $d_n = d_{n-1}.[\mathrm{OPP}, y].[\mathrm{PRO}, z]$, for $|S| + 1 \leq n \leq N$, for some $y \in R^-(\mathrm{PRO}(d_{n-1})) \setminus R^+(\mathrm{PRO}(d_{n-1}))$ and $z \in S \cap R^-(y)$. Lemma 2 proves that such a sequence can be defined, and that d_N is a dialogue for S won by PRO.   □

Notice that another winning criterion defined by [13] (the *winning strategy*) could be used in order to design proofs in which one can see precisely how any argument of a proof (not only an argument of the set S) is defended against its attackers.

Let us now describe how this type of dialogue can be used as a proof theory for the sceptical acceptance problem. Suppose that we want to prove that some argument x of an argumentation system (A, R) is in every extension of (A, R). According to the results of the preceding section, all we need to do is find an admissible set P that contains x, and then find a dialogue for $\{P\}$ won by PRO with respect to the argumentation system $(\mathcal{A}_x, R_x)$.

In order to find the initial admissible set P that contains x, Prop. 3 says that we can look for a dialogue d for $\{x\}$ won by PRO w.r.t. (A, R): we can then take $P = \mathrm{PRO}(d)$. In order to establish that x is in every extension of the theory, we then start a dialogue with the move $[\mathcal{PRO}, P]$, where $\mathcal{PRO}$ denotes the player that tries to establish the acceptability of P in the meta-graph. In fact, a more detailed dialogue can start with the move $[\mathcal{PRO}, d]$, showing not only P but the entire dialogue that established the admissibility of P.

In order to continue the meta-dialogue, we need a move of the form $[\mathcal{OPP}, d_1]$, where $\mathcal{OPP}$ denotes the player who tries to establish that P is not credulously accepted in the meta-graph, and where d_1 must be a dialogue in (A, R) for an argument that R-attacks P.

$\mathcal{PRO}$ must then put forward a dialogue for $\mathrm{PRO}(d_1) \cup \{x\}$ won by PRO, thereby showing that the admissible set found by $\mathcal{OPP}$ in the preceding move can be "returned" in favor of $\mathcal{PRO}$.

This type of meta-dialogue is best illustrated on an example.

Example 5. Consider the following system:

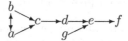

A meta-dialogue proving that d is in every extension of the theory is depicted below (note that the moves of the dialogues in (A, R) are in columns, whereas the moves of the meta-dialogue in $(\mathcal{A}_x, R_x)$ are in line):

$$\begin{bmatrix} \mathcal{PRO}, [\mathrm{PRO}, d] \\ [\mathrm{OPP}, c] \\ [\mathrm{PRO}, a] \end{bmatrix} \qquad [\mathcal{OPP}, [\mathrm{PRO}, b]] \qquad \begin{bmatrix} \mathcal{PRO}, [\mathrm{PRO}, d] \\ [\mathrm{PRO}, b] \end{bmatrix}$$

$\mathcal{PRO}$'s first move shows that $\{a, d\}$ is admissible	$\mathcal{OPP}$ then plays an admissible set $\{b\}$ that attacks $\{a, d\}$	$\mathcal{PRO}$ concludes by proving that $\{b, d\}$ is admissible in (A, R)

We close this section with a remark about the possibilities for $\mathcal{PRO}$ to defend itself. Rule 3 of the definition of a dialogue says that the $1 + i$th argument b_{2i} put forward by $\mathcal{PRO}$ must be in $R_x^-(b_{2i-1}) \setminus (\mathcal{P}_i \cup R^{\pm}(\mathcal{P}_i) \cup \mathrm{Refl}(\mathcal{A}_x, R_x))$, where $\mathcal{P}_i = S \cup \{b_2, b_4, \dots, b_{2i-2}\}$ is the set of arguments put forward by $\mathcal{PRO}$ so far. However, since the graph $(\mathcal{A}_x, R_x)$ is bipartite, $\mathrm{Refl}(\mathcal{A}_x, R_x) = R^{\pm}(\mathcal{P}_i) \cap R_x^-(b_{2i-1}) = \emptyset$.

5 Conclusion

The complexity of the credulous/sceptical acceptance problems has been studied in [14,2,15]. The credulous acceptance problem is shown to be NP-complete, the sceptical acceptance problem is Π_2^p-complete. This is in accordance with our characterization of sceptical acceptance in terms of meta-credulous acceptance. Note that the notion of dialogue is also implicit in several theorem provers that have been proposed by e.g. [16,17,18] for circumscription or to check membership in every extension of a default theory, two notorious instances of sceptical reasoning. Our presentation can be seen as an abstraction of one aspect of these provers.

In this paper, we have defined what can be proofs that an argument x is in every extension of an argumentation system. Proofs that an argument x is in at least one extension have been proposed in e.g. [7,8,9,10]. To complete the study, it would be interesting to define proofs that an argument is *not* in every extension of the theory: if x is not in every extension, why is it so? Which part of the argumentation system can be seen as an explanation of that? [9,10] show that such a proof can be an attacker y of x together with a proof that y is in at least one extension: in this case, x cannot be in that extension. However, this proof theory is not complete: when the graph has odd cycles, x may not be in every extension although its attackers are in no extension at all.

Proofs of credulous acceptance, like those of [7,8,9,10], can also be used as proofs of sceptical acceptance when the argument system only has one extension. This is in particular the case when the graph has no cycle at all.

An important perspective is to design an algorithm that computes sceptical proofs, thereby answering queries of the form: is a given argument in every extension of the system? This can be done using for example the algorithm for answering queries about credulous acceptance of [10]: this algorithm returns a proof that an argument is in at least one extension. It can be used at the meta-level, and calls itself at the base-level (however, at the base-level, the algorithm needs to be slightly modified in order to find *all* minimal proofs that an argument is in some extension of the base system). Such an algorithm could be combined with an algorithm looking for proofs that an argument is not in every extension, thus providing proofs in both cases, at least when the graph has no odd cycle. A complete characterization of proofs that an argument is not in every extension when there are odd cycles remains to be done.

Acknowledgements. We wish to thank the referees, whose comments helped improve the paper. Sylvie Doutre is grateful for partial support from the European Commission, through the ASPIC Project (IST-FP6-002307).

References

1. Bondarenko, A., Dung, P., Kowalski, R., Toni, F.: An abstract, argumentation-theoretic approach to default reasoning. Artificial Intelligence **93** (1997) 63–101
2. Dimopoulos, Y., Torres, A.: Graph theoretical structures in logic programs and default theories. Theoretical Computer Science **170** (1996) 209–244
3. Dimopoulos, Y., Magirou, V., Papadimitriou, C.: On kernels, Defaults and Even Graphs. Annals of Mathematics and AI (1997) 1–12

4. Berge, C.: Graphs and Hypergraphs. North-Holland Mathematical Library, North-Holland (1973)
5. Dung, P.: On the acceptability of arguments and its fundamental role in non-monotonic reasoning, logic programming and n-person games. Artificial Intelligence **77** (1995) 321–357
6. Kakas, A., Toni, F.: Computing Argumentation in Logic Programming. Journal of Logic and Computation **9** (1999) 515–562
7. Prakken, H., Sartor, G.: Argument-based logic programming with defeasible priorities. Journal of Applied Non-Classical Logics **7** (1997) 25–75
8. Amgoud, L., Cayrol, C.: A reasoning model based on the production of acceptable arguments. Annals of Mathematics and Artificial Intelligence **34** (2002) 197–215
9. Vreeswijk, G., Prakken, H.: Credulous and Sceptical Argument Games for Preferred Semantics. In: Proc. JELIA'2000, LNAI 1919 (2000) 239–253
10. Cayrol, C., Doutre, S., Mengin, J.: On Decision Problems related to the preferred semantics for argumentation frameworks. Journal of Logic and Computation **13** (2003) 377–403
11. Doutre, S., Mengin, J.: On sceptical vs credulous acceptance for abstract argument systems. In: Tenth International Workshop on Non-Monotonic Reasoning (NMR2004). (2004) 134–139
12. Doutre, S.: Autour de la sémantique préférée des systèmes d'argumentation. PhD Thesis, Université Paul Sabatier, Toulouse (2002)
13. Jakobovits, H., Vermeir, D.: Dialectic Semantics for Argumentation Frameworks. In: Proc. ICAIL'99, ACM Press (1999) 53–62
14. Dimopoulos, Y., Nebel, B., Toni, F.: On the Computational Complexity of Assumption-based Argumentation for Default Reasoning. Artificial Intelligence **141** (2002) 57–78
15. Dunne, P., Bench-Capon, T.: Coherence in Finite Argument Systems. Artificial Intelligence **141** (2002) 187–203
16. Baker, A.B., Ginsberg, M.L.: A theorem prover for prioritized circumscription. In: Proceedings of the 11th International Joint Conference on Artificial Intelligence, Morgan Kaufmann (1989) 463–467
17. Poole, D.L.: Explanation and prediction: an architecture for default and abductive reasoning. Computational Intelligence **5** (1989) 97–110
18. Przymusinski, T.: An algorithm to compute circumscription. Artificial Intelligence **38** (1989) 49–73

Line-Based Affine Reasoning in Euclidean Plane*

Philippe Balbiani[1] and Tinko Tinchev[1,2]

[1] Institut de recherche en informatique de Toulouse
[2] Sofia University

Abstract. We consider the binary relations of parallelism and convergence between lines in a 2-dimensional affinespace. Associating with parallelism and convergence the binary predicates P and C and the modal connectives $[P]$ and $[C]$, we consider a first-order theory based on these predicates and a modal logic based on these modal connectives. We investigate the axiomatization/completeness and the decidability/complexity of this first-order theory and this modal logic.

1 Introduction

In recent years, there has been an increasing interest in spatial reasoning and important applications to practical issues such as geographical information systems have made the field even more attractive [15]. Historically, topological spaces were among the first mathematical models of space applied to spatial information processing and they occupy the central position in the subject. The work of Randell, Cui and Cohn [12], who brought in the region connection calculus, was influential at the early stages. A major impetus for studying topological spaces in general and the region connection calculus in particular was the fact that, within the framework of constraint satisfaction problems, qualitative spatial reasoning can be easily automated [3,13]. In the second half of the 1990's, this work was continued by others and their efforts generated many results concerning different kinds of spatial relationships between different types of spatial entities [1,7,8,10, 11].

Plane affine geometry, one of the most prominent mathematical models of space, arises from the study of points and lines by means of properties stated in terms of incidence. In plane coordinate geometry, lines are sets of points satisfying linear equations. Completely determined by two of their points, they can also be considered as abstract entities. They have certain mutual relations like parallelism and convergence: two lines are parallel iff they never meet whereas they are convergent iff they have exactly one common point. Lines are to be found in many axiomatizations of plane affine geometry — however we had great difficulty finding any examples of qualitative forms of spatial reasoning based solely on them. To confirm this claim, we have not been able to find any explicit reference to a first-order language or to a modal language devoted to the study

---

* Our research is partly supported by the *Centre national de la recherche scientifique*, the RILA project 06288TF and the ECONET project 08111TL.

J.J. Alferes and J. Leite (Eds.): JELIA 2004, LNAI 3229, pp. 474–486, 2004.

of parallelism and convergence, the only possible relationships between lines in plane affine geometry.

Associating with parallelism and convergence the binary predicates P and C, this paper is about the completeness and the complexity of a first-order theory based on these predicates. Linking the modal connectives $[P]$ and $[C]$ with parallelism and convergence, this paper is interested in the completeness and the complexity of a modal logic founded on these modal connectives. The paper has two major parts. The first introduces a first-order theory of lines based on the binary predicates P and C and applies the technique of model theory to it. It mainly proves that the first-order theory of parallelism and incidence in plane affine geometry is a complete first-order theory whose membership problem can be decided in polynomial space. In the second part of the paper we turn to the following question: what is the modal logic of lines with the modal connectives $[P]$ and $[C]$? Our modal logic of parallelism and convergence is a complete modal logic whose membership problem can be decided in nondeterministic polynomial time. In all parts, completeness means completeness with respect to the Euclidean plane.

2   First-Order Theory

It is now time to meet the first-order languages we will be working with. What we would like to do in this section is study structures consisting of lines in a space of dimension 2. We assume some familiarity with model theory. Readers wanting more details may refer, for example, to [6]. Our line-based first-order theory is based on the idea of associating with parallelism and convergence the binary predicates P and C, with the formulas $P(x,y)$ and $C(x,y)$ being read "x is parallel to y" and "x is convergent with y". The *formulas* are given by the rule:

$$\phi ::= P(x,y) \mid C(x,y) \mid x = y \mid \neg\phi \mid \phi \vee \psi \mid \forall x \phi,$$

where x and y range over a countable set of *individual variables*. Let the *size of* ϕ, denoted $|\phi|$, be the number of symbols occurring in ϕ. We adopt the standard definitions for the remaining Boolean operations and for the existential quantifier.

2.1   Parallelism and Convergence

A *line-based affine plane* is a relational structure of the form $\mathcal{F} = (L, P, C)$ where L is a nonempty set of *lines* and P and C are binary relations on L. We shall say that an affine plane $\mathcal{F} = (L, P, C)$ is *standard* iff it satisfies the following sentences:

IRREF $\forall x \neg P(x, x)$
         $\forall x \neg C(x, x)$
TRANS $\forall x \forall y \forall z (P(x,y) \wedge C(y,z) \rightarrow C(x,z))$
UNIV $\forall x \forall y (x = y \vee P(x,y) \vee C(x,y))$

$DENS_n$ $\forall x \forall y_1 \ldots \forall y_n (P(x, y_1) \wedge \ldots \wedge P(x, y_n) \rightarrow \exists z (P(x, z) \wedge P(z, y_1) \wedge \ldots$
$\qquad \wedge P(z, y_n)))$
$\qquad \forall x \forall y_1 \ldots \forall y_n (C(x, y_1) \wedge \ldots \wedge C(x, y_n) \rightarrow \exists z (C(x, z) \wedge C(z, y_1) \wedge \ldots$
$\qquad \wedge C(z, y_n)))$

Notice first that:

Proposition 1. *Equality and convergence are first-order definable with P in any standard affine plane.*

Proof. It suffices to observe that the sentences $\forall x \forall y (x = y \leftrightarrow \forall z (P(x, z) \leftrightarrow P(y, z)))$ and $\forall x \forall y (C(x, y) \leftrightarrow \neg P(x, y) \wedge x \neq y)$ are true in all standard affine planes. $\dashv$

Let $\mathcal{F} = (L, P, C)$ be a standard affine plane. It is a simple matter to check that the following sentences $\forall x \forall y (P(x, y) \rightarrow P(y, x))$, $\forall x \forall y (C(x, y) \rightarrow C(y, x))$, $\forall x \forall y \forall z (\neg C(x, y) \wedge C(y, z) \rightarrow C(x, z))$ and $\forall x \forall y \exists z (C(x, z) \wedge C(z, y))$ are true in $\mathcal{F}$. Consequently $\neg C$ is an equivalence relation on L such that every equivalence class in L modulo $\neg C$ is made up of infinitely many lines whereas the partition of L modulo $\neg C$ consists of infinitely many equivalence classes. In the sequel the following notation will be used, for all lines a in L: $[a] = \{b : \neg C(a, b)\}$. Obviously, the axioms as above have models in each infinite power. We should consider, for instance, the affine plane $\mathcal{F}_{\mathbb{R}}^2$. Its set of lines consists of all lines in the Euclidean plane. A countable structure approximating $\mathcal{F}_{\mathbb{R}}^2$ is $\mathcal{F}_{\mathbb{Q}}^2$: its set of lines is made up of all lines in the Euclidean plane containing at least two points with rational coordinates. Clearly, both affine planes are standard. To illustrate the value of countable standard affine planes, we shall prove the following proposition:

Proposition 2. *Let $\mathcal{F}$ and $\mathcal{F}'$ be standard affine planes. If $\mathcal{F}$ is countable then $\mathcal{F}$ is elementary embeddable in $\mathcal{F}'$.*

Proof. Let $\mathcal{F} = (L, P, C)$ and $\mathcal{F}' = (L', P', C')$ be standard affine planes. Suppose that $\mathcal{F}$ is countable, we demonstrate that $\mathcal{F}$ is elementary embeddable in $\mathcal{F}'$. We need to consider an injective mapping g on the partition of L into the partition of L'. For each equivalence class $[a]$ in the partition of L, we also need an injective mapping $h_{[a]}$ on $[a]$ into $g([a])$. Now let f be the mapping on L into L' defined with $f(a) = h_{[a]}(a)$. To see that f is an elementary embedding of $\mathcal{F}$ into $\mathcal{F}'$, we invite the reader to show by induction on the complexity of formulas $\phi(x_1, \ldots, x_n)$ in $x_1, \ldots, x_n$ and P, C and $=$, that for all lines $a_1, \ldots, a_n$ in L, $\mathcal{F} \models \phi(x_1, \ldots, x_n)[a_1, \ldots, a_n]$ iff $\mathcal{F}' \models \phi(x_1, \ldots, x_n)[f(a_1), \ldots, f(a_n)]$. $\dashv$

As a corollary we obtain that:

Proposition 3. *Any two standard affine planes are elementary equivalent.*

The *first-order theory SAP of standard affine planes* has the following list of axioms: $IRREF$, $TRANS$, $UNIV$, $DENS_0$, $DENS_1$, $\ldots$. There are several results about SAP:

Proposition 4. (i) *SAP is ω-categorical;* (ii) *SAP is not categorical in any uncountable power;* (iii) *SAP is maximal consistent;* (iv) *SAP is complete with respect to $\mathcal{F}_{\mathbb{R}}^2$ and $\mathcal{F}_{\mathbb{Q}}^2$;* (v) *SAP is decidable;* (vi) *the membership problem in SAP is PSPACE-complete;* (vii) *SAP is not axiomatizable with finitely many variables, and hence, it is not finitely axiomatizable.*

Proof. See the extended abstract.

2.2   Convergence Alone

The first-order language of the discussion above is inextricably tied up with the properties of P, C and $=$. Of course, there is nothing against investigating the pure C-fragment only; the pure P-fragment being equivalent to the full language. All the more so since:

Proposition 5. *Equality and parallellism are not first-order definable with C in any standard affine plane.*

Proof. Let $\mathcal{F} = (L, P, C)$ be a standard affine plane. We demonstrate that equality and parallellism are not first-order definable with C in $\mathcal{F}$. Seeing that $\mathcal{F} \models \forall x \forall y (P(x,y) \leftrightarrow (x \neq y \land \neg C(x,y)))$, it is sufficient to show that equality is not first-order definable with C in $\mathcal{F}$. Assume that there is a formula $\phi(x,y)$ in x, y and C, such that $\mathcal{F} \models \forall x \forall y (x = y \leftrightarrow \phi(x,y))$. Let a be a line in L. We need to consider a surjective mapping g on $[a]$ into itself. Now let f be the mappping on L into itself defined as follows:

$$f(b) = \begin{cases} b & b \notin [a], \\ g(b) & b \in [a]. \end{cases}$$

As a simple exercise we invite the reader to show by induction on the complexity of formulas $\psi(x_1, \ldots, x_n)$ in x_1, ..., x_n and C, that for all lines a_1, ..., a_n in L, $\mathcal{F} \models \psi(x_1, \ldots, x_n)[a_1, \ldots, a_n]$ iff $\mathcal{F} \models \psi(x_1, \ldots, x_n)[f(a_1), \ldots, f(a_n)]$. Hence, for all lines a, b in L, $\mathcal{F} \models \phi(x,y)[a,b]$ iff $\mathcal{F} \models \phi(x,y)[f(a), f(b)]$. It follows that for all lines a, b in L, $\mathcal{F} \models x = y[a,b]$ iff $\mathcal{F} \models x = y[f(a), f(b)]$. If g is not injective then we can find lines a and b in L such that $\mathcal{F} \not\models x = y[a,b]$ and $\mathcal{F} \models x = y[f(a), f(b)]$, a contradiction. $\dashv$

This observation leads us to consider a line-based first-order theory based solely on C, i.e. C will be the unique predicate symbol considered from now on in this section. A *weak line-based affine plane* is a relational structure of the form $\mathcal{F} = (L, C)$ where L is a nonempty set of *lines* and C is a binary relation on L. We shall say that a weak affine plane $\mathcal{F} = (L, C)$ is *standard* iff it satisfies the following sentences:

$IREF^-$ $\forall x \neg C(x,x)$
$TRANS^-$ $\forall x \forall y \forall z (\neg C(x,y) \land C(y,z) \rightarrow C(x,z))$
$DENS_n^-$ $\forall x \forall y_1 \ldots \forall y_n (C(x,y_1) \land \ldots \land C(x,y_n) \rightarrow \exists z (C(x,z) \land C(z,y_1) \land \ldots \\ \land C(z,y_n)))$

Let $\mathcal{F} = (L, C)$ be a standard weak affine plane. It is easy to see that the sentences $\forall x \forall y(C(x, y) \rightarrow C(y, x))$ and $\forall x \forall y \exists z(C(x, z) \wedge C(z, y))$ are true in $\mathcal{F}$. Hence $\neg C$ is an equivalence relation on L such that the partition of L modulo $\neg C$ consists of infinitely many equivalence classes. Examples of standard weak affine planes are $\mathcal{F}_{\mathbb{R}}^{2-}$ and $\mathcal{F}_{\mathbb{Q}}^{2-}$, the pure C-fragments of $\mathcal{F}_{\mathbb{R}}^{2}$ and $\mathcal{F}_{\mathbb{Q}}^{2}$. To study standard weak affine planes more precisely, the concept of quotient will be of use to us. Let $\mathcal{F} = (L, C)$ be a standard weak affine plane. The *quotient of $\mathcal{F}$ modulo* $\neg C$ is the standard weak affine plane $\mathcal{F}/[\cdot] = (L/[\cdot], C/[\cdot])$ defined as follows:

$$L/[\cdot] = \{[a]: a \in L\},$$
$$C/[\cdot] = \{([a], [b]): C(a, b)\}.$$

Observe that for all lines a, b in L, $C/[\cdot]([a], [b])$ iff $[a] \neq [b]$. A straightforward consequence of our definition is that:

Proposition 6. *Let $\mathcal{F}$ and $\mathcal{F}'$ be standard weak affine planes. If $\mathcal{F}$ is countable then $\mathcal{F}/[\cdot]$ is elementary embeddable in $\mathcal{F}'$.*

Proof. See the extended abstract.

As a corollary we obtain that:

Proposition 7. *Any two standard weak affine planes are elementary equivalent.*

The *first-order theory SAP^- of standard weak affine planes* has the following list of axioms: $IRREF^-$, $TRANS^-$, $DENS_0^-$, $DENS_1^-$, ... There are several results about SAP^-:

Proposition 8. (i) SAP^- *is not ω-categorical;* (ii) SAP^- *is not categorical in any uncountable power;* (iii) SAP^- *is maximal consistent;* (iv) SAP^- *is complete with respect to $\mathcal{F}_{\mathbb{R}}^{2-}$ and $\mathcal{F}_{\mathbb{Q}}^{2-}$;* (v) SAP^- *is decidable;* (vi) *the membership problem in SAP^- is PSPACE-complete;* (vii) SAP^- *is not axiomatizable with finitely many variables, and hence, it is not finitely axiomatizable.*

Proof. See the extended abstract.

The reader may easily verify that every theorem of SAP^- is also a theorem of SAP. We will now prove the converse result, that is to say:

Proposition 9. SAP *is a conservative extension of SAP^-.*

Proof. By item (iv) in proposition 4 and item (iv) in proposition 8. $\dashv$

3   Modal Logic

It is now time to meet the modal languages we will be working with, generalizing the modal languages introduced by Balbiani and Goranko [2]. What we would like to do in this section is study a modal logic of lines in a space of dimension 2. We assume some familiarity with modal logic. Readers wanting more details may refer, for example, to [4] or to [5]. Our line-based modal logic is based on the idea of associating with parallelism and convergence the modal connectives $[P]$ and $[C]$, with the formulas $[P]\phi$ and $[C]\phi$ being read "for all parallel lines, ϕ" and "for all convergent lines, ϕ". The *formulas* are given by the rule:

$$\phi ::= p \mid \neg\phi \mid \phi \vee \psi \mid [P]\phi \mid [C]\phi,$$

where p ranges over a countable set of *propositional variables*. Let the *size of ϕ*, denoted $\mid \phi \mid$, be the number of symbols occurring in ϕ. We adopt the standard definitions for the remaining Boolean operations and for the diamond modality. The concept of *subformula* is standard, the expression $Sf(\phi)$ denoting the set of all subformulas of formula ϕ.

3.1   Parallelism and Convergence

A *Kripke model* is a pair $\mathcal{M} = (\mathcal{F}, V)$, where $\mathcal{F} = (L, P, C)$ is an affine plane and V is a *valuation on $\mathcal{F}$*, i.e. a function assigning to each line a in L a set $V(a)$ of propositional variables. If $\mathcal{M} = (L, P, C, V)$ is a Kripke model and a is a line in L then the relation "ϕ is *true in $\mathcal{M}$ at a*", denoted $\mathcal{M}, a \models \phi$, is defined inductively on the complexity of formulas ϕ as usual. In particular:

$\mathcal{M}, a \models [P]\phi$ iff for all $b \in L$ with $P(a,b)$, we have $\mathcal{M}, b \models \phi$,
$\mathcal{M}, a \models [C]\phi$ iff for all $b \in L$ with $C(a,b)$, we have $\mathcal{M}, b \models \phi$.

Formula ϕ is *true in Kripke model $\mathcal{M}$*, in symbols $\mathcal{M} \models \phi$, iff $\mathcal{M}, a \models \phi$ for all $a \in L$. ϕ is said to be *valid in affine plane $\mathcal{F} = (L, P, C)$*, in symbols $\mathcal{F} \models \phi$, iff $\mathcal{M} \models \phi$ for all models $\mathcal{M} = (L, P, C, V)$ based on $\mathcal{F}$. The following formulas are valid in all standard affine planes:

$\phi \to [P]\langle P \rangle\phi$,
$\phi \to [C]\langle C \rangle\phi$,
$\phi \wedge [P]\phi \to [P][P]\phi$,
$[C]\phi \to [P][C]\phi$,
$\phi \wedge [P]\phi \wedge [C]\phi \to [C][C]\phi$,
$\langle P \rangle\phi_1 \wedge \ldots \wedge \langle P \rangle\phi_n \to \langle P \rangle(\langle P \rangle\phi_1 \wedge \ldots \wedge \langle P \rangle\phi_n)$,
$\langle C \rangle\phi_1 \wedge \ldots \wedge \langle C \rangle\phi_n \to \langle C \rangle(\langle C \rangle\phi_1 \wedge \ldots \wedge \langle C \rangle\phi_n)$.

Let $ML(SAP)$ be the smallest normal modal logic, in the language just described, that contains the above formulas as proper axioms. It is a simple exercise in modal logic to check that if ϕ is a theorem of $ML(SAP)$ then ϕ is valid in every standard affine plane. Now we come to prove the converse proposition: if ϕ is valid in every standard affine plane then ϕ is a theorem of $ML(SAP)$. Let $\mathcal{F} = (L, P, C)$ be a generated subframe of the canonical frame for $ML(SAP)$. Seeing that the proper axioms of $ML(SAP)$ are all Sahlqvist formulas, it is easy to get information about the structure of $\mathcal{F}$:

$\forall x \forall y (P(x,y) \to P(y,x))$,
$\forall x \forall y (C(x,y) \to C(y,x))$,

$\forall x \forall y \forall z(P(x,y) \wedge P(y,z) \to x = z \vee P(x,z)),$
$\forall x \forall y \forall z(P(x,y) \wedge C(y,z) \to C(x,z)),$
$\forall x \forall y \forall z(C(x,y) \wedge C(y,z) \to x = z \vee P(x,z) \vee C(x,z)),$
$\forall x \forall y_1 \ldots \forall y_n(P(x,y_1) \wedge \ldots \wedge P(x,y_n) \to \exists z(P(x,z) \wedge P(z,y_1) \wedge \ldots \wedge P(z,y_n))),$
$\forall x \forall y_1 \ldots \forall y_n(C(x,y_1) \wedge \ldots \wedge C(x,y_n) \to \exists z(C(x,z) \wedge C(z,y_1) \wedge \ldots \wedge C(z,y_n))).$

This motivates the following definition. A rooted affine plane $\mathcal{F} = (L, P, C)$ is said to be *prenormal* iff it satisfies the above first-order conditions. Two simple observations. First, the Sahlqvist formula $[C]\phi \to [C][P]\phi$ corresponds to the first-order condition $\forall x \forall y \forall z(C(x,y) \wedge P(y,z) \to C(x,z))$ which is true in all prenormal affine planes. Hence it is a theorem of $ML(SAP)$. Second, a prenormal affine plane $\mathcal{F} = (L, P, C)$ where P and C are irreflexive relations on L is standard. As an immediate consequence of the Sahlqvist completeness theorem, we obtain that if ϕ is valid in every prenormal affine plane then ϕ is a theorem of $ML(SAP)$. We will now show that:

Proposition 10. *Every prenormal affine plane is a bounded morphic image of a standard affine plane.*

Proof. Our first claim is that every prenormal affine plane is a bounded morphic image of a prenormal affine plane $\mathcal{F}' = (L', P', C')$ where P' is an irreflexive relation on L'. Our second claim is that every prenormal affine plane $\mathcal{F} = (L, P, C)$ where P is an irreflexive relation on L is a bounded morphic image of a standard affine plane. To prove our first claim, consider a prenormal affine plane $\mathcal{F} = (L, P, C)$. The affine plane $\mathcal{F}' = (L', P', C')$ where:

- $L' = \{(a,0): a \in L\} \cup \{(a,i): a \in L, i \geq 1 \text{ and } P(a,a)\}$,
- For all a, b in L and for all $i, j \geq 0$, $P'((a,i),(b,j))$ iff $P(a,b)$ and either $a \neq b$ or $i \neq j$,
- For all a, b in L and for all $i, j \geq 0$, $C'((a,i),(b,j))$ iff $C(a,b)$,

is obviously prenormal. What is more, its relation P' is irreflexive on L'. Now, let f be the mapping from L' to L defined as follows for all a in L and for all $i \geq 0$, $f((a,i)) = a$. We claim that f is a bounded morphism from $\mathcal{F}'$ to $\mathcal{F}$, as the reader is asked to show. To prove our second claim, consider a prenormal affine plane $\mathcal{F} = (L, P, C)$ where P is an irreflexive relation on L. The affine plane $\mathcal{F}' = (L', P', C')$ where:

- $L' = \{(a,0): a \in L\} \cup \{(a,i): a \in L, i \geq 1 \text{ and } C(a,a)\}$,
- For all a, b in L and for all $i, j \geq 0$, $P'((a,i),(b,j))$ iff $P(a,b)$ and $i = j$,
- For all a, b in L and for all $i, j \geq 0$, $C'((a,i),(b,j))$ iff $C(a,b)$, either $a \neq b$ or $i \neq j$ and either $\neg P(a,b)$ or $i \neq j$,

is obviously prenormal. What is more, its relations P' and C' are irreflexive on L'. Now, let f be the mapping from L' to L defined as follows for all a in L and for all $i \geq 0$, $f((a,i)) = a$. We claim that f is a bounded morphism from $\mathcal{F}'$ to $\mathcal{F}$, as the reader is asked to show. $\dashv$

Hence prenormal affine planes and standard affine planes validate the same formulas. These considerations prove that:

Proposition 11. *The following conditions are equivalent:* **(i)** ϕ *is a theorem of* $ML(SAP)$; **(ii)** ϕ *is valid in every standard affine plane;* **(iii)** ϕ *is valid in every prenormal affine plane.*

By proposition 11, $ML(SAP)$ is sound and complete with respect to the class of all standard affine planes, a first-order definable class of affine planes. Hence, $ML(SAP)$ is also sound and complete with respect to the class of all countable standard affine planes. By proposition 3, we obtain that any two standard affine planes are elementary equivalent. We will now show that any two standard affine planes are modally equivalent. In order to prepare for the proof, let us consider a formula ϕ and a countable model $\mathcal{M} = (L, P, C, V)$. Restricting our discussion to the propositional variables actually occurring in ϕ, let $\mathcal{V}$ be the set of all sets of sets of propositional variables. Remark that $Card(\mathcal{V}) \leq 2^{2^{|\phi|}}$. Define the functions γ and δ from the partition of L into $\mathcal{V}$ as follows:

$$\gamma([a]) = \{V(b): \neg C(a,b) \text{ and } V(b) \neq V(c) \text{ for each line } c \text{ such that } P(b,c)\},$$
$$\delta([a]) = \{V(b): \neg C(a,b) \text{ and } V(b) = V(c) \text{ for some line } c \text{ such that } P(b,c)\}.$$

For our purpose, the crucial properties of γ and δ are the following:

– We can find $\varXi$ in $\mathcal{V}$ such that $\gamma([\omega]) \cup \delta([\omega]) = \varXi$ for countably many equivalence classes $[\omega]$ in the partition of L,
– For all equivalence classes $[a]$ in the partition of L, $\delta([a]) \neq \emptyset$.

Proposition 12. *Any two standard affine planes are modally equivalent.*

Proof. Let $\mathcal{F} = (L, P, C)$ and $\mathcal{F}' = (L', P', C')$ be standard affine planes. We demonstrate that $\mathcal{F}$ and $\mathcal{F}'$ are modally equivalent. Without loss of generality, we may assume that $\mathcal{F}$ is countable. If $\mathcal{F}$ and $\mathcal{F}'$ are not modally equivalent then there are two cases: either there is a formula ϕ such that $\mathcal{F} \models \phi$ and $\mathcal{F}' \not\models \phi$ or there is a formula ϕ such that $\mathcal{F} \not\models \phi$ and $\mathcal{F}' \models \phi$. In the first case, there is a formula ϕ such that $\mathcal{F} \models \phi$ and $\mathcal{F}' \not\models \phi$. Hence, ϕ is valid in every countable standard affine plane and ϕ is not a theorem of $ML(SAP)$, a contradiction. In the second case, there is a formula ϕ such that $\mathcal{F} \not\models \phi$ and $\mathcal{F}' \models \phi$. We restrict our discussion to the set of all propositional variables actually occurring in ϕ. Let $\mathcal{V}$ be the set of all sets of sets of propositional variables. Since $\mathcal{F} \not\models \phi$, then there is a model $\mathcal{M} = (\mathcal{F}, V)$ based on $\mathcal{F}$ such that $\mathcal{M} \not\models \phi$. In order to contradict $\mathcal{F}' \models \phi$, we need to define a valuation V' on $\mathcal{F}'$ such that $(\mathcal{F}', V') \not\models \phi$. By proposition 2, there is an elementary embedding f of $\mathcal{F}$ into $\mathcal{F}'$. Let a' be a line in L'. If a' belongs to $f(L)$ then there is a line a in L such that $f(a) = a'$ and define $V'(a') = V(a)$. Otherwise, there are two cases: either a' is parallel with $f(a)$ for some line a in L or a' is convergent with $f(a)$ for each line a in L. In the first case, a' is parallel with $f(a)$ for some line a in L. Reminding that $\delta([a]) \neq \emptyset$, select a set λ of propositional variables in $\delta([a])$ and define $V'(a') = \lambda$. In the second case, a' is convergent with $f(a)$ for each line a in L.

Seeing that we can find Ξ in $\mathcal{V}$ such that $\gamma([\omega]) \cup \delta([\omega]) = \Xi$ for countably many equivalence classes $[\omega]$ in the partition of L, select an equivalence class $[\omega]$ such that $\gamma([\omega]) \cup \delta([\omega]) = \Xi$. First, remark that we can find sets $\theta_1, \ldots, \theta_m$ of propositional variables such that $\gamma([\omega]) = \{\theta_1, \ldots, \theta_m\}$. Fix lines $a'_1, \ldots, a'_m$ in $[a']$ and define $V'(a'_1) = \theta_1, \ldots, V'(a'_m) = \theta_m$. Second, notice that we can find sets $\lambda_1, \ldots, \lambda_n$ of propositional variables such that $\delta([\omega]) = \{\lambda_1, \ldots, \lambda_n\}$. Let $\{B'_1, \ldots, B'_n\}$ be a partition of $[a'] \backslash \{a'_1, \ldots, a'_m\}$ such that $B'_1, \ldots, B'_n$ are infinite subsets of L' and define $V'(a'_1) = \lambda_1$ for each line a'_1 in $B'_1, \ldots, V'(a'_n) = \lambda_n$ for each line a'_n in B'_n. As a simple exercise we invite the reader to show by induction on the complexity of formulas ψ in $Sf(\phi)$ that for all lines a in L, $\mathcal{M}, a \models \psi$ iff $(\mathcal{F}', V'), f(a) \models \psi$. Since $\mathcal{M} \not\models \phi$, then $(\mathcal{F}', V') \not\models \phi$. ⊣

An important related result is that (for the proof see the extended abstract):

Proposition 13. *The following conditions are equivalent:* **(i)** ϕ *is a theorem of* $ML(SAP)$; **(ii)** $\mathcal{F}_{\mathbb{R}}^2 \models \phi$; **(iii)** $\mathcal{F}_{\mathbb{Q}}^2 \models \phi$.

Our next result deals with the relationship between $ML(SAP)$ and finite prenormal affine planes.

Proposition 14. $ML(SAP)$ *has the polysize frame property with respect to the set of all finite prenormal affine planes.*

Proof. The fundamental construction underlying our proof is that of selective filtration. Take a formula ϕ such that ϕ is not a theorem of $ML(SAP)$. Hence, there is a countable standard affine plane $\mathcal{F} = (L, P, C)$ such that $\mathcal{F} \not\models \phi$. It follows that there is a model $\mathcal{M} = (\mathcal{F}, V)$ based on $\mathcal{F}$ such that $\mathcal{M} \not\models \phi$. We start our selective filtration of $\mathcal{M}$ through $Sf(\phi)$ by selecting a line a in L such that $\mathcal{M}, a \not\models \phi$. Reminding that $\delta([a]) \neq \emptyset$, choose a set λ of propositional variables in $\delta([a])$ and select a new line $a^\star$ in L such that $a^\star$ belongs to $[a]$ and $V(a^\star) = \lambda$. Seeing that we can find Ξ in $\mathcal{V}$ such that $\gamma([\omega]) \cup \delta([\omega]) = \Xi$ for countably many equivalence classes $[\omega]$ in the partition of L, select a new line ω in L such that $[a] \cap [\omega] = \emptyset$ and $\gamma([\omega]) \cup \delta([\omega]) = \Xi$. Recalling that $\delta([\omega]) \neq \emptyset$, choose a set λ of propositional variables in $\delta([\omega])$ and select a new line $\omega^\star$ in L such that $\omega^\star$ belongs to $[\omega]$ and $V(\omega^\star) = \lambda$. Now we define an infinite sequence $L_0, L_1, \ldots$ of subsets of L such that for all positive integers i, the following conditions are satisfied:

$C_1(i)$ For all positive integers j, if $i > j$ then for all lines b in L_j and for all formulas $[P]\psi$ in $Sf(\phi)$, if $\mathcal{M}, b \not\models [P]\psi$ then we can find a line c in L_i such that $P(b, c)$ and $\mathcal{M}, c \not\models \psi$,

$C_2(i)$ For all positive integers j, if $i > j$ then for all lines b in L_j and for all formulas $[C]\psi$ in $Sf(\phi)$, if $\mathcal{M}, b \not\models [C]\psi$ then we can find a line c in L_i such that $C(b, c)$ and $\mathcal{M}, c \not\models \psi$,

$C_3(i)$ $a \in L_i$.

Let $L_0 = \{a, a^\star, \omega, \omega^\star\}$. Note that the conditions $C_1(0)$, $C_2(0)$ and $C_3(0)$ are satisfied. Let i be a positive integer. Given L_i such that the conditions $C_1(i)$, $C_2(i)$ and $C_3(i)$ are satisfied, we let L_{i+1} be the subset of L defined by the following algorithm:

```
    begin
    L_{i+1} := L_i;
    for all lines b in L_i and for all formulas [P]ψ in Sf(φ) do
        if M, b ⊭ [P]ψ and there is no line c in L_{i+1} such that P(b, c) and
        M, c ⊭ ψ then
            begin
            select a line c in L such that P(b, c) and M, c ⊭ ψ;
            L_{i+1} := L_{i+1} ∪ {c}
            end;
    for all lines b in L_i and for all formulas [C]ψ in Sf(φ) do
        if M, b ⊭ [C]ψ and there is no line c in L_{i+1} such that C(b, c) and
        M, c ⊭ ψ then
            begin
            select a line c in L such that C(b, c) and M, c ⊭ ψ;
            L_{i+1} := L_{i+1} ∪ {c};
            if there is no line d in L_{i+1} such that P(c, d) then
                begin
                choose a set λ of propositional variables in δ([c]);
                select a line d* in L such that P(c, d*) and V(d*) = λ;
                L_{i+1} := L_{i+1} ∪ {d*}
                end
            end
    end.
```

It follows immediately from the definition of the algorithm that the conditions $C_1(i+1)$, $C_2(i+1)$ and $C_3(i+1)$ are satisfied. The affine plane $\mathcal{F}' = (L', P', C')$ where:

$L' = L_0 \cup L_1 \cup \ldots$,
$P'(b, c)$ iff either $P(b, c)$ or b and c are one and the same starred line,
$C'(b, c)$ iff either $C(b, c)$ or b belongs to $[\omega]$ or c belongs to $[\omega]$,

is obviously prenormal. Define n_1 to be the number of $[P]$-boxed formulas in $Sf(\phi)$ and n_2 to be the number of $[C]$-boxed formulas in $Sf(\phi)$. We claim that $Card(L') \leq (2 \times n_1 + n_2 + 2) \times (2 \times n_2 + 2)$, as the reader is asked to show. To complete the proof we show by induction on the complexity of formulas ψ in $Sf(\phi)$ that for all lines b in L', $\mathcal{M}, b \models \psi$ iff $(\mathcal{F}', V'), b \models \psi$ where V' is the restriction of V to L'. The base case follows from the definition of V'. We leave the Boolean cases to the reader. It remains to deal with the modalities. The right to left direction is more or less immediate from the definition of L'. For the left to right direction, a more delicate approach is needed.

Consider a formula $[P]\psi$ in $Sf(\phi)$. Let b be a line in L'. Suppose $\mathcal{M}, b \models [P]\psi$, we demonstrate $(\mathcal{F}', V'), b \models [P]\psi$. Let c be a line in L' such that $P'(b, c)$. Hence, either $P(b, c)$ or b and c are one and the same starred line. In the first case, $P(b, c)$. Therefore, $\mathcal{M}, c \models \psi$ and, by induction hypothesis, $(\mathcal{F}', V'), c \models \psi$. In the second case, b and c are one and the same starred line. Therefore, $\mathcal{M}, c \models \psi$ and, by induction hypothesis, $(\mathcal{F}', V'), c \models \psi$.

Consider a formula $[C]\psi$ in $Sf(\phi)$. Let b be a line in L'. Suppose $\mathcal{M}, b \models [C]\psi$, we demonstrate $(\mathcal{F}', V'), b \models [C]\psi$. Let c be a line in L' such that $C'(b, c)$. Hence, either $C(b, c)$ or b belongs to $[\omega]$ or c belongs to $[\omega]$. In the first case, $C(b, c)$. Therefore, $\mathcal{M}, c \models \psi$ and, by induction hypothesis, $(\mathcal{F}', V'), c \models \psi$. In the second case, b belongs to $[\omega]$. Therefore, $\mathcal{M}, c \models \psi$ and, by induction hypothesis, $(\mathcal{F}', V'), c \models \psi$. In the third case, c belongs to $[\omega]$. Therefore, $\mathcal{M}, c \models \psi$ and, by induction hypothesis, $(\mathcal{F}', V'), c \models \psi$. $\dashv$

An important related corollary is that:

Proposition 15. *The membership problem in $ML(SAP)$ is NP-complete.*

3.2   Convergence Alone

The remainder of this section is devoted to studying the pure $[C]$-fragment of our line-based modal logic; the pure $[P]$-fragment being studied by Balbiani and Goranko [2]. A *Kripke model* is now a pair $\mathcal{M} = (\mathcal{F}, V)$ with $\mathcal{F}$ a weak affine plane and V a valuation on $\mathcal{F}$. The notion of a formula ϕ being true in a Kripke model $\mathcal{M} = (L, C, V)$, where $\mathcal{F}$ is a weak affine plane, at a line a in L, notation $\mathcal{M}, a \models \phi$, is defined inductively as for the full language. It is a simple matter to check that the following formulas are valid in all standard weak affine planes:

$$\phi \to [C]\langle C \rangle \phi,$$
$$[C]\phi \to [C][C](\phi \vee [C]\phi),$$
$$[C][C]\phi \to [C][C][C]\phi,$$
$$\langle C \rangle \phi_1 \wedge \ldots \wedge \langle C \rangle \phi_n \to \langle C \rangle (\langle C \rangle \phi_1 \wedge \ldots \wedge \langle C \rangle \phi_n).$$

Let $ML(SAP^-)$ be the smallest normal modal logic, with $[C]$, that contains the above formulas as proper axioms. It is a simple exercise in modal logic to check that if ϕ is a theorem of $ML(SAP^-)$ then ϕ is valid in every standard weak affine plane. Now we prove the converse proposition: if ϕ is valid in every standard weak affine plane then ϕ is a theorem of $ML(SAP^-)$. Let $\mathcal{F} = (L, C)$ be a generated subframe of the canonical frame for $ML(SAP^-)$. The proper axioms of $ML(SAP^-)$ are all Sahlqvist formulas. Hence, $\mathcal{F}$ satisfies the following conditions:

$$\forall x \forall y (C(x, y) \to C(y, x)),$$
$$\forall x \forall y \forall z \forall t (C(x, y) \wedge C(y, z) \to (\neg C(x, z) \wedge C(z, t) \to C(x, t))),$$
$$\forall x \forall y \forall z \forall t (C(x, y) \wedge C(y, z) \wedge C(z, t) \to \exists u (C(x, u) \wedge C(u, t))),$$
$$\forall x \forall y_1 \ldots \forall y_n (C(x, y_1) \wedge \ldots \wedge C(x, y_n) \to \exists z (C(x, z) \wedge C(z, y_1) \wedge \ldots \wedge C(z, y_n))).$$

Let $\mathcal{F}$ be a rooted weak affine plane. We shall say that $\mathcal{F}$ is *prenormal* iff it satisfies the conditions above. Remark that a prenormal weak affine plane $\mathcal{F} = (L, C)$ where C is an irreflexive relation on L is standard. Unsurprisingly, if ϕ is valid in every prenormal weak affine plane then ϕ is a theorem of $ML(SAP^-)$. We now make the following claim:

Proposition 16. *Every prenormal weak affine plane is a bounded morphic image of a standard weak affine plane.*

Proof. See the extended abstract.

Hence prenormal weak affine planes and standard weak affine planes validate the same formulas. These considerations prove that:

Proposition 17. *The following conditions are equivalent:* **(i)** ϕ *is a theorem of* $ML(SAP^-)$; **(ii)** ϕ *is valid in every standard weak affine plane;* **(iii)** ϕ *is valid in every prenormal weak affine plane.*

By proposition 17, $ML(SAP^-)$ is sound and complete with respect to the class of all standard weak affine planes, a first-order definable class of weak affine planes. Hence, $ML(SAP^-)$ is also sound and complete with respect to the class of all countable standard weak affine planes.

Proposition 18. $ML(SAP)$ *is a conservative extension of* $ML(SAP^-)$.

Proof. See the extended abstract.

By item **(i)** in proposition 8, we obtain that we can find two countable standard weak affine planes that are not isomorphic. However, we can prove:

Proposition 19. *We can find two countable standard weak affine planes that are not modally equivalent.*

Proof. The proof that for all propositional variables p, $\mathcal{F}_Q^{2-} \not\models p \wedge [C]p \rightarrow \langle C \rangle [C]p$ and $\mathcal{F}_Q^{2-}/[\cdot] \models p \wedge [C]p \rightarrow \langle C \rangle [C]p$, which is not difficult, is left as an exercise. $\dashv$

It is nevertheless true that:

Proposition 20. *The following conditions are equivalent:* **(i)** ϕ *is a theorem of* $ML(SAP^-)$; **(ii)** $\mathcal{F}_R^{2-} \models \phi$; **(iii)** $\mathcal{F}_Q^{2-} \models \phi$.

Proof. See the extended abstract.

Rather like the proof of proposition 14 one can prove that:

Proposition 21. $ML(SAP^-)$ *has the polysize frame property with respect to the set of all finite prenormal weak affine planes. Hence, the membership problem in* $ML(SAP^-)$ *is NP-complete.*

4   Conclusion

We now naturally ask the question: what is the first-order theory of lines in space geometry and what is the corresponding modal logic? For a start, note that two lines in space geometry may have the following mutual relations: they are parallel if they lie in the same plane and never meet, they are convergent if they lie in the same plane and have exactly one common point and they are separated if they are not coplanar. These relations bring a new array of questions. Which mutual relations can first-order define the two others in the Euclidean space? Is the real line-based affine space an elementary extension of the set of all rational lines? With respect to parallelism, convergence and separation, what is the first-order theory of the real line-based affine space? These first-order theories are decidable since they can be embedded in elementary algebra; little seems to be known as regards their complete axiomatizations or their complexity. A systematic exploration of the properties of a first-order theory based on the relations of parallelism, convergence and separation in space affine geometry and a thorough examination of the modal logic it gives rise to require further studies.

References

1. Balbiani, P., Condotta, J.-F., Fariñas del Cerro, L.: Tractability results in the block algebra. Journal of Logic and Computation **12** (2002) 885–909.
2. Balbiani, P., Goranko, V.: Modal logics for parallelism, orthogonality, and affine geometries. Journal of Applied Non-Classical Logics **12** (2002) 365–377.
3. Bennett, B.: Determining consistency of topological relations. Constraints **3** (1998) 213–225.
4. Blackburn, P., de Rijke, M., Venema, Y.: Modal Logic. Cambridge University Press (2001).
5. Chagrov, A., Zakharyaschev, M.: Modal Logic. Oxford University Press (1997).
6. Chang, C., Keisler, H.: Model Theory, 3rd ed. Elsevier (1990).
7. Cristani, M.: The complexity of reasoning about spatial congruence. Journal of Artificial Intelligence Research **11** (1999) 361–390.
8. Gerevini, A., Renz, J.: Combining topological and qualitative size constraints for spatial reasoning. In Maher, M., Puget, J.-F. (Editors): Proceedings of the Fourth International Conference on Principles and Practice of Constraint Programming. Springer-Verlag (1998).
9. Kutz, O., Sturm, H., Suzuki, N.-Y., Wolter, F., Zakharyaschev, M.: Axiomatizing distance logics. Journal of Applied Non-Classical Logics **12** (2002) 425–439.
10. Ligozat, G.: Reasoning about cardinal directions. Journal of Visual Languages and Computing **9** (1998) 23–44.
11. Moratz, R., Renz, J., Wolter, D.: Qualitative spatial reasoning about line segments. In Horn, W. (Editor): Proceedings of the Fourteenth European Conference on Artificial Intelligence. Wiley (2000).
12. Randell, D., Cui, Z., Cohn, A.: A spatial logic based on regions and connection. In Brachman, R., Levesque, H., Reiter, R. (Editors): Proceedings of the First International Conference on Principles of Knowledge Representation and Reasoning. Morgan Kaufman (1992).
13. Renz, J., Nebel, B.: On the complexity of qualitative spatial reasoning: a maximal tractable fragment of the region connection calculus. Artificial Intelligence **108** (1999) 69–123.
14. Stockmeyer, L.: The polynomial-time hierarchy. Theoretical Computer Science **3** (1977) 1–22.
15. Vieu, L.: Spatial representation and reasoning in AI. In Stock, O. (Editeur): Spatial and Temporal Reasoning. Kluwer (1997).

Measure Logics for Spatial Reasoning

Mehmet Giritli

Albert-Ludwigs-Universität, Freiburg, Germany.
mgiritli@informatik.uni-freiburg.de

Abstract. Although it is quite common in spatial reasoning to utilize topology for representing spatial information in a qualitative manner, in this paper an alternative method is investigated which has no connection to topology but to measure theory. I propose two logics to speak about measure theoretic information. First I investigate a highly expressive, first-order measure logic and besides providing models which with respect to this logic is sound and complete, I also show that it is actually undecidable. In the second half of the paper, a propositional measure logic is constructed which is much less expressive but computationally much more attractive than its first-order counterpart. Most importantly, in this propositional measure logic we can express spatial relations which are very similar to well-known topological relations of RCC-8 although the most efficient known logic system to express these topological relations is propositional intuitionistic logic which is undoubtedly harder than propositional measure logic.

1 Introduction

In the field of qualitative spatial reasoning the focus has mainly been on exploiting topological knowledge to represent and reason about relationships between spatial entities. With this work, I will present an alternative approach which does not exploit topology but rather has its roots in measure theory.

The measure theoretic approach gives an alternative representation of ambiguity in information from topology. The conclusions of this paper suggest that we can develop a theory which is computationally no harder than reasoning with classical propositional logic and yet express relations between spatial entities that are quite similar to certain sets of relations appearing in well-known approaches like RCC-8 [1]. It is important to note that the most efficient logic formalism known to express these relations is propositional intuitionistic logic as shown in [2].

A measure is a non-negative set function μ which maps sets from a σ-algebra (for the moment, it is sufficient to think σ-algebra as a set of subsets of a given universe) into $\mathbb{R}^+ \cup \{0\} \cup \{\infty\}$ such that $\mu(\emptyset) = 0$ and μ is countably additive over disjoint sets. The measure of a set is the value it gets under the function μ. A set is said to be a null-set whenever its measure is zero and it is different from the empty set. Therefore, a measure enables us to have an extra piece of information about a set which could be very useful in describing the spatial relationships between sets.

J.J. Alferes and J. Leite (Eds.): JELIA 2004, LNAI 3229, pp. 487–499, 2004.

For example, let A and B be sets such that $A \cap B \neq \emptyset$ and $\mu(A \cap B) = 0$, the intersection of A and B is non-empty and has measure 0. If we are after expressing the relationships between sets then we would want to interpret this situation as A and B are *almost* disjoint, although they are not. Actually, one could also interpret the relationship of the sets A and B as they are touching. This can be regarded similar to the topological notion of 'external connection' where two sets are disjoint but their closures share at least one point.

I present two logics in this paper. First I describe a first-order axiomatic approach to represent and reason about measure theoretic information. The axiomatic presentation of the theory enjoys a formal semantic front-end which the first-order syntactic theory is proved to be sound and complete with respect to.

To accept a spatial logic as credible, seeking an interpretation with respect to which the logic is sound and complete is the first step. In [3] Lemon discusses about spatial logics which have no known formal interpretations. Lemon presents examples of spatial logics which have elements that can not be realized in any of the informal models intended to interpret those logics. I supply the first-order logic developed in this paper with an interpretation which the logic is shown to be sound and complete with respect to.

Besides supplying our first-order theory with formal semantics, I show that (not surprisingly) this logic is undecidable. Some discussion concerning the expressive capabilities is also present exploring the spatial representation related questions.

In the second half of the paper, I construct a propositional language that is computationally much more attractive. Naturally, the expressive strength of the propositional language is much less than its first-order counterpart but we show that an important set of relations, similar to RCC-8 relations, are expressible in this language. This enables us to use the algorithms of classical propositional logic in the name of spatial reasoning.

The general organization of the paper is as follows: In section 2 I present the first-order measure logic with an axiomatic approach and show that it is undecidable. In section 3 I supply semantics for the logic developed in section 2 and prove that the formalism is sound and complete with respect to its semantics. In section 4 the less expressive propositional measure logic is constructed and the methods for reasoning with it are investigated. Paper ends with the conclusions in section 5.

1.1   Measure Theory Background

In this section I summarize some useful measure theoretic information for the coming sections. The objective of this sub-section is to make the reader familiar with concept of measures. Lemma 1 gives a good hint about how the measure function behaves over arbitrary σ-algebras.

Definition 1. *Let X be a set. A σ-algebra S is a non-empty collection of subsets of X, $S \subseteq 2^X$, such that the following hold*

1. $X \in S$
2. If $A \in S$ then $\sim A \in S$
3. If A_n is a sequence of elements of S then $\bigcup A_n \in S$.

If F is any collection of subsets of X, then we can always find a σ-algebra containing F, namely 2^X. By taking the intersection of all σ-algebras containing F, we obtain the smallest such σ-algebra. We call the smallest σ-algebra containing F the σ-algebra generated by F. Note that a σ-algebra is a ring of sets closed under countable unions and contains the universe, X.

Definition 2. *Let X be a set, μ be a function and S a σ-algebra over X such that $\mu : S \to \mathbb{R}^+ \cup \{0\} \cup \{\infty\}$. μ is called a measure iff $\mu(\emptyset) = 0$ and if A_n is a countable sequence of sets in S such that A_ns are pairwise disjoint then*

$$\sum_{n=1} \mu(A_n) = \mu(\bigcup_{n=1} A_n).$$

The triple $\langle X, S, \mu \rangle$ is called a measure space.

A set $A \in S$ is called a null-set iff $\mu(A) = 0$. Note that if X is a null-set then so is every other set from S. I will say that a measure space has the strict-null-property whenever $\forall A \in S$ we have that $\mu(A) = 0$ iff $A = \emptyset$.

Lemma 1. *Let $\langle X, S, \mu \rangle$ be a measure space. The following holds*

1. *If $A, B \in S$ and $A \subset B$ then $\mu(A) \leq \mu(B)$*
2. *If $A, B \in S$ and $A \subset B$ and $\mu(B) < \infty$ then $\mu(B \setminus A) = \mu(B) - \mu(A)$*
3. *If $A, B \in S$ and $\mu(A \cap B) < \infty$ then $\mu(A \cup B) = \mu(A) + \mu(B) - \mu(A \cap B)$.*

2 First-Order Measure Logic

2.1 Structures for Logic of Measures

Let X be a set, we define the structure $\mathcal{MS}_M = \langle Y, m, \cdot^{\delta(a)} \rangle$ such that

1. $M = \langle X, Y, m \rangle$ is a measure space
2. $X, \emptyset \in Y$
3. If $A \in Y$ then $\sim A \in Y$
4. If $A, B \in Y$ then $A \cup B \in Y$
5. If $A, B \in Y$ then $A \cap B \in Y$
6. $\forall A \in Y \ m(\emptyset) \leq m(A)$
7. $A, B \in Y$ and $A \subseteq B$ then $m(A) \leq m(B)$

$\cdot^{\delta(a)}$ is a denotation function assigning the terms of $\mathcal{L}_{ML}$ (defined in next sub-section) to the elements of Y for a given assignment a of free-occurring variables in terms to the elements of Y. The denotation of constants in Y is simply obtained by the function $\cdot^\delta$. Note that from condition 1 it is trivial to derive conditions 2-7 from the definition 1 and lemma 1. Nevertheless, they are present in the above list to underline their importance.

Many authors in the field of spatial-reasoning are strongly motivated to use a region-based approach as their basic ontology. I did not do that in this work. There are two arguments underlying this. First, there is a formal result establishing the fact that point-based and region-based approaches are actually equivalent [4] in terns of expressiveness. Second, in case of a region-based approach there is an additional complexity that has to be taken care of with many proofs of certain theorems, especially with the soundness and completeness theorems where one has to make sure that the corresponding semantics of the logical entities is always non-atomic or non-point.

2.2   First Order Language $\mathcal{L}_{\mathrm{ML}}$

The language of first-order theory of measures will be denoted with $\mathcal{L}_{\mathrm{ML}}$. $\mathcal{L}_{\mathrm{ML}}$ has denumerably-infinite number of non-logical variable $(p, q, r, \ldots$ etc.) and constant symbols $(a, b, c, \ldots$ etc.) and three binary non-logical relation symbols of $\iota(a, b)$ ('a is intersecting with b'), $\mu(a) \leq \mu(b)$ (the measure of a is less than or equal to the measure of b') and $\mu(a) = \mu(b)$ ('the measure of a is equal to the measure of b). I will use an abbreviation and write $\mu(\cdot) > \mu(\cdot)$ to mean $\neg\mu(\cdot) \leq \mu(\cdot)$ and $\mu(\cdot) \neq \mu(\cdot)$ to mean $\neg\mu(\cdot) = \mu(\cdot)$. Besides the usual propositional operators ($\vee, \neg$ and their derivatives) and the first order quantifiers ($\exists$ and $\forall$), $\mathcal{L}_{\mathrm{ML}}$ contains the propositional constants of verum and falsum ($\top, \bot$). Arbitrary formulae of $\mathcal{L}_{\mathrm{ML}}$ are constructed recursively as usual.

Semantics for $\mathcal{L}_{\mathrm{ML}}$. Let $t_1, t_2, \ldots$ be terms from $\mathcal{L}_{\mathrm{ML}}$ (ie. variables or constants) and α, β be arbitrary formulae of $\mathcal{L}_{\mathrm{ML}}$ constructed as described in the previous sub-section. We define the truth-relation for a $\mathcal{L}_{\mathrm{ML}}$-formula φ, $\mathcal{MS}_{\mathrm{M}} \vDash \varphi$ as follows

1. $\mathcal{MS}_{\mathrm{M}} \vDash \iota(t_1, t_2)$ iff $t_1^{\delta(a)} \cap t_2^{\delta(a)} \neq \emptyset$
2. $\mathcal{MS}_{\mathrm{M}} \vDash \mu(t_1) = \mu(t_2)$ iff $m(t_1^{\delta(a)}) = m(t_2^{\delta(a)})$
3. $\mathcal{MS}_{\mathrm{M}} \vDash \mu(t_1) \leq \mu(t_2)$ iff $m(t_1^{\delta(a)}) \leq m(t_2^{\delta(a)})$
4. $\mathcal{MS}_{\mathrm{M}} \vDash \neg\alpha$ iff $\mathcal{MS}_{\mathrm{M}} \nvDash \alpha$

First-order quantification symbols ($\exists$ and $\forall$) are interpreted as usual. I will write $\vDash_{\mathcal{MS}} \varphi$ to mean validity in every $\mathcal{MS}_{\mathrm{M}}$ model for every M.

2.3   Axiomatization and the Theory of $\mathcal{F}_{\mathrm{ML}}$

Theory $\mathcal{F}_{\mathrm{ML}}$ contains the following definitions and axioms:

(A1) $\forall x[x \neq \bigcirc \rightarrow \iota(x, x)]$
(A2) $\forall xy[\iota(x, y) \rightarrow \iota(y, x)]$

(A3) $\forall xy[\forall z[\iota(x,z) \leftrightarrow \iota(y,z)] \rightarrow x = y]$

(A1) and (A2) are the reflexivity and symmetry axioms, respectively. (A3) is the identity axiom. $\bigcirc$ stands for the empty object and it is defined with (A4).

We will need some basic definitions at this point:

(D1) $DJ(x,y) \equiv_{def} \neg\iota(x,y)$

(D2) $P(x,y) \equiv_{def} \forall z[\iota(x,z) \rightarrow \iota(y,z)]$

(D3) $PP(x,y) \equiv_{def} P(x,y) \wedge \neg P(y,x)$

(D4) $O(x,y) \equiv_{def} \exists z[P(z,x) \wedge P(z,y) \wedge \mu(z) \neq \mu(\bigcirc)]$

Now I will demonstrate how to construct new objects out of old:

(A4) $\exists x \forall z[\neg\iota(z,x)]$

(A5) $\exists x \forall z[z \neq \bigcirc \rightarrow \iota(z,x)]$

(A4) and (A5) together with (A3) entail the existence of unique objects $\bigcirc$ 'the empty object' and $\mathcal{U}$ 'the universe', respectively.

(A6) $\forall xy[\iota(x,y) \rightarrow \exists z \forall w[\iota(z,w) \leftrightarrow \exists q[P(q,x) \wedge P(q,y) \wedge \iota(q,w)]]]$

(A7) $\forall xy[\neg\iota(x,y) \rightarrow x \otimes y = \bigcirc]$

(A6) together with (A3) entails the existence of the object $x \otimes y$, 'product of x and y' for every x and y which are intersecting, (A7) turns this into a total function.

(A8) $\forall xy \exists z \forall w[\iota(z,w) \leftrightarrow [\iota(w,x) \vee \iota(w,y)]]$

(A8) together with (A3) entails the existence of the object $x \oplus y$, 'sum of x and y' for every x and y.

(A9) $\forall x[x \neq \mathcal{U} \wedge x \neq \bigcirc \rightarrow \exists z \forall w[\iota(w,z) \leftrightarrow \exists q[DJ(q,x) \wedge \iota(w,q)]]]$

(D5) $-\mathcal{U} =_{def} \bigcirc$ (D6) $-\bigcirc =_{def} \mathcal{U}$

(A9) together with (A3) entails a unique object $-x$, 'complement of x' for every x. (D5) and (D6) turn $-$ into a total function.

(D7) $x \ominus y =_{def} x \otimes (-y)$

(D7) defines the difference of x and y for every x and y. $x \ominus y$ is obviously unique.

(A10) $\forall x[\mu(\bigcirc) \leq \mu(x)]$

(A11) $\forall xy[P(x,y) \rightarrow \mu(x) \leq \mu(y)]$

(D8) $POINT(x) \equiv_{def} x \neq \bigcirc \wedge \forall y[P(y,x) \wedge y \neq \bigcirc \rightarrow x = y]$

(A12) $\forall x[x \neq \bigcirc \rightarrow \exists z[POINT(z) \wedge P(z,x)]]$

(A12) makes sure that there is a point inside every non-empty set.

Now let's see how we can "imitate" topological relations using measures:

(D9) $EC(x,y) \equiv_{def} \iota(x,y) \wedge \neg P(x,y) \wedge \neg P(y,x) \wedge \mu(x \otimes y) = \mu(\bigcirc)$

(D10) $TPP(x,y) \equiv_{def} PP(x,y) \wedge \exists z[EC(y,z) \wedge \iota(x,z)]$

(D11) $NTPP(x,y) \equiv_{def} PP(x,y) \wedge \forall z[\iota(x,z) \rightarrow O(y,z)]$

Some interesting definitions exploiting measures are listed below:

(D12) $VC(x, y) \equiv_{def} \exists z[\iota(z,x) \wedge \iota(z,y) \wedge \mu(z) = \mu(\bigcirc)]$
   x and y are very close to each other
(D13) $CON(x) \equiv_{def} \forall yz[x = y \oplus z \rightarrow VC(y,z)]$
   x is almost-one-piece. This immitates the topological notion of self-connected set.
(D14) $COMP(x, y) \equiv_{def} CON(x) \wedge P(x,y) \wedge$
   $\forall z[CON(z) \wedge P(z,y) \wedge P(x,z) \rightarrow x = z]$
   x is an almost-component of y: x is a maximal almost-one-piece part of y. This will be used in the proof of theorem 1.
(D15) $AINT(x, y) \equiv_{def} PP(x,y) \wedge \mu(x) = \mu(y)$
   x is almost-interior of y. This immitates the topological interior operator.
(D16) $AEQ(x, y) \equiv_{def} \neg \exists z[\mu(z) \neq \mu(\bigcirc) \wedge [P(z, x \ominus y) \vee P(z, y \ominus x)]]$
   x is almost-equal to y.

2.4   Undecidability

Our first result concerns the undecidability of $\mathcal{F}_{ML}$.

Theorem 1. $\mathcal{F}_{ML}$ *is undecidable.*

Proof. This is proved by showing that the arithmetic of finite sets is expressible in $\mathcal{F}_{ML}$. I will only provide a proof sketch. The details are easy to see.

Let X be a set and $\mathfrak{S} = <\wp(X), \oplus, \times, \prec, \varnothing, \approx>$ be the arithmetic of finite sets over X. It is well known that the structure $\mathfrak{S}$ can be given an interpretation as follows [5],

   (I1) X is a finite set and $\wp(X)$ is the power set of X
   (I2) $\oplus(abc)$ iff card(a) + card(b) = card(c)
   (I3) $\times(abc)$ iff card(a) · card(b) = card(c)
   (I4) $a \prec b$ iff card(b) = card(a) + 1
   (I5) $a \approx b$ iff card(a) = card(b)
   (I6) $\varnothing$ is the empty set

where $+, \cdot$ are the usual operations of addition and product over $\mathbb{N}$ and card(x) is the cardinality of set x.

Now define the structure $M = \langle X, S, m \rangle$ where X is from $\mathfrak{S}$, $S = \wp(X)$ and m is a set-function $m : S \rightarrow \mathbb{R}^+ \cup \{0\} \cup \{\infty\}$ defined as $m(x) = $ card(x). It is easy to see that S is a σ-algebra (definition 1) and m is a measure (definition 2). Hence, the structure M is a measure space.

Now define the following $\mathcal{L}_{ML}$-formulae

$$\varphi_\oplus(a,b,c) \equiv_{def} \exists xy[c = x \oplus y \wedge \neg \iota(x,y) \wedge \mu(a) = \mu(x) \wedge \mu(y) = \mu(b)]$$
$$\varphi_\times(a,b,c) \equiv_{def} \exists xy[\mu(b) = \mu(x) \wedge P(x,y) \wedge P(c,y) \wedge$$
$$\forall z[COMP(z,y) \rightarrow POINT(z \otimes x) \wedge \mu(c \otimes z) = \mu(a)]]$$
$$\varphi_\prec(a,b) \equiv_{def} \exists x[POINT(x) \wedge P(x,b) \wedge a = b \ominus x]$$
$$\varphi_\approx(a,b) \equiv_{def} \mu(a) = \mu(b)$$

Now it can be easily verified that $\mathcal{MS}_M \vDash \varphi_\oplus(a, b, c)$ iff $\oplus(abc)$, $\mathcal{MS}_M \vDash \varphi_\times(a, b, c)$ iff $\times(abc)$, $\mathcal{MS}_M \vDash \varphi_\prec(a, b)$ iff $a \prec b$ and $\mathcal{MS}_M \vDash \varphi_\approx(a, b)$ iff $a \approx b$ and that $\varnothing$ corresponds to $\bigcirc$.

Undecidability of $\mathcal{F}_{ML}$ follows from the fact that the formal system of the arithmetic of finite sets is undecidable [5,6].

3   Soundness and Completeness

3.1   Soundness

So far we have given a first-order axiomatic formalism from which a proof system can be obtained by adding the axioms and rules of inference of first-order logic: Modus Ponens and Generalization. I will call this proof system with $M_\simeq$ and adopt the notation $\vdash_\simeq \varphi$ iff there is a proof of the formulae φ in $M_\simeq$. A proof in $\vdash_\simeq$ is a finite sequence of $\mathcal{L}_{ML}$-formulae and every formulae in the sequence is either an axiom or obtained from the previous formulae by the rules of inference.

First we establish the following fact,

Lemma 2. *The following holds.*

1. $\mathcal{MS}_M \vDash P(x, y)$ *if and only if* $x^\delta \subseteq y^\delta$
2. $\mathcal{MS}_M \vDash DJ(x, y)$ *if and only if* $x^\delta \cap y^\delta = \emptyset$

Theorem 2 (Soundness). *For any φ, if $\vdash_\simeq \varphi$ then $\vDash_{MS} \varphi$.*

Proof. The proof is by induction on the length of a proof of φ in $M_\simeq$. Only the base case is presented here. To see this, it is sufficient to show that under the given semantics for ι and μ, all the axioms (A1)-(A12) of $\mathcal{F}_{ML}$ are valid in any given model $\mathcal{MS}_M = \langle Y, m, \cdot^{\delta(a)} \rangle$ satisfying the conditions in 2.1.

(A4) and (A5) can be seen straightforwardly by the fact that $\emptyset, X \in Y$. This shows that $\bigcirc^\delta = \emptyset$ and $\mathcal{U}^\delta = X$. (A1) and (A2) are completely trivial. Now let's show (A3).

(A3) $\forall xy[\forall z[\iota(x, z) \leftrightarrow \iota(y, z)] \rightarrow x = y]$: Let $x, y \in Y$ and assume that $\forall z \in Y[x \cap z \neq \emptyset \rightarrow y \cap z \neq \emptyset]$. We now show that this implies $x \subseteq y$. Let $p \in x$. Then $\{p\} \cap x \neq \emptyset$ and from the hypothesis it follows that $\{p\} \cap y \neq \emptyset$. This entails that $p \in y$. It follows that $x \subseteq y$. It is similar to show that $y \subseteq x$.

(A6) $\forall xy[\iota(x, y) \rightarrow \exists z \forall w[\iota(z, w) \leftrightarrow \exists q[P(q, x) \wedge P(q, y) \wedge \iota(q, w)]]]$: We want to show that z corresponds to $x \cap y$ or formally that $(x \otimes y)^{\delta(a)} = x^{\delta(a)} \cap y^{\delta(a)}$ for any a. So, we have to show that $\forall xy \in Y[x \cap y \neq \emptyset \rightarrow \forall w \in Y[(x \cap y) \cap w \neq \emptyset \leftrightarrow \exists q[q \subseteq x \wedge q \subseteq y \wedge q \cap w \neq \emptyset]]]$. Let $x, y \in Y$ and assume that $x \cap y \neq \emptyset$ and moreover assume that for some $w \in Y$, $w \cap (x \cap y) \neq \emptyset$. We have to find a $q \in Y$ such that $q \subseteq x \wedge q \subseteq y \wedge q \cap w \neq \emptyset$. Let $q = x \cap y$. From the other direction let $q \in Y$ such that $q \subseteq x \wedge q \subseteq y \wedge q \cap w \neq \emptyset$ for $x, y, w \in Y$. So, we have that $q \subseteq x \cap y$ and from the hypothesis it follows that $w \cap (x \cap y) \neq \emptyset$.

(A6) together with (A7) shows that the product operator '$\otimes$' corresponds to the set intersection '$\cap$'.

(A8) $\forall xy \exists z \forall w[\iota(z,w) \leftrightarrow [\iota(w,x) \lor \iota(w,y)]]$: We want to show that $(x \oplus y)^{\delta(a)} = x^{\delta(a)} \cup y^{\delta(a)}$ for any given a. We prove that $\forall x, y, w \in Y[(x \cup y) \cap w \neq \emptyset \leftrightarrow [w \cap x \neq \emptyset \lor w \cap y \neq \emptyset]]$. Let $x, y \in Y$ and assume that for some $w \in Y$ we have that $(x \cup y) \cap w \neq \emptyset$, the rest follows trivially. For the other direction, for some $w \in Y$ assume that $w \cap x \neq \emptyset \lor w \cap y \neq \emptyset$. This obviously entails that $w \cap (x \cup y) \neq \emptyset$. This shows that the addition operator '$\oplus$' corresponds to set union '$\cup$'.

(A9) $\forall x[x \neq \mathcal{U} \land x \neq \bigcirc \rightarrow \exists z \forall w[\iota(w,z) \leftrightarrow \exists q[\mathrm{DJ}(q,x) \land \iota(w,q)]]]$: Let $x \in Y$ such that $x \neq X$ and $x \neq \emptyset$. We want to show that $\forall w \in Y[w \cap \sim x \neq \emptyset \leftrightarrow \exists q[q \cap x = \emptyset \land q \cap w \neq \emptyset]]$. From the hypothesis we know that $\sim x \neq \emptyset$ and $x \neq \emptyset$. Assume that for some $w \in Y$, $w \cap \sim x \neq \emptyset$. Let $q = w \cap \sim x$. Other direction is also straightforward.

(A9) together with (D5) and (D6) show that the complement operator '$-$' corresponds to set complement '$\sim$'.

(A10) and (A11) follows directly from the model conditions in 2.1 and (A12) is straightforward.

3.2 Completeness

Showing the completeness of $\mathcal{F}_{\mathrm{ML}}$ is achieved through the so-called Henkin method. Completeness result follows mainly from three fundamental lemmas provided below. Only the Henkin lemma is supplied with a proof since other lemmas have standard proofs that can be found in, for example [7].

Lemma 3 (Lindenbaum Lemma). *Every* $\mathrm{M}_{\backsim}$*-consistent set of sentences can be extended to a maximal* $\mathrm{M}_{\backsim}$*-consistent set of sentences.*

Lemma 4 (Witness Lemma). *Every* $\mathrm{M}_{\backsim}$*-consistent set of sentences* Γ *in* $\mathcal{L}$ *can be extended to a* $\mathrm{M}_{\backsim}$*-consistent set of sentences* Γ' *in* $\mathcal{L}'$ *such that* $\mathcal{L}' = \mathcal{L} \cup C$, $\mathcal{L} \cap C = \emptyset$ *and* C *is an infinite set of constants which are witnesses for* Γ'.

Lemma 5 (Henkin Lemma). *Every maximal* $\mathrm{M}_{\backsim}$*-consistent set of sentences* Γ *which has a set of witnesses in* $\mathcal{L}$ *yields a* $\mathcal{M}_\Gamma$ *such that* $\mathcal{M}_\Gamma \vDash \varphi$ *if and only if* $\varphi \in \Gamma$.

Proof. The first step in the proof is to construct the model $\mathcal{M}_\Gamma$. After this, we only need to show that the claim: $\mathcal{M}_\Gamma \vDash \varphi$ if and only if $\varphi \in \Gamma$, holds.

By lemmas 3 and 4, given a $\mathrm{M}_{\backsim}$-consistent set of sentences Γ', we have a maximal consistent saturated set Γ. Let C be the set of constants occurring in Γ. Now define equivalence classes over the elements of C as follows: $[c] = \{d \in C \mid \Gamma \vdash_{\backsim} c = d\}$. Each class represent an element of the domain of our model and each such element will correspond to a set of points. So we have to define its points. The set of points that will correspond to every element can be set trivially as following:

$$\Pi_c = \{x \in C \mid \Gamma \vdash_{\backsim} \mathrm{POINT}(x) \land \mathrm{P}(x,c)\}, \tag{1}$$

Note that when $c \in \Gamma$ and $\Gamma \vdash_{\backsim} \mathrm{POINT}(c)$ we have $\Pi_c = \{c\}$.

Now, we can define $\mathcal{M}_\Gamma$. Let $\mathcal{D}_\Gamma = \{\Pi_c \mid c \in C\}$, α be the denotation function such that $c^\alpha = \Pi_c$ and finally a function $m : \mathcal{D}_\Gamma \to \mathbb{R}^+ \cup \{0\} \cup \{\infty\}$ such that $m(\Pi_x) = m(\Pi_y)$ iff $\Gamma \vdash_{\simeq} \mu(x) = \mu(y)$ and $m(\Pi_x) \leq m(\Pi_y)$ iff $\Gamma \vdash_{\simeq} \mu(x) \leq \mu(y)$ and also such that $m(\Pi_x) + m(\Pi_y) = m(\Pi_x \cup \Pi_y)$ whenever $\Pi_x \cap \Pi_y = \emptyset$. It is easy to show that we can always find such a function m. Finally we set $\mathcal{M}_\Gamma = \langle \mathcal{D}_\Gamma, m, \alpha \rangle$.

To complete the proof we finally need to show that $\mathcal{M}_\Gamma \vDash \varphi$ if and only if $\varphi \in \Gamma$. This can be done by an induction on the number of connectives in φ. I will present only the base case. The rest of the proof is standard and can be generated easily.

Base case: Since we have the binary primitives of $\iota(\cdot, \cdot)$, $\mu(\cdot) = \mu(\cdot)$ and $\mu(\cdot) \leq \mu(\cdot)$, it is sufficient to show that $\mathcal{M}_\Gamma \vDash \iota(x, y)$ if and only if $\iota(x, y) \in \Gamma$ and similarly $\mathcal{M}_\Gamma \vDash \mu(x) = \mu(y)$ if and only if $\mu(x) = \mu(y) \in \Gamma$ and finally that $\mathcal{M}_\Gamma \vDash \mu(x) \leq \mu(y)$ if and only if $\mu(x) \leq \mu(y) \in \Gamma$.

Assume that $\mathcal{M}_\Gamma \vDash \iota(x, y)$. Then $\Pi_x \cap \Pi_y \neq \emptyset$. Therefore, there is a point p such that $p \in \Pi_x$ and $p \in \Pi_y$ and $\mathrm{P}(p, x) \wedge \mathrm{P}(p, y) \wedge \mathrm{POINT}(p)$. Since $\mathrm{POINT}(p)$, we have $p \neq \bigcirc$ and from here we have that $\iota(p, p)$. Since $\mathrm{P}(p, x)$, we derive $\iota(p, x)$. Thus, from the fact that $\mathrm{P}(p, y)$, we get $\iota(x, y) \in \Gamma$.

To see the other direction, assume that $\iota(x, y) \in \Gamma$. From (A6) we have that $\exists q[\mathrm{P}(q, x) \wedge \mathrm{P}(q, y)]$ and it also follows that $q \neq \bigcirc$. On the other hand from (A12) we have that $\exists z[\mathrm{POINT}(z) \wedge \mathrm{P}(z, q)]$. Thus $\exists z[\mathrm{POINT}(z) \wedge \mathrm{P}(z, x) \wedge \mathrm{P}(z, y)]$. From here and from (1), we derive that $\Pi_x \cap \Pi_y \neq \emptyset$. Hence, $\mathcal{M}_\Gamma \vDash \iota(x, y)$.

The last two claims that $\mathcal{M}_\Gamma \vDash \mu(x) = \mu(y)$ if and only if $\mu(x) = \mu(y) \in \Gamma$ and $\mathcal{M}_\Gamma \vDash \mu(x) \leq \mu(y)$ if and only if $\mu(x) \leq \mu(y) \in \Gamma$ are obvious from the definition of function m in $\mathcal{M}_\Gamma$. This completes the proof of the base case.

The last step is to show that the model constructed in the proof of Henkin lemma is actually an $\mathcal{MS}$ model. This amounts to show that the conditions of section 2.1 are satisfied in $\mathcal{M}_\Gamma$. Next lemma deals with that.

Lemma 6. $\mathcal{M}_\Gamma$ is an $\mathcal{MS}$-model.

Proof. First let us create the universe, X such that $\mathcal{D}_\Gamma \subseteq 2^X$. We set $X = \cup\{\Pi_c \mid c \in C\}$. It can be trivially verified that $\mathcal{D}_\Gamma \subseteq 2^X$. It is sufficient to show that $\langle X, \mathcal{D}_\Gamma, m \rangle$ is a measure space which means that we have to show $\mathcal{D}_\Gamma$ is a σ-algebra over X and m is a measure over $\mathcal{D}_\Gamma$. First we show that $\mathcal{D}_\Gamma$ is a σ-algebra. So, we check the conditions of definition 1.

From (A5) and from (1) we derive that $\mathcal{U} \in C$ and $\mathcal{U}^\alpha = X$. Hence, $X \in \mathcal{D}_\Gamma$. This shows that condition 1 is satisfied. It similarly follows that $\bigcirc^\alpha = \emptyset$ and $\emptyset \in \mathcal{D}_\Gamma$.

Conditions 2 and 3 follow directly from the axioms (A9) and (A8). For a demonstration, I will show second condition. Let $a \in \mathcal{D}_\Gamma$ such that $\emptyset \neq a \neq X$ (otherwise we are done from (D5) and (D6)). Then there is a $a' \in C$ such that $\Pi_{a'} = a$ and $\bigcirc \neq a' \neq \mathcal{U}$. Then from (A9) it follows that $-a' \in C$. Thus, $\Pi_{-a'} \in \mathcal{D}_\Gamma$. It is sufficient to show that $\Pi_{-a'} =\sim \Pi_{a'}$ since $\sim \Pi_{a'} =\sim a$. From (A9) and (1) it follows that $\Pi_{-a'} = \{c \in C \mid \vdash_{\simeq} \mathrm{POINT}(c) \wedge \mathrm{P}(c, -a')\} = \{c \in$

$C| \vdash_{\simeq} \text{POINT}(c) \wedge \neg P(c, a')\} =\sim \{c \in C| \vdash_{\simeq} \text{POINT}(c) \wedge P(c, a')\} =\sim \Pi_{a'}$. It follows that $\mathcal{D}_\Gamma$ is a σ-algebra.

Finally we have to show that m is a measure. However, it is obvious from the definition of m in the proof of Henkin Lemma that m is a measure. Hence $\langle X, \mathcal{D}_\Gamma, m \rangle$ is a measure space. Thus, $\mathcal{M}_\Gamma$ is an $\mathcal{MS}$-model.

Finally, the goal theorem is achieved:

Theorem 3 (Completeness). *For any* φ, *if* $\models_{\mathcal{MS}} \varphi$ *then* $\vdash_{\simeq} \varphi$.

4   Propositional Measure Logic

In this section I will present a less expressive but computationally more attractive measure logic. A classical propositional language will be used to represent set-theoretic and measure-theoretic knowledge. Propositional logics can be given a set-theoretic interpretation where propositional letters represent subsets of a universe and logical operators correspond to usual set operators. Bennett [2] makes use of propositional logic in transforming some of the RCC-8 relations into a propositional language. Since propositional language is not strong enough to express all of the RCC-8 relations, Bennett uses the more expressive language of propositional intuitionistic logic to express all of the RCC-8 relations.

4.1   Propositional Language $\mathcal{L}_{\text{PML}}$

The language of propositional measure logic will be denoted by $\mathcal{L}_{\text{PML}}$. $\mathcal{L}_{\text{PML}}$ has denumerably-infinite number of non-logical constant symbols ($a, b, c, \dots$ etc.), the usual propositional operators ($\vee, \neg$ and their derivatives) and the propositional constants of verum and falsum ($\top, \bot$). Arbitrary formulae of $\mathcal{L}_{\text{PML}}$ are constructed recursively as usual. Note that $\mathcal{L}_{\text{PML}}$ is nothing but the language of the classical propositional logic. A theory Γ in $\mathcal{L}_{\text{PML}}$ is a pair of pairs which can be written as $\Gamma = \langle\langle \mathcal{M}, \mathcal{E}\rangle_s, \langle \mathcal{M}, \mathcal{E}\rangle_m\rangle$. $\langle \mathcal{M}, \mathcal{E}\rangle_s$ is the pair of model and entailment constraints corresponding to set-equations and $\langle \mathcal{M}, \mathcal{E}\rangle_m$ for the measure-equations. Each $\mathcal{M}$ and $\mathcal{E}$ is a set of $\mathcal{L}_{\text{PML}}$-formulae. This is obviously a simple extension of Bennett's propositional language in [2].

Semantics for $\mathcal{L}_{\text{PML}}$. Let X be a set. A model for the language $\mathcal{L}_{\text{PML}}$ is a triple $\mathcal{MS}_M = \langle Y, m, \cdot^\delta \rangle$ such that $M = \langle X, Y, m \rangle$ is a measure space and δ is a denotation function assigning elements of Y to the constants in $\mathcal{L}_{\text{PML}}$-formulae as follows:

1. $(\neg p)^\delta =\sim (p^\delta)$
2. $(p \wedge q)^\delta = p^\delta \cap q^\delta$
3. $(p \vee q)^\delta = p^\delta \cup q^\delta$
4. $(\bot)^\delta = \emptyset$
5. $(\top)^\delta = X$

Let $\vDash_{PC}$ be the entailment relation in propositional calculus and $\vDash_{\mathcal{MS}_M}$ the entailment in model $\mathcal{MS}_M$ for a measure space M and $\vDash_{\mathcal{MS}}$ in every model $\mathcal{MS}_M$ for every M. With the above interpretation of $\mathcal{L}_{PML}$-formulae, we have the following correspondence result:

Theorem 4 (Bennett, 94). $p_1, \ldots, p_n \vDash_{PC} p_0$ *if and only if* $p_1^\delta = X, \ldots, p_n^\delta = X \vDash_{\mathcal{MS}} p_0^\delta = X$

The above result of Bennett can be extended such that we can use $\mathcal{L}_{PML}$-formulae to talk about measure theoretic information as well. Note that we have not used the function m of $\mathcal{MS}_M$ to interpret any $\mathcal{L}_{PML}$-formulae.

First I state the following lemma which will be used in the proof of theorem 5:

Lemma 7. *If* $\vDash_{PC} \varphi$ *then* $\vDash_{\mathcal{MS}} m(\varphi^\delta) = m(X)$.

Proof. If φ is a tautology then from theorem 4 we have that $\varphi^\delta = X$. Since m is a well-defined function, $m(\varphi^\delta) = m(X)$ for every measure space M $= \langle X, Y, m \rangle$.

Now the actual extension to the Theorem 4 can be stated as follows:

Theorem 5. $p_1, \ldots, p_n \vDash_{PC} p_0$ *iff* $m(p_1^\delta) = m(X), \ldots, m(p_n^\delta) = m(X) \vDash_{\mathcal{MS}} m(p_0^\delta) = m(X)$.

Proof. To see from left to right assume that $p_1, \ldots, p_n \vDash_{PC} p_0$. Trivially, it follows that $(p_1 \wedge \ldots \wedge p_n) \rightarrow p_0$ is a tautology and hence from lemma 7 we have that $m(\sim (p_1^\delta \cap \ldots \cap p_n^\delta) \cup p_0^\delta) = m(X)$. It is obvious that $m(p_0^\delta) \leq m(X)$. On the other hand, from the disjoint additivity of m, in every model where $m(p_1^\delta) = m(X), \ldots, m(p_n^\delta) = m(X)$, we have that $m(X) = m(\sim (p_1^\delta \cap \ldots \cap p_n^\delta) \cup p_0^\delta) \leq m(\sim (p_1^\delta \cap \ldots \cap p_n^\delta)) + m(p_0^\delta) \leq m(\sim p_1^\delta) + \ldots + m(\sim p_n^\delta) + m(p_0^\delta) = m(p_0^\delta)$. Thus, it follows that $m(p_0^\delta) = m(X)$.

For the other direction, assume that $p_1, \ldots, p_n \nvDash_{PC} p_0$. Then, we can find an assignment a such that $a(p_1) = true, \ldots, a(p_n) = true$ and also $a(p_0) = false$. Now, define a denotation function $\cdot^\epsilon$ based on a as follows: $x^\epsilon = X$ iff $a(x) = true$ and $x^\epsilon = \emptyset$ iff $a(x) = false$. From the definitions of section 1.1 we have that $m(\emptyset) \neq m(X)$, it follows that $m(p_1^\epsilon) = m(X), \ldots, m(p_n^\epsilon) = m(X) \nvDash_{\mathcal{MS}} m(p_0^\epsilon) = m(X)$.

From Theorems 4 and 5 it is easy to see that propositional formulae can be given two interpretations. A propositional formula is entailed by the relation $\vDash_{PC}$ if and only if either its set-denotation in $\mathcal{MS}$ is equal to X or alternatively, measure of its set-denotation in $\mathcal{MS}$ is equal to the measure of X. Hence, for the first interpretation we use the first component of Γ and include the propositional formulae into $\mathcal{M}_s$ if its set-denotation is equal to X and include it into $\mathcal{E}_s$ if its set-denotation is not equal to X. Similarly, for the second interpretation, we use the second component of Γ and include the propositional formulae into $\mathcal{M}_m$ if measure of its set-denotation is equal to the measure of X and include it into $\mathcal{E}_m$ if measure of its set-denotation is not equal to the measure of X.

Naturally, we are now asking for an algorithm to check whether a given theory $\Gamma = \langle \langle \mathcal{M}, \mathcal{E} \rangle_s, \langle \mathcal{M}, \mathcal{E} \rangle_m \rangle$ of propositional measure logic is consistent or not.

Table 1. Translation of certain relations in propositional measure logic, including relations "imitating" RCC-8.

Relation	$\mathcal{M}_s$	$\mathcal{E}_s$	$\mathcal{M}_m$	$\mathcal{E}_m$
$\iota(x,y)$		$\neg(x \wedge y), \neg x, \neg y$		
$DJ(x,y)$	$\neg(x \wedge y)$	$\neg x, \neg y$		
$P(x,y)$	$\neg x \vee y$	$\neg x, \neg y$		
$PP(x,y)$ or $NTPP(x,y)$	$\neg x \vee y$	$x \vee \neg y, \neg x, \neg y$		
$PP^{-1}(x,y)$ or $NTPP^{-1}(x,y)$	$x \vee \neg y$	$\neg x \vee y, \neg x, \neg y$		
$PO(x,y)$		$\neg x \vee \neg y, \neg x \vee y,$ $x \vee \neg y, \neg x, \neg y$		
$EQ(x,y)$	$\neg x \vee y, x \vee \neg y$	$\neg x, \neg y$		
$EC(x,y)$		$\neg(x \wedge y), \neg x, \neg y$	$\neg(x \wedge y)$	$\neg x, \neg y$
$TPP(x,y)$		$\neg x \vee \neg y, \neg x \vee y,$ $x \vee \neg y, \neg x, \neg y$	$\neg(x \wedge \neg y)$	$\neg x, \neg y$
$AEQ(x,y)$			$\neg(x \wedge \neg y), \neg(\neg x \wedge y)$	$\neg x, \neg y$
$AINT(x,y)$	$\neg x \vee y$	$x \vee \neg y, \neg x, \neg y$	$\neg(\neg x \wedge y)$	$\neg x, \neg y$

Theorem 6 gives an answer to this question in three parts, Bennett's Theorem and its extension without the proof.

Theorem 6. *Given a theory Γ, consistency of each component of Gamma can be determined as follows:*

1. [Bennett, 94] A spatial configuration described by $\langle \mathcal{M}, \mathcal{E} \rangle_s$ is consistent iff there is no $\phi \in \mathcal{E}_s$ such that $\mathcal{M}_s \vDash_{PC} \phi$.

2. A spatial configuration described by $\langle \mathcal{M}, \mathcal{E} \rangle_m$ is consistent iff there is no $\phi \in \mathcal{E}_m$ such that $\mathcal{M}_m \vDash_{PC} \phi$.

3. A spatial configuration described by $\Gamma = \langle \langle \mathcal{M}, \mathcal{E} \rangle_s, \langle \mathcal{M}, \mathcal{E} \rangle_m \rangle$ is consistent iff $\langle \mathcal{M}, \mathcal{E} \rangle_s$ and $\langle \mathcal{M}, \mathcal{E} \rangle_m$ are both consistent and $\mathcal{M}_s \subseteq \mathcal{M}_m$ and $\mathcal{E}_m \subseteq \mathcal{E}_s$.

Table 1 gives a list of relations that can be expressed in $\mathcal{L}_{PML}$. Note that some of the rows are exactly the same as in [2] and thus such translations are not new. First-order definitions of all the relations appearing in Table 1 can be found in section 2.3 where it is probably easier to understand their meaning. Entries in the cells of Table 1 which can be determined according to Theorem 6's part 3 are omitted to prevent the table from getting more complicated.

5   Conclusion

A new method for representing spatial information in a qualitative way is investigated in this paper which has its roots in measure theory rather than topology. I explored two spatial logics in this paper: First-order measure logic and propositional measure logic. I supplied the first-order formalism with semantics which with respect to the logic is sound and complete. Although the first-order formalism is not decidable, the less expressive propositional measure logic is computationally very attractive. Moreover, I have shown that relations similar to that of topological RCC-8 relations are expressible in propositional measure logic. Thus, taking an approach based on measure theory rather than topology, we can encode more spatial configurations with classical propositional formulae.

References

1. Randell, D.A., Cui, Z., Cohn, A.G.: A spatial logic based on regions and connection. In Nebel, B., Rich, C., Swartout, W., eds.: Principles of Knowledge Representation and Reasoning (KR92), San Mateo, Morgan Kaufmann (1992) 165–176
2. Bennett, B.: Spatial reasoning with propositional logics. In Doyle, J., Sandewall, E., Torasso, P., eds.: Principles of Knowledge Representation and Reasoning (KR94), San Francisco, CA., Morgan Kaufmann (1994) 51–62
3. Lemon, O.J.: Semantical foundations of spatial logics. In Aiello, L.C., Doyle, J., Shapiro, S., eds.: Principles of Knowledge Representation and Reasoning (KR96), San Francisco, CA., Morgan Kaufmann (1996) 212–219
4. Pratt, I., Lemon, O.: Ontologies for plane, polygonal mereotopology. Notre Dame Journal of Formal Logic **38** (1997) 225–245
5. Grzegorczyk, A.: Undecidability of some topological theories. Fundamenta Mathematicae **38** (1951) 137–152
6. Tarski, A.: Undecidable Theories. Studies in logic and the foundations of mathematics. North-Holland, Amsterdam (1971)
7. Mendelson, E.: Introduction to Mathematical Logic. D. Van Nostrand, Princeton, New Jersey (1968)

Only Knowing with Confidence Levels: Reductions and Complexity

Espen H. Lian[1], Tore Langholm[2], and Arild Waaler[3,1]

[1] Dep. of Informatics, University of Oslo, Norway
[2] Dep. of Linguistics, University of Oslo, Norway
[3] Finnmark College, Norway

Abstract. A new logic of belief (in the "Only knowing" family) with confidence levels is presented. The logic allows a natural distinction between explicit and implicit belief representations, where the explicit form directly expresses its models. The explicit form can be found by applying a set of equivalence preserving rewriting rules to the implicit form. The rewriting process is performed entirely within the logic, on the object level. We prove that the problem of deciding whether there exists a consistent explicit form is Σ_2^p-complete, a complexity class which many problems of nonmonotonic reasoning belong to.

1 Introduction

The paper presents the propositional modal logic Æ, a logic in the "Only knowing" family of logical systems pioneered by Levesque [8]. Compared to other propositional systems in this family the Æ system contributes on three levels: *conceptually* by the introduction of a richer set of epistemic concepts, both for the description of the system itself and for use in representation of common-sense patterns of reasoning within Æ; *logically* by being closed under uniform substitution and being axiomatized entirely at the object-level; *by an increased expressive power* which enables the representation of a certain sort of prioritized normal defaults. It can also be used to represent recent work on priorities within the Reiter-style families of systems [1,2], although this is not addressed in this paper.

2 The Logic Æ

2.1 Syntax

The object language contains a stock of propositional letters, the constants $\top$ and $\bot$, and connectives $\neg$, $\vee$, $\wedge$, $\supset$ and $\equiv$. Modal operators are $\square$ (necessity) and, for each $k \in I$, B_k (belief) and C_k (co-belief). I is a finite index set partially ordered by $\preceq$. A formula φ is *completely modalized* if every propositional letter occurs within the scope of a modal operator. $\varphi[\psi_1/\psi_2]$ is φ with every subformula occurrence of ψ_1 substituted with ψ_2. The *substitution operator* $[\cdot/\cdot]$ distributes over connectives and modalities in the obvious way.

J.J. Alferes and J. Leite (Eds.): JELIA 2004, LNAI 3229, pp. 500–512, 2004.
© Springer-Verlag Berlin Heidelberg 2004

We will say that φ *entails* ψ if $\Box(\varphi \supset \psi)$ holds. Intuitively, each index in I corresponds to a *confidence level*, hence $B_k\varphi$ denotes belief in φ with strength k. The belief and co-belief operators are complementary. We read $C_k\neg\varphi$ as: the agent believes *at most* φ with strength k.

The expression $O_k\varphi$ abbreviates $B_k\varphi \wedge C_k\neg\varphi$ (all that is believed with strength k). A *modal atom* is a formula of the form $B_k\varphi$ or $C_k\varphi$, and a *modal literal* is either a modal atom or its negation. The *depth* of a modal atom refers to the nesting of modalities. If φ is propositional, $B_k\varphi$ has depth 1. Dual modalities: $\Diamond\varphi$ is $\neg\Box\neg\varphi$ (φ possible); $b_k\varphi$ is $\neg B_k\neg\varphi$ (φ possible and compatible with belief with strength k); c_k is $\neg C_k\neg\varphi$ (φ possible and compatible with co-belief with strength k).

2.2 Models

A *model* M for Æ can be written in the form of a quadruple (U, U^+, U^-, π) where U is a non-empty set of points called the *space of conceivability*, and U^+ and U^- are functions which assign a subset of U to each index in I. $U^+(k)$ is denoted U_k^+; U_k^- denotes $U^-(k)$. We require that $U_k^+ \cup U_k^- = U$ for each $k \in I$ and that $U_k^+ \subseteq U_i^+$ and $U_i^- \subseteq U_k^-$ for each $i \prec k$.

The model is *bisected* if $U_k^+ \cap U_k^- = \emptyset$ for each $k \in I$. Points in U^+ are called *plausible* and points in U^- *implausible*. π is a valuation function which assigns a subset of U to each propositional letter in the language. A satisfaction relation can be defined for each point x: $M \vDash_x p$ iff $x \in \pi(p)$ for a propositional letter p; $M \vDash_x \Box\varphi$ iff $\vDash_y \varphi$ for each $y \in U$; $M \vDash_x B_k\varphi$ iff $\vDash_y \varphi$ for each $y \in U_k^+$; $M \vDash_x C_k\varphi$ iff $\vDash_y \varphi$ for each $y \in U_k^-$ (and as usual for propositional connectives). Hence a proposition is necessary if and only if it holds in all conceivable states of affairs. We write $\|\varphi\|$ for the truth set of φ, i.e. the set of points at which φ is true. Observe that all points agree on the truth value of completely modalized formulae.

Persistence of beliefs. Observe that $M \vDash_x B_k\psi$ iff $U_k^+ \subseteq \|\psi\|$ and $M \vDash_x C_k\psi$ iff $U_k^- \subseteq \|\psi\|$. This, together with the model requirements imposed by the $\prec$ relation, expresses a persistence property on the modalities which strongly supports an interpretation of the preference relation $\prec$ as a relation of *greater conviction* or *stronger belief*. Where k is $\prec$-minimal, it is natural to understand B_k as a modality of full conviction.

Necessity. The modality of necessity is used to express *personal* necessities. One case in point can be analytic relationships between concepts, another the negation of statements that are strictly speaking consistent, but nevertheless seem so implausible (to the agent) that their *possibility* of being true is simply neglected. Semantically the notion is analyzed in terms of the conceivability space. The semantical constraint that U is non-empty implies that the *real* state of affairs is assumed to be conceivable, validating the truth axiom $\Box\varphi \supset \varphi$.

Belief and co-belief. The two belief modalities span the notion of necessity: a necessary proposition is, at any confidence level, both believed and co-believed, and vice versa. Intended readings of the formula $B_k\varphi$ are: the agent has *evidence* for φ, has a *justified* belief in φ, is *convinced* that φ with strength k. The set of plausible points U_k^+ are precisely those states of affairs which are both conceivable and compatible with the k-strong evidence. The points in $U \setminus U_k^+$ are also determined by the evidence: they are the conceivable states of affairs incompatible with k-evidence. In bisected models $C_k\varphi$ holds iff $\|\neg\varphi\| \subseteq U_k^+$. This means that φ is true should some of the agent's beliefs be false, since the real state of affairs lies in $U \setminus U_k^+$.

Semantically, U_k^+ defines *belief state* k: the points consistent with the evidence or beliefs which the agent possesses with strength k. The real state of affairs is not necessarily contained in U_k^+. Thus, even though it is not *plausible* for the agent that any of its beliefs are false (i.e. $\neg b_k(B_k\varphi \wedge \neg\varphi)$ is valid), situations in which some are may still be *conceivable* (i.e. $\Diamond(B_k\varphi \wedge \neg\varphi)$ is satisfiable).

We assume that the agent does not put its own beliefs into question, and this makes the beliefs and co-beliefs in a certain (restricted) sense necessary. Bringing in the notion of evidence can serve as a guide to the strong introspective principles of the logic: the formula $B_k\varphi \supset \Box B_k\varphi$ is e.g. valid. This formula does not express that the agent's beliefs are in a strong (metaphysical) sense determined, but rather that they are uniquely determined *from the agent's evidence*.

Bisected models and the O-operator. The representations that we will be interested in in this paper will be conjunctions of formulae of the form $O_k\varphi$ for each k (cnf. Sect. 4.2), and it is easy to prove that any such formula will have only bisected models: if $M \vDash O_k\varphi$, then $U_k^+ = \|\varphi\|$ and $U_k^- = \|\neg\varphi\|$. As $\|\varphi\| \cap \|\neg\varphi\| = \emptyset$, M is bisected. But if this is what we are after, why do we not have the O_k-operators as primitive, sacrificing the seemingly artificial C_k modalities? One reason is technical; it is natural to fix the extension of a belief state by approximating it from above (using B_k) and from below (using $C_k\neg$). Moreover, the use of the C_k-operator is by no means exhausted by its service for O_k, although investigations in this direction are not pursued in this paper.

2.3   Axiomatic System

Let us say that a *tautology* is a substitution instance of a formula valid in classical propositional logic (such as $\Box\varphi \supset \Box\varphi$). The logic Æ is defined as the least set that contains all tautologies, contains all instances of the following schemata for each $k \in I$:

$$\Box:\quad \Box\varphi \equiv B_k\varphi \wedge C_k\varphi \qquad\qquad T:\quad \Box\varphi \supset \varphi$$

$$K_B:\quad B_k(\varphi \supset \psi) \supset (B_k\varphi \supset B_k\psi) \quad K_C:\quad C_k(\varphi \supset \psi) \supset (C_k\varphi \supset C_k\psi)$$

$$B_\Box:\quad B_k\varphi \supset \Box B_k\varphi \qquad\qquad\qquad C_\Box:\quad C_k\varphi \supset \Box C_k\varphi$$

$$\overline{B}_\Box:\quad \neg B_k\varphi \supset \Box\neg B_k\varphi \qquad\qquad \overline{C}_\Box:\quad \neg C_k\varphi \supset \Box\neg C_k\varphi$$

$$P_B:\quad B_i\varphi \supset B_k\varphi \text{ for all } i \prec k \qquad P_C:\quad C_k\varphi \supset C_i\varphi \text{ for all } i \prec k$$

and is closed under all instances of the rules:

$$\frac{\varphi}{\Box\varphi}\ \text{(RN)} \qquad\qquad \frac{\varphi \quad \varphi \supset \psi}{\psi}\ \text{(MP)}$$

P_B and P_C are the *persistence* axioms for B and C respectively. We write $\vdash \varphi$ if φ is theorem of Æ. If $\vdash (\varphi_1 \wedge \cdots \wedge \varphi_n) \supset \psi$, we sometimes write $\varphi_1, \ldots, \varphi_n \vdash \psi$ and refer to $\varphi_1, \ldots, \varphi_n$ as *premises*. It is easy to show that the logic of $\square$ is S5, while B_k and C_k are both K45 modalities. Any formula in Æ is equivalent to one in *normal form*, i.e. without occurrences of nested modalities. This follows from the *Normal form property*: for a propositional ψ and a completely modalized β, $\vdash B_i(\psi \vee \beta) \equiv (B_i\psi \vee \beta)$ (and similarly for C_i).

Theorem 1. *Æ is sound, complete and decidable.*

Proof. Soundness is proved by routine induction on the length of proofs. The proof of completeness uses a standard canonical model construction. Decidability follows by taking the maximal filtration of the canonical model wrt. a finite filtration set; this construction collapses the canonical model into a finite set of Æ models finitely bound by the size of the filtration set [14,13]. □

3   Finite Languages

3.1   Logical Spaces

We will in the rest of this paper assume that the language has finitely many propositional letters $p_1, \ldots, p_n$. Let us say that an *atom* is a conjunction $\pm p_1 \wedge \cdots \wedge \pm p_n$ where $\pm p_i$ means either p_i or $\neg p_i$. We can interpret an atom as characterizing the material content of a state of affairs, i.e. the "external world" neglecting the agent's cognitive state. There are 2^n atoms and $1 \leq m \leq 2^n$ conceivable states of affairs in a model with different material content (i.e. which disagree on some propositional letters); let $\alpha_1, \ldots, \alpha_m$ characterize all the conceivable states of affairs by their material content. The *logical space* of the agent is defined as the formula

$$\Diamond \alpha_1 \wedge \cdots \wedge \Diamond \alpha_m \wedge \square(\alpha_1 \vee \cdots \vee \alpha_m) \ .$$

A logical space is the syntactical counterpart to the concept of a conceivability space. The propositional formula $\alpha_1 \vee \cdots \vee \alpha_m$ is a *characteristic formula* of the logical space. As $m > 0$ this formula, and hence the logical space, is always consistent. The characteristic formula need not, however, be in disjunctive normal form (DNF); any propositional formula equivalent to $\alpha_1 \vee \cdots \vee \alpha_m$ counts as a characteristic formula of the logical space, a fact which we can use to reduce the size of representations considerably (see below).

Note, incidentally, that the possibility of defining different logical spaces increases the expressive power of the language. We can e.g. define a logical space λ such that $\lambda \vdash \square(\text{penguin}(\text{Tweety}) \supset \text{bird}(\text{Tweety}))$ and thereby syntactically express a constraint on conceivability. With respect to the maximal logical space this constraint does not follow. We may, of course, state the conditional as part of the agent's beliefs, but conceptually analytic statements are expressed in a better way at the level of necessity.

The size of the logical space λ is clearly exponential in the number of propositional variables. Specifying λ can, however, be avoided by using any of its characteristic formulae, say ρ, as a basis for an *implicit* generation of λ. This can be achieved by adding the following axiom and inference rule to Æ:

$$\text{RI:} \quad \Box\rho \qquad\qquad \frac{\rho, \varphi \not\vdash_{\text{PL}} \bot}{\Diamond\varphi} \quad \text{(RC)}$$

Note that in (RC) φ is propositional. We shall call this system $Æ_\rho$ and use $\vdash_\rho$ to denote its deducibility relation. In the *maximal* logical space all atoms are possible, (i.e. m is 2^n) and $\top$ is one of its characteristic formulae. The maximal logical space is a theorem of $Æ_\top$. $Æ_\top$ with a singleton I is in fact identical to the propositional fragment of Levesque's system [8].

More generally we use $\lambda(\rho)$ to denote the function that maps a PL-consistent formula ρ to its corresponding logical space and $\rho(\lambda)$ to denote the function that gives the full DNF characteristic formula of a logical space λ. As an example, let ρ be $p \equiv q$. Since $\vdash \rho \equiv ((\neg p \wedge \neg q) \vee (p \wedge q))$ we can derive the following:

$$\frac{\rho, \neg p \wedge \neg q \not\vdash_{\text{PL}} \bot}{\vdash_\rho \Diamond(\neg p \wedge \neg q)} \qquad \frac{\rho, p \wedge q \not\vdash_{\text{PL}} \bot}{\vdash_\rho \Diamond(p \wedge q)} \qquad \vdash_\rho \Box((\neg p \wedge \neg q) \vee (p \wedge q))$$

It is easy to see that $\lambda(\rho)$ is $\Diamond(\neg p \wedge \neg q) \wedge \Diamond(p \wedge q) \wedge \Box((\neg p \wedge \neg q) \vee (p \wedge q))$ and that $\vdash \rho(\lambda(\rho)) \equiv \rho$.

Theorem 2. *Let λ be a logical space. Then $\lambda \vdash \varphi$ iff $\vdash_{\rho(\lambda)} \varphi$.*

Proof. λ is of the form $\Diamond\alpha_1 \wedge \cdots \wedge \Diamond\alpha_m \wedge \Box(\alpha_1 \vee \cdots \vee \alpha_m)$, so $\rho = \rho(\lambda) = \alpha_1 \vee \cdots \vee \alpha_m$. *Only if:* Assume $\lambda \vdash \varphi$. We need to show that $\vdash_\rho \lambda$. Instantiating RC with $\varphi = \alpha_i$ gives $\vdash_\rho \Diamond\alpha_i$ for each $1 \leq i \leq m$. $\vdash_\rho \Box(\alpha_1 \vee \cdots \vee \alpha_m)$ is the RI axiom. *If:* We need to show that the consequences of λ are the *only* additional theorems of $Æ_\rho$. This can be shown by induction over proofs, showing that RI and RC are deducible from λ in Æ. For RI this is trivial. For any $\Diamond\psi$ stemming from RC, it must be the case that $\rho \not\vdash_{\text{PL}} \neg\psi$. Assume that for all $1 \leq i \leq m$, $\alpha_i \not\vdash_{\text{PL}} \psi$. As either $\alpha \vdash_{\text{PL}} \psi$ or $\alpha \vdash_{\text{PL}} \neg\psi$, $\alpha_i \vdash_{\text{PL}} \neg\psi$, thus $\rho \vdash_{\text{PL}} \neg\psi$, a contradiction. Hence there must exists an α_i such that $\alpha_i \vdash_{\text{PL}} \psi$, thus $\Diamond\alpha_i \vdash \Diamond\psi$ and, consequently, $\lambda \vdash \Diamond\psi$. $\qquad\Box$

Corollary 1. *$\lambda(\rho) \vdash \varphi$ iff $\vdash_\rho \varphi$.*

The satisfiability problem for Levesque's system is Σ_2^p-complete [11,12], which is the same as for $Æ_\rho$ without confidence levels. From a logical point of view the RC and RI rules can be criticized since the proof checking problem for $Æ_\rho$ is NP-complete (and not linear). Moreover, these logics are not closed under uniform substitution, a property which holds for Æ and which traditionally has been used to distinguish a logic from a theory.

3.2   Explicit and Implicit Belief Representations

Let φ^I be a formula of the form $\bigwedge_{k \in I} O_k \varphi_k$. We will refer to φ^I as an O_I-*block*. If each φ_k is propositional, it is a *prime* O_I-block. Let λ be a logical space and ψ^I be a prime O_I-block. If $\lambda \wedge \psi^I$ is satisfiable, it has essentially only one model; moreover, this model can easily be defined from the formula itself. Otherwise, $\lambda \wedge \psi^I$ is inconsistent due to a clash with the persistence axioms. It follows from this that for any completely modalized β, either $\lambda \wedge \psi^I \vdash \beta$ or $\lambda \wedge \psi^I \vdash \neg\beta$ (or both if $\lambda \wedge \psi^I$ is inconsistent).

Hence, the agent's attitude towards every proposition which can be expressed in the language can be determined from $\lambda \wedge \psi^I$ when ψ^I is prime. For this reason we will say that $\lambda \wedge \psi^I$ gives an *explicit* representation of the agent's cognitive state. A more general explicit representation has the form

$$\lambda \wedge (\psi_1^I \vee \cdots \vee \psi_m^I)$$

where each ψ_i^I is a prime O_I-block. $\lambda \wedge \psi^I$ is a special case of this with $m = 1$; we call explicit representations of this form *unambiguous*. Otherwise, the formula (in general) conveys incomplete information about the agent's beliefs. Nevertheless the formula expresses that there are m models which fit the agent and provides a precise description of each of them. Note in particular that if β is either $B_k \varphi$ or $\neg B_k \varphi$ for some $k \in I$, then $\lambda, \psi_1^I \vee \cdots \vee \psi_n^I \vdash \beta$ if and only if $\lambda \wedge \psi_i^I \vdash \beta$ for each ψ_i^I. Hence, if there are propositions towards which the agent's attitude is indeterminate, the explicit representation provides a clear method for identifying these.

If ψ^I is not prime, $\lambda \wedge \psi^I$ gives an *implicit* representation of a belief state; implicit because it will in general require some work to see what its models are. All representations of non-trivial common-sense situations will be implicit representations, some of which are addressed in Sect. 4.2. Whatever form they may have, there is a modal reduction property which applies to them to the effect that their content can be analyzed and stated in an explicit form by purely formal manipulations *within* the logic. This property is manifested in the *Modal reduction theorem*:

Theorem 3. *For each logical space λ and O_I-block φ^I, for some $m \geq 0$, there are prime O_I-blocks $\psi_1^I, \ldots, \psi_m^I$ such that*

$$\lambda \vdash \varphi^I \equiv (\psi_1^I \vee \cdots \vee \psi_m^I) \ .$$

Every such ψ_k^I that is *consistent* with λ is called a λ-*expansion* of φ^I. In the case when φ^I has no λ-expansion, $\lambda \vdash \neg\varphi^I$. As each λ-expansion has a unique model, the "if" direction of the theorem states that these models are also models of φ^I. The "only if" direction states that every other model is *not* a model of φ^I. Accordingly the theorem tells us exactly which models the formula has.

4   Reductions and Complexity

The proof of the Modal reduction theorem given in Sect. 4.3 is constructive and is based on rewriting the original formula using equivalences within the logic. The formula is first *expanded*, then *collapsed*. Both steps are carried out by means of rewriting rules which all rely on provable equivalences within Æ. Both rule types substitute a lot of $\top$'s and $\bot$'s into the formula, and formally we need a rule for simplifying these. This simplification is, however, skipped in the presentation below.

4.1 Rewriting Rules

To apply the expand rule one must select a modal atom β of modal depth 1 and substitute it with $\top$ and $\bot$ in the following way:

$$O_i\varphi \to_\beta (O_i\varphi[\beta/\top] \wedge \beta) \vee (O_i\varphi[\beta/\bot] \wedge \neg\beta) .$$

Lemma 1. $\vdash O_i\varphi \equiv (O_i\varphi[\beta/\top] \wedge \beta) \vee (O_i\varphi[\beta/\bot] \wedge \neg\beta)$.

Proof. We show that $\vdash \varphi \equiv (\varphi[\beta/\top] \wedge \beta) \vee (\varphi[\beta/\bot] \wedge \neg\beta)$. This can be shown by induction on φ. *Base step:* If $\beta = \varphi$ or β does not occur as a subformula of φ, the statement holds trivially. *Induction step:* We only prove the cases for (1) $\varphi = B_k\varphi_1$, (2) $\varphi = \varphi_1 \wedge \varphi_2$ and (3) $\varphi = \neg\varphi_1$. Let (i) denote $\vdash \varphi_1 \equiv (\varphi_1[\beta/\top] \wedge \beta) \vee (\varphi_1[\beta/\bot] \wedge \neg\beta)$ and (ii), $\vdash \varphi_2 \equiv (\varphi_2[\beta/\top] \wedge \beta) \vee (\varphi_2[\beta/\bot] \wedge \neg\beta)$.

(1) The induction hypothesis is (i). Thus $B_k\varphi_1$ is equivalent to $B_k((\varphi_1[\beta/\top] \vee \beta) \wedge (\varphi_1[\beta/\bot] \vee \neg\beta))$. B_k-distribution yields $B_k(\varphi_1[\beta/\top] \vee \beta) \wedge B_k(\varphi_1[\beta/\bot] \vee \neg\beta)$. By the Normal form property this is equivalent to $(B_k(\varphi_1[\beta/\top]) \vee \beta) \wedge (B_k(\varphi_1[\beta/\bot]) \vee \neg\beta)$. The case $\varphi = C_k\varphi_1$ is similar.

(2) The induction hypothesis is (i) and (ii). Thus $\varphi_1 \wedge \varphi_2$ is equivalent to $((\varphi_1[\beta/\top] \wedge \beta) \vee (\varphi_1[\beta/\bot] \wedge \neg\beta)) \wedge ((\varphi_2[\beta/\top] \wedge \beta) \vee (\varphi_2[\beta/\bot] \wedge \neg\beta))$. On disjunctive normal form this becomes $(\varphi_1[\beta/\top] \wedge \varphi_2[\beta/\top] \wedge \beta) \vee (\varphi_1[\beta/\bot] \wedge \varphi_2[\beta/\bot] \wedge \neg\beta)$. As substitution is distributive, $((\varphi_1 \wedge \varphi_2)[\beta/\top] \wedge \beta) \vee ((\varphi_1 \wedge \varphi_2)[\beta/\bot] \wedge \neg\beta)$.

(3) The induction hypothesis is (i). Thus $\neg\varphi_1$ is equivalent to $(\neg(\varphi_1[\beta/\top]) \vee \neg\beta) \wedge (\neg(\varphi_1[\beta/\bot]) \vee \beta)$, equivalently $(\neg(\varphi_1[\beta/\top]) \wedge \beta) \vee (\neg(\varphi_1[\beta/\bot]) \wedge \neg\beta)$. As substitution is distributive, $((\neg\varphi_1)[\beta/\top] \wedge \beta) \vee ((\neg\varphi_1)[\beta/\bot] \wedge \neg\beta)$. $\qquad\square$

When the expand rule is no longer applicable, we may apply the collapse rules. In the rules below, all occurrences of φ and ψ are propositional. If $i \preceq k$, the collapse rules pertaining to B-formulae are:

$$O_i\varphi \wedge B_k\psi \to_\lambda O_i\varphi \text{ if } \lambda \vdash O_i\varphi \supset B_i\psi \qquad (B^1)$$

$$O_i\varphi \wedge \neg B_k\psi \to_\lambda \bot \text{ if } \lambda \vdash O_i\varphi \supset B_i\psi \qquad (B^2)$$

$$O_k\varphi \wedge B_i\psi \to_\lambda \bot \text{ if } \lambda \nvdash O_k\varphi \supset B_k\psi \qquad (B^3)$$

$$O_k\varphi \wedge \neg B_i\psi \to_\lambda O_k\varphi \text{ if } \lambda \nvdash O_k\varphi \supset B_k\psi \qquad (B^4)$$

and for C-formulae:

$$O_k\varphi \wedge C_i\psi \to_\lambda O_k\varphi \text{ if } \lambda \vdash O_k\varphi \supset C_k\psi \qquad (C^1)$$

$$O_k\varphi \wedge \neg C_i\psi \to_\lambda \bot \text{ if } \lambda \vdash O_k\varphi \supset C_k\psi \qquad (C^2)$$

$$O_i\varphi \wedge C_k\psi \to_\lambda \bot \text{ if } \lambda \nvdash O_i\varphi \supset C_i\psi \qquad (C^3)$$

$$O_i\varphi \wedge \neg C_k\psi \to_\lambda O_i\varphi \text{ if } \lambda \nvdash O_i\varphi \supset C_i\psi \qquad (C^4)$$

Lemma 2. *The collapse rules are sound.*

Proof. We only show soundness of B^1–B^4. For B^1 and B^2 we need to show that

$$\lambda \vdash (O_i\psi \wedge B_k\varphi) \equiv O_i\psi \text{ if } \lambda \vdash O_i\psi \supset B_i\varphi \text{ and}$$
$$\lambda \vdash (O_i\psi \wedge \neg B_k\varphi) \equiv \bot \text{ if } \lambda \vdash O_i\psi \supset B_i\varphi .$$

They are both equivalent to "$\lambda \wedge O_i\psi \vdash B_k\varphi$ if $\lambda \wedge O_i\psi \vdash B_i\varphi$", which follows from persistence. For B^3 and B^4 we need to show that

$$\lambda \vdash (O_k\psi \wedge B_i\varphi) \equiv \bot \text{ if } \lambda \nvdash O_k\psi \supset B_k\varphi \text{ and}$$
$$\lambda \vdash (O_k\psi \wedge \neg B_i\varphi) \equiv O_k\psi \text{ if } \lambda \nvdash O_k\psi \supset B_k\varphi .$$

Since $\lambda \wedge O_k\psi$ has exactly one model, they are both equivalent, and the contraposition is "$\lambda \wedge O_k\psi \vdash B_k\varphi$ if $\lambda \wedge O_k\psi \vdash B_i\varphi$", which follows from persistence. □

In some situations it is more efficient to perform the rewriting steps directly on O-formulae. If we count O-formulae among the modal atoms, the expand rule is still sound, as are the following collapse rules. The proof of this is straightforward and is left to the reader.

$$O_i\varphi \wedge O_i\psi \rightarrow_\lambda O_i\varphi \text{ if } \lambda \vdash O_i\varphi \supset O_i\psi \qquad (O^1)$$

$$O_i\varphi \wedge \neg O_i\psi \rightarrow_\lambda \bot \text{ if } \lambda \vdash O_i\varphi \supset O_i\psi \qquad (O^2)$$

$$O_i\varphi \wedge O_k\psi \rightarrow_\lambda \bot \text{ if } \lambda \nvdash O_k\psi \supset B_k\varphi \qquad (O^3)$$

$$O_i\varphi \wedge \neg O_k\psi \rightarrow_\lambda O_k\varphi \text{ if } \lambda \nvdash O_k\psi \supset B_k\varphi \qquad (O^4)$$

4.2   Example: Supernormal Defaults

The property corresponding to the statement "the proposition φ holds by default" is formalized in Æ by the formula $b_k\varphi \supset \varphi$ within the scope of an O_i-modality for a $k \preceq i$. We will refer to this formula as a *default conditional*. To demonstrate basic properties of the representation we will address an example with two defaults. Let φ_1 and φ_2 be propositional and let d_1 be $b_1\varphi_1 \supset \varphi_1$ and d_2 be $b_2\varphi_2 \supset \varphi_2$. Prioritizing defaults amounts to constraining the order in which defaults are tested. In Æ we can give the default representation a behaviour of this sort by exploiting confidence levels and the persistence property. To represent this in Æ we introduce three levels of confidence. Let $I = \{0, 1, 2\}$ and $0 \prec 1 \prec 2$. Letting the $\prec$-minimum 0 identify the modality of full conviction, the following formula Bel defines the default structure:

$$O_0\kappa \wedge O_1(\kappa \wedge d_1) \wedge O_2(\kappa \wedge d_1 \wedge d_2) .$$

The following are theorems of Æ:

$$\neg\Diamond(\kappa \wedge \varphi_1), \neg\Diamond(\kappa \wedge \varphi_2) \vdash \text{Bel} \equiv O_0\kappa \wedge O_1\kappa \wedge O_2\kappa$$

$$\neg\Diamond(\kappa \wedge \varphi_1), \Diamond(\kappa \wedge \varphi_2) \vdash \text{Bel} \equiv O_0\kappa \wedge O_1\kappa \wedge O_2(\kappa \wedge \varphi_2)$$

$$\Diamond(\kappa \wedge \varphi_1), \neg\Diamond(\kappa \wedge \varphi_1 \wedge \varphi_2) \vdash \text{Bel} \equiv O_0\kappa \wedge O_1(\kappa \wedge \varphi_1) \wedge O_2(\kappa \wedge \varphi_1)$$

$$\Diamond(\kappa \wedge \varphi_1 \wedge \varphi_2) \vdash \text{Bel} \equiv O_0\kappa \wedge O_1(\kappa \wedge \varphi_1) \wedge O_2(\kappa \wedge \varphi_1 \wedge \varphi_2)$$

If the logical space λ entails both $\Diamond(\kappa \wedge \varphi_1), \Diamond(\kappa \wedge \varphi_2)$ and $\neg\Diamond(\kappa \wedge \varphi_1 \wedge \varphi_2)$, the two defaults will be in mutual conflict if preference is not given to one of them. However, since $\lambda \vdash \Diamond(\kappa \wedge \varphi_1) \wedge \neg\Diamond(\kappa \wedge \varphi_1 \wedge \varphi_2)$, and the third case applies in the representation above (in which d_1 is given preference). There is hence no ambiguity about the belief state, a property which always holds when $(I, \prec)$ is a tree with a single default conditional attached to each modality defined over I.

We will illustrate the rewriting procedure in some detail to analyze the four cases above. First $O_1(\kappa \wedge d_1)$ and $O_2(\kappa \wedge d_1 \wedge d_2)$ are expanded wrt. $B_1\neg\varphi_1$:

$$O_1(\kappa \wedge d_1) \rightarrow_{B_1\neg\varphi_1} (O_1\kappa \wedge B_1\neg\varphi_1) \vee (O_1(\kappa \wedge \varphi_1) \wedge \neg B_1\neg\varphi_1)$$

$$O_2(\kappa \wedge d_1 \wedge d_2) \rightarrow_{B_1\neg\varphi_1} (O_2(\kappa \wedge d_2) \wedge B_1\neg\varphi_1) \vee (O_2(\kappa \wedge \varphi_1 \wedge d_2) \wedge \neg B_1\neg\varphi_1)$$

This provides us with two more formulae we need to expand.

$$O_2(\kappa \wedge d_2) \rightarrow_{B_2\neg\varphi_2} (O_2\kappa \wedge B_2\neg\varphi_2) \vee (O_2(\kappa \wedge \varphi_2) \wedge \neg B_2\neg\varphi_2)$$

$$O_2(\kappa \wedge \varphi_1 \wedge d_2) \rightarrow_{B_2\neg\varphi_2} (O_2(\kappa \wedge \varphi_1) \wedge B_2\neg\varphi_2) \vee (O_2(\kappa \wedge \varphi_1 \wedge \varphi_2) \wedge \neg B_2\neg\varphi_2)$$

Now, let

$$\begin{aligned}
\psi_1 &= O_1\kappa \wedge B_1\neg\varphi_1 & \psi_2 &= O_1(\kappa \wedge \varphi_1) \wedge \neg B_1\neg\varphi_1 \\
\psi_3 &= O_2\kappa \wedge B_2\neg\varphi_2 & \psi_4 &= O_2(\kappa \wedge \varphi_2) \wedge \neg B_2\neg\varphi_2 \\
\psi_5 &= O_2(\kappa \wedge \varphi_1) \wedge B_2\neg\varphi_2 & \psi_6 &= O_2(\kappa \wedge \varphi_1 \wedge \varphi_2) \wedge \neg B_2\neg\varphi_2
\end{aligned}$$

Then Bel fully expanded is

$$O_0\kappa \wedge (\psi_1 \vee \psi_2) \wedge (((\psi_3 \vee \psi_4) \wedge B_1\neg\varphi_1) \vee ((\psi_5 \vee \psi_6) \wedge \neg B_1\neg\varphi_1)) \ .$$

The reductions can now be defined for each of the four cases separately. To illustrate the use of the characteristic formula ρ we will in each case select a ρ such that $\lambda(\rho)$ yields the premisses of the theorem we want to prove.

Case 1. In this case we will use $\rho = \kappa \supset (\neg\varphi_1 \wedge \neg\varphi_2)$. It is easy to see that $\lambda_\rho \vdash \neg\Diamond(\kappa \wedge \varphi_1) \wedge \neg\Diamond(\kappa \wedge \varphi_2)$. We apply the collapse rules on $\psi_1 - \psi_6$:

$$\begin{aligned}
O_1\kappa \wedge B_1\neg\varphi_1 &\rightarrow_\lambda O_1\kappa & O_2(\kappa \wedge \varphi_2) \wedge \neg B_2\neg\varphi_2 &\rightarrow_\lambda \bot \\
O_1(\kappa \wedge \varphi_1) \wedge \neg B_1\neg\varphi_1 &\rightarrow_\lambda \bot & O_2(\kappa \wedge \varphi_1) \wedge B_2\neg\varphi_2 &\rightarrow_\lambda O_2(\kappa \wedge \varphi_1) \\
O_2\kappa \wedge B_2\neg\varphi_2 &\rightarrow_\lambda O_2\kappa & O_2(\kappa \wedge \varphi_1 \wedge \varphi_2) \wedge \neg B_2\neg\varphi_2 &\rightarrow_\lambda \bot
\end{aligned}$$

Bel has now been reduced to

$$O_0\kappa \wedge O_1\kappa \wedge ((O_2\kappa \wedge B_1\neg\varphi_1) \vee (O_2(\kappa \wedge \varphi_1) \wedge \neg B_1\neg\varphi_1)) \ .$$

In order to further collapse the formula, we need to put it on disjunctive normal form: $(O_0\kappa \wedge O_1\kappa \wedge O_2\kappa \wedge B_1\neg\varphi_1) \vee (O_0\kappa \wedge O_1\kappa \wedge O_2(\kappa \wedge \varphi_1) \wedge \neg B_1\neg\varphi_1)$. Since $\rho \vdash \kappa \supset \neg\varphi_1$, $O_1\kappa \wedge B_1\neg\varphi_1 \rightarrow_\lambda O_1\kappa$ and $O_1\kappa \wedge \neg B_1\neg\varphi_1 \rightarrow_\lambda \bot$. Hence $\lambda_\rho \vdash$ Bel $\equiv O_0\kappa \wedge O_1\kappa \wedge O_2\kappa$.

Case 2. Let $\rho = \kappa \supset (\neg\varphi_1 \wedge \varphi_2)$. Bel can be reduced to the following formula on disjunctive normal form:

$$(O_0\kappa \wedge O_1\kappa \wedge O_2(\kappa \wedge \varphi_2) \wedge B_1\neg\varphi_1) \vee (O_0\kappa \wedge O_1\kappa \wedge O_2(\kappa \wedge \varphi_1) \wedge \neg B_1\neg\varphi_1) \ .$$

Since $\rho \vdash \kappa \supset \neg\varphi_1$, $O_1\kappa \wedge B_1\neg\varphi_1 \rightarrow_\lambda O_1\kappa$ and $O_1\kappa \wedge \neg B_1\neg\varphi_1 \rightarrow_\lambda \bot$. Hence $\lambda_\rho \vdash \varphi \equiv O_0\kappa \wedge O_1\kappa \wedge O_2(\kappa \wedge \varphi_2)$.

Case 3. Let $\rho = \kappa \supset (\neg\varphi_1 \vee \neg\varphi_2)$. Bel reduces to

$$O_0\kappa \wedge O_1(\kappa \wedge \varphi_1) \wedge ((O_2(\kappa \wedge \varphi_2) \wedge B_1\neg\varphi_1) \vee (O_2(\kappa \wedge \varphi_1) \wedge \neg B_1\neg\varphi_1)) \ .$$

Since $\rho \nvdash (\kappa \wedge \varphi_2) \supset \neg\varphi_1$ and $\rho \nvdash (\kappa \wedge \varphi_1) \supset \neg\varphi_1$, $O_2(\kappa \wedge \varphi_2) \wedge B_1\neg\varphi_1 \rightarrow_\lambda \bot$ and $O_2(\kappa \wedge \varphi_1) \wedge \neg B_1\neg\varphi_1 \rightarrow_\lambda O_2(\kappa \wedge \varphi_1)$. Hence $\lambda_\rho \vdash \varphi \equiv O_0\kappa \wedge O_1(\kappa \wedge \varphi_1) \wedge O_2(\kappa \wedge \varphi_1)$.

Case 4. Let $\rho = \top$. Bel reduces to

$$O_0\kappa \wedge O_1(\kappa \wedge \varphi_1) \wedge ((O_2(\kappa \wedge \varphi_2) \wedge B_1\neg\varphi_1) \vee (O_2(\kappa \wedge \varphi_1) \wedge \neg B_1\neg\varphi_1)) \ .$$

Since $\rho \nvdash (\kappa \wedge \varphi_2) \supset \neg\varphi_1$ and $\rho \nvdash (\kappa \wedge \varphi_1 \wedge \varphi_2) \supset \neg\varphi_1$, $O_2(\kappa \wedge \varphi_2)) \wedge B_1\neg\varphi_1 \rightarrow_\lambda \bot$ and $O_2(\kappa \wedge \varphi_1 \wedge \varphi_2) \wedge \neg B_1\neg\varphi_1 \rightarrow_\lambda O_2(\kappa \wedge \varphi_1 \wedge \varphi_2)$. Hence $\lambda_\rho \vdash \varphi \equiv O_0\kappa \wedge O_1(\kappa \wedge \varphi_1) \wedge O_2(\kappa \wedge \varphi_1 \wedge \varphi_2)$.

4.3 Proof of the Modal Reduction Theorem

Let β be a modal atom of depth 1, and let v be either $\bot$ or $\top$. A *Boolean binding* β/v is said to be a *Boolean binding for* φ if β occurs in φ. A *modal valuation* V of φ is a sequence of Boolean bindings $\langle \beta_1/v_1, \ldots, \beta_m/v_m \rangle$ such that (1) each β_{i+1}/v_{i+1} is a binding for $((\varphi[\beta_1/v_1]) \ldots)[\beta_i/v_i]$ and (2) the result $\varphi[V] = (((\varphi[\beta_1/v_1]) \ldots)[\beta_m/v_m])$ is propositional. Two modal valuations are *equivalent* if they contain exactly the same bindings. It is straightforward to show that $\varphi[V] = \varphi[W]$ if V and W are equivalent.

Define $\text{mod}(\varphi)$ as the set of all modal atoms occurring as subformulae of φ. If $m = |\text{mod}(\varphi)|$, there are $m' = 2^j$ non-equivalent modal valuations of φ which evaluates φ differently for a $j \leq m$. Let V be a modal valuation of φ. The following function is useful:

$$\phi(V, \varphi) = \bigwedge_{\beta/v \in V} (\beta \equiv v) \ .$$

$\phi(V, \varphi)$ is equivalent to a conjunction of the modal atoms in the bindings in V, negated iff bound to $\bot$. As an example, let $\varphi = C_1(p \wedge B_2q)$, and let $V = \langle B_2q/\top, C_1(p \wedge \top)/\bot \rangle$. Then $\phi(V, \varphi) = (B_2q \equiv \top) \wedge (C_1(p \wedge \top) \equiv \bot)$, which is equivalent to $B_2q \wedge \neg C_1p$.

Lemma 3. *Let $V_1, \ldots, V_{m'}$ be a maximal sequence of non-equivalent modal valuations of φ. Then*

$$\lambda \vdash O_i\varphi \equiv ((O_i\varphi[V_1] \wedge \phi(V_1, \varphi)) \vee \cdots \vee (O_i\varphi[V_{m'}] \wedge \phi(V_{m'}, \varphi))) \ .$$

Proof. Induction on $m = |\text{mod}(\varphi)|$. If $|\text{mod}(\varphi)| > 0$, a modal atom β of depth 1 occurs as a subformula of φ. By Lemma 1, $O_i\varphi$ expands to $(O_i\varphi[\beta/\top] \wedge \beta) \vee (O_i\varphi[\beta/\bot] \wedge \neg\beta)$. *Base step:* Assume $\text{mod}(\varphi) = \{\beta\}$. Let $V_1 = \langle \beta/\top \rangle$ and $V_2 = \langle \beta/\bot \rangle$. Then $\lambda \vdash O_i\varphi \equiv ((O_i\varphi[V_1] \wedge \beta) \vee (O_i\varphi[V_2] \wedge \neg\beta))$. *Induction step:* $|\text{mod}(\varphi[\beta/\top])| = |\text{mod}(\varphi[\beta/\bot])| = k - 1$, thus there is some $\beta \in \text{mod}(\varphi)$ such that $\beta \notin \text{mod}(\varphi[\beta/\top]) \cup \text{mod}(\varphi[\beta/\bot])$. The induction hypothesis is that the lemma holds for $O_i\varphi[\beta/\top]$ and $O_i\varphi[\beta/\bot]$; the induction step now follows by a simple combinatorial argument. $\qquad\qquad\square$

Let $\varphi^I = O_1\varphi_1 \wedge \cdots \wedge O_n\varphi_n$ be an O_I-block, and let $V_1, \ldots, V_n$ be modal valuations of $\varphi_1, \ldots, \varphi_n$, respectively, such that $V = V_1 \cup \cdots \cup V_n$ is a modal valuation of $\varphi_1 \wedge \cdots \wedge \varphi_n$. If $\psi^I = O_1\varphi_1[V_1] \wedge \cdots \wedge O_n\varphi_n[V_n]$, ψ^I is said to be the *expansion candidate* of φ^I wrt. V.

Lemma 4. *Let* $\varphi^I = O_1\varphi_1 \wedge \cdots \wedge O_n\varphi_n$ *and* $m = |\text{mod}(\varphi_1) \cup \cdots \cup \text{mod}(\varphi_n)|$. *Let* $V_1, \ldots, V_{m'}$ *be a maximal sequence of non-equivalent modal valuations of* $\varphi_1 \wedge \cdots \wedge \varphi_n$ *and* $\psi_1^I, \ldots, \psi_{m'}^I$ *be the expansion candidates of* φ^I *wrt.* $V_1, \ldots, V_{m'}$, *respectively. Then*

$$\lambda \vdash \varphi^I \equiv ((\psi_1^I \wedge \phi(V_1, \varphi^I)) \vee \cdots \vee (\psi_{m'}^I \wedge \phi(V_{m'}, \varphi^I))) \ .$$

Proof. Induction on n, with the aid of Lemma 3. $\qquad\qquad\square$

We now complete the proof of the Modal reduction theorem. Let φ^I be an O_I-block. Given a logical space, φ^I is equivalent to a formula on disjunctive normal form where each conjunction consists entirely of modal literals of depth 1 and prime O_i-formula for all $i \in I$. This follows directly from Lemma 4. Because every conjunction has formulae of the form $O_i\psi$, ψ propositional, for all $i \in I$ as conjuncts, the collapse rules always apply such that the conjunction itself is either inconsistent, or every other modal literal in the conjunction is removed by a collapse.

4.4   Complexity

If a problem is at least as hard as the hardest problem in a complexity class C, it is *C-hard*. A problem in C that is also C-hard, is *C-complete*. On the first level of the *polynomial hierarchy* we find the familiar classes $\Delta_1^p = \text{P}$, $\Sigma_1^p = \text{NP}$ and $\Pi_1^p = \text{coNP}$. Propositional satisfiability and validity are NP- and coNP-complete respectively. On level 2 we find the versions of the level 1 classes that have access to an NP oracle (they can solve any problem in NP in constant time), most notably $\Sigma_2^p = \text{NP}^{\text{NP}} = \text{NP}^{\text{coNP}}$.

Testing the preconditions for the collapse rules can be carried out completely within propositional logic by using the characteristic formula ρ instead of λ.

Lemma 5. *For any propositional* φ *and* ψ:

$$\lambda_\rho \vdash O_k\varphi \supset B_k\psi \text{ iff } \rho \vdash \varphi \supset \psi$$

$$\lambda_\rho \vdash O_k\varphi \supset C_k\psi \text{ iff } \rho \vdash \neg\varphi \supset \psi$$

$$\lambda_\rho \vdash O_k\varphi \supset O_k\psi \text{ iff } \rho \vdash \varphi \equiv \psi$$

Proof. In this proof $M \vDash \xi$ means that $M \vDash_x \xi$ for every point x in the model M. Observe that for and propositional φ and any model M, $M \vDash \lambda_\rho \wedge \varphi$ iff $\rho \vdash \varphi$. $\lambda_\rho \wedge O_k \varphi$ has a unique model M. $M \vDash B_k \psi$ iff $U_k^+ \subseteq \|\psi\|$ iff $\|\varphi\| \subseteq \|\psi\|$ iff $M \vDash \varphi \supset \psi$ iff $\rho \vdash \varphi \supset \psi$. $M \vDash C_k \psi$ iff $U_k^- \subseteq \|\psi\|$ iff $\|\neg\varphi\| \subseteq \|\psi\|$ iff $M \vDash \neg\varphi \supset \psi$ iff $\rho \vdash \neg\varphi \supset \psi$. The last equivalence follows from the first two, as $M \vDash C_k \neg \psi$ iff $M \vDash \psi \supset \varphi$.   □

In order to prove Σ_2^p-membership we need an algorithm which nondeterministically generates a possible expansion, and then with a linear (in the size of the input formula) number of coNP-complete calls, determines whether it really is an expansion.

Algorithm 1. Does the O_I-block φ^I have a $\lambda(\rho)$-expansion in the logic $Æ_\rho$? Nondeterministically generate an expansion candidate ψ^I of φ^I wrt. some modal valuation V. Then determine whether (1) ψ^I is $Æ_\rho$-consistent, and if it is, determine whether (2) $\psi^I \wedge \phi(V, \varphi^I)$ is $Æ_\rho$-consistent. If both (1) and (2) are true, ψ^I is a $\lambda(\rho)$-expansion, otherwise it is not.

Theorem 4. *The problem of determining whether the O_I-block φ^I has a $\lambda(\rho)$-expansion in the logic $Æ_\rho$ is Σ_2^p-complete.*

Proof. Membership: Conditions (1) and (2) of Algorithm 1 can be checked with $|I| - 1$ and $|\text{mod}(\varphi_1) \cup \cdots \cup \text{mod}(\varphi_n)|$ propositional validity tests respectively, where $\varphi^I = O_1\varphi_1 \wedge \cdots \wedge O_n\varphi_n$. ψ^I is inconsistent iff it violates persistence. As ψ^I is of the form $O_1\psi_1 \wedge \cdots \wedge O_n\psi_n$ for propositional $\psi_1, \ldots, \psi_n$, persistence is violated iff $O_i\psi_i$ and $O_k\psi_k$ are conjuncts, $i \prec k$ and $\nvdash_\rho \psi_k \supset \psi_i$. *Hardness:* Since $Æ_T$ is equivalent to the propositional fragment of Levesque's system, determining whether a formula of the form $O_k\varphi$ is satisfiable in $Æ_T$ is equivalent to determining whether $\{\varphi\}$ has a stable expansion in autoepistemic logic [8], a problem which is Σ_2^p-hard [4].   □

5   History and Future Work

The present work was initiated by the third author's doctoral thesis [14], in which the Modal reduction theorem for the system $Æ_T$ was first established. The theorem for Levesque's system has later been discovered independently by Levesque and Lakemeyer and appears as Corollary 9.5.6 in [9]; their proof is similar in style to the proof here but with a less general transformation strategy. Details for proofs of Theorem 1 can be found in the third author's doctoral thesis and (for the single modality case) in Segerberg's response to this work [13]. The philosophical conception of the semantics is due to Johan W. Klüwer and is discussed in much more detail in [6].

In the language of $Æ$ formulated in this paper, it is not possible to express properties about indices in I or about the preference relation $\prec$ within the language. It would be interesting to see whether the techniques of term-modal logics [3] can be applied also to $Æ$, possibly with a cautious introduction of quantifiers. If the language is extended to decidable fragments of first-order logic, it can presumably still be used to represent defaults along the lines sketched in this paper. The point is that the term universe must be finite. We must also restrict the language to formulae in Σ_0^1, like $\Diamond\exists x$ bird(x), and formulae in Π_0^1 like $\Box\forall x(\text{penguin}(x) \supset \text{bird}(x))$. Such formulae do not generate new terms and hence reduce to propositional logic. In this way the system can be extended to restricted fragments of first-order logic which nevertheless are sufficient for describing a number of common-sense situations. Of course, if we extend the language to full first-order logic, the system can no longer be used to represent default reasoning along the lines sketched in this paper. In general it will then impossible be to represent the space of conceivability with a finite formula. In fact such systems suffer from a fundamental incompleteness property [5].

This paper is intended as a first publications in a series of papers with related results, including a cut-elimination theorem for a sequent calculus and extensions to multi-modal languages.

References

1. Delgrande, J. P., Schaub, T.: Expressing Preferences in Default Logic. Artificial Intelligence **123** (2000) 41–87
2. Engan, I., Lian, E. H., Waaler, A.: Reasoning with Prioritized Defaults in Only Knowing Logic. Unpublished report, University of Oslo
3. Fitting, M., Thalmann, L., Voronkov, A.: Term-Modal Logics. Studia Logica **69** (2001) 133–169
4. Gottlob, G.: Complexity Results for Nonmonotonic Logics. Journal of Logic and Computation **2** (1992) 397–425
5. Halpern, J. Y., Lakemayer, G.: Levesque's Axiomatization of Only Knowing is Incomplete. Artificial Intelligence **74** (1995) 381–387
6. Klüwer, J. W.: Contexts of Reasoning. PhD thesis, University of Oslo (forthcoming)
7. Konolige, K.: Hierarchic Autoepistemic Theories for Nonmonotonic Reasoning. Technical report, SRI International (1988)
8. Levesque, H. J.: All I Know: A Study in Autoepistemic Logic. Artificial Intelligence **42** (1990) 263–309
9. Levesque, H. J., Lakemeyer, G.: The Logic of Knowledge Bases. The MIT Press (2000)
10. Moore, R.: Semantical Considerations on Nonmonotonic Logic. Artificial Intelligence **25** (1985) 75–94
11. Rosati, R.: Complexity of Only Knowing: The Propositional Case. In: Logic Programming and Non-monotonic Reasoning. (1997) 76–91
12. Rosati, R.: A Sound and Complete Tableau Calculus for Reasoning about Only Knowing and Knowing at Most. Studia Logica **69** (2001) 171–191
13. Segerberg, K.: Some Modal Reduction Theorems in Autoepistemic Logic. Uppsala Prints and Preprints in Philosophy (1995)
14. Waaler, A.: Logical Studies in Complementary Weak S5. Doctoral thesis, University of Oslo (1994)

Time Granularities and
Ultimately Periodic Automata

Davide Bresolin, Angelo Montanari, and Gabriele Puppis

Dipartimento di Matematica e Informatica, Università di Udine
via delle Scienze 206, 33100 Udine, Italy
{bresolin,montana,puppis}@dimi.uniud.it

Abstract. The relevance of the problem of managing periodic phenomena is widely recognized in the area of knowledge representation and reasoning. One of the most effective attempts at dealing with this problem has been the addition of a notion of time granularity to knowledge representation systems. Different formalizations of such a notion have been proposed in the literature, following algebraic, logical, string-based, and automaton-based approaches. In this paper, we focus our attention on the automaton-based one, which allows one to represent a large class of granularities in a compact and suitable to algorithmic manipulation form. We further develop such an approach to make it possible to deal with (possibly infinite) sets of granularities instead of single ones. We define a new class of automata, called Ultimately Periodic Automata, we give a characterization of their expressiveness, and we show how they can be used to encode and to solve a number of fundamental problems, such as the membership problem, the equivalence problem, and the problem of granularity comparison. Moreover, we give an example of their application to a concrete problem taken from clinical medicine.

1 Introduction

The importance of managing periodic phenomena is widely recognized in a variety of applications in the areas of artificial intelligence and databases, including planning, natural language processing, temporal database inter-operability, data mining, and time management in workflow systems. One of the most effective attempts at dealing with this problem has been the addition of a notion of time granularity to knowledge and database systems. Different time granularities can be used to specify the occurrence times of different classes of events. For instance, the temporal characterizations of a flight departure, a business appointment, and a birthdate are usually given in terms of minutes, hours, and days, respectively. Furthermore, the ability of properly relating different time granularities is needed to process temporal information. As an example, when a computation involves pieces of information expressed at different time granularities, the system must integrate them in a principled way. Such an integration presupposes the formalization of the notion of granularity and the analysis of the relationships between different time granularities.

J.J. Alferes and J. Leite (Eds.): JELIA 2004, LNAI 3229, pp. 513–525, 2004.

According to a commonly accepted perspective [1], any time granularity can be viewed as the partitioning of a given temporal domain in groups of elements, where each group is perceived as an indivisible unit (a granule). In particular, most granularities of interest are modeled as infinite sequences of granules that present a repeating pattern and, possibly, temporal gaps within and between granules. Even though conceptually clean, this point of view does not address the problem of finitely (and compactly) representing granularities to make it possible to deal with them in an effective (and efficient) way. In the literature, many different approaches to the management of time granularities have been proposed (we briefly survey them in Section 2). In this paper, we outline a general framework for time granularity that generalizes the automaton-based approach originally proposed by Dal Lago and Montanari in [6] by making it possible to deal with (possibly infinite) sets of granularities rather than single granularities. We give a characterization of ω-regular languages consisting of ultimately periodic words only, and we exploit such a characterization to define a proper subclass of Büchi automata, called Ultimately Periodic Automata (UPA), which includes all and only the Büchi automata that recognize ω-regular languages of ultimately periodic words. UPA allow one to encode single granularities, (possibly infinite) sets of granularities which have the same repeating pattern and different prefixes, and sets of granularities characterized by a finite set of non-equivalent patterns (the notion of equivalent patterns is given in Section 3), as well as any possible combination of them.

The rest of the paper is organized as follows. First, we briefly survey the most relevant formalisms for time granularity proposed in the literature. Next, we define UPA and we show how to use them to represent sets of periodical granularities. Noticeable properties of (the languages recognized by) UPA are then exploited to solve a number of basic problems about sets of time granularities. We focus our attention on the following problems: (i) *emptiness* (to decide whether a given set of granularities is empty); (ii) *membership* (to decide whether a granularity belongs to a given set of granularities); (iii) *equivalence* (to decide whether two representations define the same set of granularities); (iv) *minimization* (to compute compact representations of a given set of granularities); (v) *comparison of granularities* (for any pair of sets of granularities $\mathcal{G}, \mathcal{H}$, to decide whether there exist $G \in \mathcal{G}$ and $H \in \mathcal{H}$ such that $G \sim H$, where $\sim$ is one of the usual relations between granularities, e.g, partition, grouping, refinement, and aligned refinement [1]). Successively, we briefly analyze variants and extensions of UPA. Finally, we show how to apply the proposed framework to a real-world application taken from clinical medicine. We conclude the paper with a short discussion about achieved results and future research directions.

2   Formal Systems for Time Granularity

Different formal systems for time granularity have been proposed in the literature, following algebraic, logical, string-based, and automaton-based approaches [10]. The set-theoretic/algebraic approach, that subsumes well-known formalisms

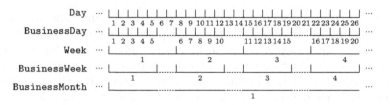

Fig. 1. Some examples of time granularities.

developed in the areas of artificial intelligence and temporal databases, such as the temporal interval collection formalism [12] and the slice formalism [15], is described in detail in [1]. It assumes the temporal domain to be isomorphic to $\mathbb{N}$, and it defines every *time granularity* as a partition $G \subseteq 2^T$ of a set $T \subseteq \mathbb{N}$ such that for every pair of distinct sets $g, g' \in G$ (hereafter called *granules*), we have that either $\forall t \in g, t' \in g'(t < t')$ or $\forall t \in g, t' \in g'(t' < t)$. This definition captures both time granularities that cover the whole temporal domain, such as Day, Week, and Month, and time granularities with gaps within and between granules, like, for instance, BusinessDay, BusinessWeek, and BusinessMonth. Figure 1 depicts some of these granularities. For the sake of simplicity, we assume that both the first week and the first month start from the first day (such an assumption can be easily relaxed).

Various relations can be defined between pairs of granularities. Let us consider, for instance, the relations of grouping, refinement, partition, and aligned refinement (a large set of granularity relations is given in [1]). We have that a granularity G *groups into* (resp. *is refined by*) a granularity H if every granule of H is the union of some granules (resp. is contained in some granule) of G; moreover, a granularity G *partitions* a granularity H if G groups into H and G refines H; finally, a granularity G is an *aligned refinement* of H if, for every positive integer n, the n-th granule of G is included in the n-th granule of H. In the case of Figure 1, we have that Day groups into BusinessMonth, BusinessDay refines Week, Day partitions Week, and BusinessWeek is an aligned refinement of Week.

A symbolic representation of a significant class of time granularities has been obtained by means of the formalism of *Calendar Algebra* (CA) [16]. Such a formalism represents time granularities as expressions built up from a finite set of basic granularities through the application of suitable algebraic operators. For instance, the granularity Week can be generated by applying the operator $Group_7$ to the granularity Day. The operations of CA reflect the ways in which people define new granularities from existing ones, and thus CA turns out to be a fairly natural formalism. In despite of that, it suffers from some non-trivial drawbacks: it does not address in a satisfactory way some basic problems of obvious theoretical and practical importance, such as the equivalence problem, and it only partially works out, in a rather complex way, other relevant problems, such as the problem of granularity conversion [11].

A string-based model for time granularities has been proposed by Wijsen [18]. Infinite granularities are modeled as infinite words over an alphabet con-

sisting of three symbols, namely, ■ (filler), □ (gap), and ≀ (separator), which
are respectively used to denote time points covered by some granule, to denote time points not covered by any granule, and to delimit granules. Wijsen
focuses his attention on the class of periodical granularities, that is, to granularities that, ultimately, periodically groups time points of the underlying temporal domain. Periodical granularities can be identified with ultimately periodic
words, and they can be finitely represented by specifying a (possibly empty)
prefix and a repeating pattern. As an example, the granularity BusinessWeek
■■■■■□□ ≀ ■■■■■□□ ≀ ... can be encoded by the empty prefix ε and the
repeating pattern ■■■■■□□≀. In order to solve the equivalence problem, Wijsen defines a suitable *aligned form*, which forces separators to occur immediately
after an occurrence of ■ (in such a case, one can encode each occurrence of the
substring ■≀ by means of a single symbol ◄). The aligned form guarantees a
one-to-one correspondence between strings and granularities, thus providing a
straightforward solution to the equivalence problem.

The idea of viewing time granularities as ultimately periodic strings establishes a natural connection with the field of formal languages and automata.
The basic idea underlying the automaton-based approach to time granularity is
simple: we take an automaton $\mathcal{A}$ recognizing a *single* ultimately periodic word
$u \in \{\square, \blacksquare, \blacktriangleleft\}^\omega$ and we say that $\mathcal{A}$ represents the granularity G if and only if u
represents G. Such an automaton-based approach to time granularity has been
proposed by Dal Lago and Montanari in [6], and later revisited by Dal Lago,
Montanari, and Puppis in [7,8]. The resulting framework views granularities
as strings generated by a specific class of automata, called Single-String Automata (SSA). In order to compactly encode the redundancies of the temporal
structures, SSA are endowed with counters ranging over discrete finite domains
(Extended SSA, ESSA for short). Properties of ESSA have been exploited to efficiently solve the equivalence and the granule conversion problems for single time
granularities. Moreover, the relationships between ESSA and Calendar Algebra
have been investigated in [7], where a number of algorithms that map Calendar
Algebra expressions into automaton-based representations of time granularities
are given. Such an encoding allows one to reduce problems about Calendar Algebra expressions to equivalent problems for ESSA. This suggests an alternative
point of view on the automaton-based framework: besides a formalism for the
direct specification of granularities, automata can be viewed as a low-level operational formalism into which high-level granularity specifications, such as those
of Calendar Algebra, can be mapped.

The choice of Propositional Linear Temporal Logic (LTL for short) as a
logical tool for granularity management has been advocated by Combi et al. [5].
Granularities are defined as models of LTL formulas, where suitable propositional
symbols are used to mark the endpoints of granules. In this way, a large set
of ω-regular granularities, such as, for instance, repeating patterns that can
start at an arbitrary time point (unanchored granularities), can be captured.
Moreover, problems like checking the consistency of a granularity specification or
the equivalence of two granularity expressions can be solved in a uniform way by

reducing them to the validity problem for LTL, which is known to be in PSPACE. An extension of LTL that replaces propositional variables by first-order formulas defining integer constraints, e.g., $x \equiv_k y$, has been proposed by Demri [9]. The resulting logic, denoted by PLTL^{mod}(Past LTL with integer periodicity constraints), generalizes both the logical framework proposed by Combi et al. and Dal Lago and Montanari's automaton-based one, and it allows one to compactly define granularities as periodicity constraints. In particular, the author shows how to reduce the equivalence problem for ESSA to the model checking problem for PLTL^{mod}(-automata), which turns out to be in PSPACE, as for LTL.

3   A New Class of Automata

In this paper, we extend the automaton-based approach to deal with (possibly infinite) sets of periodical granularities. In [6], Dal Lago and Montanari show how single granularities can be modeled by SSA, that is, Büchi automata recognizing single ultimately periodic words. In the following, we identify a larger (proper) subclass of Büchi automata that recognizes languages only consisting of ultimately periodic words, and we show how to exploit them to efficiently deal with time granularities (proof details are given in [2]).

3.1   Ultimately Periodic Automata

We first show that ω-regular languages only consisting of ultimately periodic words (periodical granularities) can be represented via suitable Büchi automata, that we call Ultimately Periodic Automata. By definition, ω-regular languages are sets of infinite words recognized by Büchi automata. They can be expressed as finite unions of sets of the form $U \cdot V^\omega$, where U and V are regular languages of finite words. From this, it easily follows that any ω-regular language is non-empty iff it contains an ultimately periodic word. (An ultimately periodic word w is an infinite word of the form $u \cdot v^\omega$, where u and v ($\neq \varepsilon$) are finite words called the *prefix* and the *repeating pattern* of w, respectively.) From the closure properties of ω-regular languages, it follows that any ω-regular language L is uniquely identified by the set $UP(L)$ of its ultimately periodic words, that is, for every pair of ω-regular languages L, L', $L = L'$ iff $UP(L) = UP(L')$.

The following theorem provides a characterization of ω-regular languages of ultimately periodic words.

Theorem 1. *An ω-regular language L only consists of ultimately periodic words iff it is a finite union of sets $U \cdot \{v\}^\omega$, where $U \subseteq \Sigma^*$ is regular and v is a finite non-empty word.*

From Theorem 1, it follows that ω-regular languages of ultimately periodic words capture sets of granularities with possibly infinitely many prefixes, but with only a finite number of non-equivalent repeating patterns (we say that two patterns v and v' are equivalent iff they can be obtained by rotating and/or repeating a finite word v'').

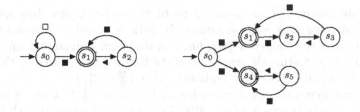

Fig. 2. Two examples of UPA.

Theorem 1 yields a straightforward definition of the class of automata that captures all and only the ω-regular languages of ultimately periodic words.

Definition 1. *An* Ultimately Periodic Automaton *(UPA) is a Büchi automaton* $\mathcal{A} = (Q, q_0, \Delta, F)$ *such that, for every* $f \in F$, *the strongly connected component of* f *is either a single transient state or a single loop with no exiting transitions.*

Theorem 2. *UPA recognize all and only the ω-regular languages of ultimately periodic words.*

Theorem 2 can be reformulated by stating that UPA-recognizable languages are all and only the ω-regular languages L such that $L = UP(L)$.

Figure 2 depicts two UPA recognizing the languages $\{\square\}^* \cdot \{\blacksquare \blacktriangleleft\}^\omega$ and $\{\blacksquare\blacksquare \blacktriangleleft\}^\omega \cup \{\blacksquare \blacktriangleleft\}^\omega$, respectively. The former represents the unanchored granularity that groups days two by two, while the latter represents two granularities that respectively group days two by two and three by three.

By exploiting the same construction methods used in the case of Büchi automata, one proves that UPA are closed under union, intersection, and concatenation with regular languages. Furthermore, it is trivial to see that UPA satisfy a weak form of closure under ω-exponentiation, namely, for every finite non-empty word v, there is an UPA recognizing the language $\{v\}^\omega$. On the contrary, from Theorem 1 it easily follows that UPA are not closed under complementation. Consider, for instance, the empty language $\emptyset$. Its complement is the set of all ultimately periodic words, which is not an UPA-recognizable language (UPA-recognizable languages must encompass finitely many non-equivalent repeating patterns).

Theorem 3. *UPA are closed under intersection, union, and concatenation with regular languages, but they are not closed under complementation.*

UPA can be successfully exploited to efficiently solve a number of problems involving sets of granularities.

- **Emptiness.** The emptiness problem is solved in polynomial time by testing the existence of a loop involving some final state (henceforth *final loop*) reachable from the initial state.

- **Membership.** The membership problem consists in deciding whether an UPA $\mathcal{A}$ recognizes a given ultimately periodic word w. Given an UPA $\mathcal{B}$ recognizing the singleton $\{w\}$, one can decide in polynomial time whether $w \in \mathcal{L}(\mathcal{A})$ by testing the emptiness of the language recognized by the product automaton $\mathcal{A} \times \mathcal{B}$ over the alphabet $\{(\genfrac{}{}{0pt}{}{\square}{\square}), (\blacksquare), (\blacktriangleleft)\}$.

- **Equivalence.** One can decide whether two given UPA $\mathcal{A}$ and $\mathcal{B}$ are equivalent by viewing them as generic Büchi automata, by computing their complements $\overline{\mathcal{A}}$ and $\overline{\mathcal{B}}$ (which are not necessarily UPA), and by testing the emptiness of both $\mathcal{L}(\mathcal{A}) \cap \mathcal{L}(\overline{\mathcal{B}})$ and $\mathcal{L}(\mathcal{B}) \cap \mathcal{L}(\overline{\mathcal{A}})$. Here we provide an alternative, direct and more efficient method for deciding the equivalence problem. The solution exploits a suitable canonical form of UPA, which turns out to be unique up to isomorphisms. Such a form is obtained by a canonization algorithm that works as follows [2]:
    1. minimize the patterns of the recognized words and the final loops (using Paige-Tarjan-Bonic algorithm [17]);
    2. minimize the prefixes of the recognized words;
    3. compute the minimum *deterministic* automaton for the prefixes of the recognized words (using Brzozowski algorithm [3]);
    4. build the canonical form by adding the final loops to the minimum automaton for the prefixes.

  Brzozowski's algorithm (used at step 3) requires exponential time and space in the worst case, but it turned out to be faster than the other available algorithms in many experiments [4]. As a result, the proposed algorithm for testing the equivalence of UPA outperforms the alternative algorithm using Büchi automata.

- **Minimization.** The minimization problem consists in computing the most compact representations for a given set of granularities. Such a problem is somehow connected to the equivalence problem, since in many cases minimal automata turn out to be unique up to isomorphisms. In the case of UPA, the minimization problem is PSPACE-complete and it may yield different solutions. A minimal UPA can be obtained by simply replacing step 3 in the canonization algorithm with the computation of a minimal *non-deterministic* automaton for the prefixes of the recognized words (using the construction developed in [14]).

- **Comparison of granularities.** Usual relations between granularities can be checked by looking at their automaton-based representations. In particular, granularity comparison problems can be easily reduced to the emptiness problem for suitable product automata. As an example, let us consider the partition relation. Let $\mathcal{A}_1$ and $\mathcal{A}_2$ be two UPA representing two sets of granularities $\mathcal{H}$ and $\mathcal{G}$, respectively. In order to check whether there exist two granularities $G \in \mathcal{G}$ and $H \in \mathcal{H}$ such that G *partitions* H, we first compute a product automaton $\mathcal{A}_3$ accepting all pairs of granularities that satisfy the 'partition' property, and then we test the emptiness of the recognized language. The automaton $\mathcal{A}_3$ is defined as follows:
    1. the set of states of $\mathcal{A}_3$ is $S_1 \times S_2 \times \{0, 1, 2\}$, where S_1 (resp. S_2) is the set of states of $\mathcal{A}_1$ (resp. $\mathcal{A}_2$);

2. the initial state of $\mathcal{A}_3$ is the tuple $(s_1, s_2, 0)$, where s_1 (resp. s_2) is the initial state of $\mathcal{A}_1$ (resp. $\mathcal{A}_2$);

3. the transition relation of $\mathcal{A}_3$ copies the transition relations of $\mathcal{A}_1$ and $\mathcal{A}_2$ in the first two components of states; it changes the third component from 0 to 1 when a final state of $\mathcal{A}_1$ occurs, from 1 to 2 when a final state of $\mathcal{A}_2$ occurs, and back to 0 immediately afterwards; finally, it constrains the recognized symbols to belong to the set $\{(\begin{smallmatrix}\square\\\square\end{smallmatrix}), (\blacksquare), (\blacktriangleleft), (\blacksquare)\}$;

4. the final states of $\mathcal{A}_3$ are all and only the tuples of the form $(s_1, s_2, 2)$.

3.2 Relaxed UPA

In the following, we introduce a new class of automata which are as expressive as UPA, but produce more compact representations of granularities. UPA structure is well-suited for algorithmic manipulation. In particular, it allows one to solve the equivalence problem by taking advantage of a suitable canonical form. However, UPA may present redundancies in their structure, due to the presence of duplicated loops encoding the same pattern. As an example, consider the automata of Figure 3. They both recognize the language expressed by the ω-regular expression $\square \blacktriangleleft^\omega \cup \square \blacktriangleleft (\blacktriangleleft\blacktriangleleft)^* \square^\omega$, but the automaton to the right has less states than the one to the left. Unfortunately, it is not an UPA, because UPA do not allow transitions to exit from final loops.

We define a new class of automata, that includes both automata of Figure 3, which only requires that, whenever an automaton leaves a final loop, it cannot reach it again.

Definition 2. *A Relaxed UPA (RUPA) is a Büchi automaton $\mathcal{A} = (Q, \Delta, q_0, F)$ such that, for every $f \in F$, the strongly connected component of f is either a single transient state or a single loop.*

The relation between UPA and RUPA is stated by the following theorem.

Theorem 4. *RUPA recognize all and only the UPA-recognizable languages.*

RUPA can be exploited to obtain more compact representations of granularities. To this end, one must take into consideration every strongly connected component S of an UPA and check whether it satisfies the following conditions:

1. S is a single loop that does not involve final states;

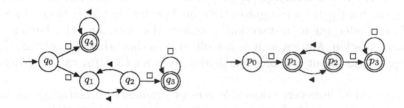

Fig. 3. UPA may present redundancies.

2. S encodes a single pattern v (up to rotations);
3. there exists a final loop C_f that encodes a pattern that is equivalent to v;
4. S and C_f have the same entering transitions.

If conditions 1-4 are satisfied, then S and C_f can be merged, preserving the recognized language. As an example, consider the UPA automaton to the left of Figure 3. The strongly connected component $\{q_1, q_2\}$ meets the above conditions: it is a single loop that does not involve final states, it encodes the single pattern ◄◄, which is equivalent to the pattern encoded by the final loop $\{q_4\}$, and $\{q_1, q_2\}$ and $\{q_4\}$ have the same entering transitions. Hence, q_4 can be removed from the automaton, provided that q_1 and q_2 become final states. The resulting RUPA automaton is exactly the one to the right of Figure 3.

Such a construction can be turned into an algorithm that transforms UPA into more compact RUPA by eliminating redundant final loops (if any). It first determines all the strongly connected components of UPA that meet conditions 1-4, and then it merges them. The algorithm turns out to be of polynomial time complexity. It must be noted that the algorithm transforms UPA into more compact, but not necessarily minimal, RUPA. The resulting RUPA are indeed not guaranteed to be of minimal size, even when the input UPA are minimal (and the minimization algorithm for UPA cannot be applied to RUPA).

3.3   Beyond (R)UPA

We conclude the section by briefly investigating possible extensions of (R)UPA. We have shown that the class of (R)UPA is the subclass of Büchi automata that recognize ω-regular languages of ultimately periodic words. As we shall illustrate in the next section, (R)UPA allow one to deal with meaningful real-world applications. Nevertheless, there are many sets of of periodical granularities which are not captured by (R)UPA.

In [2], we define a new class of automata, called *Three-Phase Automata* (3PA), which includes (R)UPA, that captures all and only the languages L for which there exists an ω-regular language L' such that $L = UP(L')$. This set of languages includes both ω-regular languages (the (R)UPA-recognizable languages) and non-ω-regular languages (the languages L such that $L = UP(L')$ $\subset L'$). In particular, unlike (R)UPA, 3PA are able to capture sets of granularities featuring an infinite number of non-equivalent repeating patterns. Computations of 3PA consist in three steps: (i) the automaton guesses the prefix of an ultimately periodic word, then (ii) it guesses its repeating pattern and stores it in a queue, and finally (iii) it recognizes the stored pattern infinitely many times. 3PA are closed under union, intersection, concatenation with a regular language, and complementation. Moreover, it is not difficult to show that the solutions to the basic problems about sets of granularities given for (R)UPA can be generalized to 3PA.

There exist, however, noticeable sets of granularities featuring an infinite number of non-equivalent repeating patterns which are not 3PA-recognizable. This is the case, for instance, of the language $\{(■^n ◄)^\omega | n \geq 0\}$ of all and only the granularities that group days n by n, with $n > 0$. All 3PA that recognize these repeating patterns must indeed also recognize all, but finitely many, combinations of them. Such a distinctive property of all 3PA-recognizable languages is captured by the following theorem [2].

Theorem 5. *Let* $L = UP(L')$ *where* L' *is defined by the* ω-*regular expression* $\bigcup_i U_i \cdot V_i^\omega$. *For any* i, *if* V_i *includes (at least) two non-equivalent patterns* v *and* v', *then* L *includes all ultimately periodic words* $u(v_o v_1 \dots v_n)^\omega$, *for all* $n \geq 0$, $u \in U_i$, *and* $v_i \in \{v, v'\}$.

4   A Real-World Application

The need of dealing with sets of time granularities arises in several application domains. We focus our attention on the medical domain of heart transplant patients. Posttransplantation guidelines require outpatients to take drugs and to submit to periodical visits for life. These requirements are usually collected in formal protocols with schedules specifying the therapies and the frequency of the check-ups. We report an excerpt of the guidelines for an heart transplant patient reported in [13]. Depending on the physical conditions of the patient, the guidelines can require, together with other treatments, an estimation of the glomerular filtration rate (GFR) with one of the following schedules:

- 3 months and 12 months posttransplantation and every year thereafter;
- 3 months and 12 months posttransplantation and every 2 years thereafter.

These protocols involve the so-called *unanchored granularities*, to manage the various admissible starting points for the scheduled therapies (and/or check-ups), as well as *sets of granularities with different repeating patterns*, to capture the set of distinct periodicities of the scheduled therapies. The ability of dealing with sets of granularities, and not only with single granularities, is thus needed to reason about protocols and patient schedules. As an example, since different protocols can be specified for the same class of patients by different people/institutions, it is a critical problem to decide whether two protocols define the same set of therapies/granularities (equivalence problem). The decidability of this problem gives the possibility of choosing the most compact, or most suitable, representation for a given protocol. Another meaningful reasoning task is that of checking whether a given therapy/granularity assigned to a patient satisfies the prescribed protocol, that is, whether it belongs to the set of therapies/granularities of the protocol (granularity comparison problem).

Let us consider this latter problem. Consider the above given (sub)set of therapies/check-ups of a protocol for hearth transplant patients. Given an UPA $\mathcal{A}$ encoding (the granularities of) such a set of therapies/check-ups and an UPA $\mathcal{B}$ representing the single granularity of the specific therapy (up to a certain date), the granularity comparison problem can be decided by checking the existence of a word in $\mathcal{L}(\mathcal{A})$ that properly relates to the one contained in $\mathcal{L}(\mathcal{B})$. For the sake of simplicity, we consider months of 30 days and years of 365 days (relaxing

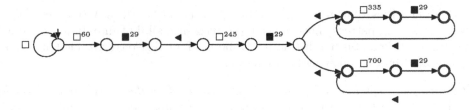

Fig. 4. The UPA-based specification of the protocol.

such a simplification is tedious, but trivial). The UPA $\mathcal{A}$ is depicted in Figure 4, where we use the shorthand $\circ \xrightarrow{a^n} \circ$ to denote a sequence of $n + 1$ states and n a-labeled transitions.

We model the granularity of the therapy assigned to the patient with a single ultimately periodic word v (equivalently, an SSA $\mathcal{B}$), where the occurrences of ◄ denote the days of the visits. We can check the consistency of the therapy with respect to the prescribed protocol by testing whether the granularity v is an *aligned refinement* of some granularity $u \in \mathcal{L}(\mathcal{A})$. Thus, the given consistency-checking problem can be seen as a particular case of granularity comparison problem. Given two words u and v that represent, respectively, granularities G and H, we have that H is an aligned refinement of G iff, for every $n \in \mathbb{N}^+$, $v[n] \in \{\blacksquare, \blacktriangleleft\}$ implies that $u[n] \in \{\blacksquare, \blacktriangleleft\}$ and that the words $v[1, n - 1]$ and $u[1, n - 1]$ encompass the same number of occurrences of ◄. Such a condition can be easily verified in polynomial time as follows. Given two UPA $\mathcal{A}$ and $\mathcal{B}$ representing two sets of granularities $\mathcal{G}$ and $\mathcal{H}$, (i) one constructs a product automaton $\mathcal{C}$ that accepts all pairs of granularities $G \in \mathcal{G}$ and $H \in \mathcal{H}$ such that H is an aligned-refinement of G, and then (ii) he/she tests the emptiness of the language recognized by $\mathcal{C}$.

As an example, consider the following instance of the temporal relation VISITS(PatientId, Date, Treatment).

PatientId	Date (MM/DD/YYYY)	Treatment
1001	02/10/2003	transplant
1001	04/26/2003	GFR
1002	06/07/2003	GFR
1001	06/08/2003	biopsy
1001	02/10/2004	GFR
1001	01/11/2005	GFR
1001	01/29/2006	GFR

By properly selecting records, we can build the granularity of GFR measurements for the patient identified by 1001. We represent this granularity as a single ultimately periodic word v (starting from 01/01/2003), in which the occurrences of ◄ denote the days of the visits. The UPA $\mathcal{B}$ recognizing v is depicted in Figure 5.

In order to check whether the granularity of GFR measurements for patient 1001 is an aligned refinement of some granularity in $\mathcal{L}(\mathcal{A})$, we must construct the

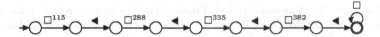

Fig. 5. The UPA representing GFR measurements for patient 1001.

product automaton for the relation of aligned refinement. Such an automaton recognizes the language

$$\left\{ (\begin{smallmatrix}\square\\\square\end{smallmatrix})^{100}(\begin{smallmatrix}\blacksquare\\\square\end{smallmatrix})^{15}(\begin{smallmatrix}\blacksquare\\\blacktriangleleft\end{smallmatrix})(\begin{smallmatrix}\blacksquare\\\square\end{smallmatrix})^{13}(\begin{smallmatrix}\blacktriangleleft\\\square\end{smallmatrix})(\begin{smallmatrix}\square\\\square\end{smallmatrix})^{245}(\begin{smallmatrix}\blacksquare\\\square\end{smallmatrix})^{29}(\begin{smallmatrix}\blacktriangleleft\\\square\end{smallmatrix})(\begin{smallmatrix}\square\\\square\end{smallmatrix})^{335}(\begin{smallmatrix}\blacksquare\\\blacktriangleleft\end{smallmatrix})(\begin{smallmatrix}\blacksquare\\\square\end{smallmatrix})^{28}(\begin{smallmatrix}\blacktriangleleft\\\square\end{smallmatrix})(\begin{smallmatrix}\square\\\square\end{smallmatrix})^{335}. \right.$$

$$\left. \cdot(\begin{smallmatrix}\blacksquare\\\square\end{smallmatrix})^{18}(\begin{smallmatrix}\blacksquare\\\blacktriangleleft\end{smallmatrix})(\begin{smallmatrix}\blacksquare\\\square\end{smallmatrix})^{10}(\begin{smallmatrix}\blacktriangleleft\\\square\end{smallmatrix})\left((\begin{smallmatrix}\square\\\square\end{smallmatrix})^{335}(\begin{smallmatrix}\blacksquare\\\square\end{smallmatrix})^{29}(\begin{smallmatrix}\blacktriangleleft\\\square\end{smallmatrix})\right)^{\omega} \right\}$$

over the alphabet $\{(\begin{smallmatrix}\square\\\square\end{smallmatrix}), (\begin{smallmatrix}\blacksquare\\\square\end{smallmatrix}), (\begin{smallmatrix}\blacktriangleleft\\\square\end{smallmatrix}), (\begin{smallmatrix}\blacksquare\\\square\end{smallmatrix}), (\begin{smallmatrix}\blacksquare\\\blacktriangleleft\end{smallmatrix}), (\begin{smallmatrix}\blacktriangleleft\\\blacksquare\end{smallmatrix}), (\begin{smallmatrix}\blacktriangleleft\\\blacktriangleleft\end{smallmatrix})\}$. Since the resulting language is not empty, we can conclude that the therapy satisfies the prescribed protocol.

5   Discussion

In this paper, we developed an original automaton-based approach to the management of sets of granularities. We defined a new class of automata, called UPA, that allow one to represent sets of granularities having possibly infinitely many different prefixes and a finite number of non-equivalent repeating patterns. We showed how well-known results coming from automata theory can be exploited to solve a number of meaningful problems about sets of granularities. In particular, we provided effective solutions to the problems of emptiness, membership, equivalence, minimization, and comparison of granularities for UPA. Furthermore, we discussed variants and extensions of UPA (RUPA and 3PA) that increase compactness and expressiveness of granularity representations. Finally, we applied the proposed framework to a case study taken from the domain of clinical medicine. More specifically, we showed that UPA can be used to specify medical guidelines and to check whether concrete therapy plans conform to them.

As for open problems, on the one hand we are looking for larger classes of languages of ultimately periodic words that extends the class of 3PA, possibly preserving closure and (some) decidability properties. On the other hand, we are currently looking for the (proper) fragment of PLTL^{mod} defining the temporal logic counterpart of UPA as well as for the logical counterpart of 3PA. Pairing the logical formalism with the automaton-based one would allow us to use the former as a high-level interface for the specification of granularities and the latter as an internal formalism for efficiently reasoning about them.

References

1. C. Bettini, S. Jajodia, and X.S. Wang. *Time Granularities in Databases, Data Mining, and Temporal Reasoning.* Springer, July 2000.

2. D. Bresolin, A. Montanari, and G. Puppis. Time granularities and ultimately periodic automata. Technical Report 24, Dipartimento di Matematica e Informatica, Università di Udine, Italy, October 2003.
3. J.A. Brzozowski. Canonical regular expressions and minimal state graphs for definite events. *Mathematical Theory of Automata*, 12:529–561, 1962.
4. C. Campeanu, K. Culik II, K. Salomaa, and S. Yu. State complexity of basic operations on finite languages. In *4th International Workshop on Implementing Automata (WIA'99)*, volume 2214 of *LNCS*, pages 60–70. Springer, 2001.
5. C. Combi, M. Franceschet, and A. Peron. Representing and reasoning about temporal granularities. *Journal of Logic and Computation*, 14(1):51–77, 2004.
6. U. Dal Lago and A. Montanari. Calendars, time granularities, and automata. In *7th International Symposium on Spatial and Temporal Databases (SSTD)*, volume 2121 of *LNCS*, pages 279–298. Springer, 2001.
7. U. Dal Lago, A. Montanari, and G. Puppis. Time granularities, calendar algebra, and automata. Technical Report 4, Dipartimento di Matematica e Informatica, Università di Udine, Italy, February 2003.
8. U. Dal Lago, A. Montanari, and G. Puppis. Towards compact and tractable automaton-based representations of time granularity. In *8th Italian Conference on Theoretical Computer Science (ICTCS)*, volume 2841 of *LNCS*, pages 72–85. Springer, 2003.
9. S. Demri. LTL over integer periodicity constraints (extended abstract). In *Proceedings of the 7th Int. Conf. on Foundations of Software Science and Computation Structures (FOSSACS)*, volume 2987 of *Lecture Notes in Computer Science*, pages 121–135. Springer, April 2004.
10. J. Euzenat and A. Montanari. Time granularity. In M. Fisher, D. Gabbay, and L. Vila, editors, *Handbook of Temporal Reasoning in Artificial Intelligence*. Elsevier, 2004.
11. M. Franceschet and A. Montanari. Time granularities in databases, data mining, and temporal reasoning, by Claudio Bettini, Sushil Jajodia, and Sean X. Wang (book review). *The Computer Journal*, 45(6):683–685, 2002.
12. B. Leban, D. McDonald, and D. Foster. A representation for collections of temporal intervals. In *AAAI National Conference on Artificial Intelligence*, volume 1, pages 367–371. AAAI Press, 1986.
13. Loma Linda University Medical Center. Pediatric heart transplantation protocol, 2002.
14. O. Matz and A. Potthoff. Computing small nondeterministic automata. In *Proceedings of the Workshop on Tools and Algorithms for the Construction and Analysis of Systems*, BRICS Notes Series, pages 74–88, 1995.
15. M. Niezette and J. Stevenne. An efficient symbolic representation of periodic time. In *International Conference on Information and Knowledge Management (CIKM)*, pages 161–168, Baltimore, MD, 1992. ACM Press.
16. P. Ning, S. Jajodia, and X.S. Wang. An algebraic representation of calendars. *Annals of Mathematics and Artificial Intelligence*, 36:5–38, 2002.
17. R. Paige, R.E. Tarjan, and R. Bonic. A linear time solution to the single function coarsest partition problem. *Theoretical Computer Science*, 40:67–84, 1985.
18. J. Wijsen. A string-based model for infinite granularities. In C. Bettini and A. Montanari, editors, *AAAI Workshop on Spatial and Temporal Granularities*, pages 9–16. AAAI Press, 2000.

Polynomial Approximations of Full Propositional Logic via Limited Bivalence

Marcelo Finger*

Computer Science Department
Institute of Mathematics and Statistics
University of São Paulo, Brazil
mfinger@ime.usp.br

Abstract. The aim of this paper is to study an anytime family of logics
that approximates classical inference, in which every step in the approximation can be decided in polynomial time. For clausal logic, this task has
been shown to be possible by Dalal [Dal96a,Dal96b]. However, Dalal's
approach cannot be applied to full classical logic.

In this paper we provide a family of logics, called *Limited Bivalence
Logics*, that approximates full classical logic. Our approach contains two
stages. In the first stage, a family of logics parameterised by a set of
formulas Σ is presented. A lattice-based semantics is given and a sound
and complete tableau-based proof-theory is developed. In the second
stage, the first family is used to create another approximation family,
in which every approximation step is shown to be polynomially decidable.

Keywords: Approximated Reasoning, Polynomial Approximations.

1 Introduction

The computational costs associated with logical reasoning have always been a
limitation to its use in the modelling of intelligent agents. Even if we restrict ourselves to classical propositional logic, deciding whether a set of formulas logically
implies a certain formula is a co-NP-complete problem [GJ79].

To address this problem, researchers have proposed several ways of approximating classical reasoning. Cadoli and Schaerf have proposed the use of approximate entailment as a way of reaching at least partial results when solving a
problem completely would be too expensive [SC95]. Their influential method is
parametric, that is, a set S of atoms is the basis to define a logic. As we add more
atoms to S, we get "closer" to classical logic, and eventually, when S contains
all propositional symbols, we reach classical logic. This kind of approximation
has been called "approximating from below" [FW04] and is useful for efficient
theorem proving.

The notion of approximation is also related with the notion of an *anytime
decision procedure*, that is an algorithm that, if stopped anytime during the

---

* Partly supported by CNPq grant PQ 300597/95-5 and FAPESP project 03/00312-0.

J.J. Alferes and J. Leite (Eds.): JELIA 2004, LNAI 3229, pp. 526–538, 2004.

computation, provides an approximate answer. Such an answer is of the form "yes" or "up to logic L_i in the family, the result is not provable". To remain inside a logic framework along the approximation process, it is necessary that every approximate logic L_i have a clear semantics, so that if the anytime process is interrupted at L_i, we know exactly where we are.

Dalal's approximation method [Dal96a] was designed such that each reasoner in an approximation family can be decided in polynomial time. Dalal's initial approach was algebraic only. A model-theoretic semantics was provided in [Dal96b]. However, this approach was restricted to clausal form logic only, its semantics had an unusual format, an no proof-theoretical presentation was given.

In this work, we generalise Dalal's approach, obtaining a polynomial approximation family for full propositional logic, with a lattice-based semantics and a tableau-based proof theory. We do that in two steps. The first step develops a family of logics of *Limited Bivalence* (LB), and provide a lattice-based semantics for it. The entailment $\models_{\Sigma}^{\text{LB}}$ is a parametric approximation on the set of formulas Σ that follows Cadoli and Schaerf's approximation paradigm. We also provide a tableau-based inference $\vdash_{\Sigma}^{\text{KELB}}$, and prove it sound and complete with respect to $\models_{\Sigma}^{\text{LB}}$. In the second step, we derive an inference $\vdash_{k}^{\text{KELB}}$ based on $\vdash_{\Sigma}^{\text{KELB}}$ and an entailment relation $\models_{k}^{\text{LB}}$ based on $\models_{\Sigma}^{\text{LB}}$, and obtain the soundness and completeness of $\vdash_{k}^{\text{KELB}}$ in terms of $\models_{k}^{\text{LB}}$. We then show that $\vdash_{k}^{\text{KELB}}$ is polynomially decidable.

This paper proceeds as follows. Section 2 presents Dalal's approximation strategy, its semantics and discuss its limitations. In Section 3 we present the family $\text{LB}(\Sigma)$; a semantics for full propositional $\text{LB}(\Sigma)$ is provided and the parametric entailment $\models_{\Sigma}^{\text{LB}}$ is presented; we also give a proof-theoretical characterisation based on KE-tableaux, $\vdash_{\Sigma}^{\text{KELB}}$. The soundness and completeness of $\vdash_{\Sigma}^{\text{KELB}}$ with respect to $\models_{\Sigma}^{\text{LB}}$ is proven in Section 4. The family of inference systems $\vdash_{k}^{\text{KELB}}$ and its semantics $\models_{k}^{\text{LB}}$ are presented in Section 5, and $\vdash_{k}^{\text{KELB}}$ is shown to be polynomially decidable.

Notation: Let $\mathcal{P}$ be a countable set of propositional letters. We concentrate on the classical propositional language $\mathcal{L}_C$ formed by the usual boolean connectives $\rightarrow$ (implication), $\wedge$ (conjunction), $\vee$ (disjunction) and $\neg$ (negation).

Throughout the paper, we use lowercase Latin letters to denote propositional letters, α, β, γ denote formulas, ϕ, ψ denote clauses and λ denote a literal. Uppercase Greek letters denote sets of formulas. By atoms(α) we mean the set of all propositional letters in the formula α; if Σ is a set of formulas, atoms(Σ) = $\bigcup_{\alpha \in \Sigma}$ atoms(α).

2   Dalal's Polynomial Approximation Strategy

Dalal [Dal96a] specifies a family of *anytime* reasoners based on an equivalence relation between formulas and on a restricted form of Cut Rule. The family is composed of a sequence of reasoners $\vdash_0, \vdash_1, \ldots$, such that each $\vdash_i$ is tractable, each $\vdash_{i+1}$ is at least as complete (with respect to classical logic) as $\vdash_i$, and for each theory there is a complete $\vdash_i$ to reason with it.

Dalal provides as an example a family of reasoners based on the classically sound but incomplete inference rule known as BCP (Boolean Constraint Propagation) [McA90], which is a variant of unit resolution [CL73]. Consider a theory as a set of clauses, where a disjunction of zero literals is denoted by **f**. Let $\sim \psi$ be the *complement* of the formula ψ obtained by pushing the negation inside in the usual way using De Morgan's Laws until the atoms are reached, at which point $\sim p = \neg p$ and $\sim \neg p = p$. The equivalence relation $=_{\mathrm{BCP}}$ is then defined as:

$$\{\mathbf{f}\} \cup \Gamma =_{\mathrm{BCP}} \{\mathbf{f}\}$$
$$\{\lambda, \sim\lambda \vee \lambda_1 \vee \ldots \vee \lambda_n\} \cup \Gamma =_{\mathrm{BCP}} \{\lambda, \lambda_1 \vee \ldots \vee \lambda_n\} \cup \Gamma$$

where λ, λ_i are literals. The inference $\vdash_{\mathrm{BCP}}$ is defined as $\Gamma \vdash_{\mathrm{BCP}} \psi$ iff $\Gamma \cup \{\sim \psi\} =_{\mathrm{BCP}} \{\mathbf{f}\}$.

Dalal [Dal96b] presents an example in which, for the theory $\Gamma_0 = \{p \vee q, p \vee \neg q, \neg p \vee s \vee t, \neg p \vee s \vee \neg t\}$, we both have $\Gamma_0 \vdash_{\mathrm{BCP}} p$ and $\Gamma_0, p \vdash_{\mathrm{BCP}} s$ but $\Gamma_0 \nvdash_{\mathrm{BCP}} s$.

This example shows that $\vdash_{\mathrm{BCP}}$ is unable to use a previously inferred clause p to infer s. Based on this fact comes the proposal of an anytime family of incomplete reasoners $\vdash_0^{\mathrm{BCP}}, \vdash_1^{\mathrm{BCP}}, \ldots$, where each $\vdash_k^{\mathrm{BCP}}$ is given by the following:

$$1. \quad \frac{\Gamma \vdash_{\mathrm{BCP}} \phi}{\Gamma \vdash_k^{\mathrm{BCP}} \phi} \qquad 2. \quad \frac{\Gamma \vdash_k^{\mathrm{BCP}} \psi \quad \Gamma, \psi \vdash_k^{\mathrm{BCP}} \phi}{\Gamma \vdash_k^{\mathrm{BCP}} \phi} \text{ for } |\psi| \leq k$$

where $|\psi|$, the size of a clause ψ, is the number of literals it contains.

The first rule tells us that every $\vdash_{\mathrm{BCP}}$-inference is also a $\vdash_k^{\mathrm{BCP}}$-inference. The second rule tells us that if ψ was inferred from a theory and it can be used as a further hypothesis to infer ϕ, and the size of ψ is at most k, then ϕ is can also be inferred from the theory.

Dalal shows that this is indeed an anytime family of reasoners, that is, for each k, $\vdash_k^{\mathrm{BCP}}$ is tractable, $\vdash_{k+1}^{\mathrm{BCP}}$ is as complete as $\vdash_k^{\mathrm{BCP}}$ and for each classically inferable $\Gamma \vdash \phi$ there is a k such that $\Gamma \vdash_k^{\mathrm{BCP}} \phi$.

In [Dal96b], a semantics for $\vdash_k^{\mathrm{BCP}}$ is proposed based on the notion of k-*valuations*. This semantics has a peculiar format: literals are evaluated to real values over the interval $[0, 1]$ but clauses are evaluated to real values over $[0, +\infty)$. A formula ψ is satisfied by valuation v if $v(\psi) \geq 1$. A k-*model* is a set V of k-valuations, such that if $\psi, |\psi| \leq k$, has a non-model in V, ie $v(\psi) < 1$, then it has a k-countermodel in V, ie $v(\psi) = 0$. It then defines $\Gamma \approx_k \psi$ iff there is no k-countermodel of ψ in any k-model of Γ. Here we simply state Dalal's main results.

Proposition 1 ([Dal96b]). *For every theory Γ and every clause ψ:*

i. $\Gamma \vdash_{\mathrm{BCP}} \psi$ iff $\Gamma \approx_0 \psi$ and $\Gamma \vdash_k^{\mathrm{BCP}} \psi$ iff $\Gamma \approx_k \psi$.

ii. $\Gamma \vdash_k^{\mathrm{BCP}} \psi$ can be decided in polynomial time.

Thus the inference $\vdash_k^{\mathrm{BCP}}$ is sound and complete with respect to $\approx_k$ for clausal form formulas and, for a fixed value of k, it can be decided in polynomial time.

Dalal's notion of a family of anytime reasoners has very nice properties. First, every step in the approximation is sound and can be decided in polynomial time. Second, the approximation is guaranteed to converge to classical inference. Third, every step in the approximation has a sound and complete semantics, enabling an anytime approximation process.

However, the method based on $\vdash_k^{BCP}$-approximations also has its limitations:

1. It only applies to clausal form formulas. Although every propositional formula is classically equivalent to a set of clauses, this equivalence may not be preserved in any of the approximation step. The conversion of a formula to clausal form is costly: one either has to add new propositional letters (increasing the complexity of the problem) or the number of clauses can be exponential in the size of the original formula. With regards to complexity, BCP is a form of resolution, and it is known that there are theorems that can be proven by resolution only in exponentially many steps [CS00].

2. Its non-standard semantics makes it hard to compare with other logics known in the literature, specially other approaches to approximation. Also, the semantics presented is impossible to generalise to non-clausal formulas.

3. The proof-theory for $\vdash_k^{BCP}$ is poor in computational terms. In fact, if we are trying to prove that $\Gamma \vdash_k^{BCP} \phi$, and we have shown that $\Gamma \nvdash_{BCP} \phi$, then we would have to guess a ψ with $|\psi| \leq k$, so that $\Gamma \vdash_k^{BCP} \psi$ and $\Gamma, \psi \vdash_k^{BCP} \phi$. Since the BCP-approximations provides no method to guess the formula ψ, this means that a computation would have to generate and test all the $O((2n)^k)$ possible clauses, where n is the number of propositional symbols occurring in Γ and ϕ.

In the following we present an approximation method that maintains all the positive aspects of $\vdash_k^{BCP}$ and avoids some of the criticism above. That is, it is applicable to all propositional formulas, whether clausal or not, and has a lattice-based semantics. This will allow non-resolution proof methods to be used in the approximation process. In particular, we present a tableaux based proof theory that is sound and complete with respect to the semantics. A family of reasoners is then built, each element of which is polynomially decidable.

3 The Family of Logics LB(Σ)

We present here the family of logics of *Limited Bivalence*, LB(Σ). This is a parametric family that approximates classical logic, in which every approximation step can be decided in polynomial time. Unlike $\vdash_k^{BCP}$, LB(Σ) is parameterised by a set of formulas Σ.

The family LB(Σ) can be applied to the full language of propositional logic, and not only to clausal form formulas, with an alphabet consisting of a countable set of propositional letters (atoms) $\mathcal{P} = \{p_0, p_1, \ldots\}$, and the connectives $\neg$, $\wedge$, $\vee$ and $\rightarrow$, and the usual definition of well-formed propositional formulas; the set of all well-formed formulas is denoted by $\mathcal{L}$. The presentation of LB is made in terms of a model theoretic semantics.

We require the parameter set Σ to be *closed under formula formation*, that is, if $\alpha \in \Sigma$ then $\neg\alpha \in \Sigma$; if $\alpha, \beta \in \Sigma$ then $\alpha \circ \beta \in \Sigma$, for $\circ \in \{\wedge, \vee, \rightarrow\}$.

3.1   Semantics of LB(Σ)

The semantics of LB(Σ) is based of a three-level lattice, $L = (L, \sqcap, \sqcup, 0, 1)$, where L is a countable set of elements $L = \{0, 1, \epsilon_0, \epsilon_1, \epsilon_2, \dots\}$ such that $0 \sqsubseteq \epsilon_i \sqsubseteq 1$ for every $i < \omega$ and $\epsilon_i \not\sqsubseteq \epsilon_j$ for $i \neq j$. The ϵ_i's are called *neutral* truth values. This three-level lattice is illustrated in Figure 1(a).

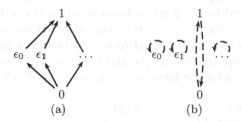

Fig. 1. The 3-Level Lattice (a) and its Converse Operation (b)

This lattice is enhanced with a *converse operation*, $\sim$, defined as: $\sim 0 = 1$, $\sim 1 = 0$ and $\sim \epsilon_i = \epsilon_i$ for all $i < \omega$. This is illustrated in Figure 1(b).

We next define the notion of an *unlimited valuation*, and then we limit it. An unlimited propositional valuation is a function $v_\Sigma : \mathcal{P} \rightarrow L$ that maps atoms to elements of the lattice. We extend v_Σ to all propositional formulas, $v_\Sigma : \mathcal{L} \rightarrow L$, in the following way:

$$v_\Sigma(\neg\alpha) = \sim v_\Sigma(\alpha)$$
$$v_\Sigma(\alpha \wedge \beta) = v_\Sigma(\alpha) \sqcap v_\Sigma(\beta)$$
$$v_\Sigma(\alpha \vee \beta) = v_\Sigma(\alpha) \sqcup v_\Sigma(\beta)$$
$$v_\Sigma(\alpha \rightarrow \beta) = \begin{cases} 1 & \text{if } v(\alpha) \sqsubseteq v(\beta) \\ \sim v_\Sigma(\alpha) \sqcup v_\Sigma(\beta) & \text{otherwise} \end{cases}$$

A *limited valuation* is a valuation that satisfies the following requirements with regards to whether a formula is or is not in the parameter set Σ:

(a) if $\alpha \in \Sigma$ then $v_\Sigma(\alpha)$ must be *bivalent*, that is, $v_\Sigma(\alpha)$ must satisfy the rules above for unlimited valuations and be such that $v_\Sigma(\alpha) = 0$ or $v_\Sigma(\alpha) = 1$;
(b) if $\alpha \notin \Sigma$ then either $v_\Sigma(\alpha)$ obeys the rules of unlimited valuations *or* $v_\Sigma(\alpha) = \epsilon_i$, for some ϵ_i.

These conditions above are called the Limited Bivalence Restrictions. The first conditions forces the elements of Σ to be bivalent. The second condition tells us that the truth value assigned to a formula $\alpha \notin \Sigma$ is not always *compositional*, for a neutral value may be assigned to α independently of the truth value of its components. This is the case so that the bivalence of $\alpha \in \Sigma$ can always be satisfied without forcing all α's subformulas to be bivalent.

If $\alpha \in \Sigma$ it is always possible to have $v_\Sigma(\alpha) \in \{0,1\}$ by making for every atom p in α, $v_\Sigma(p) \in \{0,1\}$. However, this is not the only possibility. For example, if $\beta, \gamma \notin \Sigma$ then we can make $v_\Sigma(\beta) = \epsilon_i \neq \epsilon_j = v_\Sigma(\gamma)$, so that $v_\Sigma(\beta \wedge \gamma) = 0$; similarly, we obtain $v_\Sigma(\beta \vee \gamma) = 1$ and $v_\Sigma(\beta \to \gamma) = 1$.

In the case of clausal form formulas, restriction (b) is not necessary provided we treat clauses as sets of literals [Fin04].

In the rest of this work, by a valuation v_Σ we mean a limited valuation subject to the conditions above.

A valuation v_Σ *satisfies* α if $v_\Sigma(\alpha) = 1$, and α is called *satisfiable*; a set of formulas Γ is satisfied by v_Σ if all its formulas are satisfied by v_Σ. A valuation v_Σ *contradicts* α if $v_\Sigma(\alpha) = 0$; if α is neither satisfied nor contradicted by v_Σ, we say that v_Σ is *neutral* with respect to α. A valuation is *classical* if it assigns only 0 or 1 to all proposition symbols, and hence to all formulas.

For example, consider the formula $p \to q$, and $\Sigma = \emptyset$. Then

- if $v_\Sigma(p) = 1$, then $v_\Sigma(p \to q) = v_\Sigma(q)$;
- if $v_\Sigma(p) = 0$, then $v_\Sigma(p \to q) = 1$;
- if $v_\Sigma(q) = 0$, then $v_\Sigma(p \to q) = v_\Sigma(p)$;
- if $v_\Sigma(q) = 1$, then $v_\Sigma(p \to q) = 1$;
- if $v_\Sigma(p) = \epsilon_p$ and $v_\Sigma(q) = \epsilon_q$, then $v_\Sigma(p \to q) = 1$;

The first four cases coincide with a classical behaviour. The last one shows that if p and q are mapped to distinct neutral values, then $p \to q$ will be satisfiable. Note that, in this case, $p \vee q$ will also be satisfiable, and that $p \wedge q$ will be contradicted.

3.2   LB-Entailment

The notion of a parameterised LB-Entailment, $\models_\Sigma^{LB}$, follows the spirit of Dalal's entailment relation, namely $\Gamma \models_\Sigma^{LB} \alpha$ if it is not possible to satisfy Γ and contradict α at the same time. More specifically, $\Gamma \models_\Sigma^{LB} \alpha$ if no valuation v_Σ such that $v_\Sigma(\Gamma) = 1$ also makes $v_\Sigma(\alpha) = 0$. Note that since this logic is not classic, if $\Gamma \models_\Sigma^{LB} \alpha$ and $v_\Sigma(\Gamma) = 1$ it is possible that α is either neutral or satisfied by v_Σ.

For example, we reconsider Dalal's example, where $\Gamma_0 = \{p \vee q, p \vee \neg q, \neg p \vee s \vee t, \neg p \vee s \vee \neg t\}$ and make $\Sigma = \emptyset$. We want to show that $\Gamma_0 \models_\Sigma^{LB} p$, $\Gamma_0, p \models_\Sigma^{LB} s$ but $\Gamma_0 \not\models_\Sigma^{LB} s$.

To see that $\Gamma_0 \models_\Sigma^{LB} p$, suppose there is a v_Σ such that $v_\Sigma(p) = 0$. Then we have $v_\Sigma(p \vee q) = v_\Sigma(q)$ and $v_\Sigma(p \vee \neg q) =\sim v_\Sigma(q)$. Since it is not possible to satisfy both, we cannot have $v_\Sigma(\Gamma_0) = 1$, so $\Gamma_0 \models_\Sigma^{LB} p$.

To show that $\Gamma_0, p \models_\Sigma^{LB} s$, suppose there is a v_Σ such that $v_\Sigma(s) = 0$ and $v_\Sigma(p) = 1$. Then $v_\Sigma(\neg p \vee s \vee t) = v_\Sigma(t)$ and $v_\Sigma(\neg p \vee s \vee \neg t) =\sim v_\Sigma(t)$. Again, it is not possible to satisfy both, so $\Gamma_0, p \models_\Sigma^{LB} s$.

Finally, to see that $\Gamma_0 \not\models_\Sigma^{LB} s$, take a valuation v_Σ such that $v_\Sigma(s) = 0, v_\Sigma(p) = \epsilon_p, v_\Sigma(q) = \epsilon_q, v_\Sigma(t) = \epsilon_t$. Then $v_\Sigma(\Gamma_0) = 1$.

However, if we enlarge Σ and make $p \in \Sigma$, then we have only two possibilities for $v_\Sigma(p)$. If $v_\Sigma(p) = 1$, we have already seen that no valuation that contradicts s will satisfy Γ_0. If $v_\Sigma(p) = 0$, we have also seen that no valuation that contradicts s will satisfy Γ_0. So for $p \in \Sigma$, we obtain $\Gamma_0 \models_\Sigma^{\mathrm{LB}} s$.

This example indicates that $\models_\emptyset^{\mathrm{LB}}$ behave in a similar way to $\vdash_{\mathrm{BCP}}$, and that by adding an atom to Σ we have a behaviour similar to $\vdash_1^{\mathrm{BCP}}$. As shown in [Fin04], this is not a coincidence.

An Approximation Process. As defined in [FW04], a family of logics, parameterised with a set Σ is said to be an approximation of classical logic "from below" if, increasing size of the parameter set Σ, we get closer to classical logic. That is, for $\emptyset \subseteq \Sigma' \subseteq \Sigma'' \subseteq \ldots \subseteq \mathcal{L}$ we have that,

$$\models_\emptyset^{\mathrm{LB}} \subseteq \models_{\Sigma'}^{\mathrm{LB}} \subseteq \models_{\Sigma''}^{\mathrm{LB}} \subseteq \ldots \subseteq \models_{\mathcal{L}}^{\mathrm{LB}} = \models_{\mathrm{CL}}$$

where $\models_{\mathrm{CL}}$ is classical entailment. It is clear that the family of logics $\mathsf{LB}(\Sigma)$ is an approximation of classical logic from below.

Note that the approximation of $\Gamma \models \alpha$ can be done in a finite number of steps for finite Σ, because when Σ contains all subformulas in $\Gamma \cup \{\alpha\}$ we are in classical logic.

3.3   Tableaux for $\mathsf{LB}(\Sigma)$

We present a proof theory for $\mathsf{LB}(\Sigma)$ based on KE-tableaux [DM94,D'A99], which we call $\mathsf{KELB}(\Sigma)$-tableaux. This is a variation of Smullyan's semantic tableaux [Smu68] that is more suitable to our purposes, for it incorporates the Cut rule in its expansion rules, unlike semantic tableaux which are based on cut-free formulation of logics. In fact, both $\vdash_k^{\mathrm{BCP}}$ and $\mathsf{LB}(\Sigma)$ are approximation families based on the limited validity of the Cut inference rule. Furthermore, KE-tableaux have better computational properties than semantic tableaux [D'A92].

KE-tableaux deal with T- and F-signed formulas. So if α is a formula, $T\,\alpha$ and $F\,\alpha$ are signed formulas. $T\,\alpha$ is the *conjugate formula* of $F\,\alpha$, and vice versa.

Each connective is associated with a set of *linear expansion rules*. Linear expansion rules always have a *main premiss*; two-premissed rules also have an *auxiliary premiss*. Figure 2 shows KE-tableau linear connective expansion rules for classical logic, which are the same for KELB-tableaux.

The only branching rule in KE is the *Principle of Bivalence*, stating that a formula α must be either true or false. In $\mathsf{KELB}(\Sigma)$-tableaux, this rule is *limited* by a proviso stating that it can only occur over a formula $\alpha \in \Sigma$. This *limited principle of bivalence*, $\mathsf{LPB}(\Sigma)$ is illustrated in Figure 3.

We also require a few further linear rules which are redundant in classical KE:

$$\frac{F\,\alpha \wedge \alpha}{F\,\alpha}\,(F\wedge_{\alpha\alpha}) \qquad \frac{T\,\alpha \vee \alpha}{T\,\alpha}\,(T\vee_{\alpha\alpha})$$

$$
\begin{array}{ccc}
\dfrac{\begin{array}{c} T\ \alpha \to \beta \\ T\ \alpha \end{array}}{T\ \beta}\,(T\to_1) &
\dfrac{\begin{array}{c} T\ \alpha \to \beta \\ F\ \beta \end{array}}{F\ \alpha}\,(T\to_2) &
\dfrac{\begin{array}{c} F\ \alpha \to \beta \\ T\ \alpha \end{array}}{F\ \beta}\,(F\to)
\\[3ex]
\dfrac{\begin{array}{c} F\ \alpha \wedge \beta \\ T\ \alpha \end{array}}{F\ \beta}\,(F\wedge_1) &
\dfrac{\begin{array}{c} F\ \alpha \wedge \beta \\ T\ \beta \end{array}}{F\ \alpha}\,(F\wedge_2) &
\dfrac{\begin{array}{c} T\ \alpha \wedge \beta \\ T\ \alpha \end{array}}{T\ \beta}\,(T\wedge)
\\[3ex]
\dfrac{\begin{array}{c} T\ \alpha \vee \beta \\ F\ \alpha \end{array}}{T\ \beta}\,(T\vee_1) &
\dfrac{\begin{array}{c} T\ \alpha \vee \beta \\ F\ \beta \end{array}}{T\ \alpha}\,(T\vee_2) &
\dfrac{\begin{array}{c} F\ \alpha \vee \beta \\ F\ \alpha \end{array}}{F\ \beta}\,(F\vee)
\\[3ex]
\dfrac{T\ \neg\alpha}{F\ \alpha}\,(T\neg) &
\dfrac{F\ \neg\alpha}{T\ \alpha}\,(F\neg)
\end{array}
$$

Fig. 2. KE Expansion Rules

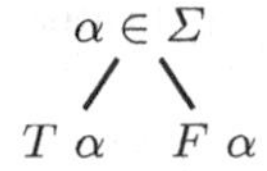

$$
\alpha \in \Sigma
$$
$$
\swarrow \qquad \searrow
$$
$$
T\ \alpha \qquad F\ \alpha
$$

Fig. 3. Limited Principle of Bivalence LPB(Σ)

The premiss and consequence of each such rule are logically equivalent, but in classical KE the consequent can only be derived with the use of the principle of bivalence, which may not be available in KELB if $\alpha \notin \Sigma$.

An expansion of a tableau branch is allowed when the premisses of an expansion rule are present in the branch; the expansion consists of adding the conclusions of the rule to the end of all branches passing through the set of all premisses of that rule. The LPB(Σ) branching rule splits a branch into two.

A branch in a KELB-tableau is *closed* if it contains $F\ \alpha$ and $T\ \alpha$. The tableau is closed if all its branches are closed. We define the inference $\vdash_{\Sigma}^{\text{KELB}}$ such that $\alpha_1, \ldots, \alpha_n \vdash_{\Sigma}^{\text{KELB}} \beta$ iff there is a closed KELB(Σ)-tableau for $T\ \alpha_1, \ldots, T\ \alpha_n, F\ \beta$.

As an example, reconsider Dalal's example given above, presented using full propositional logic. $\Gamma_0 = \{p \vee q, q \to p, p \to (s \vee t), (p \wedge t) \to s\}$. Figure 4 presents three tableaux, one for $\Gamma_0 \vdash_{\emptyset}^{\text{KELB}} p$, the second for $\Gamma_0, p \vdash_{\emptyset}^{\text{KELB}} s$ and a third one, which contains an *incremental method* to establish whether $\Gamma_0 \vdash s$.

The tableaux in Figure 4 for $\Gamma_0 \vdash_{\emptyset}^{\text{KELB}} p$ and $\Gamma_0, p \vdash_{\emptyset}^{\text{KELB}} s$ close without branching. The third tableau is actually a combination of the other two. In it we try to establish whether $\Gamma_0 \vdash_{\emptyset}^{\text{KELB}} s$; after a single expansion step, there are no expansion rules to apply, and since $\Sigma = \emptyset$, no branching is possible according to LPB(Σ); so we conclude that $\Gamma_0 \nvdash_{\emptyset}^{\text{KELB}} s$. The set Σ is then expanded to $\Sigma' = \{p\} \supset \Sigma$ so

$$
\begin{array}{c}
T\,p \vee q \\
T\,q \to p \\
T\,p \to (s \vee t) \\
T\,(p \wedge t) \to s \\
F\,p \\
\hline
T\,q \\
T\,p \\
\times
\end{array}
\qquad
\begin{array}{c}
T\,p \vee q \\
T\,q \to p \\
T\,p \to (s \vee t) \\
T\,(p \wedge t) \to s \\
T\,p \\
F\,s \\
\hline
F\,p \wedge t \\
T\,s \vee t \\
F\,t \\
T\,t \\
\times
\end{array}
\qquad
\begin{array}{c}
T\,p \vee q \quad \Sigma := \emptyset \\
T\,q \to p \\
T\,p \to (s \vee t) \\
T\,(p \wedge t) \to s \\
F\,s \\
\hline
F\,p \wedge t \\
- \qquad \Sigma := \{p\} \\
\diagup \; \diagdown \\
F\,p \quad T\,p \\
T\,q \;\; T\,s \vee t \\
T\,p \quad T\,t \\
\times \quad F\,t \\
\times
\end{array}
$$

Fig. 4. An Example of KELB-Tableaux

as to unblock the tableau, and the proof continues in the logic $\vdash^{\text{KELB}}_{\{p\}}$, in which both branches close, so we conclude that $\Gamma_0 \vdash^{\text{KELB}}_{\{p\}} s$.

This example indicates how KELB-tableaux present us with an incremental method to prove theorems, in which one moves from proving theorems in one logic to the next without having to start from square 0 at each move. It also indicates that KELB-tableaux approximate classical logic "from below", that is, for $\emptyset \subseteq \Sigma' \subseteq \Sigma'' \subseteq \ldots \subseteq \mathcal{L}$ we have that

$$
\vdash^{\text{KELB}}_{\emptyset} \;\subseteq\; \vdash^{\text{KELB}}_{\Sigma'} \;\subseteq\; \vdash^{\text{KELB}}_{\Sigma''} \;\subseteq\; \ldots \;\subseteq\; \vdash^{\text{KELB}}_{\mathcal{L}} \;=\; \vdash_{\text{KE}}
$$

where $\vdash_{\text{KE}}$ is KE-tableau for classical logic. Note that this process is finite if only subformulas of the original formulas are added to Σ. This is indeed the case if we follow the *Branching Heuristics*, that is a heuristic for branching which tells us to branch on a formula α such that either $T\,\alpha$ or $F\,\alpha$ is an auxiliary premiss to an unexpanded main premiss in the branch; according to [DM94], this heuristics preserves classical completeness. Next section shows that $\vdash^{\text{KELB}}_{\Sigma}$ is in fact correct and complete with respect to $\models^{\text{LB}}_{\Sigma}$. But before that, we comment on $\vdash^{\text{KELB}}_{\emptyset}$.

It is clear that $\Gamma \vdash^{\text{KELB}}_{\emptyset} \alpha$ if the tableau can close without ever branching. That is, only linear inferences are allowed in $\vdash^{\text{KELB}}_{\emptyset}$. Note that $\vdash_{\text{BCP}}$-inferences are one of these linear inferences, and we have the following.

Lemma 1. *Let $\Gamma \cup \{\psi\}$ be a set of clauses. Then $\Gamma \vdash_{\text{BCP}} \psi$ iff $\Gamma \vdash^{\text{KELB}}_{\emptyset} \psi$.*

4 Soundness and Completeness

Let Θ be a branch in a KELB-tableau. We say that Θ is *open* if it is not closed. We say that Θ is *saturated* if the following conditions are met:

(a) If the premisses of a linear rule are in Θ, so are its consequences.

(b) If the main premiss of a two-premissed rule is in Θ, and the formula α corresponding to the auxiliary premiss is in Σ, then $T\,\alpha$ or $F\,\alpha$ is in Θ.

In classical KE-tableaux, the second condition for saturation does not impose the restriction $\alpha \in \Sigma$. We extend the notion of valuations to signed formulas in the obvious way: $v_\Sigma(T\alpha) = 1$ iff $v_\Sigma(\alpha) = 1$, $v_\Sigma(F\alpha) = 1$ iff $v_\Sigma(\alpha) = 0$ and $v_\Sigma(X\alpha) = \epsilon$ iff $v_\Sigma(\alpha) = \epsilon$. A valuation satisfy a branch in a tableau if it simultaneously satisfy all the signed formulas in the branch.

Lemma 2. *Consider the* KELB-*tableau expansion rules.*

    i. If the premisses of a linear rule are satisfied by v_Σ, so are its consequences.

    ii. If the conjugate of an auxiliary premiss of a two-premissed linear rule is satisfied by v_Σ, so is the main premiss.

    iii. If the consequences of a linear rule are satisfied by v_Σ, so is the main premiss.

    iv. If a branch is satisfied by v_Σ prior to the application of LPB(Σ), then one of the two generated branches is satisfied after the application of LPB(Σ).

Proof. (i)–(iii) are shown by a simple inspection on the linear rules in Figure 2 and $(F\wedge_{\alpha\alpha})$ and $(T\vee_{\alpha\alpha})$. As for (iv), suppose the branching occurs over the formula α, so $\alpha \in \Sigma$. By the Limited Bivalence Restrictions, $v_\Sigma(T\,\alpha) = 1$ or $v_\Sigma(F\,\alpha) = 1$, so v_Σ satisfies one of the two branches generated by the application of LPB(Σ).

Lemma 3. *Let Θ be an open saturated branch in a* KELB(Σ)-*tableau. Then Θ is satisfiable.*

Proof. Consider the propositional valuation v_Σ such that $v(p_i) = 1$ iff $T\,p_i \in \Theta$, $v(q_j) = 0$ iff $F\,q_j \in \Theta$ and $v(r_k) = \epsilon_k$ otherwise. Clearly v_Σ is an LB(Σ)-valuation such that no two atoms are assigned to the same neutral truth value ϵ.

We prove by structural induction on α that for every $X\alpha \in \Theta$, $v_\Sigma(X\alpha) = 1$, $X \in \{T, F\}$. If α is atomic, $v_\Sigma(X\alpha) = 1$ follows from the definition of v_Σ.

If $X\alpha$ is the main premiss of a one-premissed rule R, by saturation we have both consequences of R in Θ. Then, by induction hypothesis, both such consequences are satisfied by v_Σ and by Lemma 2(iii) $v_\Sigma(X\alpha) = 1$.

If $X\alpha$ is the main premiss of a two-premissed rule; we have to analyse two cases. First, let $Y\beta$ be an auxiliary premiss for $X\alpha$ in a rule R, $Y \in \{T, F\}$, such that $Y\beta \in \Theta$, in which case R's conclusion is in Θ and, by Lemma 2(iii), $v_\Sigma(X\alpha) = 1$. Second, suppose no auxiliary premiss $Y\beta \in \Theta$, in which case there are two possibilities. If $\bar{Y}\beta \in \Theta$, where $\bar{Y}$ is Y's conjugate, by Lemma 2(ii) we obtain $v_\Sigma(X\alpha) = 1$; otherwise, by saturation, we know that all possible auxiliary premisses for $X\alpha$ are not in Σ; by saturation and rules $(F\wedge_{\alpha\alpha})$ and $(T\vee_{\alpha\alpha})$, we know that α's immediate subformulas are distinct, in which case v_Σ can assign distinct neutral values to them so as to satisfy α; that is, if $X\alpha = T\beta \vee \gamma$, make $v_\Sigma(\beta) = \epsilon_i$, $v_\Sigma(\gamma) = \epsilon_j \neq \epsilon_i$ so that $v_\Sigma(T\beta \vee \gamma) = 1$, and similarly for $F\beta \wedge \gamma$ and $T\,\beta \rightarrow \gamma$. For the latter, the special case we where $\beta = \gamma$ is dealt by the semantic definition of $v_\Sigma(\beta \rightarrow \beta) = 1$. This finishes the proof.

KELB(Σ)-tableaux have the *soundness* property if whenever a tableau for $\Gamma \vdash_{\Sigma}^{KELB} \alpha$ closes then $\Gamma \models_{\Sigma}^{LB} \alpha$. Conversely, the notion of *completeness* requires that if $\Gamma \models_{\Sigma}^{LB} \alpha$ then there is a closed tableau for $\Gamma \vdash_{\Sigma}^{KELB} \alpha$.

Theorem 1 (Soundness and Completeness). $\Gamma \models_{\Sigma}^{LB} \alpha$ *iff* $\Gamma \vdash_{\Sigma}^{KELB} \alpha$.

Proof. For soundness, we prove the contrapositive, that is, assume that $\Gamma \not\models_{\Sigma}^{LB} \alpha$, so that there is a v_{Σ} such that $v_{\Sigma}(\Gamma) = 1$ and $v_{\Sigma}(\alpha) = 0$. If there is a KELB(Σ)-tableau for $\Gamma \vdash_{\Sigma}^{KELB} \alpha$, we have that all initial signed formulas of the tableau are satisfied by v_{Σ}. By Lemma 2(i) each use of a linear expansion rule generate formulas satisfied by v_{Σ}. By Lemma 2(iv), each application of LPB(Σ) generates a branch satisfied by v_{Σ}. If this tableau closes, this means that no such v_{Σ} could exist, which is a contradiction, so $\Gamma \not\vdash_{\Sigma}^{KELB} \alpha$.

For completeness we also prove the contrapositive, so suppose that there is a KELB(Σ)-tableau for $\Gamma \vdash_{\Sigma}^{KELB} \alpha$ with an open saturated branch Θ. By Lemma 3 there is a valuation v_{Σ} that satisfies Θ, in particular $v_{\Sigma}(\Gamma) = 1$ and $v_{\Sigma}(\alpha) = 0$, and hence $\Gamma \not\models_{\Sigma}^{LB} \alpha$.

Corollary 1. *The restriction of applications of LPB(Σ) to the Branching Heuristics preserves completeness of* $\vdash_{\Sigma}^{KELB}$.

Proof. The Branching Heuristics allows only the branching over subformulas of formulas occurring in the tableau. This heuristics is actually suggested by the definition of a *saturated branch*, and aims at saturating a branch. It suffices to note that nowhere in the proofs of Lemma 3 and Theorem 1 was it required the branching over a non-subformula of a formula existing in a branch. Therefore, completeness holds for KELB-tableaux restricted to the Branching Heuristics.

The Branching Heuristics reduces the search space over which formula to branch, at the price of ruling out some small proofs of complex formulas obtained by clever branching.

The approximation family $\vdash_{\Sigma}^{KELB}$ is not in the spirit of Dalal's approximation, but follows the paradigm of Cadoli and Schaerf [SC95,CS96], also applied by Massacci [Mas98b,Mas98a] and Finger and Wassermann [FW04].

5   Polynomial Approximations

As mentioned before, the family of inference relation $\vdash_{\Sigma}^{KELB}$ does not follow Dalal's approach to approximation. We now present a family of logics based on $\vdash_{\Sigma}^{KELB}$ that is closer to that approach.

For that, let $\mathbb{S} \subseteq 2^{\mathcal{P}}$ be a set of sets of atoms and, for every $\Pi \in \mathbb{S}$, let Π^+ be the closure of Π under formula formation. We define $\Gamma \vdash_{\mathbb{S}}^{KELB} \alpha$ iff there exists a set $\Pi \in \mathbb{S}$ such that $\Gamma \vdash_{\Pi^+}^{KELB} \alpha$. We define

$$\mathbb{S}_k = \{\Pi \subseteq \mathcal{P} \mid |\Pi| = k\}.$$

That is, $\mathbb{S}_k$ is a set of sets of atoms of size k. Note that if we restrict our attention to n atoms, $|\mathbb{S}_k| = \binom{n}{k} = O(n^k)$ sets of k atoms. For a fixed k, we only have to consider a polynomial number of sets of k atoms.

We then write $\vdash_k^{\text{KELB}}$ to mean $\vdash_{\mathbb{S}_k}^{\text{KELB}}$. In terms of theorem proving, the approximation process using the $\vdash_k^{\text{KELB}}$ family performs an *iterative depth search* over KE-tableaux.

The entailment relation $\models_k^{\text{LB}}$ can be defined in a similar way: $\Gamma \models_k^{\text{LB}} \alpha$ iff $\Gamma \models_{\Pi^+}^{\text{LB}} \alpha$ for some $\Pi \in \mathbb{S}_k$. By Theorem 1, $\vdash_k^{\text{KELB}}$ is sound and complete with respect to $\models_k^{\text{LB}}$.

Lemma 4. *The family of inference systems $\vdash_k^{\text{KELB}}$ is an approximation of classical logic "from below".*

Proof. It is obvious from the definition of $\vdash_k^{\text{KELB}}$ that if $\Gamma \vdash_k^{\text{KELB}} \alpha$ then $\Gamma \vdash_{k+1}^{\text{KELB}} \alpha$, for all possible inference in the former are also possible in the latter. And for a given pair (Γ, α), we only need to consider the atoms occurring in them, so that $\vdash_{|atoms(\Gamma, \alpha)|}^{\text{KELB}}$ is actually classical KE, so $\vdash_k^{\text{KELB}}$ is an approximation of classical logic "from below".

It has been shown in [Fin04] that when Γ is a set of clauses and α is a clause, Dalal's $\vdash_k^{\text{BCP}}$ inference is sound and complete with respect to $\models_k^{\text{LB}}$. One important property of $\vdash_k^{\text{BCP}}$ is that it can be decided in polynomial time. We now prove the same result for $\vdash_k^{\text{KELB}}$.

Theorem 2. *The inference $\Gamma \vdash_k^{\text{KELB}} \alpha$ can be decided in time polynomial with respect to $n = |atoms(\Gamma, \alpha)|$.*

Proof. For a fixed k, there are at most $O(n^k)$ subsets of $atoms(\Gamma, \alpha)$ with size k, in order to decide $\Gamma \vdash_k^{\text{KELB}} \alpha$ we have to test only a polynomial number of inferences $\Gamma \vdash_{\Pi^+}^{\text{KELB}} \alpha$. The size of each such inference under the Branching Heuristics is a function of k, which is fixed, and does not depend on n, so the whole process of deciding $\Gamma \vdash_k^{\text{KELB}} \alpha$ can be done in time $O(n^k)$.

The approximation $\vdash_k^{\text{KELB}}$ performs an *iterated depth search* over the space of proofs. Comparatively, the KES_3 approximation process of [FW04], which does not guarantee polynomially decidable steps, performs a *depth-first search*.

6   Conclusion

We have created a family of tableau-based inferences systems $\vdash_0^{\text{KELB}}, \vdash_1^{\text{KELB}}, \ldots, \vdash_k^{\text{KELB}}$ that approximates classical logic, such that each step has a sound and complete lattice-based semantics and can be decided in polynomial time.

Future work involves the implementation of such an approximation system and its practical application in areas such as Belief Revision and Planning. We hope to see how well it performs in "real" situations.

References

[CL73]   C. Chang and R. Lee. *Symbolic Logic and Mechanical Theorem Proving.* Academic Press, London, 1973.

[CS96]   Marco Cadoli and Marco Schaerf. The complexity of entailment in propositional multivalued logics. *Annals of Mathematics and Artificial Intelligence,* 18(1):29–50, 1996.

[CS00]   Alessandra Carbone and Stephen Semmes. *A Graphic Apology for Symmetry and Implicitness.* Oxford Mathematical Monographs. Oxford University Press, 2000.

[D'A92]   Marcello D'Agostino. Are tableaux an improvement on truth-tables? — cut-free proofs and bivalence. *Journal of Logic, Language and Information,* 1:235–252, 1992.

[D'A99]   Marcello D'Agostino. Tableau methods for classical propositional logic. In Marcello D'Agostino, Dov Gabbay, Rainer Haehnle, and Joachim Posegga, editors, *Handbook of Tableau Methods,* pages 45–124. Kluwer, 1999.

[Dal96a]   Mukesh Dalal. Anytime families of tractable propositional reasoners. In *International Symposium of Artificial Intelligence and Mathematics AI/MATH-96,* pages 42–45, 1996.

[Dal96b]   Mukesh Dalal. Semantics of an anytime family of reasponers. In *12th European Conference on Artificial Intelligence,* pages 360–364, 1996.

[DM94]   Marcello D'Agostino and Marco Mondadori. "the taming of the cut. classical refutations with analytic cut". *Journal of Logic and Computation,* 4(285-319), 1994.

[Fin04]   Marcelo Finger. Towards polynomial approximations of full propositional logic. Technical Report RT-2004-04, Department of Computer Science, IME/USP, 2004. Available for download at www.ime.usp.br/~mfinger/publications.

[FW04]   Marcelo Finger and Renata Wassermann. Approximate and limited reasoning: Semantics, proof theory, expressivity and control. *Journal of Logic And Computation,* 14(2):179–204, 2004.

[GJ79]   M. R. Garey and D. S. Johnson. *Computers and Intractability: A Guide to the Theory of NP-Completeness.* Freeman, 1979.

[Mas98a]   Fabio Massacci. Anytime approximate modal reasoning. In Jack Mostow and Charles Rich, editors, *AAAI-98,* pages 274–279. AAAIP, 1998.

[Mas98b]   Fabio Massacci. *Efficient Approximate Deduction and an Application to Computer Security.* PhD thesis, Dottorato in Ingegneria Informatica, Università di Roma I "La Sapienza", Dipartimento di Informatica e Sistemistica, June 1998.

[McA90]   D. McAllester. Truth maintenance. In *Proceedings of the Eighth National Conference on Artificial Intelligence (AAAI-90),* pages 1109–1116, 1990.

[SC95]   Marco Schaerf and Marco Cadoli. Tractable reasoning via approximation. *Artificial Intelligence,* 74(2):249–310, 1995.

[Smu68]   Raymond M. Smullyan. *First-Order Logic.* Springer-Verlag, 1968.

Some Techniques for Branch-Saturation in Free-Variable Tableaux

Nicolas Peltier

LEIBNIZ-IMAG, CNRS
Nicolas.Peltier@imag.fr
http://www-leibniz.imag.fr/~peltier
Av. Félix Viallet, 38031 Grenoble Cedex
France

Abstract. We present a free-variable tableaux calculus that avoids the systematic instantiation of universally quantified variables by ground terms, but still permits branch-saturation (i.e. no backtracking on the applied substitutions is needed). We prove that our calculus is sound, refutationally complete, and that it is a decision procedure for function-free skolemized formulae (Bernays-Schönfinkel class). Comparison with existing works are provided, showing evidence of the interest of our approach.

1 Introduction

Tableaux are arguably the most natural proof procedure for first-order logic and play a prominent role in Artificial Intelligence and Automated Deduction. However, classical tableaux have an important drawback: one has to "guess" in advance the value of the variables when instantiating the universal formulae. Completeness can be achieved easily by enumerating the set of ground terms built on the considered signature. However, from a computational point of view, this enumeration is costly and highly redundant. The solution to this problem is well-known: it suffices to instantiate universally quantified variables by "rigid" free variables instead of concrete terms. These variables can be considered as symbols denoting "unknown" ground terms, to be instantiated later during the proof process. Unification is used to find automatically the substitutions enabling the closure of the branches. However, the use of free variables also has some drawbacks. First, this prevents branch saturation (since any universal formula can be instantiated by an arbitrary number of distinct free variables). Moreover, completeness is more difficult to achieve when free variables are used, because the rigid variables can be instantiated repeatedly with "wrong" terms during the unification process. In contrast to connection calculi [9], the procedure is still confluent, because it is always possible to generate new instantiations of the universal formulae. However it is very difficult to control the instantiation process, hence to design implementable strategies ensuring completeness (without "grounding" the terms in advance as it is done for example in [22]). Therefore, although free variable

J.J. Alferes and J. Leite (Eds.): JELIA 2004, LNAI 3229, pp. 539–551, 2004.
© Springer-Verlag Berlin Heidelberg 2004

tableaux are proof-confluent, most implementations of free variable tableaux "backtrack" on the applied substitutions: see for instance [8] for more details about this problem and [1] for an exception, implementing the method described in [15].

Various methods have been proposed to overcome this difficulty (see Section 5). In this paper, we propose another solution which is closer to the initial tableaux calculus. The idea is to restrict the γ-rule in such a way that completeness can be easily achieved and that branch saturation is made possible, but that "blind" instantiation of the universally quantified variables by ground terms is avoided.

2   Basic Notions

We briefly review the basic notions that are necessary for the understanding of our work. We assume some familiarity with the usual notions in logic and tableau-based theorem proving (see for instance [25,14] for more details).

The set of terms is built inductively on a set of function symbols Σ and a set of variables $\mathcal{X}$. Atoms are of the form $p(t_1, \ldots, t_n)$ where p is a predicate symbol of arity n and $t_1, \ldots, t_n$ are terms.

The set of first order formulae is defined inductively. A first-order formula is either $\perp$ (false), or an atom, the negation of an atom or of the form $(\phi \vee \psi)$, $(\phi \wedge \psi)$ or $(\forall x)\phi$ where ϕ, ψ are first-order formulae and x is a variable. ϕ^c is the complementary of ϕ: $\phi^c \stackrel{def}{=} \neg\phi$ if ϕ is not a negation, and $(\neg\phi)^c \stackrel{def}{=} \phi$.

We will use vectors for denoting sequences of quantifiers: for instance $(\forall \boldsymbol{x})\phi$ denotes a formula of the form $(\forall x_1) \ldots (\forall x_n)\phi$ where $\boldsymbol{x} = (x_1, \ldots, x_n)$.

Interpretations are defined as usual. We assume w.l.o.g. that all the considered interpretations are Herbrand interpretations.

A substitution is a function mapping each variable to a term. If t is a term and σ a substitution, $t\sigma$ denotes the term obtained by replacing each variable x in t by $x\sigma$. For any substitution σ we denote by $dom(\sigma)$ the set of variables x s.t. $x\sigma \neq x$.

We need to introduce the standard notion of unifier. For technical reasons we add the possibility of considering some variables as constant symbols (i.e. their value cannot be changed during the unification process). This is formalized by the following definition. A substitution σ is said to be a *unifier* of two expressions (terms or formulae) t and s *w.r.t. a set of variables* V iff $t\sigma = s\sigma$ and $dom(\sigma) \cap V = \emptyset$. The most general unifier of two terms t, s w.r.t. a set of variable V can easily be computed using existing unification algorithms [2], provided that the symbols in V are considered as constant symbols rather than variables (i.e. any instantiation of the variables in V is forbidden). We write $t \stackrel{\triangle}{=} s$ (resp. $t \stackrel{\triangle}{=}_V s$) if t is unifiable with s w.r.t $\emptyset$ (resp. t is unifiable with s w.r.t. V).

Given two expressions t and s, we write $t \bowtie s$ iff there exist two substitutions σ, θ s.t. $t\sigma = s\theta$ (obviously $t \stackrel{\triangle}{=} s$ implies $t \bowtie s$ but the converse does not hold, for instance $x \bowtie f(x)$ but $x \not\stackrel{\triangle}{=} f(x)$). If t, s are two terms or atoms, we write

$t \preceq s$ iff t is an instance of s (i.e. if there exists a substitution σ s.t. $t = s\sigma$). We write $t \prec s$ if $t \preceq s$ but $s \not\preceq t$. If σ and θ are two substitutions, then we write $\sigma \preceq \theta$ if for any variable x $x\sigma \preceq x\theta$.

An *injective* substitution η is said to be a *renaming* iff for any variable x, $x\eta$ is a variable. If σ is a substitution and η is a renaming then σ^η denotes the substitution $\{x_i\eta \to t_i\eta \mid x_i\sigma = t_i\}$. Given two expressions t, s, we write $t \sim s$ if t is a renaming of s, i.e. if there exists a renaming σ s.t. $t = s\sigma$.

Given two expressions t and s and θ a substitution, we define the substitution $qu(t, s, \theta)$ (for *quasi-unifier*) as follows: $qu(t, s, \theta) = \sigma\theta\theta^\eta$, where where η denotes an arbitrary renaming of the variables in s by variables not occurring in t and σ is a m.g.u. of t and $s\eta$.

Note that $qu(t, s, \theta)$ is not unique in general (even up to a renaming) due to the fact that there may exist several distinct most general unifiers up to a renaming. We remove this ambiguity by fixing a total precedence on the variables occurring in t and s and assuming that this precedence is compatible with the renaming η ($x\eta \prec y$ iff $x \prec y$, for any $x \in var(s), y \in var(t)$). Then m.g.u.'s are oriented according to this precedence: a mapping $u \to v$ (where u, v are variables) can only occur in the unifier if $u \succ v$. Modulo this convention, $qu(t, s, \theta)$ is *unique* (up to a renaming) and we have obviously: $qu(t, s, \theta) \sim qu(s, t, \theta)$.

3   The Proof Procedure

A *position* is a (possibly infinite) sequence of integers. ϵ denotes the empty position and $\preceq$ denotes the prefix ordering. A *tree* is a function mapping each finite position p to a set of first-order formulae. The *support* $sup(T)$ of a tree T is the set of positions p such that $T(p) \neq \emptyset$. We assume that $sup(T)$ is closed under prefix, i.e. for any position $p \in sup(T)$, and for any $q \preceq p$, we have $q \in sup(T)$. A tree is said to be *finite* iff its support is finite.

A *branch* p in T is a position s.t. there exists a position $q \preceq p$ s.t. q is a prefix-maximal position in $sup(T)$ (for technical convenience we may have $q \neq p$). We say that a formula *occurs in a branch* p iff there exists $q \preceq p$ such that $\phi \in T(q)$. The set of formulae occurring in a branch p of a tree T is denoted by $f(T, p) \stackrel{def}{=} \bigcup_{q \preceq p} T(q)$. A branch p is said to be *closed* iff $\bot$ occurs in p. A tree is said to be *closed* iff all its branches are closed.

A *tableau* is a pair $T \mid [\theta]$ where T is a tree and θ is a substitution. The tableau is said to be *closed* iff T is closed.

The notion of model is extended as follows. An interpretation $\mathcal{I}$ is said to be a *model* of a tableau $T \mid [\theta]$ iff for any instance σ of θ there exists a branch p in $\mathcal{T}$ such that for any formula ϕ occurring in p, $\mathcal{I} \models \phi\sigma$.

It is obvious that any closed tableau is unsatisfiable.

As usual the procedure is specified by a set of expansion rules allowing to extend an existing tableau. All the rules are of the following form:

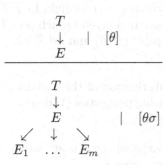

This means that a non closed branch p containing a set of formulae E in a tableau $T \mid [\theta]$ is extended by m branches $p.1, \ldots, p.m$ such that $T(p.i) \overset{def}{=} E_i$ (for any $i \in [1..m]$). The substitution part of the tableau is replaced by $\theta\sigma$ (with possibly $\sigma = id$). Initially, the tableau is of the form $T \mid [id]$ where $sup(T) = \{\epsilon\}$ and $T(\epsilon) = \{\phi\}$ (where ϕ is the consider first-order formula and id denotes the empty substitution). Clearly ϕ is satisfiable iff $T \mid [id]$ is satisfiable.

Propositional Rules

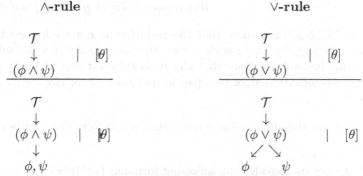

If ϕ or ψ does not occur in the branch. If ϕ and ψ do not occur in the branch.

Closure Rule

$$
\begin{array}{c}
\mathcal{T} \\
\downarrow \qquad \mid \quad [\theta] \\
\phi, \neg\psi \\
\hline
\mathcal{T} \\
\downarrow \\
\phi, \neg\psi \quad \mid \quad [\theta\sigma] \\
\downarrow \\
\perp
\end{array}
$$

If σ is a m.g.u. of $\phi\theta$ and $\psi\theta$.

∀-Rule

In order to define our version of the γ-rule, we need to introduce some terminology.

For any tableau $\mathcal{T} = (T, \theta)$, for any branch p and for any first-order formula of the form $(\forall \boldsymbol{x})\phi$ occurring in p, we denote by $IT(\mathcal{T}, (\forall \boldsymbol{x})\phi, p)$ the set of tuples $\boldsymbol{t}$ such that $\phi\{\boldsymbol{x} \to \boldsymbol{t}\} \in f(T, p)$.

Let $\mathcal{T} = T \mid [\theta]$ be a tableau. A pair (ϕ, σ) where ϕ is a formula in $f(T, p)$ and σ is a substitution is said to be a *candidate pair* in a given branch p in T iff there exist two formulae $\psi, \psi' \in f(T, p)$ s.t. $\sigma = qu(\psi, \psi'^c, \theta)$ and $\phi\theta \not\approx \phi\sigma$.

We are now in position to define our $\forall$-rule:

$$
\begin{array}{c}
T \\
\downarrow \\
(\forall \boldsymbol{x})\phi \\
\hline
T \\
\downarrow \\
(\forall \boldsymbol{x})\phi \\
\phi\sigma
\end{array}
\quad \mid [\theta]
$$

If σ is a $\preceq$-*maximal* substitution of the variables in $\boldsymbol{x}$ satisfying the following properties (V denotes the set of free variables in $(\forall \boldsymbol{x})\phi$).

- for any $\boldsymbol{s} \in IT(T, (\forall \boldsymbol{x})\phi, p)$, $\boldsymbol{x}\sigma \not\approx_V \boldsymbol{s}\theta$ (where p denotes the current branch);
- One of the following condition holds:
  - Either $IT(T, (\forall \boldsymbol{x})\phi, p) = \emptyset$ and $\sigma = id$.
  - or there exists (up to a renaming) a candidate pair $(\phi\{\boldsymbol{x} \to \boldsymbol{y}\}, \theta)$ in p s.t. $\theta \preceq \sigma$.

Remark 1. W.l.o.g. we assume that the variables in $\boldsymbol{x}$ are renamed before any application of the $\forall$-rule, in such a way that $\boldsymbol{x}$ contains no variable already occurring in the tableau. Note that the substitution σ can be easily computed by using a disunification algorithm (see for instance [12] or [23] for more efficient algorithms).

We illustrate the application of the $\forall$-rule by the following (deliberately trivial) example.

Example 1. Let us consider the following formula: $(\forall x)(p(x) \lor q(x)) \land \neg p(a) \land \neg p(b) \land \neg q(b)$. We first apply the $\land$-rule, then the $\forall$-rule on $(\forall x)(p(x) \lor q(x))$. By renaming the variable x, we introduce a new variable x_1, which yields the formula: $p(x_1) \lor q(x_1)$. Then we apply the $\lor$-rule on $p(x_1) \lor q(x_1)$ yielding two distinct branches:

- The first one containing the formulae $(\forall x)(p(x) \lor q(x)), \neg p(a), \neg p(b), \neg q(b)$ and $p(x_1)$.
- The second one containing the formulae $(\forall x)(p(x) \lor q(x)), \neg p(a), \neg p(b), q(b)$ and $q(x_1)$.

$p(x_1)$ and $p(a)$ are unifiable hence by the closure rule we can close the first branch by applying the substitution $x_1 \to a$. This leaves a unique open branch, containing the formulae$(\forall x)(p(x) \lor q(x)), \neg p(a), \neg p(b), \neg q(b)$ and $q(x_1)$ with the substitution $x_1 \to a$.

At this point, we need to apply the $\forall$-rule again on the formula $(\forall x)p(x) \lor q(x)$. To this end, we need to find a candidate pair corresponding to $p(x_1) \lor q(x_1)$. We compute the substitution $qu(q(x_1), q(b), \{x_1 \to a\}) = \{x_1 \to b\}$. $p(a)$ and $p(x_1)\{x_1 \to b\} = p(b)$ are not unifiable, thus $(p(x_1) \lor q(x_1), \{x_1 \to b\})$ is a candidate pair. Hence we can apply the $\forall$-rule with the substitution $x \to b$. We obtain the formula $p(b) \lor q(b)$. Notice that the application condition based on the use of candidate pairs prevents the $\forall$-rule to introduce other instances of $p(x) \vee q(x)$. The $\vee$-rule can be applied and the two corresponding branches can be closed by the Closure rule (using the pairs of complementary literals $(p(b), \neg p(b))$ and $(q(b), \neg q(b))$ respectively).

However, the above rules are not sufficient to achieve completeness, as evidenced by the following example.

Example 2. Let $\phi = (\forall x)p(x) \wedge (\forall x)(\neg p(x) \vee (q(x) \wedge \neg q(f(x))))$.

We first apply the $\wedge$-rule on ϕ, then the $\forall$-rule on $(\forall x)p(x)$ and $(\forall x)(\neg p(x) \vee (q(x) \wedge \neg q(f(x))))$. This yields the following formulae: $p(x_1)$ and $(\neg p(x_2) \vee (q(x_2) \wedge \neg q(f(x_2))))$. We apply the $\vee$-rule on the second formula and close the branch corresponding to $\neg p(x_2)$ by unifying x_2 with x_1. Then, we apply the $\wedge$-rule on $q(x_2) \wedge \neg q(f(x_2))$. At this point we obtain an open branch containing the following literals: $p(x_1), q(x_2), \neg q(f(x_2))$ with the substitution $x_2 \to x_1$. No rule is applicable on this branch since there is no candidate pair. For instance, we have $qu(q(x_2), q(f(x_2)), x_2 \to x_1) = \{x_2 \to f(x_3)\}$ (where x_3 is a new variable) but $f(x_3) \triangleq x_2$.

In order to handle such cases, we need a new rule, called the instantiation rule.

Instantiation Rule

$$
\begin{array}{c}
\mathcal{T} \\
\downarrow \quad \mid \; [\theta] \\
\phi, \neg\psi \\
\hline
\mathcal{T} \\
\downarrow \quad \mid \; [\theta\sigma] \\
\phi, \neg\psi
\end{array}
$$
If $\phi\theta \bowtie \psi\theta$, $\phi\theta \not\triangleq \psi\theta$ and σ is a $\preceq$-maximal substitution s.t. $\phi\theta\sigma \not\bowtie \psi\theta$

Example 3. (continued) We apply the instantiation rule on the open branch obtained in Example 2. We have to find a (maximal) substitution σ s.t. $q(x_1)\sigma \not\bowtie \neg q(f(x_1))$. We obtain the substitution: $x_1 \to a$. Afterward, we have $qu(q(x_2), q(f(x_2)), \{x_2 \to x_1, x_1 \to a\}) = \{x_2 \to f(x_3)\}$. Since $f(x_3) \not\triangleq a$, we obtain a candidate pair and the $\vee$-rule is applicable on the considered branch (on the formula $(\forall x)\neg p(x) \vee (q(x) \wedge \neg q(f(x)))$) and the substitution $x \to f(x_3)$. This eventually leads to the closure of the branch (by unifying x_3 with x_1).

We note $\mathcal{T} \rightsquigarrow \mathcal{T}'$ if $\mathcal{T}'$ is obtained from $\mathcal{T}$ by applying the $\wedge$-rule, $\vee$-rule, $\forall$-rule, Instantiation rule or Closure rule. $\rightsquigarrow^*$ denotes the reflexive and transitive closure of $\rightsquigarrow$.

A sequence $(\mathcal{T}_i)_{i \in I}$ where I is either $[0.. + \infty[$ or of the form $[0..n]$ is said to be a *derivation* iff for any $i \in I \setminus \{0\}$, $\mathcal{T}_{i-1} \rightsquigarrow \mathcal{T}_i$. A *derivation of* a first-order formula ϕ is a derivation $\mathcal{T}_0, \mathcal{T}_1, \ldots$ such that $\mathcal{T}_0$ is of the form $T \mid [id]$, where $T(\epsilon) = \{\phi\}$ and $T(p) = \emptyset$ if $p \neq \epsilon$.

A position p is a *branch in* $(\mathcal{T}_i)_{i \in I}$ where $\mathcal{T}_i = T_i \mid [\theta_i]$ iff for any $i \in I$ there exists $q \preceq p$ s.t. q is a branch in T_i. For any branch p we denote by $f(\delta, p)$ the set of formulae: $\{T_i(q) \mid q \preceq p, i \in I\}$, A derivation $\mathcal{T}_1 \rightsquigarrow \ldots \rightsquigarrow \mathcal{T}_n$ is said to be a *refutation* iff $\mathcal{T}_n$ is closed.

4   Some Properties of Our Calculus

Theorem 1. *(Soundness) Let $\mathcal{T}, \mathcal{T}'$ be two constrained tableaux s.t. $\mathcal{T} \rightsquigarrow^* \mathcal{T}'$. Any interpretation satisfying $\mathcal{T}$ must satisfy $\mathcal{T}'$.*

Proof. The proof is very standard and is not included here for the sake of conciseness. Our calculus only restricts the application of the γ-rule and adds an Instantiation rule, which obviously does not affect soundness. $\square$

Corollary 1. *If there exists a refutation from ϕ then ϕ is unsatisfiable.*

For proving refutational completeness we need to introduce a notion of *fairness*.

Intuitively a derivation is said to be *fair* if the application of the expansion rules cannot be indefinitely delayed at least in one open branch. More formally, for any tableau $\mathcal{T} = T \mid [\theta]$, and for any branch p in T, we denote by $\mathcal{C}_p(\mathcal{T})$ (set of *candidate formulae*) the set of formulae ϕ s.t. an expansion rule is applicable on ϕ in p. Given a derivation $\delta = (\mathcal{T}_i)_{i \in I}$ and a branch p, we denote by $\mathcal{PC}_p(\delta)$ (set of *persisting candidates*) the set of formulae: $\bigcup_{i \in I} \bigcap_{j \in I, j \geq i} \mathcal{C}_p(\mathcal{T}_i)$. Intuitively, ϕ occurs in $\mathcal{PC}_p(\delta)$ iff an expansion rule is applicable on ϕ in the branch p in all tableaux $\mathcal{T}_j$, for any $j \in I$ greater than a certain i. A branch p in a derivation δ is said to be *complete* iff $\mathcal{PC}_p(\delta) = \emptyset$. A *derivation* $\mathcal{T}_1 \rightsquigarrow \mathcal{T}_2 \rightsquigarrow \ldots$ is said to be *fair* iff either all the branches in δ are closed (in this case δ is a refutation) or if there exists at least one non closed complete branch.

Let $\delta = (\mathcal{T}_i)_{i \in I}$ be a derivation. $\mathcal{T}_i$ is of the form $T_i \mid [\theta_i]$. For any branch p, and any $\forall$-formula $(\forall \boldsymbol{x})\phi$ we denote by $IT(\delta, (\forall \boldsymbol{x})\phi, p)$ the set of tuples $\boldsymbol{t}$ s.t. $\phi\{\boldsymbol{x} \to \boldsymbol{t}\} \in f(\delta, p)$.

Let p be a branch in δ. We extend the notion of candidate pair to derivations: A pair (ϕ, σ) where ϕ is a formula in $f(T, p)$ and σ is a substitution is said to be a *candidate pair* in a given branch p in δ iff there exist 2 formulae $\psi, \psi' \in f(\delta, p)$ and an integer $i \in I$ s.t. $\sigma = qu(\psi, \psi'^c, \theta_i)$ and $\phi\theta_i \not\approx \phi\sigma$. Note that by definition, if σ is a candidate substitution in a branch p of δ then there exists $i \in I$ s.t. σ it is a candidate substitution in p for any tableau $\mathcal{T}_j$, with $j \geq i$.

A ground substitution σ is said to be *pure* in a branch p of δ w.r.t. a formula ϕ if there is no candidate pair (ϕ, θ) in p and δ s.t. $\phi\sigma \preceq \phi\theta$.

We denote by $I(\delta, p)$ the interpretation defined as follows: for any ground atom A, $I(\delta, p) \models A$ iff there exist an atom $B \in f(\delta, p)$ and a substitution σ non-pure w.r.t. B such that $A = B\sigma$.

Lemma 1. *Let $\delta = (T_i \mid [\theta_i])_{i \in I}$. Let $(\forall \boldsymbol{x})\phi$ be a formula with $V = var((\forall \boldsymbol{x})\phi)$. For any branch p $IT(\delta, \phi, p)$ cannot contain two tuples $\boldsymbol{t}, \boldsymbol{s}$ s.t. $\boldsymbol{t}\theta_j \overset{\triangle}{=}_V \boldsymbol{s}\theta_j$ for any $j \in I$.*

Proof. The proof follows immediately from the application condition of the $\forall$-rule (one can only use tuples that are not unifiable with the previously introduced tuples). $\square$

Lemma 2. *Let δ be a derivation. Let p be a complete open branch in δ. Let ϕ be a formula in $f(\delta, p)$. If $I(\delta, p) \not\models \phi$ then there exists a ground substitution σ non-pure w.r.t. ϕ s.t. $I(\delta, p) \not\models \phi\sigma$.*

Proof. Let $\delta = (\mathcal{T}_i)_{i \in I}$, where $\mathcal{T}_i = T_i \mid [\theta_i]$. Assume that the above property does not hold. Let $E = f(\delta, p)$, $\mathcal{I} = I(\delta, p)$. Let ϕ the smallest (w.r.t. the number of logical symbols) formula in E s.t.:

- $\mathcal{I} \not\models \phi$ and;
- for any substitution pure w.r.t. ϕ, $\mathcal{I} \models \phi\sigma$.

- If ϕ is an atom then we get an immediate contradiction with the definition of $I(\delta, p)$.
- Assume that ϕ is a negation $\neg\psi$. Then ψ must be an atom. Assume that $\mathcal{I} \not\models \phi$. Then there exists a ground substitution σ s.t. $\mathcal{I} \not\models \phi\sigma$, i.e. $\mathcal{I} \models \psi\sigma$. By definition of $\mathcal{I}$, there exist an atom $\upsilon \in E$ and a substitution σ' non-pure w.r.t. υ s.t. $\psi\sigma = \upsilon\sigma'$.
  We have $\upsilon \bowtie \phi$. If the Closure rule applies until the end of the derivation, then, since $\mathcal{PC}_p(\delta) = \emptyset$, this rule must be applied at some point, hence the branch contains $\bot$, which is impossible since the branch is open. Therefore, there exists $i \in I$ s.t. $\upsilon\theta_i \not\equiv \psi\theta_i$. Since $\theta_i \preceq \theta_j$ for $i \leq j$, this implies that for all $j \geq i$ we have $\upsilon\theta_j \not\equiv \psi\theta_j$.
  Let $j \geq i$. Since $\upsilon \bowtie \phi$, there exist two substitutions γ, γ' s.t. $\gamma = qu(\phi, \upsilon, \theta_j)$ and $\gamma' = qu(\upsilon, \phi, \theta_j)$. If there exists $j \geq i$ s.t. $\phi\gamma \not\equiv \phi\theta_j$ then the proof is completed since σ is non-pure.
  Otherwise, since σ' is non-pure w.r.t. υ, $\upsilon\gamma' \triangleq \upsilon\theta_j$.
  But $\upsilon\gamma' \sim \phi\gamma$, hence $\upsilon\theta_j \bowtie \phi\theta_j$. Since this is true for all $j \in I$, this implies that the Instantiation rule applies on the branch p in all the $\mathcal{T}_j$ ($i \leq j$) which is impossible.
- Assume that ϕ is a conjunction $\phi_1 \wedge \phi_2$. The $\wedge$-rule applies on ϕ. Since $\mathcal{PC}_p(\delta) = \emptyset$ the rule must be applied at some point in the derivation. Hence ϕ_1 and ϕ_2 must occur in $f(T_k, p)$, for some $k \in I$.
  Thus since ϕ_1 and ϕ_2 are smaller than ϕ, we deduce that either $\mathcal{I} \models \phi_1\sigma, \phi_2\sigma$ (whence $\mathcal{I} \models \phi$, which yields a contradiction) or there exist $i \in \{1, 2\}$ and a substitution σ non-pure w.r.t. ϕ_i s.t. $\mathcal{I} \not\models \phi_i\sigma$. But then we have $\mathcal{I} \not\models \phi\sigma$. Moreover, since σ is non-pure w.r.t. ϕ_i, σ is also non pure w.r.t. ϕ. Hence the proof is completed.
- Assume that ϕ is a disjunction. The proof is similar to the previous case.
- Assume that ϕ is a universal quantification $(\forall x)\psi$.
  By definition of the $\forall$-rule, $f(\delta, p)$ contains at least one renaming of ψ. In order to simplify notations we assume, w.l.o.g. that this renaming is equal to ψ. Since $\mathcal{I} \not\models \phi$, we have $\mathcal{I} \not\models \psi$. Hence, since ψ is smaller than ϕ, there exists a substitution σ non-pure w.r.t. ψ s.t. $\mathcal{I} \not\models \psi\sigma$. There exists a candidate pair (ψ, θ) s.t. $\sigma \preceq \theta$.
  We have $\mathcal{I} \not\models \phi\sigma$. If σ is also non-pure w.r.t. ϕ the proof is completed. Hence σ is pure w.r.t. ϕ. Thus $\phi\theta \triangleq \phi\theta_j$ for all $j \in I$. By definition of the notion

of candidate pair, there exists $i \in I$ s.t. $\psi\theta \not\approx \psi\theta_j$, for all $j \geq i$. This implies that $x\theta_j \not\approx_V x\theta$ (where $V = var(\phi)$).

Let T be the set of tuples $x\sigma$ in $IT(\delta, \phi, p)$ s.t. $s \overset{\triangle}{=}_V x\sigma$. Obviously, T must be finite up to a renaming, hence is finite (by Lemma 1). Thus, there exists $i \in I$ s.t. for any $j \geq i$, the $\forall$-rule is not applied on ϕ with a tuple in T in p. But then $\phi \in \mathcal{PC}_p(\delta)$, which is impossible.

$\square$

We immediately deduce the following:

Corollary 2. *Let ϕ be an unsatisfiable formula. Let δ be a fair derivation of ϕ. δ is a refutation.*

To conclude this section, we point out that our proof procedure is a decision procedure for the Bernay-Schönfinkel class (BS). A formula belongs to BS iff it contains no existential quantifiers and no function symbol of non-zero arity (BS contains the the skolem form of prenex formulae of the form $(\exists x)(\forall y)\phi$, where ϕ is quantifier-free).

Lemma 3. *Let ϕ be a formula in BS. Any derivation from ϕ is finite.*

Proof. (Sketch) It is well known that the application of the $\vee$-rule, $\wedge$-rule and Closure terminates. We prove that the number of applications of the $\forall$-rule is bounded by showing that the number of distinct instances of a formula ψ in a given branch is finite. The proof is by induction on $q(\phi) - q(\psi)$, where $q(\gamma)$ is the number of universal quantifier in γ (it is obvious that $q(\phi) \geq q(\psi)$). Assume that the property holds for any formula ψ' with $q(\psi') \geq q(\psi)$. This implies that the number of free variables occurring in the formulae ψ with $q(\psi) \leq q(\psi')$ must be finite. Moreover the number of distinct tuples built on a signature containing no function of arity greater than 0 is finite, up to a renaming. Then the proof follows from Lemma 1. Finally, the Instantiation rule strictly reduces the number of variables occurring in a given branch, hence necessarily terminates. $\square$

5   Comparison with Existing Works

In this section we briefly compare our work with existing works in tableaux-based theorem proving.

[21] (see also [11]) presents a tableaux calculus (the SATCHMO procedure, or **positive unit hyperresolution tableaux**) with no use of rigid variables, but where the systematic instantiation of variables by ground terms is avoided. The idea is to restrict branch-generation to *positive* literals, by using a kind of *macro-inference rule* combining hyperresolution with splitting of ground positive clauses. This procedure was refined in [5] by adding the possibility of handling non ground unit clauses. [17] proposes to avoid systematic grounding of variables not occurring in the negative part by adding "rigid" variables in the tableau (in the usual sense). This last procedure could be combined with our method (by adapting the notion of candidate pair to the macro-inference rule). Hence this refinement is in some sense "orthogonal" to ours.

[18] presents an instance-based theorem proving procedure, called the **hyper-linking** method, where the generation of propositional instances of the clauses is carefully restricted. The idea is the following: given two clauses $C_1 = (L_1 \lor C_1)$ and $C_2 = (\neg L_2 \lor C_2)$ where L_1, L_2 are unifiable, one generates two instance clauses $(L_1 \lor C_1)\theta$ and $(L_2 \lor C_2)\theta$ where θ is a mgu of L_1 and L_2. These clauses are added to the initial clause set and the process is repeated. When checking for propositional satisfiability, all the remaining variables are instantiated to the same ground term. This idea is refined in [24] where the possibility of using semantic information, equality reasoning and ordering constraints is considered.

Building on this idea, [10] devises a proof procedure, called the **Disconnection Calculus**, whose basic idea is to combine the use of hyper-linking (used for generating propositional instances) with a tableaux calculus (used for checking the satisfiability of these propositional instances). The generation of clause instances and the satisfiability check are not separated anymore, but combined in the same procedure. This calculus was further improved in [19], and practical results show that it is in general much more efficient than the original hyper-linking method. A somewhat related approach is proposed in [16], but where auxiliary clauses are generated during proof search.

The calculus presented in [3] can be seen as a combination of the disconnection calculus with hyper-tableaux. It combines the hyper-linking procedure with the macro-inference rule used by model generation theorem provers.

In [6] a calculus is presented (based on a previous work described in [4]) for lifting the standard DPLL procedure (initially devoted to propositional logic) to the first-order case. This yields the definition of the Model Evolution calculus, a proof procedure somehow related to the hyper-linking and disconnection calculi, but where the branching is performed on *complementary literals* (as in the original Davis and Putnam procedure [13]) rather than on the subformulae.

The disconnection calculus (and the related proof procedures) has the same goal than our work, namely allowing branch-saturation and avoiding ground instantiation of the clauses. However, in contrast to disconnection calculi, our calculus still uses "rigid" variables, hence is closer to standard free-variable tableaux. Moreover, the formulae we consider are not necessarily in clausal form. In order to better emphasize the difference between the disconnection calculus (and all the approaches related to hyper-linking) we present the following example.

Example 4. We consider the following set of formulae:

$$S = \begin{array}{c} \neg p(a, f(a)) \\ (\forall x, y)\neg p(x, y) \lor p(x, f(y)) \\ (\forall x)p(f(x), a) \\ (\forall x, y)p(x, y) \lor \neg p(x, f(y)) \end{array}$$

It is easy to see that the disconnection calculus (as the hyper-tableaux or the resolution calculus[1]) does not terminate on S. For instance, the hyper-linking

---

[1] Without ordering restriction.

rule generates an infinite number of instances of the second clause, of the form $\neg p(f(x), f^n(a)) \vee p(f(x), f^{n+1}(a))$. We present a **finite** derivation for S.

We first apply the $\forall$-rules on $\neg p(a, f(a))$, $(\forall x, y)\neg p(x, y) \vee p(x, f(y))$, $(\forall x)p(f(x), a)$ and $(\forall x, y)p(x, y) \vee \neg p(x, f(y))$, yielding the formulae $\neg p(a, f(a))$, $\neg p(x_2, y_1) \vee p(x_2, f(y_1))$, $p(f(x_3), a)$ and $p(x_4, y_2) \vee \neg p(x_4, f(y_2))$. The $\vee$-rule is applied on $\neg p(x_2, y_1) \vee p(x_2, f(y_1))$ leading to two distinct branches. The branch corresponding to $p(x_2, f(y_1))$ is closed by unifying x_2 and y_1 with a. Then the $\vee$-rule is applied again on $p(x_4, y_2) \vee \neg p(x_4, f(y_2))$, and the branch corresponding to $p(x_4, y_2)$ is closed by unifying x_4 and y_2 with a.

This yield a unique open branch containing the literals: $\neg p(a, f(a))$, $\neg p(x_2, y_1)$, $p(f(x_3), a)$ and $\neg p(x_4, f(y_2))$ with the substitution $\{x_2 \to a, y_1 \to a, x_4 \to a, y_2 \to a\}$.

Obviously the Closure rule is not applicable.

There is a candidate substitution of the form $(\neg p(x_2, y_1), \{x_2 \to f(x_3), y_1 \to a\})$. Thus the $\forall$-rule is applicable on the formula $(\forall x, y)\neg p(x, y) \vee p(x, f(y))$. We have to replace x, y by a tuple of terms (t, s) not unifiable with $(x_2, y_1) = (a, a)$ and s.t. $(f(x_3), a) \preceq (t, s)$.

We choose a *maximal* pair (according to $\preceq$) having this property. We obtain two distinct solutions: $(f(x_5), y_3)$ and $(a, f(y_4))$, yielding the formulae $\neg p(f(x_5), y_3) \vee p(f(x_5), f(y_3)$ and $\neg p(a, f(y_4)) \vee p(a, f(f(y_4)))$.

Then, the $\vee$-rule is applied on these two formulae, which yields in particular the following branch: $\neg p(a, f(a))$, $\neg p(x_2, y_1)$, $p(f(x_3), a)$, $\neg p(x_4, f(y_2))$, $p(f(x_5), f(y_3))$, $\neg p(a, f(y_4))$, with the substitution $\{x_2 \to a, y_1 \to a, x_4 \to a, y_2 \to a\}$.

Similarly, we generate two new instances of the $(\forall x, y)p(x, y) \vee \neg p(x, f(y))$, which yields the formulae: $p(f(x_6), y_5) \vee \neg p(f(x_6), f(y_5))$ and $p(a, f(y_6)) \vee \neg p(a, f(f(y_6)))$ and after application of the $\vee$-rule, the branch:

$\neg p(a, f(a))$, $\neg p(x_2, y_1)$, $p(f(x_3), a)$, $\neg p(x_4, f(y_2))$, $p(f(x_5), f(y_3))$,

$\neg p(a, f(y_4))$, $p(f(x_6), y_5)$, $\neg p(a, f(f(y_6)))$ with the substitution $\{x_2 \to a, y_1 \to a, x_4 \to a, y_2 \to a\}$.

By computing all the candidate pairs, one can easily check that no rule is applicable on this branch. Hence the procedure *terminates* and detects the satisfiability of the original formula. The considered branch is complete hence this strategy is fair. Notice that if the closure rule is applied for closing the other branches, then y_4 for instance could be instantiated with a whence the $\forall$-rule will be applicable again on $(\forall x, y)\neg p(x, y) \vee p(x, f(y))$, leading to a potentially infinite branch. In order to ensure termination, all the remaining branches have to be left open. This shows that the termination is not guaranteed: it depends on the strategy for choosing the extension rule. This example shows that our method can detect the satisfiability of formulae for which other approaches do not terminate.

[20] presents a refinement of the disconnection calculus allowing a more efficient treatment of universal variables. The basic idea is to avoid the instantiation of the variables occurring in only one literal in a given clause. This may reduce the proof complexity, and in particular, it is no more bounded by the

Herbrand complexity of the clause set. In our case, since we deal with non-clausal formula, such cases can easily be handled by using miniscoping. Note that the miniscoping rule can be applied statically on the original formula, but *also* in a dynamic way on the formula generated during proof search. This principle has one significant advantage w.r.t. the method in [20]: it is not restricted to the case of variables occurring only in one literal. We can also handle clauses of the form: $\neg P(x) \vee \neg P(f(x)) \vee \neg Q(y) \vee Q(f(y))$, that are reduced to: $(\forall x)(P(x) \vee \neg P(f(x))) \vee (\forall y)(\neg Q(y) \vee Q(f(y)))$, which is not possible (to the best of our knowledge) with the technique in [20][2].

[15] presents a fair procedure to find the closing instantiation of a given tableau. The idea is to compute the whole set of closure instantiations in an incremental way, avoiding to commit to certain substitutions. In contrast, our procedure does instantiate the free variable, hence is closer to the usual tableaux.

[7] proposed another solution, based on a concept of tableau subsumption and on a partial ordering of literals, allowing to avoid generating repeatedly the same literals and sub-tableaux. However, this strategy is "global", in the sense that it requires keeping the whole tableau, which is avoided in our approach.

Of course, additional work is required to estimate the performances of our proof procedure. In particular, the calculus has to be further developed (including redundancy criteria, pruning mechanisms etc.). An efficient implementation of the method and practical experimentations are mandatory.

Acknowledgments. The author would like to thank the anonymous referees for their precise and pertinent comments.

References

1. W. Ahrendt, T. Baar, B. Beckert, R. Bubel, M. Giese, R. Hähnle, W. Menzel, W. Mostowski, A. Roth, S. Sclager, and P. H. Schmitt. The KeY tool. *Software and System Modeling*, 2004. To appear.
2. F. Baader and W. Snyder. Unification theory. In A. Robinson and A. Voronkov, editors, *Handbook of Automated Reasoning*, volume I, chapter 8, pages 445–532. Elsevier Science, 2001.
3. P. Baumgartner. Hyper Tableaux — The Next Generation. In H. de Swaart, editor, *Automated Reasoning with Analytic Tableaux and Related Methods*, volume 1397 of *LNAI*, pages 60–76. Springer, 1998.
4. P. Baumgartner. FDPLL – A First-Order Davis-Putnam-Logeman-Loveland Procedure. In D. McAllester, editor, *CADE-17 – The 17th International Conference on Automated Deduction*, volume 1831 of *LNAI*, pages 200–219. Springer, 2000.
5. P. Baumgartner, U. Furbach, and I. Niemelä. Hyper-tableaux. In *Logics in AI, JELIA '96*. Springer, 1996.
6. P. Baumgartner and C. Tinelli. The Model Evolution Calculus. In F. Baader, editor, *CADE-19 – The 19th International Conference on Automated Deduction*, volume 2741 of *LNAI*, pages 350–364. Springer, 2003.

---

[2] We ignore if the method of [20] can be extended to handle such cases.

7. B. Beckert. Depth-first proof search without backtracking for free-variable clausal tableaux. *Journal of Symbolic Computation*, 36:117–138, 2003.

8. B. Beckert and J. Posegga. Lean-TAP: Lean tableau-based deduction. *Journal of Automated Reasoning*, 15(3):339–358, 1995.

9. W. Bibel. On matrices with connections. *Journal of the Association of Computing Machinery*, 28:633–645, 1981.

10. J.-P. Billon. The disconnection method: a confluent integration of unification in the analytic framework. In *Tableaux'96*, volume 1071 of *LNAI*, pages 110–126. Springer, 1996.

11. F. Bry and A. Yahya. Minimal model generation with positive unit hyper-resolution tableaux. In *Proceeding of Tableaux'96*, LNAI 1071, pages 143–159. Springer, 1996.

12. H. Comon and P. Lescanne. Equational problems and disunification. *Journal of Symbolic Computation*, 7:371–475, 1989.

13. M. Davis and H. Putnam. A Computing Procedure for Quantification Theory. *Journal of the ACM*, 7(3):201–215, July 1960.

14. M. Fitting. *First-Order Logic and Automated Theorem Proving*. Texts and Monographs in Computer Science. Springer-Verlag, 1990.

15. M. Giese. Incremental Closure of Free Variable Tableaux. In *Proc. Intl. Joint Conf. on Automated Reasoning, Siena, Italy*, number 2083 in LNCS, pages 545–560. Springer-Verlag, 2001.

16. J. Hooker, G. Rago, V. Chandru, and A. Shrivasta. Partial instantation methods for inference in first order logic. *Journal of Automated Reasoning*, 28:371–396, 2002.

17. M. Kühn. Rigid hypertableaux. In G. Brewka, C. Habel, and B. Nebel, editors, *KI'97*, LNAI. Springer, 1997.

18. S. Lee and D. A. Plaisted. Eliminating duplication with the hyper-linking strategy. *Journal of Automated Reasoning*, 9:25–42, 1992.

19. R. Letz and G. Stenz. Proof and model generation with disconnection tableaux. In *Logic for Programmaing, Artificial Intelligence and Reasoning (LPAR)*, pages 142–156. Springer, 2001.

20. R. Letz and G. Stenz. Universal variables in disconnection tableaux. In M. Cialdea Mayer and F. Pirri, editors, *Tableaux'03*, volume 2796 of *LNAI*, pages 117–133. Springer, 2003.

21. R. Manthey and F. Bry. SATCHMO: A theorem prover implemented in Prolog. In *Proc. of CADE-9*, pages 415–434. Springer, LNCS 310, 1988.

22. F. Oppacher and H. Suen. HARP: A tableau-based theorem prover. *Journal of Automated Reasoning*, 4:69–100, 1988.

23. R. Pichler. On the complexity of equational problems in CNF. *Journal of Symbolic Computation*, 36(1-2):235–269, 2003.

24. D. A. Plaisted and Y. Zhu. Ordered semantic hyperlinking. *Journal of Automated Reasoning*, 25(3):167–217, October 2000.

25. R. M. Smullyan. *First-Order Logic*. Springer, 1968.

Semantic Knowledge Partitioning

Christoph Wernhard

Institut für Informatik, Universität Koblenz-Landau, D-56070 Koblenz, Germany,
wernhard@uni-koblenz.de

Abstract. Some operations to decompose a knowledge base (considered as a first order logic formula) in ways so that only its semantics determines the results are investigated. Intended uses include the extraction of "parts" relevant to an application, the exploration and utilizing of implicit possibilities of structuring a knowledge base and the formulation of query answers in terms of a signature demanded by an application. A semantic framework based on Herbrand interpretations is outlined. The notion of "model relative to a scope" is introduced. It underlies the partitioning operations "projection" and "forgetting" and also provides a semantic account for certain formula simplification operations. An algorithmic approach which is based on resolution and may be regarded as a variation of the SCAN algorithm is discussed.

1   Introduction

We investigate some operations to decompose a knowledge base in ways so that solely its semantics determines the results. We regard a knowledge base as represented by a logic formula and confine ourselves here to classical propositional logic and classical first order clausal logic. A decomposition operation takes a formula as input and returns one or several other formulas that are in some sense "parts" of the original one. "Semantics" can be understood in the standard sense for these logics, here however a specific notion based on Herbrand interpretations is used. This fits with automated deduction techniques and is easily accessible to a full formalization which in turn may be automatically processed.

A knowledge base can be large, can integrate further knowledge bases and is possibly designed and maintained by someone else than its user. It should be accessed through an interface of operations that are characterized purely in terms of the semantics of the knowledge base and query expressions. Some types of such operations can be straightforwardly expressed as theorem proving tasks, others require different modes of reasoning such as model generation, decision procedures, abduction, partial deduction or knowledge compilation. Semantic knowledge partitioning can be understood as such a reasoning mode. Outputs can be again inputs to reasoning in this or some other mode.

Semantic knowledge partitioning should be a means to compute the following kinds of operations:

J.J. Alferes and J. Leite (Eds.): JELIA 2004, LNAI 3229, pp. 552–564, 2004.

- Extraction of an application relevant portion from a large knowledge base.
- Exploration and utilizing of implicit possibilities of structuring a knowledge base: Computing definitional dependency of predicates and functions. Computing ways of decomposition into mutually independent sentences.
- Expressing a theorem in terms of a certain signature, which characterizes for example those terms which are "understood" in some way or handled efficiently by a human or machine client.
- Removing information from an answer for security reasons.

2   Notation and Preliminaries

We consider first order formulas in Skolemized clausal form: A *formula* (or *matrix*) is a set of clauses; a *clause* is a set of literals; a *literal* is a pair of an atom and a sign. If A is an atom, we write $+A$ $(-A)$ for the positive (negative) literal with atom A. The *dual* of a literal L is written $\overline{L}$. Occasionally we use logic connectives in formulas or formula schemas, which can be understood as straightforward abbreviations of the respective matrix form.

We use a semantic framework based on Herbrand interpretations. A *function signature* Σ is a finite set of function symbols $Name/Arity$ that includes at least one constant symbol. For a syntactic object F, $\Sigma(F)$ is the set of function symbols in F. The *base* of a formula F and a function signature $\Sigma \supseteq \Sigma(F)$, in symbols $\mathcal{B}(F, \Sigma)$ is the set of ground atoms obtained by instantiating all atoms in F with terms constructed from Σ. An *interpretation* over a base $\mathcal{B}$ is a set of ground literals that contains for each $A \in \mathcal{B}$ exactly one of $+A$ or $-A$ and no other elements. To avoid notational clutter we assume an implicit function signature that includes all function symbols in formulas we consider. Thus we speak of *the base of a formula* F, in symbols $\mathcal{B}(F)$. For interpretations we assume an implicit base that is a superset of the bases of all considered formulas.

A clause C *contradicts* an interpretation I if and only if there is a ground instance C' of C such that the dual of each literal in C' is in I. An interpretation I is a *model* for a formula F, in symbols $I \models F$, if and only if F contains no clause that contradicts I. A formula F *implies* a formula G, in symbols $F \Rightarrow G$, if and only if for all interpretations I holds that if $I \models F$ then $I \models G$. Two formulas F and G are *equivalent*, in symbols $F \Leftrightarrow G$, if and only if $F \Rightarrow G$ and $G \Rightarrow F$.

Definition 1 (Essential Base). The *essential base of a formula* F, in symbols $\mathcal{E}(F)$, is the set of all ground atoms A such that there exists an interpretation I for which exactly one of $(I - \{-A\}) \cup \{+A\} \models F$ or $(I - \{+A\}) \cup \{-A\} \models F$ does hold.

For example $\mathcal{E}(p \wedge (q \vee \neg q)) = \{p\}$. For a propositional logic formula F, $\mathcal{E}(F)$ is the unique smallest signature such that there exists a formula equivalent to F which has this signature. Intuitively the essential base of a formula may be regarded as the set of ground atoms about which the formula does "express something."

3   Model Relative to a Scope

A *scope* is a set of ground atoms. The notion of *model relative to a scope* is the central concept in this work. It is used to specify partitioning operations semantically. It also provides semantics for certain formula simplification which do not preserve equivalence.

Definition 2 (Equality of Interpretations Relative to a Scope). For all scopes S, and interpretations I and J, I *is equal to* J *relative to* S, in symbols $I =_S J$, if and only if I and J assign the same values to all atoms in S.

Definition 3 (Model Relative to a Scope). For all interpretations I, formulas F and scopes S, I *is a model of* F *relative to* S, in symbols $I \models_S F$, if and only if there exists an interpretation I' such that $I' \models F$ and $I' =_S I$ hold.

Definition 4 (Equivalence Relative to a Scope). For all formulas F, G and scopes S, F *and* G *are equivalent relative to* S, in symbols $F \Leftrightarrow_S G$, if and only if for all interpretations I holds that $I \models_S F$ if and only if $I \models_S G$.

The following proposition shows simple connections between the model relationship relative to a base, the general model relationship, the essential base of a formula and the subset relationships between scopes.

Proposition 1. *For all formulas F, scopes S, S' and interpretations I it holds that 1. if $I \models F$ then $I \models_S F$, 2. if $\mathcal{E}(F) \subseteq S$ and $I \models_S F$ then $I \models F$, 3. if $S' \subseteq S$ and $I \models_S F$ then $I \models_{S'} F$, 4. if $I \models_{\mathcal{E}(F) \cap S} F$ then $I \models_S F$.*

4   Projection and Forgetting

Projection and *forgetting* are the core operations for this approach to semantic knowledge partitioning. They are defined as ternary relationships $\mathsf{project}(F, S, F')$ and $\mathsf{forget}(F, S, F')$, where F and F' are formulas and S is a scope. F and S are considered as input and F' as result. Intuitively projection means that F' is equivalent to F with respect to the atoms in S but provides no information about other atoms (like a database relation can be "projected" onto a given set of attributes). Forgetting means intuitively that F' is equivalent to F, except that F' does not provide any information about the atoms in S.

Definition 5 (Projection). For all formulas F, F' and scopes S, F' is a *projection of F onto S*, in symbols $\mathsf{project}(F, S, F')$, if and only if for all interpretations I holds that $I \models F'$ if and only if $I \models_S F$.

Definition 6 (Forgetting). For all formulas F, F' and scopes S, F' is a *forgetting about S in F*, in symbols $\mathsf{forget}(F, S, F')$, if and only if $\mathsf{project}(F, \mathcal{E}(F) - S, F')$.

Projection and forgetting are dual to each other in the sense that also project(F, S, F') is equivalent to forget($F, \mathcal{E}(F) - S, F'$). Projection and forgetting are "semantic" operations, i.e. for all formulas F, G, F', G' and scopes S it holds that if $F \Leftrightarrow G$, project(F, S, F') and project(G, S, G') then $F' \Leftrightarrow G'$ (and similarly for forget).

The following propositions show alternate characterizations of projection and forgetting in terms of essential base and relative equivalence:

Proposition 2. *For all formulas F, F' and sets of atoms S holds* project(F, S, F') *if and only if $\mathcal{E}(F') \subseteq S$ and $F \Leftrightarrow_S F'$.*

Proposition 3. *For all formulas F, F' and scopes S holds* forget(F, S, F') *if and only if the following three conditions hold: 1. $F \Leftrightarrow_{\mathcal{E}(F)-S} F'$, 2. $\mathcal{E}(F') \cap S = \emptyset$ and 3. $\mathcal{E}(F') \subseteq \mathcal{E}(F)$.*

Only the intersection of the given scope with the essential base of the input formula is relevant for the results of projection and forgetting: For all formulas F, F' and scopes S holds: project(F, S, F') if and only if project($F, \mathcal{E}(F) \cap S, F'$) (and similarly for forget). Since for all formulas F $\mathcal{E}(F) \subseteq \mathcal{B}(F)$, in the mutual characterizations of one operator in terms of the other instead of the $\mathcal{E}$ operator also the $\mathcal{B}$ operator can be used, which may be easier to handle computationally. For example project(F, S, F') holds if and only if forget($F, \mathcal{B}(F) - S, F'$) holds.

The following proposition related to proposition 3 is useful to show correctness of methods that compute forgettings if they do not introduce new predicate or function symbols to the result formula:

Proposition 4. *For all formulas F, F' and scopes S it holds that if $\mathcal{E}(F') \subseteq \mathcal{B}(F)$, $F \Leftrightarrow_{\mathcal{B}(F)-S} F'$ (which strengthens condition (1) in proposition 3) and condition (2) in that proposition are satisfied, then also condition (3) in that proposition holds.*

Example 1. Consider the matrix $F = \{\{\mathsf{p(a)}\}, \{\neg\mathsf{p}(x), \mathsf{q}(x)\}, \{\neg\mathsf{q}(x), \mathsf{r}(x)\}\}$ along with the function signature $\Sigma = \{\mathsf{a}/0, \mathsf{b}/0, \mathsf{c}/0\}$. The following table shows the results of forgettings about the set of all ground atoms with predicate symbol q and about the unit sets of the atoms q(a), p(a), p(b) and r(a) respectively:

$$\mathsf{q} : \{\{\mathsf{p(a)}\}, \{\neg\mathsf{p}(x), \mathsf{r}(x)\}\}$$
$$\mathsf{q(a)} : \{\{\mathsf{p(a)}\}, \{\neg\mathsf{p(a)}, \mathsf{r(a)}\}, \{\neg\mathsf{p(b)}, \mathsf{q(b)}\}, \{\neg\mathsf{p(c)}, \mathsf{q(c)}\},$$
$$\{\neg\mathsf{q(b)}, \mathsf{r(b)}\}, \{\neg\mathsf{q(c)}, \mathsf{r(c)}\}\}$$
$$\mathsf{p(a)} : \{\{\mathsf{q(a)}\}, \{\neg\mathsf{p(b)}, \mathsf{q(b)}\}, \{\neg\mathsf{p(c)}, \mathsf{q(c)}\}, \{\neg\mathsf{q}(x), \mathsf{r}(x)\}\}$$
$$\mathsf{p(b)} : \{\{\mathsf{p(a)}\}, \{\neg\mathsf{p(a)}, \mathsf{q(a)}\}, \{\neg\mathsf{p(c)}, \mathsf{q(c)}\}, \{\neg\mathsf{q}(x), \mathsf{r}(x)\}\}$$
$$\mathsf{r(a)} : \{\{\mathsf{p(a)}\}, \{\neg\mathsf{p}(x), \mathsf{q}(x)\}, \{\neg\mathsf{q(b)}, \mathsf{r(b)}\}, \{\neg\mathsf{q(c)}, \mathsf{r(c)}\}\}$$

Example 2. In this example a toy knowledge base in description logic is given. Forgetting is applied to the matrix of its standard translation. The results are then converted back to description logic. The input knowledge base contains the following axioms:

$$\text{document} \doteq \text{text} \sqcup \text{image}.$$
$$\text{web\_document} \doteq \text{document} \sqcap \text{has\_uri}.$$
$$\text{wd}_1, \text{wd}_2, \text{wd}_3 \ : \ \text{web\_document}.$$

The result of forgetting document is:

$$\text{web\_document} \doteq (\text{text} \sqcup \text{image}) \sqcap \text{has\_uri}.$$
$$\text{wd}_1, \text{wd}_2, \text{wd}_3 \ : \ \text{web\_document}.$$

The result of forgetting web_document is:

$$\text{document} \doteq \text{text} \sqcup \text{image}.$$
$$\text{wd}_1, \text{wd}_2, \text{wd}_3 \ : \ \text{document} \sqcap \text{has\_uri}.$$

The result of forgetting web_document(wd_1) is:

$$\text{document} \doteq \text{text} \sqcup \text{image}.$$
$$\text{wd}_1 \ : \ \text{document} \sqcap \text{has\_uri}.$$
$$\text{wd}_2, \text{wd}_3 \ : \ \text{web\_document} \sqcap \text{document} \sqcap \text{has\_uri}.$$

The result of forgetting has_uri is:

$$\text{document} \doteq \text{text} \sqcup \text{image}.$$
$$\text{web\_document} \sqsubseteq \text{document}.$$
$$\text{wd}_1, \text{wd}_2, \text{wd}_3 \ : \ \text{web\_document}.$$

5   Forgetting for Propositional Logic

For propositional formulas F and atoms A a function $\mathsf{forget}(F, A)$ such that $\mathsf{forget}(F, \{A\}, \mathsf{forget}(F, A))$ holds can be defined as $\mathsf{forget}(F, A) = F[A \backslash \mathsf{true}] \vee F[A \backslash \mathsf{false}]$ where $F[A \backslash G]$ denotes F with all occurrences of A substituted by G.

Algorithm 1 (DNF-Forget).
INPUT: A propositional formula F and propositional atom A.
OUTPUT: A formula F' such that $\mathsf{forget}(F, \{A\}, F')$ holds.
METHOD: Convert F to non-complementary disjunctive clausal normal form (NC-DNF).[1] Remove all literals with atom A from these clauses and return the corresponding propositional formula.

It is easy to see that applying the schema $F[A \backslash \mathsf{true}] \vee F[A \backslash \mathsf{false}]$ to a formula F in NC-DNF amounts to the method of the algorithm. Correctness of the algorithm can also be easily shown by considering F converted to NC-DNF, since for all formulas F in this form and interpretations I it holds that $I \models F$ if and only if there exists a clause $C \in F$ such that $C \subseteq I$. So it is not hard to prove $F \Leftrightarrow_{\mathcal{B}(F)-\{A\}} \mathsf{forget}(F, A)$. Hence condition (1) of Proposition 3 holds. Condition (2) does obviously hold and condition (3) follows from Proposition 4.

Another way to compute forgettings for propositional formulas is algorithm pattern-forgetting which will be described in Sect. 7. For propositional inputs the preprocessing steps of that algorithm have no effect and can be skipped.

---

[1] *Non-complementary* means that no clause contains a literal and its dual.

6   Properties of and Constructions with Projection

In this section we outline some applications of projection together with the properties and constructions underlying them. We assume that the respective projections can be computed and hence write the projection operator as a binary function, as we did in the section on forgetting for propositional logic.

Justification of Knowledge Base Preprocessing. The following proposition ensures that $\mathsf{project}(F, \mathcal{B}(G))$ can be regarded as a knowledge base extract that can be used to answer all queries whose base is a subset of $\mathcal{B}(G)$:

Proposition 5. *For all formulas F and G it holds that $F \Rightarrow G$ if and only if $\mathsf{project}(F, \mathcal{B}(G)) \Rightarrow G$.*

Justification of Cheap Decomposition. A decomposable negation normal form (DNNF) is a negation normal form in which no atom is shared between any two conjuncts [6]. One of the motivations for using a DNNF as a target language for knowledge compilation is that for a DNNF projection on a set atoms can be computed in linear time [6], which can be seen from the following propositions:

Proposition 6. *For all formulas F, G and scopes S holds*
 (1) $\mathsf{project}(F \vee G, S) \Leftrightarrow \mathsf{project}(F, S) \vee \mathsf{project}(G, S)$,
 (2) *If $\mathcal{B}(F) \cap \mathcal{B}(G) = \emptyset$ then $\mathsf{project}(F \wedge G, S) \Leftrightarrow \mathsf{project}(F, S) \wedge \mathsf{project}(G, S)$.*

Preservation of Satisfiability. The next proposition implies that a formula F is satisfiable if and only if $\mathsf{project}(F, \emptyset)$ is satisfiable. This suggests that such methods for computing projection which ensure that the base of their result is a subset of the projection scope — and hence literally return true or false if the scope is empty — can be used to compute satisfiability.[2]

Proposition 7. *For all formulas F and scopes S it holds that F is satisfiable if and only if $\mathsf{project}(F, S)$ is satisfiable.*

Definability and Construction of Definitions. If F is formula, A a ground atom and S is a set of ground atoms not containing A, then A is called *definable in terms of S within F* if and only if F implies a formula $A \leftrightarrow D$ where $\mathcal{B}(D) \subseteq S$. Definability can be expressed using projection: A is definable in terms of S within F if and only if $\mathsf{project}(F \wedge A, \ S) \wedge \mathsf{project}(F \wedge \neg A, \ S)$ is unsatisfiable.

---

[2] Actually for a propositional clause set F, forgetting about the atoms in $\mathcal{B}(F)$ one by one using the replace-by-resolvents algorithm described in Sect. 7 combined with restricted application of the equivalence preserving simplifications *removal of subsumed clauses* and *subsumption resolution* amounts to the Davis Putnam method [7]. The *rule for eliminating atomic formulas* and, as will be shown in Sect. 7.5, the *affirmative-negative rule* both correspond to applications of replace-by-resolvents.

If definability holds for F,A and S, then definitions can be constructed in two ways: 1. $A \leftrightarrow \mathsf{project}(F \wedge A,\ S)$ and 2. $A \leftrightarrow \neg\mathsf{project}(F \wedge \neg A,\ S)$. Both constructed definitions may not be logically equivalent. Consider for example $F = (\mathsf{p} \leftrightarrow \mathsf{q} \wedge \mathsf{r}) \wedge (\mathsf{q} \vee \mathsf{r})$. These two definitions of p in terms of $\{\mathsf{q},\mathsf{r}\}$ are constructed: 1. $\mathsf{p} \leftrightarrow \mathsf{q} \wedge \mathsf{r}$ and 2. $\mathsf{p} \leftrightarrow (\mathsf{q} \leftrightarrow \mathsf{r})$.

Lossless Decomposition. A set of scopes $\{S_1, S_2, ..., S_n\}$ is a n-ary lossless decomposition of F iff $\bigwedge_{i=1..n} \mathsf{project}(F, S_i) \Rightarrow F$.

7   Computation of Forgetting by Resolution

In propositional logic the forgetting about an atom can — as an alternative to Algorithm 1 — be computed by successively replacing all clauses containing a literal with the atom to be forgotten by the resolvents upon that literal. In this section we discuss an approach to transfer this method to first order matrices. Also, instead of forgetting about a single ground atom, the method for first order logic allows to forget about all ground instances of a given pattern. The pattern has to be *linear*,[3] since a certain clause instantiation procedure is involved, which, as we will see in Sect. 7.2, is guaranteed to have finite solutions only for linear patterns.

Before we discuss the sub-procedures of the method in detail we give an overview of the overall procedure.

Algorithm 2 (Pattern Forgetting).
INPUT: A first order matrix F, a linear atom P (the "pattern") and a function signature $\Sigma \supseteq \Sigma(F) \cup \Sigma(P)$.
OUTPUT: A matrix that is the forgetting about all ground instances of P in F, or an "approximation" of the forgetting, as will be discussed in Sect. 7.6.
METHOD:

1. Preprocessing: F is assigned the result of applying *diff* expansion and *break* transformation to the input arguments.
2. Core loop: While F contains a clause C with a literal L whose atom is an instance of P, assign to F the result of eliminating C with replace-by-resolvents applied to F, C and L. Between the rounds of this loop equivalence preserving *simplifications* may be performed on F.
3. Postprocessing: Try to reduce F and to remove auxiliary literals introduced by the *break* transformation with *simplifications*. Output the modified F.

In the following subsections we discuss the sub-procedures of this algorithm, starting with the core procedure.

---

[3] An atom is *linear* if and only if it does not contain multiple occurrences of the same variable.

7.1   Replace-by-Resolvents

Algorithm 3 (Replace-by-Resolvents).

INPUT: A first order matrix F, clause C and literal L with $L \in C$ and $C \in F$.

OUTPUT: If the algorithm terminates, the matrix F with C replaced by the saturation of resolvents upon L.

METHOD: While a resolvent[4] D upon L and C with some clause from F exists such that D is not tautological and not subsumed by $F - \{C\}$ add D to F. Output $F - \{C\}$.

Theorem 1. *For all matrices F, clauses C and literals L with $L \in C$ and $C \in F$ it holds that if each resolvent upon literal L and clause C with a clause in F is tautological or subsumed by a clause in $F - \{C\}$ then, for all scopes S not containing an instance of the atom of L holds $F \Leftrightarrow_S F - \{C\}$.*

For propositional matrixes this theorem can be proved straightforwardly by properties of literals, clauses and interpretations. For first order matrixes an inductive proof over an enumeration of ground instances C_i, $i \geq 1$ of C can be given: Let F_0 be $F - \{C\}$ and F_n be $F_{n-1} \cup \{C_n\}$ for $n \geq 1$. The induction step ensures that $F_{n+1} \Leftrightarrow_S F_n$ for all $n \geq 0$ by means of the theorem for propositional matrixes and the *lifting lemma*.[5]

7.2   Preprocessing Operation: *Diff* Expansion

The input matrix for a pattern forgetting operation can contain literals with atoms that are unifiable with the pattern but not instances of it. replace-by-resolvents can not be directly applied to such a matrix to forget the instances of a pattern. If the pattern is linear, however any matrix can be transformed into a form without such literals, by *diff* expansion:[6]

Algorithm 4 (Diff-Expansion).

INPUT: A first order matrix F, a linear atom P that does not share variables with F and a function signature $\Sigma \supseteq \Sigma(F) \cup \Sigma(P)$.

OUTPUT: A finite set of instances of clauses of F that has the same Herbrand expansion as F over Σ and does not contain a literal L such that the atom A of L is unifiable with P and $A \not\geq_s P$.

---

[4] *Resolvent* is understood as in [5]. We extend the notion of *literals resolved upon* from binary resolvents to resolvents: A clause C is a resolvent of clause C_1 with clause C_2 *upon* literal L_1, if $L_1 \in C_1$ and C is a binary resolvent of C_1 upon L_1 or C is a binary resolvent of a factor $C_1\sigma$ of C_1 upon $L_1\sigma$.

[5] We need here a slightly strengthened version of the lifting lemma in [5] in which we also consider a *literal resolved upon*: If C_1', $L_1' \in C_1$ and C_2' are instances of C_1, $L_1 \in C_1$ and C_2 respectively, and if C' is a resolvent of C_1' upon L_1' and C_2', then there is a resolvent C of C_1 upon L_1 and C_2 such that C' is an instance of C.

[6] In this subsection we use the following notation: $A \geq_s B$ stands for A *is an instance of* B. $\circ$ denotes composition of substitutions, where the substitution on the left side is applied first. Application of substitution is expressed by postfix notation. $\mathsf{mgu}(A, B)$ is the most general unifier of A and B. $\mathsf{vars}(A)$ is the set of variables in A.

METHOD: While F contains a clause C with a literal L such that the atom A of L is unifiable with P and $A \not\geq_s P$ replace C in F by $C\sigma$ for all $\sigma \in$ diff-substitutions(A, P, Σ). Output the modified matrix F.

Algorithm 5 (Diff-Substitutions).
INPUT: An atom A, a linear atom P that does not share variables with A and is unifiable with A and a function signature $\Sigma \supseteq \Sigma(A) \cup \Sigma(P)$.
OUTPUT: A set of substitutions S such that 1. there is no $\sigma \in S$ such that $A\sigma$ is unifiable with P and $A\sigma \not\geq_s P$ and 2. for all clauses C with $\Sigma(C) \subseteq \Sigma$ it holds that the Herbrand expansions of C and $\{C\sigma \mid \sigma \in S\}$ over Σ are identical.
METHOD: Let S be a set of substitutions initialized to $\{\epsilon\}$.

  While S contains a substitution σ such that $A\sigma$ is unifiable with P and $A\sigma \not\geq_s P$ do the following steps:

- Choose a variable X from vars$(A\sigma)$ such that (X)mgu$(A\sigma, P)$ is not a variable. (The existence of such a X follows from the while condition.)
- Remove σ from S.
- For each function symbol f/n in Σ generate n fresh variables $X_1, X_2, ..., X_n$ and add $\sigma \circ \{X \mapsto f(X_1, X_2, ..., X_n)\}$ to S.

  Output S.

Actually in each round there is exactly one element $A\sigma \in S$ that is unifiable with P. The algorithm may produce different outputs depending on the choice of X in each round. The cardinality of the result of the algorithm applied to inputs A, P and Σ is $1 + (|\Sigma| - 1) * \sum_{X \in \text{vars}(A)} |\text{ocfs}((X)\text{mgu}(A, P))|$ where $|\text{ocfs}(T)|$ is the number of occurrences of function symbols in term T.

Example 3. Consider $F = \{\{p(x, y)\}\}$, $P = p(f(u), a)$ and $\Sigma = \{a/0, \ b/0, \ f/1\}$. A *diff* expansion is $\{\{p(a, x)\}, \ \{p(b, x)\}, \ \{p(f(x), a)\}, \{p(f(x), b)\}, \ \{p(f(x), f(y))\}\}$.

For a non-linear pattern P a finite set of substitutions satisfying the output conditions of Algorithm 5 may not exist. Consider for example $A = p(x, y)$, $P = p(u, u)$, $\Sigma = \{a/0, f/1\}$. Among the required instances of clause $\{p(x, y)\}$ there are all $\{p(f^n(f(x_n)), f^n(a)))\}$ for $n \geq 0$.
An alternative to the *diff* expansion transformation would be the use of disequality constraints, which we do not pursue here, since it has two features that we want to avoid: Symbols to be "forgotten" are retained "negatively" in the constraints and the straightforward framework of first order logic is left.

7.3   Preprocessing Operation: *Break* Transformation

replace-by-resolvents terminates if each clause contains only a single literal whose atom is weakly unifiable with L. Any matrix can be brought into this form by replacing clauses with more than one such literal with fragments of them that are linked with auxiliary definitional literals, for example if $p(X)$ is the pattern, the clause $\{\neg p(Y), p(f(Y))\}$ can be replaced by the clauses $\{\neg p(Y), \neg break_1(Y)\}$ and $\{break_1(Y), p(f(Y))\}$ where $break_1$ is a new auxiliary predicate whose arguments are the variables shared between the two fragments of the original clause. The original and the transformed matrix are equivalent relative to scopes not containing instances of "*break* atoms", i.e. atoms of these auxiliary literals.

If the *break* transformation is applied before *diff* expansion, the possible generation of an exponential number of clause instances at the *diff* expansion phase is avoided.

7.4   Simplifications

In the context of theorem proving, operations that can be performed fast (typically in linear time), can be applied only a number of times that is polynomial (typically linear) in the size of the formula and reduce the refutation task in some sense while preserving satisfiability are known as *simplifications* or *reductions* [4].

Some simplifications preserve the equivalence of the input formula, for example *removal of tautological clauses*, *removal of subsumed clauses*, *subsumption resolution* and *condensation*. Other simplifications are commonly applied in theorem proving since they preserve satisfiability. A closer look at some of them however shows that they actually preserve equivalence relative to certain scopes which justifies that they can be used for knowledge base preprocessing and model generation.

For the pattern forgetting method discussed in this section simplifications play a twofold role: Equivalence preserving simplifications are applied to reduce the results and intermediate results of **replace-by-resolvents**. Along with equivalence preserving simplifications, simplifications that preserve all scopes that do not include *break* atoms are applied to delete *break* literals as far as possible from the final output of the forgetting algorithm.

7.5   Simplifications Preserving Equivalence Relative to Certain Scopes

We first consider two special cases of **replace-by-resolvents**. Let $L \in C$ be the literal occurrence to be resolved upon. L is called *pure*, if the matrix does not contain a literal that is weakly unifiable[7] with $\overline{L}$. The effect of **replace-by-resolvents** upon a pure L is just that C is deleted. This is a first order generalization of the *pure literal rule* (originally called *affirmative-negative rule*) of the Davis Putnam method. Another special case is that a first application of **replace-by-resolvents** replaces C by resolvents with partner clauses which then in turn can be removed by the purity simplification just discussed. This is a first order generalization of the *ISOL* and *ISOL** reductions in [3]. That they can be described as special

---

[7] Two atoms are *weakly unifiable* if and only if they are unifiable after their variables have been standardized apart.

cases of replace-by-resolvents shows that these simplifications do not only preserve satisfiability of the input matrix but also equivalence relative to all scopes not containing instances of the literals resolved upon.

An *extended purity reduction rule* is given in [13]: If the matrix does not contain two clauses such that literals with a predicate P occurs only positively in one and only negatively in the other, then all clauses containing a literal with predicate P are deleted. This simplification preserves equivalence relative to all scopes that do not contain atoms with predicate P.

A further simplification is the *deletion of an isolated satisfiable clause group*: If the input matrix can be split into two disjoint subsets F_1 and F_2 such that there are no weakly unifiable literals L_1 and L_2 with L_1 in F_1 and $\overline{L_2}$ in F_2, then if F_1 is satisfiable, the clauses of F_1 are deleted. The result matrix preserves equivalence relative to all scopes not including the instance of an atom from F_1.

7.6   Correctness of the Pattern Forgetting Algorithm

Algorithm pattern-forgetting terminates for all inputs — the *diff* and *break* transformations terminate, replace-by-resolvents terminates since the *break* transformation has been applied and simplifications naturally do terminate.

If the result of applying algorithm pattern-forgetting to F and P does not contain any *break* literals, it is indeed the supposed forgetting: *diff* expansion preserves equivalence of the matrix in the sense that it preserves its Herbrand expansion. The *break* transformation preserves equivalence with respect to all scopes not including *break* atoms. For replace-by-resolvents, Theorem 1 ensures condition (1) of Proposition 3, condition (2) is obviously satisfied. That also condition (3) is satisfied can be shown with the help of Proposition 4. Finally simplifications in the postprocessing phase are either preserving equivalence or equivalence relative to all scopes not containing *break* atoms.

If *break* literals remain in the result, then condition (3.) might be violated. Depending on the application such results might nevertheless be useful.[8]

8   Related Work

Algorithm pattern-forgetting is similar to the core part of the SCAN algorithm, in which clauses are "resolved away" by C-resolution [8]. This algorithm goes back to W. Ackermann [1]. Similar algorithms and a completeness property of SCAN are described in [12,13,9]. SCAN was motivated by applications in correspondence theory for modal logics. Also interpolation (i.e. knowledge base preprocessing) and the computing of circumscription are shown as applications in [8].

C-factoring (C-resolution) with *constraint elimination* [9] corresponds to "standard" factoring (binary resolution) [5] if the matrix for the standard operations includes predicate substitutivity axioms for $\approx$: For each n-ary predicate

---

[8] Our characterization of forgetting is not sufficient to distinguish "solutions" with residual *break* literals that are in some sense "necessary" from trivial solutions by just renaming the predicate to be forgotten. This is an issue for future work.

Q a clause $\{\neg Q(x_1, ..., x_n), x_1 \not\approx y_1, ..., x_n \not\approx y_n, Q(y_1, ..., y_n)\}$ can be derived by binary resolution. As can easily be seen, a C-factoring (C-resolution) step then corresponds to a binary resolution step with such a clause followed by a factoring (binary resolution) step. A factoring (binary resolution) step corresponds to a C-factoring (C-resolution) step followed by an application of the *constraint elimination* rule.

We mention some apparent differences between pattern-forgetting and SCAN, but the details and practical relevance of them have not yet been worked out: Since pattern-forgetting can also be applied to matrixes without predicate substitutivity axioms, it may have a broader range of applicability. pattern-forgetting can not only be used to forget about predicates, but also to forget about instances of patterns. By *diff* expansion, in the result signature of pattern-forgetting function symbols that are to be "forgotten" do not appear, but on the other hand this result signature is related to the "absolute signature" which is input at *diff* expansion. By the introduction of *break* literals in pattern-forgetting, processing is separated into two terminating phases. Where SCAN does not terminate, the output of pattern-forgetting does include residual *break* literals. By the use of arbitrary decision procedures in simplification *deletion of an isolated satisfiable clause group* pattern-forgetting may terminate for more inputs than SCAN. In SCAN only C-resolutions between *different* clauses are allowed. The condition "tautological or subsumed by a clause in $F - \{C\}$" in Theorem 1 may be related to that restriction, but the precise relationship has not yet been worked out.

Lin and Reiter [11] describe the semantics of forgetting about ground atoms and predicates for first order logic in standard model theoretic terms. Their work is motivated by the need of an autonomous agent to "forget" knowledge about past states.

There are a number of more or less related works with different backgrounds: In the context of knowledge compilation, applications of propositional projection to knowledge base preprocessing, planning, model-based diagnosis and circuit compilation are shown [6]. Aside from disjunctive normal form and DNNF [6], ordered binary decision diagrams provide a normal form in which propositional forgetting is an operation of low complexity. Propositional forgetting corresponds to existential boolean quantification. Partition-based logical reasoning [2] is a framework for distributed theorem proving based on consequence finding in signature restricted knowledge base partitions. Projection can be considered as a special case of marginalization, one of the fundamental operations in the "local computation" framework [10,14].

9   Next Steps

We consider the resolution based pattern forgetting algorithm as a first approach to get a deductive grip on projection/forgetting for first order logic and will investigate further techniques. One direction there are adapted model generation methods, which generate implicants of the results of projection one by one and thus can be plugged to client systems that process them one by one.

Properties and constructions like those in Sect. 6 have to be further worked out along with example scenarios.

For propositional logic project(F, S) corresponds to $\Diamond_S F$ in a multi-modal logic where $=_S$ (see Definition 2) is the accessibility relation for modality S. This approach to projection and the possibility of using processing methods for modal logics have to be investigated.

We intend to explore possibilities of making projection/forgetting available to other languages that can be embedded in first order logic, as we have outlined in Example 2 for a description logic.

Instead of sets of atoms as scopes, also sets of literals could be used (corresponding to the Lyndon interpolation theorem). This may be useful for knowledge base preprocessing, since the knowledge base extract could be significantly smaller and in queries often predicates are used only with a single polarity.

References

1. W. Ackermann. Untersuchungen über das Eliminationsproblem der mathematischen Logik. *Mathematische Annalen*, 110:390–413, 1935.
2. E. Amir and S. A. McIlraith. Partition-based logical reasoning. In *Princ. of Knowl. Repr. and Reasoning*, pages 389–400, 2000.
3. W. Bibel. *Deduktion — Automatisierung der Logik*. Oldenbourg, München, 1992.
4. W. Bibel and E. Eder. Methods and calculi for deduction. In D. M. Gabbay, C. J. Hogger, and J. A. Robinson, editors, *Handbook of Logic in Artif. Int. and Logic Programming*, volume 1, chapter 3, pages 67–182. Oxford University Press, 1993.
5. C.-L. Chang and R. C.-T. Lee. *Symbolic Logic and Mechanical Theorem Proving*. Academic Press, Boston, 1973.
6. A. Darwiche. Decomposable negation normal form. *JACM*, 48(4):608–647, 2001.
7. M. Davis and H. Putnam. A computing procedure for quantification theory. *JACM*, 7(3):201–215, 1960.
8. D. Gabbay and H. J. Ohlbach. Quantifier elimination in second-order predicate logic. In *KR'92. Princ. of Knowl. Repr. and Reasoning*, pages 425–435, 1992.
9. V. Goranko, U. Hustadt, R. A. Schmidt, and D. Vakarelov. SCAN is complete for all Sahlqvist formulae. In *Relational and Kleene-Algebraic Methods in Computer Science (RelMiCS 7)*, pages 149–162, 2004.
10. J. Kohlas, R. Haenni, and S. Moral. Propositional information systems. *Journal of Logic and Computation*, 9(5):651–681, 1999.
11. F. Lin and R. Reiter. Forget It! In R. Greiner and D. Subramanian, editors, *Working Notes, AAAI Fall Symposium on Relevance*, pages 154–159, Menlo Park, California, 1994. American Association for Artificial Intelligence.
12. A. Nonnengart, H. J. Ohlbach, and A. Szalas. Quantifier elimination for second-order predicate logic. In H. Ohlbach and U. Reyle, editors, *Logic, Language and Reasoning. Essays in Honor of Dov Gabbay, Part I*, pages 159–181. Kluwer, 1999.
13. A. Szałas. On the correspondence between modal and classical logic: An automated approach. *Journal of Logic and Computation*, 3(6):605–620, 1993.
14. N. Wilson and J. Mengin. Logical deduction using the local computation framework. In *Int. Workshop on First-Order Theorem Proving, FTP'97*, RISC-Linz Report Series No. 97-50, pages 135–139. Johannes Kepler Universität, Linz, 1997.

Negative Hyper-resolution as Procedural Semantics of Disjunctive Logic Programs

Linh Anh Nguyen

Institute of Informatics, University of Warsaw
ul. Banacha 2, 02-097 Warsaw, Poland
nguyen@mimuw.edu.pl

Abstract. We prove that negative hyper-resolution is a sound and complete procedure for answering queries in disjunctive logic programs. In our formulation, answers of queries are defined using disjunctive substitutions, which are more flexible than answer literals used in theorem proving systems.

1 Introduction

Resolution can be used not only to prove theorems but also to answer questions. This was first shown by Green in [5], where he introduced *answer literals* and a planning method using resolution. His technique has become popular in AI.

Since resolution was introduced by Robinson [13] in 1965, many refinements of resolution have been proposed by researchers in the field in order to cut down the search space and increase efficiency. One of the most important refinements of resolution is hyper-resolution, which was also introduced by Robinson [12] in the same year 1965. Hyper-resolution constructs a resolvent of a number of clauses at each step. Thus it contracts a sequence of bare resolution steps into a single inference step and eliminates interactions among intermediary resolvents, and interactions between them and other clauses.

There are many completeness results in the literature for various refinements of resolution, but these results usually derive refutation completeness, i.e. the empty clause will be derived if the input clauses are inconsistent. For question-answering systems, we want a stronger result called *answer completeness*: for every correct answer there exists a more general computed answer.

A refinement of resolution for the Horn fragment, called SLD-resolution in [1], was first described by Kowalski [6] for logic programming. It is a sound and complete procedure for answering queries in definite logic programs. In [9], Lobo et al gave a linear resolution method with a selection function, called SLO-resolution, for answering goals in disjunctive logic programs. SLO-resolution is an extension of SLD-resolution, and both of them are answer complete under any selection function.

SLO-resolution extends SLD-resolution in a natural way, and in our opinion, it is a potential framework for developing efficient proof procedures. However, queries and derivations formulated in SLO-resolution allow only definite answers,

J.J. Alferes and J. Leite (Eds.): JELIA 2004, LNAI 3229, pp. 565–577, 2004.

and in fact, SLO-resolution is answer complete only for a certain class of queries. Consider an example of [9] : given the program $P = \{p(a) \lor p(b) \leftarrow\}$ and the query $Q = \leftarrow p(x)$, there is no computed answer in SLO-resolution for $P \cup Q$, while there exists a disjunctive answer $\{\{x/a\}, \{x/b\}\}$. Of course, if we rewrite Q to $Q' = \leftarrow p(x) \lor p(y)$ then there is a computed answer $\{x/a, y/b\}$, but if the considered program is larger, it is difficult to know when and where we need to rewrite goals, and furthermore, rewriting goals is inconvenient for users.

There are also other goal oriented proof procedures proposed for disjunctive logic programming: nearHorn-Prolog procedures by Loveland [10], SLI-resolution by Lobo et al [8], and restart model elimination (RME) by Baumgartner et al [2]. The nearHorn-Prolog procedures extend SLD-resolution and Prolog style for disjunctive logic programs, but they are of interest only when the considered program contains very few non-Horn clauses. Both of SLI-resolution and RME are variants of the model elimination procedure. SLI-resolution is related to SLO-resolution, while RME is related to hyper tableaux.

In our opinion, it is very difficult for programmers to imagine behaviors of disjunctive logic *programs* as is possible when writing Prolog programs. Perhaps we should adopt the approach by Loveland and use mechanisms of theorem proving for non-Horn fragments of disjunctive logic programs. But as mentioned before, the nearHorn-Prolog procedures proposed by Loveland have advantages only for logic programs containing very few non-Horn clauses. For general cases, why don't we just use strongest theorem provers as proof procedures for disjunctive logic programming?

In this work, we formulate a negative hyper-resolution calculus as a proof procedure for disjunctive logic programming. In our formulation, every clause set can be divided into a disjunctive logic program, which consists of non-negative clauses, and a query. We define answers as disjunctive substitutions. To each goal appearing in a derivation we attach a disjunctive substitution keeping bindings of variables of the initial query. Our definition of answers is more flexible than answer literals used in theorem proving systems. In [3], Brass and Lipeck also defined disjunctive answer as a set of normal substitutions, but they did not give further properties of disjunctive substitutions as we do. Our definition of correct answers is compatible with the semantics of answer literals given by Kunen [7]. The theory of answer literals was discussed earlier in [5,11,4], but in those works the authors assume that answer literals appear only in one clause.

As far as we know, answer completeness of negative hyper-resolution in our setting of queries has not previously been studied. Here, we prove that negative hyper-resolution is a sound and complete procedure for answering queries in disjunctive logic programs.

This paper is organized as follows: In Section 2, we give definitions for disjunctive substitutions, disjunctive logic programs, queries, and correct answers. In Section 3, we specify a negative hyper-resolution calculus as procedural semantics of disjunctive logic programs. In Section 4, we prove answer soundness of that calculus. We give a *reverse* fixpoint semantics for disjunctive logic programs in Section 5 and use it in Section 6 to prove answer completeness of the calculus. The relationship between disjunctive substitutions and answer literals is considered in Section 7. Section 8 concludes this work.

2   Preliminaries

First-order logic is considered in this work and we assume that the reader is familiar with it. We now give the most important definitions for our work.

By $\forall(\varphi)$ we denote the *universal closure* of φ, which is the closed formula obtained by adding a universal quantifier for every free variable of φ.

An *expression* is either a term or a formula. If E is an expression, then by $Var(E)$ we denote the set of all variables occurring in E.

The *Herbrand universe* U_Γ of a formula set Γ is the set of all ground terms that can be formed from the constants and function symbols in Γ : if no constants occur in Γ then some arbitrary constant is used instead.

The *Herbrand base* B_Γ of a formula set Γ is the set consisting of all ground atoms that can be formed from the predicate symbols in Γ and the terms in U_Γ. When Γ is clear from the context, for $M \subseteq B_\Gamma$, we write $\overline{M}$ to denote the set $B_\Gamma - M$.

2.1   Disjunctive Substitutions

A *normal substitution* is a finite set $\theta = \{x_1/t_1, \ldots, x_n/t_n\}$, where $x_1, \ldots, x_n$ are different variables, $t_1, \ldots, t_n$ are terms, and $t_i \neq x_i$ for all $1 \leq i \leq n$. By ε we denote the *empty normal substitution*. The set $Dom(\theta) = \{x_1, \ldots, x_n\}$ is called the *domain* of θ. By $Ran(\theta)$ we denote the set of all variables occurring in $t_1, \ldots, t_n$. Define $Var(\theta) = Dom(\theta) \cup Ran(\theta)$. For a set X of variables, the *restriction* of θ to X, denoted by $\theta_{|X}$, is the substitution $\{x/t \mid x/t \in \theta$ and $x \in X\}$.

Let $\theta = \{x_1/t_1, \ldots, x_n/t_n\}$ be a normal substitution and E be an expression. Then $E\theta$, the *instance* of E by θ, is the expression obtained from E by simultaneously replacing each occurrence of the variable x_i in E by the term t_i, for $1 \leq i \leq n$.

Let $\theta = \{x_1/t_1, \ldots, x_n/t_n\}$ and $\delta = \{y_1/s_1, \ldots, y_m/s_m\}$ be normal substitutions. Then the *composition* $\theta\delta$ of θ and δ is the substitution obtained from the set $\{x_1/t_1\delta, \ldots, x_n/t_n\delta, y_1/s_1, \ldots, y_m/s_m\}$ by deleting any binding $x_i/t_i\delta$ for which $x_i = t_i\delta$ and deleting any binding y_j/s_j for which $y_j \in \{x_1, \ldots, x_n\}$.

If θ and δ are normal substitutions such that $\theta\delta = \delta\theta = \varepsilon$, then we call them *renaming substitutions* and use θ^{-1} to denote δ (which is unique w.r.t. θ).

A *disjunctive substitution* Θ is a finite and non-empty set of normal substitutions. Define $Dom(\Theta) = \bigcup_{\theta \in \Theta} Dom(\theta)$, $Ran(\Theta) = \bigcup_{\theta \in \Theta} Ran(\theta)$, and $Var(\Theta) = Dom(\Theta) \cup Ran(\Theta)$. For $X \subseteq Dom(\Theta)$, the *restriction* of Θ to X is denoted by $\Theta_{|X}$ and defined as $\{\theta_{|X} \mid \theta \in \Theta\}$. We treat a normal substitution θ also as the disjunctive substitution $\{\theta\}$.

If φ is a formula then $\varphi\Theta =_{def} \{\varphi\theta \mid \theta \in \Theta\}$. If Γ is a set of formulas then $\Gamma\Theta =_{def} \{\varphi\theta \mid \varphi \in \Gamma, \theta \in \Theta\}$. The *composition* $\Theta\Delta$ of disjunctive substitutions Θ and Δ is the disjunctive substitution $\{\theta\delta \mid \theta \in \Theta, \delta \in \Delta\}$.

A disjunctive substitution Θ is *more general* than Δ if there exists a normal substitution σ such that for $X = Dom(\Theta) \cup Dom(\Delta)$, $(\Theta\sigma)_{|X} \subseteq \Delta$.

As some properties of disjunctive substitutions, for an expression E and disjunctive substitutions Θ, Θ_1, Θ_2, Θ_3, we have: $\Theta\varepsilon = \varepsilon\Theta = \Theta$, $(E\Theta_1)\Theta_2 = E(\Theta_1\Theta_2)$, and $(\Theta_1\Theta_2)\Theta_3 = \Theta_1(\Theta_2\Theta_3)$.

2.2   Disjunctive Logic Programs and Queries

A *clause* is a formula of the form

$$\forall x_1 \ldots \forall x_h (A_1 \vee \ldots \vee A_n \vee \neg B_1 \vee \ldots \vee \neg B_m)$$

where $x_1, \ldots, x_h$ are all the variables occurring in the rest of the formula, $n \geq 0$, $m \geq 0$, and A_i and B_j are atoms. We write such a clause in the form

$$A_1 \vee \ldots \vee A_n \leftarrow B_1 \wedge \ldots \wedge B_m$$

We call $A_1 \vee \ldots \vee A_n$ the *head* and $B_1 \wedge \ldots \wedge B_m$ the *body* of the clause. If $n = 0$ and $m = 0$ then the clause is *empty* and denoted by $\bot$. If $n = 0$ and $m > 0$ then the clause is a *goal*. If $n > 0$ and $m = 0$ then the clause is *positive*. If $n > 0$ then the clause is a *(disjunctive) program clause*.

A *(disjunctive) logic program* is a finite set of disjunctive program clauses. A *(disjunctive) query* is a finite set of goals.

Let P be a logic program and $Q = \{ \leftarrow \varphi_1, \ldots, \leftarrow \varphi_n \}$ be a query. We say that a disjunctive substitution Θ with $Dom(\Theta) \subseteq Var(Q)$ is a *correct answer* of $P \cup Q$ if $P \models \forall(\bigvee_{i=1}^{n} \bigvee_{\theta \in \Theta} \varphi_i \theta)$.

For example, if $P = \{ p(f(x)) \vee p(g(x)) \leftarrow \}$ and $Q = \{ \leftarrow p(y) \}$, then $\Theta = \{\{y/f(x)\}, \{y/g(x)\}\}$ is a correct answer of $P \cup Q$.

In [7], Kunen characterized the semantics of answer literals used in theorem proving systems by the following theorem: Let Σ be a set of sentences, $\exists \overline{x}\, \varphi(\overline{x})$ be a sentence, and $\Sigma' = \Sigma \cup \forall(ans(\overline{x}) \leftarrow \varphi(\overline{x}))$. If each $\overline{\tau}_i$, for $i = 1, \ldots, k$, is a tuple of terms of the same length of $\overline{x}$, then $\Sigma' \models \forall(ans(\overline{\tau}_1) \vee \ldots \vee ans(\overline{\tau}_k))$ (this specifies an answer) iff $\Sigma \models \forall(\varphi(\overline{\tau}_1) \vee \ldots \vee \varphi(\overline{\tau}_k))$.

Our definition of correct answers is compatible with the semantics of answer literals by Kunen. To see the compatibility, take $\Sigma = P$, assume that $\varphi_1, \ldots, \varphi_n$ have disjoint sets of variables, and let $\varphi = \varphi_1 \vee \ldots \vee \varphi_n$.

3   Negative Hyper-resolution Semantics

An *informative goal* is a pair $\varphi : \Theta$, where φ is a goal and Θ is a disjunctive substitution. Informally, Θ keeps the disjunctive substitution that has been applied to variables of the initial query in the process of deriving φ. We will ignore the word "informative" when it is clear from the context. An informative goal $\varphi : \Theta$ is said to be *ground* if φ is ground.

Let $\varphi = A_1 \vee \ldots \vee A_n \leftarrow B_1 \wedge \ldots \wedge B_m$ be a program clause (i.e. $n > 0$) and $\varphi_1 : \Theta_1, \ldots, \varphi_n : \Theta_n$ be goals. Let $\varphi_i = \leftarrow \xi_i \wedge \zeta_i$, for $1 \leq i \leq n$, where ξ_i is a non-empty set of atoms called the *selected* atoms of φ_i. If there exists an mgu σ such that $A_i\sigma = A'_j\sigma$ for every $1 \le i \le n$ and every $A'_j \in \xi_i$, then we call the goal

$$\leftarrow (B_1 \wedge \ldots \wedge B_m \wedge \zeta_1 \wedge \ldots \wedge \zeta_n)\sigma : (\Theta_1 \cup \ldots \cup \Theta_n)\sigma$$

a *hyper-resolvent* of φ and $\varphi_1 : \Theta_1, \ldots, \varphi_n : \Theta_n$.

Note that "factoring" is hidden in our definition.

Before defining derivation and refutation we specify the process of standardizing variables apart. Denote the original set of variables of the language by $\mathcal{X}$, and assume that variables occurring in the given logic program, the given query, or considered correct answers all belong to $\mathcal{X}$. Let $\mathcal{X}'$ be an infinite set of variables disjoint with $\mathcal{X}$. We will use elements of $\mathcal{X}'$ for renaming variables.

Let φ be a program clause and $\varphi_1 : \Theta_1, \ldots, \varphi_n : \Theta_n$ be goals. A *standardized variant* of the set $\{\varphi, \varphi_1 : \Theta_1, \ldots, \varphi_n : \Theta_n\}$ is a set $\{\varphi\delta, \varphi_1\delta_1 : \Theta_1\delta_1, \ldots, \varphi_n\delta_n : \Theta_n\delta_n\}$ where $\delta, \delta_1, \ldots, \delta_n$ are renaming substitutions such that $Dom(\delta) = Var(\varphi)$ and $Ran(\delta) \subset \mathcal{X}'$, $Dom(\delta_i) = Var(\varphi_i) \cup Ran(\Theta_i)$ and $Ran(\delta_i) \subset \mathcal{X}'$ for all $1 \le i \le n$, and the sets $Ran(\delta)$, $Ran(\delta_1)$, $\ldots$, $Ran(\delta_n)$ are disjoint. Assume that standardizing variants is done by some unspecified deterministic procedure.

Let P be a logic program and Q a query. A *derivation* from $P \cup Q$ is a sequence $\varphi_1 : \Theta_1, \ldots, \varphi_n : \Theta_n$ of goals such that for each $1 \le i \le n$:

1. either φ_i is a clause of Q and $\Theta_i = \varepsilon$;
2. or $\varphi_i : \Theta_i$ is a hyper-resolvent of a program clause φ' and goals $\varphi'_{i,1} : \Theta'_{i,1}$, $\ldots, \varphi'_{i,n_i} : \Theta'_{i,n_i}$, where $\{\varphi', \varphi'_{i,1} : \Theta'_{i,1}, \ldots, \varphi'_{i,n_i} : \Theta'_{i,n_i}\}$ is a standardized variant of $\{\varphi, \varphi_{i,1} : \Theta_{i,1}, \ldots, \varphi_{i,n_i} : \Theta_{i,n_i}\}$, φ is a program clause of P, and $\varphi_{i,1} : \Theta_{i,1}, \ldots, \varphi_{i,n_i} : \Theta_{i,n_i}$ are goals from the sequence $\varphi_1 : \Theta_1, \ldots, \varphi_{i-1} : \Theta_{i-1}$.

For simplicity, Condition 2 of the above definition will be also stated as $\varphi_i : \Theta_i$ is a hyper-resolvent of a standardized variant of a program clause φ of P and standardized variants of some goals from $\varphi_1 : \Theta_1, \ldots, \varphi_{i-1} : \Theta_{i-1}$.

A *refutation* of $P \cup Q$ is a derivation from $P \cup Q$ with the last goal of the form $\perp : \Theta$. The disjunctive substitution $\Theta_{|Var(Q)}$ is called the *computed answer* of $P \cup Q$ w.r.t. that refutation.

Example 1. Let P be the program consisting of the following clauses:

(1) $s(x, a) \leftarrow p(x)$
(2) $s(x, b) \leftarrow q(x)$
(3) $p(x) \vee q(x) \leftarrow r(x)$
(4) $r(c) \leftarrow$

and let Q be the query consisting of the only following goal:

(5) $\leftarrow s(x, y)$

Here is a refutation of $P \cup Q$:

(6) $\leftarrow s(x,y) : \varepsilon$ from (5)

(7) $\leftarrow p(x_2) : \{x/x_2, y/a, x_1/x_2, y_2/a\}$ (1),(6)

(8) $\leftarrow q(x_4) : \{x/x_4, y/b, x_3/x_4, y_4/b\}$ (2),(6)

(9) $\leftarrow r(x_5) : \{\{x/x_5, y/a, x_1/x_5, y_2/a, x_2/x_5, x_6/x_5, x_7/x_5\},$

       $\{x/x_5, y/b, x_3/x_5, y_4/b, x_4/x_5, x_6/x_5, x_7/x_5\}\}$ (3),(7),(8)

(10) $\perp : \{\{x/c, y/a, x_1/c, y_2/a, x_2/c, x_6/c, x_7/c, x_5/c, x_8/c\},$

       $\{x/c, y/b, x_3/c, y_4/b, x_4/c, x_6/c, x_7/c, x_5/c, x_8/c\}\}$ (4),(9)

The computed answer is $\{\{x/c, y/a\}, \{x/c, y/b\}\}$.

4   Answer Soundness

In this section, we show that for every logic program P and every query Q, every computed answer of $P \cup Q$ is a correct answer of $P \cup Q$.

Lemma 1. *Let $\leftarrow \psi : \Theta$ be a hyper-resolvent of a program clause φ and goals $\leftarrow \varphi_1 : \Theta_1, \ldots, \leftarrow \varphi_n : \Theta_n$ with σ being the involved mgu. Let M be a model of φ. Then $M \models \bigvee_{i=1}^{n}(\psi \to \varphi_i \sigma)$. In particular, if ψ is empty then $M \models \bigvee_{i=1}^{n} \varphi_i \sigma$.*

Proof. Let $\varphi = A_1 \vee \ldots \vee A_n \leftarrow B_1 \wedge \ldots \wedge B_m$ and $\varphi_i = \xi_i \wedge \zeta_i$, where ξ_i is the set of selected atoms of $\leftarrow \varphi_i$, for $1 \leq i \leq n$. Then $\psi = (B_1 \wedge \ldots \wedge B_m \wedge \zeta_1 \wedge \ldots \wedge \zeta_n)\sigma$. Let V be an arbitrary variable assignment. Suppose that $M, V \models \psi$. Because M is a model of φ and $M, V \models \psi$, it follows that $M, V \models (A_1 \vee \ldots \vee A_n)\sigma$. Hence $M, V \models \bigvee_{i=1}^{n}(A_i \wedge \zeta_i)\sigma$, since $M, V \models \psi$. Thus $M, V \models \bigvee_{i=1}^{n} \varphi_i \sigma$. Since V is an arbitrary variable assignment, we conclude that $M \models \bigvee_{i=1}^{n}(\psi \to \varphi_i \sigma)$.

Lemma 2. *Let P be a logic program, $Q = \{\leftarrow \varphi_1, \ldots, \leftarrow \varphi_n\}$ be a query, and $\leftarrow \psi : \Theta$ be the last goal in a derivation from $P \cup Q$. Let M be a model of P. Then $M \models \bigvee_{i=1}^{n} \bigvee_{\theta \in \Theta}(\psi \to \varphi_i \theta)$. In particular, if ψ is empty then $M \models \bigvee_{i=1}^{n} \bigvee_{\theta \in \Theta} \varphi_i \theta$.*

Proof. We prove this lemma by induction on the length of the derivation. The case when $\leftarrow \psi$ is a clause of Q and $\Theta = \varepsilon$ is trivial. Suppose that $\leftarrow \psi : \Theta$ is derived as a hyper-resolvent of a standardized variant of a program clause φ and standardized variants of goals $\leftarrow \psi_1 : \Theta_1, \ldots, \leftarrow \psi_m : \Theta_m$. Let σ be the involved mgu and $\delta, \delta_1, \ldots, \delta_m$ be the involved renaming substitutions. By the inductive assumption, we have $M \models \bigvee_{i=1}^{n} \bigvee_{\theta \in \Theta_j}(\psi_j \to \varphi_i \theta)$ for all $1 \leq j \leq m$. Thus $M \models \bigvee_{i=1}^{n} \bigvee_{\theta \in \Theta_j}(\psi_j \delta_j \sigma \to \varphi_i \theta \delta_j \sigma)$, and hence $M \models \bigvee_{i=1}^{n} \bigvee_{\theta \in \Theta_j \delta_j \sigma}(\psi_j \delta_j \sigma \to \varphi_i \theta)$, for all $1 \leq j \leq m$. Note that $\Theta_j \delta_j \sigma \subseteq \Theta$. By Lemma 1, $M \models \bigvee_{j=1}^{m}(\psi \to \psi_j \delta_j \sigma)$. These two assertions together imply that $M \models \bigvee_{i=1}^{n} \bigvee_{\theta \in \Theta}(\psi \to \varphi_i \theta)$.

Theorem 1 (Soundness). *Let P be a logic program, Q a query, and Θ a computed answer of $P \cup Q$. Then Θ is a correct answer of $P \cup Q$.*

Proof. Let $Q = \{\leftarrow \varphi_1, \ldots, \leftarrow \varphi_n\}$ and let $\perp : \Theta'$ be the last goal in a refutation of $P \cup Q$ such that $\Theta = \Theta'_{|Var(Q)}$. Let M be an arbitrary model of P. By Lemma 2, $M \models \bigvee_{i=1}^{n} \bigvee_{\theta \in \Theta'} \varphi_i \theta$, and hence $M \models \bigvee_{i=1}^{n} \bigvee_{\theta \in \Theta} \varphi_i \theta$. Since M is an arbitrary model of P, we derive $P \models \forall(\bigvee_{i=1}^{n} \bigvee_{\theta \in \Theta} \varphi_i \theta)$, which means that Θ is a correct answer of $P \cup Q$.

5   Reverse Fixpoint Semantics

The fixpoint semantics of definite logic programs was first introduced by van Emden and Kowalski [14] using the direct consequences operator T_P. This operator is monotonic, continuous, and has the least fixpoint $T_P \uparrow \omega = \bigcup_{n=0}^{\omega} T_P \uparrow n$, which forms the least Herbrand model of the given logic program P. In [9], Lobo et al extended the fixpoint semantics to disjunctive logic programs. Their direct consequences operator, denoted by T_P^I, iterates over model-states, which are sets of disjunctions of ground atoms. This operator is also monotonic, continuous, and has a least fixpoint which is a least model-state characterizing the given program P.

In this section, we study a reversed analogue of the "direct consequences" operator called the *direct derivation operator*. The results of this section will be used to prove *answer completeness* of the negative hyper-resolution semantics.

Let P be a logic program, Q a query, and Γ the set obtained from $P \cup Q$ by replacing every positive clause $(A_1 \vee \ldots \vee A_n \leftarrow)$ by $(A_1 \vee \ldots \vee A_n \leftarrow \top)$, where $\top$ is a special atom not occurring in P and Q.

The *direct derivation operator* D_Γ is a function that maps a set G of informative goals to another set of informative goals that can be directly derived from Γ and G. It is formally defined as follows: $D_\Gamma(G)$ is the set of all goals $\varphi : \Theta$ such that either φ is a clause of Q and $\Theta = \varepsilon$ or $\varphi : \Theta$ is a hyper-resolvent of a program clause ψ' and goals $\psi'_1 : \Theta'_1, \ldots, \psi'_n : \Theta'_n$, where $\{\psi', \psi'_1 : \Theta'_1, \ldots, \psi'_n : \Theta'_n\}$ is the standardized variant of $\{\psi, \psi_1 : \Theta_1, \ldots, \psi_n : \Theta_n\}$, ψ is a program clause of Γ, and $\psi_1 : \Theta_1, \ldots, \psi_n : \Theta_n$ are goals from G.

Lemma 3. *The operator D_Γ is monotonic, compact, and hence also continuous. It has the least fixpoint $D_\Gamma \uparrow \omega = \bigcup_{n=0}^{\omega} D_\Gamma \uparrow n$, where $D_\Gamma \uparrow 0 = \emptyset$ and $D_\Gamma \uparrow (n+1) = D_\Gamma(D_\Gamma \uparrow n)$.*

The first assertion of the above lemma clearly holds. The second assertion immediately follows from the first one, by the Kleene theorem.

Let G_Γ denote the set of all ground goals φ such that there exists an informative goal $\varphi' : \Theta' \in D_\Gamma \uparrow \omega$ such that φ is a ground instance of φ' (i.e. φ is obtained from φ' by uniformly substituting variables by terms from U_Γ).

A *negated representative* of G_Γ is a set Φ of pairs (φ, A) such that: $\varphi \in G_\Gamma$ and A is an atom of φ; and for every $\psi \in G_\Gamma$, there exists exactly one atom B of ψ (a negated representative of ψ) such that $(\psi, B) \in \Phi$.

Clearly, every G_Γ has at least one negated representative.

Let Φ be a negated representative of G_Γ. A set M of ground atoms is called a *minimal refinement* of Φ (w.r.t. G_Γ) if the following conditions hold:

1. for each $A \in M$ there exists $(\varphi, A) \in \Phi$ for some φ;
2. for each $\varphi \in G_\Gamma$ there exists $A \in M$ such that A is an atom of φ;
3. for each $A \in M$ there exists $\varphi \in G_\Gamma$ such that for every atom B of φ different from A, we have $B \notin M$.

Condition 1 states that members of M come from Φ. Condition 2 states that every Herbrand model disjoint with M satisfies G_Γ; in particular, $\overline{M} \vDash G_\Gamma$. Condition 3 states that M is a minimal set satisfying the two preceding conditions.

Lemma 4. *Every negated representative Φ of G_Γ has a minimal refinement.*

Proof. Start from $M = \{A \mid (\varphi, A) \in \Phi$ for some $\varphi\}$ and keeping in mind that M will always satisfy the first two conditions of the definition of minimal refinement, do the following: if M is not a minimal refinement of Φ due to some A that violates the last condition of the definition, then remove that A from M. This operator has a fixpoint which is a minimal refinement of Φ.

Theorem 2. *Let Φ be a negated representative of G_Γ and M a minimal refinement of Φ. Then $\overline{M}$ is a maximal Herbrand model of Γ.*

Proof. Since M is a minimal refinement of Φ, due to Condition 3 of its definition, it is sufficient to prove that $\overline{M}$ is a model of Γ. Let $\varphi = A_1 \vee \ldots \vee A_n \leftarrow B_1 \wedge \ldots \wedge B_m$ be a ground instance of some clause φ' of Γ by a substitution σ. It suffices to show that $\overline{M} \models \varphi$. Suppose that $\overline{M} \not\models A_1 \vee \ldots \vee A_n$. We show that $\overline{M} \not\models B_1 \wedge \ldots \wedge B_m$.

Since each A_i is a ground atom and $\overline{M} \not\models A_1 \vee \ldots \vee A_n$, we must have $A_i \in M$ for all $1 \leq i \leq n$. Since M is a minimal refinement of Φ, it follows that for every $1 \leq i \leq n$ there exists $(\varphi_i, A_i) \in \Phi$ such that φ_i can be written as $\leftarrow A_i \wedge \zeta_i$ and ζ_i is false in M. Since Φ is a negated representative of G_Γ, for all $1 \leq i \leq n$, there exist a goal $\varphi'_i : \Theta'_i \in D_\Gamma \uparrow \omega$ and a substitution σ_i such that $\varphi_i = \varphi'_i \sigma_i$. For $1 \leq i \leq n$, let ξ'_i be the set of all atoms A''_i of φ'_i such that $A''_i \sigma_i = A_i$, and let ζ'_i be the set of the remaining atoms of φ'_i. We have $\varphi'_i = \leftarrow \xi'_i \wedge \zeta'_i$.

Let $\{\varphi'', \varphi''_1 : \Theta''_1, \ldots, \varphi''_n : \Theta''_n\}$ be the standardized variant of $\{\varphi', \varphi'_1 : \Theta'_1, \ldots, \varphi'_n : \Theta'_n\}$ with $\delta, \delta_1, \ldots, \delta_n$ being the involved renaming substitutions. For $1 \leq i \leq n$, let ξ''_i be the set of atoms of φ''_i originated from ξ'_i. Let $\psi' : \Theta'$ be a hyper-resolvent of the program clause φ'' and the goals $\varphi''_1 : \Theta''_1, \ldots, \varphi''_n : \Theta''_n$ with ξ''_i as the set of selected atoms of φ''_i. Thus $\psi' : \Theta' \in D_\Gamma \uparrow \omega$. We have $\varphi = \varphi'\sigma = \varphi''\delta^{-1}\sigma$ and $\varphi_i = \varphi'_i\sigma_i = \varphi''_i\delta_i^{-1}\sigma_i$, for all $1 \leq i \leq n$. Hence $\psi = \leftarrow B_1 \wedge \ldots \wedge B_m \wedge \zeta_1 \wedge \ldots \wedge \zeta_n$ is a ground instance of ψ'.

Since $\psi' : \Theta' \in D_\Gamma \uparrow \omega$, we have $\psi \in G_\Gamma$. By Condition 2 of the definition of minimal refinement, we have $\overline{M} \models G_\Gamma$. It follows that $\overline{M} \models \psi$, which means that $\overline{M} \models \neg B_1 \vee \ldots \vee \neg B_m \vee \neg \zeta_1 \vee \ldots \vee \neg \zeta_n$. Since ζ_i is false in M for all $1 \leq i \leq n$, it follows that $\overline{M} \models \neg B_1 \vee \ldots \vee \neg B_m$, and hence $\overline{M} \not\models B_1 \wedge \ldots \wedge B_m$.

Corollary 1. *Every maximal model of G_Γ is a model of Γ.*

Sketch. Every maximal model of G_Γ is the compliment of a minimal refinement of some negated representative of G_Γ, and hence is a model of Γ.

6   Answer Completeness

In this section, we show that for every correct answer Θ of $P \cup Q$, where P is a logic program and Q is a query, there exists a computed answer of $P \cup Q$ which is more general than Θ.

Lemma 5 (Lifting Lemma). *Let P be a logic program, Q a query, and Θ a disjunctive substitution. Let $\varphi'_1 : \Theta'_1, \ldots, \varphi'_k : \Theta'_k$ be a derivation from $P \cup Q\Theta$. Then there exist a derivation $\varphi_1 : \Theta_1, \ldots, \varphi_k : \Theta_k$ from $P \cup Q$ and substitutions σ_i, for $1 \le i \le k$, such that $\varphi_i \sigma_i = \varphi'_i$ and $(\Theta_i \sigma_i)_{|\mathcal{X}} \subseteq (\Theta \Theta'_i)_{|\mathcal{X}}$.*

Proof. Simulate the derivation $\varphi'_1 : \Theta'_1, \ldots, \varphi'_k : \Theta'_k$ from $P \cup Q\Theta$ for $P \cup Q$ so that, for $\psi \in Q$ and $\theta \in \Theta$, the goal $\psi\theta \in Q\Theta$ is replaced by ψ. Let the resulting derivation be $\varphi_1 : \Theta_1, \ldots, \varphi_k : \Theta_k$.

We prove the assertion of this lemma by induction on i. The case when φ_i is a clause from Q and $\Theta_i = \varepsilon$ is trivial. Suppose that $\varphi_i : \Theta_i$ is derived as a hyper-resolvent of a standardized variant of a program clause $\varphi = A_1 \vee \ldots \vee A_n \leftarrow B_1 \wedge \ldots \wedge B_m$ of P and standardized variants of goals $\varphi_{j_1} : \Theta_{j_1}, \ldots, \varphi_{j_n} : \Theta_{j_n}$, where $j_1, \ldots, j_n$ belong to $1..(i-1)$. Let $\delta, \delta_1, \ldots, \delta_n$ be the involved renaming substitutions (for standardizing variants) and σ be the involved mgu. Let $\varphi_{j_t} = \leftarrow \xi_{j_t} \wedge \zeta_{j_t}$ with ξ_{j_t} as the set of selected atoms, for $1 \le t \le n$. We have $A_t \delta \sigma = A'_t \delta_t \sigma$ for every $1 \le t \le n$ and every atom A'_t of ξ_{j_t}. The hyper-resolvent $\varphi_i : \Theta_i$ is equal to

$$\leftarrow (B_1 \delta \wedge \ldots \wedge B_m \delta \wedge \zeta_{j_1} \delta_1 \wedge \ldots \wedge \zeta_{j_n} \delta_n)\sigma : (\Theta_{j_1} \delta_1 \cup \ldots \cup \Theta_{j_n} \delta_n)\sigma$$

By the inductive assumption, $\varphi_{j_t} \sigma_{j_t} = \varphi'_{j_t}$, for all $1 \le t \le n$. Hence $\varphi'_i : \Theta'_i$ is a hyper-resolvent of a standardized variant of φ and standardized variants of $\varphi_{j_1} \sigma_{j_1} : \Theta'_{j_1}, \ldots, \varphi_{j_n} \sigma_{j_n} : \Theta'_{j_n}$. Let $\delta', \delta'_1, \ldots, \delta'_n$ be the involved renaming substitutions (for standardizing variants) and σ' be the involved mgu. We have $A_t \delta' \sigma' = A'_t \sigma_{j_t} \delta'_t \sigma'$ for every $1 \le t \le n$ and every atom A'_t of ξ_{j_t}. The hyper-resolvent $\varphi'_i : \Theta'_i$ is equal to

$$\leftarrow (B_1 \delta' \wedge \ldots \wedge B_m \delta' \wedge \zeta_{j_1} \sigma_{j_1} \delta'_1 \wedge \ldots \wedge \zeta_{j_n} \sigma_{j_n} \delta'_n)\sigma' : (\Theta'_{j_1} \delta'_1 \cup \ldots \cup \Theta'_{j_n} \delta'_n)\sigma'$$

Let γ be the normal substitution specified as below

$$\gamma = (\delta^{-1} \delta')_{|Dom(\delta^{-1})} \cup (\delta_1^{-1} \sigma_{j_1} \delta'_1)_{|Dom(\delta_1^{-1})} \cup \ldots \cup (\delta_n^{-1} \sigma_{j_n} \delta'_n)_{|Dom(\delta_n^{-1})}$$

Let $1 \le t \le n$ and let A'_t be an atom of ξ_{j_t}. We have $A_t \delta \gamma = A_t \delta'$ and $A'_t \delta_t \gamma = A'_t \sigma_{j_t} \delta'_t$. Since $A_t \delta' \sigma' = A'_t \sigma_{j_t} \delta'_t \sigma'$, it follows that $A_t \delta \gamma \sigma' = A'_t \delta_t \gamma \sigma'$. Because σ is an *mgu* such that $A_t \delta \sigma = A'_t \delta_t \sigma$ for every $1 \le t \le n$ and every atom A'_t of ξ_{j_t}, there exists σ_i such that $\gamma \sigma' = \sigma \sigma_i$.

For $1 \le s \le m$, we have $B_s \delta \sigma \sigma_i = B_s \delta \gamma \sigma' = B_s \delta' \sigma'$, and for $1 \le t \le n$, we have $\zeta_{j_t} \delta_t \sigma \sigma_i = \zeta_{j_t} \delta_t \gamma \sigma' = \zeta_{j_t} \sigma_{j_t} \delta'_t \sigma'$. Hence $\varphi_i \sigma_i = \varphi'_i$.

For all $1 \le t \le n$, we have $(\Theta_{j_t} \delta_t \sigma \sigma_i)_{|\mathcal{X}} = (\Theta_{j_t} \delta_t \gamma \sigma')_{|\mathcal{X}} = ((\Theta_{j_t} \delta_t \gamma)_{|\mathcal{X}} \sigma')_{|\mathcal{X}} = ((\Theta_{j_t} \sigma_{j_t} \delta'_t)_{|\mathcal{X}} \sigma')_{|\mathcal{X}} = (\Theta_{j_t} \sigma_{j_t} \delta'_t \sigma')_{|\mathcal{X}}$. By the inductive assumption, $(\Theta_{j_t} \sigma_{j_t})_{|\mathcal{X}} \subseteq (\Theta \Theta'_{j_t})_{|\mathcal{X}}$, and hence $(\Theta_{j_t} \sigma_{j_t} \delta'_t \sigma')_{|\mathcal{X}} \subseteq (\Theta \Theta'_{j_t} \delta'_t \sigma')_{|\mathcal{X}}$. We also have $\Theta'_{j_t} \delta'_t \sigma' \subseteq \Theta'_i$, which implies that $(\Theta \Theta'_{j_t} \delta'_t \sigma')_{|\mathcal{X}} \subseteq (\Theta \Theta'_i)_{|\mathcal{X}}$. Hence $(\Theta_{j_t} \delta_t \sigma \sigma_i)_{|\mathcal{X}} \subseteq (\Theta \Theta'_i)_{|\mathcal{X}}$. Therefore $(\Theta_i \sigma_i)_{|\mathcal{X}} \subseteq (\Theta \Theta'_i)_{|\mathcal{X}}$, which completes the proof.

Theorem 3 (Completeness). *Let P be a logic program, Q a query, and Θ a correct answer of $P \cup Q$. Then there exists a computed answer Θ' of $P \cup Q$ which is more general than Θ.*

Proof. Let $Q = \{\varphi_1, \ldots, \varphi_n\}$ and $Y = Var(Q) \cup Ran(\Theta)$. For each $x \in Y$, let a_x be a fresh constant symbol. Let $\delta = \{x/a_x \mid x \in Y\}$ and $Q' = Q\Theta\delta$. Since Θ is a correct answer of $P \cup Q$, it follows that $P \cup Q'$ is unsatisfiable.

Let P' be the set obtained from P by replacing every positive clause $(A_1 \vee \ldots \vee A_n \leftarrow)$ by $(A_1 \vee \ldots \vee A_n \leftarrow \top)$, and let $\Gamma = P' \cup Q'$. Since $P \cup Q'$ is unsatisfiable, we have $\Gamma \vDash \neg\top$.

We first show that $(\leftarrow \top) \in G_\Gamma$. Suppose oppositely that for every $\varphi \in G_\Gamma$, $\varphi \neq (\leftarrow \top)$. Then there exists a negated representative Φ of G_Γ which does not contain $\top$. Let M be a minimal refinement of Φ. We have that $\overline{M}$ contains $\top$. By Theorem 2, $\overline{M} \vDash \Gamma$, which contradicts with $\Gamma \vDash \neg\top$.

The above assertion states that there exists a derivation from Γ with the last goal of the form $\leftarrow \top : \Delta$. By simulating that derivation for $P \cup Q'$ with each $(A_1 \vee \ldots \vee A_n \leftarrow \top)$ replaced by $(A_1 \vee \ldots \vee A_n \leftarrow)$, we obtain a refutation with $\bot : \Delta$ as the last goal.

Since $Q' = Q\Theta\delta$, by Lemma 5, there exists a refutation of $P \cup Q$ with the last goal of the form $\bot : \Theta''$ and a substitution σ'' such that $(\Theta''\sigma'')_{|\mathcal{X}} \subseteq (\Theta\delta\Delta)_{|\mathcal{X}}$. We have that $\Theta' = \Theta''_{|Var(Q)}$ is a computed answer of $P \cup Q$. Since $\mathcal{X}' \cap \mathcal{X} = \emptyset$, we have $Var(\Delta) \cap Var(Q) = \emptyset$ and $Var(\Delta) \cap Var(\Theta\delta) = \emptyset$. Since $(\Theta''\sigma'')_{|\mathcal{X}} \subseteq (\Theta\delta\Delta)_{|\mathcal{X}}$, it follows that $(\Theta''\sigma'')_{|Var(Q)} \subseteq (\Theta\delta)_{|Var(Q)}$. Now treat each a_x as a variable and δ as a renaming substitution. Then we have $(\Theta''\sigma''(\delta^{-1}))_{|Var(Q)} \subseteq (\Theta\delta(\delta^{-1}))_{|Var(Q)}$. Since each a_x occurs neither in Θ nor in Θ'', for $\sigma' = (\sigma''\delta^{-1})_{|Dom(\sigma'')}$, we can derive that $(\Theta''\sigma')_{|Var(Q)} \subseteq \Theta$. Hence $(\Theta'\sigma')_{|Var(Q)} \subseteq \Theta$ and Θ' is more general than Θ.

7   Keeping Information for Computed Answers

In this section, we first modify the definition of derivation so that disjunctive substitutions in informative goals keep only necessary information without violating soundness and completeness of the calculus. We then show that informative goals can be simulated by normal goals using answer literals. We also study cases when it is possible to make computed answers more compact.

Let P be a logic program, Q a query, and $X \subseteq Var(Q)$. A *derivation restricted to* X from $P \cup Q$ is a modification of a derivation from $P \cup Q$ in which each newly derived hyper-resolvent $\varphi : \Theta$ is replaced *immediately* by $\varphi : \Theta_{|X}$. (Note that such a replacement affects the remaining part of the derivation.) A *refutation restricted to* X of $P \cup Q$ is a derivation restricted to X from $P \cup Q$ with the last goal of the form $\bot : \Theta$.

Example 2. Reconsider Example 1. Here is a refutation restricted to $\{x, y\}$ of $P \cup Q$:

(6)	$\leftarrow s(x, y) : \varepsilon$	from (5)
(7)	$\leftarrow p(x_2) : \{x/x_2, y/a\}$	(1),(6)
(8)	$\leftarrow q(x_4) : \{x/x_4, y/b\}$	(2),(6)
(9)	$\leftarrow r(x_5) : \{\{x/x_5, y/a\}, \{x/x_5, y/b\}\}$	(3),(7),(8)
(10)	$\bot : \{\{x/c, y/a\}, \{x/c, y/b\}\}$	(4),(9)

Lemma 6. *Let P be a logic program, Q a query, and $X \subseteq Var(Q)$. Let $\varphi_1 : \Theta_1,$ $\ldots, \varphi_n : \Theta_n$ be a derivation from $P \cup Q$ and $\varphi_1 : \Theta'_1, \ldots, \varphi_n : \Theta'_n$ be its version restricted to X. Then $\Theta'_i = \Theta_{i|X}$ for all $1 \leq i \leq n$.*

This lemma can be proved by induction on i in a straightforward way.

The following theorem states that we can save memory when searching for refutations by restricting kept disjunctive substitutions to the set of interested variables. The theorem immediately follows from the above lemma.

Theorem 4. *Let P be a logic program, Q a query, and $X \subseteq Var(Q)$. If $\bot : \Theta'$ is the last goal of a refutation restricted to X of $P \cup Q$, then there exists a computed answer Θ of $P \cup Q$ such that $\Theta' = \Theta_{|X}$. Conversely, for every computed answer Θ of $P \cup Q$, there exists a refutation restricted to X of $P \cup Q$ with the last goal $\bot : \Theta'$ such that $\Theta' = \Theta_{|X}$ (in particular, $\Theta' = \Theta$ when $X = Var(Q)$).*

We can simulate disjunctive substitutions by answer literals as follows.

For each variable x, let "x" be a constant symbol for keeping the name of x. We use "x"$/t$, where $/$ is an infix function symbol, to keep the binding x/t. Let ans be a special predicate symbol which can have different arities. Atoms of this predicate symbol will be always denoted either explicitly as $ans(\ldots)$ or using a prefix Ans. A literal $ans(\text{"}x_1\text{"}/t_1, \ldots, \text{"}x_n\text{"}/t_n)$ is called an *answer literal* if $x_1, \ldots, x_n$ are different variables. This answer literal can be treated as $\{x_1/t_1, \ldots, x_n/t_n\}$. By deleting from this set pairs x_i/t_i with $t_i = x_i$ we obtain a normal substitution, which is called the *substitution corresponding to the answer literal* $ans(\text{"}x_1\text{"}/t_1, \ldots, \text{"}x_n\text{"}/t_n)$. If $\varphi = Ans_1 \vee \ldots \vee Ans_m$ and θ_i is the substitution corresponding to Ans_i, for $1 \leq i \leq m$, then we call $\{\theta_1, \ldots, \theta_m\}$ the *disjunctive substitution corresponding to* φ. Assume that ε is the substitution corresponding to the empty clause.

A *goal with answer literals* is a clause of the following form, with $n, m \geq 0$:

$$Ans_1 \vee \ldots \vee Ans_n \leftarrow B_1 \wedge \ldots \wedge B_m$$

Let $\varphi = A_1 \vee \ldots \vee A_n \leftarrow B_1 \wedge \ldots \wedge B_m$ be a program clause ($n > 0$), and $(\psi_1 \leftarrow \varphi_1), \ldots, (\psi_n \leftarrow \varphi_n)$ be goals with answer literals (i.e. each ψ_i is a disjunction of answer literals). Let $\varphi_i = (\xi_i \wedge \zeta_i)$ for $1 \leq i \leq n$, where ξ_i is a non-empty set of atoms *selected* for φ_i. If there exists an mgu σ such that $A_i \sigma = A'_i \sigma$ for every $1 \leq i \leq n$ and every atom A'_i of ξ_i, then we call the goal

$$(\psi_1 \vee \ldots \vee \psi_n \leftarrow B_1 \wedge \ldots \wedge B_m \wedge \zeta_1 \wedge \ldots \wedge \zeta_n)\sigma$$

a *hyper-resolvent (with answer literals)* of φ and $(\psi_1 \leftarrow \varphi_1), \ldots, (\psi_n \leftarrow \varphi_n)$. Note that such a hyper-resolvent is also a goal with answer literals.

Let P be a logic program, $Q = \{\varphi_1, \ldots, \varphi_n\}$ a query, and $X \subseteq Var(Q)$. For each $1 \leq i \leq n$, let $Var(\varphi_i) \cap X = \{x_{i,1}, \ldots, x_{i,k_i}\}$, $\varphi_i = \leftarrow \xi_i$, and $\varphi'_i = ans(\text{"}x_{i,1}\text{"}/x_{i,1}, \ldots, \text{"}x_{i,k_i}\text{"}/x_{i,k_i}) \leftarrow \xi_i$ if $k_i > 0$, or $\varphi'_i = \varphi_i$ if $k_i = 0$. Let $Q' = \{\varphi'_1, \ldots, \varphi'_n\}$. A *derivation from $P \cup Q$ with answer literals for X* is a sequence $\psi_1, \ldots, \psi_m$ of goals with answer literals such that for each $1 \leq j \leq m$, either $\psi_j \in Q'$ or ψ_j is a hyper-resolvent with answer literals of a standardized variant of a program clause of P and standardized variants of some goals from $\psi_1, \ldots, \psi_{j-1}$, where a *standardized variant* is a renaming of all the variables in the original clause so that it does not contain variables of the other involved variants. Such a derivation is called a *refutation of $P \cup Q$ with answer literals for X* if the last goal ψ_m is either the empty clause or a positive clause (consisting of only answer literals).

Example 3. Reconsider Example 1. Here is a refutation of $P \cup Q$ with answer literals for $\{x, y\}$:

(6) $ans(``x"/x, ``y"/y) \leftarrow s(x, y)$ from (5)
(7) $ans(``x"/x_2, ``y"/a) \leftarrow p(x_2)$ (1),(6)
(8) $ans(``x"/x_4, ``y"/b) \leftarrow q(x_4)$ (2),(6)
(9) $ans(``x"/x_5, ``y"/a) \vee ans(``x"/x_5, ``y"/b) \leftarrow r(x_5)$ (3),(7),(8)
(10) $ans(``x"/c, ``y"/a) \vee ans(``x"/c, ``y"/b)$ (4),(9)

Theorem 5. *Let P be a logic program, Q a query, and $X \subseteq Var(Q)$. If ψ is the last goal of a refutation of $P \cup Q$ with answer literals for X, then there exists a computed answer Θ of $P \cup Q$ such that $\Theta_{|X}$ is the disjunctive substitution corresponding to ψ. Conversely, for every computed answer Θ of $P \cup Q$, there exists ψ as the last goal of a refutation of $P \cup Q$ with answer literals for X such that $\Theta_{|X}$ is the disjunctive substitution corresponding to ψ.*

Proof. Given a refutation of $P \cup Q$ with answer literals for X, simulate it by a refutation restricted to X of $P \cup Q$. For the converse direction, do it analogously. Let $\zeta_i \leftarrow \psi_i$ and $\leftarrow \psi_i : \Theta_i$ be the goals number i in the two corresponding refutations. By induction on i, it is easy to see that Θ_i is the disjunctive substitution corresponding to ζ_i. This together with Theorem 4 proves this theorem.

Keeping information for computed answers by using answer literals is just one of possible techniques, which is not always optimal. For example, $ans(``x"/a, ``y"/y) \vee ans(``x"/a, ``y"/b) \vee ans(``x"/a, ``y"/c)$ can be better represented as the composition of $\{x/a\}$ and $\{\varepsilon, \{y/b\}, \{y/c\}\}$.

We say that $\Theta = \{\theta_1, \ldots, \theta_n\}$ has a *conflict w.r.t. x* if there exist bindings $x/t_1 \in \theta_i$ and $x/t_2 \in \theta_j$ for some i, j from $1..n$ such that $t_1 \neq t_2$. Suppose that Θ is a computed answer of $P \cup Q$ and Θ has no conflicts w.r.t. any variable. Then the normal substitution $\theta = \bigcup \Theta$ is also a correct answer of $P \cup Q$. Despite that θ is "tighter" than Θ, from the point of view of users, θ is more intuitive and sufficient enough.

Consider a more general case. Suppose that $\Theta = \{\theta_1, \ldots, \theta_n\}$ is a computed answer of $P \cup Q$, $x \in Dom(\Theta)$, and Θ has no conflicts w.r.t. x. Let x/t be the binding of x that belongs to some θ_i, $1 \leq i \leq n$. Let $\theta_j' = \theta_j - \{x/t\}$ for $1 \leq j \leq n$. Then $\{x/t\}\{\theta_1', \ldots, \theta_n'\}$ is also a correct answer of $P \cup Q$. This kind of extraction can be applied further for $\{\theta_1', \ldots, \theta_n'\}$, and so on. The resulting composition is a correct answer "tighter" than Θ but it is more compact and still acceptable from the point of view of users.

8   Conclusions

We have proved that negative hyper-resolution is a sound and complete procedure for answering queries in disjunctive logic programs. This is a fundamental theoretical result for the intersection of theorem proving, disjunctive logic programming and AI. Our completeness proof is short and based on our reverse fixpoint semantics of disjunctive logic programs.

We have also introduced disjunctive substitutions to represent answers of queries. Our definition can be looked at as a formulation on the semantic level, while answer literals used in theorem proving systems are defined on the syntactical level. Our formulation extracts the meaning of answers from representation and in some situations allows a better encoding.

As a future work, we will study answer completeness of negative hyper-resolution under ordering refinements.

Acknowledgements. The author would like to thank Dr. Rajeev Goré and the anonymous reviewers for helpful comments.

References

1. K.R. Apt and M.H. van Emden. Contributions to the theory of logic programming. *Journal of the ACM*, 29(3):841–862, 1982.
2. P. Baumgartner and U. Furbach. Calculi for disjunctive logic programming. In Jan Maluszynski, editor, *Proc. of ILPS 1997*, pages 229–243. The MIT Press, 1997.
3. S. Brass and U.W. Lipeck. Generalized bottom-up query evaluation. In G. Gottlob A. Pirotte, C. Delobel, editor, *Advances in Database Technology — EDBT'92, 3rd Int. Conf.*, volume LNCS 580, pages 88–103. Springer-Verlag, 1992.
4. C.-L. Chang and R. C.-T. Lee. *Symbolic Logic and Mechanical Theorem Proving.* Academic Press, 1973.
5. C.C. Green. Theorem proving by resolution as basis for question-answering systems. *Machine Intelligence*, 4:183–205, 1969.
6. R.A. Kowalski. Predicate logic as a programming language. *Information Processing Letters*, 74:569–574, 1974.
7. K. Kunen. The semantics of answer literals. *Journal of Automated Reasoning*, 17(1):83–95, 1996.
8. J. Lobo, J. Minker, and A. Rajasekar. *Foundations of Disjunctive Logic Programming.* MIT Press, 1992.
9. J. Lobo, A. Rajasekar, and J. Minker. Semantics of Horn and disjunctive logic programs. *Theoretical Computer Science*, 86(1):93–106, 1991.
10. D. Loveland. Near-Horn Prolog. In J.-L. Lassez, editor, *Proc. of the 4th Int. Conf. on Logic Programming*, pages 456–469. The MIT Press, 1987.
11. D. Luckham and N.J. Nilsson. Extracting information from resolution proof trees. *Artificial Intelligence*, 2:27–54, 1971.
12. J.A. Robinson. Automatic deduction with hyper-resolution. *International Journal of Computer Mathematics*, 1:227–234, 1965.
13. J.A. Robinson. A machine-oriented logic based on the resolution principle. *Journal of the ACM*, 12(1):23–41, 1965.
14. M.H. van Emden and R.A. Kowalski. The semantics of predicate logic as a programming language. *Journal of the ACM*, 23(4):733–742, 1976.

Discovering Anomalies in Evidential Knowledge
by Logic Programming

Fabrizio Angiulli[1], Gianluigi Greco[2], and Luigi Palopoli[3]

[1] ICAR-CNR, Via P. Bucci 41C, 87030 Rende (CS), Italy
angiulli@icar.cnr.it
[2] Dip. di Matematica - Università della Calabria, Via P. Bucci 30B, 87030 Rende (CS), Italy
greco@mat.unical.it
[3] DEIS - Università della Calabria, Via P. Bucci 41C, 87030 Rende (CS), Italy
palopoli@deis.unical.it

Abstract. The development of effective knowledge discovery techniques has become in the recent few years a very active research area due to the important
impact it has in several relevant application areas. One interesting task thereof is
that of singling out anomalous individuals from a given population, e.g., to detect
rare events in time-series analysis settings, or to identify objects whose behavior is
deviant w.r.t. a codified standard set of "social" rules. Such exceptional individuals
are usually referred to as *outliers* in the literature.
Recently, outlier detection has also emerged as a relevant KR&R problem in the
context of default logic [2]. For instance, detection algorithms can be used by
rational agents to single out those observations that are anomalous to some extent
w.r.t. their own, trustable knowledge about the world encoded in the form of a
suitable logic theory.
In this paper, we formally state the concept of outliers in the context of logic
programming. Besides the novel formalization we propose which helps in shed-
ding some lights on the real nature of outliers, a major contribution of the work
lies in the exploitation of a minimality criteria in their detection. Moreover, the
computational complexity of outlier detection problems arising in this novel setting is thoroughly investigated and accounted for in the paper as well. Finally,
we also propose a rewriting algorithm that transforms any outlier problem into an
equivalent answer set computation problem, thereby making outlier computation
effective and realizable on top of any answer set engine.

1   Introduction

1.1   Statement of the Problem

Enhancing the reasoning capabilities of rational agents is a quite active area of research.
In fact, there is a growing body of proposals aiming at facilitating the mutual interaction of agents in multi-agent environments and at devising effective strategies for the
achievement of their own goals. Usually, each agent is assumed to have its own, trustable
knowledge about the world often encoded in the form of a suitable logic theory (call it
the *background* knowledge), which is used for taking the most appropriate decision after
some *observations* has been obtained on the actual status of the "external" environment.

J.J. Alferes and J. Leite (Eds.): JELIA 2004, LNAI 3229, pp. 578–590, 2004.

r_1 : connected(s).
r_2 : connected(Y) ← wired(X, Y), up(X).
r_3 : wired(s, a). ⋯ wired(g, t).
r_4 : down(X) ← computer(X), not connected(X).
r_5 : up(X) ← computer(X), not down(X).
r_6 : computer(s). computer(a). ⋯ computer(t).
r_7 : up(s).

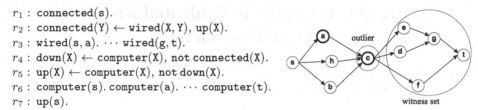

Fig. 1. Computer network example.

Clear enough, the effectiveness of the decision process depends on the ability the agent has in exploiting such observations for inferring both useful information about its environment and clues about the behavior of the other agents which it is possibly interacting with. Actually, some of the observations may result to be completely irrelevant to the agent decision process; others might instead be of a great interest, for they put into evidence the presence of some situations possibly requiring an alert or a quick reaction.

Given that observations might be a considerable number, a quite interesting problem is that of singling out those observations that look anomalous, and, as such, might provide the agent with additional information for a better understanding of the environment or of the behavior of the agents which the agent is interacting with.

The isolation of such anomalous observations (which we shall call *outliers* in the following), e.g., rare events in time-series analysis settings, or objects whose behavior is deviant w.r.t. a codified standard set of "social" rules, clearly offers a potential useful source of additional knowledge that can be exploited with the interaction among agents or simply for optimizing the way an agent carries out its activities. Further interesting and more specific applications range from fraud detection to network robustness analysis to intrusion detection.

It is worth pointing out that *outlier detection* problems come in several different flavors within different applicative settings, mainly investigated in the area of Knowledge Discovery in Databases [3,9,14,4,1]. However, only recently it has emerged as a relevant knowledge representation and reasoning problem, in the context of default logic [2]. Following such an approach, in this paper, we formally state the concept of outliers in the context of logic programming. This means that the agent background knowledge, that is, what is known in general about the world, and the agent observations, that is, what is currently perceived about (possibly a portion of) the world, are encoded in the form of a logic program (called the *Rule Component*) and a set of facts (called the *Observation Component*), respectively. In order to make the framework we are dealing with clear, we first look at the following example.

1.2 Example of Outlier Detection

Consider an agent A^N that is in charge of monitoring the connectivity status of the computer network $\mathcal{N}$ shown on the right of Figure 1. Indeed, some of the computers of $\mathcal{N}$ may be offline, hereby potentially breaking the required source-to-terminal connectivity. The agent's background knowledge is modelled by a logic program P^N, which is used by A^N for deciding whether the computer s is connected to t even though some computers are not properly working.

Program P^N (*Rule Component*) consists of the rules shown on the left of Figure 1. In P^N, each computer, say X, is represented by an atom computer(X), and connections among computers are represented by means of the binary relation wired. Then, the program states that a computer is up only if it is reachable from s by means of a path of computers that are up in their turn.

In order to monitor the net, A^N observes the actual status of *each* computer X in the net. Specifically, if the computer X is offline (resp. online) then the fact down(X) (resp. up(X)) comes true with such observations. Hence, the agent A^N has such evidences modelled in the *Observation Component* by means of a set of facts, say F^N, over the predicates down and up.

Armed with this knowledge, the agent is interested in singling out the observations that are anomalous according to the "normal" behavior of the system, modelled by P^N.

Assume, for instance, that F^N comprises the facts $\{down(a), up(b), down(c), up(d), up(e), up(f), up(g), up(h), up(t)\}$ — in the figure, we have marked in bold the computers observed to be down. Then, A^N might notice that there are some strange aspects in its observations. Specifically, if A^N had not observed that computers d, e, f, g, and t are up, he would have inferred exactly the opposite conclusions by exploiting its knowledge of the world (program P^N), since the failure of c suffices for breaking the s-t connectivity. Formally, let $\mathcal{W}$ be the set $\{up(d), up(e), up(g), up(f), up(t)\}$, then the program $P_{\mathcal{W}} = P^N \cup F^N \setminus \mathcal{W}$ entails $\neg\mathcal{W}$, denoted by $P_{\mathcal{W}} \models \neg\mathcal{W}$. Under this perspective, A^N might be induced in doubting of the observation down(c). And, in fact, the removal of the observation down(c) suffices for explaining the actual behavior of the network, since the program $P_{\mathcal{W},\{down(c)\}} = P_{\mathcal{W}} \setminus \{down(c)\}$ is such that $P_{\mathcal{W},\{down(c)\}} \not\models \neg\mathcal{W}$.

In the framework we are going to present, the computer c is precisely recognized to represent an outlier, while the set $\mathcal{W}$ is an outlier witness, i.e., a set of facts which can be explained by the rule component if and only if the outliers are not trusted in the observations. Hence, as we shall show in detail, computing an outlier amounts also to the discovery of its associated witness.

We conclude this discussion by putting into evidence that the computational core of the outlier detection problems share some characteristics with the computational core of abductive reasoning tasks. Indeed, if A^N knows in advance the set $\mathcal{W}$, he might single out the computer c precisely by trying to justify such anomalous set of observations. However, since $\mathcal{W}$ is in general not known, agent A^N must spent some efforts in discovering it. And, in fact, the activity of identifying the witness sets constitutes the main source of computational complexity in outlier detection problems as well as their main distinguishing characteristic.

1.3 Contribution and Plan of the Paper

With the framework outlined above, the contribution of this paper is basically three-fold. First of all, in Section 3, we formally define the notion of outlier in the context of logic programming based Knowledge systems, and we thoroughly investigate the computational complexity of some natural outlier detection problems.

Second, in Section 4, we formalize several cost-based generalizations of outlier detection problems, accounting for a number of interesting applicative situations in which the computation of just *any* outlier is not what we are really looking for. Moreover, we also study how this generalizations influences the complexity of outlier detection.

Finally, in Section 5, we present a sound and complete algorithm for transforming any outlier problem into an equivalent answer set computation problem. Since answer sets represent the solution of the outlier problems, the transformation can be used for implementing a prototype tool for outlier detection on top of any available answer set engine (e.g., [8,10,12]).

2   Preliminaries

Logic Programs. A *rule* r is a clause of the form: $a \leftarrow b_1, \cdots, b_k, \text{not } c_1, \cdots, \text{not } c_n.$, where $k, n \geq 0$, and $a, b_1, \cdots, b_k, c_1, \cdots, c_n$ are atoms. The atom a is the *head* of r, while the conjunction $b_1, \ldots, b_k, \text{not } c_1, \cdots, \text{not } c_n$ is the *body* of r. A rule with $n = 0$ is said *positive*. A rule with an empty body (i.e. $n = k = 0$) is called a *fact*.

A *logic program* (short: LP) P is a finite set of rules. P is *positive* if all the rules are positive. Moreover, P is *stratified*, if there is an assignment $s(\cdot)$ of integers to the atoms in P, such that for each clause r in P the following holds: if p is the atom in the head of r and q (resp. *not* q) occurs in r, then $s(p) \geq s(q)$ (resp. $s(p) > s(q)$).

For a program P, the stable model semantics assigns to P the set $\mathcal{SM}(P)$ of its *stable models* [6]. It is well known that stratified programs have a unique stable model.

Let $\mathcal{W}$ be a set of facts. Then, program P *bravely entails* $\mathcal{W}$ (resp. $\neg \mathcal{W}$), denoted by $P \models_b \mathcal{W}$ (resp. $P \models_b \neg \mathcal{W}$), if there exists $M \in \mathcal{SM}(P)$ such that each fact in $\mathcal{W}$ is evaluated true (resp. false) in M. Moreover, P *cautiously entails* $\mathcal{W}$ (resp. $\neg \mathcal{W}$), denoted by $P \models_c \mathcal{W}$ (resp. $P \models_c \neg \mathcal{W}$), if for each model $M \in \mathcal{SM}(P)$, each fact in $\mathcal{W}$ is true (resp. false) in M.

Computational Complexity. We recall some basic definitions about complexity theory, particularly, the polynomial time hierarchy (see, e.g., [13]).

The class P is the set of decision problems that can be answered by a deterministic Turing machine in polynomial time. The classes Σ_k^P and Π_k^P, forming the *polynomial hierarchy*, are defined as follows: $\Sigma_0^P = \Pi_0^P = \text{P}$ and for all $k \geq 1$, $\Sigma_k^P = \text{NP}^{\Sigma_{k-1}^P}$, and $\Pi_k^P = \text{co-}\Sigma_k^P$. Σ_k^P models computability by a nondeterministic polynomial time Turing machine which may use an oracle, that is, loosely speaking, a subprogram, that can be run with no computational cost, for solving a problem in Σ_{k-1}^P. The class of decision problems that can be solved by a nondeterministic Turing machine in polynomial time is denoted by NP, while the class of decision problems whose complementary problem is in NP, is denote by co-NP. The class D_k^P, $k \geq 1$, is defined as the class of problems that consist of the conjunction of two independent problems from Σ_k^P and Π_k^P, respectively. Note that, for all $k \geq 1$, $\Sigma_k^P \subseteq D_k^P \subseteq \Sigma_{k+1}^P$. Finally, for any of the above classes, say C, FC denotes its functional version, containing the search analogues of decision problems in C.

We conclude these preliminaries, by noticing that we are considering propositional programs. For instance, in the introductory example, the input to the outlier detection problems is the ground version of P^N, i.e., the program obtained by applying to each rule all the possible substitutions from its variables to the set of all the constants in P^N.

3 Defining Outliers

In this section, we introduce the notion and the basic definitions involved in the framework we are going to depict and we formalize the main problems we shall next study.

3.1 Formal Framework

Let P^{rls} be a logic program encoding general knowledge about the world, called *rule program*, and let P^{obs} be a set of facts encoding some *observed* aspects of the current status of the world, called *observation set*. Then, the structure $\mathcal{P} = \langle P^{\mathrm{rls}}, P^{\mathrm{obs}} \rangle$, relating the general knowledge encoded in P^{rls} with the evidence about the world encoded in P^{obs}, is said to be a *rule-observation pair*, and it constitutes the input for outlier detection problems.

Indeed, given $\mathcal{P}$, we are interested in identifying (if any) a set $\mathcal{O}$ of *observations* (facts in P^{obs}) that are "anomalous" according to the general theory P^{rls} and the other facts in $P^{\mathrm{obs}} \setminus \mathcal{O}$. Quite roughly speaking, the idea underlying the identification of $\mathcal{O}$ is to discover a *witness set* $\mathcal{W} \subseteq P^{\mathrm{obs}}$, that is, a set of facts which would be explained in the theory if and only if all the facts in $\mathcal{O}$ were not observed. Such an intuition is formalized in the following definition.

Definition 1. Let $\mathcal{P} = \langle P^{\mathrm{rls}}, P^{\mathrm{obs}} \rangle$ be a rule-observation pair and let $\mathcal{O} \subseteq P^{\mathrm{obs}}$ be a set facts. Then, $\mathcal{O}$ is an *outlier*, under the cautious (resp. brave) semantics, in $\mathcal{P}$ if there exists a non empty set $\mathcal{W} \subseteq P^{\mathrm{obs}}$, called *outlier witness* for $\mathcal{O}$ in $\mathcal{P}$, such that:

1. $P(\mathcal{P})_{\mathcal{W}} \models_c \neg \mathcal{W}$ (resp. $P(\mathcal{P})_{\mathcal{W}} \models_b \neg \mathcal{W}$), and
2. $P(\mathcal{P})_{\mathcal{W},\mathcal{O}} \not\models_c \neg \mathcal{W}$ (resp. $P(\mathcal{P})_{\mathcal{W},\mathcal{O}} \not\models_b \neg \mathcal{W}$).

where $P(\mathcal{P}) = P^{\mathrm{rls}} \cup P^{\mathrm{obs}}$, $P(\mathcal{P})_{\mathcal{W}} = P(\mathcal{P}) \setminus \mathcal{W}$ and $P(\mathcal{P})_{\mathcal{W},\mathcal{O}} = P(\mathcal{P})_{\mathcal{W}} \setminus \mathcal{O}$. □

Notice that, in the above definition, we have distinguished between brave and cautious semantics. Indeed, the semantics is part of the input, and it is provided by the designer of the rules encoding the general knowledge of the world. Obviously, if P^{rls} has a unique stable model (for instance, in the case it is positive or stratified), then the two semantics coincide. In the rest of the paper, for stratified or positive programs we do not distinguish among the semantics - for instance, we shall simply say that P entails a set $\mathcal{W}$. The following example shows, instead, a simple scenario in which the two notions differs.

Example 1. Assume that in the network of Figure 1, it is not known whether the computer s is properly working. To model this scenario, we build a program $P^{N'}$ by replacing in P^N the fact in r_7 with the rules: r'_7 : up(s) ← not down(s). and r''_7 : down(s) ← not up(s). It is easy to see that $P^{N'}$ has two different models, each one associated with a possible status of s. If the agent A^N still observes $F^N = \{\mathrm{down(a), up(b), down(c), up(d), up(e), up(f), up(g), up(h), up(t)}\}$, it might conclude that the fact down(c) is an outlier under the brave semantics, since it is witnessed by the model in which up(s) is true. Conversely, under the cautious semantics there are no outliers. In fact, even though down(c) is an "anomalous" observation in the case s is up, it cannot affect the reachability of d, e, f, g, and t when s is down. Hence, because of condition 2 in Definition 1, under skeptical reasoning, agent A^N cannot conclude that down(c) is an outlier. □

The set of all the outliers under the cautious (resp. brave) semantics for a given pair $\mathcal{P}$ is denoted by $\mathcal{O}[\mathcal{P}]_c$ (resp. $\mathcal{O}[\mathcal{P}]_b$). Following the previous example and even though the two notions does not coincide, one may wonder whether $\mathcal{O}[\mathcal{P}]_c \subset \mathcal{O}[\mathcal{P}]_b$. This relationship seems to be quite natural, but it does not hold in general, as can be verified exploiting symmetry of Definition 1 under brave and cautious semantics.

3.2   Basic Results

Now that the notion of an outlier has been formalized, we next turn to the study of the most basic problem arising in this setting. Given in input a rule-observation pair $\mathcal{P} = \langle P^{\mathrm{rls}}, P^{\mathrm{obs}} \rangle$ we denote by EXISTENCE the problem of deciding the existence of an outlier in $\mathcal{P}$. Obviously, the complexity of EXISTENCE strictly depends on what type of logic program P^{rls} is. A very simple case is where P^{rls} is a positive logic program.

Theorem 1. *Let $\mathcal{P} = \langle P^{\mathrm{rls}}, P^{\mathrm{obs}} \rangle$ be a rule-observation pair such that P^{rls} is positive. Then, there are no outliers in $\mathcal{P}$.*

Let us now consider a more involved scenario, in which P^{rls} is stratified. Even though in logic programming adding stratified negation does not increase the complexity of identifying the unique minimal model, we next show that negation (even in the stratified form) does indeed matter in the context of outlier detection. Indeed, the EXISTENCE problem becomes more difficult in this case, and even unlikely to be solvable in polynomial time.

Theorem 2. *Let $\mathcal{P} = \langle P^{\mathrm{rls}}, P^{\mathrm{obs}} \rangle$ be a rule-observation pair such that P^{rls} is stratified. Then EXISTENCE is NP-complete.*

Proof (Sketch). (Membership) Given a rule-observation pair $\mathcal{P} = \langle P^{\mathrm{rls}}, P^{\mathrm{obs}} \rangle$, we must show that there exist two sets $\mathcal{W}, \mathcal{O} \subseteq P^{\mathrm{obs}}$ such that $P(\mathcal{P})_{\mathcal{W}} \models \neg \mathcal{W}$ (query q') and $P(\mathcal{P})_{\mathcal{W},\mathcal{O}} \not\models \neg \mathcal{W}$ (query q''). Then, we can build a polynomial-time nondeterministic Turing machine that guesses both the sets $\mathcal{W}$ and $\mathcal{O}$ and then solves queries q' and q''. The result follows by observing that the two latter tasks are indeed P-complete, since P^{rls} is stratified.

(Hardness) Recall that deciding whether a Boolean formula in conjunctive normal form $\Phi = c_1 \wedge \ldots \wedge c_m$ over the variables $X_1, \ldots, X_n$ is satisfiable, i.e., deciding whether there exists truth assignments to the variables making each clause c_j true, is an NP-hard problem, even if each clause contains at most three distinct (positive or negated) variables [13]. Then, we define a rule-observation pair $\mathcal{P}(\Phi) = \langle P^{\mathrm{rls}}(\Phi), P^{\mathrm{obs}}(\Phi) \rangle$ such that: (i) $P^{\mathrm{obs}}(\Phi)$ contains exactly the fact $falseX_i$ for each variable X_i in Φ, and facts sat and $disabled$; (ii) $P^{\mathrm{rls}}(\Phi)$ is

$$\left. \begin{array}{l} c_j \leftarrow \sigma(t_{j,1}), \; not \; disabled. \\ c_j \leftarrow \sigma(t_{j,2}), \; not \; disabled. \\ c_j \leftarrow \sigma(t_{j,3}), \; not \; disabled. \end{array} \right\} \quad \forall 1 \le j \le m, \; \text{s.t.} \; c_j = t_{j,1} \vee t_{j,2} \vee t_{j,3}$$

$$sat \leftarrow c_1, \; \ldots, \; c_m.$$

where σ is the following mapping: $\sigma(t) = \begin{cases} not \; falseX_i \, , \text{if } t = X_i, 1 \le i \le n \\ falseX_i \qquad , \text{if } t = \neg X_i, 1 \le i \le n. \end{cases}$

Clearly, $P(\Phi)$ is stratified and can be built in polynomial time. Moreover, it is not difficult to see that Φ is satisfiable if and only if there exists an outlier in $\mathcal{P}(\Phi)$.   □

We next study the complexity of the EXISTENCE problem in the most general setting. The following theorem shows that, under the brave semantics, the problem for general programs lies one level up in the polynomial hierarchy w.r.t. the complexity associated with stratified programs.

Theorem 3. EXISTENCE *under the brave semantics is* Σ_2^P*-complete.*

Proof (Sketch). (Membership) Given a pair $\mathcal{P} = \langle P^{\text{rls}}, P^{\text{obs}} \rangle$, we must show that there exist two sets $\mathcal{W}, \mathcal{O} \subseteq P^{\text{obs}}$ such that $P(\mathcal{P})_{\mathcal{W}} \models_b \neg \mathcal{W}$ (query q') and $P(\mathcal{P})_{\mathcal{W},\mathcal{O}} \not\models_b \neg \mathcal{W}$ (query q''). Query q' is NP-complete, while query q'' is co-NP-complete. Then, EXISTENCE can be solved by guessing both the sets $\mathcal{W}$ and $\mathcal{O}$ and then solving queries q' and q'' by two calls to the oracle.

(Hardness) Let $F = \exists X_1, \ldots X_n \forall Y_1, \ldots Y_q \Phi$ be a quantified Boolean formula in disjunctive normal form, i.e., Φ has the form $d_1 \vee \ldots \vee d_m$, over the variables $X_1, \ldots X_n, Y_1, \ldots Y_q$. Deciding the validity of such formulas is a well-known Σ_2^P-complete problem. W.l.o.g., assume that each disjunct d_j contains three literals at most. We associate with Φ the rule-observation pair $\mathcal{P}(\Phi) = \langle P^{\text{rls}}(\Phi), P^{\text{obs}}(\Phi) \rangle$ such that: (i) $P^{\text{obs}}(\Phi)$ contains exactly a fact x_i for each variable X_i in Φ, and the facts sat and $disabled$; (ii) $P^{\text{rls}}(\Phi)$ is

$$y_i \leftarrow not\ b_i. \qquad\qquad\qquad\qquad\quad 1 \le i \le q$$
$$b_i \leftarrow not\ y_i. \qquad\qquad\qquad\qquad\quad 1 \le i \le q$$
$$sat \leftarrow \sigma(t_{j,1}), \sigma(t_{j,2}), \sigma(t_{j,3}),\ not\ disabled. \quad 1 \le j \le m\ \text{s.t.}\ d_j = t_{j,1} \wedge t_{j,2} \wedge t_{j,3}$$

where σ is the following mapping: $\sigma(t) = \begin{cases} not\ x_k, & \text{if } t = x_k, 1 \le k \le n \\ x_k, & \text{if } t = \neg x_k, 1 \le k \le n. \\ not\ y_i, & \text{if } t = y_i, 1 \le i \le q \\ y_i, & \text{if } t = \neg y_i, 1 \le i \le q. \end{cases}$

Clearly, $\mathcal{P}(\Phi)$ can be built in polynomial time. Moreover, we can show that Φ is valid if and only if there exists an outlier in $\mathcal{P}(\Phi)$. □

Whereas, for most reasoning tasks, switching from brave to cautious reasoning implies the complexity to "switch" accordingly from a certain class C to the complementary class co-C, this is not the case for our EXISTENCE problem.

Theorem 4. EXISTENCE *under the cautious semantics is* Σ_2^P*-complete.*

Up to this point, we have focused our attention to outlier decision problems. Turning to outlier computation problems, the following result can be established by noticing that in the proofs above, solving a satisfiability problem is reduced to computing an outlier.

Corollary 1. *Let* $\mathcal{P} = \langle P^{\text{rls}}, P^{\text{obs}} \rangle$ *be a rule-observation pair. Then, the* COMPUTATION *problem, i.e., computing an arbitrary outlier in* $\mathcal{P}$*, is (i) FNP-complete, for stratified rule components, and (ii)* $F\Sigma_2^P$*-complete, for general rule components.*

3.3 Computational Complexity of Outlier Checking Problems

We next study the complexity of some further problems related to outlier identification. In particular, given a rule-observation pair $\mathcal{P} = \langle P^{\mathrm{rls}}, P^{\mathrm{obs}} \rangle$, we shall look at the following problems:

- WITNESS − CHECKING: given $\mathcal{W} \subseteq P^{\mathrm{obs}}$, is $\mathcal{W}$ a witness for any outlier $\mathcal{O}$ in $\mathcal{P}$?
- OUTLIER − CHECKING: given $\mathcal{O} \subseteq P^{\mathrm{obs}}$, is $\mathcal{O}$ an outlier for any witness set $\mathcal{W}$?
- OW − CHECKING: given $\mathcal{O}, \mathcal{W} \subseteq P^{\mathrm{obs}}$, is $\mathcal{O}$ an outlier in $\mathcal{P}$ with witness $\mathcal{W}$?

The following three theorems state the complexity of the problems listed above.

Theorem 5. *Let* $\mathcal{P} = \langle P^{\mathrm{rls}}, P^{\mathrm{obs}} \rangle$ *be a rule-observation pair. Then,* WITNESS − CHECKING *is (i)* NP*-complete, for stratified* P^{rls}, *(ii)* Σ_2^P*-complete under brave semantics for general* P^{rls}, *and (iii)* D^P*-complete under cautious semantics for general* P^{rls}.

Proof (Sketch). Let us consider point *(i)*. As for the membership, given $\mathcal{W} \subseteq P^{\mathrm{obs}}$, we can guess a set $\mathcal{O}$ and check that it is an outlier in $\mathcal{P}$ with witness $\mathcal{W}$. To this aim we have to verify that conditions $P(\mathcal{P})_{\mathcal{W}} \models \neg \mathcal{W}$ and $P(\mathcal{P})_{\mathcal{W},\mathcal{O}} \not\models \neg \mathcal{W}$ holds. Since $P(\mathcal{P})$ is stratified this check is feasible in polynomial time.

As for the hardness, we can exploit a similar reduction as the one of Theorem 2, in which given a formula $\varPhi$ we build a rule-observation pair $\mathcal{P}(\varPhi) = \langle P^{\mathrm{rls}}(\varPhi), P^{\mathrm{obs}}(\varPhi) \rangle$ such that there exists an outlier in $\mathcal{P}(\varPhi)$ if and only if the formula is satisfiable. Actually, by carefully working with the reduction we can show that outliers in $\mathcal{P}(\varPhi)$ (in correspondence with satisfying truth assignments) have witness $\mathcal{W} = \{sat\}$. Then, $\{sat\}$ is a witness for any outlier if and only if the formula $\varPhi$ is satisfiable.

Point *(ii)* can be proven by exploiting a line of reasoning analogous to that used in the point above with the reductions used in Theorem 3 and Theorem 4.

Finally, as for point *(iii)*, we have to verify that both conditions $P(\mathcal{P})_{\mathcal{W}} \models_c \neg \mathcal{W}$ and $P(\mathcal{P})_{\mathcal{W},\mathcal{O}} \not\models_c \neg \mathcal{W}$ holds for some set $\mathcal{O}$. The former condition can be checked in co-NP, whereas the latter amounts to guess both an outlier $\mathcal{O}$ and a model for $P(\mathcal{P})_{\mathcal{W},\mathcal{O}}$, and, as such, it is feasible in NP. As for the hardness, given two boolean formulas ϕ' and ϕ'' the result can be obtained exploiting a rule-observation pair $\mathcal{P} = \langle P^{\mathrm{rls}}, P^{\mathrm{obs}} \rangle$ with $P^{\mathrm{obs}} = \{w, o\}$ and P^{rls} encoding both ϕ' and ϕ'', such that satisfying truth assignment of ϕ' (resp. ϕ'')) are in one-to-one correspondence with models in $\mathcal{SM}(P_{\{w\}})$ (resp. $\mathcal{SM}(P_{\{w\},\{o\}})$). Moreover, program P^{rls} can be built such that w is a witness for o if and only if ϕ' is satisfiable and ϕ'' is not. $\square$

We point out that the complexity of WITNESS − CHECKING depends on the semantics adopted for the logic programs. This is not the case for the other two problems listed above.

Theorem 6. *Let* $\mathcal{P} = \langle P^{\mathrm{rls}}, P^{\mathrm{obs}} \rangle$ *be a rule-observation pair. Then,* OUTLIER − CHECKING *is (i)* NP*-complete, for stratified* P^{rls}, *and (ii)* Σ_2^P*-complete (under both brave and cautious semantics) for general* P^{rls}.

Theorem 7. *Let* $\mathcal{P} = \langle P^{\mathrm{rls}}, P^{\mathrm{obs}} \rangle$ *be a rule-observation pair. Then,* OW − CHECKING *is (i)* P*-complete, for stratified* P^{rls}, *and (ii)* D^P*-complete (under both brave and cautious semantics) for general* P^{rls}.

4   Minimum-Size Outlier Detection

There are several practical situations in which the computation of just *any* outlier is not what we are really looking for. For instance, it often happens that we are interested in computing outliers of *minimum-size*. Consider again the network example. We have already highlighted that down(c) is an outlier. Actually, every subset of {down(a), up(h), up(b)} union {down(c)} is an outlier in its turn, even though it does not provide the agent A^N with additional useful information w.r.t. the case that just down(c) is detected.

Hence, in this section we shall study the outlier detection problems with the additional constraint of minimizing the outlier size. This applicative setting is indeed consistent with what is generally required for minimal diagnosis [15].

A first natural problem that comes into play is to decide the existence of outliers of bounded size. Actually, we next show that bounding the size of the outlier we are looking for does not increase the complexity of the EXISTENCE problem.

Theorem 8. *Given a rule-observation pair* $\mathcal{P} = \langle P^{\mathrm{rls}}, P^{\mathrm{obs}} \rangle$, *and a natural number* k, *the* EXISTENCE[k] *problem of deciding the existence of outlier* $\mathcal{O}$ *of size at most* k *(*$|\mathcal{O}| \leq k$*) in* $\mathcal{P}$ *is (i)* NP-*complete, for stratified* P^{rls}, *and (ii)* Σ_2^P, *for general* P^{rls}.

Similarly, we can formalize an analogous version of the problem WITNESS − CHECKING: given $\mathcal{W} \subseteq P^{\mathrm{obs}}$ and a fixed natural number k, is $\mathcal{W}$ a witness for any outlier $\mathcal{O}$ in $\mathcal{P}$, such that $|\mathcal{O}| \leq k$? We shall call this problem WITNESS − CHECKING[k]. Interestingly, this time bounding the size of outlier indeed influences the complexity associated with the problem. In fact, for general LPs it becomes D^P-complete (rather than Σ_2^P-complete), and for stratified LPs it becomes even feasible in polynomial time, as the following theorem proves.

Theorem 9. *Let* $\mathcal{P} = \langle P^{\mathrm{rls}}, P^{\mathrm{obs}} \rangle$ *be a rule-observation pair. Then,* WITNESS − CHECKING[k] *is (i)* P-*complete, for stratified* P^{rls}, *and (ii)* D^P-*complete (under both brave and cautious semantics) for general* P^{rls}.

As already done in the Section 3.2, we next concentrate on computation problems. Specifically, we are interested in the COMPUTATION[min] problem: computing the outlier whose size is the minimum over the sizes of all the outliers — we denote by $min(\mathcal{P})$ such minimum value. Notice that in the case no outlier exists, $min(\mathcal{P})$ is undefined. To this aim we preliminarily study the computational complexity of a variant of the OW − CHECKING problem, denoted by OW − CHECKING[min], in which we focus our attention on checking minimum-size outliers only: given $\mathcal{O}, \mathcal{W} \subseteq P^{\mathrm{obs}}$, is $\mathcal{O}$ an outlier in $\mathcal{P}$ with witness $\mathcal{W}$, such that $min(\mathcal{P}) = |\mathcal{O}|$?

Theorem 10. *Let* $\mathcal{P} = \langle P^{\mathrm{rls}}, P^{\mathrm{obs}} \rangle$ *be a rule-observation pair. Then, the problem* OW − CHECKING[min] *is (i)* co-NP-*complete, for stratified* P^{rls}, *and (ii)* Π_2^P-*complete (under both brave and cautious semantics), for general* P^{rls}.

Then, one may exploit the above result for computing in $\mathrm{F}\Sigma_2^P$ and $\mathrm{F}\Sigma_3^P$ a minimum-size outlier in stratified and general pairs, respectively, by first guessing it and then verifying that it is indeed minimal. But, we can actually do better then thus by defining a more efficient computation method based on identifying the actual value of $min(\mathcal{P})$ and, then, guessing an outlier whose size is indeed $min(\mathcal{P})$.

Theorem 11. *Given a rule-observation pair* $\mathcal{P} = \langle P^{\mathrm{rls}}, P^{\mathrm{obs}} \rangle$, *computing the value* $min(\mathcal{P})$ *(if defined) is (i)* $\mathrm{F}\Delta_2^P[O(\log |\mathcal{P}|)]$-*complete, for stratified* P^{rls}, *and (ii) in* $\mathrm{F}\Delta_3^P[O(\log |\mathcal{P}|)]$ *(under both brave and cautious semantics), for general* P^{rls}.

Using the result demonstrated above, it is not difficult to see that given a rule-observation pair $\mathcal{P}$, we can compute an outlier of minimum size in polynomial time with the help of an NP (resp. Σ_2^P) oracle for stratified (resp. general) logic programs. Indeed, the problem can be solved by first computing the value $min(\mathcal{P})$ and then checking whether there exists an outlier $\mathcal{O}$ with $min(\mathcal{P}) = |\mathcal{O}|$. This latter problem amounts to solve the EXISTENCE[k] problem presented above, with $k = min(\mathcal{P})$, and, as such, it is feasible with an extra NP (resp. Σ_2^P) oracle call for stratified (resp. general) logic programs. Hence, the following result follows.

Theorem 12. *Given a rule-observation pair* $\mathcal{P} = \langle P^{\mathrm{rls}}, P^{\mathrm{obs}} \rangle$, *computing an arbitrary outlier* $\mathcal{O}$ *such that* $min(\mathcal{P}) = |\mathcal{O}|$ *is (i) in* $\mathrm{F}\Delta_2^P[O(\log |\mathcal{P}|)]$, *for stratified* P^{rls}, *and (ii) in* $\mathrm{F}\Delta_3^P[O(\log |\mathcal{P}|)]$ *(under brave and cautious semantics), for general* P^{rls}.

One may wonder whether the computation problem is, in fact, complete for the above complexity classes. For the case of stratified LPs, we are able to sharpen the simple membership result by assessing its precise complexity. We preliminary recall some further basic complexity issues. An NP *metric Turing machine* MT is a polynomial-time bounded nondeterministic Turing machine that on every computation branch halts and outputs a binary number. The result computed by MT is the maximum over all these numbers. The class OptP contains all integer functions that are computable by an NP metric Turing machine, whereas OptP$[O(\log n)]$ is a subclass containing all functions f, whose value $f(x)$ has $O(\log n)$ bits, where $n = |x|$. A well known problem in OptP$[O(\log n)]$ is computing the size of a maximum clique in a graph. We can show that COMPUTATION[min] is complete for the class FNP//OptP$[O(\log n)]$, where $n = |\mathcal{P}|$ is the size of the rule-observation pair, and which contains (see [5]) all (partial) multi-valued functions g for which a polynomially-bounded nondeterministic Turing machine T and a function $h \in \mathrm{OptP}[O(\log n)]$ exist such that, for every x, T computes the value $g(x)$, provided that both x and $h(x)$ are taken in input. The following result can be proven by constructing a parsimonious reduction involving the problem X-MAXIMAL MODEL: Given a formula ϕ in conjunctive normal form on the variables $Y = \{Y_1, ..., Y_n\}$ and a subset $X \subseteq Y$, compute a satisfying truth assignment M for ϕ whose X-part is maximal, i.e., for every other satisfying assignment M' there exists a variable in X which is true in M and false in M'.

Theorem 13. *Given a stratified rule-observation pair* $\mathcal{P} = \langle P^{\mathrm{rls}}, P^{\mathrm{obs}} \rangle$, *computing an arbitrary outlier* $\mathcal{O}$ *such that* $min(\mathcal{P}) = |\mathcal{O}|$ *(if any) is* FNP//OptP$[O(\log n)]$-*complete.*

5 Implementing Outliers in Answer Set Paradigm

Now that our framework for outlier detection has been illustrated and its complexity has been investigated, we can focus our attention to the problem of devising some effective strategies for its implementation. Specifically, we next exhibit a sound and complete algorithm that transforms any rule-observation pair $\mathcal{P}$ into a suitable logic program $\mathcal{L}(\mathcal{P})$ such that its stable models are in a one-to-one correspondence with outliers in $\mathcal{P}$.

Besides the declarative modelling features of answer set programming, the most interesting aspect of this transformation is that, since answer sets represent the solution of the outlier problems, it is possible to implement a prototype tool for finding outliers with the support of efficient answer set engines such as GnT [8], DLV [10] and *Smodels* [12]. Actually, reformulating in terms of answer set programs has been already exploited in the literature for prototypically implementing reasoning tasks such as abduction, planning, and diagnosis.

Our rewriting algorithm *OutlierDetectionToASP* is shown in Figure 2. It takes in input a pair $\mathcal{P} = \langle \mathcal{P}^{\mathrm{rls}}, \mathcal{P}^{\mathrm{obs}} \rangle$ and outputs a logic program $\mathcal{L}(\mathcal{P})$, which is built according to the following ideas. Each fact obs_i in P^{obs} is associated with two new facts o_i and w_i, where, intuitively, o_i (resp. w_i) being true in a model means that obs_i belongs to an outlier (resp. witness) in $\mathcal{P}$. In other words, truth values of facts o_i and w_i in any model for $\mathcal{L}(\mathcal{P})$ uniquely define an outlier and a witness set for it, respectively.

The program is such that it guesses the values for each o_i and w_i and verifies that both conditions in Definition 1 are satisfied. To this aim, the rules in P^{rls} are inserted into $\mathcal{L}(\mathcal{P})$ (step 1) along with a suitable rewriting of P^{rls}, in which each predicate, say p, is replaced by the symbol p^{in} (step 2).

Roughly speaking, the modified version of P^{rls} is used for checking Condition 1, and the original program for checking Condition 2. In more detail, the algorithm inserts the rules guessing both outlier and witness set in step 3.(a) and 3.(b), respectively. Then, the rules inserted in step 3.(c) impose that any obs_i cannot be an outlier and witness at the same time — notice, in fact, that a rule of the form p ← a, not p. acts as a constraint imposing that a must be false in any model. Rule 3.(d) guarantees that obs_i is true in the program if it is neither an outlier nor a witness. Similarly, 3.(e) guarantees that obs_i^{in} is true if w_i is not. Notice that such rules simulate the removal of the outlier and the witness which is needed for verifying Conditions 2 and 1, respectively. The remaining rules of step 3 define the atom $\mathrm{satC2}$ to be true if a fact obs_i is true even if assumed to be a witness (w_i true), i.e., if Condition 2 in Definition 1 is satisfied in the model, and similarly define $\mathrm{badC1}$ to be true if obs_i^{in} is true but obs_i is a witness, i.e., if Condition 1 is not satisfied in the model.

Then, 4.(b) imposes that we are only interested in answer set in which $\mathrm{satC2}$ is true, and in the case the program is stratified, step 5.(a) imposes that we are only interested in answer set in which $\mathrm{badC1}$ is false. Indeed, in the case of unstratified rule-observation pair, the constraint imposed by rule 5.(a) would not suffice for ensuring the satisfaction of Condition 1. And, in fact, the outlier detection problem, which has been shown to be complete for the second level of the polynomial hierarchy in the case of general rule component, cannot be expressed by exploiting logic programs under the stable model semantics, that are indeed able to express only problems at the first level of the polynomial hierarchy.

In order to deal with this problem, the algorithm exploits in step 6 a rewriting into a *disjunctive* logic program accounting for outliers under the cautious semantics — a similar rewriting for brave semantics can be obtained as well. We recall that disjunctive programs allow clauses to have both disjunction (denoted by $\vee$) in their heads and

---

Input: A rule-observation pair $\mathcal{P} = \langle P^{\mathrm{rls}}, P^{\mathrm{obs}} \rangle$, where $P^{\mathrm{obs}} = \{\mathrm{obs}_1, ..., \mathrm{obs}_n\}$;
Output: A logic program $\mathcal{L}(\mathcal{P})$;
Method: Perform the following steps:

1. $\mathcal{L}(\mathcal{P}) := P^{\mathrm{rls}}$;
2. **for each rule** $r \in P^{\mathrm{rls}}$ of the form $\mathtt{a} \leftarrow \mathtt{b_1}, \cdots, \mathtt{b_k}, \mathtt{not\ c_1}, \cdots, \mathtt{not\ c_n}$, **insert into** $\mathcal{L}(\mathcal{P})$ the rule
   a) $\mathtt{a^{in}} \leftarrow \mathtt{b_1^{in}}, \cdots, \mathtt{b_k^{in}}, \mathtt{not\ c_1^{in}}, \cdots, \mathtt{not\ c_n^{in}}$.
3. **for each** $\mathrm{obs}_i \in P^{\mathrm{obs}}$, **insert into** $\mathcal{L}(\mathcal{P})$ the following rules
   a) $\mathtt{o_i} \leftarrow \mathtt{\overline{o}_i}. \qquad \mathtt{\overline{o}_i} \leftarrow \mathtt{o_i}.$
   b) $\mathtt{w_i} \leftarrow \mathtt{\overline{w}_i}. \qquad \mathtt{\overline{w}_i} \leftarrow \mathtt{w_i}.$
   c) $\mathtt{p} \leftarrow \mathtt{o_i}, \mathtt{w_i}, \mathtt{not\ p}.$
   d) $\mathtt{obs_i} \leftarrow \mathtt{not\ o_i}, \mathtt{not\ w_i}.$
   e) $\mathtt{obs_i^{in}} \leftarrow \mathtt{not\ w_i}.$
   f) $\mathtt{badC1} \leftarrow \mathtt{w_i}, \mathtt{obs_i^{in}}.$
   g) $\mathtt{satC2} \leftarrow \mathtt{w_i}, \mathtt{obs_i}.$
4. **insert into** $\mathcal{L}(\mathcal{P})$ the rules
   a) $\mathtt{satC1} \leftarrow \mathtt{not\ badC1}.$
   b) $\mathtt{p} \leftarrow \mathtt{not\ satC2}, \mathtt{not\ p}.$
5. **if** P^{rls} is stratified **then insert into** $\mathcal{L}(\mathcal{P})$ the rule
   a) $\mathtt{p} \leftarrow \mathtt{badC1}, \mathtt{not\ p}.$
6. **else for each** predicate $p \in P^{\mathrm{rls}}$, **insert into** $\mathcal{L}(\mathcal{P})$ the rules   *//*** general logic programs*
   a) $\mathtt{p^{in}} \vee \mathtt{p^{out}}.$
   b) $\mathtt{p^{in}} \leftarrow \mathtt{badC1}.$
   c) $\mathtt{p^{out}} \leftarrow \mathtt{badC1}.$
   d) $\mathtt{badC1} \leftarrow \mathtt{p^{in}}, \mathtt{p^{out}}.$

Fig. 2. Algorithm *OutlierDetectionToASP*.

negation in their bodies. Their semantics is given by the set of the answer set of P, defined in [7], as suitable extension of stable models for disjunction-free programs. Under this semantics, disjunctive programs allow to express every property of finite structures that is decidable in the complexity class Σ_2^P. Therefore, disjunctive logic programming is strictly more expressive than disjunction-free programs, unless the polynomial hierarchy collapses.

Roughly speaking, the disjunctive rewriting constrains $\mathtt{badC1}$ not to be inferred not only in the model which satisfies Condition 2, but also in all the models of program $P(\mathcal{P})_{\mathcal{W}}$, for the witness set $\mathcal{W}$ associated with the facts of the form $\mathtt{w_i}$. The following theorem accounts for the correctness of the algorithm.

Theorem 14. *Let* $\mathcal{P} = \langle P^{\mathrm{rls}}, P^{\mathrm{obs}} \rangle$ *be a rule-observation pair, and let* $\mathcal{L}(\mathcal{P})$ *be the rewriting obtained by the algorithm in Figure 2. Then,*
- *for each outlier* $\mathcal{O}$ *with witness* $\mathcal{W}$ *in* $\mathcal{P}$*, there exists an answer set* $\mathcal{M}$ *of* $\mathcal{L}(\mathcal{P})$ *such that* $\{o_i \mid o_i \in \mathcal{M}\} = \mathcal{O}$ *and* $\{w_i \mid w_i \in \mathcal{M}\} = \mathcal{W}$*, and*
- *for each answer set* $\mathcal{M}$ *of* $\mathcal{L}(\mathcal{P})$*, there exists an outlier* $\mathcal{O}$ *with witness* $\mathcal{W}$ *in* $\mathcal{P}$*, such that* $\{o_i \mid o_i \in \mathcal{M}\} = \mathcal{O}$ *and* $\{w_i \mid w_i \in \mathcal{M}\} = \mathcal{W}$*.*

Finally, in order to model also outlier problems requiring minimality of the solutions, we might exploit the approach used in the DLV system relying on *weak constraints*. Weak constraints, represented as rules of the form $\mathtt{:\sim\ b_1}, \cdots, \mathtt{b_k}, \mathtt{not\ b_{k+1}}, \cdots, \mathtt{not\ b_{k+m}}$, express a set of desiderata conditions that may be violated and their informal semantics is to minimize the number of violated instances. And, in fact, the stable models of any program can be ordered w.r.t. the number of weak constraints that are not satisfied: The *best stable models* are those which minimize such a number. Thus, the algorithm in Figure 2 is modified by inserting into $\mathcal{L}(\mathcal{P})$ the constraint $\mathtt{:\sim\ o_i}.$ for each $\mathrm{obs}_i \in P^{\mathrm{obs}}$. Letting $\mathcal{L}^{\sim}(\mathcal{P})$ to be the transformed program resulting from applying the modified algorithm, it can be proven that minimum-size outliers in $\mathcal{P}$ are in one-to-one correspondence with best stable models of $\mathcal{L}^{\sim}(\mathcal{P})$.

Acknowledgments. We gratefully thank Rachel Ben-Eliyahu-Zohary since the original concept of outlier stems from one intuition of hers. This research was partially funded by MIUR in the framework of the COFIN'03 project "Tecniche di induzione di regole, metaquerying ed estrazione di pattern strutturati su database biologici".

References

1. C. C. Aggarwal and P.S. Yu. Outlier detection for high dimensional data. In *Proc. ACM Int. Conf. on Managment of Data*, pages 37–46, 2001.
2. F. Angiulli, R. Ben-Eliyahu-Zohary, and L. Palopoli. Outlier detection using default logic. In *Proc. of the Int. Joint Conf. on Artificial Intelligence*, pages 833–838, 2003.
3. A. Arning, R. Aggarwal, and P. Raghavan. A linear method for deviation detection in large databases. In *Proc. Int. Conf. on Knowledge Discovery and Data Mining*, pages 164–169, 1996.
4. M. M. Breunig, H. Kriegel, R.T. Ng, and J. Sander. LOF: Identifying density-based local outliers. In *Proc. ACM Int. Conf. on Managment of Data*, pages 93–104, 2000.
5. Z. Chen and S. Toda. The complexity of selecting maximal solutions. *Information and Computation*, 119(2), pp. 231-239, June 1995.
6. M. Gelfond and V. Lifschitz. The stable model semantics for logic programming. In *Fifth Int'l Conf.Symp. on Logic Programming*, pages 1070–1080. Seattle, 1988.
7. M. Gelfond and V. Lifschitz. Classical negation in logic programs and disjunctive databases. *New Generation Computing*, 9:365–385, 1991.
8. T. Janhunen, I. Niemelä, P. Simons, and J.-H. You. Partiality and disjunctions in stable model semantics. In *KR*, pages 411–419, 2000.
9. E. Knorr and R. Ng. Algorithms for mining distance-based outliers in large datasets. In *Proc. Int. Conf. on Very Large Databases*, pages 392–403, 1998.
10. N. Leone, G. Pfeifer, W. Faber, T. Eiter, G. Gottlob, S. Perri, and F. Scarcello. The dlv system for knowledge representation and reasoning. *ACM Transactions on Computational Logic. To Appear.*
11. F.Lin and J.H. You, Abduction in logic programming: a new definition and an abductive procedure based on rewriting. *Artificial Intelligence.* 140(1-2), pages 175–205, 2002.
12. I. Niemelä and P. Simons. Smodels: An implementation of the stable model and well-founded semantics for normal LP. In *Proc. of the 4th Int. Conf. on Logic Programing and Nonmonotonic Reasoning*, volume 1265 of *LNAI*, pages 420–429, Berlin, 1997. Springer.
13. C. H. Papadimitriou. *Computatational Complexity*. Addison-Wesley, Reading, Mass., 1994.
14. S. Ramaswamy, R. Rastogi, and K. Shim. Efficient algorithms for mining outliers from large data sets. In *Proc. ACM Int. Conf. on Managment of Data*, pages 427–438, 2000.
15. R. Reiter. A Theory of Diagnosis from First Principles. *Artificial Intelligence*, 32(1), pages 57–96, 1987.

Logic Programming Infrastructure for Inferences on FrameNet

Peter Baumgartner[1] and Aljoscha Burchardt[2]

[1] MPI Saarbrücken, `baumgart@mpi-sb.mpg.de`
[2] Saarland University, `albu@coli.uni-sb.de`

Abstract. The growing size of electronically available text corpora like companies' intranets or the WWW has made *information access* a hot topic within Computational Linguistics. Despite the success of statistical or keyword based methods, deeper Knowledge Representation (KR) techniques along with "inference" are often mentioned as mandatory, e.g. within the Semantic Web context, to enable e.g. better query answering based on "semantical" information. In this paper we try to contribute to the open question how to operationalize semantic information on a larger scale. As a basis we take the *frame* structures of the Berkeley FrameNet II project, which is a structured dictionary to explain the meaning of words from a lexicographic perspective. Our main contribution is a transformation of the FrameNet II frames into the *answer set programming paradigm* of logic programming.

Because a number of different reasoning tasks are subsumed under "inference" in the context of natural language processing, we emphasize the flexibility of our transformation. Together with methods for automatic annotation of text documents with frame semantics which are currently developed at various sites, we arrive at an infrastructure that supports experimentation with semantic information access as is currently demanded for.

1 Introduction

The growing size of electronically available text corpora like companies' intranets or the WWW has made *information access* a hot topic within Computational Linguistics. Without powerful search engines like Google the WWW would be of much lesser use. But there are obvious limitations of the current pure word-based methods. If one is e.g. searching for information about BMW buying Rover one might enter a query like (1) into a search engine.

   (1) *BMW buy Rover.*

On inspection of some of the thousands of hits returned, two problems become visible:

Problem 1. Low Precision: Numerous irrelevant pages are returned like car sellers' pages that mention the query words in unintended contexts.

Problem 2. Low Recall: Even if the search engine does some linguistic processing to include results that are formulated e.g. in finite form (*BMW buys Rover*), relevant pages using semantically similar words like *purchase* instead of *buy* are missing.

J.J. Alferes and J. Leite (Eds.): JELIA 2004, LNAI 3229, pp. 591–603, 2004.

There exist approaches that address problem 2. For example, some IR systems use the WordNet [Fel98] lexicon to try synonymous words in queries, while other approaches use learning techniques to detect and utilize similarities between documents. But apart from the fact that these systems rely heavily on redundancy among the text collections to be searched, they mostly do not address problem 1 at all.

A principled method is to analyze documents (and queries) in terms of *semantic* predicates and role relations. As we will explain in more detail in Section 2, the linguistically motivated *frame* structures of the Berkeley FrameNet II project [BFL98] are a suitable theoretical means for such an analysis. How to operationalize such information on a large scale is still an open research question. In order to avoid the pitfalls of the 1970's KR attempts, we do neither propose a new representation language nor a new formalization of "the world". Instead, we take the frame structures of the Berkeley FrameNet II project as a base and transform them into "logic". This idea of proposing logic for representing and reasoning on information stemming from natural language texts is by no means new and has in fact been heavily investigated in computational linguistics (CL) [HSAM93,BK00,dNBBK01,KK03,Bos04, e.g.]. In contrast to the mainstream, which relies on monotonic logic KR languages, we put forward the (nonmonotonic) *answer set programming paradigm* of logic programming. We exploit "nonmonotonicity" primarily as a tool to realize *default values* for role fillers. They allow to reason with defeasible information, which can be retracted when additional contextual information is provided, e.g. in incremental semantic interpretation.

Our main contribution is a transformation of the FrameNet II frames into normal logic programs to be interpreted under the stable model semantics. We have chosen this framework because of its good compromise between expressive power and computational complexity, its declarative nature and the availability of efficient interpreters for large programs [NS96,EFLP00,Wer03].

Our approach goes beyond the formalization of FrameNet I in a description logic in [NFBP02], as we are more concrete about "useful" inference based *reasoning services*. Together with methods for automatic annotation of text documents with frame semantics that are currently developed at various sites, we arrive at an infrastructure that addresses both problems mentioned above in a principled way. We emphasize the modularity and flexibility of our approach, which is needed to support experiments in our "soft" domain of reasoning on information from natural languages sources.

The rest of this paper is structured as follows. After recapitulating some notions from logic programming, we summarize in Section 2 FrameNet, thereby focussing on aspects relevant here. Section 3 is the main part: the translation of FrameNet frames to normal logic programs. Section 4 contains some conclusions and points to future work.

Preliminaries from Logic Programming. We assume the reader familiar with basic concepts of logic programming, in particular with the stable model semantics of normal logic programs [GL88]. See [Bar03] for a recent textbook.

A *rule* is an expression of the form $H \leftarrow B_1, \ldots, B_m, \text{not } B_{m+1}, \ldots, \text{not } B_n$, where $n \geq m \geq 0$ and H and B_i (for $i = 1, \ldots, n$) are atoms over a given (finite) signature with variables. We assume the signature contains no function symbol of arity greater than 0 (i.e. the only function symbols are constants).[1] A rule is implic- itly universally quantified and thus stands for all its (finitely many) ground instances. The operator "not" is the default negation operator. A *normal logic program* (or *pro- gram* for short) consists of finitely many rules. The programs derived below are *domain restricted*[2] or can be turned into domain restricted form easily, so that systems like KRHyper [Wer03] or smodels [NS96] can be applied to compute their stable mod- els. Finally, the head H of a rule may be the special symbol $\perp$, which is intended to mean "false". We assume a rule $A \leftarrow \perp$, not A, where A is a nullary predicate symbol not occurring elsewhere (with this rule, no stable model of any program can satisfy $\perp$).

2 FrameNet

The FrameNet project [BFL98] provides a collection of linguistically motivated so- called *frames* that describe typical situations and their participants[3] and link these to linguistic realizations. A word (or linguistic construction) that *evokes* a frame is called *frame-evoking element* (*FEE*). The participants (or roles) of the frame are called *frame elements* (*FEs*). These are local to particular frames.

Frame: ACQUIRE	
FE	**Example**
RECIPIENT	**Hornby** *obtained* his first patent in 1901.
SOURCE	You may *get* more money **from the basic pension.**
THEME	We *acquired* **a darts board.**

Frame: COMMERCE_GOODS-TRANSFER	
FE	**Example**
BUYER	**Jess** *bought* a coat.
GOODS	This young man *rented* **the old lady 's room.**
MONEY	Pat *paid* **14 dollars** for the ticket.
SELLER	**Kim** *sold* the sweater.

Fig. 1. Example Frame Descriptions.

Figure 1 shows two frames together with example sentences from the FrameNet data. The frame ACQUIRE is described as *A Recipient acquires a Theme.* [...] *The Source causes the Recipient to acquire the Theme.* [...]. This frame can be evoked by FEEs like *acquire.v, acquisition.n, get.v, obtain.v*.

The second example frame COMMERCE_GOODS-TRANSFER is described as the frame in which [...] *the Seller gives the Goods to the Buyer (in exchange for the Money).* [...]. The FEEs include *buy.v, purchase.v, purchaser.n, rent.v*.

Disregarding some details we will present below, all of the following sentences found on the WWW can be analyzed as instances of COMMERCE_GOODS-TRANSFER with BUYER *BMW* and GOODS *Rover*.

(2a) *BMW bought Rover from British Aerospace.*

---

[1] With this (common) restriction, all reasoning tasks relevant for us are decidable.

[2] Every variable occurring in a rule must also occur in some non-negated body atom (i.e. in one of $B_1, \ldots, B_m$ in the above notation).

[3] In linguistic terms one should speak of *predicates* and *semantic roles*.

(2b) *Rover was bought by BMW, which financed [. . .] the new Range Rover.*

(2c) *BMW's purchase of Rover for $1.2 billion was a good move.*

(2d) *BMW, which acquired Rover in 1994, is now dismantling the company.*

Note that such an analysis solves problem 1 and 2 (from Section 1). First, it generalizes over linguistic variations such as word class or active/passive voice: a query like (1) would match documents containing any of these sentences (given frame annotation). Second, the query would not match documents containing sentences like (3) because in this case the BUYER role is filled with *Ford*.

(3) *Ford's deal to buy Land Rover from BMW is completed.*

Aim of FrameNet. The term *frame* might remind the reader of early approaches in AI as well as CL that did not fully achieve their aim of modeling the world in terms of conceptual structures. Repeating any "ad hoc" modeling is not the aim of FrameNet. Instead, the aim of the FrameNet project is to provide a comprehensive frame-semantic description of the core lexicon of English. The current on-line version of the frame database contains almost 550 frames and 7,000 lexical entries with annotated examples from the British National Corpus.

Frame Relations. Frames can be subdivided into two classes: "small" frames that have a linguistic realization and "big" frames that are more abstract or script-like and serve for structuring the resource. The frame COMMERCIAL_TRANSACTION described above is in fact of the latter kind. It is (via another intermediate frame) related to two *perspectivized* frames COMMERCE_BUY and COMMERCE_SELL that do have realizations in words like *buy.v, purchase.v, purchaser.n* and *price.n, retail.v, sale.n, sell.v,* respectively. The latter two frames share only some FEs with COMMERCIAL_TRANSACTION. E.g. BUYER and MONEY in the case of COMMERCE_BUY. This modeling is based on linguistic theory: sentences like (4) or (5) are linguistically complete in contrast to e.g. (6).

(4) *BMW buys Rover.*

(5) *Daimler-Chrysler sold Mitsubishi.*

(6) ** BMW buys.*

In the latest FrameNet release, a number of relations between frames have been defined and already partly been annotated. Of particular interest for us are the following:

Relation	Example
Inherits From	COMMERCE_BY inherits from GETTING.
Uses	COMMERCE_BUY uses FEs BUYER and GOODS from COMMERCE_GOODS-TRANSFER (but not e.g. MONEY).
[Is] Subframe of	COMMERCIAL_TRANSACTION has subframes COMMERCE_GOODS-TRANSFER and COMMERCE_MONEY-TRANSFER.

Inherits From: All FEs of the parent frame are inherited by the child frame, e.g. the frame COMMERCE_BUY inherits the FEs RECIPIENT and THEME from GETTING (modulo a renaming into BUYER and GOODS, respectively[4]).

---

[4] To keep things simple, we ignore such renamings here. As will become obvious below, our approach includes a renaming facility for roles which can easily be generalized to cover cases like this.

Uses: The Uses relation links a frame to related "background" frames. In most cases it describes partial inheritance as in the example above where COMMERCE_BUY inherits only the FEs BUYER and MONEY from COMMERCIAL_TRANSACTION.

Subframe of: The Subframe relation holds between a frame that stands for a complex event and frames that describe (temporally ordered) sub-events.

These definitions are provided as glosses to human readers. Naturally, from a logical or machine perspective, these specifications are comparatively vague. Our current goal is not to provide once-and-for-all interpretations of these relations (and of roles). Instead, we want to come up with a formalization that supports further research by allowing to experiment with different interpretations. It is by no means obvious whether e.g. a frame instance of a frame N that is a subframe of another frame M automatically evokes an instance of M or e.g. N's siblings. Neither is there a global answer as to which FEs may or must be filled given a concrete instance of a frame. Such decisions may well differ among applications (Section 3.2 discusses some usage scenarios).

The question how natural language sentence are mapped into frame structures is beyond the scope of this paper. It is the central issue of the SALSA project [EKPP03] we are affiliated with.

3   Transformation of FrameNet to Logic Programs

This section contains our main result, the transformation of FrameNet frames to logic programs. To initiate a running example, consider the COMMERCE_BUY frame. This is what FrameNet gives us about it:

Frame: COMMERCE_BUY	
Inherits From	GETTING
FEs	BUYER, GOODS
Subframe of	–
Uses	COMMERCE_GOODS-TRANSFER
FEEs	*buy.v, lease.v, purchase.v, purchase_act.n, purchaser.n, rent.v*

We find it easiest to describe our transformation by starting with a description logic (DL) view of frames (see [BCM+02] for a comprehensive textbook on DL). A natural DL definition – a TBox axiom – of the COMMERCE_BUY frame (neglecting the "Uses" relation) is as follows:

COMMERCE_BUY $\equiv$ GETTING

$\sqcap\ \exists$ COMMERCE_BUY_BUYER.$\top\ \sqcap\ \exists$ COMMERCE_BUY_GOODS.$\top$

$\sqcap\ \exists$ FEE.$\{buy.v, lease.v, purchase.v, purchase\_act.n, purchaser.n, rent.v\}$

Some comments seem due: the role names, such as COMMERCE_BUY_BUYER are prefixed now by the frame name they belong to. This reflects the mentioned local namespace property, which implies that the same role name used in different frames may denote different relations.

Because of using the top concept $\top$, roles may be filled with arbitrary elements — FrameNet does not *yet* provide more specific typing information.[5]

---

[5] Recently, FrameNet has started to annotate semantic types to frames, FEs, and even FEEs. But this task is far from trivial and the set of types is still preliminary.

The range of FEE is an explicitly defined concept which consists precisely of the stated strings. Such set expressions are available in some DLs.

Our transformation can basically be seen to follow the standard predicate logic semantics of the indicated DL reading of frames. As a significant difference, however, the existential quantifier are treated as *integrity constraints*. Under this view, populating the COMMERCE_BUY class without, say, supplying a filler for the GOODS role will result in an inconsistency, and the currently considered model candidate will be retracted. In contrast, any DL reasoner would then fill the role with a Skolem term in order to satisfy the role restriction. However, with *default values* as introduced in Section 3.2, the effect of existentially quantified roles can be simulated to some degree.

The following description of our transformation is separated into three parts, each one treating a different aspect.

3.1 Basic Frame Transformation

For the purpose of this paper, we describe a frame named N as the sets $IsA(N)$, $FE(N)$, $Uses(N)$, and $FEE(N)$, which are precisely the frame names listed as "Inherits From" at N, the role names listed as "FE", the frame names listed as "Uses", and the strings listed as "FEE", respectively. Each set may be empty. In particular, if $FEE(N)$ is empty, this indicates that N is a "big" frame without linguistic realization.

We also need the following (recursive) definition. For a given frame N, $FE^\star(N)$ consists of all roles of N, including the ones to be inherited. Formally, define

$$FE^\star(N) = FE(N) \cup \{FE^\star(M) \mid M \in IsA(N)\} \ .$$

To describe our main transformation "basic", we found it helpful to single out a certain aspect, viz., mapping of specific roles between two frames N and M[6]:

Transformation: partialRoleMapping(N, M, FEs)
Input: N, M: frames names; FEs: set of role names
Output: the following rules:

$(N \Rightarrow M)$ $(M \Rightarrow N)$

For each $FE \in FEs$ the rule   For each $FE \in FEs$ the rule

$\quad M\_FE(x,y) \leftarrow N(x), N\_FE(x,y)$ $\quad N\_FE(x,y) \leftarrow M(x), M\_FE(x,y)$

The partialRoleMapping transformation maps the fillers of roles of the frame N (if present) to fillers of roles of the frame M, and vice versa. Such a mapping is needed because of the local namespace property of roles of frames (as explained above). It "translates" roles with the same names between frames by following the convention to include in a role name the frame it belongs to. Based on this transformation, we can now introduce the announced basic transformation.

---

[6] Notational conventions: x, y, z denote object-level variables, *italic* font is used for schematic variables of transformations, and sans serif font is used for names to be taken literally.

Transformation: basic(N)
Input: N: frame name
Output: the following rules:

($\Rightarrow$-*direction (1)*)

For each M $\in$ *IsA*(N) the rule

$$M(x) \leftarrow N(x)$$

($\Rightarrow$-*direction (2)*)

For each $FE \in FE^\star(N)$ the rule

$$\bot \leftarrow N(x), \text{not some\_}N\text{\_}FE(x)$$

($\Rightarrow$-*direction (3)*)

If $FEE(N) \neq \emptyset$, the rule

$$\bot \leftarrow N(x), \text{not some\_}N\text{\_FEE}(x)$$

($\Leftarrow$-*direction*)

Let $FE(N) = \{FE_1, \ldots, FE_k\}$, for some $k \geq 0$.
Let $IsA(N) = \{M_1, \ldots, M_n\}$, for some $n \geq 0$.

The rule

$$
\begin{aligned}
N(x) \leftarrow & \text{ some\_}N\text{\_}FE_1(x), \ldots, \\
& \text{ some\_}N\text{\_}FE_k(x), \\
& M_1(x), \ldots, M_n(x), \\
& \text{ some\_}N\text{\_FEE}(x)
\end{aligned}
$$

(If $FEE(N) = \emptyset$, then the body atom some_N_FEE(x) is omitted)

(*Role inheritance*)

For each M $\in$ *IsA*(N), the result of partialRoleMapping($N, M, FE^\star(M)$)

(*Auxiliary definitions (1)*)

For each $FE \in FE^\star(N)$ the rule

$$\text{some\_}N\text{\_}FE(x) \leftarrow N\text{\_}FE(x, y)$$

(*Auxiliary definitions (2)*)

For each $FEE \in FEE(N)$ the rule

$$\text{some\_}N\text{\_FEE}(x) \leftarrow N\text{\_FEE}(x, FEE)$$

Some comments: the $\Rightarrow$-*direction (1)* rule should be obvious. The $\Rightarrow$-*direction (2)* rules express the integrity constraint viewpoint of existentially quantified roles. The some_N_FE predicate used there is defined under *Auxiliary definitions (1)*. There, in the body atom N_$FE(x, y)$, the variable x stands for a frame instance (token) and y stands for the role filler. The test for whether the roles are filled or not has to be done for all roles, including the inherited ones. This explains the use of $FE^\star(N)$ there. The $\Rightarrow$-*direction (3)* rules are similar to the rules under $\Rightarrow$-*direction (2)*, this time testing for the presence of a FEE filler (if N prescribes FEEs at all); it uses the rules under *Auxiliary definitions (2)*. There, in the body atom N_$FEE(x, y)$, the variable x again stands for a frame instance (token).

The $\Leftarrow$-*direction* rule derives that an individual x is an instance of N if (i) all its roles $FE(N)$ are filled (and also $FEE(N)$ if present), and (ii) x belongs to all the frames that N inherits from. Notice it is not necessary in the rule body to test if *all* the roles $FE^\star(N)$ of N are filled for x, because the inherited ones *must* have been filled due to (ii) when the rule is applied. The *Role inheritance* rules map the role fillers of inherited roles to role fillers for instances of N, as explained. Notice that the partialRoleMapping transformation realizes this mapping in the converse direction, too. Indeed, because it is applied to the inherited roles only, this is what is expected.

3.2   Default Values

Depending on the frame and concrete application, it may be useful to *not* consider a "missing" role filler as an indication of inconsistency in the current model candidate. For instance, an utterance like *BMW bought [at high risk]*. might well be taken to fill a COMMERCE_BUY frame. In order to achieve consistency, the GOODS role of the COMMERCE_BUY instance populated by a linguistic text analysis component in reaction to this sentence has to be filled, and a dummy value, say, unspecified_FE could be used as a substitute for a more specific, preferable one. This suggests to use *default values*. Fortunately, default values can be incorporated without effort in our setting by the following transformation.

Transformation: defaultValue(N, FE)
Input: N: frame name; FE: a role name
Output: the following rules, with the free predicate symbol default_N_FE:

(Choice of fill with default value or not)	*(Case of waiving default value)*
$N\_FE(x,y) \leftarrow$ not not_$N\_FE(x,y),$ $\quad N(x),$ $\quad$ default_$N\_FE(x,y)$	$\perp \leftarrow N(x),$ $\quad$ default_$N\_FE(x,y),$ $\quad N\_FE(x,y),$ $\quad N\_FE(x,z),$ $\quad$ not equal(y,z)
not_$N\_FE(x,y) \leftarrow$ not $N\_FE(x,y),$ $\quad N(x),$ $\quad$ default_$N\_FE(x,y)$	

The left rules represent an even cycle through default negations, similar as in the propositional program $A \leftarrow$ not B, $B \leftarrow$ not A. For this program there are exactly two stable models: one where A is true and B is false, and one the other way round. Using such even cycles as a "choice" operator is a well-known programming technique. Here, it realizes two models, one where $N\_FE(x,y)$ is true, and one where it is false. The right rule expresses that there cannot be a default value as a role filler in presence of another, different (default) role filler[7].

The transformation for default values is completed by the following two rules. They express that there must be at least one role filler for the considered role:

$$\perp \leftarrow N(x), \qquad\qquad \text{some}\_N\_FE(x) \leftarrow N\_FE(x,y)$$
$$\text{not some}\_N\_FE(x)$$

However, because these rules are readily obtained from the basic transformation when applied to N, they need not be generated and thus are excluded from the transformation.

Notice the resulting program does not include rules to define the default_N_FE predicate. Such rules are external to the transformation and should be supplied to provide default values as appropriate[8]. If none is supplied, then the rules obtained from the defaultValue transformation are vacuously true and hence are insignificant for the result (the stable models). This suggests to apply the defaultValue transformation along with the basic transformation, for all roles, and nothing will be lost.

The usefulness of our approach clearly depends on its flexibility to interact with other components of a larger system. As the following considerations show, we expect

---

[7] The "equal" predicate, which means syntactic equality, can be defined as equal$(x, x) \leftarrow$.

[8] A designated constant like unspecified_FE can be taken to supply a uniform default value by adding facts default_$N\_FE(x,$ unspecified_FE$)$ for certain frames N and roles FE.

the defaultValue facility to be particularly important in this regard. In general, it is flexible enough to express domain-independent, domain-dependent, frame-dependent, or situation-dependent default values.

(1) If the application is such that the, say, GOODS role must be filled in order to meaningfully process a COMMERCE_BUY frame, then no default value should be supplied.

(2) Specific settings might allow for plausible default values. For instance, in a stock market domain, a uniform default value could be supplied as

$$\text{default\_COMMERCE\_BUY\_GOODS}(x, \text{share}) \leftarrow \text{COMMERCE\_BUY}(x) \ ,$$

where share is an instance of an appropriate frame representing shares.

(3) Consider again the *BMW bought at high risk* example. The anaphora resolution component of a NLP inference system[9] might find out that either rover or chrysler would be a suitable role filler for the GOODS role. This disjunctive information can be represented by the following two facts (suppose e is an instance of the COMMERCE_BUY frame we consider):

$$\text{default\_COMMERCE\_BUY\_GOODS}(e, \text{rover}) \leftarrow$$
$$\text{default\_COMMERCE\_BUY\_GOODS}(e, \text{chrysler}) \leftarrow \ .$$

An analysis of the resulting program shows there are two stable models: one with rover as the only GOODS role filler for e, and chrysler in the other model. The existence of the two stable models thus represents the uncertainty about the role filler in question; it has the same effect as disjunctively assigning the two fillers to the GOODS role (if disjunction were available in the language). [10]

(4) It may make sense to supply default values for more than one role. A sentence like *The purchase was risky.* may give rise to populate a COMMERCE_BUY frame where both the BUYER and the GOODS role are filled with, say, a default value unspecified_FE.

(5) The assumption that the FEEs listed in a frame is a linguistically exhaustive listing might be too strong. For instance, instead of a FEE listed, some anaphoric expression might be present. A possible solution is to include in the FEEs an additional element, say, unspecified_FEE that acts as a default value. The realization is through the default value transformation applied to N and FEE, defaultValue(N, FEE) (thus treating FEE as a role), and adding a rule default_N_FEE(x, unspecified_FEE) $\leftarrow N(x)$.

3.3   The Uses Relation

For a human reader, the Uses relation links a frame under consideration to other frames that are relevant to understand the situation it describes. For example, to understand a buying situation, one has to be aware of what a goods transfer situation is. From a

---

[9] Anaphora resolution based on deductive methods is investigated e.g. in [BK00,dNBBK01].

[10] This approach thus is in line with those logic-based approaches in computational linguistics that represent a dialogue by a collection of models, which can be further pruned as more information becomes available. See e.g. [KK03,Bos04] for recent work. As a difference, we are working with a *nonmonotonic* logic instead of classical logic.

formal perspective, it seems to mean a partial inheritance relation, where inheritance is restricted to the roles common to a frame and a frame it is in the Uses relation with. We propose the following transformation[11]:

Transformation: uses(N)
Input: N: a frame name
Output: the following rules:

(N ⇒ Uses(N) (1))

For each $M \in Uses(N)$ the rule

$$M(x) \leftarrow N(x)$$

(N ⇒ Uses(N) (2))

For each $M \in Uses(N)$,
for each $FE \in FE^{\star}(M) \setminus FE(N)$ the rule

default_M_$FE(x, \text{unspecified\_}FE) \leftarrow N(x)$

(Partial role inheritance)

For each $M \in Uses(N)$, the result of partialRoleMapping($N, M, FE^{\star}(M) \cap FE(N)$)

(Uses(N) ⇒ N)

Let $FE(N) \setminus \{FE^{\star}(M) \mid M \in Uses(N)\}$
$\qquad = \{FE_1, \dots, FE_k\}$, for some $k \geq 0$.
Let $Uses(N) = \{M_1, \dots, M_n\}$, for some $n \geq 0$.
The rules

$$N(x) \leftarrow \text{some\_}N\_FE_1(x), \dots,$$
$$\text{some\_}N\_FE_k(x),$$
$$M_1(x), \dots, M_n(x),$$
$$\text{some\_}N\_\text{FEE}(x)$$

(If $FEE(N) = \emptyset$, then the body atom
some_N_FEE(x) is omitted)

This transformation treats the Uses relation in a similar way as the basic transformation treats the Inherits From relation. The Uses relation also defines an inheritance hierarchy of roles, in parallel to the Inherits From relation, however where only explicitly stated roles are inherited. These are precisely those roles in $FE(N)$ that are also roles of some concept M that N uses. The set $\{FE_1, \dots, FE_k\}$ mentioned under $Uses(N) \Rightarrow N$ therefore is the complementary set of roles, those that are *not* inherited. Only those have to be tested for being filled, in analogy to what the rule under $\Leftarrow$-*direction* in the basic transformation does (see explanation there).

The rules under *Partial role inheritance* are mappings precisely for the inherited roles, individually for each frame M that N uses, i.e. the roles $FE^{\star}(M) \cap FE(N)$. By definition of partialRoleMapping, these roles are mapped also "upwards", from N to a frame M that N uses. The remaining roles of such a frame M are the roles $FE^{\star}(M) \setminus FE(N)$, and for these roles default values are supplied by the $N \Rightarrow Uses(N)$ (2) rules. Together, thus, and in conjunction with the rule under $N \Rightarrow Uses(N)$ (1), this has the effect that M will be populated with all roles filled whenever N is populated. Finally, notice that some definitions for rules mentioned can be skipped, because they are part of the basic transformation.

We would like to point out that the transformation for the Uses relation is not meant to be conclusive. Experiments on real data may suggest a different treatment of the Uses relation. It will also be interesting to devise suitable transformations of the Subframe relation.

---

[11] There is no *precise* description of the Uses relation available yet. FrameNet is considering a subdivision of this relation.

3.4 Usage Scenarios

The transformations described so far are intended to be applied to the whole FrameNet. More precisely, if $\mathcal{N}$ is a set of frames, such as those of FrameNet II, then we consider the logic program $P(\mathcal{N}) = \bigcup_{N \in \mathcal{N}} \mathrm{basic}(N) \cup \{\mathrm{defaultValue}(N, FE) \mid FE \in FE^{\star}(N)\} \cup \mathrm{uses}(N)$, possibly additionally equipped with default values for specific roles as discussed in Section 3.2 and additional facts stemming from linguistic text analysis components. We have chosen to transform into normal logic programs, because its associated answer set programming paradigm provides a good compromise between expressive power and computational complexity, its declarative nature and the availability of suitable, state-of-the-art interpreter like KRHyper [Wer03] or smodels [NS96][12]. These systems are made to cope with programs far larger than the ones resulting in our case[13]. They are capable of enumerating the stable models of $P(\mathcal{N})$, which can be inspected by other system components to determine the result of the overall computation.

In the usage scenarios we have in mind, "small" frames, those that have a linguistic realization (i.e. those having a FEE property), shall be populated as a result of textual analysis. By the way the transformation is defined, the information in these frame instances is combined by transferring it up the Inherits from and Uses hierarchies, thereby providing default values as needed. This way, explicitly presented knowledge shall be completed to get more abstract views on it. To make this a little more concrete, probably the most basic class of inference covers systematic syntax-near cases a (linguistic) automatic frame assignment system cannot cover. Take e.g. the following two sentences.

(7a) *Mary promised to purchase a BMW.*

(7b) *Mary promised the purchase of a BMW.*

The second sentence might in many cases be equivalent in meaning to the first sentence. But most linguistic (syntactic) theories don't have the means to describe this equivalence. The problem is that the subject of this sentence *Mary* fills the subject position of the verb *promise*. But *Mary* is also understood as subject of the verb *purchase* and (probably) as the actor acting in the event described by the noun *purchase*. For the verb case, linguistic theory has an answer in terms of subject sharing of so-called *subject control verbs* like *promise, offer, deny*. Here, the subject of the control verb is know to be identical with the subject of the embedded verb. But in the second sentence, there is no embedded verb and nouns are not considered to have a subject.

In contrast, in a FrameNet analysis both, verb and noun evoke a COMMERCE_BUY frame. But as we argued only in the verb case, syntax based methods can fill the BUYER role with *Mary*. Here, a defeasible inference could fill the respective role in the noun case. This inference is defeasible because the sentence might continue as follows.

(8) *Mary promised the purchase of a BMW by her husband before the vacations start.*

In such cases where an actual filler is available, the inference mechanism should fill the respective role with that.

---

[12] In particular, the resulting programs are domain-restricted, as required by these systems or can easily be made conforming.

[13] The number of rules in $P(\mathcal{N})$ is quadratic in $|\mathcal{N}|$. The quadratic component derives from the partialRoleMapping transformation, which, fortunately, results in very simple rules that can be worked off deterministically.

A more ambitious kind of inference is involved in the following example. The phrase (9) is a real corpus example from a text talking about questions of possession in the former GDR.

(9) *Owner of two-family houses which have bought before 1989* [...].

For this example, automatic syntax-based methods would return two frames, POSSESSION with OWNER *Owner of two-family houses* and POSSESSION *two-family houses*, and COMMERCE_BUY with BUYER *which*. Depending on the depth of the linguistic analysis, *which* might have already been resolved to *Owner of two-family houses*. But in any case, the GOODS of the COMMERCE_BUY were empty. At this point an heuristic inference could infer that the GOODS are the houses. If additional knowledge was available about the relation of buying and possession (e.g. by FrameNet's Causative relation), this should be used here as well. Once again, the inference is defeasible as the context might tell us that the text is about owner of two-family houses which have bought, say a car, before 1989.

4 Conclusion and Outlook

In this paper we have argued that reasoning services on the basis of FrameNet's frames can satisfy the growing demand of integrating semantic information in order to improve large scale natural language processing, such as document searching.

Our aim was to arrive at an infrastructure that supports testing different formalizations of the frame relations on a larger amount of corpus data. To this end, we gave transformations of the lexicographic frame and frame relation definitions into a logic programming setting, which we expect to be feasible also with respect to practical efficiency considerations. Although our translation of the frames and frame hierarchy are in the spirit of description logics, we have argued that both, the vague specification of the frame relations and the defeasible character of the kinds of inferences we are interested in do not lead naturally to characterization within description logics.

It has to be stressed that what we presented here is work in progress. The transformations proposed are not too difficult to implement, and we will conduct a number of pilot studies within different settings. Once e.g. the SALSA [EKPP03] project will supply methods for automatic frame assignment to natural text, we have a basic architecture for semantics-based natural language processing as described in the introduction of this paper. We are well aware that our system might undergo a number of changes underway not only because the FrameNet resource itself is still developing.

The kinds of inference we want to model on the basis of what we present here cannot be characterized by criteria such as soundness or completeness with respect to a readily defined semantics of FrameNet[14]. Their appropriateness or usefulness primarily depends on such factors as the application at hand and on additional linguistic or extra-linguistic evidence available.

---

[14] In fact, our transformation *equips* FrameNet with a precise, declarative semantics by means of the transformations proposed. Nevertheless, some interesting properties of our transformation can be proven. For instance, that arguable reasonable properties of "inheritance" are realized. We did not do so here for lack of space.

Our long-term goals include a treatment of selectional *preferences* (rather than *restrictions*) which will enable a more fine-grained modeling of e.g. sortal information about the filler of particular roles. For example, in Fig 1 *from the basic pension* fills the role SOURCE of frame ACQUIRE which is perfectly acceptable for a human. This example shows that a formalization of sortal information will have to include mechanisms for dealing with preferences and type casting (e.g. to deal with typical linguistic patterns like metonymies as in *Washington announces a new drug policy*). Including preferences would also make it possible to formulate *heuristic inferences* beyond our current assignment of default values.

Acknowledgements. We thank the anonymous referees for their helpful comments. The detailed comments and suggestions we found very valuable to improve the paper.

References

[Bar03]   C. Baral. *Knowledge representation, reasoning and declarative problem solving.* Cambridge University Press, 2003.

[BCM$^+$02] F. Baader, D. Calvanese, D.L. McGuinness, D. Nardi, and P.F. Patel-Schneider, editors. *Description Logic Handbook.* Cambridge University Press, 2002.

[BFL98]   C. F. Baker, Charles J. Fillmore, and John B. Lowe. The Berkeley FrameNet project. In *Proc. of COLING-ACL-98*, Montreal, Canada, 1998.

[BK00]   P. Baumgartner and M. Kühn. Abducing Coreference by Model Construction. *Journal of Language and Computation*, 1(2):175–190, 2000.

[Bos04]   J. Bos. Computational semantics in discourse: Underspecification, resolution, and inference. *Journal of Logic, Language and Information*, 13(2):139–157, 2004.

[dNBBK01]   H. de Nivelle, P. Blackburn, J. Bos, and M. Kohlhase. Inference and computational semantics. *Studies in Linguistics and Philosophy, Computing Meaning*, 77(2):11–28, 2001.

[EFLP00]   T. Eiter, W. Faber, N. Leone, and G. Pfeifer. Declarative problem-solving using the DLV system. In *Logic-based artificial intelligence*, pages 79–103. Kluwer, 2000.

[EKPP03]   K. Erk, A. Kowalski, S. Pado, and M. Pinkal. Towards a resource for lexical semantics: A large German corpus with extensive semantic annotation. In *Proc. of ACL-03*, Sapporo, Japan, 2003.

[Fel98]   C. Fellbaum, editor. *WordNet. An electronic lexical database.* MIT Press, Cambridge/Mass., 1998.

[GL88]   M. Gelfond and V. Lifschitz. The stable model semantics for logic programming. In Robert Kowalski and Kenneth Bowen, editors, *Proc. of 5th ICLP*, 1988.

[HSAM93]   J. R. Hobbs, M. E. Stickel, D. E. Appelt, and P. Martin. Interpretation as abduction. *Artificial Intelligence*, 63(1-2):69–142, 1993.

[KK03]   M. Kohlhase and A. Koller. Resource-adaptive model generation as a performance model. *Logic Journal of the IGPL*, 11(4):435–456, 2003.

[NFBP02]   S. Narayanan, C. J. Fillmore, C. F. Baker, and M. R. L. Petruck. FrameNet Meets the Semantic Web: A DAML+OIL Frame Representation. In *Proc. of AAAI*, 2002.

[NS96]   I. Niemelä and P. Simons. Efficient implementation of the well-founded and stable model semantics. In *Proc. of JICSLP*, Bonn, Germany, 1996. The MITPress.

[Wer03]   C. Wernhard. System Description: KRHyper. Fachberichte Informatik 14–2003, Universität Koblenz-Landau, 2003.

An Answer Set Programming Encoding of Prioritized Removed Sets Revision: Application to GIS

Jonathan Ben-Naim[3], Salem Benferhat[2], Odile Papini[1], and Eric Würbel[1]

[1] Laboratoire SIS, université du Sud Toulon -Var. BP 132. 83957 La Garde Cedex.
{papini, wurbel}@univ-tln.fr
[2] CRIL-CNRS, université d'Artois. Rue Jean Souvraz. 62307 Lens Cedex. France.
benferhat@cril.univ-artois.fr
[3] LIF-CNRS, CMI technopôle de Château Gombert. 13353. Marseille cedex 13. France.
jbennaim@lif.univ-mrs.fr

Abstract. Geographical information systems are one of the most important application areas of belief revision. Recently, Würbel and colleagues [32] have applied the so-called "removed sets revision" (RSR) to the problem of assessment of water heights in a flooded valley. The application was partially satisfactory since only a small part of the valley has been handled. This paper goes one step further, and proposes an extension of (RSR) called "Prioritized Removed Sets Revision" (PRSR). We show that (PRSR) performed using answer set programming makes possible to solve a practical revision problem provided by a real application in the framework of geographical information system (GIS). We first show how PRSR can be encoded into a logic program with answer set semantics, we then present an adaptation of the smodels system devoted to efficiently compute the answer sets in order to perform PRSR. The experimental study shows that the answer set programming approach gives better results than previous implementations of RSR and in particular it allows to handle the whole valley. Lastly, some experimental studies comparing our encoding with implementations based on SAT-solvers are also provided.

1 Introduction

In many applications, intelligent agents face incomplete, uncertain and inaccurate information, and often need a revision operation in order to manage their beliefs change in presence of a new item of information. The agent's epistemic state represents his reasoning process and belief revision consists in modifying his initial epistemic state in order to maintain consistency, while keeping new information and removing the least possible previous information. Different strategies have been proposed for performing revision [30], [22]. Most of the revision approaches have been developed at the theoretical level, except few applications [31] and it turns out that in the general case the theoretical complexity of revision is high [8] [16]. An example of belief revision system is Removed Sets Revision which has been proposed in [21], [13], [15] for revising a set of propositional formulas. This approach stems from removing a minimal number of formulas, called removed set, to restore consistency.

Recently, Würbel and colleagues [32] have applied the so-called "removed sets revision" (RSR) to the problem of assessment of water heights in a flooded valley. The

J.J. Alferes and J. Leite (Eds.): JELIA 2004, LNAI 3229, pp. 604–616, 2004.
© Springer-Verlag Berlin Heidelberg 2004

application was partially satisfactory since only a small part of the valley has been handled. This paper considers a prioritized form of Removed Sets Revision, called Prioritized Removed Sets Revision (PRSR). It shows how the encoding of PRSR using answer set programming allows us to solve a practical revision problem coming from a real application in the framework of geographical information system. In particular this paper focuses on the following three issues:

- The notion of priority is very important in the study of knowledge-based systems [10]. When priorities attached to pieces of knowledge are available, the task of coping with inconsistency is greatly simplified, since conflicts have a better chance to be solved. Gärdenfors [11] has proved that upon arrival of a new piece of propositional information, any revision process of a belief set which satisfies natural requirements, is implicitly based on a priority ordering. In this paper we generalize the Removed Sets Revision, to revise prioritized belief bases, called Prioritized Removed Sets Revision.
- In the last decade, answer set programming is considered as one of convenient tools to handle non-monotonic reasoning systems. Logic programs with answer sets semantics can be equivalently described in terms of reducing logic programs to default logic, autoepistemic logic or circumscription. Morever, several efficient systems have been developed [9], [4], [24], [20], [17]. We propose to formalize the Prioritized Removed Sets Revision in terms of answer set programming and to adapt the smodels system in order to compute preferred answer sets which correspond to prioritized removed sets.
- When dealing with GIS we face incomplete and uncertain information. Since the data come from different sources characterized by various data qualities, they may conflict and require belief revision operations. Moreover, geographic information systems are characterized by a huge amount of data. In [33], [32] three different implementations of Removed Sets Revision have been experimented and compared on application on geographic information system concerning the flooding problem. The result was that an adaptation of Reiter's algorithm for diagnosis [25] gave the best results. Moreover, the Removed Sets Revision has been translated into a SAT problem and an implementation has been performed using an efficient SAT-solver MiniSat [7]. However, these approaches were not able to handle the whole geographical area (composed of 120 compartments) and only a part of it composed of 20 compartments for the adaptation of Reiter's algorithm and composed of 40 compartments for the SAT translation has been considered.

  In this paper we apply our answer sets programming encoding of PSRS to the framework of Geographic Information Systems. An experimental study shows that our approach gives better results than the adaptation of Reiter's algorithm for diagnosis and than an implementation based on a SAT-solver. These good results hold even if no priority is introduced. The introduction of priorities allows to handle the whole area.

The paper is organized as follows. Section 2 gives a refresher on Removed Sets Revision. Section 3 presents the Prioritized Removed Sets Revision. Section 4 shows how Prioritized Removed Sets Revision is encoded into logic programming with answer sets semantics. Section 5 presents an adaptation of the smodels system for computing answer sets for performing Prioritized Removed Sets Revision. In section 6 we perform an experimental study which illustrates the approach on a real application, *the flooding problem*, provided by CEMAGREF. We show that the answer set programming implementation gives better results than the one obtained using an adaptation of Reiter's algorithm and than an implementation based on a SAT-solver. Section 7 concludes the paper.

2   Background

2.1   Removed Sets Revision

We briefly recall the Removed Sets Revision [32] which deals with the revision of a set of propositional formulas by a set of propositional formulas. Let K and A be finite sets of clauses. The Removed Sets Revision focuses on the minimal subsets of clauses to remove from K, called *removed sets*[21], in order to restore consistency of $K \cup A$. More formally:

Definition 1. *Let K and A be two sets of clauses such that $K \cup A$ is inconsistent. R a subset of clauses of K, is a* removed set *of $K \cup A$ iff (i) $(K \cup A) \backslash R$ is consistent; ii) $\forall R' \subseteq K$, $R' \neq R$, if $(K \cup A) \backslash R'$ is consistent then $\mid R \mid < \mid R' \mid$*[1].

It can be checked that if R is a removed set then $(K \cup A) \backslash R$ is a so-called cardinality-based maximal consistent subbase of $(K \cup A)$ [1], [13], [15]. Würbel et al.[32] adapted the Reiter's algorithm for diagnosis stemming from hitting sets [25] and implemented this adaptation to efficiently compute the removed sets. Note also that there are several recent compilations and implementations of removed sets revision, like the ones proposed in [2], [18], [5]. However, in our application, we need to compute all preferred removed sets which is not possible with these recent implementations.

2.2   Removed Sets Revision Translated into a SAT Problem

The Removed Set Revision can be translated into a SAT problem using the transformation proposed by De Kleer for ATMS [14]. Each clause c of K is replaced by the formula $\phi_c \rightarrow c$, where ϕ_c is a new variable, called hypothesis variable. If ϕ_c is assigned true then $\phi_c \rightarrow c$ is true iff c is true, this enforces, c, on contrast if ϕ_c is assigned false then $\phi_c \rightarrow c$ is true whatever the truth value of c, the clause c is ignored. Let $\mathcal{H}(K)$ be the transformed set of clauses. The Removed Set Revision of K by A corresponds to the problem of looking for models of the set of clauses $\mathcal{H}(K) \cup A$ which minimize the number of falsified hypothesis variables ϕ_c. This leads to the definition of a preference relation between interpretations. Let first introduce some notations. H_K denotes the set of hypothesis variables, i. e. $H_K = \{\phi_c \mid \phi_c \rightarrow c \in \mathcal{H}(K)\}$ and let ω be an interpretation, $NI(\omega)$ denotes the number of hypothesis variables that are falsified by the interpretation ω, i. e. $NI(\omega) = \mid \{\phi_c \in H_K \mid \omega \not\models \phi_c\} \mid$[2].

Definition 2. *Let ω be an interpretation, ω is a H_K-preferred model of $\mathcal{H}(K) \cup A$ iff (i) $\omega \in Mod(\mathcal{H}(K) \cup A)$; (ii) $\forall \omega' \in Mod(\mathcal{H}(K) \cup A)$, $\omega' \neq \omega$, $NI(\omega) \leq NI(\omega')$.*

---

[1] $\mid R \mid$ denotes the number of clauses of R.

[2] For the sake of simplicity, we identify an hypothesis variables and a propositional formula.

The link between removed sets and models of $\mathcal{H}(K) \cup A$ is made by the following definition which assign each removed set R a set of models of $\mathcal{H}(K) \cup A$ denoted by $\mathcal{M}_R$.

Definition 3. *Let R be a removed set of $K \cup A$ the set of models of $\mathcal{H}(K) \cup A$ generated by R, denoted by $\mathcal{M}_R$, is a subset of $Mod(\mathcal{H}(K) \cup A)$ such that (i) $\forall c \in R$, $M \not\models \phi_c$ where $M \in \mathcal{M}_R$; (ii) $\forall c \in \mathcal{H}(K) \cup A \backslash R$, $M \models \phi_c$ where $M \in \mathcal{M}_R$.*

And the following proposition holds:

Proposition 1. $\forall M \in \mathcal{M}_R$. *$R$ is a removed set iff M is a H_K-preferred model of $\mathcal{H}(K) \cup A$.*

Performing Removed Set Revision of K by A amounts to looking for the H_K-preferred models of $\mathcal{H}(K) \cup A$. This can be achieved using a SAT-solver. In order to compare different implementations of Removed Set Revision we used the SAT-solver MiniSat[7] which is a simplified version of the solver SATZOO that won the last SAT 2003 competition.

3   Prioritized Removed Sets Revision

We now present the Prioritized Removed Set Revision (PRSR) which generalizes the Removed Set Revision presented in section 2.1 to the case of prioritized belief bases. Let K be a prioritized finite set of clauses, where K is partitioned into n strata, i. e. $K = K_1 \cup \ldots \cup K_n$, such that clauses in K_i have the same level of priority and have higher priority than the ones in K_j where $j > i$. K_1 contains the clauses which are the most prioritary beliefs in K, and K_n contains the ones which are the least prioritary in K [1], see also [13].

When K is prioritized in order to restore consistency the principle of minimal change stems from removing the minimum number of clauses from K_1, then the minimum number of clauses in K_2, and so on. We generalize the notion of removed set in order to perform Removed Sets Revision with prioritized sets of clauses. This generalization first requires the introduction of a preference relation between subsets of K.

Definition 4. *Let K be a consistent and prioritized finite set of clauses. Let X and X' be two subsets of K. X is preferred to X' iff (i) $\exists i$, $1 \leq i \leq n$, $| X \cap K_i | < | X' \cap K_i |$; (ii) $\forall j$, $1 \leq j < i$, $| X \cap K_j | = | X' \cap K_j |$.*

Prioritized removed sets are now defined as follows:

Definition 5. *Let K be a consistent and prioritized finite set of clauses and let A be a consistent finite set of clauses such that $K \cup A$ is inconsistent. R, a subset of clauses of $K \cup A$, is a prioritized removed set iff (i) $R \subseteq K$; (ii) $(K \cup A) \backslash R$ is consistent; (iii) $\forall R' \subseteq K$, if $(K \cup A) \backslash R'$ is consistent then R' is not preferred to R.*

4   Encoding PRSR in Answer Set Programming

We now show how we construct a logic program, denoted by $P_{K \cup A}$, such that the preferred answer sets of $P_{K \cup A}$ correspond to the prioritized removed sets of $K \cup A$. We first construct a logic program in the same spirit of Niemelä in [19], and then define the notion of preferred answer set in order to perform PRSR.

4.1 Translation into a Logic Program

Our aim in this subsection is to construct a logic program $P_{K \cup A}$ such that the answer sets of $P_{K \cup A}$ correspond to subsets R of K such that $(K \cup A) \backslash R$ is consistent. For each clause c of K, we introduce a new atom denoted by r_c and V denotes the set of atoms such that $V = V^+ \cup V^-$, with $V^+ = Atom(K \cup A) \cup \{r_c \mid c \in K\}$ and $V^- = \{a' \mid a \in Atom(K \cup A) \cup \{r_c \mid c \in K\}\}$ where $Atom(K \cup A)$ denotes the set of atoms occurring in $K \cup A$. The construction of $P_{K \cup A}$ stems from the enumeration of interpretations of V and the progressive elimination of interpretations which are not models of $(K \cup A) \backslash R$ with $R = \{c \in K \mid r_c$ is satisfied $\}$. This construction requires 3 steps: the first step introduces rules such that the answer sets of $P_{K \cup A}$ correspond to the interpretations of the propositional variables occurring in V, the second step introduces rules that constraint the answer sets of $P_{K \cup A}$ to correspond to models of A, the third step introduces rules such that answer sets of $P_{K \cup A}$ correspond to models of $(K \cup A) \backslash R$. More precisely:

(i) The first step introduces rules in order to build a one to one correspondence between answer sets of $P_{K \cup A}$ and interpretations of V^+. For each atom $a \in V^+$ we introduce two rules : $a \leftarrow not\ a'$ and $a' \leftarrow not\ a$ where $a' \in V^-$ is the negative atom corresponding to a.

(ii) The second step rules out answer sets of $P_{K \cup A}$ which correspond to interpretations which are not models of A. For each clause $c \in A$ such that $c = \neg a_0 \vee \cdots \vee \neg a_n \vee a_{n+1} \vee \cdots \vee a_m$, the following rule is introduced: $false \leftarrow a_0, \cdots, a_n, a'_{n+1}, \cdots, a'_m$ and in order to rule out $false$ from the models of A: $contradiction \leftarrow false, not\ contradiction$.

(iii) The third step excludes answer sets S which correspond to interpretations which are not models of $(K \cup A) \backslash C_i$ with $C_i = \{c \mid r_c \in S\}$. For each clause c of K such that $c = \neg b_0 \vee \cdots \vee \neg b_n \vee b_{n+1} \vee \cdots \vee b_m$, we introduce the following rule: $r_c \leftarrow b_0, \cdots, b_n, b'_{n+1}, \cdots, b'_m$.

The steps (i) and (ii) are very similar to the ones proposed by Niemela, but the third one (iii) is new and is introduced for revision.

We denote by R_K the set $R_K = \{r_c \mid c \in K\}$ and R_K^+ (resp. R_K^-) denotes the positive (resp. negative) atoms of R_K. We denote by CL the mapping from R_K^+ to K which associates to each atom of R_K^+ the corresponding clause in K. More formally, $\forall r_c \in R_K^+$, $CL(r_c) = c$. The following result holds.

Proposition 2. *Let K be a consistent and prioritized finite set of clauses and let A be a finite consistent set of clauses. S is an answer set of $P_{K \cup A}$ iff $(K \cup A) \backslash CL(S \cap R_K^+)$ is consistent.*

In order to compute the answer sets corresponding to prioritized removed sets we introduce the notion of preferred answer set.

4.2 Preferred Answer Sets

Let $K = K_1 \cup \ldots \cup K_n$. For $1 \leq i \leq n$, the set R_{K_i} denotes $R_{K_i} = \{r_c \mid r_c \in R_K,$ and $c \in K_i\} \cup \{r'_c \mid r'_c \in R_K,$ and $c \in K_i\}$. The positive and the negative part of R_{K_i} are respectively denoted by $R_{K_i}^+ = \{r_c \mid r_c \in R_K$ and $c \in K_i\}$ and $R_{K_i}^- = \{r'_c \mid r'_c \in R_K$ and $c \in K_i\}$.

Definition 6. *Let K be a consistent and prioritized finite set of clauses. Let S and S' two sets of literals. S is preferred to S' iff*
$$(i)\ \exists i,\ 1 \le i \le n,\ \mid S \cap R^+_{K_i} \mid < \mid S' \cap R^+_{K_i} \mid;\ (ii)\ \forall j,\ 1 \le j < i,\ \mid S \cap R^+_{K_j} \mid = \mid S' \cap R^+_{K_j} \mid.$$

We are now able to define the notion of preferred answer set.

Definition 7. *Let S be a set of atoms. S is a preferred answer set of $P_{K \cup A}$ iff (i) S is an answer set of $P_{K \cup A}$; (ii) $\forall S'$ an answer set of $P_{K \cup A}$, S' is not preferred to S .*

The following result generalizes proposition 2.

Proposition 3. *Let K be a consistent and prioritized finite set of clauses and let A be a finite consistent set of clauses. R is a prioritized removed set of $K \cup A$ iff there exists a preferred answer set S such that $CL(S \cap R^+_K) = R$.*

In order to get a one to one correspondence between preferred answer sets and prioritized removed sets, instead of computing the set of preferred answer sets of $P_{K \cup A}$ we compute $\mathcal{X}$ the set of subsets of literals of R_K which are interpretations of R_K and that lead to preferred answer sets. More formally: $\mathcal{X} = \{X$ an interpretation of $R_K \mid \exists S$, a preferred answer set, such that $X \cap R_K = S \cap R_K\}$.

5   Adaptation of Smodels for PRSR

We now present the computation of Prioritized Removed Sets Revision based on the adaptation of the smodels system; for more details see [12], [20], [28]. This is achieved using two algorithms. The first algorithm, Prio, is an adaptation of the smodels system algorithm which computes the set of subsets of literals of R_K which lead to preferred answer sets and which minimize the number of clauses to remove from each stratum. The second algorithm, Rens, computes the prioritized removed sets of $K \cup A$, applying the principle of minimal change defined in 5 for PRSR, that is, stratum by stratum.

5.1   Prio: An Adaptation of Smodels System

Let $K = K_1 \cup \ldots \cup K_n$. Consider the stratum k. Let L be a subset of literals which is an interpretation of $R_{K_1 \cup \ldots \cup K_{k-1}}$ leading to an answer set and let $\mathcal{X}$ be the set of subsets of literals which are interpretations of $R_{K_1 \cup \ldots \cup K_k}$ leading to an answer set and such that they remove the same number of clauses from K_k. More formally: $\forall X, Y \in \mathcal{X}$, $\mid X \cap R^+_{K_1 \cup \ldots \cup K_k} \mid = \mid Y \cap R^+_{K_1 \cup \ldots \cup K_k} \mid$. The algorithm $Prio(P_{K \cup A}, L, k, \mathcal{X})$ returns the sets of literals which are interpretations of $R_{K_1 \cup \ldots \cup K_k}$ that either contain L or belong to $\mathcal{X}$ and that minimize the number of clauses to remove from K_k, that is the number of r_c such that $c \in K_k$. The Prio algorithm constructs a set of literals L' from L where, as in the construction of smodels, several cases hold:

(i) if L' is inconsistent then L' does not lead to an answer set therefore $\mathcal{X}$ is returned.
(ii) if L' is consistent then again several cases hold:
    (1) if L' removes more clauses from K_k than an element of $\mathcal{X}$ then $\mathcal{X}$ is returned.

(2) if L' leads to the same answer set than an element of $\mathcal{X}$ then $\mathcal{X}$ is returned.

(iii) if L' is consistent and covers $Atom(P_{K \cup A})$ then

    (3) if L' removes less clauses from K_k than any element of $\mathcal{X}$ then $\mathcal{X}$ is cancelled and $L' \cap Lit(R_{K_1 \cup \ldots \cup K_k})$ is returned else $L' \cap Lit(R_{K_1 \cup \ldots \cup K_k})$ is added to $\mathcal{X}$

(iv) if L' is consistent and does not cover $Atom(P_{K \cup A})$ then using some heuristics a new atom $a \in Atom(P_{K \cup A})$ is selected such that $a \notin L'$. The algorithm starts again with $L' \cup \{a\}$ and keeps in $\mathcal{X}'$ the sets of literals of $R_{K_1 \cup \ldots \cup K_k}$ that minimize the number of clauses to remove from K_k and strarts again with $L' \cup \{\neg a\}$.

algorithm $Prio(P_{K \cup A}, L, k, \mathcal{X})$
L and L' are sets of literals, a is an atom
begin
$L' \leftarrow Expand(P_{K \cup A}, L)$
if L' is inconsistent **then**
  return $\mathcal{X}$
else
  if (1) $\exists X \in \mathcal{X}, | L' \cap R^+_{K_1 \cup \ldots \cup K_k} | > | X \cap R^+_{K_1 \cup \ldots \cup K_k} |$ **then**
    return $\mathcal{X}$
  else
    if (2) $L' \cap Lit(R_{K_1 \cup \ldots \cup K_k}) \in \mathcal{X}$ **then**
      return $\mathcal{X}$
    else
      if L' covers $Atom(P_{K \cup A})$ **then**
        if (3) $\exists X \in \mathcal{X}, | L' \cap R^+_{K_1 \cup \ldots \cup K_k} | < | X \cap R^+_{K_1 \cup \ldots \cup K_k} |$ **then**
          return $\{L' \cap Lit(R_{K_1 \cup \ldots \cup K_k})\}$
        else
          return $\mathcal{X} \cup \{L' \cap Lit(R_{K_1 \cup \ldots \cup K_k})\}$
        end if
      end if
    end if
  end if
else
  $a \leftarrow Heuristic(P_{K \cup A}, L')$
  $\mathcal{X}' \leftarrow Prio(P_{K \cup A}, L' \cup \{a\}, k+1, \mathcal{X})$
  return $Prio(P_{K \cup A}, L' \cup \{\neg a\}, k+1, \mathcal{X}')$
end if
end

The main adaptations of the original smodels algorithm consist in: (1) avoiding all the subsets of literals of $R_{K_1 \cup \ldots \cup K_k}$ leading to an answer set which removes more clauses from K_k than those in $\mathcal{X}$; (2) not computing several times the same subsets of literals of $R_{K_1 \cup \ldots \cup K_k}$ leading to an answer set; (3) comparing each new subset of literals of $R_{K_1 \cup \ldots \cup K_k}$ leading to an answer set with the elements of $\mathcal{X}$, if the new subset removes less clauses from K_k than those in $\mathcal{X}$ then $\mathcal{X}$ is replaced by it.

5.2 Rens: An Algorithm Computing the Prioritized Removed Sets

We finally present the algorithm which computes the prioritized removed sets of $K \cup A$. The idea is to proceed stratum by stratum using the Prio algorithm defined in the previous subsection. We start with the empty set and we first compute, the subsets of literals of R_{K_1} leading to an answer set which minimize the number of clauses to remove from K_1, then among these subsets we compute the subsets of literals of $R_{K_1 \cup K_2}$ leading to an answer set which minimize the number of clauses to remove from K_2, and so on. From a stratum to another, the algorithm $Prio$ described in the previous subsection provides the subsets of literals of $R_{K_1 \cup ... \cup K_k}$ leading to an answer set which minimize the number of clauses to remove from K_k. The algorithm is the following:

> **algorithm** $Rens(P_{K \cup A})$
> $\mathcal{X}$ and $\mathcal{Y}$ are two sets of sets of literals, k is an integer
> **begin**
> $k \leftarrow 1$
> $\mathcal{X} \leftarrow \{\emptyset\}$
> **while** $k \leq n$ **do**
> $\mathcal{Y} \leftarrow \{\emptyset\}$
>   **while** $\mathcal{X} \neq \emptyset$ **do**
>   choose an element $X \in \mathcal{X}$
> $\mathcal{Y} \leftarrow Prio(P_{K \cup A}, X, k, \mathcal{Y})$
> $\mathcal{X} \leftarrow \mathcal{X} \backslash \{X\}$
>   **end while**
> $\mathcal{X} \leftarrow \mathcal{Y}$
> $k \leftarrow k + 1$
> **end while**
> return $\{CL(X \cap R^+_{K_1 \cup ... \cup K_k}) \mid X \in \mathcal{X}\}$
> **end**

And the following proposition holds.

Proposition 4. *Let K be a consistent and prioritized finite set of clauses and let A be a finite consistent set of clauses. R is prioritized removed set of $K \cup A$ iff $R \in Rens(P_{K \cup A})$.*

6 Application in the Framework of GIS

6.1 Description of the Application

The aim of the application is to assess water height at different locations in a flooded valley. The valley is segmented into compartments in which the water height can be considered as constant. We want to assess a minimum/maximum interval of water height for each compartment in the valley. We have two sources of information about these compartments (aside from the knowledge of their geographical layout), see figure 1.

The first source of information (S_2) is a set of hydraulic relations between neighbouring compartments. This source is incomplete (not all neighbouring compartments are connected) and quite certain. The second source of information (S_1) consists of a set of initial assessments of minimal and/or maximal submersion heights for *some* compartments (i.e. this source in incomplete). This information is uncertain. For more details see [23] and [32].

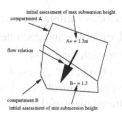

initial assessment of max submersion height
compartment A

A+ = 1.3m

flow relation

B- = 1.3

compartment B
initial assessment of min submersion height

Fig. 1. Visual description of the sources of information in the flooding application.

6.2   Representation with a Logic Program

The available knowledge is translated into a set of propositional formulas. The description of the variables (water heights) and their domains leads to n-ary positive clauses (enumeration of possible values) and binary negative clauses (mutual exclusion of the values). The initial assessments of water heights for some compartments are translated into a set of monoliteral clauses representing the assessed heights. In the following, we denote by S_1 the set of clauses describing the initial assessments.

Concerning hydraulic relations, we have seen that they are expressed in terms of inequalities on the bounds of the water height. They are translated into binary negative clauses representing the exluded tuples of values. In the following, we denote by S_2 the set of clauses containing the clauses representing the hydraulic relations and the variable descriptions. S_1 is consistent, and S_2 is consistent, but $S_1 \cup S_2$ can be inconsistent. We want to drop out some of the initial assessments of S_1 in order to restore consistency. This leads to the revision of S_1 by S_2.

Example 1. Let A and B be two compartments, defining the following variables : A^+ and A^- for maximal and minimal submersion height for compartment A, and B^+ and B^- for the same counterparts for B. These variables are defined on a domain $D = \{1, 2, 3\}$. There is a flow pouring from A to B and there are assessments telling us that the maximum submersion height is 2 for A and 3 for B. The translation leads to a set S_2 containing : (a) clauses describing the variables,

$$\left\{ \begin{array}{l} A_1^+ \vee A_2^+ \vee A_3^+, \neg A_1^+ \vee \neg A_2^+, \neg A_1^+ \vee \neg A_3^+, \neg A_2^+ \vee \neg A_3^+, \\ A_1^- \vee A_2^- \vee A_3^-, \neg A_1^- \vee \neg A_2^-, \neg A_1^- \vee \neg A_3^-, \neg A_2^- \vee \neg A_3^-, \\ B_1^+ \vee B_2^+ \vee B_3^+, \neg B_1^+ \vee \neg B_2^+, \neg B_1^+ \vee \neg B_3^+, \neg B_2^+ \vee \neg B_3^+, \\ B_1^- \vee B_2^- \vee B_3^-, \neg B_1^- \vee \neg B_2^-, \neg B_1^- \vee \neg B_3^-, \neg B_2^- \vee \neg B_3^- \end{array} \right\},$$

and (b) the clauses describing the inequalities representing the flow relation (i.e. $A^+ \geq B^+, A^- \geq B^-, A^+ > B^-$),

$$\left\{ \begin{array}{l} \neg A_1^+ \vee \neg B_2^+, \neg A_1^+ \vee \neg B_3^+, \neg A_2^+ \vee \neg B_3^+, \\ \neg A_1^- \vee \neg B_2^-, \neg A_1^- \vee \neg B_3^-, \neg A_2^- \vee \neg B_3^-, \\ \neg A_1^+ \vee \neg B_1^-, \neg A_1^+ \vee \neg B_2^-, \neg A_1^+ \vee \neg B_3^-, \dots, \neg A_3^+ \vee \neg B_3^- \end{array} \right\}.$$

The set S_1 contains the initial assessments, that is, $S_1 = \{A_2^+, B_3^+\}$. In practice, of course, the problem is compactly encoded by means of cardinality constraints.

For each clause $c \in S_1$ we introduce a new atom r_c and we construct a logic program $P_{S_1 \cup S_2}$ according to the translation proposed in section 4.1.

Example 2. Considering the previous example, the encoding is as follows: The generation rules for each propositional variables and each new atom r_c: (i) $A_1^+ \leftarrow not\ A_1^{'+}$, $A_1^{'+} \leftarrow not\ A_1^+$, etc. One rule for each clause of S_2. The translation of the set S_2 begins as follows : (ii) $false \leftarrow not\ A_1^+, not\ A_2^+, not\ A_3^+, false \leftarrow A_1^+, A_2^+$, etc. and the contradiction detection rule : $contradiction \leftarrow not\ contradiction, false$. One rule for each clause of S_1. The translation of the set S_1 gives the following rules: (iii) $r_{A_2^+} \leftarrow A_2^{'+}, r_{B_3^+} \leftarrow B_3^{'+}$

6.3   Experimental Study and Comparison

This subsection presents a summary of experimental results provided by our answer set programming (ASP) encoding of RSR and PRSR. The tests are conducted on a Pentium III cadenced at 1GHz and equipped with 1GB of RAM.

Comparison between ASP encoding and REM algorithm. We first compare our ASP encoding to the REM algorithm presented by Würbel and al. in [32] which computes the removed sets by using a modification of Reiter's algorithm for the computation of minimal hitting sets.

Due to the lack of space we do not reproduce the tests provided in [32] by the REM algorithm, we just recall that REM was only able to handle 25 compartments (see [32] for more details). We compared ASP encoding to REM algorithm and we observed that until 20 compartments, the two approaches behave similarly. However, from 25 compartments, the answer set approach is significantly better than REM approach. Moreover ASP encoding can handle the whole area of 120 compartments.

Comparison between ASP encoding and SAT encoding. We now compare the ASP encoding to a SAT encoding implemented with an efficient SAT-solver, MiniSat. The test deals with an increasing number of compartments from ten (210 variables, 2387 clauses) to sixty four compartments (1381 variables, 18782 clauses). The aim of this test is to compare the two approaches performances on the application and to identify their limits. Ten tests have been performed for a same number of compartments and an average running time on the ten tests is given.

Until 35 compartments, the two approaches behave similarly. From 40 compartments, the ASP encoding begins to give better results, and from 45 compartments the ASP encoding is significantly better than the SAT encoding. From 50 compartments the SAT encoding reaches a limit in CPU time (10 hours). The ASP encoding can deal with 60 compartments with a reasonable running time (few minutes) and reaches a limit in CPU time around 64 compartments. This is illustrated in figure 2.

Benefit of adding priorities. Prioritized Removed Set Revision is performed with a stratification of S_1 induced from the geographic position of compartments. Compartments located in the north part of the valley are preferred to the compartments located in the south of the valley. Using a stratification of S_1 table 2 shows that Rens significally reduces the running time.

In the flooding application we have to deal with an area consisting of 120 compartments and the stratification mentioned above is useful to deal with the whole area. Using the stratification table 2 shows that Rens can deal with the whole area with a reasonable running time.

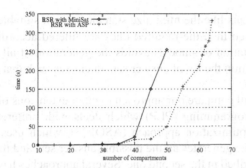

Fig. 2. Comparison between ASP encoding and SAT encoding in the flooding application.

Table 1. Gains induced by Rens.

# of compartments	#strata	time Rens (s)	# of variables	# of clauses
64	2	55	1381	18782
64	3	21	1381	18782
64	4	24	1381	18782
64	5	19	1381	18782

Table 2. Gains induced by Rens on an area containing 120 compartments.

# of compartments	#strata	time Rens (s)	# of variables	# of clauses
120	2	24132.49	2343	33751
120	3	3047.55	2343	33751
120	4	1698.67	2343	33751
120	5	424.62	2343	33751

7   Concluding Discussion

This paper generalized Removed Sets Revision to prioritized belief bases (Prioritized Removed Sets Revision) and shows that PRSR can be successfully encoded into answer set programming. An implementation stemming from smodels system is proposed and an experimental study in the framework of GIS shows that the answer set approach gives better results than the REM algorithm based on the adaptation of Reiter's algorithm for diagnosis and than an implementation based on an efficient SAT-solver MiniSat. Indeed, it first allows to deal with the whole area if priorities are provided, and even if there are no priorities, it can deal with 64 compartments, which is impossible with the REM algorithm nor with the SAT approach. It is important to note that both ASP encoding and SAT encoding introduce new variables (basically associated to clauses of the knowledge base).

In order to compute answer sets corresponding to prioritized removed sets we introduced the notion of preferred answer set, an interesting question to investigate is how to directly encode this notion of preference in the logic program in order to get a direct one to one correspondence between answer sets and prioritized removed sets.

In [29], Extended language of smodels has been proposed as well as optimization statements for the smodels system. In PRSR we use cardinality constraints for encoding the data more compactly, however a first experimentation shows that the use of the optimization statements like the minimize statement is not suitable because all answer sets are first generated then the required ones are filtered according to the minimize statement. The adaptation of smodels avoids the generation of all answer sets and the Rens algorithm partition the set of answer sets in classes such that only one answer set is computed by class.

A future work will compare our approach to other extensions of ASP. Among them, Prioritized Logic Programming (PLP) which deals with preferences among literals [26]. Answer Set Optimization approach (ASO) [3], which uses two different logic programs, the first one generates all the possible answer sets and the context dependent preferences are described in the second one. Several approaches have been proposed for dealing logic programs with preferences where the preference relation is a preference among rules like in [6]. A comparative study [27] has shown that these approaches can be characterized in terms of fixpoints, order preservation and translation into standard logic programs. Most of these approaches first generate all answer sets for a program then select the preferred ones. On contrast, we adapted the smodels algorithm in order to directly compute the preferred answer sets.

Acknowlegment. This work was supported by European Community project IST-1999-14189 REVIGIS.

References

1. S. Benferhat, Cayrol C, D. Dubois, J. Lang, and H. Prade. Inconsistency management and prioritized syntax-based entailment. In *Proceedings of IJCAI93*, pages 640–645, 1993.
2. S. Benferhat, S. Kaci, D. Leberre, and M. Williams. Weakening Conflicting Information for Iterated Revision and Knowledge Integration. In *Proceedings of Seventeenth International Joint Conference on Artificial Intelligence (IJCAI'01)*, pages 109–115, 2001.
3. G. Brewka, I. Niemelä, and M. Truszczynski. Answer Set Optimization. In *Proceedings of Eighteenth International Joint Conference on Artificial Intelligence (IJCAI'03)*, pages 867–872, 2003.
4. P. Cholewinski, V. Marek, A. Mikitiuk, and M. Truszczynski. Computing with default logic. *Artificial intelligence*, 112:105–146, 1999.
5. S. Coste-Marquis and P. Marquis. Knowledge compilation for circumscription and closed-world reasoning. *Logic and Computation*, 11:579–607, 2001.
6. J. P. Delgrande, T. Schaub, and H. Tompits. A Framework for Compiling Preferences in Logic Programs. *To appear in Theory and Practise of Logic Programming*, 2004.
7. N. Eén and N. Sörensson. An Extensible SAT-solver. In *Proceedings of 6th International Conference on Theory and Applications of Satisfiability Testing*, 2003.
8. T. Eiter and G. Gottlob. On the complexity of propositional knowledge base revision, updates and counterfactual. *Artificial Intelligence*, 57:227–270, 1992.
9. T. Eiter, N. Leone, C. Mateis, G. Pfeifer, and F. Scarcello. the kr system dlv: progress report, comparison and benchmarks. In *Proceedings of KR'98*, pages 406–417, 1998.
10. R. Fagin, J. D. Ullman, and M. Y. Vardi. On The Semantic of Updates in Databases. In *Proceedings of the 2nd ACM Symp. on Principles of Data Base Systems*, pages 352–365, 1983.
11. P. Gärdenfors. *Knowledge in Flux: Modeling the Dynamics of Epistemic States*. Bradford Books. MIT Press, Cambridge, 1988.

12. M. Gelfond and V. Lifschitz. The stable model semantics for logic programming. In *Proceedings of the International Conference on Logic Programming*, pages 1070–1080, 1988.
13. De Kleer J. Using crude probability estimates to guide diagnosis. *Artificial Intelligenc*, 45:381–392, 1990.
14. J. De Kleer. An assumption-based TMS. *Artificial Intelligence*, 28:127–162, 1986.
15. D. Lehmann. Belief revision revisited. In *Proceedings of 14th Int. Joint Conference on Artificial Intelligence*, pages 1534–1539, 1995.
16. Paolo Liberatore and Marco Schaerf. The complexity of model checking for belief revision and update. In *AAAI'96*, pages 556–561, 1996.
17. T. Linke. More on nomore. In *Proceedings of NMR'02*, 2002.
18. P. Marquis and N. Porquet. Resource-bounded paraconsistent inference. *Annals of Mathematics and Artificial Intelligence*, 39:349–384, 2003.
19. I. Niemelä. Logic programs with stable semantics as a constraint programming paradigm. In *Proceedings of the workshop on computational Aspect of Non Monotonic Reasoning*, pages 72–79, 1998.
20. I. Niemelä and P. Simons. An implementation of stable model and well-founded semantics for normal logic programs. In *Proceedings of LPNMR'97*, pages 420–429, 1997.
21. Odile Papini. A complete revision function in propositionnal calculus. In B. Neumann, editor, *Proceedings of ECAI92*, pages 339–343. John Wiley and Sons. Ltd, 1992.
22. Odile Papini. Knowledge base revision. *The Knowledge Engineering Review*, 15(4):339–370, 2000.
23. D. Raclot and C. Puech. Photographies aériennes et inondation : globalisation d'informations floues par un système de contraintes pour définir les niveaux d'eau en zone inondée. *Revue internationale de géomatique*, 8(1):191–206, Février 1998.
24. P. Rao, K. Sagonas, Swift, D. S. Warren, and J. Friere. Xsb: A system for efficiently computing well-founded semantics. In *Proceedings of LPNMR'97*, pages 430–440, 1997.
25. Raymond Reiter. A theory of diagnosis from first principles. *Artificial Intelligence*, 32:57–95, 1987.
26. C. Sakama and K. Inoue. Prioritized logic programming and its application to commonsense reasoning. *Artificial Intelligence*, 123(1-2):185–222, 2000.
27. T. Schaub and K. Wang. A Comparative Study of Logic Programs with Preference. In *Proceedings of Seventeenth International Joint Conference on Artificial Intelligence (IJCAI'01)*, pages 597–602, 2001.
28. P. Simons. *Extending and implementing the stable model semantics*. PhD thesis, Helsinky university of technology, 2000.
29. P. Simons, I. Niemelä, and T. Soininen. Extending and implementing the stable model semantics. *Artificial Intelligence*, 138(1-2):181–234, 2002.
30. Lea Sombe. *Revision and updating in knowledge bases*. International Journal of intelligent Systems. J. Wiley, New York, 1994.
31. M. A. Williams and D. Williams. A belief revision system for the world wide web. In *Proceedings of the IJCAI workshop of the Future of Artificial Intelligence and the Internet*, pages 39–51, 1997.
32. Eric Würbel, Robert Jeansoulin, and Odile Papini. Revision : An application in the framework of gis. In Anthony G. Cohn, Fausto Giunchiglia, and Bart Selman, editors, *Proceedings of the Seventh Internationnal Conference about Principles of Knowledge Representation and Reasoning, KR2000*, pages 505–516, Breckenridge, Colorado, USA, April 2000. KR, inc., Morgan Kaufmann.
33. Eric Würbel, Robert Jeansoulin, and Odile Papini. Spatial information revision : A comparison between 3 approaches. In *Proceedings of the Sixth European Conference on Symbolic and Quantitative Approaches to Reasoning with Uncertainty, ECSQARU 2001*, pages 454–465, Toulouse, France 2001. Springer Verlag.

Automatic Compilation of Protocol Insecurity Problems into Logic Programming*

Alessandro Armando[1], Luca Compagna[1], and Yuliya Lierler[2]

[1] AI-Lab, DIST – Università di Genova,
{armando,compa}@dist.unige.it
[2] AI, Erlangen-Nürnberg Universität,
yuliya.lierler@informatik.uni-erlangen.de

Abstract. In this paper we show how protocol insecurity problems expressed in a multi-set rewriting formalism can be automatically translated into logic programming problems. The proposed translation paves the way to the construction of model-checkers for security protocols based on state-of-the-art solvers for logic programs. We have assessed the effectiveness of the approach by running the proposed reduction against a selection of insecurity problems drawn from the Clark & Jacob library of security protocols: by running state-of-the-art solvers against the resulting logic programming problems most of the (known) attacks on the considered protocols are found in a few seconds.

1   Introduction

Security protocols are communication protocols that aim at providing security guarantees (such as authentication of principals or secrecy of information) through the application of cryptographic primitives. In spite of their apparent simplicity security protocols are notoriously error-prone. Quite interestingly, many attacks can be carried out without breaking cryptography. These attacks exploit weaknesses in the protocol that are due to unexpected interleavings of different protocol sessions as well as to the possible interference of malicious agents. Since these weaknesses are very difficult to spot by simple inspection of the protocol specification, security protocols received growing attention by the Formal Methods and Automated Reasoning communities as a new, challenge application domain.

In the last decade we thus witnessed the development of a large number of new techniques for the analysis of security protocols. While some techniques (e.g., [21,15,7]) are tailored to the analysis of security protocols, others reduce the analysis of security protocols to some general purpose formalism such as CSP [14], rewriting logic [9], logic programming [1], or propositional logic [6]. While techniques in the first camp usually exhibit better performance, techniques in the second camp are normally simpler to adapt in response to changes or extensions to the underlying model.

In this paper we show how protocol insecurity problems expressed in a multi-set rewriting formalism can be automatically translated into logic programs with answer set

---

* We are grateful to Joohyung Lee and Vladimir Lifschitz for the comments and discussions related to the topic of the paper. This work was partially funded by FET Open EC Project "AVISPA: Automated Validation of Internet Security Protocols and Applications" (IST-2001-39252) and by the FIRB Project no. RBAU01P5SS. The last author was partially supported by Texas Higher Education Coordinating Board under Grant 003658-0322-2001.

J.J. Alferes and J. Leite (Eds.): JELIA 2004, LNAI 3229, pp. 617–627, 2004.
© Springer-Verlag Berlin Heidelberg 2004

semantics. The proposed translation paves the way to the construction of model-checkers for security protocols based on state-of-the-art solvers for logic programs. We implemented our ideas within SATMC,[1] a model-checker for security protocols developed in the context of the AVISPA Project,[2] a platform that aims at supporting the development of large-scale Internet security-sensitive protocols. We assessed the effectiveness of the approach by running the proposed reduction against a selection of problems drawn from Clark & Jacob library of security protocols [8]. By running a state-of-the-art answer set solver (e.g. CMODELS or [13] SMODELS [17]) against the resulting logic programming problems most of the (known) attacks on the considered protocols are found in a few seconds.

Outline of the paper. We start in Section 2 by introducing security protocols via a well-known (flawed) authentication protocol. In Section 3 and Section 4 we define the notions of protocol insecurity problems and logic programs, respectively. Section 5 is devoted to the description of the proposed reduction of protocol insecurity problems into logic programming. Experimental results are discussed in Section 6. We conclude in Section 7 with some final remarks.

2   The Needham-Schroeder Public-Key Protocol

Let us consider the well-known Needham-Schroeder Public-Key (NSPK) authentication protocol. In the common Alice&Bob notation, the NSPK protocol can be represented as:

$$
\begin{aligned}
(1) \quad & A \rightarrow B : \{A, Na\}_{Kb} \\
(2) \quad & B \rightarrow A : \{Na, Nb\}_{Ka} \\
(3) \quad & A \rightarrow B : \{Nb\}_{Kb}
\end{aligned}
$$

where A and B are the roles involved in the protocol; Ka and Kb are the public keys of A and B, respectively; Na and Nb are nonces[3] generated, respectively, by A and B. Step (1) of the protocol denotes A sending B a message comprising the identity of A and the nonce Na encrypted with Kb. Since $\{A, Na\}_{Kb}$ can only be deciphered by means of the private key Kb^{-1} and the latter is (by assumption) only known by B, then the effect of Step (1) is that only B can possibly learn the value of Na. In Step (2) agent B proves to A his participation in the protocol and, by sending Nb, asks A to do the same. In Step (3) agent A concludes by proving to B her own participation in the protocol. Thus successful execution of the NSPK protocol should give evidence to A and B that they talked to each other. The rationale is that, under the perfect cryptography assumption (see Section 3), only B and A could compose the appropriate response to the messages issued in (1) and (2), respectively.

Note that the above specification is parametric in the variables A, B, Ka, Kb, Na, Nb. Thus, if we denote the above protocol specification by $NSPK(A, B, Ka, Kb, Na, Nb)$, then $NSPK(alice, i, ka, ki, na, ni)$ and $NSPK(alice, bob, ka, kb, na2, nb)$ denote two sessions whereby *alice* executes the protocol with i (the intruder) and *bob* respectively.[4]

---

[1] http://www.ai.dist.unige.it/satmc

[2] http://www.avispa-project.org

[3] *Nonces* are numbers randomly generated by principals and are intended to be used *only once*.

[4] Here and in the rest of the paper we use capitalized identifiers for variables and lowercase identifiers for constants.

By using messages from one session to form messages in the other as illustrated below, i deceives *bob* into believing that he is talking to *alice* whereas he is talking to i:

$$
\begin{array}{llll}
(1.1) & alice & \rightarrow \quad i & : \quad \{alice, na\}_{ki} \\
(2.1) & i(alice) & \rightarrow \quad bob & : \quad \{alice, na\}_{kb} \\
(2.2) & bob & \rightarrow \quad i(alice) & : \quad \{na, nb\}_{ka} \\
(1.2) & i & \rightarrow \quad alice & : \quad \{na, nb\}_{ka} \\
(1.3) & alice & \rightarrow \quad i & : \quad \{nb\}_{ki} \\
(2.3) & i(alice) & \rightarrow \quad bob & : \quad \{nb\}_{kb}
\end{array}
$$

where $i(alice)$ indicates the intruder pretending to be *alice*.

3   Protocol Insecurity Problems

We model the concurrent execution of security protocols by means of a state transition system specified in declarative language based on multi-set rewriting [2]. In this paper we assume that the network is controlled by the very general Dolev-Yao intruder [10]. In this model the intruder has the ability to eavesdrop, divert, compose, decompose, encrypt, and decrypt messages. Furthermore we make the standard assumptions of *perfect cryptography* i.e. an encrypted message can be decrypted only with the appropriate decryption key, and of *strong typing* i.e. agents accept only well-typed messages.

A *protocol insecurity problem* is a tuple $\Xi = \langle \mathcal{F}, \mathcal{L}, \mathcal{R}, \mathcal{I}, \mathcal{G} \rangle$ where $\mathcal{F}$ is a set of atomic formulae of a sorted first-order language called *facts*, $\mathcal{L}$ is a set of function symbols called *rule labels*, and $\mathcal{R}$ is a set of (rewrite) rules of the form $L \xrightarrow{\ell} R$, where L and R are finite subsets of $\mathcal{F}$ such that the variables occurring in R occur also in L, and ℓ is an expression of the form $l(x)$, called *rule name*, where $l \in \mathcal{L}$ and x is the vector of variables obtained by ordering the variables occurring in L lexicographically. Let $L_1 \xrightarrow{\ell_1} R_1 \in \mathcal{R}$ and $L_2 \xrightarrow{\ell_2} R_2 \in \mathcal{R}$; we require that $\ell_1 = \ell_2$ if and only if $L_1 = L_2$ and $R_1 = R_2$. This additional requirement ensures that rule names are in one-to-one relation with the rewrite rules in $\mathcal{R}$; thus in the sequel we will often use rule names and rewrite rules interchangeably for the sake of brevity. $\mathcal{I}$ is a subset of $\mathcal{F}$ representing the initial state. In this setting, a *state* is denoted by the set of ground facts $S \subseteq \mathcal{F}$ that are true in it. (The ground facts that do not occur explicitly in S are considered to be false.) It is also possible to denote a state by the conjunction of facts that are true in it. Finally $\mathcal{G}$ is a boolean combination of facts in disjunctive normal form (DNF), whose disjuncts represent the bad states of the protocol.

Let S be a state and $(L \xrightarrow{\ell} R) \in \mathcal{R}$. If σ is a substitution such that $L\sigma \subseteq S$, then one possible next state is $S' = (S \setminus L\sigma) \cup R\sigma$ and we indicate this with $S \xrightarrow{\ell\sigma} S'$. A *solution to (or attack on) a protocol insecurity problem* Ξ is a sequence of rules $\ell_0\sigma_1, \ldots, \ell_{k-1}\sigma_{k-1}$ where $\sigma_1, \ldots, \sigma_{k-1}$ are grounding substitutions[5] such that $S_i \xrightarrow{\ell_i\sigma_i} S_{i+1}$ for $i = 0, \ldots, k-1$ with $S_0 = \mathcal{I}$ and $S_k \models \mathcal{G}$ (where $\models$ denotes entailment in classical logic).

It is convenient to relax the definition of the transition relation associated with a protocol insecurity problem by allowing parallel executions of rules while preserving the

---

[5] A substitution is *grounding* if it maps every variable of the language to a ground term.

interleaving semantics. Let $L_1 \xrightarrow{\ell_1} R_1$ and $L_2 \xrightarrow{\ell_2} R_2$ be in $\mathcal{R}$ and let σ_1 and σ_2 be grounding substitutions such that $\ell_1 \sigma_1 \neq \ell_2 \sigma_2$. We say that $\ell_1 \sigma_1$ *conflicts with* $\ell_2 \sigma_2$ if and only if $L_1 \sigma_1 \cap (L_2 \sigma_2 \setminus R_2 \sigma_2) \neq \emptyset$ or $L_2 \sigma_2 \cap (L_1 \sigma_1 \setminus R_1 \sigma_1) \neq \emptyset$. Let S be a state, $L_i \xrightarrow{\ell_i} R_i \in \mathcal{R}$ for $i = 1, \dots, m$, $L = (\bigcup_{i=1}^{m} L_i \sigma_i)$, $R = (\bigcup_{i=1}^{m} R_i \sigma_i)$, and $\Lambda = \{\ell_1 \sigma_1, \dots, \ell_m \sigma_m\}$, then we define $S \xrightarrow[\mathrm{P}]{\Lambda} S'$ if and only if $S' = ((S \setminus L) \cup R)$, $(L \setminus R) \cap (R \setminus L) = \emptyset$ and for each $i, j = 1, \dots, m$ with $i \neq j$, we have that $\ell_i \sigma_i$ does not conflicts with $\ell_j \sigma_j$.

A *partial-order solution to (or partial-order attack on) a protocol insecurity problem* Ξ is a sequence of sets $\Lambda_0, \dots, \Lambda_{k-1}$ such that $S_i \xrightarrow[\mathrm{P}]{\Lambda_i} S_{i+1}$ for $i = 0, \dots, k-1$ with $S_0 = \mathcal{I}$ and $S_k \models \mathcal{G}$. The length of a partial-order attack is given by the number of sets in the sequence.

4   Logic Programming

A literal is an expression of the form a or $\neg a$ where a is an atom. A *logic rule* (lp-rule) is an expression

$$l_0 \leftarrow l_1, \dots, l_m, not\ l_{m+1}, \dots, not\ l_n \tag{1}$$

where l_0 is a literal or the symbol $\perp$ for falsehood, and $l_1, \dots, l_n$ are literals for $0 \leq m \leq n$. The literal l_0 is called *head* of the lp-rule whereas $l_1, \dots, l_m, not\ l_{m+1}, \dots, not\ l_n$ is the *body*. If the head of an lp-rule is $\perp$ then the lp-rule is called *constraint* and it is written $\leftarrow l_1, \dots, l_m, not\ l_{m+1}, \dots, not\ l_n$. If the body of an lp-rule is empty then lp-rule is called *logic fact* (lp-fact). A *logic program* is a finite set of lp-rules.

We interpret logic programs via the answer set semantics [11,12,19]. Let Π be a logic program comprising lp-rules with $n = m$ (i.e. Π is a program without any occurrence of *not*) and let X be a consistent set of literals; we say that X is *closed* under Π if, for every lp-rule in Π, $l_0 \in X$ whenever $\{l_1, \dots, l_m\} \subseteq X$. We say that X is an *answer set for* Π if X is the smallest set closed under Π. Now let Π be an arbitrary logic program and let X be a consistent set of literals. The *reduct* Π^X *of* Π *relative to* X is the set of rules $l_0 \leftarrow l_1, \dots, l_m$ for all lp-rules in Π such that $X \cap \{l_{m+1}, \dots, l_n\} = \emptyset$. Thus Π^X is a program without *not*. We say that X is an *answer set for* Π if X is an answer set for Π^X.

We finally extend the class of lp-rules with *choice lp-rules*, i.e. expressions of the form:

$$\{l_0\} \leftarrow l_1, \dots, l_m, not\ l_{m+1}, \dots, not\ l_n \tag{2}$$

where $l_0, \dots, l_n$ are literals. For the lack of space here we do not provide the precise definition of the semantics of logic programs with choice lp-rules. (For a precise definition of an answer set for logic programs with choice lp-rules please see [18].) However, for the purposes of the present paper, it suffice to give the following, informal explanation. We say that the body of lp-rules of the form (1) or (2) is satisfied by X if $\{l_1, \dots, l_m\} \subseteq X$ and $\{l_{m+1}, \dots, l_n\} \cap X = \emptyset$. If, on the one hand, an lp-rule prescribes that if the body is satisfied by the answer set then its head must be in the answer set too. A choice lp-rule, on the other hand, prescribes that if its body is satisfied by the answer set, its head *may or may not* be in the answer set.

To illustrate, let us consider the program composed by lp-rules $a \leftarrow$, $\{b\} \leftarrow a$, and $c \leftarrow b$. It has two answer sets $\{a\}$ and $\{a, b, c\}$. Clearly the body of the first rule is satisfied therefore a shall be part of all answer sets. The body of the second choice lp-rule is also satisfied hence b may be in the answer set. The satisfaction of the body of the last rule depends on weather b is in the answer set or not. By adding the constraint $\leftarrow c$ to the example program we can eliminate the second answer set.

For simplicity in the sequel we will use the term lp-rules in a broad sense so to encompass also choice lp-rules.

5   Protocol Insecurity Problems as Logic Programs

Let $\Xi = \langle \mathcal{F}, \mathcal{L}, \mathcal{R}, \mathcal{I}, \mathcal{G} \rangle$ be a protocol insecurity problem with finite $\mathcal{F}$ and $\mathcal{R}$[6] and let k be a positive integer. In this section we will show how to build a logic program Π_{Ξ}^{k} such that any answer set of Π_{Ξ}^{k} corresponds to a partial-order attack on Ξ of length k. The basic idea of our translation is to add a time stamp i to rule names and facts. Facts are thus indexed by 0 through k and rule name by 0 through $k - 1$. If p is a fact or a rule name and i is a time stamp in the appropriate range, then p^i is the corresponding atom. Program Π_{Ξ}^{k} is the union of the following lp-rules modeling the initial state, the goal, the execution of rewrite rules, the law of inertia, and mutual exclusion of conflicting rules.

For brevity we describe the translation by showing its application to the protocol insecurity problem Ξ_{NSPK} that models the two sessions of the NSPK authentication protocol informally introduced in Section 2. The facts in Ξ_{NSPK} are:

- $ik(T)$, meaning that the intruder knows the message T;
- $fresh(N)$, meaning that the nonce N has not been used yet;
- $m(J, S, R, T)$, meaning that S supposedly sent message T to R at step J;
- $w(J, S, R, [T_1, \ldots , T_k], C)$, meaning that R knows messages $T_1, \ldots , T_k$ at step J of session C, and—if $J \neq 0$—also that a message from S to R is awaited for step J of session C to be executed.

Initial State. The set $\mathcal{I}$ contains facts that encode the initial state. For each $f \in \mathcal{I}$ there is a corresponding lp-fact $f^0 \leftarrow$. For instance, the initial state of Ξ_{NSPK} is:[7]

$$w(0, a, a, [a, i, ka, ka^{-1}, ki], 1) \tag{3}$$

$$\textbf{.}\, w(0, a, a, [a, b, ka, ka^{-1}, kb], 2) \textbf{.}\, w(1, b, a, [b, a, kb, kb^{-1}, ka], 2) \tag{4}$$

$$\textbf{.}\, fresh(nc(n1, 1)) \tag{5}$$

$$\textbf{.}\, fresh(nc(n1, 2)) \textbf{.}\, fresh(nc(n2, 2)) \tag{6}$$

$$\textbf{.}\, ik(i) \textbf{.}\, ik(a) \textbf{.}\, ik(b) \textbf{.}\, ik(ki) \textbf{.}\, ik(ki^{-1}) \textbf{.}\, ik(ka) \textbf{.}\, ik(kb) \tag{7}$$

Fact (3) states that honest agent a plays the role of initiator in session 1 and knows her own identity, the agent she would like to talk with (the intruder), her public and private keys, and the intruder public key. Facts (4) represent the initial state of the honest agents

---

[6] For simplicity of the description of translation we assume $\mathcal{F}$ and $\mathcal{R}$ to be ground.

[7] To improve readability we use the "$\textbf{.}$" operator as set constructor. For instance, we write "$x \textbf{.} y \textbf{.} z$" to denote the set $\{x, y, z\}$.

a and b and specify their involvement as initiator and responder (resp.) in session 2. Facts (5) and (6) state the initial freshness of the nonces. Facts (7) represent the information known by the intruder. The lp-rules corresponding to the initial state are:

$$w(0, a, a, [a, i, ka, ka^{-1}, ki], 1)^0 \leftarrow$$
$$\vdots$$
$$ik(kb)^0 \leftarrow$$

Goal. We recall that the goal if a formula in DNF specifying the set of bad states, whose reachability implies a violation of the desired security property. (For simplicity, here we assume that $\mathcal{G}$ contains only positive facts.) For each disjunct $g_1 \wedge \ldots \wedge g_n$ of $\mathcal{G}$ we generate the lp-rule $goal \leftarrow g_1{}^k, \ldots, g_n{}^k$. The constraint $\leftarrow not\ goal$ is also included in the output logic program. It restricts the answer sets to contain $goal$.

For example, successful execution of NSPK should ensure authentication of the responder with the initiator and vice versa. The attack situation can be easily modeled by the goal formula $w(1, a, b, [b, a, kb, kb^{-1}, ka], s(2)) \wedge w(0, a, a, [a, b, ka, ka^{-1}, kb], 2)$ that represents all the states in which b believes to have completed a session with a, while a did not start this session with him. The corresponding lp-rules are:

$$goal \leftarrow w(1, a, b, [b, a, kb, kb^{-1}, ka], s(2))^i,$$
$$w(0, a, a, [a, b, ka, ka^{-1}, kb], 2)^i$$
$$\leftarrow not\ goal$$

Inertia. For each $f \in \mathcal{F}$ there is an lp-rule of the form $f^{i+1} \leftarrow f^i, not\ \neg f^{i+1}$. Such lp-rule states that if some fact f is true at time i it is also true at time $i + 1$ unless it is inferred to be false at time $i+1$. For instance, the inertia for the facts modeling the intruder knowledge is modeled by:

$$ik(T)^{i+1} \leftarrow ik(T)^i, not\ \neg ik(T)^{i+1}$$

Rewrite Rule Execution. For each rewrite rule $(L \xrightarrow{\ell} R) \in \mathcal{R}$ with $L = \{l_1, \ldots, l_m\}$, we generate the following lp-rules:

$\{\ell^i\} \leftarrow l_1{}^i, \ldots, l_m{}^i,$
$f^{i+1} \leftarrow \ell^i$, for each $f \in R \setminus L$, and
$\neg f^{i+1} \leftarrow \ell^i$, for each $f \in L \setminus R$.

The first rule states that if elements of L are satisfied at time i then rule ℓ might be applied at the same time. The last two rules state that if the rule ℓ is applied at time i then at $i + 1$ the facts that belong to $R \setminus L$ hold and the ones which belong to $L \setminus R$ do not hold. In the last rule we introduce $\neg f^{i+1}$ for all facts $f \in L \setminus R$. When combined with the lp-rules modeling the inertia this forces f to not hold at time $i + 1$.

We call the rules modeling the behavior of honest agents *protocol rules* and rules representing the intruder *intruder rules*. Here for the sake of brevity we present only one rewrite rule for each type and their corresponding compilation.

The following protocol rule models the activity of sending the first message of the NSPK:

$$fresh(nc(n1, S)) \centerdot w(0, A, A, [A, B, Ka, Ka^{-1}, Kb], S) \xrightarrow{step_0(A,B,Ka,Kb,S)}$$

$$w(2, B, A, [nc(n1, S), A, B, Ka, Ka^{-1}, Kb], S)$$

$$\centerdot m(1, A, B, \{A, nc(n1, S)\}_{Kb})$$

The lp-rules corresponding to this rewrite rule are:

$$\{step_0(A, B, Ka, Kb, S)^i\} \leftarrow fresh(nc(n1, S))^i,$$
$$w(0, A, A, [A, B, Ka, Ka^{-1}, Kb], S)^i$$
$$w(2, B, A, [nc(n1, S), A, B, Ka, Ka^{-1}, Kb], S)^{i+1} \leftarrow step_0(A, B, Ka, Kb, S)^i$$
$$m(1, A, B, \{A, nc(n1, S)\}_{Kb})^{i+1} \leftarrow step_0(A, B, Ka, Kb, S)^i$$
$$\neg fresh(nc(n1, S))^{i+1} \leftarrow step_0(A, B, Ka, Kb, S)^i$$
$$\neg w(0, A, A, [A, B, Ka, Ka^{-1}, Kb], S)^{i+1} \leftarrow step_0(A, B, Ka, Kb, S)^i$$

The following intruder rule models the ability of the intruder to decrypt messages:

$$ik(\{M\}_K) \centerdot ik(K^{-1}) \xrightarrow{decrypt(K,M)} ik(\{M\}_K) \centerdot ik(K^{-1}) \centerdot ik(M) \qquad (8)$$

It states that if the intruder knows both the cypher-text $\{M\}_K$ and the decryption key K^{-1}, then he can learn M. The lp-rules corresponding to this rewrite rule are:

$$\{decrypt(K, M)^i\} \leftarrow ik(\{M\}_K)^i, ik(K^{-1})^i$$
$$ik(M)^{i+1} \leftarrow decrypt(K, M)^i \qquad (9)$$

Conflicts Exclusion. For each pair of conflicting rules ℓ_1 and ℓ_2 we generate a constraint of the form

$$\leftarrow \ell_1{}^i, \ell_2{}^i$$

In this way we forbid the parallel execution of conflicting rewrite rules.

For instance, $step_0(a, b, ka, kb, 2)$ and $step_0(a, i, ka, ki, 2)$ are conflicting rules in Ξ_{NSPK} since they would use simultaneously the same fresh nonce $nc(n1, 2)$. This is encoded in logic programming by means of the constraint $\leftarrow step_0(a, b, ka, kb, 2)^i, step_0(a, i, ka, ki, 2)^i$.

Let A is an answer set for the logic program Π^k_Ξ and let $\Lambda_i = \{\ell\sigma : \ell\sigma^i \in A$ and $(L \xrightarrow{\ell} R) \in \mathcal{R}\}$ for $i = 0, \dots, k-1$, then it can be shown that $\Lambda_0, \dots, \Lambda_{k-1}$ is a partial-order attack on Ξ.

It is worth pointing out that while the above reduction paves the way to an automatic compilation of protocol insecurity problems into logic programs, its direct application is not viable as the resulting logic programs can be of unmanageable size even for simple protocols. To overcome this difficulty in [3] we introduced a number of (attack preserving) optimizing transformations on protocols insecurity problems that make the approach both feasible and effective on many protocols of interest.

6   Experimental Results

SATMC is a SAT-based Model-Checker for security protocol analysis. Given a protocol insecurity problem Ξ, as a preliminary step SATMC applies the optimizing transformations presented in [3] to Ξ thereby obtaining a new protocol insecurity problem Ξ' such that any attack on Ξ' corresponds to an attack on Ξ and vice versa. Then SATMC generates a SAT formula $\Phi^k_{\Xi'}$ (for increasing values of k) such that any model of $\Phi^k_{\Xi'}$ corresponds to an attack on Ξ' (and hence to an attack on Ξ). Models of SAT formulae are automatically found by invoking state-of-the-art SAT solvers.

In order to assess the effectiveness of the reduction described in this paper we have developed a prototype implementation of the translation described in Section 5. As a consequence, SATMC can now also translate the optimized protocol insecurity problem Ξ' into a logic program $\Pi^k_{\Xi'}$ (for increasing values of k). The logic program $\Pi^k_{\Xi'}$ is then fed to the grounder LPARSE[8] and then to a state-of-the-art solver. (Currently both SMODELS and CMODELScan be used to this end.) Once an answer set is found, SATMC transforms it into a partial-order attack that is reported to the user.

We ran SATMC against a selection of flawed security protocols drawn from the Clark & Jacob library [8]. For each protocol we built a corresponding protocol insecurity problem modeling a scenario with a bounded number of sessions in which the involved principals exchange messages on a channel controlled by the most general intruder based on the Dolev-Yao model.

Table 1 reports the experimental results obtained by compiling to logic programs (**LP** sub-table) and by compiling to SAT[9] (**SAT** sub-table). We used CMODELS as solver for logic programs and Chaff [16] as SAT solver. Experiments were carried out on a PC with a 1.4 GHz CPU and 1 GB of RAM.

For each protocol we give the smallest value of k at which the attack is found (**K**). We also give the time spent for generating the logic program (IF2LP) and the time spent by LPARSE for grounding it (LPARSE),[10] the number of lp-atoms (**LP ATs**) and lp-rules (**LP Rules**) in the logic program (in thousands), the time spent by CMODELS for solving the logic program (**LP SolT**)[11] together with the number of atoms (**ATs**) and clauses (**CLs**) in the SAT formula generated by CMODELS in this solving phase (in thousands). Moreover, we give the time spent by SATMC for generating the SAT formula (**EncT**), the number of propositional variables (**ATs**) and clauses (**CLs**) in the SAT formula (in thousands), and the time spent by Chaff to solve the SAT formula (**SolT**).

Since CMODELS[13] reduces the problem of finding answer sets of logic programs by reduction to SAT, it is interesting to compare the number of atoms and clauses directly generated by SATMC with that generated by CMODELSby compiling the logic program obtained by applying the reduction technique described in this paper. SATMC uses a noticeably smaller number of atoms, while the number of clauses generated often speaks

---

[8] http://www.tcs.hut.fi/Software/smodels/lparse.ps.gz

[9] SATMC supports a variety of techniques for compiling protocol insecurity problems to SAT. The experiments described in this paper are obtained by using the linear encoding technique. See [4] for a survey of the encoding techniques supported by SATMC.

[10] The time spent for generating the ground logic program (**LP EncT**) is the sum of IF2LP and LPARSE.

[11] The results obtained by running SMODELS on this application domain are really comparable with those of CMODELS.

Table 1. Experimental results.

Pb	K	Reduction to Logic programming (LP)						Reduction to SAT (SAT)			
		LP EncT (IF2LP / LPARSE)	LP ATs	LP Rules	CMODELS ATs	CMODELS CLs	CMODELS LP SolT	EncT	ATs	CLs	SolT
ISO-CCF-1 U	4	0.10 / 0.28	< 1	2	< 1	1	0.02	0.04	< 1	< 1	0.00
ISO-CCF-2 M	4	0.18 / 1.12	2	7	2	3	0.05	0.32	< 1	6	0.01
ISO-PK-1 U	4	0.19 / 0.95	1	4	1	2	0.03	0.12	< 1	2	0.00
ISO-PK-2 M	4	0.50 / 3.87	4	17	4	4	0.14	0.89	2	17	0.00
ISO-SK-1 U	4	0.09 / 0.29	< 1	2	< 1	1	0.02	0.04	< 1	< 1	0.00
ISO-SK-2 M	4	0.25 / 1.65	4	11	4	4	0.11	0.38	< 1	3	0.00
NSPK	7	0.46 / 7.54	12	80	12	14	0.65	2.31	7	51	0.09
NSPK-server	8	2.74 / 26.54	17	198	17	19	1.47	8.03	9	212	0.22
SPLICE	9	1.79 / 72.44	27	333	27	32	2.47	4.63	14	91	0.21
Swick 1	5	0.97 / 14.81	11	36	11	11	0.32	1.03	4	17	0.02
Swick 2	6	1.63 / 51.81	16	148	16	18	1.11	3.18	8	59	0.08
Swick 3	4	0.38 / 24.36	6	12	6	7	0.13	0.82	5	12	0.02
Swick 4	5	1.85 / 137.98	20	62	20	21	0.59	11.05	15	64	0.18
Stubblebine rep	3	1.40 / 371.00	29	2,010	29	30	14.37	82.93	13	2,048	0.63

in favor of CMODELS. The difference in the number of atoms can be explained by the advantage of the grounder of SATMC tuned to the protocol insecurity problems over the general purpose grounder LPARSE. As far as the number of clauses is concerned, the difference is due to the fact that CMODELS performs some reductions on the logic program before translating it into a propositional formula.[12]

As far are the timings are concerned, the experimental results indicate that the **SAT** approach outperforms the **LP** approach. But this is mainly due to the time spent by the grounder LPARSE that largely dominates the other times.

In [5] an optimized intruder model is proposed that leads in many cases to shorter attacks. The key idea is to model the ability of the intruder to decompose messages by means of axioms instead of rewrite rules. (An axiom is a formula that states a relation between the facts and that holds in all reachable states.) However, this requires non trivial extensions to the SAT-reduction techniques, whereas its application to the approach described in this paper is considerably simpler. For instance, the axiom

$$(ik(\{M\}_K) \wedge ik(K^{-1})) \supset ik(M) \tag{10}$$

states that, every time the intruder knows both a message encrypted with the key K and the decryption key K^{-1}, then he also knows M *at the very same time step.* This can me mimicked in logic programming by the lp-rules:

$$ik(M)^i \leftarrow ik(\{M\}_K)^i, ik(K^{-1})^i$$
$$\neg ik(K^{-1})^i \leftarrow \neg ik(M)^i, ik(\{M\}_K)^i \tag{11}$$
$$\neg ik(\{M\}_K)^i \leftarrow \neg ik(M)^i, ik(K^{-1})^i$$

---

[12] The details on the reduction can be found at http://www.cs.utexas.edu/users/tag/cmodels/cmodels-1.ps

By modeling the intruder rules by means of axioms and by changing the encoding described in this paper accordingly, preliminary experiments indicate that SATMC finds attacks which are up to 3 steps shorter therefby saving up to 44% atoms and clauses when applied to the problems in the Clark & Jacob library.

Axioms are also useful to model specific algebraic properties of cryptographic operators. For instance, the Diffie-Hellman protocol relies on the following property of exponentiation:

$$(g^X)^Y = (g^Y)^X$$

Such a property can be modeled as a set of axioms representing equivalence classes over facts. For instance, the axioms

$$ik((g^X)^Y) \supset ik((g^Y)^X) \quad \text{and} \quad ik((g^Y)^X) \supset ik((g^X)^Y)$$

state that $ik((g^X)^Y)$ and $ik((g^Y)^X)$ are in the same equivalence class. By adopting the above approach we have been able to generate with SATMC a logic program whose answer set corresponds to a (known) attack on the Diffie-Hellman protocol.

7   Conclusions

The work presented in [1] is closely related to ours. In that paper the authors put forward the idea of formalizing protocol insecurity problems (modeled according to Paulson's inductive model [20]) in logic programming and of using solvers for logic programs for automating the analysis of security protocols. In this paper we have described an approach to the automatic compilation of security protocol specifications (in a multi-set rewriting formalism) into logic programs. This reduction, combined with the optimizing transformations introduced in [3], paves the way to the construction of model-checkers for security protocols based on state-of-the-art solvers for logic programs. We have also thoroughly assessed the effectiveness of the proposed reduction by running our prototype implementation against a selection of flawed security protocols drawn from the Clark & Jacob library [8] and using CMODELS to solve the resulting logic programs. A comparison with the approach of compiling protocol insecurity problems into SAT, indicates that even if the reduction to SAT exhibits better performance, the reduction to logic programming can readily take into account specific algebraic properties of cryptographic operators. Moreover we expect a considerable gain in performance by using the SATMC grounder instead of LPARSE for grounding the resulting logic programs.

References

1. L. Carlucci Aiello and F. Massacci. Verifying security protocols as planning in logic programming. *ACM Trans. on Computational Logic*, 2(4):542–580, October 2001.
2. A. Armando, D. Basin, M. Bouallagui, Y. Chevalier, L. Compagna, S. Mödersheim, M. Rusinowitch, M. Turuani, L. Viganò, and L. Vigneron. The AVISS Security Protocol Analysis Tool. In *Proceedings of CAV'02*, LNCS 2404, pages 349–354. Springer-Verlag, 2002.
3. A. Armando and L. Compagna. Automatic SAT-Compilation of Protocol Insecurity Problems via Reduction to Planning. In *Proc. of FORTE 2002*, LNCS 2529. Springer-Verlag, 2002.

4. A. Armando and L. Compagna. Abstraction-driven SAT-based Analysis of Security Protocols. In *Proc. of SAT 2003*, LNCS 2919. Springer-Verlag, 2003.

5. A. Armando and L. Compagna. An optimized intruder model for sat-based model-checking of security protocols. To appear in the Proc. of ARSPA 2004., 2004.

6. A. Armando, L. Compagna, and P. Ganty. SAT-based Model-Checking of Security Protocols using Planning Graph Analysis. In *Proc. of FME 2003*, LNCS 2805. Springer-Verlag, 2003.

7. D. Basin, S. Mödersheim, and L. Viganò. An On-The-Fly Model-Checker for Security Protocol Analysis. In *Proc. of ESORICS'03*, LNCS 2808. Springer-Verlag, 2003.

8. J. Clark and J. Jacob. A Survey of Authentication Protocol Literature: Version 1.0, 17. Nov. 1997. URL: www.cs.york.ac.uk/~jac/papers/drareview.ps.gz.

9. Grit Denker, Jose Meseguer, and Carolyn Talcott. Formal specification and analysis of active networks and communication protocols: The Maude experience. In *Proc. of DISCEX'00*, pages 251–265. IEEE Computer Society Press, 2000.

10. D. Dolev and A. Yao. On the Security of Public-Key Protocols. *IEEE Transactions on Information Theory*, 2(29), 1983.

11. M. Gelfond and V. Lifschitz. The stable model semantics for logic programming. In Robert Kowalski and Kenneth Bowen, editors, *Logic Programming: Proc. Fifth Int'l Conf. and Symp.*, pages 1070–1080, 1988.

12. Michael Gelfond and Vladimir Lifschitz. Classical negation in logic programs and disjunctive databases. *New Generation Computing*, 9:365–385, 1991.

13. Yuliya Lierler and Marco Maratea. Cmodels-2: Sat-based answer set solver enhanced to nontight programs. In *Proc. LPNMR-04*, pages 346–350, 2004.

14. G. Lowe. Casper: a Compiler for the Analysis of Security Protocols. *Journal of Computer Security*, 6(1):53–84, 1998.

15. J. K. Millen and V. Shmatikov. Constraint solving for bounded-process cryptographic protocol analysis. In *Proc. of CCS'01*, pages 166–175, 2001.

16. M. W. Moskewicz, C. F. Madigan, Y. Zhao, L. Zhang, and S. Malik. Chaff: Engineering an Efficient SAT Solver. In *Proceedings of the 38th Design Automation Conference (DAC'01)*, 2001.

17. Ilkka Niemelä and Patrik Simons. Smodels—an implementation of the stable model and well-founded semantics for normal logic programs. In *Proc. 4th Int'l Conference on Logic Programming and Nonmonotonic Reasoning (Lecture Notes in Artificial Intelligence 1265)*, pages 420–429. Springer-Verlag, 1997.

18. Ilkka Niemelä and Patrik Simons. Extending the Smodels system with cardinality and weight constraints. In Jack Minker, editor, *Logic-Based Artificial Intelligence*, pages 491–521. Kluwer, 2000.

19. Ilkka Niemelä, Patrik Simons, and Timo Soininen. Extending and implementing the stable model semantics. *Artificial Intelligence*, 138:181–234, 2002.

20. L. C. Paulson. The Inductive Approach to Verifying Cryptographic Protocols. *Journal of Computer Security*, 6(1):85–128, 1998.

21. D. Song. Athena: A new efficient automatic checker for security protocol analysis. In *Proc. of the 12th IEEE Computer Security Foundations Workshop (CSFW '99)*, pages 192–202. IEEE Computer Society Press, 1999.

Exploiting Functional Dependencies in Declarative Problem Specifications

Marco Cadoli and Toni Mancini

Dipartimento di Informatica e Sistemistica
Università di Roma "La Sapienza"
Via Salaria 113, I-00198 Roma, Italy
{cadoli|tmancini}@dis.uniroma1.it

Abstract. In this paper we tackle the issue of the automatic recognition of functional dependencies among guessed predicates in constraint problem specifications. Functional dependencies arise frequently in pure declarative specifications, because of the intermediate results that need to be computed in order to express some of the constraints, or due to precise modelling choices, e.g., to provide multiple viewpoints of the search space in order to increase propagation. In either way, the recognition of dependencies greatly helps solvers, letting them avoid spending search on unfruitful branches, while maintaining the highest degree of declarativeness. By modelling constraint problem specifications as second-order formulae, we provide a characterization of functional dependencies in terms of semantic properties of first-order ones. Additionally, we show how suitable search procedures can be automatically synthesized in order to exploit recognized dependencies. We present OPL examples of various problems, from bio-informatics, planning and resource allocation fields, and show how in many cases OPL greatly benefits from the addition of such search procedures.

1 Introduction

Reasoning on constraint problems in order to change their formulations has been proven to be of fundamental importance in order to speed-up the solving process. To this end, different approaches have been proposed in the literature, like symmetry detection and breaking (cf., e.g., [1,8]), the addition of implied constraints (cf., e.g., [24]), and the use of redundant models, i.e., multiple viewpoints synchronized by channelling constraints, in order to increase constraint propagation [7,26,18]. Many of these approaches either are designed for a specific constraint problem, or act at the instance level, and very little work has been performed at the level of problem specification (also called "model"). Indeed, many of the properties of constraint problems amenable to optimizations, e.g., symmetries, existence of "useful" implied constraints, or of multiple viewpoints, strongly depend on the problem structure, rather than on the particular input instance considered. Hence, their recognition at the instance level, where the problem structure has been almost completely hidden, may easily become not convenient and expensive.

Moreover, almost all state-of-the-art systems for constraint modelling and programming (e.g., AMPL [14], OPL [25], DLV [12], SMODELS [22], and NP-SPEC [5])

J.J. Alferes and J. Leite (Eds.): JELIA 2004, LNAI 3229, pp. 628–640, 2004.
© Springer-Verlag Berlin Heidelberg 2004

exhibit a clear separation between problem specification and input instances, allowing the user to focus on the declarative aspects of the problem model before instantiation, and without committing *a priori* to a specific solver. In fact, some systems, e.g., AMPL [14], are able to translate –at the request of the user– a specification in various formats, suitable for different solvers.

Taking advantage of this separation, the goal of our research is to detect and exploit those properties of constraint problems amenable to optimizations that derive from the problem structure, at the symbolic level, before binding the specification to a particular instance, thus leading to the automatic reformulation of specifications.

In related work, we tackle the issues of highlighting some of the constraints of a specification that can be ignored in a first step, and then efficiently reinforced (i.e., without performing additional search, the so-called "safe delay" constraints) [3], and that of detecting structural (i.e., problem-dependent) symmetries, and breaking them by adding symmetry-breaking constraints to the problem specification [2]. We additionally show that these tasks can be performed automatically by computer tools, e.g., first-order theorem provers or finite model finders [4].

In this paper we exploit another interesting property of constraint problems, i.e., the functional dependencies that can hold among predicates in problem specifications. Informally, given a problem specification, a predicate is said to be functional dependent on the others if, for every solution of any instance, its extension is determined by the extensions of the others.

The presence of functional dependencies is common in problem specifications for different reasons: as an example, to allow the user to have multiple views of the search space, in order to be able to express the various constraints under the most convenient viewpoint, or to maintain aggregate or intermediate results needed by some of the constraints, as the following example shows.

Example 1 (The HP 2D-Protein folding problem [20]). This problem specification models a simplified version of one of the most important problems in computational biology. It consists in finding the spatial conformation of a protein (i.e., a sequence of amino-acids) with minimal energy. The simplifications with respect to the real problem are twofold: firstly, the 20-letter alphabet of amino-acids is reduced to a two-letter alphabet, namely H and P. H represents *hydrophobic* amino-acids, whereas P represents polar or *hydrophilic* amino-acids. Secondly, the conformation of the protein is limited to a bi-dimensional discrete space. Nonetheless, these limitations have been proven to be very useful for attacking the whole protein conformation prediction protein, which is known to be NP-complete [9] and very hard to solve in practice.

In this formulation, given the sequence (of length n) of amino-acids of the protein (the so called primary structure of the protein), i.e., a sequence of length n with elements in {H,P}, we aim to find a connected shape of this sequence on a bi-dimensional grid (which points have coordinates in the integral range Coord $= [-(n-1), (n-1)]$, the sequence starting at $(0,0)$), which is not overlapping, and maximizes the number of "contacts", i.e., the number of non-sequential pairs of H amino-acids for which the Euclidean distance of the positions is 1 (the overall energy of the protein is defined as the opposite of the number of contacts).

Different alternatives for the search space obviously exist: as an example, we can guess the position on the grid of each amino-acid in the sequence, and then force the obtained shape to be connected, non-crossing, and with minimal energy. A second approach is to guess the shape of the protein as a connected path starting at $(0,0)$, by guessing, for each position t of the sequence, the direction that the amino-acid at the t-th position in the sequence assumes with respect to the previous one (directions in the HP-2D model can only be North, South, East, West). It is easy to show that the former model would lead to a search space of $(2n)^{2n}$ points, while the latter to a much smaller one (4^n points).[1]

However, choosing the latter model is not completely satisfactory. In fact, to compute the number of contacts in the objective function, absolute coordinates of each amino-acid in the sequence must be computed and maintained. It is easy to show that these values are completely defined by (i.e., functionally dependent on) the sequence of directions taken by the protein.   □

Given a problem like the HP 2D-Protein folding one, if writing a procedural program, e.g., in C++, to solve it, possibly using available libraries for constraint programming, a smart programmer would avoid predicates encoding absolute coordinates of amino-acids to be part of the search space. Extensions for these predicates instead, would be *computed* starting from extensions of the others.

On the other hand, when using a declarative language for constraint modelling like, e.g., OPL, the user looses the power to distinguish among predicates which extension has to be found through a true search, from those which can be computed starting from the others, since all of them become of the same nature. Hence, the search space actually explored by the system can be ineffectively much larger, and additional information should be required from the user to distinguish among them, thus greatly reducing the declarativeness of the specification. To this end, the ability of the system to *automatically recognize* whether a predicate is functionally dependent on (or defined from) the others becomes of great importance from an efficiency point of view, since it can lead to significant reductions of the search space, although retaining the highest level of declarativeness.

The technique of avoiding branches on dependent predicates has already been successfully applied at the instance level for solving, e.g., SAT instances. As an example, it is shown in [16] how to modify the Davis-Putnam procedure for SAT so that it avoids branches on variables added during the clausification of non-CNF formulae, since values assigned to these variables depend on assignments to the other ones. Moreover, some SAT solvers, e.g., EQSATZ [21], have been developed in order to appropriately handle (by means of the so-called "equivalence reasoning") equivalence clauses, which have been recognized to be a very common structure in the SAT encoding of many hard real-world problems, and a major obstacle to the Davis-Putnam procedure.

We believe that looking for dependent predicates at the specification level, rather than after instantiation, can be much more natural, since these issues strongly depend on the structure of the problem. To this end, our approach is to

---

[1] Actually, as for the second model, possible directions of each amino-acid with respect to the previous one can be only three, because of the non-crossing constraint. Nonetheless, we opt for the simpler model to enhance readability.

give a formal characterization of functional dependencies suitable to be checked by computer tools, and ultimately, to transform the original problem specification by automatically adding an explicit search strategy that exploits such dependencies, avoiding branches on dependent predicates. Moreover, in those cases in which functional dependencies derive from the adoption of multiple viewpoints of the search space, we could choose the best maximal set of independent predicates to branch on, depending on the amenability of the relevant constraints to propagation (cf., e.g, [18]).

2   Preliminaries

In this paper, we use *existential second-order logic* (ESO) for the formal specification of problems, which allows to represent all search problems in the complexity class NP [13]. Actually, constraint modelling systems like those mentioned in Section 1 have a richer syntax and more complex constructs. However, all of them are extensions of ESO on finite databases, where the existential second-order quantifiers and the first-order formula represent, respectively, the *guess* and *check* phases of the constraint modelling paradigm. Yet, examples using the syntax of the implemented language OPL are shown in Section 4. We observe that these examples present also arithmetic constraints.

Coherently with all state-of-the-art systems, we represent an instance of a problem by means of a *relational database*. All constants appearing in a database are *uninterpreted*, i.e., they don't have a specific meaning.

An ESO specification describing a search problem π is a formula ψ_π:

$$\exists \boldsymbol{S} \ \phi(\boldsymbol{S}, \boldsymbol{R}), \tag{1}$$

where $\boldsymbol{R} = \{R_1, \dots, R_k\}$ is the relational schema for every input instance (i.e., a fixed set of relations or given arities denoting the schema for all input instances for π), and ϕ is a quantified first-order formula on the relational vocabulary $\boldsymbol{S} \cup \boldsymbol{R} \cup \{=\}$ ("=" is always interpreted as identity).

An instance $\mathcal{I}$ to the problem is given as a relational database over the schema $\boldsymbol{R}$, i.e., as an extension for all relations in $\boldsymbol{R}$. Predicates (of given arities) in the set $\boldsymbol{S} = \{S_1, \dots, S_n\}$ are called *guessed*, and their possible extensions (with tuples on the domain given by constants occurring in $\mathcal{I}$ plus those occurring in ϕ, i.e., the so called Herbrand universe) encode points in the search space for problem π. Formula ψ_π correctly encodes problem π if, for every input instance $\mathcal{I}$, a bijective mapping exists between solutions to $\pi(\mathcal{I})$ and extensions of predicates in $\boldsymbol{S}$ which verify $\phi(\boldsymbol{S}, \mathcal{I})$. It is worthwhile to note that, when a specification is instantiated against an input database, a CSP in the sense of [10] is obtained.

Example 2 (Graph 3-coloring [15, Prob. GT4]). In this NP-complete decision problem the input is a graph, and the question is whether it is possible to give each of its nodes one out of three colors (red, green, and blue), in such a way that adjacent nodes (not including self-loops) are never colored the same way. The question can be easily specified as an ESO formula ψ on the input schema $\boldsymbol{R} = \{edge(\cdot, \cdot)\}$:

$$\exists RGB \quad \forall X \ R(X) \vee G(X) \vee B(X) \ \wedge \tag{2}$$

$$\forall X \quad R(X) \to \neg G(X) \ \land \tag{3}$$

$$\forall X \quad R(X) \to \neg B(X) \ \land \tag{4}$$

$$\forall X \quad B(X) \to \neg G(X) \ \land \tag{5}$$

$$\forall XY \ X \neq Y \land R(X) \land R(Y) \to \neg edge(X,Y) \land \tag{6}$$

$$\forall XY \ X \neq Y \land G(X) \land G(Y) \to \neg edge(X,Y) \land \tag{7}$$

$$\forall XY \ X \neq Y \land B(X) \land B(Y) \to \neg edge(X,Y). \tag{8}$$

Clauses (2) and (3-5) force every node to be assigned exactly one color (covering and disjointness constraints), while (6-8) force nodes linked by an edge to be assigned different colors (good coloring constraints).   □

3   Definitions and Formal Results

In this section we give the formal definition of functionally dependent guessed predicate in a specification, and show how the problem of checking whether a set of guessed predicates is dependent from the others reduces to check semantic properties of a first-order formula.

Definition 1 (Functional dependence of a set of predicates in a specification). *Given a problem specification* $\psi \doteq \exists SP \ \phi(S, P, R)$, *with input schema* R, P *functionally depends on* S *if, for each instance* $\mathcal{I}$ *of* R *and for each pair of interpretations* M, N *of* (S, P) *it holds that, if*

1. $M \neq N$, and
2. $M, \mathcal{I} \models \phi$, and
3. $N, \mathcal{I} \models \phi$,

then $M_{|S} \neq N_{|S}$, *where* $\cdot_{|S}$ *denotes the restriction of an interpretation to predicates in* S.

The above definition states that P functionally depends on S, or that S functionally determines P, if it is the case that, regardless of the instance, each pair of distinct solutions of ψ must differ on predicates in S, which is equivalent to say that no two different solutions of ψ exist that coincide on the extension for predicates in S but differ on that for predicates in P.

Example 3 (Graph 3-coloring, Example 2 continued). In the 3-coloring specification, one of the three guessed predicates is functionally dependent on the others. As an example, B functionally depends on R and G, since, regardless of the instance, it can be defined as $\forall X \ B(X) \leftrightarrow \neg(R(X) \lor G(X))$: constraint (2) is equivalent to $\forall X \ \neg(R(X) \lor G(X)) \to B(X)$ and (4) and (5) imply $\forall X \ B(X) \to \neg(R(X) \lor G(X))$. In other words, for every input instance, no two different solutions exist that coincide on the set of red and green nodes, but differ on the set of blue ones.   □

Example 4 (Not-all-equal Sat [15, Prob. LO3]). In this NP-complete problem the input is a propositional formula in CNF, and the question is whether it is possible to assign a truth value to all the variables in such a way that the input formula is satisfied, and that every clause contains at least one literal whose truth value is false. We assume that the input formula is encoded by the following relations:

- $inclause(\cdot,\cdot)$; tuple $\langle l,c \rangle$ is in $inclause$ iff literal l is in clause c;
- $l^+(\cdot,\cdot)$ (resp. l^-); a tuple $\langle l,v \rangle$ is in l^+ (resp. l^-) iff l is the positive (resp. negative) literal relative to variable v, i.e., v itself (resp. $\neg v$);
- $var(\cdot)$, containing the set of propositional variables occurring in the formula;
- $clause(\cdot)$, containing the set of clauses of the formula.

A specification for this problem is as follows (T and F represent the set of variables whose truth value is true and false, respectively):

$$\exists TF \; \forall X \; var(X) \leftrightarrow T(X) \vee F(X) \quad \wedge \tag{9}$$

$$\forall X \; \neg(T(X) \wedge F(X)) \quad \wedge \tag{10}$$

$$\forall C \; clause(C) \rightarrow$$
$$\left[\exists L \; inclause(L,C) \wedge \forall V \left(l^+(L,V) \rightarrow T(V) \right) \wedge \left(l^-(L,V) \rightarrow F(V) \right) \right] \quad \wedge \tag{11}$$

$$\forall C \; clause(C) \rightarrow$$
$$\left[\exists L \; inclause(L,C) \wedge \forall V \left(l^+(L,V) \rightarrow F(V) \right) \wedge \left(l^-(L,V) \rightarrow T(V) \right) \right]. \tag{12}$$

Constraints (9–10) force every variable to be assigned exactly one truth value; moreover, (11) forces the assignment to be a model of the formula, while (12) leaves in every clause at least one literal whose truth value is false.

One of the two guessed predicates T and F is dependent on the other, since by constraints (9–10) it follows, e.g., $\forall X \; F(X) \leftrightarrow var(X) \wedge \neg T(X)$.   □

It is worth noting that Definition 1 is strictly related to the concept of *Beth implicit definability*, well-known in logic (cf., e.g., [6]). We will further discuss this relationship in Section 5. In what follows, instead, we show that the problem of checking whether a subset of the guessed predicates in a specification is functionally dependent on the remaining ones, reduces to semantic properties of a first-order formula (proofs are omitted for lack of space). To simplify notations, given a list of predicates $\boldsymbol{T}$, we write $\boldsymbol{T}'$ for representing a list of predicates of the same size with, respectively, the same arities, that are fresh, i.e., do not occur elsewhere in the context at hand. Also, $\boldsymbol{T} \equiv \boldsymbol{T}'$ will be a shorthand for the formula

$$\bigwedge_{T \in \boldsymbol{T}} \forall \boldsymbol{X} \; T(\boldsymbol{X}) \equiv T'(\boldsymbol{X}),$$

where T and T' are corresponding predicates in $\boldsymbol{T}$ and $\boldsymbol{T}'$, respectively, and $\boldsymbol{X}$ is a list of variables of the appropriate arity.

Theorem 1. *Let $\psi \doteq \exists \boldsymbol{SP} \; \phi(\boldsymbol{S},\boldsymbol{P},\boldsymbol{R})$ be a problem specification with input schema $\boldsymbol{R}$. $\boldsymbol{P}$ functionally depends on $\boldsymbol{S}$ if and only if the following formula is valid:*

$$[\phi(\boldsymbol{S},\boldsymbol{P},\boldsymbol{R}) \wedge \phi(\boldsymbol{S}',\boldsymbol{P}',\boldsymbol{R}) \wedge \neg(\boldsymbol{SP} \equiv \boldsymbol{S}'\boldsymbol{P}')] \rightarrow \neg(\boldsymbol{S} \equiv \boldsymbol{S}'). \tag{13}$$

Unfortunately, the problem of checking whether the set of predicates in $\boldsymbol{P}$ is functionally dependent on the set $\boldsymbol{S}$ is undecidable, as the following result shows:

Theorem 2. *Given a specification on input schema $\boldsymbol{R}$, and a partition $(\boldsymbol{S},\boldsymbol{P})$ of its guessed predicates, the problem of checking whether $\boldsymbol{P}$ functionally depends on $\boldsymbol{S}$ is not decidable.*

Even if Theorem 2 states that checking functional dependencies in a specification is an undecidable task, in practical circumstances it can be effectively and often efficiently performed by automatic tools, such as first-order theorem provers and finite model finders (cf. [4] for details and some experiments).

4 Further Examples

In this section we present some problem specifications which exhibit functional dependencies among guessed predicates. Due to their high complexity, we don't give their formulations as ESO formulae, but show their specifications in the well known language for constraint modelling OPL.

Example 5 (The HP 2D-Protein folding problem, Example 1 continued). As already stated in Example 1, rather than guessing the position on the grid of each amino-acid in the sequence, we chose to represent the shape of the protein by a guessed predicate Moves[], that encodes, for each position t, the direction that the amino-acid at the t-th position in the sequence assumes with respect to the previous one (the sequence starts at $(0,0)$). An OPL specification for this problem is shown in Section A.1. The analogous of the instance relational schema, guessed predicates, and constraints can be clearly distinguished in the OPL code. To compute the number of contacts in the objective function (not shown in the OPL code for brevity), absolute coordinates of each amino-acid in the sequence must be calculated (predicates X[] and Y[]).

As for the non-overlapping constraint, an *all-different* constraint for the set of positions of all amino-acids in the sequence is needed. Unfortunately, OPL does not admit global all-different constraints to be stated on multi-dimensional arrays. So we decided to use an additional guessed predicate Hits[] in order to maintain, for every position on the grid, the number of amino-acid of the protein that are placed on it at each point during the construction of the shape (instead of using $\mathcal{O}(n^2)$ binary inequalities). For all of them, this number cannot be greater than 1, which implies that the string does not cross.

From the considerations above, it follows that guessed predicates X[], Y[], and Hits[], are functionally dependent on Moves[].   □

Example 6 (The Sailco inventory problem [25, Section 9.4, Statement 9.17]). This problem specification, part of the OPLSTUDIO distribution package (as file sailco.mod), models a simple inventory application, in which the question is to decide how many sailboats the Sailco company has to produce over a given number of time periods, in order to satisfy the demand and to minimize production costs. The demand for the periods is known and, in addition, an inventory of boats is available initially. In each period, Sailco can produce a maximum number of boats (capacity) at a given unitary cost (regularCost). Additional boats can be produced, but at higher cost (extraCost). Storing boats in the inventory also has a cost per period (inventoryCost per boat). Section A.2 shows an OPL model for this problem. From the specification it can be observed that the amount of boats in the inventory for each time period $t > 0$ (i.e., inv[t]) is defined in terms of the amount of regular and extra boats produced in period t by the following relationship: inv[t] = regulBoat[t] + extraBoat[t] - demand[t] + inv[t-1].   □

Example 7 (The Blocks world problem [23,27]). In the Blocks world problem, the input consists of a set of blocks that are arranged in stacks on a table. Every block can be either on the table or onto another block. Given the initial and the desired configurations of the blocks, the problem amounts to find a minimal sequence of moves that allows to achieve the desired configuration. Every move is performed on a single clear block (i.e., on a block with no blocks on it) and moves it either onto a clear block or on the table (which can accommodate an arbitrary number of blocks). It is worth noting that a plan of length less than or equal to twice the number of blocks always exists, since original stacks can all be flattened on the table before building the desired configuration. In our formulation, given in Section A.3, we assume that the input is given as an integer `nblocks`, i.e., the number of blocks, and functions `OnAtStart[]` and `OnAtGoal[]`, encoding, respectively, the initial and desired configuration. As for the guessed functions, `MoveBlock[]` and `MoveTo[]` respectively state, for each time point `t`, which block has been moved at time point `t-1`, and its new position at time `t`. Moreover, we use guessed functions `On[]`, that states the position (which can be either a block or the table) of a given block at a given time point, and `Clear[]`, that states whether a given block is clear at a time point. We observe that guessed functions `On[]` and `Clear[]` are functionally dependent on `MoveBlock[]` and `MoveTo[]`.   □

5   Exploiting Functional Dependencies

Once a set P of guessed predicates of a problem specification $\psi \doteq \exists SP\ \phi(S, P, R)$ has been recognized to be functionally dependent on the others, different approaches can be followed in order to exploit such a dependence: the most simple and elegant one is to force the system to branch only on defining predicates, i.e., those in S, avoiding spending search on those in P. An alternative approach is to substitute in the specification all occurrences of predicates in P with their definition, and we will briefly discuss it in the following.

As already observed in Section 3, the concept of functional dependence among guessed predicates expressed in Definition 1 is strictly related to the one of *Beth implicit definability* (cf., e.g, [6]). In particular, given a problem specification $\psi \doteq \exists SP\ \phi(S, P, R)$, guessed predicates in set P functionally depend on those in S if and only if the first-order formula $\phi(S, P, R)$ implicitly defines predicates in P (i.e., if every $\langle S, R \rangle$-structure has at most one expansion to a $\langle S, P, R \rangle$-structure satisfying $\phi(S, P, R)$). It is worth remarking that, since we are interested in finite extensions for guessed predicates, Beth implicit definability has to be intended *in the finite*. Now, the question that arises is whether it is possible to derive, once a functional dependence (or, equivalently, an implicit definition) has been established, a formula that *explicitly defines* the dependent predicates in terms of the others. This formula, then, could take the place of all occurrences of those predicates in the problem specification. Although such a formula always exists in unrestricted first-order logic, this is not the case when only finite models are allowed. This is because first-order logic does not have the *Beth property in the finite* (cf., e.g., [11], and the intrinsically inductive definition of guessed function `inv[]` in Example 6). Nonetheless, in some cases such a formula indeed exists (cf., e.g., Examples 3 and 4). On the other hand, a second-order explicit definition of a dependent predicate would not be adequate, since new quantified predicates have to be added to the specification, and, moreover, the obtained specification may not be in ESO any more. Hence, we follow the first approach, i.e., forcing the system to avoid branches on dependent predicates, in order to save search. We also observe that, ultimately, this achieves exactly the same goal the second alternative would reach: in both cases, the search space actually explored is the one defined by predicates in S only.

In this section we show how an explicit search strategy that avoids branches on dependent predicates can be automatically synthesized. To this end, we assume to face with languages that allow the user to provide an explicit search strategy, and, in particular, since its description may depend on the particular solver, we present examples by focusing on the constraint language OPL. OPL does not require a search strategy (called, in the OPL syntax, "search procedure") to be defined by the user, since it automatically uses default strategies when none is explicitly defined. On the other hand, it provides the designer with the possibility of explicitly programming in detail how to branch on variables, and how to split domains, by adding a **search** part in the problem specification.

The simplest way to provide a search procedure is by using the **generate()** construct, which receives a guessed predicate as input and forces OPL to generate all possible extensions for it, letting the policy for the generation to the system defaults. Of course, multiple occurrences of **generate()** (with different guessed predicates as arguments) are allowed. OPL also allows for more explicit search procedures, in which the programmer can explicitly choose the order for the generation of the various extensions for that predicate (cf. [25]). However, these topics require an accurate knowledge of the particular problem at hand, and are out of the scope of this paper, since they are less amenable to be generalized and automated.

Hence, given a problem specification in which a set P of the guessed predicates is functionally dependent on the others (set $S = \{S1, \ldots, Sm\}$), a search procedure that forces OPL to avoid branches on predicates in P is the following:

```
search { generate(S1);   ...   generate(Sm); };
```

Search procedures added to the OPL specifications of HP 2D-Protein folding, Sailco inventory, and Blocks world problems in order to deal with the above described dependencies are, respectively, the following ones:

```
search { generate(Moves); };
search { generate(regulBoats);   generate(extraBoats); };
search { generate(MoveBlock);   generate(MoveTo); };
```

It is worth noting that, for some specifications, sets S and P are interchangeable. This intuitively happens when the user adopts multiple viewpoints of the search space (cf., e.g., Example 5, in which set $\{X, Y\}$ depends on $\{Moves\}$ and vice versa). In those cases, a first choice for deciding which set should be regarded as "defining" (i.e., S), may involve the size of the associated search space.

To test the effectiveness of adding such search procedures, we made an experimentation of the above problems with OPL. In particular, we made the following experiments:

Table 1. OPL solving times for some of the 44 benchmark instances of the HP 2D-Protein folding problem, with and without search procedure. ('–' means that OPL did not terminate in one hour.)

	Time		
Length	w/out search proc.	with search proc.	Saving %
14	–	1	99.9
30	–	6	99.9
36	3078	13	85.1
37	3386	17	93.6
45	–	99	>97.3
48	–	156	>95.7
50	–	215	>94.0
57	–	69	>98.0
60	–	128	>96.4
64	–	233	>93.5
102	1242	1007	18.9
123	914	913	0.0
136	761	760	0.0

Table 2. OPL solving times for some benchmark instances of the Blocks world problem, with and without search procedure. ('–' means that OPL did not terminate in one hour.)

		Minimal	Time		
Instance	Blocks	plan length	w/out search proc.	with search proc.	Saving %
bw-sussman	3	3	12	<1	>91.7
bw-reversal4	4	4	1	1	∼0
bw-4.1.1	4	6	882	<1	>99.9
bw-4.1.2	4	5	1879	<1	>99.9
bw-5.1.1	5	8	–	1	>99.9
bw-5.1.3	5	7	935	27	97.1
bw-large-a	9	12	–	–	–

- The HP 2D-Protein folding problem, on 44 instances taken from [17];
- The Blocks world problem, on structured instances, some of them used as benchmarks in [19];
- The Sailco inventory problem on random instances.

For both HP 2D-Protein folding and Blocks world, adding a search procedure that explicitly avoids branches on dependent predicates always speeds-up the computation, and very often the saving in time in very impressive. Tables 1 and 2 report typical behaviors of the system. On the other hand, for what concerns the Sailco inventory problem, no saving in time has been observed. This can be explained by observing that the problem specification is linear, and the linear solver automatically chosen by the system (i.e., CPLEX) is built on different technologies (e.g., the simplex method) that are not amenable to this kind of program transformation.

6   Conclusions

In this paper we discussed a semantic logical characterization of functional dependencies among guessed predicates in declarative constraint problem specifications. Functional dependencies can be very easily introduced during declarative modelling, either because intermediate results have to be maintained in order to express some of the constraints, or because of precise choices, e.g., redundant modelling. However, dependencies can negatively affect the efficiency of the solver, since the search space can become much larger, and additional information from the user is today needed in order to efficiently cope with them. We described how, in our framework, functional dependencies can be checked by computer, and can lead to the automated synthesis of search strategies that avoid the system spending search in unfruitful branches. Several examples of constraint problems that exhibit dependencies have been presented, from bioinformatics, planning, and resource allocation fields, and experimental results have been discussed, showing that current systems for constraint programming greatly benefit from the addition of such search strategies.

References

1. C. A. Brown, L. Finkelstein, and P. W. Purdom. Backtrack searching in the presence of symmetry. In T. Mora, editor, *Proc. of 6th Intl. Conf. on Applied Algebra, Algebraic Algorithms and Error Correcting codes*, pages 99–110. Springer, 1988.
2. M. Cadoli and T. Mancini. Detecting and breaking symmetries on specifications. In *Proc. of the CP'03 Intl. Workshop on Symmetry in CSPs*, pages 13–26, 2003.
3. M. Cadoli and T. Mancini. Automated reformulation of specifications by safe delay of constraints. In *Proc. of KR'04*, pages 388–398. AAAI Press, 2004.
4. M. Cadoli and T. Mancini. Using a theorem prover for reasoning on constraint problems. In *Proc. of the ETAPS'04 CP+CV Int. Workshop*, pages 17–31, 2004.
5. M. Cadoli and A. Schaerf. Compiling problem specifications into SAT. In *Proc. of ESOP'01*, volume 2028 of *LNCS*, pages 387–401. Springer, 2001.
6. C. C. Chang and H. J. Keisler. *Model Theory, 3rd ed.* North-Holland, 1990.
7. B. M. W. Cheng, K. M. F. Choi, J. H.-M. Lee, and J. C. K. Wu. Increasing constraint propagation by redundant modeling: an experience report. *Constraints*, 4(2):167–192, 1999.
8. J. M. Crawford, M. L. Ginsberg, E. M. Luks, and A. Roy. Symmetry-breaking predicates for search problems. In *Proc. of KR'96*, pages 148–159, 1996.
9. P. Crescenzi, D. Goldman, C. H. Papadimitriou, A. Piccolboni, and M. Yannakakis. On the complexity of protein folding. *J. of Comp. Biology*, 5(3):423–466, 1998.
10. R. Dechter. Constraint networks (survey). In *Encyclopedia of Artificial Intelligence, 2nd edition*, pages 276–285. John Wiley & Sons, Inc., 1992.
11. H. D. Ebbinghaus and J. Flum. *Finite Model Theory*. Springer, 1999.
12. T. Eiter, N. Leone, C. Mateis, G. Pfeifer, and F. Scarcello. The KR system dlv: Progress report, Comparisons and Benchmarks. In *Proc. of KR'98*, pages 406–417, 1998.
13. R. Fagin. Generalized First-Order Spectra and Polynomial-Time Recognizable Sets. In R. M. Karp, editor, *Complexity of Computation*, pages 43–74. AMS, 1974.
14. R. Fourer, D. M. Gay, and B. W. Kernigham. *AMPL: A Modeling Language for Mathematical Programming*. International Thomson Publishing, 1993.

15. M. R. Garey and D. S. Johnson. *Computers and Intractability—A guide to NP-completeness*. W.H. Freeman and Company, San Francisco, 1979.
16. E. Giunchiglia and R. Sebastiani. Applying the Davis-Putnam procedure to non-clausal formulas. In *Proc. of AI*IA'99*, volume 1792 of *LNAI*, pages 84–94. Springer, 2000.
17. W. Hart and S. Istrail. HP Benchmarks. Available at http://www.cs.sandia.gov/ tech_reports/compbio/tortilla-hp-benchmarks.html.
18. T. Hnich and T. Walsh. Why Channel? Multiple viewpoints for branching heuristics. In *Proc. of the CP'03 Int. Workshop on Modelling and Reformulating CSPs: Towards Systematisation and Automation*, 2003.
19. H. Kautz and B. Selman. Pushing the envelope: Planning, propositional logic, and stochastic search. In *Proc. of AAAI'96*, pages 1194–1201, 1996.
20. K. F. Lau and K. A. Dill. A lattice statistical mechanics model of the conformational and sequence spaces of proteins. *Macromolecules*, 22:3986–3997, 1989.
21. C. M. Li. Integrating equivalency reasoning into Davis-Putnam procedure. In *Proc. of AAAI'00*. AAAI/MIT Press, 2000.
22. I. Niemelä. Logic programs with stable model semantics as a constraint programming paradigm. *Ann. of Mathematics and Artificial Intelligence*, 25(3,4):241–273, 1999.
23. N. J. Nilsson. *Principles of Artificial Intelligence*. Tioga Publishing Co., 1980.
24. B. M. Smith, K. Stergiou, and T. Walsh. Using auxiliary variables and implied constraints to model non-binary problems. In *Proc. of AAAI'00*, pages 182–187, 2000.
25. P. Van Hentenryck. *The OPL Optimization Programming Language*. The MIT Press, 1999.
26. T. Walsh. Permutation Problems and Channelling Constraints. In R. Nieuwenhuis and A. Voronkov, editors, *Proc. of LPAR'01*, volume 2250 of *LNAI*, pages 377–391. Springer, 2001.
27. D. H. D. Warren. Extract from Kluzniak and Szapowicz APIC studies in data processing, no. 24, 1974. In *Readings in Planning*, pages 140–153. Morgan Kaufman, 1990.

Appendix: OPL Code for the Examples

A.1   The HP 2D-Protein Folding Problem

```
int+ n = ...;                          // Part of the inst. schema: string length
enum Aminoacid {H,P};
range Pos [0..n-1];
range PosButLast [0..n-2];
Aminoacid seq[Pos] = ...;              // Part of the inst. schema: amino-acid seq.
enum Dir {N,E,S,W};
range Coord [-(n-1)..n-1];
range Hit [0..n/2];

// Guessed predicates
var Dir Moves[PosButLast];             // Protein shape
var Coord X[Pos], Y[Pos];              // Absolute coordinates
var Hit Hits[Coord,Coord,Pos];

maximize ...                           // Objective function (omitted)
subject to {
    X[0] = 0;   Y[0] = 0;              // Pos. of initial elem. of the seq.
    forall (t in Pos: t > 0) {         // Chann. constr's for position
        Moves[t-1] = N => (X[t] = X[t-1]     & Y[t] = Y[t-1] + 1);
        Moves[t-1] = S => (X[t] = X[t-1]     & Y[t] = Y[t-1] - 1);
        Moves[t-1] = E => (X[t] = X[t-1] + 1 & Y[t] = Y[t-1]);
        Moves[t-1] = W => (X[t] = X[t-1] - 1 & Y[t] = Y[t-1]);
    };
    forall (x,y in Coord : x<>0 \/ y<>0)    // Constraints for Hits
```

```
            Hits[x,y,0] = 0;              // Initially, no cell has been hit...
    Hits[0,0,0] = 1;                      // ...but the origin
    forall (t in Pos, x,y in Coord: t > 0) // Chann. constr's for Hits
        ( (x = X[t] & y = Y[t]) => (Hits[x,y,t] = Hits[x,y,t-1] + 1) ) &
        ( (not (x = X[t] & y = Y[t])) => Hits[x,y,t] = Hits[x,y,t-1] );
    // Each cell is hit 0 or 1 times (string does not cross)
    forall (x,y in Coord, t in Pos) Hits[x,y,t] <= 1;
};
```

A.2   The Sailco Inventory Problem

```
int+ nbPeriods = ...;            range Periods 1..nbPeriods;
float+ demand[Periods] = ...;    float+ regularCost = ...;
float+ extraCost = ...;          float+ capacity = ...;
float+ inventory = ...;          float+ inventoryCost = ...;

var float+ regulBoat[Periods];   var float+ extraBoat[Periods];
var float+ inv[0..nbPeriods];

minimize ...                     // Objective function (omitted)
subject to {                     // Constraints
    inv[0] = inventory;
    forall(t in Periods) regulBoat[t] <= capacity;
    forall(t in Periods) regulBoat[t]+extraBoat[t]+inv[t-1] = inv[t]+demand[t];
};
```

A.3   The Blocks World Problem

```
int nblocks = ...;
range Block 1..nblocks;                range BlockOrTable 0..nblocks;
BlockOrTable TABLE = 0;                range Time 1..2*nblocks;
range TimeWithZero 0..2*nblocks;       range bool 0..1;
BlockOrTable OnAtStart[Block] = ...;   BlockOrTable OnAtGoal[Block] = ...;

// MoveBlock[t] and MoveTo[t] refer to moves performed from time t-1 to time t
var Block MoveBlock[Time];
var BlockOrTable MoveTo[Time];
var BlockOrTable On[Block, TimeWithZero];      // Dependent guessed function
var bool Clear[BlockOrTable, TimeWithZero];    // Dependent guessed function
var TimeWithZero schLen;                       // Schedule length (to minimize)

minimize schLen
subject to {
    forall (b in Block) On[b,0] = OnAtStart[b]; // Initial state (time = 0);
    forall (b in Block, t in TimeWithZero) {    // Chann. constr's for Clear
        ( ( sum(b_up in Block) (On[b_up,t]=b) ) > 0 ) <=> (Clear[b,t] = 0); };
    forall (t in TimeWithZero) { Clear[TABLE,t] = 1; };

    forall (t in Time) {                        // Moves
      (MoveBlock[t] <> MoveTo[t]);
      (MoveTo[t] <> On[MoveBlock[t],t-1]);      // No useless moves
      (t <= schLen) => (
        (Clear[ MoveBlock[t], t-1 ] = 1) &      // Moving block must be clear
        (Clear[ MoveTo[t], t-1 ] = 1 ) &        // Target pos. must be clear
        (On[ MoveBlock[t], t ] = MoveTo[t]) );  // Chann. constr's for On
      forall (b in Block) {                     // Chann. constr's for On
        (t <= schLen) => (                      // (frame conditions)
          (b <> MoveBlock[t]) => (On[b,t] = On[b,t-1]) ) };
    };
    forall (b in Block) { On[b,schLen] = OnAtGoal[b]; }; // Final state
};
```

Combining Decision Procedures
for Sorted Theories

Cesare Tinelli[1] and Calogero G. Zarba[2]

[1] Department of Computer Science, The University of Iowa, USA
[2] LORIA and INRIA-Lorraine, France

Abstract. The Nelson-Oppen combination method combines decision procedures for theories satisfying certain conditions into a decision procedure for their union. While the method is known to be correct in the setting of unsorted first-order logic, some current implementations of it appear in tools that use a sorted input language. So far, however, there have been no theoretical results on the correctness of the method in a sorted setting, nor is it obvious that the method in fact lifts as is to logics with sorts. To bridge this gap between the existing theoretical results and the current implementations, we extend the Nelson-Oppen method to (order-)sorted logic and prove it correct under conditions similar to the original ones. From a theoretical point of view, the extension is relevant because it provides a rigorous foundation for the application of the method in a sorted setting. From a practical point of view, the extension has the considerable added benefits that in a sorted setting the method's preconditions become easier to satisfy in practice, and the method's nondeterminism is generally reduced.

1 Introduction

The problem of combining decision procedures for logical theories arises in many areas of computer science and artificial intelligence, such as constraint solving, theorem proving, knowledge representation and reasoning. In general, one has two theories T_1 and T_2 over the signatures Σ_1 and Σ_2, for which validity of a certain class of formulae (e.g., universal, existential positive, etc.) is decidable. The question is then whether one can combine the decision procedures for T_1 and for T_2 into a decision procedure for a suitable combination of T_1 and T_2.

The most widely applied and best known method for combining decision procedures is due to Nelson and Oppen [8]. This method is at the heart of the verification systems CVC [9], ARGO-LIB [6] and SIMPLIFY [1], among others.

The Nelson-Oppen method allows one to decide the satisfiability (and hence the validity) of quantifier-free formulae in a combination T of two first-order theories T_1 and T_2, using as black boxes a decision procedure for the satisfiability of quantifier-free formulae in T_1 and a decision procedure for the satisfiability of quantifier-free formulae in T_2. The method is correct whenever the theories T, T_1, and T_2 satisfy the following restrictions: (i) T is logically equivalent to

J.J. Alferes and J. Leite (Eds.): JELIA 2004, LNAI 3229, pp. 641–653, 2004.

$T_1 \cup T_2$, (ii) the signatures of T_1 and T_2 are disjoint, and (iii) T_1 and T_2 are both stably infinite.

While the Nelson-Oppen method is defined in the context of unsorted first-order logic (with equality), more recent verification tools that rely on it have a sorted input language. However, strictly speaking, it is not clear how correct these verification tools are, because it is not clear whether the Nelson-Oppen method does in fact lift to a sorted setting. The common consensus among the researchers in the field is that, at least for standard many-sorted logic, "the method should be correct" as is. But to our knowledge there is no formal proof of this conjecture, nor is it obvious that the conjecture holds. In fact, a crucial requirement for the correctness of the method is that the signatures of the component theories share no function or predicate symbols (except equality). Now, in a sorted context, the method is only useful for theories whose signatures Σ_1 and Σ_2 share, if not function/predicate symbols, at least one sort. Otherwise, the only well-sorted $(\Sigma_1 \cup \Sigma_2)$-terms are either Σ_1-terms or Σ_2-terms, with Σ_1-terms sharing no variables with Σ_2-terms, which makes the combination problem trivial. Sharing sorts however essentially amounts to sharing predicate symbols, something that the original Nelson-Oppen method does not allow.

We prove in this paper that the method can indeed be lifted to sorted logics, provided that its applicability conditions are adjusted appropriately. For standard many-sorted logic, the only significant adjustment is to define stable infiniteness with respect to a set of sorts. The added benefit of using a sorted logic then becomes that it is easier to prove that a sorted theory is stably infinite over a certain sort s, than it is to prove that its unsorted version is stably infinite as a whole.[1] Also, one can now combine with no problems theories with sorts admitting only finite interpretations, say, as long as these sorts are not shared.

For *order*-sorted logics, the situation is in general considerably more complicated, requiring substantial additions to the method (see Section 5 for more details). There is however a useful special case in which the many-sorted version of the method works just as well with order-sorted theories: the case in which the shared sorts are pairwise *disconnected* i.e., do not appear in the same connected component of the subsort relation. Because of this we present our correctness results directly for order-sorted logic. Or more accurately, since there exist several, inequivalent order-sorted logics, we present our results for a fairly general version of first-order order-sorted logic based on a well developed and studied equational order-sorted logic by Goguen and Meseguer [5].

We introduce our order-sorted logic in Section 2. Then we present a version of the Nelson-Oppen combination method for this logic in Section 3, and prove it correct in Section 4. The correctness proof is based on a suitable order-sorted version of the model theoretic results used in [12,15] to prove the correctness of the (unsorted) Nelson-Oppen method. We conclude the paper in Section 5 with some directions for further research. The interested readers can find the complete proofs and more details in [13].

---

[1] Intuitively, one has to worry only about what the theory says about s, and can ignore what it says about other sorts.

2   An Order-Sorted Logic with Decorated Symbols

We will assume some familiarity in the reader with many-sorted and order-sorted algebras and logics with equality (denoted here by $\approx$) as defined for instance in [5]. We will mostly follow the notation used in [5]. The logic we present here is inspired by the order-sorted equational logic proposed by Meseguer in [7] as a successor of the logic in [5]. One main difference will be that our logic uses a vocabulary of *decorated* symbols, that is, function and predicate symbols that carry a sort declaration explicitly in them.

For any set S we denote by S^* the set all words over S, including the empty word ϵ. For the rest of the paper, we fix four countably-infinite sets: a set $\mathcal{F}$ of *function* symbols, a set $\mathcal{P}$ of *predicate* symbols, a set $\mathcal{S}$ of *sort* symbols, and a set $\mathcal{X}$ of *variables* that is disjoint with $\mathcal{F}$, $\mathcal{P}$ and $\mathcal{S}$.

A *decorated function symbol*, written as $f_{w,s}$, is a triple $(f, w, s) \in \mathcal{F} \times \mathcal{S}^* \times \mathcal{S}$. A *decorated constant* is a decorated function symbol of the form $f_{\epsilon,s}$. A *decorated predicate symbol*, written as p_w, is a pair $(p, w) \in \mathcal{P} \times \mathcal{S}^*$. A *decorated variable*, written as x_s, is a pair $(x, s) \in \mathcal{X} \times \mathcal{S}$.

An *order-sorted (decorated) signature* Σ is a tuple $\Sigma = (S, \prec, F, P)$ where $S \subseteq \mathcal{S}$ is a set of sorts, $F \subseteq (\mathcal{F} \times \mathcal{S}^* \times S)$ is a set of decorated function symbols, $P \subseteq (\mathcal{P} \times S^*)$ is a set of decorated predicate symbols, and $\prec$ is a binary relation over S. We denote by $\sim$ the symmetric closure of $\prec$, and by $\prec^*$ and $\sim^*$ the reflexive, transitive closure of $\prec$ and $\sim$, respectively. We say that a sort s_1 is a *subsort* of a sort s_2 iff $s_1 \prec^* s_2$, and that s_1 and s_2 are *connected* iff $s_1 \sim^* s_2$. If $w_1, w_2 \in S^*$, we write $w_1 \prec^* w_2$ iff w_1 and w_2 have the same length and each component of w_1 is a subsort of the corresponding component of w_2. (Similarly for $w_1 \sim^* w_2$.) When convenient, we will write Σ^{S} for S, Σ^{F} for F, and Σ^{P} for P. For simplicity, we will consider only signatures with a *finite* set of sorts.

In the following, we fix an order-sorted signature $\Sigma = (S, \prec, F, P)$.

We say that two distinct decorated function symbols $f_{w,s}$ and $f_{w',s'}$ of Σ are *subsort overloaded* (in Σ) if $ws \sim^* w's'$. Otherwise, we say that they are *ad-hoc overloaded*. (Similarly, for predicate symbols.) As we will see, the logic's semantics will allow ad-hoc overloaded symbols to stand for completely unrelated functions/relations, but will require subsort overloaded symbols to stand for functions/relations that agree on the intersection of their domains.

Definition 1 (Order-sorted Terms). *Let $X \subseteq \mathcal{X}$ be a set of variables. For all $s \in S$, the set $\mathcal{T}_s(\Sigma, X)$ of order-sorted Σ-terms of sort s over X is the set defined as follows by structural induction:*

- *every decorated variable $x_{s'} \in (X \times S)$ with $s' \prec^* s$ is in $\mathcal{T}_s(\Sigma, X)$;*
- *if $f_{s_1 \cdots s_n, s'} \in F$, $t_i \in \mathcal{T}_{s_i}(\Sigma, X)$ for $i = 1, \ldots, n$, and $s' \prec^* s$, then $f_{s_1 \cdots s_n, s'}(t_1, \ldots, t_n)$ is in $\mathcal{T}_s(\Sigma, X)$.*

We denote by $\mathcal{T}_w(\Sigma, X)$ with $w = s_1 \cdots s_n$ the set $\mathcal{T}_{s_1}(\Sigma, X) \times \cdots \times \mathcal{T}_{s_n}(\Sigma, X)$.

We say that a Σ-term has *nominal sort* s if it is a variable of the form x_s or its top symbol has the form $f_{w,s}$. Note that the nominal sort of a term t is always the least sort of t.

While decorated terms are cumbersome to write in practice, at the theoretical level they dramatically simplify or eliminate a number of problems that vex more standard definitions of sorted logics. For instance, with full decoration of symbols, sort inference is trivial, terms have a least sort, and the union and the intersection of two sorted signatures, crucial operations in combination settings, can be defined in a straightforward way as component-wise union and intersection. Of course we do not advocate that decorated signatures and terms be used in practice. They are just a way to abstract away the usual parsing, sort inference, and signature composition problems that arise when working with sorted languages, but that are not relevant for the essence of our combination results.

Definition 2 (Order-sorted atoms). *A Σ-atom is either an expression of the form $p_w(\mathbf{t})$ where $p_w \in P$ and $\mathbf{t} \in \mathcal{T}_w(\Sigma, X)$, or one of the form $t_1 \approx t_2$ where $(t_1, t_2) \in \mathcal{T}_{s_1 s_2}(\Sigma, X)$ for some $s_1, s_2 \in S$ such that $s_1 \sim^* s_2$.*

Order-sorted (first-order) Σ-formulae are defined on top of Σ-atoms as in the unsorted case, but with the difference that quantifiers bind decorated variables. Following [7], and contrary to [5] which allows only equations between terms of comparable sorts, we allow equations between terms of connected sorts.[2] This makes the logic both more general and more robust—see [7] for a discussion.

A *many-sorted Σ-structure* is a pair $\mathcal{A} = (A, I)$ where $A = \{A_s \mid s \in S\}$ is an S-indexed family of sets, *domains*, and I is a mapping of the decorated symbols of Σ to functions and relations over the carrier sets. Specifically, for each word $w = s_1 \cdots s_n \in S^*$, let A_w denote the set $A_{s_1} \times \cdots \times A_{s_n}$. Then I maps each decorated function symbol $f_{w,s} \in F$ to a (total) function $f_{w,s}^{\mathcal{A}} \in (A_w \to A_s)$, and each decorated predicate symbol $p_w \in P$ to a relation $p_w^{\mathcal{A}} \subseteq A_w$.

Definition 3 (Order-sorted Structure). *An order-sorted Σ-structure is a many-sorted (S, F, P)-structure $\mathcal{A} = (A, I)$ such that*

1. *For all $s, s' \in S$ such that $s \prec^* s'$, $A_s \subseteq A_{s'}$.*
2. *For all $f_{w,s}, f_{w',s'} \in F$ such that $ws \sim^* w's'$, the functions $f_{w,s}^{\mathcal{A}}$ and $f_{w',s'}^{\mathcal{A}}$ agree on $A_w \cap A_{w'}$.[3]*
3. *For all $p_w, p_{w'} \in P$ such that $w \sim^* w'$, the restrictions of $p_w^{\mathcal{A}}$ and of $p_{w'}^{\mathcal{A}}$ to $A_w \cap A_{w'}$ coincide.*

This definition of order-sorted structure is modeled after the definition of order-sorted algebra in [7]. As in [7], the given semantics supports subsort overloading of function symbols by requiring that, whenever $ws \sim^* w's'$, the functions denoted by $f_{w,s}$ and $f_{w',s'}$ coincide on the tuples shared by their domains. (Similarly for predicate symbols.)

Satisfiability of Σ-*sentences* (i.e. closed Σ-formulae) in an order-sorted Σ-structure $\mathcal{A}$ is defined similarly to the unsorted case. As usual, we say that $\mathcal{A}$ is a Σ-*model* of a set Φ of Σ-sentences if $\mathcal{A}$ satisfies every sentence in Φ.

---

[2] So, for instance, we allow an equation between two terms of respective sort s_1 and s_2 if they have a common subsort, even if neither $s_1 \prec^* s_2$ nor $s_2 \prec^* s_1$.

[3] Where $A_w \cap A_{w'}$ denotes the component-wise intersection of the tuples A_w and $A_{w'}$.

Definition 4 (Order-sorted Morphisms). *Let $\mathcal{A}$ and $\mathcal{B}$ be two order-sorted Σ-structures. A order-sorted Σ-homomorphism $h : \mathcal{A} \to \mathcal{B}$ of $\mathcal{A}$ into $\mathcal{B}$ is an S-indexed family $\{h_s : A_s \to B_s \mid s \in S\}$ of functions such that:*

1. *for all $f_{w,s} \in F$ with $w = s_1 \cdots s_n$ and all $a_i \in A_{s_i}$ with $i = 1, \ldots, n$,*
   $$h_s(f_{w,s}^{\mathcal{A}}(a_1, \ldots, a_n)) = f_{w,s}^{\mathcal{B}}(h_{s_1}(a_1) \ldots, h_{s_n}(a_n));$$
2. *for all $p_w \in P$ with $w = s_1 \cdots s_n$ and all $a_i \in A_{s_i}$ with $i = 1, \ldots, n$,*
   $$(a_1, \ldots, a_n) \in p_w^{\mathcal{A}} \Rightarrow (h_{s_1}(a_1), \ldots, h_{s_n}(a_n)) \in p_w^{\mathcal{B}}.$$
3. *for all $s, s' \in S$ with $s \sim^* s'$, the functions h_s and $h_{s'}$ agree on $A_s \cap A_{s'}$.*

A Σ-isomorphism h of $\mathcal{A}$ into $\mathcal{B}$ is an order-sorted Σ-homomorphism $h : \mathcal{A} \to \mathcal{B}$ for which there exists an order-sorted Σ-homomorphism $h' : \mathcal{B} \to \mathcal{A}$ such that $h' \circ h = \{id_s : A_s \to A_s \mid s \in S\}$ and $h \circ h' = \{id_s : B_s \to B_s \mid s \in S\}$.[4]

We write $\mathcal{A} \cong \mathcal{B}$ if there is an order-sorted Σ-isomorphism from $\mathcal{A}$ onto $\mathcal{B}$. We prove in [13] that $\cong$ is an equivalence relation over Σ-structures. We also prove that isomorphic Σ-structures satisfy exactly the same Σ-formulae.[5] As in the unsorted case, a crucial consequence of these results, which we use later, is that isomorphic order-sorted structures can always be identified.

If $\Sigma_1 = (S_1, \prec_1, F_1, P_1)$ and $\Sigma_2 = (S_2, \prec_2, F_2, P_2)$ are two order-sorted signatures, the *union* and the *intersection* of Σ_1 and Σ_2 are the order-sorted signatures defined as follows:

$$\Sigma_1 \cup \Sigma_2 = (S_1 \cup S_2, \prec_1 \cup \prec_2, F_1 \cup F_2, P_1 \cup P_2)$$
$$\Sigma_1 \cap \Sigma_2 = (S_1 \cap S_2, \prec_1^* \cap \prec_2^*, F_1 \cap F_2, P_1 \cap P_2).$$

It is easy to see that $\Sigma_1 \cup \Sigma_2$ and $\Sigma_1 \cap \Sigma_2$ are well defined, and thus are indeed order-sorted signatures. We will consider only unions of signatures that are *conservative* in a strong sense with respect to subsort overloading.

Definition 5 (Conservative Union of Signatures). *The order-sorted signature $\Sigma = (S, \prec, F, P)$ is a conservative union of an order-sorted signature $\Sigma_1 = (S_1, \prec_1, F_1, P_1)$ and an order-sorted signature $\Sigma_2 = (S_2, \prec_2, F_2, P_2)$ iff $\Sigma = \Sigma_1 \cup \Sigma_2$ and the following hold:*

1. *For all $p_{w'} \in P_i$ and $p_{w''} \in P_j$ with $\{i, j\} \subseteq \{1, 2\}$ and $w' \sim^* w''$, there is a $p_w \in P_i \cap P_j$ such that $w' \prec_i^* w \sim_j^* w''$ or $w'' \prec_j^* w \sim_i^* w'$.*
2. *For all $f_{w',s'} \in F_i$ and $f_{w'',s''} \in F_j$ with $\{i, j\} \subseteq \{1, 2\}$ and $w's' \sim^* w''s''$, there is a $f_{w,s} \in F_i \cap F_j$ such that $w's' \prec_i^* ws \sim_j^* w''s''$ or $w''s'' \prec_j^* ws \sim_i^* w's'$.*

The idea of the definition above is that if two symbols are subsort overloaded in the union signature, that is only because either they were already subsort overloaded in one of the component signatures (case $i = j$ in Conditions 1 and

---

[4] Where *id* denotes the identity function.

[5] Note that these two facts are not granted for a sorted logic. For instance, invariance of satisfiability under isomorphism does not hold in general for the logic in [5].

2) or, when the two symbols belong to different component signatures, each was subsort overloaded in its signature with a same *connecting* symbol belonging to the shared signature (case $i \neq j$).

An *order-sorted Σ-theory* is a pair $T = (\Sigma, Ax)$ where Ax is a set of Σ-sentences. A *model* of T is a Σ-structure that models Ax. A set Φ of Σ-sentences is *T-satisfiable (resp. T-unsatisfiable)* if it is satisfied by some (resp. no) model of T. The *combination* of two order-sorted theories $T_1 = (\Sigma_1, Ax_1)$ and $T_2 = (\Sigma_2, Ax_2)$ is defined as $T_1 \cup T_2 = (\Sigma_1 \cup \Sigma_2, Ax_1 \cup Ax_2)$.

In this paper we consider for convenience expansions of order-sorted signatures to sets of new constants. Formally, we will fix a countably-infinite set $\mathcal{C}$ of *free constants*, symbols that do not occur in any of the symbols sets $\mathcal{F}$, $\mathcal{P}$, $\mathcal{S}$ and $\mathcal{X}$ defined earlier. Then, for every order-sorted signature $\Sigma = (S, \prec, F, P)$, we will denote by $\Sigma(\mathcal{C})$ the signature $\Sigma = (S, \prec, F \cup (\mathcal{C} \times \{\epsilon\} \times S), P)$.[6]

The *quantifier-free satisfiability* problem for an order-sorted Σ-theory T is the problem of determining whether a ground $\Sigma(\mathcal{C})$-formula is T-satisfiable.

As we will see, the decidability of the quantifier-free satisfiability problem is modular with respect to the union of order-sorted theories whenever the signatures of theories satisfy certain disjointness conditions and the theories are *stably infinite* with respect to the sorts they share.

Definition 6 (Stably Infinite Theory). *A Σ-theory T is* stably infinite with respect to S' *for some $S' \subseteq \Sigma^S$ if every ground $\Sigma(\mathcal{C})$-formula φ that is T-satisfiable is satisfied by a $\Sigma(\mathcal{C})$-model $\mathcal{A}$ of T such that $|A_s| \geq \aleph_0$ for all $s \in S'$.*

We point out that the logic defined here is a proper extension of conventional many-sorted logic, obtainable from ours by considering only signatures with empty subsort relation $\prec$. All the results presented here then apply for instance to the many-sorted logics used by the verification systems described in [9,6].

3   The Combination Method

In this section we present a method for combining decision procedures for order-sorted theories whose signatures may share sorts, but no function or predicate symbols. We will further impose the restriction that the union of the two signatures is conservative (cf. Definition 5). The method is closely modeled after the non-deterministic version of the Nelson-Oppen combination method (for unsorted theories) as described in [11] and [15], among others.

For the rest of this section, let $\Sigma_1 = (S_1, \prec_1, F_1, P_1)$ and $\Sigma_2 = (S_2, \prec_2, F_2, P_2)$ be two order-sorted signatures such that

1. $F_1 \cap F_2 = P_1 \cap P_2 = \emptyset$,
2. $\Sigma_1 \cup \Sigma_2$ is a conservative union of Σ_1 and Σ_2,
3. for all distinct $s, s' \in S_1 \cap S_2$, $s \not\prec_1^* s'$ and $s \not\prec_2^* s'$.

---

[6] All the signature-dependent notions we have introduced so far extend to signatures with free constants in the obvious way.

Condition 1 corresponds to the original restriction in the Nelson-Oppen method that the two theories share no function or predicate symbols. In our case, however, the restriction is on *decorated* symbols. This means, for instance, that we allow one signature to contain a symbol f_{w_1,s_1}, while the other contains a symbol f_{w_2,s_2}, provided that $w_1 s_1 \neq w_2 s_2$. By Condition 2, the two symbols become *ad hoc* overloaded in the union signature, because that condition implies that $w_1 s_1 \not\sim^* w_2 s_2$, where $\sim$ is the symmetric closure of $\prec = \prec_1 \cup \prec_2$. Note that Condition 2 and 3 are immediately satisfied in the many-sorted case, i.e., when both $\prec_1$ and $\prec_2$ are the empty relation.

The problem. We are interested in the quantifier-free satisfiability problem for a theory $T_1 \cup T_2$ where T_i is a Σ_i-theory, for $i = 1, 2$, and both T_1 and T_2 are stably infinite over $S_0 = S_1 \cap S_2$.

Here are two examples of theories satisfying (or not) the conditions above.

Example 7. Let T_1 be an order sorted version of linear rational arithmetic, with Σ_1 having the sorts Int and Rat, the subsorts Int $\prec$ Rat, and the expected function and predicate symbols, say 0: Int, 1: Int, $+$: Int $\times$ Int $\to$ Int, $+$: Rat $\times$ Rat $\to$ Rat, $<$: Int $\times$ Int, and so on.[7] Then let T_2' be the theory of a parametric datatype such as lists, with signature Σ_2' having the "parameter" sort Elem (for the list elements), the list sorts EList, NList (for empty and non-empty lists respectively), and List, the subsorts EList, NList $\prec$ List, and the expected function symbols, say, $[\,]$: EList, hd: NList $\to$ Elem, tl: List $\to$ List, cons: Elem $\times$ List $\to$ NList.

Then consider a renaming T_2 of T_2' in which Elem is renamed as Rat, so that $T_1 \cup T_2$ then becomes a theory of rational lists. Where Σ_2 is the signature of T_2 and $S_0 = \{$Rat$\}$, it is easy to see that Σ_1 and Σ_2 satisfy Conditions 1–3 above. The stable infiniteness of T_1 over S_0 is trivial because in all models of T_1 Int is infinite (as the theory entails that all successors of zero are pairwise distinct). As discussed in [13], the stable infiniteness of T_2 over S_0 is not hard to show.

Example 8. Let T_1 be as in Example 7. Then let T_2' be an order-sorted theory of arrays, with signature Σ_2' having the "parameter" sorts Index and Elem (for the array indexes and elements, respectively), the array sort Array, the subsorts Index $\prec$ Elem, and the usual function symbols select: Array $\times$ Index $\to$ Elem and store: Array $\times$ Index $\times$ Elem $\to$ Array. Then consider a renaming T_2 of T_2' in which Elem is renamed as Rat and Index as Int, so that $T_1 \cup T_2$ then becomes a theory of arrays with integer indeces and rational elements. Where Σ_2 is the signature of T_2, it is immediate that Σ_1 and Σ_2 do not satisfy Condition 3 above because the shared sorts, Int and Rat, are comparable.

While perfectly reasonable in practice, $T_1 \cup T_2$ is a combined theory that the combination method cannot accommodate at the moment (but see Section 5 for possible extensions in this direction).

---

[7] For readability, we use here a more conventional notation for decorated symbols, instead of $0_{\epsilon,\text{Int}}$, $+_{\text{Int Int,Int}}$, etc.

We remark that a perhaps more natural combination of the two signatures would be the one in which no renamings are applied but Int becomes a subsort of Index and Rat a subsort of Elem. This kind of combination, however, is not achievable by a simple union of signatures and theories, and as such is out the scope of combination methods *a la* Nelson-Oppen.

The method. When the quantifier-free satisfiability problem for T_1 and for T_2 is decidable, we can decide the quantifier-free satisfiability problem for $T_1 \cup T_2$ by means of the combination method described below and consisting of four phases.

To simplify the presentation, and without loss of generality, we restrict ourselves to the $(T_1 \cup T_2)$-satisfiability of conjunctions of literals only.

First phase: Variable abstraction. Let Γ be a conjunction of ground $(\Sigma_1 \cup \Sigma_2)(\mathcal{C})$-literals. In this phase we convert Γ into a conjunction Γ' satisfying the following properties: (a) each literal in Γ' is either a $\Sigma_1(\mathcal{C})$-literal or a $\Sigma_2(\mathcal{C})$-literal, and (b) Γ' is $(T_1 \cup T_2)$-satisfiable if and only if so is Γ.

Properties (a) and (b) can be enforced with the help of new auxiliary constants from $\mathcal{C}$. For instance, in the simplest kind of transformation, Γ can be *purified* by applying to it to completion the following rewriting step, for all terms t of nominal sort $s \in S_0 = S_1 \cap S_2$ occurring in Γ that are not free constants: if t occurs as the argument of an non-equality atom in Γ, or occurs in an atom of the form $t \approx t'$ or $t' \approx t$ where t' is not a free constant, or occurs as a proper subterm of an atom of the form $t_1 \approx t_2$ or $t_2 \approx t_1$, then t is replaced by $c_{\epsilon,s}$ for some fresh $c \in \mathcal{C}$, and the equality $c_{\epsilon,s} \approx t$ is added to Γ. It is easy to see that this transformation satisfies the properties above.[8]

Second phase: Partition. Let Γ' be a conjunction of literals obtained in the variable abstraction phase. We now partition Γ' into two sets of literals Γ_1, Γ_2 such that, for $i = 1, 2$, each literal in Γ_i is a $\Sigma_i(\mathcal{C})$-literal. A literal with an atom of the form $c_{\epsilon,s} \approx c'_{\epsilon,s'}$ with $c, c' \in \mathcal{C}$, which is both a $\Sigma_1(\mathcal{C})$- and a $\Sigma_2(\mathcal{C})$-literal, can go arbitrarily in either Γ_1 or Γ_2.

Third phase: Decomposition. Let $\Gamma_1 \cup \Gamma_2$ be the conjunction of literals obtained in the variable abstraction phase. The only decorated symbols shared by Γ_1 and Γ_2, if any, are decorated free constants of a shared sort—constants of the form $c_{\epsilon,s}$ with $c \in \mathcal{C}$ and $s \in S_0$. For all shared sorts $s \in S_0$, let C_s be the set of constants of sort s shared by Γ_1 and Γ_2. We choose nondeterministically a family $E = \{E_s \subseteq C_s \times C_s \mid s \in S_0\}$ of equivalence relations E_s.

Intuitively, in this phase we guess for each pair of shared constant in C_s, whether they denote the same individual or not. In essence, partitioning the shared free constants into sorted classes and considering identifications only of constants of the same sort is the only difference with respect to the unsorted version of the Nelson-Oppen method, where all pairs of constants are considered for possible identification.

Fourth phase: Check. Given the equivalence relations $E = \{E_s \mid s \in S_0\}$ guessed in the decomposition phase, this phase consists of the following steps:

---

[8] But see [12], among others, for a more practical kind of abstraction process that minimizes the number of fresh constants introduced.

1. Construct the *arrangement* of $C = \{C_s \mid s \in S_0\}$ induced by E, defined by

$$arr(C, E) = \{u \approx v \mid (u, v) \in E_s \text{ and } s \in S_0\} \cup$$
$$\{u \not\approx v \mid (u, v) \in (C_s^2 \setminus E_s) \text{ and } s \in S_0\}.$$

2. if $\Gamma_1 \cup arr(C, E)$ is T_1-satisfiable and $\Gamma_2 \cup arr(C, E)$ is T_2-satisfiable, output succeed; else output fail.

In Section 4 we will prove that this combination method is sound and complete in the following sense. If there exists an arrangement $arr(C, E)$ of C for which the check phase outputs succeed, then Γ is $(T_1 \cup T_2)$-satisfiable. If instead the check phase outputs fails for every possible arrangement $arr(C, E)$ of C, then Γ is $(T_1 \cup T_2)$-unsatisfiable.

4   Correctness of the Method

To prove the combination method correct, we first need a couple of basic model-theoretic results. The first is an order-sorted version of the Downward Löwenheim-Skolem Theorem, whose proof can be found in [13]. The second is an order-sorted version of a general combination result given in [12,15] for unsorted theories.

Theorem 9 (Order-sorted Löwenheim-Skolem Theorem). *Where Σ is an order-sorted signature, let Φ be a satisfiable set of Σ-formulae, and let $\mathcal{A}$ be a Σ-structure satisfying Φ. Then there exists a Σ-structure $\mathcal{B}$ satisfying Φ such that $|A_s| \geq \aleph_0$ implies $|B_s| = \aleph_0$, for each sort $s \in \Sigma^S$.*

If $\mathcal{A}$ is an order-sorted Σ_1-structure and $\Sigma_0 = \Sigma_1 \cap \Sigma_2$ for some signature Σ_2, we denote by $\mathcal{A}^{\Sigma_0}$ the Σ_0-structure with domains $\{A_s \mid s \in \Sigma_0^S\}$ that interprets the function and predicate symbols of Σ_0 exactly as $\mathcal{A}$ does.

Theorem 10 (Order-Sorted Combination Theorem). *Let $\Sigma_A = (S_A, \prec_A, F_A, P_A)$ and $\Sigma_B = (S_B, \prec_B, F_B, P_B)$ are two order-sorted signatures, and let Φ_A and Φ_B be two sets of Σ_A- and Σ_B-sentences, respectively. When $\Sigma_A \cup \Sigma_B$ is a conservative union of Σ_A and Σ_B, $\Phi_A \cup \Phi_B$ is satisfiable iff there is a Σ_A-structure $\mathcal{A}$ satisfying Φ_A and a Σ_B-structure $\mathcal{B}$ satisfying Φ_B such that $\mathcal{A}^{\Sigma_A \cap \Sigma_B} \cong \mathcal{B}^{\Sigma_A \cap \Sigma_B}$.*

Proof. Let $\Sigma_C = \Sigma_A \cap \Sigma_B$, and $\Sigma = \Sigma_A \cup \Sigma_B = (S, \prec, F, P) = (S_A \cup S_B, \prec_A \cup \prec_B, F_A \cup F_B, P_A \cup P_B)$.

Next, assume that $\Phi_A \cup \Phi_B$ is satisfiable, and let $\mathcal{D}$ be a Σ-structure satisfying $\Phi_A \cup \Phi_B$. Then, by letting $\mathcal{A} = \mathcal{D}^{\Sigma_A}$ and $\mathcal{B} = \mathcal{D}^{\Sigma_B}$, we clearly have that $\mathcal{A}$ satisfies Φ_A, $\mathcal{B}$ satisfies Φ_B, and $\mathcal{A}^{\Sigma_C} \cong \mathcal{B}^{\Sigma_C}$.

Vice versa, suppose there exists a Σ_A-structure $\mathcal{A}$ satisfying Φ_A and a Σ_B-structure $\mathcal{B}$ satisfying Φ_B such that $\mathcal{A}^{\Sigma_C} \cong \mathcal{B}^{\Sigma_C}$. Then, as observed in Section 2, we can assume with no loss of generality that $\mathcal{A}^{\Sigma_C} = \mathcal{B}^{\Sigma_C}$. We define a Σ-structure $\mathcal{D}$ by letting for each $s \in S$, $f_{w,s} \in F$, and $p_w \in P$:

$$
D_s = \begin{cases} A_s, & \text{if } s \in S_A \\ B_s, & \text{if } s \in S_B \setminus S_A \end{cases}
$$

$$
f_{w,s}^{\mathcal{D}} = \begin{cases} f_{w,s}^{\mathcal{A}}, & \text{if } f_{w,s} \in F_A \\ f_{w,s}^{\mathcal{B}}, & \text{if } f_{w,s} \in F_B \setminus F_A \end{cases}
\qquad
p_w^{\mathcal{D}} = \begin{cases} p_w^{\mathcal{A}}, & \text{if } p_w \in P_A \\ p_w^{\mathcal{B}}, & \text{if } p_w \in P_B \setminus P_A \end{cases}
$$

Because $\mathcal{A}^{\Sigma_C} = \mathcal{B}^{\Sigma_C}$, it is clear that $\mathcal{D}$ is well defined as a many-sorted Σ-structure. To show that $\mathcal{D}$ is also a well defined order-sorted Σ-structure, we start by showing that in $\mathcal{D}$ the denotation of a sort includes the denotations of its subsorts.

In fact, let $s, s' \in S$ be two distinct sorts such that $s \prec^* s'$. Since $\prec = \prec_A \cup \prec_B$ (and S is finite), there is a sequence $s = s_0, s_1, \ldots, s_n, s_{n+1} = s'$ such that for all $i = 0, \ldots, n$ either $s_i \prec_A s_{i+1}$ or $s_i \prec_B s_{i+1}$. It is enough to show then that $D_{s_i} \subseteq D_{s_{i+1}}$ for all $i = 0, \ldots, n$. Recall that, since $\mathcal{A}^{\Sigma_C} = \mathcal{B}^{\Sigma_C}$, $D_{s_i} = A_{s_i} = B_{s_i}$ whenever $s_i \in S_A \cap S_B$. Now, if $s_i \prec_A s_{i+1}$ we have by construction of $\mathcal{D}$ and definition of $\mathcal{A}$ that $D_{s_i} = A_{s_i} \subseteq A_{s_{i+1}} = D_{s_{i+1}}$. (Similarly, if instead $s_i \prec_B s_{i+1}$.)

It remains to show that $\mathcal{D}$ respects the subsort overloading of function and predicate symbols.[9] This is true for every two symbols of F_A or of P_A because (i) $\mathcal{D}^{\Sigma_A} = \mathcal{A}$, trivially, and (ii) since $\Sigma = \Sigma_A \cup \Sigma_B$ is a conservative union of Σ_A and Σ_B, if two symbols are subsort overloaded in Σ then they are subsort overloaded in Σ_A. The argument is symmetric for the symbols of F_B and P_B. Finally, $\mathcal{D}$ respects the possible subsort overloading of a symbol of F_A (P_A) and a symbol of F_B (P_B) because again Σ is a conservative union of Σ_A and Σ_B, and $\mathcal{A}$ and $\mathcal{B}$ agree on their shared symbols.

In fact, for illustration, assume that $p_{w'} \in P_A$, $p_{w''} \in P_B \setminus P_A$, and $w' \sim^* w''$. Then, by Definition 5, there is a $p_w \in P_A \cap P_B$ such that $w' \prec_A^* w$ and $w \sim_B^* w''$, say. Let $\mathbf{d} \in D_{w'} \cap D_{w''}$. We show that $\mathbf{d} \in p_{w'}^{\mathcal{D}}$ iff $\mathbf{d} \in p_{w''}^{\mathcal{D}}$. Observing that $D_{w'} = A_{w'} \subseteq A_w = B_w$ and $B_{w''} = D_{w''}$ by construction of $\mathcal{D}$ and definition of $\mathcal{A}$ and $\mathcal{B}$, it is not difficult to see that $\mathbf{d} \in A_{w'} \cap A_w$ and $\mathbf{d} \in B_w \cap B_{w''}$. Then $\mathbf{d} \in p_{w'}^{\mathcal{D}}$ iff $\mathbf{d} \in p_{w'}^{\mathcal{A}}$ (by construction of $\mathcal{D}$) iff $\mathbf{d} \in p_w^{\mathcal{A}}$ (as $w' \sim_A^* w$ and $\mathbf{d} \in A_{w'} \cap A_w$) iff $\mathbf{d} \in p_w^{\mathcal{B}}$ (as $p_w^{\mathcal{A}} = p_w^{\mathcal{B}}$ by $\mathcal{A}^{\Sigma_A \cap \Sigma_B} = \mathcal{B}^{\Sigma_A \cap \Sigma_B}$) iff $\mathbf{d} \in p_{w''}^{\mathcal{B}}$ (as $w \sim_B^* w''$ and $\mathbf{d} \in B_w \cap B_{w''}$) iff $\mathbf{d} \in p_{w''}^{\mathcal{D}}$ (by construction of $\mathcal{D}$). The other cases are proven similarly.

Now, given that $\mathcal{D}$ is well defined, and that $\mathcal{D}^{\Sigma_A} = \mathcal{A}$ and $\mathcal{D}^{\Sigma_B} = \mathcal{B}$ by construction, it is immediate that $\mathcal{D}$ satisfies $\Phi_A \cup \Phi_B$. $\qquad\square$

Let us now consider again the order-sorted signatures Σ_1, Σ_2 and the theories T_1, T_2 from Section 3.

Theorem 11. *For $i = 1, 2$, let Φ_i be a set of $\Sigma_i(\mathcal{C})$-sentences. For each $s \in S_0$ let C_s be the set of decorated free constants $c_{\epsilon,s}$ shared by Φ_1 and Φ_2, with $c \in \mathcal{C}$.*

---

[9] That is, $f_{w,s}^{\mathcal{D}}(\mathbf{d}) = f_{w',s'}^{\mathcal{D}}(\mathbf{d})$ for all $f_{w,s}, f_{w',s'} \in F$ with $ws \sim^* w's'$ and $\mathbf{d} \in D_w \cap D_{w'}$, and $\mathbf{d} \in p_w^{\mathcal{D}}$ iff $\mathbf{d} \in p_{w'}^{\mathcal{D}}$ for all $p_w, p_{w'} \in P$ with $w \sim^* w'$ and $\mathbf{d} \in D_w \cap D_{w'}$.

Then, $\Phi_1 \cup \Phi_2$ is satisfiable iff there exists a $\Sigma_1(\mathcal{C})$-structure $\mathcal{A}$ satisfying Φ_1 and a $\Sigma_2(\mathcal{C})$-structure $\mathcal{B}$ satisfying Φ_2 such that:

(i) $|A_s| = |B_s|$, for all $s \in S_0$;
(ii) $u^{\mathcal{A}} = v^{\mathcal{A}}$ if and only if $u^{\mathcal{B}} = v^{\mathcal{B}}$, for all $u, v \in C_s$ and $s \in S_0$.

Proof. Let $\Sigma_0 = \Sigma_1 \cap \Sigma_2 = (S_0, \prec_0, F_0, P_0) = (S_1 \cap S_2, \prec_1^* \cap \prec_2^*, F_1 \cap F_2, P_1 \cap P_2)$. Clearly, if there exists a $(\Sigma_1 \cup \Sigma_2)(\mathcal{C})$-structure $\mathcal{D}$ satisfying $\Phi_1 \cup \Phi_2$, then the only if direction holds by letting $\mathcal{A} = \mathcal{D}^{\Sigma_1(\mathcal{C})}$ and $\mathcal{B} = \mathcal{D}^{\Sigma_2(\mathcal{C})}$.

Concerning the if direction, assume that there exists a $\Sigma_1(\mathcal{C})$-structure $\mathcal{A}$ satisfying Φ_1 and a $\Sigma_2(\mathcal{C})$-structure $\mathcal{B}$ satisfying Φ_2 such that both (i) and (ii) hold. We define a function family $h = \{h_s : C_s^{\mathcal{A}} \to C_s^{\mathcal{B}} \mid s \in S_0\}$ by letting $h_s(u^{\mathcal{A}}) = u^{\mathcal{B}}$, for every $u \in C_s^{\mathcal{A}}$ and $s \in S_0$. Note that each function h_s is well defined and bijective thanks to property (ii). As a consequence, we have that $|C_s^{\mathcal{A}}| = |C_s^{\mathcal{B}}|$ for all $s \in S_0$. By property (i) then, we can extend each function h_s to a bijective function $h_s' : A_s \to B_s$.

Let $\mathcal{C}_0$ be the set of all constants in $\{C_s \mid s \in S_0\}$. Since the signature $\Sigma_0(\mathcal{C}_0)$ has only constant symbols (from $\mathcal{C}_0$) and all of its sorts are pairwise disconnected, it is clear that the family $h' = \{h_s' : A_s \to B_s \mid s \in S_0\}$ is an order-sorted $\Sigma_0(\mathcal{C}_0)$-isomorphism of $\mathcal{A}^{\Sigma_0(\mathcal{C}_0)}$ into $\mathcal{B}^{\Sigma_0(\mathcal{C}_0)}$. Therefore, by Theorem 10 we obtain the existence of a $(\Sigma_1 \cup \Sigma_2)(\mathcal{C})$-structure $\mathcal{D}$ satisfying $\Phi_1 \cup \Phi_2$. □

Proposition 12 (Correctness). *Let Γ_1 and Γ_2 be conjunctions of ground $\Sigma_1(\mathcal{C})$-literals and ground $\Sigma_2(\mathcal{C})$-literals, respectively, and for all shared sorts $s \in S_0$, let C_s be the set of free constants shared by Γ_1 and Γ_2. The following are equivalent:*

1. *The conjunction $\Gamma_1 \cup \Gamma_2$ is $(T_1 \cup T_2)$-satisfiable.*
2. *There is a family $E = \{E_s \mid s \in S_0\}$ of equivalence relations E_s over C_s such that $\Gamma_i \cup arr(V, E)$ is T_i-satisfiable, for $i = 1, 2$.*

Proof. We only prove that 2 implies 1, as the other direction is straightforward. Assume there exists a family $E = \{E_s \mid s \in S_0\}$ of equivalence relations E_s over C_s such that $\Gamma_i \cup arr(V, E)$ is T_i-satisfiable, for $i = 1, 2$.

Since T_1 is stably infinite with respect to S_0, we can assume that $\Gamma_1 \cup arr(V, E)$ is satisfied by a model $\mathcal{A}$ of T_1 such that A_s is infinite for each $s \in S_0$. By the Order-sorted Löwenheim-Skolem Theorem we can further assume that A_s is *countably* infinite for each $s \in S_0$. Similarly, we can assume that $\Gamma_2 \cup arr(V, E)$ is satisfied by a model $\mathcal{B}$ of T_2 such that B_s is countably infinite for each $s \in S_0$. But then we obtain a model $\mathcal{A}$ of $T_1 \cup \Gamma_1$ and a model $\mathcal{B}$ of $T_2 \cup \Gamma_2$ such that (i) $|A_s| = |B_s|$, for each $s \in S_0$, and (ii) $u^{\mathcal{A}} = v^{\mathcal{A}}$ iff $u^{\mathcal{B}} = v^{\mathcal{B}}$, for each $u, v \in C_s$ and $s \in S_0$. By Theorem 11 it follows that $(T_1 \cup \Gamma_1) \cup (T_2 \cup \Gamma_2)$ is satisfiable, which is equivalent to saying that $\Gamma_1 \cup \Gamma_2$ is $(T_1 \cup T_2)$-satisfiable. □

Combining Proposition 12 with the observation that the nondeterminism of the decomposition phase of the sorted Nelson-Oppen method is finitary, we obtain the following modular decidability result for order-sorted theories T_1 and T_2 defined as in Section 3.

Theorem 13 (Modular Decidability). *If the quantifier-free satisfiability problems of T_1 and of T_2 are decidable, then the quantifier-free satisfiability problem of $T_1 \cup T_2$ is also decidable.*

5   Conclusions and Further Research

We addressed the problem of modularly combining order-sorted first-order theories and their decision procedures. For that, we first defined a fairly general version of order-sorted logic. Then we presented and proved correct a method for combining decision procedures for two order-sorted theories that have no function or predicate symbols in common and are stably infinite with respect to a set of shared, disconnected sorts.

The method is a direct lifting to the given order-sorted logic of the Nelson-Oppen method for combining theories in (unsorted) first-order logic. The main difference with the unsorted version is that the introduction of sorts helps reduce the nondeterminism of the decomposition phase—because the guessing of equalities between shared constant is limited to constants with the same nominal sort—and allows one to limit the stable infiniteness requirement to just the shared sorts.

We used the assumption that the shared sorts are disconnected in order to obtain a method that is as close as possible to the Nelson-Oppen method for unsorted logic. When the shared sorts are connected, the combination problem becomes considerably more complex model-theoretically, and consequently so does any corresponding combination method. More in detail, consider the case of two theories T_1 and T_2 sharing two sorts s_1, s_2, with $s_1 \prec^* s_2$ (in both theories), and assume that u is a shared free constant of nominal sort s_2. Then, in a combination method for T_1 and T_2, the component decision procedures also need to share the information on whether u "is in s_1" or not—that is, whether u could be interpreted as an element of the set denoted by s_1 or not. Thinking of the problem in terms of Venn diagrams for the denotations of the sorts, a combination procedure also has to guess the portion of the diagram to which u belongs, and generate a *sort membership* constraint to that extent. Such constraints are easily expressible in our logic—to say that u is [not] in s_1, one simply writes $[\neg](\exists x_{s_1} \; x_{s_1} \approx u)$—but involve quantifiers.

Clearly, membership constraints increase the complexity of the combination procedure because there is much more to guess. Furthermore, since some of added constraints are (inherently) non-quantifier-free, they add to the complexity of the component decision procedures as well. Finally, the requirements that the two component theories be stably infinite over their shared sorts is not enough anymore—at least if one wants to use an extension of the proofs given here.[10]

Another limitation of the current method is that it does not apply to component theories that share function or predicate symbols. The problem of extending the Nelson-Oppen method to theories with symbols in common has recently received much attention [3,4,10,12,14]. Concurrently with the work presented here,

---

[10] See [13] for a discussion on this last point.

the specific approach of [3,4] has been adapted in [2], with comparable results, to many-sorted logic (with no subsorts). An important direction for future research then would be to see how those results, which allow shared symbols but no subsorts, can be combined with the ones presented here, which allow subsorts but no shared function or predicate symbols.

Acknowledgments. We would like to thank José Meseguer for his insightful comments and suggestions on the order-sorted logic presented here.

The second author was supported in part by the project GECCOO in the context of the French national research program *ACI Sécurité Informatique*.

References

1. D. Detlefs, G. Nelson, and J. B. Saxe. Simplify: A theorem prover for program checking. Technical Report HPL-2-3-148, HP Laboratories, Palo Alto, CA, 2003.
2. V. Ganesh, S. Berezin, C. Tinelli, and D. Dill. Combination results for many sorted theories with overlapping signatures. Technical report, Department of Computer Science, Stanford University, 2004.
3. S. Ghilardi. Quantifier elimination and provers integration. In I. Dahn and L. Vigneron, editors, *First Order Theorem Proving*, volume 86.1 of *Electronic Notes in Theoretical Computer Science*. Elsevier, 2003.
4. S. Ghilardi. Model theoretic methods in combined constraint satisfiability. *Journal of Automated Reasoning*, 2004. (To appear).
5. J. A. Goguen and J. Meseguer. Order-sorted algebra I: Equational deduction for multiple inheritance, overloading, exceptions and partial operations. *Theoretical Computer Science*, 105(2):217–173, 1992.
6. F. Maric and P. Janičić. ARGO-LIB: A generic platform for decision procedures. In *International Joint Conference on Automated Reasoning*, Lecture Notes in Computer Science. Springer, 2004.
7. J. Meseguer. Membership algebra as a logical framework for equational specification. In *Recent Trends in Algebraic Development Techniques*, volume 1376 of *Lecture Notes in Computer Science*, pages 18–61. Springer, 1998.
8. G. Nelson and D. C. Oppen. Simplification by cooperating decision procedures. *ACM Transactions on Programming Languages and Systems*, 1(2):245–257, 1979.
9. A. Stump, C. W. Barrett, and D. L. Dill. CVC: A cooperating validity checker. In E. Brinksma and K. G. Larsen, editors, *Computer Aided Verification*, volume 2404 of *Lecture Notes in Computer Science*, pages 500–504, 2002.
10. C. Tinelli. Cooperation of background reasoners in theory reasoning by residue sharing. *Journal of Automated Reasoning*, 30(1):1–31, 2003.
11. C. Tinelli and M. T. Harandi. A new correctness proof of the Nelson-Oppen combination procedure. In F. Baader and K. U. Schulz, editors, *Frontiers of Combining Systems*, volume 3 of *Applied Logic Series*, pages 103–120. Kluwer, 1996.
12. C. Tinelli and C. Ringeissen. Unions of non-disjoint theories and combinations of satisfiability procedures. *Theoretical Computer Science*, 290(1):291–353, 2003.
13. C. Tinelli and C. G. Zarba. Combining decision procedures for sorted theories. Technical Report 04-01, The University of Iowa, 2004.
14. C. G. Zarba. C-tableaux. Technical Report RR-5229, INRIA, 2004.
15. C. G. Zarba. *The Combination Problem in Automated Reasoning*. PhD thesis, Stanford University, 2004.

Meta-level Verification of the Quality of Medical Guidelines Using Interactive Theorem Proving*

Arjen Hommersom[1], Peter Lucas[1], and Michael Balser[2]

[1] Institute for Computing and Information Sciences, University of Nijmegen,
{arjenh,peterl}@cs.kun.nl
[2] Institut für Informatik, Universität Augsburg,
balser@informatik.uni-augsburg.de

Abstract. Requirements about the quality of medical guidelines can be represented using schemata borrowed from the theory of abductive diagnosis, using temporal logic to model the time-oriented aspects expressed in a guideline. In this paper, we investigate how this approach can be mapped to the facilities offered by a theorem proving system for program verification, KIV. It is shown that the reasoning that is required for checking the quality of a guideline can be mapped to such theorem-proving facilities. The medical quality of an actual guideline concerning diabetes mellitus 2 is investigated in this way, and some problems discovered are discussed.

1 Introduction

Health-care is becoming more and more complicated at an astonishing rate. On the one hand, the number of different patient management options has risen considerably during the last couple of decades, whereas, on the other hand, medical doctors are expected to take decisions balancing benefits for the patient against financial costs. There is a growing trend within the medical profession to believe that clinical decision-making should be based as much as possible on sound scientific evidence; this has become known as *evidence-based medicine* [12]. Evidence-based medicine has given a major impetus to the development of guidelines, documents offering a detailed description of steps that must be taken and considerations that must be taken into account by health-care professionals in managing a disease in a patient to avoid substandard practices or outcomes. Their general aim is to promote standards of medical care.

Researchers in artificial intelligence (AI) have picked up on these developments, and some of them, for example in the Asgaard project [10], are involved in the design of computer-oriented languages, tools and systems that support the design and deployment of medical guidelines. AI researchers see guidelines as good real-world examples of highly structured, systematic documents that are amenable to formalisation.

---

* This work has been partially supported by the European Commission's IST program, under contract number IST-FP6-508794 PROTOCURE II.

J.J. Alferes and J. Leite (Eds.): JELIA 2004, LNAI 3229, pp. 654–666, 2004.

There are two approaches to checking the quality of medical guidelines: (1) the *object-level* approach amounts to translating a guideline to a formal language, such as Asbru [10], and next applying techniques from program verification to the resulting representation in establishing partial or total correctness; (2) the *meta-level* approach, which consists of formalising general properties to which a guideline should comply, and then investigating whether this is the case. Here we are concerned with the meta-level approach to guideline-quality checking. For example, a good-quality medical guideline regarding treatment of a disorder should preclude the prescription of redundant drugs, or advise against the prescription of treatment that is less effective than some alternative. Carrying out such checks could be valuable, in particular during the process of *designing* medical guidelines.

In this paper we explore the route from an informal medical guideline to its logical formalisation and verification. Previously we have shown that the theory of abductive diagnosis can be taken as a foundation for the formalisation of quality criteria of a medical guideline [7]. In this paper we study the use of logical deduction using temporal logic to formally establish whether a guideline fulfils particular quality requirements. For this purpose use was made of the theorem prover KIV [1]. This is a somewhat unusual approach, as KIV and its underlying logics are especially targeted at the verification of parallel programs, whereas here we are concerned with a type of reasoning that comes from AI.

The paper is organised as follows. In the next section, we start by explaining what medical guidelines are, and a method for formalising guidelines by temporal logic, including the logic supported by the theorem prover KIV, are briefly reviewed. In Section 3 the formalisation of guideline quality using a meta-level schema which comes from the theory of abductive diagnosis is described. The guideline on the management of diabetes mellitus type 2 that has been used in the case study is given attention to in Section 4 and a formalisation of this is given. The approach to checking the quality of this guideline using the deductive machinery offered by KIV is presented in Section 5. Finally, Section 6 discusses what has been achieved and suggests some future plans for research.

2   Preliminaries

2.1   The Design of Medical Guidelines

The design of a medical guideline is far from easy. Firstly, the gathering and classification of the scientific evidence underlying and justifying the recommendations mentioned in a guideline is time consuming, and requires considerable expertise in the medical field concerned. Secondly, medical guidelines are very detailed, and making sure that all the information contained in the guideline is complete for the guideline's purpose, and based on sound medical principles is hard work. An example of a tiny portion of a guideline is shown in Fig. 1; it is part of the guideline for general practitioners about the treatment of diabetes mellitus type 2. This guideline fragment is used in this paper as a running example.

One way to use formal methods in the context of guidelines is to automatically verify whether a medical guideline fulfils particular properties, such

- Step 1: diet
- Step 2: if Quetelet Index (QI) $\leq$ 24, prescribe a sulfonylurea drug; otherwise, prescribe a biguanide drug
- Step 3: combine a sulfonylurea drug and biguanide (replace one of these by a α-glucosidase inhibitor if side-effects occur)
- Step 4: one of the following:
  - oral antidiabetics and insulin
  - only insulin

Fig. 1. Tiny fragment of a clinical guideline on the management of diabetes mellitus type 2. If one of the steps $k = 1, 2, 3$ is ineffective, the management moves to step $k+1$.

as whether it complies with quality *indicators* as proposed by health-care professionals [8]. For example, using particular patient assumptions such as that after treatment the levels of a substance are dangerously high or low, it is possible to check whether this situation does or does not violate the guideline. However, verifying the effects of treatment as well as examining whether a developed medical guideline complies with global criteria, such as that it avoids the prescription of redundant drugs, or the request of tests that are superfluous, is difficult to impossible if only the guideline text is available. Thus, the capability to check whether a guideline fulfils particular medical objectives may require the availability of more medical knowledge than is actually specified in a medical guideline, i.e. *background knowledge* is required.

Table 1. Used temporal operators; t stands for a time instance.

Notation	Interpretation	Formal semantics
$H\varphi$	φ has always been true in the past	$t \vDash H\varphi \Leftrightarrow \forall t' < t : t' \vDash \varphi$
$G\varphi$	φ is true at all future times	$t \vDash G\varphi \Leftrightarrow \forall t' \geq t : t' \vDash \varphi$

2.2 Using Temporal Logic for Guideline Representation

As medical management is a time-oriented process, diagnostic and treatment actions described in guidelines are performed in a temporal setting. It has been shown previously that the step-wise, possibly iterative, execution of a guideline, such as the example in Fig. 1, can be described precisely by means of temporal logic [8]. This is a modal logic, where relationships between worlds in the usual possible-world semantics of modal logic is understood as time order, i.e. formulae are interpreted in a *temporal structure* $\mathcal{F} = (\mathbb{T}, <, I)$. We will assume that the progression in time is *linear*, i.e. $<$ is a strict linear order. For the representation of the medical knowledge involved it appeared to be sufficient to use rather abstract temporal operators as proposed in literature [7]. The language of standard logic, with equality and unique names assumption, is augmented with the modal operators G, H, P and F, where the temporal semantics of the first two operators

Table 2. Used temporal operators; t stands for a time instance.

Notation	Interpretation	Formal semantics
$\Box\, \varphi$	φ will always be true	$t \vDash \Box\, \varphi \Leftrightarrow \forall t' \geq t : t' \vDash \varphi$
$\Diamond\, \varphi$	φ will eventually be true	$t \vDash \Diamond\, \varphi \Leftrightarrow \exists t' \geq t : t' \vDash \varphi$
φ **until** ψ	φ holds until ψ eventually holds	$t \vDash \varphi$ **until** ψ $\Leftrightarrow \exists\, t' \geq t : \quad t' \vDash \psi$ $\qquad \land\, \forall\, t \leq t'' < t' : t'' \vDash \varphi$
φ **unless** ψ	φ holds unless ψ holds	$t \vDash \varphi$ **unless** ψ $\Leftrightarrow \forall\, t' \geq t : \quad t' \vDash \varphi$ $\qquad \lor\, \exists\, t \leq t'' \leq t' : t'' \vDash \psi$
$\circ\, \varphi$	execution does not terminate and the next state satisfies φ	$t \vDash \circ\, \varphi \Leftrightarrow \exists\, t' \in \mathrm{succ}(t) : t' \vDash \varphi$
$\bullet\, \varphi$	either execution terminates or the next state satisfies φ	$t \vDash \circ\, \varphi \Leftrightarrow \forall\, t' \in \mathrm{succ}(t) : t' \vDash \varphi$
last	the current state is the last	$t \vDash$ **last** $\Leftrightarrow \mathrm{succ}(t) = \emptyset$

is defined in Table 1. The last two operators are simply defined in terms of the first two operators:

$$\vDash \mathsf{P}\varphi \leftrightarrow \neg\mathsf{H}\neg\varphi \quad \text{(somewhere in the past)}$$

$$\vDash \mathsf{F}\varphi \leftrightarrow \neg\mathsf{G}\neg\varphi \quad \text{(somewhere in the future)}$$

This logic offers the right abstraction level to cope with the nature of the temporal knowledge in medical guidelines required for our purposes. However, more fine-grained temporal operators can be added if needed. For a full axiomatisation of this logic, see Ref. [11].

Even though this logic was shown to be suitable for representation purposes, we had to map it to the temporal logic underlying KIV, which we had chosen as the system to be used for formal verification. As a consequence, in the next section, this temporal logic is briefly described. The mapping is given in Section 5.1.

2.3   Temporal Logic in KIV

The interactive theorem prover KIV offers support for future-time linear temporal logic [2]. Reactive systems can be described in KIV by means of state-charts or parallel programs; here we use parallel programs. A state of a system can be described by first-order logic. Furthermore, static variables v, which have the same values at each time point, are distinguished from dynamic variables V. A specialty of KIV is the use of primed and double-primed variables: a primed variable V' represents the value of this variable after a system transition, the double-primed variable V'' is interpreted as the value after an environment transition. System and environment transitions alternate, with V'' being equal to V in the successive state.

The supported future-time temporal operators include the operators from Table 2, where $\mathrm{succ}(t)$ is the set of zero or one successors of t. Note that all formulae are interpreted with respect to the first point of time. Let e denote an arbitrary (first-order) expression, then constructs for parallel programs include: $V := e$ (*assignments*), **if** ψ **then** ϕ_1 **else** ϕ_2 (*conditionals*), **while** ψ **do** ϕ (*loops*), **var** $V = e$ **in** ϕ (*local variables*), **patom** ϕ **end** (*atomic execution*), $\phi_1 \parallel \phi_2$ (*interleaved execution*), and $p(e, V)$ (*call to procedure p with value parameters e and var parameters V*).

A temporal logic property for a parallel program is verified in KIV by symbolic execution with induction. Hence, there is a major difference between the temporal logic underlying KIV and the one discussed in the previous section, both in intention and in expressive power.

3   Application to Medical Knowledge

It is assumed that two types of knowledge are involved in detecting the violation of good medical practice:

- Knowledge concerning the (patho)physiological mechanisms underlying the disease, and the way treatment influences these mechanisms. The knowledge involved could be causal in nature, and is an example of *object-knowledge*.
- Knowledge concerning good practice in treatment selection; this is *meta-knowledge*.

Below we present some ideas on how such knowledge may be formalised using temporal logic (cf. [5] for earlier work).

We are interested in the prescription of drugs, taking into account their mode of action. Abstracting from the dynamics of their pharmacokinetics, this can be formalised in logic as follows:

$$(G\,d \wedge r) \to G(m_1 \wedge \cdots \wedge m_n)$$

where d is the name of a drug or possibly of a group of drugs indicated by a predicate symbol (e.g. $SU(x)$, where x is universally quantified and 'SU' stands for sulfonylurea drugs, such as Tolbutamid), r is a (possibly negative or empty) *requirement* for the drug to take effect, and m_k is a mode of action, such as decrease of release of glucose from the liver, which holds at all future times.

The modes of action m_k can be combined, together with an *intention* n (achieving normoglycaemia, i.e. normal blood glucose levels, for example), a particular patient *condition* c, and *requirements* r_j for the modes of action to be effective:

$$(Gm_{i_1} \wedge \cdots \wedge Gm_{i_m} \wedge r_1 \wedge \cdots \wedge r_p \wedge Hc) \to Gn$$

Good practice medicine can then be formalised as follows. Let $\mathcal{B}$ be background knowledge, $T \subseteq \{d_1, \ldots, d_p\}$ be a set of drugs, C a collection of patient conditions, R a collection of requirements, and N a collection of intentions which the physician has to achieve. A set of drugs T is a *treatment* according to the theory of abductive reasoning if [9,6]:

(M1) $\mathcal{B} \cup GT \cup C \cup R \nvDash \bot$ (the drugs do not have contradictory effects), and

(M2) $\mathcal{B} \cup GT \cup C \cup R \vDash N$ (the drugs handle all the patient problems intended to be managed)

If in addition to (1) and (2) condition

(M3) $O_\varphi(T)$ holds, where O_φ is a meta-predicate standing for an optimality criterion or combination of optimality criteria φ,

then the treatment is said to be *in accordance with good-practice medicine*. A typical example of this is subset minimality $O_{\subset}$:

$$O_{\subset}(T) \equiv \forall T' \subset T : T' \text{ is not a treatment according to (1) and (2)}$$

i.e. the minimum number of effective drugs are being prescribed. For example, if $\{d_1, d_2, d_3\}$ is a treatment that satisfies condition (3) in addition to (1) and (2), then the subsets $\{d_1, d_2\}$, $\{d_2, d_3\}$, $\{d_1\}$, and so on, do not satisfy conditions (1) and (2). In the context of abductive reasoning, subset minimality is often used in order to distinguish between various solutions; it is also referred to in literature as *Occam's razor*. Another definition of the meta-predicate O_φ is in terms of minimal cost O_c:

$$O_c(T) \equiv \forall T', \text{with } T' \text{ a treatment: } c(T') \geq c(T)$$

where $c(T) = \sum_{d \in T} cost(d)$; combining the two definitions also makes sense. For example, one could come up with a definition of $O_{\subset, c}$ that among two subset-minimal treatments selects the one that is the cheapest in financial or ethical sense.

4   Management of Diabetes Mellitus Type 2

4.1   Diabetes Type 2 Background Knowledge

It is well known that diabetes type 2 is a very complicated disease. Here we focus on the derangement of glucose metabolism in diabetic patients; however, even that is nontrivial. To support non-expert medical doctors in the management of this complicated disease in patients, access to a guideline is really essential.

One would expect that as this disorder is so complicated, the diabetes mellitus type 2 guideline is also complicated. This, however, is not the case, as may already be apparent from the guideline fragment shown in Fig. 1. This indicates that much of the knowledge concerning diabetes mellitus type 2 is missing from the guideline, and that without this background knowledge it will be impossible to spot the sort of flaws we are after. Hence, the conclusion is that a deeper biological analysis is required, the results of which are presented below.

The protein hormone insulin, which is produced by the *B cells* in the Langerhans islets of the *pancreas*, has the following major effects:

- it increases the uptake of glucose by the liver, where it is stored as glycogen, and inhibits the release of glucose from the liver;
- it increases the uptake of glucose by insulin-dependent tissues, such as muscle and adipose tissue.

At some stage in the natural history of diabetes mellitus type 2, the level of glucose in the blood is too high (hyperglycaemia) due to the decreased production of insulin by the B cells.

Treatment of diabetes type 2 consists of:

- Use of *sulfonylurea* (SU) drugs, such as tolbutamid. These drugs stimulate the B cells in producing more insulin, and if the cells are not completely exhausted, the hyperglycaemia can thus be reverted to normoglycaemia (normal blood glucose levels).
- Use of *biguanides* (BG), such as metformin. These drugs inhibit the release of glucose from the liver.
- Use of *α-glucosidase inhibitors*. These drugs inhibit (or delay) the absorption of glucose from the intestines. We omit considering these drugs in the following, as they are only prescribed when treatment side-effects occur.
- Injection of *insulin*. This is the ultimate, causal treatment.

The background knowledge concerning the (patho)physiology of the glucose metabolism as summarised above is formalised using temporal logic, and kept as simple as possible. The specification is denoted by $\mathcal{B}_{DM2}$:

(1) $G\,Drug(insulin) \rightarrow G\,(uptake(liver, glucose) = up \wedge$
$$uptake(peripheral\text{-}tissues, glucose) = up)$$

(2) $G(uptake(liver, glucose) = up \rightarrow release(liver, glucose) = down)$

(3) $(G\,Drug(SU) \wedge \neg capacity(B\text{-}cells, insulin) = exhausted) \rightarrow$
$$G\,secretion(B\text{-}cells, insulin) = up$$

(4) $G\,Drug(BG) \rightarrow G\,release(liver, glucose) = down$

(5) $(G\,secretion(B\text{-}cell, insulin) = up \wedge$
$capacity(B\text{-}cells, insulin) = subnormal \wedge$
$QI \leq 27 \wedge H\,Condition(hyperglycaemia))$
$\rightarrow G\,Condition(normoglycaemia)$

(6) $(G\,release(liver, glucose) = down \wedge$
$capacity(B\text{-}cells, insulin) = subnormal \wedge$
$QI > 27 \wedge H\,Condition(hyperglycaemia))$
$\rightarrow G\,Condition(normoglycaemia)$

(7) $((G\,release(liver, glucose) = down \vee$
$G\,uptake(peripheral\text{-}tissues, glucose) = up) \wedge$
$capacity(B\text{-}cells, insulin) = nearly\text{-}exhausted \wedge$
$G\,secretion(B\text{-}cells, insulin) = up \wedge$
$H\,Condition(hyperglycaemia))$
$\rightarrow G\,Condition(normoglycaemia)$

(8) $(G\,uptake(liver, glucose) = up \wedge$
$G\,uptake(peripheral\text{-}tissues, glucose) = up) \wedge$
$capacity(B\text{-}cells, insulin) = exhausted \wedge$
$H\,Condition(hyperglycaemia))$
$\rightarrow G(Condition(normoglycaemia) \vee Condition(hypoglycaemia))$

(9) (Condition($normoglycaemia$) $\oplus$ Condition($hypoglycaemia$)
$\oplus$ Condition($hyperglycaemia$))

where $\oplus$ stands for the exclusive OR. Note that when the B-cells are exhausted, increased uptake of glucose by the tissues may not only result in normoglycaemia but also in hypoglycaemia (something not mentioned in the guideline).

4.2   Quality Check

As insulin can only be administered by injection, in contrast to the other drugs which are normally taken orally, doctors prefer to delay prescribing insulin as long as possible. Thus, the treatment part of the diabetes type 2 guideline mentions that one should start with prescribing oral antidiabetics (SU or BG, cf. Fig. 1). Two of these can also be combined if taking only one has insufficient glucose-level lowering effect. If treatment is still unsatisfactory, the guideline suggests to: (1) either add insulin, or (2) stop with the oral antidiabetics entirely and to start with insulin.

The consequences of various treatment options were examined using the method introduced in Section 3. Hypothetical patients for whom it is the intention to reach a normal level of glucose in the blood (normoglycaemia) are considered, and treatment is selected according to the guideline fragments given in Fig. 1:

- Consider a patient with hyperglycaemia due to nearly exhausted B-cells:

$$\mathcal{B}_{\mathrm{DM2}} \cup \mathsf{G}\,T \cup \{\,capacity(\,B\text{-}cells,\,insulin) = nearly\text{-}exhausted\} \cup$$
$$\{\mathsf{HCondition}(hyperglycaemia)\} \vDash \mathsf{GCondition}(normoglycaemia)$$

  holds for $T = \{\mathrm{Drug(SU)}, \mathrm{Drug(BG)}\}$, which also satisfies the minimality condition $O_{\subset}(T)$.
- Prescription of treatment $T = \{\mathrm{Drug(SU)}, \mathrm{Drug(BG)}, \mathrm{Drug(insulin)}\}$ for a patient with exhausted B-cells, as is suggested by the guideline, yields:

$$\mathcal{B}_{\mathrm{DM2}} \cup \mathsf{G}\,T \cup \{\,capacity(\,B\text{-}cells,\,insulin) = exhausted\} \cup$$
$$\{\mathsf{HCondition}(hyperglycaemia)\} \vDash$$
$$\mathsf{G}(\mathrm{Condition}(normoglycaemia) \vee \mathrm{Condition}(hypoglycaemia))$$

In the last case, it appears that it is possible that a patient develops hypoglycaemia due to treatment; if this possibility is excluded, then the minimality condition $O_{\subset}(T)$, and also $O_{\subset,c}(T)$, do not hold since insulin by itself is enough to reach normoglycaemia. In either case, good practice medicine is violated, which is to prescribe as few drugs as possible, taking into account costs and side-effects of drugs. Here, three drugs are prescribed whereas only two should have been prescribed (BG and insulin, assuming that insulin alone is too costly), and the possible occurrence of hypoglycaemia should have been prevented.

5 Quality Checking Using Symbolic Execution with Induction

In the previous section we have seen that temporal logic can be used to formally check a medical guideline, but so far only from a theoretical point of view. Here we will study how such proofs can be constructed semi-automatically in terms of symbolic execution with induction using the theorem prover KIV.

5.1 Translation to KIV

In this paper we will only discuss the translation of the constructs that were employed in the formalisation in the previous section. Firstly, the universal quantification of the axioms over all points in time is made explicit. Secondly, the modal operators have to be translated. The only modal operators that were used were G and H. The operator G is semantically equivalent to KIV's □ operator. However, KIV does not support past-time operators, but as Gabbay et al. have shown [4], it is possible to translate any temporal formula with past-time operators to an equivalent temporal formula with only future-time operators that includes 'until'. This implies that after translation it is possible, at least in principle, to verify the temporal formulas introduced in sections 3 and 4. Axioms hold over all points in time of which the the ones with past-time formulas are of the following fixed form (see section 3):

$$(\varphi \land \mathsf{H}\,\mathrm{Condition}(hyperglycaemia)) \to \psi$$

We can rewrite this semantically and obtain a pure future-time formula, i.e. a formula with only future-time operators, as follows:

$$
\begin{aligned}
&\forall t : t \vDash (\varphi \land \mathsf{H}\,\mathrm{Condition}(hyperglycaemia)) \to \psi \\
\Leftrightarrow\ &\forall t : t \vDash (\varphi \to \psi) \lor \neg\,\mathsf{H}\,\mathrm{Condition}(hyperglycaemia)) \\
\Leftrightarrow\ &\forall t : t \vDash \varphi \to \psi \text{ or } t \nvDash \mathsf{H}\,\mathrm{Condition}(hyperglycaemia)) \\
\Leftrightarrow\ &\forall t : t \vDash \varphi \to \psi \text{ or } \neg \forall t' < t : t' \vDash \mathrm{Condition}(hyperglycaemia) \\
\Leftrightarrow\ &\neg \exists t : t \vDash \neg(\varphi \to \psi) \text{ and } \forall t' < t : t' \vDash \mathrm{Condition}(hyperglycaemia) \\
\Leftrightarrow\ &\neg\,(\mathrm{Condition}(hyperglycaemia) \text{ until } \neg\,(\phi \to \psi))
\end{aligned}
$$

5.2 Specification in KIV

In KIV datatypes are expressed in a many-sorted algebra with possibilities for parameterisation, allowing the creation of specific sorts by defining constraints on the parameters. The sorts with associated data elements required to create a specification of the domain of diabetes mellitus type 2 are listed in Table 3.

In KIV, functions and predicates are static, i.e. they do not change over time. Therefore, for the formalisation in KIV functions and predicates were mapped to dynamic variables. For example, *secretion(B-cells, insulin)* was mapped to a dynamic variable named `BsecretionI`. Since variables in axioms of algebraic specifications are universally quantified, a procedure with name 'patient' was used to bind these variables. This gives each relevant variable a context and prohibits instantiations of axioms with variables that have different names.

Table 3. Data specifications.

Specification	Data elements
capacity	exhausted, nearly-exhausted, subnormal
condition	hyperglycaemia, hypoglycaemia, normoglycaemia
updown	up, down
drug	SU, BG, glucosidase, insulin
setdrugs	set of elements of sort drug
setsetdrugs	set of elements of sort setdrugs

The axioms (3), (4) and (7) were selected and translated to KIV's syntax as indicated in Section 5.1. In addition, a number of variables were primed to deal with the consistency condition mentioned in Section 3, as will be discussed in Section 5.4. This yielded the following three sequents, denoted by $\mathcal{A}$:

[patient(; Drugs, Condition, UptakeLG, UptakePG, ReleaseLG
  BcapacityI, BsecretionI, QI)] ⊢
□ ((($\Box$ SU ∈ Drugs) ∧ BcapacityI ≠ exhausted) → □ BsecretionI′ = up);

[patient(; Drugs, Condition, UptakeLG, UptakePG, ReleaseLG
  BcapacityI, BsecretionI, QI)] ⊢
□ (($\Box$ BG ∈ Drugs) → ($\Box$ ReleaseLG′ = down));

[patient(; Drugs, Condition, UptakeLG, UptakePG, ReleaseLG
  BcapacityI, BsecretionI, QI)] ⊢
¬(Condition = hyperglycaemia until
  ¬(((($\Box$ ReleaseLG′ = down) ∨ ($\Box$ UptakePG = up))
    ∧(BcapacityI = nearly-exhausted) ∧ $\Box$ BsecretionI′ = up)
    → ($\Box$ Condition′ = normoglycaemia)));

Now define $\mathcal{B}'_{\mathrm{DM2}}$ as the conjunction of the right-hand-sides of $\mathcal{A}$. We will show how the meta-level properties follow from these right-hand-sides. The procedure patient only acts as a placeholder.

5.3 Proof

Again, consider a patient with hyperglycaemia due to nearly exhausted B-cells and $T = \{\mathrm{Drug(SU)}, \mathrm{Drug(BG)}\}$. The following sequent, which corresponds to condition M2 from section 3, was proven by KIV in about 50 steps:

[patient(; Drugs, Condition, UptakeLG, UptakePG, ReleaseLG
  BcapacityI, BsecretionI, QI)]
⊢ ¬(Condition = hyperglycaemia until
    ¬((($\Box$ Drug = {SU, BG}) ∧ BcapacityI = nearly-exhausted)
      → ($\Box$ Condition′ = normoglycaemia)));

The proof relies on the fact that the axioms can be inserted with the appropriate (program-)variables, after which the patient procedure can be removed from the sequent and the real work starts. Hence, the consequent of the sequent is deduced from the axioms $\mathcal{B}'_{\mathrm{DM2}}$. This yields:

$\mathcal{B}'_{\text{DM2}} \vdash \neg(\texttt{Condition} = \texttt{hyperglycaemia until}$
$\qquad \neg(((\Box \, \texttt{Drug} = \{\texttt{SU}, \texttt{BG}\}) \wedge \texttt{BcapacityI} = \texttt{nearly-exhausted})$
$\qquad \rightarrow (\Box \, \texttt{Condition}' = \texttt{normoglycaemia})));$

An outline of this proof follows. The proof obligation $\Gamma \vdash \Delta$, $\neg(\varphi \textbf{ until } \psi)$ is equivalent to Γ, $\varphi \textbf{ until } \psi \vdash \Delta$. The sequent is proved by induction over the number of steps it takes to satisfy ψ. For this, introduce a fresh dynamic variable N and generalise the sequent to $(N = N'' + 1 \wedge \phi) \textbf{ until } \psi$, $\Gamma \vdash \Delta$. The equation $N = N'' + 1$ ensures that N decreases in each step. Now, we can perform induction with induction term N which yields

$$(N = N'' + 1 \wedge \phi) \textbf{ until } \psi, \ \Gamma, \ N = n, \ \Box(N < n \rightarrow \mathsf{IndHyp}) \vdash \Delta$$

where $\mathsf{IndHyp} = ((N = N'' + 1 \wedge \phi) \textbf{ until } \psi) \wedge \bigwedge \Gamma \rightarrow \bigvee \Delta$ and n is a new static variable. We move to the next state by symbolically executing the temporal formulae. For example,

$$\phi \textbf{ until } \psi \Leftrightarrow \psi \vee (\phi \wedge \circ(\phi \textbf{ until } \psi))$$

is used to execute the **until** operator. In this case, the induction hypothesis can be applied in all possible successive states.

5.4   Disproofs

The final part of this section we will show disproofs of properties that do not follow from $\mathcal{B}'_{\text{DM2}}$ by using program verification techniques. In the previous section we reasoned with the given axioms $\mathcal{A}$, but here we use a more extensive implementation of the **patient** procedure as shown in Fig. 5.4, which not only binds variables, but implements part of the therapeutic reasoning.

Now define the theory

$$M = \{[\texttt{patient}(\dots)]\} \cup \bigcup_{x \neq \textbf{Drugs}} \{\Box \, x' = x''\}$$

where the last term denotes that variables, except for **Drugs**, are not altered by the environment, but only by the program itself. In about 400 steps using KIV it was proved that $M \vdash \mathcal{B}'_{\text{DM2}}$, which implies $M \vDash \mathcal{B}'_{\text{DM2}}$ assuming KIV is sound. From this and the fact that M is consistent (since a program is consistent and the environment is not altered), we have shown that $\mathcal{B}'_{\text{DM2}} \nvDash \bot$ and therefore condition M1. The number of steps shows that this proof was significantly harder. The reason is that in many cases an invariant could only be defined after an initial symbolic execution. This caused an explosion of states that had to be considered. Furthermore, the invariants that had to be formulated were less straightforward.

Now showing that this set of drugs is a minimal treatment (condition M3), as discussed in Section 4, we construct for all $T' \in \wp\{\texttt{SU}, \texttt{BG}\}$, $T' \neq \{\texttt{SU}, \texttt{BG}\}$:

$M_{T'} = M \cup \{\Box \, \texttt{Drugs}' = \texttt{Drugs}'', \texttt{Condition} = \texttt{hyperglycaemia},$
$\qquad \texttt{BsecretionI} = \texttt{down}, \texttt{BcapacityI} = \texttt{nearly-exhausted},$
$\qquad \texttt{ReleaseLG} = \texttt{up}, \texttt{UptakePG} = \texttt{down}, \texttt{Drugs} = T'\}$

```
patient(var Drugs, Condition, UptakeLG, UptakePG,
          ReleaseLG, BcapacityI, BsecretionI, QI)

begin
  var oncebcapi = false, hchyper = true, nownormal = false in
    while true do
      patom
        if SU ∈ Drugs ∧ (BcapacityI ≠ exhausted ∨ oncebcapi) then
        begin
          BsecretionI := up;
          oncebcapi   := true
        end;
        if BG ∈ Drugs then ReleaseLG := down;
        if (ReleaseLG = down ∨ UptakePG = up) ∧ BsecretionI = up ∧
            ((Bcapacity = nearly-exhausted ∧ hchyper) ∨ nownormal) then
        begin
          nownormal := true;
          hchyper   := false;
          Condition := normoglycaemia
        end
      end
end
```

Fig. 2. Declaration of the patient procedure.

Again, $M_{T'}$ is consistent. It was proved in about 25 steps with KIV that:

$$M_{T'} \vdash (\text{Condition} = \text{hyperglycaemia until}$$
$$\neg(((\Box\, \text{Drugs} = T') \land \text{BcapacityI} = \text{nearly-exhausted})$$
$$\rightarrow (\Box\, \text{Condition}' = \text{normoglycaemia})));$$

Because of monotony of temporal logic and $M \vDash \mathcal{B}'_{\text{DM2}}$, we have $M_{T'} \vDash \mathcal{B}'_{\text{DM2}}$. Since $M_{T'}$ is consistent, we can conclude:

$$\mathcal{B}'_{\text{DM2}} \nvDash \neg(\text{Condition} = \text{hyperglycaemia until}$$
$$\neg(((\Box\, \text{Drugs} = T') \land \text{BcapacityI} = \text{nearly-exhausted})$$
$$\rightarrow (\Box\, \text{Condition}' = \text{normoglycaemia})));$$

Hence, $T = \{\text{Drug(SU)}, \text{Drug(BG)}\}$ is a minimal treatment. As one might expect, it shows that after the construction of the appropriate countermodel, disproofs are fairly easy.

6   Discussion

The quality of guideline design is for the largest part based on its compliance with specific treatment aims and global requirements. To this purpose, use was made of the theory of abductive, diagnostic reasoning, i.e. we proposed to diagnose potential problems with a guideline using logical abduction [6,9]. This is a meta-level characterisation of the quality of a medical guideline. What was diagnosed were problems in the relationship between medical knowledge, suggested treatment actions in the guideline text and treatment effects; this is different from traditional abductive diagnosis, where observed findings are explained in terms of diagnostic hypotheses. This method allows us to examine fragments of a guideline and to prove properties of those fragments.

In this paper, we have made use of the interactive theorem prover KIV [1] to actually quality check a medical guideline using the theory of quality of guidelines developed previously [7]. This complements the earlier work on object-level verification of medical guidelines using KIV [8]. About half of the steps that were needed to complete the proofs had to be done manually. Fortunately, most of the interactive steps were rather straightforward. We are confident that with more specific heuristics, the proposed meta-level approach can be almost fully automated in KIV.

References

1. Balser M, Reif W, Schellhorn G, and Stenzel K. KIV 3.0 for provably correct systems. In: Current Trends in Applied Formal Methods, Lecture Notes in Computer Science 1641, Springer-Verlag, Berlin, 1999.
2. Balser M, Duelli C, Reif W, and Schellhorn G. Verifying Concurrent Systems with Symbolic Execution. Journal of Logic and Computation 2002; 12(4): 549–560.
3. Gabbay DM. The declarative past and imperative future: executable temporal logic for interactive systems. In: H. Barringer (ed.). Temporal Logic in Specification, Lecture Notes in Computer Science 398, Springer-Verlag, Berlin, 1989. pp. 409–448.
4. Gabbay D, Pnueli A, Shelah S, and Stavi J. The Temporal Analysis of Fairness. Pros. 7th ACM Syrup. on Principles of Programming Languages, Las Vegas, 1980, 163–173.
5. Lucas PJF. Logic engineering in medicine. The Knowledge Engineering Review 1995; 10(2): 153–179.
6. Lucas PJF. Symbolic diagnosis and its formalisation. The Knowledge Engineering Review 1997; 12(2): 109–146.
7. Lucas PJF. Quality checking of medical guidelines through logical abduction. In: F. Coenen, A. Preece, A.L. Mackintosh (eds.). Proceedings of AI-2003 (Research and Developments in Intelligent Systems XX), Springer, London, pp. 309–321, 2003.
8. Marcos M, Balser M, Ten Teije A, and Van Harmelen F. From informal knowledge to formal logic: a realistic case study in medical protocols. Proceedings of the 12th EKAW-2002, 2002.
9. Poole D. A methodology for using a default and abductive reasoning system. International Journal of Intelligent Systems 1990, 5(5), 521–548.
10. Shahar Y, Miksch S, and Johnson P. The Asgaard project: a task-specific framework for the application and critiquing of time-oriented clinical guidelines. Artificial Intelligence in Medicine 1998; 14: 29–51.
11. Turner R. Logics for Artificial Intelligence. Ellis Horwood, Chichester, 1985.
12. Woolf SH. Evidence-based medicine and practice guidelines: an overview. Cancer Control 2000; 7(4): 362–367.

Towards a Logical Analysis of Biochemical Pathways

Patrick Doherty, Steve Kertes, Martin Magnusson, and Andrzej Szalas

Department of Computer and Information Science, SE-581 83 Linköping, Sweden,
{patdo,g-steke,marma,andsz}@ida.liu.se

Abstract. Biochemical pathways or networks are generic representations used to model many different types of complex functional and physical interactions in biological systems. Models based on experimental results are often incomplete, e.g., reactions may be missing and only some products are observed. In such cases, one would like to reason about incomplete network representations and propose candidate hypotheses, which when represented as additional reactions, substrates, products, would complete the network and provide causal explanations for the existing observations.

In this paper, we provide a logical model of biochemical pathways and show how abductive hypothesis generation may be used to provide additional information about incomplete pathways. Hypothesis generation is achieved using weakest and strongest necessary conditions which represent these incomplete biochemical pathways and explain observations about the functional and physical interactions being modeled. The techniques are demonstrated using metabolism and molecular synthesis examples.

Keywords: Abduction, biochemical pathways, hypotheses generation, weakest sufficient and strongest necessary conditions.

1 Introduction

Biochemical pathways or networks are generic representations used to model many different types of complex functional and physical interactions in biological systems. For example, metabolism can be viewed and modeled in terms of complex networks of chemical reactions catalyzed by enzymes and consisting of reactive chains of substrates and products (see, e.g., [1,2]).

Often these models are incomplete. For example, reactions may be missing and only some products are observed. In such cases, one would like to reason about incomplete network representations and propose candidate hypotheses, which when represented as additional reactions, substrates, products, or constraints on such, would complete the network and provide causal explanations for the existing observations.

In this paper, we provide a logical model of biochemical pathways (Section 2) and show how abductive hypothesis generation may be used to provide additional information about incomplete pathways. Hypothesis generation is achieved using weakest and strongest necessary conditions for restricted fragments of 1st-order theories which represent these incomplete biochemical pathways and explain observations about the functional and physical interactions being modeled (see Section 3). Quantifier elimination techniques (see [3,4,5]) are used to automatically generate these hypotheses, using the technique described in [6].

J.J. Alferes and J. Leite (Eds.): JELIA 2004, LNAI 3229, pp. 667–679, 2004.

Part of the modeling process includes the use of approximate databases [7], where when queries are viewed as inferences, questions can be asked about the generated hypotheses (see Section 4).

These techniques are demonstrated in Section 5, using metabolism and molecular synthesis examples.

Comparing to other approaches, e.g., that presented in [8,9], we focus on modeling reactions in the classical first-order logic and then on hypotheses generation, using approximations provided by strongest necessary and weakest sufficient conditions, and on evaluation of queries using approximate databases, where queries are tractable.

This paper is an extended version of extended abstract [10].

2   Data Models for the Analysis of Biochemical Pathways

2.1   Preliminaries

The analysis of biochemical pathways has been considered in numerous papers (see, e,g, [1,2]). In this paper, a bipartite graph representation of chemical reactions will be used (see, e.g., [2]).

It is assumed that any reaction is specified by:

$$n : c_1 + \ldots + c_k \xrightarrow{\alpha(n)} c'_1 + \ldots + c'_l,$$

where:

- n is a label (name) of the reaction
- $c_1, \ldots, c_k$ are reactants (inputs for n)
- $c'_1, \ldots, c'_l$ are products of n and $\alpha(n)$ is a formula that specifies additional conditions necessary for the reaction, such as temperature, pressure, presence of catalyzers, etc.

In a bipartite graph there are two types of nodes: *compound nodes* (depicted by circles) and *reaction nodes* (depicted by rectangles). An edge from a compound node to a reaction node denotes a substrate. An edge from a reaction node to a compound node denotes a product of the reaction. We additionally allow conditions placed in the boxes, if these are specified for particular reactions (see Figure 1).

2.2   Representing Reactions in Logic

The language. In the paper, the classical first-order logic is used for specifying reactions.

Reaction nodes will be represented explicitly, while information about available compounds will be given via a suitable relation. Consequently, it is assumed that the following symbols are available:

1. constants and variables:
   - constants representing (naming) reactions (denoted by n, n'), compounds (denoted by $c, c', h2o, co2$ etc.), and reaction nodes (denoted by r, r')
   - variables representing reactions, denoted by N, N', compounds (C, C'), and reaction nodes (R, R');

   for constants and variables we also use indices, when necessary

$n_1 : c_1 + c_2 \xrightarrow{\alpha} c_3$

$n_2 : c_3 \rightarrow c_4$

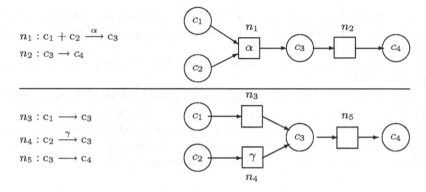

$n_3 : c_1 \longrightarrow c_3$

$n_4 : c_2 \xrightarrow{\gamma} c_3$

$n_5 : c_3 \longrightarrow c_4$

Fig. 1. Examples of bipartite graphs.

2. relation symbols reflecting static information:
    - $in(C, N)$ meaning that compound C is needed for reaction N
    - $out(N, C)$ meaning that compound C is a product of reaction N
3. relation symbols reflecting dynamic information:
    - $prec(R, R')$ meaning that reaction node R precedes reaction node R'
    - $notExcl(R, R')$ meaning that precedence $prec(R, R')$ is not excluded[1]
    - $chain(R, R')$ meaning that there is a chain of reactions $R, R_1, R_2, \ldots, R_k, R'$ such that $prec(R, R_1), prec(R_1, R_2), \ldots, prec(R_{k-1}, R_k), prec(R_k, R')$
    - $react(N, R)$ meaning that reaction N actually happened in reaction node R
    - $av(C, R)$ meaning that compound C is available for reaction represented by reaction node R.

Specifying Reactions in Logic. Let e, t be any expressions and s any subexpression of e. By $e(s/t)$ we shall mean the expression obtained from e by substituting each occurrence of s by t.

It is assumed that any formula is implicitly universally quantified over all its variables that are not bound by a quantifier.

Any reaction of the form

$$n : c_1 + \ldots + c_k \xrightarrow{\alpha(n)} c_1' + \ldots + c_l', \tag{1}$$

is translated into the formula $react(n, R)$, where the following integrity constraints are assumed:

- static information about reaction n:

$$in(c_1, n) \wedge \ldots \wedge in(c_k, n) \wedge$$
$$out(n, c_1') \wedge \ldots \wedge out(n, c_l')$$

---

[1] $notExcl(R, R')$ is useful for constraining the hypothesis generation process.

– linking nodes in graphs with reactions

$$react(n, R) \rightarrow \qquad\qquad\qquad\qquad\qquad\qquad (2)$$
$$\alpha(n/R) \wedge$$
$$\forall C. \{in(C, n) \rightarrow av(C, R)\} \wedge$$
$$\forall R', C'. \{[prec(R, R') \wedge out(n, C')] \rightarrow av(C', R')\}.$$

Observe that the above formula can be more efficiently expressed according to the schema:

$$react(n, R) \rightarrow \qquad\qquad\qquad\qquad\qquad\qquad (3)$$
$$\alpha(n/R) \wedge$$
$$av(c_1, R) \wedge \ldots \wedge av(c_k, R) \wedge$$
$$\forall R'. \{prec(R, R') \rightarrow av(c_1', R')\} \wedge$$
$$\ldots \wedge$$
$$\forall R'. \{prec(R, R') \rightarrow av(c_l', R')\}.$$

However, in order to link to an existing biochemical database one would most probably have to use the previous version with suitable syntactic adjustments.

3 Strongest Necessary and Weakest Sufficient Conditions

3.1 Preliminaries

The strongest necessary and weakest sufficient conditions, as understood in this paper and defined below, have been introduced in [11] and further developed in [6]. Observe that the weakest sufficient condition corresponds to the weakest abduction expressed in terms of a chosen vocabulary.

Definition 3.1. *By a necessary condition of a formula α on the set of relation symbols P under theory T we shall understand any formula ϕ containing only symbols in P such that $T \models \alpha \rightarrow \phi$. It is the* strongest necessary condition, *denoted by* $\mathrm{SNC}(\alpha; T; P)$ *if, additionally, for any necessary condition ψ of α on P under T, $T \models \phi \rightarrow \psi$ holds.* □

Definition 3.2. *By a sufficient condition of a formula α on the set of relation symbols P under theory T we shall understand any formula ϕ containing only symbols in P such that $T \models \phi \rightarrow \alpha$. It is the* weakest sufficient condition, *denoted by* $\mathrm{WSC}(\alpha; T; P)$ *if, additionally, for any sufficient condition ψ of α on P under T, $T \models \psi \rightarrow \phi$ holds.* □

The set P in the definitions for wsc's and snc's is referred to as the *target language*. The following lemma has been proven in [6].

Lemma 3.3. *For any formula α, any set of relation symbols P and theory T such that the set of free variables of T is disjoint with the set of free variables of α:*

$$\mathrm{SNC}(\alpha; T; P) \equiv \exists \bar{\Phi}. [T \wedge \alpha] \qquad\qquad\qquad (4)$$
$$\mathrm{WSC}(\alpha; T; P) \equiv \forall \bar{\Phi}. [T \rightarrow \alpha], \qquad\qquad\qquad (5)$$

where $\bar{\Phi}$ consists of all relation symbols appearing in T and α but not in P. □

The above characterizations are second-order. However, for a large class of formulas, one can obtain logically equivalent first-order formulas[2] (see, e.g., [3,4]) or fixpoint formulas[3] (see, e.g., [5]) by applying techniques for eliminating second-order quantifiers. The algorithms given in [3,4] are implemented and are available online. The algorithm based on [5] is implemented, as described in Section 4.

3.2   Hypotheses Generation Using Snc's and Wsc's

Snc's and Wsc's provide a powerful means of generating hypotheses using abduction. Suppose one is given a (incomplete) specification of a set of interacting reactions of the form shown in equation (1). We would use this set of formulas as the background theory T. Suppose additionally, that a number of observations are made referring to reactions known to have occurred, or compounds known to be available for participation in a reaction, etc. Let α denote the formula representing these observations. Generally, it will not be the case that $T \models \alpha$ because T only provides an incomplete specification of the reactions.

We would like to generate a formula (candidate hypotheses) ϕ in a restricted subset of the language of reactions P such that ϕ together with the background theory T does entail the observations α. It is important that we do not over commit otherwise we could just as easily choose α itself as the hypothesis which wouldn't do much good. In fact, the $\mathrm{Wsc}(\alpha; T; P)$ does just the right thing since we know that $T \wedge \mathrm{Wsc}(\alpha; T; P) \models \alpha$ and it is the weakest such formula by definition.

$\mathrm{Wsc}(\alpha; T; P)$ actually represents alternative hypotheses for explaining α. If it is put in disjunctive normal form, each of the disjuncts makes $\mathrm{Wsc}(\alpha; T; P)$ true and represents a weakest hypothesis. To reason about what each candidate hypothesis might imply in terms of completing the reaction representation, one would simply add both the background theory T and the candidate hypothesis α' to the approximate database described in Section 4 and query the database as desired.

Technically, if the wsc/sns in question can be expressed using the classical first-order logic,[4] one would then perform the following steps:

1. replace any quantifier $\forall X. \alpha(X)$ by the conjunction $\alpha(X/a_1) \wedge \ldots \wedge \alpha(X/a_k)$, where $a_1, \ldots, a_k$ are all constants occurring in the database of the type compatible with the type of X
2. replace any quantifier $\exists X. \alpha(X)$ by the disjunction $\alpha(X/a_1) \vee \ldots \vee \alpha(X/a_k)$, where $a_1, \ldots, a_k$ are as above
3. transform the resulting formula into prenex normal for with the quantifier-free part transformed into the disjunctive normal form.

Observe that two first steps are of linear complexity wrt size of the database. However, the third step might be of exponential complexity wrt the size of the formula obtained

---

[2] The class of formulas includes, e.g., all non-recursive semi-Horn formulas - see, e.g., [12].

[3] Fixpoint formulas are obtained for semi-Horn formulas, a formalism substantially more expressive than the Horn fragment of first-order logic.

[4] E.g., second-order quantifier elimination results in a first-order formula.

in previous steps. One can, however, generate suitable disjuncts one at a time, not all of them at once.

Each disjunct is a conjunction of literals and represents a possible set of facts making a given snc or wsc true. It could then be used to update the database containing the background theory. One could then query database, using the language outlined in Section 4 in order to verify certain properties of the generated hypotheses (e.g., whether the obtained chain of reactions is cycle-free or is acceptable by experts).

In the case when the wsc and snc are fixpoint formulas, one can use the standard characterization of fixpoints as disjunctions/conjunctions of iterations of fixpoint operators. However, the complexity of the resulting formula might in this case be unacceptable.

3.3 Applications of Snc's and Wsc's in the Analysis of Biochemical Pathways

Observe that:

- wsc corresponds to a weakest abduction expressed in a given target language. For example, consider

  $$\text{Wsc}(av(fin, so3); Th; L),$$

  where Th is the theory expressing properties of given reactions, as constructed in Section 2.2. Then
  - if the target language L consists of av only, the resulting wsc expresses what compounds availability makes the required output of reaction node fin feasible
  - if the target language consists of $react$, then the resulting wsc expresses reactions necessary to make the required output of fin feasible
- snc allows to infer facts from a negative information. In fact, snc expresses what would be possible under a given set of hypotheses. For example, if a certain side product has not been observed, a reaction can be excluded from the set of hypotheses.

4 Approximate Databases

4.1 Introduction

An approximate database is based on the standard concept of a deductive database but with a number of modifications that enable reasoning about incomplete and approximate knowledge.

The basis for the representation of data are approximate relations. An approximate relation, say R, is given by:

- a *lower approximation*, denoted by R_+, containing objects known to satisfy the relation
- an *upper approximation*, denoted by $R_\oplus$, containing objects that may satisfy the relation.

We also allow in the language R_-, consisting of tuples which are known not to satisfy R, $R_\ominus$ consisting of tuples that may not satisfy R and $R_\pm$, called the *boundary of* R, consisting of tuples for which it is unknown whether they satisfy R. Of course, $R_\oplus = R_+ \cup R_\pm$ and $R_\ominus = R_- \cup R_\pm$.

Queries to the database are approximate formulas, where all relations are approximate. In the case of a query containing free variables, the result of the query is a list of substitutions for those variables that satisfy the query. In the case of a query without free variables, the result is true, false or unknown.

A prototype implementation of the approximate database management system that functions as a front-end to the PostgreSQL database has been developed. The architecture of implemented layers is depicted in Figure 2.

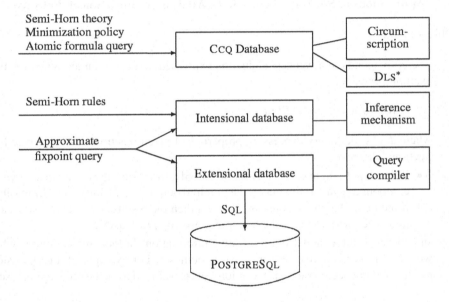

Fig. 2. The architecture of the knowledge database.

An extensional database layer (EDB) defines object constants and relations, including information about argument types, and explicitly stores positive (R_+) and negative (R_-) information for each relation R. The Boundaries of any approximate relation can be generated by combining its explicit information with all possible tuples of constants constrained by the argument types. A query compilation mechanism translates any approximate fixpoint formula into standard SQL and returns bindings of free variables using results from the PostgreSQL database.

An intensional database layer (IDB) contains deductive rules in the form of approximate formula implications and infers new positive or negative information by applying the inference mechanism on data in the EDB.

Finally, a contextually closed query layer (the CCQ layer) provides functionality for local closed world assumptions by circumscribing a definition of the query in the context of a minimization/variation policy (see, [7]). The circumscription generates a second order formula, which can often be reduced into a logically equivalent fixpoint formula that can be evaluated by the EDB. This is achieved through application of the DLS* algorithm (described, e.g., in [13]).

4.2 Using Approximate Databases for Representing Biochemical Pathways

Bipartite graphs describing chemical reactions can be represented and reasoned about using queries to an approximate database with the language presented in Section 4.1. As is often the case, the reaction graph may be incomplete, in which case querying may be insufficient to draw any conclusions at all. In this case we propose the application of Wsc's and Snc's in order to hypothesize additional reaction pathways before querying.

According to the definitions of Wsc's and Snc's they are equivalent to second order formulas. Using the DLS* algorithm, which is part of the CCQ layer, these can often be reduced into equivalent first order of fixpoint formulas.

When a hypothesis has been generated, as described in Section 3.2, it can be added to the database together with the background theory and initial conditions regarding the availability of compounds. Any consequences of the hypothesis can then be investigated by querying the database.

For example one might want to find compounds that are available as a result of the reactions in the hypothesis by performing the query:

$$\exists N, R \, [react_+(N, R) \wedge out_+(N, C)].$$

The compound variable C is unbound and the query will return any compounds that resulted from any reaction that actually took place. If one of these compounds could not be found after performing the experiment, this might be a reason to exclude the hypothesis.

Consider now relations described in Section 2.2.

We assume that relations in and out are in the knowledge database or, alternatively, that the database contains definitions of reactions prepared according to schema (2) or (3) (see Section 2.2). In what follows we assume for simplicity that schema (3) is used whenever possible.

Relations $prec$, $chain$, $react$ and av are often known only partially on the basis of observations. In such a case, in order to find the missing information, we will project out those relation symbols using the methodology of approximations based on weakest sufficient and strongest necessary conditions (see Section 3). We will assume the following set of formulas, reflecting the partial knowledge:

– if it is known that $react(n, r)$ holds, where n and r are constants, and n is specified by (1), then one adds to the database formula

$$[N = n \wedge R = r] \to react_+(N, R)$$

– if $prec(r, r')$ is known, then one adds formula

$$[R = r \wedge R' = r'] \to prec_+(R, R'),$$

and similarly for $chain$

– if $av(c, r)$ is known, then one adds formula

$$[C = c \wedge R = r] \rightarrow av_+(C, R).$$

If some reaction nodes are missing then one has to make sure that database domain has some extra constants for such nodes. These constants can eventually be used in hypothesis generation (see Section 3.2).

One also adds the following formulas:

– sufficient condition for *prec*:

$$\exists C, N. [react_+(N, R) \wedge out_+(N, C) \wedge \qquad\qquad (6)$$
$$av_+(C, R') \wedge notExcl_\oplus(R, R')] \rightarrow prec_+(R, R')$$

– necessary condition for *prec*

$$prec_+(R, R') \rightarrow \qquad\qquad\qquad\qquad (7)$$
$$\exists C, N. [react_+(N, R) \wedge out_+(N, C) \wedge av_+(C, R')].$$

Remark 4.1. All the formulas considered so far allow one to compute weakest sufficient and strongest necessary conditions as classical first order formulas, provided that additional conditions expressed by formula α in all reactions (see Equation (1)) are non-recursive.   □

The following formulas are sometimes[5] required, but should be avoided whenever possible, since computing weakest sufficient and strongest necessary conditions in their presence results in fixpoint formulas which are much more complex to handle during the hypothesis generation stage.[6]

– definition of *chain*:

$$chain_+(R, R') \overset{\text{def}}{\equiv}$$
$$prec_+(R, R') \vee$$
$$\exists R_1. [prec_+(R, R_1) \wedge chain_+(R_1, R')].$$

– no cycles:
$$\forall R. [\neg chain_+(R, R)] \text{ (or, alternatively, } \forall R. [chain_\ominus(R, R)]).$$

One can also describe the availability of certain compounds and some other conditions. For example, $\forall R. [av_+(h2so4, R)]$ specifies that $H2SO4$ is known to be available for any reaction node.

---

[5] When the reasoning concerns chains of reactions of not bounded a priori length .

[6] In fact, from the point of view of complexity, it is better to use these formulas as integrity constraints to rule out certain hypotheses (see discussion in Section 3.2).

5 Examples

5.1 A Metabolism Example

Consider a fragment of the aromatic amino acid pathway of yeast, shown in Figure 3 (this is a fragment of a larger structure used in [1]). Rectangles are labelled with enzyme names, meaning that a respective enzyme is to be available for reaction, i.e., that av holds. For example, $av(ydr127w, r)$ is necessary, when the label of r is "YDR127W".

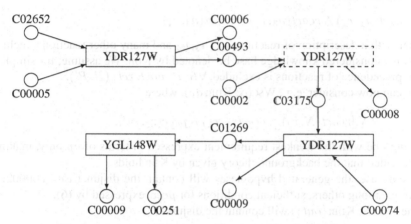

Fig. 3. A fragment of the aromatic amino acid pathway of yeast.

Figure 3 depicts the following reactions:

$$n_1 : C02652 + C00005 \overset{YDR127W}{\longrightarrow} C00006 + C00493$$
$$n_3 : C03175 + C00074 \overset{YDR127W}{\longrightarrow} C01269 + C00009$$
$$n_4 : C01269 \overset{YGL148W}{\longrightarrow} C00009 + C00251.$$

It is assumed that reaction

$$n_2 : C00493 + C00002 \overset{YDR127W}{\longrightarrow} C03175 + C00008$$

depicted by the dashed box is, in fact, missing.

The above set of reactions is expressed by formulas as defined in Section 2.2. For example, the first reaction is expressed by:

$$\begin{aligned}
react(n_1, R) &\rightarrow \\
&av(ydr127w, R) \wedge \\
&av(c02652, R) \wedge av(c00005, R) \wedge \\
&\forall R'. [prec(R, R') \rightarrow av(c00006, R')] \wedge \\
&\forall R'. [prec(R, R') \rightarrow av(c00493, R')].
\end{aligned}$$

The missing reaction is also present, among many other reactions, in the database, and is expressed by:

$$react(n_2, R) \rightarrow$$
$$av(ydr127w, R) \wedge$$
$$av(c00493, R) \wedge av(c00002, R) \wedge$$
$$\forall R'. [prec(R, R') \rightarrow av(c03175, R')] \wedge$$
$$\forall R'. [prec(R, R') \rightarrow av(c00008, R')].$$

We assume that the underlying database contains partial information about the observed chain of reactions:

$$react(n_1, r_1) \wedge react(n_3, r_3) \wedge react(n_4, r_4)$$

together with a description of reactions n_1, n_3, n_4 and many other reactions, including n_3. Let the considered knowledge base be denoted by KDB. We assume, for simplicity, that no precedence of reactions is excluded, $\forall R, R'. notExcl_\oplus (R, R')$.

We can now consider, e.g., $\text{WSC}(\alpha; \text{KDB}; av)$, where

$$\alpha \stackrel{\text{def}}{\equiv} \exists N. [react(N, r_2) \wedge prec(r_1, r_2) \wedge prec(r_2, r_3)],$$

providing one with the weakest requirement expressed in terms of av only, making α true, provided that the background theory given by KDB holds.

In our case, the generated hypotheses will contain the disjunct $av_+ (c00002, r_2)$, reflecting, among others, sufficient conditions for $prec$, expressed by (6).

The $\text{SNC}(\alpha; \text{KDB}; \{out\})$ will contain the disjunct

$$out_+ (N, c03175) \wedge out_+ (N, c00008),$$

reflecting, among others, necessary conditions for $prec$, expressed by (7). If one of the compounds $c03175, c00008$ has not been observed during the reaction chain, one can reject the hypothesis that reaction N in node r_2 was n_2.

5.2   Synthesis of 3-bromo-4propylphenol from Benzene

This example shows how to express additional conditions on reactions.

Consider the following reactions for synthesis of 3-bromo-4propylphenol from benzene (see [14]):[7]

n_1: C6H6 + C3H5OCl + AlCl3 $\longrightarrow$ C9H10O
n_2: C9H10O + Zn(H5) + HCl $\longrightarrow$ C8H12
n_3: C9H12 + HNO3 + H2SO4 $\longrightarrow$ C9H11NO2
n_4: C9H11NO2 + Br2 + FeBr3 $\longrightarrow$ C9H10NO2Br
n_5: C9H10NO2Br + Sn + HCl $\longrightarrow$ C9H12NBr
n_6: C9H12NBr + NaNO2 + H2SO4 + H2O $\xrightarrow{0^\circ C + heat}$ C9H11OBr

In order to express the condition "$0^\circ C$ + heat", one has to extend the language by adding the following relations:

---

[7] The condition in reaction n_6 is intended to mean that the reaction has to start at a temperature of $0^\circ C$ and then the reactants are to be heated.

- $temp(R, T)$ meaning that the temperature in node R is initially T
- $heat(R)$ meaning that compounds in node R are heated.

Now "0°C + heat" is expressed by $temp(R, 0) \land heat(R)$ and the reaction n_6 is expressed by:

$$react(n_6, R) \rightarrow$$
$$temp(R, 0) \land heat(R) \land$$
$$av(c9h12nbr, R) \land av(nano2, R) \land$$
$$av(h2so4, R) \land av(h2o, R) \land$$
$$\forall R'. [prec(R, R') \rightarrow av(c9h11obr, R')].$$

The hypotheses generated here might also have to be expressed in terms of a richer language. For example, the weakest sufficient condition for reaction n_6 to react in node r would involve $temp(r, 0) \land heat(R)$. In fact, no condition expressed in terms of relations introduced in Section 2.2 would make n_6 feasible, since none of them implies $temp(r, 0)$ or $heat(R)$.

6   Conclusions

In the paper we have presented a logical model of biochemical pathways and have shown how abductive hypothesis generation may be used to provide additional information about incomplete pathways. Hypothesis generation is achieved using weakest and strongest necessary conditions which explain observations about the functional and physical interactions being modeled.

The language for expressing knowledge about biochemical pathways that permits second-order quantifier elimination is quite broad and includes semi-Horn formulas (see [12]), a formalism substantially more expressive than the Horn fragment of the first-order logic. However, if one uses non-recursive semi-Horn formulas, the resulting formalism is much more efficient.

One can extend the approach in various directions. In particular, one can model much more complicated conditions required for reactions as well as time dependencies.

The approximate database implementation as well as our earlier work on snc's and wsc's has been supported in part by the WITAS project grant under the Wallenberg Foundation, Sweden.

References

1. Bryant, C., Muggleton, S., Oliver, S., Kell, D., Reiser, P., King, R.: Combining inductive logic programming, active learning and robotics to discover the function of genes. Linkoping Electronic Articles in Computer and Information Science 6 (2001)
2. Deville, Y., Gilbert, D., van Helden, J., Wodak, S.: An overview of data models for the analysis of biochemical pathways. Briefings in Bioinformatics 4 (2003) 246–259
3. Doherty, P., Łukaszewicz, W., Szałas, A.: Computing circumscription revisited. Journal of Automated Reasoning 18 (1997) 297–336

4. Gabbay, D.M., Ohlbach, H.J.: Quantifier elimination in second-order predicate logic. In Nebel, B., Rich, C., Swartout, W., eds.: Principles of Knowledge Representation and Reasoning, KR 92. (1992) 425–435
5. Nonnengart, A., Szałas, A.: A fixpoint approach to second-order quantifier elimination with applications to correspondence theory. In Orłowska, E., ed.: Logic at Work: Essays Dedicated to the Memory of Helena Rasiowa, Springer Physica-Verlag (1998) 307–328
6. Doherty, P., Łukaszewicz, W., Szałas, A.: Computing strongest necessary and weakest sufficient conditions of first-order formulas. International Joint Conference on AI (IJCAI'2001) (2000) 145 – 151
7. Doherty, P., Kachniarz, J., Szałas, A.: Using contextually closed queries for local closed-world reasoning in rough knowledge databases. In Pal, S., Polkowski, L., Skowron, A., eds.: Rough-Neuro Computing: Techniques for Computing with Words. Cognitive Technologies, Springer–Verlag (2003) 219–250
8. Chabrier, N., Fages, F.: Symbolic model checking of biochemical networks. In: Proceedings of the First International Workshop on Computational Methods in Systems Biology CMSB'03. Volume 2602 of LNCS., Springer-Verlag (2004) 149–162
9. Chabrier-Rivier, N., Fages, F., Soliman, S.: The biochemical abstract machine BIOCHAM. In: Proceedings of the Second International Workshop on Computational Methods in Systems Biology CMSB'04. LNCS, Springer-Verlag (2004)
10. Doherty, P., Kertes, S., Magnusson, M., Szałas, A.: Towards a logical analysis of biochemical pathways (extended abstract). In: Proceedings of the European Conference on Artificial Intelligence ECAI'2004. (2004) to appear.
11. Lin, F.: On strongest necessary and weakest sufficient conditions. In Cohn, A., Giunchiglia, F., Selman, B., eds.: Principles of Knowledge Representation and Reasoning, KR'2000. (2000) 167–175
12. Doherty, P., Łukaszewicz, W., Szałas, A.: A reduction result for circumscribed semi-Horn formulas. Fundamenta Informaticae **28** (1996) 261–271
13. Doherty, P., Łukaszewicz, W., Szałas, A.: General domain circumscription and its effective reductions. Fundamenta Informaticae **36** (1998) 23–55
14. Pine, S., Hendrickson, J., Cram, D., Hammond, G.: Organic Chemistry. McGraw-Hill, Inc. (1980)

Abductive Logic Programming with CIFF: System Description

U. Endriss[1], P. Mancarella[2], F. Sadri[1], G. Terreni[2], and F. Toni[1,2]

[1] Department of Computing, Imperial College London
{ue,fs,ft}@doc.ic.ac.uk
[2] Dipartimento di Informatica, Università di Pisa
{paolo,terreni,toni}@di.unipi.it

1 Introduction

Abduction has long been recognised as a powerful mechanism for hypothetical reasoning in the presence of incomplete knowledge. Here, we discuss the implementation of a novel abductive proof procedure, which we call CIFF, as it extends the IFF proof procedure [7] by dealing with Constraints, as in constraint logic programming. The procedure also relaxes the strong allowedness restrictions on abductive logic programs imposed by IFF. The procedure is described in detail in [6]. It is currently employed to realise a number of reasoning tasks of KGP agents [8] within the platform for developing agents and agent applications PROSOCS [12]. These tasks include (partial) planning in a dynamic environment [9,5], reactivity to changes in the environment [5], temporal reasoning in the absence of complete information about the environment [2,1], communication and negotiation [11], and trust-mediated interaction [10]. Some details on an earlier version of the system and the planning application can be found in [5]. Although the implementation of CIFF that we describe here has been tested successfully within PROSOCS in a number of settings, this is an initial prototype and more research into proof strategies and heuristics as well as fine-tuning are required to achieve satisfactory runtimes for larger examples.

2 Abductive Logic Programming with CIFF

An *abductive logic program* is a triple $\langle P, I, A \rangle$, where P is a *normal logic program* (with constraints à-la CLP), I is a finite set of sentences in the language of P (called *integrity constraints*), and A is a set of *abducible* atoms in the language of P. A *query* Q is a conjunction of literals, possibly containing (implicitly existentially quantified) variables. An *abductive answer* to a query Q for a program $\langle P, I, A \rangle$, containing constraint predicates defined over a structure $\Re$, is a pair $\langle \Delta, \sigma \rangle$, where Δ is a set of ground abducible atoms and σ is a substitution for the variables in Q such that $P \cup \Delta\sigma \models_{\Re} I \wedge Q\sigma$. In our case, $\models_{\Re}$ represents entailment with respect to the *completion semantics* [4], extended à-la CLP to take the constraint structure into account.

J.J. Alferes and J. Leite (Eds.): JELIA 2004, LNAI 3229, pp. 680–684, 2004.
© Springer-Verlag Berlin Heidelberg 2004

Like IFF [7], CIFF uses an alternative representation of an abductive logic program $\langle P, I, A \rangle$, namely a pair $\langle Th, I \rangle$, where Th is a set of iff-definitions, $p(X_1, \ldots, X_k) \Leftrightarrow D_1 \vee \cdots \vee D_n$, obtained by *selectively completing* P [4,7] with respect to all predicates except *special* predicates (*true*, *false*, constraint and abducible predicates). CIFF deals with integrity constraints I which are implications: $L_1 \wedge \cdots \wedge L_m \Rightarrow A_1 \vee \cdots \vee A_n$, with L_i literals and A_j atoms. Any variables are implicitly universally quantified with scope the entire implication.

In CIFF, the search for abductive answers for queries Q amounts to constructing a proof tree, starting with an initial tree with root consisting of $Q \wedge I$. The procedure then repeatedly manipulates a currently selected node by applying equivalence-preserving *proof rules* to it. The nodes are sets of formulas (so-called *goals*) which may be atoms, implications, or disjunctions of literals. The implications are either integrity constraints, their residues obtained by propagation, or obtained by rewriting negative literals *not p* as $p \Rightarrow$ *false*.

IFF requires abductive logic programs and queries to meet a number of allowedness conditions (avoiding certain problematic patterns of quantification). CIFF relaxes these conditions checking them *dynamically*, i.e. at runtime, by means of a *dynamic allowedness rule* included amongst its proof rules. This rule labels nodes with a problematic quantification pattern as *undefined*. Undefined nodes are not selected again. In addition to the dynamic allowedness rule, CIFF includes, e.g., the following proof rules (for full details and other rules see [6]):

- *Unfolding:* Replace any atomic goal $p(\vec{t})$, for which there is an iff-definition $p(\vec{X}) \Leftrightarrow D_1 \vee \cdots \vee D_n$ in Th, by $(D_1 \vee \cdots \vee D_n)[\vec{X}/\vec{t}]$.
- *Propagation:* Given goals $[p(\vec{t}) \wedge A \Rightarrow B]$ and $p(\vec{s})$, add $[(\vec{t} = \vec{s}) \wedge A \Rightarrow B]$.
- *Constraint solving:* Replace a node with unsatisfiable constraints by *false*.

In a proof tree for a query, a node containing *false* is called a *failure node*. If all leaf nodes in a tree are failure nodes, then the search is said to *fail*. A node to which no more proof rules can be applied is called a *final node*. A non-failure final node not labelled as *undefined* is called a *success node*. CIFF has been proved *sound* [6]: it is possible to extract an abductive answer from any success node and if the search fails then there exists no such answer.

3   Implementation of CIFF

We have implemented the CIFF procedure in Sicstus Prolog [1] relying upon its built-in constraint logic programming solver over finite domains (CLPFD) [3]. Our implementation includes a simple module that translates abductive logic programs into completed logic programs, which are then fed as input to CIFF. The main predicate of our implementation is `ciff/4`:

```
ciff( +Defs, +ICs, +Query, -Answer).
```

The first argument is a list of iff-definitions, the second is a list of integrity constraints, and the third is the list of literals in the given query. Alternatively, the first two arguments may be replaced with the name of a file containing an

---
[1]   The system is available at http://www.doc.ic.ac.uk/~ue/ciff/

abductive logic program. The `Answer` consists of three parts: a list of abducible atoms, a list of restrictions on variables, and a list of (arithmetic) constraints (the latter two can be used to construct the σ component in an abductive answer). Iff-definitions are terms of the form A `iff` B, where A is an atom and B is a list of lists of literals (representing a disjunction of conjunctions). Integrity constraints are expressions of the form A `implies` B, where A is a list of literals (representing a conjunction) and B is a list of atoms (representing a disjunction). The syntax chosen to represent atoms is that of Prolog. Negative literals are represented as Prolog terms of the form `not(`P`)` Atoms can be (arithmetic) constraints, such as `T1 #< T2 + 5`. The available constraint predicates are `#=`, `#\=`, `#<`, `#=<`, `#>`, and `#>=`, each of which takes two arguments that may be any arithmetic expressions over variables and integers (using any arithmetic operation that CLPFD can handle [3]). Note that, for equalities over terms that are not arithmetic terms, the usual equality predicate `=` should be used (e.g. `X = bob`). The Prolog predicate implementing the proof rules is:

```
sat( +Node, +EV, +CL, +LM, +Defs, +FreeVars, -Answer).
```

`Node` is a list of goals, representing a conjunction. `EV` is used to keep track of existentially quantified variables in the node (to assess the applicability of some of the proof rules). `CL` (for constraint list) is used to store the constraints accumulated so far. The next argument, `LM` (for loop management), is a list of expressions of the form $A:B$ recording pairs of formulas that have already been used during a computation allowing us to avoid loops that would result if rules, for instance the *propagation* rule, were applied over and over to the same arguments. `Defs` is the list of iff-definitions in the theory. `FreeVars` is used to store the list of variables appearing in the original query. Finally, running `sat/7` will result in the variable `Answer` to be instantiated with a representation of the abductive answer found by the procedure. Each proof rule corresponds to a Prolog clause in `sat/7`. E.g., the *unfolding rule* (for atoms) is implemented as follows:

```
sat( Node, EV, CL, LM, Defs, FreeVars, Answer) :-
   member( A, Node), is_atom( A), get_def( A, Defs, Ds),
   delete( Node, A, Node1), NewNode = [Ds|Node1], !,
   sat( NewNode, EV, CL, LM, Defs, FreeVars, Answer).
```

`is_atom(A)` succeeds if `A` is an atomic goal. `get_def(A,Defs,Ds)` will instantiate `Ds` with the list of lists according to the iff-definition for `A` in `Defs` whenever there *is* such a definition (i.e. the predicate will fail for abducibles). Once `get_def(A,Defs,Ds)` succeeds we know that the unfolding rule is applicable: there exists an atomic conjunct `A` in the current `Node` and it is not abducible. The cut in the penultimate line ensures that we will not backtrack over the *order* in which rules are being applied. We generate the successor `NewNode` deleting the atom `A` from `Node` and replacing it with the disjunction `Ds`. The predicate `sat/7` then recursively calls itself with the new node.

The proof rules are repeatedly applied to the current node. Whenever a disjunction is encountered, it is split into a set of successor nodes (one for each disjunct). The procedure then picks one of these successor nodes to continue the search and backtracking over this choicepoint results in all possible successor nodes being explored. In theory, the choice of which successor node to explore next is taken nondeterministically; in practice we simply move through nodes from left to right. The procedure terminates when no more proof rules apply (to the current node) and finishes by extracting an answer from this node. Enforced backtracking will result in the next branch (if any) of the proof tree being explored, i.e. in any remaining abductive answers being enumerated.

The Prolog clauses in the implementation of sat/7 may be reordered almost arbitrarily (only the clause used to implement answer extraction has to be listed last). Each order of clauses corresponds to a different proof strategy. This feature of our implementation allows for an experimental study of which strategies yield the fastest derivations. With respect to the implementation in [5], the current implementation integrates rules (that humans would combine automatically) into more complex rules avoiding to waste time checking for their applicability. E.g. rewriting a disjunction consisting of one disjunct as that very disjunct has been integrated into the *unfolding* rule as we have noted that rewriting unary disjunctions often occurs after an unfolding step. Another improvement concerns the *propagation* rule: we now only allow for propagation with respect to the leftmost atom in the antecedent of an implication. This refinement does not affect soundness and can reduce the number of implications in nodes. We plan to explore further optimisation techniques in the future.

Acknowledgments. This work was partially funded by the IST programme of the EC, FET under the IST-2001-32530 SOCS project, within the GC proactive initiative. The last author was also supported by the Italian MIUR programme "Rientro dei cervelli". We thank M. Gavanelli and M. Milano for suggestions on the constraint solver.

References

1. A. Bracciali, N. Demetriou, U. Endriss, A. Kakas, W. Lu, P. Mancarella, F. Sadri, K. Stathis, G. Terreni, and F. Toni. The KGP model of agency for GC: Computational model and prototype implementation. In *Proc. Global Computing 2004 Workshop*, LNCS. Springer Verlag.
2. A. Bracciali and A. C. Kakas. Frame consistency: Computing with causal explanations. In *Proc. NMR2004*.
3. M. Carlsson, G. Ottosson, and B. Carlson. An open-ended finite domain constraint solver. In *Proc. PLILP97*.
4. K. L. Clark. Negation as failure. In *Logic and Data Bases*. Plenum Press, 1978.
5. U. Endriss, P. Mancarella, F. Sadri, G. Terreni, and F. Toni. Abductive logic programming with CIFF: Implementation and applications. In *Proc. CILC04*.
6. U. Endriss, P. Mancarella, F. Sadri, G. Terreni, and F. Toni. The CIFF proof procedure for abductive logic programming with constraints. In *Proc. JELIA04*.
7. T. H. Fung and R. A. Kowalski. The IFF proof procedure for abductive logic programming. *Journal of Logic Programming*, 33(2):151–165, 1997.
8. A. C. Kakas, P. Mancarella, F. Sadri, K. Stathis, and F. Toni. The KGP model of agency. In *Proc. ECAI2004*.

9. P. Mancarella, F. Sadri, G. Terreni, and F. Toni. Planning partially for situated agents. Technical report, SOCS, 2004.
10. F. Sadri and F. Toni. A logic-based approach to reasoning with beliefs about trust. In *Proc. ARSPA04, Workshop affiliated to IJCAR04*, 2004.
11. F. Sadri, F. Toni, and P. Torroni. An abductive logic programming architecture for negotiating agents. In *Proc. JELIA2002*, volume 2424 of *LNCS*. Springer-Verlag.
12. K. Stathis, A. C. Kakas, W. Lu, N. Demetriou, U. Endriss, and A. Bracciali. PROSOCS: A platform for programming software agents in computational logic. In *Proc. AT2AI-2004*.

The DALI Logic Programming Agent-Oriented Language*

Stefania Costantini and Arianna Tocchio

Università degli Studi di L'Aquila
Dipartimento di Informatica
Via Vetoio, Loc. Coppito, I-67010 L'Aquila - Italy
{stefcost,tocchio}@di.univaq.it

1 The DALI language

DALI [3] [2] is an Active Logic Programming Language designed in the line of [6] for executable specification of logical agents. A DALI agent is a logic program that contains a particular kind of rules, reactive rules, aimed at interacting with an external environment. The reactive and proactive behavior of a DALI agent is triggered by several kinds of events: external, internal, present and past events. All the events and actions are timestamped, so as to record when they occurred. The new syntactic entities, i.e., predicates related to events and proactivity, are indicated with special postfixes (which are coped with by a pre-processor) so as to be immediately recognized while looking at a program.

The external events are syntactically indicated by the postfix E. When an event comes into the agent from its "external world", the agent can perceive it and decide to react. The reaction is defined by a reactive rule which has in its head that external event. The special token :>, used instead of : −, indicates that reactive rules performs forward reasoning. The agent remembers to have reacted by converting the external event into a *past event* (time-stamped). Operationally, if an incoming external event is recognized, i.e., corresponds to the head of a reactive rule, it is added into a list called EV and consumed according to the arrival order, unless priorities are specified.

The internal events define a kind of "individuality" of a DALI agent, making her proactive independently of the environment, of the user and of the other agents, and allowing her to manipulate and revise her knowledge. An internal event is syntactically indicated by the postfix I, and its description is composed of two rules. The first one contains the conditions (knowledge, past events, procedures, etc.) that must be true so that the reaction (in the second rule) may happen.

Internal events are automatically attempted with a default frequency customizable by means of directives in the initialization file. The user directives can tune several parameters: at which frequency the agent must attempt the internal events; how many times an agent must react to the internal event (forever, once, twice,...) and when (forever, when triggering conditions occur, ...); how long the event must be attempted (until some time, until some terminating conditions, forever).

* We acknowledge support by the *Information Society Technologies programme of the European Commission, Future and Emerging Technologies* under the IST-2001-37004 WASP project.

J.J. Alferes and J. Leite (Eds.): JELIA 2004, LNAI 3229, pp. 685–688, 2004.

When an agent perceives an event from the "external world", it does not necessarily react to it immediately: she has the possibility of reasoning about the event, before (or instead of) triggering a reaction. Reasoning also allows a proactive behavior. In this situation, the event is called present event and is indicated by the suffix N.

Actions are the agent's way of affecting her environment, possibly in reaction to an external or internal event. In DALI, actions (indicated with postfix A) may have or not preconditions: in the former case, the actions are defined by actions rules, in the latter case they are just action atoms. An action rule is just a plain rule, but in order to emphasize that it is related to an action, we have introduced the new token :<, thus adopting the syntax $action$:< $preconditions$. Similarly to external and internal events, actions are recorded as past actions.

Past events represent the agent's "memory", that makes her capable to perform future activities while having experience of previous events, and of her own previous conclusions. Past events, indicated by the suffix P, are kept for a certain default amount of time, that can be modified by the user through a suitable directive in the initialization file.

The DALI language has been equipped with a communication architecture consisting of three levels. The first level implements a FIPA-compliant [5] communication protocol and a filter on communication, i.e. a set of rules that decide whether or not to receive or send a message. The DALI communication filter is specified by means of meta-level rules defining the distinguished predicates *tell* and *told*. The second level includes a meta-reasoning layer, that tries to understand message contents, possibly based on ontologies and/or on forms of commonsense reasoning. The third level consists of the DALI interpreter.

The declarative and procedural semantics of DALI, is defined as an *evolutionary semantics*, so as to cope with the evolution of an agent corresponding to the perception of events [3]. The semantics has been generalized so as to include the communication architecture by resorting to the general framework RCL (Reflective Computational Logic) [1] based on the concept of reflection principle.

Following [7] and the references therein, the operational semantics of communication is defined [4] by means of a formal dialogue game framework that focuses on the rules of dialogue, regardless the meaning the agent may place on the locutions uttered. This means, we do not want to refer to the mental states of the participants.

2   The DALI Interpreter

The DALI interpreter has been implemented in Sicstus Prolog, and includes a FIPA-compliant communication library. The DALI interpreter is in principle able to interoperate with other FIPA-compliant platforms. Presently, we have implemented interoperability with JADE, which is one of the best-known non-logical middleware for agents (namely, it is written in java). DALI agents can be distributed on the web, as the implementation of the communication primitives is based on TCP/IP.

The interpreter is composed of three main modules: (i) the *DALI active_server* module, that manages the community of DALI agents; (ii) the *DALI active_user* module, that provides a user interface for the user to interact with the agents; (iii) the *active_dali* module, that is automatically activated by the active_server whenever an agent is created (then, there are as many copies of the *active_dali* module running as the existing agents).

The DALI/FIPA communication protocol consists of the main FIPA primitives, plus few new primitives which are peculiar of DALI. The code implementing the FIPA primitives is contained in the file *communication_fipa.txt*, imported by agents as a library. The DALI/FIPA communication protocol is implemented by means a piece of DALI code including suitable *tell/told* rules. Whenever a message is received, with content part *primitive(Content,Sender)* the DALI interpreter automatically looks for a corresponding *told* rule that specifies whether the message should be accepted. Symmetrically, whenever a message should be sent, with content part *primitive(Content,Sender)* the DALI interpreter automatically looks for a corresponding *tell* rule that specifies whether the message can be actually issued. The DALI code defining the DALI/FIPA protocol is contained in a separate predefined file, *communication.txt*, imported by agents as a library. In this way, both the communication primitives and the communication protocol can be seen as "input parameters "of the agent. It is important to notice that the file *communication.txt* can modified by the user by adding new rules to the default ones. Typically, a user will add new application-dependent *tell/told* rules to the file *communication.txt*. Possibly however, both library files can be replaced by different ones, thus specifying a different communication protocol.

Each DALI agent must be generated by specifying the following parameters. (a) The name of the file that contains the DALI logic program (a .txt file). (b) The name of the agent. (c) The ontology the agent adopts (a .txt file); (d) The language (e.g., Italian or English etc.) used in the communication acts; (e) The name of the file containing the communication constraints, a .txt file; as mentioned, a predefined standard version *communication.txt* is provided. (f) The name of the communication library, a .txt file; as mentioned, a standard version *communication_fipa.txt* is provided. (g) The skills that the agent means to make explicit to the community of DALI agents (e.g., profession, hobbies, etc.). Below is an example of activation of an agent.

agent('demo/program/prog',gino,'demo/pippo_ontology.txt',italian,
['demo/communication'],['demo/communication_fipa'],[tourist]).

From the program file, say *prog.txt*, a pre-processing stage extracts three files. (1) The file *prog.ple*, that contains a list of the special tokens occurring in the agent program, denoting internal and external events, goals, actions, etc. (2) The file *prog.plf*, that contains a list of user-defined directives, that the DALI environment provides for *tuning* the behavior of an agent: the user can decide for instance: the priority among events; how long to keep memory of past events, and/or upon which conditions they must be removed; the starting and terminating conditions for attempting internal events, and the frequency. (3) The file *prog.pl* which contains the code of the agent; it must be noticed that all variables are reified, so as to guarantee safe communication and reliable meta-reasoning capabilities.

3   Case Studies

We are able of course to show many simple examples, aimed at illustrating the basic language features. More complex case studies can however be demonstrated.

To demonstrate the usefulness of the "internal event" and "goal" mechanisms, we have considered as a case-study the implementation of STRIPS-like planning. We can show that it is possible in DALI to design and implement this kind of planning without defining a meta-interpreter. Rather, each feasible action is managed by the agent's proactive behavior: the agent checks whether there is a goal requiring that action, sets up the possible subgoals, waits for the preconditions to be verified, performs the actions (or records the actions to be done if the plan is to be executed later), and finally arranges the postconditions.

We can generalize this example to dynamic planning, where an agent is able to recover from unwanted or unexpected situations by suitably modifying its plan.

To explain how the filter level works, we have implemented and experimented a case-study that demonstrates how this filter is powerful enough to express sophisticated concepts such as expressing and updating the *level of trust*. Trust is a kind of social knowledge and encodes evaluations about which agents can be taken as reliable sources of information or services. We focus on a practical issues: namely, how the level of Trust influences communication and choices of the agents.

References

1. J. Barklund, S. Costantini, P. Dell'Acqua e G. A. Lanzarone, *Reflection Principles in Computational Logic*, Journal of Logic and Computation, Vol. 10, N. 6, December 2000, Oxford University Press, UK.
2. S. Costantini. Many references about DALI and PowerPoint presentations can be found at the URLs:
   http://costantini.di.univaq.it/pubbls_stefi.htm and
   http://costantini.di.univaq.it/AI2.htm.
3. S. Costantini and A. Tocchio, *A Logic Programming Language for Multi-agent Systems*, In S. Flesca, S. Greco, N. Leone, G. Ianni (eds.), *Logics in Artificial Intelligence, Proc. of the 8th Europ. Conf., JELIA 2002*, (held in Cosenza, Italy, September 2002), LNAI 2424, Springer-Verlag, Berlin, 2002.
4. S. Costantini, A. Tocchio and A. Verticchio, *Semantic of the DALI Logic Programming Agent-Oriented Language*, submitted.
5. FIPA. *Communicative Act Library Specification*, Technical Report XC00037H, Foundation for Intelligent Physical Agents, 10 August 2001.
6. R. A. Kowalski, *How to be Artificially Intelligent - the Logical Way*, Draft, revised February 2004, Available on line, URL
   http://www-lp.doc.ic.ac.uk/UserPages/staff/rak/rak.html.
7. P. Mc Burney, R. M. Van Eijk, S. Parsons, L. Amgoud, *A Dialogue Game Protocol for Agent Purchase Negotiations*, J. Autonomous Agents and Multi-Agent Systems Vol. 7 No. 3, November 2003.

Qsmodels: ASP Planning in Interactive Gaming Environment*

Luca Padovani[1] and Alessandro Provetti[2]

[1] M^2AG: Milan-Messina Action Group
DSI–Università degli studi di Milano. Milan, I-20135 Italy
luca@mag.dsi.unimi.it.
http://mag.dsi.unimi.it/
[2] M^2AG: Milan-Messina Action Group
Dip. di Fisica–Università degli studi di Messina. Messina, I-98166 Italy
ale@unime.it

Abstract. Qsmodels is a novel application of Answer Set Programming to interactive gaming environment. We describe a software architecture by which the behavior of a bot acting inside the Quake 3 Arena can be controlled by a planner. The planner is written as an Answer Set Program and is interpreted by the Smodels solver.

This article describes the Qsmodels project, which grew out of a graduation project [3] is currently under development. The aim of this project is twofold.

First, we want to demonstrate the viability of using *Answer Set Programming* [1] (ASP) in an interactive environment. The chosen environment is the *Quake 3 Arena* (Q3A) game from *id Software;* recently most of the source codes have been released to the public. *Q3A* is a *first person shooter*: the player's goal is to kill enemies using weapons and upgrades found inside the game field (normally a labyrinth). The human-like enemies found within *Q3A* are called *BOTs*. Like in the most computer games, Q3A bots behave according to the rules of a finite-state automaton (FSM) defined by expert game programmers.

The second objective is to implement and experiment with the high-level agent architecture described by Baral, Gelfond and Provetti [2]. Such schema consists in the following loop: *Observe–Select Goal–Plan–Execute.*

The Qsmodels architecture consists of two layers: a *high level,* responsible for mid- and long-term planning, and a *(low level)* in charge of plan execution and emergency state reactions. The high level has been developed mainly in ASP on the Smodels platform. I.e., smodels computes the *answer sets* of a logic program which characterizes all successful plans of a given length, following the more or less standard encoding found in [1]. The computed answer set is passed to the low-level layer that inspects it, extracts relevant syntactic informations and *executes* the required actions.

* Work supported by the Information Society Technologies programme of the European Commission, Future and Emerging Technologies under the IST-2001-37004 WASP project.

J.J. Alferes and J. Leite (Eds.): JELIA 2004, LNAI 3229, pp. 689–692, 2004.

The high-level layer of our project realizes a *Q3A* agent which, starting with the knowledge about the game field similar to that of an intermediate-level human player, tries to beat his opponents by facing them only when in a better condition for the attack. To achieve this result, we have added to the planner a very simple learning system which keeps track of opponent's behavior in order to better guess future moves.

Even though we are still in the experimental phase, we submit that our architecture has several advantages over the traditional schema for the *AI* part of games. Namely, our solution is easier to develop and keeps the AI at higher level of abstraction. The easiness in development is reached by keeping the planning rules separated from the *world model description* rules, so that they can be written even by AI beginners. Also, Qsmodels could be used for virtual-reality AI experiments; the use of a computer game as the laboratory environment allows choosing the level of abstraction of the physical model while, -at the same time- giving a useful visual feedback of agent's actions.

Finally, this project may help in evaluating the feasibility of using `smodels` in near real-time applications and environments. Indeed, we noticed a high computational demand to achieve realistic real-time behaviors. More code analysis and optimization is in demand.

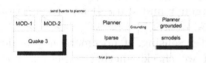

Fig. 1. The Qsmodels Architecture

The Qsmodels software components can be divided in 3 parts: i) the ASP planner, ii) the *Q3A C++* interface, which implements *sensing* and plan execution, and iii) the *C++* low-level AI. The execution model of Q3A, shown in Fig. 1, is summarized as follows. First, MOD-1 does the *sensing* phase by inspecting some *Q3A* memory areas; then, the computed informations is translated into high-level *fluent values* and added to the planner. The planner is first grounded by `lparse` then passed to `smodels`, which computes one of its answer sets. Finally, MOD-2 extracts the plan from the answer set and executes it by calling the relative *Q3A traps*.

Methodology

Our implementation required a lot of work and experiments in order to interface the existing software components, *Q3A* and `smodels`. The development of the agent required getting an in-depth knowledge of *Q3A* internal functions, most of which are not documented. `Smodels`, on the other hand, has been used as an external process, invoked by system calls. We are planning to switch to an API interface soon.

The two layers of Q3A work are executed concurrently: while the high level does the planning the low level is responsible for plan execution and reactive behavior in emergency situations. Events are deemed unforeseen when their occur makes the status of the domain incompatible with the assumptions made during the planning phase. It should be noticed that the low-level layer *inherits* some powerful functionality from *Q3A*, such as the *combat* and *shooting* actions, which are seen as atomic from the upper level.

To make our agent act realistically in its domain, we set the frequency of *sensing* at ten times per second. This measure has to do with the way actions are executed: each action may consists of several repeated calls, until the *goal* of the specific action is reached. So, since the plan execution is more associated with the *frame frequency* of the game than with the plan actions, sensing needed to be executed even during action execution.

To realize a *reaction behavior,* we have introduced so-called *pre-emption rules* which describe emergency behaviors in accordance with the environment and status of the plan. Pre-emption rules will be described in later sections.

Execution Cycle

The execution cycle of our application is shown in Figure 2. The first step is *sensing,* where we access *Q3A* memory searching for informations such as the agent state (position, health level ...) and availability of bonuses (health and ammunition tokes). Then, we check whether any emergency is happening, e.g., the agent is under attack, or he/she is facing the enemy, or he/she is behind the enemy etc. If any of these situations holds, then we execute the *pre-emption rules* to find those that apply to the present emergency and state. If no pre-emption rule applies then the execution cycle resumes.

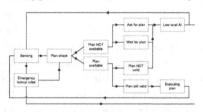

Fig. 2. Execution Cycle.

After sensing, if no emergency is detected we check whether a plan is currently available; if not, then we ask for a new one. Thus, we first translate the *Q3A* memory states in *fluents,* which are add as facts to the planner itself. Finally, we pass the augmented logic program to the external component *QsmodelsServer,* which is in charge of the smodels interface. The information embodied in the new fluents includes the agent's position, it's health and weapons state and the positions of known active objects. We include also a couple of atoms describing the *last known enemy position — expected new enemy position* to try to find usual routes taken by the enemy.

If a plan is available, then we have to check if any of the agents or enemies actions have invalidated the assumptions made at the planning phase. Indeed, since actions take some seconds to be executed and also the smodels computation can take several seconds, this situation would frequently happen, e.g., if the enemy takes a weapon that the agent was supposed to go get, the plan has to be invalidated since the weapon is not available anymore.

Let now consider plan execution. Each action available to the agent has been associated to a *trap* to *Q3A* system calls. The available actions are of course at very high level. This way, we have been able to reuse most of the basic AI work made by id Software: such as path finding and aiming. So, the available actions are: move_towards – pick_health – pick_ammo – attack and elude. All these actions except for **attack** are variations of **move_towards**, since to get an object we have to reach it. Action **attack** simply passes the control to the low-level AI in a situation where the agent will certainly has to attack the enemy.

The Use of Pre-emption Rules

The game field of Q3A can be described as very dynamic. So, it would be unfeasible to recompute the plan each time some aspect of the environment changes. In this sense, the introduction of the so called *Pre-emption rules* has probably been the most important step toward the realization of believable Q3A bots,

Pre-emptive rules allows describing a high-level reaction system in which we specify the reaction behavior of the agent and let **smodels** compute the actual reaction rules linked to the current plan. For each considered emergency situation and each time frame of the generated plan we get an appropriate reaction rule.

When an emergency happens our modification to *Q3A* searches the corresponding rule (time and event) through the rules and executes the action inside the body of the rule. As a result, pre-emption rules dictate a behavior somewhat similar to that of a FSM. However, in our case, the reaction is integrated in the planner and evaluated by the same inferential engine. Therefore, we couple a time-consuming planning system for long-term reasoning to a more efficient reaction system for quick reactions.

Application Experience

Our testing platform consists of a set of *Q3A* standard game levels in which our agent engages a duel against a human player. We require the game server (in our case an Intel P4 2.0GHz)to be run on a separate machine than that of the human player, due to the high computational power required by **smodels**.

The plan extraction phase can require up to 6/7 seconds, depending on the plan length. This delay is almost transparent to the human opponent, since during the planning our agent tries to hide. Should the agent meet the enemy then, the *pre-emption rules* together with the low-level AI will make it act quickly, usually avoiding the confrontation.

In Qsmodels plans the last action is always **attack** since the overall goal is to kill the enemy. However, the last action seldom gets executed since when emergency situations happen the *pre-emption rules* take control of the bot, canceling the residual part of the plan.

References

1. C. Baral, 2003. *Knowledge Representation, Reasoning and Declarative Problem Solving.* Cambridge University Press.
2. C. Baral M. Gelfond and A. Provetti, 1997. *Representing Actions: Laws, Observations and Hypotheses.* Journal of Logic Programming, 31(1-3).
3. L. Padovani, 2004. *Answer Set Programming in Interactive Gaming Environment.* Graduation project in Informatics (in Italian). University of Milan. Available from *http://mag.usr.dsi.unimi.it/*
4. Web location of the **smodels** solver: *http://www.tcs.hut.fi/Software/smodels/*

A System with Template Answer Set Programs[*]

Francesco Calimeri, Giovambattista Ianni, Giuseppe Ielpa,
Adriana Pietramala, and Maria Carmela Santoro

Department of Mathematics, University of Calabria - 87030 Rende (CS), Italy
{calimeri,ianni,ielpa,pietramala,santoro}@mat.unical.it

Abstract. Although ASP systems have been extended in many directions, they still miss features which may be helpful towards industrial applications, like capabilities of quickly introduce new predefined constructs or to deal with compound data structures and module. We show here an implementation on top of the DLV system of DLP^T language, which features increased declarativity, code readability, compactness and reusability.

1 Introduction

ASP has recently found a number of promising applications, like information integration and knowledge management (even in some projects funded by the European Commission [14,13]). Indeed, the ASP community has produced several extensions of non-monotonic logic languages, aimed at improving readability and easy programming; in order to specify classes of constraints, search spaces, data structures, new forms of reasoning, new special predicates [1,6,15,3,2,7].

We describe here the DLP^T system as an extension of ASP with template constructs. ASP systems developers are enabled to fast prototype, making new features quickly available to the community, and later to concentrate on efficient (long lasting) implementations. Template predicates allow to define intensional predicates by means of generic, reusable subprograms, easing coding and improving readability and compactness. For instance, a template program is like

```
#template max[p(1)](1) {
    exceeded(X) :- p(X),p(Y), Y > X.
    max(X) :- p(X), not exceeded(X). }
```

The statement above defines the predicate max, which computes the maximum value over the domain of a generic unary predicate p. A template definition may be instantiated as many times as necessary, through *template atoms* (or *template invocations*), like in :-max[weight(*)](M),M>100. Template definitions may be unified with a template atom in many ways. The above rule contains a *plain* invocation, while in :-max[student(Sex,$,*)](M),M>25. there is a *compound* one.

The DLP^T language has been successfully implemented and tested on top of the DLV system [9]. Anyway, the proposed paradigm does not rely at all on DLV special features, and is easily generalizable.

---

[*] This work was partially supported by the European Commission under projects IST-2002-33570 INFOMIX, and IST-2001-37004 WASP.

J.J. Alferes and J. Leite (Eds.): JELIA 2004, LNAI 3229, pp. 693–697, 2004.

2 Syntax

A DLP^T program is an ASP program[1] containing (possibly negated) *template atoms*. A template definition D consists of two parts; *(i)* a template header, #**template** $n_D[f_1(b_1), ..., f_n(b_n)](b_{n+1})$, where each $b_i(1 \leq i \leq n + 1)$ is a nonnegative integer value, $f_1, ..., f_n$ are predicate names (called *formal predicates*), and n_D is called *template name*; *(ii)* an associated DLP^T subprogram enclosed in curly braces; n_D may be used within the subprogram as predicate of arity b_{n+1}, whereas each predicate $f_i(1 \leq i \leq n)$ is intended to be of arity b_i. At least a rule having n_D in the head must be declared. For instance, the following (defining subsets of the domain of a given predicate p) is a valid template definition: #**template** subset[p(1)](1) { subset(X) v -subset(X) :- p(X). }.

A template atom t is of the form: $n_t[p_1(\mathbf{X}_1), ..., p_n(\mathbf{X}_n)](\mathbf{A})$, where $p_1, ..., p_n$ are predicate names (*actual* predicates), and n_t a template name. Each $\mathbf{X}_i(1 \leq i \leq n)$ is a list of *special* terms. A special list of terms can contain either a variable name, a constant name, a '$' symbol (*projection term*) or a '*' symbol (*parameter term*). Variables and constants are *standard* terms. Each $p_i(\mathbf{X}_i)(1 \leq i \leq n)$ is called *special* atom. $\mathbf{A}$ is a list of *standard* terms called *output list*. Given a template atom t, let $D(t)$ be the corresponding template definition. It is assumed there is a unique definition for each template name.

Briefly, projection terms ('$' symbols) indicate which attributes of an actual predicate have to be ignored. A *standard* term within an actual atom indicates a 'group-by' attribute, whereas parameter terms ('*' symbols) indicate attributes to be considered as parameter. An example of template atom is max[company($,State,*)](Income). Intuitively, the extension of this predicate consists of the companies with maximum value of the Income attribute (the third attribute of the *company* predicate), grouped by State (the second attribute), ignoring the first attribute. The computed values of Income are returned through the output list.

3 Knowledge Representation

A couple of examples now follows. For instance it is possible to define aggregate predicates [16]. They allow to represent properties over sets of elements. The next template predicate counts distinct instances of a predicate p, given an order relation succ defined on the domain of p. Moreover, this definition does not suffer from semantic limitations [3] and can be invoked also in recursive components of the programs. We assume the domain of integers is bounded to some finite value.

```
#template count[p(1),succ(2)](1) {
    partialCount(0,0).
    partialCount(I,V) :- not p(Y), I=Y+1, partialCount(Y,V).
    partialCount(I,V2) :- p(Y), I=Y+1, partialCount(Y,V), succ(V,V2).
    partialCount(I,V2) :- p(Y),I=Y+1, partialCount(Y,V), max[succ(*,$)](V2).
    count(M) :- max[partialCount($,*)](M). }
```

---

[1] We assume the reader to be familiar with basic notions concerning with ASP syntax and semantics; for further information please refer to [5].

A ground atom `partialCount(i,a)` means that, at the stage i, a has been counted up; `count` takes the value counted at the highest (i.e. the last) stage value.

It is worth noting how `max` is employed over the `partialCount` predicate, which is binary. The last rule is equivalent to the piece of code:

```
partialCount'(X) :- partialCount(_,X).
count(M) :- max[partialCount'(*)](M).
```

Templates may help introducing and reusing definitions of common search spaces.

```
#template permutation[p(1)](2). {
    permutation(X,N) v npermutation(X,N) :- p(X),#int(N),count[p(*),>(*,*)](N1),N<=N1.
    :- permutation(X,A),permutation(Z,A), Z <> X.
    :- permutation(X,A),permutation(X,B), A <> B.
    covered(X) :- permutation(X,A).
    :- p(X), not covered(X). }
```

Such kind of constructs enriching plain Datalog have been proposed, for instance, in [11,1]. The above predicate ranges permutations over the domain of a given predicate p. In this case a ground atom `permutation(x,i)` tells that the element x (taken from the domain of p), is at position i within the currently guessed permutation. The rest of the template subprogram forces permutations properties to be met.

4   Informal Semantics

Semantics are given through a suitable "explosion" algorithm. Given a DLP^T program P, the *Explode* algorithm replaces each template atom t with a standard atom, referring to a fresh intensional predicate p_t. The subprogram d_t (which may have associated more than one template atom), defining the predicate p_t, is computed according to the template definition $D(t)$. The final output of the algorithm is a standard ASP program P'. Answer sets of the originating program P are constructed, *by definition*, from answer sets of P'. A full description of the "explosion" algorithm as well as many more details are available in [12].

5   System Architecture and Usage

The DLP^T language has been implemented on top of the DLV system [8,9,10], creating DLT system. The current version is available on the web [4,12].

The overall architecture of the system is shown in Figure 1. The *Core* controls the whole process and interacts with frontend modules. A *Pre-parser* performs syntactic checks and builds an internal representation of the DLP^T program. The *Inflater* performs the *Explode* Algorithm and produces an equivalent DLV program P' which is piped towards the DLV system. The models $M(P')$ of P', computed by DLV, are then filtered out by the *Post-parser* in order to remove previously added internal information.

The DLV system is continuously enriched with new features; thus, the user is allowed to exploit the *ASITIS* directive in order to exclude from parsing some

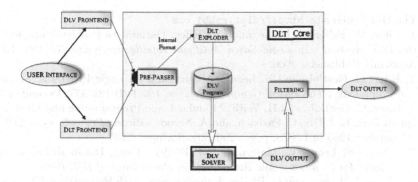

Fig. 1. Architecture of DLT system

piece of code (containing constructs DLT is not aware of, but recognized by the underlying system). This allows to adapt DLT to other ASP systems with different syntax.

6   Current Work

We are working extending the framework *a)* generalizing template semantics for safe forms of recursion between invocations, *b)* introducing new forms of template atoms in order to improve reusability of the same template definition in different contexts, *c)* extending the template definition language using standard languages, such as C++.

Some experiments are being performed in order to have an idea about the overhead due to the "exploded" code. Encodings of well-known (e.g. *K-clique, hamiltonian path, 3-colorability*, etc.) problems have been tested: "pure" ASP against *exploded* DLP^T ones (originally written exploiting templates). Overhead of the latter is never higher than 5%. However, performances are strictly tied to performances of resulting ASP programs; and it is worth remarking that this work, aiming at introducing fast prototyping techniques, does not consider time performances as a primary target[2].

References

1. M. Cadoli, G. Ianni, L. Palopoli, A. Schaerf, and D. Vasile. NP-SPEC: An executable specification language for solving all the problems in NP. *Computer Languages, Elsevier Science, Amsterdam (Netherlands)*, 26(2-4):165–195, 2000.
2. W. Chen, M. Kifer, and D. S. Warren. Hilog: A foundation for higher-order logic programming. *Journal of Logic Programming*, 15:187–230, 1993.
3. T. Dell'Armi, W. Faber, G. Ielpa, N. Leone, and G. Pfeifer. Aggregate Functions in Disjunctive Logic Programming: Semantics, Complexity, and Implementation in DLV. In *Proceedings IJCAI-2003*, Acapulco, Mexico, Aug. 2003.

---

[2] We would like to thank Nicola Leone and Luigi Palopoli for their fruitful remarks.

4. The DLP^T web site. http://dlpt.gibbi.com.
5. T. Eiter, W. Faber, N. Leone, and G. Pfeifer. Declarative Problem-Solving Using the DLV System. In *Logic-Based Artificial Intelligence*, pages 79–103. Kluwer Academic Publishers, 2000.
6. T. Eiter, G. Gottlob, and N. Leone. Abduction from Logic Programs: Semantics and Complexity. *Theoretical Computer Science*, 189(1–2):129–177, December 1997.
7. T. Eiter, G. Gottlob, and H. Veith. Modular Logic Programming and Generalized Quantifiers. In J. Dix, U. Furbach, and A. Nerode, editors, *Proceedings of LPNMR-97*, number 1265 in LNCS, pages 290–309. Springer, 1997.
8. W. Faber, N. Leone, C. Mateis, and G. Pfeifer. Using Database Optimization Techniques for Nonmonotonic Reasoning. In *Proceedings of DDLP'99*.
9. W. Faber, N. Leone, and G. Pfeifer. Experimenting with Heuristics for Answer Set Programming. In *Proceedings of IJCAI 2001*, pages 635–640, Seattle, WA, USA.
10. W. Faber and G. Pfeifer. DLV homepage, since 1996. http://www.dlvsystem.com/.
11. S. Greco and D. Saccà. NP optimization problems in datalog. *International Symposium on Logic Programming. Port Jefferson, NY, USA*, pages 181–195, 1997.
12. G. Ianni, F. Calimeri, G. Ielpa, A. Pietramala, and M. C. Santoro. Enhancing answer set programming with templates. In *Proceedings of NMR 2004*.
13. The ICONS web site. http://www.icons.rodan.pl/.
14. The Infomix web site. http://www.mat.unical.it/infomix.
15. G. M. Kuper. Logic programming with sets. *Journal of Computer and System Sciences*, 41(1):44–64, 1990.
16. K. A. Ross and Y. Sagiv. Monotonic aggregation in deductive databases. *Journal of Computer and System Sciences*, 54(1):79–97, 1997.

New DLV Features for Data Integration*

Francesco Calimeri[1], Manuela Citrigno[1], Chiara Cumbo[1], Wolfgang Faber[2],
Nicola Leone[1], Simona Perri[1], and Gerald Pfeifer[2]

[1] Department of Mathematics, University of Calabria - 87030 Rende (CS), Italy
{calimeri,citrigno,cumbo,leone,perri}@mat.unical.it
[2] Institut für Informationssysteme, TU Wien - A-1040 Wien, Austria
faber@kr.tuwien.ac.at, gerald@pfeifer.com

Abstract. The DLV system is currently employed in projects on data integration – a challenging application area for Answer Set Programming. The present system description illustrates some new optimization techniques, which significantly enhance the general performance of DLV, and especially in the context of data integration.

1 Introduction

The integration of (possibly inconsistent) data from different sources is one of the most promising applications of Answer Set Programming [5,1,3,14]. Recent studies [2,10,4,7,5] showed that query answering in data integration is often complete for the complexity class co-NP, or even for Π_2^P. This high computational complexity is mainly due to the necessity of handling inconsistencies (e.g., violations of key constraints) in the "integrated" database DB, which are due to conflicting data coming from different sources.

The (consistent) answer to a query $q(X)$ over a (possibly inconsistent) Data Integration System DB can be obtained by generating a logic program LP such that the stable models of LP yield the repairs[1] of DB. Answering the query $q(X)$ over the data integration system then amounts to cautious reasoning over the logic program LP [5,14,3], which can be performed by an ASP engine.

At the time being, the DLV system [12] is the most "database oriented" ASP engine, and it seems to be the best-suited ASP system for data-integration tasks. The suitability of DLV for data integration is backed by its use in relevant works in data integration, like [5,14,3] and by an IST project funded by the European Commission focusing on the exploitation of DLV for information integration (INFOMIX project, IST-2001-33570). Furthermore, in the experiments reported in [3], which also considered QBF, SAT, and CLP systems, DLV outperforms the compared systems on database repairing in the majority of cases.

However, as observed also in [5], DLV would be much more effective in database applications if it could take advantage of suitable optimization methods that speed up the evaluation of queries expressed as logic programs.

---

* This work was supported by the European Commission, under projects INFOMIX (IST-2001-33570), and WASP (IST-2001-37004).

[1] Intuitively, a repair is a maximal *consistent* subset of the database.

The present system description illustrates some recent enhancements in this direction [8,11], which have not been demonstrated to a broader audience yet. In particular, we focus on the following optimization techniques.

(i) Query oriented techniques for binding propagation (Magic Sets) [8]. Intuitively, the adoption of binding propagation techniques in Disjunctive Logic Programming (DLP) allows us to exploit constants appearing in the query and the program, reducing the size of the instantiation by avoiding "a priori" the generation of many ground instances of the rules which cannot contribute to the derivation of the query goal.

(ii) Backjumping techniques for the program instantiation [11]. The application of a new, structure-based backjumping method to the instantiation process of DLV significantly reduces the instantiation time and, very importantly, limits the size of the instantiation by generating, for each program rule, only a relevant subset of all its possible ground instances.

The design and implementation of these optimizations is an important step towards the concrete use of ASP systems in real-life applications.

2   Improving DLP Instantiators for Larger Data Manipulations

The kernel modules of most ASP systems operate on a ground instantiation of the input program [9]. Any input program P is first submitted to an instantiation process, which may be computationally very expensive. Thus, having a good instantiator is a key feature. It should produce a ground program P' having the same answer sets as P such that: (i) P' can be computed efficiently from P, and (ii) P' is as small as possible.

The main reason for large ground programs even for small input programs is that each atom of a rule in a program $\mathcal{P}$ may be instantiated to many atoms in the Herbrand base, which leads to a combinatorial explosion. However, most of these atoms may not be derivable whatsoever, and hence such instantiations do not render applicable rules. A good instantiator thus generates ground instances of rules containing only atoms which *might* be derivable from $\mathcal{P}$.

At each step of an instantiation by DLV, there is a number of predicates, called *solved*, such that the (total) truth values of all their ground instances have already been determined by the instantiator. For instance, all predicates defined only by facts are solved. Occurrences of these predicates can be safely omitted from the resulting ground program; it suffices to include asserting facts for each true ground instance of solved predicates.

In other words, we are not interested in all "consistent" substitutions for all variables, but rather in their restrictions to the variables that occur in literals over unsolved predicates. To this end, we designed and implemented a new backjumping-based instantiation method. In particular, given a rule r to be instantiated, our algorithm exploits both the semantical and the structural information about r in order to compute only a relevant subset of all its possible ground instances (see [11] for a detailed illustration).

Example 1. Consider the rule r_1 below, where predicates q_3, q_4 and q_5 are solved. The following are all applicable ground instances of r_1.

$r_1 : a(X, Z) :- q_1(X, Z, Y), q_2(W, T, S), q_3(V, T, H), q_4(Z, H), q_5(T, S, V).$

$a(x_1, z_1) :- q_1(x_1, z_1, y_1), q_2(w_1, t_1, s_1), q_3(v_1, t_1, h_1), q_4(z_1, h_1), q_5(t_1, s_1, v_1).$
$a(x_1, z_1) :- q_1(x_1, z_1, y_1), q_2(w_1, t_1, s_1), q_3(v_2, t_1, h_1), q_4(z_1, h_1), q_5(t_1, s_1, v_2).$

$$\vdots$$

$a(x_1, z_1) :- q_1(x_1, z_1, y_1), q_2(w_1, t_1, s_1), q_3(v_{100}, t_1, h_{100}), q_4(z_1, h_{100}), q_5(t_1, s_1, v_{100}).$

All these 10000 rules are semantically equivalent to a single instance, which is the only one computed by our algorithm: $a(x_1, z_1) :- q_1(x_1, z_1, y_1), q_2(w_1, t_1, s_1).$

3   Magic Sets for DLP

The Magic Sets method [13] is a strategy for simulating the top-down evaluation of a query using a bottom-up evaluation procedure. It modifies the original program by means of certain rules, that act as filters for the relevant information. Roughly, the goal is to use the constants appearing in the query and the program in order to reduce the size of the instantiation by eliminating "a priori" some ground instances of the rules which are irrelevant for the query goal.

In [8] the Magic Set algorithm has been extended to DLPs. While in non-disjunctive programs, bindings are propagated only head-to-body, any rewriting for DLPs has to propagate bindings also head-to-head in order to preserve soundness. For instance, consider the rule $p(X) \vee q(Y) :- a(X, Y), r(X)$ and the query $p(1)?$ on a program Π. Even though the query propagates the binding for the predicate p, in order to correctly answer the query, we also need to evaluate the truth value of $q(Y)$, which indirectly receives the binding through the body predicate $a(X, Y)$. If the program contains facts $a(1, 2)$, and $r(1)$, then atom $q(2)$ is relevant for the query, since the truth of $q(2)$ would invalidate the derivation of $p(1)$ from the above rule (because of minimality in the semantics). This shows that the bindings also have to be propagated head-to-head.

An extension of Magic Sets to DLP has been implemented in DLV, resulting in an algorithm called DMS [8].

Example 2 (Strategic Companies [6]). A collection C of companies produces some goods in a set G; each company $c_i \in C$ is controlled by a set of other companies $O_i \subseteq C$. $C' \subset C$ is a *strategic set* if it is a minimal set of companies producing all the goods in G, such that if $O_i \subseteq C'$ for some $i = 1, \ldots, m$ then $c_i \in C'$ must hold. This scenario can be modeled by means of a program $\mathcal{P}_{sc}$:

$r_1 : sc(C_1) \vee sc(C_2) :- produced\_by(P, C_1, C_2).$
$r_2 : sc(C) :- controlled\_by(C, C_1, C_2, C_3), sc(C_1), sc(C_2), sc(C_3).$

Moreover, given a company $c \in C$, we consider a query $\mathcal{Q}_{sc} = sc(c)$ asking whether c belongs to some strategic set of C. The output of DMS is the following program, which in general is much more efficient for answering $\mathcal{Q}_{sc}$ [8].

$magic\_sc^b(c).$

$magic\_sc^b(C_2) :\!- magic\_sc^b(C_1), \ produced\_by(P, C_1, C_2).$

$magic\_sc^b(C_1) :\!- magic\_sc^b(C_2), \ produced\_by(P, C_1, C_2).$

$magic\_sc^b(C_1) :\!- magic\_sc^b(C), \ controlled\_by(C, C_1, C_2, C_3).$

$magic\_sc^b(C_2) :\!- magic\_sc^b(C), \ controlled\_by(C, C_1, C_2, C_3).$

$magic\_sc^b(C_3) :\!- magic\_sc^b(C), \ controlled\_by(C, C_1, C_2, C_3).$

$r'_{1_m} : \ sc(C_1) \text{ v } sc(C_2) :\!- magic\_sc^b(C_1), \ magic\_sc^b(C_2), \ produced\_by(P, C_1, C_2).$

$r''_{1_m} : \ sc(C_2) \text{ v } sc(C_1) :\!- magic\_sc^b(C_2), \ magic\_sc^b(C_1), \ produced\_by(P, C_1, C_2).$

$r_{2_m} : \ sc(C) :\!- magic\_sc^b(C), \ controlled\_by(C, C_1, C_2, C_3), \ sc(C_1), \ sc(C_2), \ sc(C_3).$

4   Conclusions

We have described some of the most recent enhancements of DLV. These have been motivated by applications in data integration, where large amounts of data are to be processed and scalability is a very important issue. Their practical impact has been assessed by many experiments [8,11], with very positive results.

References

1. INFOMIX project (IST-2001-33570). http://www.mat.unical.it/infomix/.
2. M. Arenas, L. E. Bertossi, and J. Chomicki. Specifying and querying database repairs using logic programs with exceptions. pp. 27–41, 2000.
3. O. Arieli, M. Denecker, B. Van Nuffelen, and M. Bruynooghe. Database repair by signed formulae. In *Proceedings of FoIKS 2004*, LNCS 2942, pp. 14–30, 2004.
4. P. Barceló and L. Bertossi. Repairing databases with annotated predicate logic. NMR 2002.
5. L. Bravo and L. E. Bertossi. Logic Programs for Consistently Querying Data Integration Systems. In *Proceedings of IJCAI'03*, pp. 10–15, 2003.
6. M. Cadoli, T. Eiter, and G. Gottlob. Default Logic as a Query Language. *IEEE TKDE*, 9(3):448–463, 1997.
7. A. Calì, D. Lembo, and R. Rosati. Query rewriting and answering under constraints in data integration systems. In *Proceedings of IJCAI 2003*, pp. 16–21.
8. C. Cumbo, W. Faber, G. Greco, and N. Leone. Enhancing the Magic Set Method for Disjunctive Datalog Programs. In *Proceedings of ICLP 2004*. To appear.
9. T. Eiter, N. Leone, C. Mateis, G. Pfeifer, and F. Scarcello. A Deductive System for Nonmonotonic Reasoning. In *Proceedings of LPNMR 1997*, n.1265, LNAI, pp. 363–374.
10. G. Greco, S. Greco, and E. Zumpano. A logic programming approach to the integration, repairing and querying of inconsistent databases. v.2237 of *LNAI*, pp. 348–364, 2001.
11. N. Leone, S. Perri, and F. Scarcello. Backjumping Techniques for Rules Instantiation in the DLV System. In *Proceedings of NMR2004*, pp. 258–266.
12. N. Leone, G. Pfeifer, W. Faber, T. Eiter, G. Gottlob, S. Perri, and F. Scarcello. The DLV System for Knowledge Representation and Reasoning. *ACM TOCL*, 2004. To appear. Available via http://www.arxiv.org/ps/cs.AI/0211004.
13. J. D. Ullman. *Principles of Database and Knowledge Base Systems*, 1989.
14. D. Lembo, M. Lenzerini, and R. Rosati. Source Inconsistency and Incompleteness in Data Integration. KRDB 2002.

Profiling Answer Set Programming:
The Visualization Component of the noMoRe System

Andreas Bösel, Thomas Linke, and Torsten Schaub

Institut für Informatik, Universität Potsdam, Postfach 90 03 27, D–14439 Potsdam

Abstract. Standard debugging techniques, like sequential tracing, fail in answer set programming due to its purely declarative approach. We address this problem by means of the graph-oriented computational model underlying the noMoRe system. Although this is no generic solution, it offers a way to make the computation of answer sets transparent within the noMoRe framwork. Apart from the visualization of answer sets in terms of their generating rules, the computation can be animated in different ways.

1 Introduction

Effective programming needs supporting tools, like debuggers and profilers. In fact, for sequential programming languages, debugging can be done by step-wisely following the execution of a program. This also applies to Prolog and its procedural semantics expressed by SLD-trees. In general, such an approach is inapplicable to answer set programming due to its extremely declarative approach. Rather one has to commit to a particular computational model for making the computation of answers sets transparent.

To this end, we advocate the graph-oriented computational model of the noMoRe system [2,1]. This model is based on a rule dependency graph (RDG), whose nodes are given by the ground rules of the program and whose edges reflect positive and negative dependencies among rules. There is a positive edge from rule r to r', if $head(r) \in body^+(r')$; accordingly there is a negative edge from rule r to r', if $head(r) \in body^-(r')$. The computation of answer sets is then accomplished by gradually coloring the nodes of the graph by two colors (eg., green and red), reflecting the applicability status of the respective rule. Green nodes indicate applied rules, while red ones stand for inapplicable ones, relative to a possibly partial, putative answer set. Answer sets are represented in terms of their generating rules.

For profiling answer set programming, we put forward a graphical approach by dynamically visualizing the coloration of RDGs. For this purpose, we extended noMoRe by a visualization module. This module has an interface (API) to the graph visualization system daVinci [3]. This part of noMoRe's architecture is given in Figure 1. So noMoRe is no black box anymore but rather a vitreous one. Furthermore, the animated coloring sequences may be used for debugging ground logic programs under answer set semantics, because the user gets access to the full construction process of the answer sets. In particular, we are able to detect rules generating specific answer sets. For animation, one may chose among different levels of granularity. That is, the animation may be stopped and interactively resumed after coloring a single node, employing a particular

J.J. Alferes and J. Leite (Eds.): JELIA 2004, LNAI 3229, pp. 702–705, 2004.

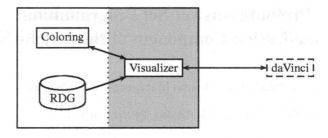

Fig. 1. Overview of the visualization of noMoRe.

operation, like a choice operation, for coloring or only when a coloring expressing an answer set is obtained. (Stopping at particular rules is currently under implementation.) Other parameters influencing the visualization, like animation speed or node layout, are explained in Section 2 and summarized in Table 1.

For illustration, let us consider a program consisting of the following rules:

$$
\begin{aligned}
r_1 &: \quad b \leftarrow p \\
r_2 &: \quad f \leftarrow b, not\ f' \\
r_3 &: \quad f' \leftarrow p, not\ f \\
r_4 &: \quad p \leftarrow \\
r_5 &: \quad w \leftarrow b
\end{aligned}
\tag{1}
$$

For later reference, assume this program is contained in a file named penguin.lp. The full sequence of coloring steps, leading to the two answer sets $\{p, b, w, f\}$ and $\{p, b, w, f'\}$ is given in Figure 2. This is the most fine-grained setting displaying each subsequent coloration step. Nodes of supposedly applied rules are colored in green; those standing for blocked ones in red. Whenever an answer set is obtained, as in the 6th and 10th instance, it is also printed by noMoRe. Nodes colored by choice operations are indicated by a double circle. The only such node is colored green in the 5th instance and red in the 9th one. Each choice leads to a different answer set. All other colorations are obtained through forward propagation. The animation capacities of daVinci also allow for visualizing and animating much larger graphs. Even graphs not fitting on a computer screen (in a certain resolution) can be animated, since daVinci automatically centers the considered node by horizontal and vertical scrolling. Although the detailed information obtained for very large examples is questionable, one can figure out which parts of a program are problematic due to extensive backtracking.

2   Using Visualization in noMoRe

The flags show and animate influence the visualization component of the noMoRe system [1]. By setting flag show the visualization is activated, which enables noMoRe to use daVinci as output tool for RDGs and their colorings. After calling the command nomore/2 (or nomore/4) the daVinci API is used to draw the actual RDG. By setting the flag animate the daVinci API is used to animate the noMoRe coloring procedure

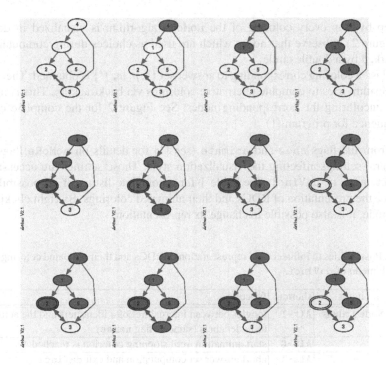

Fig. 2. The visualization of the complete coloring sequence for program (1).

during run time. Let's demonstrate the visualization component by computing the answer sets of program (1):

1. Start ECLiPSe, load noMoRe and ensure that set flag show is set by set_flag(show). This activates the visualization tool. Furthermore, ensure that the flag animate is set by set_flag(animate), since we are interested in an animated coloring sequence. Observe that due to flag dependency handling it is sufficient to set flag animate; then flag show is set automatically.
2. Continue by typing nomore('penguin.lp',0). After noMoRe has computed the RDG of Program (1) it is translated in the daVinci term representation. Then daVinci is started as a child process and the translated RDG is send to daVinci. See also Figure 2.
3. Now daVinci takes control and awaits an input by the user in order to process a number of coloring steps (a coloring step is the coloring of exactly one node.). The number of coloring steps which are performed without interruption depends on the setting of the Edit sub menu Stop At of daVinci. By default it is set to Every Node, which causes the noMoRe coloring procedure to stop after each single coloring step. However, via daVinci's Edit menu we are able to change some daVinci specific settings, such as node presentation, dependency graph representation, stopping criterion for animated colorings and animation speed. For a complete description of the possible daVinci settings see Table 1. Finally, to continue the computation type Alt-G or click the Go-icon on the upper left side of the daVinci window.

4. Step by step every coloring of the noMoRe algorithm is visualized in daVinci (Figure 2). Observe that nodes which are used as choices during computation are marked by a double circle.
5. At last, a coloring corresponding to answer set $\{b, p, w, f'\}$ is obtained. The noMoRe algorithm tries to compute alternative colorings via backtracking. This is modeled by uncoloring the corresponding nodes. See Figure 2 for the complete coloring sequence for program (1).

Apart from the flags show and animate (see [1] for details on noMoRe flags) there are several settings affecting the visualization style. Those settings are accessible via the Edit menu of daVinci. See Table 1 for a complete listing of all possibilities to influence the presentation of RDGs and their animated colorings. By right clicking on a single node, it is also possible to change its representation.

Table 1. Possibilities to influence the representation of RDGs and their animated colorings via the Edit sub menu of daVinci.

Edit menu items	shortcut	function
Toggle Node Labels	Alt-T	toggles between internal noMoRe identifiers and the actual rules as node labels (same as flag names)
Go	Alt-G	start animation until stopping criterion is reached
Abort	Alt-A	abort answer set computation and exit daVinci
Stop At	no	sub menu for choosing one of the following as stopping criterion for the animation: Choices, Each Node, Full Coloring, No Stop
Animation Speed	no	sub menu for choosing the speed of animation, possible choices are: Slow, Normal, Fast

noMoRe also represents different dependency graphs, so–called *body-head (BH-)* and *rule-head (RH-) graphs*. They can be used for visualization. Each body and head (rule and head) is represented through a single node in BH-graphs (RH-graphs). Finally observe that for every partial model the generating rules can be easily computed. Hence any ASP solver may use (partial) colored RDGs together with some graph drawing tool for visualizing its intermediate partial models as described in this paper.

References

1. C. Anger, K. Konczak, and T. Linke. NoMoRe: Non-monotonic reasoning with logic programs. In G. Ianni and S. Flesca, editors, *Eighth European Workshop on Logics in Artificial Intelligence (JELIA'02)*, volume 2424 of *Lecture Notes in Artificial Intelligence*. Springer Verlag, 2002.
2. T. Linke. Graph theoretical characterization and computation of answer sets. In B. Nebel, editor, *Proceedings of the International Joint Conference on Artificial Intelligence*, pages 641–645. Morgan Kaufmann Publishers, 2001.
3. M. Werner. davinci v2.1.x online documentation, 1998.

The PLP System

Toshiko Wakaki[1], Katsumi Inoue[2], Chiaki Sakama[3], and Katsumi Nitta[4]

[1] Shibaura Institute of Technology, twakaki@sic.shibaura-it.ac.jp
[2] National Institute of Informatics, ki@nii.ac.jp
[3] Wakayama University, sakama@sys.wakayama-u.ac.jp
[4] Tokyo Institute of Technology, nitta@dis.titech.ac.jp

1 Introduction

Prioritized Logic Programs (PLPs) [7] introduce explicit representation of priorities to logic programs. They realize various types of (prioritized) commonsense
reasoning in artificial intelligence including *preference abduction* [5]. Recently,
the authors realize a sound and complete procedure for computing *preferred
answer sets* of a PLP [8]. The procedure uses techniques of *answer set programming* (ASP) [6], and also extends the original PLP by accommodating *dynamic
preferences* in the language. The PLP procedure is implemented on top of the
ASP solver DLV [3] using C++, and is now running under the Linux/Windows
operating systems as "the PLP system". The system is available at the URL:
http://www.ailab.se.shibaura-it.ac.jp/comppas.html, which provides bi-
naries of the current release and the instruction on how to use the system. Some
examples are also found there.

This paper overviews the system. In Section 2 we review the framework
of PLPs and Section 3 presents the algorithm on which the system is based.
In Section 4 we solve Gordon's perfected shipping problem in the system, and
address brief comparison with related work.

2 Prioritized Logic Programs

A PLP is defined as a pair (P, Φ) where P is a program and Φ is a set of
priorities. A program P is a *general extended disjunctive program* (GEDP)
[4] which is a set of rules of the form:[1] $L_1; \cdots; L_k; not\, L_{k+1}; \cdots; not\, L_l \leftarrow$
$L_{l+1}, \ldots, L_m, not\, L_{m+1},$
$\ldots, not\, L_n$ $(n \geq m \geq l \geq k \geq 0)$, where each L_i is a positive/negative literal,
";" represents disjunction, and *not* represents negation as failure. A program
is *consistent* if it has a *consistent answer set*; otherwise a program is inconsistent. Let Lit be the set of all ground literals in the language of a program, and
$\mathcal{L} = Lit \cup \{\, not\, L \mid L \in Lit \,\}$. The pre-order relation $\preceq$ is defined over $\mathcal{L}$. For
any $e_1, e_2 \in \mathcal{L}$, $e_1 \preceq e_2$ (called a *priority*) means that e_2 *has a higher priority
than* e_1. We write $e_1 \prec e_2$ if $e_1 \preceq e_2$ and $e_2 \not\preceq e_1$. Given a set Φ of priorities, we

---

[1] In the system, negation as failure in the head is not used in a program due to the
syntactical restriction of DLV.

J.J. Alferes and J. Leite (Eds.): JELIA 2004, LNAI 3229, pp. 706–709, 2004.
© Springer-Verlag Berlin Heidelberg 2004

assume that Φ implicitly involves priorities which are reflexively and transitively derived by those in Φ.

The semantics of a PLP (P, Φ) is given by *preferred answer sets* defined as follows. Let S_1 and S_2 be two answer sets of P. Then, S_2 is *preferable* to S_1 with respect to Φ (written as $S_1 \sqsubseteq S_2$) if for some element $e_2 \in S_2 \setminus S_1$, (i) there is an element $e_1 \in S_1 \setminus S_2$ such that $e_1 \preceq e_2$ is in Φ; and (ii) there is no element $e_3 \in S_1 \setminus S_2$ such that $e_2 \prec e_3$ is in Φ. The relation $\sqsubseteq$ is defined as reflexive and transitive. An answer set S of P is called a *preferred answer set* of a PLP (P, Φ) if $S \sqsubseteq S'$ implies $S' \sqsubseteq S$ for any answer set S' of P. A preferred answer set S is called *strict* if $S \not\sqsubseteq S'$ for any preferred answer set S'. By the definition, preferred answer sets of (P, Φ) are answer sets of P. In particular, preferred answer sets coincide with answer sets when $\Phi = \emptyset$.

3   Computing Preferred Answer Sets

To compute preferred answer sets, we first construct a logic program $T[P, \Phi, S]$ which is obtained from a PLP (P, Φ) and any answer set S of P. The transformation is modular and is done in polynomial-time. We refer the reader to [8] for details of the transformation. The program $T[P, \Phi, S]$ has the following properties.

Theorem 3.1. [8] *Let $T[P, \Phi, S]$ be a program obtained from (P, Φ) and S.*

1. *If $T[P, \Phi, S]$ has a consistent answer set E, then $S' = E \cap \text{Lit}$ is an answer set of P satisfying $S \sqsubseteq S'$. Conversely, if there is an answer set S' of P such that $S \sqsubseteq S'$, then $T[P, \Phi, S]$ is consistent.*
2. *$T[P, \Phi, S]$ is inconsistent iff S is a strictly preferred answer set of (P, Φ).*

Given the set $\mathcal{AS}$ of all answer sets of P, we define a bijection $id : \mathcal{AS} \to \Omega$, which maps every answer set $S \in \mathcal{AS}$ to a constant $s \in \Omega$. s is called the *answer set ID* of S. The procedure *CompPAS* computes preferred answer sets of a PLP based on a *generate-and-test* mechanism. Given a PLP (P, Φ), the procedure first computes all answer sets of P using DLV. Second, for each answer set S of P, the procedure checks whether S is preferred or not, using $T[P, \Phi, S]$ and the result of Theorem 3.1. Finally it outputs every preferred answer set of the input PLP. The procedure is illustrated in Figure 1.

4   Example: Gordon's Perfected Shipping Problem

In this section we show how the PLP system can solve *Gordon's Perfected Shipping Problem*. The problem is described as follows [1]: A person wants to find out if her security interest in a certain ship is perfected. According to the Uniform Commercial Code (UCC), a security interest in goods may be perfected by taking possession of the collateral. On the other hand, according to a federal law called the Ship Mortgage Act (SMA), a security interest in a ship may only be perfected by filing a financing statement. She currently has possession of the ship, but a statement has not been filed. Now a question is whether the UCC or the SMA takes precedence in this case.

Procedure: $CompPAS(P, \Phi, \Delta)$

Input : a PLP (P, Φ);
Output : the set Δ of all preferred answer sets of (P, Φ).

1. Compute the set $\mathcal{AS}$ of all answer sets of P.
2. If $\Phi = \emptyset$, return $\Delta = \mathcal{AS}$; otherwise, do:
   (a) Set $\Sigma := \emptyset$.
   (b) For each $S \in \mathcal{AS}$, if $T[P, \Phi, S]$ is consistent, do the following steps:
      i. for each answer set E of $T[P, \Phi, S]$, put $S' = E \cap Lit$ and find the answer
         set ID $s' \in \Omega$ for S' where $S' \in \mathcal{AS}$ by Theorem 3.1;
      ii. put $\Sigma := \Sigma \cup \{ \sqsubseteq (s, s') \leftarrow \}$.
3. Compute an answer set U of the program: $\Psi \cup \Sigma \cup \{ as(s) \leftarrow \mid s \in \Omega \}$ where Ψ
   consists of the following five rules:

$$\sqsubseteq (x, x) \leftarrow as(x), \quad \sqsubseteq (x, z) \leftarrow \sqsubseteq (x, y), \sqsubseteq (y, z), \quad \sqsubset (x, y) \leftarrow \sqsubseteq (x, y), not \sqsubseteq (y, x),$$
$$worse(x) \leftarrow \sqsubset (x, y), \quad p\text{-}as(x) \leftarrow as(x), not\ worse(x).$$

4. Return $\Delta = \{ S \mid S \in \mathcal{AS} \text{ s.t. } s = id(S) \text{ and } p\text{-}as(s) \in U \}$.

Fig. 1. The procedure CompPAS

The situation is represented by the program:
```
perfected :- poss, not ab1.
-perfected :- ship, -file, not ab2.
poss.    ship.    -file.
ab1 :- not ab2.    ab2 :- not ab1.
ucc :- not ab1.    sma :- not ab2.
```
Two answer sets: $S_1 = \{ \texttt{poss}, \texttt{ship}, -\texttt{file}, \texttt{ab1}, -\texttt{perfected}, \texttt{sma} \}$ and $S_2 = \{ \texttt{poss}, \texttt{ship}, -\texttt{file}, \texttt{ab2}, \texttt{perfected}, \texttt{ucc} \}$ are computed by DLV, which represents two conflicting solutions.

To resolve conflict, the principle of *Lex Posterior* gives precedence to newer laws. In this example, the UCC is newer than the SMA. On the other hand, the principle of *Lex Superior* gives precedence to laws supported by the higher authority. The SMA is a federal law and has higher authority here. These priority knowledge is encoded in Φ as *priorities with preconditions* as follows:
```
moreRecent(ucc,sma).    fed(sma).    state(ucc).
lp(Y,X) :- moreRecent(X,Y).    ls(Y,X) :- fed(X), state(Y).
preceq(Y,X) :- lp(Y,X), not conf1(X,Y).
preceq(Y,X) :- ls(Y,X), not conf1(X,Y).
```
Here $\texttt{preceq}(Y, X)$ means $Y \preceq X$ and $\texttt{conf1}$ is a predicate for resolving conflict between legal principles. The last two rules express *dynamic preferences* which enable us to specify context-dependent preferences [1]. With these additional rules, S_1 and S_2 become two *tie-preferred* answer sets, i.e., $S_1 \sqsubseteq S_2$ and $S_2 \sqsubseteq S_1$.

Finally, we add additional priority information to Φ that states *Lex Superior* has precedence to *Lex Posterior*:
```
conf1(Y,X) :- lp(X,Y), ls(Y,X), not conf2(X,Y),
```
where $\texttt{conf2}$ is a predicate for resolving conflict which is one level higher than $\texttt{conf1}$. With this rule $\texttt{conf1}(\texttt{ucc}, \texttt{sma})$ is derived, which blocks the derivation of

preceq(sma, ucc). As a result, preceq(ucc, sma) is derived, and we get the single preferred answer set S_1 as the solution.

The above PLP program gordon is set as an input to the system, then compplp computes the preferred answer sets as follows:

```
$ compplp -timec gordon
Total Number of Answer Sets of P:2
{-file, -perfected, ab1, poss, ship, sma}
{-file, ab2, perfected, poss, ship, ucc}

Total Number of Preferred Answer Sets of (P,Phi):1
{-file, -perfected, ab1, poss, ship, sma}
Time: 10msec
```

We finally address brief comparison with related work. Brewka *et al.* [2] develop *logic programs with ordered disjunction* (LPOD) using an answer set solver. Their implementation is based on two logic programs, a generator and a tester to compute preferred answer sets. According to [2], an LPOD with the *Pareto-preference* is effectively encoded in a PLP, but the converse direction, computing preferred answer sets of a PLP in terms of an LPOD, is unlikely possible in general. The difficulty of reverse encoding is justified from the complexity viewpoints: reasoning tasks in LPODs lie at the second level of the polynomial hierarchy, while those in PLPs lie at the third level. Reasoning tasks in PLPs are thus generally hard, but as shown in the above example, the system performance is encouraging in many real world problems.

Acknowledgments. The authors thank Yosuke Kiwada at Shibaura Institute of Technology for his assistance of implementing the system.

References

1. G. Brewka. Well-founded semantics for extended logic programs with dynamic preferences. *J. Artificial Intelligence Research* 4, pp. 19–36, 1996.
2. G. Brewka, I. Niemelä, and T. Syrjänen. Logic programs with ordered disjunction. *Computational Intelligence* 20, pp. 335-357, 2004.
3. T. Eiter, W. Faber, N. Leone, and G. Pfeifer. Declarative problem solving using the DLV system. *Logic-Based Artificial Intelligence*, Kluwer, pp. 79–103, 2000.
4. K. Inoue and C. Sakama. Negation as failure in the head. *J. Logic Programming* 35(1), pp. 39–78, 1998.
5. K. Inoue and C. Sakama. Abducing priorities to derive intended conclusions. *Proc. IJCAI-99*, Morgan Kaufmann, pp. 44–49.
6. V. Lifschitz. Answer set programming and plan generation. *Artificial Intelligence* 138, pp. 39–54, 2002.
7. C. Sakama and K. Inoue. Prioritized logic programming and its application to commonsense reasoning. *Artificial Intelligence* 123, pp. 185–222, 2000.
8. T. Wakaki, K. Inoue, C. Sakama, and K. Nitta. Computing preferred answer sets in answer set programming. *Proc. 10th Int'l Conf. Logic for Programming, Artificial Intelligence, and Reasoning (LPAR'03)*, LNAI 2850, Springer, pp. 259–273, 2003.

The MyYapDB Deductive Database System

Michel Ferreira and Ricardo Rocha*

DCC-FC & LIACC, University of Porto
Rua do Campo Alegre, 823, 4150-180 Porto, Portugal
Tel. +351 226078830, Fax. +351 226003654
{michel,ricroc}@ncc.up.pt

Abstract. We describe the MyYapDB, a deductive database system coupling the Yap Prolog compiler and the MySQL DBMS. We use our OPTYap extension of the Yap compiler, which is the first available system that can exploit parallelism from tabled logic programs. We describe the major features of the system, give a simplified description of the implementation and present a performance comparison of using static facts or accessing the facts as MySQL tuples for a simple example.

1 Introduction

Logic programming and relational databases have common foundations based on First Order Logic [4]. The motivation for combining logic with relational databases is to provide the efficiency and safety of database systems in dealing with large amounts of data with the higher expressive power of logic systems. This combination aims at representing more efficiently the extensional knowledge through database relations and the intensional knowledge through logic rules.

In the specific field of deductive databases [6], a restriction of logic programming, Datalog [9], is commonly used as the query language. Datalog encapsulates the set-at-a-time evaluation strategy and imposes a first normal form compliance to the attributes of predicates associated to database relations. Datalog queries are evaluated by combining top-down goal orientation with bottom-up redundant computation checking. Redundant computations are resolved using two main approaches: the magic-sets rewriting technique [1] and tabling [5], a technique of memoisation successfully implemented in XSB Prolog [8], the most well known tabling Prolog system, and also in the OPTYap Prolog system [7].

The main concern in MyYapDB is in performance. Both Yap and MySQL are systems known for their performance. MyYapDB explores specific features of Yap and MySQL to build an external module which uses the C API's of each system to obtain an efficient deductive database coupled engine. OPTYap is also the first available system that can exploit parallelism from tabled logic programs, which seems interesting to further improve performance through the concurrent evaluation of database queries. Applications of our system include areas such as Knowledge Based Systems, Model Checking or Inductive Logic Programming.

* This work has been partially supported by APRIL (POSI/SRI/40749/2001) and by funds granted to LIACC through the Programa de Financiamento Plurianual, Fundação para a Ciência e Tecnologia and Programa POSI.

J.J. Alferes and J. Leite (Eds.): JELIA 2004, LNAI 3229, pp. 710–713, 2004.
© Springer-Verlag Berlin Heidelberg 2004

2   Basic Description of the System

In coupled deductive database systems, the communication between the Prolog engine and the relational database is usually done via a SQL query. MySQL answers to a SQL query with a structure called a *result set*, which includes the selected tuples and meta-data about these tuples. Following MySQL alternatives, MyYapDB allows for the result set to be copied to the Yap client process, or to be left in the MySQL server [3]. The tuples of this local or remote result set are then made available as Prolog facts in a tuple-at-a-time basis via backtracking.

A very important issue in terms of performance is to be able to transfer as much *unification* as possible from the Prolog engine to the database engine in the evaluation of database goals. Relational database engines traditionally have more powerful indexing schemes than Prolog engines and thus are able to solve more efficiently relational operations such as selections and joins. Dynamic SQL query generation based on the bindings of logical variables is thus fundamental in order to select exactly the tuples that unify with the Prolog goal calling pattern. Conjunctions and disjunctions of database goals should also be translated into a single SQL query, replacing a less efficient *relation-level* access for what is known as *view-level* access. MyYapDB allows for the explicit declaration of views and we plan to automatically replace constructs such as database goals conjunctions by compiler created views.

In MyYapDB the dynamic SQL query generation is done using a generic Prolog to SQL compiler written by Draxler [2]. This compiler defines a `translate/3` predicate, where the database access language is defined to be a restricted sublanguage of Prolog equivalent in expressive power to relational calculus (no recursion is allowed). The first argument to `translate/3` defines the projection term of the database access request, while the second argument defines the database goal which expresses the query. The third argument is used to return the correspondent SQL select expression. Because this compiler is entirely written in Prolog it is easily integrated in the pre-processing phase of Prolog compilers.

In MyYapDB, the association between a Prolog predicate and a database relation is defined using a directive such as ':- db_import(edge_r,edge,my_conn)', where `edge_r` is a MySQL relation, `edge` is a Prolog predicate and `my_conn` is a connection to a MySQL server. This directive asserts the following Prolog clause:

```
edge(A,B) :-
    translate(proj_term(A,B),edge(A,B),SqlQuery),
    db_query(my_conn,SqlQuery,ResultSet),
    db_row(ResultSet,[A,B]).
```

Predicates `db_query/3` and `db_row/2` are external predicates written in C. The first is a deterministic predicate that sends a SQL query to MySQL and stores the result set. The later is a backtrackable predicate that fetches a tuple at a time from the result set and unifies the tuple with a list of variables.

When we call 'edge(A,1)', the `translate/3` predicate constructs a specific query to match the call: 'SELECT source,1 FROM edge_r WHERE dest=1', where `source` and `dest` are the attributes names of relation `edge_r`.

The definition of views is similar. When programmers use a directive such as
':- db_view((edge(A,B),edge(B,A)),direct_cycle(A,B),my_conn)', the following clause is asserted:

```
direct_cycle(A,B) :-
    translate(proj_term(A,B),(edge(A,B),edge(B,A)),SqlQuery),
    db_query(my_conn,SqlQuery,ResultSet),
    db_row(ResultSet,[A,B]).
```

If later we call 'direct_cycle(A,B)', translate/3 constructs the query:
'SELECT A.source,A.dest FROM edge_r A,edge_r B WHERE B.source=A.dest
AND B.dest=A.source'. This is clearly more efficient than if we define a predicate
direct_cycle/2 in Prolog using relation level access:

```
direct_cycle(A,B) :- edge(A,B), edge(B,A).
```

Using the table directive of OPTYap allows the efficient evaluation of recursive predicates including database goals. For example, assuming edge/2 defined as above, the following tabled predicate computes its transitive closure.

```
:- table path/2.
path(X,Y) :- edge(X,Y).
path(X,Y) :- path(X,Z), edge(Z,Y).
```

3   Performance Evaluation

We want to evaluate the overhead of accessing Prolog facts in the form of MySQL tuples compared to statically compiled Prolog facts. We also want to evaluate the advantages allowed by using MySQL indexes schemes compared to the simple indexing scheme of Prolog. We used Yap 4.4.3 and MySQL server 4.1.1-alpha versions running on the same machine, an AMD Athlon 1400 with 512 Mbytes of RAM. We have used two queries over the edge_r relation of the examples above. The first query was to find all the solutions for the edge(A,B) goal, which correspond to all the tuples of relation edge_r. The second query was to find all the solutions of the edge(A,B),edge(B,A) goal, which correspond to all the direct cycles. We measured the execution time using the walltime parameter of the statistics built-in predicate, in order to correctly measure the time spent in the Yap process and in the MySQL process.

Table 1 presents execution times (in seconds) for Yap with edge/2 facts as statically compiled facts and indexed on the first argument (this is the available indexing scheme in Yap 4.4.3), and for MyYapDB with edge/2 facts fetched from the edge_r relation with a secondary index on *(source)* and a primary index on *(source,dest)*. Note that first argument indexing is the only available indexing scheme on almost all Prolog systems. XSB is one of the most well-know exceptions. The current development version of Yap, version 4.5, is also being improved to build indices using more than just the first argument. Further evaluation should experiment with these systems.

As expected, Table 1 confirms that view-level access is much more efficient than relation-level access. For queries that access sequentially a set of tuples, the

Table 1. Performance evaluation

System/Query	Tuples (Facts)		
	50,000	100,000	500,000
Yap (*index on first argument*)			
edge(A,B)	0.02	0.03	0.17
edge(A,B),edge(B,A)	5.97	24.10	132.15
MyYapDB (*secondary index on (source)*)			
edge(A,B)	0.18	0.37	1.95
edge(A,B),edge(B,A) (*relation level*)	39.88	119.84	1,779.26
edge(A,B),edge(B,A) (*view level*)	6.94	26.18	142.14
MyYapDB (*primary index on (source,dest)*)			
edge(A,B)	0.22	0.44	2.18
edge(A,B),edge(B,A) (*relation level*)	23.29	69.81	1,272.81
edge(A,B),edge(B,A) (*view level*)	0.35	0.82	4.78

overhead of MyYapDB compared to Yap accessing compiled facts is a factor of 10. For queries which take advantage of indexing schemes, an interesting comparison is the time taken by Yap and by MyYapDB using an equivalent indexing scheme. Results show a small overhead of 10% on MyYapDB using view-level access. The most interesting result for potential users of MyYapDB is the ability to use the available indexing capabilities of MySQL on the database predicates, which can allow very important speed-ups, like a factor of 25 for our example by using a primary index on both attributes. Further evaluation must also be done for different programs and queries.

References

1. C. Beeri and R. Ramakrishnan. On the Power of Magic. In *ACM SIGACT-SIGMOD Symposium on Principles of Database Systems*, 1987.
2. C. Draxler. *Accessing Relational and Higher Databases Through Database Set Predicates*. PhD thesis, Zurich University, 1991.
3. M. Ferreira, R. Rocha, and S. Silva. Comparing Alternative Approaches for Coupling Logic Programming with Relational Databases. In *Colloquium on Implementation of Constraint and LOgic Programming Systems*, 2004. To appear.
4. H. Gallaire and J. Minker, editors. *Logic and Databases*. Plenum, 1978.
5. D. Michie. Memo Functions and Machine Learning. *Nature*, 218:19–22, 1968.
6. Jack Minker, editor. *Foundations of Deductive Databases and Logic Programming*. Morgan-Kaufmanm, 1987.
7. R. Rocha, F. Silva, and V. Santos Costa. On a Tabling Engine that Can Exploit Or-Parallelism. In *International Conference on Logic Programming*, number 2237 in LNCS, pages 43–58. Springer-Verlag, 2001.
8. K. Sagonas, T. Swift, and D. S. Warren. XSB as an Efficient Deductive Database Engine. In *ACM SIGMOD International Conference on the Management of Data*, pages 442–453. ACM Press, 1994.
9. Jeffrey D. Ullman. *Principles of Database and Knowledge-Base Systems*. Computer Science Press, 1989.

InterProlog: Towards
a Declarative Embedding of Logic Programming in Java

Miguel Calejo

Declarativa
Rua da Cerca 88, Porto, Portugal
mc@declarativa.com http://www.declarativa.com/interprolog

Abstract. InterProlog is the first Prolog-Java interface to support multiple Prolog systems through the same API; currently XSB and SWI Prolog, with GNU Prolog and YAP under development – on Windows, Linux and Mac OS X. It promotes coarse-grained integration between logic and object-oriented layers, by providing the ability to bidirectionally map any class data structure to a Prolog term; integration is done either through the Java Native Interface or TCP/IP sockets. It is proposed as a first step towards a common standard Java + Prolog API, gifting the Java developer with the best inference engines, and the logic programmer with simple access to *the* mainstream object-oriented platform.

1 Introduction

InterProlog (http://www.declarativa.com/interprolog) is an open source library for developing Java + Prolog applications. It's been introduced elsewhere [1,2,3], and in addition to academic use it supported the development of a substancial Java GUI system for Prolog tools [7]. Whereas some Java - Prolog interfaces taste like objectified versions of the underlying Prolog/C interfaces, requiring explicit building of term structures prior to querying, InterProlog provides a higher-level API directly mapping Java objects to Prolog terms, inducing a more concise and declarative programming style.

This short paper introduces its new multiple Prolog implementation support, intended to provide a common API for bridging the most relevant representatives of the object-oriented and logic programming paradigms. As of writing, InterProlog supports XSB and SWI Prolog. When you read this it may already support also GNU Prolog and YAP. InterProlog is the only Java-Prolog interface API supporting more than one Prolog implementation. Lack of space prevents a comparison with other systems, but a list (with some comments) can be found in [5].

Linking Java and Prolog is relevant both for the industry and academia fields: to the first because "real-world" applications demand full-blown real logic engines, such as those produced by the logic programming community over the last decades, instead of toy engines or inferior technology; and to the second too, because reusing

J.J. Alferes and J. Leite (Eds.): JELIA 2004, LNAI 3229, pp. 714–717, 2004.
© Springer-Verlag Berlin Heidelberg 2004

Java's GUI infrastructure and other functionality liberates the logic programming community from wasting resources into condemned "Prolog driven" ecosystems. Prolog's survival is in large part dependent on the simplicity of its embedding into Java and other "real world" language environments.

We'll next review the overall functionality of InterProlog with some examples, and conclude with future plans and room for collaboration.

2 The InterProlog System

InterProlog is middleware for Java and Prolog, providing method/predicate calling between both, either through the Java Native Interface or sockets; the functionality is basically the same in both cases. InterProlog's innovation to this problem is its mapping between (serialized) Java objects and their Prolog specifications, propelled by the Java Serialization API which does most of the work on the Java side; the Prolog side is built upon a DCG that analyses/generates (the bytes of) serialized objects:

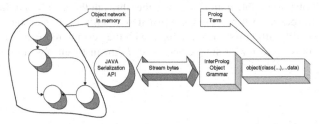

In order to support multiple Prologs, two things were done recently:

- The Prolog layer was revised to be compatible with "de facto" ISO Prolog; it now has a small part dedicated to each Prolog system (XSB and SWI; GNU and YAP under development).
- The Java class hierarchy was restructured; each Prolog system has a specific PrologEngine subclass, as well as a subclass of (an abstract class) PrologImplementationPeer, where most system-dependent knowledge is.

To understand InterProlog we'll start from two viewpoints: Java and Prolog.

2.1 Java Programming Perspective

InterProlog brings to the Java developer a simple API to access the power of full blown logic engines. The next fragment allows a Java programmer to use a Prolog file bundled into a jar file, and perform a simple query:

```
PrologEngine engine = new SWISubprocessEngine();
engine.consultFromJar("test.pl");
// or consultRelative (to the class location), or consultAbsolute(File),...
Object[] bindings =
    engine.deterministicGoal("descendent_of( X, someAncestor )","[string(X)]");
if(bindings!=null){// succeeded
  String X = (String)bindings[0];
  System.out.println( "X = " + X);
}
```

The only SWI Prolog dependence is the first line, so by changing it (e.g. XSBSub-processEngine) a different Prolog will be used. Complex structures can be passed in both directions with customized class objects, understoodable on the Prolog side by their InterProlog term specifiers, see [4].

2.2 Prolog Programming Perspective

The main InterProlog contribution for Prolog programming is the javaMessage predicate shown below, but it also provides a simple "Prolog listener" window: a traditional "console" front-end, where it is easy to experiment access to Java. The following invokes the message toString() to the Java PrologEngine in use:

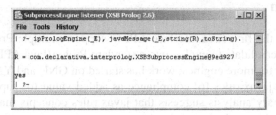

The next goal causes a window to appear:

```
javaMessage('javax.swing.JFrame',W,'JFrame'(string(myTitle))),
javaMessage(W,C,getContentPane),
javaMessage('javax.swing.JLabel',L,
   'JLabel'(string('Hello Prolog, greetings from Swing:-)'))),
javaMessage(C,add(string('Center'),L)),
javaMessage(W,pack), javaMessage(W,show).
```

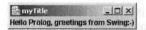

The above example illustrates how easy it is to message Java objects (and classes), but is a bit too procedural. Depending on the project at hand, rather than "writing Java constructors in Prolog" as above, it may be best to specify visual hierarchies with Prolog terms that are "interpreted" on the Java side, as in the XJ system [7]; parts of the interface may be populated later by lazily calling Prolog goals, e.g. the term specifies a lazy data structure / GUI fragment (such as when visually browsing a large Prolog structure).

A simplified variant of this principle can be experienced with the browseTerm term visualizer bundled in InterProlog; a Prolog term acts as a complete (eager) specification for a tree of TermModel objects on the Java side, which constitute a (Swing) model for a JTree (tree visualization) widget, see [5].

These approaches encourage a more coarse-grained approach to Java+Prolog system development (as opposed to "redoing Java constructors in Prolog"), which is good for performance, debugging and code maintenance.

On to another subject: the next clause allows a Prolog system to call another through Java, by using the PrologEngine method deterministicGoal(TermModel g):

```
callAnotherProlog(Engine,G) :- buildTermModel(G,GM),
   javaMessage(Engine,SM,deterministicGoal(GM)), recoverTermModel(SM,G).
```

The goal is transformed in a `TermModel` object tree specification GM; on invoking the Java method it materializes as a Java tree, which is them converted to a TermModel specification on the other engine, from which the solution term is recovered to a Java `TermModel` tree, etc. The next XSB goal finds operators defined in XSB and not in SWI:

```
javaMessage('com.declarativa.interprolog.SWISubprocessEngine',
   SWI,'SWISubprocessEngine'),
callAnotherProlog(SWI, findall(op(P,T,Name), current_op(P,T,Name), SWIops)),
findall(op(XSBP,XSBT,XSBO),
   ( current_op(XSBP,XSBT,XSBO), not(member(op(XSBP,XSBT,XSBO),SWIops) ),
   XSBonly).
```

3   Conclusion

We've reviewed the first Java interface API to support multiple Prolog implementations, and thus a candidate to evolve into a standard Prolog/Java API. Future work:

- Support for more engines; work has started on GNU and YAP.
- Provide javax.rules [6] compliance as added value for supported Prologs; a preliminary analysis suggests that javax.rules concepts map largely into InterProlog concepts.
- Use Prolog threads; currently InterProlog supports Java multiple threads for deterministic goals. Prolog threads will allow (a) multiple solution support and (b) light (multiple) engine creation, e.g. for server applications.
- Optimization of some call patterns. The serialization-based primitives provide maximum flexibility. But it may be the case that, with more applications being developed, a need arises to speed beyond the 3 mS/call currently measurable on a typical PC; thus being the case, specialized treatment of some call patterns can be tuned to avoid (generic) serialization.

References

1.   Calejo, M.: InterProlog, a declarative Java-Prolog interface, in Procs. Logic Programming for Artificial Intelligence and Information Systems (thematic Workshop of the 10th Portuguese Conference on Artificial Intelligence), Porto, December 2001
2.   Calejo, M.: InterProlog: a simple yet powerful Java/Prolog interface, Computational Logic Magazine, Dec 1998, http://www.cs.ucy.ac.cy/compulog/dec98update/projects/interprolog.htm
3.   Calejo, M.: Java+Prolog: A land of opportunities, in Procs. The First International Conference on The Practical Application of Constraint Technologies and Logic Programming, ISBN 1 902426 01 0, London 1999
4.   Declarativa: Java+Prolog Systems, http://www.declarativa.com/interprolog/systems.htm
5.   Declarativa: Prolog API, http://www.declarativa.com/interprolog/systems.htm
6.   Toussaint, A. et. al.: JSR 94: JavaTM Rule Engine API, http://www.jcp.org/en/jsr/detail?id=094, June 6 2004
7.   XSB, Inc.: XJ Platform, http://www.xsb.com/techPlatforms.html, June 6 2004

IndLog — Induction in Logic

Rui Camacho

LIACC, Rua do Campo Alegre, 823, 4150 Porto, Portugal
FEUP, Rua Dr Roberto Frias, 4200-465 Porto, Portugal
rcamacho@fe.up.pt
http://www.fe.up.pt/~rcamacho

Abstract. IndLog is a general purpose Prolog-based Inductive Logic Programming (ILP) system. It is theoretically based on the Mode Directed Inverse Entailment and has several distinguishing features that makes it adequate for a wide range of applications. To search efficiently through large hypothesis spaces, IndLog uses original features like *lazy evaluation* of examples and Language Level Search. IndLog is applicable in numerical domains using the *lazy evaluation* of literals technique and Model Validation and Model Selection statistical-based techniques.
IndLog has a MPI/LAM interface that enables its use in parallel or distributed environments, essential for Multi-relational Data Mining applications. Parallelism may be used in three flavours: splitting of the data among the computation nodes; parallelising the search through the hypothesis space and; using the different computation nodes to do theory-level search.
IndLog has been applied successfully to major ILP literature datasets from the Life Sciences, Engineering, Reverse Engineering, Economics, Time-Series modelling to name a few.

Keywords: Inductive Logic Programming

1 Introduction

The objective of an ILP system is the induction of logic programs. As input an ILP system receives a set of examples ($E = E^+ \cup E^-$) of the concept to learn (divided in positive, E^+, and negative examples, E^-), and sometimes some prior knowledge (or *background knowledge*, B). Both examples and background knowledge are usually represented as arbitrary definite logic programs. An ILP system attempts to produce a logic program (H - set of hypotheses) where positive examples succeed and the negative examples fail.

The problem of ILP is to find a consistent and complete theory, ie a set of hypotheses that "explain" all given positive examples and is consistent with the given negative examples. An ILP system performs a search through the permitted *hypotheses space* to find a set with the desired properties.

The hypotheses generated during the search are evaluated to determine their quality. Coverage is quite often used to estimate the quality of an hypothesis. The *coverage* of an hypothesis h is the number of positive (*positive cover*) and

J.J. Alferes and J. Leite (Eds.): JELIA 2004, LNAI 3229, pp. 718–721, 2004.
© Springer-Verlag Berlin Heidelberg 2004

negative examples (*negative cover*) derivable from $B \wedge h$. The time needed to compute the coverage of an hypothesis depends primarily on the cardinality of E and on the theorem proving effort required to evaluate each example using the background knowledge.

2 The *IndLog* System

IndLog [4] is an empirical ILP system written in Yap Prolog [8]. In the line of MIS, *IndLog* traverses the generalisation lattice in a top-down fashion. However, *IndLog* improves on both MIS and FOIL by using available or user supplied knowledge to traverse the generalisation lattice efficiently. *IndLog* differs from MIS and FOIL by explicitly generating the bottom of the generalisation lattice. This technique of building an initial clause to reduce the search space is characteristic of the technique of Mode Directed Inverse Entailment. The use of the bottom clause of the lattice together with further uses of knowledge either provided by the user or deduced from the available data leads to major efficiency improvements.

IndLog can handle non-ground background knowledge, can use nondeterminate predicates, uses a strong typed language and makes use of explicit bias declarations such as mode, type and determination declarations.

IndLog differs from other ILP systems, like Progol or Aleph, in the use of the Incremental Language Level Search strategy [2] and in a special feature to handle large datasets called *lazy evaluation* of examples. Lazy evaluation of literals together with Model Validation and Model Selection techniques enable IndLog to handle properly numerical domains. An interface to MPI/LAM enabled the development of a distributed/parallel module of IndLog adequate for Multi-Relational Data Mining applications.

3 IndLog Specific Features

3.1 Lazy Evaluation of Examples

Language bias may be used to avoid the generation, and therefore, the evaluation of a significant number of hypotheses. However, once an hypothesis has been generated the problem then is how to evaluate it efficiently using the available data (examples and background knowledge). IndLog uses *lazy evaluation of examples* [1] as a way to avoid unnecessary use of examples and therefore speed up the evaluation of each hypothesis. We distinguish between lazy evaluation of positive examples, lazy evaluation of negative examples and total laziness. Total laziness is based on the fact that generating hypotheses is very efficient and although we may generate more hypotheses we may still gain by the increase in speed of their evaluation process. This technique may be very useful in domains where the evaluation of each hypothesis is very time-consuming. It consists in making a lazy evaluation of negatives, and then only evaluate the positives is the hypothesis is consistent with the negatives.

3.2   Incremental Language Level Search

We define a partition of the definite clauses $\mathcal{D} = \bigcup_{i=0}^{\infty} \mathcal{L}_i$. Each subset $\mathcal{L}_i$ is called
a *language level* and is defined as:
$\mathcal{L}_i = \{$clause | maximum number of occurrences of a predicate symbol in the body of clause is $i\}$
where the *level* i of a language $\mathcal{L}$ is the maximum number of occurrences of a predicate symbol in the body of the clauses belonging to the language $\mathcal{L}$.

The maximum number of occurrences of predicate symbols in the body of the clauses determines to which subset the clause belongs. The language $\mathcal{L}_0$ is composed of definite clauses with just the head literal. The language $\mathcal{L}_1$ is composed by definite clauses whose literals in the body have no repeated predicate symbols. The language $\mathcal{L}_2$ will contain clauses whose literals in the body have a maximum number of occurrences of the same predicate symbol of two.

IndLog searches one language at a time starting at language level 0 and progressing incrementally one level at a time. One very important property of the partitioning by language level is that all clauses in language $\mathcal{L}_{i+1}$ are subsumed by at least one clause in language $\mathcal{L}_i$. An advantage of the search by language levels is that the most probable sub-lattices are searched first.

3.3   Cost Search

For some applications the target predicate may be modelling a functional relation whose output value is a numerical value. Constructing the model for such function involves the minimisation of a cost function other than coverage. *IndLog* uses *lazy evaluation* of literals [5] as a basic technique to handle numerical domains. It also improves over other ILP system by means of statistical-based Model Validation and Model selection tests. These latter techniques revealed very important in noisy datasets. IndLog uses and interface to the R-project library providing to the user a large number of numerical and statistical methods to be used as ILP background knowledge.

3.4   Parallel/Distributed Execution

A parallel implementation of an ILP algorithm may: i) improve the quality of the solutions found by searching more space in the same time of the sequential execution and/or; process larger datasets distributing the examples among the computing nodes (loading all of then in a single node may be impossible in some cases) or; get the same solution of the sequential execution much faster.

Using a MPI/LAM interface IndLog [6] has a module for parallel or distributed execution, essential for Multi-relational Data Mining applications. In IndLog, parallelism may be used in three flavours: splitting of the data among the computation nodes; parallelising the search through the hypothesis space and; using the different computation nodes to do theory-level search, that is generating different theories in different computation nodes and choosing the best one.

4   The Applications

IndLog was successfully applied to major datasets from the ILP literature. It is currently being applied to the problem of Protein Folding (predicting the secondary and tertiary structure of proteins). In the first stage of this study IndLog induces rules to predict the start and end points of an α-helix. It is being applied to two "Structure-Activity Relationship" problems: understanding of anti high blood pressure drugs and; anti malaria drugs. The parallel and distributed module is of capital importance to process very large datasets. IndLog is currently being used in the analysis of the firewall logs of a university campus. In this application approximately 50 MB of data is generated per day. It has been successfully applied to Time-Series prediction problems [7] and Reverse Engineering tasks [3]. IndLog automatically computed the thresholds of a TAR model, used in Time-Series applications.

References

1. Camacho, Rui, As lazy as it can be, 8th Proceedings of the Scandinavian Conference on AI, ed. Biornar Tessen et al. IOS press, 47-58, (2003).
2. Camacho, R, Improving the efficiency of ILP systems using an Incremental Language Level Search, Twelfth Belgian-Dutch Conference on Machine Learning (Benelearn 2002), The Netherlands, 2002.
3. Camacho, R. e Brazdil, P., Improving the robustness and encoding complexity of behavioural clones, Twelfth European Conference on Machine Learning (ECML-01), Freiburg, Germany, 2001
4. Camacho, R., Inducing Models of Human Control Skills using Machine Learning Algorithms, Dep. Electrical Engineering and Computation, Univ. Porto, (2000).
5. Srinivasan, A. and Camacho, R., Numerical Reasoning with an ILP System Capable of Lazy Evaluation and Customized Search, Journal of Logic Programming, 2-3, Vol. 40, pp 185-213, 1999.
6. Rui Camacho, "From sequential to Parallel Inductive Logic Programming" 6th International Meeting on high performance computing for computational science VECPAR 2004, Valencia, Espanha, Junho 2004
7. Alves, A., Camacho, R., Oliveira, E., "Learning Time Series Models with Inductive Logic Programming", European Symposium on Intelligent Technologies, Hybrid Systems and their implementation on Smart Adaptive Systems (EUNITE 2003), 10 - 12 July 2003 in Oulu, Finland
8. Costa, V. and Damas, L. and Reis, R. and Azevedo, R., YAP Prolog User's Manual, Universidade do Porto, (1989).

OLEX – A Reasoning-Based Text Classifier

Chiara Cumbo[2], Salvatore Iiritano[1], and Pasquale Rullo[1,2]

[1] Exeura s.r.l., iiritano@exeura.it
[2] Dip. di Matematica, Unical, 87030 Rende, Italy, {cumbo,rullo}@mat.unical.it

Abstract. This paper describes OLEX, a prototypical system for text classification. The main characteristics of OLEX are: using ontologies for the formal representation of the domain knowledge; employing the pre-processing technologies for a symbolic representation of text features; exploiting the expressive power of logic programming to extract concepts from documents. The proposed approach allows us to perform a high-precision document classification.

1 System Overview

OLEX is intended as a corporate classification system supporting the entire process life-cycle: document storage and organization, ontology construction, pre-processing and classification. It has been developed as a client-server application based on jsp-pages. Figure 1 summarizes the basic components of OLEX.

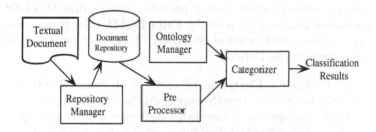

Fig. 1. OLEX Basic Components

The **Repository Manager** (RM) provides all functionalities needed for document storage and organization. It relies, on the client side, on a standard FTP web-client whereby the knowledge engineer can download and upload text files, add, remove, copy or move documents and folders.

The **Ontology Manager** (OM) supports the specification of ontologies based on a powerful visual interface. Ontologies provide the domain knowledge needed for high-precision classification. The ontology specification language supports the following basic constructs: Concepts, Attributes, Taxonomic and Non-Taxonomic binary associations, Association cardinality constraints, Concept Instances, Synonyms. Internally, an ontology is stored as a set of facts of the following type: *concept(language)*, *instance_of(language, datalog)*, etc.

J.J. Alferes and J. Leite (Eds.): JELIA 2004, LNAI 3229, pp. 722–725, 2004.

The **Pre-processor** is in charge of generating a machine-readable representation of documents [1]. This module supports two tasks: (*a*) Pre-Analysis based on three main activities: Normalization, Structural Analysis and Tokenization, and (*b*) Linguistic Analysis, which in turn consists of a Lexical Analysis (stemming and PoS-Tagging, the latter based on the Hepple Tagger [2]) and a Quantitative Analysis. The output of the Pre-Processor is a set of facts representing the relevant information about the processed document. In particular, we have (1) PoS facts of the form $p(Id, Token)$, where p is either one of *noun*, *properNoun*, *verb*, *adjective*, and Id is the position of *Token* within the text; (2) formatting facts, like *title(first-Id,last-Id)*, *section(first-Id,last-Id)* and *paragraph(par-Id,first-Id,last-Id)* and (3) frequency facts, like $frequency(Token, Number)$ and $numberOfTokens(Number)$.

Finally, the **Categorizer** is the module performing the task of classifying (pre-processed) documents w.r.t. an ontology – that is, it associates to each concept C of the given ontology all documents that are recognized to be relevant for C. From the architectural point of view, we can see the Categorizer as Control+DLV system [3]. In the following section, we will provide a brief description of the techniques underlying the Categorizer.

2   Classification Techniques

In order to classify documents w.r.t. an ontology O, we equip each concept C of O with a *categorization program* used to provide evidence that D is relevant for C. A categorization program is essentially a stratified Datalog program extended by *aggregate functions* and *external predicates* [4]. Throughout this paper, we refer to such a language as Datalog^f.

Example 1. EEL (Exeura Electronic Library) is an ontology on Knowledge Management built in order to classify papers on the various topics of this area; examples of *EEL* concepts are "knowledge discovery", "text mining", "ontology", etc. Next we show some Datalog^f rules aimed at discovering such concepts.

$$r_1 : p_1(I) : -noun(I, text), verb(J, mining), same\_par(K, I, J).$$
$$r_2 : p_2 : -N = \#count\{I : p_1(I)\} > t.+$$

Rule r_1 above "verifies" if the words "text" and "mining" occur in some paragraph of the given text. Rule r_2, in turn, "counts" the number N of times r_1 succeeds (using the aggregate function $\#count()$) and states p_1 true if N is greater than a given threshold t. Note that *noun* and *verb* are *PoS* predicates. Rule r_3 below can be used to match an expression of the form "... discover(ing) knowledge within text(s)...".

$$r_3 : \ p_3(K) :- \ verb(I, X), same\_stem(X, discover), noun(J, knowledge),$$
$$J = I + 1, noun(K, Y), same\_stem(Y, text), K > J,$$
$$same\_par(N, I, J), same\_par(N, J, K).$$

where *same_stem*() is an external predicate, based on the Porter algorithm [5], which determines whether two words have the same stem or not.
Finally, the following rule shows how the concept "ontology" can be detected within a text talking of ontology languages (such as OWL, RDF, etc.)

$$r_4 : p_4(X, F) :- \quad instance\_of(language, X),$$
$$association(onto\_language, X, ontology), frequency(X, F).$$

Here, X is an ontology specification language and F the number of times it occurs within the given text. It is worth noting how rule r_4 above exploits the knowledge provided by the EEL ontology through the predicates $instance\_of()$ and $association()$ (indeed, X is an instance of "language" linked to the concept "ontology" through the association "onto-language"). □

We define the categorization program P_C of a concept C as a totally ordered set of components $(c_1, .., c_n, < *)$, where c_i, $1 \leq i \leq n$, is a Datalog^f program and $< *$ is such that $c_i < *c_j$, for any i, j with $i < j$. Informally, each component groups rules capable to recognize concepts that are possibly inaccessible to the "previous" ones. We call c_1 the *default component* of C, as it is automatically generated by the system. Roughly speaking, the default component of C consists of rules that, exploiting the ontological knowledge (such as synonyms, relevant terms, instances, contextual knowledge, etc.) try to discover whether C occurs in the title, or in some section title, or throughout the text. Now, given a document D, the evaluation of P_C (w.r.t. D) starts from c_1 and, as soon as a component c_i, $1 \leq i \leq n$, "succeeds", the process stops successfully – i.e., D is recognized to be relevant for C; if no such a component is found, the classification (of D w.r.t. C) fails. The evaluation of each component is performed by the DLV system. As regards the classification of D w.r.t. an ontology O, OLEX relies on an ontology-driven approach which exploits the presence of taxonomic hierarchies. This technique is based on the principle that if a document is relevant for a concept then it is so for all of its ancestors within an is-a taxonomy (unless the contrary is explicitly stated). This allows us to drastically reduce the "classification space".

3 Preliminary Experimental Results

Some preliminary tests of the current implementation have been carried out on a 2.2GHz Linux PC with 512 MB RAM DDR.
Using the various modules of OLEX, we have first conducted the following preparatory steps: (1) we have gathered 71 documents on the various topics of Knowledge Management from people within Exeura; all these papers are pdf documents written in English and ranging from a minimum of 800 words to a maximum of 58.500 words, with an average length of 7150 words; (2) then, documents have been pre-processed according to the steps described in Section 1; (3) finally, the EEL ontology has been created.
Besides, we have manually classified the training database (71 texts) w.r.t. the EEL concepts (that are 12). At this point, we have ran the classifier using only

Table 1. Classification results

Concept	Precision	Recall
Knowledge Representation and Reasoning	0.69	1.00
NLP	1.00	0.73
Text Mining	0.86	0.80
Language	0.73	0.92
Ontology	0.84	0.77
Pre-processing	0.75	1.00
Summarization	1.00	1.00
Semantic Web	0.73	0.96

the default components automatically generated by the system (i.e., we haven't added any manual knowledge, so completely delegating the system in the task of classification). Using OLEX, classification is very fast: cpu time for the classification of one document (w.r.t. the whole ontology) ranges from 0.04 seconds (for a document of 800 words) to 3.62 seconds (for a document of 58.500 words). The time needed to classify the entire corpus w.r.t. all the ontology concepts is of 30 seconds, with an average time of 0.42 seconds/document. We plan to significantly improve performances by optimizing DLV calls. Concerning the quality of classification, results concerning a subset of the ontology concepts are summarized in table 1. Here, we have used the standard definitions of Precision and Recall, namely

$$Precision = \frac{|R_C \cap A_C|}{|R_C|}, \quad Recall = \frac{|R_C \cap A_C|}{|A_C|}$$

where R_C is the set of relevant documents for concept C (i.e., those manually associated to C) and A_C is the answer set for C. Clearly, these tests are very preliminary, and only a deeper experimentation can lead to firm conclusions.

References

1. Yang: A comparative study on feature selection in text categorization. In: International Conference on Machine Learning, ACL (1997) 412–420
2. Hepple, M.: Independence and Commitment: Assumptions for Rapid Training and Execution of Rule-based POS Taggers. In: Proceedings of the 38th Annual Meeting of the Association for Computational Linguistics (ACL-2000), Hong Kong (2000) 278–285
3. Faber, W., Pfeifer, G.: DLV homepage (since 1996) http://www.dlvsystem.com/.
4. Dell'Armi, T., Faber, W., Ielpa, G., Leone, N., Pfeifer, G.: Aggregate Functions in Disjunctive Logic Programming: Semantics, Complexity, and Implementation in DLV. In: Proc. IJCAI 2003, Acapulco, Mexico, Morgan Kaufmann Publishers (2003)
5. Porter, M.: An algorithm for suffix stripping. Program **3** (1980) 130–137

VERDI: An Automated Tool for Web Sites Verification[*]

M. Alpuente[1], D. Ballis[2], and M. Falaschi[2]

[1] DSIC, Universidad Politécnica de Valencia, Camino de Vera s/n, Apdo. 22012,
46071 Valencia, Spain. alpuente@dsic.upv.es.
[2] Dip. Matematica e Informatica, Via delle Scienze 206, 33100 Udine, Italy.
{demis,falaschi}@dimi.uniud.it.

Abstract. VERDI is a system for the automated verification of Web sites which can be used to specify integrity conditions for a given Web site, and then automatically check whether these conditions are actually fulfilled. It provides a rule-based, formal specification language which allows us to define syntactic/semantic properties of the Web site as well as a verification facility which computes the requirements not fulfilled by the Web site, and helps to repair the errors by finding out incomplete/missing Web pages.

1 Introduction

The increasing complexity of Web sites calls for tools which are able to aid Web designers in the construction and maintenance of Web sites. Systematic, formal approaches can bring many benefits to quality Web sites development, giving support for automated Web site verification [2]. In [3] a formal, declarative verification algorithm is proposed, which checks a particular class of integrity constraints concerning the Web site's structure (syntactic properties), but not the contents (semantic properties) of a given instance of the site. The framework XLINKIT [2] allows one to check the consistency of distributed, heterogeneous documents as well as to fix the (possibly) inconsistent information. Its specification language is a restricted form of first order logic combined with Xpath expressions [8]. This paper presents the prototype VERDI (Verification an Rewriting for Debugging Internet sites) which provides a rule-based language for the specification and the verification of syntactic as well as semantic properties on collections of XML/HTML documents. The prototype is based on the theoretical framework we proposed in [1] and enjoys the effectiveness of rule-based computation.

We use rewriting-based technology both to specify the required properties and to formalize a verification technique, which is able to check them.

[*] This work has been partially supported by MCYT under grants TIC2001-2705-C03-01, HU2003-0003, by Generalitat Valenciana under grant GR03/025 and by ICT for EU-India Cross Cultural Dissemination Project under grant ALA/95/23/2003/077-054.

```
<members>                               members(
    <member status="professor">            member(status(professor),
        <name> mario </name>                   name(mario),
        <surname> rossi </surname>             surname(rossi)
    </member>                               ),
    <member status="technician">           member(status(technician),
        <name> franca </name>                  name(franca),
        <surname> bianchi </surname>           surname(bianchi)
    </member>                               )
</members>                              )
```

Fig. 1. An XML document and its corresponding encoding as a ground term.

2 Denotation of Web Sites

In our framework, a *Web page* is either an XML[7] or an HTML[6] document.
Since Web pages are provided with a tree-like structure, they can be straightforwardly translated into ordinary terms of a given term algebra as shown in
Figure 1. Note that XML/HTML tag attributes can be considered as common
tagged elements, and hence translated in the same way. Therefore, *Web sites*
can be represented as finite sets of (ground) terms.

3 Web Specification Language

Web specifications formalize conditions to be fulfilled by a given Web site.
Roughly speaking, a Web specification is a finite set of rules of the form $l \rightharpoonup r$,
where l and r are terms. Some symbols in the right-hand sides of the rules may
be marked by means of the symbol $\sharp$. Marking information of a given rule r is
used to select the subset of the Web site in which we want to check the condition
formalized by r. Intuitively, the interpretation of a rule $l \rightharpoonup r$ w.r.t. a Web site
W is as follows: if (an instance of) l is recognized in W, also (an instance of) r
must be recognized in W.

In the following we present an example of Web specification.

Example 1. Consider the following Web specification, which models some required properties of a research group Web site containing information about
group members affiliation, scientific publications and personal data.

$$\text{hpage}(\text{status}(\text{professor})) \rightharpoonup \sharp\text{hpage}(\sharp\text{status}(\sharp\text{professor}), \text{teaching})$$
$$\text{member}(\text{name}(X), \text{surname}(Y)) \rightharpoonup \sharp\text{hpage}(\text{name}(X), \sharp\text{surname}(\sharp Y), \text{status})$$
$$\text{pubs}(\text{pub}(\text{name}(X), \text{surname}(Y))) \rightharpoonup \sharp\text{member}(\text{name}(X), \sharp\text{surname}(\sharp Y))$$

First rule states that, whenever a home page of a professor is recognized, then
that page must also include some teaching information. Here, for instance, marks
are used to check the condition only on professor home pages. Second rule for-
malizes the following property: if there is a Web page containing a member list,
then for each member, a home page exists containing (at least) the name, the
surname and the status of this member. Finally, the third rule specifies that,

whenever there exists a Web page containing information about scientific publications, each author of a publication should be a member of the research group.

4   The Verification Technique

Our verification technique allows us to verify a Web site w.r.t. a given Web specification in order to detect incomplete and/or missing Web pages. Moreover, by analyzing the requirements not fulfilled by the Web site, we are also able to find out the missing information which is needed to repair the Web site. Since reasoning on the Web calls for formal methods specifically fitting the Web context, we developed a novel, rewriting-based technique called *partial rewriting* [1], in which the traditional pattern matching mechanism is replaced by tree *simulation* [4] in order to provide a much more suitable mechanism for recognizing patterns inside semistructured documents, which is (i) independent of the order of the tagged elements contained in a Web page and (ii) able to efficiently extract the partial information of a Web page we need to check.

Basically our verification technique works in two steps. Given a Web site W and a Web specification I, we first compute a set of requirements (that is, information that should be present in the Web site) by generating the set of all possible Web pages that can be derived from W via I by partial rewriting. Then, we check whether the computed requirements are satisfied by W using simulation and marking information. Requirements which are not fulfilled allow us to detect missing or incomplete Web pages and provide the information which is necessary to fix the Web site.

Example 2. Consider the Web specification I of Example 1 and the following Web site W:

```
W = {(1)  members(status(professor),member(name(mario),surname(rossi)),
               member(status(technician),name(franca),surname(bianchi)),
               member(status(student),name(giulio),surname(verdi))),
     (2)  hpage(name(mario),surname(rossi),phone(333),status(professor),
               hobbies(hobby(reading),hobby(gardening))),
     (3)  hpage(name(franca),surname(bianchi),status(technician),phone(555)),
     (4)  hpage(name(anna),surname(blu),status(professor),phone(444),
               teaching(course(algebra))),
     (5)  pubs(pub(name(mario),surname(rossi),title(blahblah1),year(2003)),
               pub(name(anna),surname(blu),title(blahblah2),year(2002))))}
```

Then, by running the VERDI system on Web site W and Web specification I, we compute the following set of requirements

```
{(a)♯hpage(name(mario), ♯surname(♯rossi),status),
 (b)♯hpage(name(franca), ♯surname(♯bianchi),status),
 (c)♯hpage(name(giulio), ♯surname(♯verdi),status),
 (d)♯hpage(♯status(♯professor),teaching),
 (e)♯member(name(mario), ♯surname(♯rossi)),(f)♯member(name(anna), ♯surname(♯blu)),
 (g)♯hpage(name(anna), ♯surname(♯blu),status)}
```

During the analysis of the set of requirements, our system tries to recognize the structure and the contents of each requirement inside W, yielding the following outcomes: (i) requirement (c) is missing in Web site W, (ii) Web page (1) is incomplete w.r.t. requirement (f), and (ii) Web page (2) is incomplete w.r.t. requirement (d).

Informally, the outputs tell us that (i) the home page of Giulio Verdi is missing in W, (ii) Anna blu should be a member of the research group and (iii) professor Mario Rossi should add some teaching information to his personal home page.

5   Implementation

The basic methodology presented so far has been implemented in the prototype VERDI (VErification and Rewriting for Debugging Internet sites), which is written in DrScheme v205 [5] and is publicly available together with a set of tests at http://www.dimi.uniud.it/~demis/#software.

The implementation consists of about 80 function definitions (approximately 1000 lines of source code). VERDI includes a parser for semistructured expressions (i.e. XML/HTML documents) and Web specifications, and several modules implementing the user interface, the partial rewriting mechanism and the verification technique. The system allows the user to load a Web site consisting of a finite set of semistructured expressions together with a Web specification. Additionally, he/she can inspect the loaded data and finally check the Web pages w.r.t. the Web site specification. The user interface is guided by textual menus, which are (hopefully) self-explaining. We tested the system on several Web site examples which can be found at the URL address mentioned above. In each considered test case, we were able to detect the errors (i.e. missing and incomplete Web pages) efficiently. For instance, the verification of the Web site of Example 2 w.r.t. the Web specification of Example 1 is performed almost instantaneously on a standard desktop computer.

References

1. M. Alpuente, D. Ballis, and M. Falaschi. A Rewriting-based Framework for Web Sites Verification. In *Proc. of RULE'04*. ENTCS, Elsevier, 2004. To appear.
2. L. Capra, W. Emmerich, A. Finkelstein, and C. Nentwich. xlinkit: a Consistency Checking and Smart Link Generation Service. *ACM Transactions on Internet Technology*, 2(2):151–185, 2002.
3. M. Fernandez, D. Florescu, A. Levy, and D. Suciu. Verifying Integrity Constraints on Web Sites. In *Proc. of IJCAI'99*, vol. 2, pp. 614–619. Morgan Kaufmann, 1999.
4. M. R. Henzinger, T. A. Henzinger, and P. W. Kopke. Computing simulations on finite and infinite graphs. In *Proc. of IEEE FOCS'95*, pp. 453–462, 1995.
5. PLT. DrScheme web site. Available at: http://www.drscheme.org.
6. World Wide Web Consortium (W3C). HyperText Markup Language (HTML) 4.01, 1997. Available at: http://www.w3.org.
7. World Wide Web Consortium (W3C). Extensible Markup Language (XML) 1.0, second edition, 1999. Available at: http://www.w3.org.
8. World Wide Web Consortium (W3C). XML Path Language (XPath), 1999. Available at: http://www.w3.org.

SATMC: A SAT-Based Model Checker for Security Protocols*

Alessandro Armando and Luca Compagna

AI-Lab, DIST – Università di Genova
Viale Causa 13, 16145 Genova, Italy.
{armando,compa}@dist.unige.it

1 Introduction

We present SATMC (SAT-based Model Checker), an open and flexible platform for SAT-based bounded model checking [8] of security protocols. Under the standard assumptions of *perfect cryptography* and of *strong typing*, SATMC performs a bounded analysis of the problem by considering scenarios with a finite number of sessions whereby messages are exchanged on a channel controlled by the most general intruder based on the Dolev-Yao model [12].

Given a positive integer k and a protocol description written in a rewrite-based formalism, SATMC automatically generates a propositional formula by using sophisticated encoding techniques developed for planning (see [13] for a survey); state-of-the-art SAT-solvers taken off-the-shelf are then used to check the propositional formula for satisfiability and any model found by the solver is turned into a partially ordered set of transitions of depth k whose linearizations correspond to attacks on the protocol. If the formula is found to be unsatisfiable, then k is incremented and the whole procedure is iterated until either a termination condition is met or a given upper bound for k is reached.

Experimental results indicate that the approach is very effective: SATMC takes a few seconds to analyze and detect flaws on 22 protocols of the Clark&Jacob library [10].

2 Bounded Model Checking of Security Protocols

A security problem associated to a given security protocol consists of determining whether some undesirable states can be reached starting from some initial states by using the legal protocol steps and the admissible actions of the intruder.

Like other SAT-based model checkers, SATMC tackles the (bounded) reachability problem by generating SAT formulae of the form: $\Phi_\Pi^k = I_0 \wedge \bigwedge_{i=0}^{k-1} T_i^{i+1} \wedge G_k$ where I_0, T_i^{i+1}, and G_k are the boolean formulae representing the initial state, the transition relation, and the goal states, respectively. The main difference

* This work was partially funded by the FET Open EC Project "AVISPA: Automated Validation of Internet Security Protocols and Applications" (IST-2001-39252) and by the FIRB Project no. RBAU01P5SS.

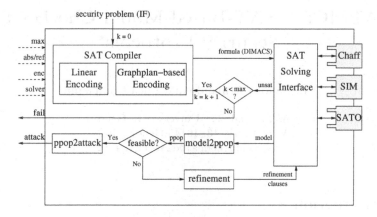

Fig. 1. Architecture of SATMC

between the encoding techniques used by SATMC and those employed in other bounded model checkers (e.g. NuSMV [9]) is in the way the formula that encodes the transition relation, i.e. T_i^{i+1}, is generated. Two encoding techniques are currently implemented in SATMC: the first belongs to the family of so-called *linear encodings* [3], the second is the more sophisticated *graphplan-based encoding* [6].

3   SATMC

The architecture of SATMC is shown in Figure 1. SATMC takes as input a security problem expressed in a rewrite-based formalism called IF [2] and the following parameters: `max`, an integer to be used as upper-bound for iterative deepening; `abs/ref`, a boolean parameter used to enable the abstraction/refinement strategy introduced in [4]; `enc`, the selected SAT reduction encoding technique (*linear* and *graphplan* are currently supported); `solver` (Chaff, SIM, and SATO are currently supported). SATMC returns either an attack or reports that no attack has been found on the input security problem by using up to `max` unfoldings of the transition relation.

The SAT Compiler first translates the IF specification into a SATE specification[1] and then applies the selected encoding technique to the SATE specification for increasing values of k. The formula generated at each step is fed to the selected state-of-the-art SAT solver through the SAT Solving Interface. As soon as a satisfiable formula is found, the corresponding model is translated back (by the model2ppop module) into a partially ordered set of transitions of depth k (also called pseudo partial-order plans) potentially representing a set of attacks on the protocol. The tool then checks whether there exists a linearization of the

---

[1] SATE is the native STRIPS-like language used in SATMC.

Table 1. Experimental data on the Clark-Jacob's library [10]

Protocol	K	A	CL	ET	ST	Protocol	K	A	CL	ET	ST
Andrew	9	442	1,365	0.14	0.01	*KLS rep.*	7	1,634	23,190	3.89	0.03
EKE	5	394	1,337	0.12	0.00	*NSCK*	9	435	1,406	0.12	0.00
ISO-CCF-1 U	4	102	295	0.00	0.00	*NSPK*	7	411	1,279	0.09	0.00
ISO-CCF-2 M	4	115	311	0.02	0.00	*NSPK-server*	8	847	2,702	0.23	0.00
ISO-PK-1 U	4	149	418	0.03	0.00	*SPLICE*	9	951	3,168	0.32	0.00
ISO-PK-2 M	4	129	363	0.02	0.00	*Swick 1*	5	192	554	0.06	0.00
ISO-SK-1 U	4	93	265	0.01	0.00	*Swick 2*	6	257	838	0.08	0.00
ISO-SK-2 M	4	117	314	0.02	0.00	*Swick 3*	4	171	498	0.05	0.01
KaoChow 1	7	426	1,781	0.18	0.01	*Swick 4*	5	215	634	0.04	0.00
KaoChow 2	9	726	3,393	0.32	0.00	*Stubblebine rep*	3	146	478	0.04	0.00
KaoChow 3	9	990	6,118	0.66	0.03	*Woo-Lam M*	6	481	1,539	0.19	0.00

partially ordered set of transitions.[2] If no linearization exists, then the associated attack is computed and returned, otherwise the refinement module refines the encoding by adding new clauses and the whole procedure is iterated. As soon as a linearizable partial-order sequence of transitions is found, the ppop2attack module translates it into an attack which is reported to the user.

Thanks to a recent extension [7], SATMC now also compiles protocol security problems into logic programs which are in turn fed into a state-of-the-art solver for logic programs.

4   Experiments

We have thoroughly tested SATMC against a large number of security protocols of the Clark&Jacob library [10]. Table 1 reports the results of our experiments.[3] For each protocol we give the smallest value of k at which the attack is found (**K**), the number of propositional variables (**A**) and clauses (**CL**) in the SAT formula, the time spent to generate the SAT formulae (**ET**), and the total time spent by the SAT solver (**ST**). Notice that the solving times are negligible for all problems and that the encoding time is less than 1 second for all problems but one. These results confirm the effectiveness of approach and pave the way to the application of SATMC to protocols of industrial complexity.[4]

The SATMC tool and all the IF specifications of the security problems used in our experiments can be found at http://www.ai.dist.unige.it/satmc.

---

[2] If the abstraction/refinement strategy is disabled (i.e. abs/ref=false), the linearization is guaranteed to exists and the check is avoided. See [4] for the details.

[3] Experiments have been carried out on a PC with a 1.4 GHz CPU, 1 GB of RAM, and with max=10, abs/ref=false, enc=graphplan, and solver=chaff.

[4] SATMC is one of the back-ends of the AVISPA Tool (http://www.avispa-project.org), a platform for the development of large-scale Internet security protocols.

5   Related Work

A large number of techniques for the analysis security protocols are available. While some techniques (e.g., [16,15]) are tailored to the analysis of security protocols, others reduce the analysis of security protocols to some general purpose formalism such as CSP [14], rewriting logic [11], or logic programming [1]. SATMC, by performing a reduction to propositional logic, clearly belongs to the second camp and similarly to all techniques in the this camp, it can be easily adapted in response to changes or extensions to the underlying model (e.g. as when properties of cryptographic operators or different models of the intruder are to be taken into account—see, e.g., [5]). Additionally—thanks to the efficiency of state-of-the-art SAT solvers—SATMC performance comparable to that of techniques in the first camp [2].

References

1. L. C. Aiello and F. Massacci. Verifying security protocols as planning in logic programming. *ACM Trans. on Computational Logic*, 2(4):542–580, Oct. 2001.
2. A. Armando, D. Basin, M. Bouallagui, Y. Chevalier, L. Compagna, S. Mödersheim, M. Rusinowitch, M. Turuani, L. Viganò, and L. Vigneron. The AVISS Security Protocol Analysis Tool. In *Proc.of CAV'02*, LNCS 2404. Springer-Verlag, 2002.
3. A. Armando and L. Compagna. Automatic SAT-Compilation of Protocol Insecurity Problems via Reduction to Planning. In *Proc.of FORTE 2002*. 2002.
4. A. Armando and L. Compagna. Abstraction-driven SAT-based Analysis of Security Protocols. In *Proc.of SAT 2003*, LNCS 2919. Springer-Verlag, 2003.
5. A. Armando and L. Compagna. An Optimized Intruder Model for SAT-based Model-Checking of Security Protocols. In *Proc. of ARSPA Workshop*. 2004.
6. A. Armando, L. Compagna, and P. Ganty. SAT-based Model-Checking of Security Protocols using Planning Graph Analysis. In *Proc.of FME'2003*. 2003.
7. A. Armando, L. Compagna, and Y. Lierler. Automatic Compilation of Protocol Insecurity Problems into Logic Programming. In this volume, 2004.
8. A. Biere, A. Cimatti, E. Clarke, and Y. Zhu. Symbolic Model Checking without BDDs. In *Proc.of TACAS'99*, LNCS 1579. Springer-Verlag, 1999.
9. A. Cimatti, E. Clarke, F. Giunchiglia, and M. Roveri. NuSMV: A New Symbolic Model Verifier. *LNCS 1633*, 1999.
10. J. Clark and J. Jacob. A Survey of Authentication Protocol Literature: Version 1.0, 17.Nov.1997. URL: www.cs.york.ac.uk/~jac/papers/drareview.ps.gz.
11. G. Denker, J. Meseguer, and C. Talcott. Protocol specification and analysis in Maude. In *Proc.of the Workshop on Formal Methods and Security Protocols*. 1998.
12. D. Dolev and A. Yao. On the Security of Public-Key Protocols. *IEEE Transactions on Information Theory*, 2(29), 1983.
13. H. Kautz, H. McAllester, and B. Selman. Encoding Plans in Propositional Logic. In *Proc.of KR'96*, 1996.
14. G. Lowe. Casper: a Compiler for the Analysis of Security Protocols. *Journal of Computer Security*, 6(1):53–84, 1998.
15. J. K. Millen and V. Shmatikov. Constraint solving for bounded-process cryptographic protocol analysis. In *Proc. of the CCS'01*, pages 166–175, 2001.
16. D. Song. Athena: A new efficient automatic checker for security protocol analysis. In *Proc.of 12th Computer Security Foundation Workshop*, pages 192–202, 1999.

tabeql: A Tableau Based Suite for Equilibrium Logic

Agustín Valverde

Dept. of Applied Mathematics
University of Málaga, Spain

Abstract. Equilibrium logic is a formal system of nonmonotonic reasoning proposed by D. Pearce [6,7] that generalises the stable model and answer set semantics for logic programs [1]. The program tabeql included several systems that are related to *equilibrium logic* and are based on tableau methodology: an equilibrium model generator [8], a checker for strong equivalence between theories [4] and a checker for uniform equivalence [9].

1 Introduction

Equilibrium logic is a formal system of nonmonotonic reasoning proposed and discussed by D. Pearce in [6,7]. It is currently defined for propositional logic and can therefore be applied also to grounded (quantifier-free) theories in a first-order predicate language. This logic is based on a 5-valued logic called *here-and-there with strong negation* and denoted by N_5. One of the interesting features of equilibrium logic is that it generalises the stable model and answer set semantics for logic programs, as developed in [1]. In fact the equilibrium models of a theory coincide with its stable models or answer sets if the theory in question has the syntactic form of a logic program (for which the latter models are defined). It therefore offers a means to extend the reasoning mechanism associated with stable model semantics beyond the syntactic limitations of logic programs.

Although tableau calculi have been developed in the past for systems of nonmonotonic logic, these have mainly been based on classical logic. However, in our systems, we use standard techniques for many-valued logics and in particular, we take truth-value sets as signs in the tableau.

Our main aim is not that of providing a more efficient implementation of stable model semantics than others in the literature such as DLV [3], GnT [2], and smodels [10]. These provide special purpose algorithms that are tailored to the specific syntax of logic programs and are therefore likely to be more efficient in this restricted setting. By contrast, the more general theorem proving techniques used in our system apply to the case of full propositional logic and are therefore likely to be of interest to those seeking to extend stable model reasoning beyond the language of logic programs as, for instance, programs with nested expressions [5]. Finally our system includes an implementation of checkers for equivalence between programs. Specifically, a system for strong equivalence checking based

J.J. Alferes and J. Leite (Eds.): JELIA 2004, LNAI 3229, pp. 734–737, 2004.

on the results in [4] and a system for uniform equivalence checking presented in [9] are included.

2   Equilibrium Logic

Equilibrium logic is a non-monotonic reasoning system defined over the here-and-there logic, $\mathbf{N}_5$. The propositional language is defined over a set of propositional variables and connectives $\wedge$, $\vee$, $\rightarrow$, $\neg$ and $\sim$. The set of truth values for $\mathbf{N}_5$ is $\mathbf{5} = \{-2, -1, 0, 1, 2\}$ and 2 is the designated value; the connectives are interpreted as follows: $\wedge$ is the minimum function, $\vee$ is the maximum function, $\sim x = -x$,

$$x \rightarrow y = \begin{cases} 2 & \text{if either } x \leq 0 \text{ or } x \leq y \\ y & \text{otherwise} \end{cases} \quad \text{and} \quad \neg x = \begin{cases} 2 & \text{if } x \leq 0 \\ -x & \text{otherwise} \end{cases}$$

Let Π be a set of formulas; in $\mathbf{N}_5$, the ordering $\sigma_1 \trianglelefteq \sigma_2$ among models σ_1 and σ_2 of Π holds iff for every propositional variable p occurring in Π the following properties hold:

1. $\sigma_1(p) = 0$ if and only if $\sigma_2(p) = 0$.
2. If $\sigma_1(p) \geq 1$, then $\sigma_1(p) \leq \sigma_2(p)$
3. If $\sigma_1(p) \leq -1$, then $\sigma_1(p) \geq \sigma_2(p)$

This order allow us to introduce the notion of total model and equilibrium model:

- A model σ of Π in $\mathbf{N}_5$ is a *total model* if $\sigma(p) \in \{-2, 0, 2\}$ for every propositional variable p in Π.
- A model σ of Π in $\mathbf{N}_5$ is in *equilibrium* if it is total and minimal under $\trianglelefteq$ among all of its models.

Equilibrium logic is the logic determined by the equilibrium models of a theory. Part of the interest of equilibrium logic arises from the fact that on a syntactically restricted class of theories it coincides with a well-known nonmonotonic inference relation studied in logic programming. Formally, when a consistent theory has the syntactic shape of a (disjunctive, extended) logic program, its equilibrium models coincide with its answer sets in the sense of [1].

In the main areas where logic programming is applied, it may be important to know when different logic programs representing a given problem or state of affairs are equivalent and lead to essentially the same solutions (answer sets or equilibrium models). Very often one would like to know that the equivalence is also robust, since two programs may have the same answer sets yet behave very differently once they are embedded in some larger context. For a robust or modular notion of equivalence one should require that programs behave similarly when extended by any further programs. This leads to the following concept of *strong* equivalence: programs Π_1 and Π_2 are strongly equivalent, in symbols $\Pi \equiv_s \Pi_2$, if and only if for any X, $\Pi_1 \cup X$ is equivalent to (has the same answer sets as) $\Pi_2 \cup X$. The concept of strong equivalence for logic programs in ASP was introduced and studied in [4] and has given rise to a substantial body of further work looking at different characterisations.

Theorem 1 ([4]). *Any two theories Π and Π' are strongly equivalent iff they are logically equivalent in $\mathbf{N}_5$, ie. $\Pi \equiv_s \Pi'$ iff $\Pi \equiv \Pi'$.*

Besides strong equivalence one may consider weaker concepts that still permit one program to be substituted for another in certain well-defined settings. One such notion is that of *uniform* equivalence, defined as above but restricted to the case where X is a set of atoms. This concept is of interest when one is dealing with a fixed set of rules, or intensional knowledge base, and a varying set of facts or extensional knowledge component. In [9] the uniform equivalence between theories is characterize using the relation $\trianglelefteq$:

Theorem 2 ([9]). *Two theories Π_1 and Π_2 with the same total models are u-equivalent if and only if the following conditions hold:*

(a) If σ is a non-total model of Π_1 then there exists a non-total model τ of Π_2 such that $\sigma \trianglelefteq \tau$.

(a) If τ is a non-total model of Π_2 then there exists a non-total model σ of Π_1 such that $\tau \trianglelefteq \sigma$.

3   Description of `tabeql`

The system `tabeql` has been implemented using Objective CAML version 3.06. Although the main work has been done under Mac OS X, the system can be straightforwardly ported to any Unix-like platform. Caml programs can easily be interfaced with other languages, in particular with other C programs or libraries; two compilation modes are supported, compilation to byte-code (for portability) and to native assembly code (for performance). The native code compiler generates very efficient code, complemented by a fast, unobtrusive incremental garbage collector. Finally, as we have mentioned above, the programs can be compiled on most Unix platforms (Mac OS X, Linux, Digital Unix, Solaris, IRIX) and well as under Windows.

The allowed syntax of the command line to call the program is the following:

- `tabeql -m` *<textfile>*   generates the equilibrium models of the formula described in *<textfile>*.
- `tabeql -e` *<textfile1>* *<textfile2>* checks if the formulas in *<textfile1>* and *<textfile2>* are either strongly equivalent or uniform equivalent.

In the text files, any string not starting with numbers can be used as atoms, and the following ASCII symbols are used to represent connectives: the conjunction, &, and the disjunction, |, can be used with any arity; -> is used for implication; - is used for (weak) negation, and ~ is used for strong negation. Every subformula must be enclosed by parentheses, except the negation of literals. This is an example of the content of a valid input file:

```
((a -> ( f -> g)) & ((f -> g) -> a)) ->
((g -> a) & (-f -> a) & ((f & a) -> g) & (f | -g | a))
```

The main part of the program is the operator that constructs a terminated tableau and generate the set of models. After that a test of minimality or maximality is applied depending of the selected option:

- tabeql -m $<textfile>$: if φ is the formula in $<textfile>$, then (1) a terminated tableau is constructed from $\{2\}\varphi$; (2) the set of total models of φ is generated; (3) the maximal models, ie. the equilibrium models are selected.
- tabeql -e $<textfile1>$ $<textfile2>$: if φ_1 is the formula in $<textfile1>$ and φ_2 is the formula in $<textfile2>$, then (1) two terminated tableau are constructed, T_1 from $\{\{2\}\varphi_1, \{-2,-1,0,1\}\varphi_2\}$ and T_2 from $\{\{2\}\varphi_2, \{-2,-1,0,1\}\varphi_1\}$; (2) if T_1 and T_2 are both closed, then the formulas are strongly equivalentes; otherwise, (3) every model generated from T_1 is checked to find a greater non-total model for φ_2 and every model generated from T_2 is checked to find a greater non-total model for φ_1. In the third step, new tableaux are used, the auxiliary tableaux described in [9].

References

1. M. Gelfond and V. Lifschitz. Classical negation in logic programs and disjunctive databases. *New Generation Computing*, 9:365–385, 1991.
2. T. Janhumen, I. Niemelä, D. Seipel, P. Simons, and J.-H. You. Unfolding partiality and disjunctions in stable model semantics. CoRR: cs.AI/0303009, March 2003.
3. N. Leone, G. Pfeifer, W. Faber, T. Eiter, G. Gottlob, S. Perri, and F. Scarcello. The dlv system for knowledge representation and reasoning. CoRR: cs.AI/0211004, September 2003.
4. V. Lifschitz, D. Pearce, and A. Valverde. Strongly equivalent logic programs. *ACM Transactions on Computational Logic*, 2(4):526–541, October 2001.
5. V. Lifschitz, L. Tang and H. Turner. Nested Expressions in Logic Programs. *Annals of Mathematics and Artificial Intelligence*, 25(3-4): 369-389, 1999.
6. D. Pearce. A new logical characterisation of stable models and answer sets. In *Proc. of Non-Monotonic Extensions of Logic Programming, NMELP 96*, LNCS 1216, pages 57–70. Springer, 1997.
7. D. Pearce. Stable inference as intuitionistic validity. *Journal of Logic Programming*, 38:79–91, 1999.
8. D. Pearce, Inma P. de Guzmán, and A. Valverde. A tableau calculus for equilibrium entailment. In *Proc. of TABLEAUX 2000*, LNAI 1847, pages 352–367, St. Andrews, Scotland, 2000. Springer.
9. D. Pearce and A. Valverde. Uniform equivalence for equilibrium logic and logic programs. In *Proc. 7th Int. Conf. on Logic Programming and Nonmonotonic Reasoning (Fort Lauderdale, FL, USA)*, LNAI 2923, pages 194–206. Springer, 2004.
10. P. Simons, I. Niemelä, and T. Soininen. Extending and implementing the stable model semantics. *Artificial Intelligence*, 138(1–2):181–234, 2002.

tascpl: TAS Solver
for Classical Propositional Logic

M. Ojeda-Aciego and A. Valverde

Dept. Matemática Aplicada. Universidad de Málaga.
{aciego,a_valverde}@ctima.uma.es

Abstract. We briefly overview the most recent improvements we have incorporated to the existent implementations of the TAS methodology, the simplified Δ-tree representation of formulas in negation normal form. This new representation allows for a better description of the reduction strategies, in that considers only those occurrences of literals which are relevant for the satisfiability of the input formula. These reduction strategies are aimed at decreasing the number of required branchings and, therefore, control the size of the search space for the SAT problem.

1 Overview of TAS

TAS denotes a family of refutational satisfiability testers for both classical and non-classical logics which, like tableaux methods, also builds models for non valid formulas. So far, we have described algorithms for classical propositional logic [6,1], finite-valued propositional logics [3] and temporal logics [2].

The basis of the methodology is the alternative application of reduction strategies over formulas and a branching rule; the included reduction strategies are based on equivalence or equisatisfiability transformations whose complexity is at most quadratic; when no more simplifications can be applied, then the branching strategy is used and then the simplifications are called for. The power of the method is based not only on the intrinsically parallel design of the involved transformations, but also on the fact that these transformations are not just applied one after the other, but guided by some syntax directed criteria.

1.1 Δ-Trees

The improved version of the TAS satisfiability tester for classical propositional logic, tascpl, presented here uses and alternative representation of the boolean formulas: the simplified Δ-tree representation [6]: in the same way that conjunctive normal forms are usually interpreted as lists of clauses, and disjunctive normal forms are interpreted as lists of cubes, we interpret negative normal forms as *trees* of clauses and cubes. In Fig. 1 an example is given in which a negation normal formula together with its Δ-tree representation are shown:

The part of the algorithm which obtains benefit from this more compact representation of negation normal formulas is the module of reduction strategies.

J.J. Alferes and J. Leite (Eds.): JELIA 2004, LNAI 3229, pp. 738–741, 2004.
© Springer-Verlag Berlin Heidelberg 2004

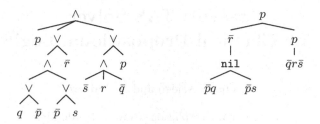

Fig. 1.

1.2 Reductions

Two types of reduction transformations to decrease the size of a negation normal form A at (at most) quadratic cost can be applied by a TAS system: meaning- and satisfiability-preserving transformations.

Restricted form. This is a generalization of the restricted form for cnfs; those subtrees in a Δ-tree which can be detected to be either valid, or unsatisfiable, or equivalent to literals are simplified.

Complete reduction. Literals in the root of a Δ-tree can be assumed true, and an equisatisfiable formula is obtained.

Pure literals deletion. Literals that always appear either positively or negatively are made true, obtaining again an equisatisfiable formula.

Subreduction. With this meaning-preserving transformation, we obtain Δ-trees such that in every branch of it there is at most one ocurrence of every atom.

1.3 Branching Process

If no simplification can be applied, then the satisfiability checking process is splitted using the following Davis-Putnam branching rule: if p is an atom in T, then T is satisfiable if and only if either $T[p/\top]$ is satisfiable or $T[\overline{p}/\top]$ is satisfiable. So, the problem is divided into two independent sub-problems that can be studied in parallel.

Although some heuristics to select the literal in the branching process have been investigated, [4], there is no yet conclusive difference in the use of either of them and thus none is applied actually in the system and the first atom of the formula is used.

1.4 Construction of Models

As tableaux systems, TAS algorithms not only check for the satisfiability, but also, if the input formula is satisfiable, a model is supplied. Models are constructed by using the deleted literals in the complete reduction, pure literal deletion and in the branching process.

2   The System for Classical Logic

The system `tascpl` has been implemented using Objective CAML version 3.06. Although the main work has been done under Mac OS X, the system can be straightforwardly ported to any Unix-like platform.

A functional language has been chosen because this is the more natural way to write the operations involved in the algorithm. On the other hand, Caml programs can easily be interfaced with other languages, in particular with other C programs or libraries; two compilation modes are supported, compilation to byte-code (for portability) and to native assembly code (for performance). The native code compiler generates very efficient code, complemented by a fast, unobtrusive incremental garbage collector. Finally, as we have mentioned above, the programs can be compiled on most Unix platforms (Mac OS X, Linux, Digital Unix, Solaris, IRIX) and well as under Windows.

2.1   The Main Program: `tascpl`

As stated previously, TAS methods are satisfiability testers (this allows also to check for validity by refutation). As a result, the required input to execute `tascpl` is a text file with the formula we want check if it is valid or satisfiable.

The command line to call the program admits a flag to turn on or off the negation of the input formula:

- `tascpl -sat <textfile>`   checks the satisfiablity of the formula described in <*textfile*>; the possible outputs are "`Unsatisfiable`" or "`Model:` <*list of literals*>", where <*list of literals*> describes a model of the input formula (if satisfiable).
- `tascpl -val <textfile>`   checks the validity of the formula in <*textfile*>; the possible output are: "`Valid`" or "`Countermodel:` <*list of literals*>", where <*list of literals*> describes a countermodel for the input formula, provided it is not valid.

This is an example of the content of a valid input file:

```
((s1 <-> (-a | d)) &
(o010 <-> (b & s1)) &
(s2 <-> (-c | d)) &
(o020 <-> (b & s2)))
->
((o010 <-> o020) | ((a & b & -c) | (-a & b & c & -d)))
```

Any string non starting by numbers can be used as atoms, and the following ASCII symbols are used to represent connectives: the conjunction, &, and the disjunction, |, can be used with any arity; - is used for negation, -> is used for implication, and <-> is used for biimplication. Every subformula must be enclosed by parentheses, except the negation of literals.

2.2 The dtree Utility

We have included this small utility to help understanding the Δ-tree representation.

- dtree <*textfile*> returns a T$_E$X file containing the Δ-tree representation of
  the formula in <*textfile*>; if this file is compiled with L^{A}T$_E$X, a pretty-printed
  version of the tree is obtained. Obviously, this utility is only interesting for
  small formulas, even although it supports larger inputs.

3   Some Comments on Performance

It is worth to say that the use of this more compact representation of formulas
not only has resulted in a simpler and more straightforward implementation of
the method, but also in a better performance when applied to formulas taken
from the libraries of satisfiability problems.

When comparing to other propositional satisfiability testers, the first problem
we faced is that only the system HeerHugo [5] is genuinely non-clausal (see
http://www.satlive.org), the comparison with other provers on families of
non-clausal formulas has been done indirectly through a preprocessing step in
order to obtain the clause form of the problems.

TAS generally outperforms for families of formulas which are not directly
stated in clause form (for instance, formulas containing a number of connectives
of bi-implication) whereas the performance it not as good when applied to formulas already in clause form. This is natural, for TAS methods were designed
primarily as non-clausal theorem provers.

References

1. G. Aguilera, I. P. de Guzmán, M. Ojeda-Aciego, and A. Valverde. Reductions for
   non-clausal theorem proving. *Theoretical Computer Science*, 266(1/2):81–112, 2001.
2. I. P. de Guzmán, M. Ojeda-Aciego, and A. Valverde. Implicates and reduction
   techniques for temporal logics. *Annals of Mathematics and Artificial Intelligence*,
   27:2–23, 1999.
3. I.P. de Guzmán, M. Ojeda-Aciego, and A. Valverde. Restricted Δ-trees and reduction theorems in multiple-valued logics. *Lecture Notes in Artificial Intelligence*
   2527:161–171, 2002.
4. E. Giunchiglia, M. Maratea, A. Tacchella, and D. Zambonin. Evaluating search
   heuristics and optimization techniques in propositional satisfiability. *Lecture Notes
   in Computer Science* 2083:341–363, 2001.
5. J. F. Groote and J. P. Warners. The propositional formula checker HeerHugo. In I.
   Gent, H. van Maaren, and T. Walsh, editors, *SAT2000: Highlights of Satisfiability
   Research in the year 2000*, Frontiers in Artificial Intelligence and Applications, pages
   261–281. Kluwer Academic, 2000.
6. G. Gutiérrez, I.P. de Guzmán, J. Martínez, M. Ojeda-Aciego, and A. Valverde.
   Satisfiability testing for Boolean formulas using Δ-trees. *Studia Logica*, 72:33–60,
   2002.

Author Index